A GUIDE TO THE BOOKS OF WILLIAM BLAKE
FOR INNOCENT AND EXPERIENCED READERS

A GUIDE TO THE BOOKS
OF WILLIAM BLAKE
FOR INNOCENT
AND EXPERIENCED
READERS

with notes on interpretive
criticism 1910 to1984

Henry Summerfield

COLIN SMYTHE
Gerrards Cross, 1998

First published in 1998 by Colin Smythe Limited,
P.O.Box 6, Gerrards Cross, Buckinghamshire SL9 8XA, UK

British Library Cataloguing in Publication Data

A catalogue record for this book is available from the British Library

ISBN 0-86140-408-4

Distributed in North America by Oxford University Press
198 Madison Avenue, New York, NY 10016

Produced in Great Britain
Printed and bound by the Guernsey Press Company Ltd.
Vale, Guernsey GY1 3BW

To C. K. Seshadri and Patrick Grant,
explorers of the wisdoms of East and West

Contents

CONTENTS 10

Preface

Many of Blake's lyrics have the power to cast an instant enchantment over readers who encounter them for the first time, yet those who are prompted to investigate Blake's later productions can initially find themselves intimidated by the prophetic books. Nevertheless persistence in exploring these mythological writings, along with the vigorous prose and multifarious paintings and engravings, often leads to a lifelong fascination. The primary purpose of this book is to provide for the serious reader of poetry, for the student, and for the scholar who is not a Blake specialist, a bridge between an initial joy in poems of exquisite and poignant beauty and a larger engagement, at once aesthetic and intellectual, with the lifework of a great author and artist.

In the twelve chapters I have given an account of Blake's beliefs, concepts and development and an exposition of those of his productions that can reasonably be classified as "books." For the most part the exposition is confined to a single reading of the text and designs, but the Notes on Criticism survey the interpretation of these works from 1910 through 1984. These Notes are intended for use with Geoffrey Keynes's edition of the *Complete Writings*, David V. Erdman's edition of *The Complete Poetry and Prose*, the latter's reproductions of texts and designs in *The Illuminated Blake*, and any edition of the *Illustrations of The Book of Job*. Critics' interpretations of the relatively inaccessible drawings in the manuscript of *The Four Zoas* are not given. I intend the Notes—and this is the secondary purpose of the book—to constitute a record of how Blake's works came to be understood and to show how successive interpretations, while they can be irritatingly or amusingly contradictory, often complement each other bringing out the richness of the poetry.

In 1910 Joseph Wicksteed initiated modern Blake scholarship with his *Blake's Vision of the Book of Job*, and such advances were made during the three-quarters of a century that followed that in 1978 Christine Gallant was able to write, "Blake criticism has now reached a point where the foundation of understanding has been laid,"[1] and in the same year Brian Wilkie and Mary Lynn Johnson could observe, "Most of Blake's basic ideas are now fairly well understood and agreed upon," and refer confidently to "the consensus of Blakeans."[2] By this time, indeed, there had evolved a body of criticism which showed that, despite quite fierce polemics, there did exist a widespread near-consensus on the nature and meaning of most of Blake's works. This holds true even though on any single point of interpretation there will probably be some dissenters, and no commentator will endorse every detail of the consensus. Thus the majority of Blakeans agree that the heroine of *The Book of Thel* refuses the passage from Innocence to Experience and that "The Mental Traveller" concerns the phases of the historical cycle. There remain, however, some issues on which there is no consensus—such as whether Thel is on one level a soul awaiting birth and whether the poet sides with the clay in "The Clod and the Pebble."

Major contributions to the understanding of Blake include but are not limited to the following: Wicksteed's elucidation of *Illustrations of The Book of Job* (1910); Keynes's bibliographical and editorial work begun in 1921 and its continuation by Erdman and Bentley; Damon's early demonstration that Blake's work is rich in philosophical, occult, literary and historical reference (1924); Sloss and Wallis's annotated edition of the prophetic books, in which they admit there is much they do not understand (1926, but mostly prepared by 1912); Plowman's discovery of the structure of *The Marriage of Heaven and Hell* (1927); Percival's exposition of Blake's use of philosophy and ancient symbolism (1938); Bronowski's, Schorer's and Erdman's proof that his work is nevertheless intimately related to the life and events of his age (1944, 1946, 1954); the contrasting researches of Frye and Raine into the unexpectedly traditional roots of his creations (1947, 1968 [for 1969]); Blunt's introduction of art history into the study of Blake (1959) and its further exploitation by Hagstrum (1964), Bindman (1977), Butlin (1981) and Warner (1984); perceptive readings of many poems and passages by Gleckner (1959), Bloom

---

[1] *Blake and the Assimilation of Chaos* (Princeton: Princeton UP, 1978), p. 3.
[2] *Blake's Four Zoas: The Design of a Dream* (Cambridge, Mass., and London: Harvard UP, 1978), p. viii.

(1963, 1965) and Adams (1963); definitions of terms and symbolic names in Damon's *Blake Dictionary* (1966); many carefully worked out arguments in articles—especially those of Chayes, Grant, Miner, Nurmi, Paley, Rose and Tolley—in the 1960s and 1970s; Essick's analyses from the 1970s onwards of Blake's engravings; the annotated editions of Stevenson (1971) and Ostriker (1977); Lindberg's study of the traditional content of the *Job* illustrations (1973); Fox's investigation of the structure of *Milton* (1976); Mitchell's scrutiny of Blake's synthesis of text and design (1978); Damrosch's examination of his relationship to the whole of Western philosophy (1980); Hilton's uncovering of the polysemous nature of many of his terms (1983); and Paley's discovery of the structure of *Jerusalem* (1983).

The quantity of Blake scholarship during the period I am considering is so vast that I have necessarily been selective in my citations, especially in the case of criticism of *Songs of Innocence and of Experience*. I have considered mainly those books and articles recognised by Blake scholars as worth drawing on or worth refuting, and I have taken into account a few studies of psychoanalytical and Marxist bent that may be regarded as outside the consensus, particularly volumes by Crehan, DiSalvo and Webster. The Notes on Criticism cover views both of the general thrust of each work and of many of its details. In annotating the latter, I have concentrated primarily on those which are controversial and secondarily on those likely to seem obscure. On finding a difficult name or term not glossed, the reader should consult the Selective Index to Names and Terms. Thus the symbol of the weights of a loom is indexed under "weights," and the phrase "the seven diseases of the Soul" under "diseases." A passage on which there is no note may be commented on in the appropriate chapter.

Quotations from Blake are taken from *The Complete Poetry and Prose of William Blake* edited by Erdman, and, as is customary, I have repunctuated them where appropriate since the poet's own punctuation is highly erratic. I take as the text of each book what Erdman prints as such and ignore passages relegated to his Textual Notes as well as the discarded plates of *America*. Brief accounts of *An Island in the Moon* and *A Descriptive Catalogue* are included at the appropriate places, but critical views of them are not given.

My own observations include a few repeated from my art-
icles "Blake's *The French Revolution* and the Bible" *(University of
Dayton Review*, XVII [Winter 1985-86], 29-37), and "Beards,
Disputations and Revelry: Observations on Blake's *Job* Engrav-
ings" (*Colby Library Quarterly*, XXIII [June 1987], 89-98).

During the years in which I have worked on this book, I
have received much intellectual and practical help. Some insights I
owe to Ms. Kathleen Raine and to Dr. Patrick Grant. Dr. Lionel
Adey, Dr. Thomas Cleary, Ms. Leonora MacNeil, Mr. Harbindar
Sanghara, and Ms. Ann Shaw are among those from whose con-
versation I have benefited. Dr. Michael Best, Dr. Elizabeth Grove-
White and Dr. Arnold Keller have given me essential advice about
the use of computers. The University of Victoria, B. C., has
granted me two study leaves, and I have enjoyed the assistance of
the University librarians—especially Mr. Howard Gerwing, Mr.
Chris Petter, Mr. Dietrich Bertz and Ms. Betty Gibb. To my wife,
Marian, and our daughter, Elizabeth Katchen, I am indebted for
their admirable patience during the book's composition.

Abbreviations

Editions of Blake's Works

E David V. Erdman, ed., *The Complete Poetry and Prose of William Blake* (Berkeley and Los Angeles: University of California Press, 1982).

IB David V. Erdman, ed., *The Illuminated Blake: All of William Blake's Illuminated Works with a Plate-by-plate Commentary* (Garden City, NewYork: Anchor Press/ Doubleday, 1974).

K Blake, *Complete Writings with variant readings*, ed. Geoffrey Keynes, reprinted (Oxford: Oxford University Press, 1972).

Titles of Blake's Writings

A	*America*
ARO	*All Religions Are One*
BA	*The Book of Ahania*
BL	*The Book of Los*
BU	*The [First] Book of Urizen*
E	*Europe*
FR	*The French Revolution*
FZ	*The Four Zoas*
GA	*The Ghost of Abel*
GP	*For the Sexes: The Gates of Paradise*
J	*Jerusalem*
Job	*Illustrations of The Book of Job*
M	*Milton*
MHH	*The Marriage of Heaven and Hell*
NNR	*There Is No Natural Religion*
SE	*Songs of Experience*
SI	*Songs of Innocence*
SL	*The Song of Los*

Thel	*The Book of Thel*
VDA	*Visions of the Daughters of Albion*

Other Abbreviations

AV	Authorised Version of the Bible
BCCE	Northrop Frye, ed., *Blake: A Collection of Critical Essays* (Englewood Cliffs, N. J.: Prentice Hall, 1966.
BIQ	*Blake: An Illustrated Quarterly* (formerly *Blake Newsletter*)
BN	*Blake Newsletter*
BNYPL	*Bulletin of the New York Public Library*
BRH	*Bulletin of Research in the Humanities* (formerly *Bulletin of the New York Public Library*
BS	*Blake Studies*
BSA	Stuart Curran and Joseph Anthony Wittreich, Jr., ed., *Blake's Sublime Allegory: Essays on* The Four Zoas, Milton, Jerusalem (Madison: U of Wisconsin P, 1973)
BT	Robert N. Essick and Donald Pearce, ed., *Blake in His Time* (Bloomington and London: Indiana UP, 1978)
BVFD	David V. Erdman and John E. Grant, ed., *Blake's Visionary Forms Dramatic* (Princeton: Princeton UP, 1970)
CI	*Critical Inquiry*
CL	*Comparative Literature*
CLQ	*Colby Library Quarterly*
Cr	*Criticism*
DV	Vivian de Sola Pinto, ed., *The Divine Vision: Studies in the Poetry and Art of William Blake* (London: Gollancz, 1957)
EC	*Essays in Criticism*
ECS	*Eighteenth Century Studies*
ELH	Not an abbreviation but the title of a journal (the letters stand for "English Literary History")
ELN	*English Language Notes*
ESC	*English Studies in Canada*
Ex	*Explicator*

FQ	Edmund Spenser, *The Faerie Queene*
HLQ	*Huntington Library Quarterly*
InB	Michael Phillips, ed., *Interpreting Blake* (Cambridge: Cambridge UP, 1978)
JAAC	*Journal of Aesthetics and Art Criticism*
JEGP	*Journal of English and Germanic Philology*
JWCI	*Journal of the Warburg and Courtauld Institutes*
MLN	*Modern Language Notes*
MLQ	*Modern Language Quarterly*
MLR	*Modern Language Review*
MP	*Modern Philology*
NQ	*Notes and Queries*
OED	*Oxford English Dictionary, 2nd edition*
PL	John Milton, *Paradise Lost*
PLL	*Papers on Language and Literature*
PMLA	*Publications of the Modern Language Association*
PQ	*Philological Quarterly*
RES	*Review of English Studies*
rpt	*reprinted*
SAQ	*South Atlantic Quarterly*
SECC	*Studies in Eighteenth-Century Culture*
SEL	*Studies in English Literature 1500-1900*
SP	*Studies in Philology*
SR	*Studies in Romanticism*
TLS	*Times Literary Supplement*
TSLL	*Texas Studies in Language and Literature*
UP	University Press
VH	Robert N. Essick, ed., *The Visionary Hand: Essays for the Study of William Blake's Art and Aesthetics* (Los Angeles: Hennessey and Ingalls, 1973)
WBED	Alvin H. Rosenfeld, ed., *William Blake: Essays for S. Foster Damon* (Providence: Brown UP, 1969)
WBEK	Morton D. Paley and Michael Phillips, ed., *William Blake: Essays in honour of Sir Geoffrey Keynes* (Oxford: Clarendon Press, 1973)
WR	*Wascana Review*

Note on Format of References

Where possible, references to Blake's text consist of the abbreviation for the title followed by plate and line numbers (in the case of *Tiriel*, section and line numbers; in the case of *The Four Zoas*, manuscript page and line numbers, then the page number for David V. Erdman's edition *The Complete Poetry and Prose of William Blake*, and finally the Night and line numbers for Blake, *Complete Writings with variant readings*, ed. Geoffrey Keynes). In references to designs in the Notes on Criticism, "*IB*" after the title abbreviation indicates that the plate number is the one given in Erdman's *The Illuminated Blake*. Erdman's plate numbers are also employed in all references to the designs in the chapters.

Cross-references in the Notes on Criticism follow the pattern "see *Thel* 6:1n." In the citations, the abbreviation "n" followed by a number refers to an endnote; a footnote is treated as part of the text of its page. When a sentence in the Notes contains only a single reference and this comes at the beginning or end, that reference indicates the source of the entire sentence.

For readers interested in the history of Blake studies, I have given the original 1954 page numbers in references to David V. Erdman's pioneering study *Blake: Prophet Against Empire*, then, in square brackets, the 1969 numbers (unchanged in the 1977 edition).

Chapters of the Bible (Authorised Version) are designated by lower case Roman numerals to avoid confusion with references to Blake's text. ("Jer." stands for Jeremiah, not *Jerusalem*.)

Prologue

To publish a detailed account of the work of Blake is inescapably to engage in a polemic. Unfortunately Damrosch's complaint about "the exceptional extent of ill-humored controversy in Blake studies"[1] is fully justified. By selective quotation or by insisting on finding irony in improbable places, scholars can make out that Blake is essentially a humanist,[2] an evangelical[3] or a radical[4] Christian, a Berkeleyan,[5] or a Christian Neoplatonist.[6] A fair and comprehensive study shows that whatever measure of truth there may be in all these claims, no label is adequate to circumscribe him. The man who smilingly dismisses the decease of his friend Flaxman with the words "I cannot think of Death as more than the going out of one room into another,"[7] who asserts that "Nothing is displeasing to God but Unbelief & Eating of the Tree of Knowledge"[8] and who attributes the limitation mercifully

---

[1] Leopold Damrosch, *Symbol and Truth in Blake's Myth* (Princeton: Princeton UP, 1980), p. 8.

[2] Alfred Kazin, Introduction to *The Portable Blake* (1946; rpt. New York: Viking Press, 1966), pp. 1-55.

[3] Kathryn Kremen cited in Florence Sandler, review of *The Imagination of the Resurrection: The Poetic Continuity of a Religious Motif in Donne, Blake, and Yeats*, by Kathryn R. Kremen, *Blake Studies* VI.1 (1973), 96-98.

[4] Thomas J. J. Altizer, *The New Apocalypse: The Radical Christian Vision of William Blake* (n. p.: Michigan State UP, 1967), p. xi.

[5] Stuart Curran, "Blake and the Gnostic Hyle: A Double Negative," *Blake Studies*, IV.2 (1972), 117-33 (see 119).

[6] George Mills Harper, *The Neoplatonism of William Blake* (Chapel Hill: U of North Carolina P, 1961), pp. 240, 266-71, and *passim*.

[7] G. E. Bentley, Jr., *Blake Records* (Oxford: Clarendon Press, 1969), p. 548.

[8] *The Complete Poetry and Prose of William Blake*, ed. David V.

imposed on the Fall to divine intervention (e.g. *J* 49:52-55) is neither a materialist nor an atheist. Although he tries in *The Marriage of Heaven and Hell* to show that "Man has no Body distinct from his Soul" (E34/ K149), later (and earlier) he distinguishes between the two:

> ...Vala produc'd the Bodies. Jerusalem gave the Souls
> (*J* 18:7)

> The Natural Body is an Obstruction to the Soul
> or Spiritual Body
>   (E664/ K775)

> Many Persons such as Paine & Voltaire with some of the Ancient Greeks say we will not Converse concerning Good & Evil; we will live in Paradise & Liberty. You may do so in Spirit but not in the Mortal Body as you pretend till after the Last Judgment for in Paradise they have no Corporeal & Mortal Body
>   (E564/ K615-16)

Damrosch notes that there are in Blake scores of passages to this effect, but that his distinction between mind and flesh is Pauline, not Cartesian: in Eternity we will have bodies, but these will be spiritual.[9]

How far or even whether Blake moved away from the non-dualism of *The Marriage of Heaven and Hell* is much disputed.

Erdman (Berkeley and Los Angeles: U of California P, 1982), p. 564 (henceforward referred to as E followed by a page number) or Blake, *Complete Writings with variant readings*, rev., ed. Geoffrey Keynes (Oxford: Oxford UP, 1979), p. 615 (henceforward referred to as K followed by a page number). For further references to Blake's writings, given in parentheses in the text, see also Note on Format of References above. There are also parenthetical references to Spenser's *The Faerie Queene* (*FQ*), Milton's *Paradise Lost* (*PL*), and the Authorised Version of the Bible.

[9] *Symbol and Truth*, p. 166.

Some of his interpreters, such as Percival, Frye, Gleckner and Adams, consider that his beliefs were essentially unaltered from the time that he wrote *Songs of Innocence* till his death about four decades later, though Frye recognises "some changes in emphasis in later poems."[10] Others, such as Margoliouth, Hagstrum, Paley and Mellor, have discerned far-reaching changes in his values and philosophy. While the *Marriage*'s enthusiasm for the body and for political revolution disappears from his later works, its insistence on the humanness of God is echoed in plate 91 of *Jerusalem*, its rebellious Jesus resembles the Christ of "The Everlasting Gospel" (*c.* 1818), and its opposition to chastity and abstinence—those "Gods of the Heathen" (?*c.* 1820—E275/ K776)—is something Blake never abandoned. Paley's claim that the poet "was a monist who found his mythology entrapping him in a dualistic position,"[11] like Raine's suggestion that he vacillates between Neoplatonic dualism and the Hermetic view that the lower and higher worlds are essentially akin,[12] suggests there may have been an unresolved contradiction in his mind; however, Damrosch's belief that he "is a dualist who wishes he were a monist"[13] corresponds well with his later world view and his slighting reference in *Jerusalem* (91:34-35) to the Smaragdine Table of Hermes. Even if, from the highest standpoint, the mortal body is only an illusion arising from a wrong perception of the spiritual body, the phantom flesh takes on an autonomous and terrible existence of its own. It is "the Vile Body" (Blake borrows the phrase from Paul [Phil. iii.21]) guilty of "Enmities against Mind," and in the last analysis it is the "Dust & Clay" that the serpent Satan devours and the "Foolish Body" that

---

[10] Northrop Frye, "The Keys to the Gates" (1966; rpt. *The Stubborn Structure: Essays on Criticism and Society* [Ithaca, N. Y.: Cornell UP, 1970], pp. 175-99 [quotation p.195]).

[11] Morton D. Paley, "The Figure of the Garment in *The Four Zoas*, *Milton*, and *Jerusalem*," in *Blake's Sublime Allegory: Essays on* The Four Zoas, Milton, Jerusalem, ed. Stuart Curran and Joseph Anthony Wittreich, Jr. (Madison: U of Wisconsin P, 1973), pp. 119-39 (quotation p. 123).

[12] Kathleen Raine, *Blake and Tradition* (Princeton: Princeton UP, 1968), I, 100.

[13] *Symbol and Truth*, p. 166.

stands over against "The Real Man" (E667/ K784; E523 [l. 95]/ K755 [l.95]; E783/ K878). Erdman, it may be noted, traces Blake's distinguishing between mortal and spiritual body as far back as the 1793 emblem book *For Children: The Gates of Paradise.*[14]

There is, however, another side to Blake's doctrines. Despite his kind words for Fénelon, Mme. Guyon and St. Teresa (*J* 72:50-52), he is no puritanical quietist, or world-renouncing mystic. He remains convinced that bodily love, "On which the Soul Expands its wing" (E522 [l. 68]/ K755 [l. 68], affords the beginnings of escape from imprisonment in the flesh, while asceticism only intensifies the confinement.[15] Moreover, the arts, not prayer and meditation, are for him the highest activity of fallen beings and the means by which "to open the immortal Eyes/ Of Man inwards into the Worlds of Thought: into Eternity" (*J* 5:18-19). While the life of Eternity is only *fully* attainable after physical death, its fourfold vision can and should be enjoyed in this life:

> Now I a fourfold vision see
> And a fourfold vision is given to me.
> 'Tis fourfold in my supreme delight
> And three fold in soft Beulah's night
> And twofold Always. May God us keep
> From Single vision & Newton's sleep.
> (E722/ K818)

Moreover, such vision should assist us to ameliorate the conditions of life on earth. Though Blake lost faith in political revolution, he never became a reactionary or a royalist or ceased to oppose the horrors of the Industrial Revolution:

> And all the Arts of Life they chang'd into the Arts of
> Death in Albion,
> The hour-glass contemn'd because its simple
> workmanship

---

[14] David V. Erdman, *The Illuminated Blake* (New York: Anchor Books/ Doubleday, 1974), p. 275.

[15] Cf. Northrop Frye, *Fearful Symmetry: A Study of William Blake* (1947; rpt. Boston: Beacon Press, 1962), p. 194.

Was like the workmanship of the plowman, & the water
  wheel,
That raises water into cisterns, broken and burn'd with
  fire
Because its workmanship was like the workmanship of the
  shepherd.
And in their stead, intricate wheels invented, wheel
  without wheel,
To perplex youth in their outgoings, & to bind to labours
  in Albion
Of day & night the myriads of eternity that they may grind
And polish brass & iron hour after hour, laborious task!
Kept ignorant of its use...
  (*J* 65:16-25)

At the end of *Milton*, when Blake has seen the fourfold
being of his hero restored, he brings the reader back to earth,
where

Los listens to the Cry of the Poor Man: his Cloud
Over London in volume terrific, low bended in anger.
  (42:34-35)

Where the physical eye sees cloud, the Imagination sees
the wrath of a prophetic spirit that beholds the suffering which
human beings inflict on their kind.

PART I

The Books of William Blake

An Introduction

1
Biographical Outline

When Alexander Gilchrist published his *Life of William Blake* in 1863, he provided the Victorians with a classic example of the genius who struggles heroically against incomprehension and indigence to leave a glorious heritage to posterity. The future poet and artist was born on 28th November, 1757, the third son of James and Catherine Blake, who kept a hosiery shop at 28 Broad Street in London. An extraordinary child, he beheld visions from his early days, and on one of the occasions when he claimed to have seen angels in a tree, his father, who is likely to have been an Anglican but may have had Moravian leanings,[1] was only dissuaded by Mrs. Blake's pleading from beating him for lying. According to Gilchrist, he told how, when he was four, God peeped in at the window and frightened him and how he saw angels among the haymakers. The boy spent his pocket money on prints and plaster casts, and from 1768 to 1772 attended Pars's Drawing School. He wanted to be an artist, so his father, apparently unable to pay for the necessary training, apprenticed him, when he was fourteen years old, to the able though old-fashioned engraver James Basire. At one time it was the boy's task to draw monuments in Westminster Abbey, and all his life he retained his adoration of Gothic art. In 1775, in the middle of the seven years of his apprenticeship, the American War of Independence broke out, and he had the experience of living in an angry society torn between liberal sympathisers with the rebels and their conservative opponents, though a politician as essentially conservative as Burke could be pro-American. Blake was already a poet, and his early ballad "Gwin, King of Norway" expresses a love of liberty.

---

[1] Alexander Gilchrist, *Life of William Blake*, ed. Ruthven Todd, rev. (London: Dent; New York: Dutton, 1945), p. 6; David V. Erdman, *Blake: Prophet Against Empire*, rev. (Princeton: Princeton UP, 1969), p. 142.

After his apprenticeship ended in 1779, Blake undertook some studies at the Royal Academy, which was still under the presidency of Sir Joshua Reynolds. He also found employment engraving plates for booksellers, who were not yet distinct from publishers. In 1782, he married Catherine Boucher, an illiterate young woman, who, Gilchrist reports, pitied him because he had recently been jilted. He was the only one of the Blake siblings, of whom five reached adulthood, to marry, and he had no children. A year later, one or more of a group of friends whose salon he frequented paid to have a collection of his juvenilia printed under the title *Poetical Sketches*. The salon was at the house of the Reverend and Mrs. Anthony Stephen Mathew, and the printing was probably arranged by Flaxman.[2] The anonymous Preface informs the reader that the contents are "the production of untutored youth, commenced in his twelfth, and occasionally resumed by the author till his twentieth year" (E846/ K883). According to Benjamin Heath Malkin, a later acquaintance of Blake, the latter wrote "How sweet I roam'd from field to field" before he was fourteen.[3] The bound volumes were not offered for sale but given to the author to distribute as he pleased.

From 1784 to 1785, Blake was in partnership with James Parker, who had been his fellow apprentice under Basire, and for a brief period he enjoyed hopes of prosperity as they jointly ran a print shop at 27, Broad Street, next door to the Blake family firm, which had by now been taken over by William's businesslike elder brother, James. It was probably late in 1784 that he wrote *An Island in the Moon*, a narrative satire on a group of intellectuals.[4] In 1785 he and his wife left Broad Street for 28 Poland Street.[5] The death in 1787 of his beloved nineteen-year-old brother Robert, who had also been an artist, was a grievous affliction for Blake—in 1800 he wrote to his patron Hayley:

> Thirteen years ago, I lost a brother & with his
> spirit I converse daily & hourly in the Spirit. &

---

[2] Michael Phillips, "William Blake and the 'Unincreasable Club': The Printing of *Poetical Sketches*," *BYNPL*, 80 (Autumn 1976), 6-18.

[3] G. E. Bentley, Jr., *Bake Records* (Oxford: Clarendon Press, 1969), p. 428.

[4] See Textual Notes, E849.

[5] Erdman, *Prophet* (1969), p. 116.

See him in my remembrance in the regions of my
Imagination. I hear his advice & even now write
from his Dictate...
   (E705/ K797)

 During the remainder of his life, he drafted poems and
drew sketches in the famous "Notebook" which had belonged to
Robert. (It is sometimes called the Rossetti Manuscript after the
poet Dante Gabriel Rossetti, to whom for a time it belonged.) The
unfolding of Blake's genius was catalysed by his encounter in the
late 1780s with the writings and followers of the Scandinavian
mystic Swedenborg, who had rebelled, as Blake himself was about
to do, against the semi-materialistic philosophy so widespread in
the eighteenth century. In 1788 (whether before or after he had
begun to read Swedenborg is uncertain), he engraved and printed
All Religions Are One and *There Is No Natural Religion*—brief
tractates consisting of illustrated prose aphorisms and designed to
expose the fallacies of Locke's unspiritual conception of the
human being. These are the first examples of the invention that
Blake called Illuminated Printing.
 As Bindman has explained,[6] a number of artists at this
time, including Blake's friend George Cumberland, were seeking a
way of conveying a text onto a metal plate without the expense of
using moveable type. Blake believed that his deceased brother
Robert revealed the solution of the problem to him in a vision.
After writing and drawing on copper with an acid-proof substance,
he immersed the plate in corrosive acid, which soon left the words
and design standing out in relief ready to be cleaned and inked for
printing. Essick[7] gives strong reasons for believing that Blake—as
Linnell and probably Cumberland report[8]—learnt to write in
reverse on the metal. The resulting page he usually coloured by
hand, making each copy different and sometimes altering or add-
ing details. While the process enabled Blake to be his own pub-
lisher, it limited his market to well-to-do collectors. Their pur-

---

[6] David Bindman, *Blake as an Artist* (Oxford: Phaidon; New York: Dutton, 1977), pp.
41-43.
[7] Robert N. Essick, *William Blake Printmaker* (Princeton: Princeton UP, 1980), pp.
89-92.
[8] Bentley, *Blake Records*, pp. 212, 460.

chase consisted of a packet of numbered leaves, which they could have bound.[9] Usually but not invariably, each page was printed only on one side.

This system of relief etching allowed Blake to create a modern equivalent of a mediaeval manuscript: instead of a text and illustrations, he fashioned words and design into an integrated whole which is the product of two arts, even though the text seems to have given rise to the designs. In 1803 he writes to Butts of his epic allegory, which will "be progressively Printed & Ornamented with Prints"; fifteen years afterwards he complains of having to issue illustrations divorced from "Poetical Personifications & Acts without which Poems they never could have been Executed" (E730, 771/ K825, 867).

For the rest of his days, Blake laboriously published his own works, beginning with the radiant *Songs of Innocence* and the enigmatic *Book of Thel* in 1789. The contrast between the rhymed stanzas of the former and the unrhymed heptameters of the latter is typical of the stylistic hiatus between his lyrics and his so-called "prophetic books" (the term is not his own) that is apt to bewilder newcomers to Blake. He produced most of his shorter prophetic books at 13, Hercules Buildings, in the district of Lambeth, a pleasanter and more spacious part of London than he had previously lived in, though it was the site of the symbolically oppressive palace of the Archbishop of Canterbury. He and his wife resided there, enjoying a garden with a vine that he insisted on leaving unpruned, from autumn 1790 till 1800.[10] In the central part of this period, he enjoyed his most prosperous years and for a time even kept a servant. Some of his poems suggest that Catherine was at times jealous, and his letter to Hayley dated 23 October, 1804, confirms that there was friction between husband and wife before they settled in later life into a harmonious relationship.

The outbreak of the French Revolution in 1789 was the beginning of an historical phenomenon as astonishing to the Romantic age as the Bolshevik Revolution was to the twentieth century. While Burke refused to extend his sympathy for the American rebels to the French Third Estate, Blake may have worn the

---

[9] Geoffrey Keynes, "An Undescribed Copy of Blake's *Songs of Innocence and of Experience*," *The Book Collector*, XXX (Spring 1981), 39-42.
[10] Bentley, *Blake Records*, p. 560.

revolutionaries' red cap in the streets of London, and he associated with Thomas Paine and other radicals clustered around the publisher Joseph Johnson.[11] In 1791 Johnson had a proof copy printed of the first instalment of Blake's *The French Revolution. A Poem in Seven Books*, but was not so brave—or rash—as to proceed to publication.

Blake's enthusiasm for the Revolution with its anticlerical component seems to have generated a strenuous antinomianism in his own thought, and in 1790 he began and possibly completed *The Marriage of Heaven and Hell*, his supreme work in prose and a masterpiece of illuminated printing. In this book he championed reason against energy, denied the reality of a distinction between soul and body, and strained to interpret Christianity as a religion that imposed no fixed moral laws on believers. For the remainder of his days, he rejected the rules and ideal of chastity. Returning to unrhymed verse in 1793 in *Visions of the Daughters of Albion*, he called for the freedom of slaves, children, women, and the victims of arranged marriages. In the same year he published *America*, the first instalment of an historical myth continued in *Europe* (1794) and concluded in *The Song of Los* (1795)—a myth encompassing the history of the human species and highlighting the American and French Revolutions as its turning point. In common with no small number of his contemporaries, he appears to have regarded the French Revolution, and later the Napoleonic Wars, as heralding the end of the world.

The interweaving of philosophical, psychological and social levels of meaning in *Visions of the Daughters of Albion* marked an essential step towards the evolution of Blake's epics. Equally necessary was the genesis of the myth of creation and fall, which initially appears in *The First Book of Urizen* (1794). In this book, as in *America* and *Europe*, Urizen is the god of law and reason who is opposed by Orc, the spirit of energy and revolt, but at this stage of his career Blake could not devise a satisfactory scheme of redemption: he was unable to complete his myth, and there was no "Second Book of Urizen."

Meanwhile the French Revolution had degenerated into an orgy of tyranny and bloodshed beginning with the September Mas-

---

[11] Gilchrist, *Life*, p. 81; Erdman, *Blake: Prophet Against Empire* (Princeton: Princeton UP), 1954 , pp. 139-42 [153-58].

sacres of 1792. After the work of the guillotine had betrayed Blake's hopes in the upheaval, he endured a period of pessimism during which he concentrated on the woes of the fallen world. Some of the poems in *Songs of Experience* and in his Notebook suggest that his feeling may have been aggravated by marital friction involving his wife's jealousy.

As *The Book of Ahania* shows, his political disillusion begins at the latest in 1795. In this year of famine, drought, and Pitt's harsh suppression of free speech and the press, he also produced *The Song of Los*, *The Book of Los*, and a series of twelve large colour prints that portray with extraordinary power and splendour the suffering that characterises the mortal realm. From 1795 to 1797 he devoted much of his energy to painting and engraving an immense series of watercolours commissioned by Richard Edwards to illustrate a new edition of Young's *Night Thoughts* (1742-45), a book-length blank verse meditation on death, bereavement and immortality. This gave Blake a promising opportunity to aim at commercial success—there was a lucrative market for finely illustrated editions of such classics as Shakespeare and Milton—while concentrating on his now favourite subject of human suffering. Unfortunately, while he completed 537 paintings, only forty-three of them reached publication as engravings, for an economic crisis destroyed the market for such enterprises and only the first volume was issued. Blake did, however, find a patron who commissioned and bought many paintings from him. Thomas Butts was a clerk in the office of the Muster-master General, who was responsible for keeping the records of the strength of each regiment; Butts was not a rich man, but his purchases and friendship helped Blake to survive years of neglect.

With the failure of his political hopes and the collapse of his financial prospects, Blake had ample excuse for depression if not despair, yet he did not wholly lose faith in the Christian promise of the ultimate redemption of the world. If *The Book of Ahania* and *The Book of Los* seem entirely dark, prophecy of deliverance is implicit in *The Song of Los*, in the last of the large colour prints—*Christ Appearing to the Apostles*—(which bears no date)—and in the lyrical images of Christ found in such of the *Night Thoughts* paintings as nos. 1, 378, and 512.

In 1797 Blake began to prepare in copperplate hand a manuscript, perhaps for sale, of an epic poem named *Vala*, which encompassed both fall and redemption. Gradually he abandoned his attempt to keep the copy saleable and piled revision on revision. After many years he put the unfinished work aside in favour of *Milton* and *Jerusalem*, and in old age he gave the manuscript to the artist John Linnell.

In the summer of 1800, the well meaning poetaster William Hayley, the friend and later the biographer of Cowper, invited the Blakes to occupy a cottage he possessed near his home at Felpham on the coast of Sussex. They arrived in September 1800 and remained till September 1803. Much of *Vala* seems to have been written here: Margoliouth points to passages that are not late revisions and that reflect an intimate acquaintance with the sea, and Mellor notes the marked similarities between some of the accompanying sketches and misericords in Chichester Cathedral and St. Mary's Hospital, which were near Felpham.[12]

The Blakes' new life began blissfully but gradually became troubled. While they delighted in the sea, the country, the clear sky, and their small cottage, Catherine's health suffered from the moist atmosphere. After a time Hayley, incapable of understanding his protégé, started urging him to confine himself to financially profitable tasks—illustrating books and painting miniature portraits. Unable to make any impression on him, Hayley redirected his advice to Catherine—with equal unsuccess judging by the poet's line "And when he could not act upon my wife" (E506/ K544). Blake's increasing frustration, however, did not prevent him from relishing the study of Latin, Greek and Hebrew, though his knowledge of Hebrew, at least, never amounted to more than a smattering.[13]

On 10 January, 1803, Blake wrote to Butts confiding that he was "under the direction of Messengers from Heaven Daily & Nightly" (E724/ K812), so that he dare not neglect his "duty...as a Soldier of Christ" to create works of spiritual art. Three and a half months later he disclosed that he had written down an epic poem dictated to him by spirits and that he believed he had been brought

---

[12] H. M. Margoliouth, ed., *William Blake's* Vala: *Blake's Numbered Text* (Oxford: Clarendon Press, 1956), p. xxiv; Anne Kostelanetz Mellor, *Blake's Human Form Divine* (Berkeley: U of California P, 1974), pp. 167-76.

[13] Arnold Cheskin, "The Echoing Greenhorn: Blake as Hebraist," *BIQ,*, XII (Winter 1978-79), 178-83. See also E727/ K821.

to Sussex for the sake of this work (E728-29/ K823). His letters, taken together with the Preface to chapter one of *Jerusalem*, show that he wrote the first drafts of his epic poetry in bursts of inspiration which yielded him "twelve or sometimes twenty or thirty lines at a time without Premeditation" (E729/ K823), but though he considered himself to be no more than "the Secretary" to whom the Authors "in Eternity" dictated their "Sublime Allegory" (E730/ K825), the 'dictation' amounted to what is ordinarily called 'inspiration,' for he declares on plate 3 of *Jerusalem*,

> When this Verse was first dictated to me I consider'd a Monotonous Cadence like that used by Milton & Shakespeare & all writers of English Blank Verse...to be a necessary and indispensible part of Verse. But I soon found that in the mouth of a true Orator such monotony was...as much a bondage as rhyme itself. I therefore have produced a variety in every line, both of cadences & number of syllables.
> (E145-46/ K621)

As the much revised manuscript of *The Four Zoas* shows, its author regarded the verbal expression of what the spirits disclosed and the organisation of the epic as his responsibility.

During his three years at Felpham, as his letters show, Blake experienced a spiritual regeneration, which left him, after he had "fought thro a Hell of terrors & horrors...in a Divided Existence" (E758/ K935), full of zeal to proclaim his allegiance to Christianity. Moreover, he credited his inner metamorphosis with eliminating the friction in his marriage, for the "spectrous Fiend" whom he had subdued within himself was "the enemy of conjugal love" (E756/ K852). His 'conversion' and the accompanying development in his theory of art are discussed in chapter seven.

On 12 August, 1803, a month before his return to London, Blake was surprised to find a soldier named John Schofield at work in his cottage garden. When the man, who had been invited by the authorised gardener, refused to leave, Blake pushed him out. Schofield conspired with his fellow trooper John Cock to charge Blake with cursing the King and his subjects and stigmatising his soldiers as slaves, and the poet had to revisit Felpham in the following January to face a serious though not capital charge of sedition[14] as well as an indictment for assault. With the aid of Samuel Rose, a lawyer hired by Hayley, and the evidence of neighbours, Blake was acquitted by the jury, but his peril had sunk deep into his mind, for Schofield, Cock and other men associated with it figure in his myth among the twelve demonic Sons of Albion.

In London, where Blake and his wife took up residence at 17, South Molton Street, he suffered grievously from want of work. His style of engraving was old-fashioned, and the renewed war with France had cut off the continental market for British prints.[15] To add to his despondency, he was at last disillusioned with Napoleon when the latter crowned himself Emperor in May 1804 finally destroying his pose as the champion of revolutionary principles. Like Beethoven's, Blake's gullibility ended here: that of the politician Charles James Fox, a sympathiser with the Revolution who was expelled from the Privy Council in 1798 (and in some danger of imprisonment in the Tower of London), lasted until 1806, when, as Foreign Secretary in the Ministry of All the Talents, he attempted to conduct peace negotiations with the French Government. Erdman suggests, however, that Blake lost some of his admiration for the dictator when the latter swept aside the French constitution in November 1799 by taking the title of Chief Consul.[16]

The year after Napoleon's final fall from grace, the engraver and publisher Robert Cromek, assuming a mask of friendly admiration, commissioned Blake to draw and then engrave a set of illustrations for Robert Blair's morbid poem *The Grave* (1743), but on receiving the designs he handed them to the fashionable engraver Schiavonetti. Engraving being much more highly paid than drawing, Blake was outraged. In 1806, Cromek committed a second injustice against Blake. Seeing in a room his drawing of Chaucer's Canterbury pilgrims, he recognised that here was a promising subject not yet treated by an artist, and in order to obtain an engraving of it which would not be Blake's, he commis-

---

[14] J. Bronowski, *William Blake 1757-1827: A Man Without a Mask* (London: Secker and Warburg, 1944), p.78-79; Erdman, *Blake: Prophet* (1954), p. 291 [316-17].

[15] Erdman, *Prophet* (1954), p. 405 [436-37].

[16] David V. Erdman, *Blake: Prophet Against Empire*, 3rd ed. (Princeton: Princeton UP, 1977), pp. 316-317.

sioned a painting of the subject by the forgettable Thomas Stothard
and had it engraved by William Bromley.

In his poverty, Blake decided to appeal directly to the
public by holding an exhibition in the family shop at 28, Broad
Street, which had long been run by his elder brother James. His
printed Catalogue, with its scintillating criticism of Chaucer and
its incisive prose, delighted Charles Lamb, who visited the exhibi-
tion on the recommendation of the diarist Henry Crabb Robinson.
Robinson struck up a friendship with Blake and recorded invalu-
able specimens of his conversation. Tragically, few visitors to the
exhibition were as appreciative as Lamb, and the *Examiner*, a per-
iodical owned and edited by Leigh and John Hunt, carried an art-
icle by their brother Robert denouncing it as the work of "an
unfortunate lunatic, whose personal inoffensiveness secures him
from confinement" and describing the Catalogue as "a farrago of
nonsense, unintelligibleness, and egregious vanity, the wild effus-
ions of a distempered brain."[17]

Under the pressure of misfortune, Blake lapsed for a time
into a state of paranoia. Alluding to Leigh Hunt's editorial symbol,
a closed fist with pointing index finger, he made Hand the eldest
of the twelve malign Sons of Albion in his myth, while he resolved
to rout out the "nest of villains" in his forthcoming epic (E572/
K592); in his private notebook, he even accused Hayley, who had
generously hired the lawyer he so sorely needed, of sending
Schofield to entrap him.

During the ensuing years of poverty, Blake completed the
composition and engraving of the fifty-plate *Milton* and the hun-
dred-plate *Jerusalem*, occasionally making changes in the text or
designs and inserting new pages.[18] Unable to sell a single copy of
his longest work (the Scottish poet Allan Cunningham reports that
"this disappointment sank to the old man's heart"),[19] he made a
desperate effort to deliver his message to the public in brief form
through the pamphlet *For the Sexes: The Gates of Paradise* (*c.*
1818), the print *Laocöon* (*c.* 1820), the leaflet containing *On
Homer's Poetry* and *On Virgil* (*c.* 1820), and the miniature drama
The Ghost of Abel (1822). In 1821, just after he and his wife had

---

[17] Bentley, *Blake Records* (1969), p. 216.
[18] See E806, 809.
[19] Bentley, *Blake Records*, p. 501.

moved from South Molton Street to 3, Fountain Court, off the Strand, he found himself forced to sell his collection of prints, accumulated since boyhood, to the firm of Colnaghi.

In spite of his sufferings, Blake's last years were lightened by the friendship of a group of young artists who partly recognised his genius: well acquainted with *The Pilgrim's Progress*, they dubbed his home "The House of the Interpreter." The first of his new friends was John Linnell, whom he met in 1818; among the others, Edward Calvert, George Richmond and Samuel Palmer are especially notable for their communications to Gilchrist. To Calvert, Blake seemed "a new kind of man" and to Palmer "a man without a mask"; sixteen-year-old Richmond felt that conversing with him was like "talking to the prophet Isaiah." "I can still trace," writes Gilchrist, "something of the mystic poet's influence surviving the lapse of more than thirty years, in all who ever knew and loved Blake; as of men who once in their lives had, as it were, entertained an angel *not* unawares."[20]

To John Linnell, posterity owes Blake's last completed masterpiece, for in 1823 he commissioned the *Illustrations of The Book of Job* (1826). Later he commissioned also the magnificent illustrations to Dante's *Divine Comedy*, which remained unfinished. On 12 August, 1827, Blake died immediately after "Singing of the things he Saw in Heaven." George Richmond, who so reported in a letter written before the funeral, added, "In truth He Died like a Saint as a person who was standing by Him Observed." The person must have been the "humble female neighbour," Mrs. Blake's sole companion, who afterwards declared, "I have been at the death, not of a man, but of a blessed angel."[21]

William Blake's genius as poet and artist is now recognised, and, as Hagstrum observes, there is "testimony that Blake attained in his later years a kind of radiant sainthood."[22] It should also be remembered that he was in daily life a compassionate man with a strong feeling for human dignity. Frederick Tatham relates[23] how he once saw from his window a boy chained by his foot to a heavy log as though he were a slave. Rushing out in a fury he

---

[20] Gilchrist, *Life*, pp. 299-301.
[21] *Ibid.*, p. 353.
[22] Jean H. Hagstrum, "Christ's Body," in *WBGK*, pp. 129-56 (quotation p. 143).
[23] Mona Wilson, *The Life of William Blake* (London: Nonesuch Press, 1927), pp. 39-40

secured the boy's release, and shortly afterwards the latter's employer came to his house to berate him for intervening. Blake, however, must have made him see the justice of his objection, for after a long quarrel the two men parted on good terms.

2
Rationalism Rejected: *Poetical Sketches*; *All Religions Are One*; *There Is No Natural Religion*; *Tiriel*; *Songs of Innocence*; *The Book of Thel*

In the high Augustan period of English literature, which faded out about three decades before Blake entered his teenage years, the imaginations of the great writers had played most freely when they turned to mock forms or light-hearted modes—Swift's mock-treatise *A Tale of a Tub* and his mock-travel book playfully ascribed to Gulliver, Pope's mock-epics *The Rape of the Lock* and *The Dunciad*, and Gay's "Newgate pastoral" *The Beggar's Opera*. The readers of these satiric masterpieces, however, were also invited by lesser poets of the era to contemplate the beauty and even the violence of nature: such poems as Ambrose Philips's "A Winter-Piece," Winchilsea's "A Nocturnal Reverie," Dyer's "Grongar Hill," and Thomson's encyclopaedic sequence *The Seasons* provided a foretaste of the more romantic writings which were to nourish Blake's boyhood imagination. These include the odes of Collins and Gray, the allegedly fifteenth-century verse composed by the boy poet Chatterton, and the bogus Gaelic epics 'translated' into rhythmic prose by Macpherson, who attributed the (non-existent) originals to the bard Ossian. Deserving of mention as a group are the works of the Graveyard School with their stern moralising and 'Gothic' horror: Blair's *The Grave*, Young's *Night Thoughts*, Hervey's prose *Meditations Among the Tombs*, and—the one lasting success of the movement—Gray's "Elegy Written in a Country Church-yard." The poets of the Pre-Romantic Age—or, to adopt Frye's more judicious term, the Age of Sensibility—found non-classical poetic models in the

Authorised Version of the Old Testament, Milton's introspective "L'Allegro" and "Il Penseroso," Elizabethan lyrics delightfully free from eighteenth-century poetic diction, and the native British ballad. The collection of old ballads and lyrics alongside modern imitations in Percy's *Reliques of Ancient English Poetry* was especially popular.

The juvenilia assembled in Blake's *Poetical Sketches* are the product of a young mind saturated in but not choked by the favourite modes and styles of the Age of Sensibility. Its poets and the literature those poets delight in are among Blake's favourite reading. Moreover, as Michael Phillips has shown,[1] John Nichols, who probably printed *Poetical Sketches*, was not only an associate of James Basire, to whom Blake was apprenticed, but a member of the Unincreasable Club, where he enjoyed the companionship of such enthusiastic students of Elizabethan and Jacobean literature as Isaac Reed and Edmund Malone, both editors of Shakespeare.

Containing little that is obscure, *Poetical Sketches* does not require extensive comment. Unfortunately, critics can only conjecture the order in which its contents were written. The collection opens with four short poems on the four seasons, and as these are in blank verse they cannot but recall *The Seasons* of James Thomson—they are arranged (by Blake or another) in the same order as Thomson's poems, and the closing line of "To Winter," with its reference to Iceland's Mount Hecla, echoes line 888 of the "Winter" of the earlier writer. In his personifications, however, Blake shows an imaginative power far surpassing Thomson's and suggesting rather Collins's or even Keats's. "To the Evening Star" both echoes and rivals Collins's "Ode to Evening" with the delicate lights and shadows of its exquisite word-painting. In "To the Muses" Blake deploys eighteenth-century poetic diction as tactfully as Collins or Gray at their rare best, and "My silks and fine array" may owe something to Chatterton's "Mynstrelles Songe." He tries his hand at the melancholy of the Graveyard School in "The Couch of Death," at the ballad in the more rough-hewn "Gwin, King of Norway," and, less successfully, at Gothic horror in the quatrains of "Fair Elenor," which should have been rhymed. "Mad Song" recalls the six mad songs in Percy's *Rel-*

---

1 "William Blake and the 'Unincreasable Club': The Printing of *Poetical Sketches*," *BNYPL* LXXX (1976) 6–18.

iques. In a series of lyrics, Blake brilliantly recaptures the spirit and simplicity of Elizabethan pastoral, while in the incomplete drama "King Edward the Third" he imitates the prose and verse of Shakespeare's *Henry V.* The meditations in poetic prose that conclude the book suffer from monotony—like their prototype, Macpherson's *Ossian*; one, "Contemplation," takes up the fashion for superabundant personifications which mid-century poets adopted when, in their search for a new direction, they took "L'Allegro" and "Il Penseroso" as models for their own work.

The contents of Blake's first book show that he is not yet intellectually or morally a rebel. Like other pastoral poets, he praises rural life, and in "Fresh from the dewy hill, the merry year" he is not embarrassed to let his speaker praise the maiden purity of his beloved, in whose presence "Each field seems Eden" (E416/K9). "Blind-man's Buff" concludes by proclaiming the value of laws, and "The Couch of Death" teaches that sin must be followed by repentance. In the Prologues to the unwritten or unprinted "King Edward the Fourth" and "King John," the sin of tyranny by the powerful draws down heavenly vengeance in an Old Testament spirit. The six scenes of "King Edward the Third"—the most controversial piece in *Poetical Sketches*—show that Blake has perceived the subtle interplay of viewpoints in Shakespeare's *Henry V*; like Shakespeare, he appears to be ardently patriotic yet sensitive to the tension between the interests of rulers and ruled and between esteem for military valour and recognition that war is an atrocity. The fifth and sixth scenes end, as does "Prologue to King John," with a vision of a peaceful, happy and prosperous England. Nevertheless, if the dramatic piece was written after the quarrel with the American colonies had become a crisis, Erdman may be right in supposing that Blake planned to follow historians who saw the Black Death as a punishment for England's aggression. Unlike Shakespeare, the young poet gave no explanation of his hero's (or villain's) dynastic claim to the French throne. "Gwin, King of Norway" celebrates the bloody overthrow of a tyrant, and it, too, may reflect sympathy with the Americans.

For all the conventionality of the values expressed in *Poetical Sketches*, readers are justified in detecting there foreshadowings of the later Blake. It is a critical commonplace that the personification in "Winter" prefigures the tyrannical god Urizen, and "How sweet I roam'd from field to field" proves that the poet was early aware of the cruelty of possessiveness in love. "Samson," which draws on both the Book of Judges and Milton's *Samson Agonistes* as well as on the tradition that Samson is a type of Christ, points to Blake's later treatment of the seductive female principle, while Frye finds the germ of the sinister Blakean spectre in the speaker of "Mad Song,"[2] who is tormented even more by light than by darkness. Above all, the division between metrical verse and poetic prose adumbrates the contrast that obtains between the lyrics and the prophetic books from *Songs of Innocence* to *Jerusalem.*

After the printing of *Poetical Sketches* in 1783, it was five years before Blake again made an appearance as an author. In 1784 he wrote but left in manuscript[3] a narrative—a Menippean satire rather than a novel—making sharp fun of a variety of intellectual activities ranging from mathematics, chemistry and anatomy to antiquarianism and philosophy, both materialist (Epicurean) and idealist (Pythagorean). Moreover the reputation of a performing monkey, ladies' fashions, and common male and female weaknesses are not beneath his notice: "she was thinking of the shape of her eyes & mouth & he was thinking, of his eternal fame" (E449/ K44). Though pleasantly amusing, *An Island in the Moon* would have remained unknown had its author not become famous for other works. The characters are not crisply enough drawn for memorable caricatures, and Blake has not yet developed his distinctively pungent and incisive prose style. In view of his later loathing of natural science, literary neoclassicism, religious scepticism, and Locke's theory of knowledge, it is significant that he refers to the pioneer anatomist and embryologist John Hunter (1728-93), abuses Dr. Johnson, and introduces the name of the sceptical philosopher David Hume in his punning version of the title of Locke's great work—"An Easy of Huming Understanding" (E456/ K52). Years later he recalled the abhorrence with which he read Locke's *Essay* "when very Young" (E660/ K476). Perhaps Blake's humanity informs the song "To be or not to be," which is put into the mouth of the mathematician Obtuse Angle and which upholds the superiority of the practical philanthropist Thomas Sut-

---

[2] Northrop Frye, *Fearful Symmetry: A Study of William Blake* (1947; rpt. Boston: Beacon, 1962), p. 179.

[3] See above p. 23n4.

ton (1532-1611), founder of Charterhouse school and hospital, over Newton, Locke, and the eminent preachers Robert South (1634-1716) and William Sherlock (1641-1707), who were at loggerheads about the Trinity. (Erdman, however, emphasises the limits of Obtuse Angle's judgment: Sutton, too, may be suspect in Blake's eyes.)[4]

In the last pages of *An Island in the Moon*, the mood briefly changes while three characters sing touching songs of childhood later incorporated in *Songs of Innocence* as "Holy Thursday," "Nurse's Song" and "The Little Boy Lost." Not only was Blake continuing to write verse, he was trying his hand at a new kind of poetry. Four years, however, were to pass before he would venture on a fresh area of prose composition with sufficient confidence to publish the results. *All Religions Are One* (1788) and the two booklets both entitled *There Is No Natural Religion* (1788) consist of three series of philosophical aphorisms and are the first examples of his illuminated printing. Apart from the frontispieces and three title pages, each leaf contains one aphorism fitted in a framework of visual art.

The philosophy in the three tractates is intended to expose Locke's claim that all human knowledge (except that of one's own and one's creator's existence) is derived from perception through the five senses and by reasoning about what the senses perceive. It is also directed against the Deists' notion of natural (as opposed to revealed) religion—that is, religion which is not supernaturally bestowed but which is deduced from the existence, harmony and majesty of the created world: the evidence of our senses, runs the argument, shows us that the universe must be the work of an omnipotent, benevolent creator.

In *All Religions Are One*, Blake adopts a position congenial to the modern religious liberal. Every religion, he maintains, and all "sects" of philosophy, originate in God's revelation, but revelation is always filtered through a human consciousness, so each creed takes on an individual, human character superimposed on its divine essence (Principles 3, 5, 7). God he refers to as the "universal Poetic Genius" (Principle 4), who is present or reflected at the centre of each human being. Within each person, this divine presence or image acquires an individual face, just as each human

---

[4] *Blake: Prophet Against Empire* (Princeton: Princeton UP,1954), p. 109 [119-20].

body is unique without failing to be like all other human bodies (Principle 2). In 1788, Blake adheres to a kind of dualism: he draws a firm distinction between the Poetic Genius or "true Man" within and "the body or outward form," and holds that the Poetic Genius gives birth to the body (Principle 1); this derivation, however, implies that the body has a high status. He insists, without citing real evidence, that the Old and New Testaments can only be the product of revelation (Principle 6).

In his miniature illuminations, Blake portrays diverse forms of human and spiritual existence—such as the true Man (pl. 4), philosophers beside Greco-Roman columns (pl. 6), the Spirit of Prophecy (pl. 8 below), the man confined to sensory perception (pl. 9 below), and the Poetic Genius dazzling earthbound mortals (pl. 10 above).

Blake appears to respect the Scriptures with little reservation. The tablets of the Mosaic Law, that he was later to abominate, appear in positions of honour on the title page and the penultimate plate. Moreover the images of the Spirit moving over the waters (Gen. i.2) on pl. 10, of Eve separating from Adam's side on pl. 5, and of the Poetic Genius as Creator on pl. 4 all testify to Blake's ready acceptance of the first two chapters of Genesis with their praise of creation. Later—for example in pl. 8 of *America*—the image of the Creator on pl. 4 of this tractate has become a likeness of Urizen, the lawgiving tyrant who "created the heaven and the earth" (Gen. i.1). On the frontispiece a prophetic figure pointing with both hands directs the reader towards the title page. Beneath his feet, a phrase that St. John the Baptist applied to himself—"The Voice of one crying in the Wilderness" (Matt. iii.3; E1/K98)—reflects Blake's early sense of his own isolation in a world where all claims to inspiration are suspect.

In the two series of *There Is No Natural Religion*, Blake looks more closely at the limitations of the human mind as Locke conceives it, able to acquire knowledge only through the senses. Human beings, Locke insists, have no inborn moral sense, and insofar as they are the products of nature, Blake agrees. But the six propositions that follow reiterate how confined the consciousness of such beings would be. In fact, claim the seven propositions of the second series, the human spirit is more than nature's offspring, for it has impulses that do not arise from sense experience and that make it long for the infinite. The implication is that the

"Education" from which, the two men agree, moral concepts derive, involves experience attained through the "Poetic or Prophetic character," which transcends perception through the five senses. Blake's aphorisms introduce two of his important terms: the mill (i.e. factory) full of machinery is an emblem both of the oppression of the Industrial Revolution and of the mechanical cosmos of Newton's followers; the ratio is the restricted knowledge of a severely limited consciousness tyrannised over by reason—in the eighteenth century the predominant ratio is the world-view of the Lockean materialist—he knows only of what is perceptible to the senses and what can be rationally deduced from this. The Conclusion, like the fourth proposition, emphasises that the universe of such a person, however vast, is finite and must therefore ultimately become wearisome. In an Application, Blake contrasts the artist, "who sees the Infinite in all things," with the rationalist, who sees only the outward appearances that can be measured (the man in the accompanying drawing is handling a pair of compasses), and the final, Christian sentence explains the Incarnation as God's coming to free humanity from the tyranny of false perception.

The common title page of the two series—resplendent, despite its tiny size, with mediaeval tracery, sculpture and pinnacles—celebrates Gothic architecture, which Blake already regards as an expression of true vision. The first frontispiece represents the natural mind by a clothed elderly couple and the inspired mind by two naked youths; the second portrays a prophetic figure raising the natural man from the ground before two trefoil Gothic arches. In the other designs there are similar contrasts between self-imprisoned and aspiring figures, and in the first series soaring birds and climbing vines symbolise the spirit that transcends the senses.

Evidence of Blake's views at this time is found in approving notes he scribbled delightedly on the unbound pages of his friend Fuseli's translation of the Swiss physiognomist Lavater's *Aphorisms on Man*, probably as it came hot off the press in mid-1788.[5] Blake opposes the scientist's "Philosophy of Causes & Consequences" (E601/ K88) and takes an anti-materialist view of his own species, for "human nature is the image of God" (E597/ K83). Indeed, he sees only two alternatives—the second, the Lockeans',

---

[5] Richard J. Schroyer, "The 1788 Publication Date of Lavater's Aphorisms on Man," *BIQ*, 11 (Summer 1977), 23-26.

quite unthinkable: "man is either the ark of God or a phantom of the earth & of the water" (E596/ K82). God Himself is everywhere present and everywhere loving; He "is in the lowest effects as well as in the highest causes for he is become a worm that he may nourish the weak" (E599/ K87), and He constitutes the hidden souls of all things, for "every thing on earth...in its essence is God" (*ibid.*). For all his emphasis on love and sweetness, Blake shows for the first time a sign of revolutionary fervour. Insisting that real vice is negative, he refers with some scorn to "what the laws of Kings & Priests have call'd Vice" (E601/ K88), and, while he endorses the sixth and eighth commandments, expresses doubt about at least one, the seventh:

> Murder is Hindering Another.
> Theft is Hindering Another....
> But the origin of this mistake in Lavater & his
> cotemporaries, is, They suppose that Woman's
> Love is Sin.
> (E601/ K88)

(Neither Testament, however, brands sexual love as in itself sinful.) Blake also rejects literal belief in everlasting punishment, for "hell is the being shut up in the possession of corporeal desires" (E590/ K74). Late in life, he expresses a similar view in the Preface to the fourth chapter of *Jerusalem*: "What are the Pains of Hell but Ignorance, Bodily Lust, Idleness & devastation of the things of the Spirit [?]" (E232/ K717).When he annotates Lavater, he already abhors idleness (E594/ K79) as he continues to for the rest of his life.

About 1789, Blake took his first recorded steps towards the creation of a mythology and began to engrave his earliest poetical illuminated volumes, *The Book of Thel* and *Songs of Innocence*, both of which show the influence of Swedenborg. Contemporary with these is the verse narrative *Tiriel*, which has several of the characteristics though few of the virtues of the later prophetic books.

Blake must have been dissatisfied with this grotesque poem since he left it unpublished, though he prepared twelve illustrations of the narrative. Written in loose heptameters, *Tiriel* presents heroic characters and action and is punctuated by rhetorical speeches. The echoes of Sophocles' *Oedipus at Colonus* and Shakespeare's *King Lear*, together with the names, drawn from such sources as the Bible, Norse mythology and Cornelius Agrippa's *Occult Philosophy* show how Blake is already drawing together elements from diverse places to create his myths. The poem's main literary interest lies in the poem's gradual disclosure of past events and of the relationships between the characters.

The blind monarch Tiriel, a literary descendant of Winter and of Gwin in *Poetical Sketches*, is a Lear more sinning than sinned against. Like his prototype, he calls on the forces of nature to avenge him against his children; his "Serpents not sons" (1:21) echoes Lear's "Tigers, not daughters" (IV.ii.40). In Tiriel's case, his children have risen against his tyranny, and his youngest daughter, Hela—his Cordelia—who leads him in his blindness, denounces him as an "accursed man of sin" (6:13). His brother Zazel, whom he has chained, and his brother Ijim, who sees him as an evil force taking, Proteus-like, many forms, likewise abhor him. The narrative relates Tiriel's two journeys to his lost palace in the West and his two journeys to the vales of Har. It slowly becomes apparent that all the other characters but Mnetha are descendants of the ancient Har and Heva, who live under Mnetha's care. This Adam and Eve (Heva is the Latin form of Eve) have become old without outgrowing childhood, so that their innocence has decayed into feebleness, and Mnetha acts as their nursemaid. Her name suggests that she is related to Mnemosyne, the Greek goddess Memory, mother of the Muses, and appropriately Har stands allegorically for decadent poetry—he sings "in the great cage" of the heroic couplet (3:21), while Heva probably represents degenerate painting. Another fairly clear allegorical element is Tiriel's killing of his four daughters—four of his senses—and his hideous transformation of the youngest by turning her hair into serpents. She is touch, the sexual sense, cursed by this moralist, but freed from her affliction at his death as the last illustration shows.

In the concluding twenty-five lines of the poem, which are probably a late addition and which constitute by far its finest passage, Tiriel's understanding is awakened. He recognises that humanity is in a fallen condition, "bound beneath the heavens in a reptile form,/ A worm of sixty winters creeping on the dusky ground," where "one law," a universal moral code, is "given to the

lion & the patient Ox" and the father "scourges off all youthful
fancies from the newborn man"; this, he realises, is why he him-
self degenerated and became "subtil as a serpent in a paradise"
(8:8-24).

Tiriel shows no clear sign of Blake's growing interest in
the teachings of Emanuel Swedenborg. It is uncertain whether the
poet first began to read this sage in 1787, 1788 or 1789,[6] but by
April of 1789 he was sufficiently enthusiastic to attend the first
General Conference of his London followers and to sign a state-
ment acknowledging the divine origin of the doctrines contained
in his writings including his endorsement of the Ten Command-
ments. Emanuel Swedenborg (1688-1772) was a brilliant Swedish
inventor and scientist, who made important discoveries in astron-
omy, mineralogy and the study of the brain. In middle age he had
many visitations—sometimes while in a state of trance, sometimes
while in full possession of his faculties—visitations in which, he
believed, he conversed with angels and devils and travelled in the
spirit to distant planets and Heaven and Hell. God, he was per-
suaded, had commissioned him to bring the Christians of his time
back to an awareness of the spiritual realities transcending the
material world and of the spiritual sense underlying the literal
meaning of Scripture. As committed as Dr. Johnson to the combin-
ation of religion and reason, he insisted that ignorant acceptance
of the surface meaning of the Bible led to belief in such absurdities
as bodily resurrection, which drove thinking people into scepti-
cism. He broke off his scientific career to write voluminously, and,
aided by his modest demeanour and by the obvious power of his
intellect, he acquired an extensive following in Europe and Amer-
ica among those dissatisfied with a Christianity cut off from the
depths of spiritual experience by a narrowly conceived rationalism.
He acquired followers of some intellectual standing including
Blake's friend the artist John Flaxman; Coleridge spoke in his
Table Talk (1 Sep. 1832) of Swedenborg's having a great mind,
and Emerson in his Representative Men referred to him as a "col-
ossal soul."

Swedenborg drew a sharp distinction between body and
soul, and between the spiritual and natural worlds. He grieved that
modern humanity could think only in the natural terms (congeneal

---

6 Erdman, op. cit., 1954, p. 125 [139].

to Locke and the scientists) of time, space, and cause and effect, and not in the spiritual terms (employed by angels) of degree and state.

According to Swedenborg, three worlds emanate successively from the invisible God, who manifests Himself as Christ, the Divine Humanity. The first is the inner or celestial heaven; the second is the outer or spiritual heaven; and the third and furthest is the inert natural world, where space and time are fixed and measurable. Here vegetable and animal life can arise only as a result of divine influx. The relationship between higher and lower is one of correspondence: everything on a lower plane has its counterpart on a higher plane, and this counterpart is its cause. Thus heat corresponds to love and light to wisdom, and as wisdom unaccompanied by love does not issue in virtuous action, so winter sunlight, unaccompanied by heat, does not nurture vegetable growth. Every spirit descends to live the life of nature on one of the planets before it becomes an angel or a damned soul.

Everything in the natural and spiritual worlds is characterised by continuous and discrete degrees. Continuous degrees, like those between light and shade or heat and cold, are gradations without clear borders; discrete degrees are sharply divided categories, usually arranged in such triads as natural, spiritual and celestial, of which the third is nearest to God and the first most nearly confined to the outworks. A human is born a natural being, in whom only the natural degree is open, but acquisition of love of one's neighbour opens the second degree and that of love of God opens the third. To rise to these planes, one must absorb love and wisdom, the primal divine qualities, which radiate from God through the three worlds. The more one absorbs them, the more human one becomes, for humanness is not the quality of the natural creature but of the Creator. For Swedenborg, the human form has a special sacredness since it is the outward form of such qualities as love, mercy, goodness and truth; it is the shape of each society of angels, and it is the shape of the totality of Heaven, which these societies constitute.

The angels are free from the delusions of materialism. They understand the Scriptures in the spiritual sense and think in terms of degrees and states. When they appear to change their position in space and time, the change really takes place in their inner state. It was, Swedenborg conceived, by a change in his own inner state, that he was able to visit distant parts of the universe as well as Heaven and Hell.

To convey his message, Swedenborg wrote an immense commentary, *Arcana Coelestia*, on Genesis and Exodus. Subsequently he extracted his main doctrines and published them in shorter works. Blake read and annotated English translations of the Latin originals of some of these. In his notes in *The Wisdom of Angels, concerning Divine Love and Divine Wisdom*, probably written in 1789, the poet shows himself an enthusiastic but critical reader, though it is not clear how far his argument is with Swedenborg himself as opposed to his followers "in the society" (E608/ K96). He endorses Swedenborg's stress on the humanness of God, on humanity's relationship to the three degrees, and on the importance of freeing one's thought from the conceptions of time and space. However, he sharpens the mystic's contrast between nature and the higher world and loudly protests at any tendency to look on the human mortal as a fallen, helpless, degraded creature. To Blake, "meer Nature" is not just the inert outwork or "Ultimate" of creation, it is "Hell" (E605/ K93); like the Neoplatonists, who hold that the material world visible to the senses is a mirage, a shadowy imitation of the real or "intelligible" world perceptible to pure intellect, he declares, "the dead [i.e. material] Sun is only a phantasy of evil Man" (E605/ K92) and "the Natural Earth & Atmosphere is a Phantasy" (E607/ K94). While the natural person cannot comprehend the divine, all will receive influxes through the spiritual and celestial degrees unless they "destroy" or "close" them in themselves (E605/ K93); even the natural love in a human being "was not created impure & is not naturally so" (E608/ K96), though it can be either corrupted or elevated.

On one point Blake flatly contradicts Swedenborg and in doing so expounds his conception of God as the universal essence underlying and giving rise to all particular identities. Replying to Swedenborg's argument against polytheism, the poet denies that Essence and Identity are synonymous, for "from one Essence may proceed many Identities as from one Affection may proceed many thoughts." The one Essence is God—"That there is but one Omnipotent Uncreate & God I agree"—and the many Identities are the products of creation, which, whatever Swedenborg may say, partake of the infinite, "for if all but God is not Infinite they shall come to an End which God forbid" (E604/ K91). Here Blake enunciates in abstract terms his conception of the Deity, a conception he never departs from though he elaborates it.

Blake was already engaged with Swedenborg's teaching when he employed his invention of illuminated printing to make his first appearance before the public as master of two arts. Both *Songs of Innocence* and *The Book of Thel* bear the date 1789. (Blake inscribed on a title page the year when he began to engrave the book rather than the date of its completion.) In *Songs of Innocence*, his art of illumination has already reached a magnificent maturity. The drawings and decorations, ranging in size from the full-page frontispiece to minute figures between lines and inside letters, immeasurably enrich both the beauty and the meaning of the volume. Every time that Blake painted one of his illuminated books, he gave it a scheme of colouring peculiar to itself, but in the case of *Songs of Innocence* each copy issued independently of *Songs of Experience* is also unique in the arrangement of its plates. (Plate numbers cited here are those of Copy Z of the composite book, which are the numbers employed in Erdman's *The Illuminated Blake*.)

In 1715 Isaac Watts, a Nonconformist clergyman, who, according to Johnson's *Lives of the Poets*, "taught the Dissenters to court attention by the graces of language," published his *Divine Songs Attempted in Easy Language for the Use of Children*. He headed the second part of the collection "A Slight Specimen of Moral Songs, Such as I wish some happy and condescending Genius would undertake for the Use of Children, and perform much better." This modest profession may have stimulated Blake to produce his *Songs of Innocence*.

The three starting points of the poet's conception of Innocence are the mind of the young and happy child, the pastoral tradition, and the consciousness of Adam and Eve before their fall. This last component is evident from the title page with its tell-tale apple tree embraced by a serpent-like vine. As Blake conceives them, happy children know they are loved and cherished by the adult world, they share their joys with animals and plants, and they trust that God and His angels are guarding earth and heaven. They have as yet no sharp consciousness of themselves as distinct individuals separated by clear boundaries from other people and from nature. Yet Innocence is a state that adults, too, can participate in—witness the speaker of "Nurse's Song." The simple faith of childhood, however, is reflected in Blake's language, free—save for the "painted birds" of "Laughing Song"—from eighteenth-century poetic diction. However, the poetry, with its variety of verse forms more reminiscent of the metaphysical poets than of the Augustans, is subtler than it seems. It ranges, moreover, from the melodious murmur of "A Cradle Song" to the chant of "Holy Thursday" and the flowing quatrains of "The Little Black Boy." There is a wide variety of juvenile and adult speakers such as a boy lost in a marsh, a chimney sweeper's apprentice, a nursemaid, and a shepherd poet. Sometimes the author creates a speaker who quotes a third person, and one piece—"Infant Joy"—is a duologue. As the reader progresses, words and pictures transmute a familiar world of trees, flowers, sheep, newborn babies, village greens, and child chimney sweepers into the world of Innocence, where the natural, the human and the supernatural easily mingle. To evoke such a world, Blake draws on the pastoral tradition with its double root in the Classics and the Bible. In text and designs we encounter shepherds and sheep, cottages, rivers, animal and vegetable life. "Spring" presents birds, children and flute as contributors to one harmony, while the woods, stream, hill and meadows of "Laughing Song" share the happiness of the girls, song birds and insects. The flower of "The Blossom" is a matron-like figure inhabited by spirits of joy and cherishing both the merry and the sad. The shepherd piper, that familiar symbol of the poet going back to the *Idylls* of Theocritus and the *Eclogues* of Virgil, blends into the divine shepherd of the twenty-third Psalm and Christ, the Good Shepherd (John x.14); the lamb that he cares for is both a real animal and Christ, the Lamb of God (John i.29). The child's awareness of Christ pervades the book. In "The Little Girl Lost" he is the "maker meek," and the infant in "The Lamb" asks, "Little Lamb who made thee[?]" and rejoices that

> I a child & thou a lamb,
> We are called by his name.

In "On Another's Sorrow," the line "He becomes an infant small" is followed by "He becomes a man of woe" alluding to Isaiah's prophecy that the Messiah would be "a man of sorrows" (liii.3). The lion of "Night," translated to heaven, attributes the welfare of all there to his "meekness" and "health." Moreover, from the title page onwards, Christ appears symbolically in plate after plate as "the true vine" of John xv.1 wound round tree trunks and saplings and sometimes bearing grapes. (Years later Blake twice alludes to the biblical passage [E536, 555/ K571, 606]). Yet Blake's outlook is not narrowly sectarian, and in "The Divine Image" he rebuts the crude claim of Isaac Watts's "Praise for the Gospel"—

> Lord, I ascribe it to thy Grace,
> And not to chance, as others do,
> That I was born of Christian race
> And not a Heathen, or a Jew

—in his nobler declaration of faith:

> And all must love the human form,
> In heathen, turk or jew.
> Where Mercy, Love & Pity dwell,
> There God is dwelling too.

Other recurring visual images besides the vine contribute to the depiction of a blessed state. On several pages two tree trunks harmoniously embrace or intertwine. The sheltering, umbrella-shaped oak (not a sinister Druidic tree) of "The Ecchoing Green" reappears in "The Lamb" and "Laughing Song," and lily-like flowers in plates 5, 10 and 18 speak as clearly as the vine of divine graciousness. The letters of titles streaming out into foliage reinforce the impression of gentle fertility made everywhere by curling tendrils. In "The Blossom," "A Divine Image" and "Infant Joy," leaves or petals can also be flames—but the fire is creative, not devouring. The ascending bird of paradise that speaks of a heavenly presence as it blazes in the sky of "The Shepherd" has many counterparts elsewhere, counterparts that are no less significant if they are birds of different species like the eagle above the first line of "A Dream" or minute like the creature beside the fifth line of "The Little Black Boy."[7]

---

[7] Cf. David V. Erdman, ed., *The Illuminated Blake* (New York: Anchor Press/ Doubleday, 1974), pp. 19-20.

After 1794, when Blake expanded his book by adding *Songs of Experience,* he usually transferred "The Little Girl Lost" and "The Little Girl Found" to the latter; often he moved "The School Boy" along with them and sometimes also "The Voice of the Ancient Bard." Although *Songs of Innocence* celebrates joy and "happy" is one of its key words, the collection is not without its shadows, even when it has lost the four poems mentioned. Three of the lyrics deal with current abuses. In the apparently serene "Holy Thursday," the severely rectilinear letters of the title, the division between the boys above and the girls below, and the semi-military regularity of the procession are tell-tale signs that Blake is assailing regimentation. Only the children at some little distance behind the beadles or matron dare to converse, yet with their innocence the children have a "radiance all their own" and a spiritual might denied to their guardians. In a similar ironical spirit, Blake makes the final line of "The Chimney Sweeper" a statement of what the children's master wants them to believe: "So if all do their duty, they need not fear harm." The reader is left to ponder whether "all" includes those whose "duty" is clearly unfulfilled when tiny children are sold to men who make them live in soot and force them up chimneys where they may be maimed or killed. In Blake's poem, which enchanted Charles Lamb, another supporter of the climbing boys, the father sells his child to a master sweep leaving him to find his only real father in heaven. "The Little Black Boy," which portrays the psychology of the oppressed, was potentially a contribution to the work of the Society for Effecting the Abolition of the Slave Trade, founded in 1787. "The School-Boy" introduces pupils bullied by a teacher, and the young people in "The Voice of the Ancient Bard" are subject to leaders blinded by rationalism and tradition. On the natural level, there are evening dews in "Nurse's Song," a lost ant in "A Dream," and carnivorous beasts in "Night."

Blake does not forget that for Christians evil in society and in nature is the result of the Fall. The apple tree on the title page and the vine around it, serpentine enough to suggest the presence of the tempter as well as of Christ, hint that the book takes us into an Eden that will not last for ever.

Despite the presence of suffering or injustice, consciousness of a transcendent beneficence, natural or supernatural, can keep the oppressed in the state of Innocence. This beneficence

oversees the happy outcome of the pilgrimage glimpsed in
"Night," where the lion, having "wash'd in life's river," can lie or
graze beside the lamb in the "immortal day" of heaven that they
share—an echo of Isaiah's prophecy (xi.6-7). A fuller explanation
of the way from the Innocence of the infant mind to what emerges
as the higher Innocence of the mature soul is given in "The Little
Black Boy," where the child's mother tells him

>   we are put on earth a little space,
>   That we may learn to bear the beams of love,

before the body vanishes allowing the soul to live like a lamb with
God, its shepherd. Meanwhile the cloud or "shady grove" of the
body protects us from too much exposure to the beams from the
sun, where

>   God does live
>   And gives his light, and gives his heat away.

But the poem has another dimension, for the boy and his mother
seek consolation in this doctrine for the inferior status that humil-
iates and enslaves them in this world. As in *All Religions Are One*,
Blake takes a dualistic view of body and soul, but does not reject
the body. Indeed, "Infant Joy" may celebrate the event of birth, for
the design shows mother, babe and spirit perched inside a womb-
like flower. Similarly in "The Blossom," the spirits in tongues of
flame-like vegetation may represent a life cycle in which courtship
and amorous embrace are followed by giving birth, infancy, and
the education that endows the soul with wings.

The most enigmatic poems in *Songs of Innocence* concern
the soul's pilgrimage. "The Little Girl Lost" opens with two pre-
liminary quatrains alluding to Isaiah's prediction that "the desert
shall...blossom as the rose" (xxxv.1); the soaring bird of paradise
beside these stanzas confirms their message, but the threatening
snake underneath shows that evil times must precede the proph-
ecy's fulfilment. The narrative begins with seven-year-old Lyca in
a paradise of sunshine and song birds which abruptly turns into a
"desert wild." A young soul ready to accept entry into the world of
darkness, she invokes moonlight and sleep, and her Innocence

makes harmless the carnivores who disrobe her and carry her
down to their underworld. However, the prospect of her misguided
parents' distress has troubled her, and in "The Little Girl Found"
they scour the desert tortured by false dreams of their starving
child but devoted to each other. Eventually a terrifying lion over-
throws their unbelief with his gentleness, and this kingly "vision"
leads them to his palace, where they live happily near their daugh-
ter, though it is not stated that she wakes.

     The illuminations tell a somewhat different story from the
poem. At the beginning adolescent lovers embracing under the
willows and tendrils of pastoral Innocence show that safe passage
through Experience will require the acceptance of sexual love. On
the second page, the movement from a leafy wood to an almost
barren tree illustrates the contrast between what is seen by illumi-
nated and by unilluminated vision. Finally, the image of children
playing with lions alludes, like "Night," to the prophecy of Isaiah
xi and obscurely signifies that imaginative vision removes fear by
showing how God provides a way through Experience.

     The Christianity that gives life to the joyous pastoral of
Songs of Innocence has affinities with the Christianity of Sweden-
borg. The image in "The Little Black Boy" of God sending out His
heat and light is Swedenborgian, and the lesson that souls are em-
bodied to learn to bear His love recalls Section 525 of *Heaven and
Hell*, in which Swedenborg tells how spirits who enter heaven
unprepared flee in torment from the Divine heat and light, which
are love and wisdom. The release of the children from black
coffins in "The Chimney Sweeper" echoes Swedenborg's account
in Section 79 of *The Earths in the Universe* of spirits on Jupiter
who appear like chimney sweepers but in heaven exchange their
black garb for angelic garments. Most fundamentally, the
humanness of God in "The Divine Image" is close to the spirit of
Swedenborg. In their inmost essence, identical with "the true
Man" of *All Religions Are One*, human beings share God's
attributes:

> For Mercy Pity Peace and Love,
> Is God our father dear:
> And Mercy Pity Peace and Love,
> Is Man his child and care.

While Blake's concept of Innocence has its seed in the infant mind, it has come to signify an intense consciousness of heavenly good and a dim consciousness of the earthly evil that this good thwarts. Such a consciousness enables one to survive for a time oppression and hardship, like that of the apprentice sweep or the lost girl, with faith in God, nature and humankind untainted. The young, however, who stay too long in Innocence decay into the premature senility of Har and Heva in *Tiriel*. By passing through Experience—a full awareness of suffering, especially suffering inflicted by humans—one can reach the mature Innocence that fully recognises pain and injustice but sees, transcending them, God's provision for turning evil ultimately to good.

Songs of Innocence, the happiest of Blake's illuminated books, is contemporary with another that exhibits in its designs and text the same pastoral imagery of trees, flowers, birds, and shepherding. The title page of *The Book of Thel* has a marked resemblance to the first plate of "The Little Girl Lost," and *Thel* reworks much of the subject matter of that poem and its sequel but is superior to them in clarity, beauty, and coherence. Thel is a young girl who, unlike Lyca, cannot nerve herself to leave Innocence for the necessary passage through adulthood and Experience; she is also a soul who retreats from the prospect of birth into a mortal body—this is synonymous, according to the Neoplatonic symbolism employed, with death from the happier prenatal world. Fearful of losing her beauty and her identity, she hopes that her death or change of state will at least be gentle. Her successive conversations with a Lily of the Valley, a Cloud, and a Clod of Clay do not give her the strength to endure what she encounters when she accepts the Clay's invitation to enter her house, which is the world of the flesh and of Experience. At this point the prevailing atmosphere of sweet and delicate melancholy abruptly changes to claustrophobic horror; the pleasant ripple of the preceding verse is overpowered by a raging torrent, and Thel flees back to clutch her former Innocence.

While Blake's earlier narrative poem *Tiriel*, written in the same loose measure, reflects a variety of influences, *Thel* shows Blake creatively synthesising, in a way that is to become characteristic of him, materials and concepts from sources as diverse as the Bible, Spenser's *The Faerie Queene*, Young's *Night Thoughts*, the ancient Neoplatonist philosopher Porphyry, the

Renaissance occultist Cornelius Agrippa, Emanuel Swedenborg, and Erasmus Darwin's *The Loves of the Plants* (1789)—this last being an illustrated poem in heroic couplets about vegetable sexuality.

Before the narrative begins, Thel's Motto poses two questions: one concerns the realms of the sky and the underworld, the other love and wisdom, which according to Swedenborg proceed from God and pervade all creation.

> Does the Eagle know what is in the pit?
> Or wilt thou go ask the Mole:
> Can Wisdom be put in a silver rod?
> Or Love in a golden bowl?

Thel and her sisters are shepherdesses in the Vales of Har, which are identified with the skyey realm, for Thel is a "virgin of the skies" (3:25). Blake equates the luminous and fertile Vales both with the biblical Eden (for it is a garden where God walks [1:14; cf. Gen. iii.8]) and with Spenser's Garden of Adonis (*FQ* III.vi); the latter, which is paradisal but subject to the ravages of time, is inhabited by souls awaiting birth. The name Adonis is turned into the feminine form Adona to be applied to the river that Thel lingers beside. The porter at the gates of Spenser's Garden appears in the first line of Blake's sixth plate. Here he governs "the northern bar," a version of the Neoplatonic northern entrance through which souls descend to assume mortal bodies in Porphyry's *The Cave of the Nymphs*, an allegorical interpretation of a passage in Book 13 of Homer's *Odyssey*.

The Lily, Cloud and Clay who attempt to console Thel enjoy the vision of Innocence, which assures them that God lovingly oversees that when they perish bodily they pass on to a richer existence in "heaven" or "eternal vales," a place of "tenfold life" (1:19, 25; 3:11)—which, however, the poet makes no attempt to describe: it is an object of faith, not of perception. The Clay, living in Innocence in the Vales of Har, is able to contemplate with equanimity the underworld she contains, confident that individuals can pass through it unharmed: "'tis given thee," she promises Thel, "to enter,/ And to return" (5:16-17). But Thel lacks the vision of the full cycle from Innocence through Experience to renewed life and does not learn from her consecutive encounters with the virgin Lily, the bridal Dew, and the matron Clay to accept the normal stages of corporeal womanhood. Given a preview of Experience, she can see in the Clay's house only the horror of a life dominated by perception through the five fleshly senses. Here, the voice of her future self complains from the grave of her body, one's hearing and sight are assailed by slander and hypocritical smiles, one's tongue and ear become voracious, and one's nostrils distend with fear. Using images from Renaissance poetry about the pains of love, the voice asks why these familiar miseries of Experience should be, and when it speaks of touch, the sexual sense, it asks why society imposes a "curb" of frustration on the youth and why the "curtain" of a finite body constricts and torments the imprisoned libido. Thel can detect only suffering in the lower world, where each has his or her "pit" (6:10), and the degradation of life in a physical body. The sixth plate, which expresses the agony of Experience, may be a late addition replacing a lost plate in a different mood dating from 1789.

One of Swedenborg's central doctrines, expressed in Sections 220, 296-97 and 307-08 of *Divine Love and Divine Wisdom*, which Blake annotated about this time, is that all created things and beings exist for the sake of service to others or "uses," and it is incumbent on human beings that their love, supported by their wisdom, issue in such "uses."

Thel, however, contrasts with the Lily, who goes "to mind her numerous charge" (2:18), in that she is a shepherdess who deserts her sheep and then complains that she lives "without a use" (1:1-2; 3:22). Already she has a glimmering of what the Cloud tries to teach her—"every thing that lives,/ Lives not alone, nor for itself" (3:26-27)—but she cannot see that to be after death "the food of worms" (3:23) is, as the Cloud insists, to be of great service. While the Clod of Clay lives by her faith—"But how this is, sweet maid, I know not, and I cannot know" (5:5)—Thel reasons. Her timorous questions about her passing away reflect a lack of faith in the God of the Old Testament, who clothes the Lily with light and feeds her with manna, and loves the lowly Clod of Clay and anoints her with oil, or she would know that He also rescues the afflicted soul from its pit in the underworld (1:23—cf. Job xxv.3, Exod. xvi; 5:1—cf. Ps. cxxxviii.6, xxiii.5; 6:10—cf. Job xxxiii.29-30). Along with lack of faith, Thel is guilty of recoiling from the sexuality of the mortal body, which, for Blake, is one of the channels by which corporeal man can commune with Eternity. Self-surrender in sexual union he here equates with the self-sacrifice in the service of others that the Lily and the Cloud commend to Thel in vain. She will not give herself to nourish another.

The designs do much to emphasise Thel's failings. On the title page, she is a shepherdess observing a male advancing amorously to a somewhat alarmed female, while soaring birds and tiny climbing figures silently proclaim that sexual love can lead heavenwards. After Thel abandons her relaxed pose on pl. 2 to express compassion for another—the Worm—on plates 4 and 5, she vanishes from the designs. On pl. 6, instead of her flight, Blake has engraved three small children riding a large serpent controlled by a bridle. Rejecting faith in God, service to others and sexual love, Thel recoils from the terrors of Experience, which they could have enabled her to endure and which for her are unillumined by any surviving light of Innocence.

In childhood and youth, Blake wrote highly accomplished poems in modes and genres popular in the Age of Sensibility. As an engraver, artist and printseller at the beginning of what looked like a prosperous career, he turned his hand to ribald prose satire. At about the age of thirty he discovered in Swedenborg a powerful ally against the earthbound philosophy of Locke, and a year or two later the poet who had been something of a child wonder at last found vehicles of expression for his genius. Using his technique of illuminated printing to become his own publisher, he created a children's book in which poetry and painting were fused into one art and a 'prophetic book' which brought together the sublimity and pathos so highly valued in the age of Gray and Cowper. He was soon to evolve a prose that would bite like his engraver's acid. *Songs of Innocence* was his first great book; *The Marriage of Heaven and Hell* was to be his second.

3

In Praise of Energy: *The French Revolution; The Marriage of Heaven and Hell*

During the eighteenth century, English travellers in France had recognised a society rapidly approaching a point of no return. "The King," wrote Lord Chesterfield to his son on Christmas Day, 1753,

> is despised and I do not wonder at it; but he has brought it about to be hated at the same time....The people are poor, consequently discontented....The clergy never do forgive; much less will they forgive the parliament; the parliament never will forgive them....The French nation reasons freely, which they never did before, upon matters of religion and government...in short, all the symptoms, which I have ever met with in history previous to great changes and revolutions in government, now exist, and daily increase, in France.

In 1765, during the same King's reign, Smollett describes in the thirty-sixth letter of his *Travels Through France and Italy*, the mismanagement of the French finances and the officials' plundering of the people:

> There is at present a violent fermentation of different principles among them, which, under the reign of a very weak prince...may produce a great change in the constitution. In proportion to the progress of reason and philosophy, which have made great advances in this kingdom, superstition loses ground; ancient prejudices give way: a spirit of freedom takes the ascendant.

In the summer of 1789 Louis XVI, who had been on the throne for fifteen years, was nearly bankrupt and in despair, he summoned the States-General (the French Parliament). When the process of constitutional change began that summer, and the Paris mob captured the Bastille, the symbol of arbitrary imprisonment, liberals and radicals in Britain looked on with high hopes for the spread of liberty. "Shall France alone," exclaimed the young Coleridge in "Destruction of the Bastille," "a Despot spurn?" As the royal family were imprisoned in the Tuileries, and the Assembly made free with the property of the Church, British opinion became sharply divided, and the statesman Edmund Burke led the opposition, warning in his *Reflections on the Revolution in France* (1790) that sound constitutions were of slow growth and accurately prophesying the emergence of a dictatorship. In *The Rights of Man* (1791), Thomas Paine replied to Burke pointing to the example of America and advocating representative government, but the British authorities, alarmed by the multiplication of societies sympathetic to the Revolution across the Channel, moved within months to suppress the book.

The excitement generated among those who saw the Revolution as a joyful turning point in human history is recorded in Wordsworth's recollection of his feelings as he landed at Calais in July 1790:

> ...'twas a time when Europe was rejoiced,
> France standing on the top of golden hours,
> And human nature seeming born again.
> (*The Prelude* [1850], VI, 352-54)

Biographical tradition[1] confirms the evidence in his own works that the fall of the Bastille and the waxing power of the French commoners kindled Blake's revolutionary enthusiasm; in spite of checks, it was to burn for sixteen years. The first known literary product of his zeal is a poem in unrhymed anapaestic heptameters on political events in France during the June and July of 1789. It survives in a single proof copy printed for Joseph Johnson,

---

[1]Alexander Gilchrist, *Life of William Blake*, ed. Ruthven Todd, rev. (London: Dent; New York: Dutton, 1945), pp.80-81.

who drew back at the last minute from issuing Volume I of Paine's *The Rights of Man*. The proof of Blake's work is dated 1791, and it bears an Advertisement stating,"The remaining Books of this Poem are finished, and will be published in their Order" (E286/ K134). Whether the other books were in fact written there is no means of knowing, but the extant portion was withdrawn before publication, presumably because either Johnson or Blake feared prosecution for sedition.

The matter and manner of Blake's poem *The French Revolution* foreshadow much that is to come in his prophetic books. Defending republicanism, flaying militarism and praising energy, it holds up an image of semi-pastoral simplicity adorned by the arts of peace, a state which once existed, for the dawn marking its return will be "ancient" (l. 7). An uneven poem that has been lauded or damned as critics have concentrated on its merits or defects, its style ranges from the repetitious and obscurely abstract to the concrete and precise. Most of the best writing is found in the speeches, especially the noble pleas of the Duke of Orleans and the Abbé de Sieyès.

The poem portrays the tussle for power in June and July 1789 between Louis XVI's reactionary counsellors and the new National Assembly; it ends with the withdrawal of the army, at the Assembly's demand, ten miles from Paris. The reformers consist of the elected representatives of the commoners and a few liberal aristocrats and clergy, especially Count Mirabeau and the above mentioned Orleans and Sieyès. Blake takes some liberties with the facts, mainly by compressing happenings of some weeks into a single day, locating the court at Paris instead of Versailles, and inventing a Duke of Burgundy as principal spokesman for the die-hard majority of the nobles.

Mingling historical events with visions, the narrator describes on the one hand the prisoners in the Bastille, the dismissal of the reforming finance minister Necker, and the campaign for the removal of the troops; on the other hand he tells of Louis XVI angered by the ghosts of dead kings and their counsellors, the Archbishop of Paris infuriated by his vision of a lamenting God, and the army haunted by apparitions of dispossessed monks and the long dead liberal monarch Henry of Navarre. Later the Archbishop is reduced to hissing incoherence in lines that allude to Sat-

an's transformation into a serpent in *Paradise Lost*, X, 517-21 (ll.
176-78).

   According to Josephine Miles,[2] it is in *The French Revol-
ution* that Blake first displays his mature prophetic style, which is
marked by an abundance of nouns and adjectives and a paucity of
active finite verbs. The imagery of the poem is largely drawn from
nature and often has a biblical as well as an Ossianic flavour; the
excessive use of this imagery has done the book's reputation some
harm. "Behold," Jeremiah warns his people of their foe (iv.13),
"he shall come up as clouds," and Blake describes soldiers loyal to
the *ancien régime* "breathing red clouds of power and dominion"
(1.20); "As the mountains are round about Jerusalem," the Psalmist
comforts the Israelites (cxxv.2), "so the Lord is round about his
people," and Blake tells us, "The King lean'd on his mountains"
(1. 105). Unfortunately the repetition of the images and their
intermittent vagueness is reminiscent of Horace Walpole's stricture
on Macpherson's *Ossian*. In a letter to George Montagu of 8 Dec-
ember, 1761, Walpole complains, "It tires me to death to read how
many ways a warrior is like the moon, or the sun, or a rock, or a
lion, or the ocean." Yet Blake often anticipates his later practice of
making one symbol carry contrary meanings according to context.
Mountains usually represent extreme royalists, but the mountains
of lines 5 and 6—"mild" and "flourishing" when they are not
"bruise[d]," though ailing in the King's eyes—stand for the
French people. Louis XVI's armies, urges the Duke of Burgundy,
are mighty "starry hosts" (1. 100), and the existing society devel-
oped over six millenia is a "starry harvest" (1. 90), but the Duke of
Orleans compares true nobility of character to stars (1. 181), and
the Assembly's ambassador, Aumont, walks "Like the morning
star arising above the black waves, when a shipwreck'd soul sighs
for morning" (1. 255). Similarly fires of "The enormous dead" can
give new energy to the autocratic cause, while for Orleans fire,
being an expression of creative energy, "delights in its form" (ll.
302-03, 189). Indeed, Orleans himself clarifies the meaning of the
symbol when he optimistically addresses his peers as "princes of
fire, whose flames are for growth, not consuming" (1. 179).

---

[2] *Eras and Modes in English Poetry*, 2nd ed. (Berkeley and Los Angeles: U of
California P, 1964), pp. 85, 89.

A surprising number of Blake's later symbols and views are adumbrated in *The French Revolution*. The powerful and at first sight mysterious lines 211-16 describe the horror of the fall of the universe into material existence when the sun and moon became globes in the sky and human souls, shut off from Eternity, were imprisoned in bodies, bound to the worship of frightful gods, and oppressed by cruel rulers. The fallen condition of history is represented as a sleep of either five thousand (ll. 7-8) or six thousand (l. 90) years; the night of this condition is equated with dark caves (l. 218), and liberation is seen as the dawn of a new morning (ll. 7-8, 216-17)—an image that is to remain a favourite with Blake. As Orleans urges, humankind must embrace energy to hasten the dawn; in an antinomian, compassionate and egalitarian spirit, one must respect the uniqueness of each individual and not presume to prescribe rules for another since into another's consciousness one cannot enter. Anticipating Blake's *Marriage of Heaven and Hell*, the Duke seems to draw on a doctrine of Boehme and Swedenborg that Adam's lost paradise is the body,[3] for he refers to "the soul whose brain and heart/ Cast their rivers in equal tides thro' the great Paradise" (ll. 183-84). In a speech fired by Blake's anti-militarism, the Abbé de Sieyès evokes a picture of the harmonious world of villages and gardens, of arts, crafts, agriculture and human honesty that antinomianism and the liberation of energy will bring about.

Blake's hostility to powerful churches becomes apparent early in the poem, when the fourth of the Bastille's seven towers is honoured with the name "Religion"; later he credits the anticlerical spirit of the Deists Rousseau and Voltaire with the overthrow of the Church's monastic communities (ll. 274-77). He envisages that the struggle for liberty will be international, for the narrator rejoices that "Kings are sick throughout all the earth" (l. 61), while the Duke of Burgundy looks to the royal resistance to "rouze up the ancient forests [i. e. long established despotisms] of Europe" (l. 101). There are even hints that Blake already associates Newtonian science with oppression, for he links "attraction" (gravity) with the breakdown of sanity (ll. 49-50), makes the Abbé de Sieyès ask of the redeemed world "where is space!" (l. 219),

---

[3] Kathleen Raine, *Blake and Tradition*, 2 vols. (Princeton: Princeton UP, 1968), I, 337-38.

and allows Burgundy, in drawing a parallel between chaos in society and in nature, to group "eternal reason and science" with the army, the monarchy, the law and religion (ll. 94-96).

As the biblical allusions show, *The French Revolution* reflects a crisis in Blake's view of the Scriptures. No longer easy with the Old Testament God in whom Thel lacked a saving faith, he now distinguishes the lawgiver and punisher of the Pentateuch, who reappears in later books, including Jude and Revelation in the New Testament, from the true God who inspired the Psalmist and the prophets and sent Christ the Redeemer. The God of the Archbishop of Paris is the lawgiving punisher of sin of the Old Testament—the being that Blake was soon to name Urizen. A Urizenic "aged form, white as snow, hov'ring in mist, weeping" (l. 131), he appears to the Archbishop in a vision modelled on the biblical vision of Eliphaz, who graphically describes it to bolster his false assumption that his friend Job has sinned (Job iv); this deity is full of self-pity as he laments the loss of his clergy and nobles, the cessation of time-honoured rites, and the oblivion of his "holy law" (l. 139), and he seems to refer to the cloud in which the Lord manifests in the Old Testament (e. g. Exodus xvi.10) when he complains "my cloud and vision [will] be no more" (l. 143). His servant the Archbishop urges the King to seal up the rebels in the "everlasting chains" reserved for the fallen angels (Jude 6). On the other hand, Orleans, Mirabeau, the Abbé de Sieyès and the apparition of Henry of Navarre are aligned with the true God. Thus Orleans' "nor be you dismay'd with sorrows which flee at the morning" (l. 180) reiterates the promise of Psalms xxx.5, Mirabeau rises to speak with "A rushing of wings around him" (l. 260) that evokes Ezekiel's vision (iii.13), the Abbé de Sieyès is compared to "a voice of God following a storm" (l. 202) like the divine voice Elijah heard in the desert (I Kings xix.11-12) and to the morning star, to which Christ compares himself (l. 255; Rev. xxii.16), and King Henry's spirit ascends to heaven in the manner of Elijah's (ll. 200-01; II Kings ii.11).

In 1789 and 1790, support for the French Revolution was not unusual in Britain (even Burke admitted in his *Reflections* that reform was needed in France), but by July 1791 a reactionary mob could sack the house of the Birmingham scientist Joseph Priestley on account of his revolutionary sympathies and destroy his laboratory and irreplaceable manuscripts. In September 1792, the now

Republican French, facing the invading Duke of Brunswick's threat to destroy Paris if the King were not reinstated, resorted to the infamous massacres that ushered in the Reign of Terror; four months later they used the guillotine to rid themselves of Louis XVI and Marie Antoinette, whom they suspected of favouring the enemy. By now Burke's views overwhelmingly prevailed in Britain, and the French Revolution was regarded with much the same half fascinated horror as the Bolshevik Revolution a century and a quarter later. On 6 January, 1793, the historian Gibbon wrote to his friend Lord Sheffield about his prospective journey across the Continent: "I have even a sort of curiosity to spend some days at Paris, to assist at the debates of the Pandemonium, to seek an introduction to the principal devils, and to contemplate a new form of public and private life, which never existed before, and which I devoutly hope will not long continue to exist." Even those who refused to relinquish the principles of the Revolution were apt to deplore its excesses. Thomas Paine, now an honorary French citizen, was very nearly executed in Paris for arguing that the King, misled since his youth, should be exiled to the United States instead of being put to death. Charles James Fox, the leader of the small pro-Revolutionary party in the British Parliament, was as much appalled by the King's fate as by the Duke of Brunswick's campaign to destroy the Republic. According to Gilchrist's unconfirmed statement,[4] Blake was similarly infuriated by the September Massacres; more confidently, we can say that *The Book of Ahania* of 1794 shows that he was deeply anguished by Robespierre's evolution into a bloodthirsty dictator. Nevertheless, when the revolutionary Government seized control of the Netherlands and provoked Britain, despite Fox's opposition, to a declaration of war in February 1793, Blake remained firmly pro-French. He could not, however, safely express his opinions in public. While Fox was free to speak his mind till 1798, when he was expelled from the Privy Council for maintaining that sovereignty was vested in the British people, men of lower rank risked prison and transportation if they campaigned for reform.

The great work which Blake began and perhaps completed in 1790, *The Marriage of Heaven and Hell*, says little explicitly about contemporary politics except in its conclusion, "A Song of

---

[4] *Life*, p. 81.

Liberty," but it is much concerned with its author's religious views. In *The French Revolution* of 1791, Blake already combines an animus against the established authority of church and state with an anti-industrial ideal, a deep suspicion of natural science, a preoccupation with the Fall, and an antinomian Christian commitment.

During the English Revolution of the seventeenth century, there appeared among the more extreme religious radicals groups of antinomians whose influence on Blake has been capably explored by A. L. Morton.[5] These antinomians held that the entire ceremonial and moral law—including the Ten Commandments—was abrogated, that God had His existence in humankind and in all created things, and that He would reveal a hitherto unknown spiritual sense of the Bible to the hearts of men, after which external churches would be abolished. This belief in a new era of spiritual liberty descends from the twelfth-century Italian abbot Joachim of Fiore (or Flora), who taught that the Age of the Father and the Old Testament had been succeeded by the Age of the Son and the New Testament, which was about to be superseded by the Age of the Spirit and the Everlasting Gospel.

Morton has shown how closely some of the antinomians' beliefs and language anticipate Blake's and has pointed out that certain of the smaller seventeenth-century sects survived in London, especially among artisans and petty tradesmen, into Blake's lifetime. When the French Revolution erupted with its anticlerical fervour and egalitarianism, Blake had already been stirred by Swedenborg's repudiation of all existing churches and probably by his devotion to the spiritual sense of the Bible. He now seems to have embraced the central doctrines of the antinomians, most of whom had been political egalitarians or "levellers."

Despite his rejection of the churches, Swedenborg is neither a revolutionary nor an antinomian—indeed, he attaches great importance to the Ten Commandments—and Blake now begins to feel that the former scientist's rebellion against religious rationalism is half-hearted and that there is an element of the absurd in what he supposes to be his personal experiences of remote parts of the cosmos and of heaven and hell. The poet's annotations in the

---

[5] *The Everlasting Gospel: A Study in the sources of William Blake* (London: Lawrence and Wishart, 1958).

1790 edition of Swedenborg's *Wisdom of Angels Concerning the Divine Providence* accuse him of upholding priestcraft and predestination and of teaching that "Cursed Folly!" that one must purify oneself from evil. The Memorable Fancies in *The Marriage of Heaven and Hell* are engaging parodies of the Memorable Relations in *The True Christian Religion*, in which Swedenborg narrates his journeys in the spirit: Blake, indeed, has acutely spotlighted the most vulnerable area of the latter's writings. In his rejection of the sage's moralising, Blake sheds for a time his old distrust of the natural man as he adopts the quite widespread hope that the French upheaval heralds a nobler world in which humanity will construct a Utopian society.

As his faith in Swedenborg breaks down, Blake turns to an earlier thinker, the German theosophist Jakob Boehme (or Behmen), with whose work he may have been acquainted for some years (E707-08/ K799). Although Boehme (1575-1624), a meagrely educated shoemaker usually regarded as the greatest of Protestant mystics, lived before the triumph of the scientific world picture and had therefore an easier task in expounding the intellectual vision of creation that was revealed to him, he was a Lutheran who suffered harsh persecution from his pastor, Gregorius Richter. Despite the patronage of admiring noblemen, he was examined for heresy by high-ranking theologians who, however, declared that they could not condemn what they did not understand. "May God convert the man," exclaimed Dr. Meissner, "if he is in error. He is a man of marvellously high mental gifts, who at present can be neither condemned nor approved." Intellectually Boehme was Blake's equal, though he lacked both the latter's artistic genius and the eccentricity that allowed him to swallow uncritically the wild speculations of contemporary antiquarians and mythologists.

In abstruse though often moving treatises, Boehme describes how, by an intricate process involving the production of seven successive qualities or "Forms," the Trinity is generated, and so, on different levels, are Paradise, the angels, the physical universe, and the child in the womb. Through this same process, human beings, corrupted by Original Sin, can undergo a spiritual rebirth. Intensely conscious of the power of evil in this world and driven to account for it, Boehme daringly presses his vision of the sundering of the primal unity in which there was no room for evil back into the Godhead Itself, where the First Principle, the Father, divides from the Second Principle, the Son. The Father is Fire or Wrath; the Son is Light or Love. The Fire separated from the Light becomes the Flames of Hell, yet without the Fire nothing could exist. Boehme tells in a dramatic way how Lucifer in pride recoiled from the meekness of the Light which illuminated him and rose up in the First Principle, in which he is for ever locked, unable to reach the Son, whom he would destroy. After Lucifer's rebellion, God decreed the emergence of the Third Principle—nature or the material universe—from the First Principle to manifest His power and wisdom and to provide a place where humankind would be able to recover from its fall. With Adam's fall, human beings, whose souls come from the First Principle, lost the Light of the Second and became imprisoned in the Third. By holiness or repentance, they can be reborn in the Second Principle, in the Light.

Jakob Boehme was a strict and orthodox moralist, and at this stage of his life Blake's admiration for him was still limited. In *The Marriage of Heaven and Hell*, he couples him with the Renaissance occultist Paracelsus and rates both these writers far above Swedenborg but well below Dante and Shakespeare (*MHH*, pl. 22). He has no scruples about distorting what he borrows from Boehme—the opposition between the Fire of the Father and the Light of the Son. In Blake's hands these two qualities are transmuted into Energy and Reason; the former is ascribed to the whole Trinity and the latter to Satan—the real Satan, mistaken for Christ by most contemporary Christians, who falsely identify reason with good and passion with evil. The term "Marriage" points to an integration of these contraries, but though Blake recognises the necessity of the synthesis, emotionally he sides with energy and against reason just as Boehme emotionally prefers the Son to the Father.

At the top of pl. 4, the heading "The voice of the Devil" warns us that we are about to be offered the philosophy of one of the contraries—energy. Nevertheless Blake himself clearly endorses most of the philosophy of this monistic spirit, though it marks a shift in emphasis and perhaps in substance from the dualistic element in *All Religions Are One* and in the annotations to Lavater's *Aphorisms*. The body, said in the former to be "derived from the Poetic Genius" (or soul), is now said to be the "portion of Soul" (E1/ K98; *MHH*, pl. 4) perceptible to the five senses in our fallen condition and the only source of energy. Subsequent plates (especially number 14) make it clear that most of us see little but the "finite & corrupt" universe of illusion into which the human species was plunged at its expulsion from Eden, but gifted prophets like Isaiah and Ezekiel and their pagan counterparts, including Diogenes and certain American Indians, can still perceive the "infinite and holy" creation that proceeded from God (pl.14); in this creation, our bodies, too, must have been free from mortal limitations. The Devil's position is not materialist—he says that we have no body distinct from soul, not no soul distinct from body—and Blake is not afraid to attribute to Leviathan, a symbol of revolution, "all the fury of a spiritual existence" (E41/ K156).

As poet, artist and engraver, Blake labours to expand our shrivelled powers of perception, and he provocatively identifies their expansion with the "improvement of sensual enjoyment":

> If the doors of perception were cleansed every
> thing would appear to man as it is: infinite. For
> man has closed himself up, till he sees all things
> thro' narrow chinks of his cavern.
>   (pl. 14)

Blake's cavern is descended from Plato's famous image of the cave in which mortals are imprisoned in such a way that they perceive only the shadows of models of real things and mistake these for reality. However, while Plato—like Christian mystics who follow the negative way—believes that reality is found by relinquishing sense perception in a quest for a higher faculty, Blake seeks escape from enslavement to illusion through the enhancement of that same sense perception. According to his Ezekiel, the Hebrews' monotheism is based on a recognition that their God, the Poetic Genius, is "the first principle" of "human perception" and the origin of all other deities (pls. 12-13). In later years, Blake speaks of expanded visual perception as seeing *through*, not *with* the eye (e.g. E566/ K617): where the material eyeball itself sees the "finite & corrupt" appearance, the Poetic Genius peering *through* the physical organ reaches the "infinite and holy" reality that Adam beheld in Paradise (pl. 14).

The Poetic Genius, the Divine Humanity or the Imagination is the Essence of all that exists—the one Essence that, according to Blake's notes to Swedenborg's *Divine Love and Divine Wisdom*, gives rise to many identities (E604/ K91). Within and through those identities, He or It can act. Hence, in words to be echoed long after in pl. 91 of *Jerusalem*, Blake declares in the *Marriage* that "God only Acts & Is, in existing beings or Men" (pl. 16). This Essence is the Holy Spirit that appears in the faces of those in Eternity as "the breath of the Almighty" (*M* 30:18) as well as the Invisible God whose image is Jesus (*M* 2:12, alluding to Col. i.15). As the Divine Hand or the unfallen Jehovah, He intervenes in the epics to limit the Fall and make redemption possible (e.g. *J* 31[35]:1-16, 49:52-58).

Despite its theological, philosophical, and even literary critical content, *The Marriage of Heaven and Hell* is primarily a great work of art. Whereas *The French Revolution* is a didactic poem expressing pro-revolutionary and anti-ecclesiastical views, the *Marriage* is a teasingly enigmatic and exuberantly fantastic satire—the last great satire of the eighteenth century. Its wit is part of its message, and its readers are left to determine the seriousness as well as the sense of each of its outrageous pronouncements. They will increase their profit and delight if they scrutinise the text in a facsimile edition, for Blake has brought the composite art of *Thel* to a new stage by enriching his pages not only with large designs but with significant though often minute interlinear scenes and figures that serve as a kind of gloss to the verbal text. For a detailed commentary on these, I must refer the reader to David V. Erdman's indispensable volume of annotated reproductions, *The Illuminated Blake* (1974).

Max Plowman was the first critic to realise that *The Marriage of Heaven and Hell* is not, as Damon supposed, "a scrapbook," but a carefully planned work consisting of six prose chapters and a prologue and epilogue, both in free verse—almost, as Damon remarked, the first free verse in English.[6] Each chapter begins and ends with a large design, and its text consists of a set of propositions followed by a more fanciful portion with a sub-heading—"The voice of the Devil" or "A Memorable Fancy." It is the

---

[6] "Note" in William Blake, *The Marriage of Heaven and Hell, Reproduced in Facsimile* (London and Toronto: Dent; New York: Dutton, 1927), pp. 5-21; S. Foster Damon, *William Blake: His Philosophy and Symbols* (1924; rpt. Gloucester, Mass.: Peter Smith, 1956), pp. 88, 90.

first set of propositions, which are not ascribed to an imaginary speaker, that expresses most clearly Blake's admission that both contraries are necessary.

On the title page—though it varies greatly from copy to copy—oblique, unconstricted flames leap upwards to transmute with their energy the sterile scene above, as the soaring bird, which has counterparts on the title pages of *Innocence* and *Thel*, confirms. The embrace of two nude figures—one emerging from the "clouds of reason" (E31/ K126), the other from the fire of energy—signifies the "marriage" that will be consummated.

A cryptic Argument in free verse presents the narrative of the just man's fate. Steering a true course through "The vale of death" (the fallen world), he has made his "perilous" route so pleasant that the hypocritical villain, who sounds like one of Blake's priests, has seized it from him and has left him to roar his righteous anger in the wilderness. His prophetic rage is mirrored in the fury of Rintrah, a revolutionary spirit who roars (in the present tense) overhead. The hypocrite is not going to be dominant for long, for the fertile scene engraved contains ascending birds and fruit.

In the third plate Swedenborg is shot down with the first instalment of Blake's satirical prose—lucid, precise, playful, and deadly. The sage had announced—for example in *The True Christian Religion* (section 722)—that a Last Judgment in heaven had caused the birth of a new church on earth in 1757, which happened to be the year of Blake's birth. But Blake has discovered that Swedenborg mistook a rationalist's heaven for a supernal paradise; much more paradisal is the 'hell' of flaming energies, whose revival was ushered in by Christ at his Resurrection, for it also revived thirty-three years (the traditional span of Jesus' life) after the Swedenborgian Judgment, and left the modern teacher's writings as the discarded shroud at the empty tomb.

The revival of hell is synonymous with Adam's return into his forfeited Garden of Eden, which, Raine observes, stands in esoteric tradition for the body.[7] The body, moreover, is alluded to in the name "Edom," Hebrew for "red," which signifies here the "Red clay" of the Argument, the matter of which the flesh is composed. Blake refers us to Isaiah xxxiv and xxxv, which tell how the

---

[7] *Blake and Tradition*, I, 337-38.

Lord will lay waste Idumea (another name for Edom) and how He will restore the desert. Imagery from these chapters contributes to the Argument.

The last sentences on the third plate upbraid the religious for dubbing the negative commands of reason Good and the active energy of passion Evil. Despite Blake's devotion to energy, however, he admits that reason also is "necessary to Human existence," for "Without Contraries is no progression." In the lower part of the design a woman gives birth to a spirit of energy who will be the "new born wonder" of "A Song of Liberty" and the Orc of subsequent books.

"The voice of the Devil"—the heading has a guard of honour of three angel-like trumpeters suggesting the speaker's divine status—launches into a defence of energy against moralists who reject the flesh. The voice finds a function for reason: it provides "the bound or outward circumference of Energy" endowing it with form (the fire on the title page has no boundary). The first error denounced is illustrated by a tiny soul flying from its body, and the contrary truth is accompanied by an image of their reunion. Their separation and reintegration are similarly depicted on later pages.) The large design shows a devil in flames chained (in most copies) to the sea and unable to reach the newborn Orc struggling in the arms of an angel of reason.

The next plate begins with a picture of an energetic warrior falling into flames. After the Devil's expression of scorn for those whose desire is weak enough to be restrained by reason, a famous piece of literary criticism identifies the Satan of the Book of Job with the Messiah of *Paradise Lost*. These two embodiments of reason are opposed to energy in the form of the Trinity. Jehovah, the Father, "dwells in flaming fire"—Deuteronomy iv.24, quoted in Hebrews xii.29, proclaims, "For the Lord thy God is a consuming fire"—the Son becomes this fire after his crucifixion, and he prays (John xiv.26) for the Holy Spirit, or desire, to provide non-empirical knowledge as working material for reason.

In the first of the Memorable Fancies, which parody Swedenborg's accounts of his spiritual travels and colloquies, a narrator describes the hell of energy and the void perceived by the five fallen senses. Four pages of Proverbs of Hell championing creative energy against cunning and destructive reason vindicate Auden's claim that Blake is "the best English aphorist whether in verse or in prose."⁸ "The most sublime act is to set another before you" and "To create a little flower is the labour of ages" may seem to sort oddly with "Sooner murder an infant in its cradle than nurse unacted desires," but this protest against stifled passion is no more to be taken literally than "The cut worm forgives the plow," which is not about the ethics of agriculture. Several sayings express views which Blake is to expound with more emphasis later. "Eternity is in love with the productions of time" implies a happy relationship between the fallen and unfallen worlds; "The apple tree never asks the beech how he shall grow, nor the lion the horse, how he shall take his prey" affirms, in an Old Testament spirit, the unique identity of each created species; and "The head Sublime, the heart Pathos, the genitals Beauty, the hands & feet Proportion" renders Blake's sense, as artist and Christian, of the holiness of the human form and foreshadows his conception of the fourfold nature of humankind. In the illustrations, leaves, grapes, animals, birds, and running, leaping, soaring and trumpeting humans represent the fertility and energy that belong together. At the end of the sequence, the winged devil in the larger picture has just finished dictating the Proverbs to two amenuenses; the one on the left may be a reasoning angel whom the other two figures regard askance.

For three pages, Blake turns from devils and hell to God or the Poetic Genius and the subsidiary powers deriving from Him or It and present "in the human breast" (pl. 11). These powers are the heathen gods, who reappear under new names in Blake's later books. (In a letter of 1804, he clearly identifies his Urizen with the Roman Jupiter [E756/ K851-52].) Writing of antiquity, when poets were not distinguished from prophets (the Latin word *vates* denoted both), he tells how the poets projected these powers from their imaginations onto cities, nations, and natural objects until cunning reasoners reduced their works to abstract theological systems, insisted that the gods were powers external to the human mind, and established themselves as a privileged priestly class abasing their fellows. At the top of the page are nature deities or spirits, and at the bottom is the first occurrence of Blake's sinister representation of Urizen as an old bearded man hovering with arms outstretched. The Memorable Fancy that follows reveals that

⁸ W. H. Auden, "'A Mental Prince,'" *Observer* (London), 17 Nov. 1957.

the "enlarged & numerous senses" of the ancient poets of pl. 11 are shared by Isaiah, Ezekiel, the Greek philosopher Diogenes, and North American Indians. The warlike emotion displayed in the Old Testament over spilling the blood of the heathen is ingeniously explained as the celebration of the future spiritual victory of the worship of the Poetic Genius over devotion to other, derivative gods. The notion that the latter have rebelled against the Poetic Genius anticipates the central theme of *The Four Zoas*, in which each Zoa or faculty makes an attempt to usurp the throne of "The Human form Divine" (126:10/ E395/ IX, 367) and govern the whole being. The narrator of the Memorable Fancy speaks with the amusing matter-of-factness of a Gulliver, and Blake slips in a tribute to the poetic power of the Psalms as well as a hit at Locke, who had opinions about a firm persuasion very different from those of Isaiah and Ezekiel:

> if strength of persuasion be the light which must
> guide us; I ask how shall any one distinguish be-
> tween the delusions of Satan, and the inspirations
> of the Holy Ghost?...if reason must not examine
> their truth by something extrinsical to the per-
> suasions themselves, inspirations and delusions
> ...will not be possible to be distinguished.
> (*Essay Concerning Human Understanding*
> IV.xix.13-14)

Blake's Ezekiel answers but does not confute Locke. How, without a test in which reason plays some part, can Blake's coherent and intellectual vision be distinguished from the delusions of his contemporary the prophet Richard Brothers, who expected to lead the Jews back to Jerusalem and there establish a kingdom? Here, indeed, both contraries are necessary.

Blake is notably successful in maintaining continuity within a work falling into fifteen short sections. In pl. 14, the perception of the infinite promoted by Isaiah and Ezekiel and by Blake's illuminated printing is related to the energy of hell, to humanity's return into Eden, and to the Platonic image of the cavern in which the fallen soul is a prisoner. The succeeding Memorable Fancy centres on the image of the cave, which takes the form of a curiously inhabited, six-chambered printing house in hell.

Expansion of consciousness begins in the first chamber with what is probably the sexual assertiveness of the dragon-man, and it encounters a necessary check from the viper of reason, who makes patterns with the restrictive beauties of tradition. It resumes with men who receive inspiration from the Eagle of Genius, and then lions of energy melt down the fixed patterns of tradition into the flexible material of new art, which is stored in books for future generations. In the accompanying design, contraries are united in the form of an eagle lifting a serpent, these signifying perhaps inspiration and reason along with energy and nature.

The succinct piece of exposition on plates 16 to 17 is incomplete without its engraving of five figures hunched up in a prison cell. They are the five senses, still sources of energy in our fallen condition but captive to outward appearances thanks to reasoners like Locke and religious lawgivers, who cut them off from the imagination, which once did and still should perceive through them, and who confine their vision to a meagre scantling of reality. Already Blake regards the story of Noah's Flood as one version of the Fall (this is to become more obvious in *America*) and, reading Genesis vi.4 allegorically, he includes his seemingly shackled giants among those who lived before the Deluge. He also classifies people who are still dominated by their energies as creators and those who have succumbed to reason as consumers. In a fierce spirit he denies that Jesus, a manifestation of the energy stifled by rationalism since the Flood, is a peacemaker and he accuses the conventionally religious of trying to suppress the friction and conflict that make our lives human and progress possible.

The fourth Memorable Fancy pits the prolific narrator against a devouring angel, who takes him through the church of orthodoxy and the mill of natural religion to the void of Newton's infinite space, where hell is on display: the fires are like those from a city burning in an uprising, the devils appear as huge devouring spiders, and Leviathan—three degrees to the east as revolutionary Paris is from reactionary London[9]—advances "with all the fury of a spiritual existence." When the angel departs with his distorting perception, the 'hell' turns into a pleasant scene where nature harmonises with art, and interlinear figures reappear

---

[9] Martin K. Nurmi, *Blake's* Marriage of Heaven and Hell: *A Critical Study* (Ohio: Kent State University Bulletin, 1957), p. 51.

in what has been the bare text of the narrative. Now it is the poet's turn to show the angel his heaven. After carrying him to the sun, he uses Swedenborg's stodgy volumes to weigh them both down so they can finish their journey, which is the reverse of the one Satan takes in *Paradise Lost* from the edge of the universe to the earth.[10] Between Saturn and the stars they find Milton's Limbo, the home of superstitions, and in it is the orthodox church. The Bible on the altar, understood in the conventional fashion, opens up into a house of cannibalistic monkeys who embody the spirit of Aristotelian logic working only on knowledge obtained through the fallen senses. Following illustrations of the Leviathan of revolutionary energy and of the inspired narrator with his left knee on the skull of dead tradition, a coda implies that Swedenborg is still in bondage to reason and only slightly wiser than a religious monkey.

Despite the title of this book, no marriage takes place till the last and wittiest of the Memorable Fancies. Here a Christian angel is persuaded by a Christian devil that Jesus broke all of the Ten Commandments and "acted from impulse: not from rules," whereupon the angel embraces flames of energy and is "consumed" and transformed into the prophet Elijah, an opponent—like modern revolutionaries—of kingly tyranny and a counterpart of Isaiah and Ezekiel. As in pl. 14 and often in his later works, Blake here endows the verb "consumed" with overtones of "consummated" using it to mean perish and reappear in another form. The "marriage" turns out to be a conversion of one contrary into the other! As a further blow against law, Blake provides a picture of the tyrant Nebuchadnezzar reduced to insanity (Dan. iv.33) and beneath it engraves the aphorism "One Law for the Lion & Ox is Oppression." These powerful words repudiate Isaiah's prophecy "the lion shall eat straw like the ox" (xi.7).

The book concludes with "A Song of Liberty" consisting of twenty numbered verses of the biblical kind and a Chorus. The "Song" combines recent history and politics with an early version of Blake's myth involving the characters he was later to call Enitharmon, Orc and Urizen. The scene is an already fallen world, in which the Flood has created the Atlantic Ocean cutting humankind off from the mountains of Atlantis, which had provided a point of contact with the unfallen Eternity. Echoing St. Paul's

---

[10] Raine, *Blake and Tradition*, II, 59-60.

lament "For we know that the whole creation groaneth and tra-
vaileth in pain together until now" (Rom. viii.22), Blake tells how
Enitharmon's groans were heard over the whole earth as she gave
birth to Orc, the spirit of energy and revolution, who was to bring
the longed-for redemption. Orc confronts Urizen, represented both
as an earthly tyrant and as the giver of the Ten Commandments,
but this oppressor, having hurled Orc into the Atlantic, himself
falls like Milton's Satan and has to confront his young antagonist
again on earth. An anachronistic medley of creatures and objects,
including elephants, castles and slings, falls with him indicating
that he is behind the wars of all periods. Shown to be Christlike by
the time-honoured pun on "son" and "sun" in verses 13 and 19,
the redeemer Orc defies counter-revolutionary curses with his cry
of triumph and obliterates the old law. Up to Urizen's collapse
onto the earth, the story is told in the past tense, though it is inter-
rupted by a present-tense allusion to the transmission of the revo-
lutionary spirit from the American Colonies to France resulting in
the fall of the Bastille. In two passages Blake calls on Spain to
escape from the Roman Church, on that Church to cast away the
"keys of the kingdom of heaven" (Matt. xvi.19), on the Jews to
return from commerce to the pastoral life of the Old Testament,
and on the London bourgeoisie and African slaves to expand their
horizons. In the Chorus he concentrates on the sex-hating
priesthood, whose dawn is heralded by the bird of death, and he
associates it with the measuring and binding of the reasoner,
whether scientist, moralist, or improver of the Proverbs of Hell
who makes "strait roads." In the final declaration, "For every thing
that lives is Holy," the last word carries favourable, unpriestly
connotations.

Through the free verse, exposition, narratives, aphorisms
and designs of the *Marriage*, there runs one constant ele-
ment—antithesis within a pair of opposites representing reason
and energy. The pairs include, in consecutive order, the villain and
the just man, good and evil, soul and body, Satan and Messiah, the
abyss of the five senses and the fires of hell, cunning and creative-
ness, priests and poets, law and prophecy, fallen and unfallen per-
ception, obscuring caves and enlightening books, the devourers
and the prolific, angel and poet, and newborn fire and starry king.

*Songs of Innocence and of Experience, The Marriage of
Heaven and Hell* and *Illustrations of The Book of Job* are Blake's

three great works of art accessible to a public unprepared to study
his idiosyncratic vocabulary and symbolism. Combining a lyric
exuberance with excoriating satire, the *Marriage* attributes to the
reasoner a weak mind and dishonourable character yet allows that
reason has a place, for energy needs its foe: "Opposition is true
Friendship" (pl. 20). Its maze of wit challenges every reader to
decide how seriously to take outrageous statements. At one point,
indeed, Blake's nerve may have failed him, for on pl. 6 he altered
the engraving to change "the Devil" in the phrase "the Jehovah of
the Bible being no other than the Devil who dwells in flaming
fire" to the innocuous pronoun "he." Later, in powerful but abs-
truse passages in *Milton* and *Jerusalem*, he tries to convey some
notion of the fiery world of Eternity transcending the temporal
contraries, a world of energies where a redeemed reason also has
its place.

4

The Lustre Fades: *Visions of the Daughters of Albion; For Children: The Gates of Paradise; Songs of Experience*

As the awareness of divine and human protection that characterises Innocence gives way to the bitter resentment against cruelty and oppression that constitutes Experience, the spirit finds itself in a world where the necessities of life, the physical environment, and the very body and soul become chattels of parent and spouse, king and priest, slaveowner and imperial power. In *Visions of the Daughters of Albion* Blake devises a more complex successor to *The Book of Thel*, a successor in which sexual, economic and political oppression are related to human psychology and to his concept of fallen perception. As the first of his prophetic works that operates simultaneously on metaphysical, psychological and political levels, it marks an essential step in his evolution as an epic poet. While the proper names of his own invention (some derived from Macpherson's *Ossian*) may seem uncouth to the newcomer to Blake, *Songs of Experience* draws on his developing mythology without resorting to such names. This complement to *Songs of Innocence* angrily exposes the wickedness of those who have power, accounts for it in terms of the Fall, and offers a muted hope of reform and redemption.

By the early 1790s, Blake has worked out his own sexual ethic, and it is evident in both these books. Love between the sexes and its physical consummation he regards as always good, though each partner must abstain from possessiveness towards the other. He says little for or against remaining faithful to one's partner but a great deal about the wrongness of demanding fidelity from him or her. A subtler kind of possessiveness that he denounces with equal vehemence is secret indulgence in clandestine love:

O dark secret love
Doth life destroy
(E23, 793/ K175)

While he despises bodily virginity, and regards true virginity as the spirit's freedom from corruption, he says nothing in favour of loveless copulation. Indeed, in the late poem "The Everlasting Gospel" (he always continued to advocate free love), he makes Jesus ask Mary Magdalene,

What was thy love? Let me see it.
Was it love or Dark Deceit?

to which she confesses

Love too long from Me has fled
'Twas dark deceit to Earn my bread;
'Twas Covet or 'twas Custom or
Some trifle not worth caring for
(E522 [ll. 57-62]/ K755 [ll. 57-62])

Blake's indignation at the fate of the prostitute—the victim both of poverty and of an oppressive sexual morality—was lifelong.

By 1789 the abolition of the slave trade was already being debated in Parliament, and in 1792-93 Blake engraved horrific illustrations of tormented slaves for *A Narrative, of a five Years' expedition, against the Revolted Negroes of Surinam, in Guiana* by Captain John Stedman, with whom he dined several times. In *Visions of the Daughters of Albion*, dated 1793, he pours out his loathing of several kinds of slavery, including that of Africans. His heroine, Oothoon, is a more courageous Thel, positive where her predecessor is negative and undefeated in spirit though she cannot prevail over circumstances or make the blind see.

The title page, markedly different on the right and left hand sides, gives the reader a clue as to what will follow. Slightly to the right of centre, Oothoon runs over dark waves pursued by a winged, burning, angry and anguished Urizen—Blake's name for his lawgiving god first appears in this poem. On the right a male in a dark cloud pours a storm onto the waters, while on the left one female reaches down to offer help to another above a rainbow of hope and vision. The Motto, "The Eye sees more than the Heart knows," tells us that our hearts sometimes fail to recognise signs of hope, or perhaps that the heart of a wretch like Theotormon cannot comprehend what his eyes show him. In the Argument, Oothoon declares how (unlike Thel) she accepts sexual joy but then suffers the terrible thunders of a rape. The top of pl. 1 extends the lesson of the title page. The ominous first word of the text, "Enslav'd," is—quite uncharacteristically for Blake—engraved in much larger letters than what follows, and this sets up an opposition between it and the yet larger subheading "Visions," for vision can triumph over enslavement. Adorning the subheading are five spirits of energy and desire.

In the poem, Blake returns to the long line of *Thel* and *The French Revolution*, but his unrhymed verse has become more obscure, intricate and powerful, while his narrative peters out early giving way first to a dialogue and then to a monologue. The divisions between the three parts are marked by the repetition of the line "The Daughters of Albion hear her woes, & eccho back her sighs." These words allude to the refrain of Spenser's "Epithalamion," but do so ironically, for no joyful marriage takes place in Blake's book.

The Daughters of Albion, the economically and sexually enslaved women of Britain, constitute a chorus whose sorrows have much in common with those of Oothoon. The latter has several identities. Allegorically, she is at once North and South America, the spirit of liberation that sustained the American Revolution, and the human soul imprisoned in the materialist's universe and in a puritanical society; literally she is both a slave raped by her master and a woman disowned by her lover because a rapist has polluted her.

The brief action at the beginning of the poem repeats the content of the Argument, combining the plucking of a flower, a time-honoured image for the sexual act, with Thel's imaginative achievement of seeing the spiritual essence in the natural object, the worm or marigold. Unlike Thel, however, she quickly learns a twofold lesson—that an essence survives though its temporary embodiment perishes, and that the sexuality of the mortal world is not to be shunned. Robbing her of her liberty and her virginity as she goes to offer her love to Theotormon, Bromion boasts that she is a pregnant (and therefore more valuable) slave, abuses her as a whore, and mocks her lover's jealousy. Theotormon's jealousy is, indeed, lethal to Oothoon, and Blake's frontispiece (in one copy, tailpiece) illustrates the lines that describe how it accusingly binds Bromion (terror) and Oothoon (meekness) back to back in the former's caves, while he, the wronged lover, weeps at the entrance. He accepts the rapist's belief that women are men's chattels, and that a woman's virginity is her bridegroom's property. Giving Theotormon symbolic significance, a brief digression (2:7-10) makes him the patron of repressive religion that blocks the expression of sexual energy, and equates this tyranny with the oppression of slaves and (probably) apprentices. Blake tries to give the word "lust" (and in 6:4 and 7:27 its derivative "lustful") favourable connotations.

To persuade Theotormon of her inner purity and unsullied devotion, Oothoon undertakes a fearful penance akin to the punishment of Prometheus. Though noble in intent, this action is perhaps misguided and only confirms his belief that she is stained. When he is unmoved, she delivers an impassioned speech equating his morality with the perverted perception that can see only the prevailing ratio—the finite and measurable material objects that constitute Locke's reality. If Theotormon will only discard his blindfold, he will find himself in the new morning that follows the night of the Fall; in the darkness of the latter, the nightingale grieves, the eagle hunts, the human brain and heart are imprisoned in the skull and thorax, and the rising sun is no more than "a bright shadow, like an eye/ In the eastern cloud" (2:35-36). This solar eye is shown in the frontispiece, where the reader looks out from Bromion's cave of fallen perception. Through a series of rhetorical questions, Oothoon urges that bodily state (the possession of certain senses or of virginity) is not the criterion of identity, and that it is one's identity that must be the object of genuine love. Various species of animal share the same senses yet differ utterly. Her unlimited devotion and the three tender and beautiful images for the suffering soul in the last paragraph of Oothoon's speech should touch any man with a heart, but Theotormon is implacable. On pl. 4 he is portrayed with his face hidden on his lap while his blindness chains Oothoon and his jealousy overcomes her flame of desire with its black wave.

Oothoon's plea that Theotormon will open his eyes to the morning is supplemented by her insistence that different individuals have different joys and that none should condemn another, for none has ever been able to enter into another's thoughts (3:2-13). Refusing to break away from his self-torment, Theotormon replies that night and morning mean nothing to one with his griefs, and that thoughts and joys, like "woes"—Oothoon has spoken of all these (3:13, 6, 17)—are immaterial and therefore unreal and powerless to ease him. He then turns to the isolation of the intolerably afflicted and to past irrecoverable happiness.

At the beginning of the poem, Bromion, whose name seems to be derived from a Greek word for "roaring," is an arrogant and cruel man in love with power. After he has violated Oothoon, her lamenting threatens to drown his voice, but for a time he outthunders her. Eventually her argument and Theotormon's jealousy undermine his certainties, and, still bound, he tries to answer them in a lament that Blake describes as cavern-shaking. Responding to Theotormon's cry for a time or place where comfort might be obtained, he confesses that there are unknown phenomena which humans could perceive if they had more than five senses, but in spite of Oothoon's claim that the unimaginative do not see reality, he denies that there are experiences or pleasures not rooted in sense perception or material possessions. He also denies that "One Law for the Lion & Ox is Oppression" (*MHH*, pl. 24) and expresses his satisfaction that the threat of hell-fire (his caves are "religious caves" [2:5, 9]) can make his underlings (mere "phantoms of existence" [4:24]) do their duty and obey him instead of seeking Oothoon's imaginative life, where each joy is "eternal" (5:5-6).

At this point the two materialists have said all they can say; Bromion is heard of no more, and the remainder of the poem consists of a long and noble speech by Oothoon with a brief introduction and conclusion. The latter assures us that Theotormon remains locked up in his own misery, and the design on pl. 6 shows him puritanically flogging himself with three lashes tipped with the marigold of sexuality illustrated below the Argument.

Oothoon's speech begins with an apostrophe to Urizen, a god who is the patron of all who believe in one law for lion and ox, and who is here assimilated to the God of Genesis i.26, who made man after His own image. In 5:8-9 Oothoon briefly resumes her catalogue of animal species representing contrasting human identities, continues her list with literal descriptions till 5:32, and then reverts to symbolic animals. The text of pl. 1 and an illustration of a prostrate black man on pl. 2 attack slavery; the text of the last four plates draws a wide ranging picture of social and moral evils in Britain. In succinct, sharp descriptions Blake flashes before us images of the recruiting sergeant robbing farm land of its labourers, the parson collecting oppressive tithes and supporting with his abstract theology the alliance of monarchy and church, upper class women driven into mercenary marriages, and their children prematurely forced into similar marriages or perhaps whipped into studying. Pl. 5 shows a lady grieving amidst luxury.

In the sixth plate, Oothoon equates modesty and religious control of sexual life with the suppression of the natural joyful sexuality that begins in Innocence and childhood. Chastity she denounces as a system of sanctioned prostitution in which women who pretend to be desireless sell their bodies in return for marriage. After making her own claim to inner virginity, she draws a powerful picture of the auto-eroticism of the frustrated, upbraids the "Father of Jealousy" (who is Urizen), and foresees herself receding so far from Eternity as to fade into non-existence (5:3; 7:3-15). An apostrophe to true love leads her to an explicit definition of false love—a possessiveness that "drinks another as a sponge drinks water" and is in reality "self-love," which Blake personifies in an image that evokes an unforgettable shudder: "a creeping skeleton/ With lamplike eyes watching around the frozen marriage bed" (7:16-22). Less convincing is Oothoon's offer to prove her own freedom from jealousy by providing Theotormon with an unlimited supply of mistresses, but in the final paragraph of her speech she eloquently contrasts the self-torture of Theotormon along with the secrecy of the miser, the night, and covert sex with the openness of the sun, whose light blots out noxious creatures of the darkness. Theotormon, she complains, is like the storm-loving sea bird and the poisonous snake. She cannot make him understand that joy and life, not chastity and the right of possession, are holy, so their relationship is at an impasse. However, a final design shows Oothoon flying over the waves as Urizen does on the title page, for she is exalted in spirit and far happier than he, and the daughters of Albion, woebegone on the previous plate, look up to her in hope.

Visions of the Daughters of Albion has fewer readers than it deserves. Although its structure is ungainly and there are troub-

ling obscurities, the poem is magnificent in its passionate zeal for
freedom, and individual images and allusions make objects of
Blake's sympathy and indignation momentarily stand out like
cameos against the background of his compassion for oppressed
women, children and slaves.

In *Visions of the Daughters of Albion*, Oothoon asks

> Does not the worm erect a pillar in the mouldering church
> yard?
> And a palace of eternity in the jaws of the hungry grave.
> (5:41-6:1)

She may be alluding to the tomb as the gateway to eternal life. In
1793 Blake issued *For Children: The Gates of Paradise*, a book
about mortality consisting of a title page and seventeen engraved
emblems with brief inscriptions. Above the fundamental question
"What is Man!" the frontispiece shows a munching caterpillar and
a chrysalis with a child's face on oak leaves: the human is born
from physical nature but has the capacity to grow the wings of the
spirit. The baby is also found in the vegetable form of a mandrake
beneath a willow by a woman who represents some aspect of nat-
ure and collects babies in her apron. In this world, human beings
are imprisoned in each of the four traditional elements—water,
earth, air and fire—as the next four plates illustrate. However, the
man in fire has the shield, spear and energy of Milton's Satan as
he is interpreted in *The Marriage of Heaven and Hell* (a quotation
from *Paradise Lost*, I, 221-22, accompanies a preparatory sketch
for the plate on p. 91 of Blake's Notebook) and his energy points
forward to the birth of the winged human spirit from an egg.

While the first six emblems (including the unnumbered
frontispiece) deal with the soul's relationship with nature, the
remaining eleven, beginning with another image of mortal birth,
treat of its life in Experience. In this world, the embodied spirit
has much to contend with. A youth tries to snare it and separates it
from its body; grown into a youth itself, it desperately attacks its
tyrannical but grieving father, just as Absalom tried to overthrow
David, whose lament "My Son! My Son!" forms the caption (II
Sam. xviii.33). As Erdman demonstrates,[1] the next plate replies to

---

[1] David V. Erdman, *Blake: Prophet Against Empire* (Princeton: Princeton UP, 1954),

James Gillray's cartoon showing that Charles James Fox and his followers could never implement their liberal ideal because they were reaching for the moon with a short ladder. Blake shows a man at the foot of a ladder that does reach the moon and near them a pair of lovers happily embracing. The optimism is countered in the three plates that follow by a drowning man crying for help, dim-sighted "Aged Ignorance" clipping a young spirit's wings, and Dante's Count Ugolino and his family starving in a bare cell above the question "Does thy God O Priest take such vengeance as this?" At last hope reasserts itself as a family beside the corpse of an old man behold his soul or spiritual body rising from it and pointing upward: the legend reads, "Fear & Hope are—Vision." Encouraged, a striding pilgrim "hasteth in the Evening" toward eternal life, and a frail old man steps into the gateway of a massive tomb. The final engraving of a crouching figure in a shroud almost encircled by a worm bears a melancholy quotation from Job xvii.14—"I have said to the Worm, Thou art my mother & my sister," but the reader has been prepared to recognise that what looks like an underground chamber with roots and almost buried human heads is a passageway to a higher existence free from drowning waters, priests, and aged ignorance.

About the time that Blake was engraving *For the Children*, he was working in his invaluable surviving Notebook on the series of adult lyrics which became the sequel or complement of *Songs of Innocence*. In 1794, five years after he had issued his children's songs, which were untouched by the French Revolution, he offered *Songs Of Innocence and Of Experience Shewing the Two Contrary States of the Human Soul* to a Britain whose reactionary rulers tended to regard any humane reform as a step on the road to Jacobin atrocities.

Having already brought together metaphysics, psychology, ethics and social criticism in a long poem, Blake now treated these subjects separately in the lyrics of his new collection. Like the colouring, the order of the plates differs from copy to copy of *Songs*, and this allows the poet to introduce varying contrasts between adjacent plates alongside the overarching contrast between *Innocence* and *Experience*. At least six of the pieces in *Innocence* have specific counterparts in *Experience*, though the poetry in the latter

pp. 186-88 [202-04].

reappears in "My Pretty Rose Tree," in which a wife or beloved rewards fidelity with jealousy, while "The Lilly" celebrates the beautiful flower that loves without putting up emotional barriers. Occupying the same plate as these brief lyrics, "Ah! Sun-flower" mournfully identifies the grave of this world with the cruel frustration of sexual desire in youth and maiden. On the upper half of the page lies a jealous woman ignoring both her suitor and ascending birds; a similar woman—again illustrated—is the speaker in "The Angel." Repressed and coy rather than jealous, she begins by luxuriating in her pose of helplessness and ends as an old maid hiding behind a mask of self-sufficiency. Perhaps akin to these unhappy creatures is the envious, frustrated spinster of "Nurse's Song," who looks after other women's children.

Blake shows an especial sympathy with the emotionally tortured young. In contrast to the baby of "Infant Joy," the newborn child of "Infant Sorrow" knows he is thrust into the world of Experience, and the engraving shows him as a rebel spirit in his cradle. The preternatural planning of a strategy which the words describe hints at mental activity below the threshold of consciousness. In "A Little Girl Lost," addressed to children of "the future Age" when love will no longer be "thought a crime," the child is not the only victim. Her misguided father suffers cruelly from what he regards as his daughter's waywardness; because his mind is set towards the Urizenic "holy book" instead of the "holy light" of day, he cannot see the joy symbolised in the rising birds and the vines that try to clothe the almost barren tree on the right of the text with fruitful life. A particularly simple, straightforward and powerful denunciation of the law of chastity is put into the mouth of the speaker in "The Garden of Love." Again, pleasing natural things—grass and flowers—represent love's fulfilment, and it is impossible not to sympathise with the lover who finds that these have been replaced by emblems of negation: graves, tombstones, briars, and (in the design) a shaven monk leading an adolescent boy and girl in prayer.

The clash between youth and religion becomes deeper and more vicious in "A Little Boy Lost," in which the child in all innocence questions the two Old Testament commandments that Christ recognised as the greatest: "Thou shalt love the Lord thy God" and "Thou shalt love thy neighbour as thyself" (Matt. xxii.35-40). Unlike the lost boy of *Innocence*, this strayed sheep is not found. A much admired priest, driven by "zeal," burns him alive, while his weeping parents (not, in this case, among the persecutors) are powerless to save him. Blake may be asking whether destruction of the spirit parallel to this atrocity on the body is permitted in repressive Britain. The ivy leaves of the frontispiece and title page, now ominously swollen, further register his horror, but it is refreshing to find him referring favourably to reason as an opponent of the "Mystery" (or mystification) that upholds priestly power. Early and late he was capable of seeing some good in the Enlightenment's assault on authoritarian churches: in 1798 he jotted harsh annotations in Bishop Watson's A*pology for the Bible,* a reply to Paine's Deist attack on the two Testaments, and on 18 February, 1826, he told the diarist Henry Crabb Robinson that God had commissioned Voltaire to expose the natural sense of the Scriptures.[2] While defending Paine, however, he confesses that that rationalist did not know "the Everlasting Gospel" (E619/ K394), and the same is doubtless true of the martyred boy .

Images from nature are prominent in two lyrics which have counterparts in *Songs of Innocence* and which may be regarded as anti-pastorals. As "A Little Girl Lost" contrasts the genuine holiness of the sunlight with the false holiness of the religious book, the "Holy Thursday" of *Experience* asks whether the capitalist's assumption of total control over the lives of children made paupers by society is reconcilable with the supposed holiness of the charity that provides for these destitute juveniles for whom fertile Britain is like an ever wintry wilderness. They are portrayed in the design—not yet taken into care and in at least one instance apparently dead—alongside two grieving mothers. The last stanza, recalling Christ's words about the Father who "maketh his sun to rise on the evil and on the good, and sendeth rain on the just and on the unjust" (Matt. v.45), implies that God's ways are different from those of the British Establishment. The bare landscape of the plate is matched by the bleak street and wretched child in the design of "The Chimney Sweeper." As in "The Chimney Sweeper" of *Innocence,* the exploited child is allowed to voice his own feelings, but the boy of *Experience* charges the parents who sold him to his employer with using his moments of happiness to persuade themselves they have done him no wrong, and being a precocious rad-

[2] G. E. Bentley, Jr., *Blake Records* (Oxford: Clarendon Press, 1969), p. 322.

ical he ascribes their wickedness to a Tory allegiance to Church and King. What every Church should provide—warmth and ale for the body, prayer and song for the soul—is announced by the disreputable but honest speaker in "The Little Vagabond," whose claim that such clerical kindness would reconcile God and the Devil slyly attacks the church's identification of godliness with mortification and evil with sensory pleasure. The freezing family depicted at the bottom of the page is counterbalanced by the speaker at the top, where God the Father has come to comfort him among looming tree trunks like those of "The Little Boy lost"and "The Little Boy Found " in *Innocence*.

Blake's charges against society are brought together in the indictment of King, church and capitalist in his great denunciation "London." Speaking in his own person and brilliantly deploying puns, assonance, alliteration and chiming reiteration, the poet tells how he wanders over the city seeing only wretchedness and oppression. The very streets and the Thames itself have been "charter'd" in the two senses of rented out and granted to monopoly-holders. In this poem of sounds, the second stanza especially is full of cries of pain. (The word "ban" means both prohibition and curse.) In the third stanza sounds are becoming visible, for the cry of the child chimney sweeper "appalls" the "black'ning Church" —both horrifies it and covers it with a black coffin cloth—and the sigh of the soldier who is a victim of the Government's aggressive policy turns into accusing blood on the walls of the monarch. By midnight sound predominates over sight, and the curse of the woman driven to prostitution by poverty and by the consequences of the church's prohibition of free love rises up to make the respectable institution of marriage a source of spiritual death. Above the text a small boy leads a crippled old man into a doorway whence bright light shines as the one sign of hope on the page.

The attack on ecclesiastical influence is intertwined with the development of Blake's myth in "The Human Abstract," counterpart of "The Divine Image" in *Innocence*. By "Mystery," Blake means the system of ritual and dogma which the church exploits to clamp its power on the souls of believers, who are made to fear damnation in the next world and perhaps excommunication here. In "The Human Abstract," Mystery becomes a tree growing from the foot of Urizen, who is called Cruelty in the text and drawn in

the design at the base of the trunk, where he is shown trapped in
his own net of legalistic religion. Characteristically, he upholds
humility and is full of tears. The raven of death and the priestly
caterpillar inhabit the branches above him, and in the first six
lines his versions of mercy, pity, peace and love parody the genu-
ine forms of these virtues praised in "The Divine Image."

In later books, Blake makes the Tree of Mystery resemble
an indefinitely spreading banyan tree as its branches reach down
to the ground, take root, and sprout new stems. He portrays the
beginnings of this phenomenon in the design of "A Poison Tree,"
where it accompanies a poem displaying the psychological and
moral consequences of nourishing unspoken hostility. The poison-
ous but alluring apple which the suppressed anger produces recalls
the fatal fruit of Eden.

Two poems in *Songs of Experience* have proved excep-
tionally enigmatic. "The Fly," with its brief, flitting lines, probes
the deficiencies of the mind overwhelmed by Experience, while
"The Tyger," made famous by its pounding rhythms and blazing
images, confronts the Problem of Evil. The speaker in "The Fly,"
comparing his likely doom with that of an insect he has heedlessly
killed, recognises that what he lacked when he slew it was
thought. Thought, in the context of the poem, is far removed from
Urizenic (or Lockean) reasoning: it includes sympathy with others,
playfulness, and the vision of the Innocent mind. It is present even
in the gaiety of a fly, it survives death, and any creature who poss-
esses it is truly alive even when its physical body has perished. Of
the three characters in the illustration, only the infant boy looking
upwards seems to have much chance of preserving vision; his
mother or nurse bends restrictively over him while his sister hits a
shuttlecock that is suspiciously like an insect.

As the drafts in his Notebook testify, Blake worked hard to
perfect his masterpiece "The Tyger." In the first four stanzas of
this apostrophe to the fearful beast, he steadily increases the num-
ber of questions packed into each quatrain mimicking the hammer
blows of the winged smith-god who, Prometheus-like, seized fire
from an unknown depth or height—hell or heaven—and formed
its mighty organs in his furnace and on his anvil. With the fifth
stanza, trembling and doubt disturb the speaker's tone. He implies
that the tiger was created when the angels fell—those angels who,
in Milton's words, "down thir idle weapons drop'd" and who were

led by one who was soon unable to withhold "Tears such as Angels weep" (*PL*, VI, 839 and I, 620). The profound theological question that follows—"Did he who made the Lamb make thee?"—receives no reply. Blake's view of creation, as laid out in *The Book of Urizen* and later writings, does not allow for a simple answer of Yes or No, since a number of causes bring about the Fall and the limitation placed upon it, which together determine the character of the cosmos we inhabit. Here, Blake's purpose, reaffirmed in the repetition of the last stanza, is to evoke a mighty image of explosive energy harmfully constricted in a narrow frame, yet potentially, though the speaker may be too submerged in Experience to be aware of it, able to work in the world for good. This energy, burning in the forests of Experience illustrated in "The Little Vagabond," "The Little Boy lost" and "The Little Boy Found," differs from the energy flowing freely across the title page of *The Marriage of Heaven and Hell*. It may be identified on one level with the First Principle of Boehme that can exist in isolation as the fire of hell or work with the Second Principle as the creating force; on a political level it may erupt in saving revolution. The tyger of the lyric can burn "bright" or, as the contrary of the Lamb, be "deadly." It can have affinities both with the tygers of wrath (*MHH*, pl. 9) and with the fallen nocturnal tiger (*VDA* 8:5), the "Tyger fierce" that "Laughs at the Human form" (*FZ* 15:1-2/ E309/ I,402-03), and even "The Guardian Prince of Albion" who "burns in his nightly tent" and tries to overawe his colonial subjects with "His voice, his locks, his awful shoulders, and his glowing eyes" (*A* 3:1, 17).

For all its greatness as a poem, "The Tyger" has a feeble illustration. At the foot of a barren tree of Experience stands a beast looking rather like a child's stuffed animal. Though Blake may well be implying that the energy that can destroy can also be benign (there is a bird of hope above the first words of the poem), the picture is aesthetically unsuccessful.

In *Visions of the Daughters of Albion, For Children: The Gates of Paradise* and *Songs of Experience*, there is no resolution of the conflict between poetic vision and materialistic blindness, liberty and tyranny, prosperity and indigence. The aged, bearded Urizen, who has no imagination and cannot see that each human being is a unique individual, lowers over the world. Oothoon cannot prise Theotormon away from his influence as Earth cannot

snatch her own freedom. His notion of love is of the Pebble's poss-
essive kind, and through his highly respectable servants in palace
and church he imposes chastity and perpetuates poverty: the
results are war, prostitution, child exploitation, and frustrated love.

5

The Myth of History: *America*; *Europe*; *The Song of Los*

After composing *The Marriage of Heaven and Hell* and *Visions of the Daughters of Albion*, Blake began to produce two series of interconnected illuminated volumes often called his Lambeth books after the district of London in which he lived from 1791 to 1800. In these works he began to express his world-view through a complex mythology of his own invention. The form of the poetic texts, as Tannenbaum has persuasively argued,[1] owes much to the work of seventeenth- and eighteenth-century scholars like Joseph Mede and Thomas Howes, who analysed the non-Aristotelian form of literary prophecy. They defended the digressions, abrupt transitions, multiple viewpoints, and non-chronological—sometimes synchronic—arrangement that they found in such books as Ezekiel and Revelation.

In "A Song of Liberty" at the end of *The Marriage of Heaven and Hell*, Blake portrays a conflict between a god of law and reason (Urizen) and a newborn babe who represents energy (Orc). The poem foreshadows Blake's three books of historical myth—*America*, *Europe*, and *The Song of Los*, this last consisting of two portions subtitled "Africa" and "Asia." If the four parts are arranged as nearly as possible in chronological order, the series runs "Africa," "*America*," "*Europe*," "Asia." Blake conceives the history of fallen humankind as beginning in Africa, and redemption as beginning with the revolution that started in the Thirteen Colonies in 1776, moved to France in 1789, and was about to spread into Asia. He may have taken a hint from the Introduction to Part II of *The Rights of Man* (1792) by his friend Thomas Paine, who there anticipated that the freedom born in America would

---

[1] Leslie Tannenbaum, *Biblical Tradition in Blake's Early Prophecies* (Princeton: Princeton UP, 1982), pp. 28-51.

spread east to undermine the ancient tyrannies of Asia, Africa and Europe.

The text of *America* is divided between a two-plate Preludium and a fourteen-plate Prophecy. Orc is the hero of both. In the Preludium he brings new life to nature, while in the Prophecy he infuses the spirit of revolution into human society beginning with the American rebels. The earlier part of the Prophecy focuses on a furious struggle between Orc and Albion's Angel, but about pl. 11, after the spirits of the Colonies decide to resist tyranny, the action speeds up and the character of the poem changes.

Two introductory designs warn the reader that revolutionary renewal will entail great suffering. On the frontispiece, a battle has been lost, but not the war, and a winged giant sitting chained by his wrists personifies energy in bondage. The title page shows a woman desperately trying to revive a wounded man lying on top of corpses as a storm sweeps the field of slaughter. Above, child spirits attempt to give new heart to a man and woman poring over books.

The first element in the Preludium that catches the reader's eye is a drawing of a scene described only in chapter seven of *The Book of Urizen*. Poisoned by jealousy of his son Orc, the fallen Los has shackled him to a rock, while his mother, Enitharmon, laments. Below, a small Orc crouches in a subterranean hollow, but overleaf he emerges from the earth. The state of the fallen human—"A worm of sixty winters" (*Tiriel* 8:11)—is illustrated beside the crouching boy.

The verse of the Preludium describes inert and dumb material nature in the person of the "shadowy daughter," as yet "nameless," of Urthona, the god of the fallen world in "A Song of Liberty." Subsequently Blake calls her Vala (see *The Four Zoas* 91:1-16/ E363/ VIIb, 124-39). She is shadowy because matter is less real than eternal substance, endowed with iron attributes because she is terrible when she imprisons soul, and girdled with cloud because her secret parts (her inmost workings) are "veiled"—the word is a source of her later name. Orc, a fiery being entered into matter, receives physical nourishment from nature while his spirit ventures forth into air and water, onto the earth, and in underground caverns. When he reaches adolescence, he copulates with his provider, and awakens her to new life. "April," Eliot tells us, "is the cruellest month," so perhaps we

of Boston, outside which the first pitched battle was fought in 1775—denounces in precise and memorable terms the hypocritical Urizen and his Old Testament sacrifices. Literally, all the colonies rally to the support of the first rebels. Blake goes on to describe in figurative and hyperbolic language the despair of the colonial governors and the British soldiers. Apparently he refers to the reinforcements sent, for we quickly hear of hosts of imperial troops, confusingly called "Albion's Angels," darkening the mountains of the Atlantic seaboard and then "must'ring in the eastern sky" (13:13, 16). The description echoes Revelation viii and ix, for these evil beings number many millions, blow trumpets, and seek to devastate America with plagues. Fearful, though sustained by the spirit of Orc, the Americans break off their daily activities and unite; even the gifted propagandist Paine, residing in Pennsylvania, and the Virginian Jefferson, who applied his versatile genius with great success to architecture, doubted the outcome. And indeed the Fall would have been deepened and America, the least fallen part of the earth, would have been submerged like Atlantis, had not the flames of Orc driven back the plagues on Britain herself. In the mother country, the war was so controversial that a statesman as respected as Edmund Burke could be a leading pro-American, and the Preface to the *Annual Register* for 1781 could speak of the heroism on both sides in the tragic struggle. Reading in visionary terms the popular riots and merchant class protests directed against the war,[3] Blake attributes the resistance, along with desertions from the army, to the spread of the revolutionary spirit. He depicts the churches of England, Scotland, Ireland and Wales together with the officially approved poetry of Britain as stricken with a deadly pestilence. (The "Bard of Albion" may be, at least on one level, William Whitehead, Poet Laureate from 1757 to 1785.) As the ecclesiastical establishment totters, the emotionally dead women whose fate is lamented in *Visions of the Daughters of Albion* begin to experience a sexual liberation. In the last plate, however, Urizen emerges weeping from his shrine above the heavens to succour his protegés and manages to dampen the flames of rebellion for twelve years—the approximate lapse of time between the American and French Revolutions.

---

[3] David V. Erdman, *Blake: Prophet Against Empire* (Princeton: Princeton UP, 1954), pp. 5-7 [5-8].

A final verse paragraph goes back to the British reverses in the war that make, says the poet, the monarchical governments on the Continent tremble. As Orc's flames approach their kingdoms, they strive in vain to preserve the constriction of the five fallen senses and the moral and political tyranny based on fallen perception.

The struggle between Urizenic and Orcean powers is represented forcefully and often majestically in the designs. On pl. 4 the Guardian Prince of Albion, George III, who is actually named in the prudently cancelled pl. b (E58/ K204), appears as a dragon, as an aged man with a serpentine robe falling in spite of his sceptre and his book, and finally as a desperate man tearing his hair as he looks at what may be a marine mammal—perhaps a visual pun on "Orc." On the next page, the King, together with his counsellor, is condemned by a revolutionary court, complete with executioner and scales of justice. He is hurled into the spiral folds of a snake rising from flames of the energy he has spurned: its terrible character embodies his distorted conception of Orc. In pl. 6 the latter's speech about liberation is illustrated by a young male nude sitting beside the discarded skull of tradition and looking skywards. (He is almost identical to the regenerated man in pl. 21 of *The Marriage of Heaven and Hell*.) Equally blissful is the dawn scene in the next plate, which, with its drooping tree resembling some of those in *Songs of Innocence*, serves as an emblem of the post-revolutionary world that Orc foresees. The newborn Orc on pl. 9, lying under grain bent over by the storms of Albion's Angels, comes between two pages portraying as contraries a bearded, robed, aged Urizen in cloud and a clean-shaven, nude, young Orc in fire; they have right and left foot advanced respectively. Under Orc's influence Boston's Angel rides a swan near the top of pl. 11, and below, a serpent of energy safely mounted by children recalls the last design of *Thel*; ascending birds of paradise close to the swan and serpent testify that they are moving in the right direction. The next two plates remind the observer of the horrors of war by their pictures of an old man entering the Door of Death and corpses being preyed upon; the lower body, with a shell of emptiness beside its head, may represent the sleep of fallen humanity under the Atlantic flood. In pl. 14, the contrary of pl. 7 with its recovery of Innocence, a Urizenic woman with a sinister serpent between her legs gives false instruction to a youth beneath a barren tree resembling several in *Songs of Experience*; its roots reach down to an ambiguous, fire-breathing monster. Tiny signs of hope above the top line and a small bird of paradise above "Then had America been lost" (1. 17) help to counter the baneful impression, and the next page illustrates the defeat suffered by Britain's Urizenic regime. Here liberated figures sport around the first six lines, and below, as the reader's eye moves from right to left, the Daughters of Albion unfold their constricted bodies and ascend amid Orcean flames that produce fruitful vines. The flames are rising to free other women in the left-hand margin. The work awaiting them is illustrated in the final plate, which bears a giant figure bowed in the self-abasement of Urizenic religion in front of spiny, barren trees. Happily, new life springs upon it. The decoration marked "FINIS" burgeons with life—vegetable, serpentine and human.

While *Visions of the Daughters of Albion* is primarily an impassioned poem about human characters, *America* is a cross between an historical narrative and an unfulfilled prophecy (the infinite perception and sexual liberation are not achieved) dominated by mythological figures—Albion's Angel, the Angels of the colonies (including Boston's), Orc, and Urizen. Blake is capable of overworking his terms. Thus, in addition to the Angels of Albion and the colonies, there are Albion's Angels in the plural, who are George III's soldiers, men (16:14) who are angels in the sense given the word in *The Marriage of Heaven and Hell*, and the degenerating angels of "ancient heavens" (15:18), who are probably the ruling class. In a few passages the image aimed at threatens to dissolve in vague generalities that Blake has learnt from *Ossian*: thus the lines

> she...smiled her first-born smile;
> As when a black cloud shews its light'nings to the silent
>   deep
>   (2:4-5)

resemble Macpherson's

    a troubled joy rose on her mind, like the red path of the
    lightning on a stormy-cloud
    ("Oithóna")

and Blake, following Macpherson, overloads his verse, as he did in
The French Revolution, with a plethora of references to cloud. The
excessive repetition of common epithets like "terrible" (seven
times) and "fierce" (nine times and once as an adverb) also makes
for vagueness. Usually, however, clarity wins through, whether the
subject is a mythological figure—

    What crawling villain preaches abstinence & wraps
       himself
    In fat of lambs?
    (11:14-15)

—or symbolic history—

    The scribe of Pensylvania casts his pen upon the earth;
    The builder of Virginia throws his hammer down in fear.
    (14:15-16)

Moreover, the central conflict between repression and revolution is
subtly as well as powerfully conveyed in word and picture, and
through biblical allusion it is related to the antithesis between the
lawgiving and prophetic deities implicit in *The French Revolution*.
Without disguising the horror of warfare, Blake wins his reader's
sympathies for the Americans and their leaders. Though not one of
its author's greatest works, *America* is an heroic narrative in
which Atlantean myth, scriptural imagery, international history,
and a parallel between nature and humankind are synthesised into
a notable illuminated poem of protest and defiance.
    In 1794 Blake engraved *Europe*, a richer and subtler poem
than *America* adorned with designs of greater magnificence.
While expounding his underlying myth, Blake surveys Western
history from the Nativity to the French Revolution. As Susan Fox
has demonstrated, although the book includes some narrative, it
does not have a linear structure but consists of discontinuous por-

tions offering different perspectives on the same phenomenon.[4]
The theme of *Europe* is the fall from the life of Eternity into time,
space, matter and corporeality, and the consequent constricted per-
ception and life-denying morality and politics. On the frontispiece,
one of Blake's greatest artistic masterpieces, Urizen reaches out
from a circle of light to "set a compass upon the face of the depth"
(Prov. viii.27). His hair is caught by the wind of the abyss, and he
holds the compass in his left or sinister hand. (Traditionally the
right—in Latin *dexter*, hence "dexterous"—is the noble and spiri-
tual side, the left—in Latin *sinister*—the evil and ungodly: in
paintings of the Last Judgment, following Matthew xxv.33-46, the
damned always descend on Christ's left while the saved rise on his
right.) Much as Blake deplores the creation, which is an aspect of
the Fall, he clearly betrays a grudging admiration for the splen-
dour of Urizen's undertaking. Facing that creator, a huge ambigu-
ous serpent on the title page hints both at Orc, the fiery rebel, and
at "the vast form of Nature, like a Serpent" (*FZ* 42:13/ E328/ III,
97) as it rears its head and tongue with an assurance matching
Urizen's own. When the same or a similar beast furiously lifts its
seven coils up the side of the eloquent description of the Fall in pl.
10, the coils symbolise the biblical days of creation while five
horns on its crest stand for the depleted senses.

     For some unknown reason—the plate may have been a
late addition or it may have been mislaid[5]—only two of the twelve
known copies of *Europe* include the delightful introductory poem
which, in language as limpid as that of *Thel*, describes how the
narrator captures a fairy. This creature is occupied in mocking
mortals' stubborn clinging to their fallen mode of employing their
senses without vision so that they see only the delusory material
forms of things. In particular they waste their sense of touch in
secret amours and marital possessiveness instead of open, liberat-
ing sexual love. The fairy must be well read, for he alludes (and
here Blake sides with the orthodox moralist) to the harlot's come-
on "Stolen waters are sweet, and bread eaten in secret pleasant"
(Prov. ix. 17), and by choosing "a streak'd Tulip" for his seat, he
defies the neoclassical dogma that art deals with the general, not

---

[4] *Poetic Form in Blake's Milton* (Princeton: Princeton UP, 1976), pp. 10-12.
[5] David V. Erdman, ed., *The Illuminated Blake* (New York: Anchor Press/ Doubleday,
1974), p. 158.

the particular—a dogma memorably expounded in the tenth chapter of Johnson's *Rasselas*: "The business of a poet...is to examine, not the individual but the species...he does not number the streaks of the tulip..." In response to his captor's enquiries, the mocker maintains that the poetic spirit reveals the joyful and eternal reality behind the material facade of the world and shows the narrator the eternal essences of the flowers. Then, leaving simplicity behind him, he dictates the Preludium and Prophecy of *Europe*.

Two of Blake's mythological figures have their first prominent roles in *Europe* and in *The Book of Urizen*, which is also dated 1794. Los, the spirit of imaginative vision and prophecy whose unfallen form is sometimes called Urthona, divides in the fallen world into the male Los and the female Enitharmon, and Orc, energy incarnated on earth, is the first of their many Children. In *Europe*, Enitharmon is in the forefront of the action.

Traditionally, the spirit within is represented as male and nature without—the world of material phenomena—as female. In symbolic terms, for the female to rule the male is for matter or physical nature to rule spirit or energy, and this perverted dominion, which Blake later calls the female will, is just what the power of fallen Enitharmon signifies. On the social level, her reign centres on women's calculated granting and withholding of their sexual favours to make men fulfil their demands, and this, too, is denounced in *Europe*.

If the Preludium of *America* ends with the Shadowy Female's ambiguous cry (she will not let Orc go though she is in torment), that of *Europe* opens with her loud lament. Rising from her lover, she finds herself in the power of his mother, Enitharmon, who forces her to bear offspring that take hideous forms in an abominable world. She pictures herself as an inverted tree compelled through the astrological powers of the heavenly bodies to draw life down from heaven onto an earth characterised by the impermanence of all it contains and by ceaseless conflict between "Devouring & devoured" (2:5). The lower elements can give her no protection (1:12-15) as she brings forth horrors, including human "kings." In making her speak of barren mountains and forests, Blake introduces two of his favourite symbols of the fallen world, but at the end of the Preludium a touch of hope appears, for the Shadowy Female realises that the infinite cannot be permanently bound in spite of the Urizen of the frontispiece, and that

Divine Providence—as Blake's epics and his illustrations to Job will testify—does watch over it. The "shady woe" of the past will be challenged by the "visionary joy" of what is to come (2:12).

While the text of the Preludium operates on a mythical plane, the designs work on a human and political one. In pl. 1 the central figure is an assassin based on a cartoon of Burke by James Gillray.[6] Clasping a dagger, the villain is about to ambush a pilgrim making his way through this mortal life. From the daggerman's right foot a plant grows downwards and overhangs on two sides a naked victim of tyranny plummeting head foremost because a large weight is fastened to his skull. Beside him, the face of a man in anguish, perhaps a reformer, is carried forward by bat's wings. From now on these wings symbolise for Blake what he comes to call the spectre—the Urizenic reasoning power as an independent entity divorced from other human faculties.

In pl. 2 are three bald and wigless middle-aged or elderly men—probably establishment figures—one of whom is strangling the other two; a fourth, though he clutches his scalp in horror, has a healthy head of hair and has managed to escape upwards.

Having given us a perspective on the cosmos in the Preludium, Blake turns to the world of history in the Prophecy, which comprises a mythological narrative interrupted by a sequel to *America*. The mythological narrative begins with an allusion to Milton's "On the Morning of Christ's Nativity" as it tells how Jesus was incarnated only to have his message quickly distorted by a church whose presiding spirit was the fallen Enitharmon. In the last six lines of pl. 3, Los, who is also fallen, announces that the night of Urthona's sleep (i.e. of the Fall) is here again and calls on his Sons to exercise their energies within material nature. He seems to be undisturbed by the presence of Urizen, who is at loose in the north, the quarter of Satan's rebellion in *Paradise Lost* (V, 752-55). However, Urizen's Sons envy the energies of Los and see or foresee them manifested in human warfare and painful labour, in which they take much pleasure. There is an abrupt transition as Enitharmon first calls up her eldest child, Orc—who is, however, safely bound—and then welcomes the night of her happiness, in which an ascetic Christianity enthrones the female will, idealises chastity, and persuades its followers that, though they are but

---

[6] Erdman, *Blake: Prophet* (1954), pp. 201-02 [218-19].

worms, they will enjoy an everlasting reward in the next world for
their self-denial in this. Blake did not hold such a materialistic
notion of heaven.

The text in pl. 8 consists of Enitharmon's summons to her
sons Rintrah and Palamabron, warrior-king and priest, and their
wives—Ocalythron, who is commendably jealous, and Elynittria,
who is probably chaste and Diana-like. The first eighteen centuries
of Christianity are now said to be a dream of Enitharmon (9:1-5).
After indicating in two lines that the armies that determine the
shifting national boundaries are moving shadows in the goddess's
dream, Blake returns to the point in pl. 15 of *America* at which the
plagues let loose by Albion's Angel recoil on Britain. The nation's
Angels (her leaders) defy "immortal demons of futurity"—
energetic radicals to whom the future belongs—and meet in
council. Confounded at first by the pestilence, they recover suffi-
ciently to follow painfully Albion's Angel—their "fiery King" and
"ancient Guardian" (9:10; 10:2, 24). The passage echoes "A Song
of Liberty" and the collapse of "the council house" alludes to the
fall in March 1782 of Lord North's twelve-year-old Government,
which had ruled in close alliance with George III, as a result of
Britain's defeat by the American colonies. For the King and his
friends, a period of "troubled mists" and "terrors" (9:16) followed,
for he had to endure three brief administrations—the first led by
his opponent Lord Rockingham and the last including the ultra-
liberal Charles James Fox—before William Pitt, his sovereign's
ally, became Prime Minister in December 1783.

There follows a passage of remarkable beauty far removed
from the biblical and Ossianic imagery of a Palamabron "skipping
upon the mountains" or defeated politicians regaining strength "as
the stars rise from the salt lake" (8:3, 9:15). Harmoniously com-
bining concentrated imagery, scriptural and antiquarian allusions,
and his conception of the Fall, Blake draws a half dark, half lumi-
nous picture of a British serpent temple that associates primaeval
catastrophe with present repression but intimates the consoling
persistence of glimmers of Eternity. He accepts William Stukeley's
theory that the serpent temple was a Druid structure, and to him
Druidism, except in its very earliest phase, was a debased religion
of human sacrifice offered to a cruel, egotistical god. The serpent
whose form provided the pattern for its temples was a symbol of
the eternal and infinite constricted into the temporal and material,

and the temple where the British reactionaries look for succour is composed of elements from the eternal world which, for all their debasement, retain some touches of heavenly beauty. The fabric consists of pillars constructed from stones of the twelve eternal colours, which are reduced on earth to the seven of the Newtonian spectrum. (At the Fall, which was identical with Noah's Flood, some of these stones became celestial bodies.) The columns are surrounded by the sacred oaks of the Druids, and they have been fashioned, like the altars of the Old Testament lawgiving God, without metal tools (Exod. xx.25; Deut. xxvii.5). In elegiac lines Blake recalls how planets became spherical, space fixed and measurable, and the human creature a reasoning 'angel' who accepted the stellar skies for a heaven and a despot for a deity. Such an unspiritual conception of God suits Albion's Angel, who makes his way to Verulam because Baron Verulam was a title of Francis Bacon, the prophet of that natural science which culminated, Blake believed, in the materialist world-view of Newton.

In *America*, Orc is closely associated with Milton's Satan as well as with the risen Christ (8:1; 6:2). By the time Blake writes *Europe*, he seems to have turned against Milton's Devil, whom he acclaimed in *The Marriage of Heaven and Hell* as the embodiment of divine energy. In *Europe*, Orc still assumes the role of Christ—the text and designs show that "the secret child" of 3:2 is both Jesus and Blake's spirit of rebellion—but it is Urizen who occupies Satan's quarter, the north (4:12), and it is the leading reactionaries who rise, like Milton's fallen angels, as though from a lake (cf. *PL*, VII, 752-53 and I, 271-355); moreover, the descriptions of the satanic Rintrah, who "hung with all his legions in the nether deep" (12:24), and of "the myriads of Angelic hosts" falling "Yellow as leaves of Autumn" (13:6-7) echo Milton's accounts of how Satan "Fell with his flaming Legions through the Deep" (*PL*, VII, 134) and of those legions lying on the infernal lake "Thick as Autumnal Leaves that strow the Brooks" (*PL*, I, 301-02). Reaching the southern end of the temple, Albion's Angel, poised between Urizen and the kings and priests who are his mortal ministers, choose for his throne a key symbol of humanity's fallen state. The Stone of Night is primarily an image of the human head which constitutes the fleshly prison of the mind. This segment of the body was formerly in "that sweet south" (10:27) through which souls reascend to Eternity but has now sunk below the north through which they descend into the material world—a journey to which the northern bar of *Thel* alludes. Urizen's book of religious laws now covers the whole world from north to south.

In pl. 12, Blake cunningly blends myth and history in a verbal picture of the young people of Britain in the state of Experience, conscious that they are misguided by their elders, who compel them to look through unimaginative "senses that are clos'd from thought" (12:8) at the symbols of their oppression: the form of the serpent temple overshadowing the whole island and Albion's Angel erect on a fearful cliff (the Stone of Night) dominating London. They see, too, that for all his power the Angel is hard pressed by Orc's libertarian flame and seeks relief in the coming of the (Urizenic) Last Judgment. Urizen himself is "feeding his soul with pity" (12:4), for his *intentions*, as Blake shows in the book named after him, are of the best.

The poet takes particular delight in one minor victory of Orc. In June 1792, William Pitt persuaded the King to dismiss his Lord Chancellor, Lord Thurlow, who had been intriguing to have the power of the intermittently insane monarch permanently transferred to the Prince Regent. Thurlow was far more conservative than Pitt, who had denounced the war with America and who, before the outbreak of hostilities with France, had sought the reform of Parliament and the abolition of the slave trade. Blake, hater of law, has the satisfaction of describing the highest legal officer in the kingdom, the Lord Chancellor, unable to free his human self from the encumbrance of his judicial wig and gown, scurrying from the Westminster Parliament to St. James's Palace to return the Great Seal to his royal master.

Though Orc can cause Thurlow's downfall, Enitharmon's more pliable Children still oppose him—priestly Palamabron with lightning and kingly Rintrah with armies. Referring to the sleeping Enitharmon's triumphant female dominion, Blake evokes an image of Greater London as a vast prison whose inmates are shackled by the prohibitions of the moral law. Yet Albion's Angel, hard pressed by the flames of rebellion, tries in vain to blow the trumpet that will cut short his ordeal by bringing on the Last Judgment. In lines that compliment as well as accuse Newton, Blake asserts that the great scientist—stronger than the angelic patron of King, Church and Cabinet—does what the Angel cannot, ushering in a new stage of history as his physics plumbs the nadir of materialism giving (to use the poet's later phrasing) a body to error so that it can be cast out (cf. *J* 12:13).

The interlude which starts where *America* ends is now complete, and Blake resumes his mythological narrative. It is late in the eighteenth century, and Enitharmon, unconscious of the history she has dreamed into existence, wakes up and resumes her song celebrating the night which she imposed on humankind after the birth of Christ. Blake has not given us enough information to enable us to understand the significance of all the Children she names, but Leutha is a temptress who spreads the mental "pestilence" (14:12) of frustrated sexuality, and Blake identifies her spirit with the seven early churches of Revelation i to iii. While Antomon and Oothoon reject their mother's sexual puritanism, Sotha and Thiralatha apparently obey her call to soothe Orc, "the horrent fiend" (14:27—cf. 4:15), whom she summons to contribute to the oppressors' revelry that harmonises with the stars of Urizen's astronomical heavens and with all of fallen nature. But she has miscalculated. The American rebellion is the sign that dawn has at last arrived to end the night of the Fall, and to Enitharmon's horror Orc descends on France to inspire the overthrow of a moribund tyranny despite the defiance of his father, Los, and the shudder that runs through nature.

The message of this layered and compelling prophecy is driven home and expanded by designs worthy of it. Intertwined with the subtitle "A Prophecy" in pl. 3 are emblems of the energy to be released by "the secret child" of line 2 (both Orc and Jesus) pictured surrounded by flames in a small circle while his descent is announced by five birds (the five awakening senses) and their woman companion over the first line of verse. However, an ominous winged symbol of the corrupt female power broods over the text. Enitharmon, on pl. 4, lifts a blanket from Orc, who has not yet escaped from her control, while her younger Children sport above. Two powerful designs display her mighty sons Rintrah and Palamabron. Rintrah, with iron crown and scaly armour, stands at the centre of pl. 5 in front of two winged angel-women symbolising the female power he upholds; his sword, conspicuously resembling a cross, suggests that he may be a Crusader. Six pages later a magnificently sinister Palamabron represents the papal power, for he wears the pope's triple crown as he sits with bloated cheeks and spectrous bat wings on a throne decorated with Gothic tracery. His two angel-women stand before and beneath him pointing down with sceptres representing secular authority to the world which he tries to govern from the book on his knees—a book, as the lines below disclose, copied from Urizen's. Two heartrending plates without text, numbers 6 and 7, depict the famine and plague with which Urizen and Enitharmon keep humanity quiescent. The designs on the next two pages represent (probably) fire (pl. 8) and the blight for which Albion's Angel is responsible (pl. 9). The impressions of horror and cruelty are reinforced by the animal and vegetable emblems of corruption on plates 12 and 14, and by the shackled prisoner of pl. 13. On the final plate an energetic young man strives with apparent success to rescue his family from a burning building as two birds hopefully rise.

The great variety of styles in both the text and pictures of *Europe* reflects Blake's many-faceted approach to the history whose inner meanings he seeks to disclose. Within a complex but coherent artistic form, he develops a myth which explains in metaphysical and psychological terms the tragedy of Western Christendom. As the narrative proceeds, the last eighteen centuries on earth are equated with a single night of Enitharmon in the overshadowing world of the gods. The spirit of Orc, bursting out in Jesus but soon suppressed, rises again in modern revolutions, and Enitharmon, Urizen and their kin strive to contain it. Intermittently, concrete scenes of oppression, disaster and the teaching of untruth pass before the reader's eye, but while the contest remains undecided, the end of the book shows that Blake has not lost his faith that a new and better age is at hand.

Although Blake wrote *The Song of Los* (1795), consisting of "Africa" and "Asia," to complete his series of books on the four continents, it seems to have satisfied him less than *America* and *Europe*. It survives only in five copies, all apparently issued in the year of publication,[7] and like *The Book of Ahania* (1795) and *The Book of Los* (1795), which survive only in single copies, it is missing from the lists of illuminated books Blake offers for sale in 1818 and 1827 (E771, 784/ K867, 878). (However, *The Marriage of Heaven and Hell*, of which some late copies survive, is also omitted from these lists.)

---

[7] G. E. Bentley, Jr., *Blake Books* (Oxford: Clarendon Press), p. 359.

The frontispiece and title page of *The Song of Los* refer to the conflict between Urizenic and revolutionary forces. On the frontispiece a worshipper kneels in abject humility at an altar raised before a sun covered with unintelligible marks, the emblems of priestly Mystery, that cause it to resemble the pages of Urizen's book of laws as the latter is portrayed in *The Book of Urizen*. The huge flowing letters of "Los" on the title page overshadow Urizen himself as he lies stretched in the forefront of a desolate, treeless landscape with his left hand resting lovingly on the skull of deadly tradition that the redeemed man on pl. 21 of *The Marriage of Heaven and Hell* presses dismissively under his left knee. This is a very different Urizen from the majestic figure of the frontispiece to *Europe*, and the bird of paradise soaring towards the left above confirms that his reign is doomed.

Africa, *The Book of Urizen* tells us, was the original home of fallen humanity, and, wound irregularly through the name of that continent, which forms the first subtitle, is a malign boa constrictor accompanied by insects of corruption. The five introductory lines corroborate the suggestion of the title page that the Los of this book—"the Eternal Prophet"—is unfallen: he sings from an eternal standpoint, and his words reduce the power of the usurping deity Urizen, while his disclosure of the latter's tyranny horrifies Ariston, "the king of beauty" (*A* 10:10), a positive figure.

After a picture of a shepherd sleeping by his sheep—an emblem of human degeneration—the first half of Los's Song surveys the wretched history of humanity from those two symbols of the Fall, the expulsion from Eden and the Flood, to the return of hope with the rebellion of the Thirteen Colonies in the portion of the earth which is a remnant of the lost Atlantis. Confirming the narrative of *Europe*, Los admits that his own Children became the purveyors of Urizen's laws, except for the eldest, Orc, who remained in fetters. After Adam, Noah and Abram are cut off from the life of Eternity (Adam, at least, sharing the revulsion of Ariston), Urizen gives his law in its classic form to Moses, spreads puritanical doctrines through the Brahminical, Hermetic, Pythagorean and Platonic philosophies, and expresses his taste for imposing morality by violence through Islam and Germanic polytheism. (Antomon was less compliant when Blake previously wrote of him [*E* 14:15-20].) The personified Night of the fallen world gloats over humankind's hypocrisy and internecine slaughter in a mocking spirit resembling Enitharmon's in *Europe*. Although Jesus, hearing the lament of Oothoon, heroine of *Visions of the Daughters of Albion*, wishes to relieve humanity, he remains "a man of sorrows" (Is. liii.3), for her lover Theotormon imposes his ascetic religion on the early church. The next lines refer scathingly to the rise of monasticism, which prevents the finest people from having children: the institutions of society, Blake claims through Los, annihilate the very memory of the higher existence, and in short, swift, rhythmic lines he recalls how Har and Heva (these ancestors of all humanity first appear in *Tiriel*) fled from the mental contentions and the loves of the other Eternals mistaking them for "War & Lust" (4:6) and dwindled into earthbound creatures with shrivelled senses no longer able to perceive reality. Their flight is illustrated on pl. 4.

Urizen's system of a moral law imposed on a humankind cut off from the supernatural and conceiving the measurable, material universe as reality reaches its consummation in the philosophy of Locke and the mathematical, experimental science of his friend Newton. But at this point in history the counter force is crystallising around Rousseau, the apostle of equality, and Voltaire, the enemy of religious tradition and ecclesiastical tyranny. To complete the symmetry of the four continents, Blake also locates focuses of revolt in Asia (which appears to mean the Middle East) and Africa (i.e. Egypt) and concludes the passage by repeating the first line of the Prophecy of *America*.

Between "Africa" and "Asia," a wordless full-page design invites the reader to look towards Eternity, whence this world of pain derives. The fairy queen sleeps inside a lily blossom while the fairy king keeps watch on the adjacent flower. The vast space of the dark background is spangled with stars, and the earth's surface is visible only in the bottom fifth of the page. Sleep is soon to give way to waking, and lapsed souls will follow the King back into Eternity.

The destructive snake round the subtitle "Africa" on pl. 3 is matched by the storm-driven ship constructed around the letters of "Asia" on pl. 6; the waves on which she rides merge further down the page into wind-driven branches. The text suggests that the tempest represents the upheavals of a revolutionary time, and to maintain continuity more branches appear on the next plate.

If *America* is the sequel to "Africa," "Asia" is the sequel to *Europe*. The Orcean flames of the French Revolution arouse fear among the tyrannical Asian monarchs, who determine in their panic to reduce the subject to obedience by economic measures like the fixing of wages and by covert incitement to mob violence. By breaking the spirit of the people, the kings and their priests will teach them the ways of morality which will eventually bring their souls into the materialistically conceived heaven of traditional religion. Responding to the rulers' fears, Urizen flies from the West (he was above the Atlantic in pl. 11 of *Europe*) to resume his biblical position as a lawgiving god over Asian Jerusalem, but the Orcean flames melt his books of metal as he passes through the sky in fear and anguish. When he reaches the sight of his ancient temple, Orc, rising above the Alps, is more than a match for him: in a prophetic conclusion Blake pictures a Last Judgment of joyful resurrection. Rich with biblical imagery, his lines associate Orc with the redeeming God of the Old Testament and with Christ. Orc rises "like a pillar of fire above the Alps/ Like a serpent of fiery flame!" (7:27-28); the allusions are to the "pillar of fire" in which the Lord appeared to the Israelites in the desert by night (Exod. xiii.21), to Moses' brazen "fiery serpent" that was to be raised on a pole to cure those bitten by snakes (Num. xxi.8), and to Jesus' analogy between himself "lifted up" and this image (John iii.14)—an analogy that led to the brazen serpent's being considered a type of Christ on the Cross. References to the prophets follow. First "rattling bones to bones/ Join" (7:31-32) echoing Ezekiel's vision of dry bones reanimated (xxxvii.1-14), and then the grave is filled with life:

> And milk & blood & glandous wine
> In rivers rush & shout & dance,
> On mountain, dale and plain
>   (7:38-40)

The imagery is indebted to visions of Israel's redemption in Amos ix.13 and Joel iii.18. After the declaration "The SONG of LOS is Ended," the narrator adds a two-word coda: "Urizen Wept" (7:41-42). The statement alludes to John xi.35, the shortest verse in the Bible, "Jesus wept." This happened when Lazarus died, but now the Christ-force is victorious and it is Urizen's turn to grieve.

A final plate (the third wordless design) shows Los resting after forging a sun free from the cryptic signs of Mystery. In this satisfying complement to the troubling frontispiece, the human form is above instead of below the heavenly body, in which, as *The Book of Los* reveals, a portion of the eternal energies has been captured for this world.

Though the designs are less powerful than those of *America* and *Europe*, the text of *The Song of Los* has a pleasing conciseness and a satirical bite far removed from the vapory rhetoric of Macpherson. As the poetic catalogue of creeds in "Africa" is followed by the elegiac, almost metrically regular passage on Har and Heva, indignation gives way to sorrow. Then, in longer solemn lines, Blake pits the consummation of Urizen's teachings against newborn Orcean revolt. "Asia," in which proper names are less numerous, is devoted at first to points of social criticism and later to the triumphant climax of the conflict between Orc and Urizen. The six swift iambic lines which conclude Los's Song breathlessly communicate Blake's joy in his vision of humanity reborn.

Why did Blake discard *The Song of Los*? The awkwardness of duplicating the Adam of Genesis with his own Har (Heva is Latin for Eve) probably did not bother him, but even an ardent admirer of the poet can see how outrageous is the easy dismissal of so many religions and philosophies. Moreover, while the identification, hinted at in the conclusion of *The Book of Urizen*, of Israel's slavery in Egypt with humanity's fallen state does much to justify the subtitle "Africa," there is no historical foundation for the conflict in "Asia," even if Bible-hallowed western Asia is primarily meant. The poem is moving but intellectually flawed. The historical myth that springs from Blake's response to the American and French revolutions peters out for lack of a revolution in the East.

6

The Myth of Creation: *The Book of Urizen*; *The Book of Ahania*; *The Book of Los*

At the end of *The Marriage of Heaven and Hell*, Blake claimed that he possessed the Bible of Hell and promised to deliver it to the world. As a first instalment he issued in 1794 an illuminated volume entitled *The First Book of Urizen*, but next year he named its two sequels *The Book of Ahania* and *The Book of Los*. Moreover, in what is probably the latest copy of *Urizen*, he blotted the word "First" from the title page, pl. 2, and most of the running titles.[1] This key work for the student of Blake's mythology is therefore best called *The Book of Urizen*.

The volume is a Genesis describing a cosmic event which is both the creation of the natural universe and a part of the fall from Eternity. The poem is also a parody of Milton's lamentably orthodox *Paradise Lost*. Moreover, since Urizen stands for reason, his antagonist Los for imagination, and the latter's son Orc for energy, the myth has an equally important psychological dimension: it tells of the collapse of the human mind into division and inner conflict.

In the brief Preludium, Blake proposes his subject—the rebellion of Urizen—and invokes the Eternals (the unfallen dwellers in Eternity) as his muses. Like Isaiah's Lucifer (xiv.12-13) and Milton's Satan (*PL*, V, 752-53), Urizen, when he separates himself, is associated with the north. But although *The Book of Urizen*, like *Paradise Lost*, begins with the proposition characteristic of Greek and Roman epic, it is divided into chapters and verses, its text is laid out in typically scriptural double columns, and its first two chapters, like the first two chapters of Genesis, give different accounts of creation. In chapter one, Urizen, to the

---

[1]Textual Notes, E804.

horror of the other Eternals, creates (Newtonian) fixed, infinite space and clock time, both mathematically measurable. His name, though it puns on "your reason," is derived from the Greek *horizein* or *ourizein*, meaning "to limit" and is related to the English word "horizon." The result of his activity, he finds, as he cuts himself off from brotherhood with his peers and wilfully imprisons himself within his own mind, is a chaos both "petrific" and violent. Blake now introduces some of his favourite symbols of lifeless Urizenic landscape: barren mountains, forests, snow and ice. He identifies Urizen not only with Satan but with Milton's Messiah, who does the work of creation and whom he has denounced in *The Marriage of Heaven and Hell* as diabolical. As in several other books and poems, Blake draws on a cluster of Old Testament texts when he portrays Urizen (whom he sometimes nicknames Nobodaddy) as a jealous, invisible, thundering god, who hides himself in clouds and darkness. "Thou hast covered thyself with a cloud," complains Jeremiah, "that our prayer should not pass through" (Lam. iii.44), and the Psalmist declares, "He made darkness his secret place; his pavilion round about him were dark waters and thick clouds of the skies" and adds, "The Lord also thundered in the heavens" (xviii.11, 13). His thunder and clouds are also found in the account of the revelation at Sinai, where Moses is told, "I come unto thee in a thick cloud" and "there were thunders and lightnings, and a thick cloud upon the mount" (Exod. xix.9, 16). (Lowery observes that the image in Psalms xviii haunts Blake as early as "Samson" in *Poetical Sketches*.)[2]

Reverting to the timeless era before the creation of the natural world with its celestial bodies and its "attraction" (or gravity), chapter two opens with a succinct account of the deathless existence of Eternity where flexible senses exclude the possibility that things will seem to have fixed dimensions or locations in measurable space. Suddenly the Eternals find themselves clustering round a rock on which Urizen, who has condensed eternal substance into the four elements (4:14-23), has taken his stand with his Book of Brass—a scripture of Law and Mystery. As he expounds on his heroic labours, the reader learns both of his iden-

---

[2] Margaret Lowery, *Windows of the Morning: A Critical Study of* Poetical Sketches, 1783 (New Haven: Yale UP; London: Oxford UP, 1940), p.76.

tity with the lawgiving God of the Old Testament—his "I alone, even I!" (4:19) recalls the biblical deity's familiar "I, even I" (e.g. Gen. vi.17, Lev. xxvi.28)—and of his good intentions. Lapsing into time-consciousness (he speaks of "days of futurity" [4:9] and soon becomes "aged" [5:26]), he perceives Eternity's fiery energies as deadly sins and infernal flames, and its Swedenborgian freedom from fixed space and time as a fearful vulnerability to change. Denying the need for the interplay between contraries celebrated in *The Marriage of Heaven and Hell*, he seeks a uniform "joy without pain," a "solid without fluctuation" (4:10-11), and rule by a universal code of law—a law promoting peace, compassion and forgiveness as well as unity, but a law which does not allow for the different needs of the lion and the ox. By the third chapter, however, Urizen discovers that though he has tried to create a better world, he is in hell. As the Eternals rage at his folly, he falls from their realm but cannot escape from their energies, which have become to his corrupt consciousness lightless and tormenting fires. Traditionally the flames of hell give no light, as Milton reminds us in his famous phrase "darkness visible" (*PL*, I, 63).

The subject of *The Book of Urizen* is the coming into existence of the fallen world with its anguished inhabitants. Its central character has a principal antagonist, Los. Neatly symmetrical, the narrative opens with two chapters and closes with two chapters in which Los does not appear. He makes his entrance in chapter three, to stand on guard—apparently voluntarily—on behalf of the other Eternals as Urizen, trying to ward off the infernal fires, fashions a shelter which foreshadows the wombs, hearts, and circulatory systems of earthly biology. Seeing the rebel fall into material existence, the Eternals exclaim, "Urizen is a clod of clay" (6:10). While he keeps the monstrous form isolated to quarantine the mental infection that caused it, Los himself begins to fall. Though the breach Urizen has opened in Eternity heals, Urizen himself does not, and Blake's later writings suggest that he could never be redeemed were it not for Los's self-sacrificial labours in forging a body for him: "But Mercy chang'd Death into Sleep" ("To Tirzah," l. 7; cf. *M* 11:15-20).

Although Blake complains that the material world is so rigid that it can be described mathematically, he is no friend to formlessness. "A Spirit and a Vision," he writes in 1809, "are not, as the modern philosophy supposes, a cloudy vapour or a nothing:

they are organized and minutely articulated beyond all that the mortal and perishing nature can produce" (E541/ K576): hence he insists on clear outline as the prime element in drawing, painting and engraving. When Urizen becomes material—"Cold, featureless, flesh or clay" (7:5)—he is "Unorganiz'd" (6:8), loses most of his form, and lapses into "formless unmeasurable [in an artistic, not scientific sense] death" (7:9).

In the two chapters numbered four, Blake tells how, to preserve Urizen ("The eternal mind" [10:19]), Los ("the eternal Prophet" [10:7]) at the cost of great anguish hammers out for him the organs of an imprisoning yet protecting body and the units of time—"hours, days & years" (10:18)—to contain his degenerate consciousness and senses. The process takes seven ages (no actual work is done in the seventh), which on another level are a "horrible night" of separation from Eternity (10:10), for this creation adumbrates Urizen's own creation of the material world in seven biblical days. The reiterated line "And a state of dismal woe" (10:43, etc.) parodies the repeated words of Genesis i "and God saw that it was good."

While Urizen survives, fettered and oblivious of the eternal life he can no longer perceive, Los moves for a time into the centre of the narrative. The price of his dutifulness or altruism is his imprisonment in objective Newtonian space—"space undivided by existence" (13:46)—which is also the formless voidness of the earth in the second verse of Genesis—"a cold solitude & dark void" (13:39). Moreover, his emotions are drawn out in pity towards Urizen, and the narrator comments that "pity divides the soul" (13:53). Here is the germ of one of Blake's subtlest concepts—the emanation. As Los's pity, separated from the wrath he displays after completing Urizen's body (13:12), pours out of him to become an autonomous being, it condenses first into a circulatory and nervous system, then into a complete female body. Appalled at the division of Los, and a little later at the sexual reproduction which follows, the Eternals isolate the new Newtonian space. They enclose it in a tent, which, as the references to curtains, pillars and hooks show, is a form of the Tabernacle that held the Tablets of the Law (which to Blake was an abomination like the material cosmos) in the wilderness of Sinai (19:2-7; cf. Exod. xxvi-xxvii). The fabric of the curtains the Eternals call "Science," a word which often then meant "knowledge" and here denotes either knowledge of reality that can save the mind from perceiving only the illusory fallen world or, much more probably, natural science, which deceives it.

As an autonomous female, Los's consort Enitharmon becomes cruelly flirtatious and coy, but she eventually gives in to him and becomes pregnant with Orc, the spirit of energy. Blake, who was familiar with the pioneering embryological studies of the surgeon John Hunter—the Jack Tearguts of *An Island in the Moon*[3]—describes the stages through which the foetus passes, reminding the reader of the savage and suffering forms of life Urizen's blindness spawns. Orc's birth is the occasion for the Eternals to complete the severance of the temporal world from Eternity.

Los, like Enitharmon, is now deeply degenerate. Providing plentiful ammunition for lovers of the Oedipus complex, Los conceives a jealousy of his son which, for all his efforts, he cannot overcome. Despite Enitharmon's grief, the fallen Los proves chauvinist enough to make her join him in chaining Orc to a mountain top, recalling the exposure of the infant Oedipus to avert the prophecy that he would kill his father and marry his mother. Orc's power, however, is not quelled, for his voice begins to awaken "All things" in the deadly world of Urizen. The references to "the voice of the child" (20:26, 28) link Orc's mission with that of Christ.

At this point Urizen is awoken from his torpor by the stirrings in nature, and he resumes his effort to create a noble world. He employs measuring instruments, including the biblical (and Miltonic) compasses pictured on the frontispiece of *Europe*, and plants "a garden of fruits" (20:42)—the paradise of Eden. Los, acting in the possessive spirit that Blake deplores, jealously isolates Enitharmon and begets a large family, which receives no further mention in this book.

Urizen meets his inevitable disappointment. Exploring the world for which he is responsible, he finds a grim landscape where fragments of reality have become living creatures that prey upon each other:

> ...he saw that life liv'd upon death

---

[3] Carmen S. Kreiter, "Evolution and William Blake," *SR*, IV (1965), 110-18.

The Ox in the slaughter house moans
The Dog at the wintry door
(23:27-25:2)

Moreover, those Children who had emanated from him in Eternity
are reborn on earth as afflicted beings: his four eldest Sons emerge
from the four elements and his Daughters from plants and anim-
als. Blinded by his own philosophy, he transfers the blame for
these horrors onto his offspring and curses them for defying his
moral laws. While he travels over the cities of humans, he weeps
at the world's pain but spins behind him the Net of Religion, an
agent of the female domination denounced in *Europe*, and a con-
strictor, like the physical brain, of the mind.

Under the pressure of the Net, most of Urizen's Children
dwindle into the human beings of the fallen world with diminu-
tive, short-lived bodies and distorting sense organs whose false
Lockean images of their environment they mistake for reality. This
shrinking occupies the six biblical days of creation, the seventh
being an earthbound sabbath in which they forget Eternity. The
cities of the victims are so arranged as to constitute the "heart-
formed Africa" of *The Song of Los* (3:3), that Blake equates with
the Egypt of Israel's enslavement, a geographical symbol of the
fallen condition. While the more submissive citizens draw up laws
of "prudence" (28:6), a virtue scorned in the "Proverbs of Hell,"
the rebels gather under Fuzon, who was born in the element of
fire, and leave Egypt in Blake's version of the Exodus. Africa or
Egypt is further identified with the terrestrial globe suspended in
space, a concept of the scientist who reasons on the basis of the
fallen senses' perceptions. This conception the rebels transcend.

The elaborate portrait of Urizen, creator of a hell, a chaos
and this fallen world, is indebted to the antinomian Gnostic heresy
of the first three or four Christian centuries. Gnosticism taught
that the Old Testament deity, who created the material universe
and formulated the Law, was the Demiurge, a fallen spirit who
had forgotten his origin in the Pleroma, the eternal world, and
thought himself the only god. ("Demiurge" derives from the Greek
demiourgos meaning "workman.") The true God, said the Gnos-
tics, sent Christ to save souls locked up in human bodies, and they
held that knowledge of supersensual reality was a necessary cond-
ition of salvation. Accounts of Gnosticism were accessible to Blake

in, for example, Gibbon's *Decline and Fall of the Roman Empire* and Mosheim's *Ecclesiastical History* (English edition 1744), but his own beliefs are best described as semi-Gnostic, for Los's fall alongside Urizen's ensures that there is some good in creation from the beginning, and he detected the presence of the true God as well as the Demiurge in the Old Testament. In interpreting Genesis he made use of the distinction between two Hebrew terms for the Deity: "Elohim," a plural word translated as "God," and the divine name, the Tetragrammaton, traditionally transliterated as "Jehovah" and translated as "the Lord." As early as 1753, the French commentator Jean Astruc recognised that God is called Elohim in the first account of creation (Gen. i.1—ii.3) and Jehovah Elohim in the second (Gen. ii.4-25).[4] Blake identifies Elohim with the Gnostic Demiurge and Jehovah (or Jehovah Elohim) with the true God of the prophets and the Incarnation. In old age he defended his claim that Nature was the work of the Devil by insisting that the god who "created the heaven and the earth" according to the first verse of Genesis was "not Jehovah, but the Elohim."[5]

The Demiurge is powerfully imaged in many of the pictures which enrich Blake's poem. Among them, ten full-page designs without text are differently arranged in each of the seven surviving copies. (The numbers used here are those in Erdman's *The Illuminated Blake*.) Above the short Preludium, swathed in flames of eternal energy, a kindly female form guides an infant through space. (A separate copy of the picture [1796] is inscribed, but not in Blake's hand,[6] "Teach these Souls to Fly.") Plates 3 and 4 (the latter absent from four copies) show respectively an Eternal as he really is and an Eternal as Urizen sees him, while in pl. 15 three Eternals (in some copies four) look down into the newly formed abyss. Three spirits who fall with Urizen are portrayed with serpents of material nature wound round them (pl. 6), and Urizen himself appears copying with closed eyes his Book of Mystery (pl. 1), unfolding his book for the Eternals (pl. 5), imprisoned in earth (pl. 9), in water (pl. 12), in air (pl. 14), and—in copy

---

[4] Leslie Tannenbaum, *Biblical Tradition in Blake's Early Prophecies: The Great Code of Art* (Princeton: Princeton UP, 1982), pp. 203, 326n7.

[5] G. E. Bentley, Jr., *Blake Records* (Oxford: Clarendon Press, 1969), p. 545.

[6] Textual Notes, E890.

A—in fire (pl. 16); the other copies show the clean-shaven Los in this last element. Caged in a grisly skeleton in pl. 8 and with a half formed body in pl. 11, Urizen commands little respect, but in the mighty design on pl. 22 he retains something of his ancient grandeur though he is shackled and unseeing. The grandeur slowly dwindles as he explores his creation with the " globe of fire" of 20:48 (pl. 23), drags the Net of Religion through the air (pl. 27), and supports it even while it binds him to the earth (pl. 28). In plates 24 and 25 his Children emerge as the text describes.

The story of Los is also depicted. He appears in anguish at his fall (pl. 7), as a body-forging smith (pls. 11, 18), exuding the globe of blood which becomes Enitharmon (pl. 17), enduring her coyness (pl. 19) and sprouting a Urizenic beard and the Chain of Jealousy as he sees her affection for Orc (pl. 21). Orc himself is an infant in pl. 20, and Enitharmon is helping to form the sky in pl. 13—she is associated with space as Los is with time (*M* 24:68). One design, free of all mythological characters, shows a hungry child and dog "at the wintry door" (25:2) (pl. 26). In many plates the text is adorned with birds flying forward or upward as reminders of the life of Eternity, while tangled plant stems several times indicate horrors of the fallen world. A tiny corpse under the inscription "The End of the [first] book of Urizen" makes an eloquent statement to the close observer of pl. 28.

This illuminated book has great merits and serious defects. The designs range from the monumental splendour of pl. 22 to the unsatisfying grotesqueness of pl. 7. The language can combine biblical, Miltonic and scientific allusions to achieve the clipped conciseness of chapters one and seven or the troubling power of chapters two and eight. In places, however, there is a poverty of vocabulary which is not excused by the claim that Blake is parodying the grand style. In the line "Till hoary, and age-broke, and aged" (5:26), the last word is redundant; the phrase "Rage, fury, intense indignation" (4:45) is generalised and almost commonplace; and the expression "eternity on eternity" (18:5) is inflated. The narrative has, on the whole, a satisfying form, beginning and ending with the acts of Urizen and leaving the reader on a note of hope as Fuzon's rebellion erupts. The structure is especially strengthened by the implication that the forging of Urizen's body and the dwindling of humanity are both facets of the six-day creation of Genesis, and by the repeated appearance of the image of the heart, an organ into which an aspect of eternal life is compressed. Urizen's first shelter against the flames is heart-like (5:28-37), as are the globe that sinks from his spine (11:1-7), the globe that splits off from Los (13:52-59; 18:1-8), and, collectively, the cities of fallen humanity (25:43-47). On all these levels, the same process of reduction is operating.

Blake abandons his plan to produce more Books of Urizen. Instead he calls the Exodus of his Bible of Hell *The Book of Ahania* and continues the series with *The Book of Los*, which reviews from a new standpoint events he has already narrated. In both these volumes, he continues to divide the text into chapters and verses. After 1795, however, he abandons the project apparently discarding these two books, which only survive in single copies, and beginning, perhaps not till a year or two later, a poem on an epic scale named *Vala*. While *America*, *Europe* and *The Song of Los* envisage the spiritual and social redemption of humankind, the two sequels of *The Book of Urizen* seem unable to encompass this. Having portrayed the Fall powerfully and pathetically in *Urizen* and in his great series of large colour prints of 1795, he seems to have been temporarily at a loss as to how to portray the redemption. His so-called conversion during his years at Felpham may have freed him to accomplish this task.

The division of Los is recounted in *The Book of Urizen*; the more horrible division of Urizen is the principal subject of *The Book of Ahania*. In spite of some obscure and grotesque imagery and an ungainly structure, it is an intriguing and moving work.

While the frontispiece pictures Urizen gloating over Ahania in jealous seclusion and the title page shows the wraith-like emanation in solitary banishment, the poem opens with his wrathful son Fuzon, who burns with fires of energy and recognises his father as the secretive, lawgiving god poised over the waters of the second verse of Genesis. The globe of his wrath that Fuzon hurls at Urizen turns into a beam, becomes an autonomous character remembering its maker's hand and laughing scornfully at its target's shield, and metamorphoses into the pillar of fire that guided the Israelites through the wilderness at night. So far Fuzon has acted the valiant part of Moses the rebel against Pharoah's kingly authority, but believing he has killed Urizen he seeks to usurp his supposed place as supreme deity with the declaration "I am God...eldest of things!" (3:38). Abruptly he falls, slain by his father, and an allusion to his beauty and his tresses equates him with the villainous Absalom, who lost his life in a rebellion against *his* father, the Psalmist David (cf. II Sam. xiv.25-26, xviii.9). At the same time, the words "His beautiful visage...smitten with darkness" (3:41-43) recall Isaiah's reference to the Messiah whose "visage was so marred" (lii.14) and point forward to his fate when the god who begot him nails his corpse to a treetop. There he groans but is not resurrected, for he is no Christ. Indeed at the end of the book a picture of severed heads and headless trunks, the work of the guillotine, signifies that on the political level Blake identifies him with Robespierre, who decayed from honourable rebel to bloodthirsty tyrant.

If Fuzon wins the reader's sympathy only to forfeit most of it, Urizen earns his or her unremitting abhorrence. Cold, jealous and secretive, this god burns with a lust he cannot express, and Fuzon's missile, passing through his loins, cuts him off from his feelings, which he condemns as sin even while he enjoys them in secret. The lust he guiltily suppresses engenders unnatural forces, one of which, a "lust form'd monster" (3:27) in the shape of a serpent, contends with him for power. Overcoming the beast, he uses the poison of its blood to kill Fuzon with a missile very different from his own beam of wrath. In chapter three, after recapitulating the story of Urizen's establishing himself on a rock (the product of his own mental processes) and writing his books, Blake develops the motif of the Tree of Mystery, which sprouts under his heel in "The Human Abstract." Now it enormously proliferates and overhangs Newtonian space, for it represents material nature as well as ritualistic, authoritarian religion. Chapter four repeats in a backflash the narrative of Los's forming of Urizen's body and of the biological degradation of Urizen's Children, whose leader is Fuzon. This degradation goes on for forty years of subjection to Mystery—which are the forty years the Israelites spent in the wilderness, where they received the Law at Sinai, the mountain which Blake identifies with the poisoned rock that slew Fuzon. At the end of this time, reduced to reptilian status, they complete the passage from Africa to Asia (i.e. Canaan and its neighbours), which then "Arose in the pendulous deep" (4:42)—the sea upon the globe of earth suspended in space.

Blake keeps the finest poetry of this book till the end. In the fifth and final chapter, the banished Ahania of the title page, the "parted soul" (2:32) of Urizen, who has "cast" her from his "bright presence" (4:63), wanders as a shadowy being on the edge (like Oothoon) of non-existence (4:45-55; cf. *VDA* 7:14-15). In a poignant and beautiful lament, she contrasts Urizen's loathsome terrestrial landscape with the paradise of Eternity, which she evokes with images of palaces, fruits, nourishing dew and morning songs borrowed from such poetic passages of the Old Testament as Psalms xlv.8, Numbers xiii.23, Proverbs iii.20 and Job xxxviii.7. The ecstatic love between herself and Urizen was then free from all jealousy. He allowed her access to "the sons of eternal joy," while she welcomed the "eternal births" that he begot on "the daughters of life." These births and her own children—her fruits with their "infant joy"—were probably the "seed of eternal science" (that is of true knowledge) that Urizen sowed during his days of labour, for there are days in Blake's Eternity as in Milton's (5:16, 17, 22, 27, 34; cf. *PL*, V, 580-82). Freedom, love and intellect must flourish together: the constraints of fixed law and possessiveness destroy them all. In the last verse Ahania reverts to the horrible present of her exile using words and images earlier spoken by the world of "Earth's Answer" that could not rise from its fallen state.

In *The Book of Ahania*, Blake tries to contrive a symbolic poem which will correlate the story of Exodus with the course of the French Revolution, while on a psychological level it dramatises the conflict between generations and the consequences of denying the emotions their own life. Replacing the fiery Orc with the equally fiery Fuzon, the poet-artist makes him stand for the liberator Moses decayed into a lawgiver and the revolutionary Robespierre degenerated into a tyrant. Whereas Orc in *America* is linked with Christ resurrected, Fuzon is associated only with Christ crucified. His history, broken off abruptly, is succeeded by the exquisite complaint of Ahania: lightly touching on each image they introduce, the short, unrhymed lines convey a heart-wrenching nostalgia for lost perfection.

Neither Ahania nor Fuzon appears in *The Book of Los*, which reverts to the story of Urizen's and Los's collapse into temporal, spatial existence and tells it from Los's viewpoint with many cross-references to *The Book of Urizen*. Blake, who has abandoned his plan of imitating successive sections of the Bible, puts the words into the mouth of a Muse, Eno, who has guided the chariot of Leutha or sexuality "Since the day of thunders" (3:3)—the time of Urizen's fall from Eternity. (Leutha appears in a noble form in *Visions of the Daughters of Albion* [pls. iii, 1], in a corrupt state in *Europe* [pl. 14]). In recalling Eternity, Eno expounds in delicate lines Blake's antinomian doctrine that the way to convert vices into virtues is to satisfy their cravings. She remembers how four of the deadly sins were so disarmed.

Unless Eno's song ends at 3:26 (as usual, Blake shuns quotation marks), she next launches into an account of conflict between the falling Los and the energetic flames of Eternity, the "living creations" of *Urizen* 5:1, which have form and intelligence and are appalled by what they see but which, to lapsed spirits with distorted perception, seem corrosive, lightless and plague-bearing. Forced "to watch Urizen's shadow" (3:32)—i.e. the shadow of the real or eternal Urizen—he quickly comes to resemble him. (The version of this narrative in *The Four Zoas* tells us that Los "became what he beheld" [53:24/ E336/ IV, 203]). The flames are intimidated by Los's resistance to them, and some of them solidify into the rock-like "solid without fluctuation" (4:9) that Urizen had longed for (*BU* 4:11) and that now encloses Los. But his "Prophetic wrath" (4:19) survives and enables him to shatter his prison at the price of falling through the vacuum of Urizen's Newtonian space much as Milton's Satan falls from heaven (*PL*, VI, 871), his motion itself being the only measure of time and space —indeed giving them existence.

Finding himself in an abyss resembling the Miltonic Chaos rather than the Miltonic Hell, Los discovers that he has lost his form—all forms being more highly organised in Eternity than in the world of matter—and strives to give his mind and body such organisation as is possible. His former "expanding clear senses," which were fully Human, are soon confined in "finite inflexible organs" (4:10, 45). While his other parts remain formless, he produces a pair of lungs, the germ of what becomes a "white Polypus" swollen to "An immense Fibrous form" (4:57; 5:1)—a symbol in Blake's later works of proliferating formless nature swarming with predatory human beings. It seems to arise here from Los's inhaling material into his lungs from the ocean of matter through which he sinks as his spirit ebbs leaving him a prey to sleep. (According to *Paradise Lost*, VII, 276-79, which expands on Genesis i.9, the whole earth was originally covered by sea.) Rising to the surface, he regains his initiative and begins to separate the elements.

The statement "Then Light first began" (5:10) tells the reader that the narrative has arrived at the primaeval event described in the third verse of Genesis. There follows another account of Los's forging a body to preserve the fallen Urizen, but this time the artificer concentrates on fixing into the astronomical sun such particles of the Eternals' "infinite fires" (5:27) as remain accessible to him. Though this sun is only a "glowing illusion" (5:47), it has the power to drive away the waters of the deep and it preserves an element of Eternity in this world. When Los fastens Urizen's backbone to it, the latter finds its energy painful enough to make him dim its splendour with the four rivers of Eden (Gen. ii.10-14). Nevertheless, it gives the reasoning deity's body the existence of "a Human Illusion" (5:56)—of the simulacrum of an eternal being.

Though the text of this book offers little hope of redemption, there are slight signs in the engravings that Los's labours are not for nought. While the frontispiece is a dismal picture of Eno with her mouth open as though she is moaning, and the title page shows Los imprisoned in rock, the last plate concludes with an image of a free Los in triumph above his sun. Moreover pl. 3 bears an image of Urizen with a book and a papal triple crown presiding over a web on which lie a man and a woman gazing unhappily towards him, but from the woman's corner a stem runs to the "s" of "Los" hinting at the possibility of escape into the world of prophecy, while from the man's a longer stem runs above the whole design and forms itself into a series of loops suggesting the vines of Blake's Innocent world.

Although *The Book of Los* is intellectually challenging, it is not, after the first twenty-six lines, poetically rewarding. Its vocabulary and rhythms are for the most part inadequate to convey conceptions of Miltonic grandeur, and it is worth reading mainly for the light it throws on some of the author's other writings.

In 1794 Blake produced two rich and powerful works: *Europe* and *The Book of Urizen*. In 1795 he followed them with three weaker volumes: *The Song of Los, The Book of Ahania* and *The Book of Los*. However, his outstanding achievement in this year was a series of twelve large colour prints, of which eleven illustrate aspects of the Fall and the fallen world, while the twelfth shows the resurrected Christ appearing to the Apostles. With some justification, a number of critics regard these colour prints as being among Blake's greatest works.

7
Blake's Conversion

When Blake resumed the composition of mythological poetry, he began an epic entitled *Vala or The Death and Judgement of the Eternal Man, a Dream of Nine Nights.* The division into "Nights" instead of the traditional "Books" reflects his intimate involvement with Young's *Night Thoughts*, a poem of comparable length also divided into nine "Nights," to the illustration of which he devoted himself from 1795 to 1797. His illustrations and the epic both concern suffering in mortal life and Christian redemption. The inscription "The Bible of Hell, in Nocturnal Visions collected. Vol. I. Lambeth" (E818/ K897) may indicate that *Vala* is the product of Blake's second attempt to write the infernal scriptures he had promised the world early in the decade (*MMH*, pl.24).

Unfortunately the chaotic state of the manuscript of *Vala*, which was much revised but never brought to a finished state, allows no certainty as to the contents of the original version, of which Blake began to make a fine copy in 1797. If Margoliouth's endeavour to disentangle the original *Vala*[1] has been largely successful, the poem of 1797 is constructed around a number of elements that Blake has already treated separately: Urizen's first, unsuccessful attempt at creation and his rejection of Ahania; the descent of Los and Enitharmon, Los's making of a body for Urizen, and the birth and chaining of Orc; Urizen's second attempt at creation, his web, and his Tree of Mystery; Orc's confrontation with Urizen; the redemption of fallen humanity at the Last Judgment. Now, however, Blake adds new events, concepts and characters, including Vala herself, an Orc who (like Fuzon) begins as a noble rebel but is corrupted by his enemy Urizen, and a realm named Beulah intermediate between the eternal and fallen worlds.

---

[1] H. M. Margoliouth, ed., *William Blake's* Vala: *Blake's Numbered Text* (Oxford: Clarendon Press, 1956).

Though largely a new character, Vala is a development of the Nameless Shadowy Female of the Preludiums of *America* and *Europe*. She represents external, material nature, whose dazzling beauty lures the human into a lower state. The Eternal Man who is seduced is both the individual soul and collective humanity, for Blake draws on a concept found in Swedenborg's Grand Man and the Cabbalists' Adam Kadmon—an unfallen cosmic human form that contains within itself in a primal unity every individual human and every created being and thing. Within the Eternal Man (revised to Ancient Man and later named Albion [E300, 818/ K263]), Los and Urizen co-exist with two other deities or "Zoas." The Greek word "Zoa," a plural form, means "beasts," and it is applied to the four beings round the throne of the Lamb (Rev. iv.6-9), who are a New Testament version of the four "living creatures" round the divine throne in Ezekiel's vision (i.5-14). The additional Zoas are Luvah, representing the passions, especially love, and Tharmas, representing the body and the senses. Each Zoa has an occupation. As an artist who imposes form on the formless, Los is a smith. Urizen is a farmer who ploughs, harrows, and sows in heaven "The seed of eternal science" ("science" carries its eighteenth-century meaning of knowledge) (*BA* 5:34); his Plough of Ages prepares the way for the phases of history. Dionysus-like, Luvah makes and distributes the wine of passion and energy. Tharmas, patron of the body, in which all the faculties operate, is a shepherd who watches over the whole flock in the tradition of the biblical divine shepherd. As Fisher has noted,[2] the Zoas are more than allegorical personifications: thus Urizen has feelings and instincts although he is dominated by reason. However, the Zoas do represent detached portions of the human wholeness and in this epic they contend for total power over the entire person until, with the coming of the Last Judgment, they recognise their error:

If Gods combine against Man Setting their Dominion above
The Human form Divine, Thrown down from their high Station

---

[2] Peter F. Fisher, *The Valley of Vision: Blake as Prophet and Revolutionary* (1961; rpt. Toronto and Buffalo: U of Toronto P, 1971), p. 231.

In the Eternal heavens of Human Thought [*final text*
Imagination]: buried beneath
In dark oblivion with incessant pangs ages on ages,
In Enmity & war first weaken'd, then in stern repentance
They must renew their brightness & their disorganiz'd
functions
Again reorganize till they resume the image of the human,
Cooperating in the bliss of Man, obeying his Will,
Servants to the infinite & Eternal of the Human form
    (126:9-17/ E395, 844/ IX, 366-74; Margoliouth, ed.,
Vala, p. 59)

In this passage, the essential subject matter of Blake's four epics is
summarised, though the revised version of *Vala*, renamed *The
Four Zoas*, is a more ardently Christian work.

    While Blake stayed at Felpham under Hayley's well meant
patronage, he began to pass through a transforming spiritual exp-
erience sometimes referred to as his "conversion." An inkling of
his religious outlook on the threshold of this experience can be
obtained from the marginalia he wrote in 1798 in *An Apology for
the Bible*, Bishop Richard Watson's attack on Thomas Paine's
Deistic objections to the Scriptures. Blake agrees with the latter's
slashing strictures on their literal sense and finds Paine a better
Christian than the churchman. In his marginalia, the poet is
straining to agree as far as possible with the Deist—he even seems
to accept for the moment the account in Genesis of created nature
before Adam's sin as the perfect work of God, whereas in his
approximately contemporary notes on Bacon's *Essays* he protests
that "The Devil is the Mind of the Natural Frame" (E625/ K403).
Yet he admits there is a higher truth hidden in the Bible than a
mere rationalist can know: "The Bishop never saw the Everlasting
Gospel any more than Tom Paine" (E619/ K394). The phrase "the
everlasting gospel," a quotation from Revelation xiv.6, was a fav-
ourite with the seventeenth-century English sects whose antinom-
ianism, as Morton has shown, Blake appears to have inherited.[3]
Already he has adopted a belief that is to remain a lifelong conv-

---

[3] A. L. Morton, *The Everlasting Gospel: A study in the sources of William Blake*
(London: Lawrence and Wishart, 1958), pp. 36-40.

iction: "The Gospel is Forgiveness of Sins & has no Moral Precepts; these belong to Plato & Seneca & Nero" (E619/ K395).

The fervent if not fanatical profession of allegiance to Christianity of Blake's later years emerges from a protracted process of inner change which can be glimpsed in some of the most striking passages in his correspondence. The transformation has both spiritual and artistic aspects. In the first of two letters that he wrote to Butts on 22 November, 1802, he made his earliest surviving declaration of faith characteristic of his later manner. After disclosing that he has been "very unhappy" but has now "again Emerged into the light of Day," he adds,

> I still & shall to Eternity Embrace Christianity
> and Adore him who is the Express image of God
> but I have travel'd thro Perils & Darkness not un-
> like a Champion. I have Conquer'd and shall still
> Go on Conquering. Nothing can withstand the
> fury of my Course among the Stars of God & in
> the Abysses of the Accuser.
> (E720/ K815-16)

However, his inner struggle is not yet consummated, and two years later, on 23 October, 1804, he writes to Hayley:

> For now! O Glory! and O Delight! I have entirely
> reduced that spectrous Fiend to his station, whose
> annoyance has been the ruin of my labours for the
> last passed twenty years of my life. He is the
> enemy of conjugal love, and is the Jupiter of the
> Greeks, an iron-hearted tyrant, the ruiner of
> ancient Greece. I speak with perfect confidence
> and certainty of the fact which has passed upon
> me....Suddenly, on the day after visiting the
> Truchsessian Gallery of pictures, I was again
> enlightened with the light I enjoyed in my youth,
> and which has for exactly twenty years been
> closed from me as by a door and by window-shut-
> ters.
> (E756/ K851-52)

Blake is convinced that he has reintegrated the Urizen or rational power ("the Jupiter of the Greeks") within himself into his psyche just as Urizen is redeemed and restored at the end of each of his three epics (*FZ*, IX; *M* 42:18-19; *J* pl. 96). Henceforward he discards his enthusiasm for revolution (which was already cooling when he made *The Book of Ahania*) and emphasises the reform of the individual at least as much as the reform of society.

Urizen, Blake charges in the letter last quoted, has marred his labours for twenty years. In the context, "labours" refers to his art, and the recovery of the light of his youth is his return to the Neoclassical (especially Florentine) and Gothic styles of his early manhood, in which outline is primary and colour, light and shade are secondary. The opposite is true of the Venetian and the later Flemish schools and the work of Rembrandt. In August 1799 he writes to his would-be patron Dr. John Trusler, author of *The Way to be Rich and Respectable* and *Hogarth Moralized*, that the purpose of his life is "to renew the lost Art of the Greeks" but indicates that rather than drawings he would like to make for Dr. Trusler small oil paintings not "unworthy of a Scholar of Rembrant & Teniers," whom he has "Studied no less than Rafael & Michael angelo" (E701/ K792). On 2 July, 1800, referring to George Cumberland's plan for a national gallery, he exults over "the immense flood of Grecian light & glory which is coming on Europe" (E706/ K797). At Felpham, in 1801, he embarks on a reconsideration of his artistic principles, which he describes in the first of his two letters to Butts dated 22 November, 1802. For two years, he says, he has made an "intense study of those parts of the art which relate to light & shade & colour," and he quotes approvingly Reynolds' view that Venetian picturesqueness is a lesser thing than Florentine grandeur and that the two qualities cannot be combined (E718-19/ K814). As Paley convincingly argues, Blake's view in the Truchsessian Gallery of numerous fine copies of Florentine, Venetian, Flemish and Dutch paintings (and perhaps a few originals) seems to have crystallised his embrace of Florentine art and his indiscriminate rejection of Venetian, Flemish and Dutch.[4] Henceforth he intemperately damns Titian, Rubens and Rembrandt while lauding Michelangelo, Raphael, Raphael's

---

[4] Morton D. Paley, "The Truchsessian Gallery Revisited," *SR*, XVI (Spring 1977), 165-77.

disciple Giulio Romano, and the northerner Albrecht Dürer. All these artists were represented (at least by copies) in the Truchsessian collection. By about 1810 Blake can assert "To recover Art has been the business of my life to the Florentine Original" (E580/ K600). The supreme value he now attaches to form or outline is not entirely new: in *The Book of Urizen*, for example, the fallen god sinks into "formless unmeasurable death" (7:9), and he must acquire a new form to revive. On the one hand, nothing can have real and eternal existence unless it has a definite form with a clear outline, for "The Infinite alone resides in Definite & Determinate Identity" (*J* 55:64); on the other hand, "a body"—a specific form—must be given "to Falshood that it may be cast off for ever" (*J* 12:13) in what Blake calls a Last Judgment (E562/ K612-13).

Blake's assertion that the "spectrous Fiend" Urizen was "the ruiner of ancient Greece" foreshadows his turning away from Hellenic art, about which he had so enthused a year or two before. While some of his contemporaries, such as the artist Barry and even Hayley, regard the Romans as vulgar and destructive imperialists, Blake now applies these strictures also to the Greeks.[5] About this period,[6] he writes in his Notebook,

> Titus. Constantine Charlemaine
> O Voltaire Rousseau Gibbon vain
> Your Grecian mocks & Roman Sword
> Against this image of his Lord
>
> . . . .
>
> a Grecian Scoff is a wracking wheel
> Roman pride is a sword of steel...[7]

By the time he writes the Preface to *Milton*, perhaps as late as 1809,[8] he is denouncing "The Stolen and Perverted Writings of Homer & Ovid: of Plato & Cicero," which are wickedly "set up by artifice against the Sublime of the Bible." In holding the Greco-Roman arts to be inferior derivatives from those of the ancient

---

[5] Morton D. Paley, "'Wonderful Originals'—Blake and Ancient Sculpture," in *BT*, pp. 170-97 (see pp. 179, 181).
[6] David V. Erdman, ed., *The Notebook of William Blake: A Photographic and Typographic Facsimile*, rev. (New York: Readex Books, 1977), p. 55.
[7] *Ibid.*, N8; also E202, 811/ K420.
[8] Textual Notes, E 806.

Hebrews and their contemporaries and to be inspired by Muses who, as the Greeks admitted, were daughters of Mnemosyne (Memory) (E531/ K565-66), Blake is following, with some variation, the beliefs of Milton. In *Paradise Regained*, Christ, tempted by Satan, scorns the pagan philosophies and dismisses Greek poetry as a weaker imitation of the Hebrew (IV, 331-42)—the idea that all ancient learning had an Israelite origin was quite common in the seventeenth century; in a famous passage in *The Reason of Church Government*, Milton contrasts the lesser verse "obtained by the invocation of Dame Memory and her Siren daughters" with that to be earned only by "devout prayer to that eternall Spirit who can enrich with all utterance and knowledge, and sends out his Seraphim with the hallow'd fire of his Altar to touch and purify the lips of whom he pleases" (the allusion is to Is. vi.6-7).[9]

Blake's new enthusiasm for Hebraic as opposed to Greek art is accompanied by a recovered interest in the Trinity[10] and in Swedenborg,[11] as well as the emergence of a marked Pauline element in his creed and his adoption of the time-honoured mystical doctrine of self-annihilation. Along with these developments, he begins to synthesise the philosophy or world-view of his maturity, which is more complex and more Christian than the outlook embodied in his shorter prophetic books.

References to the Holy Spirit in Blake's annotations of 1798 to Watson's *Apology for the Bible* and in a letter to his brother of January 1803 are the first signs that Blake is again finding the Trinity significant as he had when he wrote *The Marriage of Heaven and Hell* (E614, 727/ K387, 822). His reconsideration of Swedenborg is not easy to date, but his account in *The Four Zoas* of how the Eternals can appear either as a multitude or as one man is indebted to Swedenborg's teaching that heaven can appear as a multitude of human-formed angels, as many men each consisting of a society of angels, or as one Grand Man (*FZ* 21:1-4/ E310-11/ I, 469-72; *Heaven and Hell*, nos. 59-77), and section

[9] *The Works of John Milton* (New York: Columbia UP), III (1931), 241.
[10] H. Summerfield, "Blake and the Names Divine," *BIQ*, XV (Summer 1981), 14-22 (see p. 15).
[11] Morton D. Paley, "'A New Heaven is Begun': William Blake and Swedenborgianism," *ibid.*, XIII (Fall 1979), 64-90 (see pp. 78-83).

VIII in the *Descriptive Catalogue* of 1809 constitutes a handsome tribute to the sage.

After about 1800 a Pauline element becomes quietly pervasive in Blake's thought and vocabulary. In a passage of Night the Ninth that Margoliouth includes in his reconstruction of a relatively early version of *Vala*, the Ancient Man complains of the "war within my members" (119:32, 120:9/ E388, 389/ IX, 99, 119) echoing Romans vii.23: "But I see another law in my members, warring against the law of my mind..." The epigraph to *The Four Zoas* is a verse from Ephesians, and Paul's Mosaic veil (II Cor. iii.13-16) becomes Blake's "Veil of Mystery" (*FZ* 104:37 and textual note/ E378, 842/ VIII, 265). The poet repeats the Apostle's claim that Jesus "brought life and immortality to light through the gospel" (II Tim. i.10, quoted E875, 664/ K757, 774), and in the Laocoön Engraving (*c.* 1820) he follows Paul (I Cor. xii. 27) in identifying Jesus as the Divine Body and asserting "we are his Members" (E273/ K776). In the same engraving he employs Paul's phrase "the natural man" that he has not used since he annotated Swedenborg's *Divine Love and Divine Wisdom* about 1789 (I Cor. ii.14; E603, 606, 273/ K90, 93, 776), and likewise Pauline is his equating the natural man with Adam (I Cor. xv.44-47; E273/ K776).

St. Paul's dualism, that pits the natural body against the spiritual body appears in "To Tirzah," a poem added to *Songs of Experience* shortly after 1800.[12] Its engraving bears a quotation from I Cor. xv.44: "It is Raised a Spiritual Body." In Night the Eighth, added comparatively late to *The Four Zoas*,[13] the natural and spiritual bodies are referred to as the "vegetated body" and "Spiritual body" (104:37-38/ E378/ VIII, 265, 267), and Blake borrows from Paul's phrase "the body of this death" (Rom. vii.24) when he writes of "the dark body of corruptible death" (108:21/ E383/ VIII, 505). The description in *Milton* of the hero's mortal frame as "that body,/ Which was on earth born to corruption" (17:14-15) echoes Paul's claim that the corpse in its grave "is sown in corruption" (I Cor. xv.42). In his very late annotations to Wordsworth's *The Excursion*, Blake even employs the Apostle's words "vile body" (Phil. iii.21) when he asks, "does not this Fit &

---

12 Textual Notes, E 800; Notes, K 894.
13 Textual Notes, E 817.

is it not Fitting...to the Vile Body only & to its Laws of Good & Evil & its Enmities against Mind" (E667/ K784). However, as Hagstrum tartly and truly remarks, neither Paul nor Blake explains what is meant by a spiritual body.[14] Nevertheless, Blake's distinction in later life between the natural body and the soul that inhabits it is frequent and clear—"(For Vala produc'd the Bodies, Jerusalem gave the Souls)" (J 18:7); he is certain that "in Paradise they have no Corporeal & Mortal Body" (E564/ K616); and he believes that the illusion of a material or natural body comes into existence as a result of distorted fallen perception: "Error or Creation will be Burned Up & then & not till then Truth or Eternity will appear. It is Burnt up the Moment Men cease to behold it" (E565/ K617).

Paul's exhortation to his followers to "put off...the old man" and "put on the new man" that "is renewed in knowledge after the image of him that created him" (Ephes. iv.22, 24; Col. iii.10) can be interpreted as a summons to the mystic's task of eliminating his or her ego so that the greater divine self buried within can replace it. The ego that the mystic seeks to overcome is the self that is apt to centre its life on fleshly desires and worldly ambitions. Adopting the ancient mystical doctrine of self-annihilation (the term is not of his own invention), Blake names the entity that is to be destroyed the selfhood and the true self that is to replace it the Humanity. In *Jerusalem* he speaks of "the Selfish Center" and "the Selfish Virtues of the Natural Heart" (71:7; pl. 52, prose), and ascribes holiness rather to the circumference or outline that defines individual identity and that, in Eternity, is within the individual and has the power of expansion, which it loses at the Fall (J 19:36, 69:41-42, 71:6-8, 98:20-22). He makes the Eternals declare that

> ...however great and glorious, however loving
> And merciful the Individuality, however high
> Our palaces and cities, and however fruitful are our fields,
> In Selfhood we are nothing, but fade away in morning's
>   breath
> (J 40[45]: 10-13)

---

[14] Jean H. Hagstrum, "Christ's Body," in *WBEK*, pp. 129-56 (see p. 143).

In the view of Murry, Davies and Damrosch,[15] Blake conceives of self-annihilation as a continuous process, not a metamorphosis.

The traditional concept of self-annihilation includes transcendence of the reason, but Blake differs from most mystics in that he usually views the selfhood as centred on the autonomous reasoning power cut off from the other activities of the mind. Such reasoning power he calls a spectre. The earliest expression of his new doctrine comes in a fragment written in 1803 or quite soon thereafter:[16]

> Each Man is in his Spectre's power
> Untill the arrival of that hour
> When his Humanity awake
> And cast his own Spectre into the Lake
> > And there to Eternity aspire
> > The selfhood in a flame of fire...
>
> (E810/ K421)

Blake first uses the term "self-annihilation" in an undatable passage of *The Four Zoas* not included in Margoliouth's text of *Vala* (85:34/ E368/ VII, 344); he specifies the essential outward expression of this inward act when he refers to "Forgiveness of Sins which is Self Annihilation" (*J* 98:23)—in 1798 he singles out forgiveness as the doctrine which distinguishes Christianity (E619/ K395). For the rest of his life, he regards self-annihilation as the key to Eternity.

The doctrine of self-annihilation has normally been a part of the negative way in mysticism. This way is based on asceticism as a means of transcending sense perception and awakening the higher faculties of the soul. It is the kind of mysticism upheld in T. S. Eliot's *Four Quartets*. Though Blake praises some traditional mystics and moralists—"Fenelon, Guion, Teresa,/ Whitefield & Hervey...with all the gentle Souls/ Who guide the great Wine-press of Love" (*J* 72:50-52)—he always remains a passionate opponent

---

[15] J. Middleton Murry, *William Blake* (1933; rpt. London and Toronto: Cape, 1936), p. 236; J. G. Davies, *The Theology of William Blake* (Oxford: Clarendon Press, 1948), p. 63; Leopold Damrosch, Jr., *Symbol and Truth in Blake's Myth* (Princeton: Princeton UP, 1980), p. 147.

[16] Erdman, ed., *Notebook*, p. 55.

of asceticism; on the Laocoön plate (*c.* 1820) he denounces "Chastity & Abstinence" as "Gods of the Heathen" (E275/ K776), and his outlook is much closer both to the affirmative way of a visionary like Thomas Traherne and to the intellectual way of the Gnostics. Like Traherne, who recalls how in his infancy "The corn was orient and immortal wheat, which never should be reaped, nor was ever sown" and for whom "you never enjoy the world aright, till the sea itself floweth in your veins,"[17] Blake, instead of withdrawing from sense perception, aspires to heighten it:

> The Light of the Morning
> Heaven's Mountains adorning
> In particles bright
> The jewels of Light
> Distinct shone & clear—
> Amaz'd & in fear
> I each particle gazed
> Astonish'd, Amazed
> For each was a Man
> Human form'd.
>   (E712/ K804)

Blake also stresses, like the Gnostics, the necessity of acquiring insight associated with arcane knowledge, in the sense not simply of information, but of an awareness of reality that illuminates the entire mind and being making one a different person:

> Men are admitted into Heaven not because they
> have curbed & govern'd their Passions or have no
> Passions but because they have Cultivated their
> Understandings. The Treasures of Heaven are not
> Negations of Passion but Realities of Intellect
> from which All the Passions Emanate Uncurbed
> in their Eternal Glory. The Fool shall not enter
> into Heaven let him be ever so Holy.
>   (E564/ K615)

---

[17] *Centuries of Meditations*, III,3, and I, 29.

"Go! put off Holiness," orders Los, "And put on Intellect" (*J* 91:55-56), and the last line of *The Four Zoas* reads "The dark Religions are departed & sweet Science reigns" (139:10/ E407/ IX, 855). ("Science" carries here its eighteenth-century sense of "knowledge.")

Since classical antiquity, the Negative Way has been associated with Platonic philosophy, which teaches that the noblest souls rise above sensory pleasures and perceptions to contemplate the eternal Ideas—the super-sensible realities of which material objects are but copies. Plato particularly prized mathematics because its abstract subject matter seemed to transcend the world of physical phenomena. In his hatred of asceticism and of an abstract concept of God, Blake said harsh things about Plato and his mathematics; he included the philosopher's works among "Stolen and Perverted Writings" and found evidence in them that "The Gods of Greece & Egypt were Mathematical Diagrams" (*M*, pl. 1; E274/ K776). Nevertheless, like Milton, who charged in *Paradise Regained* that Plato "to fabling fell and smooth conceits" (IV, 295), Blake has much in common with this pre-Christian philosopher, and the fact underlies one of the most contentious issues in Blake studies.

In the third Christian century, Plotinus and his followers developed the philosophy of Neoplatonism from Plato's teachings about the human soul, the imperfection of human knowledge, and the relative unreality of the material world. Thoroughgoing Neoplatonists hold that the human soul falls or dies from a blissful and virtuous pre-natal state into a degenerate existence in the prison or tomb of a carnal body and that attachment to the senses and sensual pleasure is a grave impediment to its return to its original happiness and purity; such a restoration, however, is largely attainable even while it is locked in the flesh. According to some Neoplatonists, as long as the soul remains unpurified it is doomed to be reborn in body after body.

The Neoplatonic view of the delusiveness of human knowledge and the illusory nature of the material universe owes much to Plato's famous allegory of the cave at the beginning of book 7 of *The Republic*. Here Socrates compares human beings on earth to lifelong prisoners in a cave so fettered that they must keep their faces turned to the wall before them. A fire casts on this wall shadows of models of men, animals and implements, these models being borne above shoulder height by a procession of people passing between the captives and the flames; the bearers themselves cast no shadows for they are hidden behind a parapet. Very naturally the prisoners mistake the shadows of models of real things for real things themselves. Similarly, argues Plato, we misinterpret the images of material objects that our senses perceive: these perishable objects are but imitations of real and eternal objects in a higher, non-material realm apprehended not by the senses but by the spirit or intellect. These realities are the unchanging Platonic Ideas of the intelligible world. Neoplatonists sometimes regard the earth and its life, all that is perceptible to the senses, as the underworld.

For close to two millenia, Neoplatonism has had a widespread influence on Western and Middle Eastern philosophy, theology, art and literature. Elements of its teaching and symbolism are prominent in the work of many who do not accept the whole doctrine. Blake encountered Neoplatonic ideas in Spenser and Milton and knew personally Thomas Taylor,[18] whose English translations of Plato's writings were published from 1792 to 1804. From about 1789, when he wrote in his annotations to Swedenborg's *Divine Love and Divine Wisdom* that "the dead Sun is only a phantasy of evil Man" (E605/ K92), Blake believed that the material world as perceived by the senses of fallen humankind had only a phantom existence. Years later, he wrote in *Milton* of the scientific view of the earth, "As to that false appearance which appears to the reasoner,/ As of a Globe rolling thro Voidness, it is a delusion of Ulro..." (29:15-16); the same passage contains a reference to "Eternity of which this vegetable Earth is but a shadow" (29:22), which may echo Milton's

> what if Earth
> Be but the shaddow of Heav'n, and things therein
> Each to other like, more then on earth is thought?
> (*PL*, V, 574-76)

---

[18] James King, "The Meredith Family, Thomas Taylor, and William Blake," *SR*, XI (1972), 153-57.

In *Jerusalem*, the Eternals explain the tragic conse-
quence—descent into the fallen world—of being deceived by the
illusion:

> It seems to Be, & is productive of the most dreadful
> Consequences to those to whom it seems to Be: even of
> Torments, Despair, Eternal Death [i.e. death from
>   Eternity]
> (*J* 32[36]:51-54)

As Damrosch observes,[19] Blake's Forms, which persist unchanged
for ever though their individual embodiments perish, have a close
affinity to Plato's Ideas:

> Whatever can be Created can be Annihilated. Forms
>   cannot.
> The Oak is cut down by the Ax, the Lamb falls by the
>   Knife
> But their Forms Eternal Exist, For-ever...
> (*M* 32:36-38)

Blake anxiously distinguishes these Forms, which are to be dir-
ectly apprehended by the imagination perceiving *through* the
senses, from Locke's concept of general terms, like the animal
"horse" or the metal "lead," which are "abstract general ideas"
constructed by "the understanding" from numerous observations of
particular horses and particular samples of the element.[20] Such are
the Urizenic abstractions of Satan's "empire of nothing,"[21]
whereas the Forms, though they exist only in particular things, are
real.[22] To prefer "General Knowledge" to "Particulars" is to detach
oneself from reality and reduce the world and its inhabitants to
faceless statistics: "Every Man has Eyes, Nose & Mouth—this
every Idiot knows—but he who enters into & discriminates most

---

[19] *Symbol and Truth*, p. 13.
[20] *An Essay Concerning Human Understanding* III.iii.13.
[21] G. E. Bentley, Jr., *Blake Records* (Oxford: Clarendon Press, 1969), p. 316, quoting
Crabb Robinson's report of Blake's conversation.
[22] Damrosch, *Symbol and Truth*, pp. 16-19.

minutely the Manners & Intentions, the Characters in all their branches, is the alone Wise or Sensible Man" (E560/ K611).

Both Blake and Milton follow the Neoplatonic tradition that the material world as the senses ordinarily perceive it is a shadow of reality. Blake also believes in the descent and return of the soul and agrees with Plato and his followers in applying the term "Intellect" to a mental faculty higher than the power of logical reasoning. For Blake, the activity of intellect is characteristic of Eternity; it weakens in humans as they fall and in some is extinguished. (See, for example, *FZ* 20:12-13/ E313/ I, 571-72 and 139:7-9/ E407/ IX, 852-54; *J* 50:1, 43[29]:36-37 and 68:65-67.) Cultivation of intellect, according to Blake, complements forgiveness of sins as the way to redemption (e.g. *J* 61:14-26, 91:53-56).

While Blake's conception of intellect, which he considers an essential component of true art, is less than synonymous with the Neoplatonists', his attitude to the senses is almost diametrically opposed to theirs. They hold that the soul recaptures its lost vision by detaching itself from the operation of the senses; Blake is convinced that the imagination or soul can perceive through the senses as through windows of flawless glass and penetrate beneath the crust of material illusion which hides reality from fallen sense perception unilluminated by mental powers.

> This Life's dim Windows of the Soul
> Distorts the Heavens from Pole to Pole
> And leads you to Believe a Lie
> When you see with not thro the Eye
> That was born in a night to perish in a night
> When the Soul slept in the beams of Light.
>   (E520/ K753)

Thus far Blake's agreements and disagreements with Neoplatonism seem comparatively clear, but the extent and even the existence of Neoplatonic symbolism in his work is the subject of persistent and even acrimonious dispute. My notes on the critical treatment of such volumes as *The Book of Thel* and *Visions of the Daughters of Albion* record the main views on both sides.

As long ago as 1863, Gilchrist noted the close affinity between some of Blake's beliefs and those of the philosopher Berkeley.[23] Early in the eighteenth century Berkeley startled his contemporaries by arguing that there was no such thing as "matter," the supposedly neutral substance which had the capacity to take on the forms, densities, colours, textures, tastes and smells of perceptible objects. These objects, he maintained, derived their existence from being perceived. All things that did exist fell into two categories—spirits, which perceived, and physical entities, which were the objects of perception. Though a material thing like a tree or a house would cease to exist if it ceased to be perceived, this in fact did not happen, for even when no creature observed it, it was perceived by the Creator. All things, in truth, existed in the Divine Mind and not in Newton's absolute, fixed space, which was an illusion.[24]

In the Preface to the first edition of his *Three Dialogues Between Hylas and Philonous...in Opposition to Sceptics and Atheists* (1713), Berkeley showed that his aims included the vindication of the senses. His system affirms that, contrary to the views of the Neoplatonists (for whom the material world is but a shadow of reality) and of the atomists (for whom apparently continuous bodies are composed of particles), the senses accurately perceive what really exists. Blake, who deplores the Neoplatonic contempt for the senses and holds that the atom is a fiction (E783/ K878), agrees with Berkeley that all sensible objects exist within mind:

> Mental Things are alone Real; what is Call'd
> Corporeal, Nobody Knows of its Dwelling Place;
> it is in Fallacy & its Existence an Imposture
>   (E565/ K617)

As Witke points out,[25] Blake's Poetic Genius or Imagination is a divine creative principle very close to mind as Berkeley conceives it. The statement in *Jerusalem* that "All Things Exist in the Hum-

---

[23] Alexander Gilchrist, *Life of William Blake*, ed. Ruthven Todd, rev. (London: Dent; New York: Dutton, 1945), p. 210.

[24] George Berkeley, *Principles of Human Knowledge*, sections 110-17.

[25] Joanne Witke, "Blake's Tree of Knowledge Grows Out of the Enlightenment," *Enlightenment Essays*, III (1972), 71-84 (see p. 80).

an Imagination" (69:25) is similar to Berkeley's claim in the third part of his *Dialogues* that "All objects are eternally known by God, or, which is the same thing, have an eternal existence in His mind..."[26] Matter, to Blake (as to Berkeley) is an illusion, and the senses that seem to perceive it are a shrivelled remnant of what they were in Eternity. Berkeley, who is wholly devoid of Blake's overpowering consciousness of the fallen state of creation, in no way shares this last belief. Unfortunately Blake's only surviving annotations to Berkeley are his comments on the late tract *Siris* (1744), written when the philosopher had moved closer to Neoplatonism and had come to feel that the awakened intellect swept away the phantoms of sense perception.[27]

Blake's 'conversion' does not, then, alter his belief that the mortal's bodily perception is stricken so that "he sees all things thro' narrow chinks of his cavern" (*MHH*, pl. 14), but it undermines his confidence that uninhibited rebellion against political oppression and moral constraints will liberate deluded minds and transform society into a harmonious pre-industrial paradise. He comes to share Paul's conviction that (in Blake's words) "The Natural Man is at Enmity with God" (E665/ K782) and to see Jesus not only as the social rebel of *The Marriage of Heaven and Hell* but also, through his voluntary Crucifixion, as the supreme exemplar of the self-annihilation which leads back to Eternity.

After his 'conversion,' Blake shares, along with the distinction between the natural man and the spiritual man and between the natural body and the spiritual body, Paul's rejection of the Law, his conviction of the fallenness of the world, and his creed that Jesus brought life and immortality to light. He utterly dissents, however, from Paul's puritanical morality, and by including the Church Paul among the seven churches that are "Dragon Forms,/ Religion hid in War" (*M* 37:41-43), he shows that he laments the Apostle's work in organizing the new religion.

Many aspects of Blake's outlook are unaffected by his 'conversion.' His hostility to industrial slavery, imperialism, and the imposition of chastity is constant and unambiguous from the period of the French Revolution till his death. However, his views

---

[26] David M. Armstrong, ed., *Berkeley's Philosophical Writings* (New York: Collier; London: Collier-Macmillan, 1969), p. 214.
[27] *Siris*, section 294.

on religion and on the Jews are ambivalent; his attitude to women, as Paley observes,[28] is inconsistent; and his attempt to make an absolute division between virtue and the distinction between good and evil is unsuccessful.

On the Laocoön plate, Blake denounces "The outward Ceremony" as "Antichrist" (E274/ K776), and on pl. 91 of *Jerusalem* he elaborates on this theme in vehement and unambiguous terms, yet in old age he confessed that he would have been uneasy to have had a child die unbaptised,[29] in *Milton* he praises Wesley and Whitefield (22:61-23:2), and in *A Descriptive Catalogue* he describes Chaucer's Parson with love and admiration (E535/ K570). Though he refuses to recognise that without the Roman Catholic Church, which he is fond of attacking (e.g. *MHH*, pl. 25, verse 5; *E*, pl. 11, design; E524 [ll. 55-57]/ K749 [ll. 57-59]), the Gothic architecture he adores would never have been created, in his last years he apparently recognises confession and absolution as a form of forgiveness of sins, for he holds that the Roman Church is the only one which preaches that doctrine.[30] In his notes of 1798 to Watson's *Apology for the Bible*, Blake maintains that Christ came "to abolish the Jewish Imposture" and that the Old Testament Law is "the basest & most oppressive of human codes" (E614, 618/ K387, 393), but in the Preface to chapter two of *Jerusalem* he pays tribute to the Jewish Cabbala, and in the Laocoön plate he contrasts "Hebrew Art" with "Deist Science" (E273/ K776). Moses he always regards as having (like Paul) two aspects: he is both leader and misleader, liberator and lawgiver. The prophet's response to the demand that he suppress prophesying by lesser men was the exclamation "Would God that all the Lord's people were prophets" (Num. xi.29), and Blake chooses these words as an epigraph for *Milton*.

In recent decades, there has been controversy over whether Blake was an anti-feminist. Sometimes his symbolic image of the rebellious emanation hardens into a protest against women misusing their sexuality to dominate men, and like a crude

---

[28] Morton D. Paley, *The Continuing City: William Blake's* Jerusalem (Oxford: Clarendon Press, 1983), p. 194.

[29] S. Foster Damon, *A Blake Dictionary: The Ideas and Symbols of William Blake*, 2nd printing, rev. (1967; rpt. Hanover and London: UP of New England for Brown UP, 1988), p. 36.

[30] Damon, *Blake Dictionary*, p. 84.

misogynist he can make the female tyrant Vala speak in scorn of
the male who is "Woman-born/ And Woman-nourish'd &
Woman-educated & Woman-scorn'd!" (*J* 64:16-17). "In Eternity,"
he declares, "Woman is the Emanation of Man; she has No Will of
her own. There is no such thing in Eternity as a Female Will"
(E562/ K613). George shows that the impression made by his por-
trayal of female characters is often at odds with his theoretically
androgynous human ideal,[31] the effect of which is diluted by the
sexism inherent in language and perhaps by his increasing hostil-
ity to the Romantic worship of (feminine) nature as opposed to
(masculine) Enlightenment reason.[32] The linguistic sexism is rein-
forced by a system in which, as Frye observes,[33] every human
being is symbolically male. On the other hand, this symbolism
endows every human, male or female, with the dignity of the
human essence. Moreover, in *Jerusalem* Blake discloses that "Man
in the Resurrection changes his Sexual Garments at will" (61:51)
and that masculine and feminine alike only have independent
existence as fragments of the whole: "Such are the Feminine &
Masculine when separated from Man" (67:14). In his last epic he
introduces masculine emanations to make it clear that creativity
and communion between individuals are not to be identified with
one gender,[34] and in *For the Sexes: The Gates of Paradise*, he
portrays both men and women as embodied souls:

> When weary Man enters his Cave,
> He meets his Saviour in the Grave;
> Some find a Female Garment there
> And some a Male, woven with care...
> ("The Keys," ll. 21-24)

A statement on the Laocoön engraving implies equality of the
sexes—"A Poet, a Painter, a Musician, an Architect: the Man Or
Woman who is not one of these is not a Christian" (E274/
K776)—and in *Jerusalem* 72:50-52 the female mystics St. Teresa

---

[31] See p. 168 below.
[32] Diana Hume George, *Blake and Freud* (Ithaca and London: Cornell UP, 1980), pp.
199-201.
[33] Northrop Frye, "The Keys to the Gates" (1966; rpt. Frye, *The Stubborn Structure:
Essays on Criticism and Society* (Ithaca: Cornell UP, 1970), pp. 175-99 (see p. 191).
[34] George, *Blake and Freud*, p. 189. See *J* 49:47, 88:11, 90:1-2.

and Mme. Guyon are ranked with three male representatives of Christianity.

Blake's admiration for the great figures of Christian tradition is tempered by his antinomianism. He insists that moral legalism, with its reasoning about the rightness and wrongness of deeds, belongs to the world of materialism and not to the Spirit, and that conscience, which is "the voice of God" and "the Word of God Universal," is the only source of right action (E613, 615/ K385/389).[35] As early as *The Marriage of Heaven and Hell*, he announces, "Jesus was all virtue, and acted from impulse: not from rules" (*MHH*, pls. 23-24). His rejection of moral law sometimes leads him to express contempt for the distinction between the good and the wicked as well as for moral virtue. Near the end of *Jerusalem*, Los proclaims in wrath,

> I care not whether a Man is Good or Evil; all that I care
> Is whether he is a Wise Man or a Fool.
> (91:54-55)

Yet Blake cares much about the difference between the righteous and the unrighteous. A good man, he says, "will abhor wickedness in David or Abraham," while a wicked one "will make their wickedness an excuse for his" (E618/ K393). He points to the "hard and wirey line of rectitude" as marking "honesty" off from "knavery," and in his Public Address he cites biblical justification for his intent to "pour Aqua fortis on the Name of the Wicked" (E550, 579/ K585, 598). He can even refer to the black sheep of his own family as "my Brother John the evil one" and console himself for worldly failure by considering how he is "beloved by the Good as a Good Man" (E721, 736/ K817, 830).

Attempting to dispense with moral virtue, which Enlightenment liberals consider the foundation of liberty, Blake objects that it entails "the Slavery of that half of the Human Race who hate what you call Moral Virtue" (E564/ K616). In view of his merciful disposition, his scorn for idleness, and his denunciations of tyranny and of clandestine liaisons, it seems that the moral virtues he rejects are primarily sexual abstinence by those in love, unfeeling adherence to duty like that which made Aeneas desert

---

[35] Cf. Fisher, *Valley of Vision*, pp. 159-60.

Dido, forbearance that inhibits the expression of anger, the shackling of others' wrath or love, and asceticism—though he once has a good word for fasting.[36] His denunciation in *Milton* 29:49 of temperance, prudence, justice, and fortitude—the four Natural Virtues attained without divine aid—is really a denunciation of the natural man who is "altogether an Evil" (*J*, pl. 52, prose). Blake may not have been a prudent man, but his temperance and fortitude were exemplary, and though he can rail against the kinds of justice responsible for the condemnation of Jesus and Socrates, he can speak of doing justice to a fellow artist and belabour Satan, the Accuser, for tormenting the just (E753, 565/ K849, 616). Since, despite all his protestations, he does prize a number of moral virtues, he cannot attain a consistent viewpoint. In 1798 he declares "The Gospel is Forgiveness of Sins & has No Moral Precepts; these belong to Plato & Seneca & Nero" (E619/ K395)—be it noted that he does not deny that some acts are sinful. About twenty years later he begins a prose fragment of "The Everlasting Gospel" with the statement "There is not one Moral Virtue that Jesus Inculcated but Plato & Cicero did Inculcate before him"; he immediately ignores this admission that Christ did teach some moral virtues by asking, "what then did Christ Inculcate?" (The question should logically have been "What else, then, did Christ inculcate?") He answers,

> Forgiveness of Sins. This alone is the Gospel &
> this is the Life & Immortality brought to light by
> Jesus, Even the Covenant of Jehovah, which is
> This: If you forgive one another your Trespasses
> so shall Jehovah forgive you...
> (E875/ K757, alluding to II Tim. i.10 and Matt.
> vi.14)

But readiness to forgive is a moral virtue. Two things, moreover, Blake seems less certain about forgiving: taking revenge for sins against oneself and oppressing, as tyrants and their agents do, whole classes of people: "Christ comes as he came at first to deliver those who were bound under the Knave, not to deliver the

---

[36] For idleness see, for example, E232, 470, 594, 724/ K717,181, 79, 812; for Aeneas E633/ K412; for fasting E274/ K776.

Knave" (E564/ K615). Night the Ninth of *The Four Zoas* offers
little hope for tyrants and their abettors, but probably they, and the
avengers who have turned their backs on the Covenant of Jehovah,
will attain forgiveness when they have passed out of the Satanic
state. Indeed Murry finds in the doctrine of states the explanation
of a harsh couplet in "The Everlasting Gospel"—

> He who loves his Enemies betrays his Friends;
> This surely is not what Jesus intends...
>   (E519 [ll. 21-22]/ K751 [ll. 25-26])

Love and forgiveness are to be extended to one's enemies but not
to the state through which they are passing,[37] or, as Damrosch puts
it, forgiveness can only dissolve enmity when self-annihilation
destroys the selfhoods that created it:[38]

> Mutual Forgiveness of each Vice:
> Such are the Gates of Paradise.
>   (*GP*, Prologue, ll. 1-2)

Blake, then, may hope and believe that he rejects moral
virtue as the idol of the legalists and as a pagan ideal derived from
nature, not revelation. In fact, as Margoliouth states, he is
"substituting his own conception of Good and Evil for the current
one."[39] He spurns certain alleged virtues together with the frame-
work of law which distorts morality; instead he relies on con-
science as the exclusive arbiter of right and wrong. But though he
esteems many virtues and prefers good people to evildoers, he is
gnostic enough to insist that goodness alone will not take a fallen
soul back to Eternity. Not only does he agree with Paul—and
Solomon—that any human claim to complete righteousness is "all
Pretension," but he maintains that "Men are admitted into Heaven
not because they have curbed & govern'd their Passions or have

---

[37] J. Middleton Murry, *William Blake* (1933; rpt. London and Toronto: Cape, 1936),
pp. 320-23.
[38] *Symbol and Truth*, p. 253-54.
[39] H. M. Margoliouth, *William Blake* (London: Oxford UP, 1951), pp. 102-03.

No Passions but because they have Cultivated their Understandings" (Rom. iii.9-20; I Kings viii.46; E619, 564/ K396, 615).

> I do not consider [he explains] either the Just or
> the Wicked to be in a Supreme State but to be
> every one of them States of the Sleep which the
> Soul may fall into in its Deadly Dreams of Good
> & Evil when it leaves Paradise following the Ser-
> pent.
>   (E563/ K614)

Blake tries to make a clearcut division between judging in terms of good and evil, which he stigmatises as "Eating of the Tree of Knowledge," and judging in terms of Truth and Error, which he upholds as "Eating of the Tree of Life" (E563/ K615), but he is not always able to stick to his principles, so the harassed critic need not feel too inadequate if he or she cannot resist applying the word "evil" to Rahab and Tirzah, the Polypus, and the Covering Cherub.

Blake's new teaching in middle age about self-annihila-tion and forgiveness of sins, and the unillumined natural man's being "altogether an Evil" (*J*, pl. 52, prose) is accompanied by a changed outlook on politics. On 19 October, 1801, on the thresh-old of the Peace of Amiens, he writes to Flaxman of his expecta-tion "that France & England will henceforth be as One Country and their Arts One," but in May 1804, when Napoleon crowns himself Emperor, Blake, like Beethoven, seems to lose all faith in him,[40] and by about 1810 he caustically observes in his Public Address, "Let us teach Buonaparte & whomsoever else it may con-cern That it is not Arts that follow & attend upon Empire but Empire that attends upon & follows The Arts" (E718, 577/ K811, 597). In the same Address, he reveals his total retreat from a revolutionary stance:

> I am really sorry to see my Countrymen trouble
> themselves about Politics. If Men were Wise the
> Most arbitrary Princes could not hurt them. If
> they are not Wise the Freest Government is com-

---

[40] Gilchrist, *Life*, p. 327.

> pell'd to be a Tyranny. Princes appear to me to be
> Fools; Houses of Commons & Houses of Lords
> appear to me to be fools; they seem to me to be
> something Else besides Human Life.
>   (E580/ K600)

Nevertheless Blake always remains a Republican;[41] he puts the blame for war on such autocrats as Louis XIV and Frederick the Great, and regards its psychological source as "energy Enslav'd," especially sexual energy (*J*, pl. 52, prose; *FZ* 120:42/ E390/ IX, 152; cf. *J* 68:63); and he continues to hope for the emergence of a free and creative society realising the pastoral ideal expressed by the Abbé de Sieyès in *The French Revolution*. His persisting hatred of industrial slavery and militarism flares out in many eloquent passages of his epics. The carefully ambiguous accounts in his *Descriptive Catalogue* of 1809 permit either a straightforward or ironic interpretation of the seemingly panegyrical paintings of Nelson and Pitt, but Erdman's reading of these pictures as sharp attacks on the statesmen best explains their symbolic details.[42] In the lyric on pl. 27 of *Jerusalem*, the worldwide human sacrifices of the Druids seem to merge into the modern bloodletting of the Napoleonic wars, while the Covering Cherub who "advances from the East" in *Milton* (23:10) may, on a political level, be Bonaparte himself.

    A potent biblical symbol that Blake charges with his anti-industrial fervour comes from Ezekiel's vision of the Divine Chariot. Describing the wheels beside the living creatures, the prophet writes, "their work was as it were a wheel in the middle of a wheel" (i.16). In Blake's eyes this image becomes the contrary of the meshing cogwheels—wheels without wheels—of industrial machinery, and he laments the dehumanising blight that the new factories have cast over the lives of the poor in Britain's cities:

> And all the Arts of Life they chang'd into the Arts of
> Death in Albion.

---

[41] Gilchrist, *Life*, pp. 80, 327.
[42] David V. Erdman, *Blake: Prophet Against Empire* (Princeton: Princeton UP, 1954), pp. 415-20 [448-55].

The hour-glass contemn'd because its simple
  workmanship
Was like the workmanship of the plowman, & the water
  wheel,
That raises water into cisterns, broken & burn'd with fire
Because its workmanship was like the workmanship of the
  shepherd,
And in their stead, intricate wheels invented, wheel
  without wheel,
To perplex youth in their outgoings, & to bind to labours
  in Albion
Of day & night the myriads of eternity that they may grind
And polish brass & iron hour after hour, laborious task!
Kept ignorant of its use, that they might spend the days of
  wisdom
In sorrowful drudgery, to obtain a scanty pittance of
  bread...
(*J* 65:16-26)

In a Foreword to the 1988 reprint of Damon's *Blake Dictionary*, Morris Eaves writes of the new image of an evolving, changing Blake that has become prominent in the twenty-two years that have elapsed since the *Dictionary*'s first publication. A critical feud continues, as I have indicated in my Introduction, betweeen those who hold that Blake has fixed beliefs and those who consider that his philosophy mutates through distinct phases. Adherents of the older view have to argue that the doctrines of the primacy of imagination, the annihilation of selfhood, the inferior and partly pernicious nature of the fleshly body, and the forgiveness of sins are not alien to the Blake who places his hopes in the French Revolution. The text that most seems to embody teachings contrary to these is *The Marriage of Heaven and Hell*, yet it is possible to claim that the concept of the Poetic Genius as the divine core of every human being implies the later worship of Imagination and that the self which Blake later insists is to be annihilated is the self which perceives with instead of through the eye. Perhaps most difficult to defend is the claim that this fiery text, which seems to uphold self-assertion, has an affinity with Christian teaching about forgiveness, although Damon[43] detects this doctrine in the aphorism "The cut worm forgives the plow" (*MHH*, pl.7), and Emery[44] believes it is implicit in Blake's ideal of a creative relationship between contraries that have previously behaved as deadly enemies.

[43] S. Foster Damon, *William Blake: His Philosophy and Symbols* (1924; rpt. Gloucester, Mass.: Peter Smith, 1958), p. 319.
[44] Clark Emery, Introduction to William Blake, *The Marriage of Heaven and Hell* (1963; rpt. Coral Gables, Florida: U of Miami P, 1972), pp. 51-55.

8

Blake's System

Blake's 'conversion' in the first years of the new century is closely associated with his completion of a mythology of fall and redemption underpinned by a philosophy and a theology. "I must Create a System," his hero Los declares, "or be enslav'd by another Man's" (*J* 10:20).

Ironically Blake, the prophet of the humanness of God, presents an image of Him or It extraordinarily free from anthropomorphism. In 1788, in his first attempts at illuminated printing, and later in *The Marriage of Heaven and Hell*, he refers to God as the Poetic Genius. After his 'conversion,' he prefers other terms, especially the Divine Humanity, a Swedenborgian phrase for the Deity. Once, however, in *Milton*, he explicity identifies the Poetic Genius with "the eternal all-protecting Divine Humanity" (14:1-2). In other places, he equates the Divine Humanity with the Imagination (*J* 70:19-20) and the Imagination with "God himself" (E273/ K776), with "the Divine body of the Saviour" (E555/ K606), whose members we are (E273/ K776), with "the Real Man" (E663, 664/ K774, 775), and with "the Soul" as opposed to "The Natural Man" (E273/ K776). Blake has built on his early conception, recorded in his annotations to Swedenborg's *Divine Love and Divine Wisdom*, of God as the "one Essence," "Omnipotent" and "Uncreate," from which all "Identities" proceed and in which they are rooted (E604/ K91). He also conceives Him as the Divine Mind containing all things, as the limiter of the Fall, and as incarnate in Jesus the Saviour.

As universal Essence, God is both the creating Divine Intellect and the indwelling sustainer. In his paintings of the Last Judgment, Blake explains, the infants in Christ's halo represent "the Eternal Creation flowing from the Divine Humanity in Jesus" or "the Eternal Births of Intellect from the divine Humanity," for "All beams from him Because as he himself has said All dwells in him" (E554, 562, 561/ K444, 613, 612; the last ten words are scored through, perhaps because the allusion is really to Acts xvii.28 rather than any speech of Christ). As the inmost essence of His creatures, God acts through them. "God only Acts & Is," says the narrator of *The Marriage of Heaven and Hell*, "in existing beings or Men" (pl. 16).[1] Within humans, Deity manifests as the Holy Spirit, for the genius of a great individual "is the Holy Ghost in Man" (*J* 91:7-10). Even more clearly, God manifests Himself in the utterances of Eternity, where

>   the Eternal Great Humanity
> To whom be Glory & Dominion Evermore Amen
> Walks among all his awful Family seen in every face
> As the breath of the Almighty, such are the words of man
> to man...
> (*M* 30:15-18)

All individual identities, consciously or unconsciously, aspire towards the one Essence which gave them birth. Most conscious of their aspiration are the Eternals. Paradoxically these are both individuals and a single collective being. As individuals, they are many; as manifestations of the universal Essence, they are one, and that one is Jesus:

> Then those in Great Eternity met in the Council of God
> As one Man...
>   ...& that one Man
> They call Jesus the Christ & they in him & he in them
> Live in Perfect harmony...
> (*FZ* 21:1-2, 4-6/ E310-11/ I, 469-70, 472-74)

When the Fall makes a rent in Eternity, God acts through the Eternals, who are collectively Jesus, to impose a limit on error and make redemption possible for the fallen:

> Then All in Great Eternity Met in the Council of God
> [A]s one Man Even Jesus...
> Upon the Limit of Contraction to create the fallen Man

---

[1] See also p. 144 above.

> The limit of Contraction now was fix'd...
> (*FZ* 99:1-3, 11/ E371-72/ VIII, 1-3, 16)

Similarly, God, "The Lord Jehovah," modifies the fallen cosmos making it a place of preparation for the fallen spirits' recovery:

> He has builded the arches of Albion's Tomb, binding the Stars
> In merciful Order, bending the Laws of Cruelty to Peace.
> (*J* 49:52-55)

Insofar as creation is the making of a material illusion encased in Newtonian space and clock time, it is the work of "a very Cruel Being" (E565/ K617); insofar as it is the imposition of a limit on this catastrophe, creation is "an act of Mercy" (E563/ K614).

Always and everywhere present—"God is within, & without! he is even in the depths of Hell!" (*J* 12:15; cf. Ps. cxxxix.8)—the Divine Essence is unseen, but in another act of mercy He takes incarnation as "Jesus, the image of the Invisible God" (*M* 2:12; cf. Col. i.15). The invisibility of the Universal Essence is to be carefully distinguished from the invisibility of jealous Urizen, who arrogantly hides himself "in clouds/ From every searching Eye" (E471/ K171). Similarly the quintessence of that humanness which issues as the "Mercy, Pity, Peace and Love" of "The Divine Image" in *Songs of Innocence*, the Essence from which spring all entities (which is also the Imagination that contains all that exists) is antithetical to the abstract First Cause of Deist worship. Whereas God, as the Divine Intellect, gives birth to Eternity, the First Cause is credited with creating the clockwork universe of external nature.

Voluntarily taking on himself in Mary's womb the body and mind of the natural man—here Blake follows Swedenborg[2]—Christ leaves it behind at his Crucifixion:

> And thus with wrath he did subdue
> The Serpent Bulk of Nature's dross
> Till he had nail'd it to the Cross;
> He took on Sin in the Virgin's Womb

---

[2] *Doctrine of the Lord*, section 35.

And put it off on the Cross & Tomb
To be Worship'd by the Church of Rome.
(E524 [ll. 52-57]/ K749 [ll. 52-54, 57-59])

He thus demonstrates to fallen humankind that there is a way back
from the temporal world. Jesus, who "Opens Eternity in Time &
Space," declares

I cannot leave them in the gnawing Grave
But will prepare a way for my banished-ones to return.
(*J* 75:22, 62:21-22)

For Blake, Jesus' sacrifice is, as Sandler states,[3] "only exem-
plary"—his position happens to coincide with Peter Abelard's; he
is disgusted by the doctrine, which Milton accepts (*PL*, III, 203-
12), that Christ had to die so that failure to impose a punishment
for humankind's sins would not leave justice unsatisfied. This doc-
trine he attributes to the fallen Albion, who erects altars for the
"sacrifice of (miscall'd) Enemies/ For Atonement" (*J* 28:20-21).
Atonement in this sense is among "the crue[l]ties of Moral Law"
(*M* 5:12). When Albion, in the course of falling, beseeches, "Will
none accompany me in my death? or be a Ransom for me...?" Los,
"not yet infected with the Error & Illusion," exclaims,

Must the Wise die for an Atonement? does Mercy endure
    Atonement?
No! It is Moral Severity, & destroys Mercy in its Victim.
(*J* 35[39]:19, 24-27)

Presumably the promise of Atonement through cruel sacrifice is
the Covenant of Priam, which Blake does not define (*J* 98:46). He
refers to "the detestable Gods of Priam" (*M* 14:15) rather than the
Greek gods, perhaps because he believes that their worship came
to Albion with the Trojan Aeneas's great-grandson Brutus, legend-
ary founder of the kingdom of Britain and of the city of

---

[3] Florence Sandler, review of *The Imagination of the Resurrection: The Poetic
Continuity of a Religious Motif in Donne, Blake, and Yeats*, by Kathryn R. Kremen,
BS, VI, 1 (Fall 1973), pp. 96-98.

Troynovant or New Troy, which became London. Unlike idolatrous atonements, the true "Atonements of Jehovah" occur by "willing sacrifice of Self" (E502/ K543; *J* 28:20). This self-annihilation is the antithesis of the Druids' sacrifices on stone altars; its outward manifestation, the forgiveness of sins, is the contrary of their retribution for trespasses.

As the fragmentation of a primal, all-containing unity, the Fall begins in the very Godhead Itself.[4] Adopting Boehme's conception of Deity generating or dividing into the incomplete Wrath or Fire of the Father and the incomplete Love or Light of the Son, Blake conceives of Jehovah separated from Jesus and, occasionally, Jesus separated from Jehovah as less than perfect. The imperfection of the Father is most clearly seen in the contrasting images of God the Father in the third and fourth of the Huntington Library set of Blake's illustrations to *Paradise Lost*;[5] here he sprouts wings and grows a Urizenic beard as he declines towards the Satanic state in which he can reduce morality to a legal code: "Jehovah's Finger Wrote the Law" (*GP*, Prologue, l. 5). Elsewhere he is the leprous Jehovah of the Seven Eyes of God (*M* 13:24; cf. E521 [l. 34]/ K754 [l. 34]), and probably the "very Cruel Being" who is "the Creator of this World" (E565/ K617). Like Boehme, Blake emotionally inclines to the Son rather than the Father, but in "The Everlasting Gospel" he makes Christ confess to error (E520 [ll. 82-84]/ K753 [ll. 88-90]), and shows that, even though the last of the Seven Eyes of God is Jesus, the seven need to unite and to merge with the Eighth, the Humanity, before they constitute "One Man, Jesus the Saviour" (*M* 42:11). He told Crabb Robinson that Christ was wrong to attack the government and submit to crucifixion, for he was capable of error since "He was not then become the father."[6] In Blake, the names Jesus and Jehovah sometimes refer to the imperfect Son cut off from the Father or the imperfect—or even Satanic—Father isolated from the Son, but usually they denote the Divine Humanity.

---

[4] H. Summerfield, "Blake and the Names Divine," *BIQ*, XV (Summer 1981), pp. 14-22.

[5] Martin Butlin, *The Paintings and Drawings of William Blake* (New Haven and London: Yale UP, 1981), plates 634, 635.

[6] G. E. Bentley, Jr., *Blake Records* (Oxford: Clarendon Press, 1969), p. 311.

Sometimes Blake employs the language of philosophy. Thus he can proclaim that the Divine Humanity

> is the Only General and Universal Form
> To which all Lineaments tend & seek with love &
>   sympathy
> (*J* 38[43]:19-21)

Yet he also admits the existence of Forms intermediate between the Divine Humanity and individual identities:

> The Oak is cut down by the Ax, the Lamb falls by the
>   Knife,
> But their Forms Eternal Exist For-ever
> (*M* 32:37-38)

In books 6 and 7 of *The Republic* (505-17), Plato explains how material objects derive their existence and form from supersensible Ideas or Forms; in their turn, these Ideas derive their own existence and form from a supreme Form—the Idea of the Good, which the human mind can only partly apprehend. Similarly Blake is maintaining that God, the Divine Humanity, is the one universal Form underlying all separate identities, individuals, or particulars.

As the One General and Universal Form, the Divine Humanity, is the Essence of the Eternals, so other "general," "universal" or "eternal" forms are the essence of individual entities within Eternity. There "All Things" exist in Jesus, the Imagination or Divine Mind, where they are "comprehended in their Eternal Forms" (E555/ K605-06). Each entity gives unique expression to a Form, and that Form shines out through its minute particulars, for it must be remembered that

> A Spirit and a Vision are not, as the modern phil-
> osophy supposes, a cloudy vapour or a nothing:
> they are organized and minutely articulated be-
> yond all that the mortal and perishing nature can
> produce.
> (E541/ K576)

Each particular is in its inmost being Human, for it derives ultimately, through its immediate Form, from the Divine Humanity.

> But General Forms have their vitality in Particulars: &
> every
> Particular is a Man; a Divine Member of the Divine Jesus.
>   (*J* 91:29-30)

At the universal regeneration at the end of *Jerusalem*, all things are "Human Forms identified, even Tree, Metal, Earth & Stone" (99:1).

The things that exist in Eternity are the supersensible equivalents of the objects we are familiar with on earth. (Swedenborg insists that the landscapes and vegetation and even the buildings and garments of this world have their more perfect counterparts in Heaven.)[7] In the fallen universe, however, lineaments and particulars become blurred and indefinite. In the Dedication of *The Ghost of Abel*, Blake proclaims:

> Nature has no Outline: but Imagination has. Nat-
> ure has no Tune: but Imagination has! Nature has
> no Supernatural & dissolves: Imagination is
> Eternity.

Exploring the interior of fallen Albion, Los discovers that

> Every Universal Form [has] become barren mountains of
>   Moral
> Virtue: and every Minute Particular harden'd into grains
>   of sand
>   (*J* 45[31]:19-20)

The unique images within the Divine Mind have come to be wrongly perceived by the fallen as compounded of uniform particles like atoms and obligated to obey general moral laws that ignore their individuality. Yet while each of their embodiments is unique, the Forms are unchanging: "A Man can never become Ass

---

[7] *Heaven and Hell*, sections 170-190.

nor Horse...Eternal Identity is one thing & Corporeal Vegetation is another thing" (E556/ K607). Hence it is that

> we see the same characters repeated again and again, in animals, vegetables, minerals, and in men...Accident ever varies, Substance can never suffer change nor decay.
> (E532/ K567)

Blake's quarrel with Reynolds, who agrees with him that the painter should portray ideal images, concerns the origin of these images. For Blake, a perfect image of tree, animal or man is not to be synthesised from numerous observations of the imperfect trees, animals and men which are actually found in the world but is to be acquired "from Imagination" (E648/ K459). In the same way, he endorses the opinion of the fourth-century pagan philosopher Themistius, cited by Berkeley, that the essences of things are forms imparted by soul, but adds that "Forms must be apprehended by Sense or the Eye of Imagination"—that is by unfallen perception working through, not with, the eye (E664/ K775).

Individuals who claim for themselves the identities of subsidiary Forms—"Universal Attributes"—are "Blasphemous Selfhoods" (*J* 90:32-33). An individual like Urizen may try to usurp the status of the Universal Essence and impose his personal laws, such as the Ten Commandments, as though they were universally valid. A code of this kind, produced by a selfhood, Blake terms an Individual Law.

> ...Satan making to himself Laws from his own identity
> Compell'd others to serve him in moral gratitude &
>   submission
> Being call'd God...
> (*M* 11:10-12)

"Alas," exclaims Satan's repentant seducer,

> what shall be done him to restore?
> Who calls the Individual Law, Holy: and despises the
>   Saviour.
> (*M* 13:4-5)

An important element in Blake's image of unfallen exist-
ence is his conception of the fourfold nature of humanness and of
the four levels of vision. This conception, which is related to the
four living creatures of Ezekiel's vision (i.5-14) and their descend-
ants, the four beasts of Revelation (iv.6-9), first appears in *Vala*
and in a letter of November 1802 to Thomas Butts. In *Vala* the
four Zoas—Los, Urizen, Luvah and Tharmas—are warring comp-
onents of the archetypal human being, and in the letter Blake
discloses,

> Now I a fourfold vision see
> And a fourfold vision is given to me.
> 'Tis fourfold in my supreme delight
> And three fold in soft Beulah's night
> And twofold Always. May God us keep
> From Single vision & Newton's sleep.
>   (E722/ K818)

Building on his earlier claims that "Energy is Eternal Del-
ight" and the habitation of Jehovah is "flaming fire" (*MHH*, pls. 4,
6), the poet conceives Eternity as the very antithesis of a calm and
static realm. There the Arrows of Intellect fly from the fourfold
bows of fourfold beings in whom the Zoas work harmoniously
within the Essence containing them, the Humanity itself. These
fourfold beings engage in mental war and mental hunting, which
are the contentions of loving friendship, as, inspired by the Holy
Spirit, they hurl at each other "Ideas"—concepts expressed
through images—in the pursuit of Truth. While they converse,
their words take shape and have a contingent existence as percep-
tible objects in a space and time that vary as the perceivers choose
that their senses shall vary. These "Visionary forms dramatic"
include "Beasts & Birds & Fishes & Plants & Minerals." The
Humanness of the Universal Essence underlies and is present
within every word, letter and living form of their speech. (*M*
30:15-20, 34:50-35:6; *J* 38[43]:31-32 and 41-42, 98: 28-40.)

As the intellects of the Eternals contend, there emanate
from them or their creations "All the Passions...Uncurbed in their
Eternal Glory" (E564/ K615). These passions include horror and
wrath as well as pity and love, and they can inspire "Giant blows

in the sports of intellect," but above all they issue in "forgiving each other's trespasses" according to "the Covenant/ Of Jehovah: If you Forgive one-another, so shall Jehovah Forgive You" (*M* 13:48, 20:45; *J* 34[38]:16 and 22, 48:15-16, 61:24-25). This Covenant is the antithesis of Priam's.

When Eternals approach each other to converse, they first make contact through their gentler emotions, which go before them as male and female emanations; if these harmonise, their "Human four-fold Forms" enter, much like the angels described by Milton's Raphael, into embraces that are "Cominglings: from the Head even to the Feet"—a feeble imitation of these survives in the debased sexual intercourse of earth, which is alluded to in the phrase "a pompous High Priest entering by a Secret Place" (*J* 88:3-11, 69:43-44; *PL*, VIII, 620-29). Touch, the faculty on which sexual intercourse is based, does not exist as a separate sense in Eternity, where there are only four senses—sight, smell, hearing, and a composite taste-touch. These Blake identifies with the unfallen Urizen, Luvah, Urthona (i.e. Los), and Tharmas respectively as well as with the four points of the compass and the four rivers of the Garden of Eden (*J* 32[36]:31, 98:16-27; Gen. ii.10-14).[8] When the eternal senses expand, they perceive the undivided Oneness that originates and sustains all things; when they contract, they perceive the separate identities in Eternity which are the first stage of the division that, harmless as yet, will in its further manifestations lead to the Fall (*FZ* 21:1-7/ E310-11/ I, 469-75; *J* 34[38]:17-21). The binding force that holds the Eternals together is brotherhood, and as Damon[9] and some later critics have observed, brotherhood and not marriage provides the model for Blake's ideal community.

In a closely reasoned argument, Ault maintains that Blake sees Newton's concept of a universe of unchangeable atoms moving in an infinite void according to mathematical laws as a parody of the structure of Eternity. Newton's atoms and voids, he claims, are identities parallel to Blake's Eternals; the mathematical laws that make them cohere are equivalent to the Divine Body within

[8] Cf. S. Foster Damon, *A Blake Dictionary: The Ideas and Symbols of William Blake*, 2nd printing (1967; rpt. Hanover and London: UP of New England for Brown UP, 1988), pp. 75, 364.
[9] *Ibid.*, p. 60.

which the Eternals exist; and the agent integrating the identities and the laws (either attractive and repulsive forces or an ether) has a counterpart in the emanations of the Eternals.[10] If this theory is correct, it reveals a new dimension of Blake's myth, but it is doubtful whether there is a real analogy between the living beings of the poet's Eternity and the scientist's matter and space. Whatever the case may be, an account in cold prose can give but a pale idea of the conception of Eternity conveyed by Blake's subtle and passionate poetry.

Blake's conception of God and Eternity enjoys a rare freedom from the anthropomorphism and wish fulfilment satirised in the fishes' paradise of Rupert Brooke's "Heaven":

> And there (they trust) there swimmeth One
> Who swam ere rivers were begun,
> Immense, of fishy form and mind,
> Squamous, omnipotent, and kind...

Though the price of this freedom is a formidable obscurity, this poet's wonderful picture of Eternity is well worth the pains required to comprehend it.

The story of humankind's fall from the untrammelled energy and undistorted perception of Eternity, its consequent sufferings, and its ultimate resurrection is the subject of Blake's three Christian epics. *The Four Zoas* presents the components of this story in largely chronological order. *Milton*, combining much of the pattern of a classical epic with synchronic narrative, focuses on the redemption of a single hero and the historical influence of his errors. Organised for the first nine-tenths of its length on a synchronic basis, *Jerusalem* portrays the fall, agony and restoration of collective humanity. To complete the mythology that would embody his encyclopaedic subject matter, Blake invented new images, symbols and terms, the most prominent of which will now be briefly introduced.

The central figure of the myth is Albion, who is at once all humankind, every individual soul, and (as his name suggests) the island and people of Great Britain. He is also, before his fall, one

---

[10] Donald D. Ault, *Visionary Physics: Blake's Response to Newton* (Chicago and London: U of Chicago P, 1974), pp. 5-9, 30-34.

of the Eternals (others are Africa and probably France [*J* 40(45):19-25, 49:48]). From Eternity, he passes into Beulah, an intermediate state created as a temporal realm of refuge and sleep for those—especially the Emanations—who need relief from the fierce strife of mental war. As Fox observes, they enter Beulah as females and return to Eternity as males (*M* 31:1-5).[11] However, the spirit that sleeps in Beulah, a hospice of dreams presided over by the moon, may, instead of waking back into Eternity, sink through its lower levels into Ulro—the desert-world of illusion oppressed by social hierarchy, moral law, materialist science, and carnivorous fauna. In *Jerusalem*, Blake distinguishes between Ulro and a fourth level, Generation, where the fallen engage in a long struggle to reascend to their pristine state. Los's toils are capable of changing the barren Ulro into the potentially fruitful Generation.

According to Blake, beings who are fully Human are androgynous. (Jewish Cabbala teaches that Adam was so before Eve was divided from him, and Boehme follows this tradition.) These beings' male spectres and female emanations split off from them; their residual portions are considered as male. The sinister and dangerous spectre is the reasoning power acting as an independent faculty unco-ordinated with the emotions and imagination and dominating over the unillumined sense perception. To the spectre, reality consists of material objects, of which images are perceived by the senses and deposited in the memory, a faculty that Blake much disparages as the repository of what Locke understands as knowledge and hence as the frequent supplanter of imagination—and as the mother of the Greek as opposed to the Hebrew Muses.[12]

> The Spectre is the Reasoning Power in Man; & when
> separated
> From Imagination, and closing itself as in steel, in a Ratio
> Of the Things of Memory, It thence frames Laws &
> Moralities

---

[11] Susan Fox, *Poetic Form in Blake's* Milton (Princeton: Princeton UP, 1976), pp. 201-02.
[12] Cf. p. 134 above.

> To destroy Imagination! the Divine Body, by Martyrdoms
> and Wars
> (*J* 74:10-13)

The female counterpart of the autonomous spectre is the emanation, usually the female aspect of the whole person, acting as an independent being. The emanation can often be identified with Jung's anima. It consists of that which goes forth from the human being and it contains the emotions by which one individual makes contact with another (*J* 39[44]:38-39) and of the projections of the imagination embodied in works of art, through which communication is also effected (cf. *FZ* 4:1-3/ E301/ I, 17-19). In *Milton*, the hero descends into mortal life, but Eternals nourish him with their emanations—intimations of the real existence from which he has departed (15:10-16). While it is usually conceived of as a wife, the emanation is sometimes identified as a daughter, and in *Jerusalem* there are three references to male emanations (49:47, 88:10-11, 90:1-2).[13] Albion's Emanation, Britannia or England, divides into Jerusalem and Vala, the latter being the "Shadow" of the former "builded by the Reasoning power in Man" (*J* 39[44]:39-40). In their fallen form, emanations can turn into hatreds and cravings for power and act as siren-like temptresses to the soul.

When the Zoas renounce their subordination to the Humanity and seek independence or sovereignty, they, too, separate from their Emanations. Vala is the Emanation of Luvah, the Zoa of passion and feeling. As the goddess of external, material nature, she covers reality with her beautiful Veil of outward appearances, but the Veil is also a net interwoven with moral law and a convenient mantle for "Mystery," the dogma and ritual which enable the authoritarian priest to maintain his power. As a tyrannical female will—the concept, though not the term, goes back to *Europe*—Vala can take the form of the Whore of Babylon, who is pictured in Revelation xvii.1-5 as riding a seven-headed beast and given the name "Mystery"—a word which Blake interprets in the sense just given. He also identifies Vala in the world of time with Rahab, who is both the Canaanite harlot who aided Israelite spies

---

[13] Cf. p. 146 above.

and an Old Testament dragon (Josh. ii; Is. li.9); in the eighty-seventh Psalm, she is linked with Babylon. Since she saved herself by betraying her city and thus resembles a sinful worshipper who seeks atonement by human sacrifice,[14] Blake sees Rahab as the religion of moral virtue and, at a late stage of history, as the ground of natural religion, which stresses ethics and minimises belief in the supernatural (e.g. *FZ* 105:10-27/ E378/ VIII, 277-94; *M* 40:17-22; *J*, pl. 52, prose and 70:31).

Blake has endowed Rahab with five daughters: Tirzah, Mahlah, Noah, Hoglah, and Milcah. Numbers xxvii.1-11 records that these sisters, having no brother, inherited their father Zelophehad's property although the right of inheritance was normally restricted to sons. In the poet's eyes, this inheritance symbolises the ascendancy of female matter over male spirit, the five sisters become emblems of the five corporeal senses, and Tirzah stands for that power in nature that makes—usually weaves—bodies for souls. She is closely associated with the womb and with the seductiveness of bodily existence, and like her mother, she is a patron of natural religion. Conveniently, her name is also the name of the capital of Israel, the rebel northern kingdom that broke away from the rule of Jerusalem, which remained the seat of Rehoboam, grandson of David, the Psalmist inspired by the Poetic Genius.

A year or two after the turn of the century, Blake took to inserting an additional poem in *Songs of Experience*. The speaker of this eloquent, compressed lyric entitled "To Tirzah" fervently repudiates the fleshly body, the part that material nature has in him and the cruel constriction she has imposed on his senses. Lamenting the division of the Human into male and female at the Fall, he contrasts Tirzah with "Mercy," or Christ, who limited the consequences of the primal error to make redemption possible, and who shows the way to achieve it through his own self-sacrifice and resurrection. The accompanying design illustrates the quotation from St. Paul with which it is inscribed: "it [i.e. the corpse] is raised a spiritual body" (I Cor. xv.44). Blake expects the reader to remember the context, in which the Apostle contrasts the perishing "natural body," which is earthy, with the immortal "spiritual body," which is heavenly. The repeated line that the speaker addresses to Tirzah—"Then what have I to do with thee"—asks a

---

[14] H. M. Margoliouth, *William Blake* (London: Oxford UP, 1951), p. 158.

question Christ addressed to his mother, whom Blake took as a symbol of material nature (John ii.4; cf. E670/ K779).

In *Milton*, Rahab and Tirzah tempt the eponymous hero by sending their sons and daughters to him in a "Twofold form Hermaphroditic" (19:32). While Blake does not use the word "androgynous" to describe the unfallen Human, he frequently employs the term "hermaphrodite" when discussing the powers of Ulro. In the fully Human inhabitants of Eternity, the male and female components are combined into a single being, much like two substances chemically combined to form a compound different from either of them. The hermaphrodite, on the other hand, is a mixture of unchanged male and female elements like a mere mixture of two substances that are chemically unaltered; it constitutes an appalling imitation of the true androgyne and is characterised by self-contradiction[15] and spiritual sterility.[16] Sometimes, in variations on the hermaphrodite, the male component masks the female—this is the biblical harlot Mystery hidden within the seven-headed beast, "Religion hid in War"—or conversely the female shrouds the male "as in an Ark & Curtains" (*J* 75:13-20).

The powers represented by Rahab and Tirzah, the hermaphrodite, and Satan come together in a culminating symbol of the selfhood and the Antichrist which Blake evokes in climactic passages near the end of *Milton* and of *Jerusalem*. He finds his inspiration in the resplendent words in which Ezekiel declares that the wisdom and beauty of the King of Tyre, who has had "every precious stone" as an adornment, who has "been in Eden the garden of God," and whom the Lord has appointed as his covering Cherub, will suffer destruction for his pride in claiming to be God and for the wickedness of his city (xxviii.1-19). In the dazzling image that is Blake's version of the Covering Cherub, all the strength of Satan and the female will is gathered, so that only self-annihilation has the power to dissolve it. However determined and sincere it may be, the ego that seeks to overthrow wickedness by its own scrupulous righteousness is doomed to become a centre of wickedness in its turn. Blake's Milton confesses,

---

[15] S. Foster Damon, *William Blake: His Philosophy and Symbols* (1924; rpt. Gloucester, Mass.: Peter Smith, 1958), p. 464.

[16] D. J. Sloss and J. P. R. Wallis, ed., *The Prophetic Writings of William Blake* (Oxford: Clarendon Press, 1926), II, 168.

> Satan! my Spectre! I know my power thee to annihilate
> And be a greater in thy place, & be thy Tabernacle,
> A covering for thee to do thy will, till one greater comes
> And smites me as I smote thee & becomes my covering.
>   (*M* 38:29-32)

On a political level,

> The hand of Vengeance found the Bed
> To which the Purple Tyrant fled;
> The iron hand crush'd the Tyrant's head
> And became a Tyrant in his stead.
>   ("The Grey Monk" [Pickering MS version], ll. 33-36)

Material nature, adored as perfect by the adherents of natural religion, continues to be represented by the "forests of night" (*E* 10:18), the Tree of Mystery, the Polypus of *The Book of Los* and the serpent. In *The Book of Urizen* and its sequels, Blake begins a programme, much augmented in his epics, of representing the fleshy materiality of mortal bodies by an imagery of proliferating or 'vegetating' nerves, veins, pipes, fibres and roots that sometimes multiply until they grow into the Polypus that threatens to obliterate all form and overrun the world. The serpent, who takes "the pestilence to adorn him with gems & gold" (*VDA* 8:7), is the same venomous but glittering creature that tempted Eve. In *Europe* Blake writes of the Urizenic mind, "Thought chang'd the infinite to a serpent" (10:16), and in *The Four Zoas* he tells how Luvah and Vala, newly fallen, saw that "the vast form of Nature like a Serpent play'd before them" (42:13/ E328/ III, 97).

The framework to which Lockean perception clings is the Sea of Time and Space, which Blake names twice in his epics and once in a letter (*FZ* 56:13/ E337/ IV, 265; *M* 15:39; E724/ K812). Appropriating an ancient and widespread symbol, he conceives the entire astronomical cosmos as the Mundane Egg. In plate 59 of *Jerusalem*, its Shell, the outer edge of the universe, is formed by the petrifaction of the Veil of Vala, and in plate 37 of *Milton* he elaborates his picture of this Mundane Shell into a symbol, fascinating in its intricacy, of the horrors of the fallen world. As Bronowski, a professional mathematician, observes, Blake's image

of the universe has more than three dimensions.[17] (Damon notes
that the same is true of the city of Golgonooza.)[18] Within the Mun-
dane Shell is Udan Adan, a formless "Lake not of Waters but of
Spaces," which carries the Satanic Mills on its banks and islands;
it is situated "in the Forests of Entuthon Benython," which are
likewise "indefinite" being the dark void of infinite space in which
the reasoners locate their world of inflexible objects and impose
their rigid moral laws (*J* 13:34-38, 7:22; *FZ* 113:23-25/ E377/
VIII, 224-26; *M* 26:25; *J* 5:56-59).

Though nature as conceived by Bacon, Newton and Locke
is for Blake ghastly and desolate, it must never be forgotten that
the created world has for him a second and merciful aspect. Modif-
ied by God's limitation of the Fall and put to its best use by Los,
the Zoa of imagination, it becomes a place where those who have
succumbed to error can work their way back to Eternity. Even the
Mundane Shell is from one viewpoint the work of Los (*M* 34:31).
Beside Udan Adan and Entuthon stands Golgonooza, Los's city of
love, forgiveness and art. The name of this sacred four-dimen-
sional metropolis echoes the name of the hill where the Redeemer
was crucified. Within it, vehicles physical and mental—bodies of
flesh and works of art—are woven for the spirit as Los and Enith-
armon labour in time to build Jerusalem, the city of Eternity. At
the centre of Golgonooza are Cathedron, on whose looms Enith-
armon beneficently weaves, and the Gate Luban, symbol of the
birth canal. (E.g. *FZ* 90:2-57/ E370-71/ VII, 433-89 and 99:24-
100:10/ E372/ VIII, 30-44; *J* 12:21-13:29.)

To explain the relation between unchanging "Individual
Identities" (*M* 32:23) and their position on the scale between
predatory selfhood and complete Humanity, Blake contrives his
doctrine of States. This sophisticated version of "Blame the sin
and not the sinner"[19] posits that beings who descend into the temp-
oral world pass through a succession of States. Both their essential
identities and the States themselves are everlasting and immutable
(E556/ K606), but the fallen beings pass from one State to another,
and in this sense "States Change" (*M* 32:23). Satan is a State (and

---

[17] J. Bronowski, *William Blake 1757-1827: A Man Without a Mask* (London: Secker and Warburg, 1944), pp. 98, 148n2.
[18] *Blake Dictionary*, p. 163.
[19] Damon, *Philosophy and Symbols*, p. 194.

therefore unredeemable) and so, in Blake's eyes, are numerous biblical characters such as Adam, Noah, Rahab, Caiaphas and Pilate—as well as Memory, Love without Imagination, and Reason, though this last does vary as the scope of human reason varies from age to age (*M* 32:10-38; E556, 558, 560/ K606, 607, 608, 611). The unimaginative person makes the error of imputing sin to individuals instead of to their temporary State:

> ...to distinguish the Eternal Human...
> ...from those States or Worlds in which the Spirit travels:
> This is the only means to Forgiveness of Enemies.
> (*J* 49:72-75; cf. *J* 25:15-16, 70:17)

To cast off the Selfhood and live from the Humanity is, in Blake's terms, to remove a garment of falsehood and a hard shell of error that disguise one's true identity. Blake mocks Satan, who does "not know the Garment from the Man," and when his hero Milton advances towards self-annihilation, he makes him denounce his reasoning Spectre:

> This is a false Body: an Incrustation over my Immortal
> Spirit, a Selfhood which must be put off & annihilated
> alway.

He will "cast off the rotten rags of Memory by Inspiration" and with Christ's aid transcend [in the spirit in this life, completely after death] "the Sexual Garments.../ Hiding the Human Lineaments as with an Ark & Curtains" (*GP*, Epilogue, 1. 2; *M* 40:35-36, 41:4 and 25-26). Elsewhere Blake describes the cutting away of the adventitious selfhood, the "Circumscribing & Circumcising" of "the excrementitious/ Husk & Covering into Vacuum evaporating revealing the lineaments of Man" (*J* 98:18-19).

Further images, applicable more to the redemption of humanity collectively than to that of the individual, come from Revelation xiv.14-20, where "the harvest of the earth" is reaped, "the clusters of the vine of the earth" are gathered, and the grapes are trodden in "the great winepress of the wrath of God." With the aid of His plough and harrow—"the Plow of Jehovah and the Harrow of Shaddai" (*J* 41[46]:14)—God prepares this world for the final Judgment when all error will be cast out. The "Human Harvest," the last Vintage, and the pressing appear in all three epics, though Blake lingers longest over them in Night the Ninth of *The Four Zoas*. Moreover, diverse changes brought about in the individual and in whole societies by the pressure of experience are represented by metamorphoses wrought by agriculture and metal work. Hence the plough, the harrow and the winepress are found alongside the furnace, the hammer and the anvil in the prophetic books. Though oppressors, too, can have their furnaces, those of Los, which are essential to bring about regeneration, are the most prominent.

The Blakean myth of redemption in time has also an historical component. After his 'conversion,' Blake introduces the pagan enemies of the Israelites as people even further removed from reality and wisdom than the followers of the Mosaic Law. But he pushes back the beginnings of the narrative to the fall of "Albion our Ancestor, patriarch of the Atlantic Continent, whose History Preceded that of the Hebrews & in whose Sleep or Chaos Creation began" (E558/ K609). To synthesise myth and history, he draws extensively on the wildly fanciful speculations of eighteenth-century students of mythology and prehistory.

In 1809 Blake asserts in his *Descriptive Catalogue* that "The antiquities of every Nation under Heaven is no less sacred than that of the Jews" and makes the sweeping and unscholarly claim that "They are the same thing as Jacob Bryant, and all antiquaries have proved" (E543/ K578). As an apprentice in the 1770s, Blake may have engraved plates for Jacob Bryant's *A New System, or an Analysis, of Ancient Mythology* (1774-76) as several of these plates are signed by his master, James Basire. Todd notes how influential was Bryant's thesis that the Greek myths were badly distorted versions of ancient historical events, the record of which was better preserved in the older relics of such peoples as the Babylonians, Egyptians and Hebrews.[20] Blake's phrase "all antiquaries" no doubt includes writers like Gian Rinaldo Carli, who believed that a submerged Atlantic continent once incorporated Europe and America, as well as Captain Wilford, who spread the idea that Britain, a remnant of this continent, was

---

[20] Ruthven Todd, *Tracks in the Snow: Studies in English Science and Art* (London: Grey Walls Press, 1946), pp. 30-33.

the site of events in Genesis that took place before the Flood.[21] Other "antiquaries" elaborated long established traditions attributing primeval wisdom to the Druids. Even Milton refers respectfully in *Areopagitica* to the belief that the wisdom of Pythagoras and the Persians originated among the Druids of Britain,[22] and the modern scholar A. L. Owen traces the proliferation of such notions in the seventeenth and eighteenth centuries. Writers claimed that the Druids went back to Abraham and Noah, that in their hands the religion of the patriarchs gradually degenerated into a polytheism demanding human sacrifice, and that they passed down a version of Old Testament history which survived in a corrupt form in the mythology and literature of Greece and Rome. William Stukeley maintained that the original Druidism, which was the first religion and universal in its time, consisted of Christianity disguised by a Mosaic veil and that the British Druids sprang from a Phoenician colony, while Rowland Jones viewed the Jewish Cabbala as a Druid inheritance and John Wood claimed that Druidism began in Britain and spread over the whole world.[23] Blake believed that the degeneration of Druidism occurred when moral self-sacrifice was reinterpreted to mean the physical sacrifice of others (*J* 28:20-21; E542-43/ K578). Fisher argues that the deity of the Druidism expounded in Edward Williams's *Poems, Lyrical and Pastoral* (1794), from which Blake quotes translations of Welsh triads (E526/ K560), is a god of nature and moral law, which accounts for the Blakean equation of Druidism with natural religion.[24]

As Damon points out, Bryant was quite conventional in his assertion that all mythologies were distortions of the same truths,[25] and both Frye and Raine have demonstrated that the poet delights in combining references to different traditions.[26] Thus he

---

[21] Edward B. Hungerford, *Shores of Darkness* (1941; rpt. Cleveland and New York: Meridian Books, 1963), pp. 30, 47.

[22] *The Works of John Milton* (New York: Columbia UP), IV (1931), 339.

[23] A. L. Owen, *The Famous Druids: A survey of three centuries of English Literature on the Druids* (Oxford: Clarendon Press, 1962)—see especially pp. 10-11, 65-72, 78, 120-23, 131-32, 157-58, 182-86, 200, 212.

[24] Peter F. Fisher, "Blake and the Druids" (1959; rpt. *Blake: A Collection of Critical Essays*, ed. Northrop Frye (Englewood Cliffs, N. J.: Prentice-Hall, 1966), pp. 156-78.

[25] *Blake Dictionary*, p. 61.

[26] Northrop Frye, *Fearful Symmetry* (Princeton: Princeton UP, 1947); Kathleen Raine, *Blake and Tradition*, 2 vols. (Princeton: Princeton UP, 1968).

identifies his Urizen with Jupiter and Odin as well as with the Hebrew Elohim, and he perceives elements of the life history of his Albion in the stories of Jacob, Jonah, Job, Lazarus, Atlas, and Arthur.

In incorporating such multicultural allusions into his system, Blake combines them with the Neoplatonic and Cabbalistic conception of the fragmentation of the primal unity containing all things. As a counterpart of the Cabbalists' Adam Kadmon, who contained the whole universe in himself, Albion suffers a fragmentation in which the heavenly bodies, the earth and his own Children fly out of his body and become external to him; in terms of perception, he learns to see them as being outside himself (*J* 21:7-10). His twelve Sons—whose names are associated with Blake's trial, for the sons of Britain arraigned the poet—become spectres; his twelve Daughters—whose names derive from the history, mostly legendary, of early Britain—collectively constitute Rahab and Tirzah.[27] As a geographical figure, Albion is the "patriarch of the Atlantic Continent" (E558/ K609), on whose mountains "Giants dwelt in Intellect" (*J* 50:1). While humankind was still close to Eternity, art flourished in "the highly cultivated states of Egypt, Moab, Edom, Aram, among the Rivers of Paradise" (E531)/ K565), but the world had not then taken on the illusory form of a three-dimensional globe—it was seen for what it was, "one infinite plane" (*M* 15:32). At that time "Albion cover'd the whole Earth, England encompass'd the Nations," while Jerusalem overspread all countries from Japan to the Atlantic Mountains and

> Mount Zion lifted his head in every Nation under heaven:
> And the Mount of Olives was beheld over the whole
> Earth...
> (*J* 24:44, 48-49)

In this world there was but one language and one aboriginal religion, "the religion of Jesus, the everlasting Gospel" (E543/ K579). The earliest, uncorrupted Druidism consisted of this creed.

The primal tragedy was Albion's sleep, during which the earth was created as a material globe and the continents and coun-

---

[27] See pp. 169-71 above.

tries dwindled and separated. As Jerusalem laments, Palestine and
its neighbours now became divided from Britain:

> Goshen hath follow'd Philistea: Gilead hath join'd with
> Og!
> They are become narrow places in a little and dark land:
> How distant far from Albion! his hills & his valleys no
> more
> Recieve the feet of Jerusalem: they have cast me quite
> away:
> And Albion is himself shrunk to a narrow rock in the
> midst of the sea!
> (*J* 79:13-17)

A flood drowned "the Atlantic Continent" and interposed between
the British Isles and America a channel which swelled into a great
ocean (*J* 39[44]:14-16). Its submerged mountains, as the poem
"The Caverns of the Grave I've seen" reveals, continue to exist in
a non-material form, though a passage put into the mouth of Erin
implies that they became part of the moon (*J* 49:19-20).

Biblical history begins with Adam and his descendants,
who are the earliest Druids, but, about the time that the Flood
forms the Atlantic Ocean, Druidism degenerates into cruel pagan
religions based on human sacrifice (E542-43/ K578; cf. *J*, pl. 27,
ll. 29-40). Those "highly cultivated states" of the ancient Middle
East become abominations (e.g. *J* 92:22-25), and their arts are
copied first by the makers of surviving Persian, Indian and Egyp-
tian works and later by the imitative sculptors and writers of
Greece and Rome (E270, 273, 531, 689/ K778, 775, 565, 785; *M*,
pl. 1, prose). Druidism, with its oak groves and sacrificial altars,
spreads from Albion or Britain over the whole earth (e.g. *J* 70:16).
In time, "a remnant of Druidism" gives rise to Greek philosophy
(*J*, pl. 52, prose).

In Blake's reading of the story of ancient Israel, history
and allegory are hardly distinguished. The slavery in Egypt and
the exile in Babylon each represent humanity's fallen condition.
Both humankind and every individual must, like the Israelites,
journey through the desert, contend with the satanic selfhoods Og,
Sihon and Anak, who bar their way, and cross the Jordan or the
Arnon into the Promised Land of Canaan, where they can work

their way towards redemption.[28] Joshua's war of extermination against the pagan inhabitants, which Blake justifiably denounces in 1798, he interprets allegorically in *Jerusalem* as a spiritual struggle against selfhood and materialism (E614/ K387; *J* 49:58-59). The pagan, Ulroic Canaan, however, is a place of tyranny and temptation (e.g. *M* 19:27-20:6). Canaan is "a Female Space" (*M* 10:6), for its prototype and origin is Beulah, the space that the Eternals create for repose (*J* 69:14-31). When it is redemptive in the fallen world, it is an Allegory and Divine Analogy on account of its likeness to that higher redemptive world (*J* 84:31-85:9).

The phases of fallen humanity's history Blake represents by two parallel symbols—the Twenty-seven Churches and the Seven Eyes of God. The Churches run from Adam to Luther in a cycle which finishes only to be repeated, though escape is possible for the individual and for humankind through the path opened up by Jesus (*J* 75:4-26). The notion of consecutive churches is Swedenborgian, though the number twenty-seven is Blake's own, while the symbol of the Seven Eyes of God derives from Zechariah iv.10 and Revelation v.6, and is perhaps combined with the tradition, going back to Augustine, that history comprises seven ages. At the fall of Albion, the Eternals appoint the Seven Eyes to watch over him during his journey through time and space (*FZ* 19:9-15/ E312/ I, 553-59 and 115: 41-50/ E381/ VIII, 397-406). Each of the first six becomes corrupted, and only the seventh can defeat the satanic powers. The first is Lucifer, the bright day star who falls through pride (cf. Is. xiv.12 and marginal gloss). The second is Moloch, symbol of cruel paganism. In *Milton* the turning point of humanity's course comes when the Divine Hand fixes the limits of the Fall between Moloch and Elohim, between the end of an appalling paganism and the beginning of a less bad Hebraic legalism relieved by flashes of prophecy (13:13-27). Elohim, Shaddai (the Almighty), Pahad (Fear) and Jehovah, all manifestations of the Old Testament deity, are the third to sixth Eyes: they are forms of the Father, who in Blake's eyes is imperfect when separated from the Son; the seventh Eye, Jesus, who suffers in the "Tabernacle" of the mortal body and is the only one ready to die "willing beneath Tirzah and Rahab" (*M* 13:26; *FZ* 115:50/ E381/ VIII, 406). Yet even this Eye is imperfect, for he is the Son separated from the

---

[28] Cf. Raine, *Blake and Tradition*, I, 237, 255; II, 171.

Father, and only when the Seven Eyes unite with the Eighth, who is the sleeping Humanity of the fallen human (or of Milton), do they become Christ in his fullness, the Divine Humanity, "One Man Jesus the Saviour" (*M* 15:2-7, 20:12-14, 39:5-9, 42:10-11).[29] As Frye observes, there is a comparable example of numerology in the way that the twenty-eight cities of Albion exceed by one the twenty-seven churches and the fifty-two counties of England and Wales number one more than the fifty-one deities of Ulro in *Milton* (37:16-18).[30]

Many of Blake's conceptions have to be gathered from passages widely dispersed in his epics and in his vigorous, incisive prose that retains the edge which distinguishes it in *The Marriage of Heaven and Hell*. This later prose, much of which he left unpublished in his Notebook, is more approachable than the three epics, two of which he engraved with enormous pains. As Damrosch confesses,[31] many readers find these huge, uneven works monotonous, and Bateson complains that all the prophetic books seem to be "written much too fast and insufficiently revised."[32] Yet as early as 1929 Thomas Wright alerted readers to the way in which "Blake's *Jerusalem* and his other prophetic works are crowded with golden sayings."[33] In their pages, great poetry jostles awkward and pedestrian writing, and while an extract can thrill even at first reading, prolonged immersion can make the newcomer yearn for an end to the long line of shifting alliances and enmities of what seem like shadowy characters. Frequently, however, close study leads to delight in gnomic wisdom, passionate rhetoric, simple beauty, and images whose multi-dimensional significance grows as they recur. Frosch may well be right to classify Blake's epic style as auditory rather than visual and designed to transcend the Urizenic limitations of the eye that is all too apt to constrain the world within the Procrustean framework of geomet-

[29] See p. 161 above.

[30] Northrop Frye, "Notes for a Commentary on *Milton*," in *DV*, pp. 97-137 (see pp. 126-27).

[31] Leopold Damrosch, Jr., *Symbol and Truth in Blake's Myth* (Princeton: Princeton UP, 1980), p. 355.

[32] F. W. Bateson, ed., *Selected Poems of William Blake* (1957; rpt. London: Heinemann, 1963), p. xxviii.

[33] *The Life of William Blake* (1929; rpt. Chicheley: Paul P. B. Minet, 1972), I, xiv.

rical perspective.[34] That a strong auditory element is prominent in later eighteenth-century poetry is an observation of Frye, who implies that the poets of the Age of Sensibility tend to lull the surface of their minds with incantatory rhythms as they dredge the unconscious.[35] Eliot's claim that the auditory imagination can fruitfully reach into remote regions below consciousness[36] suggests that reliance on this faculty need not confine an author to paddling in Ossianic shallows. To his devotees, Blake, for all his eccentricity, conveys the noble vision of life that enabled him to face his own hardships and the pain of the whole world without succumbing to despair.

[34] Thomas R. Frosch, *The Awakening of Albion: The Renovation of the Body in the Poetry of William Blake* (Ithaca and London: Cornell UP, 1974), pp. 103-23.

[35] Northrop Frye, "Towards Defining an Age of Sensibility" (1956; rpt. in Frye, *Fables of Identity: Studies in Poetic Mythology* [New York and London: Harcourt Brace Jovanovich, 1963], pp. 130-37 [see pp. 132-34]).

[36] T. S. Eliot, *The Use of Poetry and the Use of Criticism* (1933; rpt. Cambridge, Mass.: Harvard UP, n. d.), p. 111.

9

An Incomplete Structure: *The Four Zoas*; the Pickering Manuscript

In *The Book of Los*, Blake retold from a different viewpoint events that he had already related in *The Book of Urizen*. Though multiple viewpoints were to be exploited more fully in the future—most notably by Browning in *The Ring and the Book*—the device was not new, and Blake was familiar with its appearance in, for example, Richardson's *Clarissa* (E754/ K934). Tannenbaum further argues that the multiple viewpoint was already widely recognised to be a feature of biblical prophecy,[1] and Milton made some use of it in *Paradise Lost*, where brief accounts of the fall of the angels by the narrator and Satan precede the detailed narrative by Raphael. In *The Four Zoas*, the first of his poems to attain an epic length, Blake aims at a synthesis of portions of his myth he has hitherto presented in different books, at the incorporation of much new material, and at the co-ordination of multiple viewpoints with chronological narrative. This co-ordination he cannot fully achieve and therefore he eventually abandons the poem. As it stands, the excessive number of major characters—four Zoas and their four Emanations—badly obscures the line of the action. In addition to the problem of structure, the language is uneven. The metrical basis is consistent throughout. As in *Tiriel, The Book of Thel, The French Revolution, Visions of the Daughters of Albion* and *America*, it is the iambic heptameter, and though there are many variations, the pattern is sufficiently regular for Margoliouth to be able to use metrical requirements to help to determine some correct readings.[2]

---

[1] Leslie Tannenbaum, *Biblical Tradition in Blake's Early Prophecies: The Great Code of Art* (Princeton: Princeton UP, 1982), pp. 46-49.

[2] H. M. Margoliouth, ed., *William Blake's* Vala: *Blake's Numbered Text* (Oxford: Clarendon, 1956), pp. 113, 120, 138, 147.

Imperfect as a whole and variable in quality, *The Four Zoas* contains many passages of great power and beauty, but even the tragic grandeur of the penultimate book and the splendour of the one that follows did not save the poem from being the only one of his three known epics that Blake did not engrave.

Many pages of the manuscript consist of proofs of Blake's engraved illustrations to Edward Young's book-length meditation *The Complaint: or, Night-Thoughts on Life, Death, & Immortality* (1742-45). The nine divisions of Young's poem carry the subheadings "Night the First," "Night the Second," etc., and the 1797 subheading of *Vala* (before it was retitled *The Four Zoas*) was "The Death and Judgement of the Eternal Man a DREAM of Nine Nights." Although Young holds fast to the conventional morality that Blake deplores, the two poets share a faith in immortality, and while Blake borrows Young's subheadings for his nine books, his poem, unlike the earlier poet's, is a narrative.

Blake's illustrations to *Night Thoughts* are engraved around rectangular spaces left blank for Young's text, and in these spaces on copies of the proofs is found a major part of *The Four Zoas*. However, many pages without engraving (including the backs of proofs) contain alongside Blake's verse his preliminary sketches for designs to accompany his own words. In some cases erotic portions have been erased, just possibly by Blake himself in preparation for making publishable engravings, but probably by a shocked John Linnell, to whom in old age he entrusted the manuscript. Among the surviving examples are winged phalluses—the clearest example is on p. 42—and Paley believes these derive from Richard Payne Knight's *Account of the Remains of Priapus* (1786) and that they allude to the first words in Blake's final subtitle: "The torments of Love & Jealousy."[3]

The drawings range from obvious illustrations of the narrative to enigmatic grotesqueries and designs of radiant splendour. Among the most intriguing are a wonderful devouring monster with jaws open wide enough to swallow the world (p. 70), a human-faced chimera with spectrous wings and two bovine hooves (p. 100), and a fowl with human head and serpentine tail (p. 134), all of whom may be—like the Prester Serpent (p. 90)—inhabitants of Urizen's world. Large and small sketches—such as those portray-

---

[3] Morton D. Paley, *William Blake* (Oxford: Phaidon, 1978), p. 45.

ing the story of Los, Enitharmon and Orc (pp. 60, 62) and Enion groping blindly after her children (p. 9)—illustrate the themes of love and jealousy. A series of mixed animal and human forms seem to show metamorphoses of the fallen Vala (p. 26), while Urizen is pictured exploring the lower world with his globe of fire (p. 74) and perhaps, in skeletal form, meddling with Vala's Veil (p. 27). Accompanying such emblems of fallen existence are images of creative work and energy (p. 66), a rising man who may stand for Albion redeemed (p. 76), an ascending figure of uncertain gender following the last words of the poem (p. 139), and above all a serene and majestic resurrected Christ (p. 108).

Although the work moves from the fragmentation of Albion to his reintegration, Blake begins his text in the traditional epic fashion *in medias res*, which in this poem means after the Fall has taken place. He starts with the lamentable condition of Tharmas and Enion. The latter, as governor of the senses and the body, can be regarded as the co-ordinator among the Zoas, but he now finds his world has become a chaotic sea. The poet goes on to describe fluctuating relationships between the Zoas, their Spectres and their Emanations, and frequently introduces speeches and unrhymed songs containing flashbacks of the Fall. Other major events, however, he does present chronologically: Urizen constructs a beautiful astronomical world—the creation of Genesis (Night II)—which collapses in a flood equated with Noah's when he casts out Ahania (Night III), and Los then forges a body for him (Night IV). After the birth and chaining of Orc, the son of Enitharmon and Los, Enitharmon's heart begins to open (Night V). Urizen explores the remains of his creation (Night VI). He encounters Orc, who becomes a malign serpent; Los embraces his own Spectre, and these two begin to build the city of Golgonooza, through which vision is recovered; Enitharmon's heart breaks, and through it is born Vala, who is acclaimed as a queen of war, while Enitharmon co-operates with Los in work of redemption (Night VII). But Christ, who is also called the Divine Vision, must be crucified, and Rahab must dominate the world with war and religion (Night VIII), before redemption can be completed through the Last Judgment and the human harvest, in which all souls are painfully purged of error—this final event is accompanied by the reintegration of the Zoas and their Emanations in Albion (Night IX). Late additions scattered throughout the epic after Blake's 'conversion' assure the reader—and some of the characters—that, under the guidance of Christ, Divine Providence is shaping the history of every individual and of all humanity to this end. The whole of Night VIII, which includes a treatment of the Crucifixion, is among these additions.

Unfortunately one element that greatly enriches *The Four Zoas* also helps to confuse its structure because it is interwoven with other matter regardless of chronological order. Erdman demonstrates that, as in *Jerusalem*, there is a political level on which repressive, imperialist Urizen stands for Britain, and Luvah, reborn as Orc, who metamorphoses into the serpent Bonaparte, for France.[4]

The editing of the manuscript with its entangled content has been especially plagued by one problem. Two Nights are both labelled the Seventh. Are they alternatives, one of which Blake intended to discard, or did he hope to amalgamate them? Should one be relegated to an appendix? The treatment of *The Four Zoas* in this chapter is based on the text first printed in *The Complete Poetry and Prose of William Blake* (1982), edited by David Erdman, who conflates the two Nights. References are also given to Keynes's text, where they are printed consecutively as "Night the Seventh" and "Night the Seventh [b]." The editorial problem is discussed in the headnote to *The Four Zoas* in the "Notes on Criticism."

Night the First

The full title of *The Four Zoas* and the epigraph from Ephesians vi.12 announce the subject: the death or fall of Albion into this world, his sufferings here, and the judgment which brings them to an end. The sufferings are rooted in the jealousy springing from possessive love and from resentment of another's power on the internal, the individual, the international, and the cosmic levels. Albion, it is to be remembered, is simultaneously every human being, all humankind, and the island of Britain, and the conflict-

---

[4] David V. Erdman, *Blake: Prophet Against Empire* (Princeton: Princeton UP, 1954), pp. 269-374 [293-402].

ing powers are at once metaphysical, psychological, and political entities.

The second verse paragraph (ll. 4-8) and the accompanying references to John i.14 and xvii.21-23 introduce the subject of the perfect unity which belongs only to the unfallen. This unity both characterises the Eternals with their freedom from inner conflict and joins together the Father, the Son and all the unfallen. Los, or his eternal form Urthona, being the Zoa of imagination and prophecy, imparts his inspired words to the human ear. Resorting belatedly to the epic formula of proposition and invocation, Blake calls on his Muse in Beulah to sing of the fall, division and resurrection experienced by both Urthona and Albion.

The narrative proper opens with the words "Begin with Tharmas" (4:6/ E301/ I, 24). Each of the Zoas experiences the Fall in his own way and is endowed with his own symbols, which contribute to the depiction of events from his viewpoint. Unfortunately, in following, like Milton, the classical practice of beginning an epic in the middle of the action, Blake confuses the reader to whom his plot is new and strange. The first book or Night is, indeed, the worst in the poem. Awkward and cryptic transitions mar the opening lines, after which Blake launches into an unexplained conflict between Tharmas (the Zoa of the body or sensation) and his separated and jealous Emanation Enion. Although some light is cast on the Fall before Night the Seventh, it is not until then that Blake clearly discloses the initial events responsible for this catastrophe. Albion, wandering in Beulah, was dazzled by the beauty of Vala (nature seen as outside himself); he fainted and Vala gave birth to a separated Urizen (reason), then divided into Luvah (passion or feeling) and a diminished Vala. By this time, Albion was unable to rise from Beulah, where Urizen resided happily in pastoral bliss until he began to conspire with Luvah bringing about the collapse into Ulro. (See 83:7-27/ E358-59/ VII, 239-59, and cf. 58:19-59:2/ E339-40/ V, 39-47.) Scattered passages reveal that Urizen and Luvah contended for mastery over the as yet unfallen Albion—over the Human Form Divine—and Luvah, borrowing Urizen's horses to usurp his function, plummeted like Phaeton leaving Albion for a time in Urizen's power. As they fell, Luvah and Urizen brought down with them Urthona (the eternal form of Los) and Tharmas. Urthona split into a Spectre, Los, and Enitharmon. The two latter were reborn as children of Tharmas and Enion (i.e. of the body), and they in turn produced the child Orc (energy), who is Luvah reborn. In the passionately Christian revision of the original *Vala*, Jesus incarnates within Luvah, the first of the Zoas to fall and the antagonist of that Urizen who, in his corrupt state, is the antithesis of the Divine Humanity.

The narrative begins with the plight of Tharmas, who, as the Zoa of the body, the containing form within which all the functions of the human being operate, is termed "Parent power" (4:6/ E301/ I, 24). His Emanation is perhaps the body's environment. For Blake's Eternals, as for Swedenborg's spirits, the environment changes in response to the changing perceptions of the mind, but in Ulro the body's environment becomes an external envelope of space and time, and the surface of the earth is part of it. Hence during Night the First Enion gives birth to time and space in the form of Los and Enitharmon, and she herself functions as a kind of earth goddess. Her "void" is the voidness of the unformed earth of the second verse of Genesis, and it acts as a magnet to those who fall (e.g. 23:16-24:1/ E313-14/ II, 16-18).

When Albion disintegrates, the body becomes a physical entity subject to space and time; this state is chaotic compared with its state in Eternity, for "A Spirit and a Vision...are organized and minutely articulated beyond all that the mortal and perishing nature can produce" (E541/ K576). The spatial, temporal condition Blake symbolises by the fallen Tharmas's world of sea, rock and cloud governed by the imprisoning Circle of Destiny, which is the cycle of life in the physical world. Although Tharmas pities Jerusalem, the newly exiled Emanation of Albion, his consciousness has degenerated and become Urizenic so that he sees his own Emanation, Enion, as a sinful temptress and a restless inquisitor of his soul, and torments her with "stern demands of Right & Duty instead of Liberty" (4:19/ E301/ I, 37). For her part, Enion is afflicted with jealousy. Moreover, in their new and bewildering circumstances both partners fear the loss of their identity. Imitating the withdrawal of an emanation from Eternity into Beulah, Enion descends into a lower state. After a moment of vision in which he turns the temporal Circle of Destiny over her and foresees her return from Experience, Tharmas divides again. His Urizenic aspect emerges from him as an independent Spectre for which Enion weaves a body. Blake associates this completion of the Spectre and of the Circle of Destiny with the creation of the scientists' spherical earth and of the earth of Genesis with its water and dry land. This does not preclude the later attribution of creation, when seen from different viewpoints, to other Zoas.

Acting as guardians of the lower world, the Daughters of Beulah enclose the Circle of Destiny in a redemptive space, which they call Ulro; to complete their work, they close the Gate of the Tongue. The tongue belongs to Tharmas, and in the Fall it splits into the two organs of taste and touch, the senses which, as Aristotle observes in the *Nichomachean Ethics* (III, 10), the intemperate indulge. Touch, it must be remembered, is the sexual sense (cf. *M* 27:45-46). The Gate of the Tongue belongs in Tharmas's quarter, the West, where the ocean cut off the Atlantic mountains that gave access to Eternity (cf. *J* 98:17). Blake identifies it with the flaming sword that bars the way back to Eden, and with the "false tongue" of deceit which assailed the Psalmist David (*J* 14:2-9—cf. Gen. iii.24; *M* 2:10ff—cf. Ps. cxx.3); David slandered was taken by commentators as a type of Christ .[5]

In Ulro, Enion defies the moral accusations of the Spectre: she and he each claim ownership of her inner mental world—"That dark & dismal infinite" (6:14/ E303/ I, 155)—but they mingle in an unblessed hermaphroditic union, which restores a certain energy to Enion and causes her to give birth to Los and Enitharmon: imagination enters Ulro, but it assumes an autonomous, wilful and divided form, introduces the reign of fallen time and space, and saps Enion's vitality.

Again there is an intervention from above. A Daughter of Beulah named Eno expands an atom of space and a moment of time to fashion a stage for the seven thousand years of history. From this stage, glimpses into Eternity are possible. Blake implies that, imperceptibly, God is intervening through Eno (9:17/ E305/ I, 230).

Recollecting her part in Albion's collapse, Enitharmon gloatingly recalls how her possessiveness contributed to his fate and how she created a "false morning," an illusion of redemption (10:21, 11:9/ E306/ I, 272, 287). Los denounces the very act she

---

[5] Matthew Henry, *Commentary on the Whole Bible* (1708-14; rpt. 6 vols., Iowa Falls, Iowa: World Bible Publisher, [*c.* 1980]), III, 724.

vaunts, and foretells the male vengeance to be wrought by Luvah as well as her own perpetual confinement in Tharmas's world.

The depth of Enitharmon's corruption becomes apparent as she summons Urizen to reign over a world of war and tyranny from which humanness is banished. Responding to her call, he saves her from violence at Los's hand and declares himself the only god. Reason, having contended with passion (Luvah) for dominion, has achieved power over Albion, and imagination (Los), though smouldering, is temporarily subordinate to it.

Urizen blames Albion's fall on Luvah and Vala. To seduce Los into serving under him, he offers him dominion over Luvah, but when his bribe is rejected, the fallen God of Reason denounces Los's master, Jesus, as an illusion and claims, "The Spectre is the Man; the rest is only delusion & fancy" (12:29/ E307/ I, 341). For all his distrust, Los, who may be on one level the poet tempted by official patronage, succumbs to Urizen's magnificence so far as to repent his violence to the latter's ally Enitharmon and sullenly to wed her under his auspices. At this early stage of creation, before the appearance of "the bright Sun" (12:38/ E307/ I, 349), elemental spirits inhabit a still radiant nature adorned with human dwellings, but it is a nature which is soon to be drawn into both the abyss of Enion and the sinister wedding. While Luvah and Vala remain isolated above in mutual and painful jealousy, the spirits sing a nuptial song lamenting that agriculture has given way to war as a result of Albion's division—and of the conflict with Luvah, who is Napoleon's France. (Keynes's punctuation clarifies the Song: from "Awake O Brother Mountain" to "the lives of Men" is spoken by Ephraim).[6] Rehearsing some details of the Fall, the spirits describe the (imminent) birth of Luvah as Enitharmon's child and place their hopes in the Spectre of Urthona. Los, however, infected by Enitharmon's corruption, now joins her in relishing "the turning wheels of heaven & the chariots of the Slain" (16:20/ E310/ I, 441). To give a description of this world from another viewpoint, Blake allots a tender lamentation to Enion.

Albion, about to sink into Ulro, is lapsing into this-worldly consciousness on the lower border of Beulah, where Jesus

---

6 Geoffrey Keynes, ed., *The Writings of William Blake*, 3 vols. (London: Nonesuch Press, 1925), II, 15.

tends him. But Jesus is also acting in and through the Eternals, whose ambassadors return from Beulah to report on the struggle for power between Urizen and Luvah. They tell how Urizen, who cunningly urges Luvah to depart for the south, seeks to rule over Albion, the cosmic human, while "remaining in porches of the brain" (21:29/ E311/ I, 497). Luvah, however, has an equal ambition. (On a political level, the imperialist Pitt confronts the imperialist Napoleon.) The conflict, in which Luvah fights with Urizen's weapons, precipitates the division of Urthona into Enitharmon, a Spectre and Los. Tharmas's compassion to the fleeing Enitharmon provokes the jealousy of Enion, which is so prominent at the beginning of Night the First. After Los, in serpent form, has been exiled into Tharmas's world of desolation, all the inhabitants of Albion collapse into Ulro and his "exteriors are become indefinite open'd to pain"—i.e. he is doomed to life in a material body (22:40/ E312/ I, 543).

The Ambassadors' narrative of Albion's fall does not give clear or satisfying characterisations of the actors, though Urizen's title Prince of Light and his secret departure for his place in the north show that he is still the rebel tyrant of *The Book of Urizen*, who is identical with the biblical and Miltonic Lucifer and Satan (21:20, 23; 22:33-34/ E311, 312/ I, 488, 491, 536-37—cf. 12:10/ E307/ I, 321). More moving are a few lines which equate the separation and suffering of Albion's Emanation with the capture of the biblical Jerusalem and the exile of her people. While the Eternals appoint Seven Eyes of God to guard fallen Albion, the Daughters of Beulah secretly provide a resting place for Jerusalem in the porches of the oblivious, corrupted Enitharmon.

Night the Second

Almost as confusing as Night the First, Night the Second continues the story of the fall of the cosmic human and of the conflicts of the Zoas and their Emanations.

Blaming Luvah for his lapse into mundane consciousness, Albion hands the power that should remain his own to Urizen. The latter rises from the wedding feast of Los and Enitharmon to assume his new honour. Terrified at what lies ahead (for he is now conscious of past, present and future instead of the state of eternity) and appalled at the emptiness of Enion's abyss, he sets about the work of creation, which is intermittently described in the course of this Night.

For all his hostility to the material cosmos of the natural scientists, Blake's account of Urizen's creative labours reflects an artist's admiration, however qualified, of the visible universe. Picturing its architect, the poet conflates "the great Work master"—Milton's God—with the commander of the fallen angels who work with the metal ores in the soil of Milton's hell (24:5, 24:13-25:1/ E314/ II, 22, 30-33; cf. *PL*, III, 696 and I, 700-09). As the denizens of the earlier poet's infernal world are much degenerated yet still recognisable, so Urizen's spirits have animal shapes but have not lost all the beauty of their human forms. Their equipment includes numerous measuring instruments, and their works are full of geometrical shapes and orbits. Lions and tigers work with metals, spiders and worms weave atmospheres, and eagles organise the heavenly bodies. What Urizen creates is "A wondrous golden Building," the palace of the universe which is also the temple enshrining his altar, the Mundane Shell bounding the universe, and an analogue of the devils' palace in *Paradise Lost* (32:10, 15; 30:8-42/ E321, 319-20/ II, 243, 248, 166-200; cf. *PL*, I, 717-30). He has no scruples about employing slaves (30:12-14, 39/ E319-20/ II, 170-72, 197), and, as Bronowski observes, the pervasive presence of the Industrial Revolution with its workers, furnaces, factories and machines is one of the features that distinguishes the epics from the earlier prophetic books.[7]

Although it shines with splendour in the midst of the abyss and although Urizen has "Cities, Nations, Seas, Mountains & Rivers" placed in "Paradises of Delight" attached to the halls of his palace, that palace or cosmos is depicted as a prison in which "spirits mourn'd their bondage night and day" (30:15-19, 32:13/ E319, 321/ II, 173-77, 246). Echoing *The Marriage of Heaven and Hell*, Blake includes among its makers those who delight in setting cunningly baited "nets...gins & traps" to condense "strong energies into little compass" as well as beasts engaged in "Petrifying all the Human Imagination into rock & sand" (30:1-5; 25:3-6/ 319, 314/ II, 159-63, 35-38).

---

[7] J. Bronowski, *William Blake 1757-1827: A Man Without a Mask* (London: Secker and Warburg, 1944), pp. 81-85.

The progress of the building entails the separation and dispersal of the heavenly bodies and of the nations of the earth. At the river by Tyburn—a future site of the gallows—among the not yet decadent Druid temples and in the still standing Atlantic Mountains, there are premonitions of imminent doom. The inhabitants of Palestine are severed from Britain to become "Nations far remote in a little & dark Land" (25:21-24/ E314/ II, 53-56), and Jerusalem ceases to shade the whole earth as the rebellious Daughters of Albion imprison her Daughters and encourage armies to fight. Since their names are drawn from the legendary history of the ancient Britons, Albion's Daughters symbolise their nation's degeneration into a warlike people. When the earth falls, human beings divide into two categories, those who see "visions in the air" and try to preserve their brotherhood, and those who, having lost all perception of reality, engage in commerce and natural science (28:11-24/ E318/ II, 121-34).

Meanwhile, since Luvah is the antagonist of the Zoa who undermines faith with reason, and since he represents both love in many forms and, being identified with France, the ideals and energy of the French Revolution, Christ has incarnated in his "robes of blood/ Lest the state call'd Luvah should cease" (33:13-14/ E321/ II, 263-64). He takes on the flesh, moreover, in the east, the quarter occupied by Luvah in Eternity but left void when the Zoas change their positions at the Fall (74:9-29/ E351/ VI, 260-80). Because it is necessary to make ultimate redemption possible, Christ has also permitted Urizen to construct his universe:

> Thus were the stars of heaven created like a golden chain
> To bind the Body of Man to heaven from falling into the
> Abyss
> (33:16-17/ E322/ II, 266-67)

Had Blake been content to limit Night the Second to the above subject matter together with Enion's second heartbreaking lament over the pains of earthly life, it would have constituted a beautiful and moving poem despite the obscurity of certain details. Unfortunately, he tried to weave into it a narrative of cruel struggles between the Zoas.

Ignoring Albion's behest to have pity on Luvah, Urizen, fearing his fellow Zoa, allows him to be cast into the furnaces created by his—Urizen's—animal followers. Vala, having forgotten their relationship, delights in the victim's sufferings. In a cryptic passage illustrated by grotesque drawings, Luvah recalls how he nurtured Vala through her several metamorphoses from earthworm to infant, and how she eventually became the mother of his children. Deprived of her, he guiltily confesses that he sought "to deliver all the sons of God/ From [the seeming] bondage of the Human form" (27:17-18/ E318/ II, 107-08) and laments that Christ does not know of the fate of the fallen in a realm where opposing forces are left to collide by chance: it is just such a realm as Milton's Chaos (*PL*, II, 898-910). By showing Luvah in the power of Vala, Blake implies that affections and energies of the mind have become subordinate to external nature.

After many ages, Vala disintegrates into ash and Luvah is melted down in the furnaces. Meanwhile Urizen has prepared channels for the molten metal with the Plough of Ages (i.e. of historical time) pulled by Luvah's bulls. Urizen, in effect, has overcome Luvah and is in possession of his energy. Reason's triumph over passion seems to be complete.

Urizen, however, is neglecting his own feminine side symbolised by Ahania, who, in her spouse's absence, is only sustained by the burnt offerings of her children. He returns to receive her affection but discovers to his dismay that she has become an autonomous person.

Los and Enitharmon now gloat over the sufferings of Luvah, Vala, and Urizen. Not yet disintegrated, Vala is a slave at the furnaces, and she tries to placate Luvah—but in vain, for she is incapable of recognising him. At this point Blake's words convey his horror at the agonies of the workers turned into virtual slaves by the Industrial Revolution. Urizen and Ahania suffer mutual jealousy, which Los and Enitharmon purposely exacerbate by conducting "the Voice of Enion to Ahania's midnight pillow" (34:4/ E322/ II, 290). They also arouse Urizen's envy, for they retain as yet the Eternals' power to expand their senses at will and exert much control over what they perceive. In an intricate passage, Blake shows how Enitharmon, jealous of Ahania, taunts Los by referring to herself as the beloved of "the God"—namely Urizen (34:24 etc./ E323/ II, 310 etc.). Eventually she leaves her corpse—her "body of death"—in Los's arms, while her spirit takes flight (34:49/ E323/ II, 335; cf. Rom. vii.24). Los dies to be painfully revived at dawn by the newly returned Enitharmon's song, which echoes her words in *Europe* as it celebrates woman's possessiveness, her control over the nine Ptolemaic spheres, and her supposed power to promote joy in nature. Again, Los finds himself pursuing Enitharmon, and in the process he is taking possession of more space driving Enion further into the abyss and drawing Ahania to this same emptiness, to "the margin of Non Entity" (36:17/ E326/ II, 422).

There is a full cast of characters in Night the Second, and their actions are curiously interwoven, but Urizen is the dominating personality, and the most memorable of several poetically powerful passages is the all but concluding lamentation in which Enion repents what she has done and what she is made to do. Bitterly she cries out

What is the price of Experience? do men buy it for a song
Or wisdom for a dance in the street? No, it is bought with
the price
Of all that a man hath...
(35:11-13/ E325/ II, 397-99)

Night the Third

Short and coherent, the third Night contributes to the characterisation of Urizen and Ahania as it carries the story of the Fall a stage further. However, in some parts the language fails to match the conception.

When the Night opens, Ahania humbly begs the enthroned Urizen to enjoy his present lordship over a resplendent creation, but the god has an appalling vision of his future servitude to a "Prophetic boy," who, of course, will be his enemy Luvah reborn as Orc (38:6/ E326/ III, 18). His attempt to utter a "determin'd Decree" dissolves in his horrified preoccupation with the coming rebirth of Luvah and Vala as the offspring of Los and Enitharmon (38:7/ E326/ III, 19).

Ahania's response is partly to mourn over Urizen's error in allowing Luvah to borrow his horses and pervert them with his wine and partly to rehearse as a dread example the story of Albion's psychic disintegration and his descent into a state where nat-

ure is outside him. Briefly she remembers Eternity, where justice
and mercy harmonised and then reveals to Urizen (and the reader)
details of the crime of Luvah, on whom she tactfully puts most of
the blame; she witnessed that crime while Urizen slept. (As Erd-
man observes, the five lines beginning "Why roll thy clouds" are
Ahania's parenthetical comment to her consort.)[8] Taking advan-
tage of Albion's preoccupation with the external appearances of
Vala, "the sweet wanderer" (42:1/ E328/ III, 85), the wandering or
erring temptress—for inner and outer were beginning to sepa-
rate—and also of reason's reduced appeal as Urizen's energy
ebbed, Luvah (love and other passions) overshadowed Los and
Enitharmon (imagination) in the human consciousness. Fatigued
by mental exertion, Albion succumbed to the hallucination of a
holy god in his own image that seemed to rise above him clothed
in the "white linen" of biblical priesthood (40:4/ E327/ III, 51; cf.
Exod. xxviii.6, Rev. xv.6). In utter self-abasement, he used Old
Testament language to confess that he was as nothing before this
apparition; whereupon Luvah, seeking to be God indeed, descen-
ded on him from a cloud. In his bewilderment Albion, who could
hear the voice of fallen Tharmas calling for his Enion, asked how
it could be in the nature of love to play the tyrant. Luvah's
response was to battle with him and afflict him with boils as Satan
afflicted Job. But Albion proved to be the stronger, and he expelled
Luvah intending to sacrifice his passions to his holy deity. Vala
plummeted alongside Luvah, and they passed out of the heart with
its paradisal energies. As Vala contracted, they separated, and nat-
ure, coming between them, took on the serpentine shape which is
one of its familiar forms in Blake's mythology.

Among the strengths of Night the Third is the contrast
between the language of Ahania and the language of Urizen. The
latter responds to Ahania's disclosures with claims that reproduce
those of the biblical creator:

> Am I not God, said Urizen. Who is Equal to me?
> Do I not stretch the heavens abroad or fold them up like a
> garment?
>   (42:19-20/ E328/ III, 106-07; cf. Is. xlv.12, xlvi.5 and
> Heb. i.11-12)

---

[8] Textual Notes, E831.

He follows his words with a cruel deed as he throws Ahania to earth with the accusation that she is becoming like Albion's seductress, Vala. Though vehement in his denunciation of the female will, Blake is no champion of the macho male, nor does he despise the feminine qualities, and in a powerful passage he makes Urizen expose his deficiency by declaring that the role of the female is confined to giving rest to the male. Significantly, he recalls Ahania as having been a river in his breast—despicable, even (potentially) deadly, and yet refreshing. In narrating Vala's fall, Ahania describes her as shrinking "like the dark sea that leaves its slimy banks" (42:15/ E328/ III, 99). An emanation has the life-giving and life-destroying powers of water.

In casting out Ahania, Urizen commits a second fatal error. His Children leave him, the existing limits of the fallen world—"The bounds of Destiny" (43:27/ E329/ III, 135)—collapse, and the formless ocean rejoices. While Urizen drops into Ulro, a place of spiritual death and sexual reproduction, Ahania finds herself in Enion's world of vacuity. (The account of their fate, marred by poverty of vocabulary and slackness of rhythm, is stylistically the weakest passage in this Night.) Above the ocean, from the remnants of "Urizen dashed in pieces," there arises, "struggling to take the features of Man," the figure of Tharmas (44:20, 18/ E330/ III, 159, 157). Tormented by the threat of being absorbed into the waters, he is preoccupied with his agonising feelings of love and hate towards Enion. He alternately upbraids and pleads with her becoming more and more despairing, but he never comes alive as a character as Enion does in her cruel fading away till she is nothing more than a voice. At this stage Ahania has taken Enion's place as the wanderer of the abyss.

Night the Fourth

In Blake's first epic, each of the Zoas takes his turn (though in Los's case rather feebly) at assuming the role of the omnipotent Old Testament creator. In the comparatively lucid Night the Fourth, it is mainly the turn of Tharmas.

From his position above the ocean, the Zoa of the body and the senses alternately laments the pain of his division from

Enion, blames Urizen and Luvah for Albion's disintegration and his own consequent sufferings, and is drawn towards his children, Los and Enitharmon. Sometimes he longs for oblivion; sometimes, as supreme god of the watery chaos around him, he tries to compel Los to give form to the shattered universe, to fetter Urizen so that he cannot rise again, and to rebuild the latter's ruined furnaces.

The Zoa of imagination, however, is not so easily subdued. Though he and his consort were last seen when they had just descended "To plant divisions in the Soul of Urizen & Ahania" (34:3/ E322/ II, 289), Los now acknowledges that Urizen, "King of the Heavenly hosts," was their sole god, but since he has "fall'n into the Deep," Los himself is now "God over all" and "all powerful"; Urthona, his undivided heavenly self, is only, he insists, his shadow (48:15-20/ E332/ IV, 38-43).

After briefly and vindictively snatching Enitharmon away in a wave, Tharmas hands her over to the Spectre of Urthona. This new character, split off from Los, is a well meaning if stubborn reasoner whose thinking starts from a thin foundation of imagination or vision that Urizen lacks. It can probably rise to the level of metaphysics, as Damon suggests,[9] but is typically concerned with everyday survival including, insofar as Los represents Blake himself, the breadwinning task of engraving.[10] The Spectre charges Tharmas with contributing to the Fall and remembers his own agonising separation from Enitharmon and birth from Enion. At last, Tharmas realises that Los is Urthona in a new form, and he withdraws leaving the submerged Urizen in Los's care.

At this point Blake rehandles, with much verbatim repetition and some expansion, the story earlier told in *The Book of Urizen* of Los's forging a bodily form for the disintegrating lawgiver. In the new version, Los vengefully rejoices that his blows on the anvil are a torment to Enitharmon as well as to Urizen and he expresses verbally his hatred of Tharmas. Already degenerate, he becomes more so, for as he continues the work with the Spectre's help he is transformed into what he beholds (53:24, 55:22/ E336, 338/ IV, 203, 286). After repeating from the earlier book the story of the creation of Urizen's material body, Blake

---

9 S. Foster Damon, *William Blake: His Philosophy and Symbols* (1924; rpt. Gloucester, Mass.: Peter Smith, 1958), p. 379.

10 Erdman, *Prophet*, pp. 280-81 [305-06].

switches the perspective to present Albion, now shut out of Beulah and lying dead on his rock in the Sea of Time and Space. He is identified with Jonah in the fish's belly and the Lazarus whom Christ restored to life. Before his departure, Tharmas borrowed from the language of Jonah's prayer as he exulted over the irreversible death of the whole human, Albion (51:15-19/ E334/ IV, 132-36; cf. Jon. ii.5). Now the Daughters of Beulah collectively play the role of Martha and lament to Jesus, who is "cloth'd in Luvah's robes of blood" and acts through the Council of God:

> Lord, Saviour, if thou hadst been here our brother had not
> died
> And now we know that whatsoever thou wilt ask of God
> He will give it thee...

Jesus repeats the promise he made to Lazarus' sister: "If ye will Believe your Brother shall rise again" (55:10-56:3; 56:17-18/ E337/ IV, 247-55, 269-70; see John xi.21-23). As he did near the end of Night the First, Jesus intervenes in Albion's catastrophe. This time he sets boundaries to the Fall naming the limit of opaqueness to true vision Satan and the limit of physical diminutiveness Adam. Los becomes conscious of the divine intervention and feels terror.

Night the Fifth

Blake continues to retell, in a much enlarged version, the story of *The Book of Urizen*. Having completed his rival's body, Los, cursing, performs a frenzied dance on the mountains of Ulro while Enitharmon lies prostrate on the ground. Both of them have degenerated into bodily organisms with "senses unexpansive" (57:19/ E339/ V, 19); though they remain gigantic, Los has shrunk from the stature that allowed him to work at the furnaces. While melodies in the air do preserve the memory of a higher state, the night and winter of fallen existence are sweeping over the world at the very time when Enitharmon is giving birth to Orc.

As Luvah's reincarnation and embodiment of energy, the new baby is welcomed on his arrival in Ulro by a kind of anti-Nativity Song from warlike demons of the abyss. Recalling details of Albion's collapse, they include—along with the battle between Luvah and Urizen and the division of Urthona—the temptation by Vala, whose "lovely form/ ...drew the body of Man from heaven into this dark Abyss" (59:1-2/ E340/ V, 46-47). While welcoming Orc, they denounce Los and Enitharmon as monsters and call on Vala to let loose the arrows of war in this world as she once let them loose in heaven to Urthona's anguish.

During Orc's childhood, Los begins to build Golgonooza, his city of redemptive art, at the point just before total darkness begins. In the centre is Luban, the place from which the fallen are born into this world. Since on one level Luban is the birth canal, it is symbolically appropriate that Tharmas, Zoa of the body, should lay the foundation on which Los builds the superstructure, but since there has been no intimation of Tharmas's return from his flight into the abyss, his contribution is a blemish in the narrative (60:4-5, 52:7-8/ E340, 335/ V, 77-78; IV, 157-58).

Repeating from *The Book of Urizen* the story of Los's binding of the adolescent Orc with the Chain of Jealousy, Blake adds significant details. Los's fear that his son plans to murder him recalls Laius's exposure of his baby Oedipus in a vain attempt to avert the prophecy that the child would kill him: imagination fears to be displaced by passion. The Spectre—Los's share of reasoning power—now helps him to bind Orc and then stands guard. Orc himself is celebrated in a pleasing passage which makes it clear that he still possesses powers and energies of Eternity including the capacity to expand and contract his sight at will; to fallen senses, such powers can seem horrifying as well as enchanting, so that Orc radiates "terror in the nether deep" (62:8/ E342/ V, 142).

In a new episode, which marks the beginning of regeneration for Los and his Emanation, the former repents of his cruelty, but when he takes the weeping Enitharmon back to the mountain, the chain is so deeply embedded in the rocks that though they would give their lives to free their son they cannot release him: the passions and their energy are so interfused with fallen life that all the power in the world cannot separate them. The parents faint and are only revived by the practically inclined Spectre's care. As they return, Enitharmon's sorrowful heart, taught by suffering, opens and closes; within that heart, Vala begins to "reanimate" (63:13/ E343/ V, 179), and, looking into it, Enitharmon finds that she can see into the roots of the temporal, spatial realm, now threatened by the growing strength of O.c. The passage foreshadows a crisis in Night the Seventh at which Vala is reborn from Enitharmon's broken heart as the Shadowy Female first encountered in *America* and *Europe* (85:13-15/ E360/ VII, 323-25).

For the moment, however, Urthona is the dominant power in Ulro, and Urizen is said to be imprisoned in his "deep dens" (63:23/ E343/ V, 189)—this is close to the image in verse 16 of "A Song of Liberty." Mingling grief with remorse, Urizen contrasts the joys he knew in Eternity with his present plight and acknowledges that he gave way to hate and envy, forgot that all came from the creator, and wilfully withheld his steeds from God's service. While he accepts his own share of responsibility for dragging Urthona and Luvah down with him, he does not omit to mention the latter's fateful pride. His lamentation leads to a resolve to explore the underworld in which he finds himself, for he rightly suspects that in accordance with prophecy Luvah (love) is reborn in this hideous hell.

Night the Sixth

When Urizen, awakened from his torpor, begins to explore Ulro, the story diverges widely from the plot of *The Book of Urizen*, though the god retains his "Globe of fire" (70:1/ E346/ VI, 83; *BU* 20:48). The opening episode is much indebted to Satan's encounter with Sin and Death in the second book of *Paradise Lost*. Only after a threat from his spear elicits a scream from the three river goddesses who interrupt his attempt to slake his thirst, does Urizen recognise them for fallen forms of his beloved Daughters. They shrink leaving dry riverbeds. "Reason," comments Ostriker, "dries up the waters of life."[11] Like Tiriel, the hero of Blake's first prophetic book, Urizen proves adept at cursing his Children; he sees his Daughters as traitors who have given their allegiance to Tharmas and to Tharmas's follower Los. Yet the longing with which he pours out his recollections of

---

11 William Blake, *The Complete Poems*, ed. Alicia Ostriker (Harmondsworth, Middlesex: Penguin, 1977), p. 939.

Eternity shows that even now his sense of values is not utterly corrupted.

Hearing the noise of conflict, Tharmas arrives over the waters, which have been frozen solid in the Urizenic cold. The agony of this Zoa is very great, for what was the unified body is dispersed among all his marine organisms. In Night the Third he howled out,

> Fury in my limbs, destruction in my bones & marrow,
> My skull riven into filaments, my eyes into sea jellies
> Floating upon the tide wander bubbling & bubbling
> Uttering my lamentations...
> (44:23-26/ E330/ III, 162-65)

Now he complains that he cannot even escape by self-destruction:

> The Body of Man is given to me; I seek in vain to destroy
> For still it surges forth in fish & monsters of the deeps
> And in these monstrous forms I Live in an Eternal woe
> (69:11-13/ E346/ VI, 60-62)

In his despair, Tharmas proposes a suicide pact with Urizen: he will withhold Urizen's food (sense perceptions) if the latter will withhold his light (the reasoning process); then they will both perish and Albion will not revive.

Ignoring Tharmas, Urizen continues his journey. After suffering the molestations of the former's sea creatures, he reaches the region of Urthona or Los in the south (it was his own realm in Eternity) and, as in chapter eight of *The Book of Urizen*, is appalled by the sight of his Children metamorphosed into monsters and condemned to inhabit a desolate world. The narrator makes it clear that the environment of the monsters—the tormenting skies and the Urizenic landscape—emerges from their own minds, which have decayed like their father's: "Beyond the bounds of their own self their senses cannot penetrate" (70:12/ E347/ VI, 94). In a long paragraph, Blake adds a social dimension to the picture. Imprisonment, torture, slavery, underground mining and fortified cities characterise the world of "dishumaniz'd men" that comes into existence when Urizen's creation collapses (70:31/ E347/ VI, 116). So completely robbed of their perceptions and enclosed in their own anguish are the victims that they cannot reply to the god's questions. As Urizen remembers Eternity, where all things are Human and "the Cloud, the River & the Field/ Talk with the husbandman & shepherd," he realises the evil his curse has wrought (71:7-8/ E348/ VI, 137-38). That curse echoes the punishing God's curse against Israel in Ezekiel vii.8 and against the wanton daughters of Zion in Isaiah iii.16-24 (68:16-23/ E345/ VI, 35-42). Not only is Urizen powerless to commune with his victims, but he has himself become subject to the material elements.

In Blake's epics, unlike *The Book of Urizen*, there are four worlds in the fallen universe, for each Zoa lives in his own version of Ulro. Veering into the lifeless world of Luvah, Urizen falls through vacancy and is only saved from extinction by another intervention of God, who creates a bed of soil in which, like a seed, he can be buried and revive (71:25-39, 73:8-14/ E348, 350/ VI, 157-71, 221-27; cf. John xii.24, I Cor. xv.35-44). This happens again and again as God guides him on his journey, and though his temporary garments perish with each death, his metal books survive and he continues to write in them: he remains a being for whom the solution to problems is the imposition of laws. Though he persists in this delusion, Blake evokes considerable sympathy for him in his errors and sufferings. Not only is the reader indisposed to be harder-hearted than "The ever pitying one who seeth all things," but Urizen's loving memories of Eternity and his compassion towards his victims—despite his desire for a world "where none should dare oppose his will"—win some respect (71:25, 73:19/ E348, 350/ VI, 157, 232). As he journeys on, like Milton's Satan labouring through Chaos (*PL*, II, 890ff), he finds himself in a cosmos where each thing exists within its own vortex as posited by the rationalist philosopher Descartes. Urizen himself, the narrator reveals, creates vortex after vortex in his struggle not to be swept downwards in the abyss. Horrified by "this world of Cumbrous wheels" (72:22/ E349/ VI, 196), he passes from sphere to sphere (each in its vortex) through the empty air between. Whenever he looks towards the centre of a vortex, whether before or behind him, he finds himself looking upward. When he is at the centre of a vortex he has just formed, he can only look downwards. His way of escape would be by opening his imagination (symbolically, taking his repose in the "Equilibrium grey of air serene" between vortexes) but he seeks to dominate this universe from without as its independent "self sustaining" monarch or else to bypass it through a surrounding void (72:16-27/ E349/ VI, 190-201).

In his own eyes, the best he can do is to begin a new creation exploiting the metals in the ground on which he periodically falls (73:14-20/ E350/ VI, 227-33; cf. *PL*, I, 670ff). He succeeds in fashioning a Cartesian universe of vortexes in which he paralyses with fear all human souls whether they are predominantly rational or emotional—his sons or Luvah's. Soon he is the aged, white haired, long bearded god of the last chapters of *The Book of Urizen* dragging through the sky a deadly web sprung from his soul and causing the human senses to shrivel. People become wedded to their external bodies situated in fixed space, and unable to perceive the boundary of the universe in the way it is perceived by eternal vision, as a "wing like tent...surrounding all" which vanishes and reappears "at the will of the immortal man" (74:3-4/ E350-51/ VI, 254-55).

At this stage of the Fall, three of the four worlds of the Zoas change the positions they occupy in Eternity. The eastern territory of Luvah becomes the southern cave of Orc, while Urizen's realm sinks from south to west, whence Tharmas's ocean is displaced and ceases to be identified with any quarter.[12]

In an important parenthesis, Blake indicates that Providence guides Urizen, without violating the freedom of his will, into the solidified and lifeless world of Urthona, which, though deeply corrupted, retains its eternal seat in the north. There Urizen meets a fearful challenge in the form of Urthona's Spectre in alliance with Tharmas and supported by a vast army. The Spectre, who is now growing iron scales and iron hair, is reminiscent of Talus, the sinister iron man of the fifth book of *The Faerie Queene*. Recognising that four of his own Sons lead Urthona's troops, Urizen flees back into the stronghold of his web, the Net of Religion, through which he commands both his subjects and the heavenly bodies. With this confrontation between Mosaic-Newtonian (or Mosaic-Cartesian) reason, which is also the ecclesiastical legalism dominating Britain, and the potentially beneficial reason

---

[12] Cf. *M* 34:32-39 and diagram E133/ K523.

that may be brought to serve imagination, Blake arouses suspense to a degree unprecedented in this poem.

Night the Seventh

Erdman's integration of the two Nights which are numbered seventh derives from the proposals of three scholars—Lincoln, Lefebvre and Kilgore.[13] It is based on the fact that Night VIIa (Keynes's Night VII) originally ended at line 332 (85:22/ E360), which can be followed without a jar by line 1 of Night VIIb (95:15/ E360). The remainder of VIIa fits satisfactorily after the end of VIIb, though the narrative of VIIa is awkwardly interrupted.

At the conclusion of Night the Sixth, Urizen hears the howling of Orc within Urthona's world and sends his comets to circle round the young demon, absorb blood, and return; at the same time the planets, moving at his command, weave additions to his web. As Night the Seventh begins, this display of power puts to flight Tharmas and the Spectre of Urthona leaving Urizen to encounter Orc alone: the struggle is between materialist, legalistic reason and the energy of the passions, and on the historical level between reactionary Britain and revolutionary—later Napoleonic—France. In the account of the confrontation, there are sharp differences between the views of Urizen, Orc, and the narrator.

Now that the fallen world contains the fettered Orc, Urizen is appalled to see his animals, balance, plough and harrow assailed by the latter's flames. In spite of their ferocity, they can burn in Orc's "raging lamps of mercy" that consume "the adamantine scales of justice" (77:10/ E353/ VII, 10-11). Seeking stability, Urizen perches on a rock, counters the flames of energy with his own coldness, and broods over his books of legal codes upheld by Mystery. As in chapter three of *The Book of Ahania*, the Tree of Mystery springs from beneath his heel and proliferates until he himself can only just escape from its many trunks and branches.

Defying Orc, Urizen sees him as a tortured Satan on his "lake of fire" (78:28/ E354/ VII, 55; cf. Rev. xix.20); since the

---

[13] Textual Notes, E836.

demon is obviously joyful, Urizen conjectures that his mind is abstracted. To Orc, however, the cold god seems to be so shackled by the set of his own mind that he is imprisoned in a block of ice. For Urizen's "Pity," he returns "hate"—and Blake's sympathies are with the hater (78:43, 79:18/ E354/ VII, 70, 88). Claiming authority over the fallen world, Urizen urges Orc to accept his astronomical cosmos, his patronage of war, and his laws of repentance.

A melancholy paragraph dominated by images of iron, cold, frost, rain and tears describes the burden of penitence that Urizen imposes on his recently rebellious Daughters as he makes them "Knead bread of Sorrow" to subdue Orc's inward fires (79:23/ E355/ VII, 93). He adjures them to harden their hearts and fight to destroy the power of Los, Zoa of imagination: they are to acquire power over Enitharmon and use her as a lure to effect Los's subjection to his own Spectre, his most nearly rationalistic element; as yet her corruption is lamentably incomplete, for she fashions the body as a vehicle of redemption and approves of "gratified desire" (80:25/ E356/ VII, 133). In an exceptionally vivid passage, Urizen expounds his art of oppressing the poor with a pretence of benevolence that induces their gratitude—thus Blake characterises the policy of Pitt's Government that prefers commending temperance to curbing profiteers when its citizens are tormented by hunger.[14]

Succumbing to the subtle power of Urizen's hyocrisy, Orc feels himself turning from a raging fiend into a passive worm and into the scaly serpent of Eden on the Tree of Knowledge, which is also the Tree of Mystery. As Urizen recognises that Orc is a reincarnation of his former companion Luvah, the rebel spirit himself becomes a proud, Urizen-like tyrant who transmutes "affection into fury & thought into abstraction" (80:47/ E356/ VII, 155). On the historical plane, this is the Napoleon who turned dictator. Yet Orc, knowing his rival's responsibility for his transformation, remains a little wiser than Urizen, who, like Milton's Satan, is convinced of his complete autonomy and is ignorant that he can only perform such acts as heaven, for its own reasons, allows (80:51-81:1/ E356/ VII, 159-60; cf. *PL*, I, 209-20).

---

[14] Erdman, *Prophet*, pp. 341-42 [368-69].

At this time Los is so tortured by memories of the love between himself and Enitharmon in Eternity that he would prefer oblivion to his present frustrated desire for her. While she lies, corpse-like, on his knees, her Shadow can range far afield and find in nature a joy denied to him or descend to the roots of the Tree of Mystery to weep over her son and be wooed by the Spectre of Urthona (81:11-12, 82:16ff/ E356, 357-58/ VII, 170-71, 210ff). Of these two surviving vestiges of imagination, the Spectre is slightly more deluded than the Shadow. He promises her that her second parturition will be easier, for the birth will take place amidst "Sweet delusions of Vala" (82:36/ E358/ VII, 230). Enitharmon's Shadow, however, her lips unsealed by "The fruit of this delightful tree" (83:2/ E358/ VII, 234)—the Tree of Mystery and of Eden—gives the clearest account of Albion's fall in the poem. Laying the primal blame on Vala, she beseeches the Spectre to have her punished through the agency of Orc. Her account includes a brief sketch of an intermediate stage when Vala had divided into Luvah and her diminished self and had caused the way back to Eternity to be closed; at this period, however, Albion still lived a happy pastoral life in Beulah with Luvah and Urizen. Following her confession that she has forgotten how she and Los were born, the Spectre recalls Albion's loss of his Emanation and his own descent (as Urthona) to Albion's loins and Enion's womb. In Eternity, Urthona is a smith, and the Spectre confesses his responsibility for creating Los as a bodily partner for Enitharmon. He agrees to bring Vala down to Orc (though not, apparently, as a punishment) and promises to destroy Los's body so that he can reunite with the Shadow. Now that she knows he is "Her once lov'd Lord," the Shadow readily embraces the "horrible" form (85:3, 83:3/ E360, 358/ VII, 313, 235).

Although the Spectre, like Enitharmon, is infected by the "intoxicating fumes" (85:5/ E360/ VII, 315) of the Tree of Mystery, which he mistakes for a divinely appointed refuge within Ulro, his insight is sufficient to bring on a crucial if ambiguous event. In Night the Fifth, after Orc's birth, Enitharmon had felt Vala coming to life inside her heart, whose gates began to open and close "with a deadly pain" (63:12/ E343/ V, 178). Now Vala bursts through the gates, reborn as the Shadowy Female, and the gates can never again be closed. The image has a double reference and double meaning. As the gates of the Miltonic Hell could never again be closed after Satan passed through them to release evil on the earth, so the emergence of external, material nature in the form of the Shadowy Female initiates the six thousand years of humankind's sanguinary history; at the same time, many beings so fallen that they are reduced to male spectres "burst forth from the bottoms of their tombs" (the contrary of resurrection or redemption) and roam freely while they are in the satanic state. Conversely, because Enitharmon now has just such "a broken and a contrite heart" as the Psalmist prescribes, the way to the reunion of Urthona's sundered parts and to the recovery of Eternity by self-annihilation is at last open (85:13-18, 85:26-86:12, 87:26-28/ E360, 367-68, 369/ VII, 323-28, 336-69, 398-400; Ps. li.17; cf. *PL*, II, 883-84).

Interrupting the account of these matters, comes (in Erdman's edition) Night VIIb, which opens with Urizen's claim to universal power, a claim bolstered by echoes of biblical imagery (95:19-20/ E360/ VIIb, 5-6; cf. Is. xxxiv.4, Heb.i.11-12). His boast that he is "A God & not a Man" discloses his ignorance that true humanness is Godhood (95:23/ E360/ VIIb, 9; cf. E520 [ll. 71-72]/ K752 [ll. 75-76]). The account of his empire which follows comes as something of a relief amidst so many pages of cloudy and obscure language expressing the cravings and anguish of mythological figures. Explicit allusions to maritime power, commerce, child labour and the slave trade are a sharp rebuke to contemporary Britain.

As a focal point for his empire, Urizen commands his Sons to build a temple. This heart-shaped simulacrum of the biblical prototype sanctifies the key activities of its deity's rule—religion and war. With its hidden inner shrine, it symbolically brings together the secrecy of sacred Mystery, which sustains priestly power, and the secrecy which engulfs sex when it becomes a commodity for sale in the marriage market. Under Urizenic dominion, sexual desire degenerates to a loveless lust, and the human heart withers.

Los's mission in this world is associated with the sun. By its light, the imagination can see *through* the eye, but when Urizen commandeers it, as he does with his "immense machines," to glorify his temple and illuminate the fixed and empty space of "the Abyss," it divides clock day from clock night, time of war from time of religion (96:10, 15/ E361/ VIIb, 30, 35). Whether the sun is a blessing or a curse depends on how one regards it.

Blake now turns to the giant but corrupted Los and his patron Tharmas. In a grotesque parody of the relationship between God the Father and God the Son, Tharmas extends to Los his paternal protection and glorification. While the poet makes it clear that Tharmas in his anguish seeks revenge for the loss of his Emanation, and that both Tharmas and Los have become addicted to war, he fails to specify how their position at this point is connected with Urizen's.

Los's role is always closely associated with Enitharmon's. In a plaintive speech, the sundered Emanation tells how she recoils from her son Orc, now a scaly serpent, and is appalled by a Tharmas who returns hate for love. She seeks safety in the strong tower of Los, for imagination provides a refuge from perverted passion and bodily limitation as well as from tyrannic reason. Meanwhile, trees that would be "humanizing" with the aid of "their immortal energies" find that when they try to enter her beneficent world of nature, they become bloodthirsty organisms in a realm where animals are sullen or savage and Urizen's Prester Serpent serves as the spokesman of his tyranny (98:10-11/ E363/ VIIb, 101-02).

Urizenic rule now prevails "in the Caverns of the Grave & Places of human seed"—that is, in the world of natural life and spiritual death, where human bodies are formed by sexual reproduction and in the world devastated by the Napoleonic wars (91:1/ E363/ VIIb, 124). Vala, the goddess of material, constricting nature, has been born from Enitharmon's heart as the Nameless Shadowy Female. As in the Preludium of *America*, she confronts Orc, but since Blake has now adopted the symmetry of four Zoas and their four Emanations, the situation has become far more complex. Instead of a torpid nature painfully awakened by energy, the energy in the form of Orc is jealous of his Emanation Vala, who has deserted him to serve a bullying Urizen, a corrupted Los, and earthly tyrants. While his lions (the symbol is clumsy, for Urizen too has lions) are engaged in "rending the nameless shadow" (91:19/ E363/ VIIb, 142), the spirits of the elements sing a song to encourage themselves and all the Urizenic powers to stop "the rising of the glorious King" (91:30/ E364/ VIIb, 153—that is of Orc, who is well aware that Urizen's "arts of...Pity & Meek affection" have begun their deadly work making "the Serpent form" exude "from his limbs" (91:11-12/ E363/ VIIb, 134-35). The evil forces overcome Orc, who is Luvah, and, since Christ took on Luvah's "robes of blood" when Albion fell, they enact a crucifixion initiating the six thousand years of human history (33:11-15/ E321/ II, 261-65). There is political allegory, too, in the passage, for "the glorious King" is Napoleon, whose overthrow the northern nations savagely pursue, and the members of the British Parliament behave like Christ's crucifiers when they "vote the death of Luvah" or the overthrow of France, while on his part Napoleon has lost any ideals he once held (92:13/ E364/ VIIb, 166).

With the victory of the Urizenic powers, men desert the arts of peace for the cultivation of war and individual craftsman-ship for the division of labour and industrial slavery. Resuming their song (92:34/ E365/ VIIb, 187), the elemental spirits hail Vala in treacherously exquisite lines as they urge her to play the part of Mary Magdalene but to do so hypocritically: before Urizen's fall, they imply, she pretended to revulsion against war; now she should cast away the tears and dust of repentance and openly delight in bloodshed.

The spirits are successful in their urging. Though Orc deprives the Shadowy Female of form and scatters her as "a form-less indefinite" through the abyss of space (93:27/ E365/ VIIb, 217), she is ecstatic to lose altogether the precise shape she had in Eternity and she exults in the battle around her. Orc, however, is reduced to a "Serpent round the tree of Mystery" (93:24/ E365/ VIIb, 214): no more is to be hoped from the Emperor of the French.

When the Shadowy Female tries to conciliate Tharmas and prevent him from starving Urizen of sense impressions (cf. 69:15-16/ E346/ VI, 64-65), she finds herself briefly mistaken for Enion. Disillusioned, Tharmas laments his fate and disagrees with his would-be comforter about whether thoughts can be disclosed without the consent of the thinker. The Shadowy Female, while admitting to some sins, falsely blames the Emanations of the other three Zoas for changing her Luvah into "that Outrageous form of Orc," who acts as her accuser and oppressor (94:17/ E366/ VIIb, 249). Tharmas, however, well aware that she, as Vala, was Alb-ion's original seducer, flees and expresses his fury in the midst of nature in violent movements resembling earthquakes, floods, avalanches and thunderstorms. In lines that celebrate nature's wonders, the narrator tells how the Shadowy Female, unable to relish them, is reduced to "howling melancholy" throughout the dominion that she shares with Urizen and that reaches as far as the border of Beulah (94:48, 55/ E367/ VIIb, 280, 287). Orc, enraged against her, remains dead to Eternity.

Though the situation of the world and of Albion is now dismal, the Daughters of Albion, who were strengthened at the end of Night the Fourth by Christ's promise of resurrection, write this promise on the tombs and urns of those who have died into this world and are thus able to counter the unbelief spread by the Shadowy Female. However, an event that occurred when the Female was born from Enitharmon's heart is now described again: spectres without emanations descend *below* their existing graves, for, Blake now adds, they are attracted by the Female's clouds rather than the Daughters' songs (85:17-21, 95:9-14/ E360, 367/ VII, 327-31; VIIb, 296-301).

At this point Keynes's Night VIIb ends, and Erdman's edition adds the remainder of Night VIIa, which continues the story of Los, Enitharmon and the Spectre of Urthona and contains some touching and some delicate passages. After her initial revulsion, Enitharmon, in the form of a shadow, has recently embraced the Spectre (85:1-4/ E360/ VII, 311-14), and her complaints lead the fallen Los to recognise the hideous yet well intentioned being as a part of himself. The blessed recognition counters their increasing entrapment in the proliferating Tree of Mystery. Contrasting himself with those who have emerged from "the bottoms of their tombs" (85:18, 95:11/ E360, 367/ VII, 328; VIIb, 298), the Spectre asserts that these satanic beings must be annihilated and teaches Los that self-annihilation is the road to redemption. By uniting with him, the lesson continues, instead of (as formerly) subduing him, Los will allow his threefold world to open up again within him and his universe will be revived and regain its pre-eminent place over the universes of the other Zoas.

Los feels the world of reality present within him and embraces his Spectre expecting to be blissfully reunited with Enitharmon. She, however, turns away to the Tree of Mystery leaving Los to receive the Spectre's command that he destroy his own body—the body the Spectre earlier declared he would himself destroy (84:34-35/ E359/ VII, 300-01). But there is no destruction: instead, Los and the Spectre build the city of Golgonooza causing the new heaven and new earth prophesied in Revelation xxi.1 to appear within Los and evoking a sublime atmosphere—threefold though not yet fourfold—that reaches all the way down to the limits of opacity and contraction that God imposed upon the Fall. Nevertheless, Los's recovery is as yet at an early stage. Enitharmon has eaten Urizen's fruit of Mystery, which is the fruit of the biblical Tree of Knowledge of Good and Evil, and it has filled her with guilt and reduced her to despair. Seeing that "by devouring appetite/ All things subsist on one another" (87:18-19/ E369/ VII, 390-91), she perceives in the cruel balance of nature and in humans' preying upon humans a reflection of God's requirement that His Son die as a ransom for humankind—a requirement in which Blake did not believe.[15] Playing the role of Eve, Enitharmon persuades Los to eat the fruit confident that his strong faith will quench her fear. In the event, only his Spectre's comfort saves Los from despair and makes possible the ultimate reunion of the three portions of Urthona after the six thousand anguished years of history.

Looking again on the emanationless Spectres of the Dead, Urthona's Spectre begins to feel remorse for his part in Albion's division and hence in their fate. He sees that they need bodies to achieve redemption. Equally repentant, Los urges faith in Jesus and announces his "forgiveness of ancient injuries" (87:47/ E369/ VII, 419), but when he urges Enitharmon to look within and see, as he does, the Saviour coming to redeem, Enitharmon perceives a Jesus coming to condemn.

Saying no more about Christ, Blake concludes Night the Seventh by describing how Los, despite the strength of the Tree of Mystery, makes beautiful forms that are both works of art and fleshly bodies. Lovingly Enitharmon breathes into these the Spectres of the Dead to draw them upwards from the debased realms of Urizen and Orc. Los and Enitharmon hope these deeds of mercy in Golgonooza will serve to ransom their guilty selves. Among the Spectres incarnated are Orc's younger brothers Rintrah and Palamabron, who are respectively Urizen abstracted from his spectrous self and Urizen's eldest son, these being reborn as children

---

[15] See pp. 160, 211 above.

of Los and Enitharmon. Formerly warlike, they become innocent, and Orc is comforted. There is a hint of the redemptive quality in the love that makes Los and Enitharmon prefer "to meet Eternal death" rather than "destroy/ The offspring of their Care & Pity" (90:50-53/ E371/ VII, 482-85). The hint is reinforced by Los's discovery that his hatred of Urizen has turned, now that the latter is reborn as Rintrah, into paternal love.

Night the Eighth

In Night the Eighth, a late addition to the poem,[16] Blake tries with only partial success to graft onto *The Four Zoas* new elements of his myth which are prominent in *Milton* and *Jerusalem*. Being written after Blake's 'conversion,' this Night reflects the ardour of his reinforced allegiance to Christianity. By now he has acquired a firmer command of his epic idiom, and his version of the Incarnation and Crucifixion is clearer and more moving than the narratives of most of the earlier events in the epic. Later he makes Enion foretell the Second Coming and writes of the visions of St. John of the Apocalypse.

The narrator begins by exchanging his focus on works of mercy at the end of the previous Night for a broad view of the afflicted Albion seen in relation to Beulah and Eternity. While the inhabitants of Beulah collectively take the form of two protecting angels at his head and feet, the Eternals, united as Jesus, "create the fallen Man"—that is to say they establish his form so that it cannot shrink below "the Limit of Contraction" (99:3/ E371/ VIII, 3). Cradled in the loving arms of Christ, Albion briefly seems about to awaken.

Returning to the descent of the Spectres of the Dead and their embodiment by Los and Enitharmon, Blake tells how the latter see and feel the divine power of Jesus, whose "Human form" and universal presence are visible to the Daughters of Beulah (100:9/ E372/ VIII, 43). Because a way is open to the Spectres through Enitharmon's broken and pitying heart, they can be rescued from Urizen, Tharmas and "the Shadowy female's clouds" —from utter slavery to reason, the senses and material nature

---

[16] Textual Notes, E817.

(100:22/ E373/ VIII, 57). The bodies with which they are furnished open inwards to Beulah.

Urizen, in uneasy alliance with Orc, makes war on the attempts of Los and Enitharmon to save the Spectres and lays siege to their world with his "dark machines" (101:7/ E373/ VIII, 67). He is bewildered to see two Luvahs: one is that Zoa's new incarnation as Orc and the other, unknown to him, is Christ in Luvah's garments. Urizen's three Daughters are making the Shadowy Female gather the fruit of the Tree of Mystery and feed it to Orc (she was once Vala as he was Luvah). Emerging on the surface of his body as an armour of gold, silver and precious stones, the baleful food undergoes a transmutation into the gemstones of Ezekiel's satanic Covering Cherub and of the breastplate of Aaron, founder of the Hebrew priesthood (cf. 101:8-15/ E373/ VIII, 68-75 with Ezek. xxviii.13 and Exod. xxviii.15-21). The very specific phrases used to denote some of Urizen's "machines" justify Erdman's unearthing of a political meaning.[17] On this level Urizen is the British Government, which was employing newly invented weapons, while Orc is the fast degenerating Napoleon relapsing into reconciliation with priests and having the Pope officiate at his imperial coronation in May 1804. The "dark dissimulation" of the Anglo-French "Communing" associated with the fourteen-month Peace of Amiens gave way to renewed war a year before this coronation (100:32/ E373/ VIII, 96). Yet Urizen's struggle is directed principally against Golgonooza (its builder, Los, is "inspir'd by the holy Spirit" [101:39/ E374/ VIII, 108]), and the members of his war machine, who temporarily take on a human shape when they feel the gravitational pull of Los's hammers and hear the music of Enitharmon's looms, lapse into a bestial condition when the fighting ceases. The war machine itself becomes an opaque hermaphrodite masking the male god Urizen.

Long-enduring and full of fear, the Shadowy Female submits to Urizen's power as she mistakes Christ, incarnate in her Luvah's form, for Luvah's murderer. But perpetually tormented with the agony of the fallen world, she remembers Eternity and believes it can only be recovered by the resurrection of Luvah. In the absence of his resurrection, she beseeches Urizen, who has

---

17 *Prophet*, pp. 369-72 [397-400].

INCOMPLETE STRUCTURE   214

sealed up Albion for ever, "relent/ Thy furious power; be our father & our loved King" (103:12-13/ E375/ VIII, 162-63).

Nature, however, is not in harmony with the manifestations of reason. Exerting her energy through Orc, whose food she delivers, the Shadowy Female brings Urizen's worldwide "Web of Religion" (103:26/ E375/ VIII, 176) crashing down to distort its spinner's intent and trap him in his own snares. Blake contrasts the saving work of "Enitharmon's Looms & Los's Forges" with the slavery imposed by "the Spindles of Tirzah & Rahab and the Mills of Satan & Beelzeboul" (113:1-2/ E376/ VIII, 200-01). Los and Enitharmon create a world of space and time as well as the bodies in which the fallen can inhabit it; it is symbolically the Promised Land of Canaan, and the river Arnon, which the embodied Spectres cross to enter it, forms the eastern half of its southern border. However, the Mills of Satan, with Òg and Sihon, who opposed the Israelites' entry into Canaan, unwind the redemptive and hopeful bodies of the Spectres to replace them with garments of false religion imbuing the fallen with the "despair," "compunction," "indolence " and "ignorance" which will keep them imprisoned in Ulro (113:20-21/ E377/ VIII, 221-22). Opposed to Golgonooza is the Lake of Udan Adan, a lake of empty space formed from the sufferings of Urizen's victims, whether they are devotees of gloomy religion, wage slaves or soldiers. Happily the Eternals can see that the life of the Spectres embodied by Los and Enitharmon constitutes "a Universal female form" who is Jerusalem, the exiled Emanation of Albion (103:38/ E376/ VIII, 188); within her is Jesus putting off the body fashioned by Rahab, while Rahab herself tries to kill him but can only destroy that body thus helping him to open the way back to Eternity.

Christ's Incarnation coincides with the nadir of the Fall, where Jesus and Jerusalem (who is both woman and city) confront Satan and Vala. Satan—who is a state rather than an individual and who consists of "multitudes of tyrant Men" (104:29, 105:18/ E378/ VIII, 257, 285)—emerges from the hermaphroditic war machine besieging Jerusalem. He is a monstrous male form without an emanation of his own, yet, as the Mosaic Tabernacle preserves the Tablets of the Law in awesome invisibility, he shrouds within himself the goddess Vala: this is what Blake calls in his engraved epics "Religion hid in War" (*M* 37:43; *J* 75:20). Having reached her lowest state, the Shadowy Female reassumes her name of Vala and Blake identifies her with Mystery, the Whore of Babylon of Revelation xvii mounted on a seven-headed beast. This seeming feminine counterpart of Satan, who lures with a siren's beauty and upholds "the Cruelties of Holiness" (105:12/ E378/ VIII, 279), is the creation of Urizen's Synagogue of Satan, an assembly which can be seen as consisting of twelve rocky masses, lifeless and meaningless shapes corresponding to the ultimate degeneration of Albion's twelve Sons.

Creating her bodily form from the fruit of Urizen's Tree of Mystery, the Satanic Synagogue brings the Shadowy Female, who is Vala, to her lowest state. Here she becomes Rahab, who can manifest "as twelve daughters lovely & sometimes as five"—these correspond to the twelve Daughters of Albion and the five fallen senses (106:4/ E379/ VIII, 328). Among the shifting groups which she contains are the Daughters of Amalek, who are collectively Tirzah, and who sing a plaintive song addressed to the souls resisting fleshly bondage and to her sisters, whom she calls on to help in the binding.[18] The song betrays a subtle mixture of emotions: anxiety that the siblings accomplish the work for the sake of self-preservation, grief over the lost joys of Eternity, and what the singer supposes is a commitment to "mercy and truth"—a common Old Testament phrase (105:52/ E379/ VIII, 320).

When Satan in alliance with Vala crucifies Christ (it is implied that the British Parliament in declaring desperate war on post-revolutionary France re-enacts the Crucifixion), Los and Jerusalem temporarily lose their faith. Jerusalem turns to Urizen as well as to Los, and puts her trust in a religion of externals as she calls for a universal worship of death with elaborate and costly rituals: this is apparently an attack on Christian churches which attach great importance to lavish ceremonial. Los despairs "of Life Eternal" (106:16/ E379/ VIII, 340). Blake, as he makes clear through several scattered passages, equates Rahab's share in the murder of Christ's mortal body (which is her own work) with the rending at the Crucifixion of the Veil which concealed the Tablets of the Law in the Temple. The double destruction exposes the outward beauty of Rahab as the mask of a false, legalistic religion and the human natural body as the mask of the spiritual body. (See 104:36-38, 105:24-26, 113:38-41/ E378, 379-80/ VIII, 264-65,

---

[18] See pp. 160 above.

267, 291-93, 341-44; cf. Exod. xxvi.31-33; II Chron. iii.8-14, v.7-10; Matt. xxvii.50-51.)

In a long speech to Rahab, Los exhorts her to repent her pride and enmity to Christ as he has repented his own. Six thousand years ago, he declares, he fell from Eternity and divided giving rise to many children. The names of his Sons and the flight of the twelve who were the founders of the Israelite tribes reflect the way in which the state of fallen spirits declined further into the state of mortals, who passed through the ages of the Old Testament Law, the perverted Christian Church, and mediaeval militarism to the imperfect calls to reform of Luther and Milton. The list of Daughters is less revealing, but it indicates that Mary, and hence the natural body of Jesus, derives from Rahab and Tirzah.

Los continues with a condensed version of the account of the Fall given in the Bard's Song of *Milton*. He tells how pity and wrath were divided and Satan, having only the former, fell. His mother, Enitharmon, created a space in which he could survive, and Jerusalem (doing the work earlier attributed to Enitharmon and Los) gave him and his companions the bodies they needed there. At the same time the Eternals seek one who will guard the fallen and die to redeem them. In a passage that has counterparts in *Milton* and *Jerusalem*, Los lists the Seven Eyes of God and tells how six refuse the commission but the seventh accepts it. They represent seven ages starting with the lapse from Eternity when Lucifer fell and including the pagan time of Molech, the Old Testament epochs of Elohim, Shaddai, Pachad and Jehovah, and the Christian era of Jesus. Los, however, tries to make Rahab—and the reader—understand that Satan is not an individual but a state into which many individuals enter; Luvah entered this state after he was reborn as Orc and Orc became a serpent.

Far from submitting to Enitharmon and freeing Jerusalem, as Los demands, Rahab seeks the support of Urizen only to find that he is stunned by the exposure, at the time of the Crucifixion, of his secrecy-shrouded religion. He even pities the unmasked Rahab, but as he reaches out to embrace her—she is again termed the Shadowy Female—he finds himself imprisoned in the senseless and corpse-like body of a scaly monster that cannot serve as the instrument of his mind. His transformation recalls Satan's imprisonment in a serpent's body in the tenth book of *Paradise Lost*; his new shape combines those of the sea creature Leviathan ("his stony form" inhabits the waters of the abyss) and of the seven-headed dragon of Revelation xii, whose tail pulls down stars from heaven ("his folding tail aspires/ Among the stars") (106:40, 107:2-3/ E382/ VIII, 437, 447-48).

Foiled in his attempt to control the natural world—the Shadowy Female has eluded his embrace—Urizen envies the comparative freedom of Los, Los's Spectre and Tharmas and fiercely resents the rising power of the degenerate Orc. His anger arouses the wild beasts of the wilderness, the landscape with which he has most affinity. It becomes apparent that the Shadowy Female, who is also Vala and Rahab, is now the dominant power. Los, Enith-armon and Tharmas feel her numbing force and take material forms: "Thus in a living Death the nameless shadow all things bound" (107:35/ E383/ VIII, 481). For all things must assume fixed form before they can follow Jesus' example by separating from it and regaining Eternity.

Tharmas's suffering is increased by his misguided search for succour in abstraction instead of the recovery of a firm identity, and he is tormented by the voice of Urizen's Emanation. Ahania, blind to the presence of Christ in Ulro, utters rhetorical questions, some of which echo words of Oothoon in *Visions of the Daughters of Albion*. Employing stirring images and rhythms, she asks the "sons of the Murder'd One"—"The Eternal Man" round whose limbs winds "the Serpent Orc"—why they cling to death instead of awakening to life and morning (108:19, 23, 25/ E383, 384/ VIII, 503, 507, 509). She gives a haunting description of Albion lying amidst rock, water and snow while the eagle, himself weakened by the Urizenic cold, waits for him to become carrion.

Whereas Ahania cries out *to* "the Caverns of the Grave" and their inhabitants, Enion answers her *from* this underworld (108:8, 109:13/ E383, 384/ VIII, 492, 533). Taking up some of Ahania's images and reporting the response of the fertile field to the barren grave, she holds up her own passage from despair to hope and faith as an encouragement and declares that Christ "has rent the Veil of Mystery" and will come again (110:1/ /E385/ /VIII, 556): the fallen shall rise, and death into this world shall be a forgotten thing. In one of the most eloquent passages in *The Four Zoas*, she proclaims that there is a Human essence within every object in this lowest world and each essence is a part of the Eternal Man, whose fragmentation produced the cosmos and who acts continuously in the animals, the plants and the elements. But now,

> ...Man looks out in tree & herb & fish & bird & beast
> Collecting up the scatter'd portions of his immortal body
> Into the Elemental forms of every thing that grows.
> (110:6-8/ E385/ /VIII, 561-63)

Although he hears the exchange of the two Emanations, Los does not recover from his despair, and for the two millenia of Christian history a triumphant Rahab seduces Jerusalem into worshipping Urizen. The narrator tells us that St. John recorded these horrors in Revelation, where the Whore of Babylon is Rahab, her cup holds the food of Orc, kings honour her, and her dragon is Urizen. Eventually Rahab is moved by Ahania's weeping and Enion's words to leave Urizen's Synagogue of Satan. Sometimes she repents and seeks aid from Enitharmon to cast off her role; at other times she returns to Urizen only to leave him again. This is the history of Christianity, repeatedly but imperfectly reformed. Finally, Satan being divided against himself, the Church renounces Mystery and turns to the rational religion of Deism, which abomination, says Blake, is only the latest form of nature worship, a creed that existed long before Christ came.

Night the Ninth

The last and longest Night of *The Four Zoas* bears the title "Night the Ninth Being The Last Judgment." It relates the redemption of Albion as well as that of his Emanation and of the four Zoas. The resurrection proceeds by stages: the fallen must re-enter Beulah before they can rise to Eternity.

Night the Ninth opens with Los and Enitharmon building Jerusalem (who is always city as well as woman) while weeping over Jesus' corpse. They are deeply immersed in Ulro, for they see the body through "Phantom" or material eyes and think that the death of the man is his annihilation (117:1-6/ E386/ IX, 1-6). Unknown to them, the real Jesus stands beside them separating their spirits from their bodies.

There is some justice in Frye's complaint that Los's precipitation of the Last Judgment at this point is inadequately explained and hardly convincing.[19] After making his favourite Zoa's hands tear the sun and moon out of the sky, Blake bombards the reader's imagination with a series of cosmos-shattering phenomena derived from biblical images related to the Day of Doom. In the turmoil, Urizen's books of law start to disintegrate, while Rahab and Tirzah and the serpentine Orc, whose twenty-seven folds symbolise the Twenty-seven Churches, begin to be devoured by flames that pour out of Eternity to penetrate the entire universe. Though Urthona remains as yet divided (so much so that Blake awkwardly introduces a new fragment of him, the female Spectre of Enitharmon), the dead are resurrected to enjoy "mental fire"—the flexible perception and unfettered consciousness of the Eternals (118:18/ E387/ IX, 44); at the same time, oppressors find themselves powerless as they are pursued by their victims. Similarly, the birds and beasts of prey flee in terror the flames emanating from the south, the quarter of Orc's cavern (74:14/ E351/ VI, 265). In anticipation of the coming redemption, the Eternals descend into Beulah. To some extent, what Blake has so far written may be regarded as a kind of overture to Night the Ninth.

The next passage clarifies the relationship between destruction and resurrection. Mystery and its ministers are burnt and drowned. They are submerged by a downpour of black blood which falls from the sky as a second Deluge and is then dried by the same "wild flames" that, "winged with intellect/ And Reason," constitute the "mental fire" of the resurrected (118:18, 119:18-20/ E387, 388/ IX, 44, 85-87). They are the fires of Eternity that tormented Urizen in the third chapter of the book that bears his name, and they here assail his "Dragon form" (119:15/ E388/ IX, 81).

At this point, Blake turns to Albion, who is still on the Rock of Ages, where he fell asleep in Jesus' care (18:11-15/ E310/ I, 464-68). Beginning to awake, he bewails his inner conflict and the transformation of his lost paradise into the "narrow house" of "this dark world" (120:3/ E389/ IX, 113). Blake still sees Jonah in the great fish as the type of fallen Albion "Enwrapped round with

---

[19] Northrop Frye, *Fearful Symmetry: A Study of William Blake* (1947; rpt. Boston: Beacon, 1962), pp. 308-09.

weeds," and the "war" in his "members" echoes Paul's struggle against the flesh (119:29, 32/ E388/ IX, 96, 99; cf. Jon. ii.5, Rom. vii.22-24). Having just referred favourably to the form of reason that characterises the "living flames," Blake makes Albion recall the glory of that Urizen who was in Eternity the "Prince of Light"—that is Lucifer or "Light-bearer," the unfallen Satan (120:14/ E389/ IX, 124). Calling on Urizen to renounce totally abstract thought as the Word in the "Introduction" to *Songs of Experience* calls on the fallen earth or soul to rise, Albion threatens the god with everlasting separation if he disobeys, for the religion created by his perverted reason is a more fundamental cause of fallenness than the perverted passion of Luvah, which issues in war. At the end of his speech, Albion tries to distinguish sin, which can be forgiven, from error, which can only be annihilated.

Moved by the threat and the appeal, Urizen laments his blindness with a directness and clarity too rare in this poem. His words combine the substance of Jesus' bidding "Take...no thought for the morrow" with that of Blake's quatrain "He who binds to himself a joy" (Matt. vi.34; E470/ K179); they express remorse for dividing nations and families, and they glance at the co-existence of urban blight with flourishing trade and architectural grandeur. Urizen's penitential phrase "I alone in misery supreme" recalls the secret agonies of Milton's Satan "Vaunting aloud, but rackt with deep despare" (121:17/ E390/ IX, 178; *PL*, I, 126). Having asked that the rage of the other Zoas may be unimpeded, he ascends in a glorious and youthful body, but this is only the first stage in the process of his redemption. Ahania, rising to reunite with him, is slain by "Excess of Joy" (121:36/ E391/ IX, 197). Albion explains that the universal restoration has to be completed by the Saviour, who is visible within the Jerusalem in front of whom he was crucified and whom he will make the dwelling place of all souls in Eternity; when that is accomplished, Ahania, as an emanation, will sleep during winter in Beulah and return to Urizen in Eternity in spring.

Repeating a few words from the brief account of the Last Judgment at the end of *The Song of Los*, Blake tells how skeletons reassemble, each particle of matter gravitates to the earth's centre, and the spirits of all humans and animals are released from their mortal bodies—yet humans reassume the appearance their bodies had in life. Like Urizen's rejuvenation, this resurrection is the beginning, not the end of a process.

Blake now describes at length the revenge of the as yet unforgiving victims against the vainly pleading warriors, tyrants and judges. Resembling "th'Ethereal substance" of the bodies of Milton's angels, the torn flesh of the oppressors "reunit[es] in pain" (123:10/ E392/ IX, 255; cf. *PL*, VI, 330-31).

Above the spectacle, Jesus appears in cloud as foretold in Matthew xxiv.30; within the folds of this cloud are the paved work of Exodus xxiv.10, the divine throne of Ezekiel i.4-28 with its four attendant living creatures, and the twenty-four elders surrounding the throne of Revelation iv.4. Albion is now upright, but because the redemption is not yet complete, he and Urizen are unable to reach Jesus. Instead, Urizen must bring the history of fallen souls to its consummation by driving the Plough of Ages over the cosmos of the (spiritually) dead and sowing fallen souls as seed. Before the work begins, Urizen's Sons refurbish the Plough, which is in part a symbol of a true marriage of heaven and hell, of reason and energy, for the harness of its horses is "the study of angels, the workmanship of Demons" (124:12/ E393/ IX, 297). Its preparation involves the fulfilment of Isaiah's prophecy that the nations "shall beat their swords into ploughshares, and their spears into pruning-hooks" (ii.4). For the souls that constitute Urizen's seed, the process of entering the earth and germinating is painful. The souls of warriors and rulers, moreover, fall on barren ground. However, Urizen's Daughters as well as his Sons are reconciled with him, and Ahania revives. The family makes a joyful music together.

At this stage, Orc has been consumed by the flames and reborn as Luvah. Albion, who finds himself in Beulah but still unable to rise into Eternity, tenderly presents both Luvah and Vala to Urizen reminding them that Zoas and their Emanations are servants of "The Human form Divine" and if they aspire to become its masters they are in a state of rebellion (126:10/ E395/ IX, 367).

Following in the path of Urizen, Luvah and Vala experience a penultimate stage of regeneration. Again, there is an echo of the "Introduction" to *Songs of Experience*, as Luvah summons Vala at morning to "Rise from the dews of death" (126:32/ E395/ IX, 389). The drama begins to echo the myth of Eros and Psyche as Luvah, an invisible sun god, calls to Vala, who identifies herself as "the Soul" (126:37/ E396/ IX, 394). When Luvah informs Vala that she rises in the morning and folds up at night, she reacts like Thel and blames the sun for creating her when she is doomed to die. Once Luvah reassures her that she will survive, she is consoled and, again resembling Thel, serves as shepherdess to the friendly flocks of her "lower Paradise"—Luvah's phrase refers to the upper reaches of Beulah (128:30/ E397/ IX, 460). The description of Vala sleeping with "her head on the downy fleece/ Of a curl'd Ram" recalls the illustration on pl. 7 of *America* (128:25-26/ E397/ IX, 455-56). While she sleeps, Luvah causes a palace to rise around her; she sees it and him in her dream and awakes to find herself in a "bodily house" or glorious body (129:3/ E397/ IX, 470). She continues to tend her flocks, and as she bathes in a river there is an interlude in her story, for she sees the world of another Zoa.

In the realm of waters, Tharmas is still calling for his Enion; his laying his head on "the Oozy rock" and his Jonah-like complaint that "weeds of death" have "wrap'd" round him show how closely his state resembles that of Albion, the whole human (129:28, 21/ E398/ IX, 495, 488; cf. Jon. ii.5). Moved by Tharmas's plight, Vala sends her plea to Enion upwards and hears it echoed, but the echo takes the form of Vala's own plea to the invisible Luvah to make himself known to her. Without further explanation, Tharmas and Enion are reborn as children in the garden world of Vala: they, too, have entered Beulah, but even here the infant Enion frequently grieves her male companion by her flight. Yet these children "are the shadows of Tharmas & of Enion in Vala's world" and that material, natural world itself is a place "of shadowy forms" visible to the harvest workers as they rest on couches in Beulah (131:19, 22/ E400/ IX, 556, 559). The redemption of the Zoas is part of the redemption of humankind, in which the historical process plays a central part. The Book of Revelation provides Blake with favourite symbols for that process when one of its angels declares that the harvest of the earth and her grapes are ripe (xiv.15-18). To prepare for the reaping, Urizen and his Children cause the spirits of the reborn Luvah and Vala to cleanse the atmosphere (similarly the wine of Luvah—of life-giving passion—regales Albion at the feast). However painful the harvest for human beings, it is joyful for Urizen and his Sons as they reap human souls with the sickle and scythe.

Building on his earlier statement that all particles of matter were moving to the earth's centre, Blake now pictures a whirlwind and "rattling of bones" in this centre, and from this assembly of matter arises the Emanation of Tharmas, Zoa of the body and senses. In a speech of some beauty, Enion proclaims her imminent rebirth as "a Golden Moth"—an emblem, like Psyche, of the soul—now that the winter of the fallen world is giving way to a spring in which the vilest creature will burgeon with beautiful life (132:15, 21/ E400, 401/ IX, 592, 598). At last Tharmas embraces his spouse.

The viewpoint becomes yet more complex as the revived Albion is represented as one of "Many Eternal Men" who sit "at the golden feast" and look down to their "shadows" lost in the world of Ulro (133: 5, 8, 21/ E401, 402/ IX, 621, 624, 637). One of them, in words both evocative and illuminating, describes each fall as the consequence of selfishness which rejects "Brotherhood & Universal Love" as well as true "Science" (or knowledge), and explains how the Eternals plant a fallen soul as a seed, cover it with a veil, and watch over it (133:22, 15/ E402, 401/ IX, 638, 631). As they embrace Albion, however, they are "Calling the Morning into Beulah," because he has not yet reached Eternity (133:30/ E402/ IX, 646).

When the morning of the harvest arrives, Urizen threshes the grain while Tharmas provides the wind to carry away the chaff. Tharmas lets loose a chant of triumph over the defeat of Mystery, who is Babylon the Great, the Mother of Harlots, of Revelation xvii.5; in *The Four Zoas*, but not in the Bible, what this witch's cup contains is religion. Her defeat, shouts Tharmas, has brought about the overthrow of all oppressors and the freeing of all prisoners, a liberation he celebrates in eloquent lines borrowed from pl. 6 of *America*. His rejoicing is supplemented by the song of an African commemorating his return to the pastoral life of his father and brothers.

To complete the annihilation of Mystery, the work of Urizen has to be supplemented by the work of Luvah—the threshing of the human grain by the pressing of the human grapes. As the intoxicated Luvah, a Bacchic figure with a crown of thorns, leads his Sons down to the vineyards, he sings "the Song of Los" (135:25/ E403/ IX, 713). All families who have sided with Mystery fall in the wine presses and suffer the agony it must inflict before they can experience the joy of rebirth. While the souls "howl & writhe in shoals of torment," the Children of Luvah delight to inflict pain (136:22/ E404/ IX, 749). There are several clues as to the nature of their suffering. It includes the "torments of Love & Jealousy" in the epic's subtitle—here called with some irony "the sports of love" and "sweet delights of amorous play" (137:2/ E405/ IX, 769)—and the ejection from their physical bodies that the souls mistake for "Non Existence" until they learn to accept "The Pangs of Eternal birth"—of birth into Eternity (136:12, 15/ E404/ IX, 739, 742).

From the standpoint of Albion, winter returns and the work already done by Urizen and Luvah is completed by Tharmas and Urthona: every aspect of the human identity must be renewed. The four Emanations of the Zoas leave their seats at the feast to weave in joy a fabric that descends to the nations below, though its function is not made clear. Luvah and Vala are exhausted, and the former is spread out to fertilise the ground by the Sons of Tharmas and Urthona, who take away "the wine of ages," "the Human Wine"—the souls produced by history (137:27, 32/ E405/ IX, 794, 799).

Urthona, no longer divided, rises regenerate and grinds the corn in Urizen's barns (which are the nations), Tharmas gives his whirlwinds free play, and Urthona bakes "the Bread of Ages"; in his ovens, people painfully acquire the "Stern Philosophy" and "knowledge" that will replace "The dark Religions" (138:17, 15; 139:10/ E406, 407/ IX, 822, 820, 855). The morning is here that Blake spoke of so long ago in "The Voice of the Ancient Bard," the "Introduction" to *Songs of Experience, Visions of the Daughters of Albion* and *America*. Lyrical lines describe the redeemed universe visible to "The Expanding Eyes of Man," and war is conducted with words, not iron (138:25/ E406/ IX, 830).

Though the conclusion of *The Four Zoas* can evoke a glow of Messianic hope, the structure of Night the Ninth stands out in retrospect as less than satisfactory. Not only is Jesus, whose role should be central, unmentioned in the last five hundred lines, but Blake fails to distinguish clearly between consecutive events and simultaneous aspects of one process. To remedy these deficiencies, he devises the synchronic forms of *Milton* and *Jerusalem* in which he can treat the same happenings from various perspectives, and he allots Jesus a pivotal and heroic role in the final redemption of the individual and of the universe.

Meanwhile, although he printed no book of short poems subsequent to *Songs of Innocence and of Experience*, Blake prepared in middle age a fair copy, known as the Pickering Manuscript, of a selection of ten lyrics. The poems were probably written while he was at Felpham.[20]

As varied in tone as in content, the collection treats of the suffering and the historical cycles that characterise the fallen world. One piece, "William Bond," tells the story (possibly autobiographical) of a sister's compassion and a wife's or beloved's self-sacrifice when the hero's love for another woman makes him ill; the self-sacrifice wins back the husband's love to the applause of the speaker. "Long John Brown & Little Mary Bell" is a bawdy, folksy poem on the evils of a woman's sexual stand-offishness, and "The Golden Net" laments the speaker's entrapment by sexually unsatisfied, possessive females. Similarly, in the cryptic narrative "The Crystal Cabinet," the speaker is the victim of some form of erotic possessiveness in threefold Beulah, and perhaps it is by trying to rise through sexuality to Eden that he falls into Ulro. The reference in *Jerusalem* 70:17-31 to the beautiful Rahab's requiting a kiss with a threefold kiss suggests that Rahab may indeed be the treacherous maiden of this monologue. Envy is the topic of the simpler "Mary" with its tender anapaestic quatrains, which may lament the misfortunes of Mary Wollstonecraft, while "The Smile" speaks in general terms of a range of negative and positive human emotions to end with a frown that expresses unforgettable hostility and a smile that conveys a happiness that can never be lost. Reminiscent of the earlier *Songs*, "The Land of Dreams" goes back to childhood to attack the weakness of unbelief.

Three of the poems are far broader in scope. In stirring quatrains "The Grey Monk" articulates a pacifist position as it assails the cruelties of warlike tyrants, celebrates "The Hermit's Prayer & the Widow's tear," and insists that he who overthrows a tyrant becomes a tyrant—like the Fuzon of *The Book of Ahania* and the Orc of *The Four Zoas*. The most famous piece in the collection is the irresistible "Auguries of Innocence," which denounces cruelty to humans and beasts, and culminates in two fav-

---

[20] Textual Notes, E859.

ourite tenets of Blake's philosophy: that one should learn to see through instead of with the eye and that God is the essence of humanness. Finally, "The Mental Traveller," long an enigma, is now understood to survey the repeated historical cycle of this world. The messianic creative male principle—a Christ or Dionysus—is first dominated by matter or nature, which is female (ll. 9-20), but breaks away to create a rich civilisation that eventually succumbs to Urizenic tendencies; its Urizen is a collector of human suffering, whose grief, presumably at his failure to create a Utopia, drives him to guilt-inspired deeds of charity that cheer the wretched (ll. 21-42). Nature, however, is reborn and eventually drives him out (ll. 43-52) leaving him to find another version of herself, one strong enough to create a materialistic society whose universe is the Newtonian cosmos (ll. 53-68). As she plays the coy lady, he regains his youth (Blake is drawing here on Plato's *Politicus*—see Notes on Criticism below) and in time fashions a pastoral and artistic society (ll. 69-92), which must collapse when he regresses as far as babyhood and her power again prevails (ll. 93-104). The speaker in this pessimistic poem, with its succession of powerful contrasting images, ironically claims to tell of "such dreadful things/ As cold Earth wanderers never knew" (ll. 3-4). The way of escape from the cycle is not hinted at though it is profoundly explored in *Milton* and *Jerusalem*.

10
Heroic Epic: *Milton*

On 25 April, 1803, Blake writes to Thomas Butts, "But none can know the Spiritual Acts of my three years Slumber on the banks of the Ocean unless he has seen them in the Spirit or unless he should read My long Poem descriptive of those Acts" (E728/ K823). He appears to be referring to an early draft of his epic *Milton*, in which his quarrel with Hayley is treated allegorically in the narrative of Luvah's quarrel with Urizen, and in which he, as observer, tells the story of John Milton's posthumous quest for regeneration. Unlike *The Four Zoas* and *Jerusalem*, which conclude with the redemption of humanity and the universe, the plot of *Milton* extends only to the redemption of one individual, who carries an inspired message and serves as an exemplar for the remainder of humankind, that are still enslaved to the selfhood. The end of the poem challenges every reader to labour for the recovery of the individual and collective Eden.

The antithesis between truly Christian values and those which prevail in Britain is introduced in the succinct and eloquent prose of the Preface. Here Blake makes it evident that his admiration for the poet of genius who champions Cromwell's Republican revolution outweighs his opposition to the stern moralist who condemns disobedience and unchastity and countenances war. If the Greek and Roman classics are to Blake "Stolen and Perverted Writings" plagiarised from the Hebrew, Milton, alluding to the literary forms found in the Old Testament, makes Jesus suggest that "Greece from us these Arts deriv'd" (*Paradise Regained*, IV, 338). Moreover, when Blake looks forward in his Preface to the transformation of the Greek Muses, the Daughters of Memory, into the Daughters of Inspiration, he alludes to Milton's claim that a great poem is only to be created with the aid of the Holy Spirit.[1]

---

[1] See p. 134 above.

Of the four known surviving copies of *Milton*, only the two earlier (A and B) include the Preface, and these consist of forty-five plates each. To the third copy (C), Blake added pls. 3, 4, 10, 18 and 32 of the now standard text, and in the final copy (D) he inserted also pl. 5.[2] The additional plates increase the complexity of the poem by providing further glimpses of the action from different viewpoints, and if they are omitted on a first reading, the narrative is still complete and continuous.

As Fox demonstrates,[3] the structure of *Milton* is based on a parallel between its two books. Milton descends to earth in book I as does Ololon, his Emanation, in book II. On the autobiographical level, Blake is at Lambeth, in London, in book I and at Felpham, in Sussex, in book II, even though his quarrel with Hayley is represented by the conflict between Palamabron and Satan in the first book. At Lambeth, both Milton and Los enter into Blake; at Felpham, Ololon descends to him. In each book John Milton delivers a key speech of heroic resolve that is among the great passages in Blake (14:14-32; 40:29-41:28).

The epic *Milton*, however, is also an heroic narrative depicting the successful quests of a repentant genius and his equally repentant Emanation. Journeying, a major preoccupation throughout, should be understood in the Swedenborgian sense as a change of inner state, not a movement in space; the author's own journey to Sussex is, of course, an exception. The designs not only underline the parallel between the two books, but help, in spite of some departures from chronological order, to carry forward the narrative. On the title page, Milton, his back to the spectator and his right or visionary hand and foot advanced, steps out of Eternity into the cloudy indefiniteness of nature. Above the head-title to book I that immediately follows, the same figure is seen from the viewpoint of the temporal world as a star about to descend ("Then first I saw him in the Zenith as a falling star" [15:47]). The full-page design on pl. 16[4] also shows him from an earthly vantage point as he doffs the robe and girdle that symbolise his acceptance

---

[2] For the make-up of the four copies, see Textual Notes, E806.

[3] Susan Fox, *Poetic Form in Blake's* Milton (Princeton: Princeton UP, 1976), *passim*.

[4] Because the plate numbers normally used to refer to the text cannot be employed to designate the designs, I use the plate numbers in Erdman's *The Illuminated Blake* for the latter.

of a place as, he supposes, one of the Elect, and brings a new sunrise to irradiate the darkness of Ulro. (On the frontispiece, which shows him at a later stage, he is already naked.) The visual depiction of his progress continues as he enters Blake's foot in the form of a star (pls. 17, 32); overthrows—to the applause of musicians in Eternity—the Urizen he once adored and breaks, with his right foot, the "Self-hood" to which he formerly clung (pl. 18); and tenderly raises the Urizen he has overthrown (pl. 45). Significantly, in book I Milton's left foot is advanced in pls. 16, 18 and 19 as William's is in pls. 17 and 32; in book II his right foot is forward in pls. 45 and 46 as Robert's is in pl. 37.[5]

The parallels between the books are also reinforced by two full-page designs portraying the fall of the Miltonic star. The first, adorning book I, shows it entering the advanced left foot of William Blake, who is in front of three steps symbolising the threefold nature of existence in the sexual realm; the second, in book II, presents the same star reaching the advanced right foot of William's dead brother Robert, who is in front of four steps symbolising the fourfold nature of eternal or fully Human existence (pls. 32, 37). Blake omits to offer the purchaser of his book information about Robert's identity; Frye argues persuasively that with his higher degree of illumination he plays Rintrah to William's Palamabron and Hayley's Satan.[6] William must remain loyal to the spirit of Robert and not be lured by Hayley into deserting his genius to escape from poverty.

The head-title to book II (pl. 33) is accompanied by a judgment scene complementing the representation of descent in the corresponding position in book I. At the conclusion of the epic, Milton and Ololon undergo Last Judgments as each rejects error and they reunite. The observer of pl. 33 looks out through the mouth of the world-cave of Ulro as lightning flashes on either side, two damned figures fall head downwards, and one who is saved rises. The lightning, which is parallel to the falling star above the head-title of book I, represents the descent of Ololon (cf. 36:13-20). Of the two inscriptions in reverse writing, the higher—"How wide the Gulf & Unpassable! between Simplicity & Insipidity"—perhaps suggests Eternity, and the lower—"Contraries are

---

[5] Cf. Fox, op. cit., pp. 226-27.
[6] Northrop Frye, "Notes for a Commentary on *Milton*," in *DV*, pp. 97-137 (see p. 130).

Positives/ A Negation is not a Contrary"—Beulah (cf. 34:23). On
the floor of the cave mouth stand a man and an emanation, his
right foot touching her left; they have larger counterparts below
the head-title of the first book. The fallen form of Milton's sixfold
Emanation depicted in a sinister fashion in book I is matched by
its joyful unfallen counterpart in book II (pls. 19, 48). In a deliber-
ately childlike drawing, Ololon in the form of a twelve-year-old
girl steps down to the Blakes' cottage at Felpham (pl. 40). Other
females portrayed near the end of the poem are Jerusalem (or Brit-
annia), whose sleepy embrace of Albion is undisturbed by the eag-
le of inspiration; Oothoon, whose tears of compassion for suffering
humanity fall over the growing grain of the human harvest (42:32-
33), and the central figure—probably Ololon—of the final plate,
which anticipates the full ripening of that grain (pls. 42, 49, 50).

The Preface has no design, but it includes the justly fam-
ous lyric "And did those feet in ancient time," which gives a prel-
iminary clue to the complexity of the illuminated epic. It asks
whether Jesus ever walked in England and whether Jerusalem,
which covered the whole world before the Fall (*J* 24:46-50, 79:13-
17), was built there. But it goes on to enquire whether Jerusa-
lem—both the holy city and the Emanation of Albion—was raised
"Among these dark Satanic Mills," the latter being at once the
Newtonian heavens and the factories of the Industrial Revolution:
those heavens were post-lapsarian and those factories date from
the late eighteenth century. In some sense, all historical time is
simultaneous. After distancing himself and expressing his resolve
to dispel the clouds of his era with his intellectual, sexual, and
prophetic energy (the "Chariot of fire" alludes to the vehicle which
carried Elijah to heaven [II Kings ii.11]), he asserts that *he* will
not desist from mental and material struggle till *we* have
(re)constructed Jerusalem in England.

Immediately below the lyric is an epigraph from Numbers
xi.29: "Would to God that all the Lord's people were prophets."
The words recall not only the prophetic (as opposed to lawgiving)
side of Moses, who uttered them, but the patriotism of Milton,[7]
who in *Areopagitica* applied them to his countrymen. In his sum-
mons to England, the nation which was "chos'n before any other,

---

[7] Joseph Anthony Wittreich, Jr., *Angel of Apocalypse: Blake's Idea of Milton* (Madi-
son and London: U of Wisconsin P, 1975), p.243.

that out of her as out of *Sion* should be proclam'd and sounded forth the first tidings and trumpet of Reformation to all *Europ*," the earlier poet foresees "a noble and puissant Nation rousing herself like a strong man after sleep":[8] the image contributes to Blake's Albion, whose sleep is finally vanquished only in *Jerusalem*.[9]

Like *The Book of Urizen*—and *Paradise Lost*—Blake's *Milton* begins with the proposition (or statement of the subject) and the invocation of Greco-Roman epic; like the *Odyssey*, the *Aeneid* and *Paradise Lost*, it commences *in medias res*, the early part of the story—the fall of the eternal human and the universe—being narrated in the Bard's Song. The Muses Blake invokes are the Daughters of Beulah, who can transmit the inspiration of Eternity, which is above them, to Ulro, which is below them. While Blake, as always, praises the Daughters, he alludes to the ambiguous character of their realm "of shadows" and "Of terror & mild moony lustre," which can be a blessing or a curse depending on whether those who leave it rise to Eternity or fall to Ulro (2:11, 3). Smoothly fusing macrocosm with microcosm, he locates Beulah, on one level, in the human brain; it is in lower Beulah, he implies, that God, working through the Daughters, plants a paradise like those in *The Book of Thel* and Night the Ninth of *The Four Zoas*, and there gives to fallen spirits forms within which they can progress towards their re-ascent. Blake's surging Miltonic rhythm carries the reader on to an account of the contrary of this work of mercy—the treachery and rapacity of "the False Tongue," an organ formed subsequent to the division of one of the four eternal senses into taste and touch (2:10; cf. Ps. cxx.3). Its ultimate crime was to crucify Jesus in Ulro in compliance with an erroneous doctrine of atonement for sin.

The subject proposed in the second verse paragraph is the return of Milton into the fallen world in response to the song of a heavenly bard. For a century England's epic poet has been in Eternity, but Blake's Eternity is not a realm of shared vision and tranquil agreement; instead there joyfully rage among its inhabitants "the severe contentions/ Of Friendship" in "great Wars" of

---

[8] *The Works of John Milton* (Columbia UP), IV (1931), 340, 344.
[9] Cf. Frye, *Fearful Symmetry: A Study of William Blake* (1947; rpt. Boston: Beacon, 1962), pp. 159-60.

intellectual conflict (41:32-33; 30:18-24; cf.35:2-6). Here Milton has remained obedient to his own image of God and is puzzled to find that his obedience has not brought him happiness. Suffering from the absence of his Emanation, he knows only of her fallen aspect, which is visible to him in all its pain in the distant world of time. In his bewilderment he continues to ponder the problem he thought he had solved in *Paradise Lost*—how to "justifie the wayes of God to men" (I, 26). (The words are quoted on the title page of the illuminated book, and with neat irony, Blake describes Milton's meditations in words that recall the vain philosophising of the Miltonic devils.) Only after the Bard's Song has enlightened him, does Milton renounce what he had taken to be a gift of divine election assuring him his place in heaven. (See 2:16-22, 14:10-13; *PL*, II, 557-61, and III, 183-84).

A large part of book I—from 2:25 to 13:44—consists of the Bard's Song, the narrative of which is simultaneously the metaphysical story of the Fall and a psychological story of the expression and the suppression of anger and of anger's relation to pity. The Song makes clear to Milton the true nature of fallen existence and of his own unredeemed state and kindles in him a resolution to return to Ulro and complete, for himself and the world, the unfinished labours of his earthly life. The Bard's Song also tells the story of Blake and his obtuse patron William Hayley, who urged him to turn aside from his heaven-appointed task of communicating Milton's correction of his former doctrine, a doctrine which had ultimately led to "the deceits of Natural Religion" (36:25).

The narrative proper begins about 7:4; the text of the preceding plates constitutes a kind of prologue in which fragments of the action and short pieces of exposition are strangely juxtaposed. Like the first portion of Faulkner's *The Sound and the Fury*, they are only intelligible to a reader who has become acquainted with their subject matter. A valuable clue is the discrepancy between 5:1, where Palamabron has been harrowing the ground, and 6:12-13, where he and his three brothers are forging the harrow along with the plough. This is not a sequential narrative but a series of snapshot perspectives on one event—the Fall—and glimpses of the subsequent state of the world, in which Los and Enitharmon work for its redemption.

Albion falls or dies, and, since he is the cosmic human as well as every individual (and Britain), the skies separate out from his body (3:1; 6:26). With him and within him, fall Urizen and Los, the latter, as in *The Book of Urizen* and *The Four Zoas*, forging for the former a body which constricts his perceptions but preserves him from disintegration; Los, unable to retain his wholeness now he is outside of Eternity, splits into his Spectre, a diminished Los, and Enitharmon (3:6-36). These last two bear a large family beginning with Orc and Vala, the Shadowy Female (these are Luvah divided and reborn), and including the four brothers Rintrah, Palamabron, Theotormon and Bromion as well as their youngest child, Satan. While Los and Enitharmon build Golgonooza and there beneficently forge and weave bodies for souls (again, material is carried over from the previous epic), the four brothers construct and use the plough and harrow that must catalyse the process of history. Though centred in London, these labours are worldwide (6:1-3, 27-31).

While Los and his family toil to restore the fallen, counter-forces attempt to keep the latter in bondage. The primeval Jerusalem that covered the earth has been ruined and replaced by Druid oak groves and temples, while the nations have been set at odds and reduced to a state of continual war. The corrupt druidic religion prescribing human sacrifice for moral trespass also claims innumerable victims ranging from those slain on Aztec and Inca altars to executed criminals and Jesus crucified—Blake equates Calvary with the site of Tyburn gallows (4:21; 5:3; 6:11, 14-24). As the fallen Daughters of Albion make ready the victims for sacrifice and stupefy the Urizenically inclined (the Elect) with the intoxication of outward beauty, his demonic Sons utter an ironic though eloquent lament over the spirit's confinement in a body like the one that Los fashioned for Urizen (5:5-37).

Hoping that he can bring the reader to see the connections between apparently disparate phenomena, Blake frequently breaks off a description to introduce with startling abruptness what appears to be an entirely new subject. Thus Los's son Satan turns out to be Urizen, master of the astronomical heavens and proponent of Locke's materialistic philosophy; hence he is cut off from Eternity and spins his moral rule and religion of sacrificial atonement from his own brain (9:25-28; 10:1; 11:10; 13:4-5). Among the objects of his persecution are the artists who, by their inspirations or "Cherubim," create unique figures and forms as opposed to those based on uniform mathematical ratios derived from Greco-Roman antiquity (4:21-28; 5:43-44). The promotion of war being a favourite activity of Satan, "who triumphant divided the Nations" (10:21), Blake alludes to the munitions industry in the London region[10] and connects the absence of peace with the frowns of the Spectre of Albion (6:14-17, 24). Moreover, he treats Charles I as an elect Urizenic king who demands that the prophet Milton repent and atone or, possibly, seeks a reconciliation through Milton's mediation; in either case, Cromwell resists the King's design (5:39). (There is also a cryptic allusion to James I or II and perhaps to the Great Fire of London.)

Because the narrative beginning on pl. 7 is, on one level, an account of the Fall, elements of it are teasingly woven into the 'prologue.' Rintrah and Palamabron plough and harrow, Los rebukes Satan for suppressing his anger, and Satan succumbs to jealousy; his swooning is once associated with redemption through the Crucifixion and once with the happy defeat of mathematically based art (4:1-2, 6-7; 5:2-3, 43-44). However, the essential introduction to the story that follows is Los's and Enitharmon's separation of the souls they embody into three classes: the Elect, the Reprobate and the Redeemed. Mocking Calvin's doctrine of predestination and alluding to Milton's distinction between the elect, the repentant and the obdurate,[11] Blake deploys these terms ironically. His Elect are the submissive souls who give Urizen no trouble; the Reprobate are inspired poets and prophets who angrily rebel against authority; and the Redeemed are those who run some danger of being intimidated into piety by the Elect but, despite their wavering, are "redeem'd from Satan's Law" (6:27-7:3; 11:19-23; 25:32-36). It seems, moreover, that just as the fleshly body is the cruel work of Tirzah and her sisters as well as the beneficent work of Los and Enitharmon, the division into three classes is also carried out for evil purposes—perhaps to promote the domination of the Elect—by the fallen Sons and Daughters of Albion (5:38). Alluding to Ephesians i.4 and Psalms lviii.3, Blake

10 David V. Erdman, *Blake: Prophet Against Empire* (Princeton: Princeton UP, 1954), p. 368 [396].
11 Kathleen Raine, *Blake and Tradition* (Princeton: Princeton UP, 1968), II, 223, citing *PL*, III, 183-202.

ironically speaks of "The Elect from before the foundation of the World" and "The Reprobate...form'd/ To destruction from the mother's womb" (7:1-3). The Reprobate, his favourites, and the Redeemed, whom he finds bearable, he identifies with the contraries, which he has long regarded as "necessary to Human existence," but the Elect he damns as "the Reasoning Negative," which only exists in Ulro (*MHH*, pl. 3 prose; 5:13-14). At the same time, he has, in spite of their "Virtues & Cruel Goodnesses," a limited sympathy for these Elect, who have no sustaining vitality of their own and who, like the Urizen whom Los binds, would fall into non-existence if they were not 'elect' in the sense that Eternals have 'elected' to preserve them (13:30-34). To recover belief in Eternity, they must be spiritually reborn (25:32-34).

As characters, the reprobate Rintrah and redeemed Palamabron are distinguished respectively by wrath and pity (it is part of the tragedy of the Fall that these qualities should be sundered), and on the metaphysical level they are entrusted respectively with the plough and the harrow to cultivate the nations in preparation for the human harvest (6:12-13).

At 7:4, Blake suddenly embarks on what begins as a lucid and engaging narrative only slightly heightened above that of plain prose. By the next plate cryptic elements reappear along with high eloquence, and it becomes evident that the characters and the action have cosmic dimensions. From the beginning, the antagonist, Satan, far from being a conscious villain, is blind to his own error. (Urizen, in the book that bears his name, seeks to create a better world, and Hayley intended only good to Blake.) Moved by Palamabron's apparent weariness, Satan pesters him into exchanging tasks for a day, but though he himself cannot understand what is happening, his incompetence maddens Palamabron's horses and gnomes, while Palamabron's wine intoxicates the servants of Satan's mills. (Blake cannot dwindle to a painter of miniature portraits any more than Hayley can be a true poet: the harrow, according to Bloom, may represent epic.)[12]

The one day during which duties were exchanged in heaven is on earth a thousand years (cf. Ps. xc.4 and II Pet. iii.8).

---

12 Harold Bloom, "Commentary" in *The Complete Poetry and Prose of William Blake*, ed. David V. Erdman (Berkeley and Los Angeles: U of California P, 1982), pp. 849-970 (see p. 912).

When the consequent damage is revealed, Los, as a sign of mourning, puts his left sandal on his head. In itself the symbol is grotesque, but it is the first of a series of images that represent the way in which error first triumphs and is then cast out. The left side is associated with error or material creation or, according to Bloom,[13] with time; the sandal on the head indicates the reversal of the normal order of things, the order that prevails in Eternity. Later Blake, inspired by Milton's entrance into his left foot, sees that imprisoned spirit can master the material world, treat it as a place of redemption, and even find in it remnants of Eternity's beauty: hence this world is reduced to a resplendent sandal on his left foot (15:49-50; 21:12-14). When Los descends to unite with Blake, he fastens *both* his sandals, for at this stage neither Los nor the poet is more closely bound to the 'vegetable' left than to the visionary right (22:8-9).

Amidst much lamentation, Los decrees a day (a thousand years) of intermission in the normal play of nature, but the destructive flames of Moloch interfere with the merciful rain of Jehovah, the Divine Humanity—rain which, the Bible tells us, is bestowed on the just and the unjust (8:27-29; Matt. v.45). Destroyed by his unhealthy meekness, Satan erupts in anger to slay not an opponent like Michael but a friend who has gently reproved him (cf. Jude 9; Rev.xii.7). Like Cain, Satan has introduced murder into his world; he has fallen and dragged others, including Michael, with him, and while Enitharmon creates the space called Canaan in which he and "the poor infected" can be imprisoned and preserved until they work their way back, Palamabron calls the Eternals down to a conference in the fallen world (8:40-9:3; 10:4-5). Though the narrative portrays the Fall itself, the post-lapsarian world already exists—Albion is on his "Death Couch" (9:3): Blake is writing from the viewpoint of eternal consciousness, which is not confined to the sequence of past, present and future.

At the conference, as Los in his fury further disorders nature, Satan is unable to sustain the meekness he uses as a mask to hide his wrath. He accuses Palamabron of being ungrateful for his assistance, he judges him according to moral rules which have no universal validity but are his personal invention (Blake dismisses

---

13 "Commentary," p. 918.

thus the Seven Deadly Sins), and he lays the charge with anger he has borrowed from Rintrah. He distorts, Blake tells us, "the Divine voice," the voice of Jehovah, "in its entrance to the earth" (9:23) as he becomes the lawgiving, punishing, war-promoting God of the Old Testament. (The "paved terraces of his bosom" [9:31-32; depicted on pl. 10] echo the "paved work of a sapphire stone" under God's feet at Sinai in Exodus xxiv.10, as the thundering and trumpets of the text reflect Exodus xix.16 and the references to disease and war allude to divine punishments and Israel's battles.) The terrible world of Ulro opens out within Satan, who, unlike Rintrah, does not know the right way to be angry. Although Rintrah tries to protect Palamabron with the fires of his fury, Satan, in completing the separation of wrath from pity, destroys these fires at the cost of consummating his own fall: an historical allusion locates the central authority of the new satanic world in the imperial centres of Rome, Babylon and Tyre, perhaps hinting at Tyre's commercial and Rome's more modern ecclesiastical eminence. It should also be remembered that Tyre, or at least its king, is denounced by Ezekiel as the Covering Cherub (xxviii.11-19).

Blake emphasises the deadly aspect of Ulro-Canaan. It is the apparent infinite space of Newton, within which Satan, "A mighty Fiend," divides peoples and seeks to destroy Albion's Eon or Emanation (10:11). So terrible is this world, symbolised by Tyburn and its gallows and by the human sacrifices of the Druids, that when Enitharmon ventures inside it she takes on the appearance of a wrinkled, crazed old woman. As in *The Book of Urizen*, Los descends along with his antagonist, but he remains strong enough to shelter his Enitharmon in Beulah and he defies Satan in a speech which denounces the new female jealousy, the churches and monarchy.

In the deliberations of the assembly, a Blakean equivalent of the theological doctrine of the Atonement emerges. The anger that Satan's unjust accusation has generated among the Eternals must have a vent, so it falls on Rintrah, whose wrath Satan has secretly borrowed. When the truth becomes apparent, Rintrah's suffering cannot be transferred to Satan, for the latter, being of the Elect, would cease to exist if he were punished instead of protected (9:8-12; 11:15-26). In this way Blake accounts for the suffering visited on the Reprobate. Rintrah and his brother Palamabron are identified with the biblical pair of witnesses who will prophesy, be martyred, and ascend to heaven (9:8; Rev. xi.3-13).

Lines 10:1-2 have reminded the reader that Satan is also the Urizen of *The Four Zoas* and that Luvah (later Orc) and Vala share in the responsibility for his tragedy. Now, in the long confession of Leutha, his Emanation, Blake presents us with another version of his fall. Responding to the Eternals' assertion that Satan could not survive condemnation for his error, Leutha takes the guilt upon herself. She is not the Leutha of untainted sexuality found in *Visions of the Daughters of Albion* so much as the fallen sexual siren of *Europe*, the daughter and servant of a corrupt Enitharmon. Like that "Sweet smiling pestilence," that "Soft soul of flowers," that "lureing bird" with "the many colour'd bow" upon her wings (*E* 14:9-12), the Leutha of *Milton* is fair, multicoloured, treacherous, and associated with a false rainbow and with the delusive outward beauty of nature. Indeed, in the course of her fall and Satan's, she perverts Jehovah's fire—the energy of Eternity—to fashion "the Serpent/ Of precious stones & gold turn'd poisons on the sultry wastes," which is one of Blake's symbols for the natural world (12:29-30). Her confession is eloquent, containing touches of both sublimity and pathos; it is also confusing, for Blake combines the stories of his siren and of Hayley's obtuseness with the conflict between God and the Devil in the Book of Revelation and with Milton's allegory of sin. This last, in book II of *Paradise Lost*, is a personification who springs from Satan's head during his rebellion in heaven, and after his defeat he encounters her at the gate to the formless abyss dominated by "eldest Night/ And Chaos" (II, 746-67, 894-95). It is Night and Chaos that Blake's Satan unintentionally releases when he mistakes the fire of Eternity for evil (cf. *BU* 4:12-13) and makes the gnomes "throw banks of sand/ Around the fiery flaming Harrow" (12:17-18).

On the biographical level, Leutha represents the latent homosexuality or at least effeminacy of Hayley. When her advances to Palamabron are blocked by the jealousy of Elynittria, his Emanation, she enters Satan's dreams becoming a female will and paralysing his masculinity, so that *he* approaches the inspired Palamabron with a mixture of admiration and envy, and gives him bad counsel out of misplaced pity. After Satan has obtained control of Palamabron's harrow, she compounds her fault by unintentionally maddening the horses, and retreats timidly into his brain to be reborn from his head and rejected by him in a puritanical rage (12:36-48, quoting *PL*, II, 759-61). Satan, for his part, is ruined when he tries to absorb the wine or inspiration of Palamabron and becomes instead of a poet a moraliser who expels Leutha as Urizen expelled Ahania. To integrate the personal tale of his betrayal by Hayley more thoroughly with the cosmic myth of the revolt in heaven, Blake makes the harrow, wrongly driven "in Pity's paths," pull down a third of the stars as Satan, "in pride of heart," sets himself to destroy Albion and Jerusalem (12:24-28; cf. *PL*, V, 706-07 and Rev. xii.4).

When she confesses her misdeeds, Leutha's repentance earns her "the Divine Pity" (13:7). In her guilt, she identifies herself and Satan with Albion's other murderers—Luvah and Vala—and expresses her longing for the breach in Eternity to be healed. She finds protection in the kindness of Enitharmon, whose provision of a space for fallen Satan is ratified by the Eternals. The latter endow the space with the six thousand years of history and send the Seven Eyes of God[14] to watch over the now necessary passage through Experience, though none can see the process through to the end: even Jesus is confined in a "Tabernacle" which is both the mortal body and an ecclesiastical organization and doctrine.

In a brief sequel to Leutha's confession, Elynittria renounces her jealousy and admits her rival to Palamabron's embraces. But as a sundered emanation, Leutha is fallen, and—perhaps in spite of Oothoon's protection—she gives birth first (like Milton's Sin) to Death, and then to Rahab, Tirzah and Tirzah's four sisters. Religious Mystery (Rahab) and the philosophy that identifies the human being with the physical body (Tirzah) infect the Archbishop of Canterbury's palace at Lambeth and the two universities.

The Bard's Song, begun at 2:25, has now ended, and the reader should remember that it is this Song that induces Milton to return to the lower realm. It has revealed to him the real character of Satan, as opposed to the one he attributed to him in his poetry, and it has disclosed Leutha's offer to sacrifice herself to save that fallen spirit. The remainder of book I tells of Milton's descent, his reception, and his impact on the world.

---

[14] See p. 179 above.

The Bard's words disturb his fellow Eternals in the heavens above Albion, for some of them do not realise that Satan's pity and love can be rooted in selfhood. After vindicating the authority of inspiration, the Bard seeks shelter by entering into Milton—as Milton is later to enter into Blake. The implications of the Bard's Song send tremors through the sleeping Albion, and the countries of the four continents which are contained in him, for a great historical event, the return of Milton, is almost upon them. Still in Eternity, the Puritan poet arises to utter a speech of heroic grandeur and renounces the gift of election that he believes God to have granted him. Leutha's repentance has heightened his awareness both of the lower world's defects and his own imperfection, and her offering herself for a ransom inspires him to make a parallel sacrifice (cf. 11:30 with 2:20). Looking down at the scene of the Napoleonic wars, where Jesus is at best dimly perceived, he recognises that nations nominally Christian still worship the warloving "Gods of Priam" (14:15) and that their peoples cling to the selfhood instead of the Humanity; he sees, moreover, that he himself is guilty of the same error, for his selfhood flourishes, and, like Satan, he is parted from his Emanation. This last condition he links with a Greco-Roman submission to the Daughters of Memory, whose knowledge does not transcend the Lockean ratio.

In later life one of Blake's less controversial insights is his understanding that all fallen beings, instead of projecting the satanic element in themselves upon their enemies, must recognise it for their own and thus gain the power to transmute it. As Shakespeare's Prospero says of Caliban in the last scene of *The Tempest*, "this Thing of darkenesse, I/ Acknowledge mine," so Blake, speaking in his own person, confesses on pl. 27 of *Jerusalem,*

Spectre of Albion! warlike Fiend!
In clouds of blood & ruin roll'd:
I here reclaim thee as my own,
My Selfhood! Satan! arm'd in gold.

Similarly Blake's Milton declares, "I in my Selfhood am that Satan: I am that Evil One!" and adds, "to loose him from my Hells/ To claim the Hells, my Furnaces, I go to Eternal Death" (14:30-32). He sees, that is, that the fires to which he condemned Satan in *Paradise Lost* should not be a means of torture but flames of creative energy. (Cf. *MHH*, pl. 6). He descends, too, to search for the first sign of that morning of the world's redemption that is hailed in the "Introduction" to *Songs of Experience*.

As Rose observes, Milton's mission to the nineteenth-century world is hinted at in a passage of *The Four Zoas* where the story of fall and redemption is outlined in a list of the Sons of Los (113:53-115:6/ E380/ VIII, 356-62).[15] Before the first stage of the Fall, his youngest is Satan; subsequently he begets a long line of Sons who represent the history of this world, a line that concludes with the patrons of the four Christian churches—Paul, Constantine, Charlemaine, Luther—and finally with Milton.

When Blake's Milton journeys to earth, his imperfect self that has been unhappy in heaven enters his hermaphroditic twenty-seven-fold Shadow that is patterned after the Twenty-seven Churches of history. This "Shadow" of his real self is his wholly fallen self, and because of his spiritual and intellectual stature and influence it stretches from the lower border of Beulah to the depths of Ulro and especially to that Albion or Britain that was the scene of his labours for good and ill (14:36). At the same time his "real and immortal Self" remains in Eternity, though in a dormant, Beulah-like state; it is also referred to as his "Sleeping Body" and, later, his "Sleeping Humanity" (15:11, 4; 38:10). The Seven Angels of the Presence or Seven Eyes of God watch over this innermost self, and even, for a short time, give glimpses of it to the self that has just entered the Shadow.

By comparing the descending Milton to lightning and to a comet passing through Chaos, Blake implies that his journey is both instantaneous and heroic: in *Paradise Lost*, Satan traverses Chaos with equal courage on a parallel though malevolent quest (15:17-20). Milton's sacrifice includes the temporary exchange of eternal perception for the limited perception which is all that remains to those who travel through the vortexes that constitute the infinite world of the Newtonian cosmos. In an attractive but syntactically difficult passage, Blake contrasts the perceptions of the "traveller thro Eternity" (the imaginative person) with those of the "weak traveller" (the reasoner confined to the Lockean ratio) (15:21-35). To the latter, whose consciousness cannot rise above what the Renaissance called the sublunary world, the earth is only

---

[15] Edward J. Rose, "Blake's *Milton*: The Poet as Poem," *BS*, I.i (Fall 1968), 16-38 (see 17-18).

the fallen planet with the globular shape detected by the scientist (cf. 29:15-16). To the eye of imagination, however, the created world has more than a single form. If travellers like Blake's Milton come down to this world, they can choose to see the objects they have passed—the sun, moon and star-lined concave heavens—as majestic spheres or to perceive the human essences which these bodies, like all things, possess. Should they pass the earth, they could see that, too, either as a globe or as human. Even terrestrial 'travellers' need not allow the earth's vortex, which they are inside, to distort their view of the planet. If, as Blake—and Berkeley—would have them, they trust their senses, their image of their own locality will be for them a sample of the unfallen earth, which is "one infinite plane." This image Blake describes again in a passage combining domestic warmth with cosmic splendour (29:4-12).

Arriving at the earth, Milton enters a vortex to encounter the desolate loveliness of Albion, who is laid out on a rock rising above the turbulent Sea of Time and Space. With a brief switch of perspective, Blake becomes an actor in his own poem, for Milton lands in the form of a star on the tarsus of Blake's foot and enters into him as an inspiration. The pun on Saul's Tarsus indicates that Blake undergoes an enlightenment or conversion like St. Paul's, while the "black cloud redounding" that rises from his ankle and overshadows Europe symbolises the moral darkness formerly spread by the religious teachings of the Puritan poet's spectrous aspect (15:47-50). Milton has returned not only to heal himself but to dispel, through Blake, his successor, the error he disseminated. The star and cloud are shown visually on pls. 17 and 32.

In the second verse paragraph of the epic, the reader is given a glimpse of the fallen aspect of Milton's sixfold Emanation in painful exile in the lower world. Now Milton himself realises that if he had put off his selfhood in his mortal existence, he could have risen to the higher world of Beulah through his three wives and three daughters, for they embodied his Emanation; instead, clinging to his selfhood, he embittered their lives and his own (15:51-17:3). At present, he and they alike are divided, for their Humanities reside above, as does his, while their fleshly bodies must remain in Ulro till they become spiritual bodies at a Last Judgment.

Meanwhile Milton has to encounter a demonic form of his Emanation, a sixfold distorted reflection of his wives and daughters. The counterparts of those six women are on one level Tirzah, her four sisters, and Rahab, on another six "rocky masses," obstacles on the way to the Promised Land of Canaan, where the process of regeneration begins (17:17). His own body, or lowest self, is the seventh obstacle, "the Rock Sinai," where the Law of Moses was given (17:14), and he re-enacts both his own and Moses' roles by making the six females write tyrannous commands to his dictation. His contentions with them mirror those of his unhappy family life.

Between Milton's highest and lowest selves, his sleeping Humanity and his body wedded to the Law, what Blake later calls his "Redeemed portion" is journeying inside his Shadow (20:11). Like his body, but on the higher level of the Mundane Shell, this self travels in the lands bordering Canaan. The Mundane Shell, the boundary of the material creation, is both a dungeon for the spirit and a limit imposed on the Fall to allow reascent to begin. Two widely separated passages give a grimly powerful and intellectually intriguing exposition of the nature of the Shell: although from one point of view it is necessary and the work of Los (34:31), Blake's language makes it seem like the place of the damned (17:21-30; 37:47-38:4; cf. 20:41-42). It is a vast concave reflection around or above the earth containing twenty-seven heavens with their accompanying hells parallel to the Twenty-seven Churches of terrestrial history. It incorporates "Chaos and ancient Night", the forces antithetical to creation in *Paradise Lost* (II, 970), and consists largely of forty-eight caverns or "Chaotic Voids" that are "deformed Human Wonders of the Almighty"—distorted forms of divine creations (37:47, 54). The image of the Mundane Shell being more than three-dimensional,[16] there is a way to Golgonooza through the depths of the caverns, but it is closed to mortals, who must "pass inward to Golgonooza" by their own mental strivings (17:30).

Just inside the Mundane Shell are the forty-eight constellations of Ptolemy's astronomy with their division into two groups of twenty-one and twenty-seven. The former consists of Ptolemy's

---

[16] J. Bronowski, *William Blake 1757-1827: A Man Without a Mask* ([London]: Secker and Warburg, 1944), pp. 98, 148n2.

twenty-one northern constellations, and it is centred on Ophiucus, the Serpent-bearer; the latter comprises fifteen southern constellations and the twelve constellations of the zodiac, and it is centred on Orion, the Hunter. Blake draws a parallel between Canaan bordered by hostile kingdoms through which the Israelites coming from Egypt had to fight their way, and the astronomical universe surrounded by the Mundane Shell. The caverns of chaos behind the two groups of constellations constitute two of these kingdoms: behind the twenty-one is the realm of Sihon, King of the Amorites; behind the twenty-seven is the realm of Og, King of Bashan (Num. xxi.21-35). Symbolically Og and Sihon oppose the journey of the fallen towards regeneration.

Conveniently for Blake, the cities of the Levites, the priests responsible for maintaining the ritual observance of ancient Israel, also number forty-eight, so they become spots on the earth's surface corresponding to the forty-eight constellations. They are also the places where the power of the Polypus of the fallen world is concentrated (38:1-4). Blake continues to make use of the parallel between the pagan enemies of Israel and the satanic foes to the redemption of the fallen as he describes Milton's struggles on earth. In a rich medley of narrative and exposition, he interweaves accounts of Milton's elect, redeemed, and reprobate selves, of the response of the Zoas and of Albion to Milton's coming, of Ololon's descent, of Blake's own fears and his encounter with Los, and of Los's contention with his Sons. The events described are related to history.

Milton's spectrous elect self is the portion that, instead of entering Blake, rebounds from his left foot, spreads a dark cloud of religion over Europe, and hangs above the mortal body, with which it is closely associated and which has become the mountain of the Mosaic Law—Horeb or Sinai (15:47-50; 20:20-24; cf. *PL*, I, 7). The contrary to this horror, the sleeping Humanity which is "the Shadowy Eighth" and perhaps, as Damon believes,[17] the reprobate self, remains in Eternity until the Seven Eyes that guard it, driven by the anger of the Eternals at what seems to them the inexplicable division of Milton's Humanity from his redeemed self, descend with it to join Los and his loyal Sons, "the Watchers of

---

[17] S. Foster Damon, *William Blake: His Philosophy and Symbols* (1924; rpt. Gloucester, Mass.: Peter Smith, 1958), p. 416.

the Ulro" (20:43-55). The repetition of "Watchers" implies a parallel between the Sons of Los below and the Seven Eyes above.

In the abyss of Ulro, the four Zoas and some of their Emanations are aware of Milton's advent. Of Tharmas's reaction we are told little, but Urizen puts forth all his strength to stop the hero, and Los also tries to block his path, for he is alarmed by the "divine" (the epithet is ironic) Enitharmon's belief that the poet who wrote *The Doctrine and Discipline of Divorce* will release her from subordination to Los (17:31-33). She summons her daughters to share the power of the female will (cf. *E* 5:1ff). Nevertheless, Los and Enitharmon, being only partly corrupted, are co-operating on the construction of the Mundane Egg, where the four fallen worlds of the Zoas, which correspond to the four elements, intersect (19:15-26; cf. symbolic diagram, pl. 36 [reproduced E133/K523] and *J* 59:10-21).

In Ulro, Luvah and Vala are present in the form of Orc, who is bound with Los's Chain of Jealousy (19:37-38; 20:60-61), and the Shadowy Female; their relationship is much what it is in the Preludium of *America*, where the former seeks to inject his energy into the latter. With her twenty-seven heavens, that align her with the twenty-seven tyrannous churches of Ulro, the Shadowy Female seeks to dominate human life, and she utters a chant of mingled melancholy and triumph. It reveals how the suffering she inflicts on misgoverned humanity will constitute a lamentation over Milton and a terrible garment containing Rahab and Tirzah, but she will disguise her cruelty with a mask of Divine Humanity to seduce the great poet and to make Orc soften his savage courtship. In a striking application of the phrase "this Satan" (18:30), Orc applies it to her garment as he urges her to return to the subordinate role of an emanation. The choice is hers, for within her are both Jerusalem and Babylon, to whom the noble Oothoon and the siren Leutha are parallel. She leans towards Babylon-Leutha, and the conflict intensifies.

Blake links the Shadowy Female's seduction of his hero with Urizen's attempt to prevent him from crossing the river Arnon from Moab into the Promised Land. As the Urizen who freezes the clay earth into marble seeks to freeze Milton's brain, Milton tries to rehumanize Urizen by covering him with flesh of the red clay from which Adam's body was made. In the designs on pls. 18 and 45, another aspect of this process is shown: Milton overthrows

Urizen, who is both his own anti-poetic self and the same anti-poetic spirit loose in society, only in order to restore and resurrect him.

As the struggle proceeds on the eastern boundary of Canaan, Rahab watches from Mount Carmel, on the western boundary. She and Tirzah send their Children as an alluring, ever changing hermaphroditic form in which the male sometimes covers over the female and sometimes the female is the mask of the male. The task of this form is to entice Milton to enter Canaan but spurn Jerusalem; they tempt him either to join and rule the heathen Canaanites—the King of Hazor was one of their leaders (Josh. xi)—or to side with the northern kingdom of Israel that seceded from Judah. In its early days, the breakaway kingdom had its capital at Tirzah; its territories included the lands allotted to the tribes of Ephraim and Manasseh. Linking Greek poetry, natural religion, experimental science, and militarism, the hermaphrodite refers to the corruption of learning at Milton's university of Cambridge, the defeat of the uncorrupted Emanations of three Zoas, and—in delicate, exulting lines—the work of Tirzah in embalming Albion and constricting the spirit within the brain, heart and loins. These regions of the body are three "heavens" beneath Beulah, but confusingly Blake also employs the word to indicate Tirzah's attitude to the two identical testicles in which the seed is imprisoned (19:55-20:2). Quoting II Peter iii.4, the hermaphrodite jeers at the notion of a Second Coming, and it links the Urizenic dispensation with Hand, Hyle, Coban and Scofield—four of Albion's Sons (19:50, 58-59).

Milton's descent and struggle not only alarms the Zoas, but begins to awaken Albion. Revealing this, Blake tries to induce his readers to see themselves in terms of the myth:

> Seek not thy heavenly father then beyond the skies:
> There Chaos dwells & ancient Night & Og & Anak old:
> For every human heart has gates of brass & bars of
>   adamant...
>   (20:32-34)

(Anak was the chief of the Anakim, Canaanites conquered by Joshua.) Each human being, like each mortal creature, has an infinite immortal self within, but the way to it is barred by fallen aspects of the person which occupy Satan's Seat in the brain, heart and loins—three bodily regions over which the hermaphrodite has just exulted in its power (20:34-40).

In one of the occasional moods of humility which alternate with his moods of arrogance, Blake marvels that God has chosen as weak an instrument as himself to reveal truth, and he recounts how, without knowing what it was they saw, he and all people perceived the historic event of Milton's return. The implication is that all humanity forms a single body commensurate with creation, but the spirit can rise superior to the external world and Blake finds that world reduced to a sandal on his left foot; in such a role, subordinate to spirit, it is radiantly beautiful. This is a joyful event in Ulro, the reverse of Los's mournful raising of his sandal to his head at the time of the Fall, and Los now descends and enters into Blake, speaking of that moment of the Fall and filling him with prophetic strength (21:12-14; 8:11-22; 22:4-17).

Los's descent is prompted by what he and Enitharmon, shut inside the Mundane Shell, hear from an invisible source: this is the lamentation of Ololon, the unfallen aspect of Milton's Emanation, for the descent of his real self from Eternity. A "fiery circle" of Eternals who had not heard the Bard's Song looked into (lower) Beulah and while "Drunk with the Spirit," mistook the redeemed Milton for Satan journeying through Chaos; their anger against the Seven Eyes for protecting his real self drove those Seven Eyes and that real self into Ulro (20:43-50; 21:31-34).[18] The angry Eternals have now been absorbed into the mild Ololon, and their fury is transmuted into pity. Indeed they (and all Ololon), as the narrator reveals, regret the effect of their anger because they now realise the identity and greatness of the man they mistook.

The Eternals who formed the fiery circle live on the banks of a river in Eternity. This river, together with the mountains and plants beside it, is Ololon, for in Eternity nature is an emanation of the Eternals. She (Ololon may be referred to as both "she" and "they") represents in part nature as Milton responds to it and later feels some responsibility for the vogue for natural religion (40:9-16). Ignorant of the Bard's Song, she blames herself for having driven Milton back into Ulro and laments for seven days. Her

---

[18] Cf. Peter Alan Taylor, "Providence and the Moment in Blake's *Milton*," *BS*, IV.i (1971), 43-60 (see 49-50).

name derives from a Greek word for an outcry, which is the ultim-
ate source of the English "ululation." At this point Blake, referring
obscurely to Luvah's bulls hauling up the "sulphur" or material
sun at dawn, indicates that Providence, which implies the temporal
world of history, now begins (21:21-24).

    When they hear Ololon's sorrow, the Eternals or Divine
Family, unanimous despite their earlier disagreement, collect
above her as One Man, who is Jesus, and weep over her as Jesus in
Scripture wept over Lazarus (cf. 21:41-44 with John xi.32-35). As
she gazes down into Ulro, Ololon shudders at the spectacle of false
religion and resolves to match Milton's self-sacrifice. Thereupon
the Divine Family reveals that it was not only a personal defect
that recalled Milton to earth, but the demand of the age expressed
in "The Universal Dictate," and that the world needs Ololon also
(21:51-55). Exhorting her to do the work of the Holy
Spirit—"Watch over this World, and with your brooding wings,/
Renew it to Eternal Life"—Jesus unites with her to make his Sec-
ond Coming "in the Clouds" as he prophesied before his Crucifix-
ion (21:55-56—cf. *PL*, I, 17-22; 21:58-60—cf. Matt. xxiv.30).

    Los, a key figure in all three epics, reacts to the descents
of Milton's questing redeemed self, his sleeping Humanity and its
guardians, and Ololon. Fearful at Enitharmon's hope of independ-
ence, he tries to block the returned Milton's path, though Urizen is
the latter's really formidable opponent (17:31-35; pl. 19, design).
To admit the sleeping Humanity into Ulro, Los opens his three
inner gates "behind Satan's Seat," for the Humanity is one of the
"travellers from Eternity" who must travel by way of that Seat
(20:38-40, 47-50; 17:29-30), yet he is dismayed that this second
descent may portend his further division: his twelve Sons who bear
the names of the twelve tribes of Israel (two are specifically ment-
ioned here) have deserted him, and now the four who mirror the
qualities of the Zoas may follow (23:61-24:4; see *FZ* 115:12-21/
E380/ VIII, 368-77). Eventually he remembers a prophecy that
offers hope: Milton will rise from Felpham to free Orc—that is, he
will rise within Blake (who is writing at Felpham) and undo the
chaining of Orc that the repentant Los himself, as *The Four Zoas*
reveals, cannot undo (20:51-61; *FZ* 62:9-63:6/ E342/ V, 143-72).
Recalling the prophecy, he passes to Udan-Adan, and that is
where, in response to Ololon's arrival, he enters into Blake and
transports him from Lambeth to Felpham so that the prediction

may be fulfilled (20:61-21:1; 22:8-13; 36:21-25). On another plane, Los takes Blake to Golgonooza.

The lengthy remainder of book I is devoted to the activities of Los and his family. Referring to the six thousand years of history that have passed, Los discloses to Blake that the last days are at hand, and declares that he has preserved every event that has occurred in time. He faces a misguided plea from Rintrah and Palamabron, who think they are defending authentic Christianity, to destroy Milton, for they associate him with the long tradition of classicism, militarism, and punishment for sin, a tradition upholding the belief that people can be righteous by their own efforts. This tradition is strong enough to have distorted Swedenborg's visions as they descended through Beulah to Ulro, and its most modern manifestation is Deism, the creed of Voltaire and Rousseau, which denies the fundamental corruption of human nature. Yet for all their insight, the brothers see Blake's resplendent left sandal as black and fibrous. As in the Bard's Song, the two brothers are identified with the two witnesses to be martyred in the days before the Second Coming, when there shall be no faith left in the world (22:56-60; 9:8; Rev.xi.3-8; Luke xviii.8). Historically the brothers and the witnesses are manifested in Whitefield and Wesley, the mid-eighteenth-century founders of Methodism, who preached that each Christian must personally experience Christ's forgiveness for his or her sins. Addressing Albion directly, Rintrah and Palamabron call on him to awake as they announce that "The trumpet of Judgment hath twice sounded"—perhaps in the form of the American and French Revolutions (23:4). They draw attention to the contrast between the rising of Orc over the Atlantic (the American Revolution) and the advance of the Covering Cherub (the warring powers or perhaps the Emperor Napoleon) from the east (23:5-10). Milton, they believe, has joined the Cherub and allied himself with the terrible Sons and Daughters of Albion.

As a sombre epic simile shows, it is in an impassioned yet loving spirit that Los rejects this dark interpretation of the great event. He declares his own oneness with Milton, "the falling Death" (23:33) who is to free Orc, while he praises the Daughters of Beulah, who protect from puritanical accusers the beauty and gentleness of the sexual love granted to those imprisoned in bodies. Urging his four remaining Sons neither to desert him nor to oppose Milton, he points to Luther's and Calvin's untimely opposition to the papacy that dragged Europe into religious wars. His speech is also a cry of longing for an end to the world's pain and an admission that his own knowledge is imperfect: he is the Zoa whom the Eternals have appointed to "circumscribe" or limit the Fall and make the space-time in which the Seven Eyes may accomplish their task—though he does not know how they will do so (23:45-53; 24:7-9). His imperfection is also suggested by his desire for a clean separation between mercy and wrath while he himself alternates between pity and anger (23:34; 24:46).

Much of the later part of Los's speech is devoted to a retrospect of elements of the Fall. These include the desertion of twelve of his Sons who elected to assume mortal bodies woven by Tirzah; Noah's Flood (24:5); the separation of those who founded three pagan nations, enemies to Israel; the descent of Joseph into Egypt, which is a symbol of the persecution of visionaries by materialists; and the division of the Covering Cherub into the faith-perverting churches of Paul, Constantine, Charlemaine and Luther that comprehend the whole history of Christendom. (The twenty-three other churches are pre-Christian.) Referring to the raising of Lazarus as a foreshadowing of Albion's redemption, Los states that, on being resurrected by Christ, Lazarus entered the Covering Cherub to watch over the sleeping Albion but was unable to prevent the formation of the perverted churches: the time of awakening had not arrived—at the end of this epic it has still not been reached. Shortly before the speech ends, a brief passage clarifies the difference between embodiment by Tirzah, which is entirely evil, and embodiment in Enitharmon's Cathedron, which can be for good when the embodied spirit is subjected also to the activity of Los in Bowlahoola and of his Sons in Allamanda (24:35-39, 51; 27:42-44). Ultimately Rintrah's and Palamabron's dispute with their father remains unresolved, and the impasse concludes the narrative portion of book I.

In a kind of epilogue occupying more than five plates, Blake interweaves passages treating of imaginative and unimaginative sense perception, and of the meaning of mortal birth and life in the world of time (especially in these latter days of the Napoleonic wars) with particular reference to a variety of common occupations. The poet seeks to show how Los, Enitharmon and their family are active in all the business of life, for

...every Natural Effect has a Spiritual Cause, and Not
A Natural: for a Natural Cause only seems, it is a
    Delusion
Of Ulro...
    (26:44-46)

As is characteristic of Blake's prophetic books, the literary quality
of this 'epilogue' is very uneven: the complex symbolism is some-
times elaborated into grotesque allegory, yet several passages are
memorable for their superb force and beauty. This whole section of
the epic is best surveyed as a single unit.

Seen through the eye and mind of the unimaginative per-
son, the heavens and the earth, with all their natural phenomena,
are Mills of Satan—or of Theotormon, who corresponds to the sat-
anic Urizen among Los's Sons (27:49-54). But when, with the aid
of Los, mortals perceive these same objects through instead of with
the eye, their reward is a spectacle of enchanting beauty, "Visions
of Eternity," here described in flowing and lucid lines addressed
explicitly to the reader and echoed in the last words of book I:
"Thus Nature is a Vision of the Science of the Elohim" (25:66-
26:12; 29:65; cf. 28:29-43). These "Elohim" (a Hebrew plural
which means "gods" or "God") are Los and his family, who mod-
ify creation to make possible glimpses of Eden and communication
with Eternity (28:44-29:26). The terrifying yet sublime musical
workings of Los's smithy, which on an organic level are the
workings of the heart, lungs and stomach, suggest that even the
churnings of the alimentary canal have an artistic aspect when
rightly perceived. In Los's world the units of measurement are the
globule of blood and the pulsation of an artery, which contrast
with such lifeless mechanical abstractions as seconds and centime-
tres. Moreover, they stand on the border between the outer realm
of nature and the inner realm of Eternity, for moments or globules
added together can make mathematically measurable years or
miles, while a poet can be inspired in less than one pulsation and
an inward journey can be conceived as taking place from a point
smaller than a globule. On a larger scale, the sun—which gives
light, life and a natural measure of time—is parallel to the globule
of blood (29:23).

Blake accounts for the state of mortal perception, frequ-
ently but not invariably stunted, by conceiving the war between

visionary and Urizenic powers as extending into the human nerv-
ous system (29:27-46). Here he locates the Polypus, which is the
fallen aspect of Orc; it represents in the individual vague emotion
and Lockean sense perception without thought or imagination (cf.
24:37-38), and in the mass a formless multitude who share these
attributes.

Of the nerves allotted to the four original senses, those of
the tongue, belonging to Tharmas, are altogether cut off from
Eternity (cf. 2:10) and a deep corruption has infected those of the
eye because sight is the peculiar sense of Urizen, who is identified
at 10:1 as Satan.[19] As Frosch observes, sight unillumined by
imagination is the most rigid and least subjective of the senses: it
reduces the external world to fixed objects contained within the
geometrical framework of perspective.[20] The olfactory nerves,
however, are allotted to Luvah, and Christ, who incarnates in Luv-
ah's robes, chooses to impose here his limits on the Fall, while Los
employs his faculty of hearing to create beauty which can guide
souls out of the world of death.

Among the necessary activities of Los and Enitharmon
and their Children are the creation of the time, space and bodies in
which fallen spirits or "spectres"—formless beings with passions
and desires—can attain redemption (26:26-30). When some of the
spectres, racked by ferocious longings, resist incarnation in beauti-
ful forms, Theotormon and Sotha attempt to terrify them into
entering the "Human lineaments" of which they have such need
(28:10-28). They pass both through the mouth of the uterus
("Luban") and the Neoplatonic northern gate of death from Eter-
nity, which is the gate of birth into this world (28:21; 26:13-22).
Los presses his back against the east, the quarter of the Covering
Cherub, to protect the souls undergoing earthly birth as well as
those passing through the southern gate back to Eternity: "those
Three Heavens of Beulah" within the degenerate Daughters of
Albion threaten to destroy the work of Los and oppress the spect-
res (26:16-22; 23:10; 5:6-7). However, the same bodies that are
vehicles of redemption woven by Enitharmon and her Daughters
are, from another viewpoint, fiendish cages of the spirit woven by

---

[19] See p. 166.
[20] Thomas R. Frosch, *The Awakening of Albion: The Renovation of the Body in the Poetry of William Blake* (Ithaca and London: Cornell UP, 1974), p. 103-10.

Tirzah and her sisters, and one of the themes of the 'epilogue' is the opposition between the 'vegetation' or incarnation of the spectres in Los's Golgonooza and the weaving of the worldwide "black Woof of Death" or veil of flesh by the five daughters of Zelophehad (29:47-63). To be "vegetated by Tirzah" is a dire fate; her work is the antithesis of "the glorious spiritual/ Vegetation" of Eternity (25:57-61).

Much of the poetry devoted to the subjects just described is noble and eloquent. Unfortunately Blake, over anxious to elaborate his system, piles on schematic correspondences in a way that becomes bizarre. Along with Golgonooza, the awkwardly named Bowlahoola and Allamanda are places of redemptive activity. In an attempt to show that the bodily functions and recognised occupations are tributary streams of this activity, Blake equates Bowlahoola with the stomach and with law, and Allamanda with the heart[21] or nervous system[22] and with commerce or economic circulation, while Golgonooza, whose partial derivation from "Golgotha" ("the place of the skull") suggests the brain, is "nam'd Art & Manufacture by mortal men" (24: 67, 48; 34:12-14; 27:42; 24:50; cf. Matt. xxvii.33). Moreover, Blake tries to see the professions as fallen forms of the eternal arts of poetry, painting and music; in a line he wisely cancelled in the two later copies of *Milton* (27:60), he identifies religion, medicine and law respectively as the lower forms of these three arts: only in the case of poetry and religion, both dependent on inspiration, is there an evident link. On the literal level of the allegory, Golgonooza is a city, Bowlahoola a great building containing anvils and furnaces, and Allamanda is the surrounding "Cultivated land" (24:51-56; 27:42-43). Blake does not connect them with geographical places, though he does locate his Neoplatonic northern and southern gates on the map of Britain and draws them in the form of silhouettes of rocky landscapes (26:13-22; design on pl. 28).

The central symbol of the 'epilogue' is the human harvest and vintage of the Book of Revelation that is so prominent in Night the Ninth of *The Four Zoas*. All the labours of Los and Enitharmon are directed to bringing it about. An essential preliminary task is the division of human beings—and of all created things, for

---

[21] Northrop Frye, *Fearful Symmetry*, p.260.
[22] Damon, *William Blake*, pp. 181, 240.

none is without some portion of humanness—into the Reprobate, the Redeemed and the Elect (25:26-41). The Elect must be bound in separate sheaves so that they can be brought by "Miracle" to "a New Birth" and so that they do not infect the Redeemed. But Los believes that the harvest and vintage are in progress, and as they are purgative they cannot but be painful to the souls who are reaped and threshed and pressed, as they now are, Blake seems to believe, in the Napoleonic wars and in countries—apparently on both sides of the conflict—"Where Human Thought is crush'd beneath the iron hand of Power" (25:3-5). Indeed the pressing of the grapes is experienced as war and as thwarted or frenzied sexuality by mortals—probably because of their degenerate nature—but to Los it is the work of his "Printing-Press" and a means of instruction (27:8-10, 30-41). (The account of the pressing is transferred from *The Four Zoas* [27:3-42; *FZ* 136:16-137:4/ E404-05/ IX, 743-71]). It is fitting that Luvah and Urizen, whose exchange of duties did so much to precipitate the Fall, should have built Los's winepress, where souls endure sufferings symbolised by noxious and dangerous fauna and flora (27:1-29). Though the epic is named after its hero, its deepest concern is the fate of all human souls, and its last line refers not to Milton but to "the Great Harvest & Vintage of the Nations."

At the beginning of book II of *Milton*, Blake returns to Ololon, the Emanation who has learnt from the Eternals that she should obey the promptings of her remorse and follow Milton to the lower world. The Divine Family in the form of Jesus has entered into her making her descent a Second Coming. As Peter Taylor argues, the Second Coming is not only a unique event at the end of history, but an event in the life of each person who definitively rejects error in an inspired moment.[23]

Ololon passes first into Beulah, and Blake treats the reader to a soothing interlude in which he describes how this intermediate state differs from the highest. The emanations, unable to endure the unchanging, strenuous joys of Eternity, need to pass through winters of quiescence, so they lapse into a realm where consciousness knows of past, present and future. Having evoked this world of fluttering and happy shadows, Blake reminds us that Ololon passes through its darker underside, which reaches down to

---

[23] "Providence and the Moment," p. 47.

"rocky Albion"—that is, both fallen humankind and the isle of Britain (31:11). Alarmed at the signs of the Second Coming, the nations repent their unjust wars. The spirits of the four elements, however, who engage in the material conflicts of this world of struggling contraries, have no eternal essence and wail in horror at the prospect of their dissolution (31:17-26); they contrast with the beneficent "Fairy hands of the Four Elements" as Enitharmon contrasts with Tirzah (28:60). A different kind of lamentation comes from the kindly Daughters of Beulah, who respond to Ololon's mourning for Milton as she arrives among them (30:4-7; 31:8-10). Blake interrupts his long, intricate analysis of Beulah's sorrowing over Ololon with a plate added to the two later copies of the book to expound his doctrine of states.

The exposition (32:8-38) is put into the mouths of the Seven Eyes of God, who address both Milton's sleeping Humanity, which communes with the Seven in dreams, and "Hillel who is Lucifer"—"Lucifer" or "light-bearer" being a translation of Hebrew *Heylel* (32:8; Is. xiv.12). Milton's real self confesses that the dominant forms of Christianity, one of which he upheld in his mortal life, are "builded on cruelty" and that he himself is separated from his Spectre and Emanation (32:3). The Seven reveal that in their fallen condition they are states, not individuals, and that they each consist of large numbers of persons forced by Satan to take a collective form. They have been Angels of the Divine Presence—always a negative term in Blake[24]—and Druids in Annandale, which may be identified with Annwn, the Celtic underworld or Ulro.[25] However, the individuals composing them have maintained a free and brotherly relationship, so that their forms, though imperfect, contrast with the forms of those who have succumbed to Satan's love of war and his belief that reality can be mathematically defined. The marginal Hebrew, Latin and English phrases beside 32:12-15 indicate that the voice of the many can sometimes be divine. (The full Latin proverb *Vox populi, vox Dei* means "The voice of the people is the voice of God," while the English phrase translates the Hebrew words.) In the fallen world,

---

[24] S. Foster Damon, *A Blake Dictionary: The Ideas and Symbols of William Blake*, 2nd printing (1967; Hanover and London: UP of New England for Brown UP, 1988), p. 23.

[25] Raine, *Blake and Tradition*, II, 267-68.

the Seven teach Milton and the reader, individuals are doomed to pass through a series of states, all of which lack the Human wholeness or completeness of Eternity. "[Their] States Change," but their essential identity or uncreated immortal self never does (32:23). Milton is about to enter the state of annihilation from Eternity—and he will emerge from it and from other illusory states to be resurrected to the reality of Eternity. All things in the created, material universe have such identities, which are part of "the Eternal Creation flowing from the Divine Humanity in Jesus" (E554/ K444).

In 32:39-43, Blake speaks in his own voice to observe that Divine Incarnation is perpetual: God descends with those who fall into Ulro and guards them till they see the gates of heaven and understand that their mortal bodies are to be discarded like Jesus' shroud, that Peter and John found in the empty tomb (John xx.4-5).

Just before the inserted plate, Blake breaks off his account of the remorse of warring nations and the dismay of elemental spirits to address the reader directly (31:28ff). He urges each of us to apprehend the meaning of nature's beauty. Earlier in the poem, he has introduced the soaring lark, which rises where the Mundane Shell ends, as an agent of communication between this world and Eternity (17:27). Now he discloses that within the Mundane Shell the lark transmits an inspiration from Eternity that reduces the sun to awed stillness and releases the music of all other songbirds. Similarly, the sweet scent of flowers is a manifestation of eternal beauty that has passed through a point so minute—smaller, no doubt, than a globule of man's blood and invisible to the Newtonian observer—that it has eluded the watchfulness of the Urizenic guards Og and Anak. Again, Blake is asserting, in the teeth of the natural scientists, that "every Natural Effect has a Spiritual Cause, and Not/ A Natural" (26:44-45). Later he singles out thyme (with a pun on "time") as the floral counterpart of the lark.

In this part of the poem, the repetition of key phrases links contrasting phenomena (31:10-11, 15-16; 31, 10, 27; 31:45, 63). The coming of the Lord in the clouds of Ololon can be an occasion for both joy and sorrow. On the one hand, it opens a new channel between Eternity and Ulro; on the other, Ololon is lamenting the descent of Milton, and Beulah fears the unprecedented "tribulation" that is immediately to precede his return (Matt.

xxiv.21, 29). The response of Beulah's Daughters and of nations on earth is to weep, but mortals experience the weeping of Beulah as an influx of inspiration from beyond nature passing to them through birds and flowers. Since Jesus is present within Ololon, the Divine Voice can be heard within Beulah's songs of mourning, which in turn are contained in Ololon's lamentations (33:1, 24).

As God, speaking through the prophets, chides His beloved Israel when she turns to other gods, the Divine Voice berates the female principle, that ought to remain as cherishing as upper Beulah, for embracing a degraded state and becoming Babylon, Jerusalem's conqueror, whom Blake often calls Rahab. (With 33:2ff, cf. Is. lxii.4 and Jer. iii.14; with 33:4, cf. Is. xlvii.1; with 33:10, cf. Deut. xxx.19 and Ezek. xxiii.25; with 33:20, cf. Rev. xvii.5.) The fallen female, declares the Voice, has to be redeemed by the sacrifice of the male who painfully annihilates his selfhood, whereupon she will renounce her jealousy (33:11-23). The passage adds a new perspective to Blake's story—both Milton and Ololon have been guilty in the past and both are now heroic. On the literal level, Milton promoted a mischievous puritanism and bullied his wives and daughters, while they, or some of them, treated him possessively.

The songs of Beulah's Daughters (who are the Muses) not only convey glimpses of Eternity to mortals and transmit the Lord's warning and prophecy, they also comfort the sorrowing Ololon. Having wrongly seen her as a "Fiery Circle" that drove the Seven Eyes and sleeping Humanity into Ulro with "thunders & lightnings," the Daughters discover that she—or they—can "pity & forgive" Milton (34:1-7; cf. 20:43-48).

Blake now turns to the experiences of Ololon. After sinking from Eternity, she observes four states of sleeping humankind: Beulah and, apparently, three levels of Ulro. Beulah is associated with the head (cf. 2:1-8); upper, middle and lower Ulro are respectively connected with the heart, the loins, and the raging stomach and intestines. Accompanied by some of the weeping Daughters of Beulah (though a number retreat in horror), Ololon follows Milton's path through Chaos to the lowest level of Ulro; some of the multitude composing her occupy chasms in the southeast of the Mundane Shell, where Milton entered, and keep watch for the time to awaken Urizen. A diagram shows how the Chaos consists of the four ruined worlds of the Zoas, who, on one level, "lie in evil death" alongside Albion (34:45; diagram E133/ K523). In a sorrowful chant describing the Polypus in the Sea of Time and Space, Blake laments the treacherous attraction that draws souls asleep in Beulah down into the twenty-seven-fold world of history, the material bodies of Tirzah and her sisters, and the religious Mystery of Rahab, here called "the nameless Shadowy Mother" (34:24-31). In the midst of Chaos, the still active aspect of Los limits the growth of the Polypus by circumscribing it with the Shell of the Mundane Egg, in which the betrayed souls can find nourishment and eventually rebirth. The Egg being another symbol for Canaan, its border coincides with the river Arnon. Blake identifies "Arnon" with "Storge," a Greek word for parental affection implying that this emotion, too, can entrap the soul in the lower world, for which a convenient geographical symbol is the Dead Sea (34:29-30).

Taking up her station before the Gates of the Dead (34:48; cf. 26:13), Ololon delivers an account of Eternity which has been cited in chapter eight, and contrasts it with this world dominated by Rahab and by the flesh that Tirzah and her sisters weave. Blake introduces London place-names, because until this city was separated from Jerusalem it was the centre and capital of the earth.

Again, Blake celebrates the opening of a new path between Eternity and the temporal world. When Ololon (who, it should be remembered, is both singular and plural) makes her confession before the Seven Eyes and Milton's sleepwalking Humanity, they rejoice that such a path has been opened (35:26-36). Among the points at which the lower realm receives an influx from Eternity is a secret moment in each day when the thyme first emits its scent at the place where the lark rises at Golgonooza's eastern gate. From this sacred place, spring two streams; one flows through states of consciousness to reach Eternity by way of Beulah; the other flows in a circle through astronomical space and historical time to transcend Satan's seat and return to Golgonooza (35:48-53).

Early in *Four Quartets*, T. S. Eliot makes a bird declare "human kind/ Cannot bear very much reality." The same thought is expressed in Blake's explanation of his thyme and his lark as mighty spirits wearing a disguise to serve as Los's messengers in Ulro (35:54-58; 36:11-12). There are, indeed, twenty-seven larks, one to watch each church and carry inspirations to the Seven Eyes of God; a twenty-eighth lark brings a new influx from Eternity that makes escape from Ulro possible—it is parallel to the Eighth that completes the sequence of Seven Eyes at the end of the poem. Just as earth cannot endure the real forms of the thyme and the lark, it cannot endure Ololon undisguised (36:13-15); and among immortals only Jesus can unincarnate bypass the Polypus of materiality and oppresssion to see Golgonooza without fleshly embodiment and self-annihilation (35:18-25). For these two reasons, the host that is Ololon takes the form of a twelve-year-old girl as she enters the Polypus and the Mundane Shell.

Ololon's descent to earth takes place in the secret moment of the day, at the source of the two streams, and here she meets the twenty-eighth lark (35:46, 60; 36:9-10). The sacred place is also the site of Luvah's empty tomb, and since Jesus wore Luvah's garments, this tomb is Christ's and hence the place of resurrection and redemption (35:59). The age of the virgin indicates that she is in a stage of transition being, like Thel, on the verge of womanhood. Perhaps it is also meant to recall the raising of Talitha, the "damsel...of the age of twelve years" whom Jesus raised from apparent death (Mark v.38-43). Both Ololon and Milton are about to be redeemed from error and suffering.

At this point, Blake emphasises the antithesis between the temporal and eternal perspectives. He sees himself, the mortal narrator, as having been bodily transported by Los from Lambeth in London to his cottage at Felpham, so that in three years he should "write all these Visions" and expose the evil of perverted religion (36:21-25). For Ololon, however, neither time nor space exists; for her the descent to Ulro and her transformation into a girl are instantaneous and, like travel in Swedenborg's visions, involve no passage through physical space (cf. 36:17-27).

The noble final pages of this epic combine heroic speech and action; cosmic, historical and personal events; triumph, pathos, melancholy and hope. Blake's tender concern for his sick wife, his "Shadow of Delight," is expressed in his letters, and he may have received a visit from a young girl whose message he interpreted as a message from Ololon and whose simplicity is reflected in his childlike drawing commemorating the event (36:31-32; E723, 725/ K811, 819; pl. 40, design).

Ololon's enquiry for her male counterpart brings Milton's Shadow into the cottage garden, whence it reaches into the sky and presents clearly to Blake's and the reader's sight a composite image of the evils that afflict the fallen world. This giant form, alluring yet terrible, has frightened some of the Daughters of Beulah who accompanied Ololon into retreating (34:47-48). The resounding passage describing it (37:6-46) implies that in the past Milton foisted the errors of paganism onto Christianity turning it into a warlike creed that demanded satisfaction for sin and perverted the relationship between the sexes. As the most horrifying symbol of cruel sacrifice known to him, Blake selects the Germanic burnt offering of living prisoners of war in a basketwork cage.

The Shadow is a cloud which has the appearance of a human form, but its "fallacious" outside, instead of manifesting an inner Human identity defined by a clear outline, has taken over the whole being and blotted out that identity. In reality it is the Covering Cherub, and it contains Satan, Rahab, twelve gods of Israel's heathen neighbours, those gods' emanations, and the Twenty-seven Churches. In a passage that evokes a world of aesthetic allure and moral corruption such as the Elizabethans saw in contemporary Italy, the twelve gods (including Og, who was really a king) and three of their goddesses are named, and their identity with the Sons of Albion in his Druid phase affirmed. This passage owes something to Milton's more diffuse list of deities in *Paradise Lost* (I, 392-521). Of the Twenty-seven Churches, which extend from Adam's expulsion from Eden to the Reformation, the first nine, whose names come from Genesis v, are hermaphroditic monstrosities preceding the Flood. The next nine, whose names come from Genesis x-xi and Luke iii, are Female-Males—outwardly religious bodies but inwardly devoted to war. The final nine, running from Abraham to Luther, are the reverse combination, "Religion hid in War, a Dragon red & hidden Harlot"—that is the woman enthroned on the beast of Revelation xvii, Blake's Rahab. Both the gods and the Churches have their places in the horror that is the malign aspect of the Mundane Shell (37:19). As the Covering Cherub, Milton's Shadow proves to be identical with the Spectre of Albion, for Milton the Puritan and fallen Albion are guilty of the same errors, and although Milton pictures a pre-Newtonian, pre-Copernican universe, Blake locates both Shadow and Spectre in the Newtonian world of atoms moving in empty space (37:44-

47). Within Albion's Spectre, instead of the love that Luvah should emanate, is the lovelessness of Luvah's Spectre.

Milton's task on his return to earth is to enter his Shadow and annihilate it by reclaiming his selfhood. Before describing the gods, Churches and Mundane Shell, Blake tells how Milton's Shadow brings together its fibres into a form of "strength impregnable"; afterwards he applies almost the same words to Milton himself, who descends to the Felpham cottage "down a Paved work of all kinds of precious stones" (37:6-7; 38:5-8). This image should remind the attentive reader of the paved work (borrowed from Exodus xxiv.10) that appeared in the bosom of the falling Satan of the Bard's Song: the Milton who now appears, "clothed in black, severe & silent," has much of the elect Puritan in him but, as becomes evident, more of the reprobate poet—so much more, indeed, that he has become separate from his Shadow, which is standing upon the sea confronting him, a spectrous Satan, "a Twenty-seven-fold mighty Demon/ Gorgeous & beautiful" (9:30-35; 38:7-12).

A totally unexpected switch of perspective now evokes some pity even for Satan. Standing as an observer within the demon's bosom, Blake discovers there a decayed universe, "a ruin'd building of God," the place of Israel's slavery in Egypt and exile in Babylon, and the hell of *Paradise Lost* where fallen angels laboured (38:15-27).

Facing Satan, Milton refuses to annihilate him, for this would lead him to become himself a tyrant in Satan's place. He turns instead to the self-annihilation for which he left heaven (14:22)—self-annihilation "for others' good," even for Satan's (that is, for the good of those in the state Satan); this is the only alternative to punishing disobedience to moral law in the false belief that the human heart possesses the natural goodness to enable it to obey that law (38:28-49). Taking the contrary view and dismissing "the Divine Delusion Jesus," Satan proclaims himself the only God and universal judge. Immediately the Seven Eyes of God form a gigantic fiery column and to the two blasts of the trumpet of Judgment that have already sounded add a third to summon Albion to awake from the sleep of historical time and regenerate his Spectre by casting him into Los's burning lake (38:50-39:13; 23:3-5; contrast Rev.xx.10).

Satan, with his Miltonic retinue of Chaos, ancient Night, Death and Sin, thunders furiously but powerlessly. Heaven tolerates his mimicking of the Divine Humanity—he has his paved work, his cherubim, and even his Seven Eyes or angels—if he had not, those who fall into the state Satan could not survive to be redeemed—yet he cannot touch the body of Albion, which is overarched by the furnaces or redemptive instruments of Los (38:50-57; 39:14-31; cf. *PL*, II, 506-13). The reader's satisfaction in contemplating good that is even stronger than the most appalling evil is modified by a touch of compassion for the demon that fears "torment ...unendurable" (39:20).

Albion, who has done no more than stir in his dreams at the second summons to Judgment, rises only to stumble and fall again, still under Los's protection. He is not only all humankind but the country of Britain, and his heroic effort is rendered in geographical terms that allow the poet to suggest how hard it is for a slumbering giant the size of the British Isles to raise his immense body, though he achieves enough to frighten his Spectre.

It is not Albion but Milton who is the central figure of the poem, and Blake deploys a curtailed epic simile to show how his redeemed self is subdivided. It simultaneously struggles with Urizen beside the river Arnon and listens to the words of Ololon, "that mild Vision," at Felpham (40:2). She, beholding the double spectacle, is awestruck at Milton's striving with Urizen and, less prominently, with the other three Zoas, for she recognises that as an attempt at self-annihilation to redeem his fallen antagonists; nevertheless, she fears that Jerusalem's Children, the delicate emanations of Albion, will be annihilated together with him. Remorsefully Ololon blames herself, as the independently acting Emanation of an inspired man for undermining his mission to the world. Herself containing a river, mountains and plants, she feels an anguished responsibility for the eighteenth-century reverence for female nature divorced from male spirit; that reverence has infected even the Deists who scorn the churches and has given rise to the "impossible absurdity" that Blake denounces as early as 1788 in the title and text of his tract *There Is No Natural Religion* (21:15-19; 40:13). To challenge Ololon's repudiation of error, Rahab Babylon—the Mystery of St. John's Revelation—appears above the paved work of the lawgiving god and stretches over the twelve nations of Europe and Asia; in the fallen world these nations are the enemies of Israel, but in Eternity they are Israel's twelve tribes. Deism, or natural religion unmodified by revelation, is the latest form of Rahab's creed.

Moved by Ololon's penitence and spurred by Rahab's defiance, Milton utters his second great speech, the counterpart of his resolution to return to the world of death (40:29-41:28; 14:14-32). To reassure Ololon and bring her to obedience, he announces that his imminent annihilation of his selfhood will save, not destroy, Jerusalem's Children. This selfhood is centred on the spectre or reason operating apart from the authentic creations of mind or imagination. The spectre works only with the phantasms lodged in the memory through the fallen senses; unilluminated by inspiration, it corrupts arts, scholarship and government as it substitutes scepticism for knowledge of and faith in reality. The complaint that the reasoner's "whole Science is/ To destroy the wisdom of ages" reflects Blake's enmity to the intellectual revolution of the seventeenth century, which injected empiricism into science, philosophy and religion and reinforced Aristotle's mimetic theory of art (41:16-17). The poet identifies the rending of the veil in the Temple at Christ's death with the tearing away of the male or female body that, with its fallen senses, makes the soul it encloses less than Human: "The Sexual is Threefold: the Human is Fourfold" (41:25-28; 4:5; Matt. xxvii.50-51). Jesus is returning in the clouds of Ololon and, declares Milton, he will burn up and regenerate the body: it will be transmuted into the spiritual body.

As Milton has been corrupted by his spectrous "false Body," a "Not Human," "an Incrustation over [his] Immortal/ Spirit," so Ololon, as she recognises, has a "Feminine Portion" that formerly lodged in Milton's three wives and three daughters and that must be annihilated so that her "Human Power" can take its place in Eternity (40:35-41:1; 41:30-34). Her "Feminine Portion," her sterile virginity, thereupon separates and flees over the sea into Milton's Shadow. Virgin and Shadow apparently evaporate. By comparing Ololon's fleeing virginity to a dove and her Human self to an ark, Blake incorporates an allusion to Noah's Flood, one of his symbols of the Fall: like the dove when the waters are abated, the virginity departs never to return, while the real Ololon proves herself a saving ark in the deluge of Ulro.

When Milton's Shadow has departed, his redeemed self must unite with his reprobate self, which is probably in the care of

the Seven Eyes, while his elect self, being identical with the Uriz-
en he has overthrown and restored, must be merged in his redeem-
ed self. Though Blake is less than explicit on these points, he
describes how the Seven unite with Milton's Humanity and, as
"the Starry Eight," become identical with Jesus in his fullness;
Jesus, in his turn, remains within the now purged clouds of Ololon
(42:10-12). The apocalyptic event has cosmic implications, for
with the fleeing of the Virgin "a shriek/ ...ran thro all Creation,"
and now the clouds are a garment inscribed with the text of the
Bible, which is, if understood "in the Litteral expression"
(according to the natural sense), "A Garment of War" (42:3-4, 11-
15). The association of "The Word of God" with "a vesture dipped
in blood" comes from Revelation xix.13.

The conclusion of the poem concerns one man—its
author—and the whole of humankind. Though all is ready for the
Judgment and final redemption, Jesus weeps as, surrounded by the
Zoas, who are here identified with the four principal Cities of
Britain, he enters Albion. When the angelic trumpets sound, Blake
swoons and reawakens to normal consciousness. The rising of the
lark and of the [scent of the] thyme shows that there has been
communication with Eternity, but Los and the good Oothoon sor-
row over the continuing agonies of humanity, and the scene moves
back from Surrey to the Lambeth of book I, where the urban poor
still suffer. Five closing lines state that the work of the human
harvest is still progressing and still incomplete.

Blake's *Milton* has significant defects: uneven diction,
disconcerting transitions, and formidable obscurity. Much of this
obscurity arises from the poet's attempt to construct an epic in
which the hero and heroine have multiple selves and in which
Albion is at once every fallen human, the fallen cosmos and a
corrupt Britain. In spite of its faults, however, *Milton* is a great
poem with the qualities of an authentic epic: in its rich narrative,
ringing heroic speech alternates with delicate or joyous lyricism,
and simple human feeling mingles with far-reaching symbolism
and an intellectual overview of humankind and the universe. From
the Bard's exposition of the true nature of Satan and the Fall,
Milton learns why he is uneasy in Eternity. He resolves to revisit
earth both to correct the errors he disseminated in the English
Revolution of the seventeenth century and to annihilate that
element in himself which made him cleave to those errors. In

annihilating his selfhood, he will unite with the feminine self he never completely accepted, projecting it instead onto his unhappy wives and daughters. That feminine self, Ololon, which included his vision of nature, was potentially a channel of divine inspiration.

In *Milton*, Blake's Eternals are not omniscient, and the Bard, frightened by the angry doubt his song raises among his fellows, leaps into Milton for refuge. Perhaps strengthened by the Bard's presence within him, Milton descends to earth and enters his successor William Blake. Blake, inspired by Los, the universal spirit of poetry and prophecy, is able to deliver Milton's new message and disclose how his Puritan morality has given birth to eighteenth-century natural religion, a pernicious form of materialism. The last part of book I celebrates the reality of nature and human life as they are benevolently modified by Los and his family; this reality is imperceptible to the five unillumined senses.

When Milton enters into him, Blake is at Lambeth in London; when he encounters Ololon, he is at Felpham in Surrey. In her descent, Ololon brings new inspiration from Eternity to the earth, where she must cast off her sterile virginity to unite with the Milton who casts off his Shadow. As both become one with Jesus, Blake rises from a brief trance to broadcast their message of faith, hope and charity to a world not yet delivered from war and poverty.

Resettled in London, Blake had scant success in selling either his illuminated books or his art, so in 1809 he appealed to the London public by exhibiting a selection of his paintings at the Broad Street hosiery shop his brother James had inherited from their father. To enlighten and educate the viewer and prospective purchaser, Blake had his *Descriptive Catalogue* printed: it was remarkable enough to induce the diarist Crabb Robinson to purchase four copies.

In scattered and cryptic form, the *Catalogue* incorporates major elements of Blake's philosophy and myth. It proclaims the existence of a supersensual realm which it is the duty of painters, as of poets and musicians, to reveal. This realm and the spirits that inhabit it are more closely organised and clearly defined than anything in the material world and can only be rendered by an art that gives outline priority over colour. Hence Blake intemperately champions Dürer and the Florentine school while he damns the Venetians, Flemish and Dutch.

Having access to the supernal realm in his visions, Blake claims to have seen the supreme artworks of the pre-Greco-Roman world as well as the records of remotest antiquity preserved in Eden. He knows of the unfallen world, where "the religion of Jesus, the everlasting Gospel," was the universal creed (E543/ K579), before the spiritual teachings of earliest Druidism were interpreted too literally and understood to prescribe human sacrifice [instead of sacrifice of selfhood]. At the Fall, the fourfold Albion split into component elements—the gods of Blake's myth, which can be identified with those of the Greco-Roman pantheon, as his exposition of Chaucer shows. Albion himself is said to be symbolically identical with Britain's King Arthur and with the Greek giant Atlas, one of the Titans—apparently Blakean Eternals—who dwelt on the earth before the advent of Zeus-Jupiter, whom Blake equates, as one of his letters shows, with his own Urizen (E756/ K851-52). Separating from the Divine Humanity, which is Christ present in each person, the gods have become autonomous, and one or another determines the character of each individual. Though they wear the historical masks of their own age, human beings always fall into the same classes, and these classes Chaucer has perfectly portrayed in his Canterbury pilgrims.

The prose style Blake employs in his appeal to the public is lucid, concise, concrete and forceful—the style of the author of *The Marriage of Heaven and Hell* writing in an expository mode. Intermittently, however, he gives an impression of crankiness as he rages against Rubens, "a most outrageous demon" (E547/ K582), or denounces oil painting as fatal to the permanence of colour and claims to have rediscovered the lost art of fresco. The enemies who, out of "malice and envy" (E538/ K573), have undermined his reputation, deprived him of his livelihood, and impoverished English art include Mr. S[tothard], who, his reading abilities being unequal to Chaucer, has adorned his rival painting of the Canterbury pilgrims with "dumb dollies" (E539/ K574). There is a curt dismissal of Newton and Locke alongside praise of Gray, who enjoyed the gift of vision, and of Swedenborg, who recognised the reality of the spiritual world.

Beside patches of what sounds like paranoia are touches of wisdom and shrewdness. In life, Blake observes, Chaucer's good Parson is with difficulty to be distinguished from his wicked Friar or Pardoner, and ancient sculptures of Olympian gods justify modern representations of spirits in bodily form. The most memorable segment of the *Catalogue* is the noble appreciation of *The Canterbury Tales*, "the finest criticism," said Lamb,[26] "he had ever read of Chaucer's poem."

---

[26] Cited Gerald E. Bentley, Jr., *Blake Records* (Oxford: Clarendon Press, 1969), p. 538.

11

The Forgiveness of Sins: *Jerusalem*;
For the Sexes: The Gates of Paradise;
The Ghost of Abel

Blake's most devoted readers rightly regard the illuminated book *Jerusalem* as his greatest work. Unlike *The Four Zoas* and *Milton*, this epic has no chronological framework: for ninety plates the poem and designs pass to and fro between the moment of Albion's fall and the state it calamitously produces. Again and again it returns—though from varied directions and perspectives—to the same images, events and conditions. After viewing a vast panorama of suffering relieved by visitations of hope, the reader finds that Los's steadfastness and Christ's love bring about the redemption of the entire world.

This immense poem is divided into four chapters furnished with prefaces addressed successively to the Public, the Jews, the Deists and the Christians. With each chapter, the struggle between oppressive materialism and liberating vision intensifies. As Blake makes his reader steadily more aware of humanity's plight on earth, he simultaneously offers ever stronger assurances that the Divine Mercy still operates and makes itself known to the fallen in ways befitting a lapsed world. Eventually all horror is dissolved in an abstruse but overwhelming image of Eternity, which gloriously repays the labour required to comprehend it. "Not any poet, not Dante," exclaimed the Irish writer "A.E.," "imagined a Paradise which lingers longer in our imagination than that brotherhood of all living things with which Blake ended his greatest song,"[1] and Kenneth Muir records the great and unexpected success in 1930 of "a dramatic

---

[1] A.E. [George W. Russell], "The Prophetic Books of William Blake," *Irish Statesman*, 12 Mar. 1927, pp. 14-16.

recital" of the conclusion of *Jerusalem* in the music room of John Masefield, apparently before an audience well versed in the Bible.[2]

The conflict of the heavenly and the demonic is portrayed through designs as well as words. The frontispiece preceding "To the Jews" (pl. 26) shows Jerusalem, whom an inscription identifies with Liberty, shrinking from the flame-invested, serpent-bearing persecutor Hand with his cruciform posture, symbol of male tyranny. Blake may be contrasting the crucifying law of the Jews with the authentic vision of their Cabbalistic doctrines, which he refers to in the Preface immediately following. The design at the head of the chapter's text (pl. 28) shows a passionate sexual embrace such as Albion has learnt to condemn. The couple sit upon a lily—perhaps the lily of Canticles ii.1-2, for their embrace conforms to the description of ii.6 and the second line below the picture refers to the Garden of Eden. Addressing his third chapter to the Deists, Blake attacks their adoration of nature, which he portrays as an iron-crowned Vala, symbol of female tyranny, in the frontispiece (pl. 51), where she is suffering alongside Albion's Sons Hyle and Schofield, and at the head of the text (pl. 53), where she wears the papal triple crown and is enthroned on a lotus. Appropriately, the frontispiece of the chapter devoted to the Christians (pl. 76), one of Blake's most beautiful designs in both the coloured and the monochrome versions, portrays Albion in a posture of self-sacrifice adoring the crucified Christ, for he has found, thanks to Los's fidelity, this only way of escape from tyranny both male and female. In the half-page design preceding the text (pl. 78), a man—possibly a melancholy Los but perhaps Hand about to lose his power—with the head of an eagle that could symbolise either cruelty or St. John the Evangelist looks despondently at the setting sun, though a small bird of paradise rising in the margin of the next plate is a sign that redemption will come.

The first of the book's hundred plates serves as a frontispiece both to the whole epic and to the initial chapter. It shows Los bravely descending through the gateway of Ulro to sustain the light of vision and hope of salvation. Once in each chapter he is shown as a smith with his hammer (pls. 6, 32[36], 73, 100). In pl. 6 he is arguing with his Spectre, in pl. 85 trying to adjust his relationship with Enitharmon, and in pl. 44(30) gladly receiving them both. As the poem enters its concluding phase, he appears in pl. 97 as in some

---

[2] Letter to the editor, *London Review of Books*, 11 Mar. 1993, p. 4.

respects the contrary of what he was in pl. 1: he is now unclothed, his right arm raised in place of his left, and a disc or globe in his left hand instead of his right. The final plate—surprisingly bleak in the black-and-white versions—ends the book with an image of Los, his redeemed Spectre, and Enitharmon together in front of "the great City of Golgonooza" (98:55), where they labour to sustain the process of redemption in the world of time.

In a similar way, until Albion eventually rises (pl. 95) and is reunited with Jerusalem (pls. 96, 99), he is seen in various forms of the fallen state—dead or sleeping (pls. 9, 19, 94); lying in agony (pl. 91); tormented as though on a rack (pl. 67); bowed over in despair (pl. 37[41]); being disemboweled by Vala, Rahab and Tirzah (pl. 25); and tempted by Vala as she treads Jerusalem underfoot (pl. 47). In pl. 33(37) he is in process of falling but is supported by Christ, who also hovers over him in pl. 31(35), as his Emanation separates in a process that is simultaneously the creation of Eve.

Jerusalem is the sleeping heroine of pls. 2, 23 and 33(37), but in pl. 14 she is suspended above Albion, perhaps appearing as an angel in his dream, while in pl. 92 she laments and in pl. 45(31) she is being bound by Vala, whose threats or blandishments she resists in pl. 46(32). Vala may also be the witch-like sibyl in pl. 4 and the scaly underwater female of pl. 11. In the latter she is counterpointed with a swan-woman who could be either an androgynous image of the poet-artist[3] or an embodiment of the female will—though she is facing in the same hopeful direction as the revolutionary swan in the design of pl. 11 of *America*.

The plates contain many emblems of the fallen state and several of redemption. There are representations of beings taking root in the earth (pls. 15, 74); a largely darkened moon as a symbol of time (pl. 8); diagrammatic images of conflict and mutability in the fallen world (pls. 54, 72); the opening of the birth canal between spectrous wings (pl. 58); Urizen with a book (pl. 64); a Urizenic archer with a triple bow (pl. 35[39]) and the cruel Hand as a triple-headed monster (pl. 50); Luvah as a tormented giant (pl. 62); Druid priestesses engaged in human sacrifice (pl. 69) and an immense Druid trilithon (pl. 70); the twelve Daughters of Albion (pl. 81); the worm of mortality (pl. 82); the wandering, groping Enion (pl. 87); and the

[3] David V. Erdman, *The Illuminated Blake* (New York: Anchor Press/ Doubleday, 1974), p. 290.

three accusers of sin (pl. 93). The mysterious vehicle in pl. 41(46), which may be carrying a drowsy Albion and Jerusalem further from Eternity, recalls the harrow of the Almighty described in pl. 12 of *Milton* but is nevertheless a chariot. Hopeful designs include the moon as a saving ark (pl. 24); a winged, wooden ark (pl. 39[44]); three females forming a stained glass window (pl. 57)[4] and beneficently spinning (pl. 59); the reunion of male and female (pl. 18); and a wise child guiding a crippled old man past a neoclassical church to a Gothic fane (pl. 84). In two designs the heavenly and the demonic are clearly juxtaposed—cherubim hover over iron cogwheels (pl. 22) and below a row of angels Rahab and Tirzah embrace serpents (pl. 75). But only with pl. 94, at the top of which the three accusers have collapsed, do the designs begin to portray the redemption.

Running parallel to the designs, the first nine-tenths of the text consists of a vast panorama portraying both the Fall itself and the fallen world. Despite its non-chronological organisation, the subject matter of this panorama encompasses all of time—that is the 6,000, 8,000 or 8,500 years of existence outside of Eternity (e.g. 13:59, 33[37]:7, 48:36). Six thousand is the figure most commonly mentioned, and Frye plausibly suggests that a period of Druidism precedes the six millenia of history.[5] Within time, some happenings are located at specific points, while others are continuous.[6] Prominent among those that occur once though the poem returns to them many times are the descent and disintegration of the primal human, the division of Los, and the corruption and martyrdom of Luvah. The last named struggles with Urizen (as *The Four Zoas* makes clear) for mastery over Albion, is suppressed and tormented, becomes a satanic spectre promoting hate instead of love, and awaits resurrection from spiritual death. The Fall is represented primarily by Albion's descent from the repose of Beulah into the deadly sleep of Ulro but also by the history of Reuben and by the shrivelling and constriction of the human form. These phenomena are accompanied by the flood which creates the Atlantic Ocean.

---

[4] *Ibid.*, p. 336.
[5] Northrop Frye, *Fearful Symmetry: A Study of William Blake* (1947: rpt. Boston: Beacon, 1962), p. 399.
[6] Henry Lesnick, "Narrative Structure and the Antithetical Vision of *Jerusalem*," *BVFD*, pp. 391-412.

Reuben stands for the "Vegetative" (32[36]:24) or corporeal human, and the course of his life has to be pieced together from scattered references. He separates from Albion when the fibres uniting them are cut (63:12; 74:41-42; 90:25), wanders over the world (69:45; 72:36; 84:13), deliberately takes root in Bashan, east of the river Jordan, as opposed to the Promised Land of Canaan (30[34]:36, 43; 74:42-43), and sleeps on a stone (as Albion sleeps on the Rock of Ages) or in the Cave of Adam (30[34]:51; 32[36]:5; 74:33-34). In pls. 30(34) and 32(36), Los imposes a limit on Reuben's degeneration when he moulds his sense organs. To make it as clear as he can that Reuben here represents humankind, Blake interrupts the account with a parallel statement that the Divine Hand finds the nadir of fallenness in Albion's bosom (31[35]:1-2), and follows it with a description of the Zoas becoming the spirits of the four material elements (32[36]:25-38). Eventually Reuben enroots in the Promised Land (15:25; 32[36]:12-14; 85:2-5) and the Hebrews spring from him to bear the seeds of universal redemption through Christ.

There are also continuous activities and permanent conditions of the fallen world to which the poem intermittently reverts. These include the slander that Jerusalem is a harlot (18:12; 45[31]:58; 62:4; 80:12); her banishment and the slaughter of her children (5:13-15; 38[43]:65-70; 43[29]:17-24; 78:21; 79:21); the religion of law, punishment and sacrifice with its oak groves and Druid temples (e.g. 9:15-16; 25:4; 42:76; 49:24-25; 68:38-39; 70:16; 80:48-50; 90:55); the splitting and reunion of the tyrannical female will while it manifests as Vala, as Rahab and Tirzah, and as the twelve Daughters of Albion (e.g. 5:40-45; 30[34]:52; 58:1-5; 84:29-30); the constituting of the worldwide Polypus of formlessness by Albion's Sons (e.g. 15:3-5; 49:24; 67:35-40); and Los's heroic labours to transform the state of Ulro into the higher state of Generation, from which redemption becomes possible. Among his labours are the construction of the Mundane Shell from the basilisk-like Veil woven by Vala (42:77-81) or by Albion's Daughters who are contained within her (63:44-64:6), the building of Golgonooza (10:17; 53:15), and a share in the raising of a world-temple to reach the stars and provide orbits for the heavenly bodies. This structure is satanic insofar as it is the work of Albion's Sons and of Urizen but redemptive insofar as it is the work of Los (58:21-51; 65:79-66:9; 90:49-51).

In spite of its great merits, *Jerusalem* is far from faultless either in style or structure. Both Damon and Frye admit that Blake intermittently lapses into a kind of jargon or shorthand consisting of his private technical terms,[7] and it is unsatisfying that, for example, Reuben on his last appearance should face the cruelty of Albion's Daughters (90:44-46), and the relation between the malignant Bath (37[41]:1-6; 75:1-3) and the Bath who is mindful of Eternity (39[44]:43-41[46]:2) remains unclear. Nevertheless the poem has a structure: it is organised much like a famous contemporary work of fiction—*The Alexandria Quartet* of Lawrence Durrell, which consists of three novels that survey and resurvey the events of a single time-span from different viewpoints and a fourth that is a chronological sequel. The first nine-tenths of *Jerusalem* resemble a scroll painting of the falling and fallen macrocosm and microcosm. As the scroll is unrolled, scenes appear and reappear in various combinations, viewed from diverse positions, and portrayed on different scales, so that close scrutiny is often required to discern their identity when they recur. Blake's artistry ensures that with each new chapter there is a heightening of the antithesis between horror and hope till the promise is fulfilled in the rapturous narrative of Albion's redemption.

The first chapter is an introduction to the Fall and the fallen world: it touches on every aspect and symbol of that world except the winepress. Similarly the Preface, headed "To the Public," introduces themes central to the three later Prefaces addressed successively to the narrower constituencies of the Jews, Deists, and Christians. These themes are the happy "Primeval State of Man," the forgiveness of sin that is the essence of Christian ethics, and the practice of art without which human life cannot flourish. With a certain degree of wishful thinking, Blake anticipates the same kind welcome for "this more consolidated & extended Work" as his "former Giants & Fairies" have received. His claim—made in blank verse—to be inspired by the voice of Sinai's God coming to him "Even from the depths of Hell," where it sounds amidst "Thunder of Thought, & flames of fierce desire," refers to the First Principle of Boehme. Like Los's speech in pl. 91, it shows that although he now preaches forgiveness and self-annihilation, Blake retains much of the enthusiasm for energy and desire that pervades *The Marriage of Heaven and Hell*. Crabb Robinson, who did not meet the poet till 1809, testifies that he spoke

---

[7] S. Foster Damon, *William Blake: His Philosophy and Symbols* (1924; rpt. Gloucester, Mass.: Peter Smith, 1958), p. 185; Frye, *Fearful Symmetry*, p. 359.

of Boehme "as a divinely inspired man."[8] Since he writes in this Preface of helping to bring "Heaven, Earth & Hell" into "harmony," it is clear that Blake still follows Boehme in insisting that error can only be avoided when the First Principle (which in isolation becomes the infernal fire) is united with the Second (here referred to as Heaven), Earth or Nature being the Third.

The two-line epic proposition or statement of the subject which immediately follows "Chap: 1" must be clear to any reader who knows that Ulro is the lowest state of the fallen world. Beginning his poem at the point where Albion is about to collapse from unity into fragmentation, Blake allows the reader to hear the "mild song" (4:5) which Jesus dictates to him: echoing consecutively John xiv.20, Jeremiah xxiii.23 and Ephesians v.30, it consists of a plea to Albion to recognise his Saviour as the "brother and friend" of whom he is himself a portion (3:18). Since the poet hears the Saviour uttering this song each morning, it seems to be a plea made continually as long as humankind remains in its fallen state. Albion, however, repudiates Christ as no more than an hallucination, hides Jerusalem from him, and proclaims the dominion of moral legalism and war. The poet's invocation, a plea to Jesus to annihilate his selfhood and to guide his hand as he writes (5:16-26), punctuates his lament over the state of Albion, who is both the primal man and the ancient country of Britain. As his and its form is dissolved and drawn into the void of Newtonian space and of Genesis' second verse, the human identities within him (or it) shrivel, and Jerusalem (Albion's Emanation) is driven into exile with Vala, who has assumed her fallen form of a nature goddess. The Children of Jerusalem are sacrificed to pagan gods while she herself comes to resemble formless smoke as the gravity-like force of the astronomical Starry Wheels draws her towards non-existence. The Daughters of Beulah try in vain to protect her with their love. Frequently the poet evokes her sorrows through plangent words that recall the scriptural record of the Israelite exile in Babylon. Echoes of Psalms, Jeremiah, Lamentations and Ezekiel abound.

Albion's worst enemies are his twelve fallen Sons and twelve fallen Daughters. The Sons—both repressed elements in Albion's psyche and the most Urizenic elements of British society—seek to destroy the furnaces of Los, stopping the completion of Golgonooza

[8] G. E. Bentley, Jr., *Blake Records* (Oxford: Clarendon Press, 1969), p. 313.

and annihilating their father's sleeping Humanity (5:25-30). They are given names associated with Blake's personal enemies: in particular, Schofield and Cox (Cock) are the soldiers who in 1803 accused him of sedition, and Hand refers to the editorial symbol—a hand—of the Hunt brothers, whose periodical the *Examiner* blasted his Exhibition of 1809. Eleven of the Daughters are invested with names of legendary ancient British women that Blake feels can fittingly represent the malignity of the female will. They unite in two groups—five form Tirzah and seven Rahab (5:40-45), and both the Sons and Daughters turn out to be Children of Jerusalem transformed (5:65).

Harrowed by Jerusalem's lamentations, Los labours at his furnaces of regeneration, but the power of the Starry Wheels controlled by Albion's Sons (6:1) causes even him to divide. Both his Spectre and his Emanation separate from him, and though the well meaning Spectre has a true insight into the fallen condition, he holds Albion responsible for it and urges Los to take vengeance. The Spectre—"a black Horror" (5:68) growing gradually darker—insists that Albion's Sons have united with the biblical enemies of Israel; he identifies Schofield and Cox with the transgressing Adam and with Noah, whose Flood is a symbol of the Fall. Los, the monster claims, does not know what evils occur in his own furnaces: nature (Vala) has oppressed and perverted the emotions (Luvah), and Adam-Schofield, united with Kox-Noah and two of their brothers, has taken control of the remaining brethren, who have been bound by two of the Daughters in an alliance with the Church and the military. Comforting as well as threatening his Spectre, Los reassures him that Albion will be resurrected, and meanwhile physical generation, spurned by the puritanical, serves as an image of rebirth; it will, moreover, eventually lead to the Incarnation. But he also compares the Spectre to the hypocritical, self-righteous Hand and proclaims that he will compel this severed portion of himself to assist in the pounding of selfhoods on his anvil—for the sake of that very Albion who has divided him (7:52; 8:17-18). Perceiving the hypocrisy behind the Spectre's pretended obedience, Los explicitly declares that this fiend is his own "Pride & Self-righteousness" (8:30) but that it must nevertheless join him in his inspired war against the tyrannies of the Sons of Albion that oppress all Europe and Asia. Because life in the flesh is a necessary part of the regenerative process, Los's furnaces and their accessories are identified on one level with the human body (53:12-14).

The Sons are now absorbed into the form of Hand, and they have condensed their emanations—all their gentle thoughts, desires and inspirations, including the impulses of genius—into greeds and hatreds that issue in aggressive war; they ally themselves with the "pomp of religion" (9:15), and devour the labour of the peaceful farmer. Opposing "the sword of war" (9:5) with "the spiritual sword" (9:18), Los takes the sorrows of martyrs and victims (9:17—cf. pl. 52, poem, ll. 25-28) and toils with little success to soften the hearts that Hand would petrify—hoping to force the enemies of humanity to disclose their true nature and cause their own rejection (9:29-31).

In his competition with the Sons or Spectres of Albion for the possession of Jerusalem's Children (who are precious emanations of Albion), Los prevents his Spectre from deploying reasonings against these Children and against his own (10:3-5, 29-35). Such reasonings, grounded on the classification of the contraries as an acceptable good and an unacceptable evil, produce the abstract Lockean conception of an external, objective reality whose essence is unknowable. In words often applied to Blake's own intellectual activity, Los strives to "Create a System" in order "to deliver Individuals" from the systems of others (10:20; 11:5). The children he saves and makes his own enter within his furnaces into "the Spaces of Erin" (9:34; 11:10, 12)—non-mathematical spaces of imagination. (Like that other western country America, Erin or Ireland is a land of spiritual liberty.) The Spectre of Los, forced by the laws of the Urizenic god he worships to condemn as sin the Enitharmon he loves, is riven by a despair that Los's comforting cannot dissolve.

The Children of Los join their father in grieving over the vulnerability of Jerusalem before the attacks of corrupted emanations, namely Vala and the Daughters of Albion. Yet Los is sustained by faith in the omnipresent God, who ensures that the intellectual errors of Albion's Sons will stand out unmistakably (12:10-15). Happily, as Golgonooza is created the Spaces of Erin transcend the Starry Wheels, and in exquisitely allegorical lines Blake describes the ethical component—the tender virtues—of this city of art. More mechanical is the rest of the account of Golgonooza: the four-dimensional metropolis has its four-dimensional gates, its animals, and its elements—all correlated with Eternity, Beulah, Generation and Ulro. An elegiac passage surveys the environs, a characteristically Urizenic fallen landscape abounding in features familiar from Blake's earlier writings. Even here, however, the work "of mercy & love" (13:45) is found—it is this which makes objects visible to the physical eyes of the fallen.

While he contemplates the extension of British imperialism and of human degeneration, Blake introduces, as in *Milton* 20:15-24, a personal prayer: may the Holy Spirit enable him to awaken Albion (15:9-13). He observes how "the Schools & Universities of Europe" are infiltrated by the false teachings of British natural science that sustain the world of industrial machinery driven by "cogs tyrannic" that contrast with the "Wheel within Wheel" of the Divine Chariot of Ezekiel's vision (15:14-20; Ezek. i.16).

For several plates there is little narrative. The poet describes how Los, in the repressive metropolis denounced years earlier in the quatrains of "London" and indeed over the whole country of Britain, labours at his furnaces with the aid of his four eldest Sons. Correlating modern Britain with ancient Israel, Blake shows that Los is upheld in his work of liberation by a vision of the far-off redemption of Reuben and all the twelve tribes. Unfortunately the allotment of British counties to Jacob's sons seems mechanical and arbitrary. In his role as artist, Los, who preserves images of all earthly actions, is susceptible to the sensual lure of Albion's hypocritically chaste Daughters; to protect himself, he sends against them his Spectre—the reasoning element of a being not entirely fallen, "The Spectre of the Living pursuing the Emanations of the Dead" (17:13). Though it can serve in this capacity, Los fears that his nearly autonomous reason may obliterate his gentle emotions, that his Spectre may devour Enitharmon. The latter he believes to be in danger, too, from the Daughters of Albion, who covet her place as Los's spouse. Their 'love,' however, is the passion of selfhood responsible for the Fall. He has a third fear, that his Spectre will separate completely leaving Enitharmon to degenerate into his warring contrary.

Although Los tries to make Hand and Schofield serve his purposes, they and Albion's other Sons take possession of an externality that devours all interiority. Hyle and Hand brand as sin the communal joys of Eternity made possible by "self-denial" preferring "War and deadly contention" (18:20) as they seek to misappropriate for their own kind the benefits of the Crucifixion.

In pl. 19, Blake describes first the fate of Albion when he has fallen into the power of his ravenous Sons, who turn out to be the

"Double-form'd"—perhaps hermaphroditic—Spectres of his Twenty-four Cathedral Cities (19:20), and then Albion's condition as he is about to fall from lower Beulah to Ulro. (Albion's own complaint in *The Four Zoas* [119:32-120:3/ E388-89/ IX, 99-113] is here turned into a third-person account [19:1-14]). Fleeing deeper into Beulah, he encounters much beauty but is no nearer Eternity. As Vala weaves her exquisite and alluring Veil, Jerusalem pleads for her forgiveness—though it is Vala who has seduced Albion into falling. For his part, Albion blames Jerusalem, Vala and his Daughters—secret sinnners all—for his desperate condition. He perceives that the militarised British are in the state of mental blindness represented by the Israelite exile in Babylon or Chaldea and recognises the "tortures of Doubt & Despair" (21:36), but he nevertheless demands moral purity. Similarly, Vala realises she has been made to promote the war that pollutes "the Valley of Vision" (22:9), and yet she deplores sin. Only Jerusalem can see that transgressors need forgiveness and not the punishment Albion would impose even on himself. Rushing outwards where he formerly fled inwards, he becomes a demonic caricature of one of Christ's "fishers of men" (Matt. iv.19): he uses Vala's "Veil of Moral Virtue" (23:22) as a net to snare the souls of the fallen in the Atlantic and prays that God, who is forcing him into Ulro, will afflict them likewise. Suddenly, remorse overtakes him for this wicked curse and for his desertion of Jerusalem in favour of fallen Babylon. In most moving lines he recalls both cities and, indeed, the whole earth, in their unfallen state, but even the vision of the slain Jesus that appears is not sufficient to save him, and the inhabitants of Beulah mourn over him and call on Christ to deliver sinners by creating states to which their sins can be imputed.

The Preface prefixed to the second chapter of his epic Blake addresses to the followers of the Law of Moses, but unlike many critics of Hebraic legalism, he recognises that the Jews have a rich tradition of myth and mysticism in the Cabbala, a tradition that he regards as essentially one with authentic Christianity and, in fact, as the ancient form of that religion, which the Israelites inherited from the earliest, uncorrupted Druids. Drawing on the eighteenth-century theories and fantasies about the Druids mentioned in chapter eight, he declares that Jerusalem (the true Hebraic-Christian faith) is an emanation of Albion (the Britain whence this original faith spread over the world). In a great lyric poem, which combines the history of

humankind with personal devotion, he moves from an Eden that links
the notion of Jesus' presence in England with idyllic childhood
memories to such features of the fallen condition as Druid human
sacrifices, executions at Tyburn, and the Napoleonic wars as well as
the falling apart of the nations to different regions of the globe. The
turning point comes when the speaker—Blake himself—accepts that
he, too, helps to slay Christ; having cleansed his conscience, he can
identify with Albion in the final stanza and predict the latter's reunion
with all countries and with Jerusalem.

      The chapter that follows the Preface shows Albion upholding
the religion of moral law and atonement through sacrifice that the
poet considers the most oppressive aspect of Old Testament doctrine.
The word "atone" appears once in this chapter and the word
"atonement" thrice: neither word occurs elsewhere in the epic. The
text begins with a portrait of Albion as a Urizenic judge from beneath
whose heel arises the Tree of Mystery; his dim recollection of Eternity
allows him to lament his degeneration (30[34]:2-16) even while he
prepares to replace moral self-sacrifice with physical human sacrifice
(28:20-24). His Spectre, whose substitute for a heart centres on a
blank dot, proclaims the insignificance of (Lockean) humankind. The
expression of this view evokes the appearance of Vala, external
nature, with her contradictory (hermaphroditic) qualities, and her
beauty enchants Albion, even while she causes the Divine Vision to
fade. She insists that "The Imaginative Human Form" (29[33]:49) is
of *her* creation, and Los, deploring her ascendancy over Albion, opens
his furnace, where work of regeneration is done. Here Blake inserts
his first snapshot from the life of Reuben showing how Los attempts
to set him on the road to redemption, but it is cut across by two
glimpses of the tyrannies of Albion's Daughters (30[34]:46, 52). In
the next plate, Christ utters from within the opened furnaces his
promise of salvation to lawbreakers. The promise serves as a kind of
interlude in an extended account of the fallen state, of the process by
which it comes into existence, and of the way in which it is limited by
the Divine Hand (31[35]:1-2) and by Los's shaping of Reuben's sense
organs. As the Spectre cuts Reuben off from imagination (32[36]:23-
24) and illusion blots out reality (32[36]:50-54), a series of calamities
overruns the world: Albion's Children scatter over the earth—perhaps
to avoid the redemptive hammer blows of Los (32[36]:14-21); the
Zoas change their positions and become, on one level, the four
elements inhabited by the four kinds of elemental spirit; accident and

chance enter a world that passes out of the control of spirit or mind (32[36]:35, 56); and the ocean submerges Atlantis (32[36]:39-40).

While Albion refuses to relent, the Eternals, whose collective utterance is the voice of Jesus, employ poignant biblical phrases as they plead with him (34[38]:10-26). Many plates are now dominated by the image of falling Albion, whose Twenty-four Cities, frequently contained in a further four—"Verulam, London, York, Edinburgh" (41[46]:24)—are Eternals trying to hold him back from his fate, but the most they can do is to participate in Christ's sacrifice and become a ransom for Albion as they fall with him. Summoned by Los, whose invisible Gate is the exit from the world of "Moral Virtue" (35[39]:10; 39[44]:1-3) and of Satan's Mill, the Twenty-eight Cities come riding on the "Living Creatures" (36[40]:22) of Ezekiel's vision (i.4ff) to weep over him. They do not fail to blame themselves (37[41]:25), and indeed they have fallen forms: Bath is associated with healing waters and with its clergyman Richard Warner, an opponent of war with Napoleonic France, but also, as indicated by his other name, Legions (37[41]:1), with Rome's military occupation of Britain, and he has had a part in the corruption of Luvah and the persecution of Jerusalem. The Cities see the fallen Zoas sending their Wheels to work, like the Starry Wheels of his Sons, for Albion's decline (38[43]:1-5; 6:1), but when they call on God to save Albion from Druidism, Los wrathfully urges that they themselves act. In a long speech, he parallels the English with the Israelites who were beset by the heathen and then exiled through the world; they are sacrificial victims of the law and the Saxon prey of the Sons (or "Giants") of Albion (38[43]:47). Across the landscape are familiar symbols of a Urizenic world. However, because "the Will must not be bended but in the day of Divine/ Power" (39[44]:18-19), the Cities fail in their attempt to carry Albion back from the entrance to Ulro, and they appoint Los as Albion's and their own prophet and guardian in the lower world.

In a gentle lament very different from Los's angry exhortation, Bath speaks as an Eternal to other Eternals and draws the lesson that no individual that cuts itself off from the divine essence can survive. He enigmatically contrasts Albion's fall, which can be undone only by Jesus, with Africa's less profound degeneration in Beulah, which was reversed when "His friends cut his strong chains, & overwhelm'd his dark/ Machines" (40[45]:21-22). Having already mentioned seven out of Albion's Twenty-four Cities (36[40]:48-37[41]:1—Chichester is merely an emanation, not an independent metropolis), Blake enumerates the remaining seventeen, interrupting his list with a plea of Oxford, "immortal Bard!" (41[46]:7), to Albion made at the request of Bath (40[45]:30-32). The names of the four principal Cities almost conclude this segment of the poem (41[46]:23-24).

In the first chapter, Los was seen contending with his Spectre and building Goigonooza; he is now contending with Albion and building the Mundane Shell, which is identified with "the Net & Veil of Vala" (42:81)—though a delusive temptation and a cramping prison, its construction marks a necessary stage in the progress to redemption. Albion, conscious of his degradation but blaming it on sin, accuses Los of stealing his emanations or children and encouraging them to transgress, while Los insists that laws of righteousness are limits imposed to curb vision, which is potentially infinite but that the creation of woman from the shrivelled mortal body will allow the birth of the Saviour. In response, Albion vainly orders his sons Hand and Hyle to arrest Los, as they arrested, he claims, the Twenty-four Cities. Insofar as Albion is Britain at war with Napoleon, he is harshly suppressing his true friends—those who would make peace. They (the Twenty-four Cities), it turns out, have now divided into fallen selves —"Spectres of the Dead" (42:57)—who regret their former compassion, and unfallen "Human...forms" (42:66), who retain just enough consciousness to whisper, "we sleep upon our watch/ We cannot awake!" (42:72-73).

Appearing as "a Human Form" (43[29]:4) inside a setting sun, God denounces the satanic being who has reacted against Albion's goodness, constructed his own law, and remodelled Albion in his own image. He describes Albion's fate in terms recalling that of conquered Israel and announces His own coming incarnation. Meanwhile two refugees emerge from the landscape inside the fallen human to retell the version of his fall included in Night the Third of *The Four Zoas*:[9] consorting with the temptress Vala, he fell in abject worship before Luvah, a priestly Shadow hidden in a cloud; when Luvah descended, Albion struggled with him, and drove both him and Vala away, so that they separated and nature (Vala) assumed its fallen form (43[29]:33-82; cf. *FZ* 39:15-42:17/ E327-28/ III, 44-101). The refugees—Enitharmon and the Spectre of Urthona—obtain protection from Los, whom Albion fails to deprive of the Divine Vision. Praying

---

[9] See p. 195 above.

to Christ, Los laments the oppression of the British poor "in every City & Village" (44[30]:27) as well as the division of the Human into sexes in Beulah, which leads to the calamitous conditions of life in Ulro. (He knows that there is no remedy but only further evil to be found in any vengeance against the cruel.) Further exploration within the person and land of Albion shows Los how concealed agents of tyranny—including the intellectual tyranny that submerges individual identities by grouping them in classes—have treated human souls as though they were indistinguishable bricks. He sees, too, the conflict between Jerusalem, the advocate of faith, and her shadow Vala, who spurns her as a harlot and would supplant her by taking possession of Albion.

At this point Los, finding "his Furnaces in ruins" (46[32]:6), grasps his blacksmith's instruments but is challenged by the Sons of Albion, who make their father the centre of their Druid cult. On their side, "Mingl[ing] with his Victim's Spectre," is the alienated Luvah, who has entered the state Satan (47:15; 49:68); he is Albion's suppressed energies breaking free in violence that extends from the human sacrifices of ancient Germanic peoples to the slaughter of the Napoleonic wars, for on the political level "Luvah is France" and his emanation is Shiloh as Albion is Britain and his Emanation is Jerusalem (47:4-11; 66:15; 49:47-48).

Though one perspective shows Albion outstretched on the Druid couch of his Sons, another reveals that Christ has placed him on a couch protected by the pillars of the "Spiritual Verse" of Scripture—those books of the Bible which have an all-important hidden meaning (48:8). For the reader's further reassurance, the poet combines a brief narrative of Jerusalem's descent from Beulah to accompany Albion with a tender account of how Erin, a collective form of emanations of Albion's "Friends" or Cities, creates a time and space in which the salvation of Albion and Jerusalem can be wrought: the time takes visible shape as a rainbow which contains and therefore transcends the Wheels of Albion's Sons (48:27-35; 50:22).

In a long speech, Erin rehearses the horrors of the Fall and its consequences—the shrivelling of the senses and a world where all "Live by Devouring" (50:7), calls for a westward "Place for Redemption" to be cleared in the British Isles and in America (48:63), and praises the omnipresent Jehovah (the Divine Humanity), who bent "the Laws of Cruelty to Peace" (49:55), turning tyrants into protectors and giving a spiritual sense to the Law of Moses by "Divine Analogy"

(49:58). Her insistence that erring individuals be saved and only the states they have entered be condemned is accompanied by the warning that unless the Emanation of the fallen one is removed from him, even she becomes an avenging tyrant. To close the chapter, the Daughters of Beulah echo Erin's invocation of the Lamb of God as they ask him to cleanse the world of the memory of the sins that have been committed: when this vanishes, so must the desire for vengeance.

The Preface that occupies pl. 52 argues that Deism, though in appearance the progressive faith of the Enlightenment, is no more than the old religion of moral laws in a new dress. Acutely Blake recognises that this supposedly rational creed is based on an unrealistically optimistic view of human nature; less fairly, he accuses it of preaching revenge for sin, though what may be an oblique allusion to Voltaire's long flirtation with the militarist Frederick the Great gives some small backing to the charge that it promotes war. Blake is in error, however, in including among its adherents the philosopher Hume, whose *Dialogues Concerning Natural Religion* (1779) demonstrate that Deism is untenable.

After the prose denunciation comes the stirring lyric "I saw a Monk of Charlemaine," which pits the inhabitant of the cloister who lives by faith against the Greco-Roman learning and values that pervade the universities and serve as a tool of warlike emperors, even nominally Christian ones like Charlemaine and Constantine.

A key element of Deism is adoration of nature, which is held to prove the existence of an entirely good and all-powerful creator. In Blake's view this amounts to worshipping the female will, which, in the multiple form of Albion's Daughters, the binary form of Rahab and Tirzah, and especially the unitary form of the fallen Vala, dominates the third chapter.

The text begins with another view of Los constructing Golgonooza, his instruments being organs of the material body, for "the Spiritual Fourfold/ London" is continuously though invisibly being raised and worn down as human life pursues its course (53:18-20). Obscure but evocative lines declare that the emanations are preserved by being allowed to participate in Generation, and that in Eternity the emanation is the light or garment, male or female, of each divinely appointed form or identity; this light constitutes a tabernacle which, contrary to the earthly tabernacle of female possessiveness and seclusion, is the agent of communication and "Mutual Forgiveness" between individuals (54:4)

Far removed from Eternity, Albion finds himself the captive of his own Spectre, who is identified with the military ruler Arthur as opposed to the imaginative Merlin of pl. 32(36):23-24; in the name of reason and natural science, the Spectre rejects Jesus, faith and eternal life. In these circumstances Albion's Emanation—now conceived as England, who contains both Jerusalem and Vala—rejects him defiantly, but the Divine Vision appears dimly and sadly above her.

As pl. 55 opens, the scene and perspective change. Seeing Albion about to fall from Beulah, the Eternals stormily debate what action to take and end by appointing, as in the earlier epics, the Seven Eyes of God. While the Zoas, the "Living Creatures" (55:55) of Ezekiel's vision (i.4ff), spurn the generalisations of reasoners and scientists, they or the Eternals collectively direct the plough that symbolises the course of events below.

Meanwhile, an interpolated page tells us, Los laments that Albion created a female will and tries to persuade and even compel one form of this power, Albion's Daughters with their "iron Reel" (56:12), to make the product of their weaving a body which will be welcome to the descending soul. The response of the Daughters, which may be sorrowful or scornful, prompts Los to complain that the three women at the Cross blighted with female influence the church created by Paul. After another glimpse of the fall of Albion (this time *he* misguides the plough, which has become "the Plow of Nations" [57:2], as Satan misused the harrow in *Milton* [7:4-30]), we return to the Daughters of Albion, who act like female Druids when they operate with the sacrificial knife to diminish the human brain and dissect Albion's now hermaphroditic Sons. Trying to counter their depredations, Los strives "To Create a World of Generation from the World of Death" (58:18); this involves transforming what Urizen builds, namely a temple of much beauty which contains the whole earth as well as the orbits of the sun and moon. Britain and the Americas have a special place in Los's affection: the former is the centre of his creative aspect, the latter apparently the prime source of liberty.

Referring back (as though this were a chronological narrative) to 23:22-23, Blake notes that as Vala's Veil, which Albion threw into the Atlantic floodwaters, begins to harden, Los transforms it into "the beautiful Mundane Shell" to make "the Place/ Of Redemption" (59:7-9). In 59:10-21, a reworking of *Milton* 19:15-25 and 34:32-39 relates the dispositions of the fallen Zoas' worlds to the

four principal Cathedral Cities and serves as a prelude to an account
of Los's Daughters nobly weaving bodies in Cathedron for descended
souls. At the same time the Divine Vision emerges from Los's
furnaces to protect Jerusalem's Children against the sanguinary
influence of the now spectrous Luvah. Imprisoned in Babylon though
invisibly sustained by Beulah's Daughters, the exiled Jerusalem
suffers the scorn of the triumphant Vala and her religion of moral
purity.

In spite of her captivity, Jerusalem can intermittently see the
Lamb of God (60:39, 50-51). A version of his song sung by slaves of
Ulro mildly reproaches her for turning from the beauty of the whole
world, which he had given her, and building Babylon. The ensuing
dialogue between Jerusalem and Christ is a high point of the epic and
a passage of extraordinary tenderness containing a vision of Joseph
and Mary at once lyrical and dramatic: it celebrates the forgiveness of
sins as exemplified by Joseph's pardoning of the pregnant Mary.
Jerusalem declares her faith in the reality of Christ and receives a
reassurance of his power to resurrect; her vision of the acceptance of
Mary allows her to realise that however "drunken with the Sacrifice of
Idols" she may be (61:38), Jehovah (the Divine Humanity) grants her
salvation. He repeats His promise despite her resort—Christianity's
resort—in the centuries following the Crucifixion to the protection of
Rome and of European monarchs. Seeing herself as Magdalen, viewer
of Christ's "Spiritual Risen Body" (62:14), she contrasts herself with
Vala; the latter is the mother of "the Body of death" (62:13) or mortal
body, and of a line of daughters running from Cain's wife to Mary,
the history of which will culminate in the birth of the incarnate God.

Blake now proceeds from Incarnation to Crucifixion, and
concentrates on the power and allies of the female will. Because Jesus
determines to rescue the fallen Luvah and Vala (though their
respective fire and cloud torment Jerusalem), he suffers crucifixion in
the person of Luvah. Blake makes explicit the political dimension of
this part of his myth. As the female will (the power of seductive
physical nature, jealous possessiveness, and the ideal of chastity)
crucifies Luvah (energy, passion, and the sexual impulse), so Albion
or Britain, perhaps with some help from the Emperor Napoleon,
crucifies the energy of revolutionary France, and brings Luvah "To
Justice in his own City of Paris" (63:6). To do this, says the poet, is to
deny the Resurrection—that is the resurrection both of a spiritually
dead society and of the spirit that, as faith but not reason declares,

survives the mortal body. Tumbling assorted references together, Blake classifies the Norse deities as well as the supernatural beings of British folklore as Druid enemies of Jehovah-incarnate-in-Christ. These enemies increase the strength of the female will and deepen the fallen condition, which involves the flight of Reuben to avoid, as yet, entering the Promised Land of Canaaan.

As a war goddess, Vala is soon found glorying in her ascendancy over humankind. Los's defiance of her (64:18-24)—he continues to labour in hope, sorrow, and sometimes despair (62:35-42)—is of little effect: she forms an hermaphroditic union with Albion's Spectre, and together they make Luvah endure crucifixion through the six thousand years of history, and replace an economy based on agriculture and crafts with one based on wage slavery and the industrial assembly line. (The trenchant passage describing these actions [65:6-55] is repeated with slight variations from *The Four Zoas* [92:11-93:19/ E364-65/ VIIb, 164-209].) Speaking half as Vala's adorers, half as the conscripts (identified with galley slaves) of Britain's war machine, the Sons of Albion hymn their goddess but make it clear that she hypocritically conceals her love of the war to which, with the aid of her sexuality, she drives men. As they rejoice in Luvah's suffering, they refer to his exchange of functions with Urizen, hinting that the latter's horses were perverted into beasts of war. Albion's Daughters join his Sons in gloating over Luvah's fate at Stonehenge (then believed to be the work of Druids) on Salisbury Plain (65:56-71; 66:2). Identifying Stonehenge with the cosmic temple of 58:21-43, Blake tries to show how Druid human sacrifice, Old Testament legalism, Locke's empirical philosophy, natural science, the attempt to control the material world, and natural religion are all parts of the outcome of worshipping nature as the ultimate reality: such worship is the enemy of that liberty which the release of energy in the French Revolution (66:1-15) was to attain.

The appalling tortures visited on Luvah (the personification of energy), the retreat of sun and moon, the separation of the animals from the human, and the disintegration of Britain followed by wars are all elements of the Fall. The reference to "Dove & Raven" (66:70) suggests that Blake alludes to Noah's Flood as well as to the fate of a Britain that comes to resemble the Napoleonic France it crucifies. Like their victim Luvah, Albion's Sons and Daughters suffer diminished perception, and Blake again employs his evocative phrase "The Divine Vision" and the image of the dread Polypus to show how humankind dwindles into a fragmentary existence cut off from reality and devoid of brotherhood (65:75-79; 66:35-84). Looking back to the atoms and materialism of Epicurus and anticipating the atheistic materialism of the twentieth century, the Daughters, whose malign embodiment of souls produces the Polypus that covers the globe, believe that life springs from the inorganic rocks. The twelve Daughters readily combine into and re-emerge from Rahab and Tirzah. The latter, with her seven furnaces antithetical to the seven furnaces of Los, chants a grotesque and ironic love song—almost the same words are put into the mouths of the Females of Amalek in *The Four Zoas*—to the spirit she imprisons in the flesh (67:44-68:9; *FZ* 105:31-53/ E378-79/ VIII, 298-321). Moreover she laments that Albion's Sons are alienated from her, but conflict is natural to Ulro. The same is true of war, and her song is followed by the chant of victorious warriors, in whose ahistorical eyes, the sacrifice of children—perhaps the joyous impulses of the soul—to Molech is of a piece with the oppressive moral law of the Old Testament; the wars they celebrate include those of modern France and Germany (the phrasing echoes that of the prefatory poem on pl. 27). The essence of their message, however, is that their frenzy for battle is sexual in origin, for the teasing, dazzling beauty of the female arouses in them both adoration and anger. Using the singular pronoun, they declare

> I am drunk with unsatiated love:
> I must rush again to War, for the Virgin has frown'd &
refus'd.
>   (68:62-63)

After proclaiming that in the universal state of war all the males combine to constitute the Polypus, which obliterates all genuine love and is "at variance with Itself/ In all its Members" (69:6-7), Blake allows his reader a short interlude of relief while he gently sketches the contrasting relationship of the sexes in Beulah, where the female, free from jealousy, is cherished in her repose by the male, who keeps open her communication with Eternity; should she, however, be unfortunate enough to fall into Ulro, her only way of return is by "Becoming a Generated Mortal, a Vegetating Death" (69:31). Rapidly, the poet brings the reader back to Ulro, and identifies the moral law based on sexual possessiveness with Druid doctrine, and Druid doctrine with the veil of the Temple that was torn at Christ's death. He claims that sexual intercourse is but a degenerate form of the embraces of Eternity, which "are Cominglings from the Head even to the Feet" (69:43).

As the twelve Daughters can unite in Rahab and Tirzah, so the twelve Sons can unite in the three-headed Hand, one of the most prominent of themselves; and as the Polypus is at war within itself, Hand's three heads are "in contradictory council brooding incessantly" (70:5), for Blake is parodying eighteenth-century empiricists who ground knowledge on the agreement and disagreement of "Ideas" (70:7-8). From Hand arise Bacon, Newton and Locke, and deep within him abides and reigns the seductive Rahab, who implicitly denies the possibility of redemption, for she condemns those who err instead of the states they have entered.

A contrast between the material world inhabited by the twelve Sons of Albion and the spiritual world inhabited by twelve of Jerusalem's Sons, founders of the tribes of Israel, introduces a long catalogue that divides among Albion's Children regions and features of Great Britain. Ireland, however, is reserved for a special honour: its four provinces are allotted to "the Four Sons of Jerusalem that never were Generated" (71:50), namely Rintrah, Palamabron, Theotormon and Bromion, who guard what remains of Jerusalem in the British Isles; these also preside over the Scottish and English universities, in which Blake here seems to perceive some merit. To the other twelve Sons of Jerusalem are allotted the thirty-two Irish counties, which "Center in London & in Golgonooza" (72:28) and are the source of the world's thirty-two nations.

To close his third chapter, Blake provides two further perspectives on the fallen state. The first (72:45-74:13) returns to the work of Los emphasising the immense and terrifying labour at his furnaces, where Rintrah, Palamabron, Theotormon and Bromion have become, after some experience of error, his helpers. Three moving lines speak of his Gate that opens into Beulah, a gate watched over by spiritual heroes and heroines including St. Teresa and the French Quietist Fénelon.

Los has some part in the work of creation within the realm that stretches from the earth to the Mundane Shell. This dismal region is here called "Luvah's World of Opakeness" (73:22) on account of Luvah's key role in the Fall, and Voltaire is harshly rebuked for conceiving God as the imposer of cruel restrictions on this cosmos whereas in reality He is "the Remover of Limits" (73:30). Los creates

the prophets, all inspired despite their imperfections, to make possible
the redemption of the long line of biblical and British monarchs raised
up by Rahab and Tirzah; his family forms protective bodies for fallen
spirits—even the Zoas degenerate into the ghostly state of the latter.

The second perspective (74:14-75:27) is that of Blake himself
when he shares the viewpoint of Los, who moves freely in the three
dimensions of time and preserves every event in perpetuity. Again, the
poet reminds us of Babylon's ascendancy over Jerusalem; of the power
of Albion's Sons (now identified with "the Twelve Gods of Asia"
[74:22]—Middle Eastern pagan deities); of the cruelty of Albion's
Daughters, who divide Reuben and the other Sons of Jerusalem from
Albion (the division of Reuben and Benjamin was mentioned at
63:12); and of Reuben's taking root in Bashan as opposed to the
Promised Land west of the Jordan (74:41-43; 30[34]:36, 43). A mom-
ent of relief comes with a glimpse of Dinah, "the youthful form of
Erin" (74:54); it is followed by the full though intermittent revelation
of the horror of Rahab in space and time, which are fashioned for this
necessary purpose by Los (75:4-6). The list of the tyrant's Twenty-
seven Churches is slightly expanded from *Milton* 37:35-43. Their
painful progression, Blake makes clear, forms an ever repeated circle,
but a circle that is capable of propelling the spiritual captives outside
of itself, of awakening Albion and Luvah.

Chapter four is preceded by a prose address headed "To the
Christians." Alluding to the orthodox belief in a heavenly world that
awaits the redeemed after death, Blake asserts that that world is the
realm of imagination and that to exercise "the Divine Arts of
Imagination" is the responsibility of every believer. In the Protestant
tradition, he urges strenuous combat against "the Enemy" and
devotion to "the Work of the Lord," insisting that "the tortures of
repentance" are brought on not by transgressing negative
commandments but by neglecting positive duty. He castigates the
moral vices—even "fleshly desires"—as impediments to spiritual
labour, but adds that what humans see as sin is not sin in God's eyes.
This statement makes a suitable prelude to a stirring passage of blank
verse in which such "a Watcher & a Holy-One" as brought revelation
to Nebuchadnezzar in a dream (Dan. iv.13) tells the speaker that the
fiery wheel that fragments the universe and shrivels its human
inhabitants is the Wheel of Religion, the creed of the Pharisees that
Jesus gave his life to overthrow. Uncharacteristically Blake applies the
word "Nature" to the redeemed world, and in the last lines he seems

to equate Christ's liberation of fallen beings with his harrowing of
hell. The Preface closes with three rhymed quatrains calling on
England to repossess her ancient happiness, for the return of
Jerusalem and of Christ is imminent.

The lyric that concludes the Preface recalls the Bard's
summons to Earth in the "Introduction" to *Songs of Experience*, but
now, instead of hearing the negative response of the spiritual prisoner,
the reader encounters at the beginning of chapter four horrific images
of Los battling Albion's spectrous Sons as they menace their father's
"Sleeping Humanity" or real self (78:3) and bestow on their mother,
who is at once Vala and Rahab, the rulership of the world. Jerusalem
is both the ruined city whose inhabitants have been exiled to Babylon
and a female prisoner in shackles. Combining ancient and modern
geography, Blake juxtaposes her exile with the Sons' assault on Erin,
the westernmost and hence least fallen area of the British Isles. After
the somewhat mechanical manipulation of names in the opening
passage, Jerusalem launches on a long and poignant lament for the
disintegration of a world in which Britain and Canaan were one and
in which Britain and Jerusalem were present within all nations—a
"Four-fold World" of more than three spatial dimensions (79:58). She
yearningly asks why Vala insists on preserving the division between
the male and the female. Very different is Vala's short answering la-
ment, the expression of an unresolved conflict. Tormented by her
memory of Eternity, where no death was permanent, she fears lest a
revived Albion renew his fight with her Luvah—see 43(29):61ff—and
slay him.

Despite Los's attempt to dissipate their power, the Daughters
of Albion incite worldwide enmity against Jerusalem (80:46-47), and
Cambel and Gwendolen seek complete power over their counterparts
among the Sons. Cambel makes Hand create an anti-Christian body
for Jerusalem, while Gwendolen combines the fleshly imprisonment of
Hyle with the imposition upon him of moral law opposed to the spirit
of Christ and eventually reduces him, she thinks, to a helpless infant
only to find that he has become a worm, emblem of mortality. Though
Gwendolen sees "Humanity"—the unfallen essence of the human—as
"the Great Delusion" (82:42), on some plane she realises that the
present identity of the Daughters is intimately involved with
"Delusions" (82:4), and she fears annihilation—much as Vala does
(80:14-15)—if this is discovered. Concocting a "Falshood" (82:17)
that Enitharmon is plotting with Los to supplant both Albion and his

Daughters, she urges that they destroy their enemies—crucify Jesus and cut Jerusalem off from America. Similarly disposed, Cambel strives to re-create Hand "according to her will" (82:63). However, she and Gwendolen are subjected to the influence of Los's furnace and Luvah's winepress, and they begin despite themselves to learn to love (82:56-79).

While Enitharmon weaves beneficently, Los tells the Daughters of Beulah of life in the fallen world, where he must continue to labour but dreads losing his recollection of Eternity; in this lower realm, the illusory surface appearance of things that hides "the real Surface" (83:47) is controlled and manipulated by the Daughters of Albion, the inner feminine powers that distort our sensory perception. As in the first chapter, Los and his Spectre work together at his furnaces.

Terrified at the growing power of Albion's Sons, his Daughters, remembering the happy prelapsarian world, even call on Los to help them overcome these monsters. Gwendolen, however, has hidden her falsehood in her left hand intending it "To entice her Sisters away to Babylon," but she has forgotten "that Falshood is prophetic" and liable to bring about the opposite of what its user intends (82:18, 20). When her sisters take it, it grows into the space Canaan and surrounds the worm to which Gwendolen has reduced Hyle. Now Los turns a part of the "Falshood" into truth and undermines the power of the Daughters, for here he plants Reuben and sets in motion the history of Israel, which will lead to the birth of Christ. In a tender and hopeful song, Los celebrates the relationship of Albion and his faithful Jerusalem; three exquisite verse paragraphs evoke images of the "three Universes of love & beauty" in Jerusalem's "Three-fold" form—the form seen outstretched on the title page (86:2-3).

Optimism and sorrow are mingled in this part of the poem, for as in 5:66-6:4, 12:7, 17:48-58, 53:4-6, and 62:35-38, Blake describes the process of Enitharmon's separation from Los. This time, however, he goes on to recount the subsequent contention for dominion between them and tells how the independent Emanation, who plans to make Christians terrified of sex, fills the world with the "Allegoric Night of Albion's Daughters," the contrary of the "Space" and "Allegory" called Canaan (88:20, 31-33; 85:1-2). The Spectre of Urthona, although "he kept the Divine Vision in time of trouble" (44[30]:15; 95:20), is only made to labour at the furnaces—as chapter one shows—under severe duress, and it is he who sows dissension between Los and Enitharmon: the rational element of imagination cuts off its emotional element, so that its work becomes ineffective.

Blake is now building up to the crisis of his epic, and as at the end of *Milton* he introduces a climactic image of error in the form of the Covering Cherub, whom he here identifies with "the Hermaphroditic Wine-presses of Love & Wrath" (88:58)—love and wrath not synthesised but unharmoniously mingled in that oppressive form of religion that brought about the Crucifixion. (Their hermaphroditic nature is foreshadowed by the mingling of Vala with Albion's Spectre at 64:25-31.) As the hermaphroditic winepress is the antithesis of Luvah's winepress of love (72:52; 82:75), so this image of the Covering Cherub, with its three lurid yet partly alluring segments pictured in three verse paragraphs, is the satanic counterpart of the tripartite image of Jerusalem (89:14-51; 86:1-32). Whereas Los sees within Jerusalem Palestine, her neighbours, and Britain in their unfallen forms, the grieving poet observes in the Covering Cherub all the nations of a world covered with Druid temples and oak forests, a world where Israel is in exile.

For the last time, Blake describes the tyrannies of Albion's Sons and Daughters that arise from the division of the Human into male and female: they create vulnerable fleshly bodies, sever the Children of Jerusalem from the landscape of Britain, worship material nature, erect Urizen's cosmic temple of natural religion (90:49-50), and merge with the Luvah they have martyred. Punctuating the account of their enormities are prophecies of Los which fill even the Sons and their temples with fear. In philosophical language, he excoriates any individual who (like the fallen Urizen) dares to believe his existence is totally independent and not rooted in a divine essence. Such a belief makes the heretic promulgate laws of his own devising as universal moral truths; it also causes his division into male and female fragments that, longing to possess their contraries and become complete, adopt religions whose laws are based on possessiveness. Moreover, in semi-Gnostic fashion Los repudiates Christ's mortal body, with its sexual identity, as a manifestation of satanic outward nature assumed only so that it could be cast off.[10]

The Children of Albion recede into the background as Los launches into an overwhelming denunciation of ritual that echoes the

[10] Cf. pp. 159-60 above.

spirit and in places the words of *The Marriage of Heaven and Hell* and accords with the assertion on the Laocoön plate (*c*. 1820) "The outward Ceremony is Antichrist" (E274/ K776). This denunciation Los commissions his Spectre to deliver to "these Fiends of Righteousness" (91:4), but the Spectre, determined to work his own will, relates to the universe on the basis of the Hermetic philosophy, which appears to occupy an intermediate position between the Urizenic science of Newton and a Blakean world-view, seeking illumination from the empty spaces between the stars instead of from the stars themselves, he aspires, like the builders of Babel, to reach heaven with material structures, but his pillars are only "pyramids of pride" (91:43). By extreme and painful efforts, Los concludes the contention with his Spectre so prominent in the first chapter as he untwists the distortions in the latter's perception—since the Spectre is a portion of himself, the labour is, in fact, "self-subduing" (91:46). While he calls for the development of mental powers in place of holiness, Los sees the first stages of the reintegration of the divided Human, but Enitharmon, still corrupt, fears, much like Milton's Eve (*PL*, IX, 826-29), that she will be annihilated and that Los will create for himself a new partner. He reminds her that there are no sexes in Eternity, where all the jealousies and terrors of the temporal world are seen only as memories and possibilities that warn the Eternals against a descent into Ulro. Remembering her sufferings at the original Fall, Enitharmon turns her possessiveness towards her sons Rintrah and Palamabron, but their father, Los, assures them they have nothing to fear from Albion's resurrection and urges them to turn from the latest form of nature worship—natural science—which is the tribulation preceding the end of the world that Jesus foretold (Matt. xxiv).

At this point, the poem turns into a chronological narrative. Blake describes Albion in his state of sleep together with his Emanation England, who wakes at the touch of the Holy Spirit and confesses that in her jealousy she murdered Albion sacrificing him on a Druid altar. Aroused by her voice, Albion rises in anger, takes his bow, and compels the three more fallen Zoas to return to their stations. In one of Blake's most moving passages, Albion encounters Jesus in "the likeness & similitude of Los" (96:7) and laments that his selfhood still marches against his Saviour, but Jesus' gentle answer, spoken under the shadow of the Covering Cherub, a manifestation of that very selfhood, is that God must willingly die for humankind to teach them mutual love: with the words "for Man is Love,/ As God is

Love" (96:26-27), Jesus seems to echo "The Divine Image" in *Songs of Innocence*. Albion learns the lesson, for as the Covering Cherub separates them, his terror is all for Jesus-Los, and summoning the Cities he had once repudiated, he hurls himself into the place of suffering, which turns into the River of Life flowing from the Divine Humanity. Thereupon his Cities and Sons and Daughters awake, and the poet hears God within Albion calling on Jerusalem to "overspread all Nations as in Ancient Time" (97:2). Albion takes his fourfold bow, which is both male and female and contains the bows of the four Zoas, and firing an arrow of love he annihilates his Spectre. Bacon, Newton and Locke, the agents of reason, take their place in heaven beside Milton, Shakespeare and Chaucer; the four eternal senses are restored; and the illusory outward self or appearance vanishes exposing the real Human, of which the four Living Creatures of Ezekiel's vision are a part.

The Eternals, who are both individuals and a collective being, converse with words that are visible images as they speak of events in the lower world. The poet sees a vision of the words of the Covenant of Jehovah, of mutual forgiveness, borne on chariots drawn by the forms of all animals. These words, triumphantly asking where the horrors of Ulro now are, rise from everywhere on the redeemed earth. But all created identities—"even Tree, Metal, Earth & Stone" (99:1)—are revealed as Human, and when they are fatigued by Edenic existence, they take their necessary rest in temporal Beulah and return to Eternity, and all their Emanations are called Jerusalem.

Throughout Blake's three epics, there are troubling variations in the quality of his language. The greatest unevenness is found in *The Four Zoas*, in which passages as poignant as Enion's lament at the end of the second Night and as concrete and biting as Urizen's advice on how to oppress the poor in the seventh coexist with many lapses into repetitive vocabulary, prolix narrative and wordy speechifying. The characters change their alliances and enmities with bewildering frequency, and their strange divisions dizzy the minds of readers and critics, yet all is resolved in the sublime scenes and ultimate serenity of the conclusion. The style and organisation of *Milton* are much more economic, and, as George says, it is the most accessible of the epics.[11] The eloquence of the great poet's repentance, the heroism of his descent and Ololon's, and Blake's resolute yet

---

[11] Diana Hume George, *Blake and Freud* (Ithaca and London: Cornell UP, 1980), p. 147.

humble dedication to the delivery of his message are fitted into a structure that ingeniously combines classical and synchronic elements. *Jerusalem*, despite a looser organisation and a sometimes depressing concentration on the horror of life since the Fall, is extraordinarily rich in aphorisms and adorned with exquisite passages such as the dialogue between Mary and Joseph on pl. 61 and the account of the heroine on pl. 86. Its conclusion is a supreme vision of a heavenly paradise ending with a line whose simplicity mirrors the oneness that underlies all existence.

However, great as *Jerusalem* is, even Blake must have realised the futility of attempting to communicate with many of his contemporaries through so complex and difficult a work. In his old age he tried to bring the essence of his doctrine to a wider audience through an elaborated version of his early emblem book *For Children: The Gates of Paradise* and a two-page dramatic scene, *The Ghost of Abel*.

For the Sexes: The Gates of Paradise is organised around a series of seventeen emblems which were orignally drawn in Blake's Notebook, where they were accompanied by literary quotations. These designs are printed in both Keynes's and Erdman's editions of Blake's writings. The book includes also three poems—a ten-line prologue, "The Keys of the Gates" in twenty-five couplets, and an eight-line epilogue as well as drawings to adorn the title page and accompany the epilogue. The intriguing emblems conform to Blake's recommendation that a work intended to instruct should not be "too Explicit" for difficulty "rouzes the faculties to act" (E702/ K793).

The prologue to *For the Sexes* repudiates biblical law and acclaims "Mutual Forgiveness of each Vice" as the essence of Christianity and the road to bliss. "The Keys," which are of much more use to those already acquainted with Blake's concepts, are furnished with numbers to link them unambiguously to the engravings, and the whole series encompasses the story of fall and redemption. The unfallen "Eternal Man" lapses into sleep, his emanation separates from him to preside over nature with its veil and its process of physical generation. The mortal human turns into a sceptical and legalistic reasoner in the world of the four elements, and the masculine and feminine components of the self become separate, often clashing, entities. However, the soul, under the aegis of the divine presence, is incarnated as man or woman in a slightly higher state which allows it to labour through the dangerous world of Experience with some hope of regeneration. It may be killed by thoughtless depravity or escape to meet a father's oppression with vengeance; it overreaches itself to all but drown in the Ocean of Time and suffers cruelty from the unvisionary old and the authoritarian church. But if it can learn to see the spirit, the "real Human" (*M* 20:13), within the flesh, it is no longer intimidated by the physical nature that encloses it from womb to tomb. The real Human is just what Satan, the Accuser of Sin, whose mask of terror is torn off in the epilogue, is unable to see.

While *For the Sexes* teases the intellect, *The Ghost of Abel* makes a more direct appeal to the emotions. A startling dedication seems to lift Blake momentarily out of his literary isolation as it shows him reacting to the most popular of the younger generation of Romantics. He considers Byron an authentic poet and asks how an inspired man can desert the realm of vision, imagination and prophecy—which is also the realm of Jehovah—to take up residence in the wilderness of nature.

The Ghost of Abel teaches the lesson of forgiveness while admitting how hard it is to learn. In Byron's *Cain*, the drama to which Blake is responding, the protagonist, who is encouraged by Lucifer to be a reasoner, questions the justice of Jehovah to Adam and Eve and blames Him for accepting Abel's sacrifice despite the suffering it causes to animals. Eve curses the murderer, Adam spurns him, and only Adah, his wife, is forgiving. When Blake's scene begins, Adam and Eve, having just discovered what death is, are distraught beside the corpse of Abel, and will not heed the summons of Jehovah until He appears, along with Abel's vengeful ghost, before their internal vision. Thereupon Eve suspects that the ghost is not Abel himself, and soon, seeing another Abel inwardly, she urges her spouse to join her in believing vision rather than the unillumined perceptions of the senses. Meanwhile the Elohim, followers of Satan who help to form the fallen cosmos, have entered into Abel or his ghost making him spurn Jehovah's Covenant of forgiveness and the Psalmist's true sacrifice of "a broken spirit" and "a contrite heart" (li.17) in favour of the Mosaic "life for life" (Exod. xxi. 23). As Abel returns to his grave, Satan himself rises from it in the form of a royal warrior to proclaim his rule over humankind, with its Druid creed, and demand the sacrifice of Jehovah Himself, the Divine Humanity. This Jehovah Himself wills, foreseeing that even Satan will eventually achieve self-annihilation. In a triumphant close, angels laud the Divine Humanity for showing the pagan gods their error in demanding vengeance for sin and enabling them to take their places as heavenly spirits. Although the designs in *The Ghost of Abel* are not among Blake's most successful, the words of his miniature drama constitute a stirring protest against both vengeance and philosophical materialism.

12
Masterpiece in a New Kind:
Illustrations of The Book of Job

Not even the shortest and simplest combinations of text and design that Blake had produced after his 'conversion' at the beginning of the century had reached an extensive audience, and a commission he received from John Linnell offered him another opportunity to woo the neglectful public. *Illustrations of The Book of Job*, however, enjoyed no wide circulation although it is unique among the books of his maturity for its near perfection and easy approachability. Unlike his subsequent illustrations to Dante's *Divine Comedy*, it is complete; unlike his epics, it is capable of delighting the uninitiated. The dramatic conflicts of its characters, the subtle play of light and shade, and the diversity of its textures render it a masterpiece of engraving.

Blake had been fascinated by the Book of Job all his life—witness his early engraving *The Complaint of Job*[1] and the discussion of the book in *The Marriage of Heaven and Hell*. It was probably in the period 1805-10 that he first produced an extended series of illustrations to the biblical text, thanks to the patronage of Thomas Butts. In 1821, he seems to have borrowed his designs back from Butts to make a copy of them (with slight variations) for John Linnell. This young artist was so impressed that in 1823 he commissioned Blake to engrave the series, and in the course of the engraving, which he did not complete till 1826, he made many revisions and added the richly adorned and inscribed margins which contribute so much to the aesthetic quality and intellectual richness of the work. In quoting from the Authorised Version of the Bible, Blake often alters the text.

---

[1] David Bindman, *The Complete Graphic Works of William Blake* (1978; rpt. London: Thames and Hudson, 1986), pl. 6 and p. 407.

Though the designs were frequently praised in the nineteenth century—for example by Palgrave and Ruskin[2]—it was only in 1910 that Wicksteed demonstrated that they embodied Blake's symbolic interpretation of the Book of Job, which he read as a version of his own myth of Albion's—that is humankind's and every human soul's—fall and redemption.[3] Fifty-three years later, Lindberg surprised Blake's now sophisticated admirers by showing that to a great extent his reading of the biblical book nevertheless embodied a great deal of traditional Christian exegesis.[4]

Combining a tragic exploration of human suffering with a lofty evocation of the wonders of nature, the Book of Job was for the eighteenth century one of the supreme literary examples of the sublime. It tells how Satan, appearing among the Sons of God, challenges the Lord's claim that Job is perfect in his piety. To prove that this wealthy and fortunate man's devotion is not dependent on his welfare, God allows Satan first to destroy his property, then to murder his seven sons and three daughters, and finally to torment his body with boils. Three friends—Eliphaz, Bildad and Zophar, the famous "Job's comforters"—arrive to commiserate with him, but insist that he must have sinned to be so afflicted. Job, however, will neither confess to sin nor arraign God's justice. At this impasse, a young man named Elihu protests that God, the ruler of the universe, is too great and mysterious to be judged on the basis of an arithmetical moral reckoning. He also announces that God guides mortals by inspiration (such as moves Elihu himself to speak) and by "a messenger" or "interpreter," who serves as "a ransom" or "atonement," He mercifully enlightens the individual and redeems him from "the pit" (xxxiii.14-24). (The openings for Christological interpretation are obvious.) God thereupon manifests Himself in a whirlwind, chides the three friends, vindicates Elihu, and rehearses the greatness and wonder of His creation. Finally, He rewards Job's fidelity by

---

[2] G. E. Bentley, Jr., ed., *William Blake: The Critical Heritage* (London and Boston: Routledge and Kegan Paul, 1975), pp. 144-45; John Ruskin, *The Elements of Drawing in Three Letters to Beginners* (London: Smith, Elder, 1857), p. 342.

[3] Joseph H. Wicksteed, *Blake's Vision of the Book of Job* (London: Dent; New York: Dutton).

[4] Bo Lindberg, *William Blake's Illustrations to the Book of Job* (Åbo, Finland: Åbo Akademi, 1973).

making his neighbours replace his fortune and by giving him again seven sons and three daughters.

Jewish and Christian interpreters explain Job's suffering as the consequence of his initial limitations. Before his afflictions, he is one who practises religion by rote and is pious without wisdom. Christians add that at this stage he has the Law but only through his ordeal does he come to know its inner meaning, which is the Gospel. This allows Blake to interpret the earlier phase of Job's religion as the legalistic and life-denying worship of a Urizenic god.

Blake's representation of Job's agony and the enlightenment it brings him is emblematic, not realistic. While he holds that the essence of Christianity was known to the earliest, uncorrupted Druids, including Abraham, the artist who takes pains to give his Canterbury pilgrims mediaeval garments is not likely to suppose that Gothic cathedrals were built in Old Testament times (*J*, pl. 27, prose; E533/ K567). Moreover, we do not need to believe that Job moves from place to place as the objects around him change or that because the cathedral and the Leviathan in pls. 1 and 14 differ from those in pls. 4 and 15 they are not the same structure and the same monster. Job's identification with the symbolic Albion is made clear by a speech of the latter in *Jerusalem*:

> The disease of Shame covers me from head to feet: I have
>   no hope.
> Every boil upon my body is a separate & deadly Sin.
> Doubt first assail'd me, then Shame took possession of
>   me.
> Shame divides Families. Shame hath divided Albion in
>   sunder!
> First fled my Sons, & then my Daughters, then my wild
>   Animations,
> My Cattle next, last ev'n the Dog of my Gate; the Forests
>   fled,
> The Corn-fields, & the breathing Gardens outside
>   separated;
> The Sea, the Stars, the Sun, the Moon, driv'n forth by my
>   disease...
> (21:3-10)

Blake's title page points to the redemption which awaits Job. Both the Hebrew lettering above (*Sefer Yov*—"Book of Job") and the Gothic script in the centre represent imaginative vision that resists Greco-Roman classicism. The arc of seven angels who descend on the right, cross the page at the bottom, and rise on the left symbolise fall and redemption. They may be identified with the soul passing from Innocence through Experience to Eternity and perhaps with the Seven Eyes of God, emblems of the stages of history. In the hands of some, at least, are scrolls and pens, and their resemblance to the angel in the lower margin of pl. 17 suggests that they may have a further role as muses.

In the twenty-one plates that follow, Blake retells the biblical story but concentrates heavily on the beginning and the ending. As Lindberg discovered,[5] the two final plates portray incidents from the apocryphal book *The Testament of Job*, which was unknown in Europe in Blake's lifetime though some of its content had filtered through into Western art and literature.

In pl. 1 the aged and wealthy Job is seated with his wife—on a symbolic level his Emanation—under a large tree, on which hang musical instruments. They are surrounded by his flock. Beside the couple kneel their seven grown sons and in front of them their three adult daughters. The parents have open books on their laps, and the whole family is meekly reciting the Lord's Prayer, the opening of which is inscribed in the upper margin. In the top left-hand corner, the sun is setting behind a low hill; between this hill and the flocks and family are a Gothic cathedral and a row of trees with water visible[6] between their trunks. In the top right-hand corner, are a waning moon, a star, and a grass-covered hill. The entire central design is contained in a tent representing the unspoiled nomadic life, and the tent in turn is encircled by the cloud barrier which, in most of the plates, separates heavenly and internal from earthly and external scenes. In addition to the two opening verses of Job, the lower margin contains a sketch of a flaming altar inscribed with quotations from the New Testament—II Cor. iii.6 and I Cor. ii.14—which reveal the meaning of the plate: "The Letter Killeth/ The Spirit giveth Life" and "It is Spiritually Discerned." Job is locked in the fetters of uncritical

---

[5] *Ibid.*, pp. 137-38.
[6] *Ibid.*, p. 69.

obedience to the deity whose words are contained in the open books, and he is imposing his spiritual blindness on his whole family. The suspension of musical instruments unused on the tree signifies Job's neglect of the arts, and the sun's setting behind the cathedral symbolises his turning away from visionary religion, while the waning of the moon hints at the coming night of the fallen state. The crescent of the seven sons reflects the curve of the angels on the title page, and the four bearded and older sons in the middle of the crescent foreshadow the tyrannies of Experience, while the two youngest at either end carry a pipe and a lyre of Innocence in their girdles.

The most packed and perhaps the most intriguing of all the designs, pl. 2, shows how the harmony between Job and his children and between Job and heaven is broken. The symbolism of the visionary right and materialistic left[7] and of books versus scrolls begins to become important here. Books represent the Law, scrolls the Gospels.[8] As yet the right relationship between Job and his god has not been subverted, for the corporeal Job has his left foot forward, the deity his right. But the stern god with tell-tale spikes on his hair (they are to swell and multiply into the hair spikes of the satanic god in pl. 11)[9] sits on a rectilinear throne like a block of concrete and bears the book of the Law on his knees. Cruelly he permits Satan to employ his perverted energy to assail Job's faith. As Wicksteed observes,[10] the fire-swathed heads of Job and his wife on either side of Satan represent their errors, which must acquire full form to be cast out. Two sorrowful attendants deprecate Satan's project: one bears a symbolic scroll, while the other repudiates the accuser with a curious gesture of his hands (he holds his right hand higher, Satan his left). A third attendant, who carries a book, approves of Satan's attack. Of the six Sons of God present, two are depositing scrolls, or scrolls and books, before the throne: between two scrolls, a book is just visible.

---

[7] Wicksteed, *Blake's Vision* (1910), pp. 18-20.

[8] Cf. S. Foster Damon, *Blake's* Job: *William Blake's* Illustrations of the Book of Job (Providence, R. I.: Brown UP, 1966), p. 4. Damon identifies books with the Law and scrolls with inspiration.

[9] Lindberg, *Blake's Illustrations*, p. 204.

[10] Joseph H. Wicksteed, *Blake's Vision of the Book of Job*, 2nd ed. (London: Dent; New York: Dutton, 1924), pp. 56-57.

Satan's melancholy attendants have their counterparts in the two Sons, of whom likewise one has his right leg and the other his left leg advanced. The clean-shaven Sons—one nude, the other semi-nude and, like his wife, garlanded—are uncorrupted by Experience. Living in freedom and at ease, they challenge their father's devotion to the Law, though two children are studying the latter as their grandfather desires. The right thumb of Job and his standing son (and the right thumb of the spirit above who sides with Satan) point to the passage in dispute, but the winged angels to whom Job appeals carry scrolls and support his sons. A rocky hill replacing the grass-covered height of pl. 1 is visible beside Job's wife, for Job is to become alienated from nature as the poets see it. However, three trees foreshadowing the crosses on Calvary separate the sons in their spiritual liberty from the degenerating landscape behind, just as in pl. 13 a balustrade separates the awakened Job and his wife from the barren mountain looming in the background. Twined round the trees are vines that represent the Vine of Christ that Blake twice alludes to in prose but that also suggest the serpent (E536, 555/ K571, 606; cf. John xv.1). On shelves beside Job are a sheepdog and a book perhaps representing his livestock and the Law, which he takes respectively for his material and spiritual wealth.

The margin clarifies and enriches the main design. At the bottom, Job and his wife are portrayed as a shepherd and shepherdess in Innocence. At the sides, vegetable Gothic tracery rising from stems rooted in the ground is the abode of a peacock, a parrot, nesting birds, and angels weeping over the pillars of cloud and fire that guided the Israelites through Sinai (Exod. xiii.21)—pillars, here, of false guidance by a god of law. At the top is a feature unique in the Job engravings: when the two sides of the cloud barrier cross the margin, instead of merging above it they turn outwards at a point linked by threads to the Gothic tracery; the linkage indicates that the inscriptions in the outward directed portions of cloud are to be read as visionary, not Urizenic. One of these inscriptions—"I shall see God" (Job xix.26)—is fulfilled when the true deity appears to Job in pl. 17. Outside the lines of cloud altogether, the quotation "We shall awake up in thy likeness" (Ps. xvii.15) points to the interpenetration or identity of humanity and Deity treated in the inscriptions on the same later plate. However, the quotations *between* the turned back segments identify the enthroned god as the Ancient of Days (Dan. vii.9) and that Angel of the Divine Presence whom Jesus defies in "The Everlasting Gospel" charging him with creating "this Body of Mine" and "Hell's dark jaws" (E521 [ll. 30, 32]/ K754 [ll. 30, 32]). He is also named, in Hebrew, "King Jehovah," for he is the Father split off from the Son and sunk into a Urizenic state.[11]

In this and other plates, Job's god is made in his own image and his heaven is both within him and above him—"What is Above is Within" (*J* 71:6). The Angel of the Divine Presence is at once the tyrant in his psyche and the creator upon whose work the Divine Humanity that manifests in Jesus imposes a merciful limit. Job's devotion to this Angel's Law has begun to divide the family that was united in pl. 1.

The third plate shows Satan, now sprouting the bat's wings of the spectrous reasoner, gleefully emitting lightning like that of the diabolical god in pl. 11 to destroy the children of Job and their families as they feast "in their eldest Brother's house" (Job i.18). Blake deplores "the Two Impossibilities Chastity & Abstinence, Gods of the Heathen" (E275/ K776), and the spirit of the Law that Job cleaves to murders his clean-shaven antinomian sons as well as his garlanded daughter-in-law, who appeared on pl. 2. Appropriately most of the light rises from the children's level, while Satan dispenses rather the Miltonic "darkness visible" (*PL*, I, 63). In the margin, scorpions and fragments of a scaly serpent indicate a descent into a debased and hostile external nature.

On his reappearance in the margin of pl. 4, Satan walks on the curved surface of the Newtonian globe with his left leg forward and bears the sword and, projecting below his right wing, the shield of corporeal war. On the top corners of the central design are two prostrate figures, perhaps his victims, and at the bottom of the page is a thunderbolt and also devouring fire carried over from the previous plate. Sitting beside severely rectilinear columns and under a tree different from that in pl. 1, Job is receiving news of external disasters from two messengers running with left feet forward. A third, visible below the lifted knee of the first, has his right leg advanced, probably to symbolise Job's imminent spiritual fall. Job still has a few sheep left, but the forest of nature has lost

---

[11] See p. 161 above.

its water and looms larger than in the first central design, the cathedral is smaller and further away, and the mountain is now barren.

The Fall itself is depicted in pl. 5. Slipping from a throne with a curved backrest and three steps (instead of the two steps and austere rectangular block of the earlier throne), the Divine Humanity possesses both book and scroll, for in Him the Law has not yet been sundered from the Gospel, though his hold on the scroll is already precarious:

> When Satan first the black bow bent
> And the Moral Law from the Gospel rent,
>   He forg'd the Law into a Sword
> And spill'd the blood of mercy's Lord.
> (*J*, pl. 52, poem, ll. 17-20)

His halo is darkening, but He is surrounded by twelve angels instead of the six Sons of God allowed to the Angel of the Divine Presence. As Job lapses into the power of his own Selfhood, Satan—the accuser of sin and the embodiment of that Selfhood—finds himself falling from the divine circle. When he killed Job's children in pl. 3, he exulted, but although he now has the additional pleasure of tormenting Job's body, his expression is one of shock and dismay. From the little he has left, Job gives to a blind, lame beggar, but he gives self-righteously with his left hand to the approval of namby-pamby angels of self-applause. He sits on blocks resembling those of the diabolical deity's throne in pl. 2, and a Druid trilithon has replaced the Gothic cathedral of true religion. Behind the beggar, the foliage of trees may still be present, but the barren mountain is beginning to proliferate into a sterile range. In the margin are two horrified angels, tormenting flames, and parts of two or more serpents; in front of the flames, harmoniously interlacing stems—two on each side—of Urizenic vegetation underline the parallels between pls. 2 and 5 and the blood-curdling degeneration that has taken place since the testing of Job began. On each side, one stem is spiky and one smooth, for the fallen world is a world of conflicting contraries.[12]

---

[12] Kathleen Raine, *The Human Face of God: William Blake and the Book of Job* (London: Thames and Hudson, 1982), p. 72.

By pl. 6, Satan has recovered his self-possession and is happily afflicting Job with boils which make his sense of touch a source of agony; four arrows in Satan's right hand are aimed at Job's four other senses.[13] The afflicted man has exchanged his flowing robe for sackcloth, and behind him smoke billows from a burning house—perhaps his home.[14] Ruins are beginning to dot the landscape, which has turned into a treeless desert, for Blake is portraying the fall not only of an individual but of a country and all humankind. On the left, the sun is setting behind the Sea of Time and Space. No longer graced by the compassionate angels of earlier plates, the margins are inhabited by Satan's spectrous followers and by fauna and flora representing sterility and voraciousness. An emblematic broken vessel, perhaps the source of the potsherd with which Job scraped his skin (ii.8), is also there, and a piece of a broken shepherd's crook reminds us of his lost Innocence, but the inscription shows that he still insists on blessing God.

When the three friends make a dramatic entrance in pl. 7, Job is continuing to defend his Maker—"What!" reads the inscription, "shall we recieve Good at the hand of God & shall we not also recieve Evil" (ii.10)—but he is sitting slackly, his body drained with exhaustion and his face utterly dejected as he looks at a heavily outlined structure on his left: this structure appears to be a cross of which part is cut off by the margin indicating that Job has faith in a redemption that remains hidden in the future. The ruins and the barren mountains are multiplied, while the last rays of the sun blaze up from behind the range. A sorrowful shepherd and shepherdess, each under a bare tree, and two mourning women are found in the margin.

Bowed down opposite Job's wife and before an ominously heavy stone archway, the three friends—Eliphaz, Bildad and Zophar—offer Job their silent sympathy in the eighth plate while he laments that he was ever born. Enlarged mountains and smoke or smoke-like clouds occupy the background. Even the ruins, signs of former human habitation, have vanished. A little Urizenic vegetation and raindrops dripping from clouds appear in the lower margin.

---

[13] Damon, *Blake's* Job, p. 22.
[14] Lindberg, *Blake's Illustrations*, p. 223.

Eliphaz's description in Job iv of his terrifying nocturnal vision of a god of righteousness is depicted in pl. 9, but the righteousness turns out to be that of the Law, for with his left hand the speaker directs his listeners' attention to an image of a god with his own face; the divine countenance is also similar to Job's. Indeed Job, Eliphaz, Job's god, Eliphaz's god and the beggar on pl. 5 closely resemble each other. Rays from the hem of this god's robe are drawn down through the cloud barrier into the sky beside the alarmed Job and above his equally uneasy wife. In the margin, the trees are larger and barer than those of pl. 7, their bark is no longer visible, and their branches are bending to the ground, perhaps to take root and proliferate as Urizen's Tree of Mystery and Nature.

Job's corporeal friends unmask their spiritual enmity in pl. 10, which combines the themes of mortality and accusation of sin. The friends, now resembling the accusers portrayed on pl. 93 of *Jerusalem* (E253/ K740), point at Job with six hands, but his wife, tenderly touching his right arm with her right hand, will not desert him. Though pleading for compassion ("Have pity upon me! O ye my friends" [xix.21]) and self-righteous in asserting his sinlessness ("The Just Upright Man is laughed to scorn" [xii.4]), he retains the faith in God that Satan had counted on his abandoning ("when he hath tried me I shall come forth like gold" [xxiii.10]). The lowest inscription quotes words of Job on the fleetingness of human life: "he cometh up like a flower & is cut down" (xiv. 2)—there is a flower below the foremost accuser's left hand. Above Job's wife stands a large tomb with a hint of the Cross in its design. The conflict between devouring judgment and redeeming faith is carried over into the margin. Here chains appear to be attached to two figures joined by a tapering bow, and, as Wicksteed notes,[15] the images recall lines in Blake's *America* written thirty years earlier to describe British oppression of the Thirteen Colonies:

> ...look over the Atlantic sea;
> A bended bow is lifted in heaven, & a heavy iron chain
> Descends link by link from Albion's cliffs across the sea
> to bind

---

[15] Wicksteed, *Blake's Vision* (1910), p. 86.

Brothers & sons of America...
  (*A* 3:6-9)

Reinforcing the hold of the chains and the bow, spectrous wings attached to the lower corners of the central design show how far the world has declined; the wings are underpinned by what may be branchless stems from the Tree of Mystery. In the bottom margin, two birds of prey clutch a snake and a mouse—the owl's talons resemble the fingers of the accusers above—while two scrolls between the birds are signs of faith and hope.

On reaching pl. 11, the observer confronts Job at the nadir and the turning point of his suffering. The three comforters have been transformed into fiends of hell,[16] two with scales and claws and one wielding a chain from the margin of the preceding design. The sihouette of the mountains has become the upper boundary of the infernal flame behind Job, over which hangs a band of cloud luminous at the edge, very much like the cloud barrier of pls. 2, 5 and 9. The afflicted man is in the same posture as in pl. 6, where Satan covers him with boils; his feet are identically disposed, his hands again raised. The evidence that Job's faith has not been annihilated is relegated to the margin, as the desperate man twists his face away from the fearful god above him, a god who combines the spikes—now swollen into huge tufts—of the Angel of the Divine Presence,[17] the lightning which Satan poured on Job's children, short horns,[18] and the cloven hoof of the popular image of the Devil. This monster, wreathed around with the serpent of Eden and of nature, points with his right hand to a heaven centred on the Tablets of the Law and with his left to a hell of punishment for sin. Freed from the illusion that his comforters are true friends, Job can now see what God he has been obeying. Blake inscribes quotations from the New Testament—"Satan himself is transformed into an Angel of Light & his Ministers into Ministers of Righteousness" (II Cor. xi.14-15) and "Who opposeth & exalteth himself above all that is called God or is Worshipped" (II Thess. ii.4)—to confirm that one can unknowingly worship the Devil. But Job's complaints, borrowed from the Old Testament book, culmi-

---

[16] Lindberg, *Blake's Illustrations*, p. 266.
[17] See n9 above.
[18] Raine, *Human Face*, p. 198.

nate in an expression of faith that his Redeemer will "stand...upon the Earth" (xix.25) and that he himself will see God, a prophecy fulfilled on pl. 17. Though his mortal body ("wrought Image" [derived from xix.27]) will perish, his spiritual body ("my flesh" [xix.26]) will be resurrected. (Blake quotes a Pauline verse—I Cor. xv.44—about the spiritual body in the engraving of "To Tirzah" [E30/ K220], the same verse that is used to gloss Job's phrase "in my flesh" in a classical early eighteenth-century biblical commentary.)[19]

With the movement from pl. 11 to pl. 12, horror gives way to melancholy and terror to inspired teaching. Job sits subdued, his right foot advanced as it was not in pls. 8, 9 and 11, to signify his spiritual progress. While his wife, whose left foot is forward to show the correctly subordinate role of his Emanation, is still bowed down with grief, the three friends are huddled together in embarrassed silence as they smart under the rebuke of the young but inspired Elihu. This prophetic figure in a skin-tight garment, who declares that dreams can carry divine messages, comes from the left with right arm and left leg advanced: he is the contrary of the nude Satan who enters pl. 2 from the right with right leg and left arm forward. Opposite Elihu, the ominous effect of part of a massive gateway or arch is relieved by a star shining through the opening—one of twelve stars in the sky.

Although the barren mountain range is still present in pl. 12, it has begun to dwindle, and the woods last seen behind the beggar in pl. 5 reappear behind the arch. Yet this is a nocturnal scene, for although Job is partly enlightened, he has not yet cast out error and is still in the night of Experience. Accordingly his body is shown sleeping in the lower margin, where he lies with head to the right as he did in pls. 6 and 11. However, though his left hand rests on a roll of cloth enrooted in the lowly earth, his tiny emanations rise from the fabric and from a veil covering him and ascend to heaven; some carry miniature scrolls of inspiration, and those on the left are assisted by two winged angels. In the triangular space in the centre of the upper margin, a second set of twelve stars—the same divine spirit is present in both worlds.

---

[19] Matthew Henry, *Commentary on the Whole Bible* (1708-14; rpt. 6 vols. Iowa Falls: World Bible Publishers, *c.* 1980), III, 110.

Immediately above the streams of soaring emanations, are the seven stars of the Pleiades on the right and the three stars of Orion on the left. Lindberg points out that Blake, who quotes on pl. 14 the biblical verse—Job xxxviii.31—about these constellations, is following a tradition going back to St. Gregory that Orion stands for the Law, the Pleiades for the Gospels. The inscriptions selected from Elihu's speeches warn against pride, imply that it is misguided to judge God as a dispenser of rewards and punishments on the basis of moral balance sheets ("If thou sinnest, what doest thou against him, or if thou be righteous what givest thou unto him" [xxxv.6-7]), and point to the possibility of receiving heavenly inspiration. They offer, too, the hope of being redeemed from "the Pit" through "an Interpreter" and "a Ransom" (xxxiii.23-24)—that is of being liberated from Ulro through Christ.

Once he has delivered his message, Elihu's presence is no longer needed. It has reached Job's wife, too, for in pl. 13 she has recovered and shares his vision of the true God, the Divine Humanity, who has descended in a whirlwind dissolving the cloud barrier between the worlds and stretching across the design with his feet to the left, in the opposite direction to the cloven-hoofed god of Job's nightmare torment. The whirlwind's motion is clockwise, for it raises the hair of Job and of God. Unable to endure the divine manifestation, the friends bow down in terror. In the lower margin, the trees of nature reappear, now bearing some foliage but beaten to the ground by storms representing a power greater than themselves. A circle of figures in the form of the Divine Humanity is revolving in the upper margin; they face the opposite way to God in the central design but move in the same clockwise direction as the whirlwind: though God acts in both the temporal and eternal worlds, differences between them remain.

In pl. 14, a sublime representation of Eternity's mercy to caverned humanity, Blake achieves one of his greatest designs. Having taught Job the falsity of moral legalism, God reassures him that there is a higher existence to which the sufferer in the natural universe can ultimately escape. The Divine Humanity occupies the centre, His arms outstretched between two cloud barriers, for His presence is common to all realms. His advanced right foot is balanced by Job's advanced left foot, indicating a proper subordination of body to spirit, for God is within Job as well as without. The models of the creation, both temporal and eternal, that surround

Him are threefold. This holds true for the margin as well as the main design, which is based on the triple Renaissance distinction between the sublunary, the celestial and the intelligible worlds, this last transcending time and space.

From the Platonic cave, the cavern in which "man has closed himself up, till he sees all things thro' narrow chinks" (*MHH*, pl. 14), Job, his wife and the three friends look up in solemn joy through the realm of the heavenly bodies to Eternity. Here dwell "the morning Stars" or "Sons of God " (xxxviii.7), who are seen advancing with right and left feet alternately forward, for in them there is no conflict between spirit and body. Blake added the two arms cut off by the margin as an inspired afterthought to suggest that their number is infinite: in the watercolours and pencil sketches, there are only four angels.

The central design also has a psychic meaning: the cavern belongs to the senses, the sun god is probably redeemed reason riding "the horses of instruction" (*MHH*, pl. 9; *FZ* 25:3/ E314/ II, 35), while the moon goddess guides the forces of passion, and the angels represent the imaginative vision that can see Eternity.[20] Moreover, these angels advancing securely above the heads of Olympian deities proclaim Blake's conviction that Hebrew art transcends Greek.

As the lower part of the engraving is subordinate to the higher, so the side on the Divine Humanity's left has a lower status than that on His right. On the latter are the three friends in the darker half of the cavern and the lunar goddess. This goddess, silhouetted against a nocturnal background, advances her left hand and is under the left arm of the Divine Humanity, whereas the solar god is in a bright space, advances his right hand, and is under the right hand of the Divine Humanity.[21] The fingers of this hand, unlike those of His left hand, are in what Janet Warner recognises as the creative position of the equivalent members of Michelangelo's God.[22]

The margin is organised in a parallel way to the main design. The sequence of the six days of creation in Genesis allows

---

[20] Cf. Damon, *Blake's Job*, p. 38.

[21] Wicksteed, *Blake's Vision* (1924), p. 19.

[22] Janet A. Warner, *Blake and the Language of Art* (Kingston and Montreal: McGill-Queen's UP; Gloucester: Alan Sutton, 1984), p.102.

Blake to arrange his illustrations of them so that each scene is more ethereal than the one beneath,[23] and those on the Divine Humanity's right more ethereal than those on His left; on the latter side, the flames from the sea below—probably infernal flames in which "Error or Creation will be Burned Up" (E565/ K617) on pl. 16—rise higher. Corresponding to the cavern in the central design, the Sea of Time and Space in the bottom margin provides a habitat for the mighty Leviathan (a form of Satan) and, as Damon perceives,[24] surges round "a shrouded corpse" in the coils of "the worm of death." At the top of the page, a pair of winged angels, perhaps those who were horror-stricken in the margin of pl. 5, are unrolling a thread, scroll or band of cloud from beneath the Pleiades to beneath Orion symbolising the necessary resynthesis of the higher and the lower, of Gospel and Law. The angels are looking towards the two constellations, which have changed sides since pl. 12, for night has given way to the morning referred to in the title inscription, a morning associated primarily with the creation of the world of Eternity, from which the material universe condenses out in a catastrophic fall.

Having looked up to higher worlds, Job, his wife and his friends are now invited to look down so that the Divine Humanity, pointing with his left hand to the two grotesque monsters in the circle of the material globe, can persuade them that the destructive forces of this world are not unmanageable. Blake follows a well established tradition, again going back to St. Gregory, by identifying Behemoth and Leviathan, created in the beginning, as symbols of Satan before and after his Fall.[25] As the powers that govern nature, they are confined in the terrestrial sphere.[26] The bulrushes indicate that this is Egypt[27] or Africa, the continent where human history begins after the Fall (BU 28:8-10). In the cave above, the earth's surface has the flatness of the unfallen earth. Within the cave are the Pleiades and Orion—benign when they are in balance—and two angels, servants of the Divine Humanity, hover just above its upper boundary. In the margin,

---

[23] Ben F. Nelms, "Text and Designs in Illustrations of the Book of Job," BVFD, pp. 336-58 (see p. 351).

[24] Blake's Job, p. 38.

[25] Lindberg, Blake's Illustrations, p. 298.

[26] Ibid., pp. 293, 297.

[27] Damon, Blake's Job, p. 40.

Blake sketches the eagles that help Urizen to create the cosmos in *The Four Zoas* (29:8-13/ E319/ II, 150-55) and the shells and waves—"dried shells that the fish/ Have quite forsaken" (*FZ* 44:28-45:1/ E330/ III, 167-68)—that Tharmas finds in the fallen realm. On the upper corners of the central design are two winged and bearded angels recording the events of the lower world.

When we are first admitted to Job's heaven, we see a stern deity seated on a rectilinear throne pointing down with his right hand. When we have advanced from pl. 2 to pl. 16 with its mixture of serenity, violence, fear and melancholy, we find the cloud barrier between heaven and earth has dissolved and a benevolent deity on a hidden throne with round steps is giving judgment with raised right hand. In both plates the divinities have their right legs advanced and with their left hands hold the book of the Law open on their laps. In the later design, the Divine Humanity is judging Satan (who in Blake's later work is a state, not a person) according to the Law, by which he has judged others. Satan's head is wrenched back in agony as he plummets into hell accompanied by his own fire and lightning previously seen in pls. 3 and 11. Beside him fall the errors of Job and his wife, present in embryo in pl. 2 but now fully formed, recognised, and cast out. Having seen how suffering fits into the pattern of existence, the couple can lay their rebellious selfhoods to rest, and insofar as Job's wife is his Emannation, from whom he was separated at his nadir in pl. 11, from which she is absent, he is reunited with her. On either side, powerful winged angels gravely rejoice at the defeat of error.

While the deity in pl. 2 has a clear halo, God's halo in pl. 16 is populated by four infants and two winged child-spirits, the latter covering their eyes to avoid watching the horror below. These six beings should perhaps be classed with the "Infants" in Christ's halo in two of Blake's paintings of the Last Judgment, infants he describes as "representing the Eternal Creation flowing from the Divine Humanity in Jesus" and "the Eternal Births of Intellect from the divine Humanity" (E554, 562/ K444, 613).[28] The youthfulness of the four lower spirits, however, and their unsymmetrical arrangement (contrasting with what is characteristic of Blake's full representations of the Last Judgment) suggest rather the ebullience of souls newly reborn into Innocence. The distressed

---

[28] Wicksteed gives the second of these quotations (*Blake's Vision* [1910], p. 108).

winged spirits in the central panel have many counterparts in the indefinite number of unwinged figures, spirits of Eternity, covering their faces in the upper corners of the margin.

Having rejected error, Job in the next four designs alternately receives and gives—first from and to God, then from and to his fellow humans. Although he and his wife are never lifted bodily into heaven, in pl. 17 heaven descends to earth, for the cloud barrier is brought down to the level of their feet. The Divine Humanity, whose halo irradiates the still bleak scene around them, blesses Job with his right hand, and his wife or Emanation with His left. The three friends, unable to bear the sight of God since they have not yet cast out error, bow down with their backs to Him, but Bildad—it is Blake's only touch of humour in these engravings—overcomes his fear sufficiently to peep with one eye. To make it clear that the figure of the Deity is both Father and Son and that he is present within the human soul as well as being the origin of all things, Blake inscribes in the lower margin a set of texts from John x and xiv. Here the book and the scroll are reconciled and a languishing winged female holding a pen and positioned above a reference to the Third Person of the Trinity unites the classical Muse with the Christian angel, as Judaeo-Christian and Greco-Roman art were harmonised (on Blake's terms) in pl. 14. At first sight a quotation in the upper margin—"When I behold the Heavens the work of thy hands the Moon & Stars which thou hast ordained, then I say, What is Man that thou art mindful of him? & the Son of Man that thou visitest him" (Ps. viii.3-4)—seems to imply an orthodox view of creation, but "heaven," as St. Augustine believed when he expounded the first verse of Genesis (*Confessions*, xii, 13), can mean the intelligible realm, which Blake calls Eternity; Job and his wife have looked up at this realm in pl. 14, and it has become apparent on earth in pl. 17. Alternatively, Blake may be referring to God's limitation of the Fall when He bound "the Stars/ In merciful Order" (*J* 49:54-55).

Having seen God—both the Father and the Son—face to face, Job has built an altar of twelve stones, and in pl. 18, with his right leg drawn back as it was four plates earlier, he makes an offering in a cruciform posture. Now that he has cast Satan out, he discards the sackcloth that he donned when the Devil assailed him on pl. 6. The sacrificial flame rises from the level of his heart and ascends into the halo of the Divine Humanity, which constitutes the spiritual sun. Its rays pierce the cloud barrier to reach the earth—there are four rays on the side corresponding to the Divine Humanity's right, only three on the opposite side.[29] Beneath the four rays, Job's wife is bowed in prayer, her face visible in profile, like Job's, while the friends are relegated to the less favoured side and their faces are hidden. On the left, the light of the rising physical sun is just visible above the mountain top.[30] The recovery of nature continues with the reappearance of individual trees; between the trunks on the left, the water just visible on the first plate is restored.[31] As the quotations remind us, Job is following God's prescription by praying for his friends, who have incurred the divine displeasure (xlii.8). Blake takes the opportunity to inculcate his favourite Christian doctrine of forgiveness by inscribing Matthew v.44 in the lower left hand corner of the margin. Besides the book and the counterbalancing scrolls, the border is adorned with a palette and brushes, probably to indicate, as Wilson suggests, that Blake forgives the enemies who have ridiculed his art.[32] The ripe corn and the music-making angels show that it is spiritual harvest time for Job and his wife—a theme developed in the margins of the two succeeding designs.

In pls. 12 through 18, the left side (the stage right) has consistently been the more visionary. After being occupied by Elihu in number 12, it has become the side of Job's wife, while the friends have been relegated to the right. In pl. 15, the Pleiades, representing the Gospels, stand over the heads of the redeemed couple, while Orion, representing the Law, stands over the friends. In pl. 16 the large angel on the left is higher than his counterpart as Job and his wife are on higher ground than the friends, the flame which devours error rises to the left, and there are more child spirits in the left side of the divine halo. God Himself stands on the left side of pl. 17, and fertilising water is visible between the trees on the left side of pl. 18. The friends are absent from the remaining three plates, but Blake seems to take special pains to show that the right side of the final design is *not* inferior: the sun's rays reach far further than they did in pl. 1, the top of Job's harp

---

[29] Wicksteed, *Blake's Vision* (1910), p. 120-21.
[30] Lindberg, *Blake's Illustrations*, p. 326.
[31] *Ibid.*
[32] Mona Wilson, *The Life of William Blake* (London: Nonesuch Press, 1927), p. 271.

and even his left hand are raised high, and the three sons on his
left are dressed in garments like the prophetic Elihu's.

In pl. 19 the grain that stood in the borders of pl. 18 has
moved into the centre of the picture replacing the two ewes of the
parallel pl. 4. The tree, apparently bearing figs, is not the tree of
that earlier design, and the former overpowering rectilinear wall is
succeeded by lighter, less symmetrical masonry—perhaps a ruin
but high enough to give shelter from the wind. Taught by Experi-
ence, Job and his wife humbly accept charity from their peers
instead of bestowing it complacently on an inferior as Job did in
pl. 5. The inscriptions emphasise God's mercy to humans and
birds, while spirits in the margin—many, if not all, female—sow
seed above and offer abundance of fruit below, for "every Natural
Effect has a Spiritual Cause" (*M* 26:44). Eight of the spirits in an
intermediate position look happily on the scene. Two palms of
spiritual victory, accompanied by roses and lilies, send their
foliage up to the top corners and provide a counterpart to the
towering plants of the fallen world in pl. 5.

Of all the plates, the twentieth has the most exquisite
margin. The leaves, fruit and stems of four vines make a living
pattern that recalls the Gothic tracery springing from the ground
in the border of pl. 2, contrasts with the sinister interlacings at the
edges of pl. 5, and surpasses in beauty the palms of pl. 19. Two
pairs of small winged angels—one pair kissing—and a large lyre
and matching lute contribute to the atmosphere of newly achieved
blessedness, while the vine has the same relation to Christ as the
vine in pl. 2 and the lowest inscription, taken from Psalms
cxxxix.8, assures us that there is no state, not even the hell of pl.
11, from which God is absent. In the central design, Job is sitting
in a lavishly decorated round room telling his story to his daugh-
ters. Scenes on the panelled walls illustrate his words, so that
between them this design and the margin allude to the four
arts—literature, visual representation, music and architecture.
Behind Job the young Satan kills his ploughman on one side and,
with the aid of winged followers, a number of his servants on the
other. Above the patriarch's head, the Divine Humanity in His
whirlwind beckons Job and his wife to rise while He indicates with
His downturned palm displeasure with the friends.[33] At a lower

[33] Lindberg, *Blake's Illustrations*, p. 342.

level, two images of the Urizenic god of pl. 11 overshadow two
bowed figures, who may be Job and his wife; in narrow panels
above the Urizenic faces flanked by lightning are two serpents.
The inlaid floor consists of interlacing arcs belonging to circles
contained in a greater circle: this may symbolise individual identi-
ties contained in the one Divine Essence.[34]

Having begun his book with a picture of unruffled piety,
Blake closes it with a scene of sober joy. In the last plate, which is
the converse of the first, the family of ten reappears in the same
disposition and under the same tree as before, but its members are
standing instead of sitting and praising God with the musical
instruments which formerly hung unused. The words of their song,
engraved in the upper margin, are the first words of "the song of
Moses...and the song of the Lamb" from Revelation xv.3, for Old
Testament justice and New Testament mercy are no longer at
odds.[35] As Lindberg puts it, Law and Gospel are now united.[36] The
sheep which constitute Job's wealth are restored, but not the barns
and cathedral. His sheepdog is alert instead of asleep, and the
presence of lambs speaks of renewal. Being inappropriate to the
high state depicted, the trees of nature and the water behind them,
resurrected in pl. 18, have again vanished. The moon, now wax-
ing, and the sun, now rising, have changed sides: both are enhan-
ced, for the sun's rays extend beyond the tree[37] and the moon is
accompanied by two stars instead of one. Similarly the sacrificial
lamb and ox have exchanged positions in the bottom of the mar-
gin. The containing tent of pl. 1 again surrounds the main design,
and the verse inscribed on the altar (Heb. x.6) insists that true
piety is of the spirit. The family is "conversing with Paradise" by
means of the arts (E559/ K609), but a narrow barren strip at the
top level of the mountain range in the background reminds us that
while we are on this side of the grave we must remain bodily in the
world of nature.

Illustrations of The Book of Job is not merely an adorn-
ment to a literary text but a great work of art in its own right.
When Blake first portrays Job, he is still in a state of Innocence,

---

[34] Cf. pp. 71-72 and 157-58 above.
[35] Damon, *Blake's* Job, p.52.
[36] *Blake's Illustrations*, p.351.
[37] Wicksteed, *Blake's Vision* (1924), pp. 208-09.

but his devotion to the external observance of the Law has brought
him to the brink of falling. In pl. 2, battle lines are drawn both
above and below: Satan and the Angel of the Divine Presence
agree to test Job by the touchstone of the Law to the sorrow of
wiser beings in their presence; Job contends on behalf of the letter
divorced from the spirit both with his sons and with angels. Soon
Satan rejoices in slaughtering Job's antinomian sons and destroy-
ing his riches. Job, faithfully supported by his wife, continues his
piety when he gives charity as an act of obedience, and as the
Divine Humanity falls asleep within him, he descends into the
barren world of the natural scientist, while Satan—like Urizen in
the book that bears his name—finds himself outcast from heaven.
Afflicted with boils, Job is visited by the three 'comforters,' but
they turn into accusers of sin, whereupon Job discovers that the
lawgiving god he has been worshipping is a vindictive demon. He
is now ready for the wisdom of Elihu, prophet of inspiration and
redemption through Christ, who is the Interpreter and the Ransom.
Appearing in a whirlwind, God confirms Elihu's insight, shows
Job the relation of time to Eternity, and demonstrates that Behe-
moth and Leviathan, the satanic powers of destruction, can be
contained and transcended. The errors of Job and his wife are
annihilated in a Last Judgment, and the Divine Humanity—who is
Jehovah, Jesus, and the Holy Spirit—blesses them both. In a
Christlike manner, Job offers up his heart to God and prays for his
misguided friends, and he and his wife accept loving charity from
their neighbours. Nature recovers its visionary gleam, and he uses
the arts to tell the story of fall and redemption while his whole
family unites to make music in praise of the Divine Humanity.

      Most lovers of Blake first encounter him, as I did, through
the delicacy and vigour of lyrics that celebrate beauty, protest
oppression, and convey a consciousness of supernatural powers.
Initial delight can arouse a curiosity that will quickly lead the
reader not only to the rich variety of his pictures and the
incisiveness of his prose, but to the strangeness of the language
and ideas in his so-called prophetic books.

      Undeniably Blake is eccentric in his espousal of extreme
views: he scorns Venetian, Flemish and Dutch art; he recklessly

assaults natural science; he uncritically accepts ill-founded theories of Druidism; and he spurns the church without which his beloved Gothic architecture would never have been created. Yet despite years of neglect, indigence, and sometimes mockery, he defies the materialist philosophy that binds souls to earth and bodies to servitude. *The Four Zoas* is the workshop in which he overcomes his dismay at the failure of political revolution and his pessimism about the creation and lays out the universal myth that, he comes to believe, is embodied in the Bible and in all great literature and is acted out in world history, in the events of his own time, and in individual lives. Thus he can see Albion in the scriptural Jacob, Urizen in the classical Jupiter and Rahab in Chaucer's Wife of Bath.[38] Britain to him is as sacred as Palestine, and the geographies of both countries (as *Jerusalem* demonstrates in too much detail) are created by the fragmentation of the cosmic man. To his visionary eye, nature tells the same tale: Los appears in the sun, Los's Gate in a rainbow, the Plough of Nations in the constellation named the Plough, and the debates of spirits in tempests.[39] Hence he can declare, "To Me This World is all One continued Vision of Fancy or Imagination" (E702/ K793).

Blake's vision is supported by an intellectual construct drawn from elements as diverse as Gnosticism, Renaissance syncretism and seventeenth-century British antinomianism; the teachings of Boehme, Berkeley and Swedenborg; and traditional hermeneutics uncovering the 'spiritual sense' of the Bible along with Enlightenment indignation at much of its literal meaning. This enables him to achieve a synthesis of religion, metaphysics, psychology, history and aesthetics such as eludes his younger contemporary Coleridge. With its aid he not only interprets contemporary events in France and Britain but extends, in his *Milton*, the line of the English epic that runs through *Piers Plowman*, *The Faerie Queene* and *Paradise Lost*, and in the vast meditation of *Jerusalem* he plumbs the fallen state of the physical, psychic and historical worlds to reach a transcendent vision of Eternity. Fin-

---

[38] Frye, *Fearful Symmetry: A Study of William Blake* (1947: rpt. Boston: Beacon, 1962), p.364; E756/ K852; Damon, *A Blake Dictionary: The Ideas and Symbols of William Blake*, 2nd printing (1967; rpt. Hanover and London: UP of New England for Brown UP, 1988), p. 79.

[39] E722 (ll. 55-58)/ K818 (ll. 55-58); W. H. Stevenson, ed., *The Poems of William Blake* (London: Longman, 1971), pp. 694, 758, 740.

ally, combining immediate appeal with profundity, as he had in early lyrics, he shows in a well ordered series of engravings how close is much of his creed to the faith given expression in traditional interpretation of the Book of Job.

PART II

Notes on Interpretive Criticism

1910 to 1984

Notes on Criticism for Chapter 2

Poetical Sketches

Critical disagreements about this comparatively simple collection hinge on the degree of subtlety with which the young Blake can be credited, the extent to which concepts of his maturity are foreshadowed in his juvenilia, and how far his sympathy with the rebellious American colonies lies behind his treatment of war. Michael Phillips has shown that the poet retained an interest in the volume: at intervals throughout his life he presented newly hand-corrected copies to friends (1970: 41-43).

While Gleckner (1982b: 14-15) reasonably asserts that there is no evidence to show whether the order of the poems is Blake's, Phillips (1973: 25) observes that the book does move from lyrics through drama to a biblical prophetic form, and McGowan (1979: 143) perceives a distinct progression from cyclic nature myth through secular love songs and poems of political import to such expressions of personal dissatisfaction as "Contemplation."

"To Spring," "To Summer," "To Autumn," "To Winter"

Several critics follow Frye (1947: 182) in seeing the germ of Orc in Blake's Summer and of Urizen in his Winter and also endorse Bloom's (1963: 15) and Miner's (1969: 259-60) view that imagery borrowed from the Song of Songs (or Canticles) shows that Blake's Spring is the divine lover of the biblical poem. Pointing to the tradition identifying that lover with Christ, Tolley (1973: 96-103) asserts that "To Spring" hints at his coming and thus marks an escape from cyclical return. Such an escape, says Gleckner (1982b: 64-75), is hinted at both by allusions to Christ and by the synthesis in "To Autumn" of bud, blossom and fruit, and of morning and evening, but the arrival of the Antichrist in "To Winter" challenges its validity. McGowan (1979: 125-27) judiciously maintains that the clear imminence of spring at the end of "To Winter" implies that the temporal cycle will be repeated.

The abundant literary echoes in the quaternary lead Hartman (1969) to argue that its real subject is poetry: working in the recent tradition of Collins's "Ode on the Poetical Character" and

Gray's "The Progress of Poesy," Blake sees the poetic spirit mov-
ing west from the biblical realm of "To Spring" to the Britain of
"To Autumn," while "To Winter" is a tribute to the Ossianic and
Norse muse. Similarly Chayes (1972) theorizes that the speaker is
a self-satisfied neoclassical poet who insists that British writers
have nothing more to learn from the charioted Apollo who is
Summer, but he meets the English poetic tradition in "To
Autumn," which echoes Milton's "Lycidas" and Marvell's "The
Garden" and teaches that earth's products can be refined into
spirit; realising that Winter is not invincible, he sees that a yet
higher kind of poetry can be made from the suffering it inflicts,
and in "To Spring," which should be printed last, he summons the
Hebrew muse to marry the English land. In McGowan's view
(1979: 129), the seasonal phases apply not only to nature and the
arts, but to sexual desire and fulfilment and to the stages of a hum-
an life and of civilization.

　　　　Thomson's *The Seasons* (Lowery 1940: 148-55) and
Spenser's "Mutabilitie Cantos" (Gleckner 1982b: 62-63) have
been singled out as Blake's major sources: the former emphasises
the ever-repeated cycle; the latter proclaims that this cycle will be
succeeded by an eternal state (vii.59; viii.2). Bateson (1957: 97)
posits that Blake's blank verse is modelled on Akenside's.

"To the Evening Star," "To Morning"

　　　　Some critics believe that these poems portray the daily
cycle, during which the nocturnal dew offers some protection
(Nurmi 1976: 40) or the sun returns to expel the necessary evil of
night (McGowan 1979: 127-28). According to Ehrstine, the star
represents transcendence of the struggle between predator and prey
(1967: 93-94).

　　　　Other critics see a more sombre picture. Although Bloom
(1965: 968) discerns the state of Innocence in "To the Evening
Star," he detects something of the cruel nature goddess of Blake's
epics in the virgin morning who urges the sun to hunt. While
Schorer (1946: 415) perceives in the former poem nothing more
sinister than a movement from "idyllic reverie" to realistic obser-
vation, Gleckner (1982b: 86-93) emphasises the star's retreat, the
dew's feebleness, and the introduction of carnivores to dispel the
previous tranquillity. The Evening Star is the planet Venus, and

Wagenknecht (1973: 33-37, 50, 56) conceives the piece as essentially erotic and a foreshadowing of the mature poet's identification of the creation with the Fall: it opens with an impression of a bridal bed blessed by Venus, whose tears decline into the dews of fallen nature, where sexual creativeness operates in a realm of dangerous passions symbolised by savage beasts.

Lowery (1940: 97-101) locates as major sources Spenser's "Epithalamion," ll. 285-95 and 148-51; Gleckner (1982b: 78, 80, 88-89) adds *PL*, IV, 598-609, VI, 1-21, and VIII, 510-20).

"How sweet I roam'd from field to field"

In 1806 Benjamin Heath Malkin reported in *A Father's Memoirs of His Child* that Blake wrote this lyric when he was not yet fourteen (Bentley 1969: 428). Does the cage, then, symbolise the threat of apprenticeship to a fashionable artist (Bateson 1957: 99), matrimony (Damon 1924: 256), or possessive love (Knights 1971: 54-55)? Ehrstine (1967: 219) believes that the speaker recoils from physical sexuality and wrongly imagines that her lover mocks her; Simmons and J. Warner (1973: 297-98, 304) argue that a satanic Phoebus Apollo represses her desire and subjects her to the control that governs Apollonian art, an angry outburst of Dionysian inspiration being part of her reaction; Bloom (1963: 19) holds that she passes from Innocence to Experience, less persuasively that her passage represents the fall of nature. Rejecting Bloom's view (1963: 18) that the prince of love and Phoebus are the same person and her gaoler, McGowan (1979: 133-35) maintains that the speaker is a young male poet inspired by Phoebus and imprisoned by the prince of love, but that his captivity has a pleasant side for he continues to sing. Ostriker (1982: 161) regards the speaker's gender as ambiguous.

"Memory, hither come"

While Schorer (1946: 403) argues that this song combines the cheerfulness of Milton's "L'Allegro" with the melancholy of his "Il Penseroso," McGowan (1979: 137) regards it as a Penseroso poem, its Allegro counterpart being "I love the jocund dance." Blake may be mocking the speaker for passively seeking poetry in memory instead of imagination (Ehrstine 1967: 22-23), for concentrating on trivialities (Gleckner 1982b: 52-53), or for clinging in the daytime to memory that leads to self-centred nocturnal brooding (Knights 1971: 59).

"Mad Song"

The speaker has been described as one who insanely seeks in darkness instead of in imaginative perception an escape from the Newtonian world of fixed space and time (Bloom 1963: 19-20); as one who shuns the light of truth that blinded Homer and Milton and fitfully visited Lear in his madness (Phillips 1973: 8-16); as an inspired poet who rejects the day world of reason for the night world of energy and is widely reputed to be mad (Duplantier 1979); and as a member of a society that ignores his insight into the tyranny that enslaves it (Ehrstine 1967: 89-90). In the speaker's imprisonment in his own consciousness of space and time, Frye (1947: 179) sees the germ of the mature poet's concept of the spectre.

Lowery notes Blake's debt to the six mad songs of Percy's *Reliques of Ancient English Poetry* and to Edgar's impersonation of a mad beggar in Shakespeare's *King Lear* (1940: 161-65).

"Fresh from the dewy hill, the merry year"

What to Damon (1924: 258) appears a fine expression of first love seems to Gardner (1968: 39) one of a series of mediocre lyrics associated with the author's courtship and early married life. Ehrstine (1967: 14-15) regards the speaker, who must wait till darkness before society lets him call on the maid, as about to enter Experience. In McGowan's view (1979: 139-40), love awes the youth into silence during the day and inspires him to song at night, but to Tolley (1973: 105) the paradise he sings of is an illusion springing from infatuation. Agreeing with Tolley, Gleckner (1982b: 44-46) stresses that the eternal state that only "seems" (ll. 15, 16) in the first four stanzas gives way to a temporal state in the fifth.

"To the Muses"

As Holloway observes (1968: 15), Mount Ida, near Homer's Troy, alludes to Greek poetry, while the sun's "chambers of the East," echoing Ps. xix.4-5 (Bateson 1957: 95), allude to Hebrew poetry. Blake may be pointing to both as sources of the English poetic tradition (Damon 1967: 331), a tradition whose eighteenth-century decadence he laments in eighteenth-century poetic diction (Bloom 1963: 21). But it is the Greeks who recognise nine muses, daughters of Memory, and Frye (1947: 179) perceives here a foreshadowing of Blake's future rejection of that faculty in favour of inspiration. Ehrstine (1967: 5-6, 22) suggests it is to the Greek muses that the speaker, unable to compose poetry, may be misguidedly appealing.

"Gwin, King of Norway"

In addition to specifying his sources—mainly Chatterton's "Godred Crovan" of 1769 (Damon 1924: 258-59; 1967: 170) and "Hardyknute" in Percy's *Reliques* (Lowery 1940: 165-67)—critics have followed Erdman (1954a: 14-15 [15-16]) in perceiving a covert expression of sympathy with the American rebels against George III and have discussed whether the defeat of tyranny portrayed is permanent. Frye (1947: 181) thinks the question is left open, Bloom (1963: 21) that the victory is final, and Gleckner (1982b: 118) that there is no indication anything has been gained by the battle and the poem is anti-war. McGowan (1979: 142) argues that the imagery surrounding Gordred shows that he is no more admirable than Gwin .

l. 53 **Barraton**—from Berrathon in Macpherson's *Ossian* (Damon 1924: 259).

"Blind-man's Buff"

Embarrassed by the uncharacteristic moral of this poem, in which, as Schorer observes (1946: 190), Blake shows the need for law, Gleckner (1982b: 23-25) tries without much success to find glimmers of subversive intent. Ehrstine (1967: 79-82) maintains that it depicts a lapse from Innocence into a state where law prevails.

l. 49 **Hodge**—a diminutive form of Roger.

"King Edward the Third"

There are three main views of what Lowery (1940: 117) recognises as a fragmentary imitation of Shakespeare's *Henry V*—that it is jingoistic, or ironic, or expressive of mixed feelings about war and nationalism. Frye (1947: 179-80) regards it as a defence of the Whig association of economic progress with liberty, while Damon finds it pervaded by adolescent patriotism (1924: 260) and remains unconvinced (1967: 228-29) by the counter-argument of Erdman. According to the latter (1954a: 60-65, 71-73 [63-68, 74-77]), the piece echoes Gray's "The Bard," with its curse on the seed of the aggressor Edward I, and its major sources are Joshua Barnes's *History of Edward III* (1688) and Rapin de Thoyras' *History of England* (translation 1723-31), which emphasise that Edward III's cruelty in France was punished by the Black Death and civil war. Erdman's claim that Blake is subtly exposing Edward's wickedness is regarded as plausible though inconclusive by Holloway (1968: 55), partly accepted by Ostriker (1977: 874), and heartily endorsed by Ehrstine (1967: 65-74), Nurmi (1976: 42), and Gleckner (1982b: 101-10). Ostriker believes an attack on militarism co-exists with sympathy for the misguided and respect for their valour; Ehrstine sees Edward as unknowingly a tyrant and self-blinded by his rationalisations; Nurmi considers the rulers' talk about liberty too overblown to be taken seriously and the King's case to be thoroughly undermined by William; and Gleckner maintains that verbal allusions to *Paradise Lost* and *Paradise Regained* show that Edward champions the militarist values espoused by Milton's Satan and rejected by his Christ. Bloom (1963: 20) accepts the presence of irony but complains that Blake has not made it clear enough, and he suggests (1965: 969) that there may be satire of James Thomson's Whig poem *Liberty*, echoes of which are discerned by Lowery (1940: 141-48). Noting the inconsistent attitude to war, Lowery conjectures that the jingoistic passages are imitative, while Blake's own ideas are expressed in the Bishop's praise of the arts of peace in scene 2

(1940: 126-27). Erdman, however, (1954a: 75-79 [79-83]) perceives in this scene a cunning plan to enlist the merchants' support for an unjust war, and Gardner (1968: 31-32) reads it as a satire on such panegyrics of a happy, prosperous London as those in Thomson's "Summer" (1727), ll. 1457-78, and Dyer's *The Fleece* (1757), III, 625-30—the satire being directed at the alliance of George III, the Anglican hierarchy, the merchants, and the Royal Navy.

Anachronistically reading Blake's later philosophy into the minstrel's song that celebrates the defeat of primeval giants by the legendary Trojan founder of Britain, Damon (1924: 261-62) suggests it may have an allegorical level: the conqueror could be the true self escaping from reason (the Greeks) and overcoming the natural man (the island). Frye (1947: 182) sees a parallel between the Trojan refugees who overran Britain and the Israelites of the Exodus who escaped from Egypt and conquered Canaan.

"Prologue Intended for a Dramatic Piece of King Edward the Fourth"

Erdman (1954a: 27 [29]) views this Prologue as an oblique allusion to the American rebellion and argues that it first blames God for the war and then inconsistently asserts that God is liable to punish the kings and nobles who are its cause. Regarding the speaker as an invented character who is misled by Milton's attribution of warlike qualities to God and Messiah, Gleckner (1982b: 111-16) supposes Blake to imply that only the mental war waged by the voice of the prophet can bring peace.

"Prologue to King John"

According to Ehrstine (1967: 76-77), this piece ends with a vision of society in a state of Higher Innocence beyond Experience, but Gleckner (1982b: 116-17) believes it implies that tyranny and rebellion alternate in an endless cycle. Erdman (1954a: 14-15 [15-16]) again finds an allusion to the American resistance to George III.

"A War Song to Englishmen"

Critics have diligently sought for irony beneath this "dignified bit of patriotic verse" (Damon 1924: 263). While Bloom (1965: 970) finds that internal contradictions expose the poet's real intent, Gleckner (1982b: 110-11) concludes that echoes of Revelation's warning about Armageddon and of words of Milton's Satan show that the singer is fundamentally misguided. Erdman (1954a: 69 [72-73]), believing this to be one of the songs announced in scene 4 of "King Edward the Third," claims it is a parody of poems like the Laureate William Whitehead's "Verses to the People of England" (1774), which incites to emulation of the victorious Edward.

"The Couch of Death"

Erdman (1954a: 73-75 [77-79]) holds that the infected breath of mother and son is a symptom of the plague that followed Edward III's aggression, but that by transcending together the false notion that they are sinful, they attain a higher vision. Arguing that Blake here anticipates his later doctrine that forgiveness is the essence of Christianity, Nurmi (1976: 43-44) attributes the son's redemption to the self-sacrifice of his mother in taking on his sin. However, Gleckner (1982b: 121-29) considers that her self-sacrificing spirit is ineffective and that it is left to "a visionary hand" to upraise the youth while his mother and sister are left to mourn.

Gardner (1954: 153n1) sees body-soul dualism in this and the next two pieces.

"Contemplation"

The unresolved clash of two voices is interpreted by Damon (1924: 263) as a conflict between Innocence and Experience and by Gleckner (1982b: 129-36) as a competition between facile moralising and self-pitying despair. Erdman (1954a: 73 [77]) sees the speaker as one who refuses to flee from urban suffering to pastoral bliss, while McGowan (1982: 142-43) hears Blake himself lamenting that he is so changed that he cannot return to the "never never" pastoral world.

"Samson"

Damon (1924: 263) notices that "Samson" draws on Milton's *Samson Agonistes* as well as on Judg. xiii-xvi, and Lowery (1940: 80) adds that the announcement of the warrior's birth alludes to Luke i.28 and 31 or to Is. vii.14. Blake is following the tradition of treating Samson as a type of Christ (e.g. Henry 1708-14: II, 217). It would be difficult to deny Bloom's claim (1963: 22) that Dalila foreshadows the female will of Blake's later writings, but there is disagreement as to whether Samson succeeds in his mission. Nurmi (1976: 44) is confident that he saves Israel, and Phillips (1973: 16-26) argues in detail that Blake has written a complete miniature epic starting *in medias res*, containing a triumphant prophecy, and celebrating a national hero; with this figure, Blake identifies both the author of *Samson Agonistes* and himself. Contrariwise, Wittreich (1975: 63-64) asserts that the piece concludes with an angel's call for self-sacrifice in mental war as opposed to the corporeal struggle of Samson, and Gleckner (1982b: 139-47) regards Samson as a woman-trapped failure whose birth is foretold by a deceiving angel who misappropriates Christ's name of Wonderful (Is. ix.6).

Erdman notes that this is another treatment of revolt against oppression (1954a: 16, 20, 27 [18, 21, 28]).

All Religions Are One; There Is No Natural Religion

These tractates are in the tradition of the emblem book (Blunt 1959: 44). The inspiration for *All Religions Are One* may have come from Lavater's *Aphorisms on Man* (Damon 1967: 236), and the form of the text may have been suggested either by this book or (Nurmi 1976: 52) by Francis Bacon's work of the same title. As Johnson and Grant (1979: 12-13) neatly observe, *All Religions Are One* challenges the claims of the national church, while *There Is No Natural Religion* rejects the rationalism of its Deist opponents.

There is widespread agreement with Frye (1947: 14-29) that Blake's intellectual intention is to refute Locke's theory that almost all knowledge is derived from sense perception. Expounding a contrary view, Blake insists on the supreme place of "the Poetic Genius" or "Poetic or Prophetic character," which Fisher (1961: 87) explains as the imagination, which "momentarily" synthesises the mental and physical powers and is Blake's "faculty which experiences." Indeed, Blake conceives of God as "a cosmic imagination" (Nurmi 1976: 54), whose presence within allows us to share His being and to see as He sees (Mellor 1974: 15). That we can perceive the infinite implies that imagination has a role in perception, and in allowing this, says Paley (1970: 24-25), Blake anticipates the *Biographia Literaria* of Coleridge.

Although it is not disputed that Blake always continued to oppose Locke, there is controversy over whether his own philosophical position altered. Bloom (1963: 28) detects the anti-dualistic conviction of the later *Marriage of Heaven and Hell* in the declaration in *All Religions Are One* that the body derives from the Poetic Genius; at the opposite extreme, Hirsch (1964: 9-12) perceives a change of view even between the two sequences of *There Is No Natural Religion*, arguing that Series b is a revised version of Series a, not its sequel. Blake, he maintains, begins by insisting that spiritual knowledge comes from a faculty other than sense perception, but then decides that perception itself can uncover the infinite in all things. Perhaps Hirsch (1964: 301) is misled by the error—corrected by Keynes (1971)—that the Conclusion belongs in the first series rather than the second.

The main disagreements regarding the tractates, however, concern the designs. Are images strongly negative in Blake's later work to be read as positive here? Bindman (1977: 54) proposes that some of them are challengingly ambiguous.

Details

All Religions Are One

Keynes (1971) shows that this is the earliest of the tractates.
pl. 1 The inscription from Matt. iii.3 identifies the man as St. John the Baptist. Blake himself, says Raine (1968: II, 104), in the

guise of the Baptist, is the speaker throughout. As Erdman notes (1974: 24), he directs the reader to the pages ahead.

pl. 2 The winged figure may be an angel revealing the oneness of all religions to the old man (Damon 1924: 267), a muse inscribing the title (Bindman 1977: 56), or one who embraces the Tablets of the Law in the company of a priest or philosopher (Erdman 1974: 24). Howard (1984: 33) considers the angel, man and tablets to be negative—they represent the religious wilderness from which the modern Baptist cries out.

pl. 4 (Principle 1) The figure may be Jehovah, as later portrayed in *A IB* pl. 8 (Keynes 1921: 95); Urizen (Damon 1924: 267); or the spirit of the cloud who some years later becomes Urizen (Erdman 1974: 25).

pl. 5 (Principle 2) Above, Eve is created, while below, sheep represent the similarity of "all men" (Keynes 1970); the human figures above represent the "variety" of "all men" in contrast to the sameness of the sheep (Erdman, *loc. cit*).

pl. 6 (Principle 3) The viper is a sort of scroll speaking for the two philosophers, examples of men who "think" (*ibid.*).

pl. 7 (Principle 4) The traveller has been interpreted as a Lockean imprisoned in the "dull round" of the ratio (Mellor 1974: 83-84) and as an enlightened follower of the Baptist and the viper (Erdman, *loc. cit.*).

pl. 8 (Principle 5) Above are children with Christ (Damon 1924: 267) or with a teacher who transmits the Poetic Genius (Erdman 1974: 26) in teaching which eventually becomes the "Religions of all Nations" (Bindman 1977: 56). The running harper below is probably the Poetic Genius (Binyon 1926: 88) or the prophetic spirit (Bindman, *loc.cit.*), though Erdman (*loc. cit.*) suggests he represents the synthesis of space and time.

pl. 9 (Principle 6) The tablets may represent "The Jewish & Christian Testaments" of the aphorism (Erdman 1974: 26), or they may already have negative connotations of oppressive Old Testament law (Hagstrum 1964: 77). The figure below may be the Poetic Genius, white in the blackness (*ibid.*), or more likely a man groping in the darkness (Binyon 1926: 88) of the physical world (Keynes 1970) or restricted to sense impressions (Erdman, *loc. cit.*). Damon (1924: 267) describes him as Urizen searching the world of Urthona.

pl. 10 (Principle 7) Above is portrayed the Ascension of Christ (Bindman 1977: 56-57) or Christ showing himself to two people (Damon, *loc. cit.*) or the "true Man" rising (Erdman, *loc. cit.*). Below, angels are hovering (Damon, *loc. cit.*) or the Dove of the Holy Spirit is suspended over the waters (Bindman 1977: 57).

Text:- This Principle is condensed to the point of obscurity: religions, it states, are as alike and as diverse as humans, and, like all things similar to each other, religions share a common origin.

There Is No Natural Religion

Raine (1968: II, 104-06) demonstrates how closely Blake traces Locke's account of the human mind, while Howard (1984: 33-34) observes that the designs frequently challenge the Lockean views referred to in the aphorisms.

Series *a*

pl. 1 The young men may be learning authentic philosophy from their experienced elders (Keynes 1971), or the independence of the clothed couple from the standing nudes may represent the gulf between rational and prophetic thought (Erdman 1974: 27).

pl. 2 Both series now have the same title page, but Bindman (1977: 53) thinks the original title page of the first series was lost. The Gothic architecture, says Hagstrum (1964: 12), reflects Blake's belief that there is visionary though not natural religion, and Erdman (1974: 28) states that it adorns a "door of perception." Less plausible is Howard's claim (1984: 34) that it is negative, and that the four living thinkers of the frontispiece are reduced to rigid statues on this facade.

pl. 3 (Argument) A mother is teaching her two children (Damon 1924: 267); beside a vine-entwined tree, figures with books and a tablet illustrate "Education" (Erdman, *loc. cit.*).

Text:- While Erdman (1974: 25-29) regards the vine as a positive symbol in these tractates, Damon (1924: 36) holds that Blake views education as indoctrination and morality as error, and considers the educated natural man as an inadequate ideal. Glancing at the sixth proposition, Hirsch (1964: 298-300) argues that Blake agrees with Locke that there is no innate moral knowledge but insists that moral education must involve non-sensory perception.

pl. 4 (I) Expanding Hagstrum's notion (1964: 76-77) that here is a person confined to sense and reason, Erdman (1974: 28) sees natural perception in the mutual gaze of man and dog and an emblem of transcendent consciousness in the vine and birds. According to Howard (1984: 34), a downward glance symbolises Lockean perception in this and subsequent plates.

pl. 5 (II) A woman (Howard [1984: 40] says a man) is holding a child who reaches out towards a flying bird. Several critics, though in different ways, explain this design as an emblem of supra-sensory perception. Hagstrum (1964: 77) reports that the bird is being freed and the child represents imagination; Erdman (*loc. cit.*) contrasts the nearby bare tree of reason with the aspiring child, who is not permitted to touch the bird; Bindman (1977: 54) considers the bird ambiguous—it can be seen as an inspiring symbol of the infinite or a puzzling natural object; and Howard (*loc. cit.*) sees the downward gaze of the restrainer as Lockean and the wings here and in the next three plates as signs of "spiritual perception." Commenting that Blake portrays no oppressive female will before *Europe*, Wardle (1980: 9) denies that the child is being held back.

pl. 6 (III) Damon's angel preaching to a man (1924: 267) is Hagstrum's upward pointing Cupid (1964: 77) and Keynes's bearer of a revelation beyond the man's deductive powers (1971). Noting the vine, Erdman (1974: 29) believes he teaches the man to apprehend beyond sense perception. Bindman regards the man as a prophet writing to his dictation (1977: 55).

Text:- Howard's claim (1984: 40) that this proposition contradicts Locke is refuted by Raine's quotation (1968: II, 105-06) from the latter's *Essay Concerning Human Understanding* II.ii.3.

pl. 7 (IV) Following Damon's assertion (1924: 267) that the piper's plumed hat is a sign that he is subnormal, Keynes (1971) locates his trouble in the limitation of his thought to sight and hearing. Hagstrum, however, (1964: 77) sees him as a man of poetic imagination; Erdman (1974: 29), citing Essick's theory that he is a poet of the primitive time, interprets the soaring birds as a sign of his musical spirituality; and Howard (1984: 41) sees wings on his hat which show he has learnt from the angel of pl. 6.

pl. 8 (V) While Keynes (1971) classifies the boy approaching the swan as one who "desires what he sees," Hagstrum (*loc. cit.*) credits him with imagination, Erdman (*loc. cit.*) notes that he moves without restraint under the positive symbol of the vine, Gleckner (1982a: 165-66) remembers that the swan is a Renaissance emblem of poetry and prophecy, and Howard (*loc. cit.*) perceives its wings as a sign of higher perception.

pl. 9 (VI) The reader appears to Keynes (1971) to be using his intellect to expand his perception, and to Erdman (*loc. cit.*) to be studying beside the supra-rational "vine of Education." In Howard's opinion, however, (*loc. cit.*) he is looking at the ground, which shows that he is Lockean.

Series *b*

pl. 1 To Damon's vague claim (1924: 267) that a woman is inspiring a young male to stand, Keynes (1971) adds that the inspirer suggests Christ, that the young person is of uncertain sex, and that the Gothic openings show that the inspiration comes from authentic art and religion. (Erdman 1974: 30) sees a scene based on Christ's resurrection of Lazarus, and Bindman (1977: 55) proposes that the Lazarus figure represents the body being awakened to the spirit and the setting may be the front of a tomb.

pl. 3 (I) While Keynes (1971) believes the reader is learning more from the book than he could from sense perception, Hagstrum (1964: 76) considers he is a Lockean restricted to sense and reason.

pl. 4 (II) When the sleeper awakes, his knowledge will be expanded (Keynes 1971).

Text:- Blake's term "the ratio" always denotes some form of blinkered consciousness. In Damon's words (1967: 341), "A Ratio is a limited system founded on what facts are available, and organized by Reason." The facts are usually those supplied by sense perception, and the ratio commonly accepted by Blake's contemporaries is the one endorsed by Locke, with his empirical theory of knowledge. As the Application specifies, its antithesis is "the Infinite."

The term, however, is quite subtle. In Murry's view (1933: 15, 22-23), the ratio is the mental image of a thing as opposed to the thing itself; it is the scientist's abstract conception of a thing as opposed to its unique individual identity, which is perceived by the Poetic Genius. Nurmi (1957a: 210) notes that "ratio" is a favourite word of Newton in his *Principia* and that Blake uses it not only in the sense of the Latin *ratio* ("reason") but with the meaning "mathematical proportion"; Ault (1974: 121) adds that Newton's ratio is not static for it is the varying numerical relationship between two changing quantities.

pl. 7 (V) The two tiny figures may be ascending in prayer (Damon 1924: 267) or wanting "More! More!" (Erdman 1974: 31).

Text:- Those who want "More! More!" have essentially material desires.

pl. 8 (VI) Subsequent critics agree with Damon (1924: 267) that the fettered man illustrates the state of despair.

pl. 9 (VII) This figure, whose triumphant state follows on the despair shown in the previous design (Paley 1978b: 16), may be desiring (Hagstrum 1964: 77) or trying to take possession (Keynes 1971) of the infinite. Erdman (1974: 31) observes that the head of a nail in his left hand is an indication of the resurrected Christ.

Text:- In this aphorism, points out Hirsch (1964: 303), Blake abandons logic for assertion. Explicating it along with the Application, Bloom (1965: 895) understands it to signify that in order to see the infinite that God sees (which is to see God), a human must become infinite. Damrosch (1980: 129-33) explains that, taken together with the final sentence of the tractate, which implies a continuous process of Incarnation, it means that we are united with Jesus by inward revelation; this abolishes the distinction between subject and object and allows us to participate in infinity so that our desire for the infinite is gratified.

pl. 10 (Application) The man with compasses is one whose vision is restricted to the ratio (Hagstrum 1964: 77-78); he is a reasoner whose image contrasts with that of the tree carrying Blake's words (Erdman 1974: 32). Keynes (1971) mentions Michael Phillips' discovery that the source of the image is the frontispiece to Vol. 2 of the third edition of Hervey's *Meditations Among the Tombs* (1748).

Text:- Erdman (1983: 14) records John Grant's observation that logically the Application must follow the Conclusion.

pl. 11 (Conclusion) The Philosophic character is Lockean, the Experimental Newtonian (Hirsch 1964: 301).

pl. 12 Damon's anachronistic notion that this is the sleeping Albion is much less persuasive than Raine's claim (1968: II, 104) that it is the Divine Humanity in the form of Christ. The glorious dead Jesus, says Bindman (1977: 55), contrasts with the reasoner of pl. 10.

Text:- This statement deals with both God and humankind, and especially with Incarnation. To Murry (1933: 23-24), it signifies the perception of the infinite made possible when the personal self is in abeyance, and to Keynes (1971) it is the mystic's proclamation of his oneness with God (cf. Damon 1924: 37). Raine (1968: II, 108) refers to God's being both the universal mind containing all things and the human imagination. Tolley's straightforward interpretation (1973: 119) is that God becomes mortal to redeem us from mortality, while Damon (1967: 402) emphasises Blake's insistence that Incarnation is a continuous and unending process. St. Athanasius writes, "He became man that we might be made divine" (*On the Incarnation*, 54; quoted Cross and Livingstone 1974: 104).

Tiriel

Critics disagree on how far Blake's later beliefs and symbols are discernible in *Tiriel*, on what the literary prototypes of the poem are, on whether Har and Heva have any merit in the author's eyes, and on what Ijim and Zazel signify. Bogen (1970: 157-58) and Behrendt (1979: 181) are unsure whether Har and Heva are literally or only figuratively Tiriel's parents.

Damon begins (1924: 71-73, 306) by viewing Tiriel as a decaying hypocritical religion, his daughters as the five senses, and the poem as a foreshadowing of *The Book of Urizen*. Retaining the original interpretation of the daughters, he later (1967: 405-07) assumes that much of Blake's system is already present in his mind, and takes the West—and therefore Tiriel, its king—as symbolic of the body, and the narrative as the story of the final decadence of a materialistic society. Agreeing on the prominence of social content, Frye (1947: 245) interprets the sons of Zazel as the proletariat of Tiriel's empire, while Schorer (1946: 228) is inclined to see in Tiriel's slaughter of his children the suppression of heresies by reason and its authoritarian religion. Looking at Blake's later mythology, Hall (1970: 170, 175-76) detects in Mnetha a forerunner of Vala, a temptress keeping Tiriel imprisoned in material nature. Bentley, however, (1967: 5) warns against reading the later Blake back into this early book, dismissing on these grounds the identification of the five daughters with the senses. Despite the bleakness of the work, Bindman (1977: 44-47) proposes that Hela, in contrast to Har and Heva, represents true art, and through her Tiriel attains a redemption reflected in his enlightened dying speech.

Several commentators point to one or more literary sources or prototypes. For Bronowski (1944: 41), it is the affinity with Shakespeare's *King Lear* that stands out. To Raine (1968: I, 34-66), *Tiriel* seems essentially to retell in a Gothic or northern mode the story of Sophocles' *Oedipus at Colonus*; it shows the monarch, she argues, as self-loving senility unwilling to give place to the next generation because it does not believe in immortality, while the landscapes and characters he encounters reflect, on the Swedenborgian principle of correspondences, changes in his consciousness. Reading the poem as an adumbration of *The Marriage of Heaven and Hell*, Halloran (1971: 161-79) sees it as based on Gen. iii and *Paradise Lost,* and its protagonist as an attack on Milton's God the Father. (Similarly, Behrendt [1979: 178 *et al.*], to a large extent following Schorer [1946: 230], treats the conflict between Tiriel and Hela as a struggle between reason and desire.) Gleckner (1959: 147) finds something of Tamburlaine as well as elements of Oedipus and Lear in Tiriel, while Bentley (1967: 14-15) detects a parallel between his story and Joseph's, which would imply, as Beer (1969: 336) observes, that Tiriel's corruption results from his enslavement. Rather than emphasising a source, however, Gleckner (1959: 142-56) sensibly treats the book as Blake's first attempt to explore the state of Experience and suggests that God sends Tiriel back to his parents to give him an opportunity to cast off the false religion they had taught him before they retreated into Innocence.

Damon (1924: 307; 1967: 174, 405) proposes that Har and Heva represent neoclassical poetry and painting and that in addition Har is a cross between self-interest and Christian forgiveness. Interpreting the drawings, Essick (1973: 52-59) specifies features which confirm that Har and Heva represent unimaginative arts: these include their total absorption in each other as they languidly bathe and the Grecian cut of Mnetha's costume, which strengthens her association, through her name, with Mnemosyne, mother of the Muses. Other interpreters have claimed that Mnetha stands for music (Bindman 1977: 44), that the sports of Har and Heva parody the sports of real Innocence in "The Ecchoing Green" (Gleckner 1959: 150-51), that the siblings' feeble existence satirises the eighteenth-century belief in the benignness of the state of nature (Fisher 1961: 204), that Har is the god of moral law (Sloss and Wallis 1926: II, 276), that he and Heva are the Aristotelian vegetable soul (Hall 1970: 175-76), and that Har has a sexual relationship with his sister, their permissive 'mother's' (Mnetha's) double, this being Blake's fantasy of innocent Oedipal incest (Webster 1983: 33-38). Mellor, however, (1974: 28-34) feels that the aged pair preserve much of what is valuable in Innocence and will give Hela refuge after her father's death: this theory finds support in Bentley's observation (1967: 24) that in the drawings Har, Heva and Mnetha are more attractive and are perhaps lodged in a paradise.

According to Damon (1967: 194-95, 406), Ijim represents the power and superstition of the people. Though he is indeed frequently associated with superstition, Stevenson (1971: 82) describes him as a sincere puritan, Gleckner (1959: 153) as man reduced to a bestial level but still honest, Fisher (loc. cit.) as the real primitive in contrast to the Enlightenment's Noble Savage, Beer (1969: 65) as selfhood not yet deeply degenerate, Hall (1970: 175-76) as the Aristotelian animal soul, and Raine (1968: I, 61) as ecclesiastical tyranny clashing with the political oppression of Tiriel. Blake has not provided the clues necessary for a convincing interpretation of this character.

Even more varied are the explanations of Zazel and his sons. Damon (1967: 406) takes them for genius spurned, Frye (1947: 245) for the proletariat—scapegoats of Tiriel's law, and

Beer (1969: 66, 341) for the life of the earth from which Tiriel is misguidedly alienated. Behrendt (1979: 184) finds Zazel to be the equivalent of Satan in defeat (a role that Halloran [1971: 176] assigns to the Tiriel of the poem's closing section), and Gleckner (1959: 154) plausibly explains him as a mind destroyed by Tiriel's rational religion. Bogen's theory (1970: 164) that Zazel stands for Fox and Ijim for Pitt may be considered together with the parallel that Erdman (1954a: 121-24 [133-38]) finds throughout the poem between Blake's blind monarch, once King of the West, and mad George III, who has lost his American colonies.

Scholars have traced the sources of the proper names. Tiriel and Zazel appear in Cornelius Agrippa's *Three Books of Occult Philosophy* (English translation 1651) (Damon 1924: 306), but Tiriel may also be related to "tyrant," the Hebrew *el* ("God"), and the arrogant Prince of *Tyre* of Ezek. xxviii.13-16 (Bloom 1963: 30), and Zazel also may derive from the demon Azazel (Damon, *loc. cit.*) or Azazel the "scapegoat" of Lev. xvi.10 (Frye 1947: 444n20), the Hebrew being given in the margin of the AV. Ijim is Swedenborg's more pronounceable variant of the Hebrew *Iim* given in a gloss to the phrase "the wild beasts of the island" in Is. xiii.22 (Frye 1947: 242-43, 444n18). Heva is the Latin name for Eve (Damon 1924: 307) and Har is Hebrew for "mountain" (*ibid.*) and a name in Mallett's *Northern Antiquities* (English translation 1770) (Raine 1968: I, 53). Mnetha is a near-anagram of Athena (Damon, *loc. cit.*) and a derivative of Mnemosyne, the Greek goddess Memory (Bloom 1963: 33). Myratana appears to be an amalgam of Myrina and Mauritania, two names from Jacob Bryant's *A New System, or an Analysis, of Ancient Mythology* (1774-76), for which Blake probably engraved plates (Bogen 1970: 157); Myrina was Queen of Mauritania, whose inhabitants, according to Bryant, were apostates from the true primeval religion (Hall 1970: 166-67).

Details

1:5 Tiriel's sons have been explained as the arts and sciences (Damon 1924: 72), as their father's "rebellious thoughts" (Bronowski 1944: 41), as "his imaginative achievements" (Bloom 1963: 31), and as his cities (Frye 1947: 245). As complete human beings who practise the arts, they may have temporarily escaped from his rationalism (Bentley 1967: 18).

1:9 **Myratana**—Tiriel's inspiration (Damon 1924: 71) or "his powers" (Fisher 1961: 203).

1:21 **Serpents not sons**—cf. Shakespeare, *King Lear* IV.ii.40 (Stevenson 1971: 76).

2:1-2 Cf. Milton, *Samson Agonistes*, ll. 80-89 (*ibid.*: 77).

3:12—13, 20-21 The cage may represent conventional metrical verse (Damon 1924: 71-72) and the song birds neoclassical lyrics and pastorals (Ostriker 1977: 880). Bogen (1970: 165) suggests that the cage is a church and Har's feeding of his birds is religious teaching.

4:76 Orcus is the Greco-Roman underworld and Matha may be a corruption of "matter" (Damon 1924: 308). The latter name appears in Macpherson's *Ossian* (Damon 1967: 266).

6:5 **the right & ready way**—perhaps an ironic allusion to Milton's *The Ready and Easy Way to Establish a Free Commonwealth* (1660) (Ostriker 1977: 881).

6:43 **Let snakes rise**—Athena's curse against Medea (Ostriker, *loc. cit.*).

8:12-22 Damon thinks this passage is influenced by Rousseau's views on education (1967: 406).

Songs of Innocence

A discussion of critical approaches to the states of Innocence and Experience will be found in the Notes on Criticism to chapter four.

Title Page

It is difficult to consider this design without being mindful of the 1794 title page to the composite volume showing Adam and Eve expelled from Paradise. Bass (1970: 197-98) interprets the two pairs of apples hanging above the children as symbols of the knowledge of good and evil conferred by the fatal fruit of Eden. The vine around the tree and the similar vines on succeeding plates are in Hagstrum's view (1964: 80) serpent-like forms foreshadowing the Fall, but in Bindman's opinion (1977: 62) they are a traditional emblem of Christ: these readings suggest a deliberate ambiguity in the image appropriate to an Innocence that will give way to Experience. According to Leader (1981: 66-68), the mother is a partly positive and partly negative figure who protects the children but gives them knowledge that will help to take them out of Innocence. Essick (1980: 138-40) draws attention to the comparable but indoor scene on the title page of John Newbery's *A Little Pretty Pocket-Book, Intended for the Instruction and Amusement of Little Master Tommy, and Pretty Miss Polly* (1767)—and indeed to the superficial affinity of Blake's further illustrations to those in contemporary books for children.

Frontispiece

Most critics from Wicksteed (1928: 83) onwards recognise that the child represents some form of inspiration, but Leader (1981: 64) regards him as a version of Cupid, who, together with the pair of intertwining trees, gives the design a sexual dimension.

"Introduction"

The major question raised by this poem is why the child, whom several critics, following Damon's lead (1924: 268), associate both with Christ and with inspiration, first laughs, then weeps, and finally weeps with joy. Expanding Damon's suggestion (1924: 40) that there is a hint of Experience here, Gleckner (1959: 85-87) interprets the three stages as symbols of Innocence, Experience, and higher Innocence, and sees in the first weeping an allusion to the crucifixion of the Lamb. Wicksteed (1928: 61) perceives merely a foreshadowing of the mingled moods of the poems that follow, and Adams (1963: 19-20) dismisses the two sets of tears as identical sentimental reactions to the Piper's music and song. Focusing on the Piper and his music, Phillips (1973: 28) proposes that he displeases the child until he moves from the "secular pastoral" of the pipe to the "religious pastoral" of song, and Glen (1983: 65-69) defines the subject of the poem as the movement from spontaneous utterance to the deliberate creation of a work of art. Glen's contention that the child disappears because the artist's task is solitary contrasts with Wicksteed's belief (1928: 81) that the boy is an aspect of the Piper himself and becomes internalised.

Blunt traces the pattern formed by the intertwining tree trunks, which is reminiscent of the traditional Tree of Jesse displaying Christ's ancestry, to mediaeval manuscripts (1959: 48).

1.18 The water is stained when the Piper makes ink or watercolours (Bateson 1957: 111).

"The Shepherd"

This poem may not be as simple as it seems. The Shepherd, says Hirsch (1964: 28-29), represents both God and humankind, and so does the lamb. The fourth line allows Leader (1981: 76) to suppose that the Shepherd praises the relationship between lamb and ewe, and Gillham (1973: 99-100) to suggest that he praises God and may continue to do so (the tense is future) when he is still a shepherd in the hereafter. Leader (1981: 77-78) is not as confident as Erdman (1974: 46) that the sun is rising rather than setting, and he sees the flock as existing in an oasis of peace that may not last long.

"The Ecchoing Green"

This apparent celebration of rural joy, whose counterpart in *Experience* may be "The Garden of Love" or "London" (Gleckner 1961: 373), is strangely controversial. What seems to Gardner (1954: 25-26), Holloway (1968: 62-63) and Glen (1983: 137-40) a picture of perfect happiness and harmony appears to others a pastoral in which a threat or hope of change is expressed on the second page. Here, with the beginning of darkness, there is a movement under the guidance of Old John, the central figure in the lower part of the design. The movement, literally towards home (Keynes 1967a, pls. 6-7), may be symbolically towards Experience (Gleckner 1959: 93-94) or towards Eternity, of which, according to Hirsch (1964: 39-41, 177), there is a hint in John's memory of childhood. Gleckner (1959: 92-93) accuses the old folk collectively of passive indulgence in memory and spiritual emptiness, while Adams (1963: 235) and Leader (1981: 86) detect in John a potential, not yet realised, for tyrannising over the young. Grant (1968a: 52) feels that since the grapes in the second design have to be given behind his back, he is already "Mr. Parental Spoilsport."

There has been much comment on the grapes. They have been taken to represent ecstasy (Damon 1924: 272), joy (Bass 1970: 210), the Vine of Christ from which children as yet Innocent are being led away (Bindman 1977: 60-61), and, because a bunch is given by a boy to a girl, Innocent sexuality (Leader 1981: 85-86) or the approach of puberty (Keynes, pls. 6-7). Noting that grapes are out of season and referring to the grapes of the eternal spring in Milton's Eden (*PL*, IV, 257-68), Tolley (1973: 110) proposes that Blake is portraying "an eternal state of Innocence"—much in the spirit of Erdman (1974: 48), who enunciates the theme as "Eternity...in an earthly village."

Gillham finds a plausible source for the lyric in ll. 91-99 of Milton's "L'Allegro" (1966: 23).

"The Lamb"

Glen (1983: 23-25) asserts that this poem, with its emphasis on the close affinity between the infant and Christ and its delight in nature, is a response to Charles Wesley's children's hymn "Gentle Jesus, Meek and Mild," which draws a sharp distinction between the human child, the incarnate Christ, and the transcendent God. Stressing the design, Wagenknecht (1973: 80-85) interprets the pair of interlinked saplings wound round with vines and the pair of doves on the cottage roof as signs that the divine element within us is realised through erotic fulfilment; he also identifies the oak tree with fallen nature and assumes that the allusion to the Incarnation in l. 16 includes an allusion to the Crucifixion.

l. 5 **clothing of delight**—clothing that gives delight (Bateson 1957: 117); also delight metaphorically regarded as clothing (Hirsch 1964: 178).

"The Little Black Boy"

Although, Van Doren observes (1951: 113), the kind of analogy that Blake draws between clouds and bodies and between God and the sun does not usually work out perfectly in every detail, there are discrepancies in this lyric that seem to be intentional. Thus the White Boy retains his silver hair after death (*ibid.*: 115), and the Black Boy is able to give shade when he no longer has a body (Adler 1957: 414-415) and he fails to imagine real equality in the last stanza (*ibid.*). These discrepancies reflect the impact on the speaker's mental processes of his extreme and unsatisfied longing for acceptance, for which his mother tries to console him. There is disagreement as to whether Blake regards the mother's teaching as wholesome (Gillham 1966: 230-31) or as vitiated by a false belief that body and soul are separate (Bloom 1963: 48-49) and by the promise of an illusory heaven (Leader 1981: 108-10). The second design, according to Hirsch (1964: 181), shows Christ in the real heaven, where, states Grant (1968a: 52), he is the Good Shepherd suffering little children to come unto him. Over him is a willow, which, Erdman believes (1974: 50), represents both his and humanity's pain and his mercy. Those who identify the willow as a symbol of fallen nature argue either that the scene is on earth, where heaven is really to be found (Wicksteed 1928: 112-13), or, contrariwise, that it shows the Black Boy's hopes are misguided (Wagenknecht 1973: 76). Discerning even darker irony, Leader (1981: 111-16) sees the conventional weary Christ of the churches seated under a sickly tree, where he communes with the English boy but excludes the African, who stands behind. Damon (1924: 269) thinks the last stanza shows that Blake does not believe in racial equality, but Nurmi (1976: 102) argues that he shows the African, being less corrupted by civilisation, regenerated before his companion, and Wardle (1978: 330) believes he is bringing the less advanced White Boy to be taught by Christ. Erdman (1954a: 221-22 [239-40]) credits Blake with trying to show that beneath their bodily masks the children are brothers.

l. 1 **the southern wild**—An African boy likely to become a slave in the West Indies compares himself to his English counterpart (Crehan 1984: 99).

ll. 9-10 Swedenborg believed that God appeared to the angels as a perpetually rising sun, whose heat and light corresponded to His love and wisdom (Raine 1968: I, 13). Hirsch (1964: 180) considers that the mother's pagan myth illustrates the theme of *All Religions Are One*. Watts's "Grace Shining and Nature

Fainting" includes the image of the soul learning to bear sun-like love (Damon 1924: 269).

l. 12 To avoid degenerating, the Innocent should progress from the enjoyment of material comfort to the exercise of love, which is energy and creates joy (Gleckner 1959: 105-07).

l. 28 Logically the speaker, who is better prepared for heaven, should say the white boy will be like him, but he pathetically turns the statement round (Bloom 1963: 50-51).

"The Blossom"

The central question about "The Blossom" is whether, as Wicksteed (1928: 125-29) and several others are convinced, the vegetation-flames represent an erect and a limp phallus, the birds are sexual symbols, and the poem is about copulation. On the one hand, the tiny figures in the tip of the vegetation seem to be most fully explicable as a clockwise life cycle running from courtship at the left through impregnation, birth and maternal nurture to education (cf. Wicksteed 1928: 127); on the other hand, the birds have been more convincingly interpreted as representative of joy and sorrow, with both of which the flower who is the speaker expresses motherly sympathy (Adams 1963: 234). Crehan (1984: 98) argues that in relating the reception of maternal love to the development of healthy adult sexuality, Blake anticipates Freudian insight. Other opinions are that the theme is the unity of the vegetable, animal and human components of the world (Bateson 1957: 119) or nature's indifference to suffering as shown by the equal happiness of the blossom beside the merry sparrow and the weeping robin (Bloom 1963: 40). Holloway (1968: 27) considers that the speaker is a female child gathering spring flowers, Hagstrum (1964: 82) that she is a woman speaking as a wife in the first stanza (which is about sexual experience) and as a mother in the second.

There have been alternative explanations of the birds and the tiny figures. The former have been perceived as a baby who is first happy and then sad (Wicksteed 1928: 125), as a child seeking a parent (Gardner 1954: 27), and as a male before and after sexual intercourse (Gillham 1973: 12). The figures surrounding the mother and child near the top of the design have been identified as the five senses (winged) and the wingless but exulting imagination

(Erdman 1974: 52); as cherubs, including two who embrace in Innocent erotic delight (Tolley 1973: 110); as Cupids who stand for the sparrow [Venus's bird] as the mother and infant stand for the robin (Hagstrum 1964: 82); and as "neoclassical *putti* or 'winged loves'" surrounding the personified blossom who embraces her child (Mellor 1974: 7).

l. 10 Gillham (1966: 164) thinks the sobbing may express not unhappiness but overflowing emotion, and Mellor (*loc. cit.*) suggests that it indicates orgasm.

"The Chimney Sweeper"

Most critics from Wicksteed (1928: 108-10) onwards have felt that Blake respects Tom's dream-vision without in the slightest degree excusing the children's exploitation—Price, for example, (1964: 395) seeing their "naïve faith" as their way of surviving. Bloom, however, (1963: 41-42) considers that the failure to condemn the guilty shows that Innocence, touching as it is, needs to be complemented by Experience. Leader (1981: 44-47) goes much further in arguing that the way the illustration of the dream is unpleasantly crammed into a narrow strip at the foot of the page indicates the boys' error in accepting the angel's consolation. Reading the lyric as both social protest and symbolic poem, Raine (1968: I, 20-26) sees in it an assertion that the soul cannot be corrupted by immersion in matter (soot) or the body (the coffin): she also notes that Swedenborg locates on the planet Jupiter sooty-faced, black-garbed sweepers and tells of one who discards his clothing with great swiftness to become a shining angel.

l. 3 **weep**—both the child's attempt to say "sweep" and a comment that there is cause for weeping (Wicksteed 1928: 108).

l. 5 **Dacre**—Foundlings as well as adult poor lived in Lady Ann Dacre's Alms Houses (Gardner 1968: 78-79).

l. 12 The several interpretations of the coffins are not mutually exclusive. They may represent sooty bodies (Gleckner 1959: 109), dark chimneys (Adams 1963: 261), and the possible death that awaits the boys in those perilous structures as well as their harsh lives (Nurmi 1964b: 17).

l. 13 The Angel may be both the Angel of Death and a figure
parallel to the child in "Introduction" (Gleckner 1959: 109).
His key, according to Wicksteed (1928: 109), is the doctrine
that what has its existence in the mind is most real.

l. 24 The speaker fulfils his duty when he comforts Tom, but the
line has also an ironic meaning when it is understood as the
adult sweep's admonition to the children (Adams 1963: 261-
62). In the latter case, the harm may be pain inflicted to make
those children climb (Nurmi 1964b: 21). Since "all" are requi-
red to do their duty, this must include the unfulfilled duty that
the adult sweep and the upper classes have towards these
unfortunates (Glen 1983: 99-102). Lastly, everyone's duty is to
acquire vision (Gleckner 1959: 110).

"The Little Boy Lost"; "The Little Boy Found"

The boy's error has been variously defined as reasoning
and questioning (Gleckner 1959: 99), looking for God externally
instead of within (Wicksteed 1928: 105-06), seeking the conven-
tional father-god (Keynes 1967a, pl. 13), trying to conceive God as
a formless spirit (Raine 1968: I, 16-18), and mistaking a vapour
for his father (Adams 1963: 209-10). According to Damon (1924:
271), the boy stands for humankind following a false god.

Literally the child has succumbed to the real danger of
being led astray by a marsh-light (Holloway 1968: 27-28). On an-
other level, his father may have deserted him (Bloom 1963: 46-47)
or even died (Hirsch 1964: 188). Blake perhaps used the story he
found in his source—C. G. Salzmann's *Elements of Morality, for
the Use of Children*, translated by Mary Wollstonecraft (1790)—to
illustrate Swedenborg's teaching that we can only know God in a
human shape (Raine 1968: I, 15-16).

On the lower half of the first design are angels who may
stand for redemption through imagination (Keynes 1967a, pl. 13).
The boy's guide in the second design has been described as the
likeness of "a youthful angel" (Damon 1924: 273), as Christ
(Hirsch, 1964: 188), and as an androgynous image of God having
both maternal and paternal attributes (Keynes 1967a, pl. 14).
Grant (1968c: 32) reports that he is only androgynous in some
copies. The sketchy figure on the lower right is a spirit acting in
place of the boy's mother (Erdman 1974: 55).

"Laughing Song"

The diction of this poem is too mild for Hirsch (1964: 189), and Gillham (1966: 201) detects a slight touch of complacency in the speaker, but Adams (1963: 228-29) recognises how all the phenomena introduced contribute to a unified world of Innocence whose essence is laughter.

"A Cradle Song"

The mixture of smiling, moaning and weeping in this delicate and melodious poem has led to discussions of how happy and how clear-sighted the mother really is. Of the three persons involved—the mother, the baby and Christ—it is not always certain who is smiling, who is moaning and who is weeping. For analysis of the deliberate ambiguities, see Gillham 1966: 182-90 and 1973: 67-69 and Leader 1981: 97-102.

According to Gleckner (1959: 120), the poem passes from Innocence with its "moony beams" through the tears of Experience—the mother's own tears and Christ's—to the Eden or higher Innocence of Christ's smiles. Gillham (1973: 67-68) emphasises the way in which she merges her own identity with her child's; he also (1966: 187; 1973: 69) manages to detect the father in the poem, claiming that he as well as Christ qualifies as "Thy Maker," and adds that the peace of the closing line is both a divine peace and the peace succeeding the act of procreation. Crediting Blake with psychological insight ahead of his time, Glen (1983: 135-36) explains how the mother's reassurance—she may be uttering statements or hopes—establishes the infant's trust in the world. Less confident that all is well, Bloom (1963: 46) accuses the singer of failing to recognise that Jesus' infant tears did not express a baby's helplessness but sorrow for the pains of the world. Leader, the critic most hostile to the mother, relies heavily on the illustrations (1981: 40-44).

Erdman's contention (1974: 57) that the swirling vegetation and tiny figures on the first of the two plates represent happy dreams is contradicted by other commentators. Damon (1924: 272) thinks the figures may be trapped in the vegetation producing a situation which foreshadows, according to Bindman (1977: 62), the Experience awaiting the baby. Noting the heaviness of the decoration, Bass (1970: 205) conjectures that it symbolises oppression as well as protection. If it represents the baby's dream, then that dream, alleges Wagenknecht (1973: 72), is a nightmare.

A series of critics from Damon (*loc. cit.*) to Leader (1981: 42-43) have noted the severe, ominous character of the second design, in which, Bass reasons (*loc. cit.*), the heavy backcloth and stout cradle imply that the child faces danger, at least from cold. According to Wagenknecht (*loc. cit.*), the mother is both protective and sinister. Keynes, however, (1967a, pls. 16-17) remarks that the pillow is deliberately made to resemble a halo, reinforcing the allusions to Christ in the last two stanzas.

Leader (1981: 40-44, 100-02), in agreement with Bloom, Bass and Wagenknecht, notes that protectiveness can easily degenerate into possessiveness, and fears that in advancing at the end from the image of Crucifixion to a happier image of Divinity, the mother may only be turning briefly and blindly away from the reality of suffering.

ll. 5-6 The "soft down" and "infant crown" hint at the Dove of the Holy Spirit and Christ's Crown of Thorns (Gleckner 1959: 117).

ll. 12, 16, 32 The Innocent meaning of "beguiles" is "charms away"; its Experienced meaning is "tricks, deceives" (Bateson 1957: 115). In ll. 11-12, says Gleckner (1959: 118, 304n3), the mother's smiles beguile the night of Experience.

ll. 13-16 The baby's moans will not wake it because Christ's moans and smiles, which are sweeter, will counteract them (Gleckner 1959: 118-19).

l. 20 The mother weeps both for Christ's suffering and the suffering that her baby faces in the future (Gleckner 1959: 119).

ll. 31-32 The peace the mother has given to her child now returns to her (Hirsch 1964: 31).

"The Divine Image"

The second stanza of this poem has allowed commentators to claim that Blake identifies God with humankind (Bateson 1957: 122; Keynes 1967a, pl. 18), that he draws a clear distinction between them (Gillham 1966: 72), and that God as the transcendent Father is other than humanity while God as the immanent Son is identical with it (Hirsch 1964: 193). Taking up a suggestion made by Henry G. Hewlett in 1876, Glen (1983: 149, 372n66) presents the poem as a response to Pope's "The Universal Prayer," which is addressed to the remote First Cause. Blake's two concluding lines, as Hirsch observes (*loc. cit.*), can be both a statement about universality and an admonition to accept it. The peace that is absent from the last stanza is the dwelling place, in Bass's view (1970: 203), of the other three virtues, whereas according to Gleckner (1961: 373) it is love that contains all four. Reading the poem ironically, Bloom (1963: 41, 142-43) dismisses the "Image" of the title as abstract and incomplete and considers that "The Human Abstract" in *Experience* exposes the inadequacy of the four virtues.

Much of the debate about "The Divine Image" centres on the design. The flame-like vegetation has been interpreted as a symbol of holiness (Hirsch 1964: 194) and as a Jacob's ladder linking earth and heaven (Hagstrum 1964: 82). Wicksteed (1928: 100) sees it as an emblem of human life rising from the vegetable level at the bottom to the angelic realm at the top.

Unlike the similar form in "The Blossom," this fire-flower is surrounded by a vine, and Erdman (1974: 59) believes that the flower represents the divine wrath, the vine the divine mercy, the poem being an expression of the latter. At the bottom, Christ raises a man while another figure remains fallen (Damon 1924: 273) or awaits her turn (Erdman, *loc. cit.*); the pair are perhaps Adam and Eve (*ibid.*).

On the upper part of the design, two worshippers are about to receive comfort from two women (Erdman, *loc. cit.*), or from a heavenly female with a companion who prefigures the dawn (Hagstrum 1964: 194), or from a personification of the four virtues who is led by an angel (Keynes 1967a: pl. 18). Alternatively, there may be four wingless angelic figures, the one at the far left bearing bread and wine (Hirsch, *loc.cit.*), or the immanent God may be taking food and drink to worshippers who are misguidedly looking above for help (Leader 1981: 55). Bass (1970: 202) proposes that there are four persons to symbolise the four virtues, and Wagenknecht (1973: 55), drawing on Blake's later beliefs, sees in the two figures on the left the reunion of touch and taste, which were a single sense before the Fall.

"Holy Thursday"

An early version of this poem appears in *An Island in the Moon* (E462-63/ K59), where Blake puts it in the mouth of Obtuse Angle, a character whose punning given name is sufficient to imply a satirical intent. But when it reappears in *Songs of Innocence* is it still meant to be read ironically? Are the guardians really "wise"? Among those who say they are, Hirsch (1964: 194-97) views them as Christ-like shepherds of the "multitudes of lambs," Holloway (1968: 63-64) regards the children as taking on the heavenly character of the angel mentioned in the last line, and Gillham (1973: 21-25) sees a realistic description of an actual event leading to a valuable moral. For those who say they are not, there is a contrast between the guardians and their charges. The former regiment the pupils in straight lines (Keynes 1967a: pl. 19)—lines which contrast with the swirling lines of the small decorations (Essick 1980: 140)—and their wands are instruments of discipline as well as emblems of office (Bloom 1963: 44). The children, however, achieve a radiance that is indeed "all their own" as they sit spiritually as well as physically "above" their supervisors (Adams 1963: 259). Taking a middle position, Price (1964: 394) argues that the guardians with their wands are formidable figures to begin with, but at the end they have become the humble but meritorious hosts of the angel-like children. Gleckner (1956a) suggests that Blake may be opposing the favourable view of charity schools expressed in John (or Charles) Wesley's hymns written for their inmates.

It has been claimed that the speaker is Blake himself (Damon 1924: 269), a self-deceived spectator (Bloom 1963: 44), and a superficial observer whose admiration for the spectacle is tempered by an underlying fear of the number and energy of the children that makes him end by praising their governors (Leader 1981: 18-21).

Holy Thursday—Ascension Day (Erdman 1954a: 111 [121]); neither Maundy Thursday nor Ascension Day, but the day—nearly always a Thursday—of an annual service in St. Paul's Cathedral for the pupils who were being prepared in charity schools to follow menial occupations (Connolly 1975).

ll. 9-10 Cf. Acts ii.1-2 (Hirsch 1964: 196) and Rev. xiv.2-4.

l. 11 Wooden galleries were installed in the Cathedral for this service (Gleckner 1956b).

l. 12 This line has been interpreted as an oppressed child's plea to adults (Erdman 1969b: 129) and as a protest against the eagerness of the authorities to place pauper children outside their own parish (Glen 1983: 122-23). Cf. Heb. xiii.2.

"Night"

There is much dispute as to whether the "immortal day," the paradise here celebrated, is a posthumous heaven (Damon 1924: 270; Gardner 1954: 29-30; Hirsch 1964: 198) or a heaven that may be realised here through such virtues as pity and meekness (Gillham 1966: 240-41), a version of the ideal realm of traditional pastoralism, in which a lion can weep (Wagenknecht 1973: 39, 78-79), or an indication that nature itself is divine (Leader 1981: 123-24). Wicksteed (1928: 129) concludes that the animals are passions which become transformed and benign.

Hirsch (1964: 198) and Wagenknecht (1973: 51-54) contrast the two designs. The former assigns the first, with its predatory lion, to earth, and the second to Eternity. The latter sees in the first the night and nature of Generation illuminated from Beulah above and in the second Generation overshadowing Beulah, where the five figures radiate light. These figures have been taken as angels (Damon 1924: 273) who replace the lion of the previous plate (Bass 1970: 204) and are ready to receive "each mild spirit" (Keynes 1967a, pls. 20-21). Wagenknecht (1973: 55) conjectures that they are probably the five senses.

l.17 **every thoughtless nest**—Thinking does not exist in Innocence (Bateson 1957: 123); the birds are trusting (Hirsch 1964: 197-98).

ll. 37-38 **his**—Christ's (Stevenson 1971: 67).

ll. 41-42 Cf. Is. xi.6-7 (Damon 1967: 242).

l. 45 **life's river**—Experience (Gleckner 1959: 124). Cf. Rev. xxii.1 (Hirsch 1964: 198).

"Spring"

The simplicity of this poem would not seem to leave much room for argument, but critics disagree as to whether the speaker is a "shifting identity" incorporating the Piper of the "Introduction" (Gleckner 1959: 95-97), unidentified in the first two stanzas and a composite lamb-child-man in the third (Adams 1963: 226-28), the mother in the first two stanzas and the child in the third (Gillham 1973: 140), the poet accompanied by the Piper (Erdman 1974: 63), or the child in the designs (Tolley 1973: 112). Hirsch (1964: 38-39) alleges that the trumpet alludes to the Last Judgment and the cock to the one that crowed when Peter denied Christ, for the poem deals with apocalyptic as well as natural rebirth.

The designs are not quite as limpid as the text. Hirsch (1964: 199) locates the first scene on earth, the second in Eternity. Eroticism enters, argues Wagenknecht (1973: 27-29), as the boy woos the lamb, and his finding himself unprotected in the second design shows there is danger in love. On the first plate, Leader (1981: 90-91) detects a sombre overtone since the mother holds her infant back from the lamb that symbolises self-sacrifice. Tolley (1973: 112) plausibly suggests that the angels in the vegetation, two in each plate, represent the four seasons.

"Nurse's Song"

As in the case of "The Ecchoing Green," there is some argument as to whether all is harmony here, as Gardner (1954: 26) supposes, or whether Bloom (1963: 47) is right in seeing the focus as being on the inevitable death of Innocence. The last two lines, which Adams (1963: 254) thinks are spoken by the poet, signify to Leader (1981: 104) the nurse's relapse into reflection on the past, which he equates with the onset of darkness. The weeping willow in the design speaks of loving care to Wicksteed (1928: 96) but suggests the sadder side of life to Keynes (1967a, pl. 24). The bare landscape, vine-entwined tree and thick decoration above hint to Leader (1981: 107) at troubles to come.

"Infant Joy"

Commentaries based on the text describe how the mother, in what Gillham (1973: 3) regards as her "imaginary conversation with her child," reveals her awareness that Innocence will give way to Experience (e.g. Adams 1963: 236-37). Most interpretations, however, stress also the striking design, in which what may be an annunciation (Keynes 1967a, pl. 25) or a nativity scene (Erdman 1974: 66) is contained in the rose of passion (Mellor 1974: 6) or a flower representing an opened womb (Wicksteed 1928: 123-25). Holding the subject to be conception rather than birth, Wicksteed identifies the angel as the father's seed and regards the first stanza as a dialogue between the father and the two-day-old embryo, leaving only the second stanza as the utterance of the mother. However, Chayes (1970b: 232-37) observes that the so-called angel has butterfly wings identifying her as Psyche and that she holds up her arms to receive the baby and may replace its mother. Psyche is ready, thinks Leader (1981: 119-20), to guide the child into its full life cycle, perhaps including posthumous resurrection. Raine (1968: I, 108) classifies the winged being as a vegetation spirit attending a soul in a flower characteristic of Spenser's Garden of Adonis (*FQ* III.vi), where souls await birth. So young an infant, claims Hirsch (1964: 41-43), must have brought his joy with him from a higher world. The pendent bud drooping beside the flower has been accounted for as an earlier form of the blossom (Bass 1970: 203), as an unopened womb (Wicksteed 1928: 125), and as a phallic symbol (Erdman 1974: 66).

"A Dream"

The Innocent speaker sees an emmet or ant lost in the night of Experience, where she is only saved when she thinks with pity of her children (Gleckner 1959: 111-13).

1. 1 **weave a shade**—a gloomy shade (Bateson 1957: 121) or, much more convincingly, a pleasant one springing from maternal care (Gillham 1966: 208).

1.16 **watchman**—The Innocent speaker of this poem about compassion has transformed the musket-carrying watchman and the beadle into a benign glow-worm and helpful beetle (Crehan 1984: 101-02).

"On Another's Sorrow"

The speaker may be either a parent, the Piper of the "Introduction," or everyman (Gleckner 1959: 304-05n6). He is the poet (Erdman 1974: 68).

In the design, Hagstrum (1964: 81) sees serpentine forms foreshadowing Experience and reinforcing verbal allusion to the Crucifixion. The figures on the left, states Bindman (1977: 62), represent the ascent of the soul or of the poet through Experience to redemption.

The Book of Thel

Several models and anti-models have been suggested as the basis of Thel's story. Damon (1924: 75), followed by Harper (1961: 247-56), classifies Blake's heroine as a Persephone who has not yet been carried to the underworld by Dis, and he also (1967: 52) maintains that she is Blake's answer to Milton's champion of chastity, the Lady in *Comus*. Gleckner (1960) sees her as contrasted with Job, who, unlike her, accepts Experience. Drawing an intriguing comparison, Raine (1968: I, 112-14) argues that Blake found the pattern for his narrative in Johnson's *Rasselas*, while Chayes (1970b: 217-20) points to Psyche, who also descended to the underworld. But it is not over the search for sources that fierce critical controversy rages. The central issues are the identity and character of the heroine, the nature of the Vales of Har, and of the House of the Clay or "land unknown," and whether Thel is right or wrong to return to her earlier home. Erdman (Textual Notes, E790) declares that the final plate, which introduces the House of the Clay, was (like the Motto) etched not less than two years after the rest of the poem, "presumably" to replace an earlier plate. Howard (1984: 50) suggests that pl. 5 originally ended the poem.

It is widely agreed that Thel represents some kind of Innocence confronting Experience, but is she also as some critics (e.g. Damon [1924: 74-75], who emphasises the influence of Porphyry) strongly affirm and others (e.g. Max Plowman [1927a: 87]) vigorously deny, also a soul on the threshold of mortal birth? Tolley, in a valuable essay (1965), insists that while the poem may have some Neoplatonic content, its relation to Night the First of Young's pious *Night Thoughts* is more important and the Christian theme of self-sacrifice predominates. Frye (1947: 232-33) usefully asserts that Thel "could be any form of embryonic life, from a human baby to an artist's inspiration, and her tragedy could be anything from a miscarriage to a lost vision."

There is disagreement, too, as to whether Thel's Innocence is of the admirable kind (e.g. Mellor 1974: 19-39) or the false Innocence of childish selfishness (Tolley 1965: 378), a fragile Greek pastoralism (Hagstrum 1964: 87-89), or fear of adult life (Hirsch 1964: 305-09) and of giving herself both sexually and maternally (Tolley 1973: 115-16). Thel's denigrators usually contrast her inauthentic Innocence with the genuine Innocence of the Lily, Cloud and Clay, who, unlike the human girl, refrain from isolating themselves (Gardner 1954: 35-40) and have Swedenborgian "uses" (Davies 1948: 44-45). For Gleckner (1959: 167-69) Thel's questions are an ominous sign that instead of giving to others she resorts to reasoning, and for Gillham (1973: 186) they are a way of avoiding "the exercise of her moral being by dwelling on transcendental matters"; for Mitchell, however, (1978: 87-88) they make her, despite her failure to learn the lesson of self-sacrifice, the only genuinely human person in the poem. Three critics who have done much to illuminate her character charge her with pride and vanity (Gleckner 1959: 163-69), with infantile passivity (Johnson 1970b: 258-77), and with having a very weak sense of her own identity (Heppner 1977). Contrariwise, the Freudian George (1980: 92-98) diagnoses her as a narcissist unwilling to loosen her grip on her ego to love another, while Webster (1983: 53-57), another Freudian, has to insist that she takes on a male role in her descent in order to accuse Blake of expressing through her final speech a fear of castration during copulation.

At least two writers doubt Blake's respect for the Lily, Cloud and Clay. Although they call for Christ-like self-sacrifice far exceeding the benevolence beloved by the Deists, Pearce (1978) charges that they are infected with the Natural Religion that Blake detests. Levinson's view (1980: 288-89) that the Lily is coy and the Cloud complacent rests largely on her identification of the "He" of 1:19 with the wedded Cloud and an alleged inconsistency between 1:18 and 3:30.

The action of *The Book of Thel* is divided between the Vales of Har and the House of the Clay. The former has been interpreted as Eternity (Damon 1924: 75), as Beulah identified with the Garden of Eden (Frye 1947: 232-33), as analogous to both Eden and Spenser's Garden of Adonis with its porter (Bloom 1963: 53-54, 60), as this world (Margoliouth 1951: 55) or one much like it (Johnson 1970b: 259), as a garden of Innocence (Fox 1976: 7), and as the conscious mind (George 1980: 93-94). The anguished world of the Clay has been regarded as this world seen in Neoplatonic fashion as a place into which souls die and thus as the classical underworld (Damon, *loc. cit.*), as the state of spiritual death (Margoliouth 1951: 56), as the realm of the dead in a literal sense (Gillham 1973: 190-91), as Experience (Gleckner 1959: 170-73), as adult life (Bogen 1971: 28), and as the unconscious mind (George, *loc. cit.*). Wagenknecht (1973: 148) interestingly claims that all the action occurs in one place and what Thel perceives around her at any moment depends on her mode of perception, while Fox (1976: 8) notes that she fears the same thing— mortality—in Innocence and in Experience, though it seems more brutal in the latter.

As the most obscure passage in the poem, the speech from Thel's grave plot has been much discussed. Scholars have explained it as the voice of the body bewailing the condition of the senses (Damon, *loc. cit.*), the utterance of Thel's morally deficient "real self, ugly, cold, mean, dark" (Gleckner 1959: 168-70), an amplified version of her customary self-centred complaining (Johnson 1970b: 270-71), the protest of a rebellious adult the retreat of whose younger self will be temporary (Bogen 1971: 30-31), the posthumous lament in which Thel, if she does not change, will bewail her wasted life (Gillham 1973: 191), and an expression of the conflicts within her unconscious (George 1980: 93-98).

Next to the question of whether Thel is, on one level, an unborn soul, the problem of whether her retreat is to be condemned has provoked the most passionate discussion. Bloom

(1963: 62) is persuaded that she is misguidedly returning to a state that will decay into the corrupt Innocence of Har and Heva in *Tiriel*; Hirsch (1964: 309) accuses her of a cowardly withdrawal from the complexities of adulthood; Read (1982) believes that echoes of James Hervey's *Meditations Among the Tombs* (1746, 1748) show that her flight illustrates Hervey's puritan error in rejecting the pleasures of life; and Raine (1968: I, 114-24) considers that Blake sides with the Lily, Cloud and Clay, who, as Hermetists, see God at work even in the basest matter, against Neoplatonic Thel, who can see no good in the lower world. Taking a contrary view, Bullough (1968) argues on a philosophical level that Thel's retreat vindicates Neoplatonic despair of this world as opposed to Swedenborg's optimistic doctrine of "uses," while Margoliouth (1951: 56-57) praises her for at last escaping the despondency which the Lily and Cloud could not assuage, and Mellor (1974: 34-37) enthuses over her heroic cry of defiance and her return to the nobler life of the Vales of Har. Some commentators take up an intermediate position. Johnson (1970b: 271-72) suggests that for all her weakness Thel's shriek may show that she recognises, in the speech from her grave plot, her own deficiency. To Wagenknecht (1973: 161-63), her withdrawal is a retreat from reality, but her imagination has been awakened. Mitchell (1978: 83) feels that the book leaves it uncertain, as perhaps its author was, whether Thel returns to a higher life or is doomed to infantile regression.

Details

Title The name "Thel" was long held to derive from Greek *thelo* ("to desire") (Damon 1924: 310), but Tolley (1965: 380n17) suggests Greek *thelus* ("woman") as an alternative. Since Blake seems to have studied Greek only after 1800 (E727/ K821), Murray's observation (1981) about the notoriety of Martin Madan's defence of polygamy *Thelyphthora* (1780-81) makes *thelus* seem the more likely origin. Schorer (1946: 235) suggests an allusion to Lethe.

Thel's Motto The eagle and mole traditionally represent keen sight and near blindness. The silver rod and golden bowl derive from verse 6 of the eloquent meditation on senile decay in

Eccles. xii (see especially Tolley and Ferber 1976); these images were often held to represent the spinal cord and skull (Mitchell 1978: 86n). Most Blake commentators consider they are also a unit or standard of measurement. Can wisdom and love be contained in or measured by the phallus and brain (Damon 1924: 310), the phallus and womb (M. Plowman 1927a: 89), the rod of "self-appointed authority" and self-centred possessiveness (Gleckner 1959: 173), the male and female genitals (Harper 1961: 252-53), the silver and gold of commerce (Beer 1969: 72-73), or the sceptre of office and the Eucharistic chalice (Mellor 1974: 37)? Given Blake's values, the answers could be *Yes, Yes, No, Yes, No* and *No*. Closely linking the two couplets, Hirsch (1964: 305-06) considers such objects of beauty as the rod and bowl too remote from the "pit" of Experience to contain love or wisdom. According to Raine (1968: I, 118-19), the Motto expresses Thel's doubt about the Hermetists' comforting doctrine "That which is beneath is like that which is above."

1:1 "Mne Seraphim" differs by one letter from Hebrew *Bne Seraphim* ("Sons of the Seraphim"), a phrase applied in Cornelius Agrippa's *Occult Philosophy* (English translation 1651) to "the Intelligences of Venus," spirits relevant to a poem on sexuality. The initial "M" has been explained as a mistake in the engraving (Damon 1924: 310); an allusion to Mnemosyne—i.e. Memory, the Mother of the Muses (Gleckner 1959: 307n4); a feminization of *Bne* (Damon 1967: 7); a slip of Blake's memory (Tolley 1965: 383); and a sign of his ambivalent feelings about Thel (Mitchell 1978: 83). But in view of his free use of unexplained names and allusions, Beer (1969: 358n24) is probably right in tracing it to Mnetha of *Tiriel*, since Thel is headed for the decadent Vales over which Mnetha presides. Bogen's view (1971: 23-24) that "Mne" alludes to Greek *mene* ("moon") and that Mne Seraphim is a spiritual realm makes it hard to fit "Seraphim" into the syntax.

Gleckner (1959: 163) considers that Thel's sisters have already passed through Experience to reach a higher Innocence.

1:4 **the river of Adona**—This river, related to Milton's river Adonis (*PL*, I, 450), symbolises the passage from Eternity into the world of generation (Damon 1924: 310). Blake identifies it with the waters of Eden and associates it with Adam, whose name signifies "red earth" (Frye 1947: 229). Adonis may have been given a feminine ending because the river represents the primal matter of the universe, and matter is symbolically feminine (Raine 1968: I, 115-16).

1:14 According to Tolley (1973: 116), this line refers to more than Gen. iii.8: Thel is seeing Christ as the sentencer of Adam and Eve of Book X of *PL*, not as the Divine Bridegroom.

2:7 **meekin**—a past or present participle from the dialect verb "to meeken" meaning "to become meek" (cf. Bogen 1971: 70).

3:10-16 Thel needs to learn that coitus is a Christ-like sacrifice of selfhood and a giving of one's body to another (Mitchell 1978: 94).

3:15 **a golden band**—either a wedding ring or a blossom (Howard 1984: 53).

5:10-11 Tolley (1973: 115-16) maintains that Thel is evading her future responsibility to nurture when she asserts that God cares for the worm.

6:1 In claiming that the porter is not Spenserian but the officer commonly found at the entrance to a realm of evil spirits, Bogen (1971: 71) ignores the close parallels or allusions to Spenser's Garden of Adonis recorded by Raine (1968: I, 100-03, 105-06).

Damon (1924: 75) traces Blake's allusion to the northern bar to Thomas Taylor's translation of Porphyry's *On the Cave of the Nymphs* [1789]; Baine (1972) points out that the source could have been the note to *The Odyssey*, XIII, 124, in Pope's translation.

6:11-20 Max Plowman (1927a: 91) refers to the deceptions involved in carnal love; Heppner (1977: 94) compares the images of Elizabethan love poetry, e.g. those of Shakespeare's *Romeo and Juliet* I.i.206-14; in ll. 13-17 Bogen (1971: 27) finds allusions to masked enmity, ostentation, cunning words, and listening without heeding; and Mitchell (1978: 90-91), expanding a hint of Johnson (1970b: 271), describes this speech as an intensified form of Thel's sighs and questions on the two previous plates.

6:19-20 The curb and curtain have been interpreted as the physical body constricting desire (Hirsch 1964: 309), as modesty overdone and abstinence (Bogen 1971: 27), as sexual repression and mystery hiding female sexuality (Mitchell 1978: 91), and as the foreskin and hymen (Bullough 1968: 116)—the hymen has been said to symbolise the body's frustration of the soul (Chayes 1974: 73) and the boundary of the ego that sexual experience threatens to dissolve (George 1980: 97).

Designs

Title page In the exquisite design framed by a willow, which can represent either sorrow or paradise (Erdman 1974: 33), Thel watches a diminutive couple who have emerged from two anemones. Many critics follow Damon's tentative identification of them (1924: 313) with the Cloud and Dew of the text (3:10-16), but opinions differ as to whether Thel observes mutual love (Bogen 1971: 18-19, 71), "amorous pursuit and flight" (Raine 1968: I, 105), unwelcome advances (M. Plowman 1927a: 86), or even a rape (Bindman 1977: 63). Janet Warner (1984: 105) notes that raised arms can indicate either fear or welcome.

pl. 1 Although there is no corresponding image of a mole, it is natural to associate the eagle at the top of the plate with the eagle of the Motto; Damon (1924: 313) explains it as genius, and Bullough (1968: 119) as the freedom Thel would have to renounce to assume a body and acquire understanding of the pit. Erdman (1974: 35) thinks it could either enlighten Thel or prey upon her. The baby beneath Pearce (1978: 29n21) views as evolving first into the youth aspiring towards the bird of vision and then into the man armed for mental fight. In a stimulating exposition, Mitchell (1978: 99-100) describes an Adam figure awakening into consciousness and seeing above him the love between mother and child, which belongs to Innocence, and—in the armed man and his counterpart, who may be hawking—the war and hunting of Experience.

pl. 6 Critics' interpretations of the concluding design, which shows children riding a bridled serpent, vary according to their view of Thel's retreat. Most relate the serpent to Experience and the children who have it under control to Innocence, and they contrast the children's success at coping with Experience to Thel's failure. Damon (1924: 313) identifies the animal specifically with sexuality, while Binyon (1926: 98) opts for nature and Raine (1968: I, 117) reads it as a symbol of matter. Thomas Wright (1929: I, 25) sees the children of imagination happily guiding a contented serpent of reason—an emblem of the Golden Age; equally sanguine, Bogen (1971: 48) refers to the tradition—loosely based on Is. xi.6—that the lion and the lamb will lie down together. But to Wagenknecht (1973: 158-59) the relationship between Innocence and Experience seems ambiguous (which needs the other?), and to Mitchell (1978: 84) the image suggests both an advance to a higher state and infantile regression. Pearce (1978: 29n21) believes heedless children are borne by a cunning serpent—a bitter comment on Thel's error. Equating Thel with Blake's imagination, Weathers (1981: 87-88) perceives an image of the entrapment this would have suffered had it, like these children, been seduced by nature.

Notes on Criticism for Chapter 3

The French Revolution

Being a relatively straightforward poem, *The French Revolution* has required comparatively little elucidation. Damon (1924: 81), followed by Orel (1973: 38-39), praises Blake for his fairness to both sides in the conflict. Erdman (1954a: 148-59 [162-74]), in a particularly valuable account of the poem, elucidates the historical content and observes that Blake treats the brief time of the action as a "Day of Judgment or Morning of Resurrection" (150 [165]). Showing how Blake combines history, psychology and universal vision, Bloom (1963: 63-69) maintains that the text we have is essentially complete, whereas Howard (1984: 57) believes that the seven towers of the Bastille represent seven forms of oppression to each of which one book of the poem was to be devoted. In an illuminating contrast between *The French Revolution* and *America* (1793), Halliburton (1966) shows that the latter is a more successful treatment of a revolution from a visionary perspective in which all time is simultaneous: it benefits from a clear distinction between its historical and its symbolic characters, and it is not burdened by a predominant image with a confusing range of meanings like the omnipresent cloud of the earlier poem. Halliburton's strictures are not invalidated by Beer's claim (1968: 95-106) that the symbolism in *The French Revolution* is more precise than it seems or by Halloran's careful and enthusiastic study of the poem's structure (1970). Beer rightly emphasises the pervasive antithesis between darkness and light or vision, and he argues that Blake's satisfaction over the Revolution is tempered by grave anxiety about violence. Agreeing with Bloom that the work is complete and with Halliburton that the narrator's perspective is timeless, Halloran defends the poem as a prophecy modelled closely on Revelation despite its necessarily clearer plot line. Like the biblical book, which it clearly echoes, it comprises seven scenes played out on three levels—the sky, Paris, and the Bastille correspond to St. John's heaven, earth, and hell. Halloran believes that it celebrates a bloodless transformation of society and ends with a reconciliation of the opponents; he disregards the absence from the last lines of any clear change of heart in the upper class.

Much of this early poem's interest for Blake's readers lies in the germ it contains of his later habits of expression (cf. Erdman 1954a: 150 [165]). In particular, Paley (1970: 52-53) draws attention to the way in which the poet deploys night, forest and stars to represent the crumbling monarchical and aristocratic order.

Details

l. 1   The vision descends to restore the spirit of prophecy which the man in the first tower (see l. 29) has been imprisoned for expressing (Howard 1984: 57).

l. 62   The voice is that of l. 15 (Stevenson 1971: 129).

l. 80   **the central fire**—The image is based on the "fluid mass of burning lava" that Erasmus Darwin (who shared Blake's enthusiasm for the French Revolution) believed to occupy the centre of the earth (Worrall 1975: 407).

ll.87-88   These lines present Burgundy as a hideous caricature of the Sistine Madonna; his warlike policy will kill many infants (Frye 1947: 203).

l. 89   **this marble built heaven**—both the royal palace and the *ancien régime* (cf. Bloom 1963: 65).

ll. 211-14   In this description of the Fall, Beer (1968: 104) sees allusions to the stone at the mouth of Christ's tomb and Israel's slavery in Egypt, while Worrall (1975: 407-08) finds traces of Erasmus Darwin's theory that the stars and sun were ejected from chaos, around whose gravitational pull they still circle, and that the moon subsequently separated out from the sun (in one place, Darwin says from the earth). The chaos, believes Worrall, becomes Blake's stone sealing off the heavens.

l. 219   Blake's terminology is anti-Newtonian (Erdman 1954a: 158 [173]).

l. 234   **stifling...sloth**—allusions to overcrowding and unemployment (*ibid.*).

l. 276   Cloud and rock are ambivalent symbols for Voltaire and Rousseau, who oppose injustice but lack vision (Beer 1968: 105).

ll. 301-02   Frye (1947: 203) describes the resurrection as taking place by Christ's agency in a cemetery that symbolises the

physical fallen human body; Halloran (1970: 50-51) judges
that Blake is alluding to Rev. xx, and Stevenson (1971: 142)
that he has in mind a flat earth.

The Marriage of Heaven and Hell

The Marriage of Heaven and Hell is a work of such daz-
zling exuberance, challenging irony and varied subject matter that
critics searching for its central focus and its structure have tended
to concentrate on one or two of its many elements. Among these
are the play of contraries in general, the specific antithesis between
Energy and Reason, the psychological core, the revolutionary
thrust, the attitude to the body, and the satire on Swedenborg.
Even the date of its completion is disputed—Erdman (E801) bel-
ieves that Blake laboured on it from 1790 to 1792 or 1793, Bind-
man (1978: 470) that the book in its entirety is a work of 1790. (It
should be noted that Joseph Viscomi has recently presented strong
evidence that Bindman's dating is correct *[Blake and the Idea of
the Book* (Princeton: Princeton UP, 1993), pp. 236-37]).
        The idea that the strife of contraries is fundamental to the
universe is, as Nurmi observes (1976: 73), common in poetry from
Spenser to Pope, though he adds that Blake's treatment of the
subject probably owes something to Boehme also. Raine (1968: I,
426n9) notes that Blake could have known something of the Greek
roots of the tradition in Heraclitus and Empedocles through Robert
Fludd's *Mosaicall Philosophy* (1659). The most prominent con-
traries in the *Marriage* are Energy and Reason, but just what does
the poet mean by these? Nurmi (1957b: 21) proposes that Energy
can be defined as desire for creation, Reason as desire for order.
Since both contraries are necessary and yet Reason is often treated
with hostility, Schorer (1946: 255), Gardner (1954: 40-41) and
Nurmi (1957b: 21) argue that there is a false Reason that represses
Energy and a true one that co-operates with it; the text suggests,
rather, that there is one Reason that can function destructively or
creatively. Gleckner (1959: 194) tries to equate Energy with Exp-
erience and Reason with Innocence. He agrees with Max Plowman
(1927b: 8-9) that the two states are here synthesised: Gleckner

calls the resulting state the higher Innocence, while Plowman identifies it with the Imagination and Liberty of Blake's later writings. Turning to the myth as developed in the epics, Wagenknecht (1973: 144) asserts that the Energy and Reason of the *Marriage* come to be personified as Luvah and Urizen.

Confining themselves to the *Marriage* itself, commentators can easily find psychological meanings and political messages. Damon (1967: 262) maintains that Energy corresponds to the Freudian Id and Reason to the Superego, and some later critics have followed this hint. Webster (1983: 63, 66-68) accuses Blake of perceiving Reason only as a crude version of the Superego and deifying the pre-rational sensory awareness and fantasies of infancy as a supposedly expanded form of perception, while George (1980: 121-22) not only sees in the contraries an Oedipal conflict between father and son, but emphasises that socially Reason is a conservative force. Speculating more freely, Crehan (1984: 137-55) interprets Blake's heaven as an upper class that restrains its own desire and keeps its inferiors inferior, and his hell as a lower class including artisans, craftsmen, and all who contribute to the production of radical books.

Along with society, the body—or the way in which we perceive it—is to be redeemed, but opinions as to the author's view of the body vary widely. The Voice of the Devil announces that it is not "distinct from" the soul, but this voice is not necessarily identical with Blake's, and Nurmi (1957b: 35-36) suggests that it tells only part of the truth. According to Frye (1947: 194-95), who cites Phil. iii.21, Blake envisages the spiritual body blossoming from the seed of the natural body, whereas Bloom (1958: 502) insists that Pauline dualism is something that he abhors. Hoagwood (1978b) asserts that the book includes an attack on the eighteenth-century materialist philosopher Holbach, for whom soul is an element of body instead of *vice versa*; Pechey (1979: 57) detects a debt to the anti-Swedenborgian writings of Joseph Priestley, a non-dualist who viewed thought as an attribute of body; and Raine (1968: I, 360-61) believes that Blake is rejecting Neoplatonic scorn for the flesh in favour of the Hermetic conviction, prominent in Paracelsus, that happily the lower world is related to the higher as wife to husband, hence the image of the marriage; she also (*ibid.*: 337-38) states that he accepts the esoteric tradition that Adam's lost paradise is the body.

In Blake's eyes, one of Swedenborg's faults seems to be his acceptance of a sharp division between body and soul, though Howard (1970: 24-30) considers that the *Marriage* satirises not so much the sage's teachings as the decline of the English Sweden-borgians' church with its increasing drift towards priesthood, a fixed order of service, sexual puritanism, emphasis on the Ten Commandments and political conservatism. However, plates 3 and 21 refer explicitly to Swedenborg's writings, and Nurmi (1957b: 28) has a strong case for claiming that Blake is turning away from Swedenborg and towards Boehme, who, as Erdman observes (1954a: 165 [180]) finds a place for wrath in the divine essence. Blake modifies what he borrows from Boehme (e.g. Nurmi 1957b: 34), possibly denies—as Schorer maintains (1946: 265-66)—the fundamental doctrine of Original Sin, and is even accused by Hirsch (1964: 59) and Wittreich (1968: 822) of writing an anti-Christian work.

Blake was once also accused of producing in the *Marriage* a virtually formless book (Damon 1924: 88), but Max Plowman (1927b: 14) showed that it consisted of six chapters and a prologue and epilogue. More recently there have been further theories about its structure, about possible prototypes, and about the light its form can cast upon its theme. Nurmi (1957b: 28-29, 37, 45) traces a division into three parts, the first treating the contraries, the second (beginning with the initial Memorable Fancy) concerned with "spiritual perception," and the third (starting at pl. 15) returning to the contraries in the light of the perception of the infinite. Clas-sifying the Argument and "A Song of Liberty" as parts of the first and final chapters, Emery (1963: 29-30, 89, 95, 97-99) sees a movement from a focus on a division in the human entity to a study of what will heal and what will sustain that division; most usefully he observes that force fails to convert an angel in the fourth Memorable Fancy whereas argument prevails in the fifth, and the single conversion is followed by the prospect of society's redemption in the "Song." Pechey (1979: 60) theorises that the seven sections from plates 1 through 11 have their mirror image in plates 12 through 24, the fourteenth section being thematically parallel to the first, the thirteenth to the second, etc.; moreover the monologues and polemic of the first half give way to dialogues and action in the second. In Tannenbaum's view (1982: 109-10, 130-31), the text and designs consist of a series of variations on the theme of usurpation, all of them analogous to Jacob's theft of Esau's (Edom's) birthright, cunning Jacob representing reason and impulsive Esau desire and energy (see also 2:4n); Howard (1984: 95-96) adds that these robberies are reversed in "A Song of Liberty." Lipking's assertion (1976) that the *Marriage* enacts and records an initiation ceremony is less illuminating than Grant's proposition (1970b: 64) that it is about the arduous education of the prophet. Agreeing with the latter theory, Howard (1984: 62-63, 75) states that the novice first appears as the speaker in pl. 6 and that his education continues till in the last two Memorable Fancies he can first resist one angel and then convert another.

Among the models that have been suggested for Blake's unique book are the school primer (G. Taylor 1974), Milton's *The Reason of Church Government* (Wittreich 1975: 202, 206-07), and the chapbook with its mixture of tales, jokes and prophecy (Pechey 1979: 53). Jones (1977) argues that its pattern is biblical, for it begins with the Fall (Argument), and proceeds via law ("The voice of the Devil"), prophets (Isaiah and Ezekiel), the promise of redemption (plates 14-17), the temptation of the Saviour (fourth Memorable Fancy), and Jesus and the Pharisees (last Memorable Fancy) to an apocalypse ("A Song of Liberty"). Of equal interest is Wittreich's proposal (1975: 191) that the *Marriage* has the typical structure of prophecy as seen in Revelation, for it consists of a prologue, a series of visions each followed by a commentary, and an epilogue. This, however, contradicts Max Plowman's still plausible view (1927b: 14) that each chapter consists of a passage of exposition followed by a fanciful illustration—in Wittreich's language, by a vision.

The interpretation of Hirsch (1964: 64-65), who sees the ideal upheld by the *Marriage* as conformity with nature, is impaired insofar as he, like Widmer (1965), fails to recognise a fundamental principle of its organisation: the reader hears different voices speaking from different viewpoints. Sometimes one is tempted to believe with Erdman (1954a: 163-64 [178-79]), Widmer (1965: 40) and Wittreich (1975: 198) that Blake is too much in love with hell to be serious about its marriage with heaven: as Widmer rightly observes, the beliefs of the angel in the last Memorable Fancy are simply reversed. Nevertheless, this is to perceive only a portion of the book's meaning. On plates 3 and 16, without putting his words into the mouth of an invented speaker, Blake clearly specifies that both contraries are necessary. Stavrou (1955: 385) explains the poet's heavy bias towards Energy as a reaction against society's current overvaluation of Reason, and Bloom (1963: 72) points out that it is the Memorable Fancies that so ardently defend Energy while the intervening passages admit the need for Reason also.

But if there is a marriage, where does it take place and what is its nature? The great majority of critics find it portrayed on the title page and narrated in the last Memorable Fancy, when an angel embraces an infernal flame (e.g. Nurmi 1957b: 57-58), but there are dissidents: Beer (1968: 57) locates it in pl. 19, where a harper sings on a moonlit bank combining energy with harmony, and Jackson (1971: 210) finds it in pl. 3, where, she claims, the energy of hell revives within Blake, who is himself the new heaven. Those who believe in a serious marriage symbolised by the angel embracing a flame insist that his angelic nature is not annihilated but transformed so that it contributes to a vitally, not statically, harmonious state in which the contraries creatively contend (e.g. Gleckner 1959: 190; Bloom 1958: 502).

Details

Argument   This prologue outlines the background to the rebellion celebrated in the rest of the *Marriage* (Price 1964: 412-13). It may give a sketch of human history covering the banishment from Eden, the priestly sabotage of Christ's plan for its restoration, the modern expulsion of prophets into "barren climes," and the rage with which current revolutionaries are reclaiming the lost Eden (Paley 1970: 261-62). However, Bloom (1958: 501-02) considers that it describes a cycle in which prophetic inspiration and its contrary displace each other by turns (Wicksteed [1928: 173] regards such a cycle as basic to the *Marriage*): Bloom, nevertheless, admits that those who attain a completely human state can escape.

2:1   Blake is at fault for the unprofitable ambiguity that obscures the meaning of Rintrah and of the design. Most critics regard Rintrah as a positive figure expressing prophetic wrath and heralding revolution, and the presence of ascending birds above l. 21 supports their view. Thus Frye (1947: 333) identifies Rintrah with Elijah, and Gleckner (1959: 196) suggests he can be equated with the Son of Fire in "A Song of Liberty." Howard (1984: 65) implausibly proposes that he is the narrator in subsequent stanzas, and Jackson (1971: 208) conjectures that he is the just man of the Argument. The leading proponent of a tyrannical Rintrah is Erdman (1954a: 174 [189-90]), who regards him as a symbol of counter-revolution.

burden'd—with scriptures and religious laws (Gleckner 1959: 187).

2:2 **Hungry clouds**—either the contrary of Rintrah's fires (Mellor 1974: 264) or their reinforcement (Margoliouth 1951: 75).

2:4, 9 **Once...Then...**—These adverbs refer to consecutive periods according to Bloom (1958: 501) but to the same period according to Howard (1984: 65).

2:4 Not all critics are confident that the just man is entirely admirable. On the one hand Schorer (1946: 253-54) sees him as a Blakean devil, Erdman (1954a: 174-75 [190]) as the newly liberated French peasant, Hirsch (1964: 60-61) as the real Christian persecuted by Pharisaic priests, Damon (1967: 204) as Esau cheated by Jacob, and Pechey (1979: 65) as one commendably meek as opposed to hypocritically humble. On the other hand Gleckner (1959: 188, 190-92) feels that he is tainted with self-righteous holiness till he acquires energy in the wilderness, and Howard (1984: 65-66) considers him ambiguously pious from one viewpoint, 'wicked' from another. Price (1964: 413, 416) raises the possibility that the just man and the villain may be two aspects of the same person.

2:5 **The vale of death**—"this world" (Damon 1924: 90). Stevenson (1971: 103) perceives an allusion to Christian's passage through the Valley of the Shadow of Death in Bunyan's *The Pilgrim's Progress*.

2:6-13 The just man, being religious, sees only the sterility, not the fruitfulness (Gleckner 1959: 188); Blake is emphasising the co-existence of contraries (Howard 1984: 65).

2:12 **bleached bones**—both the rocks which became covered with "Red clay" and the resurrected bones of Ezek. xxxvii (Stevenson 1971: 104). These bones are a type of Christ resurrected (Lipking 1976: 231).

2:13 **Red clay**—in the traditional vowelless Hebrew script, the same letters spell *edom* ["red"] and *Adam* (Frye 1947: 391),

whose name means "red clay" (Damon 1924: 316). Edom was
a name given to Esau (Raine 1968: I, 337-38) on account of the
red pottage for which he surrendered his birthright to his
younger brother, Jacob (Gen. xxv.30 and AV marginal gloss),
and (Damon 1967: 128) it became the name of the country in-
habited by Esau's descendants. This country's devastation is
predicted in Is. xxxiv.5-15, where it is called Idumea (Bloom
1965: 896); moreover, Isaiah's question "Who is this that
cometh from Edom...?" (lxiii.1) is interpreted as a prophecy of
the Messiah (Frye 1947: 214 and 443n44). Blake can thus
make interlocking references to Adam, the second Adam (who
is Christ), and Jacob, who cheated Esau out of his birthright
and stole his blessing (Gen. xxvii.6-29). These references ext-
end to pl. 3, where he declares, "Now is the dominion of Edom,
& the return of Adam into Paradise"; here he alludes not only
to the prophecy of desolation and redemption in Is. xxxiv and
xxxv, but also (Bloom, *loc. cit.*) to Isaac's words to the cheated
Esau in Gen. xxvii.40: "it shall come to pass when thou shalt
have the dominion, that thou shalt break his [Jacob's] yoke
from off thy neck."

   The "red clay" is on one level the dust out of which Adam is
made and perhaps, by extension, it stands both for him and for
the second Adam, who comes from Edom (Bloom 1965: 897).
Its bringing forth signifies to Erdman (1954a: 175 [191]) the
rebirth of Adam initiating a new historical cycle, to Wagen-
knecht (1973: 171) the Incarnation leading to the estab-
lishment of the Church, and to Jackson (1971: 208) the
creation of works of art with material from the unconscious.

2:14   **the villain**—the hypocritical serpent who penetrates the just
   man's Eden (Damon 1924: 90); the parasite who exhausts the
   civilisation the just man has created (Jackson 1971: 208-09);
   the anti-revolutionary French priest (Erdman 1954a: 175-76
   [191-92]); the time-serving London clergyman (Gardner 1968:
   86).

2:16   **barren climes**—codified morality (Keynes 1975b: pl. 2).

pl. 3   **the Eternal Hell revives**—the eruption of revolutions in
   America and France (Keynes 1975b: xii); opposition to the inc-
   reasingly conservative English Swedenborgians from rational-
   ists and radicals associated with the publisher Joseph Johnson
   (Howard 1970: 37).

dominion of Edom—either the overthrow of Edom (Margoliouth 1948: 303) or rule by Edom (Mellor 1974: 41): the ambiguity, believes Howard (1984: 68), is deliberate. Edom, according to Frye (1947: 214), is the realm of desire which remains outside Jacob's theocracy. Bloom (1965: 896) plausibly maintains that Esau's (Edom's and France's) revolutionary spirit is about to triumph in or over Jacob's Britain, and Tannenbaum (1982: 112) adds that the allusion to Is. lxiii.1 implies that out of revolutionary France comes the Redeemer. Contrariwise, Nurmi (1957b: 30), citing Isaiah's prophecy that the nobles and princes would vanish from Idumea (xxxiv.12), interprets Edom as the existing social structure and its supporting ideology that are about to be crushed. Raine (1968: I, 338) notes Swedenborg's belief that Jacob's stolen blessing will revert to Esau and that this signifies that humans in the body will regain their original relationship with the Divine Humanity.

pl. 4 Blake knows, says Wittreich (1975: 209-10), that the Devil is wrong to claim that the Bible teaches that the body and soul are separate entities and that the body is evil.

If "Energy is the only life," deduces Stavrou (1955: 384), matter is an illusion and body is the outermost element of soul. Price (1964: 413) offers as a definition of the non-dualistic body "energy perceived as mass."

pls. 5-6 **Those who restrain desire**—members of the New Jerusalem Church, claims Howard (1970: 40), who reject Swedenborg's limited toleration of concubinage.

Messiah—The Miltonic Messiah torments Satan as the biblical Satan torments Job (Bloom 1963: 81).

he prays to the Father—See John xiv.16-17. Nurmi's claim (1957b: 36) that Jesus stands for Reason, like Stevenson's (1971: 107) that he prays to his enemy Jehovah, who is Energy, contradicts the statement in the last Memorable Fancy that "Jesus was all virtue, and acted from impulse: not from rules." Nearer the mark is Bloom's suggestion (1963: 81-82) that the Son, the Father, and the Holy Spirit are three kinds of desire —"human desire," "Desire removed from all encumbrances," and "a mediating desire binding man to his envisioned fulfillment."

he, who dwells in flaming fire—Blake's original reading, which he altered on the engraved plate, was "the Devil who dwells in flaming fire" (E801).

after Christ's death, he became Jehovah—Christians continue to worship the Old Testament God under Christ's name (Damon 1924: 318). From an historical perspective, the churches' Christ seems to take on Jehovah's vengefulness, but from an eternal perspective Jehovah takes on Christ's mercifulness (Wittreich 1975: 211-12). Blake is reversing Swedenborg's doctrine that Jehovah descended to earth as Christ (Howard 1970: 41).

of the Devil's party without knowing it—In the seventeenth century, both monarchists and republicans frequently charged their opponents with being of the Devil's party; from the royalist viewpoint, Milton is of the Devil's party and does know it (Wittreich 1975: 214-15).

pls. 6-7 (first Memorable Fancy) According to Bloom, this is Blake's response to Milton's account of the fallen angels in Book II of *PL* (1965: 898), and the act of walking among the infernal fires symbolises the creation of a poem or picture (1963: 82). In a detailed exposition, Erdman (1951a: 213-14) interprets the "mighty Devil" as Blake himself, the "flat sided steep" as his copper plate, and the "corroding fires" as his etching acid. Murry (1933: 67-68) identifies the black clouds with those of the revolutionary Rintrah in the Argument.

pls. 7-10 "Proverbs of Hell"—There is widespread agreement that Blake intended many of these proverbs to be open to multiple interpretations. They "offer," writes Schorer (1946: 256), "almost endless delights to contemplation." Nurmi, however, (1957b: 40) warns that they express only part of the truth, ignoring, for example, the need for some measure of reason. They are partly inspired by Lavater's *Aphorisms on Man* (Damon 1924: 92), and they parody the prudential maxims of the biblical Book of Proverbs (Bloom 1963: 85). The comments that follow refer to the proverbs by number.

1 The reference is both to the seasons of life and to sexual initiation rites (Bloom 1963: 85). In this sequence, Blake contrives that prudence will lead to joy (Widmer 1965: 43).

2 Tradition can fertilize (Damon 1924: 319). Do not let traditional prejudices obstruct you (Sloss and Wallis 1926: II, 52).

Engage in revitalising sexuality at the expense of convention (Bloom 1963: 85).

6 The worm is weak and cowardly (Sloss and Wallis 1926: I, 15n2). Practise forgiveness (Damon 1924: 319); revenge is not a natural instinct (Damon 1967: 329). (1) Exercise Christian forgiveness; (2) do not be unassertive like the worm (Howard 1984: 77).

7 This refers to immersion in sexuality (Bloom 1963: 86).

10-12 Creative time is contrasted with time wasted or merely endured (Bloom 1963: 86).

14 Middleman (1971) cites Dan. v.25-28 as Blake's source, while Blunt (1938: 79-80, 96n29) points to The Wisdom of Solomon xi.20, and suggests that Blake is countering Plato's view that art deludes whereas measuring, numbering and weighing lead to truth (*Republic* x.602). Particularly plausible is Frost's theory (1971) that the proverb mocks Andrew Marvell for being dazzled by the "Number, Weight and Measure" he found so praiseworthy in the blank verse of Milton (Marvell, "On *Paradise Lost*," l. 54). Bloom (1963: 86) acutely perceives an attack on conventions both social and metrical, while Damon (1924: 320) sees specific criticism of pedantic eighteenth-century poetry and Thomas Wright (1929: I, 42) detects a protest against hoarding corn in time of scarcity. Gillham, however, (1973: 164) maintains that devils, unlike angels, only exercise restraint when circumstances make it essential.

16 Your behaviour to a living person will elicit a reaction (Stevenson 1971: 109); the dead body signifies broken conventions (Bloom 1963: 87).

22-25 Everything is good in God's sight (Nurmi 1957b: 40).

27 These phenomena are too great only for the natural man, not the true man (Nurmi 1957b: 39); they are too great for the eye but not for the mind that looks *through* and not *with* it (Blackstone: 1949: 51).

29 Diverse experiences are necessary (T. Wright 1929: I, 43).

30 This proverb advocates "a fairly aggressive masculinity" (Widmer 1965: 216n16).

33 Imagination is necessary even for the achievement of rational proof (Nurmi 1957b: 40).

34 Small animals seek causes, great ones results (Damon 1924: 320). (1) Big creatures fare best; (2) each creature should act in accordance with its own nature (Howard 1984: 78).

35 The cistern represents talent, the fountain genius (Damon 1924: 320).

36 Thought signifies energy, immensity reason (Gardner 1954: 41).

41 This describes the course of a normal human life (Damon 1924: 321). It refers to vision (for which morning was traditionally regarded as favourable), the practice of art, the study of art and wisdom, and the absorption of knowledge in repose (Blackstone 1949: 405).

43 Inspiration and willpower come from calling on the deity within ourselves (Damon 1967: 334). Discussion of plans precedes the work (Stevenson 1971: 110). See also proverb 59n.

44 The tigers are admired not because they are fierce but because they fulfil their own nature; the horses are the repressed houyhnhnms of Swift's *Gulliver's Travels* (Baine and Baine 1974).

48 All nature is comprehended in humankind (Nurmi 1957b: 39); "the beard of earth" associates old age with the grave (Stevenson 1971: 110).

57 Each of the four words can be taken as either a noun or a verb: the meaning is both that one should reject what makes rigid and be thankful for what loosens, and that condemnation strengthens while blessing weakens (Johnson 1970a).

59 This may be a disparagement of prayer (Erdman 1954a: 162 [177]) or mockery of the Swedenborgian church's increasing preoccupation with the form of worship (Howard 1970: 42). Damon (1924: 321-22) interprets both 43 and 59 as meaning God only rewards those who exert themselves.

60 The most profound feelings do not express themselves (Damon 1924: 322).

64 Blake is rejecting the demands of form (Widmer 1965: 45).

67 Primarily an instance of hyperbole intended to shock, this proverb has provoked the following interpretations: nursing an unacted desire will turn it into a destructive monster (Bloom 1963: 87); nursing unacted desire and murdering an infant are two similar evils (Howard 1970: 42-43); to destroy a person's

potential is as bad as murder (G. Taylor 1973); to leave a desire unacted is to murder it in its infant state (Howard 1984: 78). Murry (1933: 118) regards the "infant" as the desire experienced in a first love.

68 Nature needs humankind to see the infinite beneath its surface appearance (Hirsch 1964: 64-65).

70 "I have said enough—indeed too much" (Damon 1924: 322). These proverbs are sufficient from the devils' viewpoint but too much from the angels' (Nurmi 1957b: 41). Too much, which is the right reaction to too little, will lead to equilibrium—i.e. enough (Emery 1963: 59). Only "Too much" *is* "Enough" (Widmer 1965: 42-43).

pl. 11 **enlarged & numerous senses**—senses not confined to a few specific bodily organs: sight, for example, that is able to operate in all directions (Frosch 1974: 143).

pls. 12-13 (second Memorable Fancy) **a firm perswasion**—an allusion to Matt. xvii.20 (Damon 1924: 93); a response to Locke's insistence in *An Essay Concerning Human Understanding* IV.xix.12 that "firmness of persuasion " and "confidence of being in the right" are no guarantee of truth (Raine 1968: II, 112).

also asked Isaiah what made him go naked...I then asked Ezekiel why he eat dung—See Is. xx.3, Ezek. iv.12. Like some acts performed by Saul and David under prophetic inspiration, Ezekiel's use of dung contravenes—to Blake's delight—the Mosaic Law (Helms 1978). Blake is showing that monotheism is not an advance over polytheism but a device for exercising power over society (Pechey 1979: 63). Isaiah and Ezekiel are objects of Blake's satire who fail to recognise that "All Religions Are One" when they defend Israelite chauvinism, then contradict themselves by praising Diogenes and American Indians (Howard 1984: 82-83). In referring to practices of these last, Blake may be thinking of young men's initiation ordeals (Stevenson 1971: 114).

pl. 14 **consumed in fire**—the fire of the American and French Revolutions (Damon 1924: 93); "the fire of intellect and art" (Bloom 1963: 88).

the cherub—Reason (Damon 1924: 93); the Covering Cherub of *Milton* and *Jerusalem* (Nurmi 1957b: 44).

his flaming sword—oppressive morality (Howard 1984: 83).

tree of life—in Damon's view, sexual love (1924: 93) or the phallus, for sex offers the readiest entrance to Eternity (Damon 1967: 410).

his cavern—the skull (Damon 1924: 324); the skull or body of the fallen human (Bloom 1963: 88).

pl. 15   (third Memorable Fancy) Most critics agree that this intriguing passage describes either the inspired artist's creative process or the stages of Blake's illuminated printing or both. Emery (1963: 78) considers the printing house to be the poet himself, Cooper (1981: 85) contrasts the energetic production of works in the five chambers of the artist's mind with their dangerously tame reception by men, and Frosch (1974: 174-76) perceives here an analogy between the making of art and an ascent from a natural to an Edenic state. According to Widmer (1965: 46), the whole account, with its six chambers, is a parody, ending in anti-climax (libraries are the grave of sensibility), of the biblical account of creation in six days. On one level, believes Rose (1972b: 143), the chambers stand for the six thousand years of history. In a Freudian reading, Webster (1983: 63) interprets the caves as the mother's body fertilised by the Oedipal son and the creative activities as bodily functions.

In the first chamber the Dragon-Man, who may be a symbol of sexuality (Damon 1924: 94, 324) or of sensual delight as viewed by the religious (Nurmi 1957b: 46), clears away "conventional laws" (Keynes 1975b: pl. 15) or worn out ideas and language (Mellor 1974: 51). According to Bloom (1965: 899), the nearby dragons expand the senses other than touch. The viper is usually considered to represent reason (Damon, *loc. cit.*), which is regarded either as one of the fruitful contraries (Nurmi 1957b: 46) or as an ominous power which tries to prevent consciousness from expanding. To do this, it exploits gold and silver, which are beautiful but lifeless (Gleckner 1959: 187), or which signify enticing but fossilised truths (Damon 1924: 324), or which represent the attractions of the natural world (Frosch 1974: 175). Commentators from Damon (*loc. cit.*) on have recognised the snake's counterpart or opponent as the Eagle of Genius of the fifty-fourth Proverb, who expands consciousness, and Bloom (1963: 89) adds that the eagle-like men have a share of this genius and are artists.

Melted down by lions—symbols of righteous anger (Damon 1924: 94), imagination (T. Wright 1929: I, 44), energy (Nurmi 1957b: 47), or the passions (Emery 1963: 80-81)—the precious metals become the material of art. (Wittreich, however, [1975: 150] interprets the eagle-like men and the lions as traditional and innovative prophets respectively.) The word "cast" means both "thrown" and "moulded" (Nurmi 1957b: 47); "forms" means both "shapes" and "frames of type ready for printing" (Emery 1963: 81).

There are minor difficulties in reading the passage as on one level a representation of Blake's mode of engraving. Erdman (1969a: 411-13) admits that the stages of the work must be jumbled, if, as he supposes, the dragon-man and dragons represent the engraver and his tools or fingers, the gold and silver stand for inks and pigments, the Eagle of Genius supplies thoughts and visions, the eagle-like men signify the inscribing hands and tools, and the fourth and fifth chambers are the sites respectively of the acid bath and the plate-making. Howard (1984: 84-85) interprets the dragon as an etching needle, the dragon-man and eagle as removers of gouged up wax, the viper as a bounding ridge to keep the acid in place, the eagle-like men as writing implements, the lions as acid, and the unnamed forms as shapeless inkers.

Eschewing detailed interpretation, Crehan (1984: 146-47) claims that this Memorable Fancy reflects the world of politically radical authors, illustrators and printers; Howard (1970: 45) proposes that it pictures specifically the Swedenborgians' view of the radicals associated with the publisher Joseph Johnson. Sutherland (1970: 247) sees in the dragons, viper, eagle and lions a foreshadowing of the four Zoas or "functions of the psyche."

pls. 16-17 **But the Prolific**—The prolific need some appreciation from the devourers (Damon 1924: 94); they can become chaotically creative if not circumscribed by reason (Bloom 1963: 90-91). Erdman (1954a: 164 [179]) notes that there is an economic reference to producers and consumers.

Note—See Matt. xxv.32-33 and x.34. The equating of reasoners with the accursed goats implies that they are lost souls (Damon 1924: 94). Erdman (1974: 114) deduces from the tiny drawings of a rearing goat and bounding horse that intel-

lectual war is referred to; Keynes (1975b: pls. 16-17) interprets
these animals as prolific and the accompanying standing horse
and grazing sheep as devouring. The sword, says Howard
(1984: 91), is on one level an engraver's burin.

The word "Antediluvians" identifies the Giants of the first
paragraph in pl. 16 and in the design above with those of Gen.
vi.1-5. According to Emery (1963: 85), Blake is reinterpreting
this passage to support his idea that the natural man, the
Devourer, vainly tries to kill the supposedly wicked Giant (who
is the real human) buried inside him. The last sentence
implies, argues Nurmi (1957b: 49), that Christ was once
classified among those the religious now regard as devils.

pls. 17-20 (fourth Memorable Fancy) **foolish young man**—
Blake parodies the warning about the hell of revolution that
Burke in his *Reflections on the Revolution in France* (1790)
recalls giving to a "very young gentleman at Paris" (Pechey
1979: 67).

eternal lot—The term "lot" here signifies "identity" (Nurmi
1957b: 50).

thro' a stable & thro' a church...—The six locations from
the stable to the void are six negative images parallel to the six
creative chambers of the printing house in pl. 15. The series
may represent six features of the materialist's world: the stable
of the reasoning horses of instruction (Damon 1924: 94); the
church of religion (Schorer 1946: 261); the church vault of
dead passion (Damon, *loc. cit.*) or of Jesus' tomb—see pl. 3
(Nurmi 1957b: 50); the mill of reasoning (Damon 1924: 94), of
Aristotelian philosophy (Damon 1967: 273); the cave and
winding way of the church's repressiveness and cunning (Sloss
and Wallis 1926: I, 21n2) or of the fallen mind (Bloom 1963:
92); and the nether void of Locke's *tabula rasa* (Ostriker 1977:
901) or of "the abyss of nature" (Bloom 1963: 92) or of the
lower world, which, according to the Hermetists, is not entirely
benighted (Raine 1968: II, 19). Sloss and Wallis (*loc. cit.*)
interpret the stable, church and vault as the birth, life and
death of Jesus. However, Paley (1970: 16-17) is probably right
to see the first four items as a chronological sequence, the
nativity in the stable being followed by the primitive church,
the later church, and the mill of Deism.

the twisted root of an oak—a Neoplatonic symbol of earthiness and materiality according to Harper (1961: 171-72); a persistent error according to Damon (1924: 94), who anticipates Blake's later association of oaks with cruel Druidism.

fungus—Angels, who spurn the body, are parasites upon it (Bloom 1963: 92).

the infinite Abyss, fiery...—in part, Swedenborg's view of the hell of energy (Nurmi 1957b: 51). Eaves (1972: 87-89, 108-09) suggests that what the Angel sees is both a Last Judgment in which Jesus is present as a black sun between the sheep and goats (or the black and white spiders) and the preparation of one of Blake's illuminated pages: the sun is the reflection of Blake's head in the copper, the spiders are his hands, the tempest is the pouring of acid, the emergence of Leviathan is the raising of the plate, and his forehead represents the print and colour on the page. Damon (1924: 94-95) sees an echo of traditional paintings of the Last Judgment, in which devils and angels (cf. the black and white spiders) contend for fallen human souls (cf. the "animals sprung from corruption").

the sun, black but shining—emits heat or wrath without light (Damon 1924: 94). Cf. Boehme's First Principle.

the black & white spiders—the Angel's categories of good and evil (Damon 1967: 240).

to the east, distant about three degrees—descriptive of Paris's position in relation to London (Nurmi 1957b: 51).

Leviathan—see note below on the design. Webster (1983: 80-82) claims that this is one of several images that Blake exploits to project the fear and rage that are really his own onto the Swedenborgian angel.

climb'd up from his station into the mill—is forced from the fungus of dogma to the mill of argument (Damon 1924: 95); seeks refuge in theology (Bloom 1963: 92); retreats to the scientist's solar system (Eaves 1972: 112-13).

a pleasant bank...a harper—The harper has been identified with the Bard of "Introduction" to *SE* (Nurmi 1957b: 52) and the scene, somewhat anachronistically, with Beulah, a higher state than either reason or energy (Beer 1969: 28, 30). Mellor (1974: 49) views Leviathan and the Harper as two manifestations of Innocence in the form of Energy.

westerly—The west [the way to America] is the direction of freedom (Damon 1924: 95), or it is the quarter of sunset and decay (Eaves 1972: 111).

above the earth's shadow—beyond philosophical materialism (Nurmi 1957b: 52).

into the body of the sun—alluding to Swedenborg's contention (*Divine Love and Divine Wisdom*, section 110) that no angel can enter the spiritual sun without being consumed, Blake implies that spirit is not prior to and the source of body (Pechey 1979: 66-67).

clothed myself in white—The white garments are a Swedenborgian symbol of truth (Nurmi 1957b: 53, citing *Heaven and Hell*, section 179), but they have also been taken to signify a shroud (Eaves 1972: 112).

the void, between saturn & the fixed stars—The journey is based on a diagram in Boehme's works (Nurmi 1957b: 53). It is the reverse of the Miltonic Satan's journey from the boundary of the universe to the earth, and the void is Milton's "Limbo...since calld/ The Paradise of Fools" (*PL*, III, 495-96) (Raine 1968: II, 59-61). In his *Letters to the Members of the New Jerusalem Church* (1791), Joseph Priestley shows that Swedenborg's alleged visionary space travel has failed to show him that beyond Saturn there exists the recently discovered Uranus (Howard 1970: 47).

the Bible...was a deep pit—that is, the Bible as the orthodox understand it (Nurmi 1957b: 55).

seven houses of brick—the seven churches of Asia of Rev. i.11 (Sloss and Wallis 1926: I, 23n1, citing Swinburne). Long after, in his Laocoön engraving (E274/ K777), Blake identified these churches with the Antichrist (Damon 1967: 24).

monkeys, baboons, & all of that species—people living under the government of 'angels' and reduced to imitating each other like monkeys (T. Wright, 1929: I, 45); the Devourers turned insane (Nurmi 1957b: 55-56); disputing theologians (Bloom 1963: 92-93); humankind as Hobbes, author of *Leviathan*, sees it (Price 1964: 419); another version of the infernal printing house, the cannibalism signifying plagiarism disguised as polemics (Eaves 1972: 115).

we impose on one another—Pechey (1979: 66) reads this as a postmodern assertion that there is no reliable access to a truth transcending the play of human language and discourse.

pls. 22-24 (fifth Memorable Fancy) **The worship of God...no other God**—Blake is not saying that humankind is God but that God is immanent in humankind (Damon 1924: 89). Blake shares the doctrine here expressed with the seventeenth-century British antinomian sect of Ranters (Morton 1958: 42). This passage is related to I Cor. xii, which proclaims that all Christians can receive the Holy Spirit and become members of the body of Christ (Tannenbaum 1982: 83-84).

great men—great artists (Bloom 1963: 94).

bray a fool in a morter—Blake makes his Devil quote Prov. xxvii. 22 (Miner 1969: 265, 467n26).

arose as Elijah—The Angel has become a composite of angel and devil, for he has undergone a Last Judgment, rejecting error and embracing truth (Nurmi 1957b: 57, alluding to E562/ K613). The Angel has stretched out his arms to unite with Christ through the senses and become a part of his body (Tannnenbaum 1982: 83-84); being Elijah, he is also St. John the Baptist and he heralds the redemption described in "A Song of Liberty" (*ibid.*: 116; cf. Matt. xi.14).

pls. 25-27 "A Song of Liberty" This composition has been described as patterned after Deborah's and Barak's victory song of Judg. v.2-31 (Bateson 1957: 131); as a parody of Moses' song after the crossing of the Red Sea, Exod. xv.1-19 (Helms 1979: 289-90); and as modelled on Rev.—especially its twelfth chapter, which ends with the Messiah triumphant (Lipking 1976: 240). Wagenknecht, however, (1973: 180-81) finds the "Song" elegiac and sees no clear indication that Orc is victorious, while Crehan (1984: 154-55) is uncertain whether the conflict between contraries, which he interprets as classes, will end. The comments below are keyed to the numbers of the verses.

1-2 Besides Enitharmon (Damon 1924: 326), the Female has been identified as the earth seeking escape from a sick creation (Schorer 1946: 263) and as in part the mother of Jesus (Gleckner 1959: 194-95). Gardner (1968: 87-88) detects in her a hint of the Roman Church.

4-5 A call for the end of the Spanish and Papal empires (Erdman 1954a: 176 [192]). Spain is made golden by riches from its American conquests (Damon 1967: 380).

7 **the new born terror**—Orc (Damon 1924: 326); both Christ and everyman (Gleckner 1959: 194).

8 **the atlantic sea**—both "fallen nature" and the chaos imposed by tyrants (Bloom 1965: 900); the sea of the west (see 13), the quarter symbolising the body, whose liberation marks the beginning of revolution (Damon 1924: 326).

12 A call to end the British slave trade (Erdman 1954a: 176 [192]).

14 Like the west, the sea represents the body, and Orc drives away the latter's physicality (Damon 1924: 326); he drives away the waters that keep humankind from fraternity (Nurmi 1957b: 62). The "eternal sleep" is spiritual dormancy [i.e. sleep from Eternity] (Jackson 1971: 217).

15 When the physical aspect of the body is transcended, Reason (Urizen) loses its throne (Damon, *loc. cit.*). Urizen suffers the fate of Milton's Satan (Helms 1979: 289). He descends to quench the new liberty of France (Nurmi, *loc. cit.*), or his fall represents Britain's defeat by the American colonies (Erdman 1954a: 176 [192]).

16 **Urthona's dens**—the realm of spirit (Schorer 1946: 263); the lowest region of spirit (Damon 1924: 326) or the subconscious (Damon 1967: 263); a subhuman condition (Erdman 1954a: 233 [253]); "primitive, brutish nature" (Bateson 1957: 131); the Greco-Roman underworld and its Ossianic equivalent U-thorno, a Neoplatonic symbol for this world (Raine 1968: I, 245)—Thomas Wright [1929: I, 23] earlier noted a connection with U-thorno; a prison holding the Zoa of art (Keynes 1975b: pls. 25-27).

"Urthona" may also derive from German *Ur* ("primitive" or "ancient") and *Thon* ("clay"), and it appears to be a play on "earth-owner" (Damon 1924: 326)—this being, conjectures Bloom (1963: 195), lived on the earth before it and he fell and he became Los. Fisher (1961: 231) suggests the name is an anagram of Greek *Thronou* ("throne") found in Rev.iv.6. Percival (1938: 36) identifies Urthona with Boehme's First Principle.

18-19   The British tyrant is horrified when the morning of revolution breaks in France (Erdman 1954a: 176 [192]).

his starry hosts—the Israelites who came out of Egypt (Damon 1967: 385); the Duke of Brunswick's army—see 20n (Erdman 1954a: 176 [192]).

beamy—nearly blinded, an allusion to the beam in the hypocrite's eye, Matt. vii.3 (Helms 1979: 290).

20 **curses**—obscurantism (Damon 1924: 326); perhaps the Duke of Brunswick's manifesto of July 1792 promising that Austria and Prussia would destroy Paris if Louis XVI were not reinstated (Erdman 1954a: 175-76 [191-92]).

loosing the eternal horses—Urizen's horses of reason (Damon 1967: 189, 420); these horses of instruction are now transformed into horses of intellect in whom energy and reason are synthesised after pure energy (the disappearing lion and wolf) has completed its work of revolution (Erdman 1954a: 179 [195]).

the dens of night—an echo of "Urthona's dens" (Jackson 1971: 217).

lion & wolf—They will no longer fight each other because they are in the state of Innocence (Schorer 1946: 263-64) or of the higher Innocence (Gleckner 1959: 196). They have been identified as respectively the guardian and enemy of the sheep (Damon 1967: 263), and as Austria and Prussia, who are no longer a threat to the French Republic after Brunswick's September defeat at Valmy (Erdman 1954a: 176 [192]).

Chorus **the Raven**—Urizen (Nurmi 1957b: 62), with an allusion to Odin's raven (Bloom 1963: 97).

his accepted brethren—the European rulers (Bloom 1963: 97).

lay the bound—Murry (1933: 85) contrasts this negative act with the creative state of being "the bound or outward circumference of Energy" (pl. 4).

that...that wishes but acts not—This is contrasted with everything that really lives and is therefore holy (Bloom 1963: 97).

every thing that lives is Holy—an ironic allusion to Rev. xv.4: "for thou [the Lord] only art holy" (Helms 1979: 291).

Designs

pl. 1   The marriage of the title, accomplished in pl. 24 when an
angel embraces an infernal flame, is here shown in the embr-
ace of a devil emerging from flame and an angel emerging
from cloud (Damon 1967: 138). The genders of both figures
are uncertain—they could be androgynous and they may differ
from copy to copy (Grant 1970b). They represent interacting
contraries (Howard 1984: 69, 74), which may include the
union of soul and body (Keynes 1975b: pl.1).

Above the hell where the marriage occurs, is a heaven of
inhibited behaviour (Howard, *loc. cit.*), or more probably, a
portion of the earth's surface, the site of "the paths of ease" of
2:14 (Nurmi 1957b: 58) or of "forests of error" (Damon 1924:
327) or of "two trees of Mystery" (Bloom 1963: 72). Mitchell
(1978: 11) contrasts the happy lovers above the devil's fire
with the frustrated suitor and unresponsive woman above the
angel's cloud. Near the top right corner, the largest bird repre-
sents the soaring imagination, the five smaller ones the senses
(Erdman 1974: 97). Small couples and single figures are rising
obliquely towards the flames in the upper scene—perhaps in
danger of losing their sexuality (Bloom 1963: 72) but perhaps
to bring new life to a barren 'heaven' (Keynes 1975b: pl. 1).

pl. 2   This design, which may be deliberately enigmatic (Erdman
1974: 99), has been very diversely interpreted. Noting its close
resemblance to the second plate of "The Ecchoing Green,"
Damon (1924: 327) regards its subject as the "joys of Inno-
cence," but Paley (1978b: 21-22, 75n5) points out that the
parallel does not guarantee that the scene is positive. The two
large figures may both be female (Keynes 1975b: pl. 2), though
Damon (*loc. cit.*) and Grant (1969: 366) refer to the upper one
as male. But is fruit (Bindman 1977: 68) or something invisi-
ble (Erdman, *loc. cit.*) being handed down, or are two empty
hands meeting in front of a leaf, the theme being the sterility of
society (Keynes, *loc. cit.*)? Erdman (*loc. cit.*) suggests that the
story of Satan's temptation of Eve is being reinterpreted as a
story of joys "stolen in secret" (cf. *E* iii:6), but several critics
follow Damon's early lead (*loc. cit.*) in identifying the tall tree
with the Tree of Life. Thus Grant (*loc. cit.*) perceives Adam
and Eve fallen by the stunted Tree of Knowledge and undoing

their fall by eating fruit from the Tree of Life. Yet the ground shown may be the desert-made-fertile of the poem (Howard 1984: 74) —or its "barren climes" (Keynes, *loc. cit.*). Margoliouth (1951: 76) sees an energetic person giving fruit to one with less initiative, and Emery (1963: 100) suggests there may be a marriage of Experience (above) with Innocence (below).

pl. 3 As Erdman (1974: 100) observes, the fire and cloud of hell on the title page reappear at the top and bottom of this plate. Above is a freed soul (Damon 1924: 327) in flames of the reviving hell (Howard 1984: 75). The picture represents an act of copulation whose product is the birth below of the baby who reappears in *IB* pl. 4 (Bindman 1977: 68). This child may be inspiration (M. Plowman 1927b: 14), Orc (Damon 1924: 327) or Esau, Orc's prototype (Raine 1968: I, 338-39). His birth may signify the beginning of the new heaven (Keynes 1960). In the bottom right corner are a pair of contraries—a running man and a reclining woman (Lipking 1976: 226); Howard (1970: 39) believes that they are Adam and Eve as they flee the Swedenborgian church, which is giving birth to doctrine on a cloud of error.

pl. 4 An Innocent angel may have just rescued a young soul (Damon 1924: 327) or may be saving it from capture by frustrated desire (Margoliouth 1951: 76) but he (or she [Erdman 1974: 102] may wrongly fear energy (Paley 1978b: 22). The devil may be the body made dangerous by enslavement (M. Plowman 1927b: 14) or energy striving to save Orc from a repressive guardian (Keynes 1975b: pl 4). However, Erdman's view (1974: 101-02) that the angel and devil are soul and body reaching towards each other gains some support from his demonstration that minute figures on this and subsequent pages seem to show how relations between body and soul fluctuate.

pl. 5 A male figure falls with a horse, sword, and cloak (Keynes 1975b) or saddlecloth and the remains of a chariot wheel (Erdman 1974: 102). A small orb near the horse's head and (in some copies) a larger one near the man's right arm may be the moon and the sun or Mars (Erdman, *loc. cit.*).

The falling figure has been taken for Orc (Damon 1924: 327), restrained, perverted desire (Margoliouth 1951: 76), and a representative man (Baine and Baine 1974). There is also an allusion to Phaeton, who fell because he could not control the chariot of the sun he had borrowed from his father (Lipking 1976: 235-36). Percival (1938: 244-45) quotes Eliphaz Levi's account of the Cabbalistic contrary of Jehovah, "an unbridled horse which overthrows its rider and precipitates him into the abyss," and Howard (1970: 40) proposes that the steed is one of the rational horses of instruction.

Smith (1933) points out that the picture shows the Miltonic Satan's fall from the angels' viewpoint, but if it is turned upside down, it shows the same event as the devil sees it; both Satan and the horse are then perceived as figures of energy, and there is an expression of exultation on the former's face.

pl. 10　Orc (Damon 1924: 327) or Satan (Keynes 1960) or one of the devils (Stevenson 1971: 111) appears to be dictating the Proverbs of Hell. The scribes on his left and right have been identified respectively as Innocence and Experience (M. Plowman 1927b: 13), as both the angel who becomes a devil in pl. 14 and Blake himself (Bindman 1977: 69), and, most plausibly, as a swift writer and an amanuensis who has fallen behind (Erdman 1974: 107). Keynes (*loc. cit.*) considers that they are women and one is looking at what the other writes, Paley (1978b: 22) that they are recording angels to whom the devil is showing his scroll, and G. Taylor (1974: 144) that they are novices whom he is instructing. Pechey (1979: 74n3) sees an allusion to Cruikshank's 1792 caricature of Paine and Priestley as a devil's pupils, and Wittreich (1975: 269-70) perceives Milton, his errors symbolised by bat's wings, turning from a daughter of inspiration to a daughter of memory.

pl. 11　Above on an island or peninsula are figures projected from the human mind. These may include a solar deity and a nude woman representing a stream (Damon 1924: 327); there is also a baby who may personify a flower or worm (Erdman 1974: 108) or a plant (Damon, *loc. cit.*) or waves (Mellor 1974: 142); Keynes and Wolf (1953: 34) regard the infant as Orc, the woman as earth, and the centre figure as the Poetic Genius.

Below is a god to whom an independent existence has been attributed: he closely resembles the Urizen of *A IB* pl. 8, and, as Mellor (*loc.cit.*) comments, he may well be the figure in the tree stump and he has a strong likeness to Nebuchadnezzar on *IB* pl. 24. There is an echo of Michelangelo's *God Creating Adam*, but the man Urizen has created is slipping away from him (Keynes 1975b: pl. 11). Damon (1924: 327) identifies the parting figure as Orc fleeing Urizen and Mellor (1974: 142) as a prostrate female nude.

pl. 14   The common interpretation is that a female figure—the emanation (Damon 1924: 347) or soul (Binyon 1926: 99)—is trying to arouse a dormant body (e.g. Keynes 1960: [3]) or (Howard 1984: 86) to expand a constricted consciousness. Paley, however, (1978b: 22) sees here an illustration of the soul's illusory separateness from the body, Bindman (1977: 70) perceives the body's eternal form rising from a corpse, and Howard, in his earlier reading (1970: 45), posits that the world is being consumed in flames to be reborn as the man on pl. 21.

pl. 15   The union of contraries depicted here, like most of the Proverbs of Hell, can have a number of valid applications. It may well simultaneously represent the Eagle of Genius elevating nature (Damon 1967: 112), imagination and reason co-operating (Nurmi 1957b: 47), and vision together with the engraver's craftsmanship that embodies it (Erdman 1974: 112-13). Howard (1984: 86), who sees here imagination raising the material body, states that the snake's five coils represent the senses; Hirst (1964: 135) classifies the figure as an alchemical symbol of the union of matter and spirit; and Lipking (1976: 224) interprets it as "the method in which knowledge is transmitted," a phrase marked with a serpent-shaped curlicue.

pl. 16   The source of this design is an episode in Dante's *Inferno*, xxxiii, in which an archbishop has Count Ugolino, his two sons, and his two grandsons starved to death (e.g. Damon 1967: 97), but the figures here are the imprisoned giants of the text representing the senses (Damon 1924: 328).

pl. 20   Critics are divided over whether the Leviathan illustrated here is a negative or a positive figure. His opponents see him as nature with a side glance at Hobbes's absolutist "great Leviathan called a Commonwealth or State" (Damon 1924: 95), as materialism victorious in the Sea of Time and Space (M. Plowman 1927b: 14), as reason in these same waters (Beer 1969: 272), and as the object of the angel's worship unmasked (Bindman 1977: 67). But since the narrator credits Leviathan with "all the fury of a spiritual existence," it seems more probable that he is a manifestation of energy who is ugly in the angel's eyes (Nurmi 1957b: 51). Beer (1968: 58) feels that the energy is in some danger of drowning in the Sea of Time and Space, and Erdman (1974: 117) notes that the tongue points in the same upward direction as the aspiring eagle's beak in *IB* pl. 15.

pl. 21   The reborn human (Damon 1924: 328) enjoys "the sunrise of Eternity" (M. Plowman 1927b: 14). A skull beneath his left knee symbolises the grave (Keynes 1960) or reason (Howard 1984: 94), and his right hand presses down on a paper that signifies rationalistic philosophy (Erdman 1974: 18).

pl. 24   Based on Dan. iv.24-33, this image of the mad emperor Nebuchadnezzar has been understood as the antithesis of the regenerate man portrayed on *IB* pl. 21 (Blunt 1959: 51), as humanity in the state of nature (M. Plowman 1927b: 14) or the age of disintegration succeeding the triumph of rationalism and natural religion (Frye 1966: 184), as the reason without vision characteristic of tyrannical kings (Erdman 1954a: 177 [193]), as the single vision that recognises only material things (Damon 1967: 297), and—in the light of the aphorism beneath —as human life brutalised by the imposition of one law on all (Nurmi 1957b: 59). Detecting the eagle feathers of Dan. iv.33 on his limbs, Preston (1944: 12) associates him with the lion and ox (of the aphorism) and the eagle and man of Ezek. i.10 and Rev. iv.7, and hence with the fallen forms of the four Zoas of Blake's first epic.

pl. 27   On either side of the subtitle "Chorus," are the liberated eternal horses; the one on the right is learning to look up like the eagle, Leviathan, and the regenerate man in *IB* pls. 15, 20 and 21 (Erdman 1974: 124).

Notes on Criticism for Chapter 4

Visions of the Daughters of Albion

The most obvious source of *Visions of the Daughters of Albion* is Macpherson's *Oithóna*, a prose poem named after its heroine (Frye 1947: 238). Her lover, in contrast to the passive Theotormon, kills her violator, and she herself prefers death to living on in supposed dishonour. To the nobility of Oithóna, Oothoon adds wisdom. Blake, as Erdman demonstrates (1954a: 213-16 [230-33]), seems to have endowed the latter also with the heroism of a young female slave whom Captain J. G. Stedman married, though he was tragically unable to secure her freedom, and whose story he told in *A Narrative, of a five Years' expedition against the Revolted Negroes of Surinam* (1796). Erdman suggests that the double vowels in Oothoon's name come from African names in Stedman's text, for which Blake engraved illustrations in 1792 and 1793. Other names in the poem derive from Tonthormod, Brumo and Lutha—characters in different pieces by Macpherson (Damon 1924: 329, citing H. G. Hewlett).

Another major influence on Blake's book is the feminism of Mary Wollstonecraft, who, like the poet, belonged to the circle of the radical publisher Joseph Johnson: Schorer (1946: 290) notes how close Blake's position is to hers. In *A Vindication of the Rights of Woman* (1792), she protests that women are not educated to be men's equals and are expected, in the name of modesty, to be subdued and prudish. Blake's British women ("the Daughters of Albion") are "Enslav'd" (1:1) in ways that Oothoon, following and expanding the complaints of Wollstonecraft, makes clear. The wider criticism of society in Oothoon's last speech echoes, as Erdman shows (1954a: 224-26 [243-45]), Wollstonecraft's *A Vindication of the Rights of Men* (1790). Murry (1933: 109) suggests that the story Blake tells is essentially Wollstonecraft's, and Wasser (1948) argues in detail that Oothoon's plight represents the suffering of Wollstonecraft when she loved and was rejected by the married artist Fuseli, while the relationship between Bromion and Theotormon mirrors Fuseli's inner conflict. Further considering the parallel with the supposedly liberated but unhappy Wollstonecraft, Hilton (1983: 31-32) accuses Oothoon of having isolated herself in a paralysing stream of rhetoric.

Several other works, as well as classical myths, may have contributed to *Visions*. Damon (1924: 105-06), who cites Thomas Taylor's *A Dissertation on the Eleusinian and Bacchic Mysteries* (*c*. 1790), sees Oothoon as a Persephone descending from Leutha's Vale into the underworld of corporeal life. Frye (1947: 240) identifies her as one of the Hesperides who guard a tree bearing golden apples in the far west and regards the marigold as the equivalent of one of the apples. Turning to Christian sources, Howard (1984: 108) proposes that Blake's book may be an "inversional transformation" of the Song of Songs, while Anderson (1984: 2) claims that in her final speech Oothoon is answering Milton's *Comus* and Wagenknecht (1973: 202) sees in her experiences allusions to those of the same poet's Eve.

The symbolic meanings of Oothoon, Theotormon and Bromion have been diversely defined. There can be little doubt that, as Erdman maintains (1954a: 210-11 [227-28]), Oothoon is at once a woman, a slave, and North and South America. Gardner's claim (1954: 49) that she is the American spirit of rebellion is also plausible. Carefully distinguishing her from an individual person, Max Plowman (1927a: 94) defines her as "the soul in Experience," but Gillham (1973: 194-99) argues that she is a complete human being in contrast to Bromion, who is all sensation, and Theotormon, who is all reason. Blackstone (1949: 315-16) views her in her relationship to Bromion as instinct enslaved by religion.

With his mixture of aggressive violence, philosophical materialism, and legalism, Bromion has been described in contradictory ways. His name has been traced to the Greek *bromios* ("roaring") (Bloom 1965: 900); to Bromius, a name of Bacchus, who, in Thomas Taylor's view, represents the limited presence of intellect in the temporal world (Damon 1924: 329); and to Macpherson's Brumo, a place of worship thought to be haunted at night by the dead (Anderson 1984: 19n8). Max Plowman (1927a: 97) views him as the legalistic restrainer of desire, and Thomas Wright (1929: I, 60) as "conventional religion." To Frye (1947: 241), he seems a Deist and a representative of the moral law and slave-based economy persisting in post-Revolution America. Bloom (1965: 901) regards him as a sadistic puritan, Hinkel

(1979: 286) as hypocritical moral law, and Duerksen (1977: 187) as one with a dogmatic, rational, scientific mentality who denies his guilt. Wagenknecht (1973: 207) classifies him and Oothoon as Theotormon's Spectre and Emanation, and Stevenson (1971: 175) thinks that with his caves and his power to raise a storm on his rival's sea he resembles the winds of classical mythology.

Unmistakably weak, jealous and self-tormenting, Theotormon has been described as desire repressed (M. Plowman 1927a: 97) and restrained by both outer pressures and his own nature (Gardner 1954: 49). Unlike Oothoon, however, he distrusts the senses (Duerksen 1977: 189), and he may represent pure reason cut off from the reality around him (Gillham 1973: 195, 198-99). Murry (1933: 109) suggests he may be the feeble desire of a man whose harsh moral judgment is personified in Bromion, and Webster (1983: 91-92) regards him as playing the part of the son in an Oedipal triangle in which Bromion is the strong father and Oothoon the desirable mother. The first syllable of his name is Greek for "God" (Damon 1924: 329); the remainder may derive from Hebrew *Torah* ("Law") (*ibid.*), Macpherson's Torman, glossed "thunder" (Raine 1968: I, 398n21), or English "torment" (Wagenknecht 1973: 194). He is probably tormented by God (*ibid.*) or by his own idea of God (Bloom 1963: 102). Geographically he represents the Atlantic overshadowed by Bromion in the form of Urizenic storm clouds (Bloom 1965: 901), and politically, claims Wagenknecht (1973: 206), he is the England which never understood the significance of unrest in her American colonies.

There has been some discussion of Oothoon's relationship to the states of Innocence and Experience. She appears to meet the marigold in Innocence and then encounter the horrors of Experience but eventually attain the vision of the higher Innocence (Murry 1932: 24; 1933: 120-21). Nurmi, however, (1976: 104) thinks that she passes from Experience into Innocence, and Gillham (1973: 193) locates her entirely in Innocence while reserving Experience for Theotormon and Bromion.

Probably the most controversial aspect of *Visions* is Oothoon's status as an ideal or less than ideal heroine. Those who would convict Blake of a high degree of male chauvinism have to undermine her standing. Damrosch (1980: 197-98, 201), who remarks that her "nets and traps" (7:23) suspiciously resemble those of the parson (5:18), holds that she remains bound because she seeks joy in surface appearances instead of the underlying spiritual realities. He finds indications that she is a masochist and voyeur (2:11-17; 7:25-26; *IB* pl.3), either because this world has corrupted her sexuality or because sexuality is inherently imperfect. (The charge of perversity is effectively answered by Ackland [1982: 181n8]). Damrosch feels that Blake is not as certain about the merits of free love as he seems to be, and Murry (1932: 23-24) argues that the total triumph of Oothoon's ideal would be unacceptable because it would eliminate the play of contraries (see *MHH*, pl.3). Other criticisms of Oothoon are that as a result of her rape she loses the vision that enabled her to see the flower as both marigold and nymph (Peterson 1973), and that she pours out words to stave off despair without ever engaging the minds of Theotormon and Bromion (Hilton 1983: 31-32). In the eyes of various defenders, Oothoon brings the knowledge and values of Eternity into the temporal world (Raine 1968: I, 166), escapes from conventional modes of thought and never ceases trying to enlighten others (Duerksen 1977: 186), perceives in Urizen's legalism the common cause of Theotormon's and Bromion's deficiencies (George 1980: 128), "defines and defends her own sexuality" (Ostriker 1982: 158), and reflects Blake's hope that women or the female mode of consciousness will promote the redemption of humanity (Mitchell 1978: 191). The most crucial issue is whether Oothoon shares the responsibility for Theotormon's failure to overcome his blindness, a failure that Wagenknecht (1973: 206) feels is not clearly explained.

Details

pl. ii **The Eye sees more than the Heart knows**—The heart may be Theotormon's and Bromion's (Bloom 1963: 102) and the visionary eye Oothoon's (Wagenknecht 1973: 209). Anderson, however, (1984: 4) thinks the latter's heart, obsessed with Theotormon, lags behind her sight, while Mellor (1974: 63) credits that heart with recognising that the stormy side of the world—see the title page design—is not all-powerful. Giving a more general application to the aphorism, Damon (1924: 332) interprets it as meaning that the cruelties of the world are incomprehensible, Fisher (1961: 206-07) as saying that the eye and heart should work together, Peterson (1973: 253, 256) as warning that the eye's perception is merely physical unless the heart sees through it, and Wardle (1978: 334) as expressing the Renaissance belief in the power of visual images to reach the intellect.

iii.4 Leutha may be a sexual temptress (Bloom 1963: 102-03), though Max Plowman (1927a: 100) views her simply as sexual attractiveness, Beer (1968: 40) as sexual freedom, and Damon (1924: 329) as Puritanism. Her vale may be a place in which to hide from one's own sexuality (Bloom 1963: 103) or her genitals (Damon 1967: 265).

1:1 DiSalvo (1983: 162) suggests that the Daughters of Albion are not British women but the inhabitants of British colonies deprived of their age-old liberty.

1:3 **the soft soul of America**—Damon (1924: 329) asserts that the west, with which Oothoon is connected, stands for the body.

1:4 **flowers to comfort her**—according to Erdman (1954a: 219 [236-37]), outbursts of rebellion: when one rising fails, another "shall spring" (1:9). Gathering flowers, claims Damon (*loc. cit.*), indicates the soul's entrapment into descent by sensible beauty.

1:5 Both the meaning and merit of the marigold are disputed. It has been interpreted as a symbol of the delusive and transient mortal body (Harper 1961: 259), Oothoon's virginity (Erdman 1954a: 217 [235]), the slave rebellion of 1791 in Santo Domingo (*ibid.*: 212, 219 [229, 236-37]), the unfallen world (Bloom 1965: 901), and Oothoon's dream of happiness with Theotormon (Anderson 1984: 9). Plucking a blossom traditionally represents the sexual act (Damon 1924: 329). The flower has been said to take Oothoon into the state of Innocence (Frye 1947: 239), but also, despite its valuable anti-materialist philosophy, to mislead her into expecting good in this world (Raine 1968: I, 170, 176). Anderson (1984: 7-8, 13-14) argues that the nymph, who represents vision and freedom, is good, but the blossom, which symbolises infatuation with Theotormon, is bad.

1:15 **reign**—an archaic word for "kingdom."

1:17 Bromion is made uneasy by a feeling of guilt (Bloom 1963: 106).

1:19   Baine (1981: 206-07) conjectures that Bromion projects his own possessive sexual drive onto the dolphins; Stevenson (1971: 175) sees them as symbols of Theotormon's jealousy.

1:20   Revolution has not been carried far enough in America, so that the Urizenic Bromion can make this claim (Bloom 1963: 107). The reference is to the European conquest of American Indian lands (DiSalvo 1983: 162-63).

1:21   **Stampt with my signet**—i.e. branded (Stevenson 1971: 175).

1:21-22   Bromion deploys the common argument that the slaves, being used to their condition, are content; he also views them as superstitious (Erdman 1954a: 220 [237-38]).

2:4   **adulterate pair**—Damon (1924: 106) first maintains that Oothoon is forced by social pressure to marry her ravisher; Frye (1947: 239) holds that she is married to Theotormon and commits adultery with Bromion. Most readers, however, agree with Damon's later view (1967: 437) that she is a single woman who is raped while travelling to meet her lover.

2:5   Theotormon appears, as Jackson says (1974: 92), to have fastened Bromion and Oothoon back to back, but Duerksen (1977: 187) posits that he has tried and failed either to wash or to hide them in the waters of his creed, and Schorer (1946: 290) claims that Bromion has bound Oothoon to himself in a forced marriage. Duerksen's denial (1972, 1974) that terror and meekness are Bromion and Oothoon is not convincing.

A number of interpretations of the bound couple are more mutually enriching than contradictory. Their union is described as unnatural (Gleckner 1959: 210) and as the bond of an embittered marriage (Deen 1983: 51—cf. Raine 1968: I, 170). It is explained as not actual but a wish-fulfilment of jealous Theotormon in whose consciousness the caves are situated (Bloom 1963: 107-08; 1965: 901); they are back to back so that they cannot copulate (Wagenknecht 1973: 207). The caves are ascribed to Bromion because he has imposed his view of sexual relations on Theotormon (Murray 1974b: 94). On another level, the slaveowner is shown to be bound to his slave (Ostriker 1977: 904) and the caves are both an American slave house and a general emblem of materialistic and priestly tyranny (Howard 1984: 101).

2:6-10   Central problems about this passage are the reason for
Theotormon's tears and whether the lust is positive or nega-
tive. Does Theotormon secretly weep for society's victims
(Erdman 1954a: 216 [234]) or is his sorrow for his own suffer-
ing (Gillham 1973: 208)? Is the lust the passion that sustains
the oppression of blacks and children (Damon 1924: 330)?
Does suppressed desire like Theotormon's find an outlet in the
exploitation of children and slaves (Stevenson 1971: 176)? Or
is the "lust" desire and energy as viewed by the devout, whose
moral system oppresses slaves and exploited children (Bloom
1963: 108)?

2:11-12 According to Bloom (1963: 109), Oothoon cannot weep
because she knows she is guiltless, and her writhings are sex-
ual and reflect her unfulfilled desire.

2:13   The eagles have been explained as simulated remorse
(Bloom 1963: 109), the products of Oothoon's imagination
(Erdman 1974: 131), Theotormon's "ideals or devices of law
and order" (Duerksen 1977: 189), and analogues of a slave-
owner's whips (Howard 1984: 103).

2:18   Theotormon's smile is sadistic (Bloom 1963: 109). Oothoon
temporarily mistakes it for a sign of acceptance (Peterson 1973:
258).

3:2ff, 5:33ff In the two portions of her catalogue of species, Ooth-
oon claims either that they have senses other than the five
familiar ones (Beer 1968: 43; Mellor 1974: 61) or knowledge
not acquired by sense perception (Damon 1924: 106; Howard
1984: 104-05).

3:13   Oothoon is asking how "old" thoughts transcending the
material world have managed to enter the human mind (How-
ard 1984: 105). She is trying to bring Theotormon's repressed
longings into consciousness (Webster 1983: 99).

3:17-20 The Lamb and the Swan symbolise Innocence according
to Damon (1924: 330), but Raine (1968: I, 177) claims the
swan as a Platonic emblem for the soul—it dips its wings in
matter, bathes, and is pure again. Contradicting Raine, Gleck-
ner (1982a: 164) takes the swan as a symbol of the "eternal
imaginative individuality" and argues that Oothoon contrasts
herself, pure and white, with the fruit, the lamb, and the earth-
stained swan. As a pregnant slave, says Erdman (1954a: 222

[240]), Oothoon maintains that both pregnancy and a dark skin are beautiful.

3:19 **our immortal river**—the Adona of *Thel* 1:4 (Frye 1947: 241).

3:21-4:11 Several critics speak of Theotormon's wavering as he responds to Oothoon's plea that he recognise the element in living creatures that transcends facts about their physical bodies. Perhaps he has an inkling of a "remote land" beyond rational understanding (Duerksen 1977: 191), but his doubts about Oothoon's claims predominate (Margoliouth 1951: 94). According to Mellor (1974: 60), he believes the only escape from despair lies in shutting oneself up in one's 'house'—that is, one's Lockean mind entirely dependent on the senses. Those who write of Theotormon's distrust of the senses also tend to see him as self-isolated. Gillham (1973: 203-05) considers that he grieves because his thoughts, though independent of sense perception, seem to be under the control of a mysterious "envier"; Wagenknecht (1973: 210) supposes that he fears both a disturbing irruption of foreign thoughts and the escape of his own thoughts into public view; and Bracher (1984: 171), enlarging on a point earlier touched on by Gardner (1954: 52), holds that he spurns what actually exists to sorrow over the irrecoverable past. In Webster's view (1983: 100-01), it is for the bliss of childhood that he grieves, though he associates its recovery with the pains of envy.

4:12-24 Beer (1968: 44) considers that Bromion is addressing Oothoon, and Gleckner (1965: 5) thinks he is contradicting her claim that there are senses other than the five of fallen humanity. However, most critics agree with Damon (1924: 330-31) that he is addressing Theotormon.

Opinion is divided as to whether or not Bromion is a complete materialist. He may suspect that a transcendent realm or dimension exists but resolve to ignore it because it is altogether unattainable (Stevenson 1971: 180) or because the physical world is all humanity requires (Bracher 1984: 172-73); he holds that here war, economic inequality, and the fear of hell are necessary to maintain the social order (Erdman 1954a: 223 [241]). Wagenknecht (1973: 208) feels that he is moving towards enlightenment but that Theotormon, at the threshold of the cave, blocks his way.

Among those who, like Duerksen (1977: 191), are convinced that Bromion believes in nothing undetectable by science, Howard (1984: 105) thinks that, as an imperialist and a materialist, he speaks of new agricultural products from the colonies and new scientific discoveries, while Raine (1968: II, 124-27) maintains that he echoes Locke's speculations on what (i.e. what material things) more acute or different senses might reveal, and Mellor (1974: 59-60) claims that in 4:14-18 he reduces Theotormon to silence by rhetorical questions implying that nothing immaterial exists. Raine's and Mellor's arguments are especially interesting.

4:16   **Unknown, not unperciev'd**—There is a reference to the title page motto here. Perhaps these are things not yet apprehended by the human heart. According to Wasser (1948: 296), "not unperceiv'd" signifies that nothing imperceptible to the senses exists.

4:24   **the phantoms of existence**—human beings ground down by the law (Fisher 1961: 208); the worlds conceived by Oothoon (Mellor 1974: 59-60).

eternal life—probably, as Fisher implies (*loc. cit.*), the imaginative life advocated by Oothoon.

5:3   **Urizen**—perhaps from the Greek *ourizein* ("to bound, to limit") (D. Plowman 1929: 17), with a pun on "your reason" (Schorer 1946: 271). Klonsky (1977: 12) suggests also Greek *ouranos* ("heaven"), the name given to the planet discovered in 1781 and first called *Georgium Sidus* after George III—this allows for a pun on "your anus."

5:7-8 Although Stevenson (1971: 180) states that the great mouth and narrow eyelids both despise generosity, these seem to be opposites, the great mouth representing one who scorns to take a bribe. Bloom (1963: 114) sees the great mouth as a positive image.

5:14   **hireling**—the recruiting officer, who takes cultivators from the land (Erdman 1954a: 226-28 [246]). Other suggestions— agent implementing enclosure (Bronowski 1944: 66), speculator (Gardner 1954: 53), and gamekeeper (Stevenson 1971: 181; cf. Murry 1933: 116)—do not account for the drum.

5:15   Troops trained on the heath (Erdman 1954a: 228 [247]).

5:19   **cold floods of abstraction**—abstract ideals like honour, loyalty, and chastity (Tayler 1973b: 78).

5:24-32 The "harsh terror" is the angry, frustrated husband; the one the child hates is first his mother, then his wife—he will detest the sex act with the latter and never experience gratified desire, "the arrows of the day" (George 1980: 130). Damon (1967: 438) detects a reference to "the ill-trained children" of loveless marriages.

5:41-6:1 Everything on earth, including corpses, helps to produce new life, and the joy of the worm admonishes humans to seize happiness (Beer 1968: 45). Raine (1968: I, 119) associates the lines with the synthesis of opposites traceable to alchemical symbolism. The worm devours the flesh to free the soul (Lindberg 1973: 261). Like Thel's worm, it is on one level a phallic symbol representing the transition from virginity to sexual life (Tolley 1973: 115-16).

6:3 **infant joys**—not childhood joys but joys uncorrupted by abstract thought or "subtil modesty" (Murry 1932: 18-19); the childlike mindset of Matt. xviii.3 (Paley 1970: 35); both newly emerged, unspoilt and of early childhood (George 1980: 142).

6:10 **com'st forth**—(1) enter the world; (2) mature inwardly (George 1980: 133).

6:11, 7:3-11 A description of unhealthy erotic brooding (Schorer 1946: 293); of auto-eroticism (George 1980: 135-37). There may also be a hint of perverse enjoyment of one's own abstinence.

6:13 **seeming sleep**—(1) the deliberate suppression of sexual desire; (2) its dormancy (George 1980: 134).

6:21 **not so**—Peterson (1973: 262-63) holds that the syntax is ambiguous: Blake hints that Oothoon is too passive to be "a virgin fill'd with virgin fancies." But cf. 6:22-7:2.

7:2 Duerksen (1977: 192) claims that Oothoon is an artist.

7:3 **The moment of desire!**—the moment when Oothoon breaks through the bonds of time to reach Eternity (Hinkel 1979: 280-81, 285, 287-88). Commending Hinkel's argument, Anderson (1984: 11-12, 21n25) contrasts Oothoon's view of the moment with Comus's *carpe diem* attitude to time (Milton, *Comus*, ll. 738-43).

7:17-22 According to Tayler (1973b: 79), possessiveness and jealousy are generated in the hearts of women forced into marital bondage.

7:23-29 Oothoon's offer has been described as "misdirected" (Hilton 1983: 44) and condemned as a descent into Urizenic low cunning (Anderson 1984: 15). Peterson (1973: 263) argues that such behaviour would be a self-enjoying of self-denial (7:8). Bloom (1963: 116) and others believe the offer has Blake's approval, and DiSalvo (1983: 162) supposes it combines economic with sexual generosity. Mona Wilson (1927: 80-81) hints with some justice that there is a touch of unintentional comedy about the passage. Blake appears to have miscalculated the effect of this over vehement repudiation of jealousy.

8:4   **thy hard furrow**—Urizen's (Stevenson 1971: 186)—or Theotormon's.

8:5   **the king of night**—perhaps the eagle, who "returns/ From nightly prey" at 2:25-26. Miner (1962: 70-71) suggests the constellation Leo.

8:6   These creatures without possessions find joy by acting according to their own natures (Beer 1968: 46). The sea bird makes protective use even of Urizen's wintry blast (Duerksen 1977: 193).

8:12   **shadows dire**—beings exclusively physical (Raine 1968: I, 176). Theotormon is taking a masochistic pleasure in his own jealousy and grief (Bloom 1963: 116).

Designs

pl. i Erdman (1974: 125-26) states that opposite the eye-like sun (the "eye/ In the eastern cloud" of 2:35-36) there is in some copies a blank, in others a closed eye, making the sky a face; that the cave is also the inside of a skull—the reader's own from which he or she looks out; that the three figures do not see the sun; and that the "black jealous waters" (2:4) have penetrated into the cavern.

The ominous sun is setting over the Sea of Time and Space (Damon 1924: 332) or the Atlantic (Erdman 1974: 136); Beer (1968: 43) holds that it symbolises the moral law. There is disagreement as to whether Oothoon is, in contrast with Bromion, lightly bound (Damon 1967: 437) or not bound at all (Mellor 1974: 63). Bindman (1977: 73-74) claims that the couple are chained "to the inhospitable rocks of Albion," and

Erdman (1974: 126) remarks that Theotormon at least thinks they are shackled back to back, Bromion being terrified by some sight outside the picture. Wagenknecht (1973: 195) finds an explanation of the design in the much later words "the Contraries of Beulah War beneath Negation's Banner" (*M* 34:23).

In copy A, this plate serves as a tailpiece instead of a frontispiece.

pl. ii It is generally agreed that the presence of the rainbow makes this plate hopeful in contrast with the frontispiece. Not all critics, however, would go as far as Duerksen (1974: 96), who maintains that Oothoon joyfully bounds in her new liberty while her pursuer is discomfited. That pursuer may be Urizen (Binyon 1926: 27), who, according to Raine (1968: I, 171), chases Oothoon across the sea of matter, or Bromion (M. Plowman 1927a: 95). He greatly suffers, remarks Erdman (1974: 126), as he tries to ward off flames with his left hand, and a sinister figure pours out a storm on the right side. Opposite, three fairies dance in the rainbow: Damon (1924: 332) feels that they are disturbed by Urizen's passage, but Anderson (1984: 7, 12-13), who sees the whole design as an illustration of Milton's *Comus*, ll. 298-300, charges them with unawareness of Thel's plight.

pl. iii From Damon (1924: 332) onward, critics have recognised that this picture of Oothoon and Leutha's Marygold seems to illustrate "He who binds to himself a joy" (E470/ K179). Keynes (1921: 129) states that the small figure is male; later he and Wolf (1953: 26) see it as Leutha emerging from her own flower.

pl. 1 There are sexual symbols at the top of this plate, while the aftermath of the rape is portrayed below. Erdman (1974: 129-30) notes that a female at the top sits astride a phallic cloud with a long tail, and that this cloud, deflated, reappears at the bottom beside Oothoon. Bindman (1977: 74) considers that the spirits above are attacking the region below.

pl. 2 While Oothoon writhes in the upper left hand margin, a prostrate slave lies below with his pickaxe (Erdman 1974: 130). Strangely, Keynes first identifies the man as Theotormon (1921: 129); later he and Wolf describe him as Bromion (1953: 26).

pl. 4 The wave in which most critics think Oothoon is chained has been interpreted as a sample of the Atlantic waters that drowned slaves being shipped to America (Erdman 1954a: 216 [233]), as Oothoon's material body (Raine 1968: I, 174), as her desire (Beer 1968: 43-44), and as one of Theotormon's waves [of jealousy] (Wagenknecht 1973: 206). Its flame shape represents the heroine's aspiring soul (Mitchell 1978: 66-67), or the spirit of rebellion (Erdman, *loc. cit.*), or both. Binyon (1926: 101) identifies the chain with jealousy, while Duerksen (1974: 96) thinks it has broken from its anchorage and represents Oothoon's earlier bondage.

pl. 5 Here is a daughter of Albion with her "night pillow" (6:11), which seems to be a version of the cloud on pl. 1 (Erdman 1974: 133). Mellor (1974: 61) thinks this victim of a forced marriage may be pregnant. Keynes (1921: 129) identifies her as Oothoon.

pl. 6 Erdman (1974: 134) judges that Theotormon—here the counterpart to Oothoon in pl. 3—is ignoring her to concentrate on scourging himself with whiplashes tipped with marigolds. Damon, however, (1924: 333) thinks that he is looking at Oothoon, Keynes (1921: 129) that he is whipping her, and Thomas Wright (1929: I, 63) that he is scarifying her verbally. In this and the previous design, with the whip-like hair and bare backed woman, Webster (1983: 103-05) sees sado-masochistic fantasy induced by the suppression of desire.

pl. 7 Damon (1924: 333) counts four despairing daughters of Albion here, Erdman (1974: 135) five.

pl. 8 The degree of optimism in this design is disputed. While Damon (1924: 333) describes the cluster of Daughters of Albion as despairing, Erdman (1974: 135) notes that two of them are looking upward to Oothoon, who may be flying above the sea like Urizen on the title page, but unlike him is not tormented. Seeing deliberate ambiguity in the parallel, Anderson (1984: 16) comments that Oothoon's posture can be described as cruciform, and Mellor (1974: 147), perceiving her arms outstretched in blessing, classifies her as a typical figure of Innocence.

For Children: The Gates of Paradise

The inspiration for the emblem book *For Children: The Gates of Paradise* may, as Damon speculates (1924: 83), have been Francis Quarles's frequently reprinted *Divine Emblems* (1635). Parisi (1978: 72) points out that by the mid-eighteenth century such books were being published only for children; this could account for the title, though Damon (*loc. cit.*) plausibly maintains that Blake's "Children" are any persons who retain the power of vision, and Kmetz (1971: 172) suggests there is an allusion to Matt. xviii.3. Salemi (1981) demonstrates that the engravings embody familiar motifs from older emblem books, though their meanings are often changed.

There has been much agreement with Damon's implied view (1967: 149) that the images portray human life as a miserable passage from foetus to corpse and that they imply happiness can only be found after death. Parisi (1978), though asserting that pl. 13 points to a higher state accessible on both sides of the grave, insists that the series represents a recurring cycle. Agreeing with this interpretation, Webster (1983: 181-202) argues that it shows the male's failure to escape from the dominion of the female, and George (1980: 188) observes that the narrative starts with one worm and ends with another. Similarly linking pls. 1 and 16, Erdman (1977a: 24, 42) argues that the child being pulled from the soil and the tiny faces in the ground expose the absurdity of the materialist's notion that humans emerge from and return to the earth.

Dissenting views are expressed by Beer and Wardle. The former (1968: 233, 238) believes that Blake begins with birth, ends by stripping death of its terror, and in between shows how energy first liberates from reason but then degenerates into sexual possessiveness (pl. 7), murderousness (pl. 8) and vain ambition (pl. 9). Wardle (1978: 345) considers that the inclusion of two births (pls. 1, 6) and the return in the final design to the worm of the frontispiece are intended to promote a non-chronological thematic reading that will make clear the opportunities for escape from nature's cycle.

For detailed remarks on the engravings, see the notes on *For the Sexes: The Gates of Paradise*.

Songs of Experience

Five years separate the title page of *Songs of Innocence* (1789) from that of the composite *Songs of Innocence and of Experience* (1794); the latter bears the subtitle *Shewing the Two Contrary States of the Human Soul*. There has been major disagreement about the nature of the two states, their relationship, and Blake's opinion of their relative value.

Several critics have agreed with Frye (1951: 177) in identifying Innocence with the paradisal aspect of the state that Blake later called Beulah and Experience with the fallen but not wholly corrupt state of Generation. Wagenknecht (1973: 47-56, 72-79) is unusual in claiming that Innocence hovers uncertainly between Beulah and Generation, so that tears are as appropriate to it as smiles. While most critics follow Damon (1924: 39, 269) in supposing that Blake meant what he said when he wrote of a posthumous heaven, Gillham (1973: 92) claims that there is not much thought about the hereafter even in *Songs of Innocence*, and Leader (1981: 108-10, 122-26), denying that Blake has any belief in the supernatural, goes so far as to maintain that the Little Black Boy's mother is a deluded figure who comforts but misguides her son and that the angel-haunted heaven of "Night" is a figurative representation of earthly nature. Interestingly, Hirsch (1964: 48-51, 107) argues that *Songs of Innocence* expresses faith in immortality, while *Songs of Experience* repudiates that faith for belief in the power of the French Revolution to transform the world, but the late insertion of "To Tirzah" marks Blake's return to Christianity after the Revolution's failure.

The characters in such songs of Innocence as "The Eccho-ing Green," "Laughing Song" and "Nurse's Song" need no revolution, for they are integrated in a harmonious community. Erdman (1954a: 251 [272]) observes that the contraries are states of society as well as of the individual soul, while Gardner (1954: 107-09) specifies conflict and isolation as characteristics of Experience. The importance of the community in Innocence is emphasised by Gillham (1973: 116-17, 144-45), Glen (1983: 137-38, 220-21) and Crehan (1984: 108) as well as by Leader (1981: 153), who sees the difference between the unity of the one state and the fragmentation of the other reflected in the contrast between the interlacing 'Gothic' curves of the designs in *Innocence* and the 'classic' rectilinear geometry and self-absorbed figures of those in *Experience*.

Several commentators, including Gleckner (1959: 45) and Bloom (1963: 39), have written of the absence in the Innocent character of the awareness of a distinct identity that separates him or her from the rest of the world. Gleckner, however, (1959: 47) finds an element of selfishness in this state, while Wicksteed (1928: 150) describes Innocence as "frankly and sweetly egotistic." Selfishness, nevertheless, seems characteristic not of Innocence, with its prominent element of community, but of Experience.

In discussing the progression from the Innocence of childhood through Experience to "a higher innocence," Wicksteed (1928: 59) establishes a useful precedent for many subsequent critics such as Gleckner (1959: 46), who regards the consciousness of the self that comes in Experience as a necessary prelude to the transcendence of that self that leads to the supreme state. Among those who challenge Wicksteed's view is Adams (1963: 272), who regards the desirable third state as a synthesis of Innocence and Experience, but others, disagreeing more profoundly, deny that any third condition exists. Bateson (1957: 112) and Holloway (1968: 53-56) regard Innocence as characterised by an optimistic outlook on life which Blake later rejected, while Wilkie (1975: 121) perceptively asserts that Innocence and Experience each possess part of the truth about life. Gillham (1973: 124) holds that Innocence is a "state of perfection"; Mellor (1974: 12-13, 53-55) and Glen (1983: 111, 370n38) maintain that it is a feasible ideal from which Experience is an avoidable lapse. In a similar way, Grant (1969: 347-48) finds evidence in the designs to the second collection that Experience need not undermine Innocence. Hagstrum (1964: 83) denies that Experience is a necessary transitional stage, and Raine (1968: I, 129, 203) protests that it is a totally worthless state of delusion afflicting the soul that has sunk into the material world.

Innocence, too, has its critics. Paley (1970: 32) notes that the Innocent chimney sweeper and charity children are oblivious to the irony planted in their poems, and Bloom (1963: 51) reasonably views the state as immature and therefore incomplete. As Gleckner (1959: 47) warns, Innocence degenerates if it is not outgrown (witness Har and Heva in *Tiriel*). It is, however, according to Gillham (1973: 35-36) and Leader (1981: 92), attainable by adults at least briefly.

Even in Innocence, children are not free from suffering, but they have no fear of death (Damon 1967: 99) and they transcend their pain through Christian vision (Erdman 1954a: 117-18 [128-29]). In Experience, their afflictions are far worse: there, in Tolley's vivid phrase (1973: 112), "winter comes out of season."

Attempts have been made to relate the contrast between the collection of 1789 and the collection of 1794 to Blake's own sorrows and to historical circumstances. Damon (1924: 43) speaks vaguely of temporary disillusion, while Wicksteed (1928: 55-56) refers to a transition from early marital happiness to marital friction. Erdman (1954a: 250-51 [270-71]) points to the failure of revolutionary change to spread to Britain, whereas Crehan (1984: 107-09) sees a reflection of the growth of industrial cities at the expense of the organic rural society.

Blake's book, Erdman's observation implies, is not to any substantial extent personal. In *Songs of Innocence* the "Introduction" makes it clear that the poet is primarily writing poems for children. Despite the opening of "A Little Girl Lost," *Songs of Experience* can hardly be intended for juveniles—what parent would approve of "London" and what child could understand "The Human Abstract"?—though England (1966: 54-55) and Glen (1983: 31-32) maintain that it is. England overlooks the Piper's reference to "happy songs" when she states that his "Introduction" applies to the whole of the double collection. Blake initially sets out, nevertheless, to produce a children's book, and *Songs of Innocence* is clearly related to Isaac Watts's *Divine Songs attempted in Easy Language for the use of children* (1715). Pinto (1957: 67-69, 78, 82) shows that Blake must have had mixed feelings about Watts, for the latter's Calvinistic moralising is tempered by a sympathetic understanding of children and a belief in divine forgiveness, and he notes the influence of Anna Letitia Barbauld's *Hymns in Prose for Children* (1781). Tolley (1973: 106) refers to Watts and Barbauld as "models...that Blake is consciously superseding." Looking into a neglected field, England (1966: 44-48) argues that *Songs* is indebted to the stanza forms, metres, rhyme words and aural effects of the hymns of Charles Wesley, who, like Blake, saw the child as holy. However, Glen (1983: 8,

18-19) claims that Blake's lyrics most clearly resemble late eighteenth-century children's poems purged of their didacticism, and Leader (1981: 1-36) maintains that Blake is combating Calvin's doctrine that every child is born deeply corrupt, Locke's opposition to exposing the young to imaginative literature, and Rousseau's conviction that education should concentrate on what the child can encounter in the here and now. Damon (1967: 274-75) believes that the pattern of contrasting sets of songs derives from Milton's "L'Allegro" and "Il Penseroso."

Whereas the Piper of the first "Introduction" is inspired by a child and writes for children, the Bard of the "Introduction" to *Experience* is inspired by God the Son and addresses the fallen soul and the fallen Earth. He is a controversial figure. Since he sees past, present and future, Gleckner (1957: 11) seems to have a strong case when he claims that he, like the Piper, is Blake himself. Grant (1969: 342) agrees that he is virtually identical with the author, in which case Erdman (1954a: 250 [270]) must be right in attributing to him all the poems in *Experience*. To Bloom, however, (1963: 132) he seems a man of limited vision who can be the author only of those songs that Bloom supposes are similarly limited—"Introduction," "The Tyger," "A Poison Tree," and "A Little Girl Lost." More radical is Leader (1981: 143, 171-76, 190-93), who considers that the Bard's vision is sufficiently corrupted through most of the book for him to be in danger of degenerating into a harsh authoritarian: he accuses him of inventing speakers like the Chimney Sweeper and the Little Vagabond, who are far too calculating in their protests, but finds him recovering faith in redemption in "The Little Girl Lost" and "The Voice of the Ancient Bard."

Title page to *Songs of Innocence and of Experience*

The bird rising from the flames has been described as a symbol of forfeited joy (Damon 1924: 284) and as the Bird of Innocence (Keynes 1967a, pl. 1). Adam's and Eve's loin-coverings are made of vine leaves (Damon, *loc. cit.*) or fig leaves (Erdman 1974: 42).

Title page to *Songs of Experience*

Two children are mourning over their parents' death bed (Damon 1924: 284), or two people are lamenting over effigies on Gothic tombs (Raine 1968: I, 129). The group of four figures has a cruciform shape (Damon, *loc. cit.*). Behind is the wall of a cemetery or garden (Erdman 1974: 71) or a church (Leader 1981: 151, 242n56). Erdman (1974: 71-72, 275) states that the children see only the mortal, not the spiritual, bodies of their parents, and that their own "true human forms" dance on either side of ivy leaves; these leaves may be positive, bringing the gift of hope from above, or negative, raising the blight of Experience from below. Leader (1981: 238-39n5) proposes that the deaths of Urizenic parents may increase the children's freedom.

Frontispiece

The Piper-shepherd of the frontispiece to *Songs of Innocence* has become the pipeless Bard (Leader 1981: 132) as he leaves the sheep of Innocence to enter Experience (Damon 1924: 284), where the inspiration symbolised by the child becomes a burden (Bindman 1977: 87). He is a St. Christopher bearing the Christ with whom he still needs to unite inwardly (Hagstrum 1973a: 146-48). However, Bateson (1957: 121) regards the child as representing the natural instincts restricted in Experience, and Tolley (1969: 78), citing Grant, suggests that the man who bears him may be his spiritually blind captor.

"Introduction"; "Earth's Answer"

Three problems are central to the debate on these poems: the status of the Bard, the identity of the Holy Word, and the intention behind the ambiguity of the syntax in "Introduction." The Bard has been regarded as Blake himself (Stevenson 1971: 209), as an uncorrupted visionary (Wicksteed 1928: 145-46; Adams 1963: 24), as a partly corrupted visionary who no longer hears the Word (Bloom 1963: 130) but is redeemable (Leader 1981: 136-37), and as profoundly fallen (Gardner 1954: 117-18). Bloom accuses him of anti-Blakean dualism since his ideal is an immaterial heaven (1963: 131), an ideal which in Holloway's view (1968: 66-67) the poet endorses. Gillham, on the contrary, (1966: 158) holds that both Blake and the Bard seek only a renewal of life on earth.

Blake's Holy Word is often identified as the Second Person of the Trinity (Damon 1924: 274), who summons the sinner Adam in *Paradise Lost* (Frye 1957a: 25) and in "Introduction" weeps as he banishes the already self-banished Adam and Eve (Adams 1963: 25-26). With about equal frequency, he is identified as a tyrannical being (Gardner 1954: 117-18), who, as the allusion to Gen. iii.8 shows, cruelly punishes Adam and Eve (Gleckner 1959: 232) and who imposes the Decalogue (Bateson 1957: 113). Other views are that he is the Poetic Genius within the individual (Price 1964: 398), the fallen divine man whose consort is the fallen earth (Beer 1968: 79-81), or the "demystified Christ" of a rationalistic Utopian Bard (Pechey 1979: 73-74).

Syntactical ambiguity in "Introduction" allows the reader to conceive of either the Bard or the Holy Word as calling the lapsed soul, weeping, and addressing Earth. If the Word is Christ and the Bard is unfallen, Christ is in some sense speaking through the Bard. He may be mourning over the fate of humankind as he did over the death of Lazarus [John xi.35] (Frye 1957a: 25), or Blake may be recalling his agony in Gethsemane, where he calls to the slumbering disciples (Tolley 1973: 100). Holding the Bard to be a true visionary, Gleckner (1959: 232-36) sees a double meaning throughout the last three stanzas of "Introduction": while the Bard weeps sympathetically and calls on Earth to rise from Experience, the Word weeps hypocritically and summons her to return to his idea of day and be forgiven for her nocturnal sin, but Earth, hearing only the Word's message, rightly rejects it. According to Gillham, however, (1973: 48) Earth mistakes the Word, who really is the Son of God, for Starry Jealousy, who is Urizen; her trouble, says Grant (1968b: 577), is that she has been waiting too long and cannot recognise the summons.

The designs have provoked less debate than the poems, but the majority view that the nude on the first plate is Earth (Wicksteed 1928: 146) is challenged by Bass (1970: 208), who regards it as the Bard, and by Erdman (1974: 72), who believes it is either the Bard or the Word. Damon (1924: 284) describes the sinister serpent on the second plate as the tempter of Eden and the symbol of priesthood; Erdman (1974: 73) explains it as the frustrated male, a counterpart to Earth, lifting his head towards inaccessible grapes.

Raine (1957a: 50-55) cites evidence that the symbolism and vocabulary of these poems is indebted to Thomas Taylor's translation of Plotinus.

"Introduction" (details)

l. 5 **the ancient trees**—the forest of an oppressive creed (Gardner 1954: 118); the trees of the Garden of Eden (Gillham 1973: 48); perhaps the Tree of Knowledge and the Tree of Life (Raine 1968: II, 28).

l. 6 The lapsed soul includes both the individual human being and all created nature (Frye 1957a: 28).

l. 7 Dew is said to represent matter (Wicksteed 1928: 145) or Experience (Gleckner 1959: 233).

l. 8 Among those to whom the potential to control the universe has been attributed are the Word (Gleckner 1959: 233-34) and the lapsed soul (Frye 1957a: 25-26). Raine (1957a: 61-62) suggests the ambiguity may be deliberate since the attribution can be to either of these and also to the voice of the Bard.

l. 11 The female figure Earth encompasses all who are redeemable, including males (Frye 1957a: 29-30).

ll. 12-15 Christ utters his summons at evening but Earth hears it at the point of daybreak; the changes of tense (e.g. ll. 5, 13, 17) imply that the two phases co-exist (Tolley 1973: 99-100).

ll. 18-20 **The starry floor/ The watry shore**—respectively reason and the Sea of Time and Space (Damon 1924: 274); a prison disguised as a blessing (Stevenson 1971: 209); a synecdoche for the beauty of the created world, which Earth rejects in defiance of the Bard (Gillham 1973: 49-50); part of the limit imposed by Divine Mercy on the Fall (Frye 1957a: 28-29), although (Grant 1968b: 576) fallen humanity cannot see that they are intended for its solace. Chayes (1974: 65-66) argues that since the human head and feet exchange places at the Fall, the stars are underfoot in Eternity and the Bard from his unfallen perspective so sees them.

l. 20 **the break of day**—a false dawn (Gardner 1954: 119); the beginning of a new age that ushered in the American and

French Revolutions (Bateson 1957: 114); the Judgment Day heralding Eternity (as distinct from the morning of the natural day, to which earth is called in the preceding stanza) (Hirsch 1964: 55-56, 211-12).

"Earth's Answer" (details)

ll. 1-4 The imagery alludes to the stone-like blind eyes of fallen Earth, "fled" being an adjective (Hirsch 1964: 214).

l. 7 **Starry Jealousy**—combines the jealous, lawgiving Old Testament God with the classical Demiurge who rules the created world through the power of the stars (Raine 1957a: 56-61).

ll. 8-10 Cf. Rom. xiii. 11-12 (Tolley 1973: 100).

l. 10 **the father of the ancient men**—Urizen (Damon 1924: 274); either the Bard or the Holy Word (Gardner 1954: 120). The ancient men may be worshippers of a tyrannical god (Frye 1957a: 30-31).

l. 21 **this heavy chain**—the flesh (Damon 1924: 275).

"The Clod and the Pebble"

Those who take this delightful poem at face value can argue that the admirable Clod describes love in Innocence, the deplorable Pebble love in Experience (Damon 1924: 279-80; Gleckner 1959: 251; Keynes 1967a, pl. 32). Others, deeming the Clod passive and the Pebble active, see the two kinds of love as contraries which require to be synthesised (M. Plowman 1927a: 143-45; Adams 1963: 251-52). A third class criticises both speakers for the absence of mutual exchange from their conceptions of love (Bloom 1963: 133; Hirsch 1964: 216-18; Gillham 1973: 119-22; Glen 1983: 176-81). Wicksteed (1928: 171-73) feels that the poem is not didactic and describes what love seems to those in Innocence and to those in Experience, while Leader (1981: 147-49) accuses the Bard (not Blake) of mistaking the Clod's position for one genuinely Innocent and of drawing an oversimplified antithesis. Wilkie (1975: 129-30) considers the speaker unable to decide which kind of love is better. Giving "heaven" and "hell" the meanings they bear in *The Marriage of Heaven and Hell*, Hagstrum (1963) compares the self-centredness of the Pebble with that of the hero of "A Little Boy Lost," equates the Clod of Clay with the clod into which Urizen dwindles (*BU* 6:10), and concludes that Blake sides with the Pebble.

In the lower part of the design, Wicksteed (1928: 173) and Keynes (1967a, pl. 32) detect creatures devouring each other, but Erdman (1974: 74) denies that the observer can see this.

"Holy Thursday"

Gillham's charge (1966: 195-97) that the speaker overindulges in generalisations instead of deciding how he should help harmonises with Glen's accusation (1983: 170-75) that he is entirely negative and offers no remedy. Both must meet the challenge of Tolley's defence (1973: 114-15) that his "honest indignation" is unstained by personal interest.

l. 4 **usurous hand**—the hand of the charity school guardian who steals from the children's allowances (Leader 1981: 162-63).

l. 8 . The poverty is both spiritual and material (Gleckner 1959: 245).

ll. 9-16 The sun and rain represent love and charity (Damon 1924: 280).

l. 12 The winter is in the children's hearts (Wicksteed 1928: 202).

l. 16 The mind that is appalled can be the child's or guardian's or even the speaker's or his auditor's (Leader 1981: 164-65).

"The Little Girl Lost"; "The Little Girl Found"

There are many explanations of these poems, but it is so difficult to account for all the details and changes of tone that Gleckner (1959: 219) may be right in thinking that Blake has not yet acquired full control over his ambiguities. What may loosely be called the standard interpretation holds that Lyca begins in Innocence and passes into Experience, a state which includes sexuality and from which her parents try to hold her back. When they follow her, they eventually discover that the passions of Experience that they feared, represented in text and designs by beasts, have a benign aspect and are not evil. Lyca ends as an independent, sexually mature person or, according to Gleckner, as a person in a higher

Innocence. For studies along these lines, see Wicksteed 1928: 115-21; Gleckner 1959: 219-28; Adams 1963: 210-18; Gillham 1966: 139-47; and Leader 1981: 38-40, 185-89.

Damon (1924: 279) and Keynes (1967a, pls. 34-36) consider that Lyca passes from mortal life to the hereafter, that the lion represents death, and that both the daughter and the parents learn that he is not to be feared but leads the way to Eternity. According to Hirsch (1964: 221-29), Blake leaves it uncertain whether Lyca's regeneration brings her and her parents to heaven or to an earthly paradise. Raine (1957a: 19-49), holding that Blake retells the story of the kidnapped Persephone as understood by Neoplatonists, maintains that Lyca descends from Eternity into the Underworld of this life in pursuit, especially, of sexual pleasure; Lyca's mother, like Demeter, is the higher uncorrupted aspect of her daughter's soul who descends to watch over her in her sleep of mortality, and the lion, corresponding to Hades, turns out to be a divine presence in the lower realm; psychologically the mother corresponds to the Jungian Self, the daughter to the ego. To Chayes (1963), Lyca incorporates not only Persephone but also such folk-tale characters as the Sleeping Beauty as well as Spenser's Una, who encounters a lion (*FQ* I. iii.5-9), and her sleep, in which she becomes the consort of the leonine Pluto, is a stage in her reascent from Experience on the way to a higher Innocence. Most pessimistic are Gardner (1954: 114-16), who maintains that she is taken to a tyrant's palace and dwells in the dell of Experience, and Wagenknecht (1973: 110-29), who believes that Lyca and her parents are left at the end in the grip of fallen nature.

The two poems are accompanied by four designs. In the first the young woman with a lover is too old for Lyca—unless Leader (1981: 39-40) is right in arguing that her seven years are purely symbolic—and she may be Ona of "A Little Girl Lost" (Damon 1924: 285). The lovers do not notice the serpent in their paradise (*ibid.*): he divides the two-stanza prelude from the story of Lyca. Keynes (pls. 34-36) comments that he turns away thwarted from the visionary lovers, whereas Erdman (1974: 76) classifies him as a prophetic creature. The two middle designs portray Lyca in a forest and with an animal—perhaps the tiger of Experience (Grant 1961b: 78). The fourth may show the fleshly sexuality of the previous pictures transformed (Wicksteed 1928: 121), the higher Innocence (Grant, *loc. cit.*) or the fulfilment of the opening prophecy (Hirsch 1964: 228-29), though Adams (1963: 210) denies that it is fulfilled. The sleeping nude has been seen as one of the parents (Damon, *loc. cit.*), as the girl in the first design (Grant 1968b: 577), and as Lyca (Raine 1957a: 33). Keynes (*loc. cit.*) notices her resemblance to Earth in the plate of "Introduction," and Raine (1957a: 26-27) identifies her on one level with the speaker of "Earth's Answer" since she is the soul of the world as well as the individual soul. The design reassures Erdman (1974: 78) that the "dell" is not really "lonely."

"The Little Girl Lost" (details)

1. 4 **Grave**—(1) engrave, (2) tomb (Adams 1963: 211); (3) sombre (Hilton 1983: 19-20).

    sentence—(1) statement, (2) punishment decreed (Adams 1963: 211).

1. 8 **Become a garden mild**—cf. Is. xxxv.1 (Raine 1957a: 26).

1. 9 **the southern clime**—a reference to Sicily, whence Hades carried off Persephone (Raine 1957a: 28).

1.13 The number may allude to the seven pomegranate seeds Persephone ate in the underworld, these being interpreted as units of time, and also to Leo's being the seventh sign of the Zodiac (Raine 1957a: 42-44). As there are seven historical ages, there may be a hint that Lyca's history is also the earth's (Adams 1963: 217). The biblical associations of "seven" suggest that Providence is in control (Hirsch 1964: 225). Cf. "Found," 1. 7.

1.16 **wild birds' song**—symbolic of imaginative infancy (Wicksteed 1928: 116-17), or freedom and sexuality (Leader 1981: 186).

1. 21 **desart**—an uncultivated area, but not necessarily barren (Hirsch 1964: 222).

ll. 29-32 Lyca invokes the night-world of mortal existence (Raine 1957a: 34-35).

1. 50 **her slender dress**—Lyca's mortal body (Damon 1924: 279); the artificial life which Lyca renounces to return to Innocent nature (Stevenson 1971: 72).

"The Little Girl Found" (details)

l. 43 **my palace**—the sacred palace of love (Wicksteed 1928: 120); a twofold entity, like the fearsome yet protective lion, capable of being either a tyrant's prison or a place of regeneration (Adams 1963: 214-16).

"The Chimney Sweeper"

To Gillham (1973: 29-31) and Leader (1981: 159-62), the sweeper seems an unnaturally sophisticated thinker and not very likable compared with his spontaneous counterpart in *Innocence*. Leader adds that the speaker is presenting the boy to the reader in an unpleasantly calculating way, and Wilkie (1975: 123-25) believes that his justified indignation makes him an unreliable reporter who puts his own phrase "notes of woe" in the child's mouth.

l. 9 On May Day, sweeps and milkmaids danced in the London streets for alms (Erdman 1954a: 254-55 [275]).
l. 12 **a heaven**—a posthumous heaven that will supposedly compensate the oppressed for their present suffering (Hirsch 1964: 230-31); a heaven of ease and comfort in this world and also any heaven that may exist hereafter (Gillham 1973: 28).

"Nurse's Song"

Glen (1983: 19-20) classifies this piece as a parody of conventional poems for children about wise adult guides. The design shows the nurse supervising a potentially rebellious youth (Keynes 1967a: pl. 38) or preparing him for entrance into adult society (Bindman 1977: 88). He and his younger sister ignore each other (Leader 1981: 153). Grapes of erotic pleasure are nearby (Tolley 1973: 110).

l. 4 **green and pale**—the hues of a repressed spinster (Keynes 1967a: pl. 38); green with envy (Gleckner 1959: 316n10).
l. 6 Adolescence approaches (Wicksteed 1928: 155).

ll. 6-8   Night represents Experience (Damon 1924: 275). Winter
and night stand for "deceit" and "hidden desire" (Wicksteed
1928: 155) or the latter part of life (Hirsch 1964: 232-33).

l. 7   The speaker regrets that she wasted her own youth in sterile
flirtation (Hirsch 1964: 232). Ironically, she really wasted it by
failing to play (Tolley 1973: 115). She condemns play as
frivolous (Gillham 1973: 38).

l. 8   **in disguise**—"repression and hypocrisy" (Keynes 1967a: pl.
38); the mask of habit (Gillham 1973: 38).

"The Sick Rose"

The main points of debate about this poem are whether the
flower shares the blame for its own suffering, what the worm sym-
bolises, and whether the speaker sees the worm for what it really
is. Bloom (1963: 135) criticises the Rose for indulging in "The self
enjoyings of self-denial" (*VDA* 7:9) on its "bed/ Of crimson joy"
before the arrival of the worm. More straightforwardly, Hirsch
(1964: 234) maintains that Blake satirises it for accepting anything
as corrupting as secret love. The worm has been interpreted as the
social ethos that fosters marriage without love (Bateson 1957: 119-
20), as "the dark *thought*...in the storm of lust-passion" Wicksteed
(1928: 157), and as the flesh corrupting the spirit—even though
love should have physical expression (Damon 1924: 280-81). It is
possible that the worm only appears destructive in the eyes of the
Experienced speaker as Cupid appeared in the eyes of Psyche's sis-
ters (Raine 1957b: 834-35; Chayes 1970b: 217; Erdman 1974: 81-
82). Wilkie (1975: 130-34) maintains that Blake's main interest is
in the speaker, whose infected consciousness can only conceive of
sexual fruition as a defilement, and who is imagining what he
admits to be invisible.

In the design the small figure below is probably the spirit
of joy escaping from the rose (Wicksteed 1928: 157), but it may be
a despairing female in the coils of the worm (Raine 1968: I, 203).
The two people on stems above may be lovers frustrated by priests
(Wicksteed 1928: 157) or persons playing the part of Psyche's sis-
ters (Erdman 1974: 81).

"The Fly"

This poem raises a series of questions for the careful reader. The drafts in the Notebook show that Blake had great difficulty in completing it, and the song itself may be defective (Bateson 1961)—perhaps in the fourth stanza (Hirsch 1964: 240-41) or the fifth (Grant 1963: 42).

Damon (1924: 275-76) laid a useful foundation for subsequent criticism when he wrote of the allusion to Gray's "Ode on the Spring," pointing out that whereas Gray implies that a man is trivial, Blake implies that a fly matters. In the last stanza, argues Bateson (1961), the speaker is trying to shuffle off his guilt, and Grant (1961a: 484) draws attention to the phrase "brush'd away" as his euphemism for "killed."

There have been many accounts of the speaker. Is he a man becoming aware of the harshness of Experience (Bloom 1963: 136)? A child (Mellor 1974: 334)? An adolescent boy (Hagstrum 1969: 369)? A man who in the last two stanzas adopts the persona of a fly to reply to his own question (Wagenknecht 1973: 109)? A speaker who restricts himself to logical argument at the expense of vision and who may be celebrating the insect's gaiety or lamenting its vulnerability (Glen 1983: 182-85)? A person who, like Tiriel's Har and Heva, has tried to prolong the thoughtless joy of childhood into maturity and who decides that life and death are governed by chance in a meaningless universe (Tolley 1969: 79-82)? Or a man so out of love with thought that he prefers to live as unreflectively as a fly (Stevenson 1971: 221)?

But what is meant by "thought"? Is the hand that lacks it of the same nature as "some blind hand" (Bloom 1963: 136) or is only the latter Urizenic (Hagstrum 1969: 374-75)? Is thought consciousness (Bateson 1961)? Is it vision, a kind of adult Innocence without which we are not really alive (Kirschbaum 1961: 158-59)? Or is it Urizenic reasoning by ignoring which we can remain Innocent and happy (Mellor 1974: 334)? Can it be a synthesis of reason and imagination, one's real essence (Adams 1963: 288)? (Is the death spoken of metaphorical—the quenching of the spirit [Hagstrum 1969: 370]?) Are the fly's playful energy and the man's thought essentially the same and both immortal (Hirsch 1964: 239-40)?

There is, at least, widespread agreement with Grant (1963: 50) that the nurse or mother in the design is hovering over the boy oppressively. Leader (1981: 244-45n27) sees in the picture a reflection of the speaker's miseducation. The shuttlecock is clearly analogous to the winged creature at the right, and the girl may be developing her own "thoughtless hand" (Erdman 1974: 82) or retaliating in kind for male possessiveness (Chayes 1970b: 228-30).

The insect of the poem may or may not be a housefly. Johnson's *Dictionary* (1755) gives as the first definition of the noun "Fly," "A small winged insect of many species." Damon (1967: 139) believes the word, here and elsewhere in Blake, denotes a butterfly. Bloom (1963: 136) suspects an allusion to Shakespeare, *King Lear* IV.i.37-38.

"The Angel"

Although Chayes (1970b: 216) argues that the rejected angel in the design is Cupid and the speaker is a Psyche who never falls from grace because she never accepts him in the first place, critics generally look on the lady's story as tragic. Gleckner (1959: 263-65) compares her shrinking from the sexuality of Experience to Thel's retreat, and Hirsch (1964: 242) views the angel as representing the aspect of herself she has repressed. In Adams' opinion (1963: 256), she begins by mistaking him for a deceiver. Erdman (1974: 83) remarks that the way she uses her outspread fingers and thumb in the design shows that, contrary to him, she regards "life as but a mortal span." Bateson (1957: 30-31) and others consider "A Dream" the corresponding poem in *Innocence*.

l. 4   Adams (1963: 256) holds that "so" should be understood before "beguil'd."

l. 10   Blushes signify debased sexuality in Blake (Bateson 1957: 122).

ll. 11-12   She has put off accepting the weapons of sex for too long (Bateson 1957: 121). The shields and spears are flirtatious tricks (Stevenson 1971: 220).

"The Tyger"

Students of Blake from Damon (1924: 277) onwards have usually classified the forests of the night as negative, but they are otherwise unable to approach a consensus on the meaning of this poem. The parallels that can be found with passages in Blake's other writings can be used to support the most diverse interpretations, especially if every mention of a tiger is held to be relevant, regardless of its date.

Any sensitive reader will recognise that there are two aspects to the animal. It is not just a cruel devourer and not just gloriously beautiful: it is both. Not all readers, however, are satisfied that the speaker can be trusted. To Bloom (1963: 137-38) he seems bewildered by the mixed character of the universe and self-abasing before the fearful beast; to Grant (1961b: 65-69) he appears redeemable though his questions reveal his ignorance and terror; and to Tolley (1967) the apparent frightfulness of the tiger is the product of his fallen mind, while Damrosch (1980: 378-79) announces that he is right to fear the presence of such energy in the mortal world. Adams (1963: 61-64) detects two perspectives in the poem, that of the speaker, who is horrified at the tiger, and that of the poet, who recognises its wrath is necessary for the world's redemption. Crehan (1984: 130, 133-36), who understands the forests as in part benighted cities, the beast as the energy of revolution and the questions as coming from a dismayed conservative, shares this opinion. Price (1964: 399-400) and Wagenknecht (1973: 91-93) see a change in the speaker: the former argues that he begins in fear and doubt but moves via the tears of the merciful stars to faith in a creator whose wrath is redemptive; the latter maintains that he loses some of his confusion between the third and fourth stanzas and goes on to concoct a fiction about a cruel creator and a kindly, tearful nature. Hilton (1983: 183) believes that the poem exposes his simple-mindedness in seeking an unequivocal, definitive answer to such a question.

As the contrary of the lamb, the tiger can be seen as destructive yet liberating—just as its creation can be seen as both a cruel constriction and part of the merciful limitation imposed on the Fall (Gleckner 1959: 277-80). (It should be noted that Damon [1967: 414] regards it not as a contrary to the lamb, which would be a positive, but as a negation.) Raine (1968: II, 5) and Paley (1970: 41) plausibly associate it with Boehme's First Principle, the terrible but necessary Fire, and Sethna (1965: 210) identifies it as a troubling and terrifying aspect of the divine, namely the Christ who defeats the rebel angels or stars. Erdman (1954a: 179 [195]), who perceives it as the energy of political revolution, observes that it must not remain wrathful when the oppressors have been overthrown, and Miner (1962: 72-73) calculates that it will cease to be destructive in a redeemed world. In a careful analysis, Grant (1961b: 75) describes Blake's savage animal as energy constricted into an evil form, yet ultimately reclaimable, while Mellor (1974: 64-66, 100) considers it as energy given the artistic form it needs to overcome starry reason though there is always a danger that a boundary or limitation will turn energy itself into a tyrant.

In a parallel way, the tiger's creator is sometimes said to have characteristics of both the visionary Los and the cruel Urizen (Grant 1961b: 68-69; Miner 1962: 65; Raine 1968: II, 23), though he has also been compared or equated with Los alone (Bateson 1957: 117; Gleckner 1959: 284-85; Adams 1963: 69-70; Paley 1970: 57-59; Deen 1983: 73-74) and with Urizen (Damon 1967: 414). Mellor (1974: 64-66) views him as the creative artist who gives form to energy, and Bloom (1963: 138-39) as the conqueror of the weeping stars.

Those stars and their tears have provoked diverse expositions. Most commentators, at least from the time of Bateson (1957: 118)—Grant (1961b: 74) is a notable exception—see them as on one level the rebel angels of *Paradise Lost*, who have become, in Blake's myth, the followers of Urizen. As such, they reappear in *The Four Zoas* in Urizen's own account of his fall:

> I went not forth. I hid myself in black clouds of my wrath.
> I call'd the stars around my feet in the night of councils dark.
> The stars threw down their spears & fled naked away.
> We fell.... (64:25-28/ E344/ V, 222-25)

Mellor (1974: 64-65) notes that "The stars threw down their cups & fled" when Blake bestirred himself on England's behalf (E500/ K187). On a literal level, Blake may be writing in "The Tyger" of the fading starlight and dew of dawn (Pottle:

1950), on a political level of defeated counter-revolutionary armies (Erdman 1954a: 178 [194]), and on a philosophical level of the reign of rationalism and science (Schorer 1946: 251). Relating the poem to the Incarnation, Wicksteed (1928: 198) explains the stars as the power of reason and war that prevailed before Christ taught compassion. Hilton produces evidence that the image of spears includes the meaning "beams of light" and associates the implied dew with their astrological influence (1983: 174-79, 288n7 citing "To the Evening Star," ll. 13-14; *M* 5:28-29; *FZ* 118:14-16/ E387/ IX, 39-41; cf. Raine 1954: 49). Emotions attributed to the stars include grief at the creation of evil (Raine 1954: 50) or at the first appearance of death (Wagenknecht 1973: 92) and the compassion they now feel having relinquished their former power (Gardner 1954: 129). Miner (1962: 70, 72) views them as warriors whose defeat is followed by regeneration of the fallen world—he sees a hint of dawn in the fifth stanza. Nurmi (1956: 37-39, 43) reads their tears as a characteristic Blakean image indicating that the tiger has destroyed their repressive power and humankind has left the forests of the night. Less optimistic, Damon (1924: 278) attributes the tears to a Urizen who is lamenting that his activities should spawn such a fearful creature, while Tolley (1967) argues that the fallen speaker is denying the Urizenic God's claim in Job xxxviii.7 that the stars sang when He created the world.

What, then, of the poem's second question? Did the same creator fashion lamb and tiger? There have been positive replies from Wicksteed (1928: 196, 198-99), Nurmi (1956: 39) and Bateson (1957: 117) and a strong negative from Raine (1954: 50), which she later withdrew (1968: II, 30), though Damon (1967: 414) upheld it. There has been Damon's earlier position (1924: 277) that Blake is not sure, which Hobsbaum (1964) supports, noting that the poem consists solely of questions. Beer's view (1968: 65-66) that the supreme God created the tiger but did not will its separation from pity and reason that occurred at the Fall seems right as far as it goes, but perhaps the most satisfying answers are those like Raine's reference (1968: II, 30) to a Yes and No of great complexity and Paley's conclusion (1970: 41,48) that the question is not meant to be answered but to excite sublime awe.

Besides the account of the rebel angels in *Paradise Lost*, sources of "The Tyger" may include a passage in Everard's translation of *The Divine Pymander* [1650], one of the Hermetic writings (Raine 1954: 45-48) and Philip Doddridge's Hymn 156 (Holloway 1968: 39). It may have been partly inspired by Stubbs's majestic painting of a tiger exhibited in 1769 (Raine 1954: 43).

The tameness of Blake's own picture of the animal has always been a puzzle. Keynes (1967a, pl.42), Wilkie (1975: 135) and Hirsch (1964: 252) report that the beast is ferocious in some copies of the book, but Erdman (1974: 84) cannot confirm this and Leader (1981: 47) denies it. Wicksteed (1928: 193) suggests that Blake may be trying to show the smile on God's face, since the tiger is His self-expression, or else he may be mocking those who think an artist can portray God's acts; Erdman (1954a: 179-80 [195-96]) posits that the tiger in the design is not the tiger of the poem but the same animal redeemed; Mellor (1974: 65-66) postulates that lamb and tiger share the same "spiritual" identity—the Innocence of the former can develop into the energy of the latter; and Grant (1961b: 76-77, 80) proposes that the image is not frightening because it is seen from a prophetic standpoint. However, as Leader rightly remarks (1981: 47-48), regardless of the intention behind it, the picture is unsatisfactory.

l. 5 **deeps or skies**—hell or heaven (Bloom 1963: 138); a hint that heaven and hell may be the same (Raine 1968: II, 19); regions that existed before the creation was fully formed (Stevenson 1971: 215).

ll. 5-8 The tiger's creator may be a subsidiary god who has obtained his material from the highest realm, which is above his own as the earth is below it (Sethna 1965: 186-87) or from distant parts of an existing universe (Gillham 1973: 7). The wings hint at the flight of Icarus, the seizure of fire at the theft of Prometheus (Adams 1963: 63-64).

l. 12 Emended in one late copy, probably by Blake himself, to "What dread hand form'd thy dread feet?" The unrevised line expresses the close kinship between creator and creature, who are both immortal (Sethna 1965: 189-90).

l. 13 Cf. "In chains of the mind locked up" (*BU* 10:25) (Gardner 1954: 127). Wicksteed (1928: 197) sees a necessary though painful imprisonment of the infinite in a finite brain. Grant (1961b: 71) notes that the chain is a Blakean symbol of tyranny, and Damrosch (1980: 378), citing *BL* 5:12-17, conjectures that it represents the spine.

l. 19   Cf. "and God saw that it was good" (Gen. i.10) (Bateson 1957: 119).

"My Pretty Rose Tree"

        As Gillham delightfully says (1966: 169), there is a humorous element in Blake's choice of the respectable but thorny rose as a symbol of marriage. The narrative, often suspected to be autobiographical (Damon 1924: 286 *et al.*), may condemn the speaker for rejecting a marvellous flower out of obedience to the moral law (Gleckner 1957: 8-9); Grant (1969: 335-37) judges that he is cowardly and that he takes masochistic pleasure in the rose-tree's thorns. The flower such "as May never bore" has been referred to as the object of a brief infatuation (Gillham 1973: 135), as one whose invitation is "an offering greater than natural" (Bloom 1963: 137), as a blossom of Innocence in contrast to the Urizenic Experienced rose (Gardner 1954: 111), and as one who would have led the speaker to the higher Innocence (Gleckner, *loc. cit.*). The rose is naturally criticised for jealousy (Damon 1924: 281), though Wicksteed (1928: 151) thinks her resistance has a stimulating aspect, for her thorns have an affinity to the infernal salutary corrosives of *The Marriage of Heaven and Hell*. Glen (1983: 377-78n22) observes that the speaker and the rose-tree seek possession of each other rather than a relationship and end by losing each other. In the design, remarks Erdman (1974: 85), the couple are turned towards the barren tree and not the ascending birds; Grant (1969: 340-41) suggests that these birds may represent missed opportunities, while Hirsch (1964: 254) comments that the woman seems pleased with herself and Leader (1981: 154) accuses both her and her rejected partner of self-absorption.

        "My Pretty Rose Tree," "Ah! Sun-flower" and "The Lilly" are a sequence of three poems on one engraved plate. Wicksteed (1928: 150) perceives a movement from the egotism of Innocence through Experience to Art, which exists independently of the artist's ego.

"Ah! Sun-flower"

Critics cannot agree on whether Blake is sympathetic towards the central character in this touching little poem, and whether it refers to a real afterlife. The sunflower has been credited with reminding us that we have within ourselves an immortal element (Holloway 1968: 45) and praised for aspiring to rise from the grave of Experience to the higher Innocence (Gleckner 1959: 79). According to Grant (1969: 334, 481n2), the youth and virgin already arise from their graves and so escape from death. Raine (1968: I, 218-22) and others notice that their longing is initially for sexual fulfilment but on another level for Eternity, while Harper (1953) finds a source in a passage of Proclus translated by Thomas Taylor, who follows ancient Neoplatonists in holding that aspiration towards the spiritual realm should not be accompanied by violent suppression of the passions.

With equal conviction the sunflower has been condemned for seeking to escape from Experience through material nature instead of through the journey inwards (Adams 1963: 245), for aspiring after a conventional posthumous heaven for which the youth and virgin may well be renouncing this world and their own sexuality (Gillham 1973: 16-18), and for failing to accept its own mortality and enter into relationships with others (Glen 1983: 186-87). Gillham and Glen note that the poem consists of one incomplete sentence without a main verb; Freeman (1948: 27-28) observes that the grammatical incompleteness and the return of the poem to its starting point mirror the circular movement of the flower as it daily follows the sun.

In a complex argument, Wagenknecht (1973: 103-06) maintains that the lines are intentionally ambiguous: the aspiration may be to a false paradise, but the youth and virgin, who are contraries and cannot fruitfully unite, may very well seek a desirable freedom from bondage to nature. The ambiguity, according to Keith (1966: 63-64), is enriching, for the poem may be read as an optimistic salute to noble aspiration or as a pessimistic meditation on hopes that will not be fulfilled. Leader (1981: 166-67) considers the speaker (the Bard) an imperfect character who is unsure whether either this sunflower or the lily of the quatrain that follows is positive or negative.

The relationship of the last line to the rest of the poem is difficult to determine, and Adams (1963: 294) believes that Blake began the line with the wrong connective. However, Grant (1974: 18-24, 29, 34-41) explains that the intensely compassionate speaker, absorbed in his meditation, ignores the requirements of grammar, though the design gives a clue to the meaning for the tiny human form of the sunflower is freeing herself from the ground.

"The Lilly"

This noble quatrain, beginning with wit and ending in serenity, celebrates the beauty of love unmarred by masks of the world of Experience. Most critics follow Wicksteed (1928: 149-51) in holding that Blake sides with the lily, Grant (1969: 343-44) adding that she resembles Oothoon and that the poem is anti-militarist. However, there are some, such as Holloway (1968: 23-24), who consider her a pretender to moral virtue, while Wilkie (1975: 122-23) suggests that the speaker makes this judgment of her but that Blake criticises him for being over suspicious of all women. Glen (1983: 31) believes that the poet refrains from moral judgment as he delights in the diversity of the world.

Erdman (1974: 85) is disturbed that the flower in the right margin droops downwards though the text describes her bliss, but Grant (1969: 348) comments that she bends down into the realm of Experience, where she will endure some suffering.

"The Garden of Love"

Straightforward readings like Hirsch's (1964: 258-59) that see the speaker's viewpoint as endorsed by Blake are opposed by those of interpreters like Leader (1981: 172-74) who hold the speaker partly responsible for his own plight. Gillham (1966: 178) accuses him of either accepting bad religious doctrines or blaming the church's puritanism for the decay of a love tainted by his selfishness. Taking a more moderate position, Adams (1963: 238) sees the speaker not as Blake but as "a sullen Orc." Tolley (1973: 115) views the poem as the counterpart of "The Ecchoing Green."

In the design Keynes (1967a, pl. 44) sees a priest teaching a boy and girl, who, according to Bindman (1977: 88), are at their parents' tomb. Briars, notes Adlard (1971), were planted to hold the turf in position over graves.

"The Little Vagabond"

Not all commentators agree with Wicksteed (1928: 180) and Hirsch (1964: 259-61) that the speaker, embraced by God in the design, sees clearly how people ought to live. What to Damon (1924: 280) is a bad poem about a naive boy is to Gillham (1966: 198-201) a piece of writing whose stylistic clumsiness reveals the immaturity of its speaker's self-indulgent creed. In the upper part of the design, Damon (1924: 285) perceives the Devil reconciled with God, Stevenson (1971: 218) detects the return of the Prodigal Son, Erdman (1974: 87) sees God comforting the boy, and Leader (1981: 115, 154), who takes little account of the old man's halo, observes a Urizenic figure imprisoning a boy in his embrace.

"London"

There has not been fierce controversy over "London." Most debate concerns the historical references and the identity of the speaker. While Erdman (1954a: 255 [275]), Adams (1963: 280) and Thompson (1978: 18) see no difficulty in identifying the speaker with Blake, Gillham (1966: 17-20) manages to find that he is too saturated in Experience to remember what love is, and Leader (1981: 196) believes him to be an isolated character mentally battered by the suffering he sees.

The design, however, is unexpectedly enigmatic. Does a beam of light protect the old man and his guide (Erdman 1974: 88)? Is the former being led towards death (Hagstrum 1964: 84)? Is he a personification of the church (Kazin 1946: 14) or of London (Thompson 1978: 14) or is he the speaker of the poem being led by Innocence (Leader 1981: 197-98)? Is his lameness one of the "marks" of the first stanza (Mellor 1974: 143)? Can he, Keynes asks (1967a, pl. 46), be Urizen, crippled by the very world he has created? Grant (1968b: 578) sees the design as optimistic in contrast to the text, for the boy—the same one who finds warmth at the fire below—does a good deed in guiding the old man and is playing the part of the little child who shall lead them (Is. xi.6). Kiralis' contention (1968: 12-13) that the fire is feeble and the man misled Grant counters (1970a) with evidence that Blake's small children never misguide old men.

With some plausibility, Bloom (1971: 78) points to a biblical source for the poem in Ezek. ix.3-4, while Thompson (1978: 11-12) insists that the mark is especially that of the beast of Rev. xiii.16-17, a mark associated with buying and selling, the merchandise in the text being the sweeper's childhood, the soldier's life and the woman's beauty.

l. 1 **charter'd**—(1) hired out, and (2) granted by right or charter, referring to rights or liberties (Hirsch 1964: 262-63). Erdman (1954a: 256 [276-77]) notes Paine's severe criticism of charters for bestowing rights on the few at the expense of the many.

ll. 3-4 The speaker himself bears the marks he describes (Thompson 1978: 11).

l. 7 **ban**—a reference to Pitt's repressive proclamations (Erdman 1954a: 256 [276-77]); curses (Bateson 1957: 126); formal denunciations, prohibitions, calls to arms and marriage banns (Hirsch 1964: 264).

l. 8 The manacles are "forged *for* the mind" (Bateson 1957: 126). They are created by the minds of both oppressor and victim (Stevenson 1971: 214). They may include the Government's hired informers, who spread fear (Erdman 1954a: 256 [277]) and even the shackles on reformers being tried like common criminals (Holloway 1968: 56-57). Glen (1983: 213) sees an allusion to current debate on whether social evils spring from human nature or from oppression by the powerful.

l. 10 **appalls**—makes appalling (Wicksteed 1928: 190); both covers with a pall and makes tremble (Bloom 1963: 141). Bateson (1957: 126) notes that the burning of coal blackened churches.

l. 12 The blood may be the soldier's own, or it may be a symbol of mutinies feared and, in 1792-93, actual (Erdman 1954a: 257 [278]). Gillham (1966: 12) thinks the blood is shed by the soldier acting under orders.

l. 14 On the symbolic level, the harlot has been identified with nature that governs the baby's organs (Bloom 1963: 142) and

with Revelation's Whore of Babylon, widely regarded by dis-
senters as official state religion (Thompson 1978: 23).

ll. 15-16   An allusion to disease (Damon 1924: 283), specifically
venereal disease transmitted through the prostitute's married
client (Kazin 1946: 16) and causing prenatal blindness (Bloom
1963: 141), and also to the harlot Nature dispensing the curse
of Urizenic possessiveness (*ibid.*: 141-42). Bateson (1957: 126)
believes the reference is to "apocalyptic horrors" and Adams
(1963: 285) regards the infant as suffering "a birth into death."
Citing "An ancient Proverb" (E475/ K184), Kiralis (1968: 10)
argues that the concluding phrase declares that marriage is
love's funeral.

"The Human Abstract"

Blake's moral position is clear in this poem, but there has
been some discussion about the meaning of the title, the viewpoint,
and the symbolism. The word "abstract" probably signifies (1)
summary (Holloway 1968: 61) and (2) "based on pure reasoning"
(Wicksteed 1928: 176) as opposed to observation or imagination.
Gleckner (1961: 376) regards the full title as naming the limited
aspect of a human being perceived by the fallen senses.

While Gillham (1973: 83) plausibly refers to Blake him-
self taking over as speaker at l. 7 from a self-justifying rationaliser,
Gleckner (1961: 377-78) argues that a fallen human and a vision-
ary Bard utter alternate stanzas beginning with the former.

In Bloom's eyes (1963: 142-43), "The Human Abstract"
casts a gloomy light back on "The Divine Image" showing how its
appealing virtues are after all rooted in natural selfishness. More
cheerfully, Glen (1983: 206-07) contrasts the account in the earlier
poem of what people really do with the mere "rational argument"
presented here. According to Raine (1968: II, 44), "The Human
Abstract" shows how good and evil cannot be disentangled in the
temporal world.

ll. 5-8   When the selfish loves increase sufficiently to topple the
balance of mutual fear, cruelty emerges and people submit to it,
contributing to their own oppression (Glen 1983: 204).

l. 6   **selfish loves**—the self-love of Pope's *Essay on Man* (Gillham
1973: 85-86).

l. 12   In Neoplatonism, the foot is the body's most materialistic organ (Harper 1961: 173, 183).

ll. 13-14   The growth of Mystery signifies domination by dogma (Gillham 1973: 88). It includes an allusion to "the Mystery of the Incarnation" (Bloom 1963: 143).

l. 15   **the Catterpiller and Fly**—priesthood (Damon 1924: 283); clerical caterpillars and political flies (Gillham 1973: 89).

l. 19   **the Raven**—symbol of violent lusts (Wicksteed 1928: 177); of death (Hirsch 1964: 268); of the fear of death (Keynes 1967a, pl. 47). Alluding to the Norse gods, whom he connects with natural religion, Blake hints at an equation of Urizen (here "Cruelty") with the Norse god Odin, whose emblem is the Raven, and who suffered sacrifice on a tree in his search for the Mystery underlying the Runes; the last stanza refers to the failure of the other gods to find the mistletoe with which Baldur was killed (Bloom 1963: 143-44).

"Infant Sorrow"

The speaker's preternatural memory is a literary fiction. Adams (1963: 239) views the adult speaker as reinterpreting his infancy from the standpoint of Experience; Gillham (1966: 181) deduces that he must be drawing on his observation of babies. Though Wilkie (1975: 126-27) remarks that the illustration shows the child is not bound or harshly treated, several critics agree that the speaker encountered parental repression at birth; they differ, however, over whether he remained a being of energy (Adams, *loc. cit.*) or whether his admirable rebellion degenerated into cunning (Gardner 1954: 104-05). Keynes (1967a, pl. 48) classifies this poem about birth as the sequel to "Infant Joy," a poem about conception. The counterpart of the design is found on the second page of "A Cradle Song" (Bass 1970: 209).

l. 1   **My mother groan'd! my father wept**—His father sympathised with his mother's birthpangs (Hirsch 1964: 273). His mother regretted that he had an independent existence, and his father was jealous of him (Gleckner 1959: 239).

ll. 3-4   Other critics follow Gleckner (1959: 240) in contrasting this child with the one in "Introduction" to *Songs of Innocence*.

l. 4 **a fiend hid in a cloud**—the spirit imprisoned in the mortal
body and fiendish because severed from the divine (Wicksteed
1928: 70); a symbol of natural instincts that Blake respects
(Bateson 1957: 116).

ll. 7-8 The child is temporarily defeated (Gillham 1973: 3). He is
reluctantly resigned to earthly conditions (Wicksteed 1928:
174).

"A Poison Tree"

Commentators are much interested in the connection bet-
ween the tree of the title and the Tree of Knowledge, which Blake
equates with his Tree of Mystery. Schorer (1946: 243) believes
that the two are identical, Erdman (1974: 91) that they are only
similar. Raine (1968: II, 38-39) observes an implied analogy bet-
ween the human speaker, who misguidedly hides his anger, and
the God who, hating humankind, conceals his wrath in the tempt-
ing Tree of Knowledge to produce poisonous fruit. The speaker,
according to Gillham (1966: 177), believes, in his self-deception,
that he is acting rightly. Both he and his thieving enemy are fallen
(Hirsch 1964: 275).

The tree pictured is, in Tolley's view (1973: 112), a dead
willow and its branches represent a pretended pity veiling anger.
Erdman (1974: 91) notes the cruciform posture of the enemy's
corpse.

l. 14 **When the night had veil'd the pole**—when the night of
the fallen creation had covered "the polar center of the soul"
(Raine 1968: II, 43).

"A Little Boy Lost"

Faced with a poem in which reason seems to be praised,
critics have taken full advantage of the textual ambiguities to offer
a rich variety of interpretations. The author's attitude to the boy
depends to a considerable extent on the meaning of the first two
stanzas: Bateson (1957: 121) implies that the opening quatrain
expresses a Swedenborgian identification between humankind and
God; Adams (1963: 270) conceives of the boy as being in Inno-
cence and identifying himself with all that he knows; Gleckner

(1959: 252-53) describes him as being in Experience but advancing towards the higher Innocence; Hirsch (1964: 278) perceives him as innocently speaking the truth of a world in which self-love co-exists with love of others; and Stuart (1979: 31) sees that he is questioning the commands to honour one's parents and to love God and one's neighbour. Wicksteed's contention (1928: 178) that Blake partly agrees with the boy seems convincing, and his view that reasoning is a necessary activity at this stage in his development is plausible. On the other hand, Damon (1924: 282) and Gleckner (1959: 253) argue that the priest is mistaken in thinking the boy a reasoner, while at the opposite extreme Gillham (1973: 108-110) claims that he has learnt rationalist doctrine and Leader (1981: 170) accuses him of being an anti-Blakean Deist.

l. 5 **Father**—God the Father (Gillham 1973: 108-09). His parent, the priest, or God (Stuart 1979: 31).

ll. 7-8 Stuart (*loc. cit.*) points out the ambiguity here: the boy may love as the bird loves (cf. Gillham 1973: 110-11) or he may love his father as he loves the bird (cf. Hagstrum 1964: 84).

l. 12 The child's parents are at first among those who "admir'd the Priestly care"; only later do they weep (Gardner 1954: 102).

l. 23 According to Gillham, the parents weep for the child's guilt as well as his fate (1966: 88).

l. 24 Blake compares the persecution of a child for thinking freely with the former burning of heretics (Wicksteed 1928: 178). He may be replying to No. XXIII of Watts's *Divine Songs*, a cruel poem about disobedience to parents (Pinto 1957: 78-79).

"A Little Girl Lost"

There is no doubt that Ona descends into (or further into) Experience in this poem, but does she start in true Innocence and does she suffer any decline before she encounters her father? Whereas Adams (1963: 219-20) sees the second and fifth stanzas as celebrating Innocence, in which fear can be assuaged and night is the night of Beulah, Gardner (1954: 103) insists that there is no fear in Innocence and that an agreement to meet at night is a concession to the secrecy of Experience. According to Gillham (1973: 55-58), Ona only falls from Innocence when she encounters her father's stare and finds her love tainted with guilt.

In the design, the barren tree is countered by the vines and birds of joy (Erdman 1974: 93).

ll. 5-14 The classical Golden Age is combined with the biblical Garden of Eden, where Adam and Eve went naked (Gillham 1973: 56).

ll. 20-24 The pair know there is suffering in the world (l. 24) but they have thought of love as a consolation (Gillham 1973: 58). Line 24 refers to the weariness which arises from humanity's division into sexes (Wicksteed 1928: 164).

l. 30 **Ona**—This name, a version of "Una," which means "One," expresses her loneliness (Wicksteed 1928: 165).

l. 34 The image suggests that the father, who introduces guilt into Una's life, is to be identified with the Tree of Knowledge of Good and Evil (Adams 1963: 220).

"To Tirzah"

(Because it is a very late addition to *Songs of Experience*, this poem is discussed in chap. 8 instead of chap. 4.)

Most but not all critics believe that the speaker and the poet are at one, though they do not agree on what the speaker means. There is widespread agreement with Wicksteed (1928: 183) that Tirzah represents physical Nature, though to this Wicksteed (*loc. cit.*) adds misguided, tearful maternal solicitude, which Gleckner (1959: 269-70) sees as the maternal protectiveness of Innocence prolonged until it has become oppressive. Adams (1963: 274) also accuses her of teaching a false distinction between soul and body. To Bateson (1957: 127), she represents asceticism as well as the materialism Blake rejects after losing hope in political reform.

Two scholars argue that the speaker's views are directly contrary to Blake's. Leader (1981: 202) claims that he is the Bard of "Introduction" and that he is here the victim of error more than anywhere else. Ignoring the late date of the poem, the meaning Blake attached to Tirzah, and his belief that the unfallen human is androgynous, Gillham (1973: 101-06) assails the speaker for his self-righteous rejection of the physical body to which St. Paul allowed its own kind of glory in I Cor. xv.40.

The figures in the design have been identified as the spirit of sacrifice, a fallen body, and their companions sexual love and maternal love (Wicksteed 1928: 186); as Joseph of Arimathea, the body of Jesus, and the two Marys (Margoliouth 1951: 60-61); as Jesus, Lazarus [and presumably Mary and Martha] (Hirsch 1964: 290); as "the natural victim," two oppressive women, and a merciful but possibly ineffective old man (Grant 1968b: 579); and very reasonably as the spiritual body rising and its comforters (Erdman 1974: 94). Leader (1981: 201-02) discusses only the old man, whom he stigmatises as an orthodox Urizenic tyrant beside his Tree of Knowledge.

ll. 1-2   The material universe is to be replaced by a spiritual one as foretold in Rev. [xxi] (Hirsch 1964: 285).

l. 4   **thee**—the younger Blake who wrote the rest of *Songs of Experience* (Hirsch 1964: 290); the speaker's fleshly body (Gillham 1973: 103).

l. 5   Pride and shame divided the human into male and female (Damon 1924: 281). Pride (like Satan's) and shame (like the naked Adam's and Eve's) caused the Fall (Hirsch 1964: 286). The speaker wrongly connects the Fall with the beginning of sexuality (Gillham 1973: 104).

l. 7   Divine mercy reduced death from Eternity into a temporary sleep (Damon 1924: 281) or commuted death to exile from Eden (Wicksteed 1928: 185). A divine limitation was imposed on the contraction that came with the Fall (Gleckner 1959: 270).

l. 9   **Thou Mother of my Mortal Part**—the fleshly mother, who constricts the child's soul (Wicksteed 1928: 185); both the speaker's fleshly mother and the earth (Gillham 1973: 103).

ll.12-13 Four senses were constricted by Nature, but touch, the sexual sense, was left uninjured (Bloom 1963: 145). All the senses except touch were granted to the embodied soul (Hirsch 1964: 283).

l. 15   Christ showed fallen humanity the way to rise again (Damon 1924: 281). Jesus is the image of "imaginative power" (Adams 1963: 274). The Atonement is the overcoming of the natural body by the imaginative body through the power of touch (Bloom 1963: 145). The death of Jesus enables the speaker to cast off error and attain freedom in spirit even in this world (Hirsch 1964: 284-85, 289).

"The School Boy"

This poem is straightforward and the design is not very puzzling. Tolley (1973: 112-14) regards the boy as an Innocent trapped in Experience, but to Gillham (1966: 211-14) he seems too self-conscious and sophisticated to be Innocent and similarly his protest appears to Leader (1981: 175-76) too clear and calculated. Damon (1924: 282-83), pointing to the boy pictured reading a book happily in a tree, aptly remarks that Blake favoured not ignorance but self-education. Expounding the design, Erdman (1974: 94, 95) describes the figures in the tree as children's spiritual bodies and mentions the game of marbles on the ground.

"The Voice of the Ancient Bard"

What is to Bateson (1957: 124) an optimistic poem seems to Gardner (1954: 117) to end in sorrow. In an otherwise enthusiastic discussion, Hirsch (1964: 47-48) confesses that the transformation of the world it predicts is rather vague, but this criticism is nothing beside the shrill attack of Gillham (1973: 123-27), who, moved by his own conservatism, is indignant at the Bard's rejection of reason and tradition: this, he declares, is "ridiculous," as Blake must have come to realise when he moved the poem from *Innocence* to *Experience* after the degeneration of revolutionary France. Leader (1981: 190-93) presents the Bard as a man who looks back on an unworthy past when he was a leader who needed to be led but whose morning of enlightenment has now arrived.

Considering the design, Wicksteed (1928: 130) sees those on the Bard's left as uncertain about his message and those on his right as having accepted it. Grant (1968b: 579-80) discerns several figures from earlier plates who have emerged from the night of Experience, including the lovers on the first page of "A Little Girl Lost" and the three girls on the second page of "Night." All the young people except the boy behind the harp seem to Leader to be inattentive (1981: 192-93).

Notes on Criticism for Chapter 5

America

The most obvious problem in *America* is the relationship between the Preludium and the Prophecy. The two-part structure is one aspect of the poem's obscurity, which, Bronowski suggests (1944: 50-52), may be in part a device to avoid a charge of sedition. In the Preludium, which Stevenson (1971: 188) classifies as a late, less politically focused addition, Orc interacts with the daughter of Urthona—probably his sibling, though he seems unaware of it (Johnson and Grant 1979: 107), rather than his virgin mother (Frye 1947: 228)—and in the Prophecy with Albion's Angel. Many critics have endorsed Damon's view (1924: 334) that Urthona's daughter is a form of material, fallen nature; the epithets "shadowy" and "nameless" have encouraged Raine (1968: I, 273) to identify her with Paracelsus' conception of nature as the mysterious cloudlike mother of all things, and have reminded Paley (1970: 76, 117) that "Where man is not, nature is barren" (*MHH*, pl. 10)—here, he believes, she is an illusion ("shadowy") with no identity ("nameless"). In view of the daughter's reference to "my American plains" (2:10), which points forward to the Prophecy, it would be difficult to deny Gardner's claim (1968: 98) that she is also the oppressed colonies (and, he adds, oppressed humankind), while Quasha (1970: 270-71) presses the point further to claim that she is a transformation of Oothoon, who is "the soft soul of America" (*VDA* 1:3), and Howard (1984: 119) notes that like Oothoon and unlike Thel she accepts life. Other accounts stress her accoutrements, which remind Damon (1924: 334) of spiritual conflict, Bloom (1963: 118) of the Iron Age, Erdman (1954a: 240 [260]) of the war and famine that prevailed before the current age of revolution, and Howard (1984: 116) of the chaste goddess Athena as well as mastery of the American continent. Fisher (1961: 155-56) sees her as the Muse of History, Beer (1968: 110) as "a caricature of Britannia," and Johnson and Grant (1979: 107) as a Diana-like virgin goddess.

The Female's ravisher or awakener is the "new born" fire of "A Song of Liberty," now endowed with the name Orc, which may derive from one or more of the following: Latin *cor* ("heart"), for he is born from the heart of Enitharmon (Damon 1924: 112, 334, citing W. M. Rossetti and *FZ* 58:16-18/ E339/ V, 36-38); Latin *Orcus* (both the classical "hell" and its ruler Pluto) (T. Wright 1929: I, 26)—carrying over, Bloom emphasises (1963: 119), the ironic meaning of "hell" [from *MHH*]; Greek *orcheis* ("testicles"), for his energy is sexual as well as political and agricultural (Erdman 1954a: 24, 241-42 [25-26, 261-62]); and English "orca" (Damon 1967: 309) or "orc" (Raine 1968: I, 339, citing *PL*, XI, 835) meaning whale or sea monster. Among Orc's suggested prototypes, some are Greco-Roman—the heroic Prometheus and the annually resurrected fertility god Adonis (Frye 1947: 207); Hyperion, Typhon and Eros (Rose 1972b: 137)—and some biblical—David facing Goliath and the dragon Satan facing the Archangel Michael (Spicer 1967: 25-29); and the red, hairy Esau, who (Gen. xxv.25) is to recover his inheritance (Raine 1968: I, 338-39), and who is identified with Edom (see *MHH* 2:13n), whence comes the Messiah (Tannenbaum 1982: 132-33, citing Is. lxiii.1). Indeed, Tannenbaum (1982: 141-42) describes his descent in the Preludium as an image of the Incarnation, though Bloom (1963: 119) sees him rather as the human identity about to detach itself from the half-formed nature that has produced it. His later conflict with Urizen, Howard (1984: 125-26) interprets as the suppression by the conscious mind of upheavals from the unconscious. Gallant (1978: 27-29) considers that in arousing his sister's sexuality he expands her powers of imagination and perception as he expands those of the revolutionaries in the Prophecy and as Blake hopes to expand the reader's. Emphasising his supposed incest, Webster (1983: 112-17, 124) sees him as a Theotormon who has shed his weakness and enacts an Oedipal revenge against father figures as he resists his own (and Blake's) inner guilt and masochistic impulses.

It is generally agreed that *America* centres on the praise of liberty, and most critics believe with Frye (1947: 209) that the revolution it portrays is a regular event in a repeated historical cycle, though for good reason there is much agreement with Paley (1970: 74) that Orc's advent offers society a chance of permanent escape into a higher state free from tyranny—see 9:19n.

Not all critics accept Damon's view (1924: 112) that the portrayal of Orc is entirely favourable. Paley (1970: 61) finds him partly human and redemptive, partly serpentine and power-hungry; Rose (1972b: 141) warns that because he is desire without imagination his work has to be supplemented by Los's; Welch (1972) considers that his association with Mars and with wife-stealing Ariston reflects Blake's doubts about his violence; and Beer (1968: 110) perceives him as a limited character whose energy is a makeshift for true vision. In his encounter with a possessive female (2:7), in his emanation of heat without light (4:11) and in the pessimism of the designs, Doskow (1979) sees a reflection of Blake's disappointment that the revolution failed to transform American society, abolish slavery, and spread to other countries. More optimistically, James (1979: 247-48, 251-52) finds the division in the Preludium between Orc's chained material self and his soaring spiritual self transcended in the Prophecy, where all such divisions as those between matter and spirit, public and private life, and politics and art are transcended. In a somewhat parallel way, Schleifer (1979: 569-71, 577, 580-82) sees the advance from Urizenic outlook to prophetic vision enacted by Orc's mutation of simile into metaphor: thus clouds that *resemble* blood can quickly *become* wheels of blood (4:5-6).

The principal source of *America* is Book V of the 1787 edition of the American poet Joel Barlow's epic in heroic couplets, *The Vision of Columbus*: this text gives Blake the images of chain, cloud, and naval bombardment, all his historical names except Paine and Hancock, and the term "Albion's Prince" (Erdman 1954b). A secondary source is the description in Joshua Barnes's *History of Edward III* (1688) of the torment of the Black Death, England's punishment for invading France, while Gray's "Descent of Odin" contributes to the Preludium (Erdman 1954a: 55-56, 71-73, 242 [58-59, 75-76, 262]). Tannenbaum (1982: 135-39) finds the poet indebted to the account of the conflict between the Messiah and his opponent in the apocryphal book II Esdras.

According to Stevenson (1960), an early draft of *America*, represented by the three surviving cancelled plates (E58-59, 802-03/ K20?-05), marked an intermediate stage between *The French Revolution* and the final version: in the early draft there was no Orc, Urizen was barely named, and Albion's Angel was merely the agent of the British government. In Damon's view (1924: 339), it is in *America* that Blake first makes his text and designs tell the same story independently, though Wardle (1968) argues that most of the designs represent states opposite to those described in the poem.

Details

1:1 **Urthona**—our spiritual element, the father of Los, who is the spirit of poetry (Damon 1924: 334). However, Sloss and Wallis (1926: I, 63) raise an important point when they observe that nowhere in the shorter prophetic books are Los and Urthona said to be related. Murry (1933: 85-86) believes that when Urthona falls he becomes Urizen.

1:2 **fourteen suns**—the age of puberty (Frye 1947: 206); from the publication of Rousseau's *The Social Contract* (1762) to the American Declaration of Independence (1776) (Erdman 1954a: 239 [258-59]); "fourteen" signifies the midpoint of the lunar month, indicating the cyclical nature of Orc's existence (Bloom 1963: 119); the exodus from Egypt occurred on the fourteenth day of the first month (Num. ix.3-5) and there are fourteen generations in each historical epoch (Matt. i.17) (Tannenbaum 1982: 142).

1:7 **clouds**—of ignorance (Damon 1924: 334); of Urizenic dogma (Bloom 1963: 126); of chastity (Gardner 1968: 99); of British oppression (Cherry 1969: 31); of delusion (Howard 1984: 116).

1:10 **dumb till that dread day**—The daughter's sexual awakening is not only a liberation but also an entrance into the "dread day" of the natural cycle (Nurmi 1976: 90). Revolution gives the colonies a voice (Doskow 1979: 173).

1:11-12 Los (the fallen Urthona) shackles energy (Orc) instead of reason and fathers fallen nature (the daughter) (Erdman 1954a: 240-41 [260]).

1:12 **tenfold chains**—the Ten Commandments (Gardner 1968: 99).

1:13-16 The eagle and lion may be respectively symbols of genius and of God's protective anger (Damon 1924: 334), or the national emblems of Mexico and Peru (Erdman 1954a: 239 [259]). The four creatures have been conceived as manifestations of Orc formidable only to those afraid of the emotions (Paley 1970: 76-77), as variants of the eagle, ox, lion and man of the evangelists (Adlard 1972: 120-21), as exemplars of liberty (Johnson and Grant 1979: 108), and as constellations which the Shadowy Female identifies with nations (Worrall 1981: 281). Gallant (1978: 28) perceives here an expression of Orc's joy in his act of copulation.

1:16 **the pillars of Urthona**—See "A Song of Liberty," 16n. Erdman holds that Orc, wound round the pillars, is protecting "the tree of liberty" (1954a: 239 [259]).

1:16-17 Orc embraces the daughter in the north, the spiritual region (Damon 1924: 334).

1:19 **red eyes**—characteristic of Macpherson's heroes (Erdman 1954a: 242 [262]).

2:7 Doskow's charge (1979: 174) that the daughter is culpably possessive (i.e. unwilling to export revolution) is challenged by Howard's assertion (1984: 239n30) that what she is unwilling to relinquish is her sexual fulfilment. Observing how closely her words echo Cant. iii.4, Tannenbaum (1982: 147) almost identifies Orc and the daughter with Christ and his Bride.

2:8-9 **Thou art...dark death**—a reference to the south, the quarter of reason (Damon 1924: 334); or to slave rebellions (Erdman 1954a: 239 [259]); or to Swedenborg's claim, annotated by Blake (E603/ K90), that Africans can only conceive of God as human (Paley 1970: 76); or to the daughter's idolatrous cleaving to Orc as a fertility god (Johnson and Grant 1979: 108); or to the escape of repressed sexual energy (Wagenknecht 1973: 183).

2:12-14 The animals may represent widespread outbreaks of revolution (Beer 1968: 112). While Gallant (1978: 27-28) praises the expansion of the daughter's consciousness that accompanies copulation, Doskow (1979: 175-76) criticises her unhealthy conception of love that contrasts with Orc's forthright images of desire and its satiation.

2:15 **thy fire & my frost**—on the historical level, the revolutionary and reactionary forces (Wagenknecht 1973: 183). The copulation which appears a rape to the eye of oppression is "a marriage of contraries" (Howard 1984: 119).

2:16 **furrows by thy lightnings rent**—possibly a reference to the use of fire to make metal implements (Erdman 1954a: 242 [261-62]).

2:17 **eternal death**—the mystical annihilation of the self (Damon 1924: 334); and both sexual congress and the spiritual death preceding rebirth (Spicer 1967: 24-25); an ironic term for life on the natural plane (Bloom 1965: 902).

   torment—the suffering caused by revolution (Erdman 1954a: 242 [262]), by its failure to mend the world (Beer 1968: 112-13), or by the imminence of the end of time, of which the Shadowy Female is "the matrix" (Tannenbaum 1982: 142).

2:18-21 These lines are blotted out in all but two of the thirteen known copies—according to Erdman (1969b: 286-87), citing G. E. Bentley, Jr., the two latest. They may record Blake's dismay at the state of Britain and her treatment of the colonies (Damon 1967: 36); at the failure of revolution and the repression of British radicalism (Erdman 1954a: 264-65 [286-87]); or at the British Parliament's opting for war with France in January 1793 (Erdman 1977c: 514). Less probable objects of his emotion are Blake's own full comprehension of what apocalypse in the fallen world involves (Wagenknecht 1973: 184-88); his failure to advance from lament to liberating vision (Quasha 1970: 283-84); his guilt at fantasizing about the vengeful, incestuous rape of an unloving nurturer (Webster 1983: 111); the non-completion of apocalypse (Tannenbaum 1982: 148); and the poet Joel Barlow's vision of a religious, rational, scientific America contrary to his own revolutionary ideal (Howard 1984: 114-15). If the Bard is an invented character, he may be ashamed at the daughter's inability to accept Orc with unmixed joy (Bloom 1963: 120). The lines may customarily be cancelled because Blake's dismay was temporary (Erdman 1969b: 286-87), or because the passage is too pessimistic for a poem which is less than hopeless (Bloom, *loc. cit.*)—in which, indeed, the end of the daughter's speech indicates that prophecy is being fulfilled (Schleifer 1979: 578-79).

2:20 **A ruin'd pillar**—the broken glory of a Britain once free and peaceful (Erdman 1977c: 514).

2:21 **the vales of Kent**—the county of Kent on the south-east coast, from which the poet perhaps thinks of moving to France (Damon 1967: 228); the Old Kent Road in London (Erdman 1954a: 264 [286]).

3:1 **The Guardian Prince of Albion**—often held to be identical (Schorer 1946: 283) or "not quite identical" (Johnson and

Grant 1979: 103) with George III. Nurmi (1976: 90-91) and Howard (1984: 120) consider the Prince to be distinct from Albion's Angel, but some critics side with Sloss and Wallis (1926: I, 44) and Erdman (1954a: 24-25, [26-27]), who hold that Prince, Angel and King are all one.

3:1ff A description of "the torment long foretold" (2:17) (Schleifer 1979: 580).

3:4 Joseph Warren (1741-1775), Boston physician and patriot general killed at the battle of Bunker Hill; Horatio Gates (1728-1806), Washington's Adjutant General and the victor of Saratoga (1777); John Hancock (1737-1793), wealthy Boston merchant and politician, first signatory of the Declaration of Independence; Nathanael Greene (1742-1786), the general who forced the British out of the Carolinas in 1781.

3:5 **glowing with blood**—from the Boston Massacre of 1770 (Damon 1967: 152).

3:7 **A bended bow**—a war threat (Erdman 1954a: 21 [22]).
    iron chain—British restrictions on the American economy (Erdman 1954a: 21 [22]) and also slavery (Stevenson 1971: 191); Los's Chain of Jealousy (Beer 1968: 114).

3:14 **eastern**—geographically, British, and psychologically, belonging to the quarter of the emotions (Damon 1924: 335).

3:16 **red meteors**—from the firing of guns (Howard 1984: 119).

4:3 Like 12:10, a reference to offshore bombardments and towns set ablaze (Damon 1967: 20).

4:5 The human body undergoes an expansion foreshadowing the liberation of 15:25-26 (Quasha 1970: 278). The blood is placental blood filling the womb prior to the birth of the "Wonder" of 4:7 (Erdman 1981: 299).

4:6-9 Paley's observation (1970: 73) that this image of Orc alludes to both the fourth figure in Nebuchadnezzar's furnace (Dan. iii.25)—[sometimes regarded as a type of Christ (e.g. Henry 1708-14: IV, 1041)]—and Robert Southwell's representation of Jesus in "The Burning Babe" is supplemented by Gallant's suggestion (1978: 29) that Blake's source is Ezek. i.27 and Tannenbaum's (1982: 135-37) that it is the vision of the Messiah coming from the sea in II Esdras xiii. But Howard (1984: 120) charges the Prince of Albion with creating the image by projecting his own ferocity onto Orc, while Ostriker (1977: 906) sees the rebel as emerging from a volcanic explosion. Gardner (1968: 100) perceptively contrasts the "Human fire" of Orc with the Urizenic "Sullen fires" of 3:2.

4:11   According to tradition, hellfire radiates heat without light—here perhaps passion without reason (Damon (1924: 335). Cf. *PL*, I, 62-63 (Bloom 1965: 902). The absent light is the freedom not achieved by an incomplete revolution (Doskow 1979: 176-77). The heat is the existing drive for liberty, the light the illumination yet to come (Howard 1984: 120).

5:1   **the Stone of night**—the tablet bearing the Ten Commandments, here associated with the Temple (Damon 1924: 335). Bloom (1963: 121), accepting Frye's identification of it (1947: 224) with Jacob's pillow (Gen. xxviii.11), regards it as the "essential building block" of the "opaque" material world, and Johnson and Grant (1979: 111) connect it with the papal power, which is founded on the pun in Matt. xvi.18. See also *E* 10:26n, 11:1n.

5:1-5   Damon's speculations that Mars represents the heart and the sun the poetic impulse (1924: 335) or that Mars stands for the state of war in which the natural man lived (1967: 263) can be compared with Beer's notion of a time when Mars's rebellious energy dominated the recently fallen universe before the merciful creation of other heavenly bodies (1968: 114, 228). More illuminating, however, is Baine and Baine's discovery (1975) that Mars is the centre of the unfallen Grand Man who constitutes heaven in Swedenborg's *Concerning the Earths in Our Solar System* (English translation 1787). Orc, therefore, like Mars, once had a less fearsome countenance, but Ferber (1981) rightly complains that the allusion does not explain "the planets three," which, he suggests, represent the Ireland, Scotland and Wales of 15:13, who desert the Mars-like Prince or Angel of Albion to join the solar Orc. Worrall (1981: 284) points out that Albion's Angel longs for the time when the now unpredictable comet was controlled by Mars.

5:6-7   **the temple**—a church stained by blood-guilt (Howard 1984: 120).

6:2   **the spices shed**—the dispersal of the spices placed on Christ's body (Stevenson 1971: 193).

6:3-4   Cf. the vision of the valley of dry bones in Ezek. xxxvii.1-10 (Stevenson 1971: 194).

6:6   Cf. Samson—see Judg. xvi.21 and Milton, *Samson Agonistes*, l. 41 (Stevenson 1971: 194). Samson is traditionally considered a type of Christ (e.g. Henry 1708-14: II, 217). The reader is obliquely reminded that the United States has retained slavery (Doskow 1979: 177).

6:15   **the Lion & Wolf**—respectively the protector and the enemy of the sheep (Damon 1924: 336). Cf. Is. xxxv.9—"No lion shall be there, nor any ravenous beast" (Tannenbaum 1982: 127).

7:3-7   Enitharmon's Children are Urizen's instruments (Sloss and Wallis 1926: II, 210). The British authorities identify American rebellion with the child-devouring dragon of Rev. xii.4; "gate" has an anatomical meaning (Margoliouth 1948: 303-04). Erdman (1954a: 24[25]) compares the Royal Proclamation of 23 Aug. 1775 against rebellion.

7:4   Enitharmon presides over the phenomenal world of innumerable material bodies (Douglas 1965: 111). Her name may come from Greek *anerithmon* ("numberless") or from "zenith" and "harmony" (Damon 1924: 336, citing W. M. Rossetti for the first and W. N. Guthrie for the second), or from Greek *enarithmios* ("numbered") (Frye 1947: 440n29). Bloom (1965: 959) suggests that she is essentially numberless in Eternity but, as goddess of space, falls prey to measure and number in the temporal world. Thomas Wright (1929: I, 144) supposes her name combines those of Enion and Tharmas, her parents in the first Night of *The Four Zoas*.

8:1   Orc is trying to overthrow the Tree of Mystery, which is identical with nature (Bloom 1963: 123). The serpent of Eden is really Messianic, for he is encouraging humans to break the evil prohibition of Eden (Damon 1967: 20); he is the serpent of John iii.14, a type of Christ (Howard 1984: 122).

8:4   **the starry hosts**—the Israelites of the Exodus, on whom Urizen imposes his legal system symbolised by the zodiac, which imprisons the (Orcean) sun (Frye 1966: 182; cf. Damon 1967: 385).

8:5   **That stony law I stamp to dust**—Beer (1968: 113) sees an allusion to Moses' breaking of the Tablets of the Law, and Miner (1969: 262) cites Dan. viii.10, but most convincing is Helms (1979: 290-91), who realises that for Blake and Orc the

Law is an object of idolatry like the grove that the pious king
Josiah "stamped...small to powder" (II Kings xxiii.6).

8:8 **the deeps shrink to their fountains**—Frye (1966: 183) cites
Rev. xxi.1, Tannenbaum (1982: 138) Is. xi.15-16, and Howard
(1984: 122) Rev. xxi.6, but the primary allusion is probably to
Gen. viii.2—"The fountains also of the deep...were stopped":
the Flood, for Blake synonymous with the Fall, will be undone.

8:9 **the stony roof**—the overarching sky (Frye 1966: 183); the
human skull (Tolley 1970a: 138); the womb-cum-tomb (Rose
1972b: 141).

8:15-17 Bloom (1963: 124) notes that in this version of the giant
of Nebuchadnezzar's dream (Dan. ii.32-35) the feet are no
longer of fragile iron and clay and the breast and head are now
of the same substance, for heart and brain are equal in the res-
urrected human, and that Blake also alludes to the men unhar-
med in the fiery furnace (Dan. iii.19-20), which signifies,
according to Frye (1966: 183), the harmless enjoyment of sex-
ual freedom among the resurrected. Tolley (1970a: 140) detects
a reference to Christ's brass-like feet in Rev. i.15.

9:2 Howard (1984: 112) claims that Albion's Angel sees Orc as
wolf or lion, but 6:15 and 7:2 suggest that he intends these
animals to represent his own power.

9:8 **the stubbed oak**—the tree of error (Damon 1924: 336) or
forests of superstition (Gardner 1968: 52), which the British
cannot induce to spread.

9:10 **lightnings**—British musket fire (Erdman 1954a: 26 [27]).

9:19 **the times are return'd**—Albion's Angel insists the histori-
cal cycle is renewed despite Orc's proclamation that "The
times are ended" (8:2)—i.e. the cycle will no longer be repeat-
ed (Paley 1970: 104).

9:20-25 Albion's Angel may suppose that Orc's mother is Nat-
ure, Urthona's daughter (Bloom 1965: 902) or the country
America (Johnson and Grant 1979: 114). Albion, says Howard
(1984: 123), is the real child-devourer, the consumer of his
own colonies. Wagenknecht (1973: 189-90) compares Mil-
ton's dogs who gnaw the innards of their mother, Sin (*PL*, II,
798-800).

10:5-12 The main sources of this inspiring but obscure passage
appear to be Plato's account in the *Critias* (113c-d) of how Pos-
eidon, ruler of the now submerged Atlantis, seized a mortal

woman, and Herodotus' account in his *Histories* (VI, 61-69) of Ariston, King of Sparta, who stole another man's wife but whose name is Greek for "best" (Damon 1924: 336-37). Damon cites also Bacon's *New Atlantis*, which identifies the drowned land with America, part of which survived Noah's Flood.

It seems clear that the lines—designed to stand out for their flowing style and use of the second person pronoun (De Luca 1970: 5-6)—describe the "perturb'd" angels' decision, after a moment of hesitation, to opt for rebellion. But are Ariston, the bride-theft, the palace, the forest, and even Atlantis itself positive or negative? To Beer (1968: 116) Ariston is a hero in whose palace lovers of liberty meet; to Damon (1924: 337) he is a mixed character who constructs a noble Gothic building in a forest of error; to Welch (1972) he is Herodotus' wife-stealer, whose act led to a power struggle in Sparta; and to Howard (1984: 110) he is a tyrant whose residence is an emblem of oppression parallel to the temple of Urizen and the Stone of Night.

Back-dating Blake's later hostility to the Greeks—and ignoring his enthusiastic reference in 1795 to their "lost Art," which it is his life's mission to restore (E701/ K792)—three critics see an anti-classical stance in the passage. Damon (1924: 337) asserts that the submergence of Greece's enemy Atlantis (Plato, *Timaeus* 24d-25d) represents the victory of rational Athens; Bloom (1963: 126) suggests that the stolen wife signifies Plato's theft of his world of Ideas and tale of Atlantis from British or Hebrew sources; and Dorfman (1979) maintains that Ariston is a Urizenic figure associated with the Greco-Roman Golden Age, with the greedy maritime imperialism of Atlantis, and (on account of his palace) with social hierarchy.

Acknowledging the seemingly contradictory connotations of the phrases, De Luca (1970: 4-9) holds that Blake is constructing "an icon" to bring about supra-rational illumination, but a plausible resolution of the difficulty has been achieved by Adlard (1972: 33-39), who presents Ariston as a positive figure in whom Poseidon and the Spartan king are conflated with the art-collector, tree-planter, and philanthropist Thomas Johnes (1748-1816), who built a Gothic mansion at Hafod in the Welsh mountains for the beautiful woman he had married secr-

retly. Johnes and Blake were both friends of the artist John
Cumberland, and Blake engraved a map of Johnes's estate in
1796.

11:3 **Boston's Angel**—perhaps Samuel Adams calling for inde-
pendence in the First Congress (1744) (Erdman 1954a: 24
[26]).

11:6 A reference to the hesitation of some colonial delegates to
declare independence from Britain (Sloss and Wallis 1926: I,
55).

11:9 **performers of the energies**—devourers of the products
(Howard 1984: 124).

12:9 **the Demon red**—one of the King's officers conducting a
naval bombardment (Erdman 1954a: 25 [26-27]) or possibly
the King himself (Erdman 1977c: 26).

13:2 Blake ignores the fact that on account of his misrule Sir
Francis Bernard (1712-1779), Governor of Massachusetts, was
recalled as early as 1769 (*ibid.*).

13:15 Albion's plagues that recoil on the mother country consist
of propaganda claiming the colonists are already free (Howard
1984: 110-11).

14:2 Ethan Allen (1748-1789), American general and Deist
writer; Richard Henry ("Light-Horse Harry") Lee (1756-1818),
cavalry commander under Washington.

14:3-5 Britain is trying to ruin the colonies' economy (Erdman
1954a: 53-54 [57]).

14:14 The "Mariners" are the Boston Sons of Liberty (Erdman
1954a: 54 [57]). The reference is probably to the Boston Tea
Party of December 1773, though possibly to Britain's subse-
quent closure of the port (Damon 1967: 55).

14: 15-16 The scribe is either Paine (Erdman, *loc. cit.*) or Frank-
lin (Johnson and Grant 1979: 117). The builder is Jefferson
(Erdman, *loc. cit.*).

14:19 **all rush together**—farmers and citizens united (Erdman
1954a: 26 [28]).

14:20-15:3 The troubles of the British Government include the
Gordon Riots of 1780 (Erdman 1954a: 6-8 [7-9]).

15:1-5 During and after the American Revolution, the British
army suffered from disease and mass desertions, and merchants
in Bristol and London loudly opposed the war (Erdman 1954a:
56-67 [60]).

15:7-8 After Britain's defeat, George III suffered depression and later (1788) madness (Erdman 1954a: 58 [61]; cf. Sloss and Wallis, 1926: I, 58).

15:9 **London's Guardian**—Lord Mansfield, the Lord Chief Justice—William Markham, Archbishop of York, was his friend (Sloss and Wallis 1926: I, 58); or the Archbishop of Canterbury (Damon 1967: 264).

15:13 During the war, there were mutinies in Ireland and Scotland (Erdman 1954a: 57 [60]).

15: 16-17 English poetry is corrupted by the recoiling pestilence (Damon 1924: 112). The Bard may be the anti-American William Whitehead, Poet Laureate 1757-1785 (*ibid.*: 338), or possibly the much ridiculed Henry James Pye, whom Pitt appointed to the office in 1790 (Sloss and Wallis 1926: I, 58). Wagenknecht (1973: 187-88) suggests he could be the Bard of 2:18-21, now suffering from Pitt's oppression.

15:19-22 In 1781 it was discovered that a flaw in the Marriage Act of 1751 rendered many marriages invalid, and Charles James Fox attempted to introduce marriage by civil registration (Erdman 1954a: 59 [62-63]).

15:23-26 The female spirits are both the resurrected and the oppressed set free; their revival is parallel to the Shadowy Female's when she first smiles (Schleifer 1979: 587). By 1793 the French Revolution had spread the idea of women's liberation (Johnson and Grant 1979: 119).

15:24 **in long drawn arches sitting**—The arches are Gothic (Damon 1924: 338). The women are confined by the church (Stevenson 1971: 204).

16:5 **grey-brow'd snows**—counter-revolutionary propaganda (Ostriker 1977: 908).

16:9 Urizen's snow and ice signify the storm of December 1775 that stopped the Americans from taking Quebec (Erdman 1970: 98).

16:9-10, 19-23 Here occurs the meeting of fire and frost of 2:15-16 (Beer 1968: 118-19).

16:14 **Angels**—i.e. reasoners, followers of Urizen.

   twelve years—between the American and French revolutions (Damon 1924: 338); perhaps from the British surrender at Saratoga in 1777 to the fall of the Bastille in 1789 (T. Wright 1929: I, 66); from the decisive British defeat at

Yorktown in 1781 to the execution of Louis XVI in 1793
(Erdman 1954a: 191-92 [208]).

16:22-23 The material world is burnt away by the flames of Orc
(Damon 1924: 110). There is a worldwide Last Judgment
(Damon 1967: 235). Wagenknecht (1973: 191) sees an allusion
to the infernal gates through which Satan escaped to fly to
earth (*PL*, II, 888-89)—for hell is here married to heaven.

Designs

pl.i The giant chained figure whose identification is the central
problem of this plate is unlikely to be Urizen (Damon 1924:
339); Albion's Angel (Binyon 1926: 102-03); the Poetic Gen-
ius in a time of classicism (Hagstrum 1964: 98-99); or "the
inchained soul" of 6:8 (Keynes 1963). Miner (1969: 467n28)
sees the form of the female genitals in his head, and Janet
Warner (1970: 193-94) declares that his wings show he has
been love or Eros and his energy has been diverted to war as
indicated by the gun barrel on the ground. Erdman, then,
(1974: 137) has excellent grounds for identifying the captive as
Orc chained in the wall of law beside Oothoon, "the soft soul of
America" (*VDA* 1:3). Making the same identification, Doskow
(1979: 170) claims that Orc blocks the way to the post-war
reform of American society and Tannenbaum (1982: 134)
assigns this "demonic Messiah" the Christ-like duty of healing
the breach between God and humankind.

pl. ii Below the title, a woman tries to revive a man left on the
field of battle (Erdman 1974: 138)—though Hagstrum (1964:
99) sees her as a woman whose kissing of a corpse signifies
sexual repression. The small figures above may be unable to
distract the adults from their study of the law (Damon 1924:
340) or encouraging them in their reading of *America*
(Erdman, *loc. cit*). The girl nearest the top right-hand corner is
an emblem of liberating mental energy (J. Warner 1984: 124-
27).

pl. 1 This design seems to illustrate *BU* 20:21-25—in the pres-
ence of Enitharmon, Los has used his Chain of Jealousy to bind
down their son Orc under the Tree of Mystery. However, Mar-
goliouth (1951: 82-83), who agrees with Damon (1924: 340)

that the couple are looking down in horror, is not sure whether Blake has yet conceived this incident, while Hagstrum (1964: 99) regards the woman as Urthona's daughter and Janet Warner (see Erdman 1970: 101) believes she is Oothoon, the personification of America. Erdman's additional identification of the pair as Adam and Eve (1974: 139) is taken up by Damrosch (1980: 109-11), who refers to "the crucifixion of sexuality" in the form of a Promethean Orc, and by Tannenbaum (1982: 134-35), who sees in the spread-eagled figure a conflation of Orc and Abel, the latter being a type of Christ.

The tree's roots, whose shape suggests people sinking deep into materiality (Damon 1924: 340)—or "a copulating couple" (Damon 1967: 21), imprison a crouching figure. The latter is either the human spirit (Keynes 1963) oppressed by Urizenic forces (Hagstrum, *loc. cit.*) or Orc (Raine 1968: I, 345) in the role of the rebel Cain (Tannenbaum 1982: 135). The six-coiled worm beside him represents mortality (Damon 1924: 340), perhaps with a hint of the human "worm of sixty winters" (*Tiriel* 8:11) (Erdman 1970: 100).

pl. 2   Later critics follow Damon (1924: 340) in identifying the figure as the liberated Orc. Erdman (1977b: 186) also perceives an illustration of *SL* 7:31-40, for a segment of the earth "clasps the solid stem" of a vine, and Paley (1978b: 29) remarks that the vine and wheat serve to link the freed Orc with Christ.

pl. 3   There is little disagreement with Damon's view (1924: 340) that the family is fleeing the flames of violence. Some of the latter are blown from a trumpet either by Albion's Angel (Damon 1967: 21) or a figure representing revolution (Doskow 1979: 177-78). As Erdman observes (1974: 141), the ears of grain, the rising birds of paradise, the ornamented letters, and the liberated Orc still dragging lengths of chain are clear signs of optimism.

pl. 4   Most commentators endorse Damon's identification (1924: 340) of the descending figure as Urizen carrying a law book, but the monster may be the dragon of war pursuing him (*ibid.*), Albion's Angel (Hagstrum 1964: 99), a basilisk (Raine 1968: I, 117, 392n65), or George III symbolised by the constellation Draco (Worrall 1981: 282-83). The human hands weakened by age, notes Erdman (1974: 142), preclude Raine's suggestion that the basilisk could be Orc. Alternately the monster, the

book-bearer, and the man holding his head may all be forms of
George, while a killer whale represents Orc and a royal adviser
protects a child (Erdman, *loc.cit.*). The King may hold his
head because he fears losing it (Erdman 1954a: 188 [204-05]).

Although no woman is present in this design, Doskow (1979:
178) claims that the figures on the ground are the family of the
preceding plate. The fallen tree behind them has been inter-
preted as error overthrown (Damon 1924: 340) and as an oak
associated with naval power (Paley 1978b: 28).

pl. 5   Damon's account (1967: 21) of a "spiritual trinity" casting
down a "material trinity" is less illuminating than Erdman's
description (1954a: 189 [205]) of a revolutionary tribunal pun-
ishing George III, who on the left falls towards fire and in the
centre into the coils of Orc, whom he perceives as a serpent.
Erdman also states (1974: 143) that the King's being held on a
cloud may indicate that his doom is not inevitable; R. E. Sim-
mons believes that the monarch passes through the snake's
spiral to re-emerge as the redeemed figure of pl. 6 (noted in
Erdman 1970: 108). Damon (*loc. cit.*) and Erdman (1970: 107)
agree that the flaming sword is Christ's—see Rev. vi.4-5.

Other critics have proposed that the man lifted up is Britain's
General Clinton about to join his colleagues Burgoyne and
Cornwallis below (T. Wright 1929: I, 65), that he is innocence
being rescued (Beer 1968: 114-15), that the tribunal represents
Britain's unjust justice (Bindman 1977: 76), and that a curly
haired Orc is being cast out of heaven to reappear, perhaps, in
pl. 6 (Doskow 1979: 180).

pl. 6   The glorious figure may be the fallen human either resur-
rected (Damon 1924: 340) or—with its echo of Michelangelo's
Adam—newly born into this world, where redemption is pos-
sible (J. Warner 1970: 191), or it may be Orc uttering the text
of the plate (Howard 1984: 120). The skull could stand for a
discarded self (T. Wright 1929: I, 65) or—along with the
plants and animals below—escape from mortality (Bindman
1977: 77). The creatures have also been interpreted as error
(Damon, *loc. cit.*), "the veil of nature" (J. Warner, *loc. cit.*),
persisting oppression (Doskow 1979: 180), and, as freely
moving organisms, liberty (Erdman 1974: 144).

pl. 7   Most commentators agree that this serene image of sleepers
at dawn represents Innocence (Paley 1978b: 30) or the state to

be achieved through the violence of Orc, whose goal is so deplorably misunderstood by Albion's Angel (Margoliouth 1951: 86; cf. Howard 1984: 121-22). Doskow, however, (1979: 181) suspects that the absence of wakefulness implies the ideal will remain a dream, while Bindman (1977: 77) dissents so far as to suggest it may represent a passive condition favoured by Albion's Angel.

According to Damon (1924: 340), the upper and lower figures are Har and Heva (poetry and painting) about to enjoy a renaissance—Keynes (1963) cites *Tiriel* 3:20-21 [22-23 in K]. Quoting *FZ* 128:25-27/ E397/ IX, 455-57, Binyon (1926: 104) identifies them as Tharmas and Enion. Johnson and Grant (1979: 112) think they are Orc and his consort, Urthona's daughter, later called Vala.

pl. 8   There can be no doubt that the figure is Urizen (Damon 1924: 340)—but, maintains Mitchell (1978: 9), it is Urizen as Orc sees him. Erdman (1974: 146) considers that the god senses he is sinking towards the waves, while Quasha (1970: 280-81) interestingly suggests he is brooding over a "stony womb" from which Orc emerges on pl. 10.

pl. 9   This simple but enigmatic design centres on a newborn baby who may be a symbol of redemption (Digby 1957: 36) or of revolution (Erdman 1974: 147), or on the corpse of a child (Keynes 1921: 134) killed (not necesssarily for ever) by the dominance of reason (J. Warner 1970: 190-91). The grain around him may be an emblem of plenty (Damon 1924: 341) or a harvest beaten down by a symbolic storm (Erdman, *loc. cit.*), the eye of which contains him (Bindman 1977: 78); the engraved lines can be seen as a network imprisoning the child (Essick 1972a: 68).

pl. 10   Though the turn of Orc's head and his gesture with his hands are similar to those of Urizen in pl. 8, in most other respects the two designs are antithetical. The parallel has been said to illustrate how Urizen sees Orc's energy as infernal (Erdman 1974: 148) and sees Orc himself in his own image (Howard 1984: 123), and how Orc is limited by the characteristics he shares with Urizen (Doskow 1979: 179-80) or will become a Urizenic tyrant in his turn (Wardle 1968). Alternatively, the movement from pl. 8 to pl. 10 may illustrate the change that takes place within the angels of the colonies as they decide on rebellion (Mitchell 1978: 9-10). Relating design to text, Paley (1978b: 30) sees here the "Human fire" of 4:8, and Bloom (1965: 905) interestingly perceives Los as he is described in the last three lines of *Europe*. Janet Warner (1984: 92-94, 102-04) maintains that the pose indicates the presence of the Poetic Genius—in a perverted authoritarian form in pl. 8—and that in both figures the downturned palms are a sign of imperfection.

pl. 11   Damon (1924: 341) describes this as an image of Innocence comprising a youth ascending on a swan and children governing "the serpent of nature," while Hagstrum (1964: 100) identifies the swan with imagination and the serpent with sex, and Margoliouth (1951: 86) observes the happiness of the snake, which he connects with the harmless asp of Is. xi.8. Thomas Wright (1929: I, 25, 66) claims the swan is reason ridden by imagination, as is the serpent in *Thel IB* pl. 6. Erdman (1974: 149) interprets both creatures as forms of Orc carrying refugees inland from the naval bombardment while birds flying in the opposite direction show there is a way back that leads to the paradisal Atlantic mountains; the swan's rider may be Samuel Adams, Thomas Paine, or Paul Revere. Noting the contrary directions in which the creatures move, Gleckner (1982a: 165-66) interprets the swan as the poetic spirit constrained by the Americans into the service of war, the loosely reined serpent as free prophecy, and its riders as those who "feel the nerves of youth renew" (15:25). Howard (1984: 124) cites evidence that the swan is "an icon of prophetic vision" and Nanavutty (1952: 260) observes that in the emblem books a swan serving as a steed promises renewal and immortality, but Doskow (1979: 181) thinks that the Urizenic stars and clouds and the lunar crescent, an attribute of the female will, cast doubt on the success of the riders. Recognising the stars on the left as the Pleiades, Worrall (1981: 292-95) considers the swan and the serpent to be Cygnus and Serpens, these three constellations having driven away the Draco (George III) of pl. 4.

pl. 12   Either this design represents some form of Experience (Damon 1924: 341)—perhaps superseding Innocence, the tree being the Tree of Mystery (Keynes 1963)—or the Urizenic oppression of Albion's Angel (Mellor 1974: 143), or else it stands for the end of pre-revolutionary life (Margoliouth 1951: 86), the decease of Urizen (T. Wright 1929: I, 66), or death as a way to regeneration (J. Warner 1970: 192). Possibly it combines negative and positive elements—the tragedy of death in war and acceptance of the winds of change (Erdman 1974: 150).

pl. 13   The preying fish and eagle have been interpreted as the oppressor (Hagstrum 1964: 101), as Albion's plagues recoiling on his own people (Beer 1968: 118), and as the viciousness of war (Erdman 1974: 151). Erdman further observes that the female—Oothoon, "the soft soul of America," carried over from *VDA IB* pl. 3—has fainted but is in a more hopeful state than the passive, starved man; the latter's hands are dehumanised and his senses are in abeyance as indicated by the five tiny fishes with closed mouths. As Beer notes (1969: 359n14), the shell by his head signifies the visionless condition of those senses. Damon (1924: 341) holds that it is through her instincts that Oothoon has escaped the worst in this Sea of Time and Space, but that she is attacked "by the Vulture of Remorse." Two texts may be relevant: Jonah ii (Tolley 1973: 117) and Blake's own account of the fallen Eternal Man in *FZ* 51:15-18, 56:13-16/ E334, 337/ IV, 132-35, 265-68 (Paley 1978b: 30).

pl. 14   Under the Tree of Mystery, says Damon (1924: 341), Rahab is teaching the serpent's natural religion to a youth reclining on the book of the Law—a youth Frye (1947: 433) identifies with Orc. Erdman (1974: 152) describes the teacher as "a death-preaching sibyl," her spread fingers as a symbol of the human life-span, and the roots of the sinister tree as opponents of the flames of energy below. Her phallic snake, according to Adlard (1972: 109), is "the sneaking serpent" of *MHH* 2:17.

Seeing the teacher as male, Doskow (1979: 178, 182) accuses him of wearing "the veil of nature" and imparting orthodox Christianity, while Howard (1984: 125) regards him as the Bard of Albion under a cowl of hypocrisy (15:16-17). Similarly citing the text, Hagstrum (1964: 101) equates the youth with the metaphorical "tender corn" of 14:6. Tannenbaum (1982: 149) alludes to Cant. viii.5, traditionally understood to refer to Eve's raising her children under the Tree of Knowledge.

A dissenting interpretation comes from Beer (1968: 254, 256), who perceives a prophetess and her serpent of organised energy reawakening a youth lost in reasoning, the source of the whole design being the images of awakened desire on the Portland Vase, which Blake engraved in 1791.

pl. 15 Expositions of this design discuss the relationship of the cleansing flames of revolution (Hagstrum 1964: 101) or desire (Damon 1924: 341) and the nudes within them to the figures in the left-hand margin, one of whom is becoming either a tree (Erdman 1970: 104) or the vine of 15:26 (Paley 1978b: 29). Where Damon (*loc. cit.*) sees only human degeneration in the margin, Erdman (1974: 154) detects Oothoon rising from the lower left-hand corner to free the women and children above her. Beer (1968: 119) perceives the vegetation itself as a humanised form of the raw lust of the flames, and Doskow (1979: 178) writes of the fleeing mother of pl. 3 ascending through hope to end in despair; however, she ignores the small eagle above, which is poised to fly and which to Bindman (1977: 79) signifies the female soul's escape to heaven.

pl. 16 There is no agreement as to whether the praying giant is the despairing (Bindman 1977: 79) or dead (Beer 1968: 119) Urizen, a tearful woman who is Urizen's victim (Hagstrum 1964: 101), Rahab (T. Wright 1929: I, 66), Earth (Binyon 1926: 106), nature (Damon 1967: 21), a combination of the pupil and the tiny bowed woman on the two previous plates (Erdman 1974: 155), or America, whose revolution has failed to create a free society (Doskow 1979: 182-83). The giant's hair, adds Erdman, constitutes Niagara Falls, which represent Urizen's "icy magazines" (16:9), but the minute figures on or beside it (including lovers and the piper of Innocence) stand for the free world of the future. However, Doskow (1979: 182) claims that all except the piper are sunk in error, and she draws attention to barren trees of nature in the upper left-hand corner.

The serpent and thorns in the colophon may signify the failure of the Revolution (Damon, *loc. cit.*), or the serpent may be prophetic (Erdman, *loc. cit.*) and the flowers emblematic of love with a sexual component (Beer, *loc. cit.*).

Europe

The underlying theme of *Europe* is the perversion of human perception and its painful accompaniments and consequences. These include "the overwhelming of mind by sense" that is "characteristically European" (Raine 1968: II, 120), the subjection of energy to reason that brings on Armageddon (Tolley 1970a: 119), and the "political, imaginative, sexual" constriction that gratifies the female will (Hilton 1983: 242). The topical context of the book is the French Revolution, to which Blake looks for liberation from two millenia of error, but while Mitchell (1978: 107) is confident that the poet foresees the rapid demise of tyranny and Bindman (1977: 83) that he hopes for it, Gardner (1968: 109) is more typical when he asserts that there is no resolution of the conflict between reaction and revolution in this "tough, intransigent poem." Thus Bloom (1963: 161) and Ward (1972: 214-15) regard the outcome of the struggle as uncertain, and Johnson and Grant (1979: 122-23), like Tannenbaum (1982: 184), believe that liberty will not be achieved. The enigmatic role of Los at the poem's conclusion is an important factor in the dispute (see notes to 15:9 and 15: 9-11). Moreover, while Tolley (1970a: 145) considers that Orc himself is not yet corrupted, Paley (1970: 79) regards him as an ambiguous character, and Raine (1968: I, 348) states that though Blake celebrates the Revolution, he recognises the demon's frightful aspect. Stevenson (1960: 501-02) suggests that, unlike *America*, *Europe* was written after the Reign of Terror had begun in France and the sedition trials in Britain, and Ward (1972: 216) feels that Blake was disturbed by the revolutionaries' deification of reason in 1793. Bloom (1963: 160) plausibly claims that he is now critical of both France and Britain. On a psychological level, Damon (1924: 343, 345, 347) reads parts of the poem in the light of the fully developed myth of the Zoas: Christ descends from Luvah's (the passions') eastern realm (3:3); Urthona's quiescence in the north allows Urizen to seize his throne (3:9-12); Urthona's spirituality becomes destructive when it is transferred to Urizen's south (10:24-31); and the French Revolution erupts when light shines in Luvah's east (14:35-15:2). Cf. also Bloom 1963: 156-57. As a Freudian, Webster (1983: 125, 129, 137, 142-43) sees behind the progress from Nativity to Apocalypse the movement from helpless infancy to rebellious adolescence; on the way there are sibling rivalry (2:3-6 and *IB* pls. 1, 2) and tyranny rooted in regression to infantile anal obsession (*IB* pl. 13 and the buttock-like knees in *IB* pl. 11).

Commentators on the Preludium have asserted that it lacks the optimism of *America* (Stevenson 1971: 223), the narrative of which it continues (Bloom 1963: 146-47), for Orc has not succeeded in liberating nature (Erdman 1954a: 244 [264]). Urthona's daughter—now called "The nameless shadowy female" (1:1)—recoils from her own fecundity while light from on high continues to fertilise her and Enitharmon imposes form on her offspring (Damon 1924: 114-15) in a sanguinary world (Damon 1967: 369); or else she tries to suppress her children as they are king-devouring revolutionaries (Gallant 1978: 32-33). Another view is that the Shadowy Female dreads losing her power and that on one plane she is humankind that needs Orc but fears his domination (Gardner 1968: 104). Nurmi (1976: 96) accuses her of having become, with "Her snaky hair" (1:2), a Medusa (corrupted nature) whose look consigns beings to Ulro, the lowest level of existence. With more plausibility, Howard (1984: 148) sees her as a caricature of the Nature of Milton's "On the Morning of Christ's Nativity," who wishes to hide her unchastity.

The opening of the Prophecy undeniably alludes to Milton's poem, its relationship with which has been much studied. Tolley (1970a: 125-27, 130, 145) sees *Europe* as primarily a recasting of Milton's work in which dawn is followed by night instead of day, in which a shameless Enitharmon corresponds to an abashed Nature, in which (as in Rev. xx.7) Satan (Urizen) is "unloos'd" for Armageddon (3:11), and which is indebted for much of its plan to the sixteenth and seventeenth stanzas of Milton's "Hymn." In Blake's view, Howard observes (1984: 148-49), Milton expels the pagan gods only to substitute the false ideal of chastity; Tannenbaum (1982: 183-84) points out that Blake replaces the Miltonic banishment of error by its maturing until it is ready for destruction.

Less illuminating are the biblical sources that have been proposed for *Europe*. To Tannenbaum (1982: 152-53), the poem seems to be based on the scriptural antithesis between bride and harlot as represented by the Shadowy Female and Enitharmon respectively. Howard (1984: 150-51) draws a parallel between, on the one hand, Revelation's two dragons, Whore of Babylon, and

woman clothed with the sun who bears a righteous king, and, on
the other hand, Blake's Rintrah and Palamabron, Enitharmon, and
Shadowy Female awaiting Christ; he also (149-50, 182) sees
something of a parody of Oberon's and Titania's power struggle in
Shakespeare's *A Midsummer Night's Dream*, and he points to *SL
IB* pl.5 for confirmation.

      The form of *Europe*, however, may not be derivative. Fox
(1976: 10-12) brilliantly suggests that it offers three perspectives
on the same subject: from the laughing fairy's eternal viewpoint, a
plucked flower seems to suffer no pain (iii:20-21); from the cosmic
perspective of the Shadowy Female, herself a plucked flower with
roots above (1:8), suffering persists through endless cycles that
"bind the infinite with an eternal band" (2:13); from an historical
viewpoint, one night of the immortals is eighteen centuries of
human agony. Nevertheless the opening plate, whether by design
or unlucky accident, is included in only two of the twelve surviv-
ing copies. Kowle (1978: 96) argues from parallels with the rest of
the poem that the account of the fairy is contemporary with the
bulk of the text. The claim that the three parts are continuous and
the notion of multiple perspectives find support in Howard's
argument (1984: 132-33) that a series of variations on the image
of cloud illuminates the connection between false belief and
tyranny: the cloud of incense (iii:22) becomes successively clouds
of primal matter representing the delusion of materialism (1:12,
2:18), the clouds to which Enitharmon's terrible Children are
compared (3:6), and the clouds of royal and ecclesiastical
oppression (10:4, 12:3).

Details

iii:5   The sexual act briefly restores the prelapsarian androgynous
      condition of the human being (Davies 1948: 150). Understand-
      ing Milton's "chose with us" ("Nativity," l. 14) to mean that
      Christ chose as we have chosen, Blake endorses his predeces-
      sor's view that Christians *choose* a lower, limited, bodily con-
      sciousness (Tannenbaum 1982: 155-56).
iii:6   This line describes the "female dream" of 9:5 (Sloss and
      Wallis 1926: I, 78). Cf. Prov. ix.13-18 (Damon 1967: 132).

Making a mystery of sex promotes unhealthy erotic excitement, possessiveness, and jealousy (Hilton 1983: 132).

iii:7   **a Fairy**—a "natural joy" (Damon 1924: 342); a manifestation of energy and desire instantly gratified (Schorer 1946: 294); a vegetation spirit (Raine 1968: II, 117); one of the beings who preside over our reproductive functions (Paley 1978b: 34). This Fairy's vision of nature is the contrary of the Shadowy Female's (Damon 1967: 132-33, 296). Blake criticises Milton's dismissal of the fairies ("Nativity," ll. 235-36) as well as his elevation of chastity (Tannenbaum 1982: 160-61).

iii:7-8 **streak'd Tulip**—In chaps. 10 and 48 of Johnson's *Rasselas*, Imlac insists that poets should concentrate on general truth, not number the streaks of the tulip, and that matter is totally inert (Adlard 1964). A red and yellow tulip is employed by Berkeley, with whose immaterialism the Fairy agrees, to assist his exposition in the first of his *Three Dialogues* (Raine 1968: II, 117).

iii:8   **from the trees**—i.e. from the forests of the night towards the Fairy's eternal realm (Kowle 1978: 95).

iii:21   **because they were pluck'd**—This phrase implies sexual defloration (Adlard 1972: 56).

1:2   **snaky hair**—a sign of the female will (Mellor 1974: 153). Despite her degenerate condition, the Shadowy Female is the "Heav'nly Muse" of "Nativity," l. 15, and the Wisdom of Prov. viii and of some apocryphal texts (Tannenbaum 1982: 157-64).

   the winds of Enitharmon—winds on which she sends souls into this world of sexual generation (Raine 1968: I, 232-34).

1:6   **travel**—travail.

1:8   **My roots are brandish'd in the heavens, my fruits in earth beneath**—Damon's assertion (1924: 342) that Blake is saying here, as he does in M 26:44, "every Natural Effect has a Spiritual Cause" is consistent with Raine's suggestion (1968: II, 34) that he is conflating the Tree of Nature with the cabbalistic tree, whose roots in heaven represent the divine origin of phenomena (its branches). Taking different perspectives, Bloom (1963: 147) maintains that the Tree of Life has been turned upside down in the fallen world; Fox (1976: 10), with an eye to iii:20-21, believes the Shadowy Female is a plucked flower; and Nurmi (1976: 96-97), interpreting "the heavens" as the ruling class, detects an attack on Burke's claim that the inheritance of privilege accords with nature.

1:12 Because she is "the spirit of earth," the waters are where she takes refuge (Erdman 1954a: 244 [264]) to escape the assaults of Orc's energy (Beer 1968: 121) or fertilisation by light—especially the light of Urizen's stars (Damon 1924: 114). Beer, indeed, regards her as painfully trapped between the power of Urizen and the power of Orc (*loc. cit.*).

1:14 In Wagenknecht's view (1973: 96, 193), the sun and moon may be Los and Enitharmon or Rintrah and Palamabron.

2:1-4 The abyss is a Neoplatonic symbol for the material world (Douglas 1965: 111-12). As well as fertilisation by the stars (see 1:12n) brought about by Enitharmon (Howard 1984: 141), the Shadowy Female's fecundity has been attributed to the Hermetic union of the abyss below and the stars above, which draws down souls (Raine 1968: II, 8-9), and to Orc's fathering her offspring (Johnson and Grant 1979: 122).

2:1 **unwilling count the stars**—Engaged in this Newton-like activity, the Female can see no escape from time (Tannenbaum 1982: 163).

2:8-10 The progeny of fires that Enitharmon stamps may be one or more of the following: the Shadowy Female's offspring on whom she imposes either form (Damon 1924: 114-15) or the seal of their individual character derived from a star (Douglas 1965: 113-14); revolutionary impulses that she tries to contain (Gardner 1968: 105); pro-American liberals whom she turns against the French Revolution (Nurmi 1976: 98); "fires of inspiration" that she deadens (Tannenbaum 1982: 162, 164); tyrants to whom she gives a seeming solidity (Howard 1984: 141).

2:12 **shady woe, and visionary joy**—emotions related to the irreconcilable opposites characteristic of the fallen condition (Wagenknecht 1973: 195). The joy may be the shadow of what real revolutionary change would bring (Gardner 1968: 105) or the happiness experienced at news of Christ's birth (Nurmi 1976: 97).

2:12-19 A parody of the Immaculate Conception [apparently a slip for the Virgin Birth], for nature is fertilised by the heavenly bodies (Nurmi 1976: 98).

2:13   It may be that Christ will bind the infinite (Damon 1967: 363, 369), or that the creator Urizen does so—"Who shall bind the Infinite" is written under a preliminary sketch of the god for the frontispiece in Blake's Notebook (Erdman 1977a: 96)—or that Enitharmon tries to do so (Kowle 1978: 93), or that the infinite cannot be bound (Howard 1984: 127-28). The question really asks, says Wagenknecht (1973: 195-96), who is going to marry the speaker, though in a comic way the binder is Newton. (Tannenbaum [1982: 163-64] opts for Bacon.)

2:14-15   These lines graft allusions to the Incarnation onto the preceding allusions to the creation. The phrase "swaddling bands" echoes Luke ii.7 and "cherish it/ With milk and honey" refers to the "butter and honey" of Is. vii.15 to be fed to the infant Messiah (Beer 1968: 122), but perhaps there is also a hint of the Promised Land, as in Exod. iii.8. The pledge of the Nativity soothes the Shadowy Female (Damon 1924: 115); Christ's coming will stop the endless repetition of nature's cycle (Paley 1970: 78-79). The French Revolution, says Erdman (1954a: 245 [265]), reassures the Female that the Second Coming is imminent.

Other critics are less sanguine: Sloss and Wallis (1926: I, 69) cite *J* 67:22, 68:30 and 82:40, to show that feeding with milk signifies dominating through morality and sense experience; Gardner (1968: 105-06) feels that Christ's teaching is diluted by binding, swaddling, and sweetness; Beer (1968: 121-22) believes that the Shadowy Female glimpses transcendence but cannot imagine the infinite incarnate; and Wagenknecht (1973: 195-96) sees in the "swaddling bands" maternal possessiveness as well as the Incarnation, while Tayler (1973b: 84-85) believes such female possessiveness to be linked to the male authoritarianism of the frontispiece through a pun on "compass."

2:18   **the secret place**—where the terrors and kings of 2:4 are generated—the roots above may be the placenta (Tolley 1970a: 121). The Shadowy Female, disillusioned with repeated incarnations, ceases to be a muse and relapses into chastity (Tannenbaum 1982: 165).

3:2   **the secret child**—The mode of his birth is unknown to Enitharmon (Howard 1984: 141). There is an allusion to the hiding of Jesus in Egypt (Matt. ii) (Tolley 1970a: 121).

The child is clearly in some sense Christ—according to Beer, however, (1968: 122) the Christ of the churches (since he is "secret"), not the infinite incarnate—but is he also Orc? The two may here be identical (Ostriker 1977: 909) or not entirely so (Tolley 1970a: 145). Fox (1976: 16-17) sees their births as eighteen centuries apart for humans but a single event for the Fairy of the Preludium. For Bloom (1963: 147) this latest of many rebirths of Orc is an element of a Second Coming.

3:4 **War ceas'd**—when Orcean revolt was stifled (Gardner 1968: 106).

shadows—a Neoplatonic image for residents of the lower world—and cf. "Nativity," l. 232 (Raine 1968: I, 247). See also 9:6.

3:6 **the crystal house**—This much disputed term has been interpreted as the unsullied heart (Damon 1924: 343); a sky spangled with stars indifferent to humankind (Frye 1947: 245); the human conception of heaven (Bloom 1963: 150); and either an alchemical symbol for matter or the Ptolemaic spheres of "Nativity," l. 125 (Raine, I, 274, 415n11). Frye (1947: 127, 234) classifies Enitharmon as a sky goddess and Queen of Heaven whose worship promotes male devotion to a remote, idealised woman.

3:7 The name "Los" is an anagram of "sol" (Wicksteed 1910: 122, citing A. G. B. Russell) and a pun on "loss" with reference to humanity's—and the undivided Urthona's—loss at the Fall (Erdman 1954a: 233-34 [253], citing *FZ* 84:27-28/ E359/ VII, 293-94). Other suggested derivations are from "loos," a Chaucerian word for fame (Frye 1957c: 100-01), "logos" (Fisher 1961: 192-93), and—since Los is a visionary and, indeed, vision itself—the interjection "lo," meaning "behold," here made into a plural (Rose 1967). Ward (1972: 215) proposes also an allusion to "soul."

possessor of the moon—Either Los is the possessor of the lunar goddess Enitharmon (Damon 1924: 343) because the sun rules the moon (Raine 1968: I, 221), or more probably—since Enitharmon seems to be dominant—Ostriker (1977: 909) is right to say he should be a sun god but has become subordinate to his consort.

3:7-10 Los may expect sensory pleasures from the Messiah (Margoliouth 1951: 87), misconceive the abeyance of imagina-

tion (Urthona) as a pleasant rest (Bloom 1963: 148), mistake
Eternity's dawn for nocturnal light (Erdman 1969b: 265),
abdicate his masculine responsibility leaving Enitharmon to be
seduced by Urizen (Webster 1983: 130), and blindly welcome a
re-enactment of the Fall (Wagenknecht 1973: 197). Beer
(1969: 78) regards him as an honest antagonist of Urizen.

On the political level, Erdman (1954a: 247 [267]) sees
Urthona as the unawakened masses.

3:9-4:14 Incompetently or teasingly, Blake leaves it unclear to
which speaker or speakers he allots these lines. Alternative
views are (1) that Los utters 3:9-14, the narrator 4:1-2, Uriz-
en's Sons 4:3-9, and Enitharmon 4:10-14 (Erdman 1954a: 246
[266]); (2) that the whole speech is spoken by Los, who quotes
Urizen's Sons at 4:3-9 (Bloom 1965: 904), in which case Los,
as he calls for sublunary music as opposed to the music of the
spheres (cf. "Nativity," ll. 125-40), is the only character who
thinks the peace permanent (Nurmi 1976: 99-100); (3) that the
whole speech may be Enitharmon's (Tolley 1970a: 126-27),
but as Erdman observes (in a note appended to Tolley's essay),
"speaking" and "his" in 3:8 refer to Los. Johnson and Grant
(1979: 126) raise the possibility that Los speaks from 3:9 to
4:2, and his Sons for the next seven lines.

3:8 **bright fiery wings**—the illuminated pages of the Prophecy
(Erdman's note to Tolley 1970a: 126-27).

3:10-12 The secrecy surrounding Christ makes Urizen's liber-
ation possible (Gardner 1968: 106). Los regards the birth as a
disturbance of the nocturnal peace (Bloom 1963: 149), or is
happy at the arrival of his son (Wagenknecht 1973: 96). Cf.
"Nativity," l. 69-76.

3:13 **strike the elemental strings**—to pervert them in the night
of Christ's peace (Howard 1984: 143).

4:2-6 Pitt, Burke, and other reactionaries repress the people
(Erdman 1954a: 247 [267-68]). These people are partly motiv-
ated by envy of the revolutionaries' "libidinous freedom"
(Webster 1983: 130).

4:10-14 Los commands and mocks Orc (Sloss and Wallis 1926: I,
64). Enitharmon needs some sort of Jacobin, preferably power-
less, as an excuse for repression (Erdman 1954a: 248 [268]).
Orc's binding is parallel to the Crucifixion (Ostriker 1977:

909). Like Christ in Rev. xix.11-15, Orc has affinities with Dionysus and Mars (Johnson and Grant 1979: 127).

5:3 Blake may have been influenced by Mary Wollstonecraft's attack on flirtatiousness in her *Vindication of the Rights of Woman* (1792) (Margoliouth 1951: 87). Christianity erred in over-idealising women (Damon 1967: 447-48, misprinting 5:1-5 as 3:1-5).

5:4 Rintrah and Palamabron have been interpreted as Pitt and George III (Bronowski 1944: 52); as Pitt and Parliament, Palamabron standing for Parliament in general and Burke in particular (Erdman 1954a: 185, 201 [201-02, 218]); as prophetic wrath and artistic pity sent to undermine the cultures of Jew and Greek with hatred of sexuality (Bloom 1963: 150-51)—their emanations help to corrupt them (Bloom 1965: 904).

5:6-7 Blake is denying that the body is resurrected (Davies 1948: 123).

8:1 **eldest born**—cf. 4:14. Orc and Rintrah are twins (Erdman 1954a: 248 [268]).

8:3 Palamabron resembles Bacchus (Damon 1967: 321). His horns are both Satan's and those the Vulgate attributes to Moses (Exod. xxxiv.29ff, 35); cf. also Cant. ii.8 (Tolley 1970a: 128-29).

8:4 **Elynittria**—Diana, goddess of chastity (Damon 1924: 344); chastity and pestilence (Howard 1984: 142).

8:7 **Ocalythron**—Judaic exclusiveness associated with the jealous God (Bloom 1963: 151); jealousy and famine (Howard 1984: 142).

9:3 The harps of 3:13 and 4:4 are unstrung while Enitharmon sleeps (Johnson and Grant 1979: 128).

9:7 **the heavens of Europe**—the continent's ruling families (Erdman 1954a: 194 [211]).

9:8-13 These lines describe the American Revolution (Damon 1924: 344).

9:10 **immortal demons of futurity**—catastrophe awaiting the ruling class (Erdman 1954a: 194 [211]).

9:14 In 1783, the [thirty-seven-week] ministry of Fox and North followed the collapse of Shelburne's government favoured by the King (Erdman 1954a: 194-95 [211]).

9:15   **the stars rise from the salt lake**—reason rises from the
lake of materialism (Damon 1924: 344). Damon later suggests
the lake is the Dead Sea (1967: 354).

10:1-23   Tolley (1970a: 135) believes pl. 10 was an interpolation
intended to add an account of the creation and the Fall. The re-
sort to the serpent temple, the prehistoric monument at Ave-
bury, to which a serpentine form was ascribed by William
Stukeley (*Abury* [1743]), signifies the restoration of ancient
Druid tyranny (Damon 1924: 344). The serpent Blake regards
as a symbol of nature (Damon 1967: 109). He conceives the
fane as extending from the east to the west coast (Erdman
1954a: 196 [213]), and its gate as being at Bacon's Verulam
(St. Albans), for Bacon and the Druids both see nature as an
ultimate reality (Johnson and Grant 1979: 130); moreover,
Blake considers Bacon an agent of imperialism, and there were
Druid ruins at Verulam (Erdman, *loc. cit.*) as well as Roman
remains and a mediaeval abbey—for the place's association
with ecclesiastical government cf. *J* 34[38]:45 (Damon 1967:
434). Blake identifies the temple, Verulam, and the "council
house" of 9:12 (Tolley 1970a: 135). According to Webster
(1983: 136), Blake here laments the departure from infant con-
sciousness, which does not distinguish self from environment,
as a disaster that produced the scientific world-view.

10:2   **The fiery King**—Albion's Angel (Stevenson 1971: 232)
retreating into the sky to the constellation Draco, the serpent
temple (Worrall 1981: 291); both the English monarch and the
most recent Druid high priest (Hilton 1983: 197).

10:3   **the Island white**—Britain, so called from the cliffs of Dov-
er.

10:4   **the Angel**—Rintrah (Pitt), who revives Druid human sacri-
fice in a political form (Erdman 1954a: 196 [212-213]).

10:5   The decline from "golden Verulam" to the "temple serpent-
form'd" marks the corruption of religion (Mellor 1974: 99).

10:7   **pillars, form'd of massy stones uncut**—an allusion to the
twelve pillars alongside Moses' altar, which had to be built
with unhewn stone—see Exod. xx.25 and xxiv.4, Deut.
xxvii.1-8, Josh. viii.30-32 (Miner 1969: 280).

10: 8-10   This is the zodiac that circumscribes Urizen's govern-
ment (Damon 1924: 344), or an emblem of the worship of false
gods (Frye 1947: 369), or a symbol of Baconian empiricism

(Bloom 1963: 155). The twelve jewels—see Exod. xxviii.15-21, Ezek. xxviii.17-21, Rev. xxi.19—have both a malign affinity with Aaron's breastplate and the arrogant Covering Cherub and a touch of the New Jerusalem's glory (Tolley 1970a: 135-36). Cf. *PL*, III, 592-601 (Miner 1981: 328-29).

10:16 **Thought chang'd the infinite to a serpent**—reason transformed Eternity into nature (Damon 1924: 345). In alchemy, the serpent is nature's raw material awaiting transformation (Percival 1938: 213). Orc, an immortal born into the temporal world, when defeated by Urizenic forces becomes a serpent (Fisher 1961: 145). The serpent is the zodiac (Miner 1981: 306-07).

10:16-18 The Lamb of pity becomes the Tiger of fire (Damon 1924: 345). The infinite nature of Eternity and eternal pity terrify the fallen mind (Beer 1968: 126). Adam and Eve come to see God as terrible and misguidedly hide from him in the Garden of Eden (Tolley 1970a: 137).

10:19 **like an ocean rush'd**—an allusion to Noah's Flood conceived as an imprisonment in fallen space (Tolley 1970a: 137).

10:21-22 The circular element in the temple, like the compasses in the frontispiece, symbolises cyclic recurrence (Kowle 1978: 94); interpreting it thus, Blake reverses Stukeley's theory that it represents a timeless eternity (Paley 1983a: 194). The constellation Draco, which is the temple, circles the Pole Star annually—cf. 12:11 (Worrall 1981: 284, 291).

10:22 **an Angel**—i.e. a reasoner (Damon 1924: 345); an allusion to Shaftesbury's excessively optimistic view of human nature (Wagenknecht 1973: 192). Morality makes people think of themselves as either angels or devils and of God as a tyrant (Howard (1984: 130).

revolutions—including political revolutions leading to renewed oppression (Bloom 1963: 156).

10:24 **the ancient Guardian**—Urizen (Damon, *loc. cit.*), who shelters in his temple within the human mind and skull (Gardner 1968: 108); Albion's Angel (Bloom 1963: 156). The arrival of this figure represents the imposition of conscience on the developing mind (Webster 1983: 137).

10:25 **trees of blackest leaf**—"a forest of error" (Bloom 1963: 156).

10:26 **the Stone of Night**—Damon (1924: 335) equates this image with the stone bearing the Ten Commandments and later (1967: 387) with the Druid belief in retribution. Sloss and Wallis (1926: I, 73), who tentatively suggest a connection with *PL*, IV, 543-48, recognise it is primarily the human skull. Finding in it a symbol of lifelessness, Frye (1947: 224) identifies it with the stone pillar that remained when Jacob's vision of a ladder between heaven and earth evaporated (Gen. xxviii) and also (1966: 187) as the contrary of the "lively stones" of the spiritual temple of I Pet. ii.5. Worrall (1981: 291-92) believes it is the earth itself, and Howard (1984: 130) that it is the northern magnetic pole. Cf. 11:1n and *A* 5:1n.

10:27 **purple flowers and berries red**—deadly nightshade (Damon 1924: 345); hint of a tropical climate associated with the unfallen mind (Bloom 1963: 157).

10:28-29 There is a reference back to iii:1-5 (Kowle 1978: 94).

10:30-31 Either the eternal human falls into this world where north is overhead instead of underfoot (Percival 1938: 181-82), or Urizen ("the dizzy enquirer") descends from Eternity (the south) through the Northern gate into the material realm—cf. *Thel* 6:1 and *M* 26:13-17 (Raine 1968: II, 92). Bloom, too, (1963: 157) refers to Urizen, who was the unfallen intellect located in the south before the mind was roofed, and asserts that Blake is caricaturing the Platonic cave.

    attractive—gravitational rather than seductive (Tolley 1970a: 138).

    A raging whirlpool—the imagination displaced (Bloom 1963: 157); astronomical orbits collectively (Beer 1968: 127).

11:1 Rintrah (Pitt) is the Albion's Angel on the Stone of Night (Erdman 1954a: 196 [213]). In addition to being a Druid altar and the human skull, this Stone is London Stone, the point from which distances in England are measured (Johnson and Grant 1979: 130). See also 10:26n and *A* 5:1n.

11:3 **brazen Book**—a book of false charity, real charity being golden (Damon 1924: 345); the Bible conventionally interpreted (Bloom 1965: 904); a standard emblem for fate, here signifying the falsity of predestination, a doctrine widespread in England (Howard 1984: 130, 240n5).

12:1-13 Urizen is the biblical pillar of cloud to Orc's pillar of fire—the images reappear in *SL*, pl. 7 (Bloom 1963: 158, 163).

12:8   **a vast rock**—the Stone of Night (Damon 1924: 345).
   by...senses...clos'd from thought—in Stevenson's view (1971: 236), by imaginative sense perception, though Sloss and Wallis (1926: I, 73) consider that "thought" has a positive meaning here and a negative one in 10:16.

12:12   The voice utters the Royal Proclamation of 21 May, 1792, against seditious publications (Erdman 1954a: 197-98 [214-15]).

12:15-20   On 15 June, 1792, Pitt had Lord Chancellor Thurlow, his fellow conservative, dismissed because the latter had ventured to call him "a mere reptile of a minister" (Erdman 1954a: 199-200 [216-17]). Cf. Nebuchadnezzar's insanity and Ovid's wicked Lycaon, who became a wolf (Tannenbaum 1982: 169-70).

12:20   **the wilderness**—one corner of St. James's Park bore this name (Erdman 1977c: 512, citing Paul Miner).

12:23-24   Palambron's lightnings may be Burke's speeches against revolutionary France, and legions in the deep may be ships of the Royal Navy (Erdman 1954a: 201 [218]). Palamabron launches a final denunciation but Rintrah is restrained (Howard 1984: 143).

12:33   **Albion's Guardian**—Albion's Angel (Tolley 1970a: 142).

13:1   **The red limb'd Angel**—Rintrah, who is both Pitt and Albion's Angel (Erdman 1954a: 195 [212]); Albion's Angel, who expects the Last Judgment to effect Orc's overthrow (Stevenson 1971: 224, 238); Orc (Blackstone 1949: 58), who vainly tries to initiate revolution by blowing the trumpet (Fisher 1961: 145).

13:3   **Thrice he assay'd**—There were three attempts to break away from the recurring historical cycle (Bloom 1963: 158); there were international crises in 1787, 1790 and 1791, during which Pitt contemplated war against France, Spain and Russia (Erdman 1954a: 195 [212]).

13:4-8   The political crisis becomes worldwide (Erdman 1954a: 206 [224]), and (Bindman 1977: 82) liberation from tyranny and constricted perception is imminent. Newton gives error a clear shape so that it can be rejected (Damon 1924: 114), and he encourages rational thought, which leads to rebellion against oppression (Beer 1968: 129). However, there is a view that the trumpet is counter-revolutionary (Hagstrum 1964: 102) and that the angel succumbs to Newtonian gravity and this Last

Judgment brings about spiritual destruction instead of resurrection (Johnson and Grant 1979: 132, citing Brian Wilkie).

Frye (1947: 254) detects a hostile reference to Newton's commentary on Revelation. In view of Blake's preoccupation with Sir Isaac, Howard (1984: 131) is probably wrong to identify the blast with the repentant ex-slave trader Rev. John Newton's *Thoughts on the Slave Trade* (1788).

13:6-8 **Angelic hosts**—the troops that fled in 3:4 (Fox 1976: 16); decaying counter-revolutionaries (Ostriker 1977: 910). Cf. "Nativity," ll. 232-36 and *PL*, I, 301-03 (Tolley 1970a: 142).

13:16 Enitharmon calls on Ethinthus to pay no attention to these puny creatures (Erdman 1974: 171) or (since she is unaware the night is over) to ignore the devouring worm that releases the soul from the corpse into the day of Eternity (Tolley 1973: 118-19); being "queen of waters"—i.e. of matter—Ethinthus is a thorough materialist (Damon 1924: 346) and the mortal body (Damon 1967: 130); she reduces Manathu-Vorcyon, a spirit of inspiration, to a "soft delusion" (Bloom 1965: 904-05). She is poverty or its effects and a coquette who is wooed by the earthworm and who excites and frustrates the desire of Manathu-Vorcyon, a councillor in Enitharmon's "halls" (Howard 1984: 144, 180).

13:16-14:26 De Luca (1978: 10-12) observes perceptively that all the names of Enitharmon's Children except Orc (the only rebel) contain elements of "Enitharmon."

14:9 **Leutha**—female sexual hypocrisy (Damon 1924: 346) that reduces Antamon from artist to sensualist (Bloom 1965: 905) or enticing modesty charged to captivate him (Howard 1984: 144); a temptress who lures souls down to the material world (Raine 1968: I, 171-72); Marie Antoinette of France to Elynittria's Charlotte of Britain (Erdman 1954a: 206 [223]).

14:15-20 **Antamon**—the artist—cf. *M* 28:13-18 (Damon 1924: 346); the sperm ("pearly dew") (Damon 1967: 132). He is sexually indulged to keep him under female control (Beer 1968: 131).

14:20 **the seven churches of Leutha**—churches established by the Apostles, who had already begun to be corrupted by Puritanism (Damon 1924: 346). Cf. Rev. i-iii (Damon 1967: 85).

14:23   **Between two moments**—outside the flow of time (Harper 1961: 148); *between* moments of desire, not *in* them (Howard 1984: 145).

14:26   **Sotha**—a musician who excites his listeners to battle (Damon 1924: 346); the war that results from thwarted sex (Damon 1967: 132); adultery, from Hebrew *sota* ("adulteress") (Howard 1984: 128, 240n1).

   Thiralatha—the erotic dream of the sex-starved (Damon 1967: 132), with which Enitharmon tries to pacify Orc (Howard 1984: 145).

14:29ff   Recognising some deficiency in her world, Enitharmon summons Orc but is dismayed at the result (Beer 1968: 132).

14:32   "All" refers to the books Blake issued before the pro-revolutionary *Marriage of Heaven and Hell* (Damon 1924: 347). Enitharmon's Children have not heard her orders (Howard 1984: 145).

14:34   **enormous**—"monstrous," not "huge" (Erdman 1977b: 186).

14:36   Enitharmon weeps at Orc's behaviour (Erdman 1954a: 249 [269]) or at her Children's deserting her for Los (Howard 1984: 145-46).

14:37   **terrible Orc**—The child of the Nativity (3:1-4) has become the fierce Christ of Revelation (Erdman 1954a: 249 [269]). An element of the Second Coming is implicit here, and Orc tends to merge with the avenging Messiah of Is. lxiii.1-6 (Tolley 1970a: 125, 143-44). As a comet heralding the French Revolution, he leaves Enitharmon's regular planetary system, and the Lions and Tigers of 15:6-7 are constellations that react to this move (Worrall 1981: 292). Miner (1981: 309) identifies him with the Dog Star, source of fierce disturbances. Blake deliberately confuses Satan's journey to earth in *Paradise Lost*, the Incarnation, and the Second Coming (Wagenknecht 1973: 191).

15:5   **chariots...with red wheels dropping with blood**—on one level, the tumbrils carrying victims to the guillotine (Gallant 1978: 35).

15:9   **snaky thunders**—a sign that Los is still fallen (Wagenknecht 1973: 198). Bloom holds that he is now only partly corrupt (Bloom 1963: 160).

15:9-11 Los has an artistic and a political aspect. In Damon's
view (1924: 114, 347), he is both poetry resisting the tyranny
of Enitharmon (inspiration perverted) and Blake himself writ-
ing his Lambeth books. Murry (1933: 106) argues that Los
supports Christ-Orc both here and at the beginning of the poem
(4:10), while Johnson and Grant (1979: 123) hold that he turns
from music to war to support revolution. Sloss and Wallis
(1926: I, 65, 78) are uncertain whether he is for or against Orc,
and Beer (1968: 132) claims that he resists the violence of the
French Revolution with similar violence. The "strife of blood"
has been identified as the English war of 1793 against France
(Bronowski 1944: 51-52), and Los's Sons have been equated
with such libertarians as Paine, Wollstonecraft, and Blake him-
self (Erdman 1954a: 247 [267]). Howard (1984: 150) looks on
the strife as another version of the wine-drinking of 4:6,
Blake's phrases referring to the "winepress" of divine wrath at
Rev. xix.15. Noting the parallel between this passage and *FZ*
96:19-27/ E361/ VIIb, 40-48, Tolley (1970a: 144-45) observes
that both draw on Rev. xix.17-18, and that the shaking of nat-
ure echoes that of earth on the Judgment Day in "Nativity," ll.
160-64. Gallant (1978: 31) identifies "the strife of blood" as
the horrific violence necessary to usher in the Last Days.

Designs

Note Blake's friend George Cumberland added helpful glosses to
the designs in the British Museum copy of *Europe* (Keynes and
Wolf 1953: 81-82).

pl. i There has been much comment on the sources and meaning
of this sublime picture. The creator is Urizen, who is shown as
God the Father in a compasses-like pose (Paley 1978b: 31) bor-
rowed from the figure of Christ in Michelangelo's *Conversion
of St. Paul* (Blunt 1938: 87), while his windblown hair comes
from Tibaldi's Neptune (*ibid.*) or James Barry's *Lear*
(Hagstrum 1964: 64-65). His compasses or dividers derive
from Prov. viii.27 (Damon 1924: 348), and from *PL*, VII, 218-
34 and mediaeval paintings of creation (Blunt 1938: 73-74, 78-
79)—perhaps also from the title page of Winckelmann's
Reflections on the Painting and Sculpture of the Greeks (trans.

Fuseli, 1765), in which case they may stand for "the propor-
tions of classical art" (Mellor 1974: 123) as well as the superi-
ority of even mathematical form over absence of form
(Damrosch 1980: 264). Mitchell, indeed, (1978: 56) maintains
that the work of creation portrayed is not evil, though Damon
(*loc. cit.*) observes that Urizen's acting with his left hand
shows that he is a materialist. Nurmi (1957a) argues that he is
a caricature of Motte's portrayal of Newton as an inspired saint
in a frontispiece to the latter's *Principia*, and Blunt (1938: 79-
80) proposes that Blake is assailing Plato's mathematical con-
cept of creation in the *Timaeus*.

Daniel vii.9-10 is a source of the white hair and beard and
[in some copies] garment (Nurmi 1957a: 211); the hair and
beard may be blown in the winds of Enitharmon (Margoliouth
1951: 87—see 1:2n), and Urizen may be in the process of
"being 'born' old" from that goddess's womb of cloud
(Erdmann 1977b: 183). He may be kneeling in the sun as its
light breaches the clouds (Tolley 1970a: 116), their division by
the wind marking "a moment in the storm of eternity"
(Erdman 1974: 156); or, as the shadows suggest, he may well
be in a hole that only looks like the sun, his figure being
illumined by a light near or beyond the right-hand margin, a
light that shines from the truly infinite world as opposed to the
dark, empty space the god is creating with his instrument
(Howard 1984: 133, 140).

pl. ii This animal is either (1) the serpent of materialism (Damon
1924: 348) and nature (Damon 1967: 133) representing what
the Urizen of the frontispiece reduces infinity to (Howard 1984:
140), or (2) Orc confronting Urizen (Bindman 1977: 80), a
being of energy and desire pointing the reader forward to the
Prophecy (Erdman 1974: 157), or (3) an ambiguous Orc (Paley
1978b: 31), perhaps energy without vision as Urizen is reason
without vision (Beer 1968: 120). Essick (1980: 144-45) argues
that the cross-hatching and white lines surrounding Urizen
show that this serpent is his rebellious contrary.

pl. 1 This design operates on two distinct levels. The human pil-
grimage through life is menaced by evil (Damon 1924: 348),
and the political liberal, dressed in the American buff and blue
adopted by the party of Charles James Fox, is ambushed by
Burke hiding in the cave of Parliament (Erdman 1974: 159)

and drawn very much as in a Gillray cartoon (Erdman 1954a: 201-02 [218-19]). Blake, however, is transferring to Burke characteristics that Gillray's cartoons habitually bestow on Fox—deficient clothing, a dagger, and (in some copies) an unshaven face (Bogen 1967). Tannenbaum (1982: 162) sees an allusion to Prov. i.10-19.

The small figure between bat's wings is perhaps Fox, and the figure dragged down by a weight may represent the fate that Burke foresees for the pilgrim (Erdman, *loc. cit.*). These images may also stand respectively for the reasoner and the lowest human condition (Beer 1968: 120, 248n21).

pl. 2 The group of three can be identified from Cumberland's gloss in the British Library's copy as "Horror, Amazement, and Despair" (Damon 1924: 347, 348). The strangler may be the mythological Rintrah and the historical Pitt "in the nether deep" (12:24), while the fourth figure could be the dismissed Lord Chancellor Thurlow in process of becoming genuinely human now he has been ejected from his office (Erdman 1974: 160-61)—or more simply a man fleeing in disgust from the spectacle of "Devouring & devoured" of 2:5 (Paley 1978b: 32). Bindman (1977: 81) conjectures that the strangler is the assassin of the previous plate.

pl. 3 The joyful figures around the title display an Innocence whose doom is indicated by the giant winged woman Cumberland's gloss identifies as a comet (Damon 1924: 349). This woman may be the Shadowy Female (Keynes 1969), Enitharmon weeping (Mellor 1974: 125), Milton's "shame-fac't night" ("Nativity," l.111) (Howard 1984: 147), or Oothoon accompanying her fellow rebel Orc, who is reborn along with Christ and enclosed in a tiny circle with his flames of desire (Tolley 1970a: 123-25). Miner (1969: 468) suspects the encircled figure is a foetus; Worrall (1981: 285, 291) associates it with Orc's role as a star, namely Algol, whose light was known to fluctuate regularly. The joys at the top of the page, however, may be what this "secret child" (3:2) will bring (Erdman 1974: 161). Thomas Wright (1929: I, 73) believes that Orc's mother is descending to him, while Webster (1983: 129) considers that she is displaying resentment against the child whose birth has violated her body.

pl. 4   Wrongly supposing this unchained Orc, formerly "the secret child," to be bound (4:13) (Erdman 1974: 163), Enitharmon wakes him while in the background her other Children sport (Damon 1924: 349). The two of these furthest to the left are Bromion and Oothoon as depicted in *VDA IB* pl. i (Tolley 1970a: 128). In this image of Enitharmon awakening sleeping energy, there is an allusion to Psyche's breaking the prohibition against looking at Cupid (Chayes 1970b: 218-20)—Enitharmon does not realise that she shares Psyche's peril (Tolley 1970a: 128). Other interpretations are that Enitharmon is hiding Orc from sight (Bindman 1977: 81) at the beginning of her reign (Worrall 1981: 287-88) and that an unnamed woman is covering a radiant child who represents full vision (Beer 1968: 124).

pl. 5   At issue is Rintrah's relationship to the female angels. Are they Pity and Compassion, on whom he turns his back (Damon 1924: 349), or are they his guides Ocalythron and Elynittria (Howard 1984: 142) and his patrons the English and French queens (Erdman 1974: 163)?

pl. 6   In the famine that follows war (Damon 1924: 350), a wealthy woman and her humbler, grieving companion prepare to eat a child who has starved (Erdman 1974: 164). Howard (1984: 142) suggests that the richer woman is about to devour the other woman's infant.

pl. 7   The plague has been bred by puritanical repression (Damon, *loc. cit.*) or war (Keynes 1969). Hagstrum (1964: 102) sees here an illustration of official, Urizenic pity.

pl. 8   Albion's Angel is holding up his hands against the recoiling plagues (Tolley 1970a: 132-33); or a kingly old man—perhaps "the yellow year" of Cumberland's gloss—is trying to ward off war (Erdman 1974: 166); or Palamabron is gazing at the famine and plague of the preceding plates (Howard 1984: 143).

pl. 9   Paley (1978b: 32) aptly notes the contrast between the grace of the design and the horror of the subject. Natural energy that has become destructive (J. Warner 1984: 124-27, 136-38) is represented by a male and female, perhaps derived from the 1614 title page of Raleigh's *History of the World* (Beer 1968: 254-55), who are broadcasting a blight analogous to the plague and famine brought about by Enitharmon's Children (Howard

1984: 143). These figures, about the size of an ear of grain, are announcing apocalypse (Erdman 1974: 167). There may be an allusion to the hail of Exod. ix.18 and the barley of Exod. ix.31 (Tolley 1970a: 131).

pl. 10   This creature may be "the infinite" reduced by reason to "a serpent" (10:16) (Damon 1924: 350), a corrupted form of the title page snake now having seven coils for the seven days of creation (Erdman 1974: 168), for the seven historical cycles or churches of Leutha (14:20) (Tolley 1970a: 136-37), or for the orbits of the planets (Chayes 1974: 66-67). Alternatively, he may be an angry Orc (Paley 1978b: 32) or Orc as he appears to Albion's Angels (Bindman 1977: 82).

pl. 11   This powerful and elegant piece of satire is a counterpart of *IB* pl. 5, with a priest in place of the warrior king. This priest, with his papal triple crown (Keynes 1921: 140) and what may be a copy of Urizen's brazen book (Binyon 1926: 109), must be Palamabron (Tolley 1970a: 128) and may also represent Urizen himself (Damon 1967: 83) as well as Albion's Angel and George III (Erdman 1974: 169). Damon's speculation (1924: 350) that the two angels are "natural joys" relinquishing their wands is refuted by Binyon (1926: 110), who observes the serpents' tails projecting from beneath their robes as evidence of their orthodoxy. Howard (1984: 142-43) identifies them as the domineering Ocalythron and Elynittria feigning subservience. Paley (1983a: 195-96) remarks that before his 'conversion' shortly after 1800, Blake occasionally associated Gothic art with priestcraft, though Damon (1924: 350) thinks the ecclesiastical figure has usurped the throne of genuine Christianity.

pl. 12   Enitharmon's web of "curses" (12:27) is really as weak as spider's threads—threads which the insects break or avoid but which imprison the shrivelled, submissive man in the bottom right-hand corner (Erdman 1974: 170)—who is also seen in female form praying in despair (Tolley 1970a: 115-16). The insects have also been seen as Enitharmon's Children (Webster 1983: 307n33), who have (Howard 1984: 145) assumed these repulsive forms as a result of the trumpet blast (13:5) while they participate in nature's "enormous revelry" (14:34). Nanavutty (1957: 169-71) considers that humankind and nature are caught in the net of the creator, who, according to a Hindu myth, is a great spider spinning the universe in the form of a cosmic web.

pl. 13 Physical imprisonment is here added to spiritual (Damon 1924: 350-51), perhaps in connection with the image of bondage in 12:25-31 (Howard 1984: 144). The prisoner, who may be appealing to the retreating guard for mercy (Mitchell 1978: 109), is more likely to be the pilgrim of *IB* pl. 1 (Erdman 1974: 159) than the printer Richard Phillips jailed in 1793 for selling Paine's *The Rights of Man* (T. Wright 1929: I, 48, 163), Orc imprisoned by Newton (Digby 1957: 45), or Newton looking at a plague-spotted man symbolising the consequences of his science and derived, like the trumpeters of *IB* pl. 9, from Raleigh's title page (Beer 1968: 129, 254-55).

pl. 14 Revolutionary flames appear among the vermin (Damon 1924: 351), which represent the destructive and to a lesser extent the creative aspect of the energies of Enitharmon's Children (Paley 1978b: 32).

pl. 15 Los's rescue of his Daughters at this Armageddon recalls Aeneas' rescue of his father and son from Troy, while the ascending eagle testifies to the positive nature of the scene (Erdman 1974: 173). Beer, however, (1969: 270) sees a Los unable to stop the devastation, and Keynes and Wolf (1953: 79) refer to flight from the revolution. The fragment of a classical column, says Damon (*loc. cit.*), is a remnant of the order that is overthrown.

The Song of Los

It has been claimed that this book, whose title puns on "laws" (Erdman 1977b: 181), continues the narrative of *The Book of Urizen* (Gallant 1978: 25-26) and that of *The Book of Los*, which ends with the creation of Adam, the Human Illusion (Damon 1967: 51). The first portion, "Africa," deals with religious tyranny and the second, "Asia," with political oppression (Schorer 1946: 282-83).

A few critics feel that the book ends ambiguously, but most believe that the Grave's ecstasy, which is on one plane clearly sexual, brings fulfilment and felicity. Damon's early opinion (1924: 127) that Orc's Last Judgment and his coupling with

the Grave are accompanied by an orgy of war seems to influence
Bloom (1963: 163), for whom the world's sanguinary disintegra-
tion leaves Orc's capacity to liberate in doubt. Tannenbaum (1982:
196-97) notes that Moses' brazen serpent, to which Orc is implic-
itly compared (7:28; Num. xxi.6-9), is not only a type of Christ
(John iii.14-15) but also an object of idolatry (II Kings xviii.4).
More radically, Beer (1968: 138) shudders at humanity's prema-
ture arrival at the grave [but in the text people are resurrected *from*
it] and the accompanying barren frenzy, sexual and revolutionary.
However, Sloss and Wallis (1926: I, 127) see desire turning the
grave into a place of joy; Schorer (1946: 284) perceives a victory
of life over death; Damon (1967: 377, 423) comes to feel the grave
is impregnated and human thought expanded; Paley (1970: 162-
63) welcomes a redemption that includes fleshly resurrection;
McCord (1984: 32) acclaims the defeat of everything Urizenic;
and Erdman (1974: 180) speaks of a happy transformation of tomb
to womb—a transformation that, in Deen's eyes (1983: 64), allows
The Song of Los to complement and complete *The Book of Thel*.

The form of the poem has scriptural associations. Howard
(1984: 181-82) observes that it parodies pious biblical songs with
historical content (e.g. Exod. xv.1-19; Is. ix-x) and is indebted to
the chronological structure of such psalms as lxxviii, cv and cvi.
He finds a specific source in Rev. xx, though in that text Satan's
Urizen-like deception of the nations is to follow Christ's thousand-
year reign.

Details

"Africa"

Title Africa is the place of Israelite and black enslavement
   (Johnson and Grant 1979: 134). The practice of attributing a
   divine origin to a legal code originated in Egypt—see William
   Warburton, *The Divine Legation of Moses* (1738-41) (Tann-
   enbaum 1982· 187-88).
3:1 Los's song is sung by a minstrel to diners (Stevenson 1971:
   242); it is being repeated by a human singer for a human audi-
   ence (Johnson and Grant 1979: 134) .
3:2 **four harps**—for the four continents (Damon 1924: 126).

3:3-4 **heart-formed**—pun on "heartland," for Africa was widely regarded as the seed-bed of all civilisation (Tannenbaum 1982: 185). The subjugation of the heart, which first occurs there (McCord 1984: 26), is followed by the separation of the head from the genitals causing the degeneration of Noah's vision into Urizen's mindset and the decay of Edenic love into Ariston's lust (Beer 1968: 133-34). Cf. *BU* 25:43-44.

3:4 Damon (1924: 337) sees Ariston as negative—a militarist Spartan king who shudders at visionary truth, Margoliouth (1951: 91) judges that he has fallen from a recoverable happiness, and Howard (1984: 180, 187) supposes him (like Urizen) formerly a tyrant, now redeemed and shocked at his own past. Referring to pl. 10 of *America*, Harper (1955: 79) asserts that Blake still associates Ariston with the lost Atlantis, which some Neoplatonists regarded as the fourth continent.

3:6-7 Adam is the natural man and Noah the imaginative man who avoids submergence in time and space (Damon 1924: 126).

3:8-9 The Children of Los [and of Enitharmon] are literally the prophets (Damon 1924: 362) or "the men of arts and letters" (Margoliouth 1951: 89). In their hands, however, symbol has degenerated into dogma (Damon 1924: 126), Los's prophecy into law (Stevenson 1971: 242). Cf. their roles in *Europe*.

3:10 Blake may be referring to Adam's and Noah's horror at Urizen's oppression (Howard 1984: 182) or to Noah's turning white and the African's turning black (Nurmi 1976: 102), the latter being a result of Noah's curse in Gen. ix.22-27 (Johnson and Grant 1972: 135) or a sign of decadence (Damon 1924: 362).

3:11 **Brama**—i.e. Brahma, the Hindu creator and author of the Vedas.

3:12-14 Relying on Blake's customary symbols and ideas, Schorer (1946: 282) asserts that the permanent forms of nature mock fallen humankind, and Mellor (1974: 99) identifies the "Human form'd spirits" as souls imprisoned in mortal bodies, but Adlard (1972: 100-01) sees the war as waged between the four elements, while Howard (1984: 180) deems the Night and Cloud antithetical to Orc's fire and emblematical of delusion. Raine (1968: I, 351-52) perceives a reference to Bhagavadgita ii, where Lord Krishna urges Arjuna to fight since souls are

immortal, though Blake regards this defence of war as hypo-
critical. Tannenbaum (1982: 186-87) finds an allusion to St.
Paul's phrase "in bondage under the elements of the world"
(Gal. iv.3), Blake's "Elements" signifying both the natural
elements and the Law.

3:15 **Noah shrunk, beneath the waters**—sank into materialism
(Damon 1924: 362) or into the state that Har and Heva
"shrunk" into (4:7) (Tannenbaum 1982: 190). Both Noah and
Abraham are identified with Urizenic morality (Percival 1938:
25).

3:18 **Trismegistus**—Thrice-greatest. The ancient Hermetic writ-
ings beloved of the alchemists were attributed to Hermes
Trismegistus.

3:21 Blake connects the myths of Prometheus and the Giant
Atlas; the latter he comes to identify with Albion, his arche-
typal man, and to associate with the Atlantic (E543/ K578) (cf.
Hungerford 1941: 46-49, 56).

3:23-24 Do these contentious lines mean that Jesus' teaching was
perverted by Theotormon (Raine 1968: I, 177-78) or by the
church (Johnson and Grant 1979: 136), that Jesus himself is
responsible for his religion's repressiveness (Sloss and Wallis
1926: I, 131; Erdman 1977b: 182), that Jesus hears both The-
otormon's gospel and Oothoon's and in a spirit of resignation
chooses the former (Stevenson 1971: 243), or that the reference
is to the fallible historical Jesus as opposed to the Jesus of the
Second Coming (Frye 1947: 448-49n56)?

3:25-29 Blake may have viewed Islam as a reaction against
Christian monasticism (Damon 1924: 127)—and a commend-
able one (Sloss and Wallis 1926: I, 127) or, contrariwise, the
cause of the tyranny over women that Wollstonecraft blamed it
for (McCord 1984: 27).

3:29 **a loose Bible**—a scripture without an epic framework like
the Bible's (Fisher 1961: 197); a second-rate scripture (Bloom
1965: 905); a scripture reputed to be a gathering of loose pages
or chapters (Damon 1967: 259, citing George Sale's *Prelimi-
nary Discourse* [1734]); a scripture promoting an unhealthy
eroticism (Beer 1968: 135).

3:30-31 Denied sexual expression, Sotha's energy bursts out in
war (Damon 1967: 378-79). Sexual frustration is also respon-

sible for Christian self-flagellation and Moslem cruelty to women (McCord 1984: 27).

4:1 **Hospitals**—residences for the poor.

4:4 In McCord's view, Eternity was obliterated because it was wrongly regarded as only a dream (1984: 27-28).

4:5 **Har and Heva**—poetry and painting (Damon 1924: 362), which fled a dogma-ridden, sanguinary world (T. Wright 1929: I, 80); possibly Noah's children (Howard 1984: 243-44).

4:6 **War & Lust**—morality's view of energy (Sloss and Wallis 1926: I, 126); the vices of the Norsemen and the Moslems respectively (Beer 1968: 135-36).

4:7 **they shrunk**—as humans did after the Flood—see Gen. vi.4 (Howard 1984: 243-44).

4:9 **in reptile flesh**—Blake's source is Ovid's *Metamorphoses*, IV, which tells how Cadmus, who denies the soul's immortality, and his wife are changed into serpents (Raine 1968: I, 49-50, 381-82n38).

4:13-15 This imposition is parallel to Los's binding of Urizen (*BU* 8:1-13:34), necessary to prevent his dissolution (Hilton 1983: 69).

4:16 **a Philosophy of Five Senses**—Deism (Paley 1970: 71).

4:17 Urizen weeps hypocritically (Bloom 1963: 162), or is grieved at such extreme degeneration (Johnson and Grant 1979: 137).

4:18 Critics disagree as to whether Rousseau and Voltaire promote liberation, as in *FR*, l. 276, or oppression, as in the Preface to chapter three of *Jerusalem*. Damon (1924: 127) takes the former view, which is confirmed by Erdman's observation (1974: 177) that a bird rises above the first name and a banner is attached to the second. Nevertheless, Sloss and Wallis (1926: I, 127) charge them with Deism. Tannenbaum (1982: 192) thinks them threatening yet potentially redemptive.

4:19-20 **the deceased Gods/ Of Asia**—Thammuz and Adonis, portrayed as dying gods of Lebanon in *PL*, I, 446-54 (Tannenbaum 1982: 192, 325n14).

4:20 **on the desarts of Africa round the Fallen Angels**—The fallen angels are compared to the barbarian invaders of North Africa in *PL*, I, 351-55 (Adlard 1972: 100); they are "the sons of God" of Gen. vi.2 (Tannenbaum 1982: 191). McCord (1984:

26) believes Rousseau, Voltaire, the Asian gods, and the fallen angels are all worthy rebels.

4:21   This line is repeated from *A* 3:1, where the tyrannical monarch "burns," but Beer (1968: 136) supposes that this Prince burns with "prophetic fires."

"Asia"

Title   "Asia" signifies hostility to the Divine Vision (*J* 74:22), but the events narrated occur in Europe (Damon 1924: 127). Blake means western Asia, the region of St. Paul's work and of the churches of Rev. i.4 (Tannenbaum 1982: 185-86).

6:1   **The Kings of Asia**—really of Europe, but Blake is wary of a charge of sedition (Margoliouth 1951: 90); foes of the biblical Israel and devotees of the Whore of Babylon (Tannenbaum 1982: 193).

6:2   **The howl**—of Albion's Angel; see *E* 12:12 [and 21] (Stevenson 1971: 245).

6:13   **prosperity**—for the ruling class (Bronowski 1944: 91).

6:18   **allegoric riches**—all the proposed minimum wage would amount to on account of inflation, and perhaps what Wesley and Whitefield promise the poor after death (Bronowski 1944: 91); forms of wealth like bonds that are accessible only to the rich (Johnson and Grant 1979: 138).

6:20   The authorities tolerated and sometimes encouraged mobs that burnt the dwellings of radicals (Johnson and Grant 1979: 138). Stevenson (1971: 246) cites the Gordon Riots of 1780 and the destruction of Joseph Priestley's Birmingham home in 1791.

6:21-22   Ruins for the poor, prosperity for the rich (Bronowski 1944: 91-92).

7:3-4   I John ii.16 condemns "the lust of the eyes, and the pride of life" (Johnson and Grant 1979: 138).

7:7-8   Perhaps references to promises of a materialistic reward after death (Sloss and Wallis 1926: I, 133).

7:9-19   Urizen is parallel to the invader Sennacherib, whose wings were to cover Judah (Is. viii.8), as Orc is parallel to her successful defender Hezekiah, who resembled "a fiery flying ser-

pent" (Is. xiv.29); the metal books melt in the flames of the
French Revolution (Tannenbaum 1982: 196).

7:14   **Books of brass, iron & gold**—of charity, war and econom-
ics (Damon 1924: 363); Damon later (1967: 424) takes brass to
represent sociology, and Ostriker (1977: 912) interprets it as
law.

7:20-23   Adam and Noah are not corrupt or fallen (Howard 1984:
243-44). They are mentioned a second time to show how, und-
er Urizen, the upright human body has decayed into a skeleton
(McCord 1984: 25). That Adam is "bleach'd" is an ironic ref-
erence to his having been fashioned from the red clay of *MHH*
2:13 (Miner 1969: 289).

7:28-34   Biblical references are given in the chapter above. Deen
(1983: 62-63) identifies the resurrected bones with those to
which Adam and Noah were reduced (7:20-21).

7:29-30   The earth may shrink as Noah, Har and Heva shrunk, or
more probably it dwindles to make room for the new heaven
and earth of Rev. xxi.1 (Tannenbaum 1982: 198).

7:33   **all flesh naked stands**—as Adam and Noah "stood" (3:6-7)
before oppression began (McCord 1984: 32).

7:35   **The Grave**—this world (Damon 1924: 127); the earth
(Schorer 1946: 285). Erdman (1977b: 186) holds that nature
(4:11), earth, and grave are the same entity differently per-
ceived.

7:38   **glandous**—a word of Blake's invention.

7:42   **Urizen wept**—because, unlike Los, he realises the world is
not redeemed (Beer 1968: 138); because he now repents
(Erdman 1974: 180), for he sees from an eternal perspective
(Howard 1984: 187).

Designs

pl. 1   This page may show human worship of an unclear sun sym-
bolising reason (Damon 1924: 363), a priest at his devotions
(Bindman 1977: 83), Moses imitating the God who will reveal
only his back parts (Exod. xxxiii.23) (McCord 1984: 23, 25),
or Urizen himself adoring a sun whose face mirrors the chaos
his own passion for order brings (Mitchell 1978: 51). However,
Erdman (1977b: 180-81) argues that while he looks at first like

a devotee of the sun and the law inscribed on it, the reader who has reached the last sentence and the last design can see him as a penitent whose body is bright.

pl. 2   Though Keynes and Wolf (1953: 91) regard the prone figure as Adam, the design probably portrays the Noah of 7:22-23 dead on Ararat (Damon 1924: 363), or perhaps dying with his hand on Adam's skull—cf. 7:20 (T. Wright 1929: I, 81), or else it displays Urizen on the Stone of Night of *E* 10:24-31, which is the skull (Binyon 1926: 115) or more probably the same god on a rolling sea or landscape (Erdman 1977b: 181-82). Erdman (*ibid.*) points to the prominence of the title, the ascending birds of paradise, and the upward direction of Urizen's (unsteady) look as signs that the *Song* promises redemption.

pl. 3   It is generally agreed that the serpent intertwined with the title is malign, but is the boy below Har (Damon 1924: 363), and do the boy and the sheep stretched out together constitute an image of Enitharmon's false paradise in *Europe* (Bindman 1977: 84) or, contrariwise, a glimpse of existence before the Fall (Paley 1978b: 34)? The serpent, says Erdman (1977b: 182), looks downward in contrast to the revolutionary and prophetic serpents of *MHH IB* pl.20, *A IB* pl. 11, and *E IB* pl. ii.

pl. 4   Damon (1924: 363) rightly identifies the fleeing couple as Har and Heva. Above them flies a winged human—"a flying genius" (Binyon 1926: 116) or a refugee (Erdman 1974: 177) or a woman about to fall onto the shrunken "vast of Nature" (4:11) (Keynes 1975a).

pl. 5   Not all commentators accept as positive this tranquil, majestic, even awe-inspiring picture of fairy monarchs reposing on lilies in a starlit night. It divides "Africa" from "Asia" and in Howard's opinion (1984: 182) is intended to mark the point where the four poems named after the continents intersect. Erdman (1977b: 184-85) plausibly argues that the bud rising above sleeping Titania, who is reminiscent of *Europe*'s dreaming Enitharmon, points to her spiritual rebirth, while Oberon, bearing his crown and sceptre without arrogance, looks ahead to the overthrow of tyranny in "Asia." Elsewhere (1974: 178) he remarks that they observe the mortal world from the viewpoint of Eternity. Less enthusiastic about the serenity of this scene below the stars, Grant (1969: 360-61) per-

ceives Luvah and Jerusalem or Jesus and earth in an interme-
diate relationship, which, the lilies signify, they will transcend.
Paley (1978b: 34) finds the beauty of the scene deeply decep-
tive and asserts that the fairies, like their counterpart in *E* iii,
are cruel or indifferent to humans; other identities suggested
for the couple are the doomed monarchs of Asia (Bindman
1977: 84) and Ariston and his bride on lilies of chastity in one
of the "Secluded places" of 3:26 (McCord 1984: 28-30). Bor-
rowing a phrase from *J* 19:42, Damon (1924: 363, 445) terms
these Lilies of Havilah—i.e. of Innocence. Ignoring the pres-
ence of a queen, Beer (1968: 136) suspects that the design
illustrates the last line of the preceding plate: "The Guardian
Prince of Albion burns in his nightly tent."

pl. 6 In this image of Orcean revolution (Keynes 1975a)—rather
than a flood (Howard 1984: 182)—the letters of the title consti-
tute a ship foundering in the political storm, the waves of
which merge into the gale-blown trees of "forests of oppres-
sion" (Erdman 1974: 179). The two figures in a kind of haven
under the trees have been interpreted as man attempting to
revive his emanation (Damon 1924: 363) and as victims of
royal oppression (Hagstrum 1964: 13). The giant nude at the
bottom may be a decapitated body—a warning to kings
(Erdman, *loc. cit.*), or a man assailed by the poverty of 6:16
(Keynes, *loc. cit.*). Hagstrum (*loc. cit.*) sees the minute nudes
around the title as portents of liberation, and Erdman (*loc. cit.*)
proposes that the shapes under the first two letters are both
discarded selfhoods and the remains of executed kings.

pl. 7 In this calmer design we see the ends of the storm-beaten
boughs of the previous plate (Erdman 1974: 180). The falling
figure may represent humankind collapsing into Urizenic anar-
chy (Keynes 1975a), the disintegration of the former society
(Bindman 1977: 84), or the reunion of bones in the resurrec-
tion of 7:31-34 (Erdman 1977b: 187).

pl. 8 In this counterpart of *IB* pl. 1, Los looks down at the sun
that he has either created (Binyon 1926: 117) or cleansed from
Urizen's mysterious writing (Erdman 1974: 181); it is the
physical sun, which Los is turning into a visionary one while
the "true sun of Imagination" well below the bottom margin
radiates the light in the background (Erdman 1977b: 188).

Keynes (1975a) regards the visible orb as the "sun of poetry," which is about to be launched.

In Tannenbaum's view (1982: 198-200), the text's ambiguous ending is followed by this optimistic picture, based on Raphael's *Astronomy*, of Los and the sphere of the universe that he has "re-created"; in contrast, McCord (1984: 32-35) describes how the poem's joyful conclusion gives way to a pessimistic design, for Los, having degenerated from "Eternal Prophet" to blacksmith, has forged the sun on which Urizen's signs are to be inscribed.

Notes on Criticism for Chapter 6

The Book of Urizen

In 1924 Damon (116) observed that *The Book of Urizen* portrays simultaneously the fall of the eternal universe into the material cosmos we call creation and the fall that is re-enacted in the psyche of every human. Although Hirsch (1964: 73-74) and apparently Ph. Butter (1971: 39, 41) deny the poem a cosmogonic level, Kroeber (1970: 11) rightly observes that Damon's view is generally accepted. Some critics, such as Gallant (1978: 17) and Howard (1984: 154), also regard Los's creative labour as an image of the artist's work, which Essick (1980: 210-11) finds parodied in Urizen's making (both here and in *The Four Zoas*) of books devoid of imagination. Less convincing is Damon's later contention (1967: 53, 248) that the first four chapters portray the formation of the child in the womb as the product of antithetical forces.

Several writers imply points of continuity and discontinuity with *The Marriage of Heaven and Hell*, which enthuses over contraries and lauds energy. Thus Emery (1966: 27) remarks on Urizen's total blindness to the need for interacting contraries, and Mitchell (1978: 131-32) discerns several signs of future redemption, including Orc's voice and Fuzon's exodus. Bindman (1977: 91), on the contrary, finds little sign of redemptive energy either in this book or in its two sequels, and Mellor (1974: 94) judges its conception of an imprisoning mortal body to be very different from Blake's earlier view of the body as "a portion of Soul" (*MHH*, pl. 4).

The structure of this book, too, has been variously described. Kroeber (1970) implies that the text is organised chronologically while the designs are synchronic, for the poem, which has only one arrangement, is a narrative in the past tense focusing on cosmogony, while the designs portray present realities, namely psychological states. Most critics treat the book as a narrative. Especially interesting is Simmons's analysis (1970) of a symmetry built around the division between the first four and a half chapters, which show Urizen's fall into subjectivity, and the remaining four and a half, which show Los believing that reality is wholly objective. (Simmons regards symmetry as characteristic of all Blake's representations of the fallen world.) Marks, on the other hand, (1975: 583, 587-88) views the poem as synchronic, arguing that it keeps returning to the same images, for example the globe and the shrinking of sight, as it treats the Fall from different viewpoints: to Eternals the Fall is one event, to mortals it seems to have stages. Expounding the same theory in more detail, Mitchell (1978: 123-30) points to the references to events in *Paradise Lost* made regardless of their chronological order, the expansion of the single day of the body's fashioning (Gen. i.26-31) to seven ages, and the condensation in chapter nine of a long period of history into the week of the biblical creation. He argues that these features collapse time to show that everything in the book happens simultaneously.

In keeping with Simmons's view of two phases, Nurmi (1976: 110) states that Urizen begins the material creation and Los completes it. Endorsing this view, Tannenbaum (1982: 203, 207) maintains that the poem, drawing on the distinction between the Elohist and Jehovist accounts of the creation (Gen. i.1—ii.3; ii.4-25), portrays the victory of the just Elohim (Urizen) over the merciful Jehovah (Los).

The characters and the narrative clearly have closely related psychological and moral meanings. Howard (1984: 152-53, 171) sees what Blake later calls "selfhood"—self-centredness and selfishness—as the driving force behind Urizen's imposition of law, Los's binding of Urizen and chaining of Orc, and Enitharmon's teasing of Los. Paley (1970: 69) regards time itself as the product of the human mind's fall into selfhood.

After Freud, it is impossible to ignore the connection between Los's treatment of Orc and the Oedipus complex. Margoliouth (1951: 106) comments on the reversal of the usual situation—here the father is jealous of the son. Using Freudian terms, Majdiak and Wilkie (1972: 94-95) identify Urizen as a tyrannical superego, the Eternals as the id which resists it, and Los as the ego that mediates between them; they note Freud's attribution of timelessness to the id as well as the ego's genesis at the period when the mind recognises the reality of the external world. Singling out the divorce between subject and object as the essence of the Fall, Simmons (1970: 151) discovers its emblem in the story of Narcissus, who fell in love with his own reflection in water, and argues that his legend is absolutely central to *The Book of Urizen*. Webster (1983: 154-58, 165-67), seeing a sympathetic portrayal of Oedipal incest in *IB* pl. 21, claims that the Urizen of the title page displays the fixation of the anally obsessed infant who makes his faeces his weapon, and identifies the cosmic void with the emptiness the baby feels during its mother's absences.

Blake's psychology can hardly be separated from his view of perception. Hirsch (1964: 74) specifies the theme of *The Book of Urizen* as the way in which our distorted perception prevents us from seeing that nature is infinite, while Kittel (1978: 133) credits the poem with demonstrating that the material world has no existence independent of mind, and Simmons (1970: 159, 166) considers that the designs show Urizen and Los as a pair of clowns foolishly afraid of a fallen world that is a mere projection of mental processes. Rosenberg (1970) finds an expression of this philosophy in the way that an image introduced by the imagination of the poet to supply a metaphor or simile can take on as much reality as the perceptible object that he is ostensibly describing (e.g. 3:31-32; 27:10 and 15).

Blake is also, according to Bloom (1963: 165, 175), criticising his own tendency to admit a Urizenic element into his work, and Crehan (1984: 161-62), expressing the same view, detects, in addition, a political allusion to Pitt's treason-hunting Committee of Secrecy set up in 1794.

The most crucial disagreements about *The Book of Urizen* centre on Blake's attitudes towards his characters. Is Los an unqualified hero whose work with hammer and tongs creates forms for Urizen's states, so that, being errors, they can be cast out (Damon 1924: 118, citing *J* 12:13)—or who supplies Urizen with sense organs when he has cut himself off from everything outside his own consciousness (Simmons 1970: 154-55)—or who saves him from an endless succession of changes (Stevenson 1971: 256, referring to 8:10)—or who prevents his annihilation (Fisher 1961: 189-90) or even the dissolution of all existence (Nurmi 1976: 110)? Is Los's hammering the creative work of the unconscious amidst flames of genius (Percival 1938: 37)? Or is Los, on the contrary, wrong to accept the authority of the Eternals (Mitchell 1978: 121), in error to impose a temporal limitation on Urizen's mind (Bloom 1963: 169-70), or guilty of wiping out the poor remnant of Urizen's life (Howard 1984: 165)? Is he degenerate because he lapses from his initial vigour into sentimental pity (Margoliouth 1951: 106), or does he take a wrong turn when he stops prophesying (Marks 1975: 584-85, alluding to 13:38-39)? Does he chain down Orc because he fails to see him as redemptive rather than diabolical (Fisher 1961: 193)? Is he selfish to sequester Enitharmon—i.e. genuine pity (Emery 1966: 32)? Mitchell (1978: 112-13) believes that there is self-criticism in Blake's portrait of Los as well as in his portrait of Urizen. Hirsch (1964: 74-75, 84) and Simmons (1970: 155, 165) seem to believe that Los is the original androgynous Human, and Deen (1983: 26, 65) regards the unfallen Los as the First Principle or Poetic Genius, who divides into Urizen, Enitharmon and Orc—reason, pity and rage—when Urizen is rent from his side.

The Eternals, too, have their admirers like Damon (1967: 54) and Stevenson (1971: 249) as well as several detractors. Sloss and Wallis (1926: II, 73) hold that from this book through *Jerusalem* Blake's Eternals are fallible. Bloom (1963: 171) accuses the Eternals of emotionally spurning Urizen and of later rejecting Los, Mitchell (1978: 133n19) blames them for indifference and fear when they close off the lower world, Gallant (1978: 15) charges them with failing to recognise that Chaos is a necessary seed-bed, and Webster (1983: 164-65) insists that they react to Orc's conception like children horrified at seeing their parents copulate. Who, moreover, are the Eternals of this early prophetic work? To Bloom (1963: 165) they are the unfallen, and to Stevenson (1971: 249) "a 'republic' of immortals," but some interpreters judge from the design on *IB* pl. 15, where the four—in some copies, three—Eternals portrayed are reminiscent of the Zoas. The picture suggests that, as Jewkes (1973: 132) supposes, there may only be four of them and that these constitute "Universal Man,"—the Albion of the epics before his fall.

Also controversial is Blake's *enfant terrible*. In the view of some critics like Fisher (1961: 193) and Howard (1984: 153-54), Orc is Eternity's gift to a world gone astray; to others, like Sloss and Wallis (1926: I, 99) and Margoliouth (1951: 105-06), he is a being very much of this lower realm.

Finally, scholars have devoted much energy to investigating the sources of *The Book of Urizen* and Blake's attitude to them. The allusions to *Paradise Lost* and the first two chapters of Genesis show that the poet is correcting the former and interpreting the latter. Damon (1924: 120-21) notes that the portrait of Urizen glances at the Demiurge or subordinate god who creates the world according to Plato's *Timaeus*. Bloom (1965: 906) judges that Blake is satirising Plato alongside Genesis and Milton, and Raine (1968: II, 59) remarks that some passages of the poem would be wretched indeed if they were not burlesque. In Saurat's view (1929: 91-106), the account of creation is indebted to Gnosticism while the division of the unfallen androgyne into the two sexes derives from Cabbala. A minor source is the account of chaos at the beginning of Ovid's *Metamorphoses* (Margoliouth 1951: 99-100); a major one may be Jakob Boehme. Damon (1967: 53) observes that in the first chapter Urizen seems to undergo the contraction, expansion and anguished rotation that characterise Boehme's First Principle, from which, says Percival (1938: 166-67), his sulphureous flames derive. Harding (1970) argues further that Los corresponds to the flash of divine light that marks the transition to the Second Principle, which manifests in love (Enitharmon) and sound (Orc), while the Third Principle, nature, is represented by Fuzon. Blake, he adds, is parodying Boehme's optimistic view of creation. However, P. H. Butter (1971: 38, 43-44) cautions that Boehme's theosophy does not provide parallels to Los or the Net of Religion, and there is a stronger case for Bindman's claim (1977: 95) that some images of Urizen parody Michelangelo's depiction of God the Father in the Sistine Chapel. Tannenbaum (1982: 222-23, 329n30) demonstrates that several of Blake's figures have originals in Michelangelo's *Last Judgment*: the creation, he theorises, is presented as a Last Judgment at which Urizen condemns his followers to live in the hell of this fallen world.

Details

3:9   **ninefold**—The number nine has traditional associations with nightmares, and the nadir of the Fall comes in the ninth chapter of this book (Bloom 1963: 166, 174). Cf. Shakespeare, *Macbeth* I.iii and *King Lear* III.iv.121.

3:27-35 Cf. Satan's secret war preparations, *PL*, VI, 520ff (Bloom 1965: 906). This is an abridgment of Milton's account of the victorious Messiah, *PL*, VI, 829-39 (Raine 1968: II, 63). Ault (1974: 99) believes ll. 30-31 allude to Newton's explanation of the tides in terms of planetary motions.

3:37 **the Immortal**—the true God (Gardner 1954: 80); the universal prelapsarian man (Bloom 1963: 167); Urizen (Beer 1969: 80).

3:38 **his**—Urizen's before his fall (Howard 1984: 158-9).

4:12 **Why will you die O Eternals?**—Urizen fails to accept death as a part of life (Gardner 1954: 81). The Eternals die practising self-sacrifice for each other (Damon 1967: 54). The Eternals may fail to recognise that death exists among them till Urizen points it out (Mitchell 1978: 134). Urizen is deluded into believing there is death in Eternity (Howard 1984: 159).

4:14-18 An allusion to the Chaos of *PL*, II, but Urizen's Chaos is inside him (Bloom 1963: 168).

4:16-17 The alchemists describe the *prima materia*, the formless first matter from which the elements spring, as dark and cold and the womb of nature (Gallant 1978: 15).

4:16-23 Blake draws on Satan's passage through Chaos in *PL*, II, and the creation of the firmament in Gen. i.6-7 (Bloom 1965: 906).

4:18 **self balanc'd stretch'd o'er the void**—cf. Gen. i.2 and *PL*, VII, 242.

4:32, 43 Citing *BA*, 3:55-58, Kittel (1978: 127) defines the Rock of Eternity as Urizen's petrified consciousness.

4:32-33, 44 The Book of Brass has been variously defined as the book "of false charity" (Damon 1924: 352), "of false ethics" (Schorer 1946: 272), of Urizen's One Law (Gardner 1954: 82), and even of cheek or impudence (Simmons 1970: 167). Howard (1984: 154, 251), citing George Richardson's *A Collection of Emblematical Figures...from the Iconology of Cavaliere Cesare Ripa* (1777-79), proposes that it is the book of destiny.

4:36-37 Confinement to one habitation precludes access to the infinite; the single habitation is symbolised by the skull (Gardner 1954: 82-83). It should be noticed that l. 36 seems to offer a choice, but the epithet "ancient" in l. 37 snatches it away.

4:38-40 This passage follows the rhetorical pattern of Ephes. iv.3-6 (Mitchell 1978: 125).

4:49 **the seven deadly sins of the soul**—Although they seem sins only in Urizenic eyes, Harper (1961: 208-09, 307n13)—

who also quotes *J* 13:17, 19:26-27 and 79:56-57—suggests that Blake follows the Neoplatonists in implying an analogy between the seven sins and the malign creation of the seven planets.

5:5 **Eternity roll'd wide apart**—According to Damon (1967: 54), this is the division of good from evil.

5:21-23 **combining**—Urizen's armies of 5:16 recombine in him (Stevenson 1971: 254). Urizen's protective earthworks allude to Milton's account of the war in Heaven (Bloom 1963: 169)—see *PL*, VI, 639-74. The passage parodies Rev. vi.14-16 (Tannenbaum 1980: 25).

5:28-37 The roof is a heavy coating of materialism (Damon 1924: 118). It is the womb in which the embryonic Urizen will develop (Damon 1967: 53). Or the embryo is the universe as Plato conceives it—like "one great animal" (Harper 1961: 209-10, citing *Timaeus*, 67c), or it is the earth gestating in a cosmic womb (Leonard 1978: 81). The image of the earth as a heart makes it parallel to Urizen's own heart later formed by Los (Gardner 1954: 88). Marks (1975: 581-82) notes the irony of womb, heart and river, which are images of life, becoming images of falling, and Emery (1966: 28) observes that Urizen's shelter seems to him like a womb but to the Eternals like a heart.

5:33 The image of the black globe hints at the emergence of astronomical space (Howard 1984: 163).

6:4 **Urizen was rent from his side**—On one level, says Simmons (1970: 153), the earth (Urizen) is torn from the sun (Los). Sloss and Wallis (1926: I, 91) suspect that the original human unity was made up of Urizen and Los, while Hirsch (1964: 77) sees here "a grisly parody of Eve's creation."

6:7-8 Failing to win over the Eternals, Urizen has become paranoid and has fallen "into a catatonic withdrawal" (Howard 1984: 152-53).

6:9-10 Urizen "is both creator and creation," and in the latter capacity he is both the microcosmic human being and the macrocosmic earth (Harper 1961: 210).

8:3-5 The references to sulphur, pitch and nitre suggest that Urizen is now himself a hell (Ostriker 1977: 916).

8:7 **nets & gins**—Blake associates these with (1) laws and religions that blot out memory of Eternity (Sloss and Wallis 1926: I,

92, citing *SL* 4:2), and (2) the constriction of joy (Gardner 1954: 90, citing *VDA* 6:11). They are negative terms, for Los is creating a "death-image" (15:2), an idol (Howard 1984: 164).

8:9-10 Despite his desire for permanence, Urizen is continually changing, and Los, the imposer of form, binds and fixes the changes (Beer 1969: 83). There is an allusion to the angel's binding of Satan in Rev. xx.1-3 (Tannenbaum 1980: 42).

8:11 Iron and brass, the metals of Urizen's books, symbolise tyranny (Gardner 1954: 82, 85, 89). The rivets correspond to the "thick set nails" with which souls are bound in bodies in Plato's *Timaeus*, 43a (Harper 1961: 213).

10:9 **sodor**—i.e. solder.

10:14 Sulphur is Boehme's symbol for the Anguish, the third manifestation of the First Principle; the Eternal Mind and every human mind are immersed for a time in solitude in the Anguish (Paley 1970: 69).

10:16-18 The beat of Los's hammer is an image for poetic metre (Ostriker 1977: 916).

10:19 **The eternal mind**—either Urizen or Urizen-Los before the Fall (Kittel 1978: 130-31).

10:22-23 **a lake.../White as the snow**—a symbol of "the Indefinite" (Damon 1924: 118) or "formlessness" (Nurmi 1976: 111); the amniotic fluid within the womb of 5:29 (Damon 1967: 53); the Stygian lake, which is both the lake of matter and Udan Adan, the Lake of Spaces (Raine 1968: II, 90); Locke's *tabula rasa* or blank tablet—an image for the empty mind of the newborn child (Ostriker 1977: 916).

10:24 **necessity**—According to Locke's *Essay Concerning Human Understanding*, II.xxi.13, necessity takes over a mind which loses the power of thought and willed action (Kittel 1978: 132).

10:25 Kittel (1978: 132) traces the phrase "chains of the mind" to Locke's "chain of consequences" (*Essay* II.xxi.52 [some editions 53], but this refers to sequences of thought in a mind that is planning. More persuasively, Hilton (1983: 67-71) argues that the chains include fallen language and fallen perception.

10:35 By binding Urizen, Los has changed his "dreamless" sleep (7:7) into a "dreamful" one (Gardner 1954: 89).

10:36-37 Blake is employing an already common image for gravity—the chain (Hilton 1983: 69-70).

10:41 **nerves of joy**—a reference to the sense of touch (Nurmi 1976: 111).

11:3 The heart is "the organ of pity" (*ibid.*).

11:4 **the Abyss**—"the human body" (Gardner 1954: 88).

11:5 **Conglobing**—according to Kreiter (1965: 114-15), contracting while remaining globular, but the *OED* gives only the usual meaning—forming a spherical shape—which is the one found in Milton (*PL*, VII, 239, 292).

11:14-16 Looking out of symbolic "caves," the eyeballs behold the symbolic "deep" or sea, to which the nostrils (13:1) are also bent (Gardner 1954: 88).

13:7 **Throat**—Urizen's fourth and last sense (Damon 1924: 353); he is given no organ of touch, the sexual sense (Emery 1966: 29).

13:12-14 His body having been completed, Urizen ironically finds himself facing west, the direction of [sunset and] death (Bloom 1963: 170).

13:12-17 After finishing Urizen's body, Los is, in effect, crucified (Simmons 1970: 155).

13:18 As well as the seven days of creation at the beginning of Genesis, the seven stages of Los's work have been traced to a suspicious variety of sources. These include the "seven times" that pass over Nebuchadnezzar in his madness (Frye 1947: 258, citing Dan. iv.16-23), the account of the body's creation in Plato's *Timaeus* (Harper 1961: 212), the seven stages of a chicken embryo's development described by William Harvey (Kreiter 1965: 115-17), the seven qualities or spirits which mark the emergence of creation in Boehme (Harding 1970: 9), and the description of an embryo's growth in Erasmus Darwin's *The Economy of Vegetation* (1791) (Leonard 1978: 79-80).

13:20-40 Los thinks he has failed in his task of preserving human wholeness (Majdiak and Wilkie 1972: 92).

13:32 **by degrees**—a reference to the temporal character of fallen perception (Fisher 1961: 191-92).

13:35-47 Los's merging with Urizen is a comment on the corruption of contemporary poetry by rationalism (Bloom 1963: 170). It suggests what happens to persons who ignore their inspiration (Stevenson 1971: 259).

13:46 **existence**—life spiritually conceived (Kittel 1978: 135-36).

13:53 Pity is apt to paralyse its object with self-doubt (Percival 1938: 169); it separates the pitier from the pitied (Nurmi 1976: 111). Los's pity and subsequent division are not entirely negative, for they break up a static state and introduce a sequence of events which will ultimately bring redemption (Ph. Butter 1971: 40-42).

13:58 **a round globe of blood**—Los's heart, which separates from him to become Enitharmon (Damon 1967: 54).

15:3-5 The transformation of the void into a wintry nocturnal sky implies the eventual coming of spring and morning (Mitchell 1978: 154).

15:13 **the globe of life blood**—a symbol of the condition of life in the natural world (Fisher 1961: 192); an allusion to the moon become as blood in Rev. vi.12 (Tannenbaum 1980: 42).

18:2-3 Blake associates roots, especially the "fibrous" roots of trees, with death (Gardner 1954: 92).

18:4 **Fibres of blood, milk and tears**—blood vessels, lacteals, and lacrymals; the two latter were the subject of research by Blake's acquaintance John Hunter (Kreiter 1965: 115).

18:7-8 The separation of male from female is an early stage in the splitting of the One into the Many in Neoplatonism (Harper 1961: 232-33). The division of Los from Enitharmon is an image of the division of the sublime from the pathetic (Beer 1969: 84). The Enitharmon whom Los goes on to woo is "fallen nature" (Erdman 1969b: 261). His marriage to her signifies his perception of the natural world as an objective reality (Price 1964: 426). Fisher (1961: 193) and others regard Blake's later explicit identification of Enitharmon with space (e.g. M 24:68) as applicable to her role in this book, where her consort is indeed on one level time.

19:1 Inspiration separated from the poet degenerates into pity as opposed to love (Damon 1924: 118).

19:2-7 The Tent is "the material sky" (Damon 1967: 54). It is identified with the Tabernacle—see Exod. xxvi.31-33 (Miner 1969: 263). Though the image is biblical, the "cords & stakes" are the spatial and temporal reference points established by scientists to standardise measurements (Raine 1968: II, 136-37). Its pillars are the pillars of the church that confine Los and

Enitharmon (Gardner 1954: 93). Its "strong curtains" are the veil of nature's outward appearance (Margoliouth 1951: 114). According to Bloom (1963: 171), the Eternals are wrong to erect the Tent as it makes space and time more substantial, but Fisher (1961: 193) sees their action as contributing to ultimate redemption.

19:9 Most critics (e.g. Fisher 1961: 193; Mellor 1974: 97) agree that in this context "Science" signifies the empirical knowledge obtained through the fallen senses, the knowledge that forms the basis of the natural sciences. Margoliouth (1951: 105) neatly defines the "curtains" of 19:5 as "the veil of this phenomenal world."

19:19-36 Kreiter (1965: 110-12) suggests that this apparent recapitulation by the embryo of the evolution of the species may derive from the researches of John Hunter, but Leonard (1978: 80-81) thinks Erasmus Darwin's *Zoonomia, Part I* (1794) a more likely source, though he notes that Blake shares none of Darwin's joy in creation. Some critics consider that he is showing Orc's corruption within the womb: Marks (1975: 587) sees the perversion of the life process leading to a doomed birth, Beer (1969: 85) perceives a descent from threefold vision to single vision, and Raine (1968: I, 202) speaks of the corruption of love when it is born into the material world. Slightly less pessimistically, Howard (1984: 171) notes that the embryonic stages are listed in reverse order in 3:16 as the animal forms with which Urizen contends; this indicates that the painful development represents a fallen form of mental processes that are superior to abstract reasoning.

The worm has been interpreted as the flesh, of which the serpent is a more dangerous variant (Damon 1924: 353), as the innocence that Orc loses before birth (Kreiter 1965: 118), and as a symbol of birth emerging out of death (Gardner 1954: 94).

19:41-42 Wagenknecht (1973: 169) sees here a grim parody of the Hymn in Milton's "On the Morning of Christ's Nativity."

19:43 **the Human shadow**—i.e. Orc, who has been identified as repressed desire (Damon 1924: 353) and as the fallen human (Schorer 1946: 274). The Eternals are wrong to see Orc, whose birth is necessary for ultimate redemption, as a Shadow (Bloom 1963: 171)—but the term is the narrator's.

19:44   **Delving earth**—passing forcibly through his mother's body (Stevenson 1971: 263).

20:17   Inside the cosmic tent, Los and Enitharmon experience joy only at night when the links of the chain are burst (Gardner 1954: 95).

20:18-21   The rock, the iron and the mountain are Urizenic emblems (*ibid.*). The chain that locks Orc and his descendants into inter-generational conflict mirrors the chain of gravity and clock time that constitutes Urizen's backbone—see 10:15-37 (Hilton 1983: 69-75).

20:21-25   The Chain of Jealousy may represent the bonds of time (Sloss and Wallis 1926: I, 99)—cf. 20:20 with 10:18; the Mosaic Law (Percival 1938: 122); and the repression of desire (Fisher 1961: 194). The rock to which Orc is chained may be the Decalogue (Damon 1924: 353). He is bound down because Los is jealous of his love for Enitharmon (Raine 1968: I, 343) or because his independence seems to both parents a threat (Price 1964: 426). Although Enitharmon weeps, the pronoun "They" (20:21, 23) supports Mellor's view (1974: 97) that she and Los both behave oppressively.

Dorothy Plowman's contention (1929: 23) that Los, fearful of being displaced by Orc, confines his education to the study of abstract conceptions may be associated with Damon's proposition (1924: 119) that Orc's rebelliousness threatens to corrupt art and Bindman's contrary suggestion (1977: 93) that Los is playing the part of a mediocre artist facing a brilliant, innovative competitor.

20:26   **The dead heard the voice of the child**—The fall of humankind, that Los has tried to stem, resumes (Gallant 1978: 20). Orc manifests as "a Christ-child" as he does in E 3:1-4 (Mitchell 1978: 127)—see John v.25-28 (Hilton 1983: 232-33); Los's jealous attempt to suppress energy has failed (Howard 1984: 171). Suppressed desire emerges and will provoke Urizen to explore nature, natural science being a substitute for sexual activity (Webster 1983: 166).

20:34   Having formerly divided his "deep world within" (3:8, 4:15), Urizen has now become an empiricist and divides the external "Abyss beneath" (Kittel 1978: 137).

20:39   **golden compasses**—cf. Prov. viii.27 and *PL*, VII, 224-31 (Bloom 1963: 172-73).

20:41 **a garden of fruits**—especially of good and evil, fruits of the Tree of Knowledge (Kittel 1978: 140-41).

20:42-44 In this obscure passage, Los may be acting selfishly in sequestrating Enitharmon (Emery 1966: 32) because his fires, which should be prophetic, have become possessive (Bloom 1963: 173); in his degenerate state he may be hiding the necessity of conflict between Urizen and Orc (Murry 1933: 134-35); or he may be hiding Enitharmon from these two to preserve her remnant of vision and the dynamic balance of contraries between himself and her (Nurmi 1976: 113). Howard (1984: 172) comments that Los's imagining he is threatened by his son and Urizen signifies that the prophet is cut off from society and nature and that imagination is cut off from reason and the prompting of the senses.

20:45 **an enormous race**—"enormous" in the obsolete sense of "monstrous," "disordered." Simmons (1970: 158) terms Enitharmon "the generative mother of the world."

20:46 **Urizen explor'd his dens**—Natural religion and the sense that reality is external are here strengthened (Frye 1966: 184).

20:48 **a globe of fire**—a lamp of intellect (Margoliouth 1951: 106); "a natural source of light" (Kittel 1978: 137); perhaps the energy that Orc's voice has evoked in Urizen (Beer 1969: 85).

23:18 **first begotten, last born**—Energy is necessary for any creation, but it is so destructive that it only emerges unmodified when creation is complete (Beer 1969: 85). Fire was the first element to appear when Urizen tried to circumscribe Eternity (Howard 1984: 172).

25:3-22 The Net of Religion is the web of creation spun by the spider-like First Cause as described in Joseph Priestley's *A Comparison of the Institutions of Moses with those of the Hindoos and other antient Nations* (Nanavutty 1957: 168-72)—but Priestley's book is dated 1799. Formed from Urizen's tears, it is a version of Noah's Flood, which in Blake's myth inundates the world with matter (Tannenbaum 1982: 216-18).

25:18 **And the Web is a Female in embrio**—Probably the web is pregnant (Stevenson 1971: 266). It is perhaps the seed of a church (Ostriker 1977: 918). It will develop into the Shadowy Female, the "vague material-maternal world" founded on fallen Urizenic perception as ll. 20-21 indicate (Hilton 1983: 104). It has a connecting function resembling that of the mother, who provides a single focus for all the infant's experiences (Webster 1983: 233).

25:19 **no wings of fire**—Not even the greatest inspired poet can destroy the Net of Religion (Bloom 1963: 174).

25:32-33 The "streaky slime" (Damon 1924: 354) and the "woven hipocrisy" (Stevenson 1971: 267) are the Net of Religion.

25:37 **in reptile forms shrinking together**—materialising (Damon 1967: 54); taking forms like that of the serpent of Eden, who was doomed to eat dust—i.e. confined to the lowest kind of sense perception (Kittel 1978: 142).

25:37-38 Cf. the antediluvian Giants of Gen. vi.4 (Stevenson 1971: 267).

25:43 **thirty cities**—thirty Sons of Urizen (Damon 1924: 354).

25:44 **In form of a human heart**—apparently a reference to the shape of Africa; see 28:8-10 and *SL* 3:3 (Sloss and Wallis 1926: I, 103). Deen (1983: 67) identifies heart-shaped Africa with Urizen's petrific roof beating like a human heart (5:28-37).

28:5 **Tombs**—graves of desire (Damon 1924: 354); the pyramids (Damon 1967: 6); a symbol of reverence for ancient authority (Kittel 1978: 143).

28:10 **Egypt**—the place of the Israelites' slavery (Sloss and Wallis 1926: I, 103); "empire" and the region where civilisation began (Schorer 1946: 276); allusion to Rev. xi.8: "the great city, which spiritually is called Sodom and Egypt, where also our Lord was crucified," Blake's Egypt being the fallen world (Tannenbaum 1982: 221).

28:11-18 Blake's version of the division of humankind at the Tower of Babel (Tannenbaum 1982: 216).

28:14-18 The hearts of the shrunken humans were hardened like Pharaoh's and (later) the Israelites' (Beer 1969: 86).

28:19 **Fuzon**—"a form of Orc or Luvah" (Damon 1924: 120); a *fusion* of energy and reason which characterises the prophetic aspect of Moses' religion (Fisher 1961: 194-95); analogous to both Nimrod and Moses (Howard 1984: 174, 177). His name may derive from French *feu* ("fire") and Greek *fusis* ("nature") (Frye 1947: 214).

28:21 **pendulous earth**—an echo of *PL*, IV, 1,000 (Damon 1924: 354).

28:23   The ocean is Blake's Sea of Time and Space (Damon 1924: 20); it is composed of the "tears & cries imbodied" (18:6) that constitute Enitharmon (Simmons 1970: 160); it is both Noah's Flood and a deluge of materialism, and it is parallel to the Tent of Science that shuts out vision (Howard 1984: 155, 174).

   englob'd—This word mirrors "Self-clos'd" (3:3) (Marks 1975: 584). Cf. pl. 28n. Simmons (1970: 159-60) argues that the book is not only symmetrical but has a circular structure that mimics the closed character of the fallen world.

Designs

pl. 1   Urizen is crouched under his Tree of Mystery (Damon 1924: 355) or under dead trees (Eaves 1973: 225) in front of the Tablets of the Law, which double as gravestones (Margoliouth 1951: 99) and also resemble wings (Hagstrum 1964: 106). A "solipsist" shut in by branches, he copies from the enrooting book of nature which he reads with his toes; one hand writes while the other engraves or paints with an etching needle or fine brush (Erdman 1974: 183). Some commentators (e.g. Simmons 1970: 148) see pens in both hands, but Mitchell (1978: 113) notes that only the left one seems to have a grip appropriate to a pen. Beer's claim (1969: 79) that there is a hillock (the tomb of authentic vision) behind the upright tablets is not confirmed by other observers. Howard (1984: 157) identifies the open book with the Book of Brass [cf. *IB* pl. 5], and Margoliouth (1951: 99) sees the misplacement of the right or spiritual foot as a sign of a fallen condition.

   This elaborate design has been diversely interpreted. It may show Urizen transcribing from a Hebrew or classical authority and making two pages out of one as he petrifies and divides his material (Eaves 1973: 225, 228-29); it may combine the tradition of reading the Book of Nature with Locke's image of the mind as an empty tablet upon which sense impressions are inscribed (Kittel 1978: 144n67); it may illustrate *BA* 3:61-67, though in both poems the god is an author, not a scribe (Mitchell 1978: 141); it may show Urizen copying the names of the saved and the damned from his brass Book of Judgment

into the Book of Life and Death, these books being referred to
at E553-54/ K443-44 (Tannenbaum 1982: 222, 329n29). This
last interpretation requires both hands to be writing.

pl. 2   In the eyes of most commentators, a young soul is being
guided by a benevolent female. The pupil and teacher may be
Orc and Enitharmon (Damon 1924: 355) or nature and a soul
entering on birth (D. Plowman 1929: 19-20). The flames, ac-
cording to Beer (1968: 256), represent gratified desire. Howard
(1984: 157) finds the woman repressive as indicated by her
bound up hair.

pl. 3   The figure is likely to be an Eternal enjoying the flames of
energy (Raine 1968: II, 64), but he may be specifically Orc
(Keynes 1921: 144), Los (Damon 1924: 355), either Los or a
young Urizen (Keynes and Wolf 1953: 70), or a deliberately
ambiguous character capable of being identified as Urizen,
Orc, Fuzon or an Eternal in flames that may be either creative
or destructive (Mitchell 1978: 145-46).

pl. 4   This puzzling plate, absent from some copies, has been
taken to represent humankind under a downpour of material-
ism (Damon 1924: 355); a baffled man tormented by rain,
vegetation or fire (Mitchell 1978: 146-47); Urizen in pain
fighting the "torrents" of 4:20 (D. Plowman 1929: 20) or
collapsed in despair (Paley 1978b: 33) or enduring the fire of
Eternity (Howard 1984: 160); or Urizen's view of how an
Eternal suffers from the fire around him (Erdman 1974: 186,
citing 4:13).

pl. 5   Urizen with his Book of Brass (see 4:31-33), though Mitch-
ell (1978: 147) suggests it may be *The Book of Urizen*, dictated
by Urizen, one of the Eternals, to Blake.

pl. 6   This much discussed design has been compared to an in-
verted Laocoön group by Bindman (1977: 91-92), and the cen-
tral figure is crucified head downwards according to Damon
(1924: 355), whose identification of the three falling individu-
als as Eternals and of the serpents as emblems of the lower
state which awaits them has been endorsed by several critics.
Erdman (1974: 188) observes that those falling may be either
rational or energetic, and Mitchell (1978: 147-48) mentions
that they could be the damned at the Last Judgment. The head-
clutching despair of the lateral figures (J. Warner 1984: 107)
contrasts with the calmness and outspread arms of the central

one, which may hint at a future resurrection (Mitchell 1978: 149), or may be the gestures of Orc or Los rallying his companions (Erdman, *loc. cit.*). The two presences dimly visible between the victims have been described as followers of Urizen expelling them (Damon, *loc. cit.*) but are more probably "the flayed heads and skins of aged, bearded kings" (Erdman, *loc. cit.*).

pl. 7 Los in agony (Damon 1924: 355). The source is an image of a tortured soul in Michelangelo's *Last Judgment* showing that Urizen's world, in which Los is now imprisoned, is hell (Tannenbaum 1980: 24). The design may illustrate 6:5-6 (Howard 1984: 164). Here, and in *IB* pl. 11, Los's body has begun to close in on itself and become somewhat Urizenic, a process carried further in *IB* pl. 21 (Mellor 1974: 148).

pl. 8 The embryonic skeletal form of Urizen (Damon 1924: 355).

pl. 9 Another portrait of Urizen. He may be exploring his dens (Binyon 1926: 112, alluding to 20:32), trapped under the stony roof of 5:28 (Emery 1966: 50), discovering that his "solid without fluctuation" (4:11) is after all threatening (Erdman 1974: 191), or blind within the earth and reduced to a catatonic state (Howard 1984: 160).

pl. 10 The figure has been identified as Urizen pressed down by the "stony sleep" of 10:2 (Emery 1966: 50) or constructing a protection against the fires of Eternity (Simmons 1970: 162); however, in view of the countenance of Urizen visible in some copies on the rock face (Erdman 1974: 192), of the similar design on the title page of *BL* (Paley 1978b: 33), and of the character's obvious energy, it appears to be Los. Holding this opinion, Damon (1924: 355) notes the cruciform posture of the arms. Mitchell (1978: 151) sees a sign of hope in the figure's resistance to the mental torpor symbolised by the rock in this design and in *IB* pls. 8 and 9.

pl. 11 It is agreed that Los is on the right and Urizen, in the body Los has made for him, on the left, but Erdman (1974: 193) notes that the details vary considerably from copy to copy. Citing 13:20 as the text illustrated, Mitchell (1978: 151) refers to "a brick dome behind Los and a stone arch behind Urizen," while Paley (1978b: 33) feels "a phallic tower" is going to fall between them. According to Webster (1983: 160-62), the frail state of the tower emerging from Los is a sign of his weakness:

both he and Urizen alternate between aggressive action and relapsing into enervating pity.

pl. 12 Urizen is submerged in the "waters of materialism" (Damon 1924: 356). The spread of his beard shows that he is neither rising nor descending (Mitchell 1978: 152), though he imagines he is doing the former (Kittel 1978: 134-35), and he could be trying to do either the former or the latter (Erdman 1974: 194). The lines illustrated may be 13:28-30 (Binyon 1926: 112) or 4:21-22 (Stevenson 1971: 252). The figure is a parody of the image of a soul rising to heaven in Michelangelo's *Last Judgment* (Tannenbaum 1980: 34).

pl. 13 The insubstantial figure pushing apart clouds—or (Erdman 1974: 195) in some copies the sun and moon—appears to be either Ahania (Keynes 1921: 145) or Enitharmon (Mellor 1974: 91)—though Hagstrum (1964: 43) identifies it as Los. Mitchell (1978: 128, 153) comments that this plate, the only one in which the design separates two blocks of text, marks the central point of the book, and he suggests that either the picture illustrates *BA* 2:38-40 or the figure is a muse, like that of *IB* pl. 2, invoked at the nadir of the Fall. Bindman (1977: 95) notes the resemblance to Michelangelo's depiction of creation.

pl 14 Most critics follow Damon (1924: 356) in identifying the figure as Urizen, though Stevenson (1971: 260) thinks he is Los. The design probably illustrates 4:18-20 (Tannenbaum 1980: 21-24); however, Paley (1978b: 33) thinks Urizen is diving in search of the dens of 20:46. Erdman (1974: 196) finds deliberate ambiguity: Urizen may be diving or doing a handstand and clutching either rocks or clouds. According to Mitchell (1978: 161), he is vainly seeking a settled position from which to govern his world. Hagstrum (1964: 46, pl. XXVIIIA, pl. XXVIIIB) points to Goltzius's engraving of Tantalus as a source, while Tannenbaum (*loc. cit.*) notes the similarity to a devil dragging a lost soul in Michelangelo's *Last Judgment* and deduces that this creator is a demon.

pl. 15 In some copies three, in others four Eternals are reaching down to cover the world with their Tent. Mitchell (1978: 155-56) finds their act ambiguous: are they bringing beneficial order or the deluge of the poem's last line? Binyon (1926: 113), citing Ellis and Yeats, suggests that they may be the four Zoas, and Erdman (1974: 197) identifies as the artist Los the one

whose left hand is drawing something over a curved sur-
face—the earth or a skull—as he shows his "dark visions"
(15:12) to his companions, and, on another level, puts flesh on
the bones of Urizen. In this figure, Tannenbaum (1980: 34-37)
detects an ironic allusion to an angel reaching down to raise a
soul in Michelangelo's *Last Judgment*.

pl. 16   A sorrowful Los is falling in fire. Paley (1978b: 33) notes
his resemblance to a foetus, and Kroeber (1970: 12) states that
he could be either Los or Urizen, the ambiguity being inten-
tional. In copy A (reproduced D. Plowman 1929), he has a
beard and may be Urizen.

pl. 17   In this depiction of the birth of Enitharmon, the details of
the nerves vary from copy to copy (Erdman 1974: 199). Damon
(1924: 356) and Stevenson (1971: 261) claim that Enitharmon
is emerging from the globe, but most commentators agree with
Binyon (1926: 113), who quotes *FZ* 50:13/ E333/ IV, 96, that
the human figure is Los. The latter, observes Mitchell (1978:
156-57), is painfully but protectively exuding his pity for Ur-
izen in the form both of a world and of a foetus. Deen (1983:
68), noting that Orc delves through earth to be born (19: 44-
46), identifies Enitharmon with the "earth, or earth-moon."

pl. 18   Los falters in his art as his inspiration fades (Bindman
1977: 92). He is now free from the suffering he endures in *IB*
pls. 7, 10, 11 and 18 (Mitchell 1978: 158)—these pages pre-
cede *IB* pl. 18 in all copies. According to Simmons (1970: 150-
51), *IB* pls. 13 and 18 taken together illustrate 18: 7-8, for they
show the "trembling and pale" Enitharmon waving before
Los's "deathy" face. However, Erdman (1974: 200) couples *IB*
pls. 17 and 18 holding that the latter shows the unselfish pity
of Los as he looks with arms in cruciform position (cf. Damon
1924: 356) at the globe that becomes Enitharmon.

pl. 19   Los turns inward (Erdman 1974: 201) or despairs
(Bindman 1977: 92) as Enitharmon rejects him. However,
Mitchell (1978: 158) sees in Los the creator of Enitharmon a
positive contrary to Los the creator of Urizen in *IB* pl. 11.

pl. 20   Orc's birth.

pl. 21   This picture focuses on jealousy, but George (1980: 119)
thinks that the tilt of Enitharmon's head indicates that she re-
tains some affection for Los. The latter's newly acquired beard
shows that he is coming to resemble Urizen (Erdman 1974:

203), and chains are a Urizenic symbol (Mellor 1974: 148). Suggested models for the design are Renaissance depictions of Venus, Cupid and Vulcan, the latter being jealous of Mars (Bindman 1977: 93, 239n17), and Michelangelo's lethargic Apollo, who seems, like Los, to have lost his creativeness (Tannenbaum 1980: 43-48).

pl. 22   This picture of the fettered, weeping Urizen may illustrate 25:3 (Damon 1924: 357) or 10: 24-25 (Stevenson 1971: 265). In Simmons's view (1970: 153), a marked antithesis between *IB* pls. 16 and 22 underlines Los's association with the sun and Urizen's with the earth, the latter perhaps being rent from the former. Howard (1984: 165) comments that the sun is setting behind.

pl. 23   Whereas Damon (1924: 357) holds that Urizen sees the lion, who in reality guards the lamb, as monstrous, Erdman (1974: 205) maintains that he is about to walk past the animal, which he sees only dimly in the feeble light of a lantern that leaves him feeling his way with his free hand. Binyon (1926: 114) believes the beast is one of those lions who are "dishumaniz'd men" (*FZ* 70:31/ E347/ VI, 116). Noting that Urizen does not actually grasp the sphere, Hilton (1983: 180, 232-34) argues that this object represents the chained Orc, who is both the light-giving sun and the Son who will arouse the "dead" (20:26), and of whom the lion is another form. Less elaborately, Mitchell (1978: 158-59) perceives Urizen as "a mock Diogenes" seeking with a useless lamp for a law-abiding man instead of an honest one.

pl. 24   While the sun sets behind the sea (Damon 1924: 357), the four senses identified with the four elements emerge (Bindman 1977: 95, 239n21); they are Urizen's Sons and take on human form—beginning, despite their father's hope of maintaining a stasis, to regenerate (Howard 1984: 172). This is an ironic version of a resurrection scene: Grodna and Utha are based on two of the resurrected dead in Michelangelo's *Last Judgment* (Tannenbaum 1980: 24-34).

pl. 25   As Erdman notes (1974: 207), the details of this confused scene vary with the copy. Damon (1924: 357) sees Urizen's Daughters appearing from the twisted form of "a winged Worm," where Raine (1968: II, 66) perceives anguished mon-

sters with human faces and Stevenson (1971: 266) an inter-
twined agglomeration of human and serpent forms.

pl. 26 This picture of a child with a howling dog partly illus-
trates 25:2. The boy's posture suggests prayer (Keynes 1921:
146) or begging (Erdman 1974: 208), and the modernity of the
scene indicates that the same fallen condition has prevailed
since creation (Bindman 1977: 95). Mitchell (1978: 162)
thinks the child is Orc, and Kroeber (1970: 13) considers that
his helplessness represents the loss of the infant Orc's energy
shown on *IB* pl. 20. Howard (1984: 157, 174) connects this
plate rather with *IB* pl. 2, suggesting that the child in the latter
now stands before a door that bars him from Eternity, while the
dog is analogous to the woman who previously misled him.
Mitchell (1978: 163) points out that Imagination (Los) as well
as Reason (Urizen) has helped to build a cruel world.

pl. 27 The obvious interpretation of this image is that Urizen is
dragging his Net of Religion through the sky. Damon (1924:
357) observes how his clothing seems to become the Net.
Making a connection with *IB* pl. 26, Emery (1966: 51) judges
that Urizen finds himself powerless to ease the pain of the boy
and the dog, while Mitchell (1978: 159, 163) asserts that he
turns hypocritically away leaving the child to be protected by
the religion he draws behind him.

pl. 28 This image of Urizen resigned to defeat (Damon 1924:
358) is a transformation of the title page. Simmons (1970: 148)
notes that he is now much stronger than in that initial design,
and Erdman (1974: 210), extending the comparison, notes that
his left foot is now advanced, his hands hold onto the Net of
Religion instead of working, his eyes are open, the funereal
Tablets of the Law serve him as arm rests, and he dominates
the world that has imprisoned him. Mitchell (1978: 141) adds
that his being trapped in his own net is a satirical stroke absent
from the text, though Damon (1967: 345) points out that it is
shown in the design to "The Human Abstract" and described in
FZ 103:26-31/ E375-76/ VIII, 176-81.

The energetic vine between the columns of verse may well, as
Erdman claims (*loc. cit.*), speak of better things to come in
spite of the tiny corpse drawn under the closing words.

The Book of Ahania

Although Howard (1984: 188, 198) emphasises the up-surge of selfhood first in Urizen and then in Fuzon and the hero-ine, *The Book of Ahania* centres primarily on the suppression of desire and emotion, on a form of the Oedipus complex, and on the psychological and social consequences of these phenomena.

Following Damon's comments (1924: 360) on the un-healthiness of detaching Pleasure (Ahania) from Reason (Urizen) and then suppressing it, Sloss and Wallis (1926: I, 115) suggest that the detachment is the result of a single outburst of passion represented by Fuzon's assault on his father, while Percival (1938: 28) recognises that in expelling Ahania, Urizen is banishing the emanation in whom he should find repose so that the rhythm of activity and rest is broken. Bloom (1963: 176-77) blames Urizen for provoking Fuzon's assault by nursing unacted desires (see "Proverbs of Hell," no. 67), and for condemning his own sexuality when his son has aroused it. Not only, argues Howard (1984: 192-93, 195), does he project onto Ahania the guilt that he feels at his own desire, but he implants in Fuzon the seed of guilt (5:46), which germinates when the latter succumbs to the temptation of pride (3:38) and causes him to groan on his Tree (4:44). Fuzon, the snake and Ahania, supposes Cramer (1984), are all potentially creative energies rising from the unconscious only to be repressed by Urizen, who should reintegrate them to restore the lost whole-ness of the psyche, which Ahania lovingly recalls.

To Damon (1967: 148), the conflict between father and son seems to echo both Oedipus's killing of his father and Saturn's castration of Uranus. Implicitly developing the former analogue, Gallant (1978: 19) notices the parallel between Urizen's treatment of Fuzon and Los's treatment of Orc. Fuzon, however, beginning as an Orc-like rebel, rapidly becomes tyrannical. While Schorer (1946: 280) sees that, nailed to the Tree of Mystery, he is a Christ crucified by his father, Erdman (1954a: 288-90 [314-15]) per-ceives that he is also a Robespierre. Scholars have found other characters alluded to in the enterprise and doom of Fuzon: Damon (1924: 360; 1967: 50) believes that the story of father and son was suggested by the relationship of Wisdom and Pleasure in the first part of Plato's *Philebus*; Frye (1947: 214) points to the death of Absalom and Bloom (1963: 176) to the agony of Prometheus; De

Luca (1982: 104n17) finds a source in the story of Thor, the serpent Midgard, the wounded Baldur, and the punished rebel Loki in the Prose Edda; and Tannenbaum (1982: 231) makes a valiant if curious attempt to relate chapters two through five to the four last books of the Pentateuch.

Blake may have discarded this book because the functions of Orc and Fuzon awkwardly overlap, though Fisher (1961: 196) considers that the former stands for emotional and the latter for intellectual rebellion, and Paley (1970: 81) feels that Fuzon allows Blake to treat energy pessimistically while leaving room for retraction. Damon (1967: 51) makes the weighty point that Passion could not be Reason's son.

Details

2:1-2 The image of the chariot refers to the beginning of the French Reign of Terror (Erdman 1954a: 288-89 [314]).

2:10-13 Erdman (1954a: 289 [314-15]) finds here a reference to Robespierre's formal deposition of the Goddess of Reason in June 1794, Bloom (1963: 176) notes the allusion to the creator of Gen. i.2, and Tannenbaum (1982: 229) observes attributes of the lawgiving God of Exod. xix.16-20 and xx.18-21. In "King of sorrow," Webster (1983: 169) sees an allusion to Christ that reflects Blake's ambivalence about him in 1795.

2:19 The beam has a phallic shape (Bloom 1963: 177). Being "hungry," it is probably the guillotine (Erdman 1954a: 290 [315]). Spherical to begin with, it is distorted by Fuzon's hate (Howard 1984: 197).

2:20-21 Referring to Exod. xiii.21, Frye (1947: 213, 215) interprets the Disk as a form of the Urizenic pillar of cloud contrasting with the Orcean pillar of fire. He detects an underlying image of the earth covering the sun's face at night (*ibid.*: 443n46).

2:23 **mills**—logical reasoning (Damon 1924: 360).

2:27 **The sounding beam**—According to Beer (1969: 88), Fuzon is remembering Eternity, where music is not distinct from light.

2:32 There have been a number of explanations of the elusive character Ahania. Damon (1924: 124) regards her as Pleasure, Sloss and Wallis (1926: II, 127) as the "emotional self," Per-

cival (1938: 25) as "the whole of the mind's desire," and Erd-
man (1954a: 233 [253]) as a personification of prelapsarian
nature. Her name has been traced to the Ossianic "a daughter
of Annia" (T. Wright 1929: I, 75), to the exclamation "aha!"
(Preston 1944: 24), and to the Greek *a-* ("without") and *ania*
("sorrow") (Pierce 1931: 396-97). Erdman (*loc. cit.*) opts for
"aha!" and "Annia." Following Fisher's hint (1961: 195) that
her name is derived from "Athena," Bloom (1963: 176) views
Ahania as a wisdom goddess while he also suggests (1965:
908) that she has some relation to the Miltonic Satan's daugh-
ter Sin. On the basis of her memory of him in Eternity, Raine
(1968: I, 150, 154-62) describes her as the goddess Earth in
whom Urizen should sow souls due to enter mortal bodies.
Tannenbaum (1982: 242-23) identifies her with God's beloved
celebrated in Canticles and—following Paley (1966:
32n20)—with the Wisdom of Prov. viii, who rejoiced with God
before creation. See also headnote to *FZ*, Night III.

2:43 **Pestilence**—the product of repressed sexuality (Paley 1966:
30).

2:46 **Five hundred years**—perhaps a reference to the supposed
five-hundred-year rule of Shepherd Kings in Egypt mentioned
in Jacob Bryant's *A New System of Mythology* (1774-76), a
period during which religious monuments were destroyed
(Sloss and Wallis 1926: I, 103); the period during which the
pillar of fire guided Egypt before Los turned it into the sun
(Stevenson 1971: 271); the time during which the pillar, then
unperverted, served the Israelites while they sojourned in Egypt
(Howard 1984: 190).

2:47 **beat in a mass**—"beat *it into* a mass" (Stevenson 1971:
271).

2:47-48 Los becomes the spirit of time, the governor of mortal
life (Sloss and Wallis 1926: I, 119); Los is preventing the
energy that proceeds from Fuzon from lapsing into
formlessness (Beer 1969: 88).

3:7-11 The allusion to creatures emerging from the Nile mud
continues the Egyptian association (Beer 1969: 88-89). Noting
the serpent at Urizen's knees, Howard (1984: 197-98) claims
that the source of the eggs is onanistic. Webster (1983: 169-71)
believes that Urizen, having cast out sexual pleasure, is left
with an infantile obsession with excrement.

3:13 **Serpent**—of materialism (Damon 1924: 124); of "material-istic science" (Blackstone 1949: 75); of mortality (Bloom 1963: 178); of nature (Damon 1967: 50).

3:23-24 Urizen's repentance for experiencing sexual desire prompts him to make the black bow (Murry 1933: 139), which stands for moral law (Paley 1966: 30). Or the bow represents Urizen's teachings while the rock symbolises his legal code; he is determined to remake Fuzon in his own mould (Howard 1984: 192).

3:41-44 Here is an allusion to the death of Absalom (II Sam. xviii.9-14) viewed as an Orc who rose against his father (Frye 1947: 214). Erdman (1954a: 289 [315]) plausibly sees also a reference to the execution of Robespierre on 27 July, 1794, a month after his dethronement of the Goddess of Reason. Bloom (1963: 179) adds that Moses the liberator is being figuratively slain by the moral law and that the darkening of the tresses symbolises nature's decline into the forests of the night. Those tresses remind Miner (1981: 308) of the constellation Coma Berenices or the Hair of Berenice.

3:45-46 Urizen's puritanical rejection of Ahania produces the Mosaic Law (Percival 1938: 25).

3:46 A quotation from Gal. iv.25, which signifies the victory of the Law (Margoliouth 1948: 304).

3:47-50 The blood and ointment, representing classification into good and evil, are the poison constituted by Experience (Bloom 1963: 179).

3:64, 73-4-1 Several scholars, such as Erdman (1954a: 289 [315]), endorse Damon's view (1924: 360) that the book of iron is the book of war; Raine (1968: II, 97) regards it as the book of the Iron Age. Urizen's other books, says Howard (1984: 194), contain his religious doctrines.

3:65-70 The proliferating Tree is defined by Damon (1924: 125, 360) as "Religion" and "the Church." The term "Mystery" de-rives from Rev. xvii.5 (Margoliouth 1951: 110). Webster (1983: 172) supposes the Tree stands for the mother's body, desired by both father and son, and the Mystery is both relig-ious and sexual. To elaborate his conception, Blake draws on *PL*, IX, 1100-14 (Frye 1947: 136) and the legend of the pois-onous Upas Tree, which was said to proliferate over a great area (Damon 1967: 411, citing Erasmus Darwin, *The Loves of the Plants*, III, 237-54, and E500, 861/ K185). According to Bloom (1963: 49, 143), Raine (1968: II, 6-8, 32-34) and Hilton (1983: 119-20, 251), it represents physical nature as well as ecclesiastical power maintained through enigmatic doctrine and ritual.

4:5   In Heb. i.6, Christ is referred to as "the firstbegotten."

4:5-8 Reason tortures passion with religion (Damon 1924: 125). There is an allusion to God the Father's requiring Atonement through the Son's crucifixion (Beer 1969: 89). The priest is putting a sinner on public display (Howard 1984: 194).

4:9   **the arrows of pestilence**—These originate in the rejected Ahania, who has turned into "The mother of Pestilence" (2:43)—revolutionary France has become authoritarian and puritanical (Paley 1966: 32-33).

4:11-16 These lines refer to the period just before Urizen's fall (Sloss and Wallis 1926: I, 122).

4:11-35 Disturbed by the fluctuation of his emotions (4:16), Urizen tries to control his mind, but he only produces pestilence-breeding clouds of delusion and inhibition, few of which Los can control (Howard 1984: 194).

4:14   Cf. *BU* 10:19-23.

4:31   **The shapes**—spiritual fragments produced by division, fragments on which Los, as poet, tries to bestow human forms (Damon 1924: 360); the remains of the Israelite people that emerged from the wilderness (Tannenbaum 1982: 239).

4:31-43 In response to the arrows of pestilence, Fuzon's body assumes a natural form (Frosch 1974: 47).

4:37   **Forty years**—spent by the Israelites in the wilderness of Sinai (Damon 1924: 360). Fuzon on the Tree of Mystery is parallel to Moses' brazen serpent [of Num. xxi] as well as to Christ on the Cross (Bloom 1963: 179).

4:41   **Asia**—the continent of tyrannical religions (Damon 1924: 125) and the homeland to be of the Hebrews (Damon 1924: 51).

5:5-7 Cf. Job xxxviii.7 (Tannenbaum 1982: 243).

5:8-9 **mountain...valleys**—punning allusions to the female anatomy (Hilton 1981: 203n6).

5:14   **harvests**—In Eternity, Urizen harvests the "Bread of Thought" (Damon 1924: 361). See also Raine's observation cited 2:32n.

5:34 **science**—"knowledge," according to Damon (1924: 361), who is giving the usual eighteenth-century meaning of the word, but Percival (1938: 21, 25) explains "eternal science" as "complete illumination" or "the higher enlightenment."

Designs

pl. i Urizen, who is about to hide the anguished Ahania, is "Kissing her and weeping over her" (2:35) (Binyon 1926: 117) in front of the mountains of Jealousy (Erdman 1974: 211). He has conflicting feelings of despair and longing (Bindman 1977: 96).

pl. 1 Cf. 2:38-43 (Binyon 1926: 118). Ahania has become a formless voice—see 4:45-49 (Erdman 1974: 211). In spite of Urizen's attempt to subjugate her shown on pl. i, she here asserts her independence (Ackland 1982: 174).

pl. 5 Contradicting the views of Damon (1924: 361), Thomas Wright (1929: I, 76), and Keynes and Wolf (1953: 94), who respectively interpret the design as fallen Urizen or fallen Albion, as Fuzon under the rock of the Decalogue, and as fallen Urizen, Erdman (1954a: 289 [315]; 1974: 213) points to the detailed signs that here are body parts left by the guillotine. Paley (1978b: 34-35) agrees, while Bindman (1977: 96) perceives the remains of defeated Titans.

The Book of Los

Most commentators agree that *The Book of Los* is to some degree a story of failure. Damon's claim (1924: 123) that the products of Los's labour are the material sun and the natural man is widely accepted. Percival (1938: 73) regards the former as a substitute for the sun of Eternity, which is the unfallen Urizen, and Howard (1984: 204-05) observes the contrast between the "Human Illusion" (5:56) with which Los is left and Eno's initial image of freedom in Eternity. Bloom (1963: 183-84) condemns Los for having created an astronomical globe that imposes cyclic time, and for having reduced Urizen to an Adamic human, while Howard (1984: 205) criticises him for joining the light of prophetic vision to "the bony links of abstraction" only to end with a solar idol. However, Beer (1969: 93-94) charges Urizen with sheltering behind his four rivers of Eden from the sun's energy and thus thwarting Los's prospect of resurrecting the fallen Human. Exceptionally, Fisher (1961: 199) argues that Los recovers lost light and heat to create the "living sun," which the fallen mind sees as the natural sun. Damon's contention (1924: 359) that Los's orb is "the Sun of Poetry" is taken up by Blackstone (1949: 76), who notes that reason darkens it. Rose (1971a: 63-64) emphasises that Los must fall to learn how to regenerate.

As Imagination, Los is impaired when Reason cuts itself off from the rest of mental life (Bloom 1963: 182). Blake is showing, says Howard (1984: 199), that it is creative imagination that determines how we perceive the world. Beer (1969: 92) describes Los's mind as producing its own void and, as it becomes better organised, causing element to replace vacuum. Gallant (1978: 23-24) commends Los for coping with the void better than Urizen: he organises it instead of striving against it (*BU* 3:13-17; *BL* 4:49-53). Similarly, Howard (1984: 199, 204-05) remarks that though there is an element of selfhood in Los's struggle, he does recover a certain amount of lost vision, and Ault (1974: 154) maintains that the glow of his illusory sun enables him to bestow a form on Urizen. In Webster's view (1983: 178-81), Los's painful experiences are essentially those of the infant ejected from its emotional paradise as it discovers it has an existence distinct from its mother's.

There is disagreement over the chronological relationship of *The Book of Urizen* and *The Book of Los*. Sloss and Wallis (1926: I, 105) and Bloom (1963: 182) agree with Damon (1924: 122) that the latter commences about the time that Los is appointed as the Eternals' watchman (*BU* 5:38), but Frye (1947: 254) specifies the fourth chapter of *Urizen* as marking the point where *Los* begins, and Gallant (1978: 22) asserts that that point comes well after *Urizen* ends. In Deen's opinion (1983: 72), there has been a change in the myth since the slightly earlier volume, for Los now acquires a material body before he binds Urizen, who formerly initiated creation.

Several sources have contributed to *The Book of Los*. According to Howard (1984: 200-05), the poem parodies both Plato's *Timaeus* and the first chapter of Genesis, implying that these ancient texts portray the same creator. Tannenbaum (1982: 251-70) finds in Los both the God of Gen. i, who moves upon the face of the waters, and the Samson of Judg. xiii-xvi, who is traditionally regarded as a solar hero. The borrowings from Genesis are combined, according to Ault (1974: 150-54), with Newton's void, his gravity that links bodies in long chains (5:13-16) and his heat-producing light, and with Descartes' vortex (5:14-17), his light-producing heat and his light-conducting fluid (5:10-11). In Paley's eyes (1970: 67-68), both Urizen and Los fall into Boehme's Dark World of the isolated First Principle that Satan entered when he rejected the Light of the Second Principle. Finally, Stevenson (1971: 282) notes that Los's fall echoes that of his fellow artisan Mulciber from heaven (*PL*, I, 740-44) as well as that of Satan through Chaos (*PL*, II, 932-34).

Details

3:1   Comparing *FZ* 6: deleted passage l. 10ff/ E820-21/ I, 139ff with *J* 48:18, 30ff, Damon (1924: 122, 359) deduces that Eno is identical with the Earth-Mother Enion. Considering her name an anagram of "one," Wicksteed (1954: 199) regards her as the chaos from which creation emerges. Bloom (1963: 182) terms her "a mother of fallen existence," while Fisher (1961: 197) holds that though she is the mother of the succession of time in the natural world, she is also a Daughter of Beulah who enjoys glimpses into Eden. Damon (1924: 367) thinks her name an anagram of "eon."

3:2   **the chariot of Leutha**—the body (Damon 1924: 359); affection combined with the desire to perpetuate one's identity by reproducing (Fisher 1961: 197-98). Leutha is a temptress, argues Bloom (1963: 182), and to guide her chariot is to participate in sexual deception, but Stevenson (1971: 279) believes she is not malign in this context. Fisher (*loc. cit.*) suggests her name comes from "Luvah" (lover) and "Lilith" (the animal qualities of the natural man).

3:3   **the day of thunders**—the time of the Fall (Damon 1924: 359).

3:4   **Oak**—error according to Damon (1924: 359) and a Neoplatonic symbol of materialistic earthiness according to Harper

(1961: 171), but Stevenson (1971: 279) suggests the epithet "eternal" may indicate that this is not a malignant Druid tree.

3:27-30 On earth, "the flames of desire" become destructive (Beer 1969: 91). They are flames of Eternity which Los stamps out because he envies their freedom (Stevenson 1971: 279). They represent Los's wish to act (Ostriker 1977: 920). Like Urizen before him (*BU* 5:12-27), Los feels they are hostile (Howard 1984: 200-01).

3:31 **bound in a chain**—of cause and effect (Damon 1924: 122). When desire is severed from affection, Los (perception) is "Compell'd to watch Urizen's shadow" (3:32) in a world become solid and opaque (Fisher 1961: 198).

4:6 Egypt stands for empire, which assails art (Damon 1924: 359). The marble of Egypt alludes to the thirty cities of *BU* 28:8-10 and to Egyptian animal idols which blasphemed against the divinity of the human form (Gallant 1978: 22-23); or to the worship of Thoth in the form of an unmarked black stone as described in Jacob Bryant's *A New System of Mythology* (1774-76) (Tannenbaum 1982: 274). Thomas Wright (1929: I, 78-79) supposes the marble to be the self-doubt to which genius is liable and from which Los breaks free only to fall into error. To Fisher (1961: 198), it is the opaque prison that obscures perception.

4:39 **our world**—Though the phrase is part of a simile, Howard (1984: 201) may be right in believing that it indicates Los is now in astronomical space. (Cf. Rosenberg 1970).

4:42 **oblique**—The direction of Los's fall changes from vertical to oblique when his "wrath" gives way to "contemplative thoughts" (Sloss and Wallis 1926: I, 105). It changes first (4:35) from perpendicular to whirling, making life in the fallen world cyclic, and then becomes oblique, after the pattern of Lucretius' atoms, whose swerve or *clinamen* initiates creation (Frye 1947: 257; see *De Rerum Natura*, II, 216-24, 292).

4:46-53 Los has fallen into the sea of matter (Raine 1968: I, 239). Space now contains fire and pieces of earth (Howard 1984: 201).

4:54 It is through the lungs, which in Swedenborg correspond to Understanding, that Los first communicates with his material environment (Damon 1924: 359). They indicate a mind buoyed up by the power of thought—that mind goes on to create a body that can live under the Sea of Time and Space (Hilton 1983: 87).

4:57 **Polypus**—a collection of vague, unorganised feminine emotions, the image of emasculating tentacles being derived from Ovid [*Metamorphoses*, IV, 366-67] (Percival 1938: 65-66); the product of bodily fibres and conduits, eventually a mass of purposeless living matter that—in Blake's epics—infects the universe (Miner 1960); undifferentiated tissue (Bloom 1963: 183); sexually generated life without a spiritual component, the description being indebted to Erasmus Darwin (Raine 1968: I, 239-41); an entity that parodies the definite form made visible by a clear outline or circumference (Welch 1978: 238); according to the French biologist Buffon (1707-88), a form intermediate between animal and plant, but also, in eighteenth-century usage, a kind of tumour sometimes found in the lungs (Hilton 1983: 88-89); at once the fecundity of nature, a caricature of human brotherhood, and proliferating uncertainty (Paley 1983b: 214-15); both a body furnished with organs and fallen humankind (Howard 1984: 202). Damon (1924: 375, 444) identifies the polypus of *The Four Zoas* and *Jerusalem* with "human society" and "the social system."

5:3-9 The heavy is comparable to Urizen, the thin to the fire of Eternity, and it is a hopeful sign that Los distinguishes between them (Sloss and Wallis 1926: I, 105-06). The separation is a parody of the separation of light from darkness in Gen. i.4 (Bloom 1963: 183); it alludes to both Plato's *Timaeus* 52e-53a and Gen. i.7-9 (Howard 1984: 202-03). The heavy is solid, the light gas (Stevenson 1971: 279).

5:11 **fluid so pure**—apparently the thin element (Sloss and Wallis 1926: I, 112); perhaps the air—cf. *PL*, VII, 263-65 (Stevenson 1971: 284).

5:12-14 Bloom (1963: 183) thinks Los's sight of Urizen's backbone a parody of Moses' sight of the back parts of God (Exod. xxxiii.23).

5:20-21 **built/ Furnaces**—acquired technique (Damon 1924: 123).

5:26 **his**—Urizen's.

5:39-40 Being infinite, the furnaces endow time with a prophetic element contrasting with the constricting power nature gives it (Rose 1971a: 58).

5:46   See *BU* 10:36-37n and 20:18-21n.

5:48   **no light**—Urizen puts out the light or truth even of this temporal sun, though he cannot assuage its heat or wrath (Damon 1924: 123). The light that is absent is "spiritual or intellectual light" (Raine 1968: I, 230).

5:52-57   This passage draws on Plato's *Timaeus*, 38c-d, 73e-74a (Howard 1984: 203). The obscured "Orb of fire" consists of energy and imagination confined "in material forms—including language" (Hilton 1983: 70).

5:53   **four rivers**—The rivers of Eden become the fallen senses, says Bloom (1963: 184)—though there are five of these. Stevenson (1971: 285) recognises that they are also blood vessels.

5:57   Urizen is still the Old Testament lawgiving God, who "made darkness his secret place" and whose "pavilion round about him were dark waters and thick clouds of the skies" (Ps. xviii.11)—see p. 118 above.

Designs

pl. 1   Eno (Damon 1924: 359).

pl. 2   Los (Damon 1924: 359) enclosed in his black marble, which is starting to break (Keynes 1976), or else in plain rocks (Bindman 1977: 96), or in his "Solid/ Without fluctuation" (4:4-5), namely the element earth (Howard 1984: 201). Erdman (1974: 214) suggests that the giant form is "metaphorically related" both to Los in his black solid and the Human Illusion of the close.

pl. 3   This intriguing but minute design challenges sharp eyes. There is no doubt that Urizen, wearing the papal triple crown (Paley 1978b: 34) and holding either an open book (Erdman 1974: 214) or the Tablets of the Law (the latter quite clearly, according to Bindman [1977: 96]), is presiding over his spiderish web; but is he himself imprisoned as well as imprisoning (Beer 1969: 94), is he, in his egg-shaped 'O,' a despairing creature awaiting birth (Erdman, *loc. cit.*), and is the web the "bowels" of Ps. xl.8 (AV marginal reading), in which the Law is contained (Miner 1981: 331)? The figures at the corners of the web may be a young man and maiden (Damon 1924: 359), "Man and Woman" (Margoliouth 1951: 109), a naked Adam

and Eve who will not avert their gaze from their master to es-
cape (Erdman, *loc. cit.*), two adoring cherubs (the whole being
a parody of ordinary sacred art) (Bindman, *loc. cit.*), oppres-
sive parents (Webster 1983: 181), or a couple trying to disen-
tangle themselves from the Net of Religion (Paley, *loc. cit.*).
Above the heading "Chap. I" is a tiny figure reading, if Keynes
(1976) is right, the Book of the Law.

pl. 5   According to one view, Los kneels, with his arms in a cruci-
form posture, looking at his sun (Damon 1924: 359), which he
is about to throw down (Keynes 1976, referring to 5:42-43).
Another opinion is that although he takes the form of the Hum-
an Illusion (Binyon 1926: 119) and is shrouded in the darkness
and clouds of the last line, he is joyful because his sun is rising
in the abyss (Erdman 1974: 215).

Notes on Criticism for Chapter 9

The Four Zoas

There can be no reasonable doubt that the subject of *The Four Zoas* is the fall and resurrection of Albion together with his constituent Zoas and their Emanations, nor can it be disputed that Albion is both every individual and humankind collectively. But why did Blake abandon the poem? It is the first prophetic book in which he makes a serious attempt to portray the course of redemption, and Frye (1947: 308-09) believes that at the crucial point it does not explain how Los causes the Last Judgment to begin (117:1-13/ E386/ IX, 1-13) and that the Spectre of Urthona does not fit into the poem's structure. Less specifically, Fisher (1961: 225-29) complains of a failure to amalgamate the themes of love's degeneration and of the transcendence of mortality, and Mellor (1974: 211-13) is troubled by the poet's inability to co-ordinate his conceptions of spiritual regeneration in this world and in the afterlife. Focusing on the transition from *Vala* to *The Four Zoas*, Sloss and Wallis (1926: II, 6-7, 241-42, 260) observe that the latter expresses a belief in Divine Providence absent from *Vala* as well as from the earlier prophetic books, and Margoliouth (1951: 115) finds that Blake insisted on adding material that belongs only in *Milton* and *Jerusalem*. Erdman (1954a: 270-71 [294-96]) was formerly confident this material consisted of a series of responses to changes in Anglo-French relations, which altered so rapidly that they eventually baffled his design, while Bentley (1963: 191) is sure the additions have nothing to do with historical events but consist of explicitly Christian passages—he also (1958: 103-08) judges that they are often incompetent and involve the neglect of literary quality in favour of intellectual content. Erdman is now (1964b: 113, 117-18) less certain that Blake was reacting to current events but believes Bentley's assessment of the revisions is coloured by some misreadings of the poet's handwriting.

Blake's failure to complete his recasting of *Vala* appears to be intimately connected with the confusion surrounding the text of Night the Seventh, which many critics from Sloss and Wallis onwards (1926: I, 138) have recognised as containing the crisis of the poem. There has been a long controversy as to whether the two Nights numbered seventh were intended to be amalgamated (Damon 1924: 159-60), whether VII was written as a replacement for VIIb (Sloss and Wallis 1926: I, 137), whether Blake composed the replacement but was uncertain about discarding the original Night (Erdman 1954a: 339-40 [366]), or whether he hesitated between the two versions (McNeil 1970: 374).

In 1956 Margoliouth (xii-xiii) recognised the importance of Blake's having added, in two instalments, a long passage to the original end of VII. (85:22/ E360/ VII, 332 was at first followed by "End of the Seventh Night"; later 85:31/ E367/ VII, 341 was followed by "The End of the Seventh Night [E837, 838-39].) This passage, as Erdman has come to agree (1978: 137), broke the continuity that previously existed between VII and VIIb: they were originally written as consecutive segments of a narrative.

The problem facing a modern editor is neatly summarised by Stevenson (1968). The original end of VII (85:22/ E360/ VII, 332) is continuous with the beginning of VIIb (95:15/ E360/ VIIb, 1), while the beginning of VIII is continuous *both* with the end of VIIb (95:14/ E367/ VIIb, 301) *and* with the new ending of VII (90:67, E371/ VII, 499). If VII is allowed to lead directly to VIII, VIIb is robbed of its place. If VIIb is omitted, the editor takes drastic action without Blake's authority and excludes important material. If VIIb is placed between VII and VIII, further complications arise.

The new ending of VII describes the transformation of Los into an unambiguous agent of redemption and shows him working harmoniously with Enitharmon. If VIIb follows, 96:19-27/ E361/ VIIb, 40-48 brings an inexplicable relapse to a warlike Los (Kilgore 1978: 109-10) and to a state of tension between him and his Emanation (Lincoln 1978: 126). Following a proposal of Lefebvre (1978), Erdman (1978) has decided to overcome this difficulty by inserting VIIb between the original conclusion of VII and its final ending. The price of this solution is the interruption of VII's continuous narrative of the redemption of Los and Enitharmon beginning with the breaking of the latter's heart gates. Blake did not do the extensive rewriting that alone could have allowed the inclusion of both VII and VIIb without leaving a significant blemish on the poem.

Margoliouth (1956: xxvi) and Bentley (1958: 106-07) believe that Blake ruined *Vala* when he attempted to turn it into a thoroughly Christian work, and DiSalvo (1983: 138) refers to it as "that brilliant shower of fragments." Nevertheless Margoliouth and DiSalvo join other critics in seeking a plan not entirely submerged in the confusion, and Frye (1947: 270) notes the dreamlike quality, which fits well with the closing words of the original title, "a DREAM of Nine Nights" (E818/ K263)—Albion, he says, is the dreamer. Damon (1967: 143) even finds in this epic the invention of the literary "dream technique."

As regards the later books, there is general agreement with Frye's view (1947: 278) that while the cycle of Orc's rise and corruption runs through the fifth to seventh Nights, the beginning of Los's regeneration in the seventh leads to the climactic appearance of the Christ and Antichrist in the eighth and apocalypse in the ninth. Several scholars also detect a chronological framework for the whole epic. In a pioneering analysis, Max Plowman (1927a: 154-58, 175) observes that each of the first four Nights focuses on the fall and division of a Zoa (the order is Tharmas, Luvah, Urizen, Urthona), that Orc's birth in the fifth completes the pre-biblical Fall, that in the sixth Urizen tries to take religion to Urthona's realm, and that the three remaining Nights incorporate the Fall of Genesis, the Crucifixion, and the Last Judgment. To this Frye (1947: 278) adds that the falls of the Zoas coincide with the endings of the Gold, Silver and Bronze Ages and, in the fourth case with the beginning of our Iron Age at the time of Adam. Other theories include that of Ostriker (1977: 923, 930), who classifies only the first Night as pre-biblical and implies that Urizen's creation in the second is a version of the one at the beginning of Genesis, and that of Margoliouth (1956: xvi), who traces a movement from the opening "cosmic fantasy" through Blake's own time in Night VIIb to the future in Night the Ninth. Percival (1938: 180, 253-55, 268) identifies the Deluge of the third Night with Noah's Flood, which, he claims, divides an ancient monistic world where Enion's web imprisons Tharmas from a dualistic world of spirit and matter, good and evil. Locating the main divisions after the third and sixth books, Wilkie and Johnson (1978: 81-82) group the Nights into three triads dealing successively with the Fall, the resultant state, and the redemption; within each triad, the first member is said to focus on instinct, the second on passion, and the third on reason. With the emphasis on characters rather than Nights, Deen (1983: 136-38) interestingly suggests that Blake contrasts the behaviour of Urizen and of Los towards Luvah, whom they both fear: whereas Urizen, though asked to pity him (23:7/ E313/ II, 7) smelts him in a furnace, Los, after binding him in his form of Orc, acquires compassion towards him and becomes a Christian poet. However, Deen's insistence that *The Four Zoas* centres on a movement from the serpentine to the human form depends on suppositions not substantiated by the text—e.g. that Urizen becomes a serpent and that Enitharmon turns into Jerusalem (1983: 124, 138, 150).

In discussing the theme, Max Plowman concentrates on psychology (1927a: 134, 137-38, 158, 175, 178). The epic, he believes, surveys the history of instinct (Orc), which survives its infant crucifixion, defies religion, and nourishes the distinctive identity of the individual in the material world; eventually it becomes overweening and is superseded by imagination, which brings the soul back to its God-like essence.

Later interpretations employ psychoanalytical terms or have a political slant. Thus Frye (1947: 300-01) equates Tharmas with the id, Urizen with the superego, and Luvah with the libido; Bloom (1965: 955) adds that Los and the Spectre of Urthona are the active and passive elements of the Ego; and Mellor (1974: 204-05) locates the ego in Tharmas and the id in Luvah. Oedipal conflict, alleged to be everywhere present in the work, dominates the exposition of Webster (1983: 203-49), who believes that Blake has come to see woman as the emasculating mother and wife exemplified by the four consorts of the Zoas, and thus no longer regards sex as a way to liberation.

Opting for Jung, Preston (1944: 12, 15) observes the striking parallel between Urizen, Luvah, Tharmas and Los and that psychologist's four functions—thinking, feeling, sensation and intuition respectively. In a detailed Jungian reading, Gallant (1978: 50-58, 64, 71-75, 106) argues that Albion, his Zoas, and the Emanations all fear the formlessness of non-existence, which is the abyss or void of the unconscious. The unconscious, she holds, is also represented by the ocean and the furnace that devour Tharmas and Luvah, and Urizen vainly tries to block it with the Mundane Shell and Tree of Mystery as Los does with Urizen's body; only its negative side appears until the construction in the seventh Night of Golgonooza, a mandala or emblem of psychic wholeness—like the Council of God, the Seven Eyes, the visions of Beulah's Daughters, and the pastoral episode in the final Night. Ostriker (1982: 158-59, 164n8) disputes Gallant's contention (1978: 53-54) that the Emanations are not sufficiently differentiated to represent the animas of the Zoas, but that they collectively consitute the feminine archetype, Enion and Ahania being positive, Vala and Enitharmon negative.

In Erdman's view, the major characters also have political meanings (1954a: 270, 273-74, 284 [294, 298-99, 309]). Albion is the oppressed English people whose utterance is divided between the outspoken, much censored journalist Tharmas and the poet Los; during his periods of silence, when Tharmas acts as his conscience, Los (in the person of the Spectre of Urthona) lives by the engraving that his smith's work symbolises, while fallen Tharmas is a satirist. Their antagonist and censor is Urizen. On the international level, Urizen stands for Britain and Luvah for France.

Treating the epic as a history of civilisation, DiSalvo (1983: 11, 15, 80-86, 139-41, 152, 164-70, 194-235) blames the conflict between Urizen and Luvah for the decline from a cultured, egalitarian, fraternal society to Urizen's tyrannical, priest-ridden monarchy (24:5-33:36/ E314-22/ II, 22-286). After the collapse of the latter (43:27/ E329/ III, 135), Los is unable to fulfil Tharmas's command that he reconstruct society (51:32/ E335/ IV, 149). Degenerating, he crucifies the Orc who brings radical Christianity (60:28/ E341/ V, 101), but when the French Revolution becomes corrupt (80:27-48/ E356/ VII, 135-56), the Spectre of Urthona restores his memory of history (85:37/ E368/ VII, 347). This endows him with a new vision that enables him and Enitharmon to guide the masses—the Spectres of the Dead (90:4ff/ E370/ VII, 435ff)—despite the Antijacobin repression of the penultimate Night, to the lost egalitarian Eden where arts and science flourish.

Crehan (1984: 52-53, 293, 303-10), who also sees Eden as an image of Blake's ideal republic, combines political with psychological exegesis. In his view, Urizen declines from a monarch of the Enlightenment into a harsh despot—this probably reflects the middle class's rejection of Enlightenment ideas on the outbreak of war with France. The neurotic fear and guilt induced by repression are especially visible in Tharmas and Enion, two halves of a split personality, whose infantile regression is represented by their rebirth (130:4/ E398/ IX, 507). Similarly, Los displays inner conflict when he nails down his earlier rebellious side (60:28/ E341/ V, 101).

Two critics doubt that the structure of *The Four Zoas* really is chronological. McNeil (1970: 385) states that the entire action may be confined to the moment after Albion's disintegration, and Evans (1972) maintains that the final Night is a mirror image of the first eight, in which much of their content reappears transfigured (see the headnote to Night the Ninth below). These commentators are eager to explain away all allusions to the supernatural: McNeil (1970: 383) regards the references to a benevolent transcendent realm as ironic, while Evans (1972: 326-27) proposes that the Council of God and Daughters of Beulah may represent human potential for the recovery of vision.

Several critics agree with Damon (1967: 142) that in Los the epic has a hero, though Margoliouth (1956: 144) has a strong case when he argues that it is only in the passages added to the original Night VII, passages in which he reunites with his Spectre and Enitharmon, that he acquires such stature. In this work, he becomes a richly complex character—the imaginative faculty, a god who creates, a poet and artist, and a fallen man who is husband and father. Of all the characters in the poem, Margoliouth rightly observes (1956: xxii), Los and Enitharmon are most like human beings.

Commenting on the complexity of the Zoas in general, Howard (1984: 211) states that each one has some attributes of the other three, and Paley (1970: 111-12) acutely notes that the fallen and unfallen Urizen represent respectively the discursive and intuitive reason of the Renaissance while he can also be tyrannical authority imposing "irrational dogma." Paley's altogether reasonable position (1970: 94-95) that the poem is a *psychomachia* or allegory of inner conflict is disputed by McNeil (1970: 374), who finds that the persons lack exact allegorical equivalents.

Albion—the name belongs to *The Four Zoas*; in *Vala* he was called only the Eternal Man—is a many-layered symbol rather than a character. Besides every individual and all humankind, he is the cosmos (Damon 1924: 143-44, 154), the English nation (Erdman 1954a: 270 [294]), a mountain rising from the postdiluvian Sea of Time and Space (Hilton 1981: 197), and, according to McNeil (1970: 375), a "frame for the action." He is even, says

Deen (1983: 17), himself a poem generated by his Zoas. Sloss and Wallis's claim (1926: II, 129), endorsed by Ostriker (1977: 922), that he is one of a company of eternals is convincing despite Stevenson's objection (1971: 452) that his containing all mortals leaves no room for any peers: by disintegrating, he gave rise to our present cosmos and its inhabitants as his former comrades have observed with horror. There has been much discussion of the differing accounts of his fall scattered through the poem. While Deen (1983: 125) believes Blake deliberately withholds a definitive account, Stevenson (1971: 291) may be right in asserting that the Ambassadors from Beulah narrate the facts accurately (21:8-19:5/ E311-12/ I, 476-549).

Frye is not the only critic to relate the Zoas who issue from the collapsing Albion to four ages. Beer (1969: 108) revises Frye's scheme by connecting Luvah with the Golden Age, Urizen with the Silver, and Tharmas with the Bronze, while Harper (1965: 113-15) links shepherd Tharmas and ploughman Urizen to the pastoral epoch, weaver Luvah and blacksmith Urthona to the urban, commercial period. Other correspondences are with levels of vision, the seasons, prescientific humours and elements, and body parts. Unlike Damon (1967: 150), who holds that Generation does not yet have a separate existence in *The Four Zoas*, Preston (1944: 15) associates Urizen, Luvah, Tharmas and Urthona respectively with the single, double, threefold and fourfold vision of Ulro, Generation, Beulah and Eden. (In Beer's paradigm [1969: 107-08], Los and Luvah change places.) Perhaps, as Frye (1947: 287) says, Luvah is associated with summer and his antagonist Urizen with winter, though Rose (1970c: 447) claims that in the first four Nights the descent of Tharmas precedes Luvah's spring and Urizen's summer, while the round of seasons that characterises the night of the Fall gives birth in Night the Ninth to an eternal day. Percival (1938: 150-61) traces a detailed but speculative correspondence between the fortunes of the Zoas and the signs of the zodiac. Fittingly enough, Crehan (1984: 301) couples Tharmas with melancholy and water, Luvah with blood and fire, Urizen with phlegm and air, and Los with choler and earth.

The action of the poem, says Stevenson (1971: 334, 336, 395), takes place from one point of view in a vast human body (cf. also Percival 1938: 15; Erdman 1954a: 285 [311]); indeed Harper (1961: 244) suggests that the myth of Albion's division may be indebted to the myth of the torn asunder and reunited Bacchus and its Neoplatonic interpretation. Frye (1947: 277) modifies Murry's assignment (1933: 189) of the head to Urizen, the heart to Luvah and the loins to Tharmas by switching the positions of Tharmas and Luvah and allotting the legs to Urthona; Damon (1967: 143) identifies Urthona with the spirit. Beer (1969: 103, 108) substitutes hands and feet for legs, while Percival (1938: 16, 20, 28, 36, 42, 299) assigns Urizen, Luvah, Los and Tharmas to the head, heart, loins and whole body respectively, and asserts that when the last named disintegrates at the Fall, the human being degenerates from a fourfold to a threefold state.

The most obvious source of *The Four Zoas* is *Paradise Lost*—Damon (1967: 422) remarks that until his repentance Urizen's career parallels quite closely the Miltonic Satan's. Damon also (1924: 166-67) conjectures that Paracelsus' *Philosophy Addressed to the Athenians* is a major influence. With its increased biblical content, the revised version of the epic, argues Raine (1968: I, 237), is not only more Christian than *Vala* but less Neoplatonic. While Helms (1974: 131) finds a biblical model for Albion in Isaiah's personification of a sick Israel, Frye (1947: 271) parallels Albion's fall with those of Nebuchadnezzar (Dan. iv.28-33), Arthur's empire, and Atlantis, and Paley (1970: 94) proposes that the sources of his collapse may include the fate of the Celestial Man of the Hermetic writings, who meets disaster when he tries to embrace his own image. Damon (1924: 143-44) derives Blake's character from the traditional personification of England, from the Grand Man who constitutes Swedenborg's heaven, and from the cosmic man of Cabbala, Adam Kadmon. This last, notes Ansari (1969: 217), is originally androgynous, as is (Percival 1938: 126, 183) Boehme's unfallen Adam. Howard (1984: 217-19) perceives in Blake's poem extensive parody of Edward Young's *Night Thoughts* and especially of Young's belief in sacrificial atonement and eternal punishment.

Night the First

The opening Night, universally admitted to be confusing, introduces two important new characters into Blake's myth. Tharmas stands for the senses and the body (Damon 1924: 155,

156). Percival (1938: 42) conceives him as the energy, partly sexual, of the physical body, and in Eternity as the energy of the androgynous body in which all things are contained and hence as a principle of cosmic unity. In a parallel way, Bloom (1963: 195) regards him as the instinct that holds together all the elements in a human being. The unfallen Tharmas gives real existence to the mind's creations (Frye 1947: 274, 278-79), and after his collapse he is fallen Innocence (Frye 1947: 284). As a shepherd, he is akin to Beulah and represents the pastoral side of Jesus (Frye 1947: 277-78, 284)—Stevenson (1971: 288) credits him with compassion; he is associated with the sea because he is liable to storms of anger (Frye 1951: 190-91). As the tongue (Frye 1947: 280-82), he is equated by Erdman (1954a: 273 [298]) with the various forms of communication, especially communication under the clamp of censorship. Raine (1968: I, 278-80, 285) believes that at one time Blake conceived of him as the Eternal Man and that much confusion arises in this Night because the poet is drawing on too many complex Gnostic and Hermetic myths of the Fall.

Enion, a more elusive character, has been explained as the earth mother and the generative instinct (Damon 1924: 156) and as the root, now unconscious, of creativity (Frosch 1974: 190). Percival's view (1938: 42-43, 172-73) that she is outward nature or its creator but is faced with the threat of degenerating into "dark, blank, abstract matter" overlaps with Raine's conviction (1968: I, 290-93) that she is indeed matter, while external, perceptible nature is represented by Vala.

The two names are probably derived from Blake's own Enitharmon (Margoliouth 1956: 159), but alternatively or also they may be connected with Hesiod's Thaumas, son of Earth and Sea and his niece the sea nymph Eione (Frye 1947: 284). Other suggested sources of the name and nature of Tharmas include the Sanskrit *Tamas* meaning "desire" (Damon 1924: 365), Thomas (Erdman 1954a: 234 [253]), Father Thames (Wicksteed 1954: 29), and the god Dionysus, who was torn apart and resurrected and whom Jacob Bryant, in his *A New System of Mythology* (1774-76), identified with Thamas or Thamuz (Raine 1968: I, 303-05). The name Enion may be an anagram of Innoe, signifying innocence (Margoliouth 1956: 142) or related to Homer's Ino, who lends Odysseus a girdle that, like Enion's web, represents the body (Raine 1968: I, 385-86n15). She also has an affinity with Demeter, who searches for her daughter Persephone (Frye 1947: 279). Miner (1958: 207) mentions the river Enion in the Sixth Song of Drayton's *Poly-Olbion*, and Erdman (1974: 366) suggests that her name puns on "anyone."

Much more puzzling than Enion is the Spectre of Tharmas, who rapidly drops out of the poem, perhaps because a limit is imposed in Night the Fourth on the chaos that he represents (Frye 1947: 283) or because he symbolises an aspect of natural life more effectively represented by Vala (Raine 1968: I, 288). Frye also (1947: 281-82) regards him as the satanic selfhood that Tharmas degenerates into, and Raine (1968: I, 279-81) identifies him with the Thaumas or "Wonder" of the *Hermetica*, a mixture of humankind and nature. Damon (1967: 123) explains him as the cruel male sex urge, while Percival (1938: 43) regards him as doubt that enters into nature as created by Enion and deprives it of a spiritual aspect it once had, and Bloom (1965: 949) accuses him of being a self-destructive drive towards chaos.

Neither Damon's theory (1924: 366) that Tharmas falls because of the repression of sexual passion (Enion) nor Bloom's claim (1963: 201) that he falls because he neglects his own duty of unifying the whole being to indulge in the pleasure of imagination (Enitharmon) contradicts Frye's thesis (1947: 279) that Night the First deals with the lapse into the temporal and natural world, where time and space are born as Los and Enitharmon. These characters Damon (1924: 156) identifies with the poet and his inspiration born in this Night out of a conflict between their father, "the Bodily Reason," and their mother, "the Generative Instinct." Later (1967: 122, 142, 399) Damon adds that the narrative is about the passage from childhood Innocence to adolescent Experience, where guilt at one's emerging sexuality helps to engender the spirit of poetry. On slender grounds, Wicksteed (1954: 29) speculates that the curious tale reflects Blake's own courtship opposed by his or his prospective bride's father. DiSalvo (1983: 159-60) believes that Tharmas and Enion and Los and Enitharmon illustrate a decline into monogamy, and Webster (1983: 203-11), emphasising drawings as well as text, theorises that Blake deals with his fear of the castrating female by showing power transferred from Enion to Tharmas.

Although the name Luvah occurs once in *The Book of Thel* (1789), Luvah and Vala are likewise effectively introduced as

new characters. According to Frye (1947: 235, 287), they symbol-
ise the sexual element of all life, and Luvah is both the energy of
nature's cycle and the blood in the body. Percival (1938: 28-33)
conceives of Luvah as the energetic emotions, which reappear in
Orc, and of Vala not as external nature (as Sloss and Wallis [1926:
II, 245] imply) but as the passive emotions, which degenerate into
cruel sexual love and into nature's inner spirit or "ethical force."
Nature's visible form Percival locates in Enion, but Vala is a much
stronger candidate for this role. Frye (1947: 234) classifies Vala as
an earth goddess, Margoliouth (1951: 114) is confident that she is
the veil or illusory outward appearance of nature, and Damon
(1967: 428) regards her as a symbol intended to show how
"everything we see is an exteriorization of our emotions." Her veil,
remarks Raine (1968: II, 174-77), has many sources, including the
veils of Isis, the Shulamite (Cant. v.7), Minerva, and Spenser's
Nature (*FQ* VII.vii.5). Thomas Wright (1929: I, 27) notes that her
very name derives from "veil," Wicksteed (1954: 24) adds as a fur-
ther possibility "vale," and Murray (1974a: 13) proposes "Luvah,"
its syllables being reversed. She is both the veil of the pudendum,
observes Ostriker (1982: 160), and the veil of the Tabernacle and
Temple, and she links debased sexuality with organised religion.
Taking a different approach, Kiralis (1959: 195) argues that the
fallen are apt to see Vala only as nature (*J* 18:29-30, 30[34]:9), but
that she is primarily Jerusalem's Shadow—i.e. the rational moral-
ity that Ulro substitutes for forgiveness as the foundation of liberty.

Damon (1924: 364-65) points to the Norse prophetess
Vala as the source of the Blakean name, but Bentley (1963: 167)
objects that the poet had no access to an edition of the *Eddas* con-
taining this name, and Margoliouth (1956: xviii) adds that Vola in
Mallet's *Northern Antiquities* is unlike Blake's character. Miner
(1958: 204) suggests as other northern sources Valkyriar
(Valkyries) and Valhalla, and Beer (1969: 110) alludes to the
ancient concept of nature as the veil of Isis. Luvah's name prob-
ably comes from "lover" (Damon 1924: 311); Erdman (1954a: 307
[333]) also sees a connection with "lava" in view of the way the
god is smelted down to molten metal (28:3-10/ E318/ II, 113-20).

Details

p. 1 *Title* **Zoa**—a Greek word in Revelation (iv.6 *et al.*) translated "beasts" in the AV. These "beasts" surround the divine throne and correspond to the "living creatures" round the Divine Chariot in Ezekiel's vision (i.5ff) (Damon 1924: 144-45). Blake treats the Greek plural as an English singular (Sloss and Wallis 1926: II, 257). While Harper (1969: 240-41) believes that Blake is also influenced by the Pythagorean reverence for *four* as a divine number, Herrstrom (1981: 76-77n16) argues that he is contrasting the fourfold Divine Humanity with the tyrannical Trinitarian deity. Summerfield, however, (1981: 15) demonstrates Blake's respect for the Trinity from 1798 onwards.

p. 2 *Motto* **Rest before Labour**—The sleep of the fallen state precedes the toil required for redemption (Wilkie and Johnson 1978: 7-8); unconscious mental preparation in a dream is the prelude to artistic creation (Schotz 1977); the passivity of Beulah comes before the creative work of Eden (DiSalvo 1983: 346). McNeil (1970: 375) thinks this motto is ironic, for the Zoas rest *after* labour.

p. 3 *Epigraph* The dark powers referred to in Eph. vi.12 may be one or more of the following: rulers like Pitt, George III and Napoleon (Erdman 1954a: 269 [293]); spiritual and temporal authority (Damon 1967: 323); the fallen Zoas (Bloom 1963: 190); the Elohim who created the natural man (Damrosch 1980: 258).

3:1-3/ E300/ I, 1-6 The Aged Mother is Eno of *The Book of Los* (Bloom 1965: 948), a muse, whose song consists of the whole epic (Damon 1967: 125)—or of three lines (3:4-6/ E300-01/ I, 9-11) (Wilkie and Johnson 1978: 13). According to Stevenson (1971: 292), the three opening lines are a subtitle. Rose (1971a: 66) claims that geographically Eno represents "a unified Britain."

3:5/ E300/ I, 10 **the Universal Brotherhood of Eden**—Brotherhood is the relationship that prevails in Eternity, from which marriage and parenthood are absent (Frye 1947: 388, 395).

3:9-4:6/ E301/ I, 14-23 There is much dispute as to whether this passage refers to Los (Damon 1924: 156), as the syntax strongly suggests, or to Albion (Fisher 1961: 229), or even to both (Wilkie and Johnson 1978: 16). Harper (1961: 228-29, 236-37), opting for Urthona-Los, claims that he is Blake's version of Bacchus or Dionysus, whose scattered fragments are reassembled and whom the Neoplatonists identify with divine intellect.

3:9/ E301/ I, 14 **the fourth immortal starry one**—the fourth figure in Nebuchadnezzar's furnace (Albion's heart)—see Dan. iii.25 (Bloom 1963: 194-95); the sun, fourth planet in the Ptolemaic system (Raine 1968: II, 26).

3:11/ E301/ I, 16 **Urthona**—As the darkness that gives birth to the light of the unfallen Urizen, Urthona is both Boehme's First Principle and the Poetic Genius (Percival 1938: 36-37). He is the imagination in the individual as opposed to Jesus, "the universal Imagination" (Damon 1967: 426).

4:1-3/ E301/ I, 17-20 Los's art of poetry appeals through the ear (Damon 1924: 365), and his emanations are the English fairies of his invention that were later worshipped as heathen gods (Ostriker 1977: 924). The nerves of the ear are the site of the Fall, for Satan whispered his temptation to Eve (Miner 1981: 311, citing *PL*, IV, 799-809).

4:3/ E301/ I, 20 **Beulah**—This name may derive from Is. lxii.4, where it means married and is applied to the restored land of Israel (Wicksteed 1910: 101), or from Bunyan's Beulah, a land beside the border of heaven in *The Pilgrim's Progress* (Sloss and Wallis 1926: II, 134). Less plausibly, Frye (1947: 390, 449n57) suggests that its origin is in Plato's *Phaedrus*, 248. Damon (1967: 42) identifies Blake's Beulah with the subconscious.

4:6/ E301/ I, 24 Tharmas is the Parent Power because in Eternity he mediates between perceiver and perceived (Fisher 1961: 235); because he is communication, and sexual communication brings parenthood (Erdman 1954a: 274 [298]); because he holds together the other Zoas (Bloom 1963: 195); or because he is Innocence and hence the parent of subsequent states (Wilkie and Johnson 1978: 20). Raine (1968: I, 280) thinks he was originally conceived as the father of the Zoas. Frosch (1974: 180) remarks that since he is the sense of touch, desire (Luvah) acts through him, so he is the first to be affected by Luvah's rebellion.

4:7/ E301/ I, 25   Lost emanations are those tragically unable to return to the whole person, who is their source (Stevenson 1971: 294). Tharmas's, says Erdman (1954a: 274-75 [299-300]), is the subject matter and inspiration of his censored writings.

4:8/ E301/ I, 26   **the Living**—the other Zoas (Bloom 1965: 948).

4:9/ E301/ I, 27   **Jerusalem**—the totality of Albion's emanations, his spiritual state when his faculties are working in harmony, and "the liberty of regenerated souls" (Percival 1938: 17)—hence "a collective figure, a 'building of human souls'" (Raine 1968: I, 207, quoting *M* 6:19); human freedom, which can only be sustained by love (Schorer 1946: 318) or by mutual forgiveness (Kiralis 1959: 195-96, citing *J* 54:3-5); human conscience (Fisher 1959: 167, 171); Albion's lost Emanation, who, as in Revelation, is both city and woman (Bloom 1963: 196, 259); Divine Immanence, blindness to which brings on the "stern demands of Right & Duty" (4:19/ E301/ I, 37) (Spector 1984: 19). In Damon's view (1967: 207), the freedom she represents is lost at puberty. Her character and vicissitudes are portrayed much more fully in the epic that bears her name.

4:10/ E301/ I, 28   The "Labyrinth" in which Jerusalem and Enion can hide from accusations of sin is both nature and natural religion, the latter teaching that human nature is good; it takes the forms of the "Shadowy semblance" of 4:24/ E301/ I, 42 and Enion's laboriously woven Circle of Destiny of 5:24/ E302/ I, 87 (Percival 1938: 172-74). Blake regards hiding someone in a maze as evil (Stevenson 1971: 295), and Tharmas has degenerated for he once took pleasure in beauty visible to all (Beer 1969: 125).

4:13/ E301/ I, 31   **It is not Love I bear to [Jerusalem]**—Keynes retains the MS. reading "Enitharmon," which is consistent with the ambassadors' statement (22:22-24/ E312/ I, 525-27) that when Urthona divided Enitharmon fled to Tharmas. Stevenson (1971: 290-91) finds in Enion's subsequent jealousy the origin of her quarrel with him. Damon (1924: 366) blames rather the suppression of sexual desire for Tharmas's and Enion's fall.

4:15-25/ E301/ I, 33-43 The elements of life taking refuge with Tharmas are those newly condemned by Albion, whose puritanism begins to infect Enion (Percival 1938: 171-72). Only with an influx from spirit (Tharmas), which she is trying to seduce with "delusive beauty," can matter (Enion) enjoy more than a ghostly existence (Raine 1968: I, 293-94, 319-20). After their first sexual experience, Tharmas and Enion feel embarrassment, guilt, and awareness of the difference between subject and object (Frosch 1974: 56-57, 60).

4:24/ E301/ I, 42 **Hide me some Shadowy semblance**—Stevenson suggests "in" or "as" should follow "me" (1971: 295). The phrase signifies "take refuge in an illusion," and is also Catherine Blake's plea that her husband will hide his dangerous opinions behind seemingly innocuous writings (Ostriker 1977: 925). See also 4:10/ E301/ I, 28n.

4:30/ E302/ I, 48 **Stalks of flax**—the matter of which the mortal body is made, which Blake associates with the flax in which Rahab hid the Israelite spies in Jericho (Josh. ii.6); for Rahab as weaver, see 113: 19/ E376/ VIII, 220 (Raine 1968: I, 286-87).

4:39-40/ E302/ I, 57-58 Tharmas wrongly sees the generative impulse as satanic though lovely (Damon 1924: 366). Enion tempts the journalist Tharmas to publish his politically suspect writings (Erdman 1954a: 275 [300]).

5:1-4/ E302/ I, 64-67 Protective outward forms (symbolically, females) perish so that the spirits (males) may wake again into Eternity (Percival 1938: 85). The underlying image of butterfly emerging from chrysalis represents the soul's death and resurrection (Chayes 1970b: 238-39).

5:3/ E302/ I, 66 Visitors from Eden take temporary finite forms in Beulah (Percival 1938: 56).

5:7/ E302/ I, 70 **A tabernacle**—perhaps the universe (Sloss and Wallis 1926: I, 145); the material body (Ostriker 1977: 925).

5:11/ E302/ I, 74 **the circle of Destiny**—the realm of cause and effect (Damon 1924: 366) and of fixed space and time (Blackstone 1949: 81), a circle Tharmas describes to preserve Enion (Harper 1961: 143); the web of bloodthirsty natural life not governed by a conscious mind—hence the waywardness of 5:21-22/ E302/ I, 84-85 (Frye 1947: 279); "the round of nature" (Percival 1938: 68), where everything runs in repeated cycles (Bloom 1965: 949); an Hermetic image for the mortal body (Raine 1968: I, 286, 385-86n15). The Tharmas initiates its motion, which is completed during Enion's nine-day labour with the result that the terrestrial globe of 5:25/ E302/ I, 88 appears (Margoliouth 1956: 161). See also 4:10/ E301/ I, 28n and 9:19-23/ E305/ I, 232-36n.

5:13-14/ E302/ I, 76-77 **the sea**—the Sea of Time and Space (Damon 1924: 366), water being a symbol, Neoplatonic in origin, of material existence (Harper 1961: 163-69). The "Woof" also suggests matter (Hilton 1983: 150).

5:15/ E302/ I, 78 **His Spectre issuing from his feet**—It comes from his lowest part (Damon 1924: 366). The absorption of Tharmas, the energy of the body, in an outward physical form marks an early step towards a materialistic view of nature (Percival 1938: 173). The Spectre is the Shadow or reflection in water mistaken for the true self (Raine 1968: I, 278, 415n22).

5:19/ E302/ I, 82 **nine days & nights**—a reference to the nine nights of the epic and the nine days and nights of "the first fall" (Bloom 1965: 949). Cf. *PL*, I, 50.

5:27/ I, 303/ I, 90 **her woven shadow**—the "Created Phantasm" of 5:53/ E303/ I, 118, *viz.* Tharmas's Spectre (Margoliouth 1956: 161). Miner (1969: 470n44) views the product of Enion's weaving as a "garment-body."

5:29-43/ E303/ I, 94-108 Bloom (1963: 198-200) blames the Daughters of Beulah for losing their nerve in the face of the Circle of Destiny and creating the deadly Ulro; also (1965: 949) for naturalising instead of humanising Tharmas's Spectre. Stevenson (1971: 298) praises them for providing a place of hope and an opportunity for the Spectre to begin regenerating.

5:37/ E303/ I, 102 **Ulro**—This name for the material fallen world may derive from one or more of the following: "ultimate error" (Margoliouth 1956: 102); "ruler" or "rule" (Fisher 1959: 168); "unrule" or "unruly" (Bloom 1963: 199); "Ur" and "low" (Ostriker 1977: 1056); "ultimate ratio" (Peterfreund 1981: 219); "roll" (Hilton 1983: 221, 293n26, citing 5:25/ E302/ I, 88—also *J* 12:51 and 42: 17-18).

5:43/ E303/ I, 108 **the Gate of the Tongue**—the capacity for self-expression and the composition of poetry (Damon 1924: 367, 369); the Edenic power of communication (DiSalvo 1983:

169). The tongue is the centre of Tharmas's sense, touch, which includes taste and which unifies the perceptions of all the senses (Frosch 1974: 131-35). Stevenson (1971: 298) cites *J* 38(43): 24—"the affectionate touch of the tongue is clos'd in by deadly teeth."

5:44-47/ E303/ I, 109-12 Matter (Enion) repents having seduced spirit (Tharmas) into descending (Raine 1968: I, 295).

7:9-13/ E304/ I, 182-87 Percival (1938: 114) holds that Tharmas's identity disappears as Enion absorbs him—i.e. the external, feminine side of Albion swallows the inner, masculine self. The mixture of colour and clearness may come from the Hermetic allegory of light (spirit), which contains the colours of the spectrum, mingling with water (matter) (Raine 1968: I, 282).

9:6/ E304/ I, 219 **Non Entity**—This phrase signifies a view of matter as totally lifeless (Percival 1938: 44) or, as Plotinus holds, deprived of any illumination from the Divine Mind (Harper 1961: 242), and as having quantity without qualities (Raine 1968: I, 291-92, citing Plotinus, *Enneads* III.vi.7).

9:9/ E304/ I, 222 As a muse who exists outside time, Eno saves the children of body (Tharmas) and earth (Enion) from dissolution (Harper 1961: 140).

9:19-23/ E305/ I, 232-36 The young poet and his inspiration (Damon 1924: 367) enjoy a brief, happy residence in Beulah (Wilkie and Johnson 1978: 30). They are also time and space born of matter (Raine 1968: I, 285). Nine is the number of the world of time and generation and ten the number of restoration to Eternity in Neoplatonic symbolism (Harper 1961: 140-42). The nine Spaces are the Ptolemaic planetary spheres (Hilton 1983: 119).

9:28/ E305/ I, 241 **desart, flood & forest**—the desert of Newtonian particles, the flood of formless matter, and the forest of nature (Raine 1968: II, 139).

10:8/ E305/ I, 259 Catherine Blake reproaches her husband for his lack of involvement in the world and for keeping her down (Damon 1924: 367).

10:11-12/ E305/ I, 262-63 Luvah and Vala move from their home in the heart to Urizen's place, the head; the passive emotions like mercy and pity represented by Vala become Albion's exclusive ideals, and the pity soon becomes self-righteous

(Percival 1938: 20, 28, 33, 168-69, 298). Luvah and Vala, rising from their home in the loins through the heart, which is Tharmas's, to the brain, impose the cyclical pattern of nature and generation upon Eden (Nurmi 1976: 129).

10:15/ E305/ I, 266   Enitharmon appears in Albion's dreams in the guise of Vala (see 10:21/ E306/ I, 272), for which he rebukes her in 10:17-25/ E306/ I, 268-78 (Wilkie and Johnson 1978: 32).

10:20-21/ E306/ I, 271-72   The veil is Vala's, and the morning is false because passion has usurped the guiding role of reason (Margoliouth 1956: 165).

11:3/ E306/ I, 281   Enitharmon has provoked Los (Margoliouth 1956: 166) by trying to make him jealous (Stevenson 1971: 306).

11:10/ E306/ I, 288   Cf. Is. i.5-6 (Helms 1974: 131).

11:12-14/ E306/ I, 299-301   These evocative but ambiguous lines may refer to Luvah's fate as a dying god and the ensuing war (Nurmi 1976: 133) or to the future crucifixion of Christ in the form of Luvah (Ostriker 1977: 926). Raine (1968: I, 186) sees a reference to Psyche, the fallen soul, whose sisters give her a knife to murder her invisible divine lover, claiming he is a demon, while Erdman (1954a: 296-97 [322]) considers that Los, rejecting Enitharmon's delusion that the French Revolution was a "false morning," warns against the crucifixion of the revolutionary spirit.

11:15-18/ E306/ I, 302-05   The "lamps" are stars and Los believes that being material they are located in Tharmas's world (Damon 1924: 367); their appearance, like that of all natural phenomena, originates in the human mind (Raine 1968: II, 70). Percival (1938: 37) asserts that Los alludes to his working harmoniously with Urizen in Eternity, but Stevenson (1971: 308) holds that Los claims the brain, normally allotted to Urizen, for himself and Enitharmon. The "bright world" and "cold expanse," suggests Hilton (1983: 95), are two views of the same location.

11:21/ E306/ I, 308   In calling on Urizen, the Muse Enitharmon commits herself to reason instead of prophecy (Ostriker 1982: 159).

11:23-24/ E306/ I, 310-11   Enitharmon foretells Napoleon's seizure of power on 9 November, 1799 (Erdman 1954a: 297 [322-

23]). She prophesies the victory of psychic chaos (Gallant 1978: 163).

12:5/ E306/ I, 316 **The Wandering Man**—the erring Eternal Man (Margoliouth 1956: 166-67).

12:6/ E306/ I, 317 The parties referred to are Los and Vala or Enitharmon (Erdman 1965: 745).

12:10/ E307/ I, 321 **the prince of Light**—the use of this title for Urizen alludes both to Satan (Lucifer or light-bearer before his fall) and—ironically—to the Enlightenment (Bloom 1965: 950).

12:18-20/ E307/ I, 331-33 Thomas Wright (1929: I, 144-45) perceives here an echo of Blake's resistance to Hayley's attempt to turn him into a conventional artist.

12:27/ E307/ I, 339 **the Divine Vision**—Jesus—see 33:11/ E321/ II, 261. The phrase signifies "the Divine Imagination" (Harper 1961: 126) or consciousness of human unity (Blackstone 1949: 63, 384-85), for from an eternal standpoint all individuals constitute the One Man who is Jesus.

12:32-33/ E307/ I, 343-44 This passage closely follows the account of Messiah's advance on Satan, *PL*, VI, 767-70 (Stevenson 1971: 309). The spirits on the wind are Britain's Mediterranean fleet, the chariots her troops about to disembark (Erdman 1954a: 294 [320]).

12:35-37/ E307/ I, 346-48 Urizen has triumphed over the other three Zoas (Ostriker 1977: 927). The blood in the heavens is the wine in the cup, and it is going to afflict the world—see Jer. xxv.15 (Hilton 1983: 180-82).

12:38-39/ E307/ I, 349-50 The sun is the sun of imagination and the shell the Mundane Shell (Damon 1924: 368). Blake refers to the stagnation of eighteenth-century art (Harper 1961: 128-29).

12:40-44/ E307/ I, 351-55 The context supports neither Damon's opinion (1924: 368) that the reunion is happy and the bread and wine represent love nor Margoliouth's supposition (1956: 168) that it is the spirits of 12:32/ E307/ I, 343 that eat and drink. More plausibly, Percival (1938: 62, 150) regards the festivity as a "Feast of Mortality" and as Urizen's vain attempt to harmonise the contraries into which Urthona has split. Bloom (1963: 203) claims that pity divides Los's soul, he falls in love, and he and Enitharmon devour the bread and wine of temporal existence, while Frosch (1974: 167) asserts that Los's pity leads to secret sex and near blindness to the Divine Vision and Ostriker (1977: 927) takes the more extreme view that this is a hideous Mass at which the bread and wine are humankind. The word "nervous" has the eighteenth-century sense of "potent" (Hilton 1983: 97).

13:1/ E308/ I, 356 **Sphery Song**—the Music of the Spheres (Stevenson 1971: 310).

13:4-10/ E308/ I, 359-65   When Luvah changes from love to hate, Jesus puts on this Zoa's robes (Sloss and Wallis 1926: II, 179) to rescue love (Blackstone 1949: 85). The robes Jesus assumes are of blood, which signifies the flesh (Damon 1924: 372) and also Luvah's prolonged suffering (Stevenson 1971: 324)—though the eternal Luvah is associated with wine, fallen Luvah is associated with blood (Howard 1984: 212, 226). The biblical allusions are to the "vesture dipped in blood" of Rev. xix.13 (*ibid.*: 223) and to Jesus' scarlet robe of Matt. xxvii.28 and Mark xv.17 (Paley 1973b: 122); the latter image Blake employs to equate Incarnation with Crucifixion and apocalypse (Damrosch 1980: 295), for he regards the Incarnation and Crucifixion as being essentially the same self-sacrifice (Altizer 1967: 78). Deen (1983: 129, 158) identifies the robes with Vala, and Frosch (1974: 167) identifies the One Man with Albion instead of Jesus.

Damon (1967: 428) states that the vision of Incarnation is meaningless to Luvah and Vala, while Wilkie and Johnson (1978: 178) assert they are not so fallen that they cannot see it.

13:11-18/ E308/ I, 366-70   According to Harper (1965: 115), this is a description of the Golden Age preceding the fall of the shepherd Tharmas. Those unwise enough to heed Enion fail to recognise what a marvel the world is (Margoliouth 1956: 168).

14:7-16:17/ E308-10/ I, 386-433   The singers are followers of Urizen (Erdman 1954a: 294 [320]), and most critics agree with Blackstone (1949: 83) that they delight in war, though Damon (1924: 368) unconvincingly claims that they treat of the good and bad sides of revolution. At the marriage of fallen time and fallen space, they rejoice, judges Raine (1968: II, 139), that the world is now in Urizen's power. Margoliouth (1956: 168) believes there may be references to contemporary wars but rejects Erdman's view (1954a: 294 [319-20]) that the song specifically celebrates Nelson's victory at the Battle of the Nile (1798) and Napoleon's failure to take Acre. Beer (1969: 160-61) detects a prophecy that the war provoked by Luvah and Vala will destroy them, while Hilton (1981: 199-200), citing Ezek. xxxix.17-19, suggests that the wedding feast combines sacrificial slaughter of enemies with a victory banquet. Gallant (1978: 55) considers the chant—and the ensuing lament of Enion—an expression of a threat of disorder from the unconscious.

14:7ff/ E308-09/ I, 386ff Ephraim and Zion represent the kingdoms of Israel and Judah respectively (Bloom 1965: 950). Ephraim's words may end with "drink the lives of Men" (Keynes 1925: II, 15) or with "the Human form is no more" (Ostriker 1977: 927).

14:15-20/ E308-09/ I, 394-99 Industry is turning to steam engines, which are classified according to their horsepower (Bronowski 1944: 64)—cf. next note. The ruling class fear rebelliousness in the villages, though there is war fever in the cities (Erdman 1954a: 295 [320-21]).

15:1/ E309/ I, 402 **The Horse**—i.e. the war horse (Erdman 1954a: 295 [321]).

15:3/ E309/ I, 404 Nanavutty (1957: 170) sees an allusion here to the Hindu myth of the Creator as a spider spinning the cosmos from his entrails.

15:7-8/ E309/ I, 408-09 **Luvah...no more**—Keynes (1925: II, 15) ascribes these words to the bow string; Stevenson (1971: 311) classifies them as part of the demons' narrative within their song. They signify that war is ungoverned passion (Ostriker 1977: 927).

15:7-15/ E309/ I, 408-16 The syntax supports Stevenson's view (1971: 312) that the sunbeam is the messenger whose report of the clamour of Luvah's triumph causes Urizen ("the Mighty Father") to advance defiantly; the presence of the sheephook supports Ostriker's opinion (1977: 927) that the stars are Urizen's troops, the sunrise his movement to battle, and "the Mighty Father" the shepherd Tharmas. Wilkie and Johnson (1978: 256) assert that the Father is either Tharmas or the sun, and DiSalvo (1983: 196) considers the first beam to be Luvah in the role of Lucifer.

16:1-3/ E309/ I, 422-24   Cf. 25:40ff/ E317/ II, 72ff; the "furrows" are channels that lead the molten metal into a mould (Stevenson 1971: 312).

16:9-12/ E309/ I, 430-33   A prophecy of Orc's birth and chaining (Stevenson 1971: 312). The singers want Orc and the Spectre of Urthona to fight each other, not Urizen (Bloom 1965: 950). They applaud the bondage, which signifies the cult of war and the exclusion of passion from art (Wilkie and Johnson 1978: 34).

18:11/ E310/ I, 464   **the Palm tree...the Oak of Weeping**—the palm of martyrdom and oak of error (Damon 1924: 368); the palm of the Holy Land and oak of Britain, and probably also the palm of life and oak of Druid sacrifice (Wilkie and Johnson 1978: 35). Erdman (1954a: 294 [320]) sees an allusion to the ground of British victories in Egypt and Palestine—see 14:7ff / E308-10/ I, 386ff and *J* 59:5-6n.

18:15/ E310/ I, 468   **The Rock of Ages**—the limit of spiritual petrifaction (Damon 1924: 368); fallen existence in time (Sloss and Wallis 1926: I, 302); geographically, England (Frosch 1974: 34). Bloom (1963: 407) comments that this is Blake's only providential rock. The phrase seems to derive from Top-lady's famous hymn of 1775 (T. Wright 1929: I, 7), but Blake gives it a completely new meaning (Margoliouth 1956: 149). It occurs as an AV marginal reading to Is. xxvi.4, and there is an allusion to the stone pillar of Gen. xxviii.11, on which Jacob dreamed of communication with heaven (Stevenson 1971: 440, 314).

21:3-7/ E311/ I, 470-74   Cf. John xvii.21-23 (Damon 1967: 105).

21:7/ E311/ I, 475   Mt. Snowdon was in the territory of the Welsh bards, preservers of patriarchal vision (Stevenson 1971: 301, 302). Some British radicals sought refuge in Wales from persecution (Erdman 1954a: 288 [313]).

21:9/ E311/ I, 477   **Shiloh**—the location of the Tabernacle [Josh. xviii.i], frequently associated with Christ (Damon 1924: 368); probably the Shiloh of Gen. xlix.10, traditionally identified with Christ (Bloom 1963: 206); a holy city, later in the northern kingdom of Israel and therefore alienated from true worship (Stevenson 1971: 301); the emanation of France, liberty—see *J* 49:48 (Erdman 1954a: 284 [309]).

21:9-10/ E311/ I, 477-78 Alluding to John xi.3, Blake implies that Albion, like Lazarus, can be raised (Margoliouth 1948: 304).

21:15/ E311/ I, 483 **Conway's Vale**—the setting of Gray's "The Bard" (Ostriker 1977: 928).

21:23/ E311/ I, 491 **the North**—the spiritual quarter [belonging to Urthona] as opposed to Urizen's own quarter, the south (Damon 1924: 369); the quarter where the rebellious Satan defied God—cf. Is. xiv.13 and *PL*, V, 689 (Bloom 1965: 951); Holland, where Britain demanded a free hand in return for accepting Napoleon's (Luvah's) occupation of Italy ("the South") (Erdman 1954a: 285 [311]).

21:29/ E311/ I, 497 **in porches of the brain**—in Britain: Blake equates the head with the British Isles, the body with continental Europe (Erdman 1954a: 285-86 [311]).

22:4-5/ E311/ I, 507-08 Damon charges Luvah with believing (1924: 369) or saying (1967: 306) that the Children of Liberty (Jerusalem) are Anak, Sihon and Ogg; Stevenson (1971: 302) holds that these three are not yet fallen.

22:7/ E311/ I, 510 **arm my sons against me in the Atlantic**—make allies of the Americans, who had been aided by France (Luvah) in their independence struggle (Erdman 1954a: 285-86 [310-12]).

22:13-14/ E312/ I, 516-17 **Luvah pour'd/ The Lances of Urizen**—France either adopted a British kind of tyranny or collaborated with Irish insurgents (Erdman 1954a: 287 [312]).

22:22-25/ E312/ I, 525-28 Cf. 4:13/ E301/ I, 31n. The body shelters pity, which is murdered by the reproductive urge (Damon 1924: 369). Enion (matter) prevents fallen Enitharmon from rising and restoring an imaginative dimension to space (Raine 1968: II, 142). Nature (Enitharmon) becomes totally inert (DiSalvo 1983: 63).

22:27-31/ E312/ I, 530-34 Damon (1924: 369-70) supposes these obscure lines to mean that when the spirit (Urthona) is fragmented, poetry resorts to sex (Enion) for inspiration and degenerates into a serpentine materialism; this world's inhabitants then thrust poetry into a low place. Apparently imagination and the prophetic spirit are immured deep in the fallen realm.

22:32-37/ E312/ I, 535-40 After the ruin of imagination, reason treacherously withdraws; passion, having no object for its anger, becomes so unruly that reason, with Albion's consent, takes over—see 23:1-6/ E313/ II, 1-6 (Stevenson 1971: 303). The British army retreated from Holland late in 1799 (Erdman 1954a: 287 [312]).

22:40/ E312/ I, 543   There is now no boundary to limit Albion's excursions into error (Damon 1924: 370).

19:4/ E312/ I, 548   A near quotation of Ps. xlv.3 (Margoliouth 1948: 305).

19:7/ E312/ I, 551   **the Universal tent**—the "tent of Eternity," of which this world is now deprived (Bloom 1963: 207).

19:9-10/ E312/ I, 553-54   Pointing to their derivation from Zech. iii.9 and Rev. iv.5 and v.6, Damon (1924: 368) describes the Seven Eyes as seven aspects of God employed to represent stages on the way to redemption. Frye (1947: 128, 343, 440n32), who adds a reference to Zech. iv.10, regards them as seven Orc cycles, and Wicksteed (1954: 84-87) views them as diverse human perceptions of the power that governs the universe. Later critics follow Percival (1938: 246-48) in identifying them explicitly with historical periods, and Paley (1983b: 120-27) equates them with the seven thousand years or world-week of Christian tradition. They are first named at 115: 42-50/ E381/ VIII, 398-406. Percival correlates the third Eye, Elohim, with the reconstruction after Noah's Flood, but Frye (1947: 360-65) aligns it with the creation of Adam and plausibly cites Exod. vi.3 to show that the departure from Egypt marks the beginning of the sixth Eye, Jehovah; this is the Hebrew dispensation, which Jesus, the seventh Eye, purges of its non-imaginative element. Contrasting the passages describing the Eyes of God with "The Mental Traveller," Paley (1970: 122-23, 138-41) sees the former as promising both the individual and the world a way of escape from the endlessly repeated historical cycles of the latter.

The Eyes also exist in Eternity, and Rose's conjecture (1970a: 54-55n8) that they are there co-existent or simultaneous is consistent with Altizer's contention (1967: 137-38) that when the first six enter time they fail in their duty and are therefore antithetical to the Seventh. Developing Altizer's notion, Summerfield (1981: 17-18) observes that M 32:10 shows that the Eyes turn out to be not individuals but corruptible states and argues that they may be aspects of God the Father cut off from God the Son. Stevenson, on the other hand, (1971: 507) is confident that they are humankind's benevolent protectors.

Damon (1924: 368) points to a concept analogous to the Eyes in Boehme, and Adlard (1969: 114-17) refers specifically to the Seven Spirits of God in that author's *Aurora* as well as finding an additional source in the Sephiroth of the Cabbala. Raine (1968: II, 210-13) identifies Blake's Seven Eyes with seven fallen Sephiroth. Cf. also Ansari 1969: 213-14.

Shaddai (the Fourth) and Pachad (the Fifth) are Hebrew for "Almighty" and for "fear" respectively. Damon (1924: 389) traces Pachad to Is. ii.10, 19, etc.; Frye (1947: 361, 447n3) believes its source is Gen. xxxi.53.

19:13/ E313/ I, 557   **wander'd in mount Ephraim**—Jesus, who came here after resurrecting Lazarus (John xi.54), will follow Albion and make it a place of regeneration (Bloom 1965: 951). According to Swedenborg, Ephraim stands for the spiritual church's understanding, Zion for its love (Raine 1968: II, 320n10). In Ps. lxxviii, Ephraim is associated with apostacy and "wander'd" connotes "strayed" (Ostriker 1977: 929).

20:1/ E313/ I, 560   **the Emanation**—probably Jerusalem but perhaps Enitharmon (Stevenson 1971: 304).

20:12-15/ E313/ I, 571-74 By fighting each other, Luvah and Urizen reverse the direction of the Divine Chariot's motion (Bloom 1965: 951, citing Ezek. i). The Eternal Wheels contrast with objects that undergo the "mathematic motion" of 33:24/ E322/ II, 274 (Nurmi 1976: 130-31). Damon (1967: 197) usefully distinguishes between intellect, "the source of ideas," and reason, "the process of logic."

Night the Second

There are cosmic, psychological and social dimensions to this Night. Sources for Luvah's usurpation of Urizen's sun are the myth of Phaeton as retold in Ovid's *Metamorphoses*, II (Percival 1938: 30), Plato's version of the story in the *Phaedrus* (Frye 1947: 285-86), and the reference to Lucifer in Is. xiv (*ibid.*). The account of Urizen's ensuing creation comes close to a parody of the account of creation in Plato's *Timaeus* (*ibid.*).

According to Percival (1983: 32-33), who cites 42:1/ E328/ III, 85, Albion's devotion to the passive feelings (Vala) brings about the sacrifice of their active counterparts (Luvah), while Frosch (1974: 181) speculates that desire (Luvah) becomes so obsessed with an existing creation that it wishes to make it external and permanent. Accepting Percival's identification of Vala, Margoliouth (1956: xx) argues that reason allies itself with the milder emotions to suppress the stronger passions, but the milder emotions then weaken and become confined to the service of duty. Damon (1967: 256) holds that the material with which Urizen's lions fashion the cosmos is the melted and solidified substance of Luvah—the visible universe is "Emotion solidified by Reason."

The description of creation is coupled with an exposé of industrial exploitation in which Luvah represents both iron ore and the fraternity of workers while Vala stands for the furnace fuel and the damage done to nature in obtaining and using it (Erdman 1954a: 307 [333]).

Details

23:3/ E313/ II, 3 **these sick'ning Spheres**—the wheels of 20:14-15/ E313/ I, 573-74, which are now the Circle of Destiny (Bloom 1963: 210). The Newtonian heavenly bodies (Raine 1968: II, 69).

23:4/ E313/ II, 4 **this Voice of Enion**—the expression of "the deeply buried instinctual sense of loss and despair" (Wilkie and Johnson 1978: 40).

23:9/ E313/ II, 9 The Feast is Los and Enitharmon's nuptial banquet (Sloss and Wallis 1926: I, 173).

24:5/ E314/ II, 22 **great Work master**—Blake lifts this term for the Creator from Bacon's *The Advancement of Learning*, Book II (Blackstone 1949: 220). Milton repeats it, *PL*, III, 696.

24:8/ E314/ II, 25 **the Mundane Shell**—the layer of matter that covers all things and is sometimes symbolised by the sky (Damon 1924: 370); the universe as it appears to unillumined sense perception and also the historical world of the Twenty-seven Churches (Sloss and Wallis 1926: II, 203); a temporary, doomed world midway between Beulah and Ulro (Percival 1938: 60); both the universe and an ancient empire based on slave labour (DiSalvo 1983: 209-11).

24:10-13/ E314/ II, 27-30 Most of the objects named are constellations (Worrall 1981: 278).

25:8/ E314/ II, 40 Tyburn was the site of public hangings in London. Frye (1947: 372) observes that Blake views it as a form of Calvary, and Damon (1967: 398) notes that Tyburn Brook is a tributary of the Thames.

25:9-14/ E314/ II, 41-46 DiSalvo (1983: 169) perceives here a descent into barbarism.

25:10/ E314/ II, 42 Damon (1924: 370) identifies the moon with Luvah and the sun with Urthona.

25:13-14/ E314/ II, 44-45 The destruction of spiritual freedom (Jerusalem) is associated with Lambeth, site of the Archbishop of Canterbury's palace (Damon 1924: 370).

25:17-18/ E314/ II, 49-50 Damon (1924: 370) suspects an allusion to Gwendolin's drowning of Sabrina and Estrildis (Geoffrey of Monmouth, *History of the Kings of Britain*, II, 4); Stevenson (1971: 316) refers to the civil war battles fought beside the Severn in 1403 and 1471.

25:21, 24/ E314/ II, 53, 56 Damon's identification of Reuben as the lowest type of corporeal human [i.e. the natural man] (1924: 370) is supplemented by Frye's observation that Blake equates their father, Jacob, with Albion (1947: 363-64). For Snowdon, see 21:7/E311/ I, 475n; Penmaenmawr, another mountain of North Wales, is associated with unbelief at *J* 21:35 (Damon 1967: 325), and, because of its fortifications, with war (Stevenson 1971: 668). The nations of 25:24/ E314/ II, 56 are the Israelite tribes (*ibid.*: 317).

25:25-32/ E314, 317/ II, 57-64 Damon (1924: 371) conceives of the Daughters of Albion (named in ll. 29-30) as natural human functions that weave the body and strip nature of her "garments of Spiritual Beauty"; Percival (1938: 69) classifies them as power-hungry counterparts of the Daughters of Beulah; and Erdman (1954a: 305-06 [332]) assails them as the British cloth industry that strips the wool from sheep ("mild demons"), exploits child labour in factories ("dungeons"), and guides armies ("the hounds of Nimrod") as far as the Orient in search of markets. As twelve females who weave war, they strikingly resemble, as Miner observes (1958: 203-06), the subject of Gray's poem "The Fatal Sisters." Stevenson (1971: 317) contrasts their artificial needlework with Jerusalem's eternal curtains, and Bloom (1963: 213, 373) notes that Nimrod [see Gen. x.8-9] is an archetypal tyrant.

25:33/ E317/ II, 65   In this accidentally truncated sentence (Erdman 1965: 748), Reason presides over Stonehenge, which is on Salisbury Plain (Damon 1924: 371), or the Anglican Church is as warlike as the Druids (Bloom 1965: 952).

25:38/ E317/ II, 70   See 28:10/ E318/ II, 120n.

25:40/ E317/ II, 72   Luvah smelted in the furnaces has been explained as love compelled to be chaste (T. Wright 1929: I, 23, 145), as the corporeal body and its energy imprisoned in Urizen's intellectual construct (Bloom 1965: 952), as a being enclosed in a body (Nurmi 1976: 135), as passion severed from the natural world—i.e. from Vala (Paley 1970: 92) or repressed into the unconscious (Gallant 1978: 58-59) and sublimated (Wilkie and Johnson 1978: 110), and as the ore and the workers exploited in factories (Erdman 1954a: 307 [333]). The "Furnaces of affliction," according to Percival (1938: 222, 323), are Los's furnaces, in which humankind passes through "the cycle of experience." Margoliouth (1956: 101) notes their connection with Is. xlviii.10.

25:41/ E317/ II, 73   Vala is a nature goddess to whom the dying god Luvah has been sacrificed (Bloom 1965: 952). She has excited and frustrated desire (Wilkie and Johnson 1978: 47). She is a mother figure co-operating with a tyrannical father (Webster 1983: 212).

26:2/ E317/ II, 78   Luvah's howling derives from the noise of an actual furnace (Stevenson 1971: 634).

26:5-27:20/ E317-18/ II, 81-110   This enigmatic passage is accompanied by drawings of the metamorphoses it refers to. The being that metamorphoses is generally believed to be Vala and therefore nature. Beginning as the worm of the flesh (Damon 1924: 371), she turns into creatures variously interpreted. The Dragon, especially, has been the subject of much guesswork having been identified as the image of Vala that sexual abstinence begets in Luvah's mind (T. Wright 1929: I, 145), as the combined Beast and Whore of Revelation (Erdman 1954a: 308 [334]—Adlard [1972: 112] remarks that from Genesis to Revelation Satan changes from serpent to dragon); as the alchemists' First Matter, which is both poisonous and regenerative (Nanavutty 1969); and as the rebellious Leviathan (nature), who, punished by the biblical Flood, emerges as though from amniotic fluid in the form of a child (nature become remote) (Wagenknecht 1973: 166-68). That child has been regarded as nature become diminutive enough in the Sea of Time and Space to be endurable (Damon 1924: 371), as spectrous (Sloss and Wallis 1926: I, 177), and as a regenerative image that becomes the temptress nature (Bloom 1963: 214-15). Bloom also (1965: 952) sees in the transformations "a natural history of natural religion."

There are strong reasons for criticising Luvah. He has been charged with mistaking the Divine Vision [i.e. Jesus] for "That Human delusion" (Damon 1924: 371), with thinking himself the creator of all animal (including human) life (Margoliouth 1956: 102), with possessive love as shown by his labyrinths (Bloom 1963: 215), with misconceiving Eternity as a chance-ruled chaos (*ibid.*), with being the passion of Albion, who loves an unworthy object in Vala, the illusory outward appearance of nature (Paley 1970: 93-94), and with gradually coming to fear and condemn sex (Wilkie and Johnson 1978: 49-51).

Psychological interpretations claim that Luvah sees Vala as a threatening phallic woman (Hagstrum 1973b: 108-09) and that he is the ego seeking independence from the threatening maternal archetype of the unconscious (Gallant 1978: 59-61).

27:15/ E318/ II, 105 In Eternity, Urizen is reason working on a foundation of perfect faith in God (Percival 1938: 21). Blake may be glancing at philosophers like Descartes who adopt doubt as a first principle.

28:1-2/ E318/ II, 111-12   Luvah (passion) ought not to be patient, and reasoning does not come from the loins (Stevenson 1971: 319). The spectre has a sexual origin (Hilton 1983: 150).

28:8/ E318/ II, 118   **the molten metal ran in channels**—Psychic energy was diverted into approved ways (Gallant 1978: 59).

28:10/ E318/ II, 120 Luvah's bulls of passion contrast with Urizen's horses of instruction (T. Wright 1929: I, 27). The feminine emotions of Luvah have usurped authority over the masculine intellect; the Plough is also the constellation so named—cf. 62:30-31/ E342/ V, 164-65 (Percival 1938: 152, 315). The bulls are Luvah's revolutionary force pulling Urizen's plough, which, like the harrow that follows, creates the political conflicts that must precede redemption; it operates painfully in Ulro (25:38/ E317/ II, 70) before it is cleared of rust in Night the Ninth (see 124:6-10/ E393/ IX, 291-95 [and n]) (Damon 1967: 175, 329).

28:26, 29:2/ E318, 319/ II, 136, 144   Howard (1984: 247n41) traces the cube and pyramid to the account of creation in Plato's *Timaeus*, [where (55d-56b) the cube is the form of earth, the pyramid of fire]. In the account of the creation of the Mundane Shell, Blake is parodying Milton's description of creation in *PL*, VII, and Plato's in the *Timaeus* (Bloom 1965: 963) as well as the work of all the theorists whose mathematics lead to exploitation (Bloom 1963: 216-17).

28:32-29:1/ E318-19/ II, 142-43   **the strong scales..rent from the faint Heart**—justice separated from love (Damon 1924: 371); the constellation Libra, which signifies a brief period of balance between reason and emotion and which marks the high point of the Mundane Shell's effectiveness (Percival 1938: 155-56); it is no longer love that estimates the value of things (Margoliouth 1956: 102).

29:4/ E319/ II, 146   Milton uses the phrase "spun out the Air" in *PL*, VII, 241 (Margoliouth 1956: 103). The metaphor was common in the eighteenth century (Hilton 1978: 80, 82).

29:6/ E319/ II, 148   The weights keep the web taut (Stevenson 1971: 321).

29:7-30:7/ E319/ II, 149-65   The corrupted emotions, symbolised by work at the looms, have a role in the work of creation (Percival 1938: 63). The "woof" and "draperies" are the woof of Locke, which contains the points in infinite space arbitrarily selected for Urizen to start his measurements from (Raine 1968: II, 137). The passage is an expansion of *BU* 19:5-9, where the veil of the Tabernacle, hung with golden hooks, is equated with the sky enclosing the cosmos; these concepts are now combined with Urizen's ensnaring Net of Religion, and the hooks are suns, the caverns mental spaces, and the eagles scientists spreading the threads of their theories, in which they are ultimately trapped—see 29:16-30:1/ E319/ II, 158-59 (Hilton 1978: 82-83). The eagles, with their "Human forms," have a positive aspect (Ackland 1983: 179).

29:12-13/ E319/ II, 154-55   In the seventeenth century, Grimaldi applied the image of wine mixed with water to the diffusion of light (Hilton 1978: 82). It hints at the Eucharist [the wine for which is mixed with water] and hence at redemption (Ackland 1983: 180).

30:2-4/ E319/ II, 160-62   Certain attractive kinds of art block the vision of Eternity (Damon 1924: 372).

30:6-7/ E319/ II, 164-65   Swedenborg conceives of three spiritual and three natural atmospheres conveying heat and light to the lowest level of nature, where they promote the production of seed; Blake's seeds and roots may be respectively new and developed thoughts (Hilton 1978: 83-84). The seeds and roots signify a potential for regeneration (Ackland 1983: 179).

30:8-14/ E319/ II, 166-72 The structure is "the Palace of Reason, the world of Science" (Damon 1924: 372). The "female slaves" are London's despised women brickmakers (Erdman 1954a: 311-12 [338]).

30:13/ E319/ II, 171 **mingled with the ashes of Vala**—perhaps an allusion to the tradition of offering a human sacrifice when the foundation of a building was laid (Margoliouth 1956: 103). Vala (nature) has lost the beauty she had in Eternity (Bloom 1965: 953-54). Scientific rationalism cannot transcend nature but only incorporate her in its structures (Ackland 1983: 182).

30:15-40/ E319-20/ II, 173-98   The Sons are the signs of the zodiac, the Daughters head, heart and loins (Damon 1924: 372). Erdman (1954a: 336 [364]) suspects an allusion to the plan for a national art gallery under the patronage of George III (Urizen). According to Raine (1968: II, 297n42), the structure is modelled on the ideal city of Plato's *The Laws*, and in Gallant's view (1978: 58) it is the Mundane Shell, which is only a useless imitation of the healing symbol of the mandala.

30:21/ E319/ II, 179 The western wall bars the way to freedom (Damon 1924: 372).

30:23/ E319/ II, 181 **His Shadowy Feminine Semblance**—Stevenson (1971: 322) thinks she is Urizen's Shadow, less substantial than his Emanation, but most critics follow Damon (1924: 372) in identifying her as Ahania. As such, she has been conceived as Urizen's sensitive, feminine side (Margoliouth 1956: 112), and as his former wisdom cut off by his obsession with systemisation (Frosch 1974: 189-90). Scholars have speculated on allusions to Nelson's tearful mistress Lady Hamilton (Erdman 1954a: 311 [337]); to Hera, the consort Zeus ejected from heaven (Raine 1968: I, 155); to the mediaeval adoration of Sophia and perhaps the French homage to the goddess Reason in 1793 (Wilkie and Johnson 1978: 53); and to the Neoplatonic veneration of a remote, pure woman (Ostriker 1982: 159).

30:29-42/ E320/ II, 187-200   There is some disagreement as to whether blame attaches to Ahania as well as to Urizen. The east is the side of error (Sloss and Wallis 1926: I, 181) associated with the tyrannies of the European continent (Stevenson 1971: 635), and Blackstone (1949: 84) maintains that Ahania has become jealous and has turned into sadistic desire. Percival, however, (1938: 178) regards her as the desire for perfection to which Urizen allots the western or Edenic side and which drives him to the suppression of his own energies, this suppression being represented by sacrifices. Erdman (1954a: 310-11 [336-37]) links the sacrificial altar with Blake's own tribute to Urizen in the form of his engraving of Flaxman's prospectus for a monument to commemorate British naval victories.

The imagery of this passage mingles allusions to the Hebrew Tabernacle and the Temple; the ten thousand slaves and one thousand men may derive from I Kings v.14 and II Kings xxiv.16 (Miner 1969: 278-79).

31:1ff/ E320-21/ II, 215ff   The suffering of the Israelite slaves in Egypt (Sloss and Wallis 1926: I, 182) is identified with those of Psyche ("the suffering soul in exile") forced to labour by Venus and with those of modern industrial workers (Raine 1957b: 834).

31:4/ E320/ II, 218   The Lord addressed appears to be God, but Wilkie and Johnson (1978: 56) are unsure whether he is Urizen, Luvah or Albion.

31:9-10/ E320/ II,229-30   Damon (1924: 372) sees Luvah's feet as the lowest part of suppressed passion. Ostriker (1977: 931) perceives an allusion to the pillar of fire that led the Israelites through the wilderness.

32:6-7/ E321/ II, 238-39   Enitharmon plans to subjugate reason by separating it from pleasure (Damon 1924: 372).

32:7/ E321/ II, 240   **the wondrous work**—It is based on Satan's Pandemonium, *PL*, I, 710ff (Raine 1968: II, 71); it is a Ptolemaic cosmos based on occult mathematics (Wilkie and Johnson 1978: 52-53).

32:9/ E321/ II, 242   The stars apparently come from Eternity (Margoliouth 1956: 104).

32:16-33:3/ E321/ II, 249-53   DiSalvo (1983: 210) sees the towers and irrigation channels as closely resembling those of Babylon.

33:5-7/ E321/ II, 255-57   Blake is contrasting the material world's seductive beauty with its deadly nature (Harper 1961: 166). The "World of Tharmas" is Milton's Chaos (Ostriker 1977: 931).

33:14/ E321/ II, 264   **Lest the state call'd Luvah should cease**— Christ is preserving love when Luvah metamorphoses into hate (Sloss and Wallis 1926: II, 179), or he is saving the passional and sexual element in the human (Nurmi 1976: 136), and France and the ideals of her Revolution (Erdman 1954a: 351 [378]). Beer (1969:141) suggests that even an imperfect church retains some truth in a rationalistic world, and Percival (1938: 230) associates this passage with the self-sacrifice of the Reprobate to save the Redeemed (*M* 11:21-23).

33:16-26/ E322/ II, 266-86   Blackstone (1949: 220-21) proposes that Blake is challenging Bacon's assertion in *The Advancement of Learning* that God, not being human, did not lay out the stars in regular and beautiful geometrical patterns.

33:16/ E322/ II, 266   **a golden chain**—the rationalism that prevents a deeper fall—cf. the "vital chains" of Plato's *Timaeus*, 38e (Damon 1924: 372); the moral law, which later becomes iron (Percival 1938: 61); cf. *PL*, II, 1051 (Margoliouth 1956: 104).

33:17/ E322/ II, 267   **the Body of Man**—all creation perceptible to the senses (Fisher 1961: 235).

34:16-22/ E322-23/ II, 302-08   Spiritual beauty disappears when the poet confuses it with pleasure (Damon 1924: 372). Enitharmon has now lost the charms of the lily and rose (Grant 1969: 350-51). She begins to act towards Los as both a spurned mother and a jealous wife (Webster 1983: 214-15).

34:24/ E323/ II, 310   **the God**—Urizen (Stevenson 1971: 326), who converts Enitharmon to Mystery (DiSalvo 1983: 63).

34:41-47/ E323/ II, 327-33   When Enitharmon turns to Urizen, Los seeks revenge (34:97-98/ E324/ II, 383-84) by depriving Urizen of Ahania: imagination attacks the domination of reason (Wilkie and Johnson 1978: 57-60).

34:54/ E323/ II, 340 The poet needs inspiration to survive (Damon 1924: 158).

34:58-92/ E323-24/ II, 344-78 Beer (1969: 128) comments that Enitharmon retains touches of vision despite her craving for power.

34:67/ E324/ II, 353 The nine spheres are the seven planets, the sun and the moon representing spirit, passions and intellect (Damon 1924: 372). The reference is to the music of the spheres (Harper 1961: 296). Cf. 64:3/ E343/ V, 200.

34:74-75/ E324/ II, 360-61 These lines describe "sexual consummation" (Wagenknecht 1973: 199).

34:80-81/ E324/ II, 366-67 The babe is Christ (Damon 1924: 372). All living things experience an infant stage (Damrosch 1980: 170).

34:97-98/ E324/ II, 383-84 See 34:4/ E322/ II, 290.

35:1-13/ E324-25/ II, 387-99 Damon (1924: 373) notes the kinship of this passage to Job xxviii, Margoliouth (1956: 106) points to the echo of verses 12-13 of that chapter in 35:11-13/ E325/ II, 397-99, and Bloom (1965: 954) notes a phrase from Zech. viii.17 in 35:2/ E325/ II, 388. The song, says Erdman (1954a: 315-16 [342-43]) laments the end-of-the-century famine caused by intermittent poor harvests and grain hoarding. Percival (1938: 174) supposes the planted oath to be the invidious belief that nature and human nature are good; Harper (1961: 176-77) identifies the dog as a Neoplatonic earthbound demon and the snake as an emblem of material existence; and Raine (1968: I, 297) adds that Enion is the dust of the earth (Gen. ii.7, iii.17-19), which nourishes weeds and the serpent. In McGann's view (1973: 17-18)—he cites Matt. xix.21— Enion misses the chance to pass through Experience to apocalypse; in Gallant's opinion (1978: 62) she is responding to power-hungry Enitharmon's song much as she responded to that of the gloating "Demons of the Deep" (16:13/ E310/ I, 434).

35:9-10/ E325/ II, 395-96 Damon (1924: 373) interprets brass as "false charity," iron as war, the moon as Enion's passions, and the sun as her inspiration; Margoliouth (1956: 106) speaks of a merciless sky, a stubborn earth, a dead moon, and a sun that brings disease. In Beer's view (1969: 129), this Urizenic world lacks the moon's threefold and the sun's fourfold light. Most useful of all is Stevenson's citation (1971: 329) of the brass heaven and iron earth of the great curse in Deuteronomy (xxviii.23).

35:12-15/ E325/ II, 398-401 Erdman (1951a: 215) perceives a dual allusion to recent famines and to Blake's "plowing" his unsold copperplate designs to Young's *Night Thoughts*. Crehan (1984: 167-68) refers to the increased pace of enclosure to boost war production.

36:7/ E325/ II, 412 There were epidemics on the Continent (Erdman 1954a: 315 [343]).

36:17-19/ E326/ II, 422-24 Enion is the earth goddess; Ahania sees that the puritanical condemnation of sensory pleasures will lead to the condemnation of all pleasure (Percival 1938: 27). Ahania is the earth and she feels threatened when she realises that matter (Enion) verges on the non-existent (Raine 1968: I, 292, 417n5).

Night the Third

Ahania now appears in a new and much more amiable role. Percival (1938: 25-26) identifies her with all the desires of the mind and also with its energy-giving periods of rest and reverie, in which it incubates new ideas; Bloom (1963: 217, 222, 229) conceives of her as intellectual delight and compares her with Athena and the Wisdom of Proverbs viii. According to Nurmi (1976: 136), Urizen rejects her because her account of Albion's worshipping another infuriates him. In Paley's view (1970: 96-97), he spurns sexual pleasure (an aspect of Ahania) in order to ward off passion but plummets into Tharmas's realm of sensation. Weiskel (1976: 72-74, 76) observes that he compares her with Vala, whom he blames for seducing Albion. What he does not appreciate, argues Brisman (1978: 254-56), is her attempt to correct his distorted perception by focusing his attention on that of Albion, who sees Urizen as faded and Luvah as a shadow. Ackland (1982: 177) sensibly remarks that Urizen falls because in rejecting Ahania he rejects some of his own major attributes. In Stevenson's eyes (1971: 330-31), both the Zoa and his Emanation are partly right and partly wrong: Urizen is arrogant and Ahania has some desire for power over him. Developing this interpretation, Webster

(1983: 217-19) asserts that Ahania seems kind and gentle, but he has reason to fear she may emasculate him (43:5-22/ E328-29/ III, 113-30) and collaborate with Orc, his potential supplanter; she and Vala undermine his defence, symbolised by an orderly universe, against female power.

Details

37:1-2/ E326/ III, 1-2 Nurmi (1976: 136) notes the reminiscence of *PL*, II, 1ff, and Gallant (1978: 64) perceives an image of an ego stubbornly refusing to recognise the unconscious.

37:3-10/ E326/ III, 3-11 Deprived of peace by Enion's lament at the end of the second Night, Ahania expresses her anxiety to Urizen (Damon 1924: 158).

38:2-6/ E326/ III, 14-18 Most critics agree with Damon (1924: 373) that the Prophetic Boy is Orc, whom Bloom (1965: 954) regards as Tharmas's (the ocean's) foster-son. However, Wagenknecht (1973: 200-01) thinks there is a suggestion of Los about him, too, and Ostriker (1977: 933) considers he is indeed Los, born from Tharmas in the first Night. Damon (1924: 158) explains "the dark Ocean" as the Sea of Time and Space.

38:7/ E326/ III, 19 **Must grow up to command his Prince**—This does not happen, but Paley (1970: 102) believes that the passage was written while Blake retained hope in the French Revolution and intended Orc to contribute to revolutionary change.

38:8-9/ E326/ III, 20-21 Space will give birth to nature, and time will beget passion (Damon 1924: 373). Within space and time, nature and her consort parody the relationship between Jesus-Albion and Jerusalem (Rose 1968b: 230). Urizen foretells the birth of the Shadowy Female and Orc (Ostriker 1977: 933).

38:15/ E326/ III, 27 **the Eternal One**—the Eternal Man, whom Ahania does not distinguish from God (Margoliouth 1956: 110).

39:6/ E326/ III, 35 The wine presses have been interpreted by Damon (1924: 373, 394, 395), who cites Rev. xiv.17-19, as war and (1967: 442) as an allusion to those intoxicated by battle. According to Bloom (1963: 278), the war includes both corporeal conflict and the loving mental strife of Eternity; the former

(Bloom 1965: 954) is an outcome of the enslavement of energy, and it makes the presses a form of the furnaces of affliction. Ostriker (1977: 933) identifies the presses with both love and war, and Margoliouth (1956: 153) asserts that they purify the passions perverted by Mystery. In this passage, claims Erdman (1954a: 278 [303]), the reference is specifically to war with France that is intended to intoxicate (i.e. distract) British intellectuals; he also (1951a: 219) observes that as the instrument of Los it is on one level a printing press and is so called at *M* 27:8—see also note to that line.

39:8-9/ E327/ III, 37-38 **they rowze thy tygers/ Out of the halls of justice**—Juries acquit writers charged with sedition; the "dens" are the repressive parliamentary acts of 1795 (Erdman 1954a: 278 [303]).

39:13/ E327/ III, 42 Ahania discloses what is in the depths of Urizen's mind (Wilkie and Johnson 1978: 71).

39:15-42:6/ E327-28/ III, 44-90 Blake has left unclear the nature of the Shadow that rises from Albion's fatigued mind to over-awe him. Much depends on its relationship to the cloud of 40:1 and 19/ III, 48 and 66. It may be the object of Albion's self-worship (Hagstrum 1973b: 108); it may contain Luvah (Damon 1924: 373), the representative of the feminised mediaeval Christianity that will succeed Urizenic religion (Percival 1938: 179); or it may be Urizen (Altizer 1967: 5) or an image of Urizen's weakness and consequent desire of power (Brisman 1978: 253, 258). If it is a manifestation of Urizen, there is much to be said for Weiskel's view (1976: 73, 75) that a white, spectrous form of this Zoa emerges from his golden unfallen self and that he allows Luvah to descend and torment Albion as God allows Satan to descend and torment Job.

Noting how closely 41:11/ E328/ III, 77 echoes 23:4/ E313/ II, 4, Wilkie and Johnson (1978: 73) observe that the Albion described here is at the point at which the second Night begins. He now realises, argues Stevenson (1971: 330, 713), that Vala has seduced him and Luvah deceived him, and that he has neglected other aspects of himself. Beer (1969: 151) thinks that Albion turns from Vala when he has lost his virility after responding sexually to a delusory vision, while Wilkie and Johnson (1978: 71) conjecture that Urizen has caught Albion and Vala in intimate conjunction. According to Weiskel's impressive analysis (1976: 75-79), it is the guilt Albion feels for his dalliance with Vala that produces the Shadow, and he tries to assuage this guilt by suppressing passion (Luvah) and cutting himself off from nature (Vala).

40:2/ E327/ III, 49 **his palace**—the Bower of 24:7/ E314/ II, 24 (Margoliouth 1956: 111).

40:4/ E327/ III, 51 **white linen pure**—priestly garment(s)—cf. Exod. xxviii.42-43, II Chron. v.12, *et al.*

40:13-18/ E327/ III, 60-65 Cf. Ps. cxliii.2, 7 (Margoliouth 1948: 305) and Ps. civ.28-29 (Weiskel 1976: 73).

41:5-9/ E327-28/ III, 72-76 Erdman (Textual Notes, E831) endorses Margoliouth's highly plausible view (1956: 112) that this passage is a parenthesis that Ahania addresses to Urizen. Bentley (1963: 41) believes that l. 10 is marked for insertion after l. 2, which would imply the speaker was Albion.

41:13/ E328/ III, 79 This line answers the question "can Love seek for dominion?" (Margoliouth 1956: 112).

41:14/ E328/ III, 80 Vala had donned a body while she tempted Albion (Stevenson 1971: 334).

41:16/ E328/ III, 82 Alludes to Job ii.7 (Damon 1924: 373).

42:10-13/ E328/ III, 94-97 Luvah and Vala went down from the brain they had seized from Urizen [10:10-12/ E305/ I, 261-63] (Deen 1983: 128), and turned the paradise in the heart, whose serpent had begun by being playful, into this fallen world (Margoliouth 1956: 112). Luvah's collapse is modelled on Phaeton's, which, according to Ovid's *Metamorphoses*, II, 173-75, aroused the polar serpent (Percival 1938: 30, 298).

42:16/ E328/ III, 100 Urizen's laws separate Luvah from Vala depriving nature of its visionary aspect (Beer 1969: 142).

42:19-20/ E328/ III, 106-07 Miner (1969: 267) cites Ps. civ.2, Ostriker (1977: 934) Job ix.8. Cf. also Is. xl.22, 25.

43:5/ E328/ III, 113 **like Vala**—who, according to Urizen's interpretation of 42:15-16/ E328/ III, 99-100, rejected Luvah (Margoliouth 1956: 113).

43:6-11/ E328-29/ III, 114-19 As an earth goddess, Ahania is only fruitful when Urizen sows human souls in her, but her passivity angers him (Raine 1968: I, 154-63). He projects his own inertia onto her (Weiskel 1976: 70); he berates her for the very obedience he insists on (Ackland 1982: 177). "Virtue" signifies (1) moral goodness, (2) the active element in a med-ical or alchemical mixture, (3) virility (Wilkie and Johnson 1978: 74).

43:12/ E329/ III, 120 **Whence is this power given to thee!**— Trying to fight his fear of the future alone, Urizen is unwilling to concede that Ahania is the source of his mental energy (Weiskel 1976: 71).

43:12-14/ E329/ III, 120-22 Ahania is the world-cave, which seems repellent to Urizen now that he rejects the body as impure (Raine 1968: I, 157-58); the sluggish current represents an early stage of the fall into generative bodily life (*ibid.*: II, 91-92). Urizen's fear of Orc's future rivalry poisons his memory of past pleasure (Weiskel 1976: 70-71). Miner (1969: 265, 467n28) notes an echo of Cant. i.7 and Milton's use of the phrase "caverns shag'd with horrid shades" in a passage about chastity (*Comus*, 1. 429). Urizen has a distorted conception of his relationship with Ahania in Eternity (Wilkie and Johnson 1978: 75).

43:17-18/ E329/ III, 125-26 Cf. 40:5/ E327/ III, 52. Percival (1938: 179) accuses Urizen of blaming Ahania instead of his own self-righteousness (30:23-42/ E319-20/ II, 181-200) for the prospect of a "watry" creed's prevailing; Ackland (1983: 182-83) claims that Ahania's disturbing image shows him he has not been able to escape from nature.

43:20-21/ E329/ III, 128-29 Vala sees love with the distorting eye of Experience (Raine 1968: I, 197).

43:25/ E329/ III, 133 Urizen's Sons are his "lesser imaginative achievements" (Bloom 1965: 954). They flee to the realms of the body (west) and the passions (east) (Damon 1924: 373), and Urizen loses his productivity (Margoliouth 1956: 113).

43:27-30/ E329/ III, 135-38 On one level reason (Urizen) is overwhelmed by a flood of sense impressions (Tharmas) (Percival 1938: 43), and on another the deluge, which is to be identified with Noah's Flood (*ibid.*: 22, 180), restores the chaos of Night the First and the limited power of Tharmas (Bloom 1963: 236). Damon (1967: 86) doubts whether the "bounds of Destiny" are connected with the Circle of Destiny (see 5:11/ E302/ I, 74n), but Ostriker (1977: 933) very reasonably equates them holding that the Circle has enclosed the sea.

44:3-4/ E329/ III, 142-43 The Caverns are the flesh (Damon 1924: 373). Fisher (1961: 195) argues that Ahania, the faith that used to guide reason, is diluted to hope and experiences despair, but Gallant (1978: 64) regards the seed and the hope as positive elements.

44:14-22/ E329-30/ III, 153-61 The human body now acquires material form (Damon 1924: 158). The shattering of nature's womb releases Tharmas from Enion's web, where his identity has been submerged (Percival 1938: 181, citing *M* 41:37-42:1). Tharmas tries to emerge from the ocean of matter and recover his human shape; 44:15/ E329/ III, 154 refers to the resurrection of bones in Ezek. xxxvii.1-10 (Raine 1968: I, 303). Webster (1983: 223-24) sees in his subsequent sufferings the trauma of the infant as it becomes separate from its mother.

44:23-45:8/ E330/ III, 162-75 The crash plunges the world into full blown duality:. Tharmas is now spirit, that condemns yet needs matter (Enion) (Percival 1938: 183-84). Tharmas, the fragmented unity that is ourselves, tries to subdue his vindictiveness towards Enion (Bloom 1963: 228).

45:13/ E330/ III, 180 **Entuthon Benithon**—abstract philosophy (T. Wright 1929: I, 147); the bodily "physical frame" (Damon 1967: 123); "the 'forests' of nature" (Raine 1968: I, 250) and matter unillumined by spirit—perhaps from Greek *entuthen benthos* ("thenceforth in the depths of the sea") (*ibid.*: I, 296); the skeleton, punning on "tooth and bone" (Erdman 1977c: 432); the personal unconscious—with reference to 62:15/ E342/ V, 149 (Gallant 1978: 67).

45:17-26/ E330/ III, 184-93 Matter (Enion) expresses remorse and fear after destroying the spirit (Tharmas), which alone adds qualities to its inherent quantity (Raine 1968: I, 293).

Night the Fourth

The collapse of reason as ruling power leaves only a surging sea of instinct (Margoliouth 1956: 115). Los's subsequent binding of Urizen under Tharmas's direction has been conceived as a curbing of Urizen's power (Damon 1924: 374); as instruction that when fallen reasoning dominates, it should be based only on limited sense perceptions (Percival 1938: 185); as the final act of separation in the course of the Fall (Schorer 1946: 322); as the imposition of a limit on chaos leaving no further room in the poem for the Spectre of Tharmas, who *is* chaos (Frye 1947: 283); as the subjugation of tyranny (Erdman 1954a: 281-82 [307]); as a malevolent act to prevent Urizen from rising (Margoliouth 1956: 119); as the creation of the fallen human being (Fisher 1961: 234), who is Adam (Bloom 1965: 953); and as the arrival of adolescent self-consciousness about the body and its imperfections as well as the creation of a body trapped in time and a universe (Wilkie and Johnson 1978: 94-95). Tharmas's aim, says Bloom (1963: 230), is the non-rational construction of a world which he can rule and which can bring back Enion.

In this Night there first appears one of Blake's most intriguing characters. Damon's suggestion (1924: 158, 379) that the Spectre of Urthona is the "Poetic Logic" that is left when the Poet (Los) is deprived of inspiration (Enitharmon) and that this sometimes takes the form of metaphysics is succeeded by Paley's comment (1970: 112) that he embodies the more imaginative manifestations of reason such as metaphysics and logic, by Mellor's idea (1974: 186) that he is Coleridge's fancy as opposed to imagination, by Wilkie and Johnson's proposition (1978: 90) that he includes a poet's craftsmanship, by Essick's theory (1980: 213) that he is the journeyman whose task is to embody the artist's creation, and by Damrosch's insistence (1980: 314-15) that he is the rational element indispensable to the creation of art. Paying attention to his temporal aspect, Raine (1968: II, 149-50) regards him as the "Masculine Portion" of "Space," which is "Death" (E563/ K614)—i.e. time past, devourer of the present, and Frye (1947: 292-93, 386) conceives of him as endless "clock time" or "linear time" contrasting with Los's creative recurrent cycles. Frye also supposes (1947: 292-93) that he is a person's drive and ambition, Margoliouth (1956: 116-17) identifies him with the everyday self that should be subordinate to the spiritual self, and Erdman (1951a: 217; 1954a: 280 [305]) perceives him as Blake the engraver, who often has to work for bread instead of serving Los, Blake's creative imagination. In a comparable but pessimistic way, Bloom (1963: 204-05) portrays him as the worldly ego that threatens the poet's dedication and power of vision and (1965: 955) as "a self-crippled and time-obsessed will" that fears the future and especially material misfortune, while Percival (1938: 41-42) considers him the fear that arises in the spirit when reason gazes on the dualistic world of its own engendering. Wilkie and

Johnson (1978: 161-62) write of his moral and intellectual doubts and uncertainties, and of his being Los's repressed aspect. While Deen (1983: 139) sees in him Los's and Enitharmon's horror of mortality, Webster (1983: 225) describes him as the imagination that needs—once infancy has passed—to attain satisfaction slowly by interacting with the external world, and DiSalvo (1983: 72-80) views him as individual subjectivity cut off from society and nature. Whereas Los is identified with the constellation Orion, the Spectre of Urthona and Urthona himself are the brutal and regenerate forms of Orion's mirror image, Hercules (Miner 1981: 314).

Details

48:2/ E332/ IV, 25 In a time of political confusion, Tharmas curses the rulers of Britain and France (Erdman 1954a: 279 [304]).

48:4-10/ E332/ IV, 27-33 This curious passage makes Percival (1938: 184) think that Tharmas is having a mortal world built to accommodate the contraries. Bloom (1965: 955) considers that Tharmas is mad, and Stevenson (1971: 340) is unsure whether he seeks revenge or the salvation of a remnant of humanity as he envisages a ceaseless round of birth and death. According to Erdman (1954a: 279 [304]), Tharmas, rendered impotent by his own fury, orders Los and Enitharmon to undertake reconstruction.

48:12/ E332/ IV, 35 The fallen being must experience material existence without being overwhelmed by it (Percival 1938: 186). Los may be repeating Canute's famous command to the waves (Damon 1924: 374) or echoing Job xxxviii.11 (Percival, *loc. cit.*).

48:15-16/ E332/ IV, 38-39 In his fallen state, Los can no longer tolerate the place of death in the universe, and in search of stability he turns to Urizen (Beer 1969: 131). Preferring reason to instinct, he diminishes himself and his art by rejecting the earth (Wilkie and Johnson 1978: 88).

48:20/ E332/ IV, 43 **Urthona is but my shadow**—Los imagines he has more power in his present (fallen) state (Erdman 1954a: 279 [305]). He rejects his true self as an artist (Wilkie and Johnson 1978: 88).

48:28/ E332/ IV, 51 The divine architect is Urizen (Bloom 1965: 955).

49:4-5/ E332/ IV, 56-57 This striking action by Tharmas has been interpreted as an attempt to teach Los that he is not supreme by taking his poetic inspiration (Damon 1924: 158, 374), a vindictive deed (Bloom 1963: 229), and, as the next two lines suggest, the re-creation of Adam and Eve after the Fall (Wagenknecht 1973: 211-14). Stevenson (1971: 338-39) states that this passage was written before Blake introduced Los's division into the first Night.

49:11ff/ E333/ IV, 63ff For the Spectre of Urthona, see the headnote to this Night. At this point, claims Damon (1967: 382), he is simply Los separated from Enitharmon.

49:13-14/ E333/ IV, 65-66 This may be the real Los's shadow bent by an unlevel surface—cf. 5:15/ E302/ I, 78 (Raine 1968: I, 415n22).

49:18-19/ E333/ IV, 70-71 Tharmas allows the reunion of Los and Enitharmon because he recalls that Urthona (the Spirit) formerly protected him (Damon 1924: 158) or in return for their obedience (Stevenson 1971: 339, 342). The bower is a foreshadowing of Golgonooza (Wagenknecht 1973: 214).

50:10-12/ E333/ IV, 93-95 Urthona's genitals become external (Wilkie and Johnson 1978: 91).

50:22-24/ E333-34/ IV, 105-07 Perhaps an allusion to the grinding of an engraver's copper plate with a moist blue stone (Erdman 1954a: 305 [331]).

51:2-3/ E334/ IV, 119-20 **this Son/ Of Enion**—Los (Damon 1924: 374).

51:5-6/ E334/ IV, 122-23 Here Tharmas seems to address Los, not the Spectre (Margoliouth 1956: 118).

51:7-9/ E334/ IV, 124-26 Erdman (1954a: 280-81 [305-06]) states that to make a living, Blake the poet (Los) must rely on Blake the engraver (the Spectre), who incises metal to make way for a tide of ink. Less specifically, Margoliouth (1956: 118) is satisfied that the Spectre gives Los "a foothold in this world."

51:12/ E334/ IV, 129 Urizen (Pitt's government) has lost his sway over people's minds (Erdman 1954a: 278-79 [303-04]). Tharmas seems chaos to the Eternal Man but provides a foundation for mortal existence (Margoliouth 1956: 118). There is a threat that mental activity will be reduced to an unorganised current of sense perceptions—see the next eight lines (Paley 1970: 101).

51:14/ E334/ IV, 131 **Urthona is My Son**—The body believes itself the source of spirit (Damon 1924: 374).

51:15-18/ E334/ IV, 132-35 Blackstone (1949: 88-89) cites an analogy by Proclus given in Berkeley's *Siris* (section 313), but cf. also Jon. ii.3-5.

51:32/ E335/ IV, 149 Tharmas has a moment of inspiration, for the fallen must pass through the reconstructed material world (Percival 1938: 186). He vainly hopes that the confinement of reason will preserve an element of prelapsarian happiness, which he has recalled in the three preceding lines (Paley 1970: 100-01).

52:2/ E335/ IV, 152 **Death choose or life**—The poet must choose between imaginative creation and spiritual death (Damon 1924: 374). Cf. Deut. xxx.19 (Ostriker 1977: 935).

52:3-4/ E335/ IV, 153-54 Tharmas remembers the prelapsarian pastoral life (Wagenknecht 1973: 212-14). The lyres will lure energetic spirits into the furnaces (Hilton 1978: 83).

52:15-17/ E335/ IV, 165-67 Los, lord of time, mends the fallen world, which Urizen created through his furnaces or planetary rulers of destiny (Raine 1968: II, 23). Los is reclaiming his own furnaces, which Urizen used in the second Night to confine Luvah and build his universe—he is rescuing art from rationalism (Wilkie and Johnson 1978: 92-93).

52:29-53:3/ E335/ IV, 179-82 Los is creating both clock time and poetic metre (Ostriker 1977: 935). He is showing that Urizen's domination is not eternal (DiSalvo 1983: 80—cf. Damon 1924: 374).

53:5-19/ E335-36/ IV, 184-98 The text says that the Spectre regrets but Los rejoices in Enitharmon's sufferings. Los may be taking revenge for her spitefulness (Stevenson 1971: 346) or for her alliance with Urizen (Wilkie and Johnson 1978: 93). However, Margoliouth (1956: 120), citing 53:25/ E336/ IV, 204, is able to argue that Los, sacrificing one good for the sake of another, has mixed feelings. Allegorically, says Damon (1924: 374), the bonds of time injure inspiration.

55:14/ E337/ IV, 251 **a Double female form**—Martha and Mary, whom Blake here identifies with the Daughters of Beulah

(Margoliouth 1948: 305-06). In 56:1-2/ E337/ IV, 254-55, there is a quotation from John xi.21-23 (Damon 1924: 375).

56:8/ E337/ IV, 260 Cf. Ps. xvii.8 (Stevenson 1971: 348).

56:19-24/ E338/ IV, 271-76 Blake's "Limit" is Boehme's term both for the nadir of the Fall and for the time of the Incarnation (Raine 1968: I, 404-06n40); it is probably in part a non-mathematical response to Newton's mathematical fluxions (Nurmi 1969: 305-07). Opacity is impermeability to "the Divine Light" (Damon 1924: 375) or "the imaginative power" (Stevenson 1971: 349)—it thickens until just before even the satanic world becomes invisible (Nurmi 1969: 306), and the result, according to Ostriker (1977: 936), is hard heartedness. Contraction takes place from infinity (Damon, *loc. cit.*), proceeds to the lowest point from which a human can be redeemed (Nurmi, *loc. cit.*), and includes the constriction of perception (Ostriker 1977: 1011). Wilkie and Johnson (1978: 97) note that Jesus *finds* the limit of contraction but *puts* a limit to the Starry Wheels—that is, imposes an end in time on natural cycles and human fallenness. The Wheels are credibly said to represent "astrological fatalism" (Damon 1924: 375) and the zodiac governed by Urizen (Bloom 1965: 956).

56:25/ E338/ IV, 277 **the Seventh furnace**—the Seventh Eye of God, Jesus, who imposes a limit on the Fall (Damon 1924: 375) or the last historical cycle (Bloom 1965: 939). God's touching the seventh furnace has been interpreted as Divinity bringing the poet's work to life (Damon 1967: 138) and as the Incarnation (Frye 1947: 253). There is an allusion to the furnace of Dan. iii.19, which was heated seven times more than usual (Bloom 1965: 956).

in terror—The binding of Urizen is both cruel and merciful; God limits it in such a way that experience of error will be regenerative (Percival 1938: 185-86).

55:16ff/ E338/ IV, 280ff Los's vision is clouded so that he cannot see that the imposition of limits is providential (Bloom 1963: 231).

55:22-23/ /E338/ IV, 286-87 Percival (1938: 319) cites Plotinus' view that souls become what they contemplate. The allegorical meaning, according to Schorer (1946: 322), is that an ignoble subject corrupts art. Wilkie and Johnson (1978: 97-99) assert that what Los creates both transforms him and wins his sympathy, but that at 53:24/ E336/ IV, 203 "he became what he beheld" signifies that he caused what he saw. Webster (1983: 226-28) alleges that, as in *BU*, Los succumbs to guilt.

55:24-27/ E338/ IV, between 287 and 288 Margoliouth (1956: 120) maintains that since Enitharmon already has an independent existence, *BU* 18:1-8 should not be inserted here despite Blake's instructions in the manuscript (E833/ K305). Wilkie and Johnson (1978: 269) approve the insertion since it emphasises that Enitharmon is a part of Los's being.

55:28-35/ E338/ IV, 288-95 The spasms may be an allusion to religious possession and are also sexual, for Los begets Orc (Nurmi 1976: 138). He is resisting descent into the unconscious, where the other Zoas now are (Gallant 1978: 66-67).

Night the Fifth

Nature has an important place in this Night. The theme, according to Bloom (1963: 232), is the cyclical repetition to which desire that will not transcend the natural world is doomed. Orc grows immense and comprehends all nature (Nurmi 1976: 138); indeed, in Wilkie and Johnson's view (1978: 101-02), he himself is fallen nature with all its savagery.

This Night carries the plot significantly forward. After finding themselves unable to release Orc from the rock to which they have bound him, Los and Enitharmon begin to acquire the spirit of self-sacrifice—imagination is learning to sympathise with the suffering (Wilkie and Johnson 1978: 109-14). Hilton (1983: 33-34) observes that this marks a departure from the essentially self-pitying lamentation that has been a substitute for action with Enion, Ahania and other characters and seems to have tempted Blake himself, since he temporarily thought of his epic as a dirge—see Erdman 1965: 739 (or Textual Notes, E819). Urizen, one of the complainers, begins to show a stubborn persistence, and noting that it continues through the next two Nights, Erdman (1954a: 338-39 [365-66]) equates it with the aggressive policy of Britain in 1801 when peace negotiations faltered and she bombarded the Danish fleet and drove Napoleon from Egypt.

Details

57:10/ E339/ V, 10 **the furious wind**—of time (Bloom 1963: 232).

57:15/ E339/ V, 15 **furnaces**—Los's power of vision in Eternity (Sloss and Wallis 1926: I, 215); symbols of suffering, often redemptive suffering (Damon 1967: 146); the seven planetary spirits who are the subordinate agents of creation or destiny in the Hermetic and other systems (Raine 1968: II, 21-23). A single furnace represents the physical body, in which one encounters experience, Los's bellows being the lungs and his hammer the heart; seven furnaces correspond to the Seven Eyes of God (Frye 1947: 253)—see *M* 24:58-59.

58:7-8/ E339/ V, 27-28 The planets, with their malign movement from west to east, the direction of the Wheel of Religion (*J*, pl. 77, blank verse, ll. 1-6), here come into existence (Percival 1938: 147, 315).

58:13/ E339/ V, 33 **a marriage chain**—Crehan (1984: 310) supposes that with this chain—composed of time, sorrow and jealousy—Los binds Orc.

58:17-18/ E339/ V, 37-38 Revolt rises from the heart of inspiration (Damon 1924: 375). When Luvah is reborn as Orc, sex dominates over love and becomes an obsession (M. Plowman 1927a: 160). Erdman (1954a: 282 and 239 [307 and 258]) equates the birth with the publication of Rousseau's *The Social Contract* in 1762, and Paley (1970: 103) identifies Orc with Boehme's First Principle.

58:21-59:20/ E339-40/ V, 41-65 The demons' song is a call for war (Nurmi 1976: 138) and an amoral "celebration of energy" (Wilkie and Johnson 1978: 104). It demands Vala's presence to complement Orc's (Margoliouth 1956: 123), for Vala has become a war goddess and Luvah-Orc manifests in the Napoleonic wars (Bloom 1965: 956).

58:21/ E339/ V, 41 This line is an ironic allusion to Charles Wesley's "Hark! the herald angels sing/ Glory to the new born king" (Paley 1970: 103).

58:22/ E339/ V, 42 Suppressed love becomes hate (Damon 1967: 256). Paley (1970: 104) detects a parody of Crashaw's "Hymn to the Name and Honour of the Admirable Saint Teresa," ll. 1-2.

58:23/ E339/ V, 43 **deep darkness**—The ignorance Urizen tries to impose on Orc (Damon 1924: 375).

58:24/ E339/ V, 44 **spears of Urizen**—possibly rational arguments (Margoliouth 1956: 123).

59:1/ E340/ V, 46 **gloomy prophet**—probably Los, possibly Orc (Wilkie and Johnson 1978: 105).

59:4/ E340/ V, 49 **secret fires**—sexual attractions (Stevenson 1971: 353).

59:12/ E340/ V, 57 **sons**—with a pun on "suns" (Hilton 1983: 234).

59:14/ E340/ V, 59 The Spirit is Los (Damon 1924: 375), or Los together with the Spectre of Urthona (Margoliouth 1956: 123), or the Spectre only (Bloom 1965: 956), or either Urizen or Orc (Wilkie and Johnson 1978: 105). Blake may be blamed for the uncertainty.

59:15-16/ E340/ V, 60-61 **And his dark wife.../Within his ribs** —both Enitharmon in Eve's pre-natal position and the moon occulting Los-Orion (Miner 1981: 319).

60:3/ E340/ V, 76 On the narrative level, Los, partly motivated by jealousy, here builds Golgonooza to protect Enitharmon from Orc (Stevenson 1971: 353-54), to hide her from him (Webster 1983: 230), or to sublimate his hostility to that boy, who is taking Enitharmon's affection from him and will displace him (George 1980: 116). Margoliouth (1956: 124) perceives an autobiographical dimension—Blake-Los is constructing *Vala* as a psychological safety valve while he is under pressure from Hayley. In more general terms, the poet in Los is born under the stimulus of revolt (Damon 1967: 164).

The city's name derives from Golgotha—"The place of a skull" (Mark xv.22)—for in order to create, the artist must follow Christ's example of self-sacrifice (Damon 1924: 375); this involves the surrender of the ego (Dilworth 1983: 24). Erdman (1954a: 356 [384]) justifiably finds the name ambivalent as it evokes both the tragedy of Golgotha and the opulence of Golconda. Other sources of the name may be the Greek *goggolon* ("round") (Miner 1981: 313) and the "noose" of Tyburn, a site Blake associates with Golgotha (Rose 1970b: 417). Raine (1968: II, 321nn34, 37) interprets Blake's coinage as "the city within the skull" or "life within the brain," Mitchell (1973b: 303) as a new consciousness developing inside the old. Hilton (1983: 235-36) asserts that its "inner form" is the *logon zooas* ("living word" or "word of life" of Phil. ii.16). Thomas Wright (1929: I, 107) believes that Golgonooza and its environs are patterned after four-gated Chichester, near Felpham. Regarding Chichester, the biblical Tabernacle and Temple, and contemporary London as models for Golgonooza, Paley (1983b: 136, 160, 164, 166) feels that its name also evokes "the primeval ooze of existence." See also 87:6-11/ E368/ VII, 378-83n.

Udan Adan is "a Lake not of Waters but of Spaces" (113:24/ E377/ VIII, 225) which Blake characterises as "indefinite" (*J* 7:22). According to Frye (1947: 380), it represents the mind that "passively reflects its sense experience," and in Damon's view (1967: 416) its leading characteristic is formlessness. Percival (1938: 68) believes that the black lake of Virgil's *Aeneid*, VI, 328, is a source; Doskow (1982: 170n8) suggests that "Adan" is an anagram of Spanish *nada* ("nothing").

60:4/ E340/ V, 77   The Limit of Translucence is higher than its contrary, the Limit of Opacity (Wilkie and Johnson 1978: 106).

Luban (in *FZ*), holds Damon (1924: 375), is a gateway into Golgonooza, and hence, says Bloom (1963: 257), a refuge from Experience; Bloom (1965: 961) adds that it is also a main entrance into New Jerusalem. Sloss and Wallis (1926: I, 258) state that in Jacob Bryant's *A New System of Mythology* (1774-76), Luban is an alternative name for "the Ararat of Moses," at the foot of which humankind first lived. Bryant's Luban, notes Raine (1968: I, 232), is a lunar symbol, and the moon governs the gate of birth into the material world. (See also next note.)

60:5/ E340/ V, 78   Tharmas has here been viewed as a corporal ally who, Los feels, can assist him in working for regeneration (Percival 1938: 43), as the Zoa of the body laying the foundations of Luban, the birth canal (Damon 1967: 254), and as instinct laying the foundation of Golgonooza, the poet's creation (Wilkie and Johnson 1978: 106).

Los works in "howling woe" because he cannot yet succeed in harmonising the psyche in Golgonooza; he still excludes certain elements from it fearing obliteration of his ego-identity by the unconscious (Gallant 1978: 71-72, 77-78).

60:19-20/ E341/ V, 92-93   Percival (1938: 191) holds that Orc is a threat to Los's Old Testament prophetic religion faced by feminine paganism in the form of Enitharmon; Paley (1970: 105) argues that the energy Los imprisons in the bonds of time actually is potentially destructive; and George (1980: 117-18) considers that Blake does not disclose whether Orc's supposed enmity is real.

60:28/ E341/ V, 101   Los nails Orc to the rock of the Law (Schorer 1946: 323). All that is not imprisoned in Urizen's body—especially a passionate desire for sensory experience—is confined here (Frosch 1974: 50-51). Los's act represents Puritan family discipline (DiSalvo 1983: 331). Los is repressing his rebellious youthful self (Crehan 1984: 310).

61:2/ E341/ V, 105   The Chain is the Mosaic Law (Percival 1938: 191). "Tenfold" may allude to the Decalogue (Margoliouth 1956: 124).

61:8/ E341/ V, 111   The labyrinth may be protective (*ibid.*) or a sign of possessiveness (Deen 1983: 134-35).

61:10/ E341/ V, 113   *Storge* is a Greek word meaning parental affection; it is found in Swedenborg's *Conjugial Love* (section 395) (Damon 1967: 388). Sloss and Wallis (1926: I, 219) state that the line can apply either to Los or the Spectre, while Damon (1924: 375) thinks "Storgous" is a euphemism for "incestuous" and it refers to the love between Orc and his mother.

61:11ff/ E341ff/ V, 114ff   This passage, which is indebted to Dan. vii.10, suggests that Orc still has regenerative potential (Paley 1970: 105-06), and his senses can as yet expand and contract like those of the Eternals (Stevenson 1971: 355). The repressed Orc reacts positively to the unconscious, which resembles the Hell of *The Marriage of Heaven and Hell* (Gallant 1978: 68). He experiences the sexuality and rebelliousness of adolescence (Wilkie and Johnson 1978: 106). The spirits attending him are comets, which were held to carry fertilising moisture (Worrall 1981: 290).

61:19/ E341/ V, 122   The mountains that are "infinite" to Orc are "iron" to Los—see 60:26/ E341/ V, 99 (Gallant 1978: 68).

61:23/ E341/ V, 126   Each planet is associated with an element; the orbs are comets (Margoliouth 1956: 124).

62:21ff/ E342ff/ V, 155ff The chaining of Orc is so disastrous that its consequences will always affect humankind (Percival 1938: 191). Los's jealousy will become the Tree of Mystery and turn Orc into Urizen (Bloom 1963: 234-35). The chaining signifies that Los has transferred his hostile emotions to the boy, in whom they have become embedded to be passed down to future generations (George 1980: 119-20).

62:27-28/ E342/ V, 161-62 According to Hilton (1982: 167), "melt," "death" and "Consummation" signify orgasm.

62:30/ E342/ V, 164 Damon (1924: 376) explains Urthona as Spirit and the Bulls as "animal ...Passion." Since the Bulls belong to Luvah, who is Orc, Margoliouth (1956: 125) thinks they may represent the latter's own efforts.

63:2-3/ E342/ V, 168-69 The "living Chain" is both the incestuously inclined boy's guilt repressed into the unconscious and the mental bond that will turn Orc into an oppressor and that frustrates every revolution (Paley 1970: 107-08). Orcean energy has penetrated Urizen's solid world as far as the focal point of Newtonian gravity (Ault 1974: 110). Orc has become a selfish or self-enclosed centre (Welch 1978: 228-29).

63:11/ E343/ V, 177 **Dranthon**—This mysterious name is associated with "repentant nature" according to Bloom (1965: 957), lamentation according to Howard (1984: 210).

63:13/ E343/ V, 179 Vala is conceived here, born in Night the Seventh (Damon 1924: 376).

63:19ff/ E343/ V, 185ff The stirrings of rebellion awaken Urizen's memories of Eternity (Ostriker 1977: 938).

63:23/ E343/ V, 189 **the deep dens of Urthona**—the world reconstructed by Los (Bloom 1965: 957; the human body that Los has fashioned (Johnson and Grant 1979: 222). Erdman (1954a: 340 [367]) sees here and in Night the Sixth an allusion to George III's madness, which may be corroborated (Margoliouth 1956: 125) by an allusion to royal swans five lines later.

63:24ff/ E343-44/ V, 190ff In Urizen's lament, silver symbolises love and gold wisdom—see 64:23/ E344/ V, 220 (Damon 1967: 373). The age of Zeus or Jupiter, the classical equivalent of Urizen, is the Silver Age; the gold crown stands for power granted from above (Raine 1968: II, 84).

63:28/ E343/ V, 194   Swans feed at a fountain guarded by the Norns, who are identical with Urizen's Daughters; the swan symbolising the soul has degenerated to a wingless creature (Raine 1968: II, 88, 91). Sacred to Apollo, the swan is a common symbol for the poet (Gleckner 1982a: 165).

64:3/ E343/ V, 200   **Nine virgins**—the seven planets, sun and moon [cf. 34:67/ E324/ II, 353] (Damon 1924: 376); or the Ptolemaic spheres (Stevenson 1971: 358); or the Nine Muses (Margoliouth 1956: 125), who are also the virgins of 63:27/ E343/ V, 193 (Ostriker 1977: 938).

64:8/ E343/ V, 205   **my wise men are departed**—George III relapsed into insanity following the resignation of Pitt and four of his ministers in February 1801 (Erdman 1954a: 337, 343 [365, 370]).

64:12, 14/ E343, 344/ V, 209, 211   **my Lord...the Lord of day**—apparently the Divine Vision, Jesus (Stevenson 1971: 358); Urizen's creator, the Divine Vision (Ostriker 1977: 938).

64:13/ E344/ V, 210   Urizen kept the intellectual faculties indolent (M. Plowman 1927a: 159).

64:15-17/ E344/ V, 212-14   George III regrets that he did not allow the public to view the art in his palaces (Erdman 1954a: 344 [371]).

64:21/ E344/ V, 218   **the mild & holy voice**—of the Eternal Man (Sloss and Wallis 1926: I, 223); of God (Percival 1938: 170) saying "Let there be light" (Gen. i.3) (Ostriker 1977: 938).

64:21-29/ E344/ V, 218-26   Reason, by choosing to govern instead of guide, has destroyed love and imagination (Stevenson 1971: 358).

64:24/ E344/ V, 221   **my Son who wanders on the ocean**—humankind (Margoliouth 1956: 126); Luvah (Beer 1969: 153); Tharmas (Crehan 1984: 312). There may be a play on words since the physical "sun" also needs guidance (Johnson and Grant 1979: 223).

64:25-28/ E344/ V, 222-25   Urizen speaks of his "councils dark" with Luvah (Ostriker 1977: 938). George III regrets he fought the Americans (Erdman 1954a: 344 [371]).

64:29-30/ E344/ V, 226-27   When reason governs, nature and the passions fade (Damon 1924: 376). Blake makes George III regret that Britain made war on France (Luvah) (Erdman 1954a: 344 [371]).

64:31/ E344/ V, 228   Luvah spread emotional delight (Percival 1938: 29). The line links him with Ganymede (Johnson and Grant 1979: 223).

65:3/ E344/ V, 232   As the Zoa of love, Luvah promulgated forgiveness of sin (Percival 1938: 28-29).

65:5-8/ E344/ V, 234-37   **the wine of the Almighty**—a draught of "love and pity" that made Urizen try to promote a moral ideal through laws (Percival 1938: 171); perhaps the wish to be all-powerful (Damon 1967: 256). Luvah got Urizen drunk to make him lend his horses (*ibid.*: 420).

65:9-12/ E344/ V, 238-41   Urizen decides to seek the hidden spiritual explanation for phenomena (Margoliouth 1951: 121), or to survey the natural world in a way that will lead to Deism (Bloom 1965: 957), or to master the world by reason (Wilkie and Johnson 1978: 120). The prophecy is of Orc's birth (38:2/ E326/ III, 14) (Margoliouth 1956: 110), or of the reunion of Urizen's light with Luvah's love (Beer 1969: 154-55).

65:12/ E344/ V, 241   **Then love shall show its root in deepest hell**—This richly ambiguous line has been taken to mean that when reason falls it encounters love turned into hate (Fisher 1961: 226); that Urizen is resolved to defend "Thought" against love (Bloom 1965: 957); that Luvah, who contributed much to the Fall, may now contribute to redemption (Paley 1970: 109); that love retains power even in the mortal world (Stevenson 1971: 359); and that Urizen displays both fear and a touch of hope (Wilkie and Johnson 1978: 116-17).

Night the Sixth

Frye (1947: 220-23) gives an admirable account of Urizen as the post-Renaissance scientific thinker attempting to understand the material universe: he perceives time as cyclic until he encounters clock time in the person of the Spectre of Urthona, and attempts to impose total uniformity on society in his fear of unpredictable change. His doctrine, says Bloom (1963: 236), is church Christianity, and Sloss and Wallis (1926: I, 225) note his discovery that he cannot free his Children from the misery of which he is himself the cause. His journey through three worlds, claims Percival (1938: 159-60), is parallel to Christ's three days in hell and is a prelude to the first stage in the long process of regeneration. Wilkie and Johnson (1978: 137) aver that it shows the ultimate frustration of the reason, to which the individual turns in adolescence and to which society resorts in the first stage of modern science.

The narrative of Urizen's travels is indebted to the account of Satan's exploration of Hell in book I of *Paradise Lost* (Beer 1969: 117) and of his passage through Chaos in book II (Damon 1924: 376, citing Saurat), and to a lesser extent to Dante's descriptions in the *Inferno* (Wilkie and Johnson 1978: 119, 271n5). The horrific picture of the fallen cosmos is indebted to the account of the world after Noah's Flood in Thomas Burnet's *The Sacred History of the Earth* (1681-89) (Nurmi 1976: 140), and it parodies the encounters of the human with the not-human in Northern mythology, which, in Blake's view, greatly overvalues the latter (De Luca 1982: 95-97).

Details

67:1-2/ E344/ VI, 1-2 Urizen is enacting the role of the warrior god Odin on his visit to a well; the river he comes to is the source of generative life (Raine 1968: II, 86-94). His spear and helmet show his intention to tyrannise over nature (Wilkie and Johnson 1978: 121), and he represents mad George III persisting in his war policy (Erdman 1954a: 344 [371]). Hilton (1983: 177, 179) suggests the spear is a metaphor for a beam of light.

67:5ff/ E345/ VI, 5ff   Urizen's Daughters are "the fallen body" (Frye 1947: 300) or a threefold form of the nature goddess Vala and Blake's version of the classical Fates (Fisher 1959: 174) and akin to the Norse Norns (Bloom 1963: 236). The water they pour is matter (Damon 1924: 377) or the water of life [Rev. xxi.6] (Ostriker 1977: 939). Urizen cannot get enough of the former (Damon, *loc. cit.*), or cannot, in his fallen condition, slake his thirst with the latter (Damrosch 1980: 79).

Damon (1924: 376-77) characterises the Daughters from eldest to youngest as the loins wearing the same "clouds of mystery" as the Shadowy Female of *America*, the heart endowed with the magnetic power of the passions, and the head bestowing form as it divides the water into the four rivers of Eden. Later commentators develop this exposition. The clouds of the first, blue of the second, and green of the third point, says Margoliouth (1956: 127), to air, water and earth, while Fisher (1959: 175) equates them with the colours of the three orders of Bards, Ovates and Druids. Bloom (1963: 236-37) proposes that the eldest is sexuality in the world of cyclic repetition and the name on her brow recalls the Mystery of Rev. xvii.5, that the blue of the middle one is an ironic allusion to the blue of the Virgin Mary, and that the youngest may be the embodied mind dividing the original unified senses into the four fallen ones. However, the fallen senses number five, and Beer (1969: 117) believes the rivers are the four eternal ones now in the power of reason. Raine (1968: II, 92-94) identifies the Daughters with Juno, who guards the fountain of descending souls; Minerva, the fountain of virtues; and Diana, the fountain of nature. The "attractive power" of the second is, according to Ault (1974: 110), gravitation. Emphasising their corruption but also its incompleteness, Wilkie and Johnson (1978: 121-22) argue that they represent both nature as Urizen, the fallen mind, views it and human feeling: the drying of the river signifies that reason's onslaught turns both nature and mind sterile. The Daughters may resist their father because Tharmas is their god [see 68:24/ E345/ VI, 43] (Bloom 1965: 957) or because they are nature and the vestiges of mental beauty resisting the power of rationalism (Wilkie and Johnson 1978: 121). Maintaining that any character can play any role or roles in the Oedipal drama, Webster (1983: 231-33, 236-37) interprets the withholding of water as "maternal deprivation" that will eventually cause the child's alienation from self and nature.

Erdman (1954a: 345 [372]) regards the Daughters as allegorically the British arts, once nourished by authority (68:6ff/ E345/ VI, 25ff) and the object of Gallic envy and the Eternals' admiration (68:14-15/ E345/ VI, 33-34).

The episode is principally modelled on Satan's encounter with Sin and Death, *PL*, II, 643-889 (Bloom 1963: 236).

67:18-19/ E345/ VI, 18-19 The four rivers of the Garden of Eden have become the four rivers of the Greco-Roman underworld (Raine 1968: II, 95).

68:5ff/ E345-46/ VI, 24ff With Urizen's curse, Margoliouth (1956: 128) compares Is. iii.16-26, and Erdman (1954a: 344-45 [371-72]) notes the parallel with the curses of Lear, who similarly bears the major responsibility for his own sufferings. Urizen may so treat his Daughters because they cannot conform to his lofty standards (Sloss and Wallis 1926: I, 227) or because they represent the power of nature, which he tried to banish when he ejected Ahania (Ackland 1983: 184-85).

68:24/ E345/ VI, 43 The Daughters make a god of the body (Damon 1924: 377), or their wateriness causes Urizen to think they let Tharmas guide them (Wilkie and Johnson 1978: 124). Tharmas and Los stand respectively for journalists like Paine and poets like Blake (Erdman 1954a: 345 [372]).

68:25/ E346/ VI, 44 **Demon of destruction**—Tharmas (Margoliouth 1956: 128); Orc (Stevenson 1971: 361).

68:28/ E346/ VI, 47 Cf. 68:2/ E345/ VI, 21 (Margoliouth 1956: 128).

69:11-12/ E346/ VI, 60-61 Bodies destroy each other but continue multiplying; only the most primitive creatures—fish—can survive in the Sea of Time and Space (Damon 1924: 377).

69:15-16/ E346/ VI, 64-65 The food is sense perception, the light reason (Paley 1970: 109-10). A materialist world view precludes an intellectual one (Howard 1984: 213).

69:26/ E346/ VI, 75 Contrast Orc's delight in "the deeps" at 61:16/ E341/ V, 119 (Gallant 1978: 69).

69:33/ E346/ VI, 82 **a world for Los**—a hell for poets to describe (Margoliouth 1956: 128).

70:1/ E346/ VI, 83 Urizen's Globe is of fire, not light; he was formerly Prince of Light but has regressed into Boehme's First Principle, and it is that Principle's "Wrath-world" he is exploring (Paley 1970: 110).

70:5-17/ E347/ VI, 87-99 According to Bloom (1963: 239), Urizen is encountering "our world." Crehan (1984: 79) thinks it is in part London under anti-Jacobin repression.

70:6/ E347/ VI, 88 **once his children and the children of Luvah**—once the British and French citizens who cherished freedom (Erdman 1954a: 345 [372]).

70:21/ E347/ VI, 106 Damon (1924: 377) and Bloom (1963: 240) see these women as female wills, but since they appear to be victims, Erdman's identification of them as female brickmakers seems nearer the mark (1954a: 346 [373]).

70:26-30/ E347/ VI, 111-15 The "myriads" are mill workers, the "multitudes" miners, and the "cities & castles" armaments factories (*ibid.*).

71:15/ E348/ VI, 147 After exploring his own quarter, the south, Urizen enters Luvah's, the east (Damon 1924: 159).

71:26/ E348/ VI, 158 **created a bosom of clay**—in imitation of the heart, Luvah's location in the body (Stevenson 1971: 365).

71:27-41/ E348-49/ VI, 159-73 Reason rapidly expires in the realm of passion and is quickly resurrected (Damon 1924: 377). This passage describes symbolically "the ups and downs of the ordering intellect" (Margoliouth 1956: 129) or the decline and rise of civilisations (Ostriker 1977: 940). Urizen's falls and his new beginnings at the infant stage are repetitions of the child's trauma when it realises it has an identity distinct from its mother's (Webster 1983: 232).

71:37/ E348/ VI, 169 **his death clothes**—different forms of the moral law (Sloss and Wallis 1926: I, 232) or different commentaries on Urizen's unchanging dogmas (Ostriker 1977: 940).

71:40/ E349/ VI, 172 Brass, iron and gold stand respectively for sociology, war and science (Damon 1967: 424). Cf. 80:1/ E355/ VII, 109n.

71:42-72:1/ E349/ VI, 174-75 The rationalist cannot avoid being a lawmaker (Schorer 1946: 324).

72:4/ E349/ VI, 178 The orbits of the planets have become irregular (Ault 1974: 148).

72:12/ E349/ VI, 186 It is Urizen who both stems and labours (Margoliouth 1956: 129).

72:13-27/ E349/ VI, 187-201 The vortices have been described as "systems of error" (Sloss and Wallis 1926: I, 225); as a product of Urizen's Newtonian view of space (Bloom 1963: 241); the vortices of which Descartes thought the universe composed (Raine 1968: II, 80-82; cf. also Damon 1967: 440), within which Urizen is barred from a comprehensive view of the cosmos (Nurmi 1969: 309-10); and as a combination of those vortices with the Newtonian void in which vortices cannot long survive (Ault 1974: 148-49).

72:20-21/ E349/ VI, 194-95 Here he could, if he would, live contented in the present moment (Wilkie and Johnson 1978: 132).

72:29/ E349/ VI, 203 **upward**—psychologically upward (that is, laborious) for in a vortex spatial direction only exists in relation to the centre and circumference (Nurmi 1969: 310).

73:14/ E350/ VI, 227 **foot**—of the compasses (Ostriker 1977: 940); both of the compasses and of the body (Wilkie and Johnson 1978: 133).

73:21-22/ E350/ VI, 234-35 Urizen establishes a restrictive scientific framework for thought (Margoliouth 1956: 130). Blake may have in mind the Enlightenment or Greco-Roman culture (Ostriker 1977: 940). Theoretical systems like Malthus's and Ricardo's ("Sciences") generate oppressive social systems ("Vortexes") (Wilkie and Johnson 1978: 134-35).

73:23/ E350/ VI, 236 The "wheels of heaven" are the constellations (Damon 1924: 377), and they "imply" industrial machines (Wilkie and Johnson 1978: 134). Rose (1972a: 45-46) relates them to the imprisoning "Circle o'er Circle" of 72:23/ E349/ VI, 197.

73:24-34/ E350/ VI, 237-46 Urizen's Children are thoughts, Luvah's emotions (Margoliouth 1956: 130). The energies of Luvah are safely contained in a Newtonian universe where all is predetermined (see 73:20/ E350/ VI, 233), and which Urizen joins to Cartesian vortexes with his Web (Ault 1974: 149-50).

73:35-39/ E350/ VI, 247-51 Stevenson (1971: 368) thinks something may have dropped out of this obscure passage, but Worrall (1981: 280) recognises that, together with the lines immediately following, it tells how the constellations Leo, Lynx and Scorpio contract and become inanimate. Miner (1981: 311) argues that these constellations are projections of the mind's own passions.

74:3-4/ E351/ VI, 254-55 These lines may describe what Vala does in Eternity (Margoliouth 1956: 131). The sky no longer appears well disposed (Wilkie and Johnson 1978: 136).

74:33-34/ E351/ VI, 284-85 Perhaps a condemnation of the eighteenth-century arts (Bloom 1965: 958).

75:3/ E351/ VI, 294 In view of 63:23/ E343/ V, 189, Wilkie and Johnson (1978: 119) think that Urizen has moved in a circle.

75:5ff/ E352/ VI, 296ff   The selfhood (Spectre) and the governor of the flesh together oppose Urizenic reason and morality (Bloom 1963: 242) and defend Orc hoping obscurely that he may help to bring on an apocalypse (Bloom 1965: 958). Erdman (1954a: 347 [374]) sees the Spectre, who resembles Spenser's iron man Talus, as representing the growing domestic hostility, monstrous in kingly eyes, to Britain's warlike and repressive policies. Margoliouth (1956: 132) compares *PL*, II, 890ff, Stevenson (1971: 370) *PL*, II, 643ff, and Miner (1969: 264, 465n22) Dan. viii.10.

75:13-14/ E352/ VI, 304-05   To Miner (1969: 264) this image suggests the constellation Orion, to which Stevenson (1971: 370) adds the hero Hercules and Ostriker (1977: 940) the god Thor. To Janet Warner (1973: 219, 221), he recalls Bunyan's Giant Despair.

75:21/ E352/ VI, 312   The fifty-two armies may be the year's fifty-two weeks and the cliffs the four elements (Damon 1924: 378), or the cliffs may be the four seasons (Sloss and Wallis 1926: I, 237). Alternatively, the armies may be rebels from the fifty-two counties of Britain [i.e. England and Wales] resisting oppression, while this epic's "four Cliffs of Urthona" are a variant of the "four cliffs of Albion" of *America*, cancelled plate c, ll. 14-17 (E59/ K205), a passage repeated almost *verbatim* here (Erdman 1954a: 347 [374]).

75:25/ E352/ VI, 316   Reason is unable to stand before the Spirit (Damon 1924: 378). The Spectre and Tharmas act as an inner censor and stop reason from continuing its quest for hidden causes (Margoliouth 1951: 122). Ostriker (1977: 941) compares Satan's retreat at *PL*, IV, 877-1015.

75: 29-31/ E352/ VI, 320-22   Newton suggested that comets refuelled stars and replenished atmospheres (Hilton 1983: 289n13).

75:33-34/ E352/ VI, 324-25   Urthona's squadrons are rendered "dismal" by Urizen, who compels them to spread his Web of superstition (Margoliouth 1956: 132), with which he overawes his restive subjects (Erdman 1954a: 347 [374]). Nanavutty (1957: 169-71) remarks that the heavenly bodies are part of the cosmic web that the Hindu creator-god spins from his entrails.

Night the Seventh

Much has already been said about Night the Seventh in the general headnote to *The Four Zoas*. Among its major events are Orc's metamorphosis, the birth of Vala from Enitharmon's heart, Urizen's war, Los's reunion with the Spectre of Urthona, and the redemptive work of Los and Enitharmon.

Sloss and Wallis (1926: I, 247, 324) believe that Orc's identification with Luvah, like the Shadowy Female's with Vala, is a late development, and Paley (1970: 90, 102) reasons that Blake's disillusion with the French Revolution causes him to equate Orc with a fallen Zoa. Psychologically, according to Gallant (1978: 70), Orc's transformation into a vicious serpent occurs because Urizen's influence stops him from seeing his caverns (the unconscious) as a storehouse of energy.

After the degeneration of the revolutionary spirit, the Spectre of Urthona unites with the Shadow of Enitharmon marking, says Frye (1947: 299), the end of the Orc cycle, and Wilkie and Johnson (1978: 156) write, "As virtually all students of Blake recognize, this embrace is the crisis of the poem." Its result is the birth of Vala, who manifests in Night the Eighth as the monstrous Rahab.

Night VIIb, which contains the account of Urizen's war, has much more political content than the psychologically and metaphysically oriented VIIa (Sutherland 1970: 254). Margoliouth (1956: 140) considers that Blake has reached the world of his own time and writes of the wars of 1792-1802 rather than, as Erdman maintains (1954a: 298-302 [323-28]), the campaigns specifically of 1799.

Urthona's Spectre also unites with Los, combining, in Frye's view (1947: 298), the former's sense of linear time with the latter's power of vision to produce the line of prophecy and art that leads to Christ. Wilkie and Johnson (1978: 161-62, 245-46) emphasise that the union shows that only with recognition of one's doubts and fears and of the Satan in oneself does inner healing become possible; Night VIIb, on the other hand, shows the futility of internal and external conflict. Erdman (1954a: 349 [376]) deduces that Blake came to believe that peace could only arrive as the gift of Providence.

It is after this (according to Lefebvre's and Erdman's arrangement of the text—see p. 204 above), that Enitharmon persuades Los to follow her example by eating the fruit of the Tree of Mystery—an obvious replay of events in the Garden of Eden. (Deen, indeed, [1983: 139-46] thinks the Spectre of Urthona performs the role of Satan the Tempter both to Enitharmon's Eve and to Los's Adam and Christ.) But, as Howard observes (1984: 222), Los and Enitharmon break precedent by co-operating afterwards instead of quarrelling. Together they create works of art that double as mortal bodies, showing, declares Mellor (1974: 208-11), that clearly outlined forms need not be Urizenic and constricting but can manifest the infinite and divine. In a post-modernist reading, Brisman (1978: 265-75) argues that the Fall is here portrayed as a distancing of the mind from immediate experience resulting in a resort to metaphorical language; the Shadow of Enitharmon and Spectre of Urthona are themselves metaphors as suggested by the polysemous word "shade" (85:3/ E360/ VII, 313), but they vanish from the scene and Los comes to recognise the illusory element in such images and is ready to create works of art, which can restore some of the lost immediacy.

Details

77:5-19/ E352-53/ VII, 1-19 Here are the horses of intellect, the lions of the furnaces, and the tigers of wrath (Margoliouth 1956: 134). Urizen sees the horses he lent to Luvah in Orc's cavern (Damon 1967: 420), where they are raging in the bonds of twofold vision (Beer 1969: 119-20). Though the tigers' wrath promotes revolution, it is limited by its blindness to the human form—cf. 15:1-2/ E309/ I, 402-03—hence "the redounding smoke" (Damon 1967: 413).

77:10-12/ E353/ VII, 10-12 Justice is Urizenic, mercy revolutionary (Ostriker 1977: 941-42). Instead of moderating the law, oil of compassion becomes destructive passion (Wilkie and Johnson 1978: 148). Margoliouth (1956: 134) endorses Keynes's punctuation (1925: II, 74), but a period could well follow "mercy."

77:14-15/ E353/ VII, 14-15 Urizen's plough and harrow are instruments for cultivating civilisation (Margoliouth 1956: 134). They are intellectual instruments misused for purposes of battle (Paley 1970: 111). Repressed sexual desire issues in war (Webster 1983: 234). See also 28:10/ E318/ II, 120n.

77:26/ E353/ VII, 26 The revolutionary idea becomes worldwide (Damon 1924: 378). The daughters are the Furies (Raine 1968: II, 89).

77:27/ E353/ VII, 27 Los, who descended into the personal unconscious of Entuthon Benithon at 62:15/ E342/ V, 149, has now reached the collective unconscious of Orc's caves (Gallant 1978: 67).

78:12/ E353/ VII, 39 **all but the book of iron**—When religion is worldly it makes use of war (Damon 1924: 378) to fight revolution (Schorer 1946: 324). Cf. 80:1/ E355/ VII, 109n.

78:25-26/ E354/ VII, 52-53 These lines refer to variously shaped particles produced by the action of vortexes in the Cartesian cosmos of the sixth Night (Raine 1968: II, 82).

78:30/ E354/ VII, 57 **Pity**—bogus pity (Sloss and Wallis 1926: I, 244); real pity (Bloom 1963: 249).

79:20-24/ E355/ VII, 90-94 Urizen's Daughters prepare the bread of materialistic ideas (Damon 1924: 160) or of the frustration of sexuality (Bloom 1963: 250) or of Gen. iii.17-19 (Ostriker 1977: 942). They are to make Orc's food bitter (Damon 1967: 421) or teach him how to endure without anger (Beer 1969: 120). France learns from British aggressiveness how to make war (Erdman 1954a: 349 [376]); Orc, with his repressed guilt, is ready to learn from Urizen, as France has imitated Britain (Paley 1970: 112).

79:25/ E355/ VII, 95 **the Rocks**—of 68:1-4/ E345/ VI, 20-23 (Margoliouth 1956: 135).

79:25-37/ E355/ VII, 95-107 The book of iron is the Mosaic Law [but see next note] and the bread is the "bread from heaven" that rained down to lie like "hoar frost" (Exod. xvi.4, 14) (Raine 1968: II, 95-97).

80:1/ E355/ VII, 109 The speech that follows supports Damon's claim (1924: 378) that Urizen's book of brass is the book of "false charity," while the book of iron is the book of war. Cf. also Damon 1967: 58, 424 (where he substitutes "sociology" for "false charity.") Ostriker (1977: 942) associates Urizen's economics with the tones like "sounding brass" of those that have no charity (I Cor. xiii.1). Cf. 71:40/ E349/ VI, 172n.

80:5ff/ E355-56/ VII, 113ff   The Shadow of Enitharmon, an unexpected new character, has been explained as measurable space (Frye 1947: 298) in an exclusively material world, where her name signifies "numbered" instead of "numberless" [see *A* 7:4n] (Bloom 1965: 959); as Enitharmon's vital energy (Ostriker 1977: 941); as a degenerate aspect of Enitharmon attracted to the basest type of male (Wilkie and Johnson 1978: 155-56); and simply as Enitharmon reduced to a shadow (Damon 1967: 299) or to mortality (Margoliouth 1956: 136).

   Damon (1967: 368-69—cf. 1924: 318) regards the Shadow as a constituent of every person—like the Spectre and Emanation: he conceives it as "the residue of one's suppressed desires." Here, however, it is the Shadow of an Emanation we encounter, and in *J* 15:17 it is the Shadow of a Spectre. Sloss and Wallis (1926: II, 221) consider the Shadow a fallen emanation; Davies (1948: 74) defines it as "the disintegrating physical perception."

80:9ff/ E355-56/ VII, 117ff   Schorer (1946: 324-25) perceives here an attack on Malthus's *Essay on the Principle of Population* (first version 1798), Erdman (1954a: 341-42 [368-69]) an attack on Pitt's speech of 11 Nov. 1800 refusing measures to help the poor.

80:22-26/ E356/ VII, 130-34   Urizen describes the embryo of the Shadowy Female (Damon 1924: 378) and expresses fear that Los's Children may consume everything (Beer 1969: 121). He claims that Orc is rebellious because his parents misused him (Wilkie and Johnson 1978: 148-49).

80:27-44/ E356/ VII, 135-52   Urizen has persuaded Orc to accept Mystery (Percival 1938: 193). Orc's turning into a serpent immediately after receiving instruction from Urizen may symbolise Napoleon's Concordat of 1801 with the Vatican (Paley 1970: 115-16). The worm and the serpent represent British and French radicalism—the former starved by repression, the latter transformed into Bonapartism (Erdman 1954a: 348 [375]). The supposed worm—Urizen's view of revolution enfeebled—becomes a serpent, which is energy misconceived as evil (Wilkie and Johnson 1978: 149-50).

80:38/ E356/ VII, 146   Cf. 63:2-3/ E342/ V, 168-69 and note. Orcean energy is subdued by Newtonian gravity (Ault 1974: 110).

80:39-48/ E356/ VII, 147-56   Revolutionaries transform reason into wrath (Damon 1924: 378). They err in resorting to rationalism to fight rationalism (Schorer 1946: 325-26) or they confess their indebtedness to the Enlightenment (Crehan 1984: 314). There is a parody of the Eucharist here (Bloom 1965: 959). Boehme's Second Principle (Light) is turned into his First (Fire), to which Orc regresses (Paley 1970: 110, 116).

81:5-6/ E356/ VII, 164-65   Cf. John xii.32 (Margoliouth 1956: 136). Citing this passage, Wilkie and Johnson (1978: 151-52) show that Urizen is unawares making Orc play the part of Christ on the Cross. Citing also John iii.14, Ostriker (1977: 943) sees revolution corrupted.

81:6/ E356/ VII, 165   The "result" is the destruction of Urizen's Tree by Orc's fire (119:4/ E388/ IX, 70) (Sloss and Wallis 1926: I, 248) or humanity's liberation from guilt by the Crucifixion in the eighth Night (Wilkie and Johnson 1978: 152).

81:7-9/ E356/ VII, 166-67   Here resumes the narrative broken off at 63:17/ E343/ V, 183 (Stevenson 1971: 377). Los`s descending thoughts "break futilely over Mystery" (Damon 1924: 379).

81:11/ E356/ VII, 170   The real Enitharmon is unable to penetrate Urizen's insubstantial, ghostlike world (Stevenson 1971: 371).

81:13-17/ E357/ VII, 172-76   Enitharmon is alive alternatively to Los and to the Spectre of Urthona (Johnson and Wilkie [not to be confused with Wilkie and Johnson] 1978: 100-01).

81:23-82:14/ E357/ VII, 184-208   Los is deprived of inspiration (Damon 1924: 379). He encounters woman's jealousy (Sloss and Wallis 1926: I, 249), or seasonal decay in Enitharmon's appearance and affection (Bloom 1965: 959). He is jealous of the rival—apparently Orc—who enjoys her visits (Webster 1983: 236).

81:29-82:3/ E357/ VII, 190-97   Los realises that a fallen material body and world cannot satisfy his needs (Frosch 1974: 48-49).

82:10/ E357/ VII, 204   Los's "winged woes" are the metaphorical birds hatched from the eggs of his melancholy (Margoliouth 1956: 136).

82:15-22/ E357-58/ VII, 209-16 The conscious selves of Los and Enitharmon above do not know that the Spectre is courting the Shadow below (Ostriker 1977: 943).

82:17-25/ E357-58/ VII, 211-19 Citing "A Poison Tree", Raine (1968: II, 40-42) argues that Boehme's First Principle, the divine Wrath, produces the Tree of Nature, which secretes the poison of love with its serpent-like fruit.

82:36/ E358/ VII, 230 **Sweet delusions**—pleasure in natural religion promised to the poet's Inspiration (Damon 1924: 379); nature's outward appearance, which seduced Albion (Raine 1968: II, 181).

83:7-16/ E358/ VII, 239-48 Albion's fathering of Urizen gives the latter an Oedipal motive for his hostility (Bloom 1963: 253). Albion enters Generation with his embrace of Vala, who represents a passive state that separates subject from object; these become inextricably intermingled in the "double form" of "Luvah & Vala" (Bloom 1965: 960). Beulah's flowers are sexual pleasure (Damon 1967: 43), and Albion moves from an erotic relationship with another person (he "Saw/ Vala") to the creation of a distorted mental image of her (Brisman 1978: 266). He exhibits infantile regression in Beulah (DiSalvo 1983: 336).

83:33/ E359/ VII, 265 **thy fiery South**—see 74:14, 28/ E351/ VI, 265, 279.

84:1-2/ E359/ VII, 267-68 **this delightful Tree**—the church seen as a refuge within Experience (Damon 1924: 379). Catherine (Enitharmon) views William's sexual desire (the Spectre) as horrific, the Spectre tempts her to shelter in conventional Christianity, and she eventually (85:17/ E360/ VII, 327) bears the child Orc (Sutherland 1970: 252). The Tree and its fruit (87:15ff/ E369-70/ VII, 387ff) bring a sense of sin, which, though misguided, will show the need for self-transformation (Wilkie and Johnson 1978: 158).

84:31/ E359/ VII, 297 **that Creation I created**—creations of the mind like time and space mistaken for objective absolutes (Paley 1970: 157); Los, whom the Spectre falsely boasts he has created (Johnson and Wilkie 1978: 101).

84:33-35/ E359/ VII, 299-301 The Spectre will subject nature to revolution and destroy the selfhood (Damon 1924: 380). At the Shadow of Enitharmon's request, he will punish Vala (Margoliouth 1956: 138). He will seek the reunion of Vala and Orc to promote the reintegration of the Eternal Man (Beer 1969: 134). He will abolish the separate existence of Los ("That body") (Stevenson 1971: 381).

84:36-40/ E360/ VII, 304-10   Aware of his deficiency but not of his potential for redemption, the Spectre couples with the Shadow begetting Vala (Bloom 1963: 253-54).

84:40/ E360/ VII, 310   For "The spectres of the Dead," see 87:35-38/ E369/ VII, 407-10n.

85:6-11/ E360/ VII, 315-21   Los is unaware that Enitharmon shrieks in sympathy with her Shadow, who is suffering birth-pangs below (Stevenson 1971: 382).

85:11-12/ E360/ VII, 321-22   Returning to Enitharmon's conscious mind above, her desire runs wild (Ostriker 1977: 943). The birth frees Enitharmon from her Shadow (Johnson and Wilkie 1978: 101).

85:13-15/ E360/ VII, 323-25   The gates of Enitharmon's heart, closed in the first Night [20:6/ E313/ I, 565], are now open (Damon 1924: 161) yielding the broken and contrite heart demanded in Scripture (Ostriker 1977: 943). The breaking of Enitharmon's heart represents the revival at the time of Christ of the emotional aspect of Los, the Poetic Genius: the feelings newly support the intellect making possible the fulfilment of the latter's vision (Percival 1938: 123, 227, 262). Surprisingly, Wagenknecht (1973: 224) regards the opening of the heart as ambivalent since it is modelled on the birth of Sin in *PL*, II, 778-85. Raine (1968: I, 235-36) finds a more convincing source in *PL*, II, 871-84.

Enitharmon's heart gives birth to Vala in the form of the Shadowy Female—i.e. space gives birth to nature (Damon 1924: 161)—cf. 63:13/ E343/ V, 179n. Stevenson (1971: 382-83) judges it is more likely the Shadow of Enitharmon than Vala, the "wonder horrible," new daughter of that Shadow, who bursts the gates. Sutherland (1970: 252) thinks it is Orc, not Vala, who is born—cf. 84:1-2/ E359/ VII, 267-68n.

85:17/ E360/ VII, 327   **a Cloud**—fast spreading materialisation (Damon 1924: 380); perhaps the expanding cloud of matter of the Hermetists (Raine 1968: I, 408n11).

85:17-19/ E360/ VII, 327-29 Damon (1924: 360) believes the "dead" fall lower; Wagenknecht (1973: 224-25) is unsure whether or not this reverse resurrection is desirable.

85:22/ E360/ VII, 332 **her**—Vala, who has now degenerated into the Shadowy Female (Damon 1924: 380); Enitharmon (Sutherland 1970: 252).

95:16/ E360/ VIIb, 2 **the Shadow**—Orc (Damon 1924: 382); Vala (Margoliouth 1956: 143).

95:20/ E360/ VIIb, 6 Cf. Ps. civ.2 (Margoliouth 1956: 143).

95:31-96:18/ E361/ VIIb, 18-38 The temple is devoted to "the Selfish Virtues of the Natural Heart" (Bloom 1965: 960, quoting *J*, pl. 52, prose). It is the centre of a religion which exalts chastity but is obsessed with sexuality (Damon 1924: 162, 382), which it insists on suppressing (Damon 1967: 420), and through which Urizen (on one level Britain) tries to subject nature to his own purposes (Erdman 1954: 313 [340]).

The "secret place" is devoted to "phallic worship" (T. Wright 1929: I, 149), the phallus being the product of the "wondrous workmanship" (Harper 1961: 174). It is the temple's Holy of Holies (Ezek. vii.22), which Blake associates with sexual secrecy and priestly power (Stevenson 1971: 391) and with the pagan abominations of Ezek. viii (Miner 1969: 284-85). It is an image of the Pentateuch hidden in the vagina (Damrosch 1980: 205).

96:7/ E361/ VIIb, 27 **cloth'd in disguises beastial**—Compulsory abstinence makes the imagination conjure up monsters (T. Wright 1929: I, 149).

96:11-14/ E361/ VIIb, 31-34 Even the material sun resists its subjection to Urizen's purposes (Raine 1968: I, 230). A theocratic monarch tries to exploit both the sun's energy and the chariot of intellect (DiSalvo 1983: 218-19). Energy is enslaved by mechanism (Crehan 1984: 554).

96:18/ E361/ VIIb, 38 **his temple**—This phrase is followed in the MS. by the deleted words "Urizen named it Pande" (Bentley 1963: 100)—i.e. Pandemonium (Erdman 1965: 763)—showing that Blake identified the temple with Satan's capital in Hell (*PL*, I, 756).

96:19-27/ E361/ VIIb, 40-48 There is some disagreement as to whether this is a thoroughly corrupt Los delighting in war for its own sake (Margoliouth 1956: 144) or a Los some way between the war poet of earlier Nights and the visionary (Bloom 1965: 960) or even prophecy resisting imperialism (Ostriker 1977: 946). The line 97:21/ E362/ VIIb, 75 supports Margoliouth's case. In Erdman's view (1954a: 298 [323-24]), Los is here a war correspondent serving Tharmas and preferring chaos to empire.

96:29/ E361/ VIIb, 50   Tharmas will destroy the anti-Napoleon coalition of 1799 (*ibid.*).

96:31-97:1/ E361/ VIIb, 52-55   Tharmas's son is Los, who almost stands for England; her motto after the Armada was "He blew and they were scattered" (Margoliouth 1956: 144).

97:28/ E362/ VIIb, 82   **thee**—Los, whom Enitharmon no longer recognises (Damon 1924: 382); Tharmas, who asked for trust at 97:1/ E361/ VIIb, 55 (Margoliouth 1956: 144); Orc, who has become a tyrant—specifically, Napoleon (Erdman 1969b: 323-24).

97:31/ E362/ VIIb, 85   **a tower upon a rock**—the "bower" of 49:19/ E333/ IV, 71 (Margoliouth 1956: 144); the pillars of 59:28/ E340/ V, 73 (Stevenson 1971: 393).

98:1/ E362/ VIIb, 92   **Shadow of Jealousy**—Orc, or, if Enitharmon is adddressing Tharmas, the Spectre of Urthona (Stevenson 1971: 393).

98:2-6/ E362/ VIIb, 93-97   Damon (1924: 382) cites Is. xxi.11, and Paley (1970: 120) Ps. cxxvii.1.

98:7ff/ E362-63/ VIIb, 98ff   Some later critics agree with Margoliouth (1956: 145) that the trees and animals have been corrupted by the war spirit.

98:17-21/ E363/ VIIb, 108-12   These lines refer to the constellations Aries, Taurus, Leo, Lynx, Serpens, Hydra and Scorpio (Worrall 1981: 279-80).

98:22-24/ E363/ VIIb, 113-15   Prester John was a monarch and a priest (Margoliouth 1956: 145). The Prester Serpent may be the final form of Orc (Wagenknecht 1973: 235) or a kind of offshoot since Orc is still fettered to the Tree (Stevenson 1971: 394)—see 93:24/ E365/ VIIb, 214. Blake is aiming at clergy who offer public prayer for military aggrandisement (Paley 1973a: 272). Most likely his cowl signifies uncircumcision (Miner 1969: 278).

98:27/ E363/ VIIb, 118   **seven Diseases**—the seven deadly sins (Margoliouth 1956: 145); "the seven deadly virtues" (Bloom

1965: 960-61)—i.e. the four cardinal virtues (prudence, temperance, fortitude, justice) and the three theological virtues (faith, hope, charity).

91:1-5/ E363/ VIIb, 124-28   The Shadowy Female, now a vortex, threatens to absorb human life (Bloom 1965: 961). She is the illusion of a mechanical nature, nameless for lack of a male partner (Paley 1970: 117-18).

91:14-15/ E363/ VIIb, 137-38   Unlike Urizen, Los and earthly monarchs, Orc does not degrade Vala by perceiving her incompletely (Schorer 1946: 329). She is classed with (Bloom 1965: 961) or identical with (Hilton 1982: 168) Mystery, the Whore of Babylon of Rev. xvii.5.

91:21-23/ E364/ VIIb, 144-46   War (Damon 1924: 162) or revolution (T. Wright 1929: I, 151) has arrived, and Orc vainly fights to liberate energy from reason (Mellor 1974: 188). The song that follows cruelly celebrates war between the Zoas (Ostriker 1977: 945). We have met the elemental gods before, when they sang the warlike nuptial song for Los and Enitharmon (13:22/ E308/ I, 377), and Stevenson (1971: 396) convincingly associates them with the demons who sing Orc's nativity song (58:21/ E339/ V, 41). Wagenknecht (1973: 228-29) believes that the singers are now fighting to help Vala suppress Orc, and Wilkie and Johnson (1978: 249) credit them with singing both of inner conflict and of physical warfare. As Stevenson observes (*loc. cit.*), their viewpoint seems inconsistent.

91:25-27/ E364/ VIIb, 148-50   Damon (1924: 382) correctly regards the north as the quarter of Urthona, whom he regularly identifies as the Spirit (e.g. 365). The "dragons of the North" have been interpreted as British dragoons (Erdman 1954a: 300 [326]), as (possibly) Russians campaigning in Holland in 1799 (Margoliouth 1956: 140), and as Urizen's warriors (Mellor 1974: 188).

91:28/ E364/ VIIb, 151   **the Eastern sea**—the Strait of Dover (Erdman 1954a: 300 [326]).

91:30/ E364/ VIIb, 153   **the glorious King**—France (Erdman 1954a: 300 [326]); either Urizen or Orc (Stevenson 1971: 396); the phrase could apply to any of the Zoas (Wilkie and Johnson 1978: 249).

92:3, 6/ E364/ VIIb, 156, 159 The "black bow" is a black gun that shoots "darts" and "arrows" and becomes "cloudy" when it smokes (Erdman 1954a: 300 [326]).

92:6-8/ E364/ VIIb, 159-61 Keynes very reasonably treats these lines as an interruption in the song (1925: II, 95).

92:11-15/ E364/ VIIb, 164-68 This vigorous piece of narrative has been said to deal with the crucifixion of the passions (Damon 1924: 382); Parliament's reactionary domestic legislation in 1799 and its simultaneously intensified campaign against France (Erdman 1954a: 300 [327]); British M.P.s of this year who are identified with Roman soldiers at Calvary (Bloom 1965: 961); what the victors did to France after Napoleon's overthrow (Damon 1967: 256); and Urizen's defeat of Luvah in the first Night and the parallel between Druid human sacrifice, the Crucifixion, and contemporary events (Stevenson 1971: 397). Frye (1947: 396) sees in Luvah nailed to a tree an image of the human being imprisoned in a fallen body.

92:16/ E364/ VIIb, 169 The sun and moon no longer have value for the imagination (Margoliouth 1956: 141).

92:17-33/ E364/ VIIb, 170-86 As Keynes's punctuation implies (1925: II, 95) and Stevenson observes (1971: 397), this is an interpolation in the war song, and Blake himself is the speaker. In Bronowski's view (1954: 29-31), Blake is complaining that the mechanism of the new machines, based on "Wheel without wheel," is far removed from that of the human body, and that such machines deaden the operators' minds. Blackstone (1949: 315-16) notes that the "intricate wheels" include those of the clock, modern counterpart of the hourglass, and, more important, Erdman (1954a: 313 [339]) sees how the poet is contrasting the horror of cogwheels with the "wheel in the middle of a wheel" of Ezek. i.16.

92:34ff/ E365/ VIIb, 187ff The demons inform Vala that war is not pretty (Erdman 1954a: 301-02 [327-28]). They are probably to some extent anti-war and sarcastic at the expense of Vala, an alluring harlot ("Magdalen") (Wilkie and Johnson 1978: 251). As Mary Magdalene attended Christ's sepulchre, Vala attends the grave of Luvah, and they urge her to enter it and use her seductive art to stop him from rising (Beer 1969: 143). Miner (1958: 203-06) remarks Vala's resemblance to the sinister supernatural weavers of Gray's "The Fatal Sisters."

93:1-5/ E365/ VIIb, 191-95 Using imagery borrowed from Is.
li.21 and lii.3, Blake celebrates Christ's forgiveness of Mag-
dalene, who may again sow the unfallen Urizen's seed
(Percival 1938: 124-25, 311). Vala's blue eyes show she is a
Valkyrie, one of the maidens of Odin who decide which warr-
iors are doomed (Paley 1983b: 193).

93:6/ E365/ VIIb, 196 **thy feigned terrors**—contrasted with the
terrors of actual fighting (Margoliouth 1956: 141); a show of
pretended chastity diverting her lovers' energies into war
(Ostriker 1977: 946). The secret couch belongs to Urizen,
whom she is seducing from his duty (Stevenson 1971: 398).

93:6-10/ E365/ VIIb, 196-200 For this description of sunrise,
Blake borrows the bow of Apollo, who, like unfallen Urizen, is
Prince of Light (Margoliouth 1956: 141).

93:21/ E365/ VIIb, 211 Orc employs Urizen's own instrument,
war, to combat his rule and transform nature (Schorer 1946:
330). He lets slip the opportunity to humanise the earth (Paley
1970: 119).

93:23, 29/ E365/ VIIb, 213, 219 Matter must be destroyed for
nature to be redeemed (Damon 1924: 383). The Shadowy Fem-
ale rejoices because her opponent shares "the cruelty by which
she reigns" (Stevenson 1971: 399).

93:25-26/ E365/ VIIb, 215-16 The French Revolution gives way
to Napoleon's imperialism (Margoliouth 1956: 142). Orc allies
himself with Urizen's stars (Paley 1970: 119).

93:31/ E365/ VIIb, 221 The British army returned from Holland
in November 1799 after suffering enormous losses (Erdman
1954a: 302 [328]). The soldiers begin to be disillusioned with
war (Wilkie and Johnson 1978: 252).

93:36-37/ E365-66/ VIIb, 226-27 The body's fury is ruining reas-
on (Damon 1924: 383). Stevenson (1971: 400) draws attention
to Tharmas's proposed suicide pact.

93:38/ E366/ VIIb, 228 The body thinks the material world is
the Earth Mother (Damon 1924: 383).

93:40/ E366/ VIIb, 230 Vala tries to win Tharmas's alliance
(Ostriker 1977: 945, 946). She mocks him (Wilkie and John-
son 1978: 252).

94:10-16/ E366/ VIIb, 242-48 Blake alludes to the traditions that
the air contains the World Memory and that lost things find a
home on the invisible face of the moon (Damon 1924: 383).

The gate of mortal birth is governed by the moon (Raine 1968: I, 232).

94:16-17/ E366/ VIIb, 248-49   Inspiration, Pleasure and Generation enclosed the passions (Luvah) in revolution (Damon 1924: 383). Vala vainly lies to hide her responsibility for Albion's fall (Stevenson 1971: 400).

94:23/ E366/ VIIb, 255   Orc broke the Chain of Jealousy at 91:17/ E363/ VIIb, 140 (Stevenson 1971: 400).

94:37-47/ E367/ VIIb, 269-79   Vala becomes melancholy under a Urizenic regime (Margoliouth 1956: 143). She is Psyche, the soul, served, as Apuleius tells, by invisible attendants, whom Blake identifies with the spirits of nature (Raine 1957b: 833). Under the influence of Tharmas, who detects error in her story, Vala starts to see in nature both her Luvah and a potential for redemption (Beer 1969: 137).

94:54-55/ E367/ VIIb, 286-87   **the Demon**—Orc, who rages under Urizenic domination (Margoliouth 1956: 143); Tharmas, whose anger is an obstacle to Urizen's gaining complete control over chaos (Wagenknecht 1973: 231-32).

95:1-2/ E367/ VIIb, 288-89   According to Damon (1924: 383), corrupt nature seeks comfort from Beulah, but more probably, as Margoliouth proposes (1956: 143), her melancholy extends even into Beulah.

95:6/ E367/ VIIb, 293   The line combines John xi.23 and xi.40 (Beer 1969: 137, 360n12). The physical body will be resurrected as a spiritual body (Mellor 1974: 189).

This is the first explicitly Christian passage in *Vala* that is not an addition to the original text (Paley 1970: 121).

95:11/ E367/ VIIb, 298   With the arrival of Vala, comes the descent of souls (Margoliouth 1956: 143). Souls 'sleeping' in graves in Beulah fall into Ulro (Damon 1967: 43).

95:14/ E367/ VIIb, 301   Satan is a subhuman condition or perhaps past wisdom that has decayed into present error (Damon 1924: 383). He is the selfhood (Bloom 1963: 245). The Daughters of Beulah give the name (Margoliouth 1956: 143).

85:26-32/ E367/ VII, 336-42   Finding Enitharmon feels for her Shadow, the Spectre of Urthona thinks Los may feel for him (Stevenson 1971: 383). Although the Spectre is renouncing his "Domineering lust" (his craving for power [Margoliouth 1951: 123]), Damon (1924: 380) supposes he is trying to impose the power of his selfhood on Los. A centre opens in Los that is the contrary of the Shadowy Female's Vortex (91:2/ E363/ VIIb, 125) (Bloom 1965: 961).

85:43-86:9/ E368/ VII, 353-66 Here Blake counsels submission to Divine Providence, which has brought about the blessed Peace of Amiens (Erdman 1954a: 350-52 [377-79]).

85:45/ E368/ VII, 355 **the fourth Universe**—that of Urthona, the Spirit (Damon 1924: 380). Cf. 123:39/ E393/ IX, 284 and *M* 19:15-18.

86:13/ E368/ VII, 370 Los is motivated by a pity that does not divide [cf. *BU* 13:53] but reunites (Nurmi 1976: 141).

87:2/ E368/ VII, 373 Los seems momentarily to be given a Spectre distinct from the Spectre of Urthona. Damon (1924: 379) recognises such a separate spectre, a personification of poetic technique.

87:3/ E368/ VII, 374 **the Center**—the earth's centre, where tradition placed hell (Stevenson 1971: 385).

87:4-5/ E368/ VII, 375-76 Los must destroy his own works, such as Urizen's body, that impose a restrictive view of the world (Evans 1972: 316).

87:6-11/ E368/ VII, 378-83 For Damon (1924: 161), the act of building Golgonooza is the act of reconstructing the universe on an ideal pattern and (1967: 164) its function is to bestow form on all that is uncreated; for Murry (1933: 199), Golgonooza is the art that embodies the Divine Vision present in the regenerating or regenerated universe. When it is finished, Frye maintains (1947: 248), it will have become Jerusalem. Agreeing with Frye, Raine (1968: II, 264-66) sees Golgonooza as being also the Jungian mandala; as such, adds Gallant (1978: 74-75), it shows that Los is now well on the way to unifying psychic contraries. With the Peace of Amiens, says Erdman (1954a: 354 [381]), Blake ceases to design Jerusalem as a model for revolutionaries, preferring to create a city of art. In Webster's view (1983: 230), the art is a disguise for Los's Oedipal attempt to possess the mother's body, which Golgonooza represents, though Harper (1961: 213) considers it to be anatomically the head and Damon (1967: 162) believes it includes or even consists of the whole human body, male and female. See also 60:3/ E340/ V, 76n and 60:5/ E340/ V, 78n.

87:8/ E368/ VII, 380 Cf. Rev. xxi. 1 (Damon 1924: 380).

87:9-12/ E368-69/ VII, 381-84 The atmosphere, being Sweden-borgian, limits perception but allows development (Hilton 1978: 84)—see 30:6-7/ E319/ II, 164-65n. The Limit of Translucence is the higher boundary of Beulah, from which one can rise to Eden or sink to Ulro (Bloom 1965: 961); this atmosphere of Golgonooza extends from threefold Beulah down to the limits of opacity (Satan) and contraction (Adam), which means that art ranges from "divine dreams...to malice and stupidity" (Ostriker 1977: 944). Contrast *J* 42:35, which states "there is no Limit of Translucence"—i.e. (Frye 1947: 448n56) no upper limit. Deen (1983: 141) supposes that the Spectre of Urthona corresponds to Satan and Los to Adam.

87:15-22/ E369/ VII, 387-94 Blake alludes to Rom. vii.7-9 in this attack on the concept of vicarious atonement (Damon 1924: 381), which Enitharmon wrongly accepts (Beer 1969: 135). She hopes Los will follow her in eating the fruit and by not succumbing to despair like hers will revive her belief in eternal life (Damon 1924: 161, 381).

87:23/ E369/ VII, 395 Sutherland (1970: 253) sees a sexual meaning: William experiences consummation and appears to tolerate conventional religion to ease the mind of Catherine, who refers to it as a ransom.

87:25/ E369/ VII, 397 Time (the Spectre) comforts the imagina-tion (Los) (Bloom 1963: 255).

87:26-28/ E369/ VII, 398-400 The error of dividing things into black and white does lead Los to despair, and the six thousand years of creation begin (Damon 1924: 161, 381).

87:35-38/ E369/ VII, 407-10 Spectres of the Dead may be "fragments of spirit" (Damon 1967: 382); spirits who have lost their connection with the divine oneness (Sloss and Wallis 1926: II, 226); mental phantoms evoked by "doubts in self accusation" (Essick 1980: 213, quoting 87:13/ E369/ VII, 385); or bodiless thoughts, memories and male sexual desires (Deen 1983: 151). Their counterparts may be emanations, which are ideals (Damon 1924: 161, 381); material bodies (Damon 1967: 382); or the Spectres' imaginative complements as Los is the Spectre of Urthona's (Bloom 1963: 255), these being works of art (Bloom 1965: 961).

87:39-44/ E369/ VII, 411-16 Los witnesses the conception (not birth) of Jesus (Damon 1924: 381).

90:5-43/ E370-71/ VII, 436-75 There is general acceptance of Damon's point (1924: 161) that Los, with Enitharmon's aid, creates works of art, but while Stevenson (1971: 388) and Paley (1973b: 121-25) conceive of these as being simultaneously bodies of flesh, Johnson and Wilkie (1978) do not. Raine (1968: I, 263-64) believes they are noble images which the Spectres will contemplate and come to resemble.

90:10-13, 24, 50-52/ E370, 371/ VII, 441-44, 455, 482-84 Enitharmon accepts Los's counsel that they follow Christ's example by sacrificing themselves for others (Beer 1969: 136). No longer sacrificing their Children (as they did Orc), they recognise self-sacrifice as the way to redemption (Wilkie and Johnson 1978: 164-65). Hostile to the Spectre of Urthona, Deen (1983: 140-44) conceives him as a Urizenic advocate of propitiatory sacrifice who believes that the Spectre is the real human.

90:20-21/ E370/ VII, 451-52 **piteous forms**—inspirations given by Enitharmon to Los (Damon 1924: 161); souls whose bodily lives are futile unless Los's works of art teach them of Eternity (Raine 1968: I, 264-65).

90:21-24/ E370/ VII, 452-55 Blake should produce saleable engravings (Essick 1980: 213).

90:28-34/ E370/ VII, 460-66 Los draws inspiration from the conflict of ideas ("Urizen's war") and from people's constrained passions (Orc's lake) and gives his art a rational foundation (Damon 1924: 381-82). He uses Orc's fire ("the energies of natural man") but draws an imaginative circle contrary to Urizenic circles (Bloom 1965: 962). The very flames of Orc that had evoked Los's Chain of Jealousy in the fifth Night now enable him to complete his mandala (Gallant 1978: 77-78). On the societal level, Blake's work draws the British and French (Urizen and Orc) from war and politics to artistic pursuits (Erdman 1954a: 355 [382]). The "furious raging flames" resemble prickly wheat stalks (Stevenson 1971: 388).

90:35-38/ E370-71/ VII, 467-70 Catherine Blake tinted her husband's pictures (Damon 1924: 382). Colours supplied by Enitharmon (who is primarily space, secondarily Catherine) convey emotions (Rose 1971a: 55). Grimes (1973: 81) proposes that the reunion of Los and Enitharmon, which is Blake's combination of text and design, enacts a union of space and time that can bring about "visionary perception."

90:44/ E371/ VII, 476   Rintrah and Palamabron are righteous wrath and pity won over and restored to Innocence (Damon 1924: 382); they stand for Pitt and Parliament (Erdman 1954a: 355 [382]).

90:55-56/ E371/ VII, 487-88   The "soft silken veils" are flesh (Damon 1924: 382) and the "Female forms" may be the Daughters of either Los or Beulah (Sloss and Wallis 1926: I, 260).

90:58-60/ E371/ VII, 490-92   The Shadow of Urizen is perhaps pity (Sutherland 1970: 254), and his creative side manifests in Rintrah while his Spectre becomes Satan in the next Night (Bloom 1963: 256). Los removes his forms from Urizen's control so that they will not become "abstract negations" (Rose 1971a: 57).

90:62/ E371/ VII, 494   **Thiriel**—not the eponymous hero of *Tiriel* but the element air [see *BU* 23:11] (Erdman 1954a: 356 [383]). Within Los, reason is not Urizenic but a form of wrath (Rose 1971a: 57-58).

90:65/ E371/ VII, 497   **he**—Los, who loves the redeemable element in Urizen (Bloom 1963: 256); Urizen (Beer 1969: 136). Britain (Urizen) has recovered Blake's good will by signing the Peace of Amiens (Erdman 1954a: 356 [383]). This is an example of Blake's doctrine of forgiveness at work (T. Wright 1929: I, 149).

Night the Eighth

Sloss and Wallis's perception (1926: I, 139) that the symbolism of this Night shows it to be a late addition is confirmed by Erdman's judgment (1954a: 367 [395]), endorsed by Margoliouth (1956: xviii), that it embodies images of the London of 1804, which was preparing to resist a French invasion.

There is widespread agreement with Damon (1924: 162) that the focus is on error, which, reaching its culmination, becomes recognisable and ready to be cast out. Wilkie and Johnson (1978: 196) emphasise the contrasts between a materialistic and a visionary or imaginative world-view, and Gallant (1978: 80-81) speaks of the powerful images of Christ and the Antichrist, which are to be synthesised in the closing Night.

Details

99:2/ E371/ VIII, 2 **Gilead & Hermon**—the Hill of Witness and the spiritual boundary of the Promised Land (Damon 1924: 383). Being east of the Jordan, they are symbols of error—cf. Hos. vi.8 (Sloss and Wallis 1926: I, 264). Hermon is associated in Ps. cxxxiii.3 with living in harmony and with everlasting life (Bloom 1965: 962). Citing Jer. viii.22, Wilkie and Johnson (1978: 273n1) mention the famous balm of Gilead.

99:4-5/ E371/ VIII, 4-5 Cf. Jon. ii.3, 5 (Miner 1969: 266).

99:8/ E372/ VIII, 8 The angelic forms guard the passions ("East") and the body ("west") (Damon 1924: 383-84).

99:12/ E372/ VIII, 17 **sneezed seven times**—like the Shunammite's son whom Elisha resurrected, II Kings iv.35 (Margoliouth 1948: 306).

99:19/ E372/ VIII, 24 This line is continuous with 99:14/ VIII, 19 (Margoliouth 1956: 176); it refers to 95:11/ E367/ VIIb, 298 (Stevenson 1971: 404).

99:24-25/ E372/ VIII, 30-31 The poet (Los) receives inspiration abundantly (Damon 1924: 384). See also *E* 1:2n.

100:3/ E372/ VIII, 37 **Cathedron**—This name for a place where nature works to redeem may be drawn from "cathedral" and "Catherine," the name of Blake's wife (Bloom 1963: 257-58, 441n16), the latter being also the name of his mother and his sister (Paley 1973b: 125). Cathedron is the female body, and especially the womb, where souls incarnate (Damon 1967: 74). Cf. *J* 13:25n.

100:4/ E372/ VIII, 38 **Bodies of Vegetation**—both physical bodies and forms of religion, two kinds of temporary refuge (Percival 1938: 229); garment bodies that are simultaneously prisons and a means of escaping to Beulah (Paley 1973b: 126-27). Cf. the images of 90:15-67/ E370-71/ VII, 446-99.

100:11-16/ E372/ VIII, 45-51 This is the visionary counterpart of Urizen's fallen view of the same state at 72:28-34/ E349/ VI, 202-08 (Evans 1972: 317-18).

101:2-5/ E373/ VIII, 62-65 Urizen is baffled to see passion as peace (Jesus) and passion as war (Orc) (Damon 1924: 162, 384).

101:5-8/ E373/ VIII, 65-68 **dark machines**—the starry wheels (Sloss and Wallis 1926: I, 266); cf. 20:14-15/ E313/ I, 573-74. Stevenson (1971: 406) notes the existence of the constellation Serpens.

101:9, 14/ E373/ VIII, 69, 74 The list comprises seven of the stones on Aaron's breastplate (Exod. xxviii.17-21), six of them being also on Ezekiel's Covering Cherub (xxviii.13) (Damon 1967: 310). Other likely sources are *PL*, IX, 497-503 (Paley 1970: 166-67) and Rev. xxi.19-20 (Stevenson 1971: 407). Paley (*loc. cit.*) also suspects an allusion to Napoleon's imperial coronation in 1804.

101:14-21/ E373/ VIII, 74-81 The fruit of the Tree is the result of oppressive moral law (Sloss and Wallis 1926: I, 267). This fruit can be both the Fiend and his fruit-like precious stones (Raine 1968: II, 42-43); Ostriker (1977: 948) suggests it also represents the wealth amassed when revolution turns into reaction.

Uveth (intellect isolated) kneads good and evil in the bowl of the skull (Damon 1924: 384). The food, with which Urizen keeps Orc in subjection (Stevenson 1971: 407), is the unleavened bread of Exod. xii.34 (Raine 1968: II, 97-98).

101:23/ E373/ VIII, 83 Britain's war-enriched iron industry influences France's behaviour (Erdman 1954a: 371 [400]).

101:26-100:31/ E373/ VIII, 86-95   Britain exploited the peace of 1802-03 to rearm, renewed the war [in May 1803], and despatched Nelson to the Mediterranean; Blake refers to newly designed weapons—the "hollow globes" contain shrapnel—and echoes Milton's account of Satan's artillery (*PL*, VI, 484-766); "the heavens of Los" are the London sky (Erdman 1954a: 369-71 [397-99]).

100:32/ E374/ VIII, 96 Orc has now been corrupted by the Tree of Mystery in the forms of Deism and Roman Catholicism (Erdman 1954a: 371 [399]). Cf. 80:27-44/ E356/ VII, 135-52n.

100:33/ E374/ VIII, 97 **Synagogue of Satan**—see Rev. iii.9 (Margoliouth 1956: 176). It is dedicated to the Ten Commandments (Damon 1924: 384), and includes the Christian Church (Johnson and Grant 1979: 230).

101:31/ E374/ VIII, 100 **Endless Destruction**—the resumed war
with France (Paley 1970: 166).

101:34/ E374/ VIII, 103 **hermaphrodite**—unreconciled contra-
dictions engendering doubt (Damon 1924: 162, 384); an entity
"spiritually sterile" owing to the fruitless mixture and conflict
of contradictory ideas like mercy and persecution (Sloss and
Wallis 1926: II, 42, 168); an Ulroic union of the reasoning
head and effeminate heart (Percival 1938: 69-70) and the
domination of emotion and sense perception over spirit, which
is masculine (*ibid.*: 103); a fruitless combination of subject and
object reduced to reflections of each other so that consciousness
knows only a world of abstractions (Frye 1947: 135, 272, 301);
an embodiment of the solipsistic state in which the subject
absorbs the object into its consciousness instead of creating it
(Bloom 1963: 258-59); sometimes a combination of two abstr-
actions or general ideas, which cannot produce a concrete
entity (Rose 1965: 591); a Human in whom the male and fem-
ale have become separate entities (Tayler 1973b: 82). Ault
(1974: 82-84) may be right in suggesting that Blake regards
Newton's combination of an indefinite, infinite void with solid,
unchangeable atoms as hermaphroditic. In Erdman's view
(1954a: 371 [399]), the hermaphrodite of this line is a mon-
strosity created by British and French tyranny, which some-
times collude (100:32/ E373/ VIII, 96).

101:36-37/ E374/ VIII, 105-06 War is concealed in religion
(Damon 1924: 384). The image expresses male fear of emascu-
lation (Webster 1983: 239-40).

101:39-40/ E374/ VIII, 108-09 The reference is to Blake's own
art (Bloom 1965: 963).

101:41/ E374/ VIII, 110 **the Gates of Death**—i.e. of rebirth
(Damon 1924: 834).

101:41-102:11/ E374/ VIII, 110-28 The animals are probably im-
ages on military banners (Margoliouth 1956: 177), and constel-
lations that subside into their present flat and limited form
(Worrall 1981: 280). Souls drawn down (or back) into bodies
by evil passions are said symbolically to assume animal forms
(Raine 1968: I, 252-53). Los compels these beings to
"humanize" so that Enitharmon can begin the work of redeem-
ing them (Stevenson 1971: 409), or their heroic ideals bring
them briefly under Los's influence (Ostriker 1977: 948).

Wilkie and Johnson (1978: 174) suspect the word "humanize" is ironic.

102:14-22/ E374-75/ VIII, 131-39 The "linked chains" are chain-shot, the "boring screws" are for attaching explosives to ships, and the "harsh instruments" provide martial music (Erdman 1954a: 369-72 [398-400]). In response to the enmity of Vala armed with Orc's energy, Urizen imbues his own "mechanical systems" with "organic life" (Ault 1974: 111-12).

103:3/ E375/ VIII, 153 Vala is seeing Orc (Bloom 1965: 963) or Jesus (Stevenson 1971: 410).

103:7-8/ E375/ VIII, 157-58 **Bondage**—for which Vala herself is responsible (Stevenson 1971: 410).

103:17-20/ E375/ VIII, 167-70 Joys survive only in the form of an allegorical [i.e. symbolic] substitute (Beer 1969: 143). Vala recognises that love, not theology, is real (Ostriker 1977: 948), and even she is redeemable (Gallant 1978: 85-86).

103:21-29/ E375-76/ VIII, 171-79 The cause of the Web's collapse has been identified as (1) Urizen's perception that his philosophy is founded exclusively on matter (Damon 1924: 162); (2) the Shadowy Female's (Vala's) introduction of Orc's power into the Web, where it stirs up new appetites (Beer 1969: 143-44); (3) the malign effect of religion on the vortexes, which providentially impose form on the fallen world (Nurmi 1969: 311-12); (4) the defeat of the abstract Newtonian mathematical system governing Urizen's world of solids by the fluctuating indefiniteness of nature (Ault 1974: 110-11, 115); (5) Vala's tears, grief being powerful enough to overwhelm a weak rational creed (Ostriker 1977: 948) and fill Urizen with guilt (Webster 1983: 240); (6) her hint of Christ's advent (Gallant 1978: 86); (7) the life-destroying character of scientific rationalism (Ackland 1983: 185-86).

104:1-4/ E376/ VIII, 190-93 **Jerusalem**—"Liberty, the Emanation (Inspiration) of all on earth" (Damon 1924: 384); Albion's counterpart (Beer 1969: 144); the aggregate of souls in quest of salvation (Stevenson 1971: 411).

104:7/ E376/ VIII, 196 **the dark Satanic body**—at once the physical body, the pain of living in the fallen world, and the religion of Mystery (Wilkie and Johnson 1978: 186).

113:2/ E376/ VIII, 201 As a harlot and "Worldly Religion," Rahab stands for both sexual licence and moral virtue, while

Tirzah is a prude and the mills represent logic (Damon 1924: 162, 191, 438); Tirzah excites male desire but frustrates it and represses her own lust (Damon 1967: 407). Blake combines Rahab the Jericho prostitute (Josh. ii) with the harlot Mystery [Rev. xvii] and the sea monster Rahab (Ps. lxxxvii.4, lxxxix.10; Is. li.9) making her a symbol of seductive nature and official religion that block out the vision of Eden (Frye 1947: 139-40, 441n58). Traditionally, Joshua's Rahab has been regarded as a type of the church (Bloom 1963: 259). The spindles represent destiny, and the mills oppress the world with their power (Bloom 1965: 963). Stevenson (1971: 403, 633-34) describes Tirzah as sadistic paganism and maternal oppressiveness and Rahab as a glamorous, power-hungry mistress, and Mitchell (1978: 188) defines the former as natural religion and the latter as natural philosophy [cf. *J*, pl. 52, prose]. See also 105:44-50/ E379/ VIII, 312-18n.

113:6-12/ E376/ VIII, 207-13 Percival (1938: 230) alleges that the Daughters draw their silk from the bowels of compassion, while Hilton (1983: 113) avers that they spin from instinct; Raine (1968: I, 254-55) associates this silk with the thread of the Fates (Plato, *Republic* 617b-d). Blake, note Wilkie and Johnson (1978: 171), here mingles images pertaining to artistic creation and to gestation. From this passage, Hagstrum (1973b: 117) deduces that the body, including its sexual element, survives in the redeemed human.

113:14/ E376/ VIII, 215 **Arnon**—the border the spectres cross to pass from the realm of reason to the Promised Land (Damon 1924: 385), which is a place of regeneration (Sloss and Wallis 1926: I, 272). See Num. xxi.14 (Percival 1938: 231-32). It has been identified with the birth canal (Damon 1967: 28) and regarded as analogous to Lethe (Raine 1968: I, 254-55, citing Plato, *Republic* 621a-b).

113:17-18/ E376/ VIII, 218-19 The unwinding exposes the victims to Urizenic vindictiveness (Damon 1924: 385) and robs them of self-respect (Wilkie and Johnson 1978: 175-76).

113:31-32/ E377/ VIII, 232-33 According to Hilton (1983: 115), the reader ("Humanity") receives Blake's text ("Integuments").

113:33/ E377/ VIII, 234 Percival (1938: 237) suspects an allusion to pre-Reformation heresies that restored some elements of genuine Christianity. The flint knife is a circumcising knife—

see Josh. v.2, AV marginal reading (Stevenson 1971: 413). Cf. *J* 66:20-34n.

113:36-37/ E377/ VIII, 237-38 See Luke vii.37-38 and John xii.3 (Miner 1969: 269). Blake follows tradition in identifying Lazarus' sister Mary with Mary Magdalene (Stevenson 1971: 413). The Daughters of Beulah are Marys, not Marthas.

104:16-17/ E377/ VIII, 244-45 See Rev. xxii.20 (Stevenson 1971: 413).

104:19ff/ E377/ VIII, 247ff The hermaphroditic war gives birth to Satan, the selfhood (Damon 1924: 385) comprising the corrupt Orc and Urizen (Murry 1933: 206-09) or the degenerate Orc and the Shadowy Female—i.e. war and religion (Beer 1969: 122).

104:27/ E377/ VIII, 255 This line illustrates Frye's observation (1947: 368) that the image of the holy ark and its curtains (Exod. xxxvi-xxxvii) represents Vala as a form of the female will. See also 110:1/ E385/ VIII, 556n.

104:33/ E378/ VIII, 261 **time after time**—The Crucifixion occurs with every victory of love and forgiveness (Sutherland 1970: 255). It is "a symbolic act" that must be performed continually (Damrosch 1980: 289-90).

104:35/ E378/ VIII, 263 Luvah's robes are the flesh; Mystery's mantle consists of the church's symbols (Damon 1924: 385). A primary meaning of the robes is the sexual desire that Christ experienced in his mortal body (Hagstrum 1973a: 140). For the equation of Mystery's mantle with the "dark Satanic body" (104:3/ E377/ VIII, 241), cf. *M* 13:25-26n.

105:3/ E378/ VIII, 270 **Amalek**—in an area in the extreme southern (Urizenic) region of Canaan (Damon 1924: 385); an enemy of Israel and therefore of Albion (Bloom 1963: 260).

105:7/ E378/ VIII, 274 See Is. liii.12, Mark xv.28, Luke xxii.37 (Damon 1924: 385).

105:9-10/ E378/ VIII, 276-77 **Twelve rocky unshap'd forms**—the Sons of Albion (Damon 1924: 386); the jury at the trial of the Lamb (Bloom 1963: 260); "unshap'd" implies unhewn, like the lawgiving God's altar stones of Exod. xx.25 (Miner 1969: 280).

105:31-53/ E378-79/ VIII, 298-321 Frosch (1974: 54) sees here "the inception of natural love" and its accompanying jealousy.

105:33/ E379/ VIII, 300 Error will disappear when people cease to believe in it (Sloss and Wallis 1926: I, 276).

105:42-43, 48/ E379/ VIII, 309-10, 316 Kanah marks the boundary between Ephraim and Manasseh (Damon 1924: 386), the latter being the ancestor of Tirzah and her sisters [see next note] (Damon 1967: 261). All three, along with Ebal, Shechem and Gilead, were in the northern kingdom, of which Tirzah was capital (Margoliouth 1956: 178). Lebanon is a place of forests, hence of error (Damon 1924: 386). For "mount of Cursing" see Josh. viii.30-34 (Damon 1967: 113-14) and Deut. xi.29 (Miner 1969: 273).

105:44-50/ E379/ VIII, 312-18 Tirzah and her four sisters represent the five senses; they were the daughters of Zelophehad, who became his heirs because he lacked sons—see Num. xxvi.33 (Damon 1924: 386). They signify "the feminine powers of the fallen world" (Miner 1961: 48), and Tirzah, the female will, is the opponent of Jerusalem because Tirzah was the capital of the breakaway northern kingdom of Israel (Frye 1947: 127).

105:53/ E379/ VIII, 321 **bound upon the Stems of Vegetation** —confined within the bounds of sense perception (Sloss and Wallis 1926: II, 251); fastened on the sacrificial altar (Hilton 1981: 200, citing the variant reading of 105:28 [E378, 842—not given in K]).

105:55-56/ E379/ VIII, 323-24 Christ redeems even the basest passions (Damon 1924: 386). Cf. Judg. xx.6 (Margoliouth 1956: 178). In his prose note to "The Fatal Sisters," Gray tells how these weavers divide their web into twelve pieces (Miner 1958: 204). Blake equates Luvah with Israel and its twelve tribes (Stevenson 1971: 418).

106:4/ E379/ VIII, 328 The twelve Daughters of Albion and five daughters of Zelophehad (Stevenson 1971: 418).

106:9-13/ E379/ VIII, 333-37 Jerusalem misguidedly recommends orthodox religion and ecclesiastical art (Wilkie and Johnson 1978: 190).

106:15-16/ E379/ VIII, 339-40 In default of a transcendental faith, Los secretes a philosophy by which he can live; the biblical parallel is with Joseph of Arimathea—see Matt. xxvii.60 (Damon 1924: 386).

113:38-43/ E379-80/ VIII, 341-46   When Jesus is killed, his ene-
mies are found to be cherished in his bosom (Damon 1924:
162, 386).

114:48/ E380/ VIII, 351   Harper suggests Blake here identifies
Los with Adam (1961: 237).

115:1-9/ E380/ VIII, 357-65   These are representative types exte-
nding from Eternity into this world well past the nadir of the
fallen state; the women's names are the more obscure, but Mil-
ton and Mary are the perfect male and female; Caina may be
intended as Cain's wife (Damon 1924: 387-88). Except for
Caina, the names from Moab to Mary are biblical (Bloom
1965: 964), perhaps because there are comparatively few emi-
nent women in history (George 1980: 201). Mary may be either
the Virgin or Mary Magdalene (Stevenson 1971: 420). All the
Sons are aspects of the one not mentioned—Orc (Damon 1967:
253). Cf. *J* 62:8-13n.

115:12-22, 38-40/ E380, 381/ VIII, 368-78, 394-96   Wrath and
pity cut Satan off from the realm of art, but inspiration guards
him in time of revolution; he uses reason to seduce humankind,
the sons of Jacob (Damon 1924: 388). The space is "clos'd
with a tender moon" because it is part of the night of illusion,
of the fallen world (Raine 1968: II, 170).

115:23-29/ E380/ VIII, 379-85   Blake conceives the doctrine of
states (such as tyranny) to explain how individuals and socie-
ties can escape from even the worst conditions (Erdman 1954a:
372 [400-01]). Love (Luvah) becomes hate (Damon 1967:
356).

115:27-30/ E380-81/ VIII, 383-86   Despite Napoleon's tyranny,
the remains of revolutionary France deserve protection (Erd-
man 1954a: 373 [401]).

115:41/ E381/ VIII, 397   The mantles are fleshly bodies created to
save the fallen from even deeper decline (Damon 1924: 388).

115:42-50/ E381/ VIII, 398-406   See 19:9-10/ E312/ I, 553-54n.
Impatience is the error of the prophet who resorts to arms (Frye
1947: 297). Pahad means "terror" and he is a god who rules by
inspiring fear—see Is. ii.10, 19, etc. (Damon 1924: 388-89).
Jehovah is leprous because he is the Father in a state of degen-
eration when separated from the Son (Summerfield 1981: 17-
18). Shaddai is Hebrew for "Almighty."

116:5-106:20/ E381/ VIII, 412-17   Urizen senses the evil in Rahab, in whom he recognises his own spiritual pride (Bloom 1963: 262). With 106:17/ VIII, 414, cf. Luke xxiii.44-45 (Margoliouth 1956: 178). The "female death" is the wound reason receives from moral virtue (Damon 1924: 390).

106:23-40/ E381-82/ VIII, 420-37   Cf. *PL*, X, 511-15 (Damon 1924: 390). Trying to embrace nature, Urizen turns into a lower animal (Ostriker 1977: 951). He divides into a petrified human form and "a scaly serpent" (Margoliouth 1956: 178), or, as Orc splits into worm and serpent (80:27-44/ E356/ VII, 135-52), he divides into a "stone man" and a dragon (Wilkie and Johnson 1978: 193-94). When his inhibitions no longer hold his impulses in check, he is paralysed (Webster 1983: 241). The phrase "Outstretch'd thro the immense" refers to the expansion of British seapower (Erdman 1954a: 373 [401]). As though there were no division, Stevenson (1971: 422) inserts a period after "around" in 106:40/ VIII, 437 and places no punctuation after "form."

106:41ff/ E382/ VIII, 438ff   Cf. the description of Leviathan in Job xli.15, 18 (Miner 1969: 266-67). Gallant (1978: 89-90) sees this Urizen as an energetic Antichrist who animates nature.

107:4-6/ E382/ VIII, 449-51   Blake is following Robert Fludd's *Mosaicall Philosophy* (1659), which tells how creation operates through cold that condenses and solidifies (Raine 1968: II, 74-77).

107:9-20/ E382/ VIII, 454-66   Orc glories in Urizen's metamorphosis into a dragon (Damon 1924: 163). Here is fulfilled the prophecy of 38:6-7/ E326/ III, 18-19 that Urizen would serve Orc (Sloss and Wallis 1926: I, 263). Britain, facing a now equally tyrannous France, retains all her ambition and (107:17-18/ VIII, 463-64) regrets her brief repentance during the Peace of Amiens (Erdman 1954a: 373 [401]). Urizen's dragon form "forgets his wisdom," which remains in his stony form (Wilkie and Johnson 1978: 194); he adopts inflexible principles to combat revolution (Damon 1924: 190).

107:20/ E382/ VIII, 466   Urizen is drawn into "the indefinite lust" of Orc—the superego has lapsed into anarchy (Bloom 1965: 964). The dark, Orcean aspect of the Antichrist threatens to dominate it (Gallant 1978: 90).

107:21-30/ E382-83/ VIII, 467-76 While Tharmas (the body) threshes around in fury, Urthona (the spirit) tries to impose order on society in the form of the Polypus (Damon 1924: 390). Unlike Ahania and Enion, who possess insight into the unconscious, Tharmas, Urthona, Los and Enitharmon lose their identities before an overwhelming manifestation of it in an archetype deriving from Orc and Urizen (Gallant 1978: 90).

107:31-38/ E383/ VIII, 477-84 Los-Blake still has the strength to expose the misdeeds of Britain and France and prepare the people for the time of the Lamb (Erdman 1954a: 373 [401-02]).

107:35-36/ E383/ VIII, 481-82 The 'Death' consists of eighteen centuries of perverted Christianity (Percival 1938: 234). The Nameless Shadowy Female (Vala) imposes a static rigidity (Stevenson 1971: 424).

108:9ff/ E383-84/ VIII, 493ff Ahania asks whether the nation will opt for freedom or tyranny (Erdman 1954a: 373-74 [402]). Ahania has no vision of immortality because her wisdom is based only on memory; Enion, who answers her, is in contact with "vegetative and instinctive life" (Fisher 1961: 35).

108:19/ E383/ VIII, 503 **the Murder'd one**—Albion (Damon 1924: 390).

108:21/ E383/ VIII, 505 **the dark body of corruptible death**—Cf. Rom. vii.24 (Tolley 1973: 117); also I Cor. xv.53 (Ostriker 1977: 951).

108:27/ E384/ VIII, 511 **the Scaly monsters**—manifestations of Albion's suppressed sexuality ejaculated by Orc (Miner 1981: 311).

108:30/ E384/ VIII, 514 Cf. Jon. ii.5 (Miner 1969: 266).

109:1-11/ E384/ VIII, 521-31 Ahania describes the Eagle of Genius, the Lion that protects the Lamb, and the Horse of Instruction (Damon 1924: 390). For the lion, cf. Judg. xiv.8 (Margoliouth 1956: 179). For the pale horse, see Zech. xii.4 (Miner 1969: 269) and Rev. vi.8 (Tolley 1973: 117-18, citing Miner).

109:13/ E384/ VIII, 533 Unlike Ahania, Enion speaks *from* the Caverns of the Grave (Margoliouth 1956: 179). She describes the condition of the world just before Albion's resurrection (Johnson and Grant 1979: 228).

109:17-19/ E384/ VIII, 537-39 According to the alchemical philosophy, both the worm and matter enjoy God's love for all their lowliness (Raine 1968: I, 297-98). Despite death's bitterness, the worm devours the body to free the spirit (Tolley 1973: 118-19). Cf. Cant. ii.11-12 (Miner 1969: 259).

109:21/ E384/ VIII, 541 See Matt. xxv.6 (Damon 1924: 390).

109:23/ E384/ VIII, 543 Enion, who represents matter, is here both grave and water, for both symbolically consume descending spirit; Ahania is the earth goddess made fruitful by Urizen, sower of souls (Raine 1968: I, 297, 154-55, 159-60).

109:28/ E384/ VIII, 548 **The furrow'd field**—an image for the silent and submissive Ahania who has been cast out by Urizen (Ostriker 1982: 159).

110:1/ E385/ VIII, 556 See Matt. xxvii.51 (Stevenson 1971: 426 and 419). Jesus tears away the veil of the shrine that conceals "the nothingness of the Pharisees' God" and that is also the veil of nature that disguises reality (Frye 1947: 266, 381). See also 104:27/ E377/ VIII, 255n.

110:7/ E385/ VIII, 562 Blake alludes to the scattered pieces of the god Dionysus (Harper 1961: 231), and to the alchemical hidden god and to the fragments of Osiris sought by Isis (Raine 1968: I, 298-99).

110:13-14/ E385/ VIII, 568-69 Blake denies the Hermetic and alchemical principle that the higher rules the lower (Damon 1924: 391).

110:19-20/ E385/ VIII, 574-75 The forgetful soul may choose reincarnation (Damon 1924: 391).

110:21-23/ E385/ VIII, 576-78 Humanity now suffers, but the context hints that the redeemed Albion will be a Christlike husbandman (Gallant 1978: 92-94).

110:33/ E385/ VIII, 596 In the modern world, the divine element is buried in the grave of philosophical materialism (Raine 1968: I, 299). The two millennia are equivalent to Christ's two days in the grave and represent the ages of church Christianity (Wilkie and Johnson 1978: 190).

111:1-24/ E385-86/ VIII, 597-620 The resolution to burn Mystery is the French Convention's endorsement of Robespierre's Feast of the Supreme Being held in 1794 (Erdman 1954a: 389-90 [418-19]). Rahab is on one level the Church of England, who sacrifices her people to the war god Urizen (Bloom 1965: 964).

111:3ff/ E385-86/ VIII, 599ff See Rev. vi.9-16, xvii.3-5 (Stevenson 1971: 427).

111:7/ E386/ VIII, 603 **press'd**—by Urizen's Daughters (Bloom 1963: 264).

111:10-11/ E386/ VIII, 606-07 **No more spirit remained in her** —Cf. I Kings x.5 and Josh. ii.6 (Margoliouth 1948: 307). Legalistic and radical periods have alternated in church history (Ostriker 1977: 951).

111:18-24/ E386/ VIII, 614-20 Blake is describing the Reformation (Percival 1938: 237). Cf. Rev. xvii.12-17 (Wilkie and Johnson 1978: 205, 276n11).

111:20/ E386/ VIII, 616 **with fire**—Percival (1938: 32, 298) considers this fire is ignited by the surviving spark of revolt in Orc—i.e. in the human heart—cf. 119:1ff/ E388/ IX, 67ff. Bloom, however, regards it as Deistical thought (1963: 265).

111:23/ E386/ VIII, 619 **as of old so now anew**—After six millenia, natural religion, which was originally disguised as the serpent that seduced Albion into leaving Paradise and was then hidden behind the mask of ecclesiastical Mystery, is seen for what it is, and humankind may either reject it or repeat the cycle (Percival 1938: 2, 237-38). There is an allusion to the Circle of Destiny named in Night I (Evans 1972: 315-16).

Night the Ninth

The first eighty-nine lines of this Night are an addition to the original text. Sloss and Wallis (1926: I, 289) comment that the latter completed the unrevised *Vala*, in which Night IX followed Night VIIb, while the new beginning is an adjustment to fit in with added passages, including Night VIII. Erdman (1954a: 350-53 [377-80]) believes that Blake wrote the later opening under the conviction that Providence had effected the Peace of Amiens and that submission to the Divine Vision, not revolution, was right.

The structure of the Night has been variously analysed. It presents, according to Evans (1972: 317-25), a series of events and images antithetical to those in Nights I through VIII. Thus Los's tearing down of the sun and moon (117:6-9/ E386/ IX, 6-9) is the converse of Urizen's erection of the Mundane Shell (24:8/ E314/

II, 25), Albion's second summons to Urizen (120:14/ E389/ IX, 124) that of his first (23:3/ E313/ II, 3), Luvah's care of Vala in lower paradise (128:28-30/ E397/ IX, 458-60) that of his sequestering her in a garden (27:5/ E317/ II, 95), Tharmas and Enion's childhood (130:4ff/ E398ff/ IX, 507ff) that of their parenting (8:1ff/ E304/ I, 191ff), the Golden Feast (132:10ff/ E400ff/ IX, 587ff) that of the nuptial banquet (13:19ff/ E308/ I, 374ff), and the bread of knowledge (138:15/ E406/ IX, 820) that of the bread of sorrow (79:23/ E355/ VII, 93). The action in Night IX, adds Evans, forms a circle contrary to the Circle of Destiny in Night I.

Less disputable is the presence of a major seasonal element. Frye (1947: 306-08) sees a progression from the winter of the (early nineteenth century) fallen world, which is given potential by revolution, through the summer of the pastoral interlude and the autumn with its human harvest to a winter of rest preceding an awakening into Eternity. This final state is seen as an eternal spring by Margoliouth (1956: 154) but as a passing stage in a recurring cycle by Gallant (1978: 114-15); Damon (1967: 176) considers that for the individual the events of the harvest and vintage immediately follow decease. (See also 138:27-31/ E406/ IX, 832-36n.)

Dividing the harvest and vintage into six stages running from ploughing to baking, Damon (1924: 163) maintains that they undo the six-day creation of Genesis to usher in the millenium. As Damon observes (1967: 434-35), Blake accepts the tradition that the vintage of Rev. xiv is war and interprets both the vintage and harvest of this chapter as catastrophes on earth but the making of eternal wine and bread in heaven. Wilkie and Johnson (1978: 222, 228-31) point out that Urizen and Luvah, former enemies, co-operate in the work and that the narrative mingles visions of fallen and redeemed humanity as it incorporates the harvest of Ps. cxxvi, the beaten swords of Is. ii and Mic. iv, and the trampled grapes of Is. lxiii as well as numerous passages in Revelation. Schorer's notion (1946: 336) that Luvah separates "the wine of humanity" from the lees is supplemented by Ackland's statement (1982: 180) that what is separated by threshing and crushing is the selfhood. In a more complex exposition, Bloom (1963: 276-79) explains that nature is humanised through the harvest and that the dying god Luvah, wrongly worshipped by participants in corporeal war as a vegetation god and as Christ, becomes the Dionysus of rebirth who presides over mental strife; the winepress represents both kinds of conflict. Gallant (1978: 95-98) understands the harvest as a ritual in which the Zoas enact the creation of cosmos out of chaos.

The pastoral interlude, with its unexpected affinity to *Thel*, has provoked much discussion. To Damon's point (1924: 163, 393) that it shows Luvah's and Vala's return to Innocence, Frye adds (1947: 307) that that Innocence is Beulah and a stage on the way to redemption. There is widespread agreement with this thesis. Stevenson (1971: 443) notes that the episode allows the reader to feel the summer is passing and Urizen's grain has time to grow; Tolley (1973: 120-22) describes it as a spring song, rich with echoes of the Song of Solomon as it celebrates a regeneration that releases from cyclical recurrence. There are several evaluations of what Blake defines as "lower Paradise" (128:30/ E397/ IX, 460). Margoliouth (1956: 149-50) views it as showing the real but limited worth of natural beauty, Gallant (1978: 103-07) praises its gentle acceptance of mutability and mortality, Mellor (1974: 190-91) claims that it shows the mode of life and faith that is right for this world, and DiSalvo (1983: 172-73) appreciates its restfulness but notes its deficiency in creativity and community. Wilkie and Johnson (1978: 225-27) contend that in it Luvah teaches Vala not to deify the sun but to see all nature as a manifestation of God and then himself acquires the character of Innocence, and Lincoln (1981: 472), in a careful analysis, shows how in the house of the body Vala's maternal instincts are aroused, how she imperfectly mends the relationship of Tharmas and Enion, and how the sensory pleasures she enjoys precede her return to Eternity—though one can also fall from this Beulah paradise into Ulro. In a hostile interpretation, Webster (1983: 239-41, 245-56) argues that Blake reduces Vala—still formidable to males in Night VIII—to meekness and that the sibling love of Tharmas and Enion shows that, with his Oedipal preoccupation, he unconsciously remains attracted to incest.

Other elements that have been discerned in the final Night include an autobiographical component in the treatment of Los and Enitharmon (Murry 1933: 164-70), stress on the Christian doctrine of the resurrection of the body (Wilkie and Johnson 1978: 209) to be followed by a millenium of peace, justice and feasting (Paley 1983b: 121-22), and a prophecy that peace and prosperity will follow George III's (Urizen's) repentance and the Peace of

Amiens, though there will be a short, ferocious dictatorship first
(Erdman 1954a: 322-31 [350-59]).

Details

117:1-9/ E386/ IX, 1-9 Los, in his fear of annihilation, rends
away the sun and moon, which represent the spirit [Urthona]
and the passions [Luvah], and this opens up the reality behind
the symbols (Damon 1924: 163, 391). No longer able to toler-
ate natural religion, Los destroys the natural sun and moon,
which have completed the work he created them to do (Percival
1938: 239). In his despair at Jesus' death, Los breaks away
from his limiting world view (Sutherland 1970: 255-56). Dam-
on (1967: 214) takes the continued presence of the crucified
body as Blake's denial of physical resurrection, while Wilkie
and Johnson (1978: 211) suppose that separating spirit from
body probably means combatting the hopelessness bred by the
belief that physical death is final. Bloom, however, (1965: 965)
follows Percival (*loc. cit.*) in associating the sun with Urizen
and the moon with Luvah, and argues that an impulsive assault
on them with merely natural "fibrous strength" cannot regen-
erate the fallen human. Los is presented, says Gallant (1978:
96), through the image of the Norse World Tree Yggdrasil,
whose branches and roots reach heaven and hell.

117:7-8/ E386/ IX, 7-8 Cf. Matt. xxiv.29-31 (Stevenson 1971:
430) and Rev. vi.12-13 (Howard 1984: 224).

117:19-23/ E387/ IX, 19-23 Blake depicts the revenge of the op-
pressed as a natural reaction; cf. Rev. vi.9-10 (Damon 1924:
391). He portrays the revenge against oppressors that will fol-
low resurrection according to the Koran (Damon 1967: 236).

117:24-118:6/ E387/ IX, 24-31 These Spectres are the (now ter-
rified) logical elements of Enitharmon and Urthona that alone
survive here (Damon 1924: 391). Stevenson (1971: 431) iden-
tifies Enitharmon's Spectre with her Shadow.

118:8-13/ E387/ IX, 33-38 According to Percival (1938: 239),
the first stage of the Last Judgment is the annihilation of error
in the flames of the liberated Orc. The flames, says Paley
(1973a: 272), devour "corrupt institutions."

118:20-22/ E387/ IX, 46-48 The families gather in large clusters to show that the true family is that of humankind (Wilkie and Johnson 1978: 214).

118:36/ E388/ IX, 62 **A terror coming from the South**—Orc (Stevenson 1971: 432).

119:1-23/ E388/ IX, 67-90 Gallant finds here an image of Antichrist that is centred on Orc, Urizen and fire and that is Christ's co-contributor to apocalypse as it burns up (1978: 96-97).

119:3-4/ E388/ IX, 69-70 Revolution no longer having a function, Orc destroys good and evil together with himself (Schorer 1946: 333). His twenty-seven coils are the cycles of history—cf. the Twenty-seven Churches (Paley 1970: 168). Cf. also 111:20/ E386/ VIII, 616n.

119:19-20/ E388/ IX, 86-87 **winged with intellect/ And Reason**—combining the attributes of Orc and Urizen (Wilkie and Johnson 1978: 214-15).

119:25-26/ E388/ IX, 92-93 The vortexes are probably the Zoas' (Stevenson 1971: 433), and they may be Cartesian (Hilton 1983: 210-11). Damon (1924: 391) identifies the rock as the Rock of Ages, and Bloom (1965: 965) locates it in the south, where Orc suffered in Nights VI and VII.

119:32/ E388/ IX, 99 The war includes the Anglo-French conflict (Sutherland 1970: 256). Cf. Rom. vii.23 and James iv.1 (Ostriker 1977: 953).

119:32-120:25/ E388-89/ IX, 99-135 Albion's speech embodies the hungry people's demand for peace moves—ignored by George III (Urizen)—in the famine year 1800 (Erdman 1954a: 316-19 [343-47]). Albion's plight is modelled on Job's (Raine 1968: II, 256-57).

120:23/ E389/ IX, 133 **dread form of Certainty**—Cf. 27:15/ E318/ II, 105 (Sloss and Wallis 1926: I, 296).

120:28/ E389/ IX, 138 Cf. Ps. cxlviii.7 (Bloom 1965: 965). Blake identifies Urizen with the Beast of Rev. xvii and Vala with the Harlot—see 120:47/ E390/ IX, 157 (Beer 1969: 146). Treating its own government as the aggressor, the British people assert that the withdrawal of the Royal Navy (Urizen as "dragon of the Deeps") will elicit a peaceful French response (Erdman 1954a: 319-20 [347-48]).

120:42/ E390/ IX, 152 It is Urizen who enslaves energy (Bloom 1963: 270).

120:49-51/ E390/ IX, 159-61 See Josh. ii.18—there is some good even in the harlot (Damon 1924: 392). The line of blood, traditionally a symbol of Christ's blood and his sacrifice which the Church has misused to block out vision ("the morning"), is now withdrawn (Bloom 1963: 270). Sin can be saved like Rahab when she displayed her scarlet thread—see Josh. ii.1-3, 6, 17-25, and Is. [l]i.9 (Beer 1969: 146, 360n16).

121:5-16/ E390/ IX, 166-77 George III's (Urizen's) confession about the nature of his maritime empire, with its reliance on wool, textiles and war (Erdman 1954a: 322-23 [350-51]). The "running Kennels" are uncovered drains (Stevenson 1971: 436).

121:24-25/ E390/ IX, 185-86 It is time to destroy the old regime, which Los has been rebuilding so that its badness becomes clear (Erdman 1954a: 323 [351]).

121:26/ E390/ IX, 187 Censorship is abolished in Britain (*ibid.*). Reason becomes nothing but doubt when passion and sensation frighten it (Ostriker 1977: 953).

121:35-38/ E391/ IX, 196-99 Raine (1968: I, 160-61) explains that Ahania, being the fallen soul and the fallen earth, must descend into the cave where the seed of the fallen is planted and the human harvest reaped. Other interpreters stress the impatience of Urizen, who has yet to unite with the faculties represented by the other Zoas (Bloom 1963: 271), support idealism (Ahania) by works as well as faith (Ostriker 1977: 953), or destroy his own tyrannical creations (Evans 1982: 320-21). Insofar as he is George III, his repentance is not enough to regenerate society—see 122:21/ E391/ IX, 225 (Erdman 1954a: 324 [352]). Citing 122:13/ E391/ IX, 217, Webster (1983: 217-19, 244) claims that Ahania sacrifices herself so that Urizen will no longer feel her power as a female threat as he did in Night III.

122:6-14/ E391/ IX, 210-18 The silken garments are the physical body; Ahania, on the natural level, goes (like Persephone) through the annual cycle of death and rebirth (Raine 1968: I, 161-62). There is a cycle in the eternal year (Stevenson 1971: 437). The cycle represents the life of Beulah, not Eternity (Damrosch 1980: 231). Cf. 5:1-4/ E302/ I, 64-67.

122:18/ E391/ IX, 222 Cf. Rev. xxi.2, 9-10 (Margoliouth 1956: 148).

122:21ff/ E391-92/ IX, 225ff Urizen's confession produces the Last Judgment (Margoliouth 1956: 148). There is a pun on Locke in 122:22/ IX, 226 (Rose 1970b: 411). According to Frosch (1974: 180-81), Urizen's function in Eternity is to lay down necessary but transient boundaries.

122:26ff/ E392/ IX, 230ff The material covering of all things is shattered by the expanding Eternity within (Damon 1924: 163, 392). Gravity ceases (Raine 1968: II, 80). Cf. Ezek. xxxvii.7 (Stevenson 1971: 438).

123:6/ E392/ IX, 251 **the Cold babe**—Christ, allowing a brief period of revenge (Erdman 1954a: 325 [353]); a symbol of oppressed children (Stevenson 1971: 438).

123:20/ E392/ IX, 265 They see the crucified Christ in their victims (Damon 1924: 392). Cf. Rev. i.7 (Margoliouth 1956: 148).

123:21-22/ E392/ IX, 266-67 Jerusalem's "little ones" are individual human beings (Damrosch 1980: 149).

123:27-29/ E393/ IX, 272-74 Cf. Rev. i.7 (Damon 1924: 392); also Luke xxi.27 and Rev. xiv.14 (Margoliouth 1956: 148).

123:30-33/ E393/ IX, 275-78 **The Cloud is Blood**—because this Judge has been unjustly judged (Wilkie and Johnson 1978: 221). The revengers act imperfectly and need purification in the human harvest and vintage (Stevenson 1971: 439).

123:34-38/ E393/ IX, 279-83 The "four Wonders" are the Zoas; cf. Rev. iv.2, 4, 6 (Damon 1924: 392). "Life's" is a plural and the translation of the Greek plural *Zoa* from Rev. iv. (AV gives "beasts") (Margoliouth 1956: 148).

124:5/ E393/ IX, 290 **could not enter**—because the Elect (or orthodox) within Albion cannot renounce their error (Percival 1938: 240); before the harvest and vintage (Bloom 1963: 272); before the physical body is changed into a spiritual body (Mellor 1974: 190).

124:6/ E393/ IX, 291 Contrast 92:17/ E364/ VIIb, 170—"Then left the Sons of Urizen the plow..." (Margoliouth 1956: 149).

124:8-9/ E393/ IX, 293-94 The field is Ahania, the earth goddess, herself (Raine 1968: I, 160). The weed is the effects of the Industrial Revolution (Harper 1965: 120).

124:6-29/ E393-94/ IX, 291-315 This passage, which draws on Is. ii.4, shows how the mind must furrow the material universe (Bloom 1965: 965), the instrument of cultivation being both the engraver's burin and the constellation of the Plough (Worrall 1981: 277). The Sons of Urizen are brain workers, the Sons of Urthona creative workers (Margoliouth 1956: 149). The "dens of death" are Urthona's dens, which are Ulro and which must be redeemed before Luvah's Generation and Tharmas's Beulah (Bloom, *loc. cit.*). Erdman (1954a: 326 [354-55]) suggests that war production is yielding to the manufacture of agricultural equipment. See also 28:10/ E318/ II, 120n.

124:12-13/ E393/ IX, 297-98 Contraries are harmonised in the harness (Gallant 1978: 103).

124:23/ E393/ IX, 308 Urizen has recovered his horses, which were still in Luvah-Orc's possession at 77:5-7/ E352-53/ VII, 5-7 (Damon 1967: 420).

125:3-11/ E394/ IX, 321-29 Cf. (1) the sowing of souls in Plato, *Timaeus*, 42d (Damon 1924: 392); (2) the parable of the sower in Luke viii.4-15 (Margoliouth 1956: 149); (3) I Cor. xv.36 (Ostriker 1977: 954). Monarchs are deprived of their economic foundation but not executed (Erdman 1954a: 327 [355]). Non-producers are discarded in favour of seed-sowing peasants (Crehan 1984: 178-79).

125:12, 23-25/ E394/ IX, 330, 341-43 The flames of Orc nourish the seeds (Stevenson 1971: 442); they represent revolution and nourish society (Erdman 1954a: 327 [355]).

126:1-8/ E395/ IX, 358-65 Orc and the Shadowy Female are regenerated as Luvah and Vala and obediently return to the loins and discover they are back in Eden (Damon 1924: 393). The brain and heart are left free for Urizen and Tharmas now that Orc, being consumed, is reborn as Luvah and Vala (Bloom 1963: 273-74). Orc is self-consumed because he no longer has a Urizen to sustain his wrath (Paley 1970: 165).

126:4-5/ E395/ IX, 361-62 The smoke is an Hermetic and Paracelsian symbol of insubstantial nature (Raine 1968: I, 273)—cf. *J* 5:46-53n; it is in part left behind by Orc's flames (Wilkie and Johnson 1978: 222). The Immortal who speaks has been identified as Urizen (Blackstone 1949: 97) but much more plausibly as Albion (Bloom 1963: 273).

126:18/ E395/ IX, 375 **Dark Urthona**—identical with "The
eternal gates' terrific porter" of *Thel* 6:1 (Raine 1968: I, 181).
Percival (1938: 240-41) supposes that Vala must descend to
create comparatively merciful religions of Beulah to preserve
the unseeing Elect after the Last Judgment.

126:19/ E395/ IX, 376 Like the Shulamite of the Song of Solo-
mon, Vala is a shepherdess who keeps a garden (Raine 1957b:
834). That garden is nature (Harper 1961: 154); Damon (1967:
385, 432) identifies it with the garden round Venus's temple in
Spenser's *The Faerie Queene* IV.x.23-27 and associates it with
the Garden of Adonis (*ibid.* III.vi.30-44). As a realm of Inno-
cence, it is a place of partly subconscious daydreams (Damon
1967: 432), and it presents an Innocent view of the mortality
that Ahania groans over at 108:8-109:12/ E383-84/ VIII, 492-
532 (Gallant 1978: 104).

126:20-25/ E395/ IX, 377-82 Unlike Thel, Vala recognises that
the material world is a temporary phenomenon existing within
the immortal soul (Raine 1968: I, 181).

126:26/ E395/ IX, 383 **those upon the Couches**—the Eternals;
Beulah dreams are authentic (Damon 1924: 393).

126:28/ E395/ IX, 385 For the rest of Night IX, Luvah is rain
and Vala the earth it fructifies; within the grape, Luvah bec-
omes wine, which is symbolically a fertility god's blood
(Erdman 1954a: 327 [355]).

126:36/ E396/ IX, 393 **Whose voice is this**—perhaps an allusion
to "the unfallen Psyche and the invisible Cupid" (Damon 1924:
393). Because Psyche (Vala) is fallen, she cannot see Cupid
(Luvah) (Raine 1968: I, 190).

127:10-15/ E396/ IX, 404-09 Luvah and Vala as yet credit the
sun with the work of Divine Mercy (Stevenson 1971: 444).
These lines proclaiming unbelief are spoken not by Luvah's
"sweet & comforting voice" of 127:28/ E396/ IX, 422 but by
the "voice of sorrow" of the next line (Lincoln 1981: 473).

127:14-15/ E396/ IX, 408-09 Cf. Ps. xc.5-6 (Damon 1924: 393).
Tolley (1973: 120) ascribes these lines to Vala, who cannot yet
believe in her immortality. The "Thou" that is awakened and
will die is, claims Ostriker (1977: 955), Vala's mortal body.

128:25-26/ E397/ IX, 455-56 These lines describe the design on
SE IB pl. 36; *A IB* pl.7; and *SL IB* pl. 3 (Damon 1924: 393).

128:29ff/ E397/ IX, 459ff Cupid, the divine lover, builds the house of the body for Psyche, the soul; Blake follows Apuleius' version of the myth (Raine 1957b: 833).

129:2-12/ E397-98/ IX, 469-79 The valley containing Vala's bodily house is inferior to the hills, for no birds sing there (Lincoln 1981: 474).

129:12-18/ E398/ IX, 479-85 Now that Vala is redeemed, holds Damon (1924: 393), she has clear vision even within the Sea of Time and Space ("the world of waters") and sees the unredeemed, who cannot see her. Raine (1968: I, 188-89) argues that the river symbolises matter, but, that unlike Thel, Vala does not identify her reflection in it (her body) with her essential self. However, Lincoln (1981: 475) identifies the seeming reflection as Enion and regards her vision of it and Tharmas as an echo of Eve's disturbing discovery of her own image (*PL*, IV, 457-75) and a warning to her against "the dangers of wilful self-absorption."

129:27/ E398/ IX, 494 The Beulah-Innocence that Vala recovers is the realm of instinct or Tharmas, whose calming of his seas marks his repentance (Bloom 1965: 966).

129:33-35/ E398/ IX, 500-02 Margoliouth (1956: 150) cites Exod. xxxiii.22, Cant. ii.14, Is. ii.21, Jer. xlix.16, and Obad. 3. Raine (1957b: 834) argues that the phrase "clefts of the rock" derives from Canticles, which Blake regards as the source of Apuleius' version of the myth of Cupid and Psyche. The phrase, Bloom acknowledges (1965: 966), probably does echo Cant. ii.14, though it is a common phrase in the Bible. Beer (1969: 138) attributes the now innocent Vala's anxiety to the continuing power of the moral law.

129:36/ E398/ IX, 503 The light signifies that the crisis of Vala's melancholy, induced by Tharmas's lament for Enion, is averted (Lincoln 1981: 475).

130:2ff/ E398ff/ IX, 505ff With the revival of Innocence, comes the rebirth of its parents, the shepherd Tharmas and his emanation Enion (Bloom 1963: 274-75). Reborn to Nature (Vala), these two are respectively earth's waters and the moon that courts them (Erdman 1954a: 327 [355-56]). Focusing on psychology, Lincoln (1981: 476) maintains that the sight of the children draws Vala back to her body and brings her consciousness from an infant to a maternal state, while Crehan (1984: 309) accuses Tharmas and Enion of infantile regression.

130:20-34/ E399/ IX, 523-37 Even the purified matter that Enion now represents is changeable (Raine 1968: I, 300). Vala teaches Tharmas and Enion that open sexuality is innocent (Frosch 1974: 126).

130:23/ E399/ IX, 526 Cf. 93:40/ E366/ VIIb, 230 (Damon 1924: 393)—now that Luvah's and Vala's realm is what it should be, as it was not in Night VIIb, Tharmas is able to recover Enion (his Innocence) (Margoliouth 1956: 151).

131:1-7/ E399/ IX, 538-44 The day and night are respectively spiritual and fleshly phases of Tharmas's existence, and the fruit tempts him towards the latter (Raine 1968: I, 317-18).

131:13-19/ E399-400/ IX, 550-56 Tharmas and Enion are still in the natural world, but this is what sex ought to be there (Damon 1967: 123).

131:35-36/ E400/ IX, 572-73 Luvah, as rain, is fertilising the human harvest, and the clouds of war disappear (Erdman 1954a: 328 [356]). Urizen's clouds and Tharmas's waters vanish in a blaze of new vision (Bloom 1965: 966).

131:40/ E400/ IX, 577 Cf. Rom. viii.22 (Margoliouth 1956: 151).

132:2-17/ E400/ IX, 579-94 Cf. Rev. xiv.14-16 (Damon 1924: 393-94). Margoliouth (1956: 151) notes that in August, Leo, part of which is sickle-shaped, is in the sun, but Bloom (1965: 966) doubts whether there are astrological references. The sickle may be in the south, Raine suggests (1968: I, 349, 425n38), because Porphyry's southern gate admits souls from the mortal to the immortal world.

132:14-17/ E400/ IX, 591-94 There is a deliberate echo of 44:14-17/ E329/ III, 153-56 (Margoliouth 1956: 151), and the arrival in a whirlwind and the noise from bones come from Ezek. [i.4, xxxvii.7] (Wilkie and Johnson 1978: 230). Damon (1924: 394) finds in this passage an assertion that physical death, though painful, is a form of rebirth, while Bloom (1965: 966) sees a joyful acclamation of the resurrection of the body—i.e. of that part of the soul the senses perceive [cf. *MHH*, pl. 4].

132:21/ E401/ IX, 598 **a Golden Moth**—Blake's equivalent of the Greek butterfly, emblem of the resurrected soul (Damon 1924: 394).

132:23-24/ E401/ IX, 600-01 An echo of the celebration of spring in Cant. ii.11-12 (Miner 1969: 259). The black mould is lowly matter, which, in the alchemical view, has a nourishing function (Raine 1968: I, 300).

132:24-36/ E401/ IX, 601-13 Instinctual creatures acquire human consciousness (Bloom 1965: 966). They symbolise "unconscious energy" (Gallant 1978: 107).

132:36-39/ E401/ IX, 613-16 Contrast the merging of Enion with Tharmas's Spectre at 7:8-13/ E304/ I, 182-87 (Margoliouth 1956: 152). Damon (1924: 394) holds that the worlds where the temporal Los is absorbed back into the eternal Urthona are his "smoking tomb"; in this connection Bloom (1965: 966) notes the identification here of Los with Jesus.

133:2/ E401/ IX, 618 The south is the site of Albion's head, the place of Urizen, and the zenith (Bloom 1965: 966). It represents the eternal realm: Proserpine dwelt in the south (Sicily) before Pluto carried her to the underworld of mortal existence (Raine 1968: I, 133). But contrast 30:29-42/ E320/ II, 187-200n.

133:8/ E401/ IX, 624 **their shadows**—i.e. "their physical manifestations" (Margoliouth 1956: 152).

133:11-22/ E401/ IX, 627-38 When a man becomes selfish, the Eternals place him in an earthly family to revive his threefold vision (Beer 1969: 167). This is the trapping of spirits and creation of seeds of 29:16-30:6/ E319/ II, 158-64 seen from an eternal viewpoint (Hilton 1978: 85). The Eternals reluctantly see the defective institution of the family with its financial "walls of Gold" as fulfilling a temporary need, but Eden is based on brotherhood between equals (DiSalvo 1983: 177, 345).

133:14/ E401/ IX, 630 Percival (1938: 53) compares *M* 30:25 and notes that when the wings are folded, the mind takes the appearances of Beulah for reality.

133:19/ E401/ IX, 635 **windows**—the five senses (Damon 1924: 394); the plates of Blake's visionary works (Rose 1968b: 223).

133:30/ E402/ IX, 646 The southern garden is Beulah; Albion has not yet got back to Eden (Bloom 1965: 966).

133:34ff/ E402/ IX, 650ff The threshing consists of wars and natural catastrophes, disastrous from a temporal standpoint but redemptive from an eternal one (Bloom 1963: 277). With his

threshing, Tharmas, the Tongue, separates truth from false-
hood (Erdman 1954a: 328 [356]) and the winnowing disperses
the latter (Damrosch 1980: 153). Bloom (1965: 967) maintains
that the winnowing is Blake's invention; he may, however,
have taken hints from Matt. iii.12 (Margoliouth 1956: 152),
from the winnowing fan of Dionysus (Raine 1957b: 833), and
from Is. xli.15-16 (Wenger 1969). Miner (1969: 288) com-
ments on the AV marginal gloss that allows the reading "valley
of threshing" in Joel iii.14.

134:5-29/ E402-03/ IX, 657-81 The prophecy of *America*, the
promise of the American Declaration of Independence, is here
fulfilled (Erdman 1954a: 328-29 [356-57]). Though Webster
(1983: 248) thinks that Blake is assailing in the person of Vala
all women who torment infant boys, Howard (1984: 224) per-
suasively asserts that it is the state of Mystery that is destroyed,
not individuals.

134:34/ E403/ IX, 686 The African, having less error to reject
than others, undergoes less suffering (Nurmi 1976: 144). The
family to which he returns is in part a metaphor for universal
fraternity (Wilkie and Johnson 1978: 230). Less technically
advanced and less emotionally inhibited peoples remember the
prelapsarian age (DiSalvo 1983: 163-64). Suggested meanings
for the mysterious name Sotha include northern enslavers of
Africans (Damon 1924: 394, referring to *SL* 3:30—Damon
later [1967: 379] notes that the element of the north is earth);
our planet as opposed to others "in the wide Universe" men-
tioned four lines earlier (Margoliouth 1956: 153); and truth
(Harper 1965: 123).

135: 21-22/ E403/ IX, 709-10 **Luvah/...drunk with the wine of
ages**—Cf. Bacchus (Margoliouth 1956: 153). The wine of lib-
erty is for a time too strong (Erdman 1954a: 329 [357]).

135:23/ E403/ IX, 711 **His crown of thorns**—Damon (1924:
395) points out that this implies both Luvah's association with
Christ and his earlier "circumscription," and Margoliouth
(1956: 153) observes that he was indeed crucified at 92:13/
E364/ VIIb, 166, while Gallant (1978: 109) feels that at this
point he becomes more like Dionysus.

135:25/ E403/ IX, 713 **the Song of Los**—just possibly Blake's
book of this name (Sloss and Wallis 1926: I, 318); probably its
last stanza (Margoliouth 1956: 153).

135:28/ E403/ IX, 716   See 39:6/ E326/ III, 35n.

135:37/ E404/ IX, 725   **human families**—families as self-centred, competing entities (Damon 1924: 395).

135:38/ E404/ IX, 726   The "Odors of life," say Sloss and Wallis (1926: I, 318), are the resurrected whose error has been purged, and Raine (1968: I, 304-05, 419n10), agreeing they are ascending souls, traces the image to the vapours that rose from the slain Titans who had rent apart Dionysus, vapours that generated humankind. Damon (1924: 395) cites Rev. xiv.20, and Miner (1969: 270) Rev. v.8-9. Stevenson (1971: 456) points out that while the sense organs identified with Urizen, Urthona and Tharmas are the eyes, ears and tongue respectively, the nose is allotted to Luvah.

136:5-15/ E404/ IX, 732-42   With the abolition of familiar religion, comes "a Dionysian reversal of history and the cosmos" (Altizer 1967: 196). After the Innocence of Vala's garden, there is a descent into the horror and the vitality of the unconscious, parallel to the fall of the Zoas, involving fear of nonexistence and of suffering like that of the victims of the Daughters of Amalek (Gallant 1978: 108, 110, citing 105:28-54/ E378-79/ VIII, 295-322).

136:6/ E404/ IX, 733   **Forsaken of their Elements they vanish** —Error vanishes, but their essences remain (Sloss and Wallis 1926: I, 319).

136:15/ E404/ IX, 742   **Eternal birth**—probably repeated reincarnation, though it is not entirely clear whether Blake believed in this (Raine 1968: I, 352-53).

136:16-20/ E404/ IX, 743-47   The leopards' and asses' skins are among Bacchus' cult objects (Raine 1968: I, 357-58). The image of lying upon them is the contrary to the image of Vala and the ram at 128:25-27/ E397/ IX, 455-57 (Wilkie and Johnson 1978: 231).

136:21-27/ E404/ IX, 748-54   The human grapes are painfully burst so that the best they contain flows into the wine of fraternity (Damon 1924: 395). People engage in physical warfare and offer sacrifices, forms of perverted sexuality, in place of intellectual contention (Bloom 1963: 278-79). Luvah's Children—sensual pleasures that are sometimes cruel—are purified in their turn at 137:28-31/ E405/ IX, 795-98 (Stevenson [1971: 457] refers also to 136:40-137:4/ E405/ IX, 767-71). Luvah, holds Webster (1983: 248), is taking revenge for Vala's cruelty to him [in Night II].

136:29-39/ E404-05/ IX, 756-66 The animals and plants have been perceived as the lesser evils of war (Damon 1924: 395); lower creatures among whom love is less painful (Margoliouth 1956: 154); ambiguous beings who may represent war and sickness but also Urizenic misconception of energy (Raine 1968: I, 355-56); innocent emotions, which are associated with wisdom (Beer 1969: 168); elements of the deep unconscious being regenerated (Gallant 1978: 111-12).

136:39/ E405/ IX, 766 **Naked in all their beauty**—i.e. "in their spiritual forms" (Damon 1924: 395).

137:5-6/ E405/ IX, 772-73 Albion asks Tharmas and Urthona to stop the sufferings in the winepresses (Bloom 1963: 279).

137:8-9/ E405/ IX, 775-76 Urthona has Vulcan's limp and hammer, the latter signifying that he is a poet or "maker," while Tharmas, with his crook, is the shepherd of Innocence (Damon 1924: 395). Urthona is among those for whom the wine of liberty is initially too intoxicating—see 135:21-22/ E403/ IX, 709-10n (Erdman 1954a: 329 [357]). As the crippled poet-artist, he leans on Innocence's instinct for unity (Bloom 1963: 279).

137:11-19/ E405/ IX, 778-86 The product of the looms is "a new nature" (Bloom 1963: 279) or the garments clothing the redeemed passions, which are the Children of Luvah (Bloom 1965: 967).

137:15/ E405/ IX, 782 **All beneath howl'd loud**—where Mystery's following is being destroyed (Stevenson 1971: 458).

137:19/ E405/ IX, 786 Passion, when left free to do so, exhausts itself (Damon 1924: 395).

137:20-21/ E405/ IX, 787-88 The unconscious threatens to overwhelm the whole person, and Luvah degenerates from an ecstatic Dionysus to a drunken Silenus (Gallant 1978: 112).

137:23/ E405/ IX, 790 The sexually driven cycles of the dying and resurrected vegetation god have ended, and the life-giving, truly human part of the emotional life survives as his wine (Bloom 1963: 280-81). The lees are states as opposed to individuals (Howard 1984: 225).

137:24/ E405/ IX, 791 **Luvah was put for dung on the ground**
—The business of erotic love is to facilitate sexual repro-

duction (Raine 1968: I, 218). Luvah's passion must supply material if Los is to create art (Hagstrum 1973: 117). Blake repudiates his own unhealthy fantasy of the sex-driven cruelty of the winepresses (Webster 1983: 248-49).

137:28-31/ E405/ IX, 795-98 At the vintage the Zoas were in Beulah, and they now begin the ascent to Eternity (Frosch 1974: 139-40).

137:30/ E405/ IX, 797 **he cast them wailing**—The man temporarily rejects troublesome passions (Damon 1924: 395). It is Luvah's Children and possibly Luvah and Vala themselves that are ejected (Tolley 1973: 122). Ostriker (1982: 160) notes Luvah's and Vala's close connection with the seasons.

137:33/ E405/ IX, 800 **vocal harmony**—the music of the spheres (Wilkie and Johnson 1978: 233).

137:35-36/ E406/ IX, 802-03   Cf. Rev. xx.13 (Damon 1924: 395). We return here to what is left of the world of Blake's own time (Bloom 1965: 967).

138:4-5/ E406/ IX, 809-10 The body supplies the energy for the spirit's mills (Damon 1924: 395).

138:13-15/ E406/ IX, 818-20 The grain being Urizen, the suffering, according to Wilkie and Johnson (1978: 233), is intellectual.

138:14-17/ E406/ IX, 819-22 Urthona makes the bread of philosophy, that philosophy being the product of Experience (Damon 1924: 163, 395). The corn of thought may complement the wine of feeling (Stevenson 1971: 456). The bread of knowledge contrasts with the "bread of Sorrow" of 79:23/ E355/ VII, 93 (Wilkie and Johnson 1978: 233). Whereas Urizen's Daughters turned his knowledge into the latter, Urthona now bakes it into the spiritual bread of prophecy (Howard 1984: 226). The baking unites all souls into the redeemed human of Eternity, who contains all humans (*ibid.*: 225); although the process is redemptive, Hilton (1983: 221) identifies Urthona's "crushing Wheels" with those of the starry mills of the Newtonian heavens.

138:19/ E406/ IX, 824 The Spirit rests after producing the bread of philosophy (Damon 1924: 395). This is the final winter of the fallen world (Bloom 1963: 281).

138:23-28/ E406/ IX, 828-33 These lines describe the unfallen view of the universe (Evans 1972: 326).

138:24-25/ E406/ IX, 829-30 In place of starlight, the internal power of perception lights up the cosmos (Wilkie and Johnson 1978: 234).

138:26/ E406/ IX, 831 **Erring Globes**—the stars before their physical husks have been threshed away (Wenger 1969); planets (Hilton 1983: 204, 290n39).

138:27-31/ E406/ IX, 832-36 That "one Sun" converses "night & day" supports Rose's contention (1970c: 447-50) that the world of time is superseded for ever and the days and seasons are simultaneous as opposed to Gallant's view (1978: 114-15) that the passage from fragmentation to unity is continually repeated like the seasons.

138:35-38/ E406/ IX, 840-43 This image of ideal human life combines craftsmanship, absence of property, reunion with nature, and cultivation of individuality (DiSalvo 1983: 310).

138:36/ E406/ IX, 841 The lions, like the furnaces, rightly belong to Urthona and not to Urizen, who possessed them in Night II (Margoliouth 1956: 155). These lions replace the tigers of "the forests of the night" (Bloom 1963: 282).

138:39-40/ E407/ IX, 844-45 People are amazed that the fire of vision frees them instead of devouring them (Beer 1969: 169).

139:3/ E407/ IX, 848 In Eternity, there is "an autumn of countless springs" (Rose 1970c: 449, 451).

139:4-8/ E407/ IX, 849-53 The life of instinct replaces poetry (Damon 1924: 396). The prophet is no longer condemned to solitude and secrecy (Erdman 1954a: 330 [358]). Urthona, the complete artist, has superseded Los, the prophet of the world of time (Bloom 1965: 967). Art is no longer required as a distinct activity, and Urthona makes the arms for intellectual combat (Wilkie and Johnson 1978: 236-37). The Spectre of Prophecy is the fallible Spectre of Urthona (Stevenson 1971: 460), who (Damrosch 1980: 336) ceases to exist separately, for this is Eden. The reader, having acquired Blake's vision, will no longer perceive only the Spectre of Prophecy in his text (Hilton 1983: 171).

139:10/ E407/ IX, 855 **sweet Science**—"spiritual knowledge" (Sloss and Wallis 1926: II, 216); the kind of knowledge contained in *The Four Zoas* (Margoliouth 1956: 155); the fullest possible knowledge of art (Bloom 1963: 283); knowledge of the immortality to be won by such virtues as love and mercy (Mellor 1974: 191).

The Pickering Manuscript

"The Smile"

According to Damon (1924: 297), the woman's mixed smile and the man's frown of frowns need to be united to reach perfection, but the perfect smile, in Holloway's view (1968: 70-71), is only an ideal to be dreamed about. Adams (1963: 152-54) identifies the smile of love and deceit as the creator's smile when he looked at the tiger, a unique smile containing all time and reflecting the duality of creation as both part of the Fall and means of redemption. Wright (1929: I, 156-57) asserts that the smiler is Vala—i.e. nature, and Margoliouth (1951: 63) mentions the poem's incorrect syntax.

"The Golden Net"

The net has been said to symbolise chastity (Damon 1924: 297), the "veil of nature" (Frye 1947: 266), natural religion (Bloom 1963: 288), the mortal body (Adams 1963: 129), the suffering that love involves (Damon 1967: 297-98), and female possessiveness (Damrosch 1980: 197). Adlard (1972: 122-23) considers that the virgins are performing a rite to evoke a glimpse of a future husband, and Holloway (1968: 71) comments on their seeming sadism evoked by the speaker's pity for their sufferings. The speaker, says, Adams (1963: 130-31), moves from Innocence to Experience as his capacity for pity is exploited.

ll. 2-3 "Alas" puns on "a lass" and "Whither" on the imperative verb "wither" (Hilton 1983: 257).
l. 10 **the Branches**—of the Tree of Knowledge, which is our fallen realm (Adams 1963: 131).

"The Mental Traveller"

In 1947, Frye (229) usefully pointed to the part played in "The Mental Traveller" by the Orc cycle, in which Orcean creative energy degenerates into Urizenic tyranny, but Sutherland (1955: 140-43) and Paley (1962: 97) recognised that this was relevant only to the first part of the poem. Its most challenging element is the fact that its principal characters can grow younger as well as older. The poem was probably first understood by Yeats (1925: 133-34), after he had worked out his own concept of twin gyres representing antithetical qualities that alternately dominate civilisation: the influence of one quality diminishes while that of the other increases till a turning point comes and they exchange roles. Yeats tentatively suggested that the same concept may have reached Blake through orally transmitted doctrine of Swedenborg, but in 1958 Raine published her discovery that Blake's source was Plato's *Politicus*, of which, as she later noted (1963: 406), the first English translation was Thomas Taylor's of 1804. In this dialogue (269c-273e), Plato speaks of alternation between peaceful periods when the world is under Saturn's government and people grow younger, and periods when the world is left to itself, there is much suffering, and people grow older.

The pattern of history, governed by the antithetical forces of spirit (male) and nature (female), is the main theme of the poem, but phases in the relationship between men and women may also be glanced at. Typically, readers find it "terrifying" (Paley 1962: 103), and shot through with "despair" (Hirsch 1964: 121, 312), though to Raine (1958) the narration seems detached and even "playful." Perhaps following a hint of Holloway (1968: 74), Paley (1970: 123-24) notes the pervasive irony of a speaker who pretends to be talking of an unknown world when he is actually describing the reader's own. That speaker has been identified as Blake himself (Sutherland 1955: 140) and as an unfallen Eternal (Bloom 1963: 290), but more importantly, Adams (1963: 78-81) emphasises the distance between his view of events and the fallen earth-dweller's.

Two subjects of dispute are whether the Female Babe is good or malign and whether there is an opportunity of escape from the ever-repeated cycle. Is this Babe, like the Woman Old, a mani-

festation of nature, who represents a threat but is sometimes con-
quered (Bateson 1957: 137), or who is essentially repressive
(Bloom 1963: 293), and who has absorbed the energy of the
unfiery male Babe as Vala absorbs Orc's in *The Four Zoas* (Ault
1974: 186-88)? Or is she perhaps the church, Rahab (Damon
1924: 131)? Alternatively, is she a positive, fertilising embodiment
of Orc's achievements (Frye 1947: 229), "the prophetic impulse"
(Adams 1963: 98), creative energy (Enscoe 1968: 407-09), or even
ambiguous (Deen 1983: 88, 98)? Frye later (1957b: 322) decides
that she is an aspect of nature, and Miner (1981: 326-27) believes
that the metamorphoses of the female principle are correlated with
the phases of the moon.

While Adams (1963: 98-99) thinks that the grown Babe
and her lover disappear midway through the poem because they
have the prophetic power to turn the fallen world into Eden and
escape from time, several interpreters see chances to escape which
are *not* taken—specifically at ll. 87-92, where art flourishes
(Bloom 1963: 296), at the Second Coming at the conclusion
(Nurmi 1964a: 115-16), and in ll. 5-8 before the male child is
given to the Woman Old (Mellor 1974: 201). Probably as common
is the view that no chance of escape is offered (e.g. Chayes 1961:
368).

Not every critic agrees that Plato's *Politicus* yields the key
to the poem, but none of the dissenters provides a convincing
explanation of time's running backwards. Twitchell (1975)
proposes that the mathematical sign for infinity, introduced in
1655, suggested to Blake the shape of his cycles. Although the
cycle is everlastingly repeated, Bouwer and McNally (1978) locate
male spirit and female nature within the individual, whose fall and
regeneration they say the poem traces. In his Marxist-Freudian
interpretation, Crehan (1984: 314-17) attributes the projection of
the scientific image of the cosmos onto the heavenly bodies to the
crumbling of the ego's boundaries and classifies the brief pastoral
paradise that precedes the discovery of the Babe as "a cosy utopian
fantasy." According to Beer (1968: 89-93), the male is the Divine
Image, which is consecutively oppressed by the law, expelled by
the female will, and immersed in a sexual relationship that some-
how leads through materialism back towards the lost paradise. To
place the emphasis on the domination of men by women and of
women by men, Enscoe (1968: 405, 411) has to claim that the

Woman Old is the male baby's mother and that the poem ends with a baby newly *born*. Finally, Deen (1983: 85-122), focusing on the competitive, even parasitic relationship between the male and the goddess Nature, who thwarts his potential, traces a series of parallels with sky and earth, Shakespeare's Adonis and Venus, Hephaestus and Pandora, and Revelation's royal child and woman clothed with the sun.

l. 6 **That was begotten in dire woe**—because the old lifestyle has to be swept away before the new one can be born (Paley 1962: 98); because of puritanical hostility to sex (Enscoe 1968: 404).

ll. 7-8 Cf. Ps. cxxvi.5 (Ostriker 1977: 961).

ll. 9-20 The Babe's sufferings echo those of Dionysus, Prometheus and Christ (Raine 1958). His five wounds are the wounds of the crucified Christ and of imprisonment in the fallen senses (Adams 1963: 89).

l. 10 **a Woman Old**—old Tirzah, who turns into the seductive young virgin Rahab (Adams 1963: 82-86); Juno and Blake's own Enion, her torture of the Babe being equivalent to Tirzah's and Rahab's (i.e. material nature's) torture of Albion [*J IB* pl. 25] (Raine 1963: 408, 410); an emblem of "the mother, society, or nature" (Mellor 1974: 199).

ll. 17-18 Division and analysis characterise the creation of the natural world (Frosch 1974: 47).

ll. 21-24 Cf. Orc and the Shadowy Female in the Preludium to *America* (Bateson 1957: 137).

ll. 25-28 These lines describe an artistic civilisation (Raine 1958), an authentic union in Beulah—as in ll. 87-92 (Paley 1962: 103), or a parody of the latter state (Bloom 1963: 292).

ll. 29ff Orc turns into Urizen (Frye 1947: 229; Paley 1962: 99-100).

ll. 33-36 These apparent treasures are the product of repression—contrast the "merry" heart and "loving" eye of "Riches" (E470/ K181) (Paley 1962: 100); they are material wealth (Mellor 1974: 200); being the works of art of an earlier, more creative period, they commemorate human suffering (Raine 1963: 411-12)—Bloom (1963: 293) notes the employment of the language of courtly love, which involves sexual repression.

Damon (1967: 324) interprets the pearls as love and the rubies as wisdom.

ll.38-40 The charity is Urizenic and comparable to that of "The Human Abstract" (Paley 1962: 100), though Beer (1968: 91) thinks it is genuine but unaccompanied by vision.

ll. 41-42   In spite of the Shadow, some people manage to be creative (Sutherland 1955: 142-43). A disillusioned poet or dying religion can still give some people satisfaction (Hirsch 1964: 317-18).

l. 46   The gems and gold are a hint of the serpent in paradise (Bouwer and McNally 1978: 188).

l. 49   Sutherland (1955: 143), who admires the Female Babe, thinks her partner may be an artist, mystic or saint.

l. 51   **Host**—Ostriker (1977: 961) detects a pun on the sacramental host.

ll. 53-58   The remains of an old civilisation fertilise a new one as Greek culture fertilised the Renaissance (Raine 1963: 412-13). Decayed imagination resorts to embracing nature (Bloom 1963: 294). The Poor Man is a husband who piled up riches, neglected his wife, and lost her to another man (Mellor 1974: 200).

ll. 57-68   A rationalistic civilisation develops in contrast to the artistic one of ll. 25-28 (Raine 1958). The old man's spousal possessiveness makes his universe dwindle to mirror his shrivelled consciousness (Enscoe 1968: 409-10).

ll. 75-84   Spirit relates to matter through scientific enquiry (Raine 1963: 415-16). Spectre and emanation engage in "courtly" amorous pursuit (Bloom 1963: 295).

l. 84   The animals are returning passions (Paley 1962: 103) or "the enemies of the spirit" (Bouwer and McNally 1978: 189).

ll. 87-92   Raine (1963: 416) regards the paradise here described as the result of a reaction against a scientific age, while Hirsch (1964: 322-23) views it as an illusory, idealised view of nature projected by a mind in the state of Beulah, and Nurmi (1964a: 115) holds that the maiden has raised the aged man from Ulro to lower Beulah. Frye (1966: 192-93) sees the desert as only partially reclaimed, for despite the man's efforts he looks for his emanation outside himself, but Beer (1969: 93) is satisfied that an urban society is happily becoming pastoral. To Wagenknecht (1973: 170-71), there seems to be only a speciously progressive society, the product of enthusiasm for nature.

ll. 97-100 Raine (1958) interprets an allusion to Uzzah, who died when he touched the Holy Ark [II Sam. vi.6-7; I Chron. xiii.6-7], as an indication that mortals cannot alter the preordained course of history. She later observes (1968: I, 321, 422n46) that King Jeroboam's hand withered when he opposed a prophet (I Kings xiii.2-4) and (1963: 417) that an echo of Rev. vi.13 in the falling fruit of l. 100 hints at an imminent Last Judgment. Rose (1966: 119-20) claims that both the arm of the Babe and the arm of the toucher are withered, both individuals being subject to the power of the cycle.

"Mary"

Raine (1968: I, 166), Damrosch (1980: 150) and Paley (1983b: 188) think that Damon's suggestion (1924: 100-01) that this poem is a defence of Mary Wollstonecraft may be correct, though Erdman (1954a: 142 [156-57]) insists that it does not fit her case. The theme, according to Holloway (1968: 70) is the inescapable fate of goodness in this world. In Adams' view (1963: 138-41), Mary is comparable to Thel, for finding herself thrust from Innocence into Experience she cannot cope and takes the false way of self-denial and restraint of desire.

"The Crystal Cabinet"

The repetition of "threefold" has led to a widespread and well founded view that the speaker enjoys sexual love in Beulah (Damon 1924: 298) until he attempts to rise to a higher, fourfold level and collapses into Generation or Ulro (Frye 1947: 234, 300). He has been charged with becoming too possessive towards the maiden (Damon, loc. cit.), with trying to apprehend the essence of existence while in Beulah and not Eden (Bloom 1963: 298-301), with wanting to make permanent a transient moment (Beer 1968: 88-89)—perhaps a glimpse of "eternal realities" (Wardle 1980: 38-39)—or reacting to it by reaching outward instead of inward (Adams 1963: 121-29), and with being totally absorbed in essentially narcissistic eroticism (Damrosch 1980: 200-01).

Blame also attaches to the maiden, who may be Vala-Rahab (T. Wright 1929: I, 159) and who entraps "a masculine soul" as do the virgins of "The Golden Net" (Margoliouth 1951: 63-64). According to Chayes (1970b: 230), possessiveness is the fault first of the maiden, then of the speaker.

Damon (1967: 95) suspects that the poem tells of an unhappy love affair—perhaps the poet's own in Lambeth, which is situated in Surrey. Gillham (1966: 167-69) interprets it as an account of the excitement of sexual intercourse followed by disappointment, and Erdman (1954a: 366-67 [394-95]) feels that it expresses Blake's disillusion with London on his return from Felpham. Observing that the alchemists recognised a feminine trinity in the lower world and a masculine trinity in the upper, Raine (1968: I, 274-77) detects an account of spirit lured down into the material world and trapped there. Adlard (1972: 65-66) refers to an alchemical notion of catching a fairy with a mirror and suggests that the poem may end with a laboratory explosion.

The cabinet itself has been identified not only as the prison of love, Raine's matter and Adlard's mirror, but as an eye and a womb that give birth to a tear and, after copulation, to the weeping woman's weeping babe (Deen 1983: 243). Following coition, according to Wardle (1980: 37), the man feels like a crying baby while the woman actually weeps.

l. 4 **Lock'd me up**—an act of copulation (Bloom 1963: 298); a pun on Locke, for whom the newborn human's mind was an empty cabinet (Hilton 1983: 63)—according to Rose (1971a: 62), Blake often puns thus on Locke's name.

"The Grey Monk"

This is a version of the poem on *J*, pl. 52.

"Auguries of Innocence"

Schorer (1946: 108-10, 239) defines the theme as universal interdependence and holds that the poem rests on the principle of correspondences between equivalent entities on different planes, a principle Blake learnt from Swedenborg. Contrariwise, Adams (1963: 159-61) maintains that the animals stand for classes of humans (for details, see below) and that the central theme is the vision attained by seeing *through* instead of *with* the eye. However, the animals may well be *both* themselves *and* symbols of human beings, and this possibility is consistent with Janet Warner's view (1976: 138, 136) that Blake is showing that the natural world can be regenerated and that entities external to ourselves—nature, other people, institutions—can become auguries, or vehicles, of the lost vision of Innocence in which all things are seen as interdependent and all things are seen as human. None of these readings can be reconciled with Holloway's opinion (1968: 70-71) that the poem portrays evil as invincible in this world.

There is disagreement over Damon's assertion (1924: 132) that Blake would have rearranged the order of some of the couplets before publication. Grant (1964: 495-96) says *Yes*; Adams (1963: 155, 159-60) and Janet Warner (1976: 126) say *No*.

Title "Innocence" signifies the unfallen state (Frye 1947: 45). The auguries may be *about* Innocence or they may be produced by those in Innocence and accessible to those in Experience; they are an alternative to the auguries of ancient Rome, often obtained by killing animals (Grant 1964: 489-90). Innocence itself has been sacrificed and only auguries of it remain in the realm of Experience (J. Warner 1976: 127).

ll. 1-4 The infinite can be seen in the non-human flower and even in that symbol of dehumanisation, a grain of sand (Bloom 1963: 301). In order to see a world, you should hold infinity... (Grant 1964: 493). The lines may be read this way, or "see" and "Hold" may be parallel infinitive verbs (J. Warner 1976: 127-28).

ll. 1-2 The wild flower implies free love—cf. "The wild flower's song" (E472/ K175, 170); the heaven is seen through love (Luvah) and the world through intellect (Urizen), and love and intellect should be synthesised by imagination (Urthona) (Grant 1964: 492, 494).

ll. 9, 11, 17 The dog represents a beggar, the horse a slave, and the cock a soldier (Adams 1963: 161).

l. 16 The singing signifies the inward possession in the lower realm of the visionary world (Adams 1963: 161).

l. 23 The lamb's submission symbolises Jesus' self-sacrifice (Adams 1963: 162).

l. 25   This bat is a human spectre (J. Warner 1976: 135).

ll. 27-28, 33-34, 36   The owl stands for the human lost in darkness who fears "an unknown god"; the boy is a negation intervening between two contraries—prolific fly and devouring spider; the weaving imprisons the soul within the Mundane Shell (Adams 1963: 162-64).

ll. 37-40   The caterpillar is the human emerging from nature's womb to become a moth or butterfly (Adams 1963: 164). Comparing *The Gates of Paradise*, Janet Warner (1976: 134-37) states that this is the first of a sequence of images which includes swaddling bands (l. 63) and winding sheet (l. 116) and represents the course of human life.

l. 42   **pass the Polar Bar**—escape to the spiritual world via the "northern bar" of *Thel* 6:1 (Damon 1924: 299).

l. 52   **Toadstools on the Miser's Bags**—an emblem of the unrestrained life of the selfhood, the source of riches and poverty (Adams 1963: 164-65).

l. 72   **Waves**—of the Sea of Time and Space (Damon 1924: 299).

ll. 91-95 The questioner who replies will be a reasoner without real knowledge (J. Warner 1976: 135). *M* 41:12-28 supports this interpretation.

l. 98   Surprisingly, Adams (1963: 165) thinks the laurel crown a crown of doubt.

l. 105   **The Emmet's Inch & Eagle's Mile**—(1) perception from close at hand and from far off; (2) physical and imaginative perception (Beer 1968: 200).

ll. 111-12   One should project one's passions to work creatively, not lock them up in oneself (Adams 1963: 167-68).

ll. 122-24   Whether one lives in "sweet delight" or in "Endless Night" depends on whether one sees through or with the eye (Mellor 1974: 216).

l. 127   **Born in a Night to perish in a Night**—an allusion to the gourd of Jon. iv.10 (Bloom 1963: 302). Blake combines the Neoplatonic view of life in the body as the sleep of the soul with the lesson that Jonah had to learn—that God is not vindictive (Grant 1964: 497-500).

l. 129   **God is Light**—to the abstract reasoner and the scientist (Schorer 1946: 110), or to humanity in its childhood as illustrated by "The Little Black Boy" in *SI* (M. Plowman 1927a: 133). This is the transcendent conception of God, with which the next couplet contrasts the imminent conception (Davies 1948: 67-69), or God as perceived in the New Testament dispensation, which will be succeeded by the Age of the Spirit when God will be entirely indwelling and fully united with humanity (Morton 1958: 37-38, citing Ranter doctrine). Blake is criticising the Quaker doctrine of the Inner Light in which God dwells but which is distinct from His transcendent essence (Mellor 1974: 215-16). He is assailing Milton's claim that "God is light" (*PL*, III, 3) (Ostriker 1977: 963).

"Long John Brown & Little Mary Bell"

Damon is clearly wrong to claim (1924: 300) that the Devil represents "the Puritan conscience" and that he rather than the fairy denounces love as a sin. More persuasive is Thomas Wright's contention (1929: I, 161) that he is sexual desire and that John is the victim of Mary's teasing inconsistency. The fourth line, Adams maintains (1963: 134-36), does not say that there was sexual intercourse, and Mary eventually suffered the unsatisfied desire she had visited on John. Margoliouth (1951: 63) believes the poem is also a parable about hostility to imagination.

"William Bond"

It is often thought that, as Damon believes (1924: 100), this poem about a William with a spouse or girlfriend and a sister is autobiographical; Hilton (1983: 242) judges the surname shows that Blake includes himself among those in bonds. In a detailed analysis, Adams (1963: 143-46) describes how William encounters Experience in the form of a church, a seductress, and angels of Providence who replace Innocent fairies; longing for the seductress, he is morally tormented until his former love selflessly renounces her claim on him, so that he learns that love involves giving and belongs to Beulah, whose symbol is the moon. The poem may tell how William renounces twofold energy for threefold vision (Beer 1968: 188) or Eros for Agape (Paley 1983b: 177).

Notes on Criticism for Chapter 10

Milton

Since 1924 (Damon: 179), it has been widely recognised that the main action of *Milton* (excluding the events of the Bard's Song) take place in a moment. But exactly what does this imply? And does the poem conclude with the redemption of all humanity in the person of Albion, as Fox (1976: 18) believes, or, as Frye (1947: 323-24) judges, is the universal redemption reserved for *Jerusalem*, to which *Milton* serves as a prelude? Frye's plausible view is endorsed by such well known scholars as Bloom (1963: 356), Paley (1970: 143), Mitchell (1973b: 282, 286), and Erdman (1974: 216). To Frye (*loc. cit.*), the Last Judgment seems still in the distant future when *Milton* ends, but to Sloss and Wallis (1926: I, 426), as to Fox (1976: 18, 222), it appears imminent.

In her careful and stimulating analysis of the poem's structure, Fox expands Damon's idea (1924: 179) that nearly all the events in the poem occur "in one moment." She claims that the entire action, including the descents of Milton and Ololon, their encounter with Blake and their union, passes in a single instant without duration, the last instant before time vanishes and Albion is redeemed (1976: 18). To argue that this is so, Fox has to maintain that that action concludes at 42:23 (1976: 182-83) and virtually ignore the subsequent shifting of the scene back to Lambeth, the continued existence of poverty, and the unfinished state of the human harvest. She also asserts that Ololon's descent to Milton is simultaneous with Milton's descent to Ololon (1976: 17, 92) although Milton, in the beginning, appears to be entirely in heaven, while his Emanation is divided between heaven and the abyss, and it is not till Milton leaves heaven that Ololon decides to make the same sacrifice. Moreover, the theory requires us to believe that the descriptions of Albion turning on his couch while "Unwaken'd," Albion awakening, and Albion beginning to walk but falling back on his couch are three increasingly detailed accounts of the same event (23:7-10; 25:23; 39:32-52; Fox 1976: 167-68). It is, however, possible that Fox is correctly describing a plan that Blake imperfectly executes. Mitchell's comment (1973b: 287) that the Bard's Song—with its obvious allusions to Cain and Abel, to the Dragon who pulls down stars, and to the Two Witnesses—functions as both a Genesis and a Revelation underlines the element of simultaneity that does exist. Stevenson (1971: 487, 550) believes that it is the action from 35:42 to 42:28 that takes place in a single moment.

Emphasising the twofold structure of the book in a different way, Erdman (1973) observes how Milton's return to earth and reascent are parallel to Blake's journey from London to Felpham and back; this movement is reflected in the division into two books and in the opposite directions in which the steps behind William and Robert face in pls. 32 and 37. The whole structure, he argues, involves the division and reunion of contraries: brothers, spouses, pity and wrath, grain and grape.

Some critics (e.g. Frye 1957c: 105; Bloom 1965: 909-28) consider that the book's twofold pattern is supplemented by the fourfold framework of Ulro, Generation, Beulah and Eden. Rieger (1973: 277) even maintains that there are "four levels of discourse," one for each realm, and each is incompletely intelligible to the world below. As should be obvious from my chapter on the work, I agree with scholars like Damon (1967: 150) and Stevenson (1971: 486) who hold that it is only in *Jerusalem* that Generation becomes a separate level.

No admirer of *Milton* could deny that it has significant flaws. In particular, there have been many references to what Paley (1970: 249) calls the one serious fault in its structure—the prophecy at 20:56-61 and 23:35-38 that Orc will be liberated from the Chain of Jealousy is neither clearly vindicated nor falsified. However, Rose (1968c: 21) regards Milton's fulfilment of his quest as implying that energy is unshackled and the Chain broken, and Damon (1924: 182) believes that the prisoner is freed when he ascends over the Atlantic at 20:6 (but cf. *A* 1:11-13, where he rises but is still bound). Perhaps more persuasive is Wittreich's contention (1975: 245-47) that the prophesy is unobtrusively fulfilled in Milton's reintegration of both Urizen and Orc into "the human psyche" at 40: 4-8. Fisch (1969: 44-45) believes that Blake is forecasting the purification of the degenerate revolutionary spirit, and James (1978: 119) supposes that the breaking of the Chain symbolises the escape of humanity from the futile cycle of political revolutions to the irreversible "poetic revolution" of Los. Erdman (1974: 265) sees Blake's return to London in 1803 to utter his own prophecies as the vindication of the prediction on a personal level.

Blake's treatment of Orc in this poem is indeed defective. Initially he represents the energies of Luvah reborn in the fallen world, where they are bound with the Chain of Jealousy but remain conscious, as his exhortation of the Shadowy Female shows, of what it is to be Human (19:37-38; 18:26-50). However, there is a strange inconsistency within the warning that Rintrah and Palamabron deliver against Los's allowing Milton to advance: he will, they declare, free Orc, whom they link with the diabolic powers—yet thirty-five lines later they implicitly praise Orc as they grieve that Albion has not awoken though Orc rises over the Atlantic—that is, the American Revolution has erupted (22:32-33; 23:3-10). It must also be noted that repressed energy eventually turns into corruption, so that Orc in his lowest state becomes the Polypus itself and his Spectre is Satan (29:27-34)—Bloom (1963: 330) views the Orc of *Milton* as the natural man in the bonds of the Chain of Jealousy.

Critics disagree as to the central theme of this epic. While Bloom (1963: 309) perceives it as the expulsion of the Puritan censor from Milton's mind, Rix (1984: 114-17) sees it as his identification with Isaiah's Suffering Servant, who, according to Blake, takes different forms in different ages. Emphasising Blake's opposition to Milton's belief that punishment should follow sin, Sloss and Wallis (1926: I, 347-48) urge that the divine mercy makes Rintrah and Leutha accept blame on Satan's behalf, Enitharmon provide his protective space, and the Eternals appoint seven spirits to watch over it.

Whether or not Milton's imperfections as man or poet lie at the heart of the work, Blake, as his Preface indicates, is anxious to unburden himself of a message about art. Raine (1968: I, 257) and Beer (1968: 185) regard the central theme as inspiration, Hagstrum (1964: 111) views it as art conceived as the road back to Innocence, and Schorer (1946: 360) defines it as "the superiority of the visionary poet over other kinds." Bindman (1977: 173-76) argues that Blake singles out the portrait of Satan in *Paradise Lost* as Milton's greatest achievement, since it gives a form to error; on his return to earth, Milton repeats this success by building a body for Urizen (19:6-14) and casting him out (*IB* pl. 45). Hilton's belief (1983: 15) that Palamabron's name derives from the Greek *palama* ("hand") may be associated with Teitelbaum's proposal (1969: 45-49) that Palamabron represents outline and Rintrah the inspiration that should inform it, while Satan is the enemy of all definite form. Taking a broader perspective, Mitchell (1973b: 297-98, 300-07) sees the character Milton as "the masculine, active imagination," which operates within an historical consciousness and which unaided can do no more than glory in the splendour of nature, its own creation, as it does in the 'epilogue' to book I; when the Eternals, who argue over the Bard's Song and expel Milton's real self, think again, they encourage the descent of Ololon, this life-giving, feminine, inspirational side of imagination which sees history from the perspective of Eternity and makes the regeneration of nature and humanity possible. Elsewhere, in an essay based on the ambiguities he finds in several of the designs (1973a: 61-63), Mitchell argues that Milton's descent is largely a failure, for he probably neither escapes from error nor unites with Ololon: she is shown without him in the final plate, where she is moving towards liberation.

There are also psychological interpretations. As a Freudian, Webster (1983: 255-71) supposes that Blake's ideal is an elaboration of the pre-sexual world of early infancy in which the ego is all-powerful, but that he tries to eliminate the mother's necessary contribution to it by insisting on the female subservience exemplified by his treatment of Ololon and the Daughters of Albion; she conjectures that his guilt feelings over his ingratitude to Hayley make him call on his literary father, Milton, for vindication. In a Jungian analysis, Gallant (1978: 116-54, especially 151-54) points to "*letting go*" as the poem's message, for Milton and Blake both cut loose from their personae to face the Satan in themselves; the former unites with his Emanation, and the latter releases his anger against Hayley, explores the unconscious, and finds the archetype of the self. Holding that the work focuses primarily on Blake himself, Cooper (1981: 90-107) asserts that it takes the form of a vortex which spirals up from the incoherent mythology of pls. 3 through 7, where the author has no identity, through his imperfect persona, the Bard, his alter ego Los, and his exemplar Milton, to the apex of the last plates, where he achieves full humanity as an individual expression of the universal Christ;

unlike Milton's, however, his psychic integration is not final because he is still in the mortal body.

Details

pl. i **To Justify the Ways of God to Men**—Rose (1968c: 25) holds that Blake quotes Milton's declaration of his intent (*PL*, I, 26) disapprovingly, for it is not the business of prophets to justify God's conduct.

pl. 1   *Poem* l. 1 Christ appeared in Britain in the form of Albion before the Fall (Saurat 1929: 85); Albion, not Christ, walked in Britain then (Bateson 1957: 134). Cf. Is. lii.7 (Hilton 1981: 201).

l. 8 **Satanic Mills**—logic (Damon 1924: 404); "any unimaginative mechanism" including factory machinery and the Newtonian model of the universe (Frye 1947: 290); specifically, works producing metal for armaments in the London of 1803 (Erdman 1954a: 367-68 [396]).

ll. 9-13 According to Murry (1933: 313-14) and Howard (1976: 159), the lyric endorses only mental war, and the arms are symbolic—Howard, perhaps developing a hint of Goslee (1974: 124), mentions, for example, the engraver's burin. Preston (1944: 27) interprets the bow as feeling, the arrows as sexuality, the spear as reason, and the chariot as intuition, while Pinto (1965: 19) understands them as the "intellect, passion, animal energy and poetic inspiration" which would animate "the community of perfected souls." Paley (1970: 259) identifies the "Chariot of fire" with the Divine Chariot of Ezekiel's vision, whereas McGann (1973: 19) equates it with that of Elijah, who was followed by Elisha as Milton is by Blake. In ll. 9-10, Rose (1971a: 65) finds a hint that the rainbow of the artist's pigments shoots his arrows of desire as weapons of mental war.

ll. 15-16 These lines anticipate Albion's reunion with his Emanation, Jerusalem (Adams 1963: 275-76). They declare Blake's determination to re-establish the pristine Druidical-Patriarchal religion of *J*, pl. 27 (Owen 1962: 225, 234-35) or to recreate the Golden Age in *Jerusalem* (Rose 1970b: 423) and to establish in that poem the essential identity of Israel and England (Adams 1975: 149-50).

2:9-10, 12   Cf. Col. i.15 and Gen. i.26. The form God gives to the fallen spirits is the one He Himself assumes when He becomes visible as Jesus. Cf. p. 159 above. Sloss and Wallis (1926: II, 227-28) consider the spectres to be abstract ideas the artist can only embody through inspiration.

2:10   **the False Tongue**—Satan's (the Accuser's) voice (Damon 1924: 404); "the doctrine of materialism" (Damon 1967: 408); the language of Blake's mythology, which can easily become a substitute for the realities it should convey (Cooper 1981: 96-97). Cf. Ps. cxx.3 (Margoliouth 1948: 308).

2:14   **the heavens of Albion**—the fallen world (Bloom 1965: 910), or the heaven of self-righteousness, a bogus Eternity that Milton renounces (Mitchell 1973a: 53-54).

2:17   Frye (1957c: 132) observes that Milton's brooding suspiciously resembles that of his own fallen angels in *PL*, II, 555-61.

2:19-20   Thomas Wright (1929: II, 2) conceives the Emanation as an embodiment of Milton's error still corrupting the world; Margoliouth (1951: 144) claims that "the deep" refers to Milton's own mind. See also 21:15-19n.

2:25   This warning, several times repeated, may be the Bard's or the poet's own. De Luca (1970: 10) holds that it applies to Milton, Blake, and the reader.

3:1-2   These lines, notes Stevenson (1971: 566), refer to Britain's materialism and rejection of imagination. Albion's mountains are the poles supporting the tent of the sky and also the Welsh highlands whither his Britons fled from the Saxons (Hilton 1981: 198).

3:14-16   Failing to perceive *through* Urizen's space and time [i.e. through, not with, the eye], Los allows Urizen's void to enter into him (Peterfreund 1981: 216).

3:35   The blue fluid contrasts with blood, the fluid of life (Bloom 1963: 312). Its blue is the blue of space, Newton's absolute space being what Los's Spectre represents (Peterfreund 1981: 217).

3:37   Knowledge of the whole proceeds from knowledge of the parts, and Golgonooza is constructed on a basis of particular forms (Teitelbaum 1969: 42, 62-63n9).

3:41   Insofar as Satan is a Son of Los, the Zoa of imagination, he represents false art (Rose 1971b: 21).

3:43   **Prince of the Starry Wheels**—governor of the planetary orbits (Raine 1968: II, 26).

4:11   **Pantocrator**—Bloom (1965: 911) credits Newton with inventing this word by combining "pantograph" (a copying machine) with "cosmocrator" (world-ruler), but Sloss and Wallis (1926: I, 429) note that it occurs in the Greek text of Rev. (e.g. i.8, iv.8).

4:22   The Cherubim have been identified as spectres that must be sacrificed to create art (Damon 1924: 406); as young British soldiers (Erdman 1954a: 368-69 [396-97]), the victims being, according to Erdman, their parents; as the spiritual protectors of the victims (Stevenson 1971: 568); and as oppressors about to be sacrificed by their own victims (Ostriker 1977: 967). James (1978: 23-24), seeing deliberate ambiguity here, pertinently asks whether the victims are preparing themselves or being prepared by the Cherubim.

5:1-3 Lacking Christ's spirit of self-sacrifice, Hayley (Satan), unable to handle the harrow—which is epic poetry—faints beneath the manifestations of Blake's poetic inspiration (Bloom 1965: 911, 912). Satan, as many fail to recognise, is not to be confused with the true God, who "fainteth not, neither is weary" (Rix 1984: 112-13, quoting Is. xl.28).

The lines move from unfallen Palamabron by way of Satanic error to redemption effected by Christ; Blake puns on "morning" (James 1978: 48-49). Accepting the doctrine of Heb. ix, Blake believes that Christ's Atonement should have stopped all further sacrifice of human beings (Mathews 1980b: 73-74).

5:7   The Heavens of Beulah are the head, heart and loins of the human who becomes threefold in Beulah instead of fourfold in Eden (Percival 1938: 57). Mortals can enter Beulah through these heavens or gates (Damon 1967: 43, 44).

5:19-37 Bloom (1965: 911-12), who attributes this song to the Daughters, sees it as ironic and the women as sadistic; Fox (1976: 40-42, 234) judges it a sincere lament chanted by the males.

5:38-44 Accepting Damon's opinion (1967: 204) that Blake is among those who blame the Catholics for the Great Fire of London of 1666, Sandler (1972: 26) argues that the elect Mil-

ton and the elect Cromwell sacrifice Charles I in an act of Uri-
zenic atonement and that Catholic James II avenges his father
by starting the Fire, which foreshadows the conflagration of the
last days; Fuller (1983: 52), agreeing with this view of James,
holds that Charles I and Cromwell are both seen as tyrants.
Bloom, on tne other hand, (1965: 912) classifies Milton as rep-
robate, Cromwell as redeemed, and James I and Charles I as
elect souls seeking to be new created through Milton's grace;
James I, he claims, repents of having fostered the mercantile
class and invokes Los's purgative fires. James (1978: 25)
believes the ambiguity of these lines is deliberate and asks, for
example, whether the atonement is to be Charles's or Milton's.

5:43   Mathematically oriented Satan falls in love with Elynittria,
the principle of harmony that works with imagination and
emotion (Sutherland 1977: 147).

5:44   **Mathematic Proportion...Living Proportion**—Mathemat-
ic form as opposed to living form derives, as Locke says our
idea of extension does, entirely from sensation and memory
(Welch 1978: 227).

6:5-7   In his prose note to "The Fatal Sisters," Gray records an
alleged sighting of twelve sanguinary goddess-like weavers
near Caithness (Miner 1958: 204). Cf. also 26:15.

6:8-13   Los's work is universal, and London stands for the cosmos
(Stevenson 1971: 491). Blake is identifying Los's creations
with his own works, for the districts named surround his home
(Carothers 1978: 123-24).

6:14-17   This is an allusion to the London munitions industry;
iron had formerly been smelted with charcoal from Surrey tim-
ber (Erdman 1954a: 368 [396]). Howard (1976: 82) detects a
possible reference to the degeneration of the (Swedenborgian)
New Jerusalem Church founded in London in the late 1780s.

6:23   **Babel**—in Blake's view, a militarist city state (Damon
1967: 33).

7:1-3   Cf. Eph. i.4. Most critics follow Damon (1924: 421) in
observing that Blake reverses the traditional—Damon says
Methodist—definitions of the Elect and the Reprobate. Frye
(1947: 442n4) suggests that the poet's threefold classification
may derive from the three Gunas described in the Bhaga-
vadgita (xiv), while Damon (1967: 409) points to *Paradise
Lost* as the source, and Raine (1968: II, 223) quotes an

appropriate passage from it (III, 183-202). Usefully, Rose (1971b: 21-22) remarks that the Elect are the Establishment, who rely on a static memory of Eternity's utopia and make outcasts of the Reprobate, whose vision of Eternity is directed towards the future, while the Redeemed possess a measure of vision and bring some improvement to society.

7:31 **the wind of Beulah**—inspiration (Bloom 1963: 318).

8:4--5 **Palamabron had serv'd/ The Mills of Satan**—Blake had resorted to "mechanical and repetitive" commercial engraving at Hayley's urging (Essick 1980: 212).

8:11-12 According to Damon (1967: 354-55), the right hand represents Urthona, and the left foot Urizen, so Los must be pausing to work the situation out rationally. Contrasting Los with the immobile fallen Albion, Rose (1971a: 61) states that when the former's sandals are on his feet they act like the winged shoes of Mercury and enable him to travel through Eternity. Miner (1981: 315) claims that the raising of the sandal signifies that Los is moving as the constellation Orion into the southern hemisphere. Hilton (1983: 236) believes the sandal corresponds to the risen sun of ll. 10 and 16, which is "Sol" and "Los" and the signal to the servants of "morning" and "mourning."

8:20-22 Mitchell (1973b: 291) asserts that Los erroneously thinks that the disruption of nature will be confined to a single day.

8:33 Damon (1967: 403) regards Thulloh as the mutual affection between Blake and Hayley.

8:39 Urizen usurps and misuses Rintrah's anger (Ault 1974: 180).

9:1-12 Satan-Hayley, Bloom plausibly maintains (1965: 913), loses his temper and inadvertently reveals himself as the Accuser of Sin, whereupon the Assembly realises it blundered in condemning Rintrah (wrathful inspiration) and exclaims sarcastically, "Satan is among the Reprobate." However, Glausser (1980: 193) is confident the judgment falls on "the Rintrah in Satan." Mitchell (1973b: 291-92) sees the Assembly as an object of satire, for it drives Los into the destructive acts of 9:13-17. In Ault's eyes (1974: 180, 215n20), these constitute a version of the Fall, and Rintrah's energy perverted by Satan is what drives Los. Cf. I Sam. x.12.

9:1 **Palamabron's tent**—Blake's cottage (T. Wright 1929: II, 3).

9:2-3 **the corner of the Atlantic**—the celestial counterpart of Britain, the home of "Druids & Bards" (Stevenson 1971: 496).

9:10-11 According to Sutherland (1977: 147, 149), Satan represents not only Hayley but also Blake's selfhood that was tempted to opt for worldly prosperity, and the quarrel between Satan and Hayley in part represents Blake's inner conflict. Gallant (1978: 124-25, 129-30) even believes that Satan's outburst expresses the poet's suppressed wrath against his patron.

9:18 Blake did not tell his wife of all the uncertainty he felt (Sutherland 1977: 150).

9:25-29 Erdman (1954a: 395 [424]) suggests that Satan stands for Cromwell, who quarrelled with Parliament (Palamabron), to which DiSalvo (1983: 272-74) adds that Rintrah represents the radical egalitarians whom both suppressed. To Howard (1976: 87-91), Satan recalls Pitt, who combined repression at home with war against France.

9:51 In pl. 37, Blake shows that the Covering Cherub, the ultimate and warlike manifestation of the Antichrist and the Selfhood, contains all false religions and their errors. Its source is Ezek. xxviii.14-16 (Damon 1924: 408). Frye (1947: 137-38) also identifies it with the cherubim of Gen. iii.24, which bar the way back to Eden, and Margoliouth (1951: 168), following a hint of Damon (*loc. cit.*), with those that veil the Mercy Seat in the Ark of the Covenant (Exod. xxv.18-21). Ezekiel's passage, Kiralis observes (1956: 151), was usually understood to describe Satan. Hirst (1964: 255-57) proposes that Blake's conception owes something to Richard Clarke's Cabbalistic *Jesus the Nazarene, Addressed to Jews, Deists and Believers* (1795), and Raine (1968: I, 330-31) specifies the poet's major source as Boehme.

10:1-2 Ault (1974: 112, 180-81) notes the relationship between these lines and *FZ* 103:21-29/ E375-76/ VIII, 171-79—the systematising, scientific Urizen has succumbed to deceptive, shadowy nature (Vala) charged with the energy (Orc) that is his enemy; he deceives Los and Enitharmon into thinking that he is Urizen unadulterated.

10:2-11 It is generally recognised that Canaan can be a place of regeneration. Thus Frye (1947: 366, 383, 402) contrasts the Promised Land with its fallen form, pagan Canaan, which is Ulro, and Damon (1967: 67) draws a triple distinction between the unfallen "Heavenly Canaan" (*J* 71:1), the Promised Land (a state really or supposedly ideal), and heathen Canaan ("the unregenerated heart"). Bloom (1965: 913) maintains that Enitharmon, being weaker than Los, aggravates the Fall by creating the space Canaan, and claims that allegorically the latter is degenerate England in need of Milton's prophetic message.

10:14-20 In Beulah the sun and moon are emanations of Los's Sons Rintrah and Palamabron respectively (Frye 1957c: 128), and their consorts, Ocalythron and Elynittria, are jealous solar and lunar goddesses (Bloom 1963: 320), though Elynittria overcomes her possessiveness (Damon 1967: 305-06). The mountains may signify the upper classes (Erdman 1954a: 374 [403]).

11:4-5 Percival (1938: 148-50, 157) holds that as the Fall deepens, the Mundane Shell, originally built at the altitude of the stars as a protective shell (*FZ* 24:8/ E314/ II, 25), sinks to the level of Tyburn, site of the gallows.

11:12 See II Thess. ii.4.

11:17 **be an Eternal Death**—never be restored to Eternity (Damon 1924: 409).

11:23 Mitchell (1973b: 292-93) considers this line ironic, for Palamabron and his class avoid punishment by letting a scapegoat suffer: Blake is blaming himself for preferring Felpham's pleasures to performing his task. More simply, Sutherland (1977: 145-46) refers to Palamabron's redemption from the orthodox satanic law.

11:30ff There is much controversy as to whether Leutha's offer of self-sacrifice is noble or misguided. Sandler (1972: 17) sees it as a parody of the vicarious atonement Blake opposes, Damrosch (1980: 217-19) as an attempt to bring about redemption by impossible means, and Mitchell (1973b: 293, 294) as an exemplary action which Milton copies. Erdman (1954a: 396-97 [425-26]) considers that her offer is good but she is unable to carry it through and hence bears Death and Rahab (13:40-41). In Webster's view (1983: 254-55), the birth of these offspring reflects Blake's guilt feelings over fantasies of incest, since Leutha, Satan and Palamabron constitute an Oedipal triangle. Thomas Wright's conjecture (1929: II, 3) that Leutha is based on Harriet Poole—Hayley's friend and Blake's patron—who temporarily antagonises Catherine Blake (Elynittria) should probably be ignored.

12:2-3 Cf. Rev. xii.4 (Damon 1967: 108).

12:4-7 There was some unconscious homosexuality in Hayley (Damon 1967: 178).

12:16-19 Lacking Elynittria's ability to bring harmony to the emotional and imaginative life, Satan loses control and resorts to oppression (Sutherland 1977: 147-48).

12:24-27 Percival (1938: 64, 304) notes the allusion to Rev. xii.4 and asserts that the stars descend to preserve a meagre light in the moral abyss.

12:28-30 The serpent's colours correspond to those of the peacock's tail, which mark a stage of the regenerative work of the alchemical furnace (Percival 1938: 206-07).

12:38 **I came forth from the head**—The female will is born from human reason (Rose 1965: 595).

12:42-44 According to Wagenknecht (1973: 247), an angry Elynittria welcomes Satan satirically.

13:8 **The Spectre of Luvah**—the "selfhood of the natural, passional man" (Bloom 1965: 914); war (Damon 1967: 382). Politically, Luvah is France, and Leutha and Satan, who constitute its Spectre, can be taken as the spirit of Marie Antoinette and the spirit of Napoleon (Erdman 1954a: 396-97 [425-26]).

13:10-11 Time is a temporary breach in Eternity brought about by a lapse into selfhood (Harper 1961: 142-43).

13:22 **Triple**—characterised by the head, heart and loins into which the four elements condense in the fallen state (Percival 1938: 211); restricted to threefold power (Damon 1967: 119).

13:25 **the Body of Death**—both the mortal flesh and official religion (Percival 1938: 141).

13:27 Cf. Is. liii.12 (Margoliouth 1948: 308).

13:35 **the fatal Brook**—Tyburn Brook, which flowed near the gallows where the Elect executed their victims (cf. 11:5). Erdman (1954a: 429-30 [465]) identifies this stream with the Serpentine of Hyde Park, Damon (1967: 413) with a brook that flowed through St. James's Park.

13:36-41 Copulation with the head (reason), from which Leutha springs, produces death (Rose 1965: 595). "Death" may signify the cycle of mortal life, which depends on the combination of female sexual magnetism (Leutha) and human emotion

(Palamabron); "delusion" and "dreams" suggest the births occur in Beulah (Sutherland 1977: 153).

13:44 Damon (1967: 308) believes Oothoon is at last compelled to resort to secrecy (cf. *VDA passim* and *E* 14:21-22), but Teitelbaum (1969: 53) thinks that Leutha will learn from her that loving without jealousy liberates.

13:48-49 Pity and love can be selfish and exploitative (Percival 1938: 217—also 171 citing *BU* 4:34-35). Hayley deserves credit for these qualities, yet has a destructive side (Margoliouth 1951: 136-37). The Eternals fail to realise that these virtues can be masks for cruelty and other evils (James 1978: 37).

14:4 **the Heavens of Albion**—"The 'heavenly' Albion," who is both a human form and a world (Stevenson (1971: 505).

14:4-9 According to Bloom (1965: 914) and Stevenson (1971: 505), it is the Eternals who suffer from "doubtfulness" (about the means and possibility of redemption); Howard (1976: 214) attributes the anxiety to Ulro and its churches.

14:9 Milton accepted the Bard's Song (Margoliouth 1951: 137).

14:13 The robe of promise and oath of God, which Digby (1957: 48-49) assigns to the rational, conscious aspect of the mind, may be the Old Testament deity's gift of Canaan to Abraham's descendants (Howard 1976: 156, 207), "covenanted religion and...the reward promised to the righteous" (Margoliouth 1948: 308), Puritanism (Bloom 1963: 321-22), or the garment of election guaranteeing a place in heaven at the Last Judgment (Teitelbaum 1969: 54); Fox (1976: 161) identifies the garment with the black cloud of 15:50 that overshadows Europe. In casting off the robe and the oath, Milton is deserting the Elect to join the Reprobate (Bloom, *loc.cit.*); Mitchell (1973a: 54-55) sees also an allusion to Christ's self-sacrificial offer in *PL*, III, 236ff.

14:30-32 Milton's hells can be either creative fires of art or destructive fires of inner conflict (Tayler 1973a: 252-53). Milton here resembles Christ, who rescued souls from hell after his crucifixion (Stevenson 1971: 506). To loose Satan from his hells is to jettison the satanic element in himself (Mathews 1980b: 77).

14:34 **he took the outside course**—Milton returns to earth without being reborn in a womb (Howard 1976: 216); as a traveller

"from Eternity," he passes "outward to Satan's seat" (17:29)
(Stevenson 1971: 506).

14:36 **his own Shadow**—variously explained as his "mortal
garment" (Bloom 1965: 915); the product of his suppressed
passion (Damon 1967: 368-69); the Polypus containing projec-
tions of his elect and redeemed selves (Mitchell 1973b: 295);
Ulro (Fox 1976: 88); his lower self and the effect of his works
on the world (Ostriker 1977: 971); a form of his Spectre, Satan
(George 1980: 175); and "the fallen aspect of his Emanation"
enclosing his lower selves in "a Female Space" (10:6) (Deen
1983: 177). See also note on *FZ* 80:5ff/ E355-56/ VII, 113ff.

15:1-20 Milton walks in Eden, sleeps in Beulah, and journeys in
Ulro (Fox 1976: 69-70, 88); angels protect him in Eden, Ema-
nations in Beulah (Stevenson 1971: 507). Damon (1924: 412)
locates the couch of death (ll. 9-10) in Beulah, but Stevenson
(1971: 508) identifies it as Albion's; Miner (1960: 200)
equates it with the uterus.

15:8-10 Damon (1967: 333) locates here, in Milton's repressed
desires, the origin of the Polypus that is to overspread the
world—see 37:60ff.

15:21-35 A central question about this contentious passage is
whether the "infinity" whose nature it describes is synonymous
with Eternity (Frye 1947: 350; Herzing 1973: 27) or whether it
is really infinity collapsed and crumbled (Frosch 1974: 72-73).
In the former case, the vortex may cause the objects of the
Eternals' perception to be present in their minds (Frye, *loc.
cit.*), and may offer every perceiver an opportunity to behold
the infinite (Mitchell 1978: 70-74); in the latter case, a vortex
may only exist between fallen perceivers and the objects from
which they separate themselves (Nurmi 1969: 311; Fox 1976:
70-74). Any argument that the vortex comes into play exclus-
ively in fallen perception (Damrosch 1980: 33), where it
clearly does determine our consciousness of time and space
(Hilton 1983: 209-10) and makes the eye see things as external
to itself (Ault 1974: 158), must take into account Blake's con-
trast between the "traveller thro Eternity" (ll. 22, 35) and "the
weak traveller confin'd beneath the moony shade" (l. 33). The
reader should also consider whether the vortex of *Milton* is
identical with the vortexes, clearly fallen, of Urizen (*FZ* 72:6-
73:34/ E349-50/ VI, 180-246) and those of Hyle's wheels (*J*

74:28-30). Finally, Descartes' theory that the universe consists of nothing but matter whirling in vortexes certainly contributes to the vortical cosmos of Urizen in *FZ*, VI (Raine 1968: II, 80-83), but has it any bearing on the vortex of *Milton*? And if so, is it combined, as Ault believes (1974: 147-60), with the Newtonian concepts of gravity and void space? (See also Bronowski 1944: 97-98, 148; Grimes 1973: 79-80; James 1978: 79-80; Welch 1978: 229-30). Damon (1967: 440) considers each vortex is an idea a person has to pass through before perceiving its significance in human terms.

15:23 **he percieves it roll backward**—He now conceives the object of his perception as existing independently outside his own mind, for "backward" is parallel to "outward" and "downward"; its "human form" (l. 27) is its "archetypal being," which it possesses in common with the perceiver (Adams 1963: 31-32).

15:32 Rose (1964a: 181) argues that Blake holds the earth is infinite and flat from the viewpoint of fourfold vision, vision that surrounds its object and is its object's circumference. Although Hilton (1983: 193, 212, 289-90n25) maintains that the earth appears an infinite plain only to fallen vision and that 29:11-12 shows that Blake does not believe the earth to be flat, 5:32-33 states that it is the sublunary "weak traveller" that cannot see the "infinite plane." How the earth would appear if it *were* an infinite plane was discussed in the eighteenth century, and Robert Smith argued in his *Compleat System of Opticks* (1738) that the sky and horizon would seem unchanged (Ault 1974: 159-60).

15:35 **A vortex not yet pass'd**—therefore still visible as an "infinite plane" (Ault 1974: 160).

15:41-46 According to Frye (1947: 350), Milton passes through the apex of the cone of his own vision, the point at which his eyebeams converge on the object, and, after this, perceived objects seem to be outside himself; according to Adams (1955: 106-09), the "infinite plane" extends back from this point of convergence (which is the vortex) into the mind of the perceiver, for the plane is mental. Bloom (1963: 326) holds that Milton has entered Albion's heart and found it under the shared dominion of Urizen (sky) and Tharmas (sea). Greenberg (1978) maintains that Milton, unlike Urizen in *FZ*, VI, is able to pass by self-annihilation through a limiting vortex (fallen Albion's), and he is then free to enter into Blake.

15:47 Cf. *PL*, I, 745 (Miner 1981: 317).

15:49-50 Mitchell (1973b: 295-96) considers that it is the redeemed portion of Milton that enters Blake while the elect portion becomes the black cloud; Erdman (1974: 248) regards the cloud as the product of the burning up of Milton's selfhood. Gallant (1978: 138) identifies the left side with the unconscious.

15:51-52, 17:1-2 Milton could have learnt to see Eternity through his wives, daughters and milder emotions (Fox 1976: 76-77).

17:1-3 Milton's Emanations could have been and still can be reunited through his renunciation of his selfhood (Damon 1924: 413 *et al.*) or through their renunciation of their selfhoods (Stevenson 1971: 510).

17:5-6 **they and/ Himself was Human**—The unsundered male and female constitute the Human (George 1980: 166).

17:6 **Death's Vale**—Cf. *MHH* 2:5 and Ps. xxiii.4.

17:6-17 It is difficult to be sure how this passage relates Milton's former existence to his present experience. Whereas Damon (1924: 414) noncommittally reminds the reader that after he became blind Milton dictated his compositions to his daughters, Bloom (1965: 916) asserts that the subject of his present dictation is the Mosaic Law while Howard (1976: 220) claims that he is denouncing the Law and teaching self-annihilation. Howard's position is consistent with Stevenson's opinion (1971: 510) that he is looking back on his life's work and seeing its defects.

17:24 According to Percival (1938: 65, 157, 235-36, 304), the three heavens of Beulah (see 5:7n) degenerate into the twenty-seven heavens and churches of Ulro; these heavens are states of error through which the soul must pass, and their number echoes the twenty-seven divisions Plato interposes between earth and Saturn in the *Timaeus* (35c) and is also related to the twenty-seven phases of the moon.

17:31 The Vehicular Los has been defined as the form Urthona, the imagination, takes in the fallen world (Percival 1938: 185) and as "the outward circumference of an individual energy" (Bloom 1965: 939). Frye (1947: 272-73) relates the vehicular to the ordinary form as the body relates to the soul whose energy it incarnates—he associates it with the Divine Chariot of Ezek. i, the vehicular form of God, and Rose (1964a: 175) understands "vehicular" as implying fourfold vision and (1971a: 61) as the contrary of "static," an epithet applicable to fallen Albion. As "the Vehicular terror," Los is, says Fox (1976: 97) "pure inspiration."

17:31-33 Bloom (1965: 916) implies that Enitharmon welcomes Milton's coming. Without explaining the phrase "to unloose my bond," Howard (1976: 220-21) comments that she fears his arrival and Satan's consequent destruction of Albion.

18:4-38 Bloom (1965: 916) identifies Orc as the natural man and the Shadowy Female as his "material environment," while Stevenson (1971: 572) sees Orc as a noble and heroic figure. Although she gloats over "Kings" as well as "Councellors & Mighty Men" (l. 15), James (1978: 81-82) suggests that the Shadowy Female is describing the tyranny of the Puritan Commonwealth. Miner (1969: 274) detects an allusion to Aaron's priestly robes, and Hilton (1983: 38) observes that the Female's garment, inscribed with words to be learnt "by rote" (l. 14)—i.e. the letter that killeth (II Cor. iii.6)—contrasts with the garment of 42:12-14.

18:28-29 **a Form...that cannot consume in Man's consummation**—a refuge, like Beulah, for an emanation (Fox 1976: 80).

18:39-45 There is much disagreement as to whether Oothoon has vision while Leutha is fallen (Raine 1968: I, 171-73) or both are fallen (Paley 1970: 251) or both are admirable (Bloom 1965: 916). Paley maintains that Oothoon lures Orc, while Leutha rejects him; Bloom contends that Leutha presages "a redeemed Babylon."

19:4 **clay now chang'd to marble**—This phrase implies oppression by the wealthy and by the churches, whose power Milton is tempted to assume (Howard 1976: 225).

19:6-14 The Milton of this passage is compared by Margoliouth (1948: 309) to Jacob wrestling with the angel near Mahanaim and then residing at Succoth (Gen. xxxii.1, 24-32; xxxiii.17), by Bloom (1963: 328-29) to Moses leading the Israelites to the bank of the Arnon (Num. xxi.13), and by Frye (1957c: 134) to Christ healing the blind man (John ix.1-7). Bloom (*loc. cit.*) notes that Beth Peor was the site of Moses' burial (Deut.

xxxiv.6), Damon (1967: 389) observes that metal ornaments for Solomon's Temple were cast in the "clay ground between Succoth and Zarthan" (I Kings vii.45-46), and Miner (1969: 288-89) recognises this clay as the clay earlier alluded to in *MHH* 2:13, the substance of which Adam's mortal body was made. Mahanaim is also associated with the crossing of the Jordan (II Sam. xvii.22-24). Miner (*loc. cit.*) sees a parody of John's baptism of Christ, with what Damrosch (1980: 79, 330) regards as the water of materiality, but whereas Miner (*loc. cit.*) credits Milton with recreating Urizen, Bindman (1977: 174) argues that in filling out the latter's body he is giving a form to error so that it can be rejected as shown in *IB* pl. 45.

19:36 Milton resembles Moses in that he does not enter the Promised Land: to pass from Egypt to Canaan would be to travel from one Ulro to another (Frye 1947: 337, 366).

19:37-39 The temptation is directed to the undergraduate Milton (Damon 1967: 18-19).

19:40 **Rephaim's Vale**—"the fallen form of lost Atlantis" (Bloom 1965: 938). The Bible associates this valley, where David fought the Philistines, with an inundation (Raine 1968: II, 321-22n50, citing II Sam. v.20). Frye (1957c: 122) mentions that Rephaim are giants or ghosts, and Damon (1967: 346), noting that the Palestinian valley was supposedly haunted but that Blake varies his Vale's location, maintains he treats it as a storehouse of ancient errors.

19:59 In *Jerusalem*, Reuben represents the fallen human or natural man.

20:3 Manasseh (Ephraim's brother) and his Syrian concubine, whom Blake considers an alien temptress, were ancestors of Tirzah and her sisters (Damon 1967: 261).

20:15-19 Though these lines seem to be spoken by Blake, Damrosch (1980: 306) supposes that Milton addresses them to Urizen.

20:33 According to Frye (1957c: 122), Og and Anak—and also Sihon (e.g. 22:33)—are intellectually beliefs derived from the sublunary world (cf. 37:50), psychologically inner censors, and politically tyrants like Pitt and Napoleon. In Tolley's view (1973: 127), Og and Anak both bar the way to Eternity and shield fallen humankind from an as yet unendurable vision of it.

20:43-50 Bloom (1965: 918) believes Blake disapproves of the Eternals' resentment of their companion's quest. Mitchell (1973b: 295) explains the anger of those who missed the Bard's Song as indignation that Milton should dare to spurn their heaven.

20:53 Bloom (1965: 918) relates Gad's and Reuben's alienation to Josh. xxii, where they seem but are not disloyal to the God of Israel. Stevenson (1971: 517) refers to *FZ* 115:18-20/ E380/ VIII, 374-76.

20:56 Wagenknecht claims that Los is desperate because he fails to distinguish Milton from Satan (1973: 217).

20:59-60 Inspiration (Milton) will free Orc (passion and enthusiasm) from the Chain of Jealousy (the normal condition of human life) (Sloss and Wallis 1926: II, 211-12).

21:3 Satan's Spectre is a censor, his Shadow suppressed desire (Bloom 1965: 918).

21:7 **the vast breach**—political revolution, which mortals cannot recognise as the outward sign of Milton's advent (Wagenknecht 1973: 218).

21:12-14 Blake suddenly enjoys a vision of the infinite pervading the material universe, a vision the selfhood blocks, as it does at 20:35 (Murry 1933: 222-25). The world of time and space provides an indispensable foundation for Blake's walk through Eternity (Grimes 1973: 60-61). His left foot can be identified with the left foot of the constellation Orion, who is a form of Los (Miner 1981: 313-14).

21:15-19 The name Ololon seems to be related to "ululation" (Frye 1947: 143) and to be associated in Blake's mind with lamenting. It may be derived from the Greek *ololugon*—an outcry, usually joyous, of women to the gods (Reiman and Kraus 1982: 82, following a hint in Fisher 1961: 248; cf. also Wagenknecht 1973: 255). There is widespread agreement with Damon (1924: 417) that Ololon is the eternal form of Milton's sixfold Emanation that comprises his wives and daughters. Some critics accept Bloom's theory (1963: 308) that she (or they) includes also Milton's poems—to which Bloom adds (1965: 918) his "potential achievement."

Ololon can appear in diverse shapes—as a river and its banks, as clouds, as a multitude, and as a twelve-year-old virgin. Only in the fallen world, argues George (1980: 174), do

"they" assume a gender and become "she." Ololon's associ-
ation with nature is as inescapable as her connection with
Milton's actions and influence. As a river, she may be
"unconscious and undifferentiated sexuality" that will produce
the male and female which recombine at the end of the book
(Reimer and Kraus 1982: 83-84); a current "of tears...and
maternal milk" whose transformations represent the turning
point when lamentation gives way to joy (Hilton 1983: 40-42);
or a stream related to the "pure river of water of life" of Rev.
xxii.1 (Bloom 1963: 332) and as such representing "Milton's
prophetic spirit and the possibility of psychic unity" (George
1980: 167). Her clouds are associated with the return of Christ
(Tayler 1973a: 252), for whose fleshly embodiment she may
bear some responsibility (implied Miner 1961: 51-52). Her
multitudinous aspect, according to Fox (1976: 92-93), is
redemptive, her sixfold aspect fallen: Rose (1964c: 48-49) even
sees her as a double threefold accuser—he compares the six
pointing hands in pl. 10 of Blake's *Job*. Peterfreund (1981:
213) believes that she represents space (in contrast to Milton,
who represents time) and that her sixfold character alludes to
Newton's six primary planets. As a twelve-year-old virgin,
observes Peter Taylor (1971: 50-51), she symbolises redeemed
nature as opposed to Rahab, who represents nature as viewed
by the Deists. Beer (1968: 159-60, 184) emphasises her role in
disclosing to the fallen world a "revelation of eternity within
the natural order"; Hagstrum (1964: 112-13) can say that she is
all the small, joyous beauties like lambs, birds and clouds; and
James (1978: 136) implies that she is in part a metaphor for
Milton's experience of nature. Digby (1957: 85) describes her
as "the unresolved conflicts" of Milton's repressed uncon-
scious, Cooper (1981: 102) as the intimacy lacking in his
relationships, and Frye (1947: 336) as the "totality of the
things he loves," which he must learn to see not as external but
as a portion of himself. Interpreting the final coalescence of
Milton and Ololon as the synthesis of prophecy and history,
Erdman (1954a: 394, 401 [423, 431]) sees her as "history-as-it-
should-have-been" and as it would have been had Milton not
perverted it. Biblical history draws the attention of Rix (1984:
108-09), who identifies her with the second Isaiah's Jerusalem,
an individual female who is also the multitude of Israel and

who is to be reconciled with her husband and creator. Frye (1947: 351-55) and Bloom (1965: 918) discern in Blake's portrait of Ololon a rebuke to Milton the male chauvinist, for, as Bloom expresses it, she is woman redeemed as he never painted her. Scrutinising the process of her redemption, Howard (1976: 231-32, 252) sees Rahab and Tirzah as her selfhood and argues that the transformation of the angry Eternals who drove out Milton into the compassionate Ololon marks the reunion of wrath and pity, which were sundered at the Fall.

21:12-14; 22:4-14 Los and Blake are "afoot with vision" (Rose 1964a: 175). Blake's tying of his sandal signifies his acceptance of the material universe as the gateway to Eternity; when Los ties Blake's sandals, he ends the day of mourning he began by placing his left sandal on his head (8:11); with both sandals fastened, Blake strides firmly forward (Fox 1976: 96). Later, (22:34-35) Rintrah and Palamabron perceive only evil in the vegetable world when they see it in the form of Milton's "fibrous left Foot black" (Sloss and Wallis 1926: I, 387).

21:18-24 Murry (1933: 234-37) believes that Providence begins for Blake immediately after his visionary moment shows him that on the path to regeneration the Selfhood must be repeatedly created, annihilated and re-created. Fox (1976: 92) argues that the seven days of Eternity are seven millenia on earth, and that when each one starts, Providence begins, for a new guardian is appointed. Cf. 7:13.

21:20-22 Damrosch (1980: 216) comments that instead of divine love moving the sun, as in the last lines of Dante's *Divine Comedy*, sexual love drags it; DiSalvo (1983: 298) finds here an image of workers, the real creators, enslaved by tyrants. While Damon (1967: 389) holds that *A* b:7 and *FZ* 28:18/ E318/ II, 128 show that the sulphur sun is the material sun, Adlard (1969: 117-19) links the sulphur sun with the creative fire-flash in Boehme's *Signatura Rerum* and associates it with Los, insisting that its rising is not mechanical and contrasting it with the Sun of Salah (23:60).

21:35-42 Comparing 15:24-27 with 21:37-42, Fox (1976: 93, 95) maintains that Ololon's prayer (21:35) makes the Divine Humanity appear in a human instead of a globular form.

21:53 **The Universal Dictate**—the decree that the whole universe will sense the imminence of the last days (Stevenson 1971: 519).

22:18-25 Unlike images deposited in the memory by sense perceptions, the images of temporal events in Los's storehouse are accompanied by the feelings that belong with them (Ault 1974: 72-74, citing also *J* 13:55-14:1).

22:26-27 Cf. Ezek. viii.2-3 (Helms 1974: 132).

22:32-33 Rintrah and Palamabron wrongly suppose that Milton will make Orc satanic by reconciling him with Urizen (Rose 1972b: 144).

22:55-23:2 The confused syntax of this passage has caused disagreement as to which words, if any, constitute the cries of the churches. Accepting Erdman's classification of "Witnesses" as a plural possessive (1965: 117), Stevenson (1971: 522) helpfully shows the "Faith in God" is theirs, while the churches, lacking true faith, demand the evidence of miracles—their cries run from l. 59 to l. 60 or 62. See Phil. ii.7-8 and Rev. xi.3, 8 (Miner 1969: 270). Beer (1968: 161) notes that the wrathful Rintrah raises the more vehement preacher.

23:10 **the East**—Cf. 9:40.

23:12 **give our Emanations**—give visionary glimpses of truth (Sloss and Wallis 1926: I, 388, citing also 15:3-15).

23:17-18 Rintrah and Palamabron are misguided in seeking to take the great Puritan captive to Bowlahoola, which "is nam'd Law" (24:48) and therefore Urizenic (Mathews 1980b: 80).

23:40 **Satan's Watch-Fiends**—perhaps on the political level Pitt's spies (Howard 1976: 131).

23:60 The Sun of Salah has been explained as "the body of error" (Hirst 1964: 216); the material sun (Damon 1967: 354); the sun of a corruptible priesthood, for Salah comes midway in the list of the Twenty-seven Churches on pl. 37 (Adlard 1969: 118-19); and Hebrew legalism, since Salah's son, Eber, was the ancestor of the Israelites (Stevenson 1971: 524, citing Gen. x.24 and Tolley's suggestion of a pun on "sun"). Bloom (1965: 919) identifies Blake's Salah with the Shelah of Gen. xxxviii. The line may mean until the material sun and the astronomical space containing it are no more.

24:3-4 To flee Los, be generated and wander with Tirzah is to reject inspiration, become material and accept laws of chastity (Damon 1967: 201).

24:6 **Menassheh**—i.e. Manasseh, whose name means "to make forget," elder son of Joseph and ancestor of Tirzah (Damon 1967: 260-61). See Gen. xli.51 with AV marginal reading and Num. xxvi.28-33.

24:17-20 Joseph is stolen from Eternity, wrapped in a body, and taken to Rahab's land of Egypt, place of generation (Miner 1969: 275).

24:26-29 These enigmatic lines have been variously interpreted. Do they focus on the contrast between flesh and spirit or the conflict between Jesus and the Covering Cherub? Damon (1967: 236) believes that Blake is attacking the spectrous doctrine of physical resurrection, and Damrosch (1980: 173) argues that when Lazarus's mortal (or "Vehicular") body disappears in the Covering Cherub his spirit is freed. Complaining that the Covering Cherub absorbed Lazarus and thwarted Jesus' redemption of Albion, Howard (1976: 196-97) differs from Bloom (1965: 919), who seems to accuse the Cherub of absorbing Albion. Stevenson (1971: 526), who takes "Vehicular Body" to mean "incarnation" or "living example," claims that Lazarus is a redeemed part of Albion who nobly enters the latter's Spectre to watch over his sleeping body; the Spectre reacts by creating churches. Frye (1957c: 120) interprets Lazarus and the Theotormon of 22:38 as symbols of Jesus, the Seventh Eye of God or seventh cycle of history; even this cycle has a corrupt element, natural religion derived from both Hebrew and Greco-Roman sources. Sloss and Wallis, too, defend Lazarus, holding that the vision which his resurrection should have preserved in the fallen world is perverted by rationalism (1926: I, 391).

24:35 **Cathedron's Looms weave only Death**—i.e. from the viewpoint of Eternity, which does not consider their redemptive aspect (Paley 1973b: 131). Miner (1958: 206) notes the resemblance of this line and the next to the last stanza of Gray's "The Fatal Sisters": both contain the phrase "web of death."

24:36 Allamanda is the heart according to Frye (1947: 260, 339), the nervous system according to Miner (1960: 200). Stevenson (1971: 530) observes that it is an agricultural area supplying the city of Golgonooza. Strangely, Johnston (1970: 430-31) classifies Allamanda and Bowlahoola as cities themselves, foils to Golgonooza, which are devoted to unimaginative commerce and law respectively (24:48; 27:42). As the stomach (24:67), say Sloss and Wallis (1926: II, 217), Bowlahoola divides essence from outer crust, "truth from error." Etymologically, the names may derive from "aliment" and "bowel" (Damrosch 1980: 72).

24:37-38 The fibres of the Polypus, in contrast to those of the human body, are unorganised (Hilton 1983: 89).

24:69-70 Time is the "Eternal Now" of Blake's comment on Lavater's Aphorism 407 (Wicksteed 1954: 16, quoting E592/ K77). It is not cyclical and hence subject to annual exhaustion and renewal but able to bring final revelation at any moment (Grimes 1973: 62-63).

25:3-7 Blake identifies the Napoleonic Wars with the vintage of Rev. xiv (described in *FZ*, IX) that is to precede the Millenium (Damon 1967: 435).

25:29 Despite this line, Blake does not deplore the existence of nations as opposed to their mutual antagonism. Before the Fall, "England encompass'd the Nations" (*J* 79:22). See Damon 1967: 294-95.

25:48-50 Erdman (1951b: 184-89) explains how Lambeth, the place of the Lamb, is occupied by the palace of the Archbishop of Canterbury, who supports the war; how Greek and Norse gods, personifications of human attributes, are the objects of worship; how the labour of the children in the Royal Asylum for Female Orphans and of the impoverished Blakes at their prophetic books has been separated from pleasure; how the latter is commercialised at the Apollo pleasure gardens on the site of the former Hercules Inn; and how Blake, living at Hercules Buildings and catering to the demands of patrons, resembles the hero Hercules reduced to spinning for Queen Omphale. Damon (1967: 232-33) emphasises that Lambeth, situated in Surrey, is to Blake "a place of inspiration," where he produced many books. Contrariwise, Sloss and Wallis (1926: I, 397-98) think he laments that even in Lambeth the heathen gods appear.

25:53 **the Polar Caves**—The north, the quarter of imagination and mental war, becomes the scene of physical war when sex is suppressed (Damon 1967: 301-02, 332).

25:60-61 **spiritual/ Vegetation**—an allusion to the Pauline spiritual body (Sloss and Wallis 1926: II, 252).

25:66ff Mitchell (1973b: 299) holds that the long description of the inner reality of creation is uttered by Los to some extent in combination with Milton and Blake.

26:10-12 Is it the vegetable (material) eye devoid of imagination that sees "only as it were the hem of their garments" or, as Bloom (1965: 920) and Damrosch (1980: 42) suppose, the imaginative eye?

26:13 See note below to the design on *IB* pl. 28.

26:16-18 Wicksteed (1910: 135-36) correctly points out that Los is described from the viewpoint of one to whom his back is turned.

26:20 The fallen world may not be able to endure the beauty of Beulah (Stevenson 1971: 535), or the cycle of birth and death may be disrupted by its form of sexuality (Bloom 1965: 920). Cf. 5:5-10, which suggests that what is life-enhancing in Beulah becomes venomous in the Daughters of Albion, though Damon (1967: 43-45) identifies the heavens in pl. 26 with the Twenty-seven Churches and contrasts them with the three gates into Beulah of 5:7.

26:37-43 Having only a selection of the characteristics of the class to which he or she belongs, each fallen individual is "imperfect" (Ault 1974: 94, alluding to E536/ K571).

27:8 There is disagreement over the meaning of the winepress and the attitude to war that it expresses. On the one hand, Blake is said to believe that some wars are righteous and purgative (Raine 1968: I, 356-59) and the winepress is described as akin to the furnaces of Bowlahoola—it destroys to regenerate (Fox 1976: 111). On the other hand, it is argued that war is here viewed as a perversion of sex (Frye 1957c: 117), that it results from the degeneration of the "full and truly human love" of Eternity (Wilkie 1970: 363-64), and that the wine of prophecy it produces can become blood when viewed by fallen perception (Howard 1976: 160). Fuller (1983: 68) with some plausibility claims that governments are accused of indulging in war to distract attention from their own oppressiveness, which is rooted in Urizen's confinement of Luvah or passion, but that Los uses that war to expose their cruel injustice. The winepress may allude to all the wars of history (Raine 1968: I, 349-50) or to the Napoleonic wars heralding apocalypse (Ostriker 1977: 978). Cf. *FZ* 39:6/ E326/ III, 35n.

27:10 **the adverse wheel**—of natural religion (Rose 1966: 116); its direction is to be reversed by Los's printing press (Rose 1972a: 45), which is the art of the fallen world (Damrosch 1980: 344) .

27:11-24 The organisms have been interpreted as seemingly noxious creatures in whom Blake sees beauty and holiness (Blackstone 1949: 243), as authors formerly infected by rationalism who now, inspired by prophetic wine, cast off their outwardly magnificent clothing (Howard 1976: 156), and as those who spurn Blake's work out of envy (Webster 1983: 265). See also *FZ* 136:29-39/ E404-05/ IX, 756-66n.

27:30-41 The tortures inflicted by Luvah's Children may represent the cruelty of external, material nature (Herzing 1973: 32) or the torments of sexual love in this world (Damrosch 1980: 295-96).

27:42-54 Urizen, the Sons of Urizen, and Theotormon work towards one goal, while Los's other Sons and their father work towards an opposite one (Bloom 1965: 921).

27:55-63 In this world, fallen architecture (Urizen's art) is divided into religion, law and surgery, the fallen forms of poetry, music and painting, these forming one of Blake's diabolical trinities (Rose 1966: 123): the engraver's burin, unlike the surgeon's knife, reveals reality (Rose 1968a: 18, 24). Alternatively, unfallen architecture becomes the source of the above mentioned substitutes for the three fallen arts (Johnston 1970: 431).

27:60 The arts are corrupted by the aggressive masculine element in creativeness (Webster 1983: 265).

28:1-5 By great mental effort, one can learn to perceive through imagination the real identities within "Indefinite" material forms (Harper 1961: 108-09). Blake is rejecting the belittling of imagination by Shakespeare's reasoner Theseus in *A Midsummer Night's Dream* V.i.16-17 (Damon 1967: 370).

28:1-43 Fox (1976: 113-15) maintains that Antamon creates the Redeemed, Sotha and Theotormon the Reprobate, and Ozoth the Elect, but that each of us contains something of all three classes.

28:1, 8 Iron and silver stand respectively for the wit combats and love themes of comedy, gold and ivory for the thought and human suffering of tragedy (Damon 1967: 198, 203).

28:21-28 These Sons of Los reveal the real nature of cruelty causing the spectres who begin by embracing it to recoil in horror (Fuller 1983: 68).

28:22, 30 Sevens succeeded by eights signify a movement towards completion (Fox 1976: 114; cf. Frye 1947: 448-49n56).

28:24-27 Although Blake mentions no antipathy between the cock and the lion, Damon (1924: 422) and Adlard (1966) allude to the mention of such enmity in ancient and modern authors. Raine (1968: I, 253-54, 428) refers to the tradition that the cock's crowing sends ghosts back to their graves at dawn, to Odin's cock that awakens the heroes of Valahalla to a day of battle, and to Proclus's account of the cock as an awe-inspiring solar animal. Stevenson (1971: 537) notes that cock-fighting was common.

28:29 The name Ozoth may derive from "Azoth," Paracelsus' universal medicine (Frye 1957c: 126) or combine this term with "optic" (Raine 1968: II, 302n36). Hilton (1983: 98-99) relates Ozoth's host of sons to the vital spirits or nerve endings of contemporary theory.

28:44-29:3 Time is here portrayed, claims Harper (1961: 147), not as absolute but as the psychological product of imaginative perception. Bloom (1965: 921-22) contrasts the passage with *E* 14:23 and states that creativeness occurs *within* a moment, whereas possessive love is indulged *between* two moments. This non-linear image of time, comments De Luca (1970: 11-12), consists of concentric elements, of which the smallest—the moments—are at the centre; these distinct units, Ault observes (1974: 135-38), contrast with the historical time that exists between them and also with the continuous, "infinitely divisible" moments of Newton.

28:58 Citing *J* 48:37, Damon (1924: 454) writes that Blake believes a great artistic genius is born once in two centuries. Fox (1976: 116-17) suggests that two hundred years—approximately the time between Milton's birth in 1608 and the completion of Blake's epic—may be a poetic generation.

29:10-12 Hilton (1983: 193-95, 203) contrasts seeing "the stars of God" (*J* 58:49) thus with seeing the forty-eight reason-created Ptolemaic constellations of *M* 37:47-38:4.

29:21, 26 The globule is the active, pulsing counterpart both of Newton's solid atom and of his planet (Ault 1974: 139). Blake is defying Locke's insistence in his *Essay Concerning Human Understanding* (II.xxiii.11) that our knowledge of the red globules in blood is very limited (Welch 1978: 236-37).

29:30-34 As the Polypus, Orc is the power behind eating and sleeping (Frye 1951: 190). Luvah (love) has degenerated into a corrupt Orc, who is hatred (Damon 1967: 333, 356). Having been absorbed by Vala (formless, unstable nature), Orc—now the Polypus—in turn absorbs the Urizenic Satan with his fixed, systematic view of the physical universe—cf. *FZ* 103:21-29/ E375-76/ VIII, 171-79 (Ault 1974: 112).

29:32-33 Reason mistakes the body's death for total extinction (Damon 1967: 315). Spectres are things seen, and the material optic nerves of the fallen have very restricted vision (Hilton 1983: 170-71).

29:35-38 Either Blake regards matter itself as accident treated as substance, real substance being spirit (Ostriker 1977: 980) or he is attacking Locke's denial that we can have a clear idea of the substance underlying colour, shape, etc. (*An Essay Concerning Human Understanding* II.xxiii.4) as Los's "I...feel a World within/ ...& in it all the real substances" (*FZ* 86:7-8/ E368/ VII, 364-65) suggests (Welch 1978: 227-28). The Saviour limits the opaqueness and indefiniteness that are the product of our distorting minds (Stevenson 1971: 539).

29:38 **by Los's Mathematic power**—Cf. *J* 12:5-15, which makes it clear that in association with Los mathematics is used to give error a definite though rigid form so that it can be cast out: this is turning Satan's weapon against himself. For the contrast between the exactness of mathematics and the indefiniteness of sense perception, see Ault 1974: 76-83.

29:40-44 The Nerves of the Ear represent poetry; love (the moon) overcomes death (Damon 1967: 286).

29:48-49 Blake assails reliance on the four cardinal or natural virtues, which, unlike the three theological virtues—faith, hope and charity—can be attained without divine assistance (cf. Hilton 1983: 123).

29:56 **Weave the black Woof of Death upon Entuthon Beny-
thon**—weave the flesh over the skeleton (Erdman 1977c: 432).

29:57 **Horeb terminates in Rephaim**—The Decalogue, given
on Horeb or Sinai, destroys the spirit (Miner 1969: 266).

29:59-63 According to Raine (1968: I, 91-92), the water that
washes the woven flesh symbolises matter. Bloom (1965: 922)
interprets the oceans as the veil of nature into which human
suffering is woven. The Erythrean (literally, Red Sea) is the
Indian Ocean (Damon 1967: 128), the eastern counterpart of
the Atlantic (Stevenson 1971: 673).

29:65 **a Vision of the Science of the Elohim**—There is dis-
agreement as to whether "Elohim" is singular (Bloom 1965:
922) or plural (Damon 1924: 423). The "Vision" has been und-
erstood as a reflection of the cruel mind of the creators, the
triple Elohim of 13:22, who assumed power at the time of
Noah's Flood (Percival 1938: 252-53), as the variable human
mode of perceiving creation (Raine 1968: II, 182), and as Los's
re-creation of Ulro (Ault 1974: 136-37). The science has been
explained as the creator's knowledge (Stevenson 1971: 540) or
perhaps his skill (Ostriker 1977: 980), and as "primarily artis-
tic technique" (Dilworth 1983: 19). Davies (1948: 107-08)
identifies Blake's Elohim with seven spirits who, in Boehme's
system, receive from God power enabling them to contribute to
creation.

30:17-20 The Eternals, according to Ault (1974: 31-32), are con-
traries engaged in mental war yet living in harmony.

30:20 **Mental forms Creating**—The forms both create and are
created (Rose 1966: 118).

31:9-63 Reasons given for the lamentation of the Daughters of
Beulah over the descending Ololon include misguided fear that
the latter is going to her destruction (Wagenknecht 1973: 252),
sorrow over the wars on earth that must precede a Last Judg-
ment (Fox 1976: 132), fear of that imminent Judgment
(Reiman and Kraus 1982: 83), and anxiety that the pleasing
maternal nature of Beulah (see 30:10-12) must be exchanged
for a higher state (Hilton 1983: 38-39). Bloom (1963: 344;
1965: 923) helpfully explains the association of joyful birds
and flowers with sorrow by remarking that Beulah's song is a
spring celebration to those in Ulro, an autumn lament to those
in Eternity—it is a lament to them, Damrosch points out

(1980: 86), because spring's arrival, joyful as it is, belongs to the cyclical fallen world; and Fox (1976: 132) states that Beulah wails over the coming release of Orc while Generation rejoices at the prospect of new birth. Erdman (1954a: 401 [431]) considers that at signs of the Second Coming the Daughters' sorrow over current events gives way to joy.

31:12-16 England repents her oppression of the American colonies and of India, Germany her wars against Napoleonic France and Italy (Erdman 1954a: 401 [431]). The Bard's Prophecy at 13:30 that the Elect will meet the Redeemed is fulfilled, for Germany and England belong to the former class, France, Italy and America to the latter (Fox 1976: 131-32).

31:17-25 The material elements grieve at the signs of the Second Coming (Tolley 1973: 125-26).

31:27-63 Unlike most Blake scholars, Fox (1976: 136-38) associates the lark with time and the thyme with space, the former being mobile and the latter stationary; she also identifies the bird with hearing and the flower with the other senses, and finds a parallel between Blake's treatment of them and his treatment of time and space at 28:44-29:26. Bloom (1963: 344), referring to *PL*, III, 38-40, detects here an acknowledgment to the nightingale (Milton) who (Fisch 1969: 54-56) has taught the lark (Blake) to sing his more transcendental song; Tolley (1973: 126) sees an allusion to the flowers of Milton's "Lycidas," which, like Blake's, are expressing not only grief but, at a deep level, joy. Drawing on Paracelsus' view of thyme as a uterine herb, on Blake's conception of it as Los's messenger, and on its traditional name of Christ's Ladder, Kauvar (1976) argues that it is a threefold symbol combining the sexuality Ololon accepts in discarding her virginity, Los's poetic creativity, and the ascension from Beulah to Eternity. See also 35:48-58n.

32:7 **by undervaluing calumny**—either by slander that disparages or by paying the evil of slander insufficient attention. Webster (1983: 268) supposes the undervaluer is Hayley.

32:8 **Hillel**—a transliteration of the Hebrew word translated as "Lucifer" in Is. xiv.12 (Wicksteed 1954: 88).

32:10-21 In their fallen state, the Seven established natural religion (Bloom 1965: 924).

32:11 **Angels of the Divine Presence**—In Blake's work, "the Angel of the Divine Presence designates Satan" (Damon 1967: 23).

Annandale—Annwn, a Celtic realm of the dead—symbolically, this fallen world (Raine 1968: II, 267-68). Annandale was the site of supposed Druid relics and perhaps oak groves (Stevenson 1971: 574).

32:24 One's own real essence or identity never perishes—even when one achieves self-annihilation (Fuller 1983: 75).

32:27 **Eternal Annihilation**—the state of one who is in the process of self-annihilation (cf. Murry 1933: 236, 246). Only "the Living" (i.e. the spiritually alive) will dare to annihilate their selfhoods (Raine 1968: II, 248).

32:33-35 Love and reason are states when, like memory, they restrict themselves to past experience and ignore the present and future (Fuller 1983: 76).

32:35 **Ratio**—here, "a rational scheme" (Stevenson 1971: 576).

33:1-23 Fallen creation will bring her rival, Jerusalem, to God and in her selflessness will cease to be fallen and separate (Tayler 1973b: 81-82). The Divine Voice addresses Jerusalem's shadow, Babylon, who is "the shadowy female Elect," and it refers to Ololon's sixfold shadow, who is Rahab; Rahab's repentance and redemption will bring about Babylon's (Fox 1976: 142-43). Alternatively, the Divine Voice, perverted by Beulah, wrongly calls Ololon Babylon, and supports polygamy, but Ololon is not deceived (Hilton 1983: 43-45).

33:15 **all his loves**—i.e. other women and the pleasures related to imagination; he is left to resort to reason and Greek and Roman literature (George 1980: 173).

33:17 **She shall relent in fear of death**—Ololon will fear that death of the spirit incurred by turning away from one's beloved out of jealousy (Tayler 1973b: 81).

34:9-13 "Or" may derive from the Cabbalistic "Or" meaning "deep, profound" as explained in J. Basnage's *History of the Jews* (1708), pp. 252-53 (Nanavutty 1937). As we move from Beulah to Or-Ulro, "ul" becomes more prominent and "a" disappears, reinforcing the impression of descent to a radically changed state (De Luca 1978: 13-14).

34:23 When they are prevented from co-existing, one contrary destroys the other (Stevenson 1971: 547).

34:24-31 Psychologically, the Polypus represents motherhood that refuses to allow its offspring independent life as well as the castrating female with smothering genitals (Gallant 1978: 146). See also *BL* 4:57n.

34:31 The Mundane Shell is first built by Urizen in a vain attempt to stem the Fall (*FZ*, I); after its disintegration, its recreation by Los is part of the process of transforming Ulro into Generation (Percival 1938: 21-22, 66, 87).

34:40-41 Harper (1955: 76-78) believes Blake adopts Plato's conception of the earth as a porous orb, the inhabited regions being at the bottom of some of its many hollows (*Phaedo* 108e-110a).

34:49 **the Heavens of Ulro**—the Twenty-seven Churches, also called the Heavens and Churches of [lower] Beulah (Damon 1967: 416-17); "the starry void around the world" (Mitchell 1973b: 303). Cf. 29:55.

35:4-7 In this world, victory over one's intellectual opponent seems more important than either fellowship with him or the finding of truth (Fuller 1983: 77).

35:7-8 Though the fallen are born from them, the females did not will the creation of Ulro (George 1980: 174). Blake refers to the exploitation of female weavers (Hilton 1983: 121).

35:8-13 The places named are all high locations around London (Sloss and Wallis 1926: I, 412).

35:22-25 One cannot create art till one has experienced human society (Damon 1967: 333).

35:35 **a wide road...to Eternity**—Blake contrasts this with the "broad way" of *PL*, X, 473, carrying evil from hell to the universe (Margoliouth 1951: 144).

35:48-60 Bloom (1965: 925) relates the two streams rising from the Rock at Golgonooza to Rev. xxii.1; he writes that the first goes via the poet's work to Eden, the second through the world of error back to Golgonooza. Blackstone (1949: 406) associates the first with sexual love as well as with art. Damon (1924: 426) identifies the first with a way to Eternity through the body ("the western gate") and the second with the emotions traversing the realm of dogma to reach the metropolis of art. In a stimulating argument, Peter Taylor (1971: 51-56) maintains that the stream that flows to Eden, the thyme, and Ololon all represent the irruption of the divine in the moment of inspiration, and the other stream, the lark, and the Seven Eyes of God signify the divine acting in history, while Jesus, appearing in the clouds of Ololon (42:11-12) and as the Seventh Eye, participates in both modes. Deen (1983: 187) equates the first stream with time passing into Eternity and the second with cyclical time. The fountain of vision, suggests Blackstone (*loc. cit.*), may spring from a rock which is the Philosopher's Stone, and this Stone is Christ.

35:59-60 Ololon represents a mourning woman at Jesus' vacant grave, the odours standing for the burial spices and the thyme for the shroud; the latter is redeemed in the clouds of 42:12 (P. Taylor 1971: 56-57). As Milton was tempted to enter Canaan, Ololon is tempted to take up residence at an empty tomb—she resembles Mary Magdalene failing to recognise that Christ has risen (Mathews 1980b: 82-83, citing John xx.15).

36:1-10 The succession of larks represents the passage of inspiration through the poets of different generations (Fox 1976: 154).

36:15 **except in a Female Form**—The emanations are male and female in Eternity but only female in the fallen world (George 1980: 174).

36:17 **a Virgin of twelve years**—Cf. Mark v.42 (Wagenknecht 1973: 270-71; see also Hilton 1983: 42). She may break the cycle of the past by not repressing her emergent sexuality (George 1980: 175).

37:1-3 Bloom (1963: 353) ascribes Ololon's remorse to her having separated herself from Milton in a spirit of chastity. George (1980: 175) sees comedy in her ignoring Blake's merely personal request.

37:9 **within**—i.e. in Satan's heart (Stevenson 1971: 553).

37:9-10 There is a visible outline of external identity on the outside and an outline of an inner identity within (Stevenson 1971: 553). Cf. *J* 18:1-4 and n.

37:11 **the Wicker Man of Scandinavia**—According to Caesar (*Gallic Wars*, VI, 16), Druids sometimes made burnt offerings of such figures after filling their limbs with living men (Damon 1924: 426). The frontispiece to Hobbes's *Leviathan* (1651) and the engraving *The Wicker Image* in Aylett Sammes's *Britannia Antiqua Illustrata* (1676) may have influenced Blake (Beer 1968: 255). Among the books that spread the idea that Druidism was practised in Scandinavia is Mallet's *Northern Antiquities* (English translation 1770) (Owen 1962: 229).

37:20-34 Citing material from Jacob Bryant and other eighteenth-century authors, Sandler (1972: 51-56) argues that Blake attributed the Jewish ideal of chastity and the Christian doctrine of sacrificial atonement to Canaanite influences. Damon (1967: 161) notes the derivation of Blake's list from *PL*, I, 391-513.

37:23-24 Cf. Num. xv.38-39—Blake seems to be equating the borders of the Veil with biblical fringes symbolising the commandments (Miner 1961: 48).

37:30-32 Bronowski (1944: 13) sees an allusion to the government spy and agent provocateur in contemporary Britain.

37:35-43 Percival (1938: 115-23, 311) argues that the three groups of churches derive from Augustine's division of history into spiritual periods in *The City of God*, xxii, 30: in the hermaphrodite period humankind is completely dominated by its feminine, corporeal element; from the Flood to Abraham's father, masculinity revolts in the form of Orc and encounters Old Testament divine vengeance; between Abraham and Luther, the pity engendered by Orc's sufferings degenerates into the Mystery dominating the Church. According to Fisher (1961: 61), from Noah to Terah passive sense perception blocks out an imaginative approach to nature, while from Abraham to Luther, the only active element in this approach is the female will, now called the will to power. The hidden male and harlot represent, in Damon's view (1967: 395), powerful unconscious motivations. Raine (1968: I, 325-30), asserting Blake's indebtedness to Boehme's and Swedenborg's historical schemes, finds in the three phases a balance between spirit and body, the veiling of the spiritual by the material, and militaristic nature worship.

37:44-46 In response to Urizen's hermaphroditic combination of solid Newtonian atoms with the Newtonian void, his contrary, Luvah, becomes a spectre in that void (Ault 1974: 178-79). Even the voids are among the oppressive Newtonian wheels (Hilton 1983: 221, citing *J* 13:37).

37:45 Stevenson (1971: 556) plausibly claims a social or political meaning for this line: contemporary Britain is dominated by perverted passions.

37:50   Orion is a giant killed by the female will in the form of Diana, goddess of chastity; Ophiucus is humanity ensnared by nature or moral law—Blake later applies the name in Greek script to Laocoön, assailed by serpents labelled "Good" and "Evil" (Damon 1967: 306, 418, citing E273/ K775).

38:1   **Cities of the Levites**—the results of false religion and the causes of society's polypus-like condition (Damon 1924: 427); manifestations of priestly religion parallel to the similarly satanic Twenty-seven Churches (Frye 1947: 366).

38:6   **a Paved work**—Moses beheld a paved work beneath God (Damon 1967: 324, citing Exod. xxiv.10).

38:8   According to Tayler (1973b: 83), it is Milton's Shadow that descends black-garbed. Bloom (1963: 353-54) treats the returning figure simply as Milton; Stevenson (1971: 557) thinks his identity is left deliberately ambiguous.

38:13-14   If Satan attacked Milton, whose Spectre he is, he would destroy himself (Stevenson 1971: 557).

38:16   Cf. II Cor. v.1 (Bloom 1965: 927).

38:17   **mountains of marble terrible**—This allusion to ecclesiastical power is followed by an attack on the Industrial Revolution (Howard 1976: 249).

38:26   **her scarlet Veil woven in pestilence & war**—Cf. Gray, "The Fatal Sisters," l. 25: "Weave the crimson web of war" (Miner 1958: 205). According to Thomas Wright (1929: I, 27), this covering is sexual allure; according to Rose (1964c: 57), who notes it is elsewhere called a scarlet robe or net, it is the physical body. Hagstrum (1964: 116) regards it as vindictive, war-fostering moral virtue.

39:22-28   Cf. *PL*, II, 508-13 (Damon 1967: 358).

39:53   Urizen faints because Albion begins to awaken (Bloom 1963: 356).

40:9-13   The Enlightenment opponents of orthodoxy are seduced by the female will, the material shadow of the supersensual reality—cf. *J* 30(34):40 (Harper 1961: 234).

40:24-25   The seven kingdoms and five Baalim, being parallel to the sevenfold Rahab and fivefold Tirzah, are associated with the female will (Frye 1947: 379-80). The Baalim are the five rulers of Philistea [see Josh. xiii.3] (Damon 1967: 326). For the seven kingdoms, see Deut. vii.1 (Stevenson 1971: 562).

40:37 **To cleanse the Face of my Spirit by Self-examination**—This resembles Christ's achievement in *Paradise Regained*, though Milton fails to show Jesus' union with his Emanation (Sandler 1972: 31-32).

41:29 **clouds of despair**—Ololon has suffered from Milton's Pauline insistence that females be subordinate and also veil their sexuality to avoid exciting males (Hilton 1983: 134-35).

41:30-35 **our**—The word may refer to Ololon (who contains a multitude) or to both Ololon and Milton (Glausser 1980: 198).

41:35 Milton and Ololon are "creative Contraries" (Bloom 1963: 357).

42:1 **a Womb**—"the womb of nature" (Percival 1938: 181).

42:5-6 The fallen aspect of Ololon (the female will) vanishes like Noah's dove in Gen. viii.12 (Frye 1957c: 119) into the fallen aspect of Milton (Tayler 1973b: 84). The dove, her virginity, plunges into the sea of fallenness (Wagenknecht 1973: 256). Ignoring the different fates in the poem of ark and dove, Mitchell (1973b: 305) sees them both as life-renewing forms Ololon takes after shedding her virginity.

42:7-23 Hagstrum's assertion (1973b: 116) that the "Garment dipped in blood" is Luvah's garment, a robe of sexual passion, may be compared with Miner's proposal (1961: 51-52) that the Garment of this passage is the womb that bears Christ's mortal body. When Ololon, says Wagenknecht (1973: 256-57), yields her virginity (the dove) to Milton, the blood she loses becomes this body, which has taken on the form of history. Associating the "Moony Ark" both with Beulah and with the Catholic concept of the Virgin Mary as the Ark of the Covenant, Nicholas Warner (1980: 55) sees the clouds as beneficent and protective.

The "War" has been classified as "spiritual" (Damon 1967: 45) or "mental" (Rose 1968c: 33); Peter Butter (1978: 160) supposes Christ and the prophets must wage such war against their attackers. Cooper (1981: 106) considers "Litteral" a triple pun—"literal," "consisting of letters," and "littoral." Bloom's perception here (1965: 928) of a Blakean conviction, shared by Milton, that body and soul must rise together should be weighed against Blake's expressions of scepticism about physical resurrection (E564/ K616; E520 [ll. 81-102]/ K753 [ll. 87-108]). Miner (1969: 274) cites Ezek. ii.9-10 and Rev. xix.13, 16.

42:10-24 Gallant (1978: 150-54) finds that here and in 39:6-9 Blake encounters the archetype of the self leaving him free to impart his wisdom to society.

42:12-14 Hilton (1983: 142-43) argues that the text is now purified from the veil of lamentations hitherto so prominent and that the reader is shown to be Jesus' garment.

42:16-17 Blake has a prevision of universal redemption in which all Albion's Cities are resurrected (Howard 1976: 255).

42:16-23 Fox (1976: 182-83) maintains that this passage describes Albion's present redemption; Howard (1976: 255-56) reads it as a prophetic vision of his future redemption.

42:18 **the Immortal Four**—the resurrected Zoas (Bloom 1963: 360). The context suggests also the four chief Cities (London, Verulam, York and Edinburgh) identified with them (cf. Damon 1967: 71).

42:20, 22, 29 **Felpham's Vale**—Blake is about to "go forth" (43:1) from the veil and vale of seductive nature (Hilton 1983: 141).

42:26-27 Deen (1983: 249) supposes that Blake, having experienced an annunciation with Ololon's arrival, re-enacts Christ's agony, death and resurrection.

42:29-31 The lark and thyme, beings of spring, herald the harvest of autumn (Tolley 1973: 128). In these lines Los and Enitharmon represent Blake and his wife re-entering London late in the summer of 1803 by way of Wimbledon in Surrey (Erdman 1954a: 367 [395]).

42:32-33 Oothoon weeps with happiness because the human harvest has come to ripeness (Bloom 1965: 928). Possibly so, says Peter Butter (1978: 161-62), but she could be grieving because that harvest is thin. Erdman's claim (1954a: 367 [395]) that she is the republican spirit lamenting the lack of support in a country facing invasion by Napoleon is plausible.

42:36-43:1 Rintrah's plough and Palamabron's harrow have accomplished their tasks, and Satan's mills have disappeared from the scene (Bloom 1963: 362).

Designs

pl. 1   The eddies into which Milton advances may be his Shadow (Damon 1924: 429), fire from his own hell that he formerly shunned (Margoliouth 1951: 131), smoke from Mt. Sinai representing the moral law (Hagstrum 1964: 111), a vortex into which the reader is drawn after him (Erdman 1974: 217) or "the nether Abyss" of 3:26 that stifles his inner self (Carothers 1978: 124). The white lines upon him suggest to Essick (1980: 154) the woven character Blake ascribes to the garment of the body. According to Wittreich (1975: 16, 22), he is identified here with the angel of Rev. ix.1 and in subsequent plates with the star of the same verse.

pl. 2   The star is the descending Milton illuminating the slumbering "spiritual forms of the bread and the wine" (Damon 1924: 429), whose human forms he will free from their vegetable state (Erdman 1974: 218).

pl. 4   The design illustrates the weaving of the three classes of men (Damon 1924: 430). The boulder represents the bony skull as well as the Shell, and it reappears in *IB* pl. 6, while the Druid trilithons foreshadow the three crosses on Calvary (Erdman 1974: 220, 222). There is a hint on the right of "a Druid form of the Tyburn gallows" (it resembles the scaffold in Hogarth's *The Idle 'Prentice Executed at Tyburn*) and a body-like shape suspended over it (Hilton 1981: 201, 204n29).

pl. 6   The man riding the horse of intellect has the task of pushing the rocking stone, which represents Satan, into the abyss (Wicksteed 1954: 69); or the rider is the imaginative man fleeing a rationalistic society (Hagstrum 1964: 54); or the horseman and shepherd represent the prophets' images of God as warrior and God as shepherd (e.g. Jer. xxi.5-6 and xxxi.10)—i.e. wrath and mercy, which are sundered in this world (Rix 1984: 110).

pl. 10   Not every critic shares Erdman's plausible view (1974: 226) that Palamabron (on the left) and Rintrah (in the centre) are watching the degenerating Satan standing on "the paved terraces" of his own bosom (9:30-32). Mitchell (1973a: 65-66) believes that the figures are intended to be ambiguous: Palamabron (in the centre) may be hesitating between a flaming Rintrah and a Satan who wishes to depart and who may be hiding anger beneath mildness. Sutherland (1977: 151) suggests Rintrah's anger is passing into Satan where their feet touch much as the Miltonic star descends to Blake's foot. Another proposal is that Los and Enitharmon exhibit dismay at the sight of the flaming Orc (Damon 1924: 430).

pl. 11 The London street in which Enitharmon appears distracted is also the cave of this world, and its dots signify the fragmentation of the Fall (Erdman 1974: 227).

pl. 15 Cain has smitten Abel (Damon 1924: 430)—or (perhaps) Satan Thulloh (Fox 1976: 226). The altar behind them is built of human skulls as well as stones, and it reappears in *IB* pl. 17 between Blake and his wife (Erdman 1974: 231, 233). This symbolic altar linking Cain to Abel, contrasts with the star that links Blake to his brother (*IB* pls. 32, 37) and to Milton (*IB* pl. 17), and with the sandal that links him to Los (Tannenbaum 1978: 28).

pl. 16 Milton's girdle is in his right hand and his robe in his left. Raine (1968: II, 249-50) states that he is shedding all his possessions in the act of self-annihilation, Bindman (1977: 173-74) finds a clear parallel with Christ resolving to descend from heaven, and Carothers (1978: 126) asserts that he has overcome Urizen and holds Jesus' garments. In copies A, B and C, claims Wittreich (1975: 22-27), Milton is discarding "the robe of the promise" (14:13), "the rotten rags of Memory" (41:4) and "the Sexual Garments" (41:25), but in copy D he is donning the garment of imagination to stand as a type of Christ. To Essick (1980: 154-55), he seems to be casting off the crosshatching of commercial copy engraving so that the human form is revealed.

pl. 18 The details of this representation of Milton grappling with Urizen are much disputed. Is this Milton with shaven head meant to recall his own Samson pulling down the Urizenic Philistine temple (Erdman 1974: 234), or is he reborn as a young poet (Tayler 1973a: 251) or intended to resemble the short-haired Blake (Mitchell 1973a: 55)? Rather than wrestling with Urizen, can he be sculpturing him "into life" (Paley 1978a: 173)? Are the dancing musicians above him the five senses liberated (Damon 1924: 430), Milton's Emanations in Beulah (Tayler, *loc. cit.*), rejoicing Eternals (Stevenson 1971:

510), or the Children of Rahab and Tirzah tempting Milton to cross the Jordan (Keynes 1967b, referring to 19:27-31)—and tempting him successfully, as *IB* pl. 45 shows, according to Mitchell (1973a: 56)? Or is the river the Arnon (Fox 1976: 225)?

pl. 19   Above, Milton's three wives avert their faces from his three dancing daughters (Damon 1924: 430); these women have yet to attain the harmony they display on *IB* pl. 48 (Erdman 1974: 235). In George's eyes (1980: 166-67), they exemplify the uniting and dividing of fallen emanations and represent both the real conduct of women and men's psychological projections upon them. Below, Los—Keynes (1921: 158) refers to the figure as a mandragora—opposes Milton's advance (17:34-36), as does Urizen, whose head is visible on the ground between them (Damon, *loc. cit.*). Erdman (1974: 236) suggests an allusion to the division of England's head and body in the Civil War, while Wittreich (1975: 259-60n46) sees a specific reference to the severed head of Milton's adversary Charles I.

pls. 21-25, 27   Erdman (1974: 237-41, 243, 256) detects in these plates several small images of Blake himself foreshadowing the self-portrayal in the engagingly naive *IB* pl. 40; especially attractive is the ecstatically dancing Blake in the centre of the right margin of pl. 24.

pl. 28   Here are profiles of the northern and southern gates of Britain (26: 13-22). Erdman (1974: 244) classifies them both as entrances for "Souls descending to the Body" and suggests they may be Druid altars in process of becoming redemptive pavements. In Neoplatonic symbolism, northern and southern gates are respectively entrances to mortality and Eternity.

pl. 31   Book I ends with a bleak representation of the Vale of Surrey, which is also the biblical Vale of Rephaim, supposedly the haunt of giants or wicked ghosts and hence an emblem of Ulro (see 19:40n.). It is to reappear filled with life in *IB* pl. 33 and bearing the human harvest in *IB* pl. 49 (Erdman 1974: 247, 249-50). Wagenknecht (1973: 275) notes Isaiah's reference to the harvest in this Vale (xvii.5) but maintains that Blake treats it as a negative symbol, perhaps of the Deluge.

pls. 32, 37   In front of three steps, William advances his left or vegetable foot; in front of four steps, Robert—who brings him inspiration—advances his right or spiritual foot (Damon 1924: 431-32); William is a Palamabron, Robert a Rintrah (Frye 1957c: 130). In pl. 32 the "black cloud" (15:50) is rising immediately after the moment portrayed in *IB* pl.17; the unhewn stones on the latter are replaced by mason's work representing art—the three steps show William is in this world, the four that his brother is in Eternity (Erdman 1974: 248, 253). In Blake's designs, straight as opposed to spiral staircases indicate painful struggle, which in these cases has led to vision (Paley 1983a: 200-01). William has given up his grip on his persona and leant back to encounter the darkness of the unconscious, in which Robert is more thoroughly at home (Gallant 1978: 153).

pl. 33   Damon (1924: 431) and Keynes (1967b) identify the descending figures as Sons and Daughters of Ololon (30:4), but Erdman (1974: 249-50) realises that the border in copy A, with trumpet-blowing angels in the upper corners, shows that the design represents a Day of Judgment; nevertheless his contention that the central figures are Milton and Ololon is less plausible, as he now agrees (1975: 40), than Fox's interpretation of the lightning as the descending Ololon of 36:17-20.

pl. 36   The egg shape of the created universe, states Damon (1924: 431), signifies the diminution of fallen life, but he later (1967: 288) adds that within it humans are prepared for hatching into Eternity. The antiquity of the symbolic cosmic egg is noted by Percival (1938: 72) and documented by Raine (1968: II, 179-82, 312n28) as well as by Nurmi (1969: 312-18), who argues that Blake is contributing to a fairly widespread attack on the implicitly deistic treatment of the concept in Thomas Burnet's *The Sacred Theory of the Earth* (1690-91).

The circular form of their worlds, asserts Harper (1961: 129), shows that the Zoas are not yet much fallen. Rose (1968c: 32) observes that these are ruined worlds in a fiery furnace, where they may be transformed, and Beer (1968: 174-75) proposes that the flames are also tentacles of the Polypus. Damon (1967: 5) interprets Adam as the conscious mind and Satan as the fiery, energy-producing subconscious, while Erdman (1974: 252) points out that Satan's region of fire contrasts with Adam's faintly circumscribed circle of earth. Dilworth (1983) contends that in the cases of copies A and C turning the image upside down reveals a pair of hands containing the satanic flame—hands sketched in to suggest the self-annihilation necessary for the creation of true art.

pl. 40 Erdman (1974: 256) emphasises the contrast between the "humility and simplicity" of the self-portrait here and the apocalyptic sublimity of the text on the following plate, while Fox (1976: 213-14) conjectures that the "homey" character of the design relates to a marital quarrel and reconciliation that may be one of the inspirations behind the epic.

pl. 42 Are the humans in this much discussed plate the poet in general and his emanation (Damon 1924: 432); the Albion and Britannia of *J* 94:15-21, which the design may illustrate (Binyon 1926: 125); Blake and his wife (T. Wright 1929: II, 6); Milton and a woman (Keynes and Wolf 1953: 100); or Milton and Ololon (Sandler 1972: 16)? Are they deliberately ambiguous—Milton and Ololon, and, at the same time, Milton's "male & female" Shadow of 14:36-38 (Mitchell 1973a: 62-63), or alternatively is the man both Milton and Albion (Wittreich 1975: 27-33)? Are they pictured in a bridal embrace (Sandler, *loc. cit.*), a post-coital slackness (Erdman 1974: 258), or a state of unsatisfied desire (Stevenson 1971: 557)? Is the male, as copy A suggests, sexually excited (Damon, *loc. cit.*)? Does the design show Milton's failure to reunite with his Emanation (Mitchell 1973a: 62)?

The eagle, too, is controversial. To some it seems a form of inspiration—the eagle of genius (Damon, *loc. cit.*), the symbol of St. John the Evangelist (Sandler, *loc. cit.*), Milton himself savagely trying to arouse Albion (Wittreich, *loc. cit.*), or the agent about to wake Albion and his partner (Fox 1976: 229-30). Erdman (*loc. cit.*) posits that in its swoop and scream all the great descents and musical moments of the epic manifest in a single instant. Interpreting it negatively, Frye (1957c: 108-09) sees it as the accusing sexual shame that disfigures the fallen world, and Bindman (1977: 176) identifies it with the famished, vulture-like eagle of *FZ* 109:1-6/ E384/ VIII, 521-26. To Mitchell (1973a: 56, 63), it seems ambiguous—a bird of prey descending on the defenceless Milton and Ololon but also Milton himself about to enter heroically his own Shadow.

pl. 45 Damon (1924: 432) holds that Milton is forgiving the kneeling Ololon, and Wittreich (1975: 14, 19, 270-71) adds that he is uniting with her, though these views correspond to nothing in the text. Binyon (1926: 125) sees the kneeling figure as an old man. Stevenson (1971: 561), Erdman (1974: 261) and Bindman (1977: 176) identify him as Urizen on the bank of the Arnon. Bindman maintains that Milton casts out the Zoa, the other two that he raises him as a defeated enemy. Ignoring the mystical meaning of self-annihilation, Webster (1983: 269-70) supposes that the concept is illustrated here and that it signifies the resolution of male conflict through one man's nurture of another, perhaps with a homosexual element.

pl. 46 Though Beer (1968: 181) perceives in this design Urizen struggling against a serpentine Orc, most critics believe the man to be Milton. The latter is variously said to be confronting "the serpent of Despair and the wolf of 'ravenous Envy' [41:17]" (Keynes 1967b), spectres conjured up by his errors (Tayler 1973a: 256), and Urizen in the form of a serpent with two heads—a cock's and a dog's (Erdman 1974: 262), and simply snakes (Bindman 1977: 176).

pl. 47 This representation of Los appearing to Blake illustrates 22:4-8 (Damon 1924: 430-31) and is not usually treated as controversial, though Beer (1968: 256) identifies the half kneeling figure as a nervous Milton and Webster (1983: 261) sees a hint of homosexuality overlaying "a deeper fantasy of merger with an idealised figure." In contrast, Marks (1976: 62-63) asserts that Blake's discovery of his twin means the release of his creative potential, which is synonymous with the ejection of his selfhood.

pl. 48 Milton's wives and daughters, portrayed in *IB* pl. 19, put in a second appearance, and Damon (1924: 432) observes that they "bathe in the Waters of Life, to wash off the Not Human" (41:1). Erdman (1974: 264) identifies the two figures furthest left and the one furthest right as the daughters. According to Fox (1976: 226-27), the six are united in Ololon following the latter's descent.

pl. 49 Keynes (1967b) interprets the weeping Oothoon as an emblem of frustrated love, Fox (1976: 229) sees her as parallel to the eagle of inspiration on *IB* pl. 42, Erdman (1974: 265) refers to her tears of joy over the maturity of the human harvest, and Grant (1976: 91-95) holds that her active benevolence is the female contribution essential to the harvest.

pl. 50   Damon (1924: 432) regards the central figure as the soul
in ecstasy, and Binyon (1926: 126) adds that she is escaping
from the flesh. Raine (1968: I, 161-62) considers her to be
Ahania, the "Vegetater happy" of *FZ* 109:23/ E384/ VIII, 543.
Most critics, however, believe that she is Ololon, whether what
she is shedding is her vegetable (material) body (Johnson 1973:
17), her virginity (Mitchell 1973a: 62), or, as suggested by her
cruciform posture, her selfhood (Erdman 1974: 266-67). The
object she steps from may be a tree trunk (Hilton 1983: 142) or
a trunk-like veil (Erdman 1974: 266). Erdman (1974: 267)
describes her as advancing to redemption in a spirit of pity that
contrasts with the wrath of the self-annihilating Milton on *IB*
pl. 1, while Grant (1976: 97-99) argues that she reflects
Blake's respect for the female since he concludes his book by
portraying her as the first human to be redeemed.

Ololon's companions have been seen as multi-winged sera-
phim (Damon, *loc. cit.*), as perhaps Rintrah and Palamabron
(Mitchell 1973a: 61), as a male and female ripening for the
harvest (Raine, *loc. cit.*), and as two human stalks that need to
contribute to their own harvesting, the one looking up towards
Oothoon, who hovers over the grain (see previous design),
being the more likely to do so (Grant, *loc. cit.*).

Notes on Criticism for Chapter 11

Jerusalem

Blake himself announces the theme of *Jerusalem* in the opening lines, and although Damon (1924: 184) and Frye (1947: 363) look on Albion as the hero and Blackstone (1949: 158-59) and Altizer (1967: 66) opt for Jesus, there is now widespread agreement with Wicksteed (1954: 13) that the book's real hero is Los. The central point of contention about the work has long been less the identity of its hero than its organising principle, which has been slowly uncovered as error after error has been discarded.

Most early critics who dare to investigate the problem search for some kind of chronological foundation. While Sloss and Wallis (1926: I, 437, 439) are resigned to finding only "a congeries of episodes" in a "chaotic" poem, Damon (1924: 187) ascribes one stage of Albion's journey to each chapter as he passes through Beulah, Generation, and the triumphal reign of error to redemption. Schorer's theory (1946: 362-84) that Albion undergoes a series of falls is succeeded by Frye's valiant attempt (1947: 357) to correlate this final epic with *The Four Zoas*: he discerns a preoccupation with the Orc cycle in the first two chapters and a parallel between the contents of Nights Seven and Eight of the *Zoas* and the treatment of Jesus and Deism in the third chapter of *Jerusalem*. Similarly, Bloom (1963: 390, 403, 416) maintains that Albion's fall into Ulro is followed by his confrontations with Los and his own Sons until, at the end of chapter three, he reaches the nadir earlier depicted at the close of Night the Eighth. Bloom also (1963: 407; 1965: 940) makes the important observation that at 57:16 Albion reaches a stationary condition in which he remains till pl. 95. This does not prevent Lesnick (1970: 392) from claiming that for more than three chapters Blake portrays consecutive stages of Albion's fall. With less than full confidence in the functioning of a narrative framework that he admits is inoperative in chapter two and all but crumbles in chapter three, Stevenson (1971: 675, 730, 762-63) records how Albion successively rejects the Divine Vision [pl. 4], submits to his Spectre [pl. 29(33)], assumes God's role [42:47-54], and embraces Vala [64:25]. As late as 1978, Ferguson (171, 190) argues that whenever a song embodies a mildness like that of Christ in pl. 4, the narrative takes a step forwards, and that Los's struggle to replace anger with mildness lasts until pl. 85.

By dividing his work into four equal chapters, setting them off with five full-page designs, and furnishing each with preface, headpiece and tailpiece, Blake leads one to expect a symmetrical work (Mitchell 1978: 171). Accordingly, several critics have sought the structural key in the quadripartite division. Attempts have been made to relate chapters two through four to the "Childhood, Manhood & Old Age" (98:33) of religion (Kiralis 1956: 147) and to the abuse of the body, of the mind and emotions, and of the imagination (Mellor 1974: 287); to allot each chapter to one of the Zoas (Rose 1963: 48-49) or to a stage in Los's development from embodiment of wrath, first to sacred watchman, then to prophet and creator, and finally to the saviour of 82:56ff (McClellan 1977); to find a correspondence between the four chapters and the four Gospels—each Gospel being traditionally regarded as addressed, as is each chapter, to a different audience (Witke 1970); to discern in each the superimposition of a satanic threefold division on a Human fourfold division (Curran 1973: 334-35); to see the chapters as focusing consecutively on division, death, sexuality, and awakening (Kroeber 1973: 361, 363), or on the vision of Golgonooza and the vision of Babylon, on the family and the law, on the contrast between cruel sacrifices and separation of truth from error, and on Atonement and Consummation (Wagenknecht 1973: 266-81), or on Golgonooza, London, Babylon and Jerusalem (Bogan 1981: 85). Detecting a two-part structure, Wyatt (1975: 114-22) asserts that in pls. 1 through 46 the text concentrates on the constriction of vision while positive elements prevail in the designs, but that in pls. 47 through 93 the text concentrates on expansion of vision while the designs are predominantly negative.

In 1976, Fox referred (14) to the "shaky consensus" among Blake scholars that *Jerusalem* is "plotted progressively," but none of the structures proposed up to that time correspond to the reader's experience of the book and most of them are based on highly selective evidence tendentiously culled from a densely packed work. One valid earlier observation, however, is Frye's statement (1947: 357) that each chapter "presents a phase of imaginative vision simultaneously with the body of error which it clarifies"—a statement usefully complemented by Bloom's perception (1963: 391) that the poem is characterised by "a progressive sharpening of spiritual conflict." But the essential discovery is that the book has a synchronic structure. This discovery has a long ancestry including claims that the text is sprinkled with topical allusions "scattered without regard for chronology" (Erdman 1954a: 431 [467]), that it is not constructed on the basis of "historical time" (Rose 1965: 602), that its coherent sequences of plates appear not to be organised into a coherent whole (Beer 1969: 172-73), that in its "multiple" universe "each event is repeated and reenacted" (Altizer 1967: xviii-xix), that each chapter presents the same subject and has the same pattern (Witke 1970: 266), and that *Jerusalem*, unlike *Milton*, lacks a "linear narrative" (De Luca 1970: 12). In 1973, Curran forthrightly declares (340), "There is no narrative progression whatsoever in the first three chapters." At this stage two steps remain to uncover the book's organising principle. In a stimulating analysis, Mitchell (1978: 165-218) conclusively shows that the narrative is not chronological, but in trying to assign a function to each chapter he does not sufficiently heed his own warning against "the modern tendency to deduce a structure based upon a judicious selection of quotations" (165), and, like Doskow (1982: 15-17), who supposes the entire poem to focus on the instant of Albion's awakening, he does not recognise the switch to narrative form near the conclusion. It has been left to Paley (1983b: 302-14) to demonstrate that the chapters do not function as distinct components of a larger structure and that, although a few occurrences, such as the appointment of the Seven Eyes of God (55:30-33), are described only once, *Jerusalem* returns over and over from different perspectives to such events and situations as Los's division, Luvah's murder, Jerusalem's fallen state, and Albion's flight from the Divine Vision, while the story of Reuben must be gathered from fragments scattered in defiance of chronology.

Such a principle of organisation allows Blake to change the arrangement of chapter two in the third and fourth of the five copies of *Jerusalem* he prints. The change consists of moving pls. 43 through 46 to a position between pls. 28 and 29, and inserting pl. 42 between pls. 37 and 38. This breaks up the sequence of six Bath plates—36 through 41 in Erdman's edition—(Wicksteed 1954: 189) and disorders the story of how the Friends, having been unable to rescue Albion, descend to their nadir in pl. 42 (Paley 1983b: 299-301), so De Luca (1983) is probably right when he follows a hint of Paley (cited Wyatt 1975: 106) and argues that the second arrangement was adopted for the superior order of the designs, which form symmetrical patterns based on repeated and complementary page layouts like those of *IB* pls. 31(35), 33(37), and 35(39) and of *IB* pls. 28 and 50.

It should be remembered, however, that the conclusion of *Jerusalem* is a continuous narrative of Albion's regeneration. The turning point (which may be earlier than the beginning of the narrative conclusion) has been located at positions ranging from 82:81 (Beer 1969: 236) to 94:18 (Paley 1983b: 230).

Bloom identifies Ezekiel as the principal model for Blake's last epic (1963: 366) and asserts that its relation to *Jerusalem* closely resembles that of Homer's epics to the *Aeneid* (1971: 66). The affinities are further traced by Helms (1974), who maintains that Blake nevertheless challenges the prophet's condemnation of Jerusalem and his belief in ritual, and by Herrstrom (1981: 64, 66, 68), who discerns in the poem a set of variations on the situation of a sleeper on a rock beside a river in a city with a temple—cf. Ezek. i and x. Even more illuminating is Paley's recognition (1983b: 286-90) of how closely the pattern of *Jerusalem* duplicates that of the Apocalypse as expounded in Joseph Mede's *The Key of the Revelation* (English translation 1643) and David Pareus' *The Authors Preface Upon the Revelation* (1644): Mede speaks of the Apocalypse's sychronic structure as a "Sychronisme of prophecies," and Pareus explains how, for example, there are seven separated descriptions of the one Last Judgment.

Other suggested models for *Jerusalem* include Milton's four-book *Paradise Regained* (Curran 1971: 147-55) and Charles Jennens' libretto for Handel's *Messiah* (Paley 1983b: 291-94). De Luca (1982) maintains that Blake's picture of the fallen world is based on so-called "sublime" Teutonic literature, especially as found in Mallet's *Northern Antiquities* (English translation 1770), which presents the ruins of a once animate universe now characterised by Druid stones, petrifying monarchs, rocky shores and stormy seas, whereas his representation of Eternity is based on the

sublimity of the Bible, which, as Robert Lowth strongly implies in
his *Lectures on the Sacred Poetry of the Hebrews* (English trans-
lation 1787) arises from verbal patterns—hence the sacredness of
words to Blake (see 95:9; 98:35-36).

For some critics, the nature of *Jerusalem* and the function
in it of Los are illuminated by the book's relationship with *Milton*.
The vision which one deceased poet achieves in the latter is won
by all humankind in its sequel (Frye 1947: 356). *Jerusalem* begins
where *Milton* ends (Rose 1963: 51) and focuses on the action pro-
ceeding from the acquisition of self-knowledge that is the preoccu-
pation of the earlier work (Ferguson 1978: 191). In particular,
there is a greatly increased emphasis on the importance of forgive-
ness (Welch 1978: 237), which Los himself has only come to und-
erstand in the course of *The Four Zoas* and *Milton* (Gallant 1978:
158-59). The very theme of *Jerusalem* has been defined as the
forgiveness of sins (Sloss and Wallis 1926: II, 66, 72), which must
be mutual (Bloom 1965: 940), and which is indivisible from
Blake's aesthetic (Rose 1971b: 15). This in turn is intimately rel-
ated to his theory of perception (Rose 1965: 595): Los, the force of
whose hammer "is eternal Forgiveness" (88:50), is himself "the
visionary faculty of the seer" (Fisher 1961: 111) or "the act of per-
ceiving" (Rose 1973: 83).

Understandably concentrating on the formidable negative
element in the poem, Beer (1969: 239-62) finds at its heart the loss
of vision when its two poles—sublimity and pathos—are sundered
at the Fall. The lost vision has been conceived in several ways that
are complementary rather than contradictory: as the ability to see
the whole human community—the universal form of 38(43):
20—in every individual (Deen 1983: 204-05); as Los's perception,
at once sequential and simultaneous, of time (Rose 1973: 95); as
Los's perception of time that contrasts with his Spectre's and
allows for an escape from cyclical repetition (Marks 1976: 59);
and as a view of the Newtonian temporal and spatial world as no
more than a part of what the imagination creates (Fisher 1961:
200-01). This last may be associated with what Damon (1924:
194) and Paley (1983b: 268-69) regard as a rise in Blake's esti-
mate of creation or nature, which he now sees as largely the work
of Los and the first step in the reascent from the nadir of the Fall.

Other critics see as the central element of *Jerusalem* the
antithesis between the transient and the eternal (Wicksteed 1954:

1); Los's separation from his Spectre and Albion's from his Emanation (Price 1964: 438); the conflict between Los and his Spectre that persists until pl. 91 (Marks 1974: 32, 37-45); the clear distinction between the desperate, guilt-induced suffering of the Spectre of Urthona and the suffering of the prophet like Los or Blake (Bloom 1971: 67, 71, 74); the metamorphosis of the material body into "the fourfold vehicular body of the imagination" (Nelson 1974: 137); and the question of whether Jerusalem or Babylon will prevail (Herrstrom 1981: 68). Wicksteed (1954: 8-9 and *passim*) emphasises the book's autobiographical element, and especially the representation of the poet and his wife in Los and Enitharmon.

A subordinate theme of *Jerusalem* is the relationship of Britain with Israel, on which Blake lavishes outpourings of geographical detail too generous for most readers. His attempt to write of his own country's towns as fervently as the prophets wrote of Israel's (Beer 1969: 176) and to create for England a mythology comparable with Ireland's (Raine 1968: II, 273) may be associated with his notion—inherited, as Saurat was the first to realise (1929: 51-85), from the seventeenth and eighteenth centuries—that British Druidism was the source of biblical religion. Johnson and Grant even consider Blake's country the real hero of the book (1979: 309). At the same time Blake is demanding that the Britain of the years leading up to Waterloo make peace with France and abstain from vengeance (Erdman 1954a: 427 [462]).

Several critics have brought psychoanalytic concepts to bear on the poem. The malign Covering Cherub, the struggling Los, and Albion's sin-obsessed Spectre Bloom identifies respectively with the id, ego, and superego (1971: 75-76). According to Gallant (1978: 155-83), Albion denies and represses the unconscious, Jerusalem faces it but is psychologically submerged and socially exploited, while Los realises one must integrate its apparent chaos in oneself. Webster (1983: 272-97) argues that Blake's own Oedipus complex causes him to project his anger against the cruel father onto the dominating female Vala-Rahab, and also to compete in the person of Los with the father-figure Albion for the possession of Jerusalem; eventually the adoption of the principle of forgiveness assuages Los's anger and allows them to share her so that Blake can escape from guilt without renouncing his incestuous impulse.

The identification (on one level) of Los with Blake and of Los's struggle against his Spectre with the inner conflict Blake suffered as a creative artist has long been a commonplace of criticism. The Spectre has been interpreted as Blake's doubts and uncertainties (M. Plowman 1927a: 174), Blake the engraver who executes commissions and makes a living (Erdman 1951a: 217-18), and the voice that urges him to make that living for himself and his wife, Enitharmon (Wicksteed 1954: 128-29) or tells him that his worldly prospects are cause for despair (Bloom 1963: 373).

Los's furnaces—the apparatus of the alchemist, who may regenerate either base metals or the fallen human soul (Percival 1938: 204; cf. Paley 1983b: 243)—are one of a number of major symbolic images in Blake's text and designs. The Veil of Vala combines moral virtue with the covering of matter that masks the essence of nature (Damon 1924: 188, 445). More precisely it is at once "the film of matter which covers all reality," the Mundane Shell, the mortal body, the moral law and the veil in the Temple (Damon 1967: 432). Raine (1968: I, 210) equates it with "nature," and Paley (1983b: 194-96) adds that it is also the hymen and that Los transforms it into something redemptive. Insofar as it is the veil concealing the Temple sanctuary, it is part of a cluster of images including the Mosaic Tent of Meeting or Tabernacle (later replaced by the Temple), the Ark of the Covenant housed there, and the Tablets of the Law within the Ark (Exod. xxvi). In a useful exposition, Miner (1961) shows how these images usually represent the descent into selfhood and sexual secrecy, and particularly the female genitals that clothe the spirit with flesh and are the key to women's power over men through the rules of chastity; he adds that sometimes, however, Blake identifies the Ark of the Covenant with Noah's saving Ark, and when the veil of secrecy is rent, as by Christ at the Crucifixion (e.g. Matt. xxvii.50-51), the sexual act can be a sacrifice reuniting the male and female sundered at the Fall, so that "Tent & Tabernacle" become the place of "Mutual Forgiveness" (7:62-67, 54:4). Miner (1969: 277) speaks of this veil as both the womb and the outer crust of matter, and Riede (1981: 553-57) associates it with the closed Temple door of Ezek. xliv.1-2 and equates Christ's rending of it with both his Nativity and his Crucifixion. The Temple veil is traditionally understood to represent the flesh, especially Christ's flesh (Poole 1685: III, 141, citing Heb. x.20; Henry 1708-14: V, 430), and, on the authority of Philo and Josephus, Hilton (1983: 136, 283n29) states that it symbolised the four elements. Miner (1969: 472-73n58) earlier draws attention to the relevant passage in Josephus. Other scholars identify the feminine Tabernacle with reason (Rose 1966: 124) and with the Newtonian void of space (Ault 1974: 119).

The materiality represented by the veil Blake conceives of as composed of fibres or (Hagstrum 1964: 115) "stems of vegetation"; Blake borrows the term "fibres" from biology to denote the hardened building blocks of the fallen world (Kroeber 1973: 360). Hilton (1983: 89-98, 274n39) explains how, unorganised, the fibres compose the Polypus (cf. *M* 24:37-38n); organised, they constitute the imprisoning body of woven vegetation (e.g. 80:65). Drawing on contemporary uses of the term, Hilton (1983: 89-98, 274n39) shows that Blake makes fibres turn into sperm and generate (e.g. 80:74-76; 86:50-58) or constitute tissues, especially the nerves, which can transmit intellect, imagination and love (e.g. 4:7-8; 98:14-18) or become hard, opaque vehicles of hatred (e.g. 15:1-2) identifiable with aggressive armies and imperialist economics (67:37-40). Paley (1983b: 66, 256-58) observes that fibres of brotherly and marital love can also carry sexual desire (86:50-51) and that Enitharmon can employ fibres to cage the spirit (87:5-7, 12-14; *IB* pl. 85) or to make this world minister to regeneration (86:40-41; 83:71-74). Since the vegetable body—like all materiality—is a product of false perception, Welch (1978: 225, 238) has a strong case for identifying the vegetation that interposes barriers between individuals and between the individual and Eternity with Lockean vision.

One way of escape from imprisonment in materiality is through what Blake calls a Centre. He contrasts the "Selfish Center" (71:7), or acme of Selfhood, with the Centre that, like Eno's atom (*FZ* 9:12/ E305/ I, 225), exists in time and space but opens into Eternity (Rose 1965: 587-89, 604-06). Frosch (1974: 76-77, 80), who holds that Centre and Circumference are only separated at the Fall, regards as Centres both objects distorted by corrupted perception and individual human beings; Welch (1978: 223, 225) agrees that individuals are Centres and regards the Circumference as Edom or Eternity. Damon (1967: 87) defines the Circumference as the bodily form (Tharmas) and the Centre as the heart (Luvah). Applying the terms to *Jerusalem* itself, Mitchell (1978: 176-78) considers its Circumference to be its total form, its Centres to be its details or minute particulars; the Circumference he relates to Golgonooza's Western Gate, closed till the end of time—or of the poem (13:11), the Centres to its Eastern Gate [12:56]. According to Raine (1968: II, 155), Blake derives the symbol of the Centre from Boehme; according to Welch (1978: 224, 232), both his Centre and his Circumference may be traceable to Swedenborg's *Divine Love and Divine Wisdom*, from which he borrows them to challenge Locke's conception of infinity as endless distance, eternity as endless time, and substance as a quantitative entity (*Essay Concerning Human Understanding* II.xvii, xxiii). Ault (1974: 51-52) thinks that by his non-scientific handling of such mathematical terms as "circumference" and "limits," Blake is defying Newtonianism.

Like the Centre, the wheel can have either positive or negative connotations. Developing Damon's point (1924: 442) that the "Wheel within Wheel" of 15:20 alludes to the wheels of Ezek. i.16, Erdman (1954a: 313 [339]) observes how Blake contrasts these wheels operated by vision with the horrific intermeshing cogs, "wheel without wheel" (15:18), of industry. The latter Rose (1972a: 36-37) identifies with the wheels of war, the fiery wheel of natural religion (pl. 77, second poem), the wheels with which Enitharmon spins or weaves the flesh, and the starry wheels of Albion's Sons; he further declares (1965: 594) that in *Jerusalem* Blake pits Ezekiel's fourfold wheels against the threefold wheels of Albion's Sons and of the Zoas, wheels that form "Harmonies of Concords & Discords" (74:24) parallel to the Lockean "agreements & disagree[me]nts of Ideas" (70:8) dominating the Enlightenment conception of human knowledge. Less convincingly, Harper (1974: 76) postulates as the source of the "Wheels within Wheels" the Spheres of Plato's cosmology (*Republic*, X), which, he alleges, Blake far prefers to the Newtonian starry wheels. Ault (1974: 90-91) believes that these latter wheels imply a universe where everything is predetermined and that they stand for the deceptive scientific astronomy used to veil the horror of Ulro's void; Bloom, however, (1963: 370-73) associates them with the Zodiac, and Ferguson (1978: 189) suggests that they may derive from Boehme's conviction that the stars govern the external world.

Albion's having twelve Sons and twelve Daughters is part of the number symbolism that pervades *Jerusalem*. Grant notes that four (the number of the chapters), twenty-eight (the number of [shorter] chapters originally planned), and one hundred (the number of the plates) all signify apocalypse (cited Erdman 1964: 7). After glancing at the contrast between imaginative fours and demonic threes and their multiples, Frye (1947: 368-69, 378-79) comments that Jerusalem's sixteen Sons plus Albion's twelve make up twenty-eight, the number of Albion's Cathedral Cities—and also the sum of the four beasts and twenty-four elders of Rev. iv.4-6. Suspecting that much of Blake's anti-scientific mathematics is traceable to Boehme, Harper (1969: 236-39, 242, 245) demonstrates how he represents the struggle between demonic and redemptive forces by a conflict between female numbers (two, three, seven, twelve and twenty-seven) and their male counterparts (one, four, sixteen, thirty-two and sixty-four) and how the fallen world reflects the unfallen in having, for example, four continents, four compass points, and, in its British Isles, four kingdoms and four principal Cathedral Cities.

Albion's Cities are among the many characters from Blake's earlier works who loom large in *Jerusalem*. Of the Twenty-eight—Geoffrey of Monmouth credits ancient Britain with twenty-eight cities, as Frye notes (1947: 130, 440n37)—the oft-mentioned Twenty-four are apt to manifest in the four principal ones. The latter, who are equated with the Zoas (Sloss and Wallis 1926: I, 500), comprise, as Bloom points out (1965: 936), the two chief cities of the Church of England (Canterbury and York), the capital of Scotland (Edinburgh), and the Roman city from which Francis Bacon took his title (Verulam). As Albion's well meaning but sometimes weak Friends, they have been perceived as centres of state religion that will return to authentic Christianity (Erdman 1954a: 439 [475]), the redemptive potential within the natural world (Bloom 1963: 396), and "humanistic achievements" (Curran 1973: 343).

If the Cities are Albion's feeble Friends, his own Children become his mighty enemies, although, as Paley remarks (1983b: 228-29), they are eventually redeemed. Collectively, explains Stevenson (1971: 622-24), they represent all Britons of all periods, including the aggressive nation of the eighteenth century, as well as the warlike ancient Israelites—eighteenth-century Britain and the Old Testament Hebrews are both components of Blake's sick Albion. In depicting the Sons' conflict with their father, Blake draws on the story of Jacob's family and on Hesiod's account of Kronos and his sons to illuminate the conflict of generations (Paley 1983b: 211-13). The Sons have been viewed as elements rising from Albion's unconscious (*ibid.*), and as manifestations of "his affections" (Damon 1967: 211), three of them—Hand, Hyle and Coban—standing for his head, heart and loins (*ibid.*: 15). The twelve have been regarded as falling into three groups of four constituting the accuser, judge and executioner (Damon 1924: 186), and have been described as a "Zodiacal jury of Urizenic Accusers" (Bloom 1963: 372-73) and as "the various types of ordinary fallen man" (Margoliouth 1951: 154). They are the Calvinist Elect (Paley 1983b: 216), and they build Druid temples, including Stonehenge (Damon 1967: 15-16).

The Sons are named after Blake's real and supposed enemies, especially those associated with his trial for sedition at Chichester in January 1804. Ives (1910: 853, 859-61) identifies Thomas Barton Bowen as a lawyer who pleaded at Sussex Sessions, William Brereton as one of the Justices of the Peace at the preliminary hearing at Petworth in October 1803, Trooper [John] Cock (Cox) as Schofield's co-concoctor of false evidence, and John Quantock (Kwantok) and John Peachey as two of the Justices of the Peace on the bench at the trial. Later Keynes (1957) discovers that Lieut. George Hulton (Hutton) preferred the criminal charges on behalf of Schofield and Cock. Coban has been explained as an anagram of Bacon (Sloss and Wallis 1926: II, 232), an allusion to Caliban (Frye 1947: 377), and the publisher Henry Colburn, who was associated with Hayley (Erdman 1969b: 459, citing Adlard). Ives (1910: 860) suggests that Hyle is a distortion of Hayley, and Damon (1924: 187, 436) deduces that he is therefore the bad artist and notes that his name is Greek for "matter," a fact that makes easy his identification with fallen nature (Frye 1947: 402) and with "spiritual nullity" (Bindman 1977: 179). Harper (1961: 184-85) remarks that Thomas Taylor personifies Hyle (i.e. matter), and Curran (1972: 124-26) quotes passages from Taylor demonising the personification. Damon (1967: 192), citing 74:28-29, proposes that Hyle is the heart severed from the head, Wagenknecht (1973: 270) finds him equivalent to Luvah-Orc, and Beer (1969: 178) sees in him the fate of humanity under the power of the female will. Given his place in Blake's history, Schofield's name is largely self-explanatory. It has been understood to signify the accuser and the natural man (Damon 1924: 187), or the Adam of Blake's time, the typical contemporary Englishman (Bloom 1965: 929, citing 7:25-26); the man devoid of imagination and, since all are accusers, the father of humankind (Damon 1967: 361, citing 7:42-43, 60:16); and the spirit of war and destruction (Bindman 1977: 179). Frye (1947: 376) associates him with Joseph, who causes the Fall, one symbol of which is Israel's descent into Egypt, but Paley (1983b: 217) more convincingly treats him as the contrary of Joseph, who forgave his brethren.

The most interesting of Albion's Sons is Hand. Already in 1924 Damon (187, 436) recognises that his name gives him an extra dimension: he is both "Rational Man" and the mechanical hand as opposed to the visionary wing. Thomas Wright (1929: II, 41-42) perceives that his three heads allude to the brothers Leigh, Robert and John Hunt, whose periodical the *Examiner* assailed first Blake's 1808 designs for Blair's *The Grave* and then his Exhibition of 1809. To this, Erdman (1954a: 423-25 [458-61]) adds that the editorial symbol in the *Examiner* is a hand and that Blake's character includes the pro-war press in general and embodies the spirit of accusation. Being corrupted reason, Bloom feels (1963: 373), he functions as Satan and as Urizen's Spectre; less convincingly, Beer (1969: 178) classifies him as "impotent desire." Rose (1964c: 51-52) stresses that he is the misused human hand and a tyrant who, under the government of the female will, keeps the imagination, Merlin, from the natural man, Reuben (32[36]:23-24), but Frye (1947: 376, 448n35) maintains that Hand himself corresponds to Reuben and serves as the agent of the imagination that reaches for power instead of wisdom.

Although they are the Emanations of Albion's Sons, all his Daughters except Gwinefred bear the names of royal women who figure in the twelfth-century 'history' of Britain by Geoffrey of Monmouth (Damon 1924: 187, 438). It has been said that they create the mortal body to detain the soul in Generation (*ibid.*: 437), that they are used by Blake to attack the code of chivalry (Kiralis 1956: 160), that they cut the fibres of Jacob's sons to make them sacrifices to nourish the Sons of Albion (Damon 1967: 202), that they seek to implement the female domination Blake believes is implicit in the adoration of the Virgin Mary (Curran 1973: 343), and that out of perverted love they torture the male sexual passion in the person of Luvah (Paley 1983b: 225-26). The most prominent Daughters are Gwendolen and Cambel, the Emanations respectively of Hyle and Hand. Gwendolen has been perceived as "Selfish Pleasure" (Damon 1924: 187), perverted imagination (Damon 1967: 169), a savage female will (Frye 1947: 373) and one who sacrifices human happiness and liberty to religion (Stevenson 1971: 761). Rooted in terror of sex, her cruelty matches that of the legendary Gwendolen, who persecuted her husband Locrine's illegitimate daughter (Paley 1983b: 227). Wicksteed (1954: 228) identifies her with Wales, and Thomas Wright (1929: I, 101, 114-15) curiously speculates that she has an original in Mrs. Chetwynd, a widow with whom Hayley (Hyle) was helplessly infatuated. Beginning by conceiving Cambel as "False Inspiration," "Restricted Sex" and the female will (1924: 187, 462), Damon later decides she is "perverted Reason" (1967: 169).

The most pathetic victim of the Daughters is Luvah. Frye (1947: 397) sees him as a version of fallen Albion, whose fragmentation his cruel sacrifice re-enacts, and also (372) as Edom, Israel's enemy whence comes the Messiah (Is. lxiii.1), and as France, fount of revolution. However, to Damon (1967: 145), he seems to be rather Napoleonic France, transformed from love to hatred. Psychologically, he is the sexual drive that, repressed by Albion, emerges in a perverted form to tear apart the individual and impel nations to war (Paley 1983b: 172-76).

In Blake's last epic, fallen Luvah's fallen Emanation, Vala, is sometimes also an Emanation of Albion (cf. Stevenson 1971: 625). Murray (1974a: 13) argues that she is Lu-vah reversed—hate, lust and revenge instead of love. Like Jerusalem, she is both a woman and a city—in her case, the city is Babylon (Stevenson 1971: 683). She remains a manifestation of nature, and Deen (1983: 196-97) describes her as communal nature worship that destroys brotherhood and promotes war. In the individual, she is the state of attachment to past achievement blocking continued creativity (Bloom 1963: 378): if one tries to give Jerusalem a fixed form, she turns into Vala (Frosch 1974: 181-82).

As Wicksteed emphasises (1954: 25-26, 165), England or Britannia, Albion's consort in Eternity, contains both Vala and Jerusalem, but with the Fall these become, Paley recognises (1983b: 178), the Hagar or Sinai and Sarah or Jerusalem of Gal.

iv.22-26. Raine, indeed, (1968: I, 204) believes that the Vala of *The Four Zoas* has split into the Jerusalem and Vala of the final epic—Vala was formerly, she alleges, both the "Sinless Soul" of *FZ* 128:25/ E397/ IX, 455 and the Shadowy Female. Murry (1933: 290) sees a link between the two in Mary, who as Vala, bears the mortal Jesus and as Jerusalem beholds his "Spiritual Risen Body" (62:14).

Both Blake and his critics like to define Jerusalem as liberty. This liberty has been explained as the antithesis of nature (Damon 1924: 188); as the liberty that co-exists with brotherhood (Sloss and Wallis 1926: II, 182) and is its foundation (Damon 1967: 211); as spiritual liberty (Blackstone 1949: 161); as social and political liberty (Erdman 1954a: 428 [463-64]); and as the redeemed human community of Is. lxv.17-18 and Heb. xiii.14 (Paley 1983b: 120, 135-36). However, these phrases give a bloodless and incomplete conception of Blake's exquisite and long-suffering heroine. She is a collective being containing all Albion's emanations (Percival 1938: 17) and a multitude of minute particulars (Blackstone 1949: 63). She is the Bride of Christ (*ibid.*: 63-64; cf. Rev. xxi.2) as well as the sister or daughter of Albion and mother of human souls (Raine 1968: I, 206). Among her antecedents, as Percival observes (*loc. cit.*), is the Shekinah, the female Divine Presence of the Cabbala. Ansari (1969: 204-05, 214-16) remarks how closely the end of the Shekinah's separation from God resembles the wandering Jerusalem's eventual reunion with Albion. Pressing the argument further, Spector (1984: 11-12, 15, 18-19) seems to assert that the Shekinah and Jerusalem, both of whom endure exile from the Fall to its reversal, are identical. Jerusalem also has affinities with the Gnostic Sophia (Percival, *loc. cit.*) and the Gnostic Mother of the Living, who sustains souls (Curran 1972: 126-27). She is sometimes (e.g. Wicksteed 1954: 1) thought of as the soul of Albion, from whom she differs in being inside Los's furnaces of affliction throughout the poem instead of entering them at the end (Erdman 1974: 372). Clearly she is an element of his being, and she has been described as his "instinctive longing for and knowledge of Eternal Life" (Margoliouth 1951: 152), the spirit of love, kindness and self-sacrifice (Wicksteed 1954: 33, 227), Albion's lost power of undistorted, immediate perception (Fisher 1961: 223-24), and the "outward form of" his "creative energies" (Marks 1976: 64). Insofar as Jerusalem is the

Emanation of Britain, she is paired with Shiloh, who, as the Emanation of France (Damon 1967: 371), represents the liberty lost under Napoleon's rule (Bloom 1963: 403).

The Children of Jerusalem may be Blake's works of art (Margoliouth 1951: 153) or human beings who have undergone a spiritual rebirth (Raine 1968: I, 207). Frye (1947: 378) writes that her sixteen Sons, who are also the Sons of Los and who consist of the four never generated (71:50-51) together with Jacob's sons, represent the ideal of human unity; her Daughters, states Paley (1983b: 184), are facets of herself or her surrogates. Among her other surrogates, Paley (1983b: 184-85) appropriately singles out Erin. With her rainbow and her protective Spaces, western Erin has been associated not only with Ireland, whose name she bears, but also with America (Damon 1924: 440), with the body (*ibid.*)—for Tharmas's quarter is the west—and with the power of vision dimmed at the Fall (Frye 1947: 380). As Ireland, she shelters Albion from the Atlantic's waters of error just as her symbol the rainbow protects him from another flood (Margoliouth 1951: 153). Like Jerusalem, she represents freedom, for Blake profoundly sympathises with Daniel O'Connell's campaign for the repeal of the 1800 Act of Union with Britain (Erdman 1954a: 445-47 [482-84]). Conveniently, Ireland has twice sixteen counties, and sixteen (four squared), as opposed to twelve (four times the demonic three), is a Blakean number of perfection. Wicksteed (1954: 142) associates Erin with the innocence of childhood and Kiralis (1959: 195) with the innocence of love and the body, while Murray (1974a: 23-24) praises her as the representative of the visionary west in the Ulroic east.

Certain characters in *Jerusalem* are absent, or almost so, from the earlier epics. Of these the most significant are Arthur, Merlin, Joseph and—most prominent—Reuben. Quoting the *Descriptive Catalogue*, which states that "The stories of Arthur are the acts of Albion" (E543/ K578), Sloss and Wallis (1926: II, 149) reasonably maintain that Arthur's death and prophesied resurrection are a version of Albion's fall and regeneration, and Worrall (1977b: 203-06) accordingly perceives Arthur as a type of the woman-dominated warrior. However, Bloom (1963: 403), closer to Damon's notion (1924: 456) that he is "enslaved Logic," asserts that the Arthur of *Jerusalem* is a different character from the Arthur of the *Catalogue* and, as the first British monarch, he is

Albion's Spectre. The legendary Merlin's succumbing to the wiles of the enchantress Vivien invites Damon's interpretation that he is imagination seduced by matter or the female will but not wholly obliterated (1924: 449). Similarly persuasive is the reading of Joseph's being sold into Egypt as the betrayal of innocence (Damon 1967: 223-24) or of vision (Beer 1969: 174-75). Blake follows tradition in treating him as a type of Christ (Paley 1973b: 137), and his famous coat may be the physical world (*ibid.*) or the flesh (Damon 1967: 224).

In Genesis, the life of Joseph is saved when Reuben dissuades their brothers from killing him, but Reuben also lies with the concubine of their father, Jacob, who calls him "Unstable as water" (xlix.4). Frye rightly conceives Blake's Reuben as the natural man (1947: 369) or "Ordinary human life" (1966: 189). In this he is endorsing Damon's perception (1924: 185, 189) that he represents the carnally minded governed by their physical bodies—bodies that Los creates to limit their fall, Reuben being the Limit of Contraction. Wicksteed (1954: 180) sees in him unsatisfied male sexuality, and Beer (1969: 174) kindness without vision. Mellor (1974: 311) blames his condition on Hand; Doskow (1982: 77) holds Vala responsible.

Blake also alludes to the tribe of Reuben, which settled east of the Jordan outside the Promised Land. By sending him across the Jordan, Los is limiting his degeneration, and by bending his senses he is giving them form, which opens a way for imagination (Bloom 1963: 393-94). Stevenson (1971: 686) holds rather that Los's treatment of Reuben's senses adjusts them for his survival in Vala's world, and Paley (1983b: 271) sees in it a parody of judicial mutilation. Paley also (305) reconstructs this character's story from Blake's scattered fragments: Reuben sleeps on a stone, grows roots, suffers the cutting of his fibres, divides, has his senses bound, wanders widely, and is guided by Los into the Promised Land, which he has hitherto fled out of an Oedipal passion for his mother (nature), to whom he gave mandrakes, a sexually symbolic plant (93:7-8, alluding to Gen. xxx.14).

A known name like Reuben or Arthur provides at least a starting point for an investigation of a character's meaning, but many of Blake's names are of his own invention. In a stimulating article, De Luca (1978) argues that these are frequently grouped in clusters within which they divide, generate each other, and metamorphose, and together with the familiar names form patterns parallel to those of the mythological narrative and of its sustaining intellectual concepts. In *Jerusalem*, he proposes, the mixture of names from diverse sources mimics Albion's fragmented state, but near the conclusion proper names drop out of sight until only Los, Albion, Jesus and Jerusalem are left, and finally only Jerusalem remains. It should be noted, however, that there are several other proper names, including Golgonooza, in pl. 98.

The ending of the poem is one of its most sharply disputed elements. Some critics accept Damon's well grounded assurance (1924: 193) that the fallen world is permanently annihilated and agree with Bloom (1963: 433) that only Eternity and Beulah remain now that, as Paley conceives it (1983b: 122), the transition is made from the Seventh Eye of God to the Eighth. (Deen, however, [1983: 230] believes another fall is always possible.) Others assert with Mitchell (1978: 180-81) that the fallen world persists and, as Gallant is convinced (1978: 181-83), the mental war for liberation must be fought again and again. A third category suppose with Kroeber (1973: 365) that *Jerusalem* treats only of this world: Blake is said to describe how with words, visual images, musical notes and gestures we create our own perceptions (Mellor 1974: 329-30); how Albion becomes the Divine Vision, all the objects he perceives are Jerusalem, reproduction has been replaced by utterance, and all environment is emanation (Frosch 1974: 100, 173-74); how language, which creates the only reality we know, should be used (Adams 1975: 165-66); and how all human activities harmonise in a society blessed with fourfold vision (Ferguson 1978: 189).

Details

1:4--6 The two rocks and the spectrous power correspond to the three stones of a Druid trilithon and to the two cherubim and Jehovah's presence in the Ark of the Covenant, the stone beneath to the Druid altar and Hebraic Mercy Seat (Miner 1961: 57-58). The rocks and stone are portions of the Door of Death in the design (Lesnick 1969: 52).

pl. 3 **SHEEP   GOATS**—This allusion to Matt. xxv.32-33 hints that Christ is conducting the Last Judgment (Wicksteed

1954: 113) and that the poem will separate the two classes (Stevenson 1971: 628). These classes constitute the public, which Albion on one level represents, and like other contraries they are to be reconciled through forgiveness (Mitchell 1978: 185, 197, 200).

Erdman (1964a: 10) implies that Blake deleted portions of the text in a mood of despondency at the neglect he suffered, Ferguson (1978: 167) that he was obliterating any suggestion of an apology since his role was like that described in Ezek. iii.8-9.

God of Fire and Lord of Love—Moses and Jesus, wrath and love (Damon 1924: 434); Jesus as the solar God of Fire nearly identical with Los (Blackstone 1949: 375); Boehme's First and Second Principles combined (Paley 1970: 257-58).

Poem l. 4 In the eighteenth century it was widely held that writing originated at the revelation on Sinai (Damon 1924: 434)—cf. Exod. xxxi.18 (Damon 1967: 374). At the end of *Jerusalem*, this writing becomes the Human speech of Eternity (Deen 1983: 226).

Greek quotation—"All power is given unto me in heaven and in earth" (Matt. xxviii.18).

When this Verse...necessary to each other—There are echoes here of Milton's defence of blank verse prefixed to *PL* and of Edward Bysshe's *The Art of English Poetry* (1702) (Damon 1924: 435). Blake refers to the tradition of high, middle and low styles (Bloom 1963: 338) and expresses a preference for the cadences of the Authorised Version (Bloom 1971: 77-78). His "terrific," "mild" and "prosaic" allude to the sublime, pathetic, and philosophical or discursive (Paley 1983b: 57, 69).

4:5 **this mild song**—Either the phrase refers to 4:6-21 (Bloom 1963: 368) or "mild" is ironic and it refers to the whole epic (Gallant 1978: 157). The singer addresses both Albion and Blake (Harper 1974: 70).

4:6 **sleeper**—fallen Albion (Lesnick 1970: 391), also Blake at Felpham (Harper 1974: 70), or Albion and Blake (Johnson and Grant 1979: 313).

4:10 **A black water**—the Sea of Time and Space (Damon 1924: 435); both Albion's shed blood and the Atlantic Ocean that submerged Atlantis (Bloom 1963: 369); perhaps an allusion to the River Blackwater at Malden, site of a Viking victory [991 A. D.] (Paley 1983b: 76, 198).

4:14-17 Cf. Prov. viii.22-30, the Wisdom there evoked being Jerusalem (Bloom 1963: 369). Jerusalem should be Jesus' Bride (Damon 1967: 211).

4:29-31 Britain, no longer part of the ancient commonwealth of the Atlantic, has become narrowly possessive (Erdman 1954a: 428 [463]). Cf. Ezek. xxix.3—Albion is aligned with Pharoah (Ostriker 1977: 998). The Wolds are serpent-shaped, Snowdon signifies the death of the last bard, and the three other peaks mark county or national borders (Paley 1983b: 197).

4:34 Blake's source is the marriage of the Thames and the Medway in *FQ* IV.xi (Bloom 1963: 370); these rivers belong to Beulah and represent wedded love (Damon 1967: 43, 267), which Albion suppresses (Paley 1983b: 198).

5:1-15 Albion undergoes psychic fragmentation (Ostriker 1977: 998), liberty ("Jerusalem") is suppressed in Britain (Schorer 1946: 365-66), and the ideas of Newton and Locke deceive Oxford, Cambridge and London (Blackstone 1949: 160).

5:28 **the eastern gate**—the gate of the emotions (Damon 1924: 437); see 13:13-14 for its strength (Paley 1983b: 215).

5:31 South and north have been identified with reason and the spirit (Damon 1924: 437) and with the Neoplatonic gate of spirits and gate of mortals (Stevenson 1971: 632-33). Ostriker (1977: 998) suggests the Sons are reborn into history from the north.

5:34 The loom weaves Vala's Veil of external nature (Damon 1924: 437); the furnace produces stony, opaque forms from nature's soft, vegetable texture (Nelson 1974: 134-35). Beryl is the colour of the wheels of Ezekiel's vision (Damon 1967: 42, alluding to i.16 and x.9). Implying that the furnace is that of the only partly fallen Los, Raine (1968: II, 25, 287n54) asserts that it is in one respect the human body; she also associates this ultimately redeeming apparatus with Paracelsus' declaration that when nature is consumed a beryl remains (1968: II, 6, 156, 287n53).

5:46-53 Paracelsus speaks of all bodies as but "coagulated smoke" (cited Damon 1924: 438-39)—cf. *FZ* 126:4-5/ E395/ IX, 361-62n. Stevenson (1971: 634) traces the image to the smoke of a blast furnace. Citing *FZ* 24:1/ E314/ II, 18, Ostriker (1977: 998-99) writes that the void of error draws in truth.

5:54-65 Jerusalem splits into her essence, guarded by Beulah's Daughters until 48:18, and a wandering cloud (Damon 1967: 207). Damon (1924: 439) and others agree "the Immortal Form" (l. 55) is Albion.

6:6-7 Los-Blake persists in serving England (Stevenson 1971: 636) despite her treatment of her prophets (Gallant 1978: 157-58).

7:14 **thy stolen Emanation**—possibly a reference to Stothard's stealing Blake's idea of a picture of Chaucer's Canterbury Pilgrims (Damon 1924: 439) or to Cromek's handing over the engraving of Blake's illustrations to Blair's *The Grave* to Schiavonetti (Erdman 1951a: 215).

7:18-26 A cruel population inhabits the world (Damon 1924: 439). Babel, Nineveh, Ashur and Aram are south, west, north and east respectively (Kiralis 1959: 207). Damon (*loc. cit.*) cites *PL*, XII, 24ff for Nimrod, whose ascendancy, Bloom remarks (1965: 930), makes war the norm. See Gen. x (Stevenson 1971: 637).

7:25-26 Schofield is an anti-saviour coming out of Edom (Bloom 1963: 373, alluding to Is. lxiii.1), whose people are vilified in Obadiah (Kiralis 1959: 208); there is something of him in all the generations of Adam (Murray 1974a: 15).

7:30-37 Christianity degenerates into natural religion, and France is martyred by England (Bloom 1965: 930). See also *FZ* 25:40/ E317/ II, 72n and *FZ* 25:41/ E317/ II, 73n.

7:44-45 Britain had fought wars for the sake of markets for its cloth (Hilton 1983: 120-21).

7:44-49 An awkward attempt, not repeated, to associate Albion's Sons with the demonic number nine (Frye 1947: 376).

7:63-64 Later critics endorse Damon's interpretation (1924: 439) that even corrupt religion preserves a vital seed of truth; Raine (1968: II, 238) observes that physical birth offers the opportunity to win redemption.

7:65 **holy Generation**—Sexual union joins contraries (Sloss and Wallis 1926: I, 455), and is central to the relationship of time and Eternity (Murry 1933: 295-96). The reference seems to be to Jerusalem, "the earthly manifestation of heaven" (Stevenson 1971: 640).

7:71-8:4   Robert Hunt, who abused Blake's art in the *Examiner*, sits at his furnace or workplace, but Blake responds with his whirling mace (Erdman 1954a: 422 [457]).

8:1-2   The brook is Tyburn Brook (Stevenson 1971: 640). The three pleasure gardens named are spectrous resorts and blots on the west or visionary region (Sloss and Wallis 1926: I, 456).

8:20   **Babel & Shinar**—The savage spirit of the Babylonians and Assyrians prevails in the contemporary world (Stevenson 1971: 641).

8:25-26   The Spectre observes from without the evil he has caused (Sloss and Wallis 1926: I, 456). The cruelty evident in history is the product of impulses from which Los himself is not immune (Webster 1983: 273).

8:27   **London Stone**—a relic of ancient Jerusalem, the principal Druid sacrificial altar, the point from which distances were measured in Roman Britain, and the contemporary place of military execution in Hyde Park (Erdman 1951b: 190).

8:32   For Blake, circumcision is "the sacrifice of the Selfhood" (Damon 1924: 439), the excision of "the Not Human" of that which veils the clear outline of identity (Rose 1968a, quoting *M* 41:1), and the sign of God's Covenant with Abraham that initiates the line of prophecy (Riede 1981: 550-51). See also 55:66n.

8:43   **Hand has absorb'd all his Brethren**—The press has corrupted the British public—9:4-5 refers to its war propaganda (Erdman 1954a: 424-25 [460]).

9:9   **a Body of Death**—a mortal body—cf. E564/ K615-16 (Sloss and Wallis 1926: II, 147). Cf. Rom. vii.24, AV marginal reading: "this body of death."

9:18-19   **the spiritual sword/ That lays open the hidden heart** —wrath that does work seemingly cruel but necessary for redemption (Price 1964: 400); the faculty in Los that makes indignant, tragic art out of life's injustices (Ostriker 1977: 999).

9:23-24   Los alludes to the jewels of Eden (Ezek. xxviii.13) and of Aaron's breastplate (Exod. xxviii.17ff) (Miner 1969: 270, 469n40); also of the New Jerusalem (Rev. xxi.19-21) (Stevenson 1971: 643).

9:26-27   These lines may refer to the fearfulness of Los's poetic themes (Bloom 1963: 375-76), or to the Children of Albion,

who, representing the life of the world, provide his raw mate-
rial (Mitchell 1978: 202), or to the imperfection of his art
(Deen 1983: 208; cf. Beer 1969: 196).

9:34 **the Spaces of Erin**—a defence against the defenders of
falsehood (Bloom 1963: 376) and "creative" deeds with powers
of preservation in the fallen world (Bloom 1965: 939).

10:7-16 A negation separates the contraries (Altizer 1967: 176).
An abstract or negation has been understood as the reason that
rejects all vision (Beer 1969: 197), as a rejection of one of the
contraries (Stevenson 1971: 644), as a perverted form of truth
(Rose 1973: 87-88), and even as a legal prohibition (Damon
1924: 440). Adams (1970: 731) believes that Blake is challeng-
ing Locke's distinction between primary and secondary quali-
ties and between objectivity and subjectivity. In l. 14 "obj-
ecting" means both saying "No" and objectifying (Hilton 1983:
251).

10:31 **my own Children**—either mortals or the products of
prophecy (Sloss and Wallis 1926: I, 460). Unlike Milton's
God, who punishes the Satan who tempts his human children,
Los comforts the Spectre who tempts his (Wagenknecht 1973:
264-66).

10:37 **thy Sins**—acts proceeding from prophecy and vision
(Ostriker 1977: 1000).

10:37-59 The now pitiable Spectre's state may be based on the
very similar state of Hayley's friend the poet Cowper, who was
convinced he was predestined to damnation (Paley 1968).
There may be echoes here of speeches by Milton's Satan (*PL*,
IV, 32ff) and Spenser's Despair (*FQ* I.ix.38-47) (Bloom 1965:
931). The Spectre is guilty of "wanhope," despair of God's
mercy, a sin denounced in Chaucer's "Parson's Tale" (J. War-
ner 1984: 109-10).

10:42-43 The Spectre laments his sins, which have the same
source as the poet's inspirations (Damon 1924: 440).

11:4 **the clay ground**—both the etcher's ground and the natural
man, the foundations of art and of the real Human (Rose 1973:
89).

11:8-15 Back in London from Felpham (Paley 1983b: 262),
Blake-Los creates in his furnaces flawless works (Damon 1924:
440) along with designs (Erdman 1974: 290). Stevenson, how-

ever, (1971: 646) considers the Father of l. 14 to be not Los but Albion.

11:19-20 Beer (1969: 198) regards Sabrina and Ignoge as positive characters, but Ostriker (1977: 1000) more convincingly deems the phrase "light and love" ironic.

11:21-23 In Gen. xxx.14-16, Reuben gives his mother, Leah, mandrakes. Since they were held to confer sexual allure and Leah had a rival in Rachel, the reference may be to family dissension (Stevenson 1971: 647). Alternatively, it may be to Reuben's representing the natural man, symbolised by the mandrakes (Bloom 1965: 931), and to his Oedipal attraction to his mother (Paley 1983b: 217); or to Schofield's undermining spiritual liberty (Bloom, *loc. cit.*) or guarding Reuben, the ordinary sensual man (Damon 1967: 361).

12:11-14 God's finger touches the seventh furnace, which is also the Seventh Eye (Jesus) to impose a limit on the Fall (Damon 1924: 440). The "mathematic power" may signify the rationalistic view of nature that will come to be seen as incredible (Wicksteed 1954: 131), the rigid fixity imposed by mathematics (Ault 1974: 70-71), or the traditional symbolism of divine numbers (Harper 1969: 236-37). For Apollyon, see Rev. ix.11 and Bunyan's *The Pilgrim's Progress*. To Damon (*loc. cit.*), the "Falshood" is untruth that must be stated to be disproved; to Percival (1938: 225), it is the error given necessary embodiment in the material world. Altizer (1967: 28) believes it is the "mathematic power" that bestows a body on error that is cast off.

12:24-13:29 Golgonooza is as yet imperfect with its closed western gate (Damon 1924: 441), its non-human images and entrances that terrify the fallen (Bloom 1963: 380-81), and its elements amenable to straightforward allegorical description (Damrosch 1980: 320-21). It is quite distinct from Jerusalem (Frosch 1974: 156-67) and may have only potential existence until in pl. 98 it is free from closed gates and sentries (Gallant 1978: 158, 178). Though it is four-dimensional (Damon 1924: 440), or more precisely a tesseract (Paley 1983b: 137), as the New Gologotha it replaces the Old Golgotha of the district around Tyburn, place of execution (Margoliouth 1951: 156), in the locality of which there is much development at this time (Erdman 1954a: 438 [474-75]) distinguished especially by

John Nash's architecture (Johnson and Grant 1979: 317). Golgonooza is a city not only of art but also of forgiveness (Blackstone 1949: 161) and of millenial liberty—hence its association through Erin with the Irish freedom struggle (Paley 1983b: 266-67). Being, as 12:25 shows, built of words, it has a close affinity with Blake's Eternity (De Luca 1982: 98-100, citing 95:9 and 98:35-36). Symbolically it is a mandala, the study of which heals psychic disintegration like Albion's (Bogan 1981: 92-93). In constructing it, Webster argues (1983: 273), Los is assuaging his anger against Albion by means of art.

12:25-26 **where was the burying-place/ Of soft Ethinthus? near Tyburn's fatal Tree?**—The theme is resurrection. Ethinthus may be an exemplar of druidic preference for secret love (Bloom 1963: 380, citing E 14:1-5), or the physical flesh, including that of the executed criminal (Damon 1967: 130-31). According to Tolley (1970b: 5-6), burying Ethinthus implies denial of resurrection.

12:27 **Zion's hill's most ancient promontory**—the site commemorated in M 4:21 (Wicksteed 1954: 254-55); a site on Mt. Moriah, scene of the sacrifice of Isaac, the Crucifixion, and God's past and imminent epiphanies (Tolley 1970b: 3-4).

12:27-28 **mournful/ Ever weeping Paddington**—Here were found Tyburn (Wicksteed 1954: 158), the place where the violated corpses of Cromwell and his colleagues were reburied (Erdman 1954a: 438 [474]), the dwellings of poverty-stricken Irish workers (*ibid.*), and St. George's Burying Ground (Miner 1969: 256).

12:38 **furniture**—perhaps Blake's Lambeth books (Sloss and Wallis 1926: I, 464).

12:48 **Each within other**—"fourfoldedness contains fourfoldedness within fourfoldedness to infinity" (Armstrong 1982: 95).

12:55-56 That it is the location of the sun's meridian suggests the identification of the zenith and the head with the south and antithetically of the nadir and the loins with the north, leaving the east where the moon rises for the centre and the heart, and the west where it sets for the circumference and the body (Percival 1938: 15). The north is also associated with ice, darkness and ancient savage creeds, the east with war and reactionary governments (Stevenson 1971: 635). The west may be linked with the circumference because it is the region of the ocean (Frye 1947: 275); the east may be unapproachable because God is seen in the sunrise (Raine 1968: II, 264) or because He passed through the visionary closed east gate of Ezek. xliv.1-2 (Miner 1969: 282).

12:61-13:19 Of the four Living Creatures of Ezekiel—man, lion, ox and eagle—traditionally identified with the Evangelists, Blake replaces St. John's eagle with cog wheels to signify the advance of Deism (Witke 1970: 276-77).

13:6-11 The Western Gate, which corresponds to the circumference, is shut until the Day of Judgment and until the end of the poem, when the artistic form is complete (Mitchell 1978: 177-78). Being Tharmas's (Bloom 1965: 932), it is closed against the [unfallen] body and its pleasures (Damon 1924: 441), but also against the Atlantic, for shutting one's Western Gate means blocking oneself off from Eden, which Blake identifies with the Western land—America or Atlantis—cut off by the Flood (Raine 1968: II, 268). The lost Eden is, in esoteric tradition, the body (*ibid.*: I, 337-38)—cf. *FR*, ll. 183-85.

13:23 **a threefold curtain of ivory & fine linen & ermine**—the body composed of bones, flesh and skin (Raine 1968: II, 270); perhaps "the veil of sexuality" (Ostriker 1977: 1001).

13:25 At the heart of the mandala, Christ is generated in the human soul and Eternity meets time (Raine 1968: II, 272). The palace represents Eternity, the looms time (Harper 1969: 244).

13:26-29 The cubing of four enhances its perfection; the spirits of the four elements are numbered in thousands (Stevenson 1971: 650).

13:38-50 Percival (1938: 67-68) believes Blake's familiar symbols of the fallen world have sources in the Bible, rabbinical writings, Dante, Virgil and Milton. Damon (1924: 441) specifies *Aeneid*, VI and the *Inferno*. The gates of Golgonooza, Armstrong observes (1982: 106-07), are fashioned by mastery over the same materials that are uncontrolled in the surrounding chaos.

13:56-14:1 Nelms (1974: 88) notes the very close association of Golgonooza with the whole content of historical time, and Ostriker (1977: 1002) adds that art must bestow a body on error.

The six thousand years of history seem to change to eight thousand at 33(37):7 and to eight thousand five hundred at

48:36 and 83:52. Damon (1924: 450) proposes that humankind spends eight thousand and Los eight thousand five hundred years outside Eternity, but that time only lasts for six millenia; Frye (1947: 399) plausibly maintains that a Druid age precedes Adam's creation, which begins those millenia; Bloom's suggestion (1965: 936) that Blake is unintentionally inconsistent receives some support from a similar discrepancy in *FR*, ll. 7-8 and 90.

14:1 Blake may be challenging Plato's contention in the *Parmenides* that there are no eternal Ideas of hair and dust (Harper 1961: 94-95).

14:4-7 The False Tongue is endowed with the chaos associated with water and the destructiveness of fire and identified with the flaming sword of Gen. iii.24 blocking the way back to Eden—see Jas. iii.6 (Frye 1947: 282).

14:16-30 Blake here describes his own works (Damon 1924: 442), which are analogous to Golgonooza as 12:45-46 indicates (Paley 1983b: 266). Their golden, ruby, iron and (closed) western gates stand respectively for sensory, emotional, intellectual and (excluded) explicit meaning (*ibid.*: 266-67). Sloss and Wallis (1926: I, 468) define Los's Children as "spiritual agents in mundane life," and Ostriker (1977: 1002) identifies their gates with "the doors of perception" of *MHH*, pl. 14. According to Stevenson (1971: 653), the "Universe within" is confined to the Daughters: women's beauty affords access to the edge of Beulah.

14:25-28 The missing fourth region (see 18:1) is probably death or Eternity (Stevenson 1971: 653-54). In the fallen world, art is imperfect (Bloom 1965: 932).

14:31 Jerusalem's good intentions do not immunise her against bad influences (Stevenson 1971: 654).

15:1-3 The accusers threaten to take over Reuben, the natural man (Bloom 1963: 383). Evil (Schofield) everywhere corrupts weakness (Reuben) (Stevenson 1971: 654).

15:7 **Shadow**—of the Spectre's frustrated desire (Damon 1924: 442).

15:14-17 The Loom of Locke, driven by the water of matter, by materialism (Harper 1961: 169) or of perverted learning (Murray 1974a: 17-18), weaves the Veil of Vala (Raine 1968: II, 183) and is associated with the cruelties of the textile industry (DiSalvo 1983: 50). Blake combines Locke's confession that the essence of the universe is unknowable with Newton's mathematical map of it (Ault 1974: 91).

15:21-25 Around Los's anvil of self-sacrifice ("death"), his Sons cut fibres to free humanity (Damon 1924: 442). The cutting is their counter-action to Reuben's enrooting—i.e. art works in opposition to nature (Bloom 1963: 384). The cutting and enrooting mark the separation of Israel from Albion—cf. 63[:41] (Stevenson 1971: 655). Los promotes commerce ("an Ox of gold"), but his Sons cut oaks from the hills to build ships for imperialist war (Erdman 1969b: 464).

15:25-28 The promise of the embodied human's (Reuben's) redemption only begins with Abram, who fled from Chaldea and became Abraham (Damon 1924: 442). His flight to establish Israel initiates the natural man's return to imagination (Bloom 1963: 384). Reuben's enrooting is the expression of an Oedipal wish to return to the womb (Paley 1983b: 305).

15:34 **the Valley of the Son of Hinnom**—the place of child sacrifice—formerly to a pagan god (Jer. vii.31-32), now to the Moloch of war (Bloom 1965: 933).

16:26 See Rom. viii.21-22 (Tolley 1973: 128).

16:30 An allusion to the Israelites who survived the Babylonian conquests of Jerusalem (Wicksteed 1954: 142-43). Stevenson (1971: 657) compares FZ 99:25ff/ E372/ VIII, 25ff.

16:31-34 An influx from Eternity enters the world through the bardic country of Wales (Stevenson 1971: 657). Wales, which resisted imperialism, is placed before England (Crehan 1984: 328).

16:28-60 There is much to be said for Damon's opinion (1924: 442) that this passage may be "the worst place in the book" and for Bloom's judgment (1963: 384) that "No defence on poetic grounds of such a list is possible." Suggested models are Num. ii (Bloom 1965: 933) and a three-page enumeration of the Twelve Tribes in John Wood's *The Origin of Building: or, the Plagiarism of the Heathens Detected* (1741) (Paley 1983b: 159). The underlying theme may be the return and redemption of the Twelve Tribes (Damon 1967: 202) or the fallen state of the counties allotted to twelve rather than sixteen patrons (Harper 1969: 245-46). Armstrong (1982: 92) comments that Los's vision of order follows Blake's vision of chaos.

16:61-69 Los's halls, which Stevenson (1971: 658) locates in Golgonooza, are not Damon's "Cosmic Memory" (1924: 443-44) but a repository of the archetypes of all earthly life (Fisher 1961: 218-19), which are found in the Bible (Bloom 1963: 385). Rose (1966: 115) identifies the sculptures with the "Visionary forms dramatic" of 98:28, though Damrosch (1980: 329) thinks their rigidity a sign that even art, an activity of the fallen world, has limitations.

17:1-15 What Los fears may be total surrender to his own inspiration (Damon 1924: 187), the seductiveness of nature's external beauty (Percival 1938: 276), participation in physical generation (Damrosch 1980: 203), or surrender to his own sexuality, which he channels into his Spectre (Paley 1983b: 255). Wicksteed (1954: 143-44) thinks Blake resists a temptation to adultery.

17:13 In this ambiguous line, the Spectre of the Living may be imagination's mask when it contends with nature (Bloom 1965: 933), Los's Spectre seduced by nature's beauty (Marks 1974: 38-39), the element in Los not cut off from the eternal world (Raine 1968: I, 264), or imaginative vision (Hilton 1983: 172).

17:23 They—the Daughters of Albion, enemies of genuine love and vision (Sloss and Wallis 1926: I, 474); women who tempt Blake (Ostriker 1977: 1003).

17:25-26 false/ And Generating Love—natural religion (Sloss and Wallis 1926: I, 474); fleshly love (Raine 1968: I, 212).

17:41-43 Armstrong (1982: 96, 102-03) holds that failure to bestow form on his Spectre at this pivotal point causes Los to divide from him and be contaminated by the realm of non-being that dominates the rest of the chapter.

17:48-56 Los is separated from Enitharmon, his inspiration (Damon 1924: 187). She is the pity of *BU* 13:53 that divides the soul (Damon 1967: 211). When the artistic mind cherishes its work as an external object, it turns from inspiration to spectral, empirical resources (Marks 1974: 34-35).

17:57 from his back—Los turns his back on his Spectre (Armstrong 1982: 103).

17:59 Bath and Canterbury have been taken to symbolise physical and spiritual healing (Damon 1924: 444), physical and spiritual enmity (Bloom 1965: 933), humanitarianism and moral law (Damon 1967: 38), and corruption and vision (Beer 1969: 220). Los will not permit druidical Schofield to identify himself with any of the cathedral cities (Armstrong 1982: 91). Blake seems to have suspected that Schofield came from Bath (Erdman 1954a: 442 [478]) and perhaps heard of his death in Canterbury in 1812 (Miner 1969: 466).

18:1-4 The Outside spread Without is the external, material world misconceived as outside the perceiver's mind (Adams 1963: 31). It is the fallen body, whereas the Outside spread Within is the fallen mind (Frosch 1974: 77-79). The identity itself is reduced to an outline (Armstrong 1982: 103). Ostriker (1977: 1003) notes that the image, like Golgonooza's, is four-dimensional. The passage appears to mean that the being has become all externals, its essence is clouded over, and its true identity (defined by outline) is blotted out by externality.

18:8 **Three Immense Wheels**—accuser, judge, and executioner (Damon 1924: 444); the childhood, manhood and old age of Vegetable Man, who lacks the fourth region, Eternity (Rose 1970c: 443-44); the endless cycles ruling the material world (Marks 1974: 36).

18:11-12, 19 For Jerusalem as harlot, see Ezek. xvi, xxiii (Margoliouth 1948: 309). For idolatry under oaks, see Ezek. [vi.13], for happiness under vine and fig tree, Mic. iv.4 (Helms 1974: 131).

18:26 **the Perfect**—the Elect of *Milton*, the angels of *The Marriage of Heaven and Hell* (Damon 1924: 444). Blake attacks the belief in atonement through an innocent sacrificial victim (Beer 1969: 221).

18:29-30 A bitter allusion to Gal. iv.26 (Helms 1974: 130).

18:32 **the Potter's field**—cemetery for strangers—see Matt. xxvii.7 (Margoliouth 1948: 309) or for paupers and criminals (Ostriker 1977: 1003).

18:39 Hand tyrannised over England (Rose 1964c: 52).

18:44-45 **rending a way in Albion's Loins**—Albion's affliction has a sexual origin (Bloom 1965: 934). The image suggests the destructive action of a celestial plough (Rose 1972a: 42). The Sons rob their father of his masculinity (Paley 1983b: 215). Albion's night is deadly, Beulah's revitalising (Stevenson 1971: 662).

19:1-14 See *FZ* 119:32-120:25/ E388/ IX, 99-135n.

19:16 **His Eon**—his Emanation (Damon 1924: 445).

19:20 **the Twentyfour**—Albion's Sons and Daughters (Damon 1924: 445); more convincingly, the Twenty-four Cathedral Cities (Stevenson 1971: 663).

19:26 **seven diseases**—Refusing to regard them as sins (Stevenson 1971: 663), Blake attributes these characteristic afflictions of spectres to unsatisfied desire (J. Warner 1984: 114).

19:27 **Luvah in his secret cloud**—concealed emotions (Damon 1924: 445). Stevenson (1971: 663) compares *FZ* 39:15ff/ E327-28/ III, 44ff.

19:36 **Circumference...Center**—senses, emotions (Damon 1924: 445); body, heart (Damon 1967: 75). First Albion's circumference is severed from Eternity, then—except in dreams—his centre (Stevenson 1971: 664).

19:39 The rivers of Albion are those of Eden (Stevenson 1971: 664). When Albion falls, his arteries become the source of the fallen world's rivers (Wagenknecht 1973: 268). His inward flight marks the separation of inner and outer, the person and the environment (Frosch 1974: 61).

19:40-47 Damon (1967: 176) perceives Havilah (Gen. ii.11) as unfallen love, Wicksteed (1954: 150) and Raine (1968: I, 209) detect a celebration of the Blakes' happy married life, and Stevenson (1971: 664) praises the harmony between Vala and Jerusalem. Contrariwise, their embrace may be a presexual but ominously unstable union that induces sexual excitement and guilt in Albion (Paley 1983b: 167-72), or a disastrous mixture of freedom and bondage (Bloom 1963: 388), to which Albion's fall is a psychological reaction (Wagenknecht 1973: 268) and which contrasts with the true union of the two Emanations in Britannia (Rose 1963: 47-48, citing 32[36]:28). The Lily of Havilah may be a symbol of Innocence (Damon 1924: 445), but Havilah means sand (Stevenson 1971: 664) and the flower may signify "sterile beauty" (Ostriker 1977: 1004) or "death and moral purity" (Rose, *loc. cit.*).

19:47 **Sighing to melt his Giant beauty**—Cramer (1984: 524) holds that Albion seeks not Blake's Eternity but Freud's infantile oceanic feeling.

20:30-41 Although Stevenson (1971: 666) considers that Vala's weaving of the net separated herself and Jerusalem from Albion, other critics, from Percival (1938: 170, 317) onwards, locate the incident before the Fall, when (Margoliouth 1951: 155) Christ bestowed on Albion unfallen Vala—i. e. the vision of nature's beauty expressed in *Milton*. His rending of the Veil has been explained negatively as indulgence in nature mysticism (Damon 1924: 445) and as beginning to take symbolism for literal truth (Sloss and Wallis 1926: I, 480-81), positively as penetrating to the reality behind the sensible appearance of nature (Raine 1968: II, 184-86), as enacting Christ's rending of the veil of the Temple (Grant 1969: 361-62), as taking Vala's virginity (Ostriker 1977: 1004), and as experiencing the unconscious (Gallant 1978: 159-60). Opposing Bloom's view (1963: 388-89) that Albion was guilty of exclusive devotion to Vala, Grant (*loc. cit.*) observes that his fault lay only in his subsequent condemnation of this sexual act, a condemnation that (Paley 1983b: 168-69) ended the "time of love." Riede (1981: 551-52) maintains that Albion's copulation with Vala is an image in the fallen world of Christ's espousal of Jerusalem.

21:13 **the deep wound of Sin**—the threatening vagina (Webster 1983: 175), which Albion associates with sin (Paley 1983b: 221).

21:14 **costly Robes**—religious rites (Sloss and Wallis 1926: I, 481).

21:16 **Luvahs's Sepulcher**—a state in which the emotions are dead (Damon 1924: 445). Albion will not allow Luvah (passion) to resume his rightful role (Stevenson 1971: 667). The tomb of the spiritually dead natural man (Raine 1968: II, 192, referring to 24:51).

21:19-27 Albion misjudges his Daughters in retrospect (Stevenson 1971: 667), abhors their infantile sexuality (Webster 1983: 275), and cannot even see the innocence of Cordella and Sabrina (Paley 1983b: 221-22).

21:35 **Penmaenmawr & Dhinas-bran**—North Welsh heights, the latter surmounted by an ancient camp (Damon 1967: 103, 325; cf. also Hilton 1981: 199).

21:36 There was much poverty in Manchester, and Liverpool prospered on the slave trade (Paley 1983b: 198).

21:37 **Malden & Colchester**—perhaps an allusion to military and naval unrest at these ports (Damon 1967: 260); the sites respectively of a Viking victory [991 A. D.] and a succession of fortifications (Paley, *loc. cit.*).

21:42-47 Damon's rather vague assertion (1924: 445) that the arks in which the slain Daughters are carried to inspire war are arks of error is clarified by Miner's perception (1961: 50-51) that they are British counterparts to the Ark of the Covenant and symbols of female power based on sexual secrecy. Stevenson (1971: 668) adds that there are allusions to Druid oaks, annually dying fertility gods, and their female equivalent Persephone. Referring to Osiris, Nicholas Warner (1980: 48) notes that Jacob Bryant's *A New System of Mythology* (1774-76) mentions the ark from which that deity was reborn. As the land Abram fled, Chaldea stands for human sacrifice (Mathews 1980a: 157). There is an allusion to the British naval song "Hearts of Oak" (Paley 1983b: 222) and perhaps to the Napoleonic wars (Damon 1967: 76). In 1979 Keynes recognised that "warshipped" is probably not an error but a pun (Kxvi).

21:50 **her scarlet Veil**—a reference to the export of textiles (Erdman 1974: 319); the mortal body (Paley 1983b: 195). Stevenson (1971: 668) thinks Vala is turning into the Scarlet Woman.

22:1-4 Humans crucify nature until Nimrod exploits her for war (Damon 1924: 445). Before taking Vala for their goddess, Albion's Sons crucify her (Damon 1967: 16). She delights in the lie that Nimrod is Jehovah (Bloom 1963: 389), which is the view of Schofield, the New Adam (Bloom 1965: 934). She claims that war (Nimrod) has rescued her from the moral accusations of Albion's Sons (Ostriker 1977: 1004). Damon (1967: 299) judges that "of" is accidentally omitted after "Huntsman"; in hunting humans, Nimrod is hunting God.

22:8-9 Cf. Is. xxii.1-5 (Sloss and Wallis 1926: I, 483).

22:26-32 See 21:16n. For the cup and knife, see 63:39-40. Albion summons physical nature to take possession of him (Raine 1968: I, 310).

22:34 **Iron Wheels of War**—the wheels of industry that sustain the conflict (Rose 1972a: 41-42).

23:2 Albion is troubled by an erotic dream of incest (Webster 1983: 276).

23:5-7 Albion confuses Jerusalem's beauty, through which Eternity shines, with Vala's deceptive beauty (Beer 1969: 202).

The freedom of Jerusalem's love from any jealousy of Vala constitutes the repair of the latter's Veil (Ostriker 1977: 1005).

23:9-10 **Embalm'd in Vala's bosom**—So embalmed, Jerusalem preserves for Albion a pittance of vision (Murray 1974a: 21).

23:27-28 **caverns of Derbyshire & Wales/ And Scotland**— Sloss and Wallis (1926: I, 485) cite E542/ K577—these are Druid caverns.

23:36-40 Albion's curse reinforces the cycle of repression and retaliation (Chayes 1970b: 242-43). Sloss and Wallis (1926: I, 486) assert that "Manhood" is Jesus and the curse is fulfilled at the Incarnation; Murry (1933: 269) holds that it is fulfilled and turned into a blessing at 96:35, where the "Manhood" is Albion himself.

24:3 **Two bleeding Contraries**—perhaps the Incarnation and Crucifixion (Sloss and Wallis 1926: I, 486); contraries like Good and Evil, wounded by the negation (Ostriker 1977: 1005).

24:4-7 This imitation of the lost prelapsarian world (Worrall 1977b: 190-91) may have taken the form of licentious witch dances at Stonehenge (Stevenson 1971: 672). The cause of shame is probably, like the cause of Adam's and Eve's, their nakedness (Ostriker 1977: 1005).

24:7 **Blue**—either ancient British woad or the colour (13:33) of the Mundane Shell (Worrall 1977b: 193). Cf. 33(37):10n.

24:11 The groans of Scandinavia's mountains foreshadow the human sacrifices of 38(43):65 (Worrall 1977b: 191).

24:44 The original, uncorrupted English Druidism spread civilisation over the world (Saurat 1929: 72).

24:47 **Hesperia**—Italy (Damon 1967: 185), for which it is a Greek name. Cf. 89:39.

24:52 **the gentlest mildest Zoa**—perhaps Albion's nostalgic illusion (Damrosch 1980: 237).

24:59 **Look not so merciful upon me**—Cf. Marlowe, *Faustus* V.ii.191 (Beer 1969: 223).

25:6 Luvah is here France, the Zoa of love, and a type of the crucified Christ (Bloom 1965: 934).

25:8 Cf. Matt. x.29 (Damon 1924: 446).

pl. 27 **the Learned**—Jacob Bryant or William Stukeley; cf. also Milton's claims for "the old philosophy of this island" in his *Areopagitica* (Sloss and Wallis 1926: I, 490). Saurat (1929:

53-73) adds Jean Bailly, the Abbé Baudeau, Edward Williams and Edward Davies, the authors respectively of *Lettres sur l'Origine des Sciences* (1777), *Mémoire à consulter pour les anciens Druides gaulois* (1777), *Poems* (1794), and *Celtic Researches* (1804). Todd (1946: 47-56) is convinced Blake took their history as literally true; Bloom (1963: 391) believes he did not. Stevenson (1971: 676) states that 38(43):69-70 and 63:41-42 show that he thought Britain and Palestine were once a single geographical entity.

Was Britain the Primitive Seat of the Patriarchal Religion?—Owen (1962: 234) cites William Cooke's *Enquiry into the Patriarchal and Druidical Religion* (1754) and the anonymous *Complete History of the Druids...with an Inquiry into their Religion and its Coincidence with the Patriarchal* (1810).

Amen! Huzza! Selah!—a mixture of Hebrew and English exclamations (Stevenson 1971: 677).

Poem ll. 1-16 According to Erdman (1954a: 437 [473]), in Blake's childhood the area specified consisted mostly of open fields but contained some inns; Gardner (1968: 143) insists it was scarred by brickfields, a huge dust pile, and a cemetery for executed soldiers.

l. 25 **those golden Builders**—of the boom in home construction in Paddington in 1811 (Erdman 1954a: 438 [474]); of John Nash's urban renewal encompassing the same area just before 1820 (Gardner 1968: 141-44). Pinto (1965: 26) interprets the builders as "the imaginative powers which produced the ecstatic vision of Blake's childhood," Miner (1981: 319) perceives them as solar Los and lunar Enitharmon hovering above the ruin, and Adams (1970: 734) credits Los with attempting to rebuild in the slum where Satan first triumphed.

l. 26 **ever-weeping Paddington**—see 12:27-28n. For Pinto (1965: 26), the epithet evokes dismal rain.

ll. 27-29 The "mighty Ruin" may be London Stone (Erdman 1954a: 429 [464-65])—see 8:27n—or the remains of gallows ("Fatal Tree") and spectator galleries at Tyburn (Pinto 1965: 27). The "Fatal Tree" must also be the Tree of Mystery.

ll. 36-48 War springs from the suppression of sex ("his Loins"), and these lines deal with Roman, British, and Napoleonic imperial wars (Erdman 1954a: 430 [465-66]). Ll. 47-48 may allude to Bonaparte's Middle Eastern machinations (Pinto 1965: 29) or British expansion in Asia (Damon 1967: 31).

ll. 41-44   The wars from 1776 to 1815 destroyed Blake's Innocent childhood vision (Pinto 1965: 28). From London, Jerusalem falls east through coastal Malden toward realms of war and superstition (Stevenson 1971: 679) or toward Palestine (Ostriker 1977: 1006).

ll. 61-64 Jesus, image of human perfection, passes from generation to generation (Pinto 1965: 29). Blake is Swedenborgian in his vision of Jesus being contained in every human (Raine 1968: II, 206).

ll. 65-88   Bateson (1957: 136) asserts that Albion is the speaker in these closing stanzas.

ll. 65-68 Pinto (1965: 29-30) sees here an allusion to Blake's recovery in 1804 of the light of his youth (E756/ K852).

ll. 78-80   Cf. Matt. x.34-36 (Damon 1924: 454) and Mic. vii.6 (T. Wright 1929: II, 57). The family may become a collective selfhood (Davies 1948: 150). Blake opposes the belief in a chosen people (Ostriker 1977: 1006). The self-contained family has replaced the biblical ideal of communal fraternity (Ferguson 1978: 174).

ll. 85-86 Stevenson (1971: 680, 673), who compares 24:42, reasonably thinks that Blake sees fraternity in commerce (cf. Erdman 1954a: 436 [472]); Johnson and Grant (1979: 323) consider that he treats financial transactions as "fallen metaphors of spiritual interchange."

If Humility...follow Jesus—Beer (1969: 202-03) equates the animals with the passions, which true humility does not reject. The Tabernacle is identified by Miner (1961: 54-55) with generation, by Rose (1963: 41) with the Temple, nature, and the uterus—it was, says Rose, "rebuilt by Jesus," which seems to mean made to contribute to redemption. Johnson and Grant (1979: 324) suppose Blake here criticises biblical preoccupation with genealogy, including Matthew's linkage of David with Christ.

28:6-7 According to Damon (1967: 196), Blake regarded incest as innocent: an emanation is usually its partner's sister and spouse. The "crimes" include the Lesbian embrace of *IB* pl. 28 (Mitchell 1978: 206-07).

28:14-15 This Tree is (Damon 1924: 447) or resembles (Bloom 1965: 935) Urizen's Tree of Mystery. It is also the Cross and Tyburn gallows (Hilton 1981: 201).

28:22 **the Potter's Furnace**—in which souls are moulded like clay (Stevenson 1971: 681).

28:25 **ransom**—an allusion to the theology of the Atonement (*ibid.*: 682).

29(33):1-2 Memory belongs to chaos, imagination to Eternity (Damon 1924: 448), for sense impressions are deposited in the memory at random (Raine 1968: II, 216-18). Blake rejects Locke's view that the collapse of memory dissolves personal identity (Damrosch 1980: 144).

29(33):6 **seventy inches long**—a reference to human stature and human longevity (Frye 1947: 378).

29(33):8 **fortuitous concourse of memorys**—In *Three Dialogues* (1713), Berkeley accuses supposed atheists of believing in "a fortuitous concourse of atoms" (Paley 1970: 254-55).

29(33):10 **a stone of the brook**—like that which killed Goliath—see I Sam. xvii.40 (Margoliouth 1948: 310).

29(33):16 **the tablet**—the *tabula rasa* or blank tablet that was Locke's image for the newborn human's mind (Raine 1968: II, 218).

29(33):19 **a white Dot call'd a Center**—Satan's heart, from which springs a polypus (Miner 1960: 202); the extreme of egoism, the antithesis of a Centre that opens (Rose 1965: 589); perhaps derived from the white dot at the focal point of Newton's spectrum (Raine 1968: II, 158-59); a void (Murray 1974a: 20); a zero that sprouts the vegetative shoots that deprive it of vision (Welch 1978: 228); the brightest star in the vast constellation Hydra is Cor Hydrae or Heart of the Polypus (Miner 1981: 329).

29(33):25-28 The Emanation that appears is Vala, who materialises as nature (Damon 1924: 448, 188). It is Jerusalem imprisoned in Vala—see 4:16 (Murray 1974a: 20-21).

29(33):28 **Sexual Reasoning Hermaphroditic**—"the doubt of self-contradiction" (Damon 1924: 448); the sterile reasoning of the sexual world that exists since the Fall (Stevenson 1971: 683).

29(33):29-34 Albion mistakes decay for harvest (Damon 1924: 448). His contemplation of the White Dot has entangled his vision (Jerusalem) in the appearance of nature (Vala) (Murray 1974a: 20-21). The passage reflects Blake's attraction to the chiaroscuro and primacy of colour that his judgment condemns (Paley 1983b: 200-01).

29(33):36 **a City & a Temple**—Babylon, but Vala lies about it (Stevenson 1971: 683).

29(33):43 **fanatic love**—natural religion's view of "the visionary ethic" (Sloss and Wallis 1926: I, 506); in reality, the false love of 17:24-26 (Paley 1983b: 192).

29(33):45-30(34):1 Vala considers the selfish love she created has an equal value with brotherhood (Wicksteed 1954: 162). Her love is fleshly love (Raine 1968: I, 212-13), which, as Vala deploys it, blots out the vision of brotherhood (Deen 1983: 198). She asserts the superiority of beauty to brotherhood (Ostriker 1977: 1007).

30(34):3-4 Albion has perspired and ejaculated in his dream (Ostriker 1977: 1007) after being deceived by Vala's speech (Paley 1983b: 201).

30(34):7-10 Having exchanged vision for natural religion (Sloss and Wallis 1926: I, 507), Albion identifies Vala with Apuleius' Isis (Raine 1968: II, 176), ranks her above Jerusalem (Beer 1969: 226), and mistakes the material world for the only reality (Stevenson 1971: 684).

30(34):11-14 Damon (1967: 75, 329-30) associates the grot and cave with the subconscious, and views the plough as an emblem of revolution, which Blake now believes to originate in England.

30(34):15 Cf. Matt. xxii.30 (Stevenson 1971: 684). Marriage is possessiveness (George 1980: 188).

30(34):25-35 Sex has a malign power in the fallen world (Sloss and Wallis 1926: I, 507), where humanity, which should serve only God (cf. *PL*, IV, 299 [Beer 1969: 184]), turns from Him to the feminine "spirit of this world" (Percival 1938: 110). Cf. I Cor. xi.3, 8, 9 (Damon 1924: 448) and iii.16 (Margoliouth 1948: 310).

30(34):36-37 For Reuben, the natural or normal man, and his treatment by Los, and for Merlin, the imagination, see pp. 272, 284 above. Bashan, land of Og, is in the territory east of the Jordan allotted partly to Reuben (Bloom 1963: 393, citing Num. xxxii.33) and partly to Manasseh, the half-tribe to which belongs Zelophehad, father of Tirzah, a symbol of the female will (Baine 1984: 243). Kept in a spectrous state by that will, Reuben is now represented by Hand (Baine, *loc.cit.*)—but see also 32(36):23-24n. By enrooting in the land of the vicious Og, the normal man degenerates (Ferguson 1978: 175-76); Merlin, the poet or prophet, is subdued by the female will (Damon 1924: 449). Beer (1969: 227) argues that the whole human has split into the earthbound fallen Reuben and the mind confined to abstractions, which is fallen Merlin, and Ostriker (1977: 1007, 1008) believes this is the beginning of an account of the conquest of Canaan, during which Reuben's power of perception dwindles as his territory increases.

30(34):39-40 Cf. *M* 40:9-13n.

30(34):45 **the Stone of Bohan**—a border stone between the territories of Judah and Benjamin (Damon 1967: 49). Succoth is east and Zareton west of the Jordan; Reuben is often associated with a stone (Stevenson 1971: 686).

30(34):46 **three Bodies**—the three spatial dimensions, and head, heart and loins (Frosch 1974: 47).

30(34):48-54 Those who flee cannot endure Los's clear image of the fallen senses; nevertheless authentic art changes a community (Ferguson 1978: 176-77).

30(34):52 This puzzling line has been related to the division "into twelve pieces" of the web woven in Gray's "The Fatal Sisters," a source of Blake's Daughters of Albion (Miner 1958: 204) and to Judg. xix.29 (Miner 1969: 471n51). Baine (1984: 244) conjectures that Gwendolen seeks to seduce the Twelve Tribes.

30(34):55-58 Citing *The Principles of Human Knowledge*, 47, Raine (1968: II, 107) observes that Blake endorses Berkeley's view that changes in our sense organs could alter only our *image* of an object. Damrosch (1980: 27) points out that he refers only to fallen perception, which, states Hilton (1983: 131), is "Sexual Organization," the perception that prevails when the Human is divided into sexes.

31(35):3-5 Cf. Dan. iii.25 (Damon 1924: 449). Cf. *A* 4:6-9n.

32(36):1 Damon (1967: 347) holds that this marks the third stage, following 30(34):46 and 52, in Reuben's conception of moral virtue, Tirzah. Others consider Tirzah Reuben's material counterpart (Beer 1969: 228), his Emanation (Adams 1970:

735), and nature's mother, herself in Eternity and therefore inaccessible here (Stevenson 1971: 688).

32(36):2   Reuben comes into this world upside down (Rose 1963: 50). Cf. 63:44n.

32(36):3   Cf. Judg. v.15-16 (Kiralis 1959: 198).

32(36):4   **the Moon of Ulro**—Damon's view that this moon is love in our fallen world (1924: 449) created to impose form on error (1967: 286) is consistent with Percival's theory (1938: 73) that Los is replacing Luvah, the lost moon of Eternity (or, according to Nicholas Warner [1980: 46], of Beulah) and with Paley's belief (1983b: 269) that it is a lunar ark conveying humankind over the Sea of Time and Space. This ark is identified by Beer (1969: 228) with a degree of vision and by Baine (1984: 245) with the body, on which Los labours throughout the human life span. Ferguson (1978: 179) sees this moon only as the clear form imposed on the physical to expose its deceptiveness.

32(36):5   **the Cave of Adam**—the skull (Damon 1967: 348); mortality (Stevenson 1971: 689). There is a city named Adam east of the Jordan—see Josh. iii.16 (Margoliouth 1948: 310); it is near the Zaretan of 30(34):45 (Stevenson, *loc. cit.*).

32(36):6   **sent him forth over Jordan**—into Ulro, represented by Canaan (Frye 1947: 366); into the region of generation, represented by Canaan (Miner 1961: 48).

32(36):10-12   Heshbon means reasoning (Frye 1947: 368). This city was given to Reuben's tribe (Stevenson 1971: 689)—see Num. xxxii.37. Gilead is east, Gilgal just west of the Jordan (Damon 1967: 157).

32(36):14   **The Seven Nations**—of Canaanites (Stevenson 1971: 689).

32(36):23-24   Reuben (the flesh) is blocked off from Merlin (imagination) by Hand (reason) (Damon 1924: 449). Frye (1947: 376) identifies Reuben, more precisely, as the natural man and Hand as the Selfhood. For Ferguson (1978: 179), Hand stands for materialism, which offers Reuben an alternative choice to imagination.

32(36):35, 56   Some judge the subject to be the natural world in which (Damon 1924: 449) the laws of chance are found to operate or in which (Stevenson 1971: 690) accident and chance are credited with what is really the work of the Divine Vision.

However, Damrosch (1980: 30) believes the subject to be perception, which only divine intervention can restore to its unfallen state; the dimensions are not "the underlying structure of reality."

32(36):41-42 Concentrating on the Fall and its consequences, critics have discerned the identity of the fallen human with the fallen imagination (Damon 1924: 450)—that is, with the surviving imaginative potential of Reuben, which is Merlin (Frye 1947: 376); Merlin is therefore the true self of fallen Reuben (Ferguson 1978: 179-80). Fisher (1959: 168) argues that creation, redemption and judgment are Ulro's Urizenic counterparts of Generation, Beulah and Eden, while Stevenson (1971: 690) maintains that Reuben accepts erroneous orthodox theology. Ostriker (1977: 1009) points to both Merlin's and Reuben's having been misled by females (see above p. 693), and Paley 1983b: 271-72) credits Los's bending of Reuben's senses for his attainment of such vision as is symbolised by Merlin. Put simply, the meaning is that the fallen imagination experiences the fallen world.

33(37):10 blue—The word probably has druidic associations (Erdman 1964a: 24), and it applies to both the Spectre and the imprisoning sky or Mundane Shell (Hilton 1983: 162-63). It refers to the woad that marks Albion as both sacrificer and sacrificed—cf. 65:9 (Paley 1983b: 204). Cf. 24:7n.

34(38):29 London; a Human awful wonder of God!—one of the Eternals (Sloss and Wallis 1926: I, 460). Here Blake begins to evoke Albion's Twenty-eight Cities (Ostriker 1977: 1009).

34(38):40-42 Blake enjoyed his imaginative vision of London before, during and after his three years in Sussex (Stevenson 1971: 693).

34(38):43 London's opening streets—a reference to John Nash's rebuilding in Blake's neighbourhood just before 1820 (Gardner 1968: 141).

34(38):45 Damon (1967: 434) holds that here, as in 41(46):24, Blake identifies Verulam with Canterbury, Stevenson (1971: 693) that Verulam, a centre of Christianity in Roman Britain, is quite distinct.

34(38):53-54 In the Antijacobin frenzy of 1793 and 1794, Scottish courts sentenced leaders of a reform movement to transportation (Erdman 1954a: 439-40 [476]).

34(38):55 **a Gate**—a gate of imagination (Damon 1924: 450), perhaps that of 72:51 (Damon 1967: 210); Los's gate of physical death leading to immortality (Raine 1968: I, 243). Standing in Oxford Street, Blake saw this Gate beyond Tyburn, most likely in a rainbow (Stevenson 1971: 694).

35(39):12-13 **Cambridgeshire**—a probable allusion to the great architecture of Ely and Cambridge (Beer 1969: 229), and the latter's graduate Milton (Stevenson 1971: 695), who is the twenty-eighth earthly representative of Los (Ostriker 1977: 1009). Los is closely related to Jesus, who ends the cycle of the Twenty-seven Churches (Damon 1967: 247).

35(39):20-21 Cf. Exod. xii.11 (Stevenson 1971: 695).

36(40):7 See 48:4-11n.

36(40):11-12 The entire world laments Albion's decease (Beer 1969: 230).

36(40):12-14 The robbers are his allies in the war against France, his friends the English radicals (Erdman 1954a: 430 [466]).

36(40):19-20 **falshoods!/ ...errors**—war propaganda (Erdman 1954a: 441 [478]).

36(40):22 The "Living Creatures" are the Zoas, "the third procession" is that of the body (Damon 1924: 451).

36(40):41-42 **Eon**—Emanation (Damon 1924: 451). Cf. *FZ* 59: 15-16/ E340/ V, 60-61n.

36(40):48-51 Damon (1924: 186) claims that Chichester, as the site of Blake's trial, is the accuser, but the city is a Friend. In 1075, the bishopric was moved from Selsey to Chichester (Sloss and Wallis 1926: I, 517), so that Selsey sacrificed its life for another (Erdman 1954a: 439 [475]).

36(40):53 **Winchester**—Hayley, patron of poets (Damon 1967: 72, citing 71:20); site of William of Wykeham's celebrated school (Paley 1983b: 229).

36(40):58-60 Universal symbols are represented by English churches with English names (Wicksteed 1954: 184). Los is continually creating language to approach nearer to a true expression of vision (Adams 1963: 41). The imagination creates language to give speech to the fallen and preserve experience (Rose 1966: 117). It lays the foundation for the visionary speech of pl. 98 (Rose 1970c: 453-54). Language gives form to Albion's world and shapes his reality (Adams 1975: 150). Using the temporal instrument of language, Los shows reality transcends time (Mitchell 1978: 167-68). Language is the imperfect foundation of thought (Damrosch 1980: 326).

36(40):61 Salisbury (being near Stonehenge) stands for reason, Bristol (Chatterton's city) for the spirit, and Exeter for the emotions (Damon 1924: 186).

37(41):1-2 Listed seventh out of the Twenty-four (Stevenson 1971: 707), Bath as a famous watering place has been identified with both bodily healing powers and excessive concentration on the body—i.e. materialism (Damon 1924: 451). "Legions" alludes partly to Mark v.2-13, Albion being full of devils, and partly to Geoffrey of Monmouth's statement (*History of the Kings of Britain* [III.x]) that the Romans called Caerose (Caerleon), which Blake here identifies with Bath, the City of Legions, (Wicksteed 1954: 174-75). Geoffrey claims it served as winter quarters for Roman troops and [IX.xii-xiii] was the site of Arthur's coronation (Damon 1967: 237). He also reports [VII.iii] Merlin's prophecy that its medicinal waters will become death-dealing and [II.x] that Bladud, founder of Bath, practised necromancy (Stevenson 1971: 698). Wicksteed (1954: 174) and Paley (1983b: 206-07) comment on the corrupt social life of Bath, and Beer (1969: 230) notes that it contains both Gothic and neoclassical buildings. Among its inhabitants, observes Erdman (1954a: 442 [478]) are both warmongers and a prominent pacifist—see next note and 39(44): 44n.

37(41):3 Bath was the home of Richard Warner, who advocated peace with France (Luvah) (Erdman 1951a: 221)—see also 39(44):44n. When Luvah becomes lustful, he joins with degenerate Bath to attack Jerusalem—cf. 54:11 (Stevenson 1971: 698). Bath takes to worshipping its Spectre as a god (Doskow 1982: 87).

37(41):4 The triple octave and those reduced to twelve may be the Spectres of the Twenty-four Cities and the sixteen Sons of Jerusalem reduced to the twelve Sons of Albion (Stevenson 1971: 699, citing 74:23ff), or the Twenty-four Cities fallen and the sixteen inspired biblical books (36[40]:7; 48:6-11) reduced to the legalism of the Twelve Tribes (Doskow 1982: 87). Damon (1924: 452) refers to an unspecified twelve deprived of their emanations, and Wagenknecht (1973: 258) argues that Bath turns Jerusalem from a universal to an institutional religion and that there are allusions to the three main Jewish festivals and the Twelve Tribes.

37(41):5-6 From the standpoint of London, the English places named are in the east, the quarter of error (Sloss and Wallis 1926: I, 518).

37(41):7-9 Britain oppresses workers and fights wars for the sake of the cloth industry and its markets (Hilton 1983: 120).

37(41):15 **a Grain of Sand in Lambeth**—the way to Eternity through nature (Damon 1924: 452); probably Blake's works (Sloss and Wallis 1926: I, 518), specifically his Lambeth books, impenetrable to the sedition-hunting Urizenic mind (Erdman 1970: 111-12); Blake's home (T. Wright 1929: I, 52); the sexual joy miscalled sin (Altizer 1967: 120-21); any sand grain perceived imaginatively—see 39(44):9-12n (Ault 1974: 146).

37(41):17 Oothoon may represent liberty as in *VDA* 1:3 (Erdman 1951b: 184); her palace may be Blake's imagination (Adams 1970: 735) or his poetry (Bloom 1965: 936). She may be a Daughter of Beulah protecting Vala and Jerusalem (Stevenson 1971: 699); the regenerating sexual love united, unlike Vala's sexuality, with imagination (Frosch 1974: 170-72); or sexual love, both physical (Vala) and spiritual (Jerusalem)—see l. 21 (Paley 1983b: 186).

Quatrain in mirror writing—The lake may be Udan Adan (T. Wright 1929: I, 28), Los's lake of fire identical with that of Rev. xix.20 (Damon 1967: 381, 231), or a lake of energy and imagination (Hilton 1983: 156).

38(43):1, 6 **They**—the Friends or Cities (Sloss and Wallis 1926: I, 522); the now perverted Zoas (Stevenson 1971: 700), who (Rose 1972a: 38-39) are a parody of the wheels of the Divine Chariot (Ezek. i).

38(43):5 **the Four Complexions**—This mediaeval and Renaissance term refers to the four main classes of temperament, each dominated by one of the four humours (Lewis 1964: 169-74—term defined without reference to Blake).

38(43):6-7 Blake associates Amerindian human sacrifice with the closing of the Western Gate (Frye 1947: 398). Britain and France tried to bar each other from trade with America; there was an Anglo-American war in 1812; in 1811 and 1813 the

Spanish shot Mexican revolutionaries (Erdman 1954a: 445 [482]).

38(43):16 **these Heavens & Hells**—the Twenty-seven Churches (Damon 1924: 452).

38(43):19-23 See p. 162 above and cf. 91:26-30. Jesus, the true universal form, preserves the peculiarities of every particular, while Lockean universals consist only of what particulars have in common (Ault 1974: 63-64). There are not a multitude of Platonic Ideas but only a single universal Form (Damrosch 1980: 19). The "minute particulars" have been defined as "little tendernesses and impulses" (Damon 1924: 448, 452), individual persons (Erdman 1954a: 433 [468]), both the individual characteristics that constitute a human and "Mutual Forgivenesses" (Bloom 1963: 399, 405).

38(43):37-39 **Oshea [Joshua] and Caleb**—the last Israelites of the Exodus to survive (Damon 1924: 452, citing Num. xxvi.65) and the only ones who entered Canaan (Bloom 1965: 937). They may fight each other—Bloom (*loc. cit.*) suspects Blake alludes to a quarrel with an old friend and fellow artist—or kill members of mixed families, for Gentile wives had seduced Israelite men into idolatry bringing on a plague at Peor (Stevenson 1971: 702, citing Num. xxv, xxxi). The prophet Balaam may be "a reconciler of enemies" (Damon 1967: 36) or "a tempter to idolatry" (Bloom, *loc. cit.*, with reference to Num. xxxi.8, 16; Rev. ii.14). His armies are his thwarted spiritual power (Stevenson, *loc. cit.*).

38(43):45-54 Blake refers to the Napoleonic wars (Wicksteed 1954: 176-77). Erdman (1954a: 430-31 [466]) detects in l. 51 an allusion to Leipzig (1813), where Saxon regiments fought the French.

38(43):47-50 Making use of the nursery rhyme in "Jack and the Bean-stalk" (Damon 1924: 453), Blake treats its giant as one of a class of aboriginal evildoers (Frye 1947: 375). The reference is appropriate to an Oedipal fantasy in which the son saves the mother (Jerusalem) from the father (Webster 1983: 280). The installation of a steam engine in 1786 turned the Albion flour mill into a London showplace (Bronowski 1944: 64).

38(43):62 Blake regarded the Canaanites as great merchants (Damon 1967: 68, citing this passage and E524 [ll. 48-49]/

K749 [ll. 48-49]). In Blake's time, most bitumen was imported from the Middle East (Stevenson 1971: 703).

39(44):1-6 The Cities try to become the Cherubim of Ezekiel's vision (Bloom 1963: 397). Erdman (1974: 318) conjectures that the would-be saviours attempt to make Albion read the Bible.

39(44):6-7 The Wheels of Albion's Sons have become Albion's Wheels (Rose 1972a: 40).

39(44):9-12 Newton attributes the opacity of matter to internal reflection of light through the void spaces between its particles (Ault 1974: 81-83).

39(44):18-19 **the day of Divine/ Power**—the moment of truth's recognition (Blackstone 1949: 386); the apocalyptic day of l. 30 (Erdman 1954a: 444 [481]).

39(44):25 **a Sexual Machine: an Aged Virgin Form**—the laws of chastity based on devotion to the Virgin Mary (Kiralis 1959: 203); a parody of Erin called religion by the spectre who creates it (Damon 1967: 128); fallen Albion and Vala, goddess of chastity (Mellor 1974: 311); the churches' two images of woman—as reproductive mechanism and as passive virgin (Doskow 1982: 94). Frosch (1974: 161) regards the Sexual Machine as the natural realm of endlessly repeated sexual reproduction; Hilton (1983: 135) believes it is the womb.

39(44):38-40 **Emanative portion**—"intuitive sympathy" (Damon 1924: 453); a projection of one's substance analogous to the projection from an object that constitutes its perceptible image according to Epicurean theory (Stevenson 1971: 705).

39(44):44 The voice is that of Richard Warner, a Bath clergyman, poet, pacifist, and anti-war pamphleteer; Bath's speech echoes his *War Inconsistent with Christianity* (1804) (Erdman 1954a: 440-42 [476-78]).

40(45):19-22 Africa's rising and binding down have been explained as the Mosaic exodus from Egypt (Damon 1924: 453), the slave revolt at Surinam described by Stedman (Damon 1967: 7), the former attempt of twofold vision to suppress fourfold and threefold (or solar and lunar) vision (Beer 1969: 186), and slave trading by Africans themselves (Paley 1983b: 207). The cutting of Africa's chains may be Parliament's abolition of the slave trade in 1807 (Erdman 1954a: 392 [421]). The "Machines" may allude to pyramid-building

(Erdman 1974: 319) and the means by which Britain oppressed Africans (Erdman 1954a: 436 [472]). The lines are tantalisingly ambiguous.

40(45):24-25 **Albion's sleep is not/ Like Africa's**—Britain's dimness of vision is less curable than Blake's own (Wicksteed 1954: 182); Britain is wedded to a materialistic philosophy more idolatrous than any African creed (Raine 1968: II, 276). In l. 25, Blake alludes to the role of the textile industry in the imperial economy (Erdman 1974: 319).

40(45):30 **take thou these leaves of the Tree of Life**—Cf. Rev. xxii.2 (Sloss and Wallis 1926: I, 528); write an introduction to Richard Warner's peace publications (Erdman 1951a: 219-23); just possibly, the reference is to early prose pamphlets of Shelley (Stevenson 1971: 707).

41(46):3-6 Hereford, Lincoln, Durham, Carlisle, and the scribe of Ely have been respectively identified as Inigo Jones (1573-1652), architect; Robert Grosseteste (*c.* 1175-1253), who resisted his King and the Pope; Thomas Sutton (1532-1611), philanthropist; William Paley (1743-1805), defender of Anglicanism against Deism; and the poet Milton (Damon 1967: 181, 72, 120). There is every reason to accept the substitution of Thomas Johnes of Hafod, whose paternal home was Croft Castle, Hereford, for Inigo Jones (Paley 1969, citing Ruthven Todd)—see *A* 10:5-12n.

41(46):7 **Oxford, immortal Bard!**—The bard appears to be "Edward, the bard of Oxford" of Blake's letter of 27 January, 1804, as Damon guesses (1924: 454)—namely Edward Marsh of Oriel (Sloss and Wallis 1926: I, 529, citing Gilchrist). Damon's conjecture (1967: 314-15) that the bard is Shelley is countered by Erdman's observation (1966: 609-11) that Shelley was hardly a trembling, fainting figure, was not at Oxford till 1810, and proclaimed himself an atheist.

41(46):24 These four Cities are the Zoas—see 74:3 (Damon 1924: 186).

42:3-4 Cf. *BU* 23:8-21 (Bloom 1965: 937). The "own beloveds" of Albion are his "little ones" (e.g. 42:21) (Ostriker 1977: 1011)—these are his "free impulses" (*ibid.*) or the offspring of his imagination (Stevenson 1971: 709). He cannot admit his responsibility for society's ills (Gallant 1978: 160).

42:24 **the Fourth**—Los, identified with the fourth man in Daniel's furnace (Bloom 1965: 937)—see *A* 4:6-9n.

42:44 **thee**—Albion's selfhood (Stevenson 1971: 710).

42:48 Damon (1967: 16) sees a reference to 19:17-32, Stevenson (1971: 710-11) to 37(41):23.

42:51 These four districts comprise the east, west, south and north of London (Stevenson 1971: 711).

42:66 The Friends' higher (unconscious) selves that do not fall watch over their lower mortal selves (Raine 1968: I, 256-57). These are liberal-minded men almost paralysed by their compromise with society's demands (Paley 1983b: 207-08).

42:78 **Los built the Mundane Shell**—to limit Albion's errors (Damon 1924: 190) or chaos (Stevenson 1971: 712).

43(29):1-3 From Tyburn the sunset would be visible over Kensington Gardens; darkness arrives at l. 27 (Stevenson 1971: 712, 713).

43(29):9-15 The Reactor has been identified as the Spectre (Sloss and Wallis 1926: I, 496); as Albion (Wicksteed 1954: 134; Kroeber 1973: 358); and as Newton, whose Third Law of Motion is echoed in ll. 14-15 (Ault 1974: 43-44). However, the quotation from II Thess. ii.3 refers to Satan (Percival 1938: 217, 322), who is, of course, the Spectre as well as (Schorer 1946: 372) the restrainer of energy. Blackstone (1949: 164) defines the Reactor as "that which *acts back* in envy against joy," Stevenson (1971: 712) charges Albion with mistaking reaction for action (l. 15), and Wagenknecht (1973: 272) cites Satan's envy of Adam and Eve in *PL*, IV. The phrase "for Obedience" signifies the exaction of obedience (Stevenson, *loc. cit.*).

43(29):18-24 **Ephratah**—see Ps. cxxxii.6 (Damon 1924: 447); it is an alternative name for Bethlehem (Damon 1967: 127). By taking it, Satan has taken Jerusalem (Bloom 1965: 938), whose remnants in Britain are all of her that survives (Stevenson 1971: 713).

43(29):28 At Witke's suggestion, E and K emend "locks" to "rocks"; Essick (1972b: 170) argues that "locks" refers to the hair of Albion, who has a human as well as a geographical form.

43(29):33-80 See notes to *FZ* 39:15-42:17/ E327-28/ III, 44-101, where the context makes it clear that the Prince of Light is

Urizen. Here, the adored Shadow is Albion's own Spectre (Paley 1983b: 175).

44(30):1-15 Perhaps an allegorical account of the Blakes' sojourn at Felpham (Sloss and Wallis 1926: I, 499).

44(30):6 **a Shadow of the Emanation**—perhaps Catherine Blake's ill health used as an excuse for leaving Felpham (Stevenson 1971: 716); a form of fallen nature (Wagenknecht 1973: 272).

44(30):8 **fleeing**—to Felpham from the warlike London described in this and the next plate (Erdman 1954a: 368 [396]); from Albion's Sons, including Schofield (Stevenson 1971: 716).

44(30):11 **Sexual Religion**—Urizen's religion of chastity and phallus-worship—see *FZ* 95:32/ E361/ VIIb, 19-38 (Damon 1924: 448); the pre-Christian religion slightly improved by Christ's teaching (Percival 1938: 226); the materialistic world-view embryonically present in Hayley's well intended advice to Blake (Stevenson 1971: 716); a religion based on guilt (Webster 1983: 281).

44(30):18 **Feminine Allegories**—doctrines based on misinterpretation of symbols (Damon 1924: 448); formal allegory that can only partly deceive Los because allegory is "Seldom without some Vision" (Rose 1970b: 418-20, quoting E554/ K604); error, including a false concept of art (Stevenson 1971: 716).

44(30):29 The reference is to prostitutes who lured young men to encounters with recruiting officers or to underpaid women whose industrial work supported the war (Erdman 1954a: 432 [467]).

44(30):33-37 The self-love in the sexual relationship in Beulah condenses into a veil-like form (Stevenson 1971: 717). Male and female are here both emanations and their self-love is a step towards the Fall (Ault 1974: 185). The adjective "double" invariably has sinister connotations in Blake (Sloss and Wallis 1926: I, 501)—it may sometimes signify duplicity.

44(30):38 By investigating mistakes involving sex, Albion begins to reject error (Damon 1967: 244). The loins are the place of circumcision or cutting away of error (Rose 1968a: 23). This is Albion's nadir (Ostriker 1977: 1012). Albion's sexuality drives the cycle of birth, reproduction and death (Paley 1983b: 202).

44(30):39-40 Although Albion's secretive union is with fallen Vala, their Children will rise from Ulro to Generation, where God's hand will free them from Vala's Veil (Stevenson 1971: 717-18). The curtains are those of the Mosaic Tabernacle (Miner 1961: 60). According to Riede (1981: 557), the rending of the Veil brings on apocalypse or the Last Judgment.

45(31):2-27 Los tours London with its "caves" (shops and hovels) to find why the people accept the human sacrifice of war (Erdman 1951b: 189-90). He seeks to distinguish appearance from reality (Rose 1963: 43) in a quest which is self-exploration (Rose 1973: 85).

45(31):5-7 **the tempters**—Instead of finding these, Los discovers that the Accusers have murdered human individuality (Bloom 1963: 399)—see 38(43):19-23n. Welch (1978: 239) asserts the minute particulars of l. 7 are imaginative perceptions, those of l. 8 Lockean sensory perceptions.

45(31):10-13 Blake describes the stages of brick-making (Stevenson 1971: 718). Los finds the workers' souls impenetrable (Erdman 1951b: 190). Heber and Terah are Abraham's idolatrous ancestor [and father] (Sloss and Wallis 1926: I, 502), here associated with the belief humans should be as alike as bricks in the Egyptian pyramids (Margoliouth 1951: 157), which are both symbols of oppression and the grave of the natural man (Bloom 1965: 938).

45(31):15-16 Leutha is associated with islands in Oothoon's Caribbean and hence with the West India Dock at the Isle of Dogs (Erdman 1951b: 190) or with prostitution at the docks (Damon 1967: 239). There is an allusion to Narrow St., a lane alongside this part of the Thames (Erdman, *loc. cit.*).

45(31):17 **the jewels of Albion**—citizens unvalued by the authorities (Erdman 1951b: 190); street children (Stevenson 1971: 718).

45(31):19-20 See pp. 162-63 above. No longer an expression of the soul, virtue is imposed through inflexible formulae (Stevenson 1971: 719). The sand grains include Newton's particles of light (Ault 1974: 146-47) and sense perceptions devoid of vision (implied Welch 1978: 239-40).

45(31):24 **Luvah**—i.e. the passions (Damon 1924: 448). Luvah is now Albion's adversary (Stevenson 1971: 719).

45(31):25-27 **Bethlehem**—Bedlam, the insane asylum (Damon 1924: 448), built from 1812 to 1815, so Blake is asking whether it yet has inmates (Erdman 1951b: 191). The Hebrew name Bethlehem means "house of bread," and bread was formerly made here from potato flour (*ibid.*: 191-92). Erdman rejects Frye's theory (1947: 372) that Lambeth, where Blake produced prophetic books, is the English counterpart of Palestine's Bethlehem, for Bedlam was outside Lambeth.

45(31):36-39 Blake worries that Britain in 1815 is about to impose oppressive terms on France (Erdman 1951b: 191). He has overcome his resentment against his personal enemies (Damrosch 1980: 313). To "hinder" is to use force, so Los substitutes "perswade" (Schorer 1946: 373).

45(31):55-57 Vala praises the battle of Waterloo that will obliterate hope of freedom (Erdman 1954a: 434 [470]). She accuses Albion of being governed by reason (Urizen) and suppressing passion (Luvah) (Stevenson 1971: 720).

46(32):13 **trembling from the bloody field**—At a late stage in the Napoleonic wars, Albion's Sons keep their father from spiritual regeneration (Wicksteed 1954: 194). This is Albion's fate as a private soldier (Erdman 1954a: 425 [460-61]).

47:3-9 War is caused by the separated emotions (Damon 1924: 454) and the suppression of sexuality (Damon 1967: 356), which is confined to the genitals at the Fall (Frosch 1974: 161-62). Cf. pl. 27, poem, ll. 37-40, 45-46 (Stevenson 1971: 722).

47:7 See *M* 37:11n.

47:12 The reason of mortals creates the illusion of matter (Damon 1924: 454). The dead may be both the spiritually deceased and war's fatalities (Stevenson 1971: 722-23)—Worrall (1977b: 210) adds those sacrificed by the Druids.

47:13-15 Cf. 58:13-20 (Sloss and Wallis 1926: II, 232).

48:4-11 The books named are those biblical books that Swedenborg believes to be inspired—see his *Arcana Coelestia*, X, 325; the Cloud is a veil of symbolism (Damon 1924: 454). The inspired books are the ones with a spiritual or symbolic sense (Damon 1967: 45).

48:13-14 Beulah is found where Eden meets both earth and Ulro (Stevenson 1971: 723) or (Ostriker 1977: 1013) both Ulro and Generation.

48:28 **an Aged pensive Woman**—Though Damon (1924: 454) thinks she is Enion, who is the "Maternal Love" of l. 18, and Beer (1969: 188) supposes she is Jerusalem, most critics follow Erdman (1954a: 444 [481]) in identifying her as Erin.

48:35 Does the rainbow represent materialistic illusion (Damon 1924: 454) or is it a happy sign that error will be annihilated (Percival 1938: 68)? Wagenknecht (1973: 275-76) proposes that its connotations include both fallenness and vision, but Erdman's intensive study of all of Blake's illuminations persuades him that the rainbow is always positive (1974: 19).

48:37-39 See *M* 28:58n.

48:41 **Perusing Albion's Tomb**—Erin is reading the Scriptures in their spiritual sense (Paley 1983b: 210).

48:48-50 Even Jerusalem begins to be corrupted (Stevenson 1971: 724). Wagenknecht (1973: 273-74) usefully notes the echo of 20:29 and cites 50:15-17.

48:55 **The Place of Holy Sacrifice!**—coition (Miner 1961: 54).

48:58 A man's children are his works (Damon 1924: 454).

49:4-5 The places named encompass the whole shoreline of Ireland (Stevenson 1971: 725).

49:10-11 A reference to the Wicker Man—see *M* 37:11n.

49:18 **a little slimy substance**—the skin (Frosch 1974: 48).

49:23 The peace party is afraid to speak out (Erdman 1954a: 443 [480]).

49:24 **Polypus**—natural religion (Sloss and Wallis 1926: I, 440); imperialist war (Erdman 1954a: 428 [463-64]).

49:31 See Job iv.18 (Ostriker 1977: 1013). Stevenson (1971: 726) holds that the sight referred to is Satan's.

49:42 **they are removed**—The Children of Albion have quit Palestine (Stevenson 1971: 727).

49:46-48 Spiritually, Shiloh, as the place of the Tabernacle, has been explained as divine inspiration (Damon 1924: 455). As the place where Samuel showed his innocence (I Sam. iii.1-10), it has been associated with the France of Voltaire, who exposed the literal sense of the Bible opening the way to its spiritual meaning (Wicksteed 1954: 201). Politically, Shiloh and Jerusalem are the corroded liberties of England and France (Erdman 1954a: 284 [309])—i.e. Napoleonic France (Bloom 1963: 403).

49:57-58 **the Body of Moses...the Body/ Of Divine Analogy**—a reference to Cabbalistic or Swedenborgian correspondences (Damon 1924: 455); perhaps the Pentateuch understood allegorically (Sloss and Wallis 1926: I, 536); the parallel between the fallen sensory forms and eternal imaginative forms of all natural objects (Frye 1947: 382); the recurring temporal, natural Circle of Destiny (*FZ* 5:11/ E302/ I, 74), which is an analogy of the life of Eternity, where every identity is unique (Fisher 1959: 163-67, 178). Damon (1967: 325) notes that God buried Moses at an unknown grave at Beth-Peor.

49:58-59 Cf. 38(43):37-39 and n.

49:60 **surfaces**—of imprisoning matter (Damon 1924: 455); of error and delusion (Sloss and Wallis 1926: I, 536).

49:73 See Ezek. xxviii.14 (Damon 1924: 454).

50:2 For Blake, "allegory" denotes some form of falsehood (Stevenson 1971: 716, 728, 813). Damon (1967: 17) defines it as "something falsified from an original"—hence degenerate, and Rose (1971b: 13-19) associates the term with satanic vision that sees generalised abstractions instead of individuals.

50:5 Cf. Rom. viii.21-22 (Tolley 1973: 128).

50:10-11 Cf. Rev. xxii.20 (Stevenson 1971: 729). The quotation from John xi.21 implies that Albion will be resurrected (Paley 1983b: 210). See *FZ* 55:14/ E337/ IV, 251n.

50:20-22 Beer's assertion (1969: 204) that the rainbow contains the unfallen Wheels of Albion's Sons is much less convincing than Worrall's claim (1977b: 198-99) that the Sons' fallen Newtonian universe is a perversion of Ezekiel's vision enclosed in a bow of hope, which (Paley 1983b: 215) limits the power of the Sons. See also 48:35n.

pl. 52 **Rahab**—natural religion, which perpetually exists under some name (M. Plowman 1927a: 73); state religion, currently orthodox Anglicanism, which is infected by Deism (Bloom 1965: 939).

the Ancients...Prophecied of Jesus—These ancients include Virgil, Hermes Trismegistus and the Sybils (Damon 1924: 455).

Man is born a Spectre or Satan—He is in his spectre's power in the mortal realm (J. Warner 1973: 223, citing quatrain, pl. 37[41]). Frosch (1974: 161) alleges this is an allusion to physical birth in the fallen world, not original sin.

Foote...all the World—In his farce *The Minor* [1750], Samuel Foote satirised the Methodists, especially Whitefield, as hypocrites (Sloss and Wallis 1926: I, 540).

Rousseau thought...no friend—Rousseau's natural man is Blake's fallen man (DiSalvo 1983: 151-52).

Poem 1. 3 **Grey Monk**—The lyric reflects the ordeal of Blake's trial in a Chichester courtroom that had been part of a Grey Friars' church (Erdman 1954a: 385-86 [414-15]).

1. 4 **infernal**—anti-angelic [angels being the orthodox] (Damon 1924: 291).

1. 8 **iron & gold**—the iron of war and gold of monarchy (Doskow 1982: 37).

53:1 **Vehicular Form**—see *M* 17:31n.

53:4 **Albion's Tree**—of 28:14-19 (Stevenson 1971: 735).

53:10 **Seven-fold**—Damon (1924: 455) identifies Los's furnaces with the Seven Eyes of God, but see also 5:34n.

53:11 **single vision**—In the late eighteenth century, the phrase referred to the materialistic explanation (e.g. in Newton's *Opticks*) of how sight through two eyes produces a single image (Nurmi 1969: 304-05).

53:19 There are no breaks in art's battle with nature (Bloom 1963: 403). As "the city of verbal form," Golgonooza is under constant threat from those who would reduce words to mere signs of external realities (Adams 1975: 150).

53:26-28 The female contrary, the first to be corrupted [e.g. Eve and Vala], is purified, submits to the male, and becomes spiritually fruitful (Percival 1938: 228-29). She is saved from becoming a Shadow like Enion in *The Four Zoas* (Stevenson 1971: 736).

53:28-29 See 28:22n. In Hinnom Valley, the site of child sacrifice (Damon 1967: 186, citing Jer. vii.31), potters worked (Ostriker 1977: 1016). The Potter's Furnace consists of Los's furnaces and the funeral urns are physical bodies (Raine 1968: II, 18), or furnace and urns are images for this world (Stevenson 1971: 736). Beer (1969: 244-45) finds an association with the breaking of a vase [Jer. xix.11] to signify the shattering of the divine image.

54:1-5 The recognition of everyone's and everything's uniqueness is true liberty (Schorer 1946: 375), and Jerusalem is differently present in every individual (Rose 1973: 85), yet in each individual the "vision of humanity" can be seen (Beer 1969: 245). The contraries, which "co-exist" in Beulah, "are identified" in Eternity (Rose 1970b: 406). Ansari (1969: 205) comments that Cabbala attributes to the unfallen human a body or garment "of the nature of light," but Damrosch (1980: 192) is uncertain whether a garment, being something external, can be wholly good. Miner (1969: 267) cites Ps. civ.2.

54:8   **the Memory between Man & Man**—a caricature of authentic brotherhood, in which emanations must participate (Paley 1983b: 200).

54:9-12 In this context, Luvah has been identified as the passions, whose embrace by Albion's Sons provokes Albion's hatred (Damon 1924: 546), as the "spiritual Hate" of l. 12 (Sloss and Wallis 1926: I, 543), and as a fierce spirit who provokes war (Stevenson 1971: 737).

54:21 See Matt. iv.2-4 (Stevenson 1971: 738).

54:24 The Spectre confuses imagination with the fantasies of wish-fulfilment (Paley 1983b: 200).

54:25-26 Blake associates British monarchy with 'Druid' pagan enemies of Israel (Bloom 1965: 939). Cf. pp. 692-93 above.

54:27-32 Albion's Emanation resists him with stars of reason and dragons of war, and the vision of liberty and nature reconciled is tormented (Damon 1924: 456).

55:1 Several critics accept Damon's identification (1924: 456) of the "Mighty-One" as Albion, though Stevenson (1971: 739) thinks he could be either Albion or Los.

55:11-12 The veil separates ruler from ruled as well as man from woman (Wicksteed 1954: 78-79). See also pp. 685-86 above.

55:13 **the Serpent**—of materialism (Damon 1924: 456); the degenerate Orc (Stevenson 1971: 740).

55:14 **plant them in One Man's Loins**—restrict them to Generation (Damon 1924: 456); a reference to a nation's eponymous ancestor (Frye 1947: 395); a hostile allusion to the concept of the Chosen People (Stevenson 1971: 740).

55:15-16 Joseph's sale into Egypt is a symbol of the Fall (Frye 1947: 381) and to make one family of contraries is to suppress their differences (Stevenson 1971: 740). Damon (1924: 456) treats Joseph's sale as an instance of family dissension, and Beer (1969: 232) writes of a war of contraries within the family.

55:22   A reference to the setting of a guard at the gate of Eden (Bloom 1965: 939).

55:23-25 Blake has seen in tempests the debates of spirits (Stevenson 1971: 740).

55:33   **the Eighth**—Jesus' Second Coming (Frye 1947: 448-49n56); the individual's essential self or Human identity (Wicksteed 1954: 81, 84); the incarnation of the Seven Eyes in every individual (Altizer 1967: 151-55).

55:36-53 Attributing the speeches to the Seven Eyes rather than the whole company of Eternals, Wicksteed (1954: 81-82) claims the former are determined to remember their own divinity while on earth. As Blake engraves (labours at the furrow) or gazes out into the morning sunshine, the inhabitants of his imagination can conceive ideas, see visions, and perceive both multiplicity and unity (Erdman 1951a: 215-17). Blake recognises the reality of earthly experience but holds it subordinate to vision (Bloom 1963: 404).

55:66   **Virginity**—abstinence, the antithesis of circumcision [see 8:32n] (Damon 1924: 456); the refusal "to exercise the Divine Arts of Imagination" (Sloss and Wallis 1926: I, 547, quoting pl. 77); the uncircumcised outer surface's hiding and disempowering of the inner identity (Rose 1968a); deliberate isolation as opposed to participation in some society (Stevenson 1971: 742).

56:7   The line alludes both to the mother's care of the infant and to her weaving of the world-view it will wear as an adult (Stevenson 1971: 742).

56:12   **the iron Reel**—The Daughters govern the iron reel of war and reel drunkenly at 58:3 and in *IB* pl. 69 (Erdman 1954a: 234 [253]).

56:18-25 Stevenson (1971: 743) attributes these thoughts to the timorous souls, who look at everything as it relates to themselves; Ostriker (1977: 1017) believes Los ironically undertakes to shape a world to suit Albion's warlike Daughters. The sun and moon, believes Damon (1924: 456), stand for the vehicle of spiritual war and a vessel of love carrying souls over the Sea of Time and Space. Contrariwise, Wicksteed (1954: 210) sees the sun as time and the moon as "Generation and Death."

56:22-25 Wicksteed (*loc. cit.*) refers straightforwardly to the mother's care of the infant; Webster (1983: 282) thinks Los wishes to substitute for female generation of the body his own creation of it in works of art.

56:26-28 This response of the Daughters of Albion has been said to declare that pleasure has degenerated into matter, imagination into the human worm (Damon 1924: 456); that maternal tenderness has disappeared (Wicksteed 1954: 210-11); that sublime sexual love has been replaced by physical sex (Beer 1969: 233); and that the maternal clay dominates the weak male worm (Webster 1983: 282). Also the Daughters may be proclaiming they see only the mortal element in humans (Stevenson 1971: 743), or Gwendolen, become clay, may both nourish seed and provide a ground for the work of imagination (Rose 1968b: 220, 227).

56:33 **while**—meanwhile (Stevenson 1971: 743).

56:39-40 Either the women cannot endure the blaze of truth (Stevenson, *loc. cit.*), or they are insincere (Paley 1983b: 223).

56:42-43 This sketch of the three Marys at the Cross may allude to neoclassical St. Paul's Cathedral, an emblem of moral virtue (Damon 1924: 456) or to the Twenty-fourth Church, the women being Vala, Rahab and Tirzah (Bloom 1965: 940). Blake may be blaming Paul for making the Church hostile to sex (Damon 1967: 323-24), for elevating the female principle in the form of the Virgin (Ostriker 1977: 1017), or for subordinating women and driving them to create a female will (Hilton 1983: 134-35).

57:2 The Plow of Nations should be used by Los or the Seven Eyes to furrow the fallen world, but Albion has usurped it (Bloom 1965: 940); the phrase "of Nations" hints at Albion's political ambition (Stevenson 1971: 744). Adams (1970: 738) thinks there is chaos in Britain.

57:6-7 At first, Damon (1924: 456) considers Henry II's hiding place for his mistress Rosamund as sheltering love from Satan; later (1967: 350-51) he regards it as an emblem of reprehensible secret love. He associates these place-names with human sacrifice (Stonehenge), embarkation of soldiers (Malden, Colchester), Gwendolen's enticement (the Peak), and justice (the Stone) (*ibid.*). It is the Cities that weep (Stevenson 1971: 744).

57:12-16 Albion is captured by his own past (Damon 1924: 456). The living and dead elements in him are mixed, and the plough divides him from his Spectre (Bloom 1963: 407), which now dominates England in the form of Deism and rationalism (Helms 1974: 138).

57:16-18 At this point, where Albion remains till pl. 95, vision is possible (Bloom 1963: 407). Cf. *M* 15:21ff (Stevenson 1971: 745).

58:1-12 The female will torments humankind with morality (Damon 1924: 456). Gwendolen—cf. the Miriam of Exod. xv. 20—divides supporters and opponents of the war (Ostriker 1977: 1017-18). The castrating females fear male sexuality (Webster 1983: 282-83).

58:3 **the Street of London**—perhaps Watling Street, a Roman road; cf. E542/ K577 (Stevenson 1971: 745-46).

58:11-12 The "Hermaphroditic Condensations" have been interpreted as mixtures of lust and chastity (Damon 1924: 457), as sterile fallen humans of neither sex (Stevenson 1971: 746), as supporters of the war (Ostriker 1977: 1018), and as "fallen male reason and fallen female sexuality" (Doskow 1982: 118). The "obdurate Forms" may be synonymous with them; Ostriker (*loc. cit.*) believes them opponents of the war.

58:15 **Two Contraries**—"Rational Philosophy and Mathematic Demonstration" and "the intoxications of pleasure & affection," the Spectres respectively of Albion and Luvah (Sloss and Wallis 1926: I, 551; II, 200-01); "Rational Philosophy" and "Mathematic Demonstration" (Damon 1967: 150); possibly the pure theorist and the experimenter (Stevenson 1971: 746).

58:19-20 Clear definition of the sexes must precede their true reunion (Paley 1983b: 269). The "comingling" may be either the Peace of Amiens (1802) or the Deism shared by England and France (Ostriker 1977: 1018).

58:22 **a Mighty Temple**—The beautiful description that follows may or may not be deceptive. The possibilities are that this is a temple of pure reason and materialism (Damon 1924: 457) and of empire hiding under an appearance of prelapsarian harmony (Ostriker 1977: 1018), or that Urizen and Los uncharacteristically co-operate (Stevenson 1971: 746-47) and even Urizen's constricting world-framework provides a foundation for Los's redemptive labour (Doskow 1982: 118-19).

58:27-32 Los may make the sun and moon radiant even in Urizen's world (Wicksteed 1954: 212), or they may be trapped in the latter's temple (Damon 1967: 285).

58:35-36 For the eight steps and the three countries named, see Ezek. xl.31 and Dan. xi.43 (Miner 1969: 281).

58:45 Creation occurred here in Britain (Stevenson 1971: 748).

59:3 **To catch the Souls of the Dead**—to make people mistake external appearances for reality (Raine 1968: II, 184).

59:5-6 Humanity is dominated by nature and the female will, for one Deborah was buried under an oak (Gen. xxxv.8) and another lived under a palm (Judg. iv.5) (Frye 1947: 362). These trees could be Adam and Eve separated by the flesh—cf. 55:11 (Miner 1969: 283-84). Cf. *FZ* 18:11/ E310/ I, 464 and n.

59:10-21 Cf. *M* 19:15-25 and 34:31-39 (Bloom 1965: 940). Rose (1965: 600) identifies the "Center" with the White Dot of selfhood (29[33]:19), and Stevenson (1971: 749) believes "the sublime Universe" of l. 21 is Golgonooza.

59:26-41 Recognising both aspects of their labour, Damon (1924: 457) represents the body-weaving of Los's Daughters as cruel yet necessary. It sustains all organic life (Bloom 1965: 940) and counters "the divisive spinnings" of Albion's Daughters (Adams 1970: 738). Frye (1947: 381-82) thinks that their cloth reveals rather than hides the shape of "the mental reality" behind the material surface. On the social level, their fate may reflect conditions in the Royal Asylum for Female Orphans (Stevenson 1971: 749) or the exploitation of women weavers who have become dehumanised, masochistic (l. 34), and the dupes of delusive dreams (Hilton 1983: 122-23).

59:42-43 The toil of the Daughters sustains even Rahab and Tirzah (Bloom 1965: 940). They may be working visionary dreams into the cushions (Stevenson 1971: 750). These women weave for the wealthy (Hilton 1983: 123).

59:48-49 The lamb and sea-fowl are Los's messengers (Sloss and Wallis 1926: I, 554). Christ becomes the Lamb (see pls. 60-61), whose wool sustains the war economy through the labour of exploited mill workers (Rose 1972a: 41-42).

59:55 We regard as sacred the appearance of the world that we ourselves weave (Hilton 1983: 124). For the allusions to the veil of the Tabernacle, see Exod. xxxvi.8-14, xxvi.1-7 (Miner 1961: 50) and Exod. xxxv.25-26 (Stevenson 1971: 750).

60:2 **Albion's Spectre who is Luvah**—These are the now satanic natural man and the corrupted Orc (Bloom 1965: 940); Urizen-within-Albion and Luvah are trapped in a recurrent cycle (Adams 1970: 738); their identity results from the "comingling" of 58:19-20 (Stevenson 1971: 750). Insofar as the Spectre is Britain making war, he is indistinguishable from Napoleonic France (Damon 1967: 382). Lines 1-4 imply that war is imminent (*ibid.*: 13).

60:11 **the Stems of Vegetation**—the phallus (Damon 1924: 457); the churches' Christianity (Sloss and Wallis 1926: I, 555); "organic fibres" (Hagstrum 1964: 115); life in this world (Stevenson 1971: 751); Jesus' mortal body (Damrosch 1980: 296). The last three interpretations may all be valid.

60:18-20 Nimrod's Tower is the Tower of Babel (Damon 1924: 457). Mizraim is both Ham's son (Gen. x.6) and [the Hebrew name for] Egypt (Sloss and Wallis 1926: I, 555). Teshina may be an error for Shinar (e.g. Gen. x.10), near Chaldea (Stevenson 1971: 751).

60:39 **the Dungeons of Babylon**—self-accusation, shortly to be countered by the story of Joseph and Mary (Bloom 1963: 407).

60:41-43 Within the mills of analysis, Jerusalem is tormented by the wheel of her own reason (Beer 1969: 215), her certainty having surrendered to doubt (Ostriker 1977: 1019). According to Rose (1972a: 40), the Wheels of all Albion's Sons have amalgamated to form the Wheel of Hand. Herrstrom's claim (1981: 71) that this is the loom of Vala, who is now dominated by Hand, is less convincing than Raine's observation (1968: I, 204-06) that Vala assumes the role of Venus enslaving Psyche, the soul.

60:60 Jerusalem contrasts scientific astronomy with visionary perception of the stars alluded to in Job xxxviii.31 (Beer 1969: 233).

60:67-69 Cf. Matt. xxviii.20, John xi[.23] (Stevenson 1971: 753), and Mark v.36 (Ostriker 1977: 1019).

61:1-2 "Elohim" signifies judgment and "Jehovah" mercy (Damon 1967: 119).

61:24-27 The allusions to I Kings viii.46, Matt. vi.14, and Matt. i.18-20 seem to have been neglected.

61:27 Mary has succumbed to 'sin' through an impulse of divine origin (Damon 1924: 457). Though she is an adulteress, Mary is "with child by the Holy Ghost" since "the babe in her womb is lifted to Eternity by the act of Forgiveness" (Murry 1933: 285-87).

61:31-33 Blake names the four rivers of Eden (Damon 1924: 457). Mary's happiness at her pardon spreads over all known lands (Ostriker 1977: 1019).

61:33-35 The voice adumbrates the reunion of Jerusalem and Vala-Babylon and shows the intimate connection of Mary with the former (Paley 1983b: 189).

61:35 **another voice**—Vala's (Damon 1924: 457); Mary's (Sloss and Wallis 1926: I, 559); Jerusalem's—cf. Ezek. xvi.5 (Margoliouth 1948: 310-11). The two voices are those of adulteresses who find hope in Mary's story (Stevenson 1971: 754-55).

61:52 Jerusalem can recover her true self (Gallant 1978: 168).

62:8-13 Many of these names have heathen associations to emphasise how the fallen world with its "feminine delusions" is made a place of regeneration (Sloss and Wallis 1926: I, 560). The adulterous mother of Christ's body is descended from non-Israelites and transgressors against the moral law (Damon 1967: 265-66). Stevenson (1971: 756) thinks this Rahab is the Rachab of Matt. i.5, but cf. the list in *FZ* 115:1-9/ E380/ VIII, 357-65, which includes also Tirzah. For "the Body of death," see *J* 9:9n.

62:15-16 Cf. Job xix.25-26 (Bloom 1965: 940) and John xi.23-27 (Stevenson 1971: 756-57).

62:25-28 The imagery is that of the journey through Sinai to Canaan (Damon 1924: 458).

62:30-31 The war that was imminent at 60:1-4 now breaks out (Damon 1967: 13). Luvah's cloud is his desire of domination (Stevenson 1971: 757).

62:35 According to Ostriker (1977: 1020), the rest of the chapter describes what Los sees in his furnaces.

63:1 See *M* 32:11n. Lines 10 and 16 support Stevenson's view (1971: 758) that Jehovah is merciful, which Beer (1969: 190) denies.

63:3-4 **the Plow**—the constellation of this name and the instrument that Albion failed to control at 57:12-15 (Stevenson 1971: 758). Beer (1969: 190) thinks it is a symbol of the law and that Albion drags it.

63:5-6 France (Luvah) suppresses Christianity (Damon 1924: 458), or popular passion ends freedom of the press (Damon 1967: 399). Britain and France share responsibility for destroying the Revolution ("Resurrection"), but Britain imposes deadly peace terms on France (Erdman 1969b: 463). The time is 1814 (Erdman 1954a: 431 [466]).

63:7-8   Vala takes the form of natural religion (Damon 1924: 458), or she imposes superstitions on Albion (Ostriker 1977: 1021). She causes Albion's harshness to France to afflict Britain also (Stevenson 1971: 759).

63:9-10   Thor and Friga are Norse deities of war and love (Damon 1924: 458), once worshipped in pre-Christian England (Stevenson 1971: 759). The chariot wheels derive from those of the Messiah when he routed Satan (Damon 1967: 445, citing *PL*, VI, 750, 847-50).

63:12   Being Jacob's eldest and youngest sons, Reuben and Benjamin signify all humankind—cf. 68:47, 90:46 (Damon 1967: 347). Their separation from a place re-enacts the division of Albion from Israel (Ostriker 1977: 1021).

63:14   **the Fairies lead the Moon**—"natural joys lead Love" (Damon 1924: 458); the moon is degraded, perhaps by paganism (Stevenson 1971: 759).

63:21, 38   **the Looking Glass of Enitharmon**—an old symbol of "Nature as the Mirror of Deity" (Damon 1924: 458); the antithesis of the imagination of 71:15-19 that sees the humanness of all things (Rose 1965: 600-01); a reflection in this world of things eternal (Damon 1967: 246); Boehme's "vegetable glass of nature," which shows that every birth is a reflection of the Incarnation (Raine 1968: I, 239); the moon, with its endless monthly cycle of birth and death (Miner 1981: 325-26). Ostriker (1977: 1021) stresses the negative character of "a mere reflection of eternity."

63:23-24   Damon associates "the Divisions of Reuben" with division into nations (1924: 458) and Cheviot with war (1967: 81)—Raine (1968: II, 321n46) suggests an allusion to "The Ballad of Chevy Chase." Sloss and Wallis (1926: I, 563) connect the Cherubim with forgiveness.

63:35   **Thames & Medway**—associated with British sea power (Beer 1969: 207).

63:38   **the Murder**—of Tharmas by Luvah (Stevenson 1971: 760); of Luvah by Albion (Ostriker 1977: 1021).

63:41-43   The east is the region of error (Sloss and Wallis 1926: I, 564); the Rhine and Danube have seen Roman and Napoleonic wars (Erdman 1954a: 432 [468]). Canaan may represent this world separated from unfallen Albion (Stevenson 1971: 761).

63:44 **head downwards**—Reuben's loins are dominant (Damon 1967: 348); he is undergoing birth (Rose 1971b: 26). Cf. 32(36):2n.

64:2-5 The Veil of Vala (Paley 1983b: 224), identified with the cherubim-adorned veil of the Tabernacle (Miner 1961: 53, citing Exod. xxvi.31), alternates between the sublime and the spectrous (Beer 1969: 207). It makes human perception range from the visionary to the exclusively material (Sloss and Wallis 1926: I, 564), or it cuts humankind off from Eternity operating sometimes within the material creation and sometimes within individuals (Stevenson 1971: 761).

64:13 **Thyself Female**—one whose main function is to contribute to sexual reproduction (Stevenson 1971: 762). Vala mocks the idea that man can ever change "his Sexual Garments at will" (61:51)—i.e. adopt the role of either sex (Webster 1983: 283).

64:14-17 The female will governs through the Pope, whose agent was Arthur, the first king (Damon 1924: 458). See p. 284 above. Arthur, the type of the woman-dominated warrior, went from his mother (Igrayne) to his wet nurse (Sir Ector's wife) to his spouse (Guinevere) (Worrall 1977b: 205); Guinevere betrayed him (Stevenson 1971: 762).

64:21 Rose (1968b: 228) connects "the Spectre's double Cave" with the cave-like eyes of fallen humans, "the caves of sleep" of mortal existence (*FZ* 133:11/ E401/ IX, 627), and the "double Spectres" of "The Keys," *GP*, l. 30.

64: 25-31 There is here an amalgamation of nature and reason (Damon 1924: 458) or an incongruous mixture of nature and spirit (Raine 1968: I, 281-82).

64:32 **Spindle**—Tirzah's Spindle of Necessity (Bloom 1963: 408).

64:34 The taxing, or inhibition of vision, may be the work of either the Daughters or Reuben (Sloss and Wallis 1926: I, 566). There is an allusion to Augustus [see Luke ii.1]—Reuben is an imperialist (Stevenson 1971: 763).

64:35, 38 There are subterranean caverns near Derby Peak, England's highest mountain (Damon 1967: 102). The Chasm, the contrary of the 'prophetic' Peak, is Poole's Hole, whose stalactites and stalagmites suggest Albion's petrifaction; East Moor (80:66; 93:6) represents the mid-level, where reason and prophecy contend (Worrall 1977a).

64:38 **the Caves of Machpelah**—burial place of the patriarchs and their spouses (Bloom 1965: 941).

65:1-4 Christianity is separated from Deism, and humanity is pitied and divided from its passions (Damon 1924: 458). Gwendolen and Ragan wish to decide who will be saved and who condemned (Stevenson 1971: 763). The Hermaphrodite punishes France but not Britain (Ostriker 1977: 1021).

65:4 **the Four Regions**—childhood, maturity, old age and death or Eternity (Stevenson 1971: 763, 653-54).

65:6-55 Cf. *FZ* 92:9-93:19/ E364-65/ VIIb: 162-209 and nn.

65:9 **poisonous blue**—woad (Damon 1924: 459), showing that Luvah is a Druid sacrifice as well as a Christlike victim (Paley 1983b: 39); nitric acid containing some copper and used in etching (Todd 1980). Lesnick (1970: 405) suggests that 33(37):10 shows that Blake associates blue with dying into this world.

65:32 **scythes**—i.e. blades attached to chariot wheels, introduced here to bring in ancient wars (Stevenson 1971: 765).

65:33-36 An allusion to the press-gang (Damon 1924: 458).

65:36 **fearing our officers more than the enemy**—something expected in a Roman soldier. This is one of several borrowings from the first chapter of Gibbon's *Decline and Fall of the Roman Empire* (Erdman 1954a: 432 [468]).

65:57 The corrupted British soldiers behave like Roman legionaries to the defeated French (Erdman 1954a: 432 [468]).

65:58-62 The Spectre devours the passions his rationality otherwise deprives him of (Percival 1938: 101). Taking over the realm that belongs to passion, reason turns into Vala's temple and (ll. 72-79) becomes crazed like Swift (Bloom 1963: 409). The British have absorbed the spirit of Napoleonic France (Erdman 1954a: 432 [468]). "Giant Dance" was reputed to be a Celtic name for Stonehenge (Margoliouth 1951: 163). See also Ezek. xxiii.4, AV marginal readings (Miner 1969: 474n68).

65:68-71 Nature is now reason's sanctum (Damon 1924: 459). Albion's Sons did not know that Vala, who rises as smoke from their victim Albion, was his Emanation (Stevenson 1971:

766). Having killed Luvah to obtain possession of Vala, they find they have internalised the latter (Webster 1983: 285).

66:1-14 The temple of Deism, begun at 58:21, is here completed (Rose 1964c: 54). Blake identifies it with the Tower of Babel that reached towards the stars (Bloom 1963: 409) and with the Ark of the Covenant (Miner 1961: 57—cf. Exod. xxv.17-20) as well as with Stonehenge on Salisbury Plain. The alignment (l. 5) of Stonehenge with the midsummer sun (Stevenson 1971: 767) links it with natural religion (Ostriker 1977: 1022). The Cove, consisting of erect stones on three sides of the altar stone (Stevenson, *loc. cit.*), mimics the cherubim over the Ark's Mercy Seat (Paley 1983a: 195). The teachings of Voltaire and Rousseau that stimulated revolution have undermined it (Erdman 1954a: 387 [416]), or their teachings were anti-revolutionary from the beginning (Damrosch 1980: 100-01).

66:15 English philosophical rationalism has submerged revolutionary passion in France (Schorer 1946: 378).

66:17-19 The High Priest put off his robe to enter the Holy of Holies on the Day of Atonement (Miner 1969: 286-87). By oppressing France, Britain corrupts herself and her women (Erdman 1954a: 431-32 [467]). Cf. also *FZ* 25:25-32/ E314, 317/ II, 57-64n.

66:20-34 The victim has been identified as the poet (Damon 1924: 459); the spirit entering the flesh (*ibid.*; cf. Raine 1968: I, 310-11); the true spirit of Christianity (Sloss and Wallis 1926: I, 570); England, whose landscape has features analogous to his veils and caverns (Frye 1966: 190); the Jesus who dies to save humankind (Mathews 1980a: 167-68); and male sexuality (Paley 1983b: 225-26). Allusions have been detected to the mockery of Christ [Matt. xxvii.37], Sisera with his chariots [Judg. iv] and Mexican human sacrifice (Frye 1947: 398; cf. Margoliouth 1948: 315); the seven shorn locks of Samson (Judg. xvi.19) (Margoliouth 1948: 311); the fate of Dionysus (Raine 1968: I, 311); and the perverted sexuality in the ritual of an execution (Frye 1966: 190).

66:41-43 The flame and fire represent wrath, the wheel fatality (Damon 1924: 459). Cf. Exod. iii.2-6, xiii.21; Ezek. i (Stevenson 1971: 768).

66:45   An allusion to the brevity of the human life span (Damon 1924: 459) and to the cycle of the dying god (Bloom 1963: 411).

66:46-56 In picturing the antithesis of his ideal of brotherhood, Blake equates the Polypus with the Tree of Mystery (Damon 1967: 333; cf. Stevenson 1971: 769).

66:62   Cf. Gray, "The Fatal Sisters," 1. 13 (Miner 1958: 205). The women are operating a loom (Stevenson 1971: 769); the fibres are human flesh (Ostriker 1977: 1022).

66:68-76 The Raven and Dove are sent out into the Sea of Time and Space [cf. Gen. viii.6-12] (Damon 1924: 459). In the chaos after the Flood, the wilderness, being fourfold, is redeemable (Harper 1969: 251-52). Beer (1969: 216) interprets the raven, serpent, dove and eagle as single, twofold, threefold and fourfold vision.

66:79   **Mona**—a Druid island—Anglesey or Man; cf. Milton, "Lycidas," 1. 54 (Stevenson 1971: 770).

67:3-5 Flesh is woven on stone looms (bones) in Porphyry's *The Cave of the Nymphs* (Raine 1968: I, 86-91). "Rock" is an old term for a distaff and its attached wool or flax (Hilton 1983: 109).

67:14-16 The rocks constitute Stonehenge (Stevenson 1971: 771), and "the bloody Veil" is the tormented body (Damon 1924: 459).

67:17-18 **Jerusalem's/ Sons**—the Twelve Tribes, who seek God in a misguided way (Stevenson 1971: 771).

67:23   An allusion to Potiphar's wife seizing Joseph's garment [Gen. xxxix.12] (Damon 1967: 202) or to his coat's being dipped in animals' blood (Gen. xxxvii.31) (Stevenson 1971: 771); the dipping in shed blood is antithetical to Christ's saving descent in robes of blood at the Incarnation (Paley 1973b: 137).

67:29   Beth Peor, where Moses repeated the Law, represents the apex of retributive religion (Sloss and Wallis 1926: I, 574).

67:31-34 The warriors incorporate their dead heroes in their religion (Damon 1967: 395). Having retreated into the distance, the objects of human perception become aggressive (Frosch 1974: 53-54).

67:35-37 Roman roads cover Britain (Damon 1924: 459). The Polypus of war creates empires, including the Roman and

British (Erdman 1954a: 428 [463-64]), and infects several of the Cathedral Cities, Albion's Friends (Stevenson 1971: 772). Francis Bacon, Baron Verulam, is the source of the nature-based philosophy (Bloom 1965: 941). The Sea of Rephaim (variously located) is a storehouse of superstitions (Damon 1967: 346). The passage connects Britain's economic imperialism with Druid sacrifices at Stonehenge on Salisbury Plain (Hilton 1983: 96).

67:41-42 Albion's Daughters limit our mental life (Sloss and Wallis 1926: I, 575). The image comes from Judg. v.26 (Miner 1969: 475n73), though Damon (1924: 459) supposes the golden pin to be the phallus.

67:44-68:9 See notes to *FZ* 105:31-53/ E378-79/ VIII, 298-321.

68:1-2 The Daughters wish to confine Joseph, the type of the Redeemer, and the destroyer Schofield in the same fleshly prison (Paley 1973b: 137).

68:18 **Double God of Generation**—perhaps an allusion to the Hermaphrodite (Damon 1924: 459) or homosexuality (Damon 1967: 376). Molech and Chemosh, to whom children were sacrificed, are sometimes identified (Stevenson 1971: 774). Blake wrongly supposes Chemosh female (Ostriker 1977: 1023).

68:19-23 An act of circumcision forms the fallen world (Wagenknecht 1973: 279). The "sheet of generation" alludes to Acts x.11-12 (Miner 1969: 275-76). The Valley of the Jebusite is the Valley of Kidron, a place of interment (Damon 1967: 205) or the Valley of Hinnom, where children were sacrificed (Miner 1969: 276, citing Josh. xv.8 and Jer. vii.31-32).

68:31 Blake combines allusions to the sacrifice of a seven-year-old bullock (Judg. vi.25-26) and of children (Is. lvii.3-5) (Miner 1969: 285-86).

68:38 **from Havilah to Shur**—land of the Ishmaelites (Gen. xxv.18) (Margoliouth 1948: 311).

68:39-40 Shaddai and Jehovah, two of the Seven Eyes of God (Sloss and Wallis 1926: I, 280, 577) vainly oppose these sacrifices (Stevenson 1971: 775).

68:41 **Twelve Stones of Power**—the twelve altars of 28:21 (Sloss and Wallis 1926: I, 577) or the twelve stones memorialising the passage of the Ark over the Jordan (Johnson and Grant 1979: 343, citing Josh. iv).

68:42 The spear is intellectual and the love "that false/ And Generating Love" (Sloss and Wallis 1926: I, 577—cf. 17:25-26 and n). Stevenson (1971: 775) notes the mingled allusions to war, religion and sex, and Hilton (1983: 134) remarks that Blake identifies the penetrating phallus with the weapon that pierced Jesus' side (John xix.34).

68:51 **Uzzah**—an Israelite struck dead for touching the Ark (Damon 1924: 459, citing I Chron. xiii.10); the type of the warrior-victim of Albion's Daughters (Bloom 1965: 941). Ostriker (1977: 1023) describes the spear and Ark as sexual.

68:52 **Great Tartary**—a probable allusion to Napoleon's invasion of Russia in 1812 (Erdman 1954a: 430 [466]).

68:55, 61 **Rehob in Hamath/ Meribah Kadesh**—the northern and southern extremities of Canaan-England; Moses' spies visited Rehob, and Meribah means "strife" (Bloom 1965: 941).

69:1-5 The "One Male" is Hand (Damon 1924: 459); "the Female" is distorted perception (Sloss and Wallis 1926: I, 578-79)—cf. 69:38n. The Polypus of empire obliterates liberty worldwide (Erdman 1954a: 428 [463]).

69:11-13 Blake refers to Laban's cheating, to jealousy between Leah and Rachel, and to Rachel's theft of images (Sloss and Wallis 1926: I, 579). He sees Jacob as Albion and Jacob's wives as manifestations of Vala (Frye 1947: 364).

69:26-37 Too long a stay in Beulah brings corruption (Beer 1969: 248-49). Beulah is infected by Ulro (Stevenson 1971: 777), its Daughters degenerate from muses to sexual temptresses (Damrosch 1980: 222-23), love is corrupted by jealousy (Damon 1967: 395), marriage suffers (Bloom 1963: 412), and the warriors who are repressed establish a repressive creed (Stevenson, *loc. cit.*). Los's world is the world of generation (Miner 1961: 56), where sexuality involves being born and dying (Ostriker 1977: 1024).

69:38 **the disobedient Female**—"the recalcitrant emotions and the world of sense" Percival (1938: 117).

69:38-44 There is no sequestered, sacred place in Eden, where all is holy (Bloom 1963: 412). The Circumference, unlike the indefinite hidden Centre, has a clear outline (Rose 1965: 604, 605). Damon (1924: 460) identifies the outline as the spiritual body, Ostriker (1977: 1024) believes Blake refers to both a total sexual communion and the entire people's free access to holiness, Paley (1983b: 201) writes of "polymorphous perversity," and Webster (1983: 286) accuses Blake of idealising "the total body sensuality of the child." Cf. Lev. xvi.2, 13-17 (Miner 1961: 56), Heb. xiii.13 and Rev.xx.9 (Wicksteed 1954: 216), and *PL*, VIII, 620-29 (Bloom 1963: 412). Paley (1983b: 150, 155-56) notes John Lightfoot's claim (*The Temple: Especially As it stood in the dayes of our Saviour* [1650], p. 254) that the four Living Creatures of Rev. iv.6 [Blake's Zoas] formed a square round the Divine Throne analogous to the Israelite camp pitched on the four sides of the Tabernacle.

70:5 Damon (1924: 460) theorises that the three heads represent the contradictory impulses of head, heart and loins.

70:8 Locke's *An Essay Concerning Human Understanding* (IV. i.2) bases knowledge on our perception of how our ideas agree and disagree (Fisher 1961: 120-21).

70:17-31 Rahab, the maiden of "The Crystal Cabinet," is here a type of the Church's seductive claim to provide the only route to salvation (Bloom 1963: 413-14). She is the feminine principle that lures souls down into the material world (Raine 1968: I, 277). Her description is a satiric parody of the eighteenth-century pathetic mode and of Burke's concept of the Beautiful (Paley 1983b: 68, 194).

71:1 **the Heavenly Canaan**—Eternity (Sloss and Wallis 1926: I, 582); Palestine, which brought redemption through Christ's Incarnation (Wicksteed 1954: 217); the paradise within the human being (Beer 1969: 249-50).

71:1-49 A development of the idea expressed at 63:41-44 (Stevenson 1971: 780). Damon (1924: 460) supposes southern Britain to correspond to the loins, central Britain to the heart, and the last four places listed to the head.

71:6-9 **Circumference...Center**—body and emotions (Damon 1924: 460). Blake adopts Boehme's teaching that the essence is above and within, the outward form below (Raine 1968: II, 157). The Selfish Centre is a minute entity outside both oneself and other people (Grimes 1973: 76). The Circumference, which sustains brotherhood, is within (Deen 1983: 212).

71:10-49 A description of the Sons and Daughters in Innocence (Damon 1967: 15); an account of Albion's former condition in Eternity (Stevenson 1971: 780). The Cities' inner spirits are the deadly Sons of Albion (Bloom 1963: 414).

71:23 Boadicea is "the Warring Female" (Damon 1967: 66) and, though culpable as such, admirable for her resistance to Rome (Paley 1983b: 229).

71:50 Cf. *M* 23:62-24:13 (Stevenson 1971: 781).

71:56-63 Blake renounces clear and open prophecy and perhaps defends the cryptic character of *Jerusalem* (Bloom 1965: 942).

72:1-27 This is the second part of the list of counties, the first being 16:28-60; the allotment of the Irish counties to the Twelve Tribes is parallel to their positioning in "the Four Camps" round the Tabernacle in Num. ii, but the allotment of Great Britain's counties is chaotic to represent the fallen state (Damon 1924: 442-43, 460). Ireland stands for the personal vision cut off when the Western Gate was closed at the Fall (Frye 1947: 380); its thirty-two counties represent the thirty-two nations (*ibid.*).

72:42-44 The nations are islands in the Sea of Time and Space (Damon 1924: 461). Though Blake seems to consider that only thirty-two nations exist, Damon (1967: 294) believes that these thirty-two are a fraternity of countries that will rule the remainder of the earth and preserve Jerusalem or freedom.

72:46-47 The earth and the Mundane Shell are both images of the historical and cosmic process of the Fall; each image is the reverse of the other (Altizer 1967: 126).

72:50-52 Unfit for the mental strife of Eternity (Bloom 1963: 415), these Quietists associated with Beulah contrast with the prophets (Fisher 1959: 169). However, Damon (1967: 449) regards the winepress they guide as spiritual war. He identifies the "Four precious stones" with those of 59:1 (1967: 388). Beer (1969: 251) observes that the Quietists regard sexual love as an image of sacred love.

73:9-14 The instruments and weapons listed represent regenerative spiritual toil (Sloss and Wallis 1926: I, 587); the rollers are those of Blake's printing press (Paley 1983b: 243).

73:16ff **Albion's Tomb**—the sky, whose stars symbolise the reason which tries to discern humanity's fate unaided by imagination and love (sun and moon) (Damon 1924: 461); the world of mortality, which Los's Sons are seeking the means of redeeming as they study the malign constellations (Stevenson 1971: 785), including Orion and Ophiucus, which are Og and Anak (Miner 1981: 310). Cf. *M* 28:25-28 (Miner 1981: 335).

73:22   **Luvah's World of Opakeness**—his materialised emana-
tion, nature (Damon 1924: 461); Ulro (Sloss and Wallis 1926:
I, 587).

73:24   **Los, who is of the Elohim**—Los is among the creators of
the material world, but he creates to promote redemption (Pal-
ey 1983b: 268-69).

73:25-26   The female is subordinated to the male for the sake of
the generation that is necessary for regeneration—cf. 53:26-28
(Percival 1938: 119-20). The emanation becomes a continu-
ously fertile female (Stevenson 1971: 786).

73:27-28   Los and Jesus are here partly (Damon 1924: 461) or
completely (Bloom 1965: 942) identified. Adam contains pairs
of conflicting contraries (Damon 1967: 5). Peleg (Gen. x.25),
Esau and Saul are visionless energy; Joktan, Jacob and David
are contracted vision (Beer 1969: 363n48).

73:29-37   Voltaire implies there is no escape from finite nature
(Percival 1938: 233), for he mistakes for harsh bonds the mer-
ciful limits imposed on her fall by Los and Jesus (Bloom 1965:
942), limits which would become poisons if Los did not break
and remake them (Damrosch 1980: 325). He supports Deist
monarchs (Beer 1969: 251). Blake deleted l. 37 as possibly sed-
itious (Erdman 1954a: 385 [413-14]) or to heed his own adm-
onition against vengeance (Erdman 1974: 352).

73:46-52   See *FZ* 90:5-43/ E370-71/ VII, 436-75n.

73:54   **Primrose Hill**—on the northwest outskirts of London.

74:23, 27   There may be a connection with the shutting of the
fourfold Western Gate (Sloss and Wallis 1926: I, 590). The
fourfold sixteen is reduced to the threefold twelve (Rose 1965:
593).

74:28   Hayley cramped Blake (Stevenson 1971: 789).

74:30   **Gog**—the conqueror of Ezek. xxxviii-xxxix, doomed to
destruction (Damon 1967: 162).

74:39   See 38(43):62n.

74:42-51   This stage of the Fall has been described as the settle-
ment of the Twelve Tribes among the Canaanites (Sloss and
Wallis 1926: I, 590-91); the enrooting of Reuben, released by
the Daughters, in a land that is petrified as he is (Bloom 1963:
415); the creation of nations (Damon 1967: 202); and the birth
of twelve Sons of Jerusalem into the material world (Stevenson

1971: 790). The forty-eight roots may be cities (*ibid.*); Sloss and Wallis (1926: I, 591) aptly cite *M* 38:1-2.

74:54 Since her brothers slew her lover, Shechem (Gen. xxxiv), Dinah has been interpreted as "violated Innocence" (Wicksteed 1954: 219), as persecuted love (Kiralis 1959: 204) analogous to oppressed Ireland (Stevenson 1971: 790), as a harbinger of violent apocalypse (Adams 1970: 739), and as the right, non-violent response to Irish suffering (Paley 1983b: 186). Rose (1965: 597) regards her as the emanation of all Israel-Albion's Sons, and Frosch (1974: 95) as an early manifestation of the emanation redeemed. Noting Boehme's understanding of Dinah as the focus of conflict between Christians, Raine (1968: II, 304-05) suggests an allusion to the Catholic-Protestant clash in Ireland.

74:57 **the Land of Cabul**—Ulro; see I Kings ix.13 (Sloss and Wallis 1926: I, 591). Note the AV marginal reading, *"Displeasing, or, Dirty"* (Margoliouth 1948: 311).

75:2-3 **Merlin & Bladud & Arthur**—the enslaved imagination, senses and reason in the possession of the fallen body, Bath, whose founder Bladud was (Damon 1924: 456, 461). Rahab is the Whore of Babylon with her cup (Bloom 1965: 942)—see Rev. xvii.4.

75:7-9 Bowlahoola digests possibilities, while Cathedron is the body of actual events (Fisher 1961: 61). Los is a John the Baptist preparing the way for Jesus—see 75:21 (McGann 1973: 19).

75:10-20 See *M* 37:35-43n.

75:23 Los bestows form on the heavens created by Rahab (Stevenson 1971: 792).

75:24-26 Los saves humanity from everlasting entrapment in a cycle (Sloss and Wallis 1926: II, 209). Three is the number of cyclic recurrence, and the *third* chapter ends where the *first* began (Frye 1947: 368). It ends where *FZ*, VIII concludes (Bloom 1963: 416).

pl. 77 **"Saul Saul"**—the Church founded by Paul (Bloom 1963: 416). The reader (Easson 1973: 315) or the nominal Christian (Ostriker 1977: 1026-27), who is, like Saul, in need of enlightenment. See Acts ix.4.

   Poem 1 l. 1 **a golden string**—the umbilical cord that leads to the world's navel, Jerusalem (Rose 1965: 597); the thread that leads from the labyrinth when the minotaur of selfhood is slain (Easson 1973: 313-14).

1. 2 Wind the recurrent cycle of nature into the sphere of perfection (Adams 1963: 80-81). The ball is the visionary sun that rises when time ends (Rose 1966: 113-14).

1. 4 When desire is not blocked by the wall of chastity (an Old Testament symbol), it becomes imagination and escapes from the Orc cycle (Rose 1963: 50).

We are told...incoherent roots—Several critics endorse Damon's view (1924: 461) that this is an ironic exposition of puritanical beliefs that Blake rejects; others hold with Sloss and Wallis (1926: II, 114) that it is an expression of his dedication. Among the latter is Tolley (1973: 100-01), who cites Rom. xiii.11-14.

the liberty both of body and mind—For Mitchell (1978: 174) this phrase just saves Blake from undermining his life-long opposition to body-mind dualism; Damrosch (1980: 213-14) more convincingly relates it to his ambivalence towards the body.

Imagination the real...the Building up of Jerusalem—Miner (1969: 270) notes the allusions to Matt. xiii.27 and vi.25; Ostriker (1977: 1027) adds Matt. xxv[.14-30], vi.19-21 and vii.7-11. Idleness, as Blackstone remarks (1949: 394), is the antithesis of the free play of energy.

Poem 2 1.1 **my valleys of the south**—The south is the intellectual quarter (Damon 1924: 462). The reference may be to "Felpham's Vale" [e. g. *M* 23:37] (Sloss and Wallis 1926: I, 594).

11. 2-3 **a Wheel/ Of fire**—the wheel of Shakespeare's *King Lear* IV.vii.47 (Frye 1947: 246); identical with the Starry Wheels of Albion's Sons (Bloom 1963: 417) and (Rose 1972a: 43) closely related to the wheels of industry; a parody of the Divine Chariot of Ezekiel (Bloom 1971: 66-67) or the fiery whirlwind of Ezek. i.4 (Ferguson 1978: 186). See also Jas. iii.6 (AV marginal reading "wheel") and 10 (Miner 1969: 271).

1. 4 **From west to east**—anticlockwise (Damon 1924: 462); from the quarter of illumination against that of error (Sloss and Wallis 1926: II, 139); from the circumference, Tharmas's Edenic quarter, to the heart, the quarter left empty by fallen Luvah—see *FZ* 71:24/ E348/ VI, 156 (Percival 1938: 244);

opposite to the sun's course or "current of/ Creation" (Bloom 1963: 417) but in the direction of the movement of the planets, early objects of idolatry (Hilton 1983: 224).

ll. 7-8 Damon, as usual, identifies the sun with imagination, the moon with love (1924: 461).

l. 12 **a Watcher & a Holy-One**—"Blake's Muse" (Schorer 1946: 380); the phrase comes from Dan. iv.13 (Margoliouth 1948: 311); in effect, Los (Rose 1966: 113); possibly Ezekiel (Bloom 1971: 67, quoting iii.17).

l. 15 **devouring sword**—the "flaming sword" of Gen. iii.24, which Boehme interprets as both the sword of judgment barring from Paradise and the sword of death that cuts off the body—less harshly since Christ broke it—to readmit the soul (Raine 1968: I, 330-32; cf. also Hilton 1983: 225-26); the sword of physical warfare (Erdman 1977c: 522).

l. 34 **For Hell is open'd to Heaven**—The movement of the wheel of fire can be reversed (Bloom 1963: 418). Cf. 75:21-22 (Rose 1965: 595).

Poem 3 l. 9 Regeneration comes at the lowest point of the Fall (Schorer 1946: 380). The time foreseen in "And did those feet in ancient time" (*M* pl. 1) has arrived (Johnson and Grant 1979: 348).

ll. 9-12 As the imagination gives form to nature, the city should provide a focus or foundation for the nation's essential form (Johnston 1970: 440). "London's towers" may be the subject of "exult" or of "Recieve"; "Recieve" may be present indicative or imperative (Tolley 1973: 97).

78:3 **his mace of iron**—the club of the constellation Orion, with whom Los is identified (Miner 1969: 264).

78:5-6 The shattered forms are types of government, church, etc. (Percival 1938: 212). Cf. Is. xxx.14 (Bloom 1963: 418).

78:7 After each hermaphroditic conjunction, Los must separate the sexes or contraries so that they may reach through conflict a union in which both survive (Percival 1938: 120-21).

78:17 **The Concave Earth**—the flesh, according to Damon (1924: 462), but *M* 17:21 shows it is the Mundane Shell.

78:21-23 Cf. Lam. i.5, 8, and ii.9; Rev. xxi.12 (Margoliouth 1948: 311).

79:3 See 32(36):10-12n.

79:7 **The mountain of blessing**—Gerizim (Deut. xi.29) (Miner 1969: 273).

79:10-13 Jesus withdrew with his disciples to Ephraim (John xi.54); Shiloh is equated with the Messiah; to follow Philistea is to practise idolatry; and in Goshen, Egypt, the Israelites were exempt from the plague of darkness (Exod. viii.22, x.21-23) (Miner 1969: 272-73). Stevenson (1971: 798) believes the Palestinian Goshen of Josh. x.41 is referred to. For Gilead, see Jer. viii.22 (Damon 1967: 157).

79:24 Liberty prevailed worldwide before empires were created (Erdman 1954a: 428 [463]).

79:35 For the river Kishon, see Judg. v.21 (Damon 1967: 229).

79:39-44 There are references to revolutionary France (Erdman 1974: 342) and Spain's St. Teresa (Damon 1967: 398).

79:54 Seraphim are traditionally characterised by love, cherubim by wisdom (Damon 1967: 80). The mountains are of Atlantis (Bloom 1963: 418-19).

79:58-59 Damon (1924: 462) perceives the cherubim of reason protecting Divinity in its Ark, where Webster (1983: 288) finds an image of female sexual liberality.

79:65 **count the bones**—a deliberate contrast with Ezekiel's resurrection of dead bones (Ferguson 1978: 190, citing Ezek. xxxvii.10).

79:70-72 The masculine aspect of Vala, the Jungian animus, has taken control of her; the same is true of Gwendolen in pls. 81 and 82 (Gallant 1978: 171-73).

79:78 **realize**—treat as real; the nets symbolise sexuality (Ostriker 1977: 1027).

80:1 **the frozen Net...the rooted Tree**—the net of matter and Tree of Mystery (Damon 1924: 462). The net is Vala's Veil (Stevenson 1971: 800).

80:8-9 The songs are heard from Israel to Babylon (*ibid.*).

80:14-15 **Woman**—either the feminine element of emotion and sense perception as ruler of the whole person (Percival 1938: 117) or woman as an independent being (Stevenson 1971: 800).

80:16-23 Possibilities are that Albion overcame his passions (Luvah) but nature (Vala) revived them and exacted retribution (Damon 1924: 462) and that beauty (Vala) slew her admirer

Albion but puts the blame on desire (Luvah), who set her on (Bloom 1963: 419).

80:27-29　As a vegetation deity, Vala awaits the resurrection of the dying god Luvah (Bloom 1963: 419), and seeks to avoid the repetition of his annual death at the hands of Albion (Adams 1970: 740); the latter must not kill what remains of passion and energy (Altizer 1967: 99-100).

80:31-36　The Spindle is Tirzah's Spindle of Necessity (Bloom 1965: 943), and the Dragon is war (Damon 1924: 462). From the Dragon and Jerusalem, Vala wishes to create a church (Ostriker 1977: 1028).

80:41-42　Wicksteed (1954: 227) believes that Los sees a redeeming element in Gwendolen and Cambel. For "Stones of power" (l. 45), see 68:41n.

80:57-66　This account of the total domination of Hand and Hyle by their seductive emanations involves geographical symbolism. Margoliouth (1951: 167) stigmatises Skiddaw and Derbyshire as unspiritual "barren masses"; Stevenson (1971: 802) regards Albion's mountains as his bones. Cf. 64:35n.

80:64　The spirit of Hand is destroying Europe (Rose 1964c: 55).

80:74-79　To subordinate Hyle, Gwendolen confines his sexuality to his testicles and subjects it to moral law (Riede 1981: 548-49)—cf. 47:3-9n.

81:2-14　Gwendolen boasts of having reduced man to "spiritual infancy" (Damon 1924: 463). She desires one more subservient than Merlin or even Reuben (Bloom 1963: 420), and line 7 expresses her fear of sex (Paley 1983b: 227). Reuben is physical and Joseph imaginative love (Beer 1969: 234), and her beloved is Hyle (Stevenson 1971: 803).

81:15-16　These lines, which express Gwendolen's thought (Stevenson 1971: 804), may belong to the design (Wicksteed 1954: 228) or serve as both a caption and part of the text (Erdman, Textual Notes, E812). In the reversed inscription, "Especially to the Female" may modify the preceding couplet or draw the attention of females to it (Stevenson, *loc. cit.*).

82:8　**Hyle is become a weeping infant**—The dominant empirical philosophy has turned the world into a womb in which it is itself reborn "into spiritual second childhood" (Bloom 1965: 943). Blake may be mocking the prophetess Joanna Southcott's claim to have been impregnated by the Holy Spirit (Paley 1983b: 134-35).

82:17-21 Margoliouth (1951: 167-68) is probably right in identifying the Falsehood as ll. 22-44 of this plate, though Damon (1924: 463) has a case for claiming it is the couplet in mirror writing—"But if you on Earth Forgive/ You shall not find where to Live"—behind the motto to which Gwendolen points in pl. 81. Frye (1947: 402) defines the Falsehood as a "perverted vision of life" imposed on Hyle and Rose (1964c: 55) as "this world."

82:26-31 Gwendolen hopes to seduce the male with a distortion of true civilisation (Mitchell 1978: 190).

82:33 **the Friend of Sinners**—Jerusalem (Wicksteed 1954: 230). Cf. Heb. xiii.12 (Stevenson 1971: 805).

82:34-35 **her secret Ark**—a sexual symbol; "permanent" signifies virgin (Stevenson 1971: 805-06).

82:43 Cf. Cant. vii.4 (Margoliouth 1948: 311-12).

82:44-45 **From Mam-Tor to Dovedale**—from breast to pubes (Wicksteed 1954: 230); a double peak and a beautiful valley, both in Derbyshire (Damon 1967: 107, 260).

82:47 **a winding Worm**—without head, heart or loins (Damon 1924: 463); entirely of the earth (Frye 1947: 402); both phallic and devouring (Ostriker 1977: 1029).

82:56 **Seventh Furnace**—Jesus (Damon 1924: 463); a hint the seventh and last cycle is now finished (Wagenknecht 1973: 283).

82:59 Los berates Cambel in foul (Billingsgate) language (Ostriker 1977: 1029).

82:65-71 Though she purposes evil (Stevenson 1971: 807), Cambel exhibits some self-sacrifice (Damon 1924: 463); her infant Hand, however, is deformed (Bloom 1965: 943).

82:72-76 The wind of inspiration from Los's bellows influences the first unambiguous change of heart in the poem (Bloom 1963: 421), namely Gwendolen's repentance (Damon 1924: 192).

82:81-84 Fallen Los here first recognises he is Urthona (Bloom 1963: 421). It may be Enitharmon who draws him down (Sloss and Wallis 1926: I, 607-08), tempting him to base his art on the external world (Frosch 1974: 43). Riede (1981: 549) thinks the "fountain of veiny pipes" is the erect phallus, which indi-

cates Los's subjection to his own sexual desire. Los-Blake ref-
uses to desert the British people (Erdman 1954a: 444 [481]);
his expatiating is verbal expression as well as physical move-
ment (Ostriker 1977: 1029).

83:5 **Enion! Tharmas!**—parents of Los and Enitharmon in *FZ*, I
(Damon 1924: 463).

83:7-8 Regardless of Jerusalem's freely given love, the British
scorn the unmarried mother (Stevenson 1971: 808).

83:10-13 The stone masses are Avebury and Stonehenge; nailing
Luvah and Vala down exposes their errors (Sloss and Wallis
1926: I, 608). Like "Found" (83:23), "determine" is an impera-
tive verb (Stevenson 1971: 808, 809).

83:25-27 **Surrey and Sussex**—the counties where Blake's Lam-
beth and Felpham are situated (Damon 1967: 391); the laby-
rinths are his poems (Miner 1969: 292, 477n85).

83:27-32 While there is general agreement that Oothoon remains
a positive, sexual figure, Antamon has been charged with hein-
ous indulgence in secret love (Worrall 1977b: 212-13), though
this "sickening sight" may be the unavoidable price of saving
the female from Hand (Damrosch 1980: 320). Oxford is the
site of Rosamund's Bower (Damon 1924: 454—see 57:6-7n);
under a veil of orthodoxy, English universities allow much
freedom of thought (Beer 1969: 218).

83:33-39 The sisters are the feminine elements that govern our
sense perception and hence our view of the universe (Percival
1938: 111, 194); Beer (1969: 218) thinks Oxford affords them
a measure of imagination. The body, the world's appearance,
and the mind's workings are all woven (Hilton 1983: 119).

83:40-41 These lines refer to the Copernican, Ptolemaic and
Blakean conceptions of the earth (Damon 1967: 418).

83:49 Albion's emanations have degenerated into female wills
(Damon 1967: 16).

83:51 **the old Parent**—possibly Albion (Sloss and Wallis 1926:
I, 609); Father Thames and perhaps Tharmas (Ostriker 1977:
1030).

83:54-56 There is danger of revolution in England (Beer 1969:
218-19).

83:59 The allusion may be to Llewelyn ab Gruffydd, last ruler of
independent Wales (1254-82) (Damon 1967: 243), or the sup-
posed twelfth-century Welsh settlement in America (*ibid.*), or

the Britons being driven into Wales to retain their freedom (Stevenson 1971: 810).

83:81 **The stars rising & setting**—souls returning to and departing from Eternity (Raine 1968: I, 173).

83:82-83 **the Dogs of Leutha**—Actaeon's devourers, who stand for Puritanism (Damon 1924: 463) or destructive passions (Damon 1967: 239); demons of the material realm or matter personified (Raine 1968: I, 173-74). Ostriker (1977: 1030) thinks the Dogs are here tame. Cf. *PL*, II, 654-58 (Miner 1981: 318).

83:84ff Though self-exiled, the Daughters are nostalgic for Jerusalem (Margoliouth 1951: 168). They are repentant but muddled (Bloom 1963: 422).

84:3 **We builded Jerusalem**—a lie (Paley 1983b: 223).

84:15-16 Damon (1967: 59, 166-67, 332) records that Blake was born at the corner of Broad Street; apprenticed to Basire of Great Queen Street, Lincolns Inn Fields, and lived at 28 Poland Street from 1785 to 1791.

84:20-30 The Daughters simultaneously appeal to Los and court Hand, then regress to unite with Rahab (Bloom 1963: 423). They have ceased repenting and want Los to help them to dominate the Sons (Stevenson 1971: 812). For "Double Molech & Chemosh," see 68:18n.

84:31-85:2 **a Space & an Allegory**—a religion that envelopes humanity with a pseudo-paradise (Damon 1924: 463-64); a fallen Canaan or perverted image of the Promised Land into which Hyle will be reborn as the safely unrebellious nature of the Deists (Frye 1947: 402); a land of moon-worship analogous to Beulah and hence possessing redemptive potential (Bloom 1963: 424); marriage, in which Reuben settles three lines later—cf. 88:30-31 (Damon 1967: 212); a theological falsehood in which Los deposits the germ of truth (Ostriker 1977: 1030); abstract concepts purporting to explain the material world but transformed by imagination into symbolism (Doskow 1982: 149).

85:4 **twelvefold**—The association of Reuben's wanderings with the Twelve Tribes, the Zodiac and the months implies that they take place in cyclical time (Rose 1971b: 27).

85:7 **Divine Analogy**—history, a distorted imitation of Eternity (Damon 1924: 464); the parallel between events from Abraham

to Jesus and the last part of Reuben's regeneration (Sloss and
Wallis 1926: II, 215-16); the events of the Old Testament,
which should be read analogically (Wicksteed 1954: 232); the
Newtonian model of the universe, which is not objective but a
mere analogy of the visionary model (Fisher 1961: 111-12);
"the whole cycle of history" (Bloom 1963: 424); both the Mun-
dane Shell and the fallen human mind (Rose 1973: 92).

85:9 **The Seeds of beauty**—the seeds of 83:55 (Doskow 1982:
148-49). Cf. 85:28.

85:12 **the East**—the region of error (Sloss and Wallis 1926: I,
612); the quarter of the dawn (Rose 1968b: 225).

85:22-86:32 This evocation of Jerusalem—and *Jerusalem*—ming-
les the earthly with the heavenly because Albion is not yet
restored (Rose 1968b: 220-21); she is only threefold because
she lacks Vala, who is nature and the body (Doskow 1982:
150-51). There are allusions to Rev.xxi.2 (Damon 1924: 464);
Rev.xxii.1-2 (Sloss and Wallis 1926: I, 614); Exod. xxviii and
Is. vi.2 (Stevenson 1971: 815, 816).

85:28 **Sisters**—the Daughters of Beulah (Sloss and Wallis 1926:
I, 613).

85:30-32 Jerusalem fell into error and imperialist ambitions bef-
ore the Israelite exile in Babylon (Stevenson 1971: 814).

86:23-25 Seraphim are held to burn with the love of God (cf.
Damon 1967: 365).

86:28-32 Earthly enemies are reconciled in Eternity (Stevenson
1971: 816). Javan is Greece (Damon 1967: 204-05).

86:42-49 The only way to redemption is through earthly life
(Sloss and Wallis 1926: I, 614), into which one is generated by
beings whose emanations weave one a body in Golgonooza
(Stevenson 1971: 816). The Daughters of Albion submit them-
selves to Los's furnaces and become his children. Beer (1969:
254) believes that to "consummate bliss" in threefold vision
provokes a fall into single vision, as in "The Crystal Cabinet."

86:46 The worm endangers the pre-biblical divine revelation
preserved, according to Swedenborg, in Tartary (Paley 1983b:
220-21).

86:50-60 When Enitharmon divides from Los for the reason
given in 86:42-43 (Wagenknecht 1973: 284), her appearance
parodies the rainbow of 86:21 and presents Los with a major
test preparatory to his union with Christ (Ferguson 1978: 173).

The "Globe of blood" is nature, which can be seen as either devouring or light-bearing (Doskow 1982: 149-50); the rainbow represents the deceptive loveliness of the material universe (Paley 1983b: 256).

86:54-57 The Spectre may disrupt artistic co-operation between Los-William and Enitharmon-Catherine (Paley 1983b: 259).

86:62-87:2 This passage recalls the rebirth of Los and Enitharmon as children of Tharmas and Enion in *FZ*, I (Damon 1924: 192), but Los has now passed from Innocence to the maturity of Experience (Bloom 1963: 425), and Enitharmon is close enough to him to reject Enion or materialism (Doskow 1982: 152).

87:6 **roots**—matter (Damon 1924: 464); outgrowths of the Tree of Mystery (Sloss and Wallis 1926: I, 615); genitality (Hilton 1983: 92-93).

87:7-11 On one level, William asks Catherine to help produce the illuminated books (Paley 1983b: 257).

87:13-14 The woman will produce and govern the children (Stevenson 1971: 818).

87:18-20, 88:2-15 Enitharmon conceives of relations between portions of beings, Los of relations between complete beings (Stevenson 1971: 816).

87:19-20 The jewels—see Ezek. xxviii.13—are contained in "symbolic semen"; cf. 9:23-25 (Miner 1969: 270).

87:24 "his Daughter"—either Jerusalem or Vala (Sloss and Wallis 1926: I, 616); Jerusalem, whom Los is trying to free (Stevenson 1971: 818).

88:2 **the starry round**—of time (Stevenson 1971: 818).

88:3-10 Cf. 39(44):38 and 71:16 (Damon 1924: 464). Despite the evidence of the latter line, Ault (1974: 185) supposes this passage describes an Eternity that has begun to fall.

88:15 **secret joy**—for Blake, reprehensible (Sloss and Wallis 1926: I, 616).

88:16-19 By idealising women, Arthur created the female will (Damon 1967: 29-30). Both Merlin and Arthur were ruined by women (Stevenson 1971: 819). Worrall (1977b: 206) proposes that the genitals where Arthur was conceived and the breasts he sucked (his mother and his nurse being chosen by Merlin) constitute the triple tabernacle.

88:23 **Sussex**—i.e. Felpham in Sussex, where Blake was parted from his inspiration (Damon 1924: 464) or had an uneasy relationship with his wife (Damrosch 1980: 210).

88:31 **Allegoric Night**—love (Damon 1924: 464); the realm, created by Albion's Daughters, that we perceive through our senses (Sloss and Wallis 1926: I, 617); the fallen world in need of transformation by the Divine Analogy of 85:7 (Rose 1965: 588); the Allegory of 85:1, namely marriage, which has now become widespread (Damon 1967: 212).

88:34-43 Experiencing both sexual desire, which imbues him with guilt, and squeamish loathing of bodily sexuality, the Spectre hates the Enitharmon who provokes his passion (Paley 1983b: 259-60).

88:37-40 **their places of joy & love**—the genitals (Beer 1969: 256), about which the Spectre creates emotional uneasiness (Frosch 1974: 163); this the older Blake partially shares (Damrosch 1980: 196).

88:47 Tainted by the Spectre's association of desire with guilt, Los isolates sexuality from the rest of life (Paley 1983b: 260).

88:51-54 **the Wheels of Enitharmon**—beneficent spinning wheels (Damon 1967: 445); demonic looms (Rose 1972a: 43). From Jerusalem influenced by Vala, comes the bodily form, linked to Urizenic religion, that Jesus enters (Wagenknecht 1973: 284).

88:56 The cup (cf. 75:3) is filled with "Moral Virtue" (Damon 1924: 464), and Jerusalem's taking it is a parody of Holy Communion (Bloom 1965: 944).

88:58 **the Hermaphroditic Wine-presses of Love & Wrath**—This perversion of Luvah's winepress (Beer 1969: 256) — "Hermaphroditic" because self-contradictory (Damon 1924: 464)—is war enjoying ecclesiastical sanction (Bloom 1965: 944).

89:1-51 The Covering Cherub may be a parody of Albion's risen body (Frosch 1974: 81-84) or of the Divine Humanity (Ferguson 1978: 191); within it Eden is transformed into the worlds of ancient paganism and modern industry (Johnson and Grant 1979: 350). Beer's accusation (1969: 255-56) that Enitharmon's drive for power is responsible for the Cherub's appearance is carried further by Mathews (1980a: 170), who charges her with creating this impersonator of Christ, and by

Riede (1981: 559-60), who claims that she crucifies him to keep the Divine Vision hidden.

The passage is threaded through with biblical allusions. Damon (1924: 464-65) points to the four rivers of Eden (Gen. ii.10-14) named in ll. 15, 25, 35 and 38. Bloom (1965: 944) notes that the "precious stones" of l. 11 recall those of Aaron's breastplate [Exod. xxviii.15-21]. Sloss and Wallis (1926: I, 619, 620) identify the Dragon of the River (l. 19) as Pharaoh (Ezek. xxix.3) and record the use of Cant. vii.4 in l. 26. Stevenson (1971: 822) observes the echoes of Ezek. i[.18] and Rev. iv.6 in the phrase "fill'd with Eyes" (l. 28). Damon (1967: 22, 122, 297, 157) comments on the Hebrew names for several classes of giant in l. 47. Johnson and Grant (1979: 350) cite Matt. xxiv.15, I John ii.18 and iv.3, and II John vii.

89:4 Love and wrath are contraries and should not be thus united (Ostriker 1977: 1031); "double" may signify that the winepress is hypocritical or that it has potential for good as well as evil (Stevenson 1971: 820).

89:6-7 The references are to the "Pharisees, Scribes, Presbytery, High Priest, Priest, and Sadducees" (Damon 1924: 464).

89:8 **Each withoutside of the other**—each consisting only of surfaces (Stevenson 1971: 821).

89:13 **the rejected corse of death**—the illusions rejected by the redeemed human being (Sloss and Wallis 1926: I, 619); the body Christ rejected on the third day (Bloom 1963: 425-26).

89:16-19 Israel's descent into Egypt represents the Fall; the brick kiln and iron furnace stand for the fallen body (Frye 1947: 364); the Sea of Rephaim is the Red Sea in which the Egyptian pursuers drowned (Bloom 1965: 944).

89:21 **Twelve ridges of Stone**—Druid altars dedicated to the Twelve Gods of Asia (Damon 1924: 464) and corresponding to the Tribes of Israel and Sons of Albion (Ostriker 1977: 1031).

89:36-37 These ribs are a parody of the rainbow of vision (Herrstrom 1981: 75).

89:43-44 Freedom (Jerusalem) is indestructible, so she is concealed in the lowest quarter (Damon 1924: 465). Jerusalem is in the Covering Cherub's stomach in the same way that Eden is in his brain (Wagenknecht 1973: 284).

89:50-51 The Giants' Causeway [consisting of basalt columns on the northeast coast of Ireland] is allegedly prior to the Sea of Time and Space (Damon 1924: 465). See also *M* 19:40n.

89:56 **multitudes innumerable**—the Israelites (Stevenson 1971: 823).

89:58-60 According to Damon (1924: 465), Alla is the state immediately beneath Beulah, and to "Burst the bottoms of the Graves" is to sink into a subhuman state.

90:1-7 The masculine and feminine emanations have been equated respectively with spectre and emanation (Damon 1924: 465) and with the activities of the Zoas and of their emanations (Bloom 1965: 944). Damrosch (1980: 183) states that they separate at the Fall. The images of veil and net give some support to Rose's contention (1971b: 22) that both the divided sexes here function as female. Hilton (1983: 143) identifies the veil of the flesh with the scarlet robe of Matt. xxvii.28.

90:11 **the Sublime...the Pathos**—male and female (Sloss and Wallis 1926: I, 621); the art expressive of the Zoas and of their emanations (Bloom 1965: 944); Los and Enitharmon (Rose 1971a: 57); Tharmas and Luvah (Wagenknecht 1973: 285).

90:14-22 Bowen and Conwenna may be seizing the region assigned to Benjamin at 16:49 (Stevenson 1971: 824). The rivers have been associated with vision (Sloss and Wallis 1926: I, 622), but also labelled Neoplatonic streams of matter or mortal life (Raine 1968: I, 82-91). The chalk alludes to Britain's white cliffs (Damon 1967: 56). Conwenna takes in semen (Hilton 1983: 91-92, 273-74n38).

90:23-24 Hand's furnace suppresses individuality, which Los's preserves (Rose 1964c: 56); "double Boadicea" may be the "Double Female" (Rahab) of 89:52 (Damon 1967: 49), both Gwendolen and Cambel (Rose, *loc. cit.*, citing 71:23), both Boadicea and Cambel (Stevenson 1971: 824-25), or heroism combined with cruelty (*ibid.*).

90:27 Here the furnace and loom are attractive but malign instruments of Albion's Children (Stevenson 1971: 825).

90:28-33 No person has a right to complete authority, secular or spiritual (Damon 1924: 465). The good attributes of any individual derive from God (Percival 1938: 98). One should realise one's individuality and not imitate even the most exalted model (Damon 1967: 196). It is wrong to worship the human nature or selfhood even of Jesus (Raine 1968: II, 232-33). One must pass through states (e.g. David or Eve), not remain in them permanently (Beer 1969: 257). No one may claim to be God, or Lordship, or Womanhood or assert that he or she embodies the ideal to which all should conform (Stevenson 1971: 825).

90:34-38 Christ's embodiment is an entrance into illusion (Damon 1924: 465) and a crucifixion (Damrosch 1980: 289). "Eve" is "a tactful slip of the pen for 'Mary'" (Damon 1967: 265); Blake is attacking the doctrine of the Immaculate Conception (Frye 1947: 393). Christ is to show that "the Satanic Body" cannot overwhelm his Divine Humanity (Stevenson 1971: 825). Altizer, however, (1967: 107) thinks Blake is spurning the rejection of the body implied by the Virgin Birth.

90:49-51 They crush the Little-ones' individuality as they use them to build the Tower of Babel, but Los preserves in them a spark of debased life (Stevenson 1971: 826).

90:53-54 For male or female, appropriating individuality is claiming to be a complete identity without the other (Murry 1933: 280-81).

90:58-59 The Sons of Albion (Ostriker 1977: 1032) erect rocking stones, then thought to be Druid monuments (Damon 1967: 110).

90:68 **Witchcrafts**—the deceptions of natural religion (Sloss and Wallis 1926: I, 624).

91:10 **the intellectual fountain of Humanity**—the inspirer of imagination (Damrosch 1980: 283). The addition of this phrase changes the meaning of the immediate context from that of the similar passage in *MHH* pls. 22-23 (Ostriker 1977: 1032). Blake's reverence for intellect is Neoplatonic (Harper 1961: 239-41).

91:26-28 See pp. 162-64 above and 38(43):19-23n. Crehan (1984: 46-47) holds that Blake is denouncing the application of scientific method "to *society as a whole*."

91:32-33 Cf. Ps. civ.2 (Miner 1969: 267). Raine (1968: II, 138) notes the parallel with *FZ* 42:20/ E328/ III, 107—the Spectre has assumed Urizen's role. He imposes a general pattern on the heavens (Fisher 1961: 172).

91:36 The stars at least yield a little rational truth (Damon 1924: 466) or a weak light (Percival 1938: 66), and Los, unlike the Spectre-scientist, appreciates their sublimity (Beer 1969: 219).

The voids are the field of operation of Newton's laws (Bronowski 1944: 86).

91:41-46 Los dissolves the illusions of sense perception (Sloss and Wallis 1926: I, 626) showing the Spectre that his apparent power is unreal (Paley 1983b: 253). Behemoth and Leviathan, emblems of tyranny in nature and society (Frye 1947: 139), are "the pyramids of pride" (Percival 1938: 270). What Los subdues is the Spectre in himself (Stevenson 1971: 829)—"his own Faustian will" (Paley 1983b: 254).

91:47-49 Los persuades the Spectre the outward creation is illusory (Raine 1968: II, 138). The Spectre recognises facts but not beauty (Stevenson 1971: 829).

91:50-52 Damon (1924: 466) explains that to alter the Spectre's ratio is to increase the knowledge available to reason so that he revises his system. Los's instrument, claims Ault (1974: 125), is his enemy's weapon, Newton's calculus, and Adams (1970: 741-42) believes the change enables Los to escape body-soul dualism. Frye (1947: 394) observes that the artist (Los) sacrifices his personal will (the Spectre) to allow the vision of the ideal to shine through him unclouded.

92:1-6 Equating the British, Saxons, Romans and Normans with west, north, south and east, Damon (1924: 466) declares that all nations are uniting in Albion. Bloom (1965: 945) credits Los with realising that English history is analogous to the story of humanity's reunification, and Rose (1971b: 30-31) adds that this passage synthesises the British and Hebrew myths. Line 5 echoes Ezek. xxx.23 (Margoliouth 1948: 312); ll. 3-5 may allude to Jacob's flight from Laban (Gen. xxxi.18-22), Joseph's being sold into Egypt (Gen. xxxvii.36), Simeon's Canaanite spouse (Exod. vi.15) and the Daughters of Canaan of 74:38ff (Miner 1969: 276-77). Through an allusion to Dryden's "To My Honour'd Friend, Dr. Charleton," Blake associates Albion's loins with English rationalism and monarchy (Worrall 1977b: 202-03).

92:12 Cf. *PL*, IX, 826-29 (Ostriker 1977: 1033).

92:13 **Los answer'd swift**—with the message that the disappearance of the separate sexes will not cause Enitharmon's annihilation (Damon 1924: 466-67).

92:15-19 These things will only be memories or warning images (Stevenson 1971: 830).

93:2-16 Enitharmon's hunger for power comes from her desire to restore her family's prelapsarian harmony (Beer 1969: 238) as she recalls how Satan usurped Palamabron's plough [actually, harrow—see *M* pl. 7] (Damon 1924: 467). She compares her Sons who fled [*M* 23:62—24:4] with those who stayed (Stevenson 1971: 832).

93:6 East Moor and Cheviot, located on Albion's spine, over-shadow England (*ibid.*: 831) or divide her (Ostriker 1977: 1033). See also 63:23-24n, 64:35, 38n.

93:7-10 See Gen. xxx.14-16 (Damon 1924: 467). The Prides that meet may be the rival sisters Leah and Rachel, but Reuben was also proud because his gift of mandrakes brought Jacob to his mother Leah's bed (Stevenson 1971: 831). Reuben may have an "Oedipal wish to enwomb himself" (Paley 1983b: 305) or his phallic gift may be seen as a submission to the female will (Webster 1983: 290).

93:18-26 **this Waking Death**—the Covering Cherub (Damon 1924: 467); Albion (Sloss and Wallis 1926: I, 629); the Spectre of Urthona (Bloom 1965: 945); the imaginative Merlin, det-ached by Los from Reuben, the natural man (Worrall 1977b: 203-04).

93:26 **Signal of the Morning**—Los alludes to Matt. xxiv.3-15 (Sloss and Wallis 1926: I, 629).

93:27 **Mam-Tor**—There are caverns and lead mines in the vic-inity of this Derbyshire height (Stevenson 1971: 832).

94:7-14 This passage treats of the depressed state of the country after Waterloo (Wicksteed 1954: 242). Albion's Rock is the island of Britain with its white cliffs (Damon 1967: 350), while the "Female Shadow" is based on British fog and cloud (Stevenson 1971: 833).

94:15 **Eagle**—infinity (Beer 1969: 238); genius frustrated by female domination (Webster 1983: 290). But see *M IB* pl. 42n.

94:18 See Rev. x.6 (Ostriker 1977: 1034).

94:20-21 Britannia repents of her imperialism as well as her imp-osition of moral law (Erdman 1954a: 447-48 [485]). Jerusalem and Vala, into whom she had divided at 32(36):28, reunite in her to redeem Albion (Stevenson 1971: 833). The phrase "who is Britannia" may signify England's base imperialism (Erdman 1974: 373), or England may be Britannia's guiding element

(Ostriker 1977: 1034). The seven faintings correspond to the seven historical ages (Doskow 1982: 161).

95:5-11 The risen Albion's entire body is sensitive to the Divine Breath, which is inspiration (Frosch 1974: 125). The flames are "the wormy Garments" of 94:17 transformed (Paley 1973b: 138), "the Words of Eternity" are unfallen language (Paley 1983b: 231), and "the Four Elements" are the Zoas (Sloss and Wallis 1926: I, 631).

95:10 **Revolutions**—including political revolutions (Frosch 1974: 202).

95:11-20 Wicksteed (1954: 246) finds here a message that the world would flourish if all fulfilled their divinely ordained duty of craftsmanship.

95:13 "He" refers to both the sun and Albion (Adams 1975: 165). For the bow, see 97:6-15n.

95:17 Luvah is a weaver because the emotions are the feminine aspect of the psyche (Percival 1938: 29).

95:18 **the Great Spectre Los**—Los himself (Sloss and Wallis 1926: II, 231), who is reintegrated with his Spectre (Paley 1983b: 254). Hilton (1983: 171-72) reminds us that a spectre is a mode (not always fallen) of seeing.

96:3-7 See Matt. xviii.12-14 and John x.11 (Stevenson 1971: 835). Blake reverses the customary image of Christ's apocalyptic appearance in heaven surrounded by angels (Altizer 1967: 206). Los, in the self-sacrifice of Atonement, takes on the identity of a universal enabling Albion to see the individual person together with the Divine Humanity (Wagenknecht 1973: 286-89). Los and the art he represents have undergone self-annihilation, art having given way to vision—see also 1.22 (McGann 1973: 19-20).

96:8-9 **my Selfhood**—the Covering Cherub (Damon 1924: 467), who is the law-giving God of Sinai (Altizer 1967: 142) or resembles the Israelite fighting force in the wilderness (Stevenson 1971: 835). Edom is a rabbinical code name for Rome, and for Blake it is the land of Deism (Doskow 1982: 170n14).

96:11-13 See The Wisdom of Solomon xviii.24 for the image of the whole world on the gem-studded robe of the high priest (Percival 1938: 206-07). Albion sees his selfhood in the form of all history (Wagenknecht 1973: 286).

96:12 **a Serpent of precious stones & gold**—an alchemical image, for Christ has suffered in the regenerating furnace (Percival 1938: 206-07).

96:18 **Overshadow'd them**—For the parallel with the cloud at the Transfiguration, see Mark ix.7 (Margoliouth 1948: 312) and Luke ix.34 (Stevenson 1971: 836).

96:23-28 Individuals must accept their own mortality before they find supreme happiness in the Human Form Divine (Wicksteed 1954: 244-45). Christ's death is continually repeated, and this seems to exclude a final universal redemption (Damrosch 1980: 339).

96:29 **the Cloud**—the Covering Cherub (Damon 1924: 467), which impairs Albion's perception of Jesus until he summons his Emanation in 97:1 and rises from threefold to fourfold vision (Wagenknecht 1973: 288-89).

96:30-31 **his Friend/ Divine**—Los-Jesus (Bloom 1963: 431); Jesus (Ostriker 1977: 1034); Los (McClellan 1977: 208). Sloss and Wallis (1926: I, 632-33) define "Self" as selfhood or spectre.

96:35-37 Easson (1973: 325) ascribes the furnaces to Los. The transformation of fire into the water of life is an alchemical symbol (Percival 1938: 213); what were the dark Atlantic waters become akin to the rivers of Eden and of Ezek. xlvii.9 (Ferguson 1978: 192-93); this fire transmuted may be wholly different from earthly water (Damrosch 1980: 79). Through a similar image, Joseph's illumination at 61:28-30 is made to foreshadow Albion's (Gallant 1978: 177). Self-sacrifice turns out to be redemption, for Resurrection is Crucifixion from another viewpoint (Marks 1974: 49), and Albion's former plight proves to have been an illusion of his own creation (Blackstone 1949: 159, 170). Stevenson (1971: 836) cites Dan. iii, John iv.10-15, Rev. xx.10 and xxi.6.

97:1-4 Cf. Cant. ii.11 (Bloom 1963: 431); Cant. ii.8-13 (Tolley 1973: 99); Gen. ix.19, Is.li.9 and 17 (Miner 1969: 258, 463n8).

97:5 **so spake in my hearing**—Here and in 98:40 and 99:5, Blake's role compares with John's in Revelation (Nelms 1974: 82).

97:6 Wicksteed (1954: 17-18) supposes that Albion, Jesus and Los are Father, Son and Holy Spirit in Blake's Trinity. According to Erdman (1974: 375), the "Universal Father" is the "Jehovah-like Albion" of the design.

97:6-15 The bow that lays "Open the hidden Heart"—cf. 9:17-19 (Sloss and Wallis 1926: I, 634)—in the transfigured version of Luvah's crucifixion (Curran 1973: 344) is the bow of "And did those feet in ancient time" (*M* pl. 1) (Bloom 1963: 431) and the contrary of Satan's black bow of "I saw a Monk of Charlemaine" (*J* pl. 52) (Damon 1967: 55). It is "spiritual warfare" (Damon 1924: 467), "a fully realized poetic art" (Bloom 1965: 945), and, being identical with the rainbow, the painter's palette (Rose 1970c: 460). Its being male and female signifies the perfect balance of the sexes in Albion giving him freedom from spectre and female will (Nelms 1974: 83) and his recovery of his prelapsarian androgyny (Paley 1983b: 232). Nelms (1974: 83) regards the hand that operates it as the regenerated Hand, and in Beer's view (1969: 45, 356n89) Albion's skill with the bow echoes the parallel mastery of Ulysses when he escapes from nature (Circe) to return to his Emanation.

98:1-3 The twenty-eight weapons of the Cities compose the four of the Zoas, which compose the single one of Albion (Damon 1967: 74). For "unreprovable," cf. Col. i.22 (Margoliouth 1948: 312).

98:6 **The Druid Spectre**—the Covering Cherub (Damon 1924: 193).

98:9-11 These threefold—i.e. mortal (Ostriker 1977: 1034) or incomplete (Stevenson 1971: 838)—geniuses form two triads ready for mental strife in Eternity (Bloom 1963: 432). Blake lists the poets in the order of their greatness (Damon 1967: 274, 369). Frosch (1974: 93) claims that the thinkers are freed from their spectres, but Rose (1970b: 413) considers that their inclusion indicates the achievement of the poets was limited—hence also the merely threefold chariots.

98:14-15 Every part of the spiritual body possesses sight (Rose 1970c: 455). Blake identifies the four rivers of Eden with the river of Rev. xxii[.1-2]; cf. also the eyes of Rev. iv.6 and the horses of Rev. vi (Stevenson 1971: 838).

98:17 **the Parent Sense**—the first to function in the newborn (Damon 1967: 399).

98:19   The lineaments are revealed because error falls away when the visionary perceives it with "the Human Nerves of Sensation" (Nelms 1974: 83-84).

98:20   **the Body of Death**—the illusion of a mortal body (Raine 1968: II, 271), and even this, if 'driven outward' or rightly conceived has a new life in Beulah (Nelms 1974: 84), where it experiences time, space and relationship in a new way (Frosch 1974: 172).

98:24-27   In Eternity (contrast 63:11 and 74:4-6), the wheels of the Zoas are synchronised (Rose 1972a: 44), and space and time have merged into an Einsteinian continuum (Peterfreund 1981: 223-24n8). Each sense perceives through all the senses, making perception a perfectly unified process (Rose 1966: 124-25). Albion's resurrected body is more like an activity than a body (Frosch 1974: 143), and the chariots are "symbols of the regeneration of life through the free play of energy in art" (Paley 1970: 258-59).

98:28-40   Altizer's explanation (1967: 16-17) that the expansion and contraction of the senses creates, transforms and dissolves worlds is complemented by Frosch's account (1974: 144-46) of interplay between the senses combined with synaesthesia in a kind of speech that is also creation. Adams (1975: 165) insists that the subject is imaginative speech that creates reality in *this* world.

98:29   **Redounded**—added (*OED* Redound *v.* 13), for each speaker's view needs to be added to the others' (Peterfreund 1981: 209). But the word seems to be used in the Spenserian sense of "flow" and "overflow."

98:30   **exemplars**—examples of errors that can lead to a fall from Eternity as 92:15-20 makes clear (Sloss and Wallis 1926: I, 636); archetypes of memory and archetypes of intellect, only the former being intelligible to reason (Kiralis 1956: 145-46); "everpresent archetypal symbols identical with that which they represent" (Rose 1965: 603); temporal phenomena granted only a brief existence so that memory and intellect retain their inferior station (Stevenson 1971: 839); the Cherubim of Ezekiel's vision, the patterns of all true art (Herrstrom 1981: 65). It should be remembered that Blake habitually denigrates memory (see p. 168 above) but prizes intellect (e.g. E564/K615).

98:31-33 Space and time are creations of the mind (Raine 1968: II, 134). When we focus on the spatial and temporal aspect of our perceptions, we participate in "the Planetary lives" of 99:3, but they are also symbolic vehicles of further vision (Mellor 1974: 329-30).

98:33-34 **Non Ens/ Of Death**—Ulro (Sloss and Wallis 1926: I, 636); earthly horrors non-existent from an eternal standpoint (Kiralis 1956: 146); "the non-human" (Altizer 1967: 214). The mind makes and unmakes death at pleasure (Bloom 1963: 432-33).

98:35-38 Some eighteenth-century theorists believed only unhealthy nerves were opaque (Ault 1974: 147). Blake opposes Newton's view that nerves are solid (Hilton 1983: 98-101).

98:39-40 **clearly seen/ And seeing**—Cf. I Cor. xiii.12 (Ostriker 1977: 1034).

98:40-41 Eschewing any transcendence of nature, Frosch (1974: 147, 202-03n9) identifies Jehovah with Albion, the Holy Place with the body and the entire universe, and the Mutual Covenant Divine with the shared humanity of perceiver and perceived. Rose (1970c: 456) equates the Covenant with the "mutual interchange" of 88:5, and Paley (1983b: 211) sees it as uniting the dispensations of the Old and New Testaments.

98:44 **the all wondrous Serpent**—nature redeemed (Damon 1924: 467-68, citing Rom. viii.21).

98:46-53 Damon (1924: 193) considers that all illusions have vanished, Gallant (1978: 181-82) thinks that they persist but that true vision shows they are insubstantial, and Lesnick (1970: 410-12) believes the world, metamorphosed by imagination, survives as the expression of Eternity. Golgonooza, according to Paley (1983b: 127), outlasts time.

98:46 **the Covenant of Priam**—the ethic and art based on the Classical ideal of the virtuous warrior (Bloom 1965: 945); the covenant of the dying god who is described at 21:42-49 (Rose 1970c: 458); military values which Blake connects with Greco-Roman and Judeo-Christian morality, Druid human sacrifice, and British imperialism (Ostriker 1977: 1034-35).

98:52 **the Triple Headed Gog-Magog Giant**—Albion's Spectre, with some reference to the triple-headed Hand of 70:1-16 (Sloss and Wallis 1926: I, 457, 637); the foremost of the aboriginal British giants defeated by Trojan Brutus (Damon 1967:

162); also a symbol of commercial exploitation, for statues of Gog and Magog stood outside the London Guildhall (Ostriker 1977: 1035). Stevenson (1971: 840) cites Ezek. xxxviii-xxxix and Rev. xx.8-9.

98:53 The Spectrous Oath may be a promise of vengeance for sin (Sloss and Wallis 1926: I, 638, citing *GA* 2:22) or the Spectre's boast that he is God (Ostriker 1977: 1035, citing 54:16). The taxing of the nations alludes to the taxing of Augustus (Luke ii.1), the taxes that helped to provoke the American and French revolutions, and the taxes of contemporary England (Margoliouth 1948: 312).

99:1-4 These lines present both a double perspective and a vision of transcendent unity. Contrasting 50:5-9, Rose (1963: 41-43) observes that the imagination now sees all things as they really are, as participants in the Human Form Divine, and (1970c: 455) that the Eternals are outside time, which they create as a medium for their utterances, so that (1973: 94) experience, which is simultaneous from an eternal standpoint, becomes sequential from a temporal one. Each Eternal, according to Stevenson (1971: 623, 841), contains all forms of existence—male and female, as well as animal, vegetable and mineral—all being human and all enjoying periods of rest from Eternity. In a more prosaic interpretation, Adams (1970: 742) asserts that "the world of work and creativity" supersedes the fallen state. See also p. 695 above.

99:1 To have Human identity is to be both an individual and a part of the universal, all-enveloping whole, which is Christ (Frye 1951: 181-83). Each Human Form is in possession of its own identity (Beer 1969: 259) or is perceptible to the sight as human (Frosch 1974: 131). Each identifies and is identified (Rose 1966: 119).

99:2 **going forth & returning**—Cf. 20:10 (Rose 1970c: 458).

99:4-5 The unity of all humans with each other and with God is effected by the imagination's forgiveness of sins, by entering into others' bosoms, by the interchange of emanations—cf. 54:1-5 and 88:3-11 (Rose 1970c: 455-57); the emanations or "mental acts" are all that remain from the world of time (Rose 1973: 94). In response to the risen Albion's speech, the Human Forms Identified utter the name of their emanations signifying the completion of one poem or world in an endless sequence

(Frosch 1974: 148, 151-52). Given a name (Jerusalem), the sum of all human aspiration can be realised (Adams 1975: 166). Jesus is the One, Jerusalem the Many (Deen 1983: 228). There may be allusions to Rev. xxi.3 (Margoliouth 1948: 312) and Ezek. xlviii.35 (Bloom 1971: 78-79).

Designs

pl. 1   In this illustration of 45(31):2-4 (Damon 1924: 468), Los-Blake (Wicksteed 1954: 104), dressed in an eighteenth-century watchman's garb (Mellor 1974: 288), steps through a Gothic doorway (Damon, *loc. cit.*). This is also Los's Gate [of 35(39):3] (Wicksteed 1954: 105) and Death's Door (Hagstrum 1964: 118), from which the wind of time issues to blow back his cloak as he encounters it from the opposite side to that shown in *GP*, pl. 15 (E267/ K769) (Lesnick 1969: 50, 54). To succour the fallen man (Digby 1957: 33-34) or in an act of self-annihilation (Mitchell 1978: 198), he enters the inner life (Damon, *loc. cit.*) or the world of mortality (Wicksteed 1954: 104-05). He is also the reader (Nelson 1973: 130-31) beginning the poem (Mitchell, *loc. cit.*) and parallels have been suggested with Christ's descent into hell (*ibid.*) and the quest of Diogenes (Paley 1983b: 239). In his hand is the Light of Eternity (*ibid.*) or a sun (Erdman 1974: 281), perhaps the spiritual sun (Raine 1968: I, 225); or it may be the lamp of imagination—including the reader's—shedding its rays on the Jerusalem of the title page he discovers inside (Latané 1983). Most probably Blake deleted the original engraved inscription to make his frontispiece match *IB* pls. 26, 51, 76 and 100 (Erdman 1964a: 8-9).

pl. 2   Damon's opinion (1924: 468) that the title page portrays five Daughters of Beulah has been superseded by Wicksteed's recognition (1954: 109-10) that the supine figure is Jerusalem imprisoned in the material world, her bracelet symbolising her bondage. She is Psyche, the soul (Raine 1968: I, iv [frontispiece caption]), and may be sleeping in Ulro (Mitchell 1978: 198) or Beulah (Paley 1983b: 182). The design pictures her as she is described at 86:1-10 and asks whether she is subsiding into a larval existence in nature or acquiring wings to escape from it (Rose 1968b: 217, 221). Upon her the heavenly bodies are represented as but "dust on the fly's wing" (91:48) (Raine, *loc. cit.*); the whole cosmos is here shown to be dormant (Mitchell 1978: 199). Wicksteed (1954: 110, 112) perceives the personified dawn—perhaps Erin—at the top of the page and Enitharmon at Jerusalem's head, whereas Erdman (1974: 282) sees two of her daughters mourning over her—a bat-winged incipient Vala and a bird-winged incipient Erin—and fairies above pointing to the first letter. Alternatively, nature spirits may be acting out the redemption as well as the fallen state (Paley 1978b: 67). Doskow (1982: 19, 30) sees Jerusalem rising through eternal death on the left to Eternity at the top in a sequence that can also be read downwards as Jerusalem falling.

pl.3 The placing of "GOATS" shows that in this book the right side of the page is the side of error (Chayes 1974: 52-53, 55-56). See also p. 694-95 above.

pl. 4 Damon's statement (1924: 468) that Jerusalem points out the moon of Beulah to children escaping Rahab is challenged by claims that Jerusalem is guiding English girls towards liberty (Paley 1978b: 67) and that the cloaked figure is Eno (Wicksteed 1954: 116) or Vala (Erdman 1974: 284). Vala's left hand may rest on a form of Albion sitting on Dover cliffs above the Net of Religion (*ibid.*). According to Doskow (1982: 19), the design depicts Albion in three states—rooted, escaping, and fully awake.

The Greek inscription—"only Jesus"—is from John viii.9 (Sloss and Wallis 1926: I, 448), where it relates to Christ's forgiveness of the adulteress. It also alludes to Luke ix.36, where the words appear in a different order and allude to Christ's superseding Moses (Wicksteed 1954: 117). In Greek and English alike, the phrase means both "no one but Jesus" and "Jesus in solitude" (Curran 1971: 148).

pl. 5 The Daughters of Albion here portrayed illustrate the passage from Innocence through Experience and from maidenhood to motherhood (Wicksteed 1954: 118-20). As Jerusalem "is scattered abroad like a cloud of smoke" (l. 13), four of her Daughters rise above her (Erdman 1974: 284). The upright figures represent visionary religion, the kneeling figures false religion (Doskow 1982: 48).

pl. 6   Over Los hovers his Spectre (Wicksteed 1910: 139). Among details that have elicited comment are Los's phallic hammer (Beer 1969: 373), the Spectre's shutting his ears and hanging so that he sees everything upside down (Murray 1974a: 14-15), his stopping Los's work with his arguments (Erdman 1974: 285), the pudendum-like appearance of his vertebrae (Mills 1980: 93), and the engraved lines hinting at a human skeleton under a bat's form (Carr 1980: 522). Herrstrom (1981: 70) considers the Spectre a Covering Cherub.

pl. 8   A child pulls the moon over clouds (Keynes 1921: 162); "A Fairy...drags the bleeding Moon of Love...through the Valley of Logic (63:14)" (Damon 1924: 468); a woman is handicapped by "pretences to Chastity" (l. 32), which the moon symbolises (Beer 1969: 196); a Daughter of Albion is tied to Vala's moon of nature and menstruation (Erdman 1974: 287); the figure may be a goddess of chastity (Mitchell 1978: 193).

pl. 9   Above are a shepherd and his flock in Innocence (Damon 1924: 469) with some wild animals (Binyon 1926: 127). From them descends a vine to become a snake which is tempted by a woman (Erdman 1974: 288) or which tempts her at the Fall (Damon, *loc. cit.*). Below, stars of reason rise above fallen Albion, whose five senses lament over him (*ibid.*). However, the females—Daughters of Zelophehad—may be his murderers (Paley 1983b: 203) or may be mourning Daughters of Beulah (Beer 1969: 196-97). Wicksteed (1954: 124) thinks the stars stand for the Innocence and Experience of the top and middle panels.

pl. 11   There is much to be said for Bindman's view (1982: 160) that there is no satisfactory explanation for these enigmatic images. Most plausible are Erdman's theory (1974: 290-92) that the swan, a traditional emblem of the poet, is the poet-artist simultaneously singing and etching (cf. l. 4) and Beer's suggestion (1969: 198) that the woman below is the female will in the person of Vala; these two, as Kemper observes (1960b: 589-90), are facing respectively in the 'right' and 'wrong' directions, and Binyon (1926: 128) truly remarks that it is difficult to believe the bejewelled nude is positive. Other interpretations propose that the upper and lower figures are respectively the female will and inspiration (Damon 1924: 469), innocence betrayed and a courtesan (Wicksteed 1954:

129-30); reason in Udan Adan and an American Indian symbolising imagination and liberty (T. Wright 1929: I, xiii, 67; II, pl. 66); just possibly Sabrina and Ignoge, Daughters of Albion (Bindman 1977: 182), and a prophetess and a woman of fashion (Mitchell 1978: 200). Kemper (1960a) thinks the swan a positive symbol of mediation between alchemical stages, whereas Paley (1978b: 68) sees her as derived from animal-headed Egyptian deities and hence representing "debased humanity"; Erdman (*loc. cit.*) identifies the swimmer or flyer as the Erin of l. 8 colouring the etcher's engraving, her jewels being the latter's bubbles transformed.

pl. 12   In this, the most intriguing of all the marginal designs, Wicksteed (1954: 136) perceives a Vala with bat-winged arms presiding over Newton, who observes the earth turning wither-shins while Jerusalem below sees it revolving clockwise. Les-nick (1969: 54-55) adds that the male sees the globe spinning in the direction of the Wheel of Religion of pl. 77 as he watches it from the viewpoint of Reuben, the natural man with head downwards (63:44). Brilliantly, Chayes (1974) identifies the upper female, with her bat-wing frills, as the "Body" and "Shade" of ll. 1 and 19, the male as reason creating the mater-ial earth, and the lower female as aspiring desire able to reach only the region labelled "west," site of the closed Edenic gate of the Tongue (ll. 52, 60). Other suggestions are that Gol-gonooza ironically attracts a fashion-conscious Jerusalem (Kemper 1960b: 593), that there may be a vortex at the base of the globe and that Newton teaches science to a woman (Erdman 1974: 292), that the whole is "an allegory of Vanity" (Bindman 1977: 183), and that Los and Enitharmon are con-structing Jerusalem among the stars (Miner 1981: 319).

pl. 14   Either Enitharmon visits the sleeping Los in Beulah (Damon 1924: 469) or Albion in his dream enjoys the visita-tion of Jerusalem (Margoliouth 1951: 152) or of Erin with her rainbow of 50:22 above the Sea of Time and Space (Paley 1983b: 92, 210). That rainbow may represent visionary art (Margoliouth 1951: 153) or a Utopian hope for society (Damon 1967: 340) or it is ambiguous—possibly a demonic wheel (Herrstrom 1981: 72). Erdman (1974: 293) argues that Albion fails to respond to the vision.

pl. 15   Abraham's flight from Chaldea is blocked by Reuben (Damon 1924: 469) or by the enrooting Hand, Hyle and Schofield of ll. 1-2 as his outstretched arms prefigure the Crucifixion (Erdman 1974: 294). The figure caught in the branches hints at the ram that was substituted as a sacrifice for Isaac, and the tiny buildings are "the Schools & Universities" of l. 14 (*ibid.*). Doskow (1982: 53) supposes that a giant academic Urizen is oppressing diminutive humanity.

pl. 18   According to Damon (1924: 469), Jerusalem and Vala, adorned with the lilies and roses of spiritual and material beauty respectively, are asleep under moons of Beulah (19:40-44). There has been widespread acceptance of Damon's identifications, though Paley (1983b: 180) reverses them, since Vala is the Lily of Havilah (19:42). The theme may be the union of body and soul (Wicksteed 1954: 147-48) that is preserved by moon-arks bearing it across the Sea of Time and Space (Grant 1969: 362-64) and also the wrongness of the quarrel between England and France (*ibid.*: 363, 489n41). Raine (1968: I, 207) points appropriately to the words "For Vala produc'd the Bodies, Jerusalem gave the Souls" (l. 7). Beer (1969: 221) perceives here Albion and Jerusalem separating while their Children approach each other, which allows Nelson (1973: 142-43) to see contrary movements of parting and coming together as well as male and female, all contributing to a "fourfold vision."

pl. 19   Damon's identification (1924: 469) of the giant as fallen Albion is generally endorsed, but are his Children fleeing (l. 1) while the sun sets and he is mourned by "the Four Senses" (*loc. cit.*)? (Binyon [1926: 129] substitutes "genii" for "Senses.") Erdman (1974: 298) explains Albion as a defeated army (cf. ll. 3-4), some of his Children being dead or crushed under his body while others practise sanguinary Druid rites above.

pl. 20   Damon's assertion (1924: 469) that the figures are Albion's Children and Beer's account (1969: 201) of flowers transformed by flames of jealousy are less illuminating than Erdman's contention (1974: 299) that men are reducing the formations of heavenly bodies to wheels. At the top of the page Albion and Vala may be meeting (Wicksteed 1954: 145) or Vala and Jerusalem may be quarrelling (Kemper 1960b: 590). Above l. 14, Hand and Hyle may be pulling and Schofield pushing the vortex of materialistic vision, which draws Vala behind it (Wicksteed 1954: 151-52), or souls may be passing through the Circle of Destiny into a vortex of fallen perception (Hilton 1983: 228-29). Beneath, writes Wicksteed (1954: 152), Jerusalem "floats serenely behind the *out*-flaming Souls of human individuality drawn forward by the fourfold Man."

pl. 21   Hand whips three Daughters of Albion (Damon 1924: 469, citing 21: 29-30) with the rationalist's "starry universe" (Rose 1964c: 49). Doskow (1982: 58-59), referring to 17:1-15, sees rather Los's Spectre using Puritanism to prevent the Daughters from tempting Los.

pl. 22   Damon (1924: 469-70) can only be right to see the lower design as an accompaniment to ll. 34-35, and Erdman (1974: 301) pertinently draws attention to 18:8-10 as well as the coupling of *three* wheels with *four* cherubim. Those wheels are assailed by furnace flames (Herrstrom 1981: 73) and water (Paley 1983b: 92). The images above have been taken for spectre and emanation (Damon 1924: 469), Vala veiling and leaving Albion (Wicksteed 1954: 145), Vala and Jerusalem (Grant 1969: 364), and a swan and (possibly) Leda (Stevenson 1971: 669). Mitchell (1978: 200) perceives Albion represented as "a netted bird."

pl. 23   Damon's simple phrase "Mankind buried in matter" (1924: 470) is complemented by Wicksteed's reference to the labouring masses (1954: 154) and Erdman's mention of coalmines (1974: 302). Above, on the Peak in Derbyshire (Paley 1983b: 182-83), lies a female whom Binyon (1926: 129) tentatively identifies as Jerusalem "Embalm'd in Vala's bosom/ In an Eternal Death" (ll. 9-10). Nanavutty (1947: 133-35) recognises this Jerusalem as a figure whose crucifixion and future redemption are symbolised by the Lily of Calvary and Star of Bethlehem at her head and feet, while her stony sepulchre is overshadowed by intestines (cf. 89: 43-44), from which Los's Spectre and Emanation escape on the right. The intestines constitute the Veil of Vala (Erdman, *loc. cit.*). Citing 43(29):81, Mills (1980: 95-97) ventures to doubt whether the winged figure is Vala or Jerusalem.

pl. 24   Though the intestinal Veil of Vala reappears in this plate (Doskow 1982: 63), the main image is the moon-ark, which, according to Damon (1924: 470), carries across the Sea of

Time and Space "the winged head of a seraph." Binyon (1926: 129) claims the passenger is really an entire cherub, while Wicksteed (1954: 146) declares it a dove and explains that Blake combines Noah's Ark with the Ark of the Covenant. Raine (1968: I, 234-35) believes it to be the pudendum or gate of birth associating the vessel depicted with Mary, the *Foederis Arca* or Ark of the Covenant, who bore the Saviour. The moon-ark has also been regarded as the Mundane Shell (Todd 1946: 37-38) and as protective Beulah (Mitchell 1978: 193). Miner (1981: 327-28) even frowns on it and its counterpart in *IB* pl. 39(44) as maleficent coffins containing the Tablets of the Law. The identification of moon and ark has been traced to George Faber's *The Origin of Pagan Idolatry* (1816) (Mitchell, *loc. cit.*) and to Jacob Bryant's *A New System of Mythology* (1774-76) (N. Warner 1980: 48).

pl. 25 Albion still incorporates the heavenly bodies (Damon 1924: 470) and so is only partially fallen (Lesnick 1970: 393, citing 24:10), though the sun and moon have been displaced from his forehead and loins (N. Warner 1980: 50, 53). While Damon (1924: 470) considers his sinister companions to be three of his Daughters, there is now little dispute with Wicksteed's labelling of these females from left to right as Rahab, Vala and Tirzah (1954: 155-56), though Mellor (1974: 293) locates Rahab on the right and Tirzah on the left. Hypnotized by Rahab, Albion becomes a Druid sacrifice under Vala's Veil (Erdman 1974: 304). His sexual guilt makes him vulnerable (Paley 1983b: 200). Nevertheless his torture in the fallen world can be seen as simultaneously a hopeful birth into that world as Tirzah is about to cut his umbilical cord (Mitchell 1978: 200-01). Alternatively, Damon (*loc. cit.*) sees a thread of 'vegetation' being unwound from his navel, and (Hagstrum 1964: 115) this is an example of the organic fibre that is a negative symbol throughout *Jerusalem*. The same fibres hang from Vala's hand (Lesnick, *loc. cit.*). The winding of the thread is a parody of the winding of the "golden thread" of the quatrain on pl. 77 (Paley 1971: 186), Albion's posture recalls that of the blasphemer in Blake's painting *The Stoning of Achan* (Digby 1957: 51), and the whole design is a parody of a deposition (Chayes 1970b: 240-41). Among the visual sources claimed are Freher's engravings of microcosmic humans in

Law's edition of Boehme (Raine 1968: II, 251-55), Van Coxe's illustrations of Apuleius' narrative of Psyche's sufferings (Chayes 1970b: 241-43), Mitelli's engraving of Poussin's *Martyrdom of St. Erasmus* (Paley 1971: 186), an engraving after Il Rosso Fiorentino's *Le Tre Parche* (*The Three Fates*) (Toomey 1971: 188-90), and images in the 1622 edition of John Speed's *History of Great Britain* of ancient Britons with heavenly bodies pictured on their flesh (*ibid.*).

pl. 26 Jerusalem looks in astonishment (Keynes 1921: 163), horror (Damon 1924: 470), pity (Margoliouth 1951: 155), or fear (Stevenson 1971: 675) on a Hand tormented by the loss of his Emanation (Beer 1969: 224) and swathed in flames of the energy he perverts (Mellor 1974: 298-99) that resemble the robe of the body (Rose 1964c: 49-50). The stigmata show him to be the "Vegetated" or corporeal Christ of 90:34 (Lesnick 1970: 393) or a parody of Christ (Paley 1978b: 67). He is wrapped round with a brazen serpent of flame [see p. 115 above] and may be trying to take Jerusalem to Hades (Erdman 1974: 305). Seeing in the flames the circle of eternity as well as the serpent, Mitchell (1978: 181-82) regards Hand as both the power of the craftsman and the tyrannical selfhood, and Doskow (1982: 21) suggests that he and Jerusalem symbolise respectively the legalistic and prophetic elements of the Old Testament. While Mellor (*loc. cit.*) suggests that Jerusalem's mild pleading is spurned, Digby (1957: 76) asserts that as the rejected anima or unconscious she is taking fiery revenge. The quatrain has been interpreted as signifying her distress at the Parisian mob's perverted concept of the liberty for which she stands (Wicksteed 1954: 156) and as both Hand's denunciation of freedom and Blake's declaration that regenerate Britons acclaim it (Mellor 1974: 299-300).

pl. 28 The figures that Damon (1924: 470) describes as the Fairy King and Queen embracing above the Sea of Time and Space, Binyon (1926: 130) plausibly identifies as Jerusalem and Vala "assimilating in one" (19:41). The assimilation takes place in Beulah (Frye 1947: 433), which is, like this design, an ambiguous realm, since it is connected both to Eternity and Ulro (Damrosch 1980: 223). What may be an innocent, prelapsarian Lesbian union (Mitchell 1978: 206-07) excites Albion but imbues him with sexual guilt (Paley 1983b: 169-72). He cannot see that "embracing in the Vision of Jesus" (29[33]:44) turns Vala's net that drapes the pair into a fertilising stamen and is not to be condemned among "unnatural consanguinities" (28:7) (Erdman 1974: 307). Wyatt (1975: 116) sees here an approval of "polymorphous sexuality."

Some critics endorse Keynes's perception (1921: 163) of the figures as male and female. Among these, Digby (1957: 79) writes of the transcendent moment of union with the soul, Damon (1967: 240-41) of the bliss of newly-weds oblivious of the net of marriage, and Grant (1969: 354-65) of Vala's union with Albion, who will be trapped by her net when he wrongly repudiates their sexuality. Stevenson (1971: 681) suggests ll. 1-2 praise the happiness of the couple, and Paley (1978b: 67-68) suspects they have merged into one androgynous Eternal. An early proof, Erdman finds (1964a: 18-20), depicts a man and woman in a position that shows they are copulating.

pl. 29(33)   Urizen may be ploughing in Generation with Luvah's bulls (Damon 1924: 470) or beasts of twofold vision (Doskow 1982: 75), or this may be Jehovah's plough (41[46]:14) pulled by Palamabron's horses (Raine 1968: II, 226). Alternatively, with reference to l. 9, the picture may illustrate the Spectre's contempt for the human, and especially for philosophers who 'plough'—i.e. engrave their visions (Erdman 1974: 308). Wicksteed (1954: 163) speculates that the subject is a land-owner's pride in his estate and his ancestors, who pull his plough.

pl. 31(35)   Over the birth of Eve—the work of Divine Mercy (42:33)—hovers Christ bearing the stigmata (Damon 1924: 470). He may be Jehovah-Jesus creating Eve (Stevenson 1971: 687), or Blake may be following Milton in attributing Eve's creation to Christ (Altizer 1967: 98). Paley (1983b: 105-06) conceives the event as the division of the original androgynous Human. From Jehovah and also from Eve (who can develop into Jerusalem) comes the Divine Voice of l. 3, the flames being those of the furnace therein mentioned (Erdman 1974: 310). Indeed Nelson (1973: 138) argues that Eve, born through Christ's wound identified with Adam's, *is* the speech towards which she ascends on the page—i.e. the Word made Flesh. Doskow (1982: 85) claims that Adam and Eve are also Albion and Vala, while Bindman (1977: 180) asserts that what rises from the supine figure (Albion) is his aspiration to be redeemed.

pl. 32(36)   Los is either forging the sun (Damon 1924: 470), fixing states to free individuals (Wicksteed 1954: 165), or constructing both the moon-ark ("the Moon of Ulro") and—"rib by rib"—Reuben, whom he sends away to the right (Erdman 1974: 311, citing ll. 3-4).

pl. 33(37)   Although Digby (1957: 40-41, 77) thinks that Los here supports Albion, there is a strong case for believing that it is Christ from whom the falling man receives assistance (Damon 1924: 470, citing 48:1-4) between the Palm of Suffering and Oak of Weeping (Binyon 1926: 131)—see 23:24-26 (Paley 1983b: 208-09). However, is the figure below the Spectre also Albion (Binyon, *loc. cit.*) or is it a female (Keynes 1921: 163-64), namely Jerusalem (Wicksteed 1954: 167-68)? Mills (1980: 89-91) points out that the garment, hair and breast support the latter identification. The winged disc may be an alchemical emblem of chaos (Wicksteed 1954: 167), or a symbol of the Father and the Holy Spirit derived from Stukeley's *Abury* (1743) (Raine 1968: II, 261-62), or the circle of eternity with wings of pity (Mitchell 1978: 182). Below, the moon's dark side is turned to the sun representing disorder (Wicksteed 1954: 168). Marks (1976: 58) emphasises the contrast or choice between defying the Spectre, as Los in the form of Jesus does, to help the fallen and surrendering to it by seeing the fallen as dead; Digby (*loc.cit.*) perceives the Spectre as hovering over the repressed unconscious.

pl. 35(39)   The archer has been identified as the Covering Cherub (Damon 1924: 471), Sagittarius, representing reason (Percival 1938: 159), satanic time (Wicksteed 1954: 169-70), and Albion's Spectre (Erdman 1974: 314).

pl. 37(41)   Though Damon (1924: 471) thinks the despairing giant is Hyle, he is much more likely to be Albion (Wicksteed 1954: 175) given the chance to read the diminutive Blake's advice in the water's reflection of the mirror writing (Erdman 1974: 316).

pl. 39(44)   Wicksteed (1954: 178) recognises the close kinship of the upper image to its counterpart on *IB* pl. 24. It has been interpreted as the preserver of Noah, "the Man of Imagination," from the inundation of time and space (Damon 1924:

471); woman, the vessel that, guided by female angels, carries
life over the sea of material existence (Raine 1968: I, 232); and
an ark in which the Zoas (Beer 1969: 210) or two of the
Friends of 38(43):74 (Erdman 1974: 318) try to return Albion
to Eden. Kemper (1960b: 590) cites l. 18 and argues that the
snake below shows the ark is moving in the wrong direction,
Miner (1981: 321-22) sees it as the moon of chastity over-
shadowing the phallic serpent of Old Testament priesthood,
and Doskow (1982: 89-90) views it as the degenerate threefold
church.

pl. 40(45) The explanations of this curious design are that Ooth-
oon is leaving vegetating Theotormon (Damon 1924: 471), the
female has ensnared the male as described in 87:3-8 (Binyon
1926: 132), Albion is being rescued from the state Reuben
(Wicksteed 1954: 180-81), Bath is emerging from vegetation
(Beer 1969: 186), and Vala is trapping Albion, whose maritime
empire is represented by the devouring fish (Erdman 1974:
319).

pl. 41(46) Three highly positive readings maintain that this des-
ign represents a sage and his inspiration in Elijah's chariot
pulled by Luvah's bulls (Damon 1924: 471), the fore part of
"the Plow of Jehovah, and the Harrow of Shaddai" (l. 14)
drawn by creatures based on the unicorns of Job xxxix.9-12
(Raine 1968: II, 226-28, citing *M* 7:17ff), and God and his
Bride (De Luca 1983: 194, 203-04n15). More negative read-
ings begin with Margoliouth's contention (1951: 159-60) that
the passengers are Albion and his sleeping Emanation, the ser-
pents materialism, and the bulls passion. Noting the hands
pointing opposite ways, Wicksteed (1954: 185-87) sees a
chariot of time carrying Albion and his Emanation from the
past that obsesses them, while the two tiny riders stand for
written history and oral tradition. Beer (1969: 187), citing ll.
25-28, perceives diminutive angels of judgment and bovine tyr-
ants that contribute to a witty assault on the concept of the
Atonement. Accepting Raine's citation of l. 14 and Job xxxix,
Erdman (1974: 320-21) blames Albion-Jehovah for not yet
guiding the vehicle that should synthesise such contraries as
the hands of Los (pointing forward) and Urizen (pointing
back), the lion and the ox, and the serpents of etching and eag-
le-winged riders of tinting. Mitchell (1978: 216), agreeing that

the vehicle is static, detects self-parody, while Herrstrom (1981: 74) believes that Blake is depicting the Covering Cherub, a parody of Ezekiel's dynamic Divine Chariot, and Doskow (1982: 91-92) suggests that passive humans are pulled in Urizen's threefold serpentine vehicle by the twofold bulls of Luvah. Particularly illuminating is Paley's argument (1983b: 107-10) that the chariot (clearly not a plough or harrow), with its wheels representing "cyclical natural energies," is drawn by Luvah's bulls (cf. *FZ* 77:16/ E353/ VII, 16) and that the laurel wreaths and pens mock Petrarchan love poetry. The human-headed bulls derive from engravings of Persian sculpture in *Ouseley's Travels* (1821) (Blunt 1959: 38). Other sources traced include an engraving of Ceres' chariot with serpent wheels in de Montfaucon's *Antiquity Explained, and Repre-sented in Sculptures* (English translation 1721-25) and an account of eagle-headed Garuda in Moor's *The Hindu Pan-theon* (1810) (Paley 1978a: 174-75, 186).

pl. 44(30) Damon's statement (1924: 470) that Los welcomes his Spectre and Emanation as described in l. 16 is endorsed by Binyon (1926: 130), who quotes ll. 1-3, and Erdman (1974: 323), who observes that the harp-like strings on Los show that the reunion enhances his creativity.

pl. 45(31) Rather than the two fallen minute particulars of Dam-on's interpretation (1924: 470), here is Vala binding Jerusalem (Wicksteed 1954: 193) in "the iron threads of love & jealousy & despair" of l. 49 (Erdman 1974: 324).

pl. 46(32) Damon (1924: 470) recognises that Vala approaches a classical fane while Jerusalem and her Daughters stand before a Gothic cathedral, and Wicksteed (1954: 196, 204-05) adds that Jerusalem is rejecting Vala's Veil, that the leaping girl may be Erin, and that the whole group stands on the English isle. Identifying the churches as St. Paul's and Westminster Abbey, Erdman (1974: 325) contradicts Wicksteed with the claim that Vala has nearly hypnotised Jerusalem in the pres-ence of her anxious Daughters. The latter Bindman (1977: 182) identifies rather as Daughters of Beulah symbolising immature arts under Jerusalem's protection. The entire design, reports Mellor (1974: 307), parodies the traditional choice of Hercules between modest virtue and naked vice; Paley (1983b:

111) observes that charity was often personified as a mother with her children.

pl. 47   It is tempting to accept Raine's reading of this grotesque picture as an illustration of the line immediately beneath: "And the Veil of Vala is composed of the Spectres of the Dead" (1968: II, 185). Other explanations stem from Damon's view (1924: 471) that it portrays Albion turning from Jerusalem and Britannia as he stands on the Sea of Time and Space. Wicksteed (1954: 197-98) maintains that he is rejecting the feminine, Erdman (1974: 326) that he has uttered his "last words" (1. 18) and spurns both Jerusalem and the luring Vala, and Paley (1983b: 200) that he errs in choosing the latter instead of the former. Binyon (1926: 133) believes the women are Daughters of Albion and one has her foot on the other's neck; Doskow (1982: 99) sees the trampler as Vala and her victim as Jerusalem.

pl. 50   Damon (1924: 471) correctly states that 70:1-16 describes the central image; he sees the emerging Sons as a two-headed Bacon, a Newton, and a pointing Locke; two-headed Janus, comments Paley (1983b: 219), is Bacon's symbol. Beer (1969: 211) strangely describes the three as deceiving females, and presumably it is the crowns that speak to Wicksteed (1954: 203) of history's "dismal tale." The whole monstrosity, says Erdman (1974: 329), represents not only Hand but Albion as "the Vortex of the Dead" (48:54) emitting Vala's Veil and the sevenfold Beast of Rev. xiii. On the right, two suns stand for the fallen and eternal perspectives (Rose 1964c: 50) or allude to ll. 27-29 (Lesnick 1970: 396). On the left, there may be a sceptre, cross and orb—emblems of human power (Beer, *loc. cit.*), lightning flashing from the beak of a devouring cormorant that symbolises retribution for trespasses (Lesnick 1970: 397), or a perversion of one of the eyes of the Divine Chariot of Ezek. (i. 18) (Worrall 1977b: 198). Possible sources include the engraving of a seven-headed Saxon war god in Aylett Sammes's *Britannia Antiqua Illustrata* (1676) (Worrall 1977b: 197) and the three heads representing Prudence, Good Counsel and Time in emblem books (Mitchell 1978: 203-05).

pl. 51   In separate prints of this design, Blake labelled the figures Vala, Hyle and Skofield (Erdman 1974: 330). Hyle may be powerless rationalism (Wicksteed 1954: 205) or may mark the

limit of contraction (Mitchell 1978: 205), and Schofield has
been viewed as an enslaved conscript (Wicksteed, *loc.cit.*),
either a lunatic or prisoner (Paley 1983b: 215), bondage to the
law (Beer 1969: 212), and more victim than accuser (Lesnick
1970: 397). The fleur-de-lys—a symbol, revived by Napoleon,
of the *ancien régime* (Paley 1978b: 68)—reveals one aspect of
what Erdman (*loc. cit.*) calls "Vala's court of despair." Steven-
son (1971: 730) cites Gilchrist's suggestion (1945: 202) that
Vala and Hyle are dejected at the failure of Schofield's prose-
cution. To Mellor (1974: 313) the group seems a parody of the
Holy Trinity, to Mitchell (1978: 206) a display of the "mutual
tyranny" of the sexes, and to Ferguson (1978: 182) a demon-
stration to Los that the fallen world needs pity, not wrath.
Erdman (*loc. cit.*) makes the important point that it is the anti-
thesis of *IB* pl. 100.

pl. 53   Identifying this imposing figure enthroned over the Sea of
Time and Space as Beulah, Damon (1924: 472) is able to clas-
sify her blocking out of the sunlight of Eternity as merciful.
However, Margoliouth (1951: 161) observes that Blake never
personifies Beulah and the woman may be "Religion hid in
War" (75:20) or Rahab, and Grant's claim (1974: 48) that she
malignly comes between Eternity and humankind is probably
correct. Moreover it is consistent with Wicksteed's view (1954:
207) that she is the beautiful temptress nature, a view that jus-
tifies Damon (1967: 390, misprinting the plate number) in
reidentifying her as Vala. Referring to *IB* pl. 2, 19:40-44, and
86:1-5, Mitchell (1978: 206-08) argues that she is an ambigu-
ous combination of Vala and Jerusalem, of natural religion and
prophecy. It is disputed whether her sunflower represents
longing for immortality (Damon 1924: 472) or whether it is an
earthbound flower (Raine 1968: I, 406n58) or a symbol of frus-
trated sexuality (Mellor 1974: 314). The astronomical images
may represent reason with a glimpse of vision (Beer 1969:
374), Albion's Sons (twelve stars) along with the winter season
(note the earth's angle) appropriate to Ulro (Lesnick 1970:
397-98), or the goddess's power over the physical universe
(Mellor, *loc. cit.*). Her coiffeur recalls the sacrificial flame on
an altar (Erdman 1974: 332). Rose (1968b: 229), who aptly
cites 78:15-16), regards this figure as a parody of Jerusalem,
and Grant (*loc. cit.*), who notes her blindness, views her throne

as a parody of seraph wings. Among the sources are an engrav-
ing of an Indian deity in Moor's *Hindu Pantheon* (1810) (Blunt
1959: 38) and perhaps portraits of Elizabeth I (Rose, *loc. cit.*).

pl. 54   Line 6 of the text shows that here is the "Rocky fragment"
Albion has become (Rose 1965: 600). Reason, Pity, Desire and
Wrath are respectively Urizen, Los-Palamabron, Luvah, and
Tharmas-Rintrah (Erdman 1974: 333). On either side are
rising the Sheep and Goats of *IB* pl. 3 (Wicksteed 1954: 207)
or "energies and aspirations" surviving Albion's collapse (J.
Warner 1984: 134) or else the Daughters of Albion are
mourning (Beer 1969: 213). Below may be the fallen Zoas
(Wicksteed, *loc. cit.*); the fallen human tormented by the
insects of reason (Beer, *loc. cit.*); three-headed Hand and a
companion (Stevenson 1971: 739); Arthur constricted into the
"Druid Rocks" of l. 26 but retaining, the stars show, a little
perception (Erdman 1974: 333); or a four-headed figure repre-
senting Arthur's defeated followers (Worrall 1977b: 199).

pl. 57   The obvious interpretation of this design seems to be
Damon's (1924: 472): worldly York and London triumph over
Jerusalem. Paley (1972: 186) usefully adds that fibres of vege-
tation from the hands of the former two seem to be ensnaring
the latter, and Wyatt (1975: 120) conceives of Blake's heroine
as trapped in Vala's Veil. Considering the buildings and the
accompanying arcs, Johnston (1970: 435) maintains that the
fallen earth is poised between sinister Romanesque and imagi-
native Gothic cities, and even Wicksteed's theory (1954: 211)
that York, London and Jerusalem represent respectively past,
present and future seems to give the last the preference.
Erdman, however, (1974: 336) perceives all three women as
worthy weavers creating a stained glass window for Cathedron,
whereas Beer (1969: 246) manages to criticise Jerusalem for
remaining asleep while her companions rise into the starry reg-
ion of vision, and Hilton (1983: 91) condemns the women as
female wills handling the stuff of the terrestrial globe.

pl. 58   Keynes's description (1921: 165) of the upper image as a
flying head is superseded by the theories that it is a spectre
(Damon 1924: 472) and that it is the entrance to Generation
(Wicksteed 1954: 212). As an opening, it takes the form of the
female genitals—the exit of the newborn child into the grave of
earthly life as indicated by the skeleton below (Raine 1968: I,

234). Mills (1980: 89-93) argues that a female will here hovers over a male victim as a male spectre hovers over a female victim in *IB* pl. 33(37). Classifying the upper image as the compressed form of a dragon, Stevenson (1971: 746-47) sees in the fiery skeleton the Urizenic world of l. 44, but Erdman (1974: 337) finds the flames creative and the prostrate form an expression of what the artist endures.

pl. 59　The women are Daughters of Los (Damon 1924: 472), whose spinning wheels, according to Wicksteed (1954: 212), represent time, digestion and reproduction, while the flames signify the emotional life and the work artistic creation. Erdman (1974: 338) conceives them as akin to the three Fates and is confident that the sister at the left is working at an unseen loom.

pl. 62　The commonest view, that the giant is Luvah in torment, goes back to Damon (1924: 472), who quotes *FZ* 31:9-10/ E320/ II, 229-30 and decides that the diminutive figure is Vala, though Erdman (1974: 341) thinks that the latter is Blake and that the eyed feathers show that Luvah, at present a victim of the Druids, may yet attain unbounded vision. Luvah is said to be "perverted love" (Doskow 1982: 122-23) and on one level the French Revolution (Erdman, *loc. cit.*). Other theories are that the giant is Albion unable to prevail against age and time though Los, as ll. 35-36 imply, can see the Divine Vision between his still unshaken feet (Wicksteed 1954: 213); that humanity is being strangled by reason and burnt by "unorganized energy" until, perhaps, it shrivels into a diminutive form (Beer 1969: 190, 372); and that the angel of Rev. x.1 is suffering the pain that comes with vision while St. John, in the shape of Los and Blake, is a witness (Mitchell 1978: 212).

pl. 63　Rejecting Wicksteed's theory (1954: 213, 228) that here is the Gwendolen of l. 32, three critics relate this design to ll. 23-26—Beer (1969: 248) interprets the eclipsed moon as the cherubim, the nude as chastity, and the worm as Reuben or physical passion; Stevenson (1971: 760) suggests that vision sees the mountain curves of Cheviot as a female and that they are rigidified like the Reuben of 30(34):43ff; Janet Warner (1977: 111) holds that the woman enwrapped by the worm of mortality represents the inescapable sexuality of nature. Alter-

natively, Erdman conceives her as France shorn and squeezed
by the British Leviathan (1954a: 428, 429 [463, 464]) and also
as a feminine counterpart of Luvah (1969b: 463, 464)—and
hence as the war goddess Vala, who causes a partial eclipse of
the sun (1974: 342). The figure echoes the reclining nude in
Titian's *Bacchanal* as well as the Ariadne on the Portland
Vase, which Blake had engraved in 1791 (J. Warner 1977:
111-14).

pl. 64   The obscure upper images have been explained as a
woman who is sleeping after studying and her dreams (Damon
1924: 472), as two females—Vala and Jerusalem—competing
for the mind of Reuben-Blake below (Wicksteed 1954: 214),
and as a downcast Jerusalem turned away from two figures in
flight (Stevenson 1971: 761). The male below may be a bene-
volent Jehovah instructing a sleeping male, namely Albion
(Nelms 1974: 89-90). More plausible is Erdman's interpreta-
tion (1974: 343) that an almost haloed (i.e. redeemable) Vala
writes on a scroll, two Daughters of Albion unfurl the Web of
ll. 2-3, and Urizen relates the marks on the Web to his text.

pl. 65   This may be the Chain of Jealousy (Damon 1924: 472),
which develops into the chain of 66:5 and shackles the victim
of *IB* pl. 67 (Erdman 1974: 344), or it may be the chain of time
(Wicksteed 1954: 214).

pl. 67   The tortured man is a victim of imperialism (Erdman
1954a: 428 [463]) and a prisoner of time accompanied by the
birds of Innocence (Wicksteed 1954: 215). The two groups of
birds also represent the now divided five senses and the man is
at once Luvah, Albion, and the "poor Human Form" of l. 44
(Erdman 1974: 346). As fallen Albion, he constitutes "a hum-
an link in a great chain" (Paley 1983b: 211).

pl. 69   In this grisly illustration of 65[:63-65] (Binyon 1926:
135), the victim may be "Man" (Wicksteed 1954: 215, citing
rather 66:16-33) or Albion (Raine 1968: I, 310-11), while the
sacrificers are Rahab with her cup and Tirzah with a knife and
scalp (Damon 1924: 472-73), though the body fragment may
be a heart (Raine, *loc. cit.*) or the product of circumcision or
castration (Hagstrum 1973b: 114). Erdman (1974: 348) notes
the cruciform position of the victim's arms. The theme has
been announced as the pain of mental conflict (Wicksteed, *loc.*

cit.), spirit sacrificed by nature (Raine, *loc. cit.*), and the torture of male sexuality (Paley 1983b: 225).

pl. 70 The figures have been identified as Urizen's Daughters—the head, heart and loins—passing through Experience (Damon 1924: 473) and as Bacon, Newton and Locke (T. Wright 1929: II, 59). The globe is usually seen as the moon, which Rose (1964c: 50) understands as imagination imprisoned in a Druid arch, but Erdman (1974: 349) views it as an eclipsed sun in the midst of the clouds of Vala's Veil.

pl. 71 Early guesses are that this is a spectre and an exhausted emanation (Damon 1924: 473) and that sex as a spiritualising force links a phallic swan to tendrils of reasoning that lead to the "flower of Human fertility" (Wicksteed 1954: 217-18). Later speculation identifies the woman as either a sleeping Jerusalem threatened by the now spectrous swan of *IB* pl. 11 (Beer 1969: 250) or Vala, whose brain is extending over the sky like Urizen's Net of Religion in *The Book of Urizen* (Miner 1960: 204) or who enacts the role of Leda, mother of Helen and thereby of war (Erdman 1974: 350). Erdman (*loc. cit.*) thinks the object by her head a sacrificial altar like that of *M IB* pl. 15.

pl. 72 Far above the serpent of nature (Damon 1924: 473), angels lament over a world tormented by fires of passion (Wicksteed 1954: 218). Erdman (1974: 351) locates the globe in Los's furnace, from which it emerges onto his anvil in the next plate. Seeing the shape at its centre as "the heart-shaped tabernacle of the universe," Miner (1981: 332) perceives the words circling round it as headed for "Jerusalem's West Gate of sexual renovation." In Beer's opinion (1969: 20-21, 250-51), the design illustrates the disintegration of the wings of vision, the sun of reason, and the serpent of energy hitherto synthesised in the form that Stukeley ascribed to the prehistoric monument at Avebury (*Abury* [1743]).

pl. 73 In this picture of Los and the solar orb (Damon 1924: 473), Wicksteed (1954: 218-19) sees a setting sun and Erdman (1974: 352) the natural sun, which Los transforms. Beer (1969: 251, 373) argues that Los must force infinite energy into this solar form to preserve Urizen's world.

pl. 74 Fibres emerge from a nude male (Keynes 1921: 166) to imprison him (Paley 1983b: 93). Blake is portraying the enrooting of Reuben (Damon 1924: 473) and also of his brothers as described in ll. 42-49 (Erdman 1974: 353); the figure contrasts with the Jerusalem of *IB* pl. 57 (*ibid.*). Stevenson (1971: 791) supposes it to be the Dinah of ll. 52-54.

pl. 75   Here, declares Damon (1924: 473), angels confront their contrary in Rahab, Tirzah and the Dragon of War below. Paley (1978b: 68) believes there is a single female, Rahab, seen from two viewpoints, and Binyon (1926: 136) refers to more than one dragon. The monster or monsters have been considered as benign embodiments of energy (Beer 1969: 192); as a seven-headed polypus representing the material world (Mellor 1974: 316); and as the Dragon of the Apocalypse (Altizer 1967: 128) in an hermaphroditic union with Rahab, the Whore of Babylon (Mitchell 1978: 208), who faces the viewer and reigns as a crowned and sexually powerful queen (Webster 1983: 286). The contrast between the angelic circles and the coils on the dragon may symbolise the contrast between brotherhood with forgiveness and government by interlocking cause and effect (Damon, *loc. cit.*), between loveless sex and limitless divine love (Wicksteed 1954: 220), and between redemption and cyclic repetition (Paley, *loc. cit.*). The parallel between the two chains of circles suggests to Erdman (1974: 354) that imagination can redeem the fallen realm and to Mitchell (1978: 209) that Jerusalem is present even within the dragon.

pl. 76   Acclaiming the greatness of this design, Damon (1924: 473) points to the cruciform posture of Albion as he adores the crucified Christ on the dead "Tree of Moral Virtue" or (Bindman 1977: 179) the biblical Tree of Knowledge. It bears apples (Damon 1967: 95) or apple-like acorns (Erdman 1974: 395) and is also a Druid oak (Hagstrum 1964: 116-17) and the Tree of Mystery (Mellor 1974: 321). The dawn on the left, noticed by Wicksteed (1954: 220), signifies the rising of the natural sun contrasted with the spiritual sun above (Damrosch 1980: 55) emanating "visionary forgiveness" (Beer 1969: 209). Blake borrows Albion's stance from his own engraving *Glad Day*, the inscription on which refers to the hero's "Dance of Eternal Death"—i.e. his self-sacrifice (Blunt 1959: 81-82) or self-annihilation (Bindman, *loc. cit.*; engraving—Bindman 1978, pl. 400). Albion—redeemed energy (Mellor 1974: 321-23)—is identified with St. John, the sole disciple said to have observed the Crucifixion (Mitchell 1978: 210). Unlike the

Jews, the Deists and his own earlier self, he recognises fallen humankind's need for an external, self-sacrificing saviour (Mathews 1980a), and he becomes what he beholds (Deen 1983: 250). A dissenting view is that Albion is misguidedly adoring the vegetated Christ of 90:34-38, the body cast off on the Cross, though the casting off is self-annihilation so the sun rising on the left is probably the eternal sun (Lesnick 1970: 399-400). Substantially sharing this view, Erdman (1974: 355) adds that the presence of both the natural sun (perhaps setting) and the spiritual sun prefigures Albion's recovery of his vision.

pl. 78   In this much disputed design, the sun may be rising (Wicksteed 1910: 139) or setting (Keynes 1921: 166) beside the Sea of Time and Space (Damon 1924: 473). Clearly the beak is a raptor's, but is the crest a cock's alluding to the dawn (Wicksteed, *loc. cit.*) or specifically to the one St. Peter heard at daybreak [e.g. Matt. xxvi.74] (Wicksteed 1954: 236), or is it a headpiece like that of the eagle-headed griffin in Blake's illustration to Dante no. 88 (Ott 1976: 50; the Dante design, Butlin 1981: pl. 973)? If the head is an eagle's, the figure may be a genius resembling the eagle-men of *MHH*, pl. 15 (T. Wright 1929: I, 38); Hand, with his "rav'ning beak" (9:13) representing all his brothers—see 8:43 (Lesnick 1970: 400); or St. John (who has traditionally been portrayed with an eagle's head deriving from Ezek. i[.10] and Rev. iv[.7]) here identified with Los (Adlard 1972: 120-21); the composite John-Los replicates the pose of Melancholy pictured as genius in Dürer's *Melancholia I* (Ott 1976).

Some expositions account for both eagle's beak and cock's comb: the bird-man may be Los suffering mixed emotions (Wicksteed 1954: 226); a combination of St. John, Los and Albion, in whom the eagle of genius is combined with the symbol of dawn (Mitchell 1978: 211-12); Hand on the threshold of Ulro's night yet bearing a pledge of morning (Lesnick 1970: 400-01); or Hand as both devourer and victim (Doskow 1982: 141-42). As a symbol of degenerate humanity, he may, like the swan-woman of *IB* pl. 11, combine incongruous elements in a mode derived from Egyptian deities (Paley 1978b: 68).

pl. 80   Whether Gwendolen is above and Cambel below (Damon 1924: 473) or vice versa (Binyon 1926: 136) is disputed. They are generating Hyle and Hand respectively (Wicksteed 1954: 228) and beginning to humanise them (Erdman 1974: 359). Doskow (1982: 147-48) suggests a woman is being metamorphosed into a worm or a worm into a woman depending on whether one reads up or down.

pl. 81 Lecturing her sisters (Damon 1924: 473), Gwendolen holds her falsehood behind her back (Margoliouth 1951: 167), while Cambel adopts the Venus Pudica pose (Damon 1967: 66), which symbolises chastity (Beer 1969: 235). Illustrating 82:10-21, this design, points out Erdman (1974: 360), is parallel to *IB* pl. 46(32), which centres on a Jerusalem whose pose contrasts with Cambel's; he asserts that six of Gwendolen's sisters have fallen and four are now doing so. Doskow (1982: 146) sees Cambel as coy, secretive love and believes the mirror writing is inscribed on Vala's Veil. See also 82:17-21n.

pl. 82 The worm to which Hand and Hyle are reduced (Binyon 1926: 137)—or just Hyle (Wicksteed 1954: 229).

pl. 84 Though Beer (1969: 253-54) claims that St. Paul's neoclassical dome dominates the commercial city, other critics detect optimism in what Damon (1924: 474) recognises as a design repeated from *SE IB* pl. 46 ("London") to illustrate l. 11 of this plate. Damon himself (*loc. cit.*) feels the cathedral shows that genuine faith has a shrine even within corrupt Babylon, Wicksteed (1954: 232) declares that the boy points to a gate in Jerusalem's wall [see quatrain, pl. 77], Johnston (1970: 418-22) believes the mixture of architectures indicates the people may choose to build Babylon or Jerusalem, and Erdman (1974: 363) is satisfied the child leads the man past the wrong door to the Gothic entrance behind which the two churches will merge under the Cross.

pl. 85 Damon (1924: 474) imagines an emanation is joining two men (one invisible) in friendship, Raine (1968: II, 174) thinks Vala is pulling nature's veil out of Albion, and Beer (1969: 254) considers Jerusalem is making fertile a man who turns from her brightness. However, most critics endorse Binyon's identification of the couple as Los and Enitharmon (1926: 137). Binyon cites 86:51, Stevenson 87:6-9 (1971: 814). Enitharmon may be giving the westward-looking Los vegetation from the Babylonian east where the sun is obscured (Wicksteed 1954: 233), the couple may be arguing though there are signs

they will co-operate (Erdman 1974: 364-65), or Enitharmon
may be weaving a malign body from the substance of Los
(Paley 1983b: 258).

pl. 87   The gist of this design is given in Damon's description
(1924: 474) of Enion pursuing Enitharmon, who clasps Los's
hand, the scene being "the fourfold/ Desarts" of ll. 1-2. How-
ever, there are disagreements about the figure in the top left
corner, who may be Tharmas (Damon, *loc. cit.*) or Urizen
(Beer 1969: 237), and the small creature below him, who may
be Ahania (Damon, *loc. cit.*), Enion's image of herself (Wick-
steed 1954: 235), or the weeping Erin of 86:42-46 (Erdman
1974: 366). Wicksteed (*loc. cit.*) thinks the subject is the old
age of woman as that of *IB* pl. 84 is the old age of man, and
Carr (1980: 533-34) asserts that the Zoas are here reduced to
indefinite forms in "wheels without wheels."

pl. 89   The figures have been interpreted as Los and Enitharmon
above the Tree of Mystery (Damon 1924: 474); Vala handing
Jerusalem a symbol of generation, which would bring about the
Incarnation (Wicksteed 1954: 236-37); the reason and desire of
IB pl. 12 almost reuniting (Chayes 1974: 75); and the Druid
priestess of the top right corner of *IB* pl. 74, perhaps reformed,
receiving a heavenly basket from a spirit above (Erdman 1974:
368). Doskow (1982: 154-55) sees the mysterious object as a
cocoon, which represents the human being's opportunity to
metamorphose from mortal worm to winged soul.

pl. 91   There is much acceptance of Damon's view (1924: 474)
that the man is Albion and the symbols are a six-pointed star
and an ear of corn signifying respectively the Old and New
Testaments, which, adds Paley (1983b: 211), are later united in
"the Mutual Covenant Divine" of 98:41. These images have
also been understood as representing a Last Judgment and
Blake's poverty (Wicksteed 1954: 237), as sublimity and path-
os (Beer 1969: 237), and as occultism and the roots of the Tree
of Mystery (Doskow 1982: 158-59). Raine (1968: II, 257) per-
ceives here the fallen human sacrificed to make nature exter-
nal.

pl. 92   Jerusalem is probably lamenting before Druid Babylon's
gates (Damon 1924: 474) in a posture of self-surrender (Paley
1983b: 183), her clothed state indicating, as in *IB* pl. 26, her
low condition (Wyatt 1975: 120-21). The four faces around her

have been read as her slain Children (Damon, *loc. cit.*), the "Briton, Saxon, Roman, Norman" of l. 1 (Binyon 1926: 138), her disintegrating pagan oppressors like Amalek (Johnston 1970: 435), both her Sons (see 71:50-52) and the Zoas (Erdman 1974: 371), and the British victims of Hengist's treachery at Stonehenge (Worrall 1977b: 200-01). Erdman (*loc. cit.*) cites Is. iii.25-26 but draws attention to the dawn sky in the background. Applying the inscription "Jerusalem" to the ruins, Bindman (1977: 182) identifies the figure as probably Enitharmon.

pl. 93   The figure below has been explained as a soul at peace in its tomb despite the presence of penal fire (Damon 1924: 474), as Enitharmon addressing her Sons (works of art) (Wicksteed 1954: 238-40, quoting ll. 1-5), as Enitharmon in the furnaces of affliction being painfully metamorphosed into Jerusalem (Erdman 1974: 372), and as Jerusalem in these furnaces at the nadir of her experience (Wyatt 1975: 121). The accusers' fingers, states Erdman (*loc. cit.*), indicate that human life is but a span and that hellfire awaits, and they try to warn us against the remaining pages of the book.

pl. 94   Damon's view (1924: 474) that the upper panel shows the accusers overthrown and the lower panel Britannia awaking on Albion's bosom (l. 20) is augmented by Binyon's comment (1926: 138) on the arrival of dawn and Erdman's perception (1974: 373) of "The Breath Divine" (l. 18) rising as sunlight. Comparing *A IB* pl. ii, Bindman (1977: 183) proposes that we see a slain warrior and his dead wife, and Paley (1983b: 230) finds this emblem of war relieved by the daybreak. To Worrall (1977b: 206), the lower scene recalls the death of Arthur, who is identified with *fallen* Albion.

pl. 95   Albion rises in the flames of wrath of l. 6, and the face by his left foot represents the body discarded in the grave (Damon 1924: 474). Blake deliberately leaves it unclear whether the figure is clothed (Paley 1973b: 138). Doskow (1982: 162) judges that the rejuvenated Albion takes Los's form here and in *IB* pl. 97.

pl. 96   The rising, embracing figures may be God and the soul (Damon 1924: 474); Albion and England (Wicksteed 1954: 243-44)—i.e. the couple of *IB* pl. 94 resurrected and now incorporating all the male and all the female characters (Erdman

1974: 375); God the Father (the Lawgiver redeemed by union with Christ) and Jerusalem (Hagstrum 1964: 117); Satan-Albion becoming spiritual and Jerusalem taking incarnation (Altizer 1967: 205-07); or two composite characters—Albion-Jehovah-the Universal Father (see 97:6) and Britannia-Vala-Jerusalem (Nelms 1974: 88-90).

pl. 97   The figure may be the poet (Damon 1924: 474), Los (Binyon 1926: 136), Albion (Beer 1969: 258), or Albion identified with Los-Urthona (Erdman 1974: 376), and he may be in moony Beulah (Damon, *loc. cit.*) or in the full light of Eternity (Nelms 1974: 86). He is the traveller of *IB* pl. 1 in a reverse posture (Wicksteed 1954: 245), no longer a common citizen but a hero (Hagstrum 1964: 118), who has shed his garments of mortality to rise from instead of entering the realm of death (Nelms, *loc. cit.*); his regenerated body emanates light (Nelson 1973: 140-41) now that he has moved from the Centre or east to the Circumference or west (Mitchell 1978: 178-79, citing 14:29-30). The globe of *IB* pl. 1 may have become the material sun, which will perish (Binyon, *loc.cit.*) or may be raised with him (Wicksteed, *loc. cit.*) when he enters Eternity. If he is Albion, he may be suppressing "the spectre sun" (Beer, *loc. cit.*) or have rescued the eternal sun from the Atlantic (Lesnick 1970: 402-04). If he is Los-Albion, he carries the sun of imagination, which is the Spectre of Urthona, and beneath this (in three copies) is his bow with gaps representing "the Arrows of Love" of l. 12 (Erdman, *loc. cit.*).

pl. 98   Interpretations of the dragon-headed worm (Damon 1924: 475) or snake (Binyon 1926: 138) range from the basest human form (Damon, *loc. cit.*) through the years, days and other units of time (Wicksteed 1954: 248) to the serpent redeemed (Beer 1969: 259). The creatures below may be earth-dwellers in the state of Beulah (Wicksteed, *loc.cit.*); humble creatures now in Eternity (Nelms 1974: 87); the minute particulars of Albion's fourfold body (Bogan 1981: 98); or the regenerated "Living Creatures" of l. 54, including the twenty-eight larks of *Milton* and a large bird symbolising imagination (Erdman 1974: 377). Doskow (1982: 171n17) thinks the twenty-eight may stand for Albion's Cathedral Cities.

pl. 99   The obvious parallel with *IB* pl. 96 leads several critics from Damon (1924: 474, 475) to Erdman (1974: 378) to consider the characters in the two designs as identical. The second portrays the consummation of the union pictured in the first (Altizer 1967: 208-09), its rectification by the addition of "joy and giving" (Erdman, *loc. cit.*), or its transcendence (Bindman 1977: 182, 183). There is a division, however, between those who regard the older figure either as Albion (Beer 1969: 260) or as both Albion and God (Erdman 1969b: 486) and those who see it as Deity embracing Jerusalem, who can now reunite Albion with Eternity (Fisher 1961: 222), or who enacts with God the union to which Albion aspires on *IB* pl. 76 (Nelson 1973: 143). Bindman (1977: 183) believes the younger figure a representation, its sex deliberately undefined, of all who seek the Spirit, while Mitchell (1978: 214) perceives in it an androgynous touch. Altizer (*loc. cit.*) posits that the figures are being transformed into each other, that their heads unite to form an icon of Christ, and that Jerusalem's arms mark out a human space to contain the divine countenance.

Blunt (1959: 80-81) identifies Martin de Vos's engraving of the Prodigal Son's return as a major source. From this, Beer (*loc. cit.*) deduces that both parties gain from the reunion and Damrosch (1980: 271-72) that a father-child relationship without repression is implied. Mitchell (*loc. cit.*), noting the lower character's cruciform posture, asserts that the forgiveness is mutual.

The flames may represent creativity, desire, wrath or purgation (Nelms 1974: 88); according to Erdman (1974: 378), they double as water illustrating 96:36-37. Wicksteed (1954: 249-50) thinks them the flames of hell, into which the Ancient of Days (in the coloured copy Jesus) descends to redeem Jerusalem.

pl. 100   As early as 1924, Damon (344, 475) recognises what are most commonly understood as the basic elements of this composition: the Spectre of Urthona moving inward, the smith Urthona [or Los], the weaver Enitharmon, and the serpentine temple that William Stukeley (*Abury* [1743]) supposed—wrongly, as Todd notes (1946: 48)—to have stood at prehistoric Avebury. However, Blake's not quite consistent nomenclature also allows the central figure and his companion to be called respectively Urthona and Los (Binyon 1926: 139). With Urthona is merged, according to Doskow (1982: 28), the red-

eemed Albion, or according to Erdman (1974: 379), the red-
eemed Urizen. The latter, however, Janet Warner (1984: 144-
45) identifies with the leaping companion—who, Mellor thinks
(1974: 331), could be the regenerated Albion. The female is
sometimes considered to be Vala (T. Wright 1929: II, 61) or
either Enitharmon or Jerusalem (Erdman 1954a: 449 [486-
87]). The tongs of Los-Urthona, said to "turn the heavens"
(Wicksteed 1954: 251), combine the reason embodied in Newt-
on's compasses with creativity (Beer 1969: 260). The phallic
hammer (*ibid.*) is credited with shattering constricting forms
and fashioning new ones (Mellor, *loc. cit.*). The leaper may
carry the astronomical sun (Ferguson 1978: 192), the renewed
sun of *FZ* 138:20/ E406/ IX, 825 (T. Wright, *loc. cit.*), the
eternal sun (Lesnick 1970: 410), the sun of imagination
(Johnston 1970: 437), or the globe on *IB* pl. 1 (Rose 1971a: 65-
66).

Clearly this design depicts activity, and most critics consider
the activity redemptive. Nevertheless readings of the scene
range from Kiralis's pessimistic account (1969: 213-14) of a
dejected Los forced to watch the constant return to Generation
indicated by the presence of a Druid structure, to Doskow's
notion (*loc. cit.*) that Urthona is in front of the lateral figures,
who are still in Generation, and Paley's happy description
(1983b: 274-77) of an image of the life of the millenium. In
question are the interpretation of the serpent temple and of the
female's spinning or weaving. Though he begins by thinking
the temple negative—as do Beer (*loc. cit.*), Bindman (1977:
184) and Ferguson (*loc. cit.*)—Wicksteed (1910: 139) believes
the sun is liberated from it by Los and carried away by his
companion. Later (1954: 251) he describes Los as poised in the
centre between the life of mortality, spun by Mother Earth, and
Eternity, into which the sun is borne. Equally optimistic is
Thomas Wright's view (*loc.cit.*) that the female is Vala per-
manently discarding her Veil. However, while Kiralis's view is
exceptionally gloomy, Damrosch (1980: 334-36) is persuaded
that Blake is showing the rather poor best that can be achieved
in this world, where Los reduces the size of the trilithons but
they retain their malignant serpentine shape; he rejects Paley's
view (1983b: 277, citing 98:44) that this shape is here unfallen.
Noting the coherent layout of these trilithons, unique in

Blake's work, Johnston (1970: 436-37) accepts Wicksteed's theory (1954: 251) that the Druidic-seeming temple *is* Golgonooza; Mellor (1974: 332) believes Urthona has just turned the former into the latter. Johnston (*loc. cit.*) adds that this city is created from the materials of nature's veil and that it is both Golgonooza and Golgonooza's fulfilment, namely Jerusalem. Nelms (1974: 86-87) suggests that, as the former city, it could be an imaginative representation of the six millenia of temporal experience.

Equally controversial is the action of the female. Kiralis (1969: 213-14) judges that she is Vala spinning her Veil while the Spectre tries to enlighten her darkness with the "golden pillar of Jerusalem" he bears; contrariwise, Mitchell (1978: 180) asserts that she is Enitharmon weaving a space and shape for the fallen realm, into which Los takes prophecy. Expanding on Erdman's observation (1954a: 449 [486-87]) that she is producing the atmospheres, Hilton (1983: 116-17) describes how she draws onto her distaff or spindle energy from the sun and fibres from the moon. His conception of atmosphere as "the medium of materialization" gives this view of Enitharmon a certain affinity with the widely accepted opinion of Damon (1924: 475) that she is the weaver of the mortal body. This body, claims Mellor (1974: 331-32), is woven with fibres from Cathedron's looms and, rightly seen, does not imprison but bestows form. Paley (1983b: 276) observes that Enitharmon's weaving is antithetical to the unravelling of the body in *IB* pl. 25. Beside Enitharmon is a crescent moon that may symbolise Beulah (Damon, *loc. cit.*) or Generation (Wicksteed 1954: 251)—or, since this female is all females, it may be Vala's blood-filled cup (Rose 1971a: 65-66), which, according to Erdman (1974: 379), is now transformed into a saving moon-ark.

This design has some relation to others in the volume, and its subject includes the book itself. Los has now finished the task he commenced in *IB* pl. 1 (Rose 1968b: 231-32), and this final design is antithetical to its static counterpart, *IB* pl. 51, which also features two males and a female (Nelms 1974: 86-87). Essick (1980: 158) remarks that one portrays a corrupt and one a redeemed triad and that there is a parallel contrast between the crucifixions on *IB* pls. 26 and 76, the second of which brings about a spiritual unfolding in Albion. The central figure of the redeemed triad is, Rose maintains (1971a: 65-66), Los looking back into the work he has just completed, and Erdman (*loc. cit.*) sees a reference to his labour in the form of an analogy between the sunlight, moonlight and stones and Blake's ink, colour and copper plates. Mitchell (1978: 180-81) identifies the hundred stones of Golgonooza with the hundred plates of *Jerusalem*.

For the Sexes: The Gates of Paradise

By changing the introductory part of his title from "*For Children*" to "*For the Sexes*," Blake indicates he is now addressing those in the state of Generation (Damon 1924: 83) or Experience (Keynes 1968: 8). The subject is both humanity collectively and the individual (Kmetz 1971: 184). While Frye (1966: 193-94, 197) sees even in the expanded work an image of a dismal life cycle relieved only by one glimpse of an immortal self (pl. 13) and Bloom (1963: 435-36) perceives a representation of the Orc cycle followed by a gently triumphant epilogue, several critics find the later book as a whole more hopeful. It has been said to focus on regeneration (Paley 1978b: 26), on an occasionally interrupted journey forwards and upwards (Erdman 1977a: 42-44), and on the Platonic cycle of descent and return (Raine 1968: I, 96-97). Mellor (1974: 227-31) argues that, unlike *For Children*, it shows that vision can bring rebirth here as well as hereafter: new captions, she points out, allude to visionary perception (pl. i) and the presence of the Divine Image (pl. 7), the "Keys" show that the shell of pl. 6 is now the Mundane Shell instead of the body, and pl. 13 concerns posthumous redemption while "To The Accuser" relates to redemption in this world.

Details

pl. i Deploying the Greek symbols of the cocoon and butterfly for the body and the soul reborn from it (Damon 1924: 83), Blake contrasts the human who is a crawling insect—governed by visionless sense perceptions (Raine 1968: II, 102, 104) or devouring error and reproducing (Damon 1924: 83-84)—with the freely flying soul he or she can become (Digby 1957: 7-8). The higher possibility is emphasised by the outline of wings added to the cocoon in *For the Sexes* (Salemi 1981: 109, 124n13), the child's as yet unconscious state being represented by the dark leaf overhead (*ibid.*). The inscription "What is Man!" (common to both versions of the book) alludes to the human littleness referred to in Job vii.17 and the human greatness touched on in Ps. viii.4 and its quotation in Heb. ii.6 (Parisi 1978: 75-76). The claim, under the revised design, that the sunlight depends on the organ that beholds it urges the reader to perceive imaginatively (Keynes 1968: 9) and indicates that the chrysalis-child will fall or rise according to the way it sees (Mellor 1974: 228).

The caterpillar, says Bindman (1977: 86), observes the child showing that human life is one of nature's processes, and the oak leaf, according to Lindberg (1973: 257), is a symbol of immortality. Webster (1983: 183-84) interprets the light and dark leaves as the beneficent and the threatening aspects of the mother, and the chrysalis and grub as the spiritual and greed-stained aspects of the child.

pl. ii The angels added in *For the Sexes* welcome the rising sun (Erdman 1974: 268) and have been said to stand for the forgiveness mentioned on the same plate (Keynes 1968: 8) and to be part of the Gates (Mellor 1974: 227).

pl. 1 Blake exploits the tradition that the human-shaped mandrake with its forked root screams when pulled from the ground. Damon (1924: 84) believes this plant signifies that the child, unlike an Eternal, has a sexual identity; Rose (1968b: 224) equates it with the human "little grovelling Root" of *J* 17:32; Frye (1947: 369) sees it as a symbol of the natural man and (1966: 193) points to its association with mothers in Gen. xxx.14. Under Eden's Tree of Knowledge (Kmetz 1971: 176), which is also the tree of nature (Raine 1968: II, 36-37), the woman—perhaps Eve (Parisi 1978: 77) or nature herself (Rose 1963: 45)—may be plucking the natural man (*ibid.*), warring against her son's sexual desire symbolised by the mandrake (Webster 1983: 184-85), or cruelly tearing children from their proper environment (Adlard 1972: 53) or from a pre-natal paradise identifiable with Beulah (Kmetz, *loc. cit.*). She stunts their development, and they lose their hair and facial features in her veil (Erdman 1974: 269)—the Veil of Vala (Keynes 1968: 10-11) or apron representing the womb (Kmetz, *loc. cit.*). The tree is a willow, which is associated with lamentation, sterility and virginity (Adlard 1972: 53-54, 137n23) and which signifies the sadness of birth into the world of the four elements (Tinker 1939: 106-07).

Mellor (1974: 69-72, 228) sees in the earlier version an unnatural mother drawing a child from Eden into this world, and in the later a sleeping soul born under Vala's dominion.

pls. 2-5 There can be no disputing Blake's dislike of the four elements, but do they clothe the foetus (Frye 1966: 193), represent the troubles of childhood (Damon 1967: 149), or imprison the adult (Mellor 1974: 72)? Digby (1957: 24-26) equates water, earth, air and fire with Tharmas, Urthona, Urizen and Luvah respectively, while Parisi (1978: 79-81) considers they stand for four states in the fallen world.

The water of pl. 2, according to Keynes (1968: 11), represents both matter and unhappiness, and its victim, says Erdman (1974: 269), is man, who is immobilised by doubt as he gazes at his reflection in it. The earth from which he tries to escape in pl. 3 is the matter of pl. 2 solidified (Erdman 1974: 270) or the Platonic prison of the body (Tinker 1939: 107).

Although Tinker (1939: 107, 110) holds that reflection has led the figure of pl. 4 to despair, Erdman (1974: 270) observes that despite its lack of faith in vision it is less confined by matter than before. Critics find clues to its meaning in the stars, which may constitute the confining cosmic bound of Newton or Urizen (Mellor 1974: 72) or may signify intellectual arrogance as they often do in earlier emblem books (Salemi 1981: 112). The latter is suggested by the quotation from Ezek. xxviii.6 beneath the preliminary sketch for the design on p. 94 of Blake's Notebook: "Thou hast set thy heart as the heart of God." This rebuke to the Prince of Tyre may imply that a desire for knowledge has led astray (Kmetz 1971: 177) or that the reasoner is arrogant (Keynes 1968: 12), or it may ambiguously allude both to the danger of pride and the need for knowledge (Erdman, *loc. cit.*).

The engraving in pl. 5 derives from a sketch on p. 91 of the Notebook marked by a quotation from *PL*, I, 221-22 describing

Satan rising from hell's burning lake. In *For the Sexes*, this engraving is substantially modified, the figure, who had looked up, being deprived of sight, and his loins and some of the flames being covered with scales. The change, says Erdman (1974: 270-71), is from an ascending to a falling figure, and, adds Keynes (1968: 13), from an unmalicious if misguided being to a tyrant trying to keep humankind within the Mundane Shell. Mellor (1974: 74-75, 230) may be right in seeing a transformation of noble rebellion powered by Satanic energy into perverted power-hunger, though Tinker (1939: 110) perceives destructive anger even in the earlier picture, and Digby (1957: 26) believes that the blindness of the final figure is being wrongly attributed to desire or energy by reason. The weapons, maintains Digby (*loc. cit.*), are those of mental or spiritual conflict, while Kmetz (1971: 177) oddly believes that the spear of imagination contends with the shield of selfhood. The figure, according to Beer (1968: 235), is the Satanic spectre.

pl. 6   On one level the infant breaking free in *For Children* may be an ambiguous figure—energy which can be either destructive desire or Eros about to harmonise the warring elements (Beer 1968: 234-35), which are contained in the Mundane Shell (Erdman 1977a: 41). However, Mellor (1974: 75, 230) believes that the egg is the imprisoning flesh in *For Children* and it only becomes the Mundane Shell in *For the Sexes*, where the body can be a beneficial garment for the psychologically liberated. From the gloomy context of the inscription—"At length for hatching ripe he breaks the shell"—in its original setting in Dryden's translation of Chaucer's "Knight's Tale" (III, 1069), Parisi (1978: 81-82) deduces that Blake is showing mortals as born under Saturn's baleful influence (cf. also Beer 1968: 238-41). Damon (1967: 456) finds a more optimistic source of Blake's design in Edward Young's "Embryos we must be, till we burst the Shell,/ Yon ambient, azure shell, and spring to Life" (*Night Thoughts*, I, 131-32), and Raine perceives in it an image of the birth of time from the cosmic egg (1968: II, 182-83, 312n28) and of the soul's rebirth into Eternity from the temporal world (1983: 230 and pl. 111).

Most commentators believe the engraving represents a stage in human development. This stage has been specified as the beginning of the Orc cycle (Rose 1963: 45), physical birth (Frye 1966: 193), the movement from Innocence into Experience (Tinker 1939: 110-11), passage from childhood to adulthood (Damon 1924: 85), and escape from early depression through sexuality (Webster 1983: 188). The wings, according to Lindberg (1973: 256-57), are inherited from a pre-existence, and Erdman (1974: 271-72) sees the attainment of freedom through becoming as a little child.

pl. 7   This enigmatic picture has drawn much comment. According to Damon (1924: 85), the youth, who has killed one joy and pursues another, abuses sex. Kmetz (1971: 179-80) compares Blake's defence of oppressed females in *Visions of the Daughters of Albion*, Beer (1968: 238) remarks that the boy who hunts butterflies will become a man who oppresses a woman, and Webster (1983: 189) argues that the fruitful sexuality of earlier plates has been perverted into cruelty. However, Digby (1957: 38) detects a reference to the female principle that habitually sacrifices itself to promote the creativity of the male principle, which in turn annihilates itself to redeem the female. Mellor (1974: 75-76, 230) distinguishes between the original plate, where the boy is either astonished at the flying child or tries to capture it, and the revised plate, where he sees the "Divine Image" of the newly added inscription in both the body below and the soul that has risen from it. These figures—butterflies in human shape—have the same form, says Wardle (1978: 339-40), to express Blake's opposition to dualism. Blackstone (1949: 174) asserts that the youth is one who defies the warning in the poet's quatrain "Eternity" (E470/K179) and "binds to himself a joy." Combining this observation with Mellor's distinction between the two versions and Rose's assertion (1963: 45) that the prone Jerusalem is dead to the protagonist, George (1980: 186-87) maintains that the innocent youth of *For Children* is surprised at the result of his attempt to bind a joy, while the sinister youth of *For the Sexes* may be a fallen human whose emanation is cast aground while his spectre flies above. Erdman (1974: 272) believes the young man may rise with the ascending figure or fall with the outstretched one, while the inscription satisfies Hilton (1983: 239) that though one female is dead, the other will escape. Frye

(1966: 193) considers that the boy tries to seize nature but a portion of it escapes him.

pl. 8   This design seems straightforward but there is controversy as to whether Blake sides with the son—an Orc attacking a Urizen (Kmetz 1971: 181), who has taught him the art of war (Mellor 1974: 231; see "Keys," ll. 31-32)—or whether the latter is becoming a tyrant in his turn (Rose 1963: 45-46) or is ungrateful (Tinker 1939: 111-12) as suggested by the inscription "My Son! my Son!" borrowed from David's lament for Absalom (II Sam. xviii.33). However, this youth's hair is short unlike Absalom's, so he may escape the latter's doom (Mellor 1974: 77). Keynes (1968: 16) comments that the despairing father offers no defence and that the son resembles Death aiming a dart at his parent Satan (*PL*, II, 728-30). While Parisi (1978: 86) compares the youth with the hero portrayed in Blake's engraving *Albion Rose* (Bindman 1978, pls. 315, 400), Erdman (1974: 242) more aptly points out that he is no longer moving forward and carries a ferocious weapon. Digby's observation (1957: 39-40) that the paternal authority is both individual and societal and that the conflict is internal as well as external should not be ignored.

pl. 9   As with pl. 8, the artist's stance is disputed. Erdman (1954a: 186-88 [202-04]) sees in the 1793 version Blake's answer to the cartoonist Gillray, who caricatured Fox's effort to promote liberty by representing it as a very short ladder pointed at the moon. He also remarks that the climber makes a promising start by looking at the nearby lovers, one of whom waves to him (1974: 273) and that he wears the same hat as the commendable traveller of pl. 14 (1977a: 43).

However, critics who believe the climber to be an object of satire also have a case. His starting with his left foot, which signifies his use of a material means of ascent, convinces Damon (1924: 86) that he cannot succeed; Tinker (1939: 112) contrasts him, as a "moonstruck youth," with the lovers, who have found the way to paradise; and Beer (1968: 237) accuses him of "crying for the moon," a body which, according to Salemi (1981: 114) is a common symbol of futile hope in emblem books. Parisi (1978: 86-90) cites such evidence of the presence of misdirected desire as the use of a common roofer's ladder and the inclusion of a comparable ladder in Dürer's *Melancholia I*.

In Mellor's view (1974: 77-79, 231), the length of the ladder may make liberation possible even in this life for the man of *For Children*, but his counterpart in *For the Sexes* should be aspiring to the sun instead of the moon. The latter Rose (1963: 46) regards as "the sexual cup of the allegoric night" of the fallen world (*J* 88:31), though Damon (1967: 285) considers it signifies the love for which the young climber longs. Miner (1981: 322) supposes the ladder to represent a frustrated phallus amidst the virgin Pleiades.

pl. 10 Here is shown the fate of the climber of pl. 9 (Damon 1924: 86), for desire is not sufficient to effect an escape (Mellor 1974: 79-80). Rose (1963: 46) insists that the protagonist is drowning in a world devoid of help, but Erdman (1974: 273) observes that unlike the victim of the downpour in pl. 2, he is aware of other people and assistance will come.

pl. 11 Tracing a continuous narrative, Damon asserts that the climber who nearly drowned in "the Ocean of Materialism" has become Aged Ignorance (1924: 86) and now mutilates his own delights (1967: 149). Similarly, Frye (1966: 194) claims that the young rebel of pl. 8 has become a tyrannical Urizen. Following along the lines of Russell (1912: 63), who identifies the winged victim as "a young Love," and Binyon (1926: 46), who calls him simply "Love," Tinker (1939: 105) states that Time, or more likely Old Age, is destroying this passion, and Erdman (1974: 274) describes the young figure as an adolescent Cupid journeying forwards (his genitals are indicated in *For the Sexes*). Webster (1983: 191-92) sees Blake's guilt feelings emerging in an ambivalent picture of sexuality and aggression punished, while Mellor (1974: 80-81) identifies the victim as unambiguously the visionary; he is located, argues Keynes (1968: 17), under the tree of material life near the setting sun of inspiration, to which, notes Blackstone (who thinks the sun is rising), Ignorance has turned his back (1949: 175). The boy's wings, according to Lindberg (1973: 257), are the wings of pl. 6.

Mellor (*loc. cit.*) believes the victim's desires are thwarted, but Erdman (1977a: 43) is confident he will travel on without wings.

pl. 12   In this attack on the church (Keynes 1968: 17-18), the climber, drowning man and Aged Ignorance of the preceding plates has, in Damon's view (1924: 86) become the ecclesiastical oppressor. Digby (1957: 46) maintains that human beings choose to degrade themselves thus by submitting to the world and its values, and Kmetz (1971: 182) reasonably suggests that the five prisoners symbolise the five fallen senses. Pointing out that oppression has now united father and son, Webster (1983: 192) supposes on the basis of associated sketches in Blake's Notebook that the old man will be driven to eat his children's bodies. The design is based on the account of Ugolino's punishment in canto 33 of Dante's *Inferno* (Russell 1912: 63).

pl. 13   According to Damon (1924: 86), the protagonist, who had been the oppressor in the preceding plates, is reawakened on seeing the soul of a friend ascend from its corpse. Damon later (1967: 149) corrects "friend" to "father," and George (1980: 188) speaks of "spiritual body" rather than "soul," while Webster (1983: 192-94), sharing Russell's belief (1912: 64) that the old figure is an apparition, finds that it elicits a look of guilt from the eldest son. The ascending spirit, Parisi argues (1987: 107), teaches the mourners how to attain vision, which transcends the alternation of hope and fear, and which is more important than the desire of pl. 6. However, Kmetz (1971: 182) credits hope and fear with giving birth to vision; cf. also Salemi 1981: 124n23.

To Percival (1938: 228), the fear and hope are emotions subjected to such stress by reason's tyranny that they undergo an abrupt and happy conversion. In Digby's view (1957: 43-47), the breakthrough to vision follows the nadir of opacity in pl. 11 and of contraction in pl. 12, and it shows that fear and hope are only relative. Erdman (1974: 275) notes the contrast between the families of this and the preceding plate and (1977a: 43) maintains that this design shows that the only way of escape from the dungeon is upwards. Damon (1924: 86) comments on Blake's memory of seeing his brother Robert's spirit rise joyously from his deathbed (see Gilchrist 1945: 51).

pl. 14   Now confident of his immortality (Damon 1924: 86), the traveller presses onwards avoiding the forest (Erdman 1974: 275) and uses his staff instead of wings (Erdman 1977a: 43).

According to Parisi (1978: 97-100), in *For Children* but not in *For the Sexes* the man is a melancholic wanderer without purpose in life; Mellor (1974: 231) credits the figure in the later book with emerging from the satanic state.

pl. 15   In 1805, when re-using this picture of Death's Door for one of his illustrations to Blair's *The Grave*, Blake places an image of the resurrected body above the tomb. His omitting to make this addition here allows Parisi (1978: 100-04) to argue that the old man, moving in the same direction as the natural wind, is among those who have not found Eternity here and therefore have little chance of doing so hereafter. However, most critics agree with Keynes (1968: 18-19) that the traveller of the previous plate enters the tomb confident of his own immortality. Erdman (1974: 276) suggests that forty years have elapsed between the two plates and the crutch now replaces the staff. It is, declares Lesnick (1969: 54), the crutch of mortality, and the wind blowing the man to the gate is the wind of time.

pl. 16   The bewildering variety of interpretations of this design, with its strange inscription "I have said to the Worm: Thou art my mother & my sister" (adapted from Job xvii.14), centres on the sex and identity of the human figure. This may be the protagonist himself, an aspect of the material world he leaves behind, or one who helps him on his way to paradise.

Plausible is Keynes's view (1968: 19-20) that the male or androgynous person is the dead traveller in his shroud, two other corpses being visible in the ground beside him. Paley (1978b: 26) adds that his staff has become useless, and Lindberg (1973: 259-60), drawing attention to his open eyes as well as to what he judges to be his unshaven male face, opines that he is about to begin his posthumous quest.

However, Russell (1912: 64) considers the figure a woman, and Erdman (1974: 276-77) could be right in deeming her both a sibyl and Death herself pointing the way up to heaven, whither the traveller has proceeded leaving her his staff and shroud. The way, Erdman notes (1977a: 44), lies not through earth, where sleeping faces are visible, but through the Door of pl. 15, a work of art.

The figure has also been interpreted as the soul looking up for a revelation (Tinker 1939: 113-14); the mother tyrannising over both father and son (Webster 1983: 198-202); Tirzah, the creator of bodies (Damon 1967: 149, 407); the goddess Nature, who domineers over the unregenerate but is accepted as mother and sister by the regenerate (Digby 1957: 50); a symbol of the earth (Beer 1968: 233); and the beneficent Matron Clay of *Thel* with the worm she fosters (Raine 1968: I, 122).

The worm may be the literal devourer of our mortal portion (Bindman 1977: 86); nature, which weaves bodies benevolently and is a skin-shedding emblem of regeneration (Kmetz 1971: 183); or the physical body itself (Damon 1967: 150), or its mortality, which the traveller, knowing his own immortality, is content to recognise as mother and sister in the temporal life (Lindberg 1973: 257), for the mortal part of the human being is the winding worm of *J* [82:47ff] (Rose 1963: 47).

[Prologue]

1. 3 **Against**—either "in opposition to," in which case Satan opposes forgiveness [and the first sentence ends at "Fire"] (Damon 1924: 83), or (less probably) "in answer to," in which case Jehovah writes the Law at Satan's desire [and the first sentence ends at "Paradise"] (Deen 1983: 221).

1. 4 **the Stones of Fire**—Satan is identified with the Covering Cherub, the arrogant ruler of Tyre who walked among these stones according to Ezek. xxviii.14 (Digby 1957: 15-16). Jehovah's Law causes the flames of energy to devour humans instead of vitalising them (Beer 1969: 36-37).

ll. 5-8 Jehovah gave the Law a form so that it could be cast out (M. Plowman 1927a: 118). He is an ambiguous figure, first a lawmaker and then sincerely (or perhaps hypocritically) repentant (Kmetz 1971: 175). The Law of Sinai had to be buried because it had been misinterpreted as a law of retribution instead of a law of forgiveness (Nelms 1974: 84). The Jehovah who writes the Law is the Father separated from the Son, while the repentant Jehovah is the Father reunited with the Son to form the wholeness of the Divine Humanity (Summerfield 1981: 17).

1. 7 **Corpse**—perhaps a pun on "corpus" (Ostriker 1977: 1039). Christians worship the corpse of the Law in the form of Christ's body (Deen 1983: 221).

l. 10   This line suggests that the Law can be equated with the Sin that Christ put off on the Cross to be worshipped by the Roman Church (Kmetz 1971: 175, citing E524 [ll. 55-58]/ K749 [ll. 57-59]).

"The Keys of the Gates"

l. 2   **Mother's Grief**—birthpangs (Keynes 1968: 9). The caterpillar weaves the mortal flesh (Miner 1981: 322, 324).

l. 7   **Serpent Reasonings**—rational dualism that comes with adolescence (Digby 1957: 23-24); the reasonings of priests (Keynes 1968: 10-11).

l. 13   **Two Horn'd...Cloven**—These epithets suggest the Lockean gulf between subject and object (Kmetz 1971: 176-77) or denote the insistence that everything is true or false, good or evil (Ault 1974: 39).

l. 15   **Hermaphrodite We stood**—one in a state of inner conflict (Digby 1957: 28), or a being "part mortal, part divine" (Raine 1968: I, 289); the human body and nature, which have become indistinguishable in Ulro (Frye 1966: 191), or the individual and nature, which is the female will, combined (Kmetz 1971: 177); the speaker, including his alienated female aspect (Tayler 1973b: 76), or the speaker and his mother combined and unable to rise above sexuality (Ostriker 1977: 1039); Satan, which is what the fallen Eternal Man has become (Deen 1983: 222). According to Rose (1963: 45), the female element, which is the female will, links the fiery Orcean with the cold Urizenic imagery in the neighbouring lines.

l. 17   **the Flaming Sword**—the analytical, dividing mind (Digby 1957: 29); an allusion to Gen. iii.24 signifying banishment from Eternity (Kmetz 1971: 178); a phallic image with which the speaker identifies (Ault 1974: 40).

l. 18   **snowy Whirlwinds**—"rationalizations and repressions" (Digby 1957: 30); a constricting force like the Wheel of Religion of *J*, pl. 77 (Hilton 1983: 225).

ll. 19-20   Raine (1968: II, 184-85) refers to the veil of outward appearance that is torn away by Christ and its symbolic association with the Temple veil rent at the Crucifixion (Matt. xxvii.51), while Ault (1974: 39-40) sees the speaker as breaking away from his hermaphroditic union with nature (for which he is partly responsible) by copulating with Vala, which is rending her Veil. Agreeing that this fabric is material nature, Tayler (1973b: 76) adds that it is also the female's hymen and her devotion to chastity. Deen (1983: 222) finds that the Eternal Man is here born as Satan and begets a child, perhaps Death, on his own mother.

ll. 20-26 Sexual desire may become obsessive and destructive (Keynes 1968: 14); sex can either liberate the fallen—there is a hint here of Christ's resurrection—or imprison them more firmly (Kmetz 1971: 178). Digby (1957: 34-37) sees the sexual garments as male and female archetypes or symbols which rescue the fallen from passion and illusion.

l. 22 **He meets his Saviour**—By Christ's power, Imagination, we can escape from our imprisonment in the Mundane Shell (Damon 1924: 85).

l. 28 The slain may be captive in the temporal world while the other one has escaped from it (Kmetz 1971: 180).

l. 30 **double Spectres**—They are double because the spectre has an "unconscious attachment to authority" (Digby 1957: 40). They are conflicting selfhoods, the spawn of abstract reasoning (Keynes 1968: 16). Rose suggests (1972b: 136) that they could be Orc and Urizen, and he (1963: 48) and Hilton (1983: 171) view them as modes of distorted perception. See also *J* 44(30):33-37n and *J* 64:21n.

ll. 45-50 Death's open door may be the eighteen centuries of Christianity (Percival 1938: 234). Worms bring new life out of death, and orgasm, for which the latter is a metaphor, can give "an intimation of immortality" (Beer 1968: 242).

ll. 46-50 The worm is the flesh, brought to birth by the female; it weaves the sexuality that produces the worm-formed foetus (Damon 1967: 452). The visionless person sees himself as no more than a mortal worm (Rose 1970c: 446). The female addressed is woman, of whom man is born, whom he espouses, and whom he fathers; as worm, she devours the flesh and frees the soul (Lindberg 1973: 260-61). The weaving worm is all that "Serpent Reasonings" (l. 7) amount to, as the enlightened speaker now sees (Deen 1983: 223).

ll. 49-50 This couplet concerns the trap of the fallen world and the opportunity to escape from it. Percival (1938: 127, 234) sees a reference to the female will's weaving the illusion of the material realm, but Keynes (1968: 19) is confident that sexual strife is now a dream and the web of life a memory, and Mellor (1974: 232-33) asserts that the traveller has escaped from the web though the female will laments over it. Pessimistically, George (1980: 188) perceives here an image of the natural cycle in which those who miss the vision opened up in pl. 13 must remain. Hilton (1983: 117-18), citing *FZ* 5:20-22/ E302/ I, 83-85, identifies the caterpillar of l. 1 with the worm of l. 50 and claims that the latter weeps because her web has assumed an independent existence and dreams of a happy state in which it remains subordinate.

"To The Accuser who is The God of This World"

The title alludes to II Cor. iv.4 (Damon 1967: 150) and Rev. xii.10. Mellor (1974: 233-35) considers the poem treats of redemption in this life, while Lindberg (1973: 260) believes the sleeping traveller of the engraving is the pilgrim of previous plates and the speaker of "The Keys" now engaged in a posthumous search.

l. 2 **the Garment**—the body (Damon 1924: 87); the state as opposed to the person (Blackstone 1949: 176). St. Paul's "Natural Man" or "Old Man" (Paley 1970: 156, citing Ephes. iv.22, 24, and Col. ii.11, iii.9).

the Man—the Imagination (Bloom 1963: 436); the Divine Image (Beer 1969: 38).

l. 7 **the Son of Morn**—Isaiah's "Lucifer, son of the morning" (xiv.12) (Rose 1964b). The spectre, being only the speaker's dream, is powerless when day succeeds night (Keynes 1968: 22). Satan has forgotten he is the Morning Star (Deen 1983: 224).

l. 8 **The lost Traveller's Dream under the Hill**—Although Raine (1968: II, 245) identifies the lost traveller as Satan and his dream as the illusion of the material world, the syntax and the drawing imply that he is the traveller of earlier plates gone astray. The Accuser is in his dream (Bloom 1963: 436), which is the nightmare in the design (Hagstrum 1964: 7). There is an allusion to the sleep that delays the progress of Bunyan's Christian on the hill Difficulty (Frye 1966: 194), and an allusion also to characters like Rip Van Winkle (Damrosch 1980: 262).

under the Hill—in the tomb or sleep of the mortal world under Golgotha-Calvary (Rose 1964b); in the hells under the hill of Purgatory in *The Divine Comedy* of Dante (Raine 1968: II, 54); "in the cave of the Selfhood" (Kmetz 1971: 184); in the abode of witches, a nocturnal delusion (Mellor 1974: 233); under Sinai, to which Mr. Worldly-Wiseman directs Bunyan's traveller Christian (Miner 1981: 328, citing also Exod. xxiv.4).

The serpent engraved under the title represents the priesthood, and his ten numbered coils stand for the Ten Commandments (Keynes 1968: 22).

In the design below, the sleeping traveller may be overshadowed by his Spectre (Keynes, *loc. cit.*) and misconceive God in a satanic image (Digby 1957: 53), but since his staff is unbroken (despite the spider's web on the top), he is capable of resuming his journey (Mellor 1974: 235).

To Tayler (1973a: 248-49), Satan seems to emerge from the traveller's penis showing that sexual repression contributes to his dream; however, Erdman (1974: 279) deduces that he is rising from within the sleeper, his wings adorned with the orbs over which he claims power, and is about to be swept away by the dawn advancing from behind the hill. Damrosch (1980: 262) adds that the sleeper is on the verge of waking, and Miner (1981: 320) that Orion on Satan's right wing vainly pursues the ever virgin Pleiades on his left wing.

The Ghost of Abel

The memorable dedication of these scenes is an address, unique in Blake's writings, to a contemporary poet. It is based on I Kings xix.9 and 13 (Damon 1967: 153). Byron, a rebel who fled from the censorious English society, is compared with Elijah, who fled the anger of Jezebel after he had exposed her religion of nature gods (Tannenbaum 1975: 351). However, Blake's attitude to both figures is mixed: though he recognises Elijah as a true prophet—see, for example, *M* 24:71 (Bidney 1979: 164), the latter's place of refuge, Mount Horeb, is associated with the giving of the Law (Stevenson 1971: 861); similarly, he hails Byron as an authentic poet, but according to Tannenbaum the vision of Jehovah that a poet can hardly doubt is the message of the Atonement through Christ (1975: 355, alluding to Byron, *Cain* III.i.85-92).

No critic can miss Blake's belief that only forgiveness can put an end to the horror arising from Abel's murder, and Damon (1967: 154) draws attention to Blake's claim elsewhere that the mark God set on Cain's forehead (Gen. iv.15) was a sign of "the Forgiveness of Sins" (E688/ K933). Comparatively elusive, however, is the relationship of Blake's brief drama to Byron's three-act *Cain*. Frye (1947: 199) holds that in place of Byron's view that genius and crime go together, Blake is asserting that genius does not participate in evil (including murder) and good (including just retribution) but transcends them. Reisner's opinion (1970: 140-41) that Blake imputes Cain's violence not to genius but to reasoning may be associated with Bidney's argument (1979) that, in the person of Jehovah, Blake introduces the power of imagination that is missing from *Cain*, for Byron's Urizenic Lucifer belongs to Ulro and his compassionate Adah to Beulah, but only imagination can restore the fallen to Eden. Tannenbaum (1975: 364) traces a progression from a primitive notion of atonement by burnt offering in Gen. iv through Elijah's and Byron's exposure of false prophets to the true conception of atonement by recognition of one's essential identity with God.

Turning in a later publication to representations of the first murder by artists contemporary with Blake, Tannenbaum (1978: 24-30) notes that the focus is normally on Abel, and that both in his painting *The Body of Abel Found by Adam and Eve* (final version *c.* 1826; Butlin 1981: pl. 971) and in his playlet, Blake defies the venerable tradition that the slain man is a type of Christ. Moreover, he adds, a series of tiny illustrations on the left-hand sides of the two plates emphasises that Cain's fall is a variation of Adam's and Eve's, for the tragic history must repeat itself until forgiveness replaces retribution.

Details

Dedication **Nature has no Outline**—Stevenson (1971: 861) perceives an allusion to the journey to the far reaches of the universe in the second act of *Cain*.

1:8 (and stage direction) The "Ghost," according to Stevenson (1971: 862), is Abel's Spectre. Whether it is taken over by Satan (Beer 1969: 41-42) or is revealed by the stage direction after 2:12 to be Satan (Bloom 1963: 434) or whether Abel himself is possessed by Satan (Ostriker 1977: 1041) or by the Elohim (Johnson and Grant 1979: 361) is perhaps not of great importance.

1:11 **Prince of the Air**—a term for Satan in Ephes. ii.2. In Damon's view (1924: 476), Blake, in order to refer to the way that acts tend to be repeated, is drawing on the occult doctrine that the atmosphere contains a universal memory .

2:13 This is a satanic distortion of Ps. l.13 and Heb. ix.12 and x.4 (Johnson and Grant 1979: 362).

2:19-21 The Incarnation and Crucifixion are here identified with the annihilation of Satan, the Urizenic God: by sacrificing His transcendence or otherness God ceases to be "afar off" (*J* 4:18) and becomes universally accessible spirit (Altizer 1967: 75-76, 82-85). Blake is interpreting Rev. xx.1-3 (Stevenson 1971: 864). Jehovah's example, when He incarnates and is crucified, may teach self-annihilation to Satan (Ostriker 1977: 1041). Satan is here both an individual and a state: Satan the individual will put off Satan the state in self-annihilation (Bidney 1979: 163). Cf. *J* 63: 16-17.

2:23 **Elohim Jehovah**—Blake is exploiting the already discovered distinction between the E[lohim] and J[ehovah] narratives in Genesis (Miner 1969: 291, 476n83). Ostriker (1977: 1041) argues that both Jehovah and Satan are "Elohim" (a plural word used for both "God" and "gods"), and Johnson and Grant (1979: 363) claim that "Elohim" is here no more than a title prefixed to "Jehovah." More usefully, Tannenbaum (1975: 356-59, 363) follows up Damon's assertion (1967: 119) that Elohim signifies justice and Jehovah mercy by contrasting Satan-Elohim (who stands for justice) with Jehovah (who teaches mercy and redeems both Satan and humankind); eventually, he maintains, these unite.

2:24 **Death O Holy!**—self-annihilation (Damon 1924: 476).

2:25-26 The heathen Elohim cease to block the Mercy Seat over the Ark (Johnson and Grant 1979: 363). They become the fixed stars (Tannenbaum 1975: 363) or planetary spirits (Bidney

1979: 164). The Chorus draws on Heb. ix (Tannenbaum, *loc. cit.*).

Designs

pl. 1   On the left side are Adam and Eve under the Tree of Knowledge, Abel's ghost visiting Eve, and Adam and Eve after they have eaten the fruit (Erdman 1974: 382). Tannenbaum (1978: 30) plausibly interprets the visiting spirit as an angel delivering a warning before the fatal act occurs.

pl. 2   On the left side are Eve bearing a coffin, Abel speaking to her against forgiveness, Satan defying Jehovah, and Satan's self-annihilation on the almost cross-shaped Tree (Erdman 1974: 383). Tannenbaum (1978: 30) interprets these miniature scenes as Cain sowing seed, Cain killing Abel, Cain arguing his case before God, and Adam and Eve, the Tree, and the serpent.

The skin-girdled figure lamenting over the hidden body of Abel at the base of the page has been identified as Eve (Keynes 1921: 171-72), Adam (Damon 1924: 477), and Cain (Damon 1967: 64). The uncertainty, thinks Tannenbaum (1978: 29), may be intended. Erdman (1974: 383) observes that Abel's apparition issues from his spilled blood, and Johnson and Grant (1979: 363) remark that the closing inscription—"The Voice of Abel's Blood"—shows that it was the demand for vengeance that prevented the recovery of Paradise.

Notes on Criticism for Chapter 12

Illustrations of The Book of Job

In searching for the interpretation of the Book of Job that he is sure must be contained in Blake's *Illustrations*, Wicksteed finds the essential first clue in his observation that Job's left foot is often in the same position as his God's right foot; comparing the disposition of right and left legs in *Milton IB* pls. 32 and 37, and remembering that Blake asks the spectator of his painting of the Last Judgment to "attend to the Hands & Feet" (E560/ K611), he concludes that the artist employs the left and right sides to represent respectively the spiritual or imaginative and the corporeal or earthly (1910: 15-20, 133-36). This symbolism, of course, must not be read mechanically or without regard to context and artistic requirements, though Lindberg (1973: 123-24) goes too far when he reacts to over reliance upon it by refusing to see any significance in the positions of the characters' feet.

Proceeding from his initial discovery to study the *Illustrations* in the light of Blake's then meagerly understood writings, Wicksteed recognises that they show how Job's apparent virtues bring about the catastrophe which reveals to him that he has been worshipping a satanic spirit; he thereupon overcomes his selfhood to attain humility, love and the vision of the Divine Humanity (1910: 35-43). It is not till more than sixty years later, however, that Lindberg (1973: 130-32, 194, *et al.*) demonstrates that Blake's interpretation is an offshoot of a continuous Christian tradition going back as far as St. Jerome (*c.* 342-420) and Gregory the Great (*c.* 540-604). This tradition holds that Job began by following the Law but was only led by his suffering to discern its inner meaning, the Gospel. Lindberg also believes that Blake enriches his engravings by alluding to the ancient belief that Job is a type of Christ—see notes on pls. 7 and 10.

Though the central theme of the series, underlined by the altar inscriptions on the first and last plates, now seems unmistakable, there are disagreements about the identity of the deities in pls. 2 and 5, the roles of Elihu and Job's wife, the significance of the cross-like forms in the architecture, the interpretation of that architecture, the significance of the books and scrolls, and the relationship between the earthly and the heavenly scenes.

Unlike most commentaries, my chapter on *Job* argues that the deities of pls. 2 and 5 are different beings. Wicksteed (1924: 93-94, 117-18) and Raine (1982: 68) believe both images represent the true God, but, unlike Lindberg (1973: 200-01, 204), neither notices in pl. 2 the turned back sections of the cloud barrier, the threads running from them, and the tiny spikes on the god's head, which are related to the tufts of his satanic counterpart in pl. 11. Holding with Hagstrum (1964: 128-29) and others that both deities are diabolical, Lindberg also agrees with Hagstrum (*loc. cit.*) that the benign God *is* the divine lawgiver transformed. Lindberg's thesis (1973: 82-88, 204, 317) that the divine-diabolical deity inclines first, up to pl. 11, to unite with his son Satan but later, in pl. 16, with his son Christ faces the obstacle that in Blake's myth Satan's brother is not Jesus but Adam (E273/ K775). Summerfield (1981: 17) proposes that the Urizenic god of pls. 2 and 11 is the Father cut off from the Son and sunk into a degenerate state, while Raine (1982: 68-69) argues that in pl. 5 the Divine Humanity is falling asleep within Job as his selfhood takes command.

The satanic selfhood's great triumph comes in pl. 11, exactly half way in the series and immediately before Job's redemption begins with the advent of Elihu. The general belief in this symmetrical construction has withstood Frye's challenge (1969: 226-28, 233-34) based on his claim that Elihu preaches natural religion—a claim made despite the emphasis in the inscriptions on inspiration, divine dreams, and the Redeemer. (For detailed refutations, see Nelms 1970: 344-50—including J. E. G[rant]'s appended note—and Paley 1978b: 70-71).

Some attempts to find more intricate symmetrical patterns in the *Illustrations* have met with justified scepticism. Damon (1924: 236; 1966: 4-7) tries to co-ordinate the plates with fourteen phases related to the Seven Eyes of God; Wicksteed (1924: 74-77) consigns five consecutive designs to each of the four stages he perceives in Job's experience and allots the remaining plate (no. 11) to both the second and third stages; and Nelms (1970: 356-58), returning to the Seven Eyes as a basis, proposes that there are seven groups consisting of three pictures each, but the relationship of the groups to the Eyes is often unconvincing. Equally dubious, as Lindberg shows (1973: 111), is Wicksteed's argument (1924:

87, 108-09, 142, 160, 181-82) that the struggle between the clockwise Current of Creation and the anticlockwise Wheel of Religion—see the blank verse of *J*, pl. 77—looms large in the book's organisation, though Percival (1938: 245) makes the interesting assertion that pls. 5 and 13 show the two movements are really one. Less schematic is Raine's contention (1982: *passim*) that allusions to the Seven Eyes and to two guardian cherubim, the four Zoas, and Blake's four worlds pervade the series. Perhaps too simple is Beer's view (1969: 269-74) that the organising thread is the story of the separation and ultimate reintegration of energy and vision.

The changing relationship between Job and his wife has also been a matter of dispute. She has been seen as suffering in plate 6 the disruption of the harmony between herself and Job, a harmony restored in pl. 12 (Wicksteed 1924: 123-27); as evolving spiritually alongside her spouse but more slowly (Lindberg 1973: 145); and as parallel with the Jerusalem who remains faithful to fallen Albion (Raine 1982: 78, 84).

Like Blake's attitude to women, his attitude to the Cross is not consistent. Sometimes he scorns it as a merely external symbol—it is cast into hell in his great drawing of the Last Judgement (E315) and associated with alleged Catholic idolatry in "The Everlasting Gospel" (E524 [ll. 55-57]/ K749 [ll. 57-59])—and sometimes speaks of it reverently (e.g. E174, 767/ K652, 863). Elaborating on his earlier observations (1924: 228-29, 235), Damon (1966: 4) sees the Cross present in the architecture of pls. 4, 7, 8, 10 and 12, where it functions as an emblem of Urizenic religion condemning those it overshadows, while Job and his wife are blessedly free from it in pl. 19. However, Andrew Wright (1972: 13) and Lindberg (1973: 230) regard it as a symbol of true faith especially evident in pl. 7.

Less striking than the divergencies in interpretations of the Cross, are disagreements over the meanings of books and scrolls. Wicksteed (1924: 95-96) does not distinguish between these, but Damon (1966: 4) holds that they represent respectively law and inspiration—Lindberg's discoveries suggest that the Law and the Gospel are equivalents at least equally valid.

What appears to be the most fundamental controversy over the Job engravings concerns the meaning of the upper world and its inhabitants. While Wicksteed (1910: 51) and Damon (1966: 3) are sure these are inside Job's soul, Lindberg (1973: 80-81, 88-89) insists that Job's God, while having an immanent aspect in the form of the Holy Spirit, is literally the Creator of the universe. Both positions are correct. Since there are two ways from the fallen world to Eternity—one outward through the caverns of the Mundane Shell that bounds the universe (*M* 37:52-56) and one inward through a human being's own soul (*J* 5:17-20), the upper world of these *Illustrations* is both a heaven transcending the material world and a realm within Job himself.

Details

Title page Wicksteed (1910: 47-48) convincingly describes the angels as representing the passage through and emergence from Experience. Several critics follow Damon (1924: 225) in further identifying them with the Seven Eyes of God, the most notable dissenter being Lindberg (1973: 190-91), who holds that they are of the same kind as the angels on pls. 2 and 5, and that they look outwards at the world and the reader, whose thoughts they record. La Belle (1973: 547) sees them as the seven angels of Rev. xv.1, who sing the song quoted at the top of pl. 21.

pl. 1 Besides the question of whether the buildings in front of the hill are houses (Lindberg 1973: 192) or barns (Wicksteed 1910: 50), commentators argue over Job's spiritual state and the meanings of the cathedral and the tree. Taking an extreme view, La Belle (1973: 529) considers Job already fallen, and Andrew Wright (1972: 5) regards the design as an indictment of his complacency, but most other scholars agree with Wicksteed (1910: 50) that he is in a pastoral state of Innocence though subject to some error. Percival (1938: 136, 139) and Frye (1969: 226) identify Job's state as Beulah, from which he has to sink before he can rise to Eden. In addition to more obvious symbolism, the sheep dog (Andrew Wright [*loc. cit.*] takes him for a dog-like sheep) is a drowsy guardian here, but is alert on pl. 21 (Nelms 1970: 355).

The oak tree in the centre has been interpreted both negatively as the institutional church (Hagstrum 1964: 132) and the Tree of Mystery (A. Wright 1972: 5) and positively as the Tree of Life (Beer 1969: 270), the symbol of Job's strength, endurance and faith (Lindberg 1973: 136), and the tree of the as yet uncorrupted Druids (Raine 1982: 37). While Lindberg (1973: 194), who is followed by Bindman (1977: 210), takes the cathedral as an emblem of the letter that kills and organised religion hiding the light of the sun, most critics from Wicksteed (1910: 50) to Paley (1983a: 204) see it as a symbol of authentic art or religion. Significantly Blake refers in an account of his lost painting of the Last Judgment to "a Gothic Church" which is "representative of true Art" (E559/ K610) and it is a hill behind the building that covers most of the sun.

pl. 2   Critics differ over what Blake has pictured in this plate as well as over its meaning. Thus the deity that looks sickly to Frye (1969: 227) seems weak to Andrew Wright (1972: 9) and Damrosch (1980: 259) and holy and august to Raine (1982: 48). Views of his identity have been discussed in the fourth paragraph of the headnote above.

Contrary to my suggestion in the chapter above but perhaps rightly, Wicksteed (1910: 52), Damon (1966: 14), Lindberg (1973: 203-05) and Raine (1982: 48, 51) hold that the angels are setting records of Job's life before the throne. According to Damon and Lindberg, Job is fearful that he or members of his family may have transgressed against the Law, but Raine argues that he cites the Law to defend his conduct. Taking a different approach, Andrew Wright (1972: 9) maintains that angels are relinquishing scrolls of artistic inspiration before the legalistic god.

On lesser matters, there is further disagreement. While Wright (*loc. cit.*) describes the deity as holding a book of Law, Raine (1982: 48) identifies the volume with "the Word of Divine Revelation" (E555/ K606) on Christ's knee in the lost painting just referred to. The same scripture, along with a scroll recording Job's life, is, she believes, in the god's possession in plate 5 [1982: 68]). The faces on either side of Satan, which most critics follow Wicksteed (1910: 52) in perceiving as those of Job and his wife, Hagstrum (1964: 132) attributes without evidence to Urizen and the Harlot of Babylon. Beside Job and his wife are two angels, who represent, in Wicksteed's view (1910: 53), his spiritual good; while he shows them the Scriptures, remarks Russell (1912: 104), the children's reading is interrupted. The dog below the bench seems to Wicksteed (1924: 96) a phallic symbol, but to Beer (1969: 270) a drowsy sentry that should be guarding the sheep.

Controversy extends to the margin. Whereas the Gothic tracery, springing from stems or trunks rooted in the ground, is generally accepted as a positive image and the angels within it are recognised as benevolent, the columns of fire and cloud have been denounced as the signs, wept over by angels, that led the Israelites to the place where the Law was given (Damon 1924: 227) but have also been hailed as "the fire of spiritual sacrifice and the incense of prayer" gladly received by the spirits above them (Raine 1982: 51). Where Damon (1966: 14) detects "the peacock of pride and the parrot of vain repetitions," Lindberg (1973: 205) observes a peacock and a pheasant emblematic of Job's wealth, and Raine (1982: 51) believes that the nesting birds in the margin represent "imaginative thoughts" and the peacock may stand for beauty. Finally, Wicksteed (1910: 54) and Damon (1924: 226) are satisfied that Job and his wife are shown as a shepherd and shepherdess in Innocence in the lower margin, where, as Lindberg says (1973: 201, 205), the dog protects the sheep, but Andrew Wright (1972: 10) finds an indication of disorder in the sleepiness of the animal and the gap in the fence.

pl. 3 There are two interpretations of this design. Wicksteed (1910: 55-63) holds that it attacks family self-sufficiency and reliance on material prosperity and sensual pleasures: the figure of Satan is distorted to bring his left foot forward and show his spiritual affinity with the son in the centre, who rises on his left foot, while the left foot on the tambourine represents the misuse of artistic gifts. Lindberg (1973: 211), who insists that Satan is no emanation from Job but the Prince of this World, supports his contention that Blake is condemning the children by quoting "We are told to abstain from fleshly desires that we may lose no time from the Work of the Lord" (*J*, pl. 77, prose)—it would, however, be equally relevant to quote from the Laocoön plate, another late text, "the Two Impossibilities, Chastity & Abstinence, Gods of the Heathen" (E275/ K776).

The contrary view is that Blake condemns Job for imposing an oppressive morality on his children. Thus Hagstrum (1964: 132) views the central figure as a hero recalling Los, Damon

(1966: 16) views Satan as a projection of puritanical Job's moral indignation, Andrew Wright (1972: 13) blames the latter's angry rejection of art and sexual pleasure, and Raine (1982: 57-59) asserts that his self-righteousness destroys the love within his family. Interestingly, Damon (*loc. cit.*) considers the children are only figuratively killed—they are dead to their father.

At the bottom of the main design are a corpse-like woman and two figures—one garlanded, one with head downwards—of uncertain sex. Damon (1966: 16), who regards both father and children as blameworthy, accuses the woman of degrading musical instruments with her feet and her left hand; Wicksteed (1924: 109) identifies her as a harlot and her garlanded neighbour as a hermaphrodite. In the upside down figure, Wicksteed (1910: 61-62) sees a reflection of Blake's charge that "The Modern Church Crucifies Christ with the Head Downwards" (E564/ K615) signifying that orthodox religion has perverted imaginative creativeness into sensuality; if Nathan (1950) is right in thinking that the sentence alludes to the execution of Jewish malefactors in this position in mediaeval Christendom, the implication in the engraving may be that the victim is an unbeliever in Satan's creed of punishment for sin. According to Andrew Wright (*loc. cit.*), the architecture is Roman. The serpent beginning to appear in the margin represents the creed of materialism for Damon (1966: 16), matter for Raine (1982: 59), and—surprisingly—money for Wicksteed (1910: 63), who quotes a phrase from the Laocoön plate: "Money, which is The Great Satan..." (E275/ K776). Lindberg (1973: 135) sees a symbol of life's brevity in the scorpions, presumably because of their poison.

pl. 4 This plate has not proved very controversial. Noting that the two prominent messengers have their left legs advanced, Wicksteed (1910: 65) observes that they are announcing only material catastrophes, so the church still stands. The distant third messenger, perceptible above the left elbow of the second, will reveal, says Damon (1966: 18), the deaths of the sons. Lindberg (1973: 58, 69), with his enthusiasm for detailed readings on the literal as well as the symbolic level, claims that Job sits outside his house, which is one of the dwellings visible in pl. 1; contrariwise Russell (1912: 105) dubs the columns behind the couple "Druid pillars." The marginal figures on the top corners of the main design have been taken for the dead children (Wicksteed 1910: 66) or perished joys (Wicksteed 1924: 112) of Job, for two girls killed by Satan (Lindberg 1973: 58), and for enervated spirits (A. Wright 1972: 17).

pl. 5   Some later critics—e.g. Lindberg (1973: 219) and Raine (1982: 68-69) agree with Wicksteed (1910: 67) that Satan has acquired power over God, but Andrew Wright (1972: 19) perceptively notices the anxiety on the fiend's countenance. Damon (1924: 228) accuses God of trying to retain His throne by gripping the Law with his right or spiritual hand. Russell, however, (1912: 106) sees Him as compassionate.

Contradicting most scholars from Wicksteed (1910: 68) onwards, Lindberg (1973: 221) finds in the trilithon which replaces the cathedral not a symbol of debased Druidism with its human sacrifice but an emblem of the uncorrupted Druidism synonymous with essential Christianity.

There has been comment on the winged angels observing Job. They have been seen as Job's own thoughts (Wicksteed 1910: 70-71) and as protectors watching over him (A. Wright 1972: 19) as he does a good deed in a spirit of obedience instead of love (Wicksteed 1910: 68-69), while his wife cautions him against such imprudent charity (Lindberg 1973: 220). Though there is no clear visual contrast between these angels, Percival (1938: 170) identifies them as Vala and Jerusalem, now divided. Andrew Wright (*loc. cit.*) points out that the grieving angels in the upper margin have more strength than their predecessors in pl. 4. The stems in the lateral borders, Raine suggests (1982: 72), are a visual allusion to Gen. iii.18: "Thorns also and thistles shall it [the ground] bring forth to thee..." There seems, however, to be only one kind of prickly plant.

pl. 6   The themes commonly observed in this plate are mortality and sexual guilt. In Lindberg's opinion (1973: 134, 225-26), the weeds in the margin symbolise worldly transience, the broken pot represents the fragility of human life, and Job has at this stage no belief in the hereafter. Damon (1966: 22) detects in the lower border images of personal decay—the grasshopper and pitcher—from Eccles. xii.5-6.

The fact that Satan's arrows aim at Job's loins and that light radiates lustfully from his lowest part, his feet, to the loins of his wife convicts Job, in Wicksteed's eyes (1924: 122), of sexual error. Damon (1924: 228), who maintains that the four arrows attack Job's sight, hearing, taste and sense of smell, observes that the boils afflict his sense of touch, his sexual sense, and Raine (1982: 76) describes Satan's scales as those of the phallic snake. Damon (1966: 22) quotes *J* 21:3-5, but whereas he emphasises the sexual guilt expressed in Albion's declaration

The disease of Shame covers me from head to feet: I have no hope;
Every boil upon my body is a separate & deadly Sin,

Lindberg (1973: 226) insists that scepticism is the fundamental error he laments as the succeeding line shows:

Doubt first assail'd me, then Shame took possession of me.

Janet Warner (1973: 222-23) is confident that Job, whose upraised hands can still protest, and his Emanation are both in the power of his Spectre, his own psyche being the scene of the action, while Wicksteed (1924: 126) holds that his wife, reacting to his sensuality, wrongly desires independence, as indicated by her uncovered right foot and the disposition of the sun's rays above her, the greater number being on the orb's stage left.

Though Lindberg (1973: 223) and Paley (1983a: 204) agree that the ruin behind Job is the remains of his house, there is controversy about other structures and about the landscape. Where Lindberg (*loc. cit.*) perceives great areas under cultivation, Raine (1982: 79-81) convincingly writes of bare rock and infertile mountains. Lindberg (1973: 69, 223) is again less persuasive than Raine (*loc. cit.*) when he discerns the remains of the cathedral visible just to the left of Job's house, while she notes three Druid altars at the foot of the mountain and conjectures that beside Satan's right calf there is a tomb perforated by the Door of Death. (For the image of the latter, see E267/ K769).

pl. 7   Job's resting his eyes on the Cross symbolises his persisting
faith (Lindberg 1973: 230). Whereas Wicksteed (1924: 131)
thinks that his wife is dismayed that her husband retains this
faith, Lindberg (*loc. cit.*) praises her for consoling him, he be-
ing a type of the dead Christ and the two of them forming a
pietà based on Michelangelo's. However, most disagreements
over pl. 7 concern the figures in the margin. Are those sitting
on the upper corners asleep (Wicksteed 1910: 75) or are they
angels weeping for Job (A. Wright 1972: 23)? Are the lower
figures a young and an old shepherd lamenting (Hagstrum
1964: 133) or a grieving shepherd and shepherdess displaying
Job-like patience (Raine 1982: 84)? Or are they Job himself
and his wife, still retaining a measure of Innocence and either
asleep (Wicksteed, *loc. cit.*) or patient in their grief (Damon
1966: 24)? Andrew Wright (*loc. cit.*) finds a Druid altar and
Druid ruins in the background.

pl. 8   The desolate atmosphere of this grim design leads Wick-
steed (1924: 134) to declare that all spiritual life is absent from
the scene. Lindberg (1973: 234) scores up a victory to Satan,
because he has made Job sin by cursing his own birth, the work
of his creator; Damon, however, (1966: 26) judges Job's anger
more commendable than his previous submission to a Urizenic
god. While the vegetation below is an unmistakable symbol of
decay, there are different views of the raindrops. These may be
emblems of corrupting pity (Wicksteed 1924: 134) or tears
from merciful heaven (Raine 1982: 86). Russell (1912: 107)
and Wright (1972: 25) see the masonry as Druid architecture.

pl. 9   Unlike most interpreters, Lindberg (1973: 59) considers Job
to be unimpressed by Eliphaz's vision. Percival (1938: 224)
and others believe, on the contrary, that Job's startled response
marks a stage in his awakening from Urizenic religion, a stage
necessary to prepare him for the revelation of pl. 11. Most
critics endorse Wicksteed's view (1910: 79) that Blake is pic-
turing Eliphaz's erroneous conception of God: Nelms (1970:
343-44) points to the dark cloud overhead as a sign of "a false
or misinterpreted vision." Uniquely, Beer (1969: 271) asserts
that the figure in the bed is Job himself terrified by the Uriz-
enic visitation. The wood across the lower margin may repres-
ent the Tree of Mystery (Raine 1982: 90) and the Forest of the

Night (Damon 1924: 229, 231) soon to be overthrown by the whirlwind.

pl. 10   Andrew Wright (1972: 29) believes that the mortuary cross in this design symbolises Job's true faith, Lindberg (1973: 244) holds that Job errs only in one way, namely his lack of belief in immortality, and Mellor (1974: 252) takes the unusual but not untenable view that he clings tenaciously to his false god. Lindberg (1973: 243) also considers that he is a type of Christ mocked. Interestingly, rather than a ruin representing crumbling faith (Wicksteed 1924: 141), Andrew Wright (*loc. cit.*) sees behind the friends Druid structures, now happily in the far background. Job's wife may be gently drawing his attention to his error, thus leading him towards the revelation in the next plate (Wicksteed 1924: 139-40), she may fear in her bewilderment that the friends have a case (A. Wright, *loc. cit.*), or she may side against the friends, for whom the position of her hands expresses abhorrence (J. Warner 1984: 57). Wicksteed (1924: 142) interprets a dark cloud overshadowing the couple as a sign of their shared grief.

There has been much disagreement about the enigmatic images in the margin. Several writers see the figures beneath the bow—one of them bearded—as struggling upwards but held back by the chains. Are they, however, angels (Damon 1966: 30), the souls of Job and his wife aspiring towards the bow of the heavens (Lindberg 1973: 245), or possibly Los and his spectre creating the chains of time (Raine 1982: 93-94)? The bow, suggests Wicksteed (1910: 86), quoting *A* 3:7-9, may itself be a symbol of oppression along with the chains. Noting that it is broader towards the right, he also proposes that the bow and chains represent the sun's daily circuit, the clean-shaven figure standing for dawn and the other for sunset.

From the lower corners of the margin, vertical wood-like columns rise to join spectrous bat's wings. Quoting "I sunk with cries of blood...rolling in tubelike forms/ Shut up within themselves descending down" (*FZ* 84:18-20/ E359/ VII, 284-86), Wicksteed (1910: 84-85) describes the columns as tubes descending from the wings in the process of division essential to the Fall. If this is so, the tubes have taken root. Between them may be the raven of death (Raine 1982: 93), a "cuckoo of slander," "the owl of false wisdom" and "adder of hate," all alluding to Blake's harsh critics (Damon 1966: 30), or simply birds of prey symbolising those who live by devouring others (Wicksteed 1910: 84).

pl. 11   In quoting Job xix.25-27, Blake made two major alterations of the AV text. For "worms destroy," he read "destroy thou," and he transformed the last phrase, "though my reins [i.e. kidneys—the seat of the passions] be consumed within me." His version runs,

> For I know that my Redeemer liveth & that he shall stand in the latter days upon the Earth & after my skin destroy thou This body yet in my flesh shall I see God whom I shall see for Myself and mine eyes shall behold & not Another tho consumed be my wrought Image.

First Job's skin is to be destroyed and then his body, but Damon (1966: 32) convincingly argues that Job has now come to believe in immortality and the survival of the Pauline spiritual body here referred to as "my flesh" (cf. *J* 62:14 and see p. 309 above). The "thou" that will destroy his physical body has been identified as satanic nature (Wicksteed 1910: 89) and has been located within himself (La Belle 1973: 537); the "wrought Image" which is to vanish—the very phrase is being consumed by the flames (Nelms 1970: 343)—is Job's "personal life" (Wicksteed, *loc. cit.*) or selfhood (Raine 1982: 196); his distorted self-image (Nelms 1970: 342-43) or the false god he has made in his own likeness (La Belle 1973: 537-38); or his natural body (Lindberg 1973: 268). Wicksteed sees the serpent as nature (1910: 88) and the chains as the bonds of materialism (1924: 145), while Percival (1938: 61) conceives the fetters as the moral law. The demons in the flames Lindberg (1973: 266) regards as the form the three friends take in Job's dream. In the modern spirit, Digby (1957: 41) interprets the god above and the demons below as representations of the conscious and unconscious minds, both corrupt.

pl. 12   Apart from Frye, whose opinion is recorded in the headnote above, the major critics agree that Elihu enlightens Job. According to Wicksteed (1924: 127), he regains a harmonious relationship with his wife, who, says Andrew Wright (1972:

29, 33), repents having doubted her husband. Wicksteed (1910: 96) and Lindberg (1973: 270, 273) note that Job has thrown down where Elihu stands the potsherd with which he scraped his boils; Wicksteed regards it as a symbol of the self-right-eousness he has overcome, Lindberg as an emblem of the final-ity of death he no longer believes in. Identifying the objects on the earth as a purse and two coins, Andrew Wright (1972: 33) associates them with Job's advance from the mechanical dis-pensing of charity in pl. 5 to the humble acceptance of it in pl. 19. The star shining through what Russell (1912: 109) desc-ribes as "the corner of a Druid temple" and Wicksteed (1924: 157-58) as still massive but no longer stable masonry is read by the latter critic as a sign of hope. Raine, however, (1982: 204) sees the stone structure as part of a house, and she remarks that ruins and tombs persist in the landscape but the altars have disappeared. The appearance of stars, says Percival (1938: 66), marks Job's emergence from Ulro.

The most disputed element of this plate is the exquisitely delicate imagery of the margin, where emanations rise from the sleeping Job to form, perhaps, a Gothic arch (Hagstrum 1964: 134) or a human tent which soars up to infinity (Nelms 1970: 349). Although they ascend above all the stars that are visible, Frye (1969: 230) regards them as the emanations of a Job still steeped in error and departing from him to form the satanic external universe. More responsive to the mixed hope and pathos of the drawing, Andrew Wright (1972: 33) deduces that Job has exchanged the nightmare of pl. 11 for dreams of angels, and his scroll is "the word made flesh, the letter spiritualized." This scroll, observes Klonsky (1977: 136), strikes roots into the ground. In a characteristically schematic interpretation, Wicksteed (1910: 94-96) maintains that there are four streams of spirits representing higher and lower spiritual and higher and lower corporeal emanations, while he sees devouring flames rather than grass at Job's head. Later (1924: 156) he identifies the four streams with single, twofold, threefold and fourfold vision, only the third and fourth being able to reach the heavens—and the third requiring the help of the two winged angels. Although the figures on both sides seem to be rising, Raine (1982: 204) theorises that they ascend on the right and descend on the left symbolising the cycle of birth and reincarnation. Damon (1966: 34), without specifying their origin, supposes that they are angels trying to rouse the sleeping Humanity of Job, and Grant (editorial note to Nelms 1970: 350) credits them with raising an aspect of Job's "emanative portion" or wife, who outwardly, in the main design, still despairs. With some plausibility, Lindberg (1973: 274) argues that since Job has ceased to rely on the Law these two winged messengers can waken and guide upwards "the creatures of his mind." Attending more closely than other commentators to Blake's details, this scholar (1973: 271) states that some of the tiny beings on top of Job sleep, some wake, and some rise. Bindman (1977: 211) could be right in conjecturing that they are raising a "mental covering" from Job in his dream.

pl. 13   While most observers, beginning with Wicksteed (1910: 97-98), recognise that Job has undergone a conversion and the God that now appears to him is the Divine Humanity, Damrosch (1980: 259) claims that it is the same Urizenic creator who is enthroned in pl. 2. Damon (1966: 36) and Bindman (1977: 211) identify him as Christ because he has a cruciform pose, and Bindman draws a specific analogy with the Jesus on pl. 31(35) of *Jerusalem*. (But here his palms do not face forwards.) There is legitimate disagreement over the number of gods in the margin—six and a hint of a seventh in the left margin (Damon 1924: 231) or five and the hand of a sixth (Lindberg 1973: 276). They represent the Eyes of God in the view of Damon (*loc. cit.*) and Raine (1982: 25-26, 216), but Lindberg (1973: 278), citing E565-66, 712/ K617, 804, interprets them as the Human reality behind the outward appearance of nature. Behind the figures stands a balcony of some elegance. For Wicksteed (1924: 162-63) it replaces the cathedral and trilithon of pls. 1, 4 and 5, and signifies the new faith of Job as it reaches beyond the picture to connect him with the wider world by Christian love. Damon (1966: 4) finds it of a piece with the Renaissance architecture of pl. 20, but Russell (1912: 109) believes it a Druid temple and Andrew Wright (1972: 35) takes it as a classical structure and optimistically but unconvincingly describes it as "recessive." Lindberg accurately refers to a lake above God's right hand (1973: 276); he also observes that the movement of the whirlwind continues into the lower margin, where it bows down the trees, which symbolise the state of the unenlightened friends (1973: 276, 279). Damon (1924: 229, 231) very reasonably identifies these trees with the oppressive ones of pl. 9, while Andrew Wright (*loc. cit.*), describes with some exaggeration three roots in one corner as almost pulled from the ground and claims that here is "the tree of life itself" in process of being restored.

pl. 14   Commentators agree that the images on this page form a kind of ladder from the lowest world to the highest and that the angels at the top of the central design are inhabitants of Eternity; the intricate parallels and numerous compartments have nevertheless elicited varied interpretations. The Deity in the centre finds His most implacable enemy in Damrosch (1980: 125-27, 259), who denounces Him as the tyrant Urizen sheltering beneath His arms an Apollo who is Satan and a Diana who is Rahab. Taking a middle position, Janet Warner (1984: 96-102) sees Him as authoritarian but benevolent and notes the positive "creative" gesture of His fingers. Many critics, however, wisely endorse Wicksteed's view (1910: 101-02) that the God who presides over such an uplifting harmony is the Divine Humanity. Russell (1912: 110) credits Him with summoning the day and sending the night into retreat.

The cave at the base of the main design (it reappears in the next plate) is the realm of corporeal sense perception (Damon 1924: 231) with Platonic overtones (Lindberg 1973: 289), and the water which burns in the lower margin is the Sea of Time and Space (Wicksteed 1910: 104). Raine (1982: 226) believes that what rises from it is Boehme's First Principle, the Fire which is essential to creation but which, divorced from the Light, becomes the flames of hell.

In the waves lies Leviathan behind a worm wound round a human body in process of formation (Russell 1912: 110), "a shrouded corpse" (Damon 1966: 38), a log (Lindberg 1973: 284), "a grave-mound" (Raine 1982: 226), or, improbably, a wave (A. Wright 1972: 37). While most interpreters share Wicksteed's view (1910: 89, 104) that the worm represents mortality (Raine [*loc. cit.*] refers to man, the "Mortal Worm" [*J*, pl. 27, poem, l. 55]), Leviathan has been understood as nature (Damon 1924: 232), chaos (Nelms 1970: 351), and the serpent of matter (Raine, *loc. cit.*). But why, if indeed it is on the same level of existence as the cave, is this Ulroic nadir relegated to the margin? According to Andrew Wright (1972: 37), Blake is showing evil to be only a subsidiary element of creation; according to Paley (1978b: 71), the monster and the worm are creatures of illusion.

Treating the sea and the cave as parallel symbols, Wicksteed (1910: 101-02, 104) detects three levels on the page—the world of time and space, the inner worlds of solar intellect and lunar love, and the eternal world of the seraphs. Correlating the compartments of the main design with the Zoas, Damon (1924: 232) finds Tharmas in the cave, Urizen in the solar god, Luvah in the lunar goddess, and Urthona in the angels. (Damrosch [1980: 125-27] maintains that the star-surrounded angels are the redeemed Zoas, who in Eternity are no longer four beings.) Seeing a continuous ascent from the waters to the row of angels, Raine (1982: 224-25) perceives Ulro, Generation, Beulah and Eden in the sea, the cave, the sun and moon, and the starry firmament. Between the angelic and the solar-lunar levels, a space, which Wicksteed (1910: 102) describes as a glimpse of "the void of Nature," works against Damrosch's theory that the central Deity is Urizen since it prevents Him from being identified with a single realm.

More challenging than the sea monster and the worm are the deities of sun and moon. Tempting as it is to follow Thomas Wright (1929: I, 30) and Damon (1966: 38) in identifying the lunar compartment with Blake's own lunar realm of Beulah, this leaves no room for its solar counterpart, which is on the same level, and whose god Damon elsewhere (1967: 189) terms the redeemed Urizen in the guise of Apollo, and whose animals Wicksteed (1910: 101) calls the Horses of Instruction. If Percival (1938: 214) were correct in thinking the moon goddess to be Vala, the sun god should be Luvah, but, as Damon points out (1967: 189), horses are Urizen's attribute; this also weakens Hagstrum's theory (1964: 134) that the deities stand for Los and Enitharmon. Accepting Wicksteed's equation (loc. cit.) of the sun god with intellect and the moon goddess with passion, Damon (1924: 231-32) dubs the former Apollo and the latter Diana. Lindberg (1973: 287-88) objects that the deities, who are Helios and Selene, and their attributes are drawn from classical mythology and Milton's "Il Penseroso" (1. 59), so the animals cannot be the Horses of Instruction and Damon's "dragons of passion" (1966: 38). (Yet Blake is quite capable of endowing borrowed symbols with his own meanings.) Percival (1938: 214) considers that the goddess's creatures are "the masculine and feminine contraries" and the snakes of good and evil portrayed on the Laocoön plate (E facing p. 273), while Mellor (1974: 263) claims them as traditional symbols of Eternity.

If one considers only the central design, it is possible to read it, as Damon prefers to (1924: 231), only as a picture of the human being showing the flesh, the intellect, the emotions and the spirit, but as soon as one takes into account the marginal images of the six days, which contrast, as Damon admits (1966: 38), with the sabbath or millenium in the centre, one sees that Frye (1969: 233) has a substantial case for acclaiming it as an image of the return to the Innocent vision of the relationship between nature and Eternity. Raine's opinion (1982: 223-24) that the six ovals reflect six aspects of the work of the Divine Imagination does not take into account Nelms's perception (1970: 351) that on each side three ovals rise from the earthbound to the celestial level. This observation corroborates Lindberg's insight (1973: 285-86, 289) into the plate's depiction of nature as a state of exile from Eternity, but an exile that allows humanity to look up from its cave and glimpse angels in the stars as an earnest of its homecoming. Lindberg (1973: 290-91) argues that Blake conceived this plate as a divinely inspired re-creation of the breastplate of Aaron along lines conceived by some of his contemporaries.

pl. 15   Commentators agree that this plate embodies an optimistic view of existence, though not of nature. Most critics largely endorse Frye's view (1969: 233-34) that the design shows how Satan, in the form of Behemoth and Leviathan, can be brought under control once he is clearly seen. Damon (1924: 232), who follows Wicksteed (1910: 105) in citing J 91:38-41, regards the monsters as powers of nature and perceives in the sea-dragon's coils a symbol of recurrent natural cycles; later (1966: 40) he locates them in the human subconscious. To Wicksteed (loc. cit.) they seem the powers at work in earth and water, to Beer (1969: 272) "brutal energy" and "the coils of Reason," to Frye (loc. cit.) social and political tyranny, and to Lindberg (1973: 295, 298) the devilish forces enclosed in "meer Nature or Hell"

(E605/ K93). Emphasising that they represent the duality of the lowest world as viewed from Generation, Raine (1982: 227-29) interprets them as the contraries Good and Evil, which are seen to exist in perfect balance as God points down into the Tabernacle of the upper quotation (the universe) containing the Holy Ark (humankind). Andrew Wright (1972: 39) judges that the presence of stars below the cloud barrier shows that the cave of the previous plate has disappeared, while Lindberg (1973: 62, 298) declares these stars a sign of the increasing insight of Job and his wife. Exceptionally, La Belle (1973: 541), discussing only the inscriptions at the top and the left, states that they express Elihu's false concept of a terrifying, comprehensible god, a concept refuted by the visual image of a benevolent deity.

The margin presents few problems. *FZ* 29:8-11/ E319/ II, 150-53 suggests that the eagles are agents of material creation (Damon 1924: 233). The bearded angels are said to represent light and intellect—as opposed to air and love symbolised by the eagles (Wicksteed 1910: 106), to be reminiscent of Urizen and his law books (Binyon 1926: 72), to be inscribing "the laws of creation" (Damon 1924: 233), to be preparing the records for the Judgment in pl. 16 (A. Wright 1972: 39), and to be spiritual forms of Job storing up the divine teaching in his memory (Lindberg 1973: 62-63). Wicksteed (1910: 106) judges that the angels, the eagles, Leviathan and Behemoth correspond respectively to light, air, water and earth, the light and air having as mental counterparts intellect and love; the coiled shells, he holds, signify "revolving and evolving life," though Damon (1966: 40) dismisses them as symbols of human bodies discarded by souls.

pl. 16   Lindberg (1973: 312-13, 317-18) observes that God and Job look at each other while God passes on Job a particular Last Judgment which foreshadows the collective Last Judgment; Satan falls into the hell pictured in the margin, while the friends occupy the traditional place of the damned. On God's knee is "the book of judgment" (Russell 1912: 111), the Book of the Law—the Law being a necessary part of existence (Damon 1966: 42), or the Book of Life of Rev. xx.12 (Lindberg 1973: 316). Most unexpected are the child-figures in God's halo: Raine (1982: 233-34) identifies the winged pair as the reborn souls of Job and his wife, the group of three as the reborn spirits of the friends, and the lone figure as the future Messiah. It should be noted that this last is on what Lindberg (1973: 313) recognises as the spiritually lower side of the design—the side on God's left, where the angel's wing tip is a little lower and the unredeemed friends recoil. Lindberg (1973: 316) proposes that the spirits covering their faces illustrate the Vulgate rendering of Job xli.25 and that they are weeping and purging themselves of misguided pity.

pl. 17   Except as regards the identity of the mysterious angel, this plate has not proved very controversial. According to Raine (1982: 241), God has descended into Job's world in the form of the Father, while Wicksteed (1910: 109-10) believes that Christ has raised the mortals above the cloud belt, and that the deity is no longer in Job's image. St. John's Gospel, the source of most of the texts, is apparently inspired by the female angel, who has been identified as Jerusalem, the Bride of the Lamb in Rev. xxi.2 and 9 (Wicksteed 1910: 109), the Comforter—i.e. the Holy Spirit (Damon 1966: 44), a combination of classical muse and Christian angel (Lindberg 1973: 83, 324), and the Wisdom of Prov. viii.22-31 (Raine 1982: 244-46). The mixture of books and scrolls, argues Damon (loc. cit.), signifies the harmonising of law and inspiration; both of them, says Raine (1982: 243), represent the Book of Life.

pl. 18   Job, in a cruciform posture (Damon 1924: 234), annihilates his selfhood (Frye 1969: 226) and through self-surrender is united to God (Wicksteed 1910: 122) and forgives his enemies (Lindberg 1973: 327-28). Lindberg (1973: 326) considers that the Spiritual Sun—the divine halo of the preceding plates—is changing nature into spirit, and Damon (1966: 46) suspects the influence of Plato's Timaeus in the design of the altar with its pyramid of flame and cube of stones symbolising respectively spirit and earth. According to Raine (1982: 247), the stones may be unhewn because they belong to the uncorrupted Druids or because only such stones were to be used to build the Lord's altars (Exod. xx.25-26). The trees may constitute a patriarchal (Lindberg 1973: 66) or a Druid (Raine 1982: 248) oak grove. Between those on the left can be seen light (Wicksteed 1910: 121) or water (Lindberg 1973: 326). The wheat in the margin indicates that prayer is the bread of the soul, the response to prayer being a divine descent into the world represented by the six angels (Damon 1966: 46). Alternatively, the angels of pl. 14 may have reappeared to show that Job can now make heavenly music (Lindberg 1973: 147). These spirits, the palette, and the writings represent three arts in the border (Lindberg 1973: 329-30). See also p. 315 above.

pl. 19   Recognising Job as both an individual and humankind, Frye (1969: 230) observes in the introduction of new people here a step towards the rebuilding of the community. Lindberg (1973: 335) conceives that Job is sitting outside the ruin of his house receiving the first of the visitors mentioned in the biblical verse xlii.11, namely a brother and his family, and also (1973: 145-46) that the spirits of Job's ten dead children cluster around the upper corners of the central design, a reflection of an episode in *The Testament of Job* in which they appear to him in a vision. The wheat Raine (1982: 250) regards as "The Bread of sweet Thought" (E709/ K800), for the gifts Job receives are in her eyes primarily spiritual. However, as Wicksteed feels (1910: 125), Blake may be acknowledging in this design the patronage he has received from Linnell.

In the margin, the two topmost spirits are sowing seed (Lindberg 1973: 334), or one is throwing up coins while the other carries what seems to be an earring, gold being symbolic of Eden (Raine 1982: 250-51). Below, two hold the fruits of husbandry (Lindberg 1973: 334), scatter them (A. Wright 1982: 47), or distribute flowers symbolising sexual love (Raine 1982: 251). Still more variously interpreted are the margin's trees and flowers. What are "palms of victory" to Damon (1924: 235) are to Wicksteed (1910: 126) an allusion to the prophecy "The righteous shall flourish like the palm tree" (Ps. xcii.12), to Lindberg (1973: 335-36) an emblem of eternal life (a traditional interpretation of the palm in the biblical verse), and to Grant (1969: 365, citing *J* 59:6) a symbol of suffering. Contrasting with this tree, says Lindberg (*loc. cit.*), the "creeping" flowers represent human mortality in this world—the tree in the central design is similarly accompanied by two humble flowers in the lower right corner. On the other hand, the roses and lilies have been understood respectively as male and female generosity (Wicksteed 1924: 199), as love and innocence (A. Wright, *loc. cit.*), and as "material and spiritual beauty" (Damon 1924: 235, comparing the roses of Vala and lilies of Jerusalem in *J IB* pl. 18). To Grant (1969: 365-66) they signify Job's regeneration, and Wardle (1980: 13) notes that they are symbols of paradise in the Boston version of Blake's painting *Satan watching the endearments of Adam and Eve* (Butlin 1981, pl. 648).

pl. 20 No one can deny that Job is here recounting his experiences to his daughters, but the many details of this engraving have evoked diverse readings. The daughters themselves have been explained as representing the sun, earth and moon (Wicksteed 1910: 129, comparing pl. 14), or poetry, painting and music (Damon 1924: 235), as Job's recovered emanations (Frye 1947: 434), and as the three Graces (Raine 1982: 257). The carved (Wicksteed 1910: 127) or painted (Lindberg 1973: 339) walls bear some obscure images. Are the bowed figures beneath the satanic god two of Job's spiritually dead sons (Wicksteed 1910: 128-29), two of the friends, the third being invisible behind Job (A. Wright 1972: 49), two likenesses of Job's wife in her former grief (Lindberg 1973: 343), or the wife and Job (Raine 1982: 259)? Lindberg acutely observes that the snakes just above have dorsal spines and move over grass towards the spectator's right. Of the three panels above, only the one behind Job's left hand gives difficulty: it seems to represent Satan killing a ploughman against a background of houses (Lindberg 1973: 340, 342), but Wicksteed (1910: 127) labels the scene a natural disaster, and Hagstrum (1965: 174-75) perceives Blake himself there in the form of a ploughman like Palamabron portrayed in the moment of inspiration as he is in *M IB* pl. 32. Gillespie (1983: 66-67) argues that the central panel illustrates the instant at which Job's false perception is corrected: the incidents are on the rim of a circle, a circumference that "still expands going forward to Eternity" (*J* 71:8), and it becomes apparent that reality does not consist of a finite, external world and heaven enclosed in the tent and cloud barriers of other plates. The interlacing circles on the floor, speculates Lindberg (1973: 342), may only be decorative but probably represent "devotion" and "the human mind." However, Damon (1924: 236) is perhaps right in his more precise suggestion that the smaller, interpenetrating circles containing four-sided figures represent "individuals entering each other's bosoms" in "the heaven of art" while the large circle stands for the One Man, Jesus, containing them all; his main implicit reference is to *J* 88:3-5. (Though Lindberg [1973: 339-40] denies that the chamber is perfectly round since he regards the area containing the paintings as a projecting apse, the edge of the circular floor is not interrupted by the upright divisions on either side of the main design.) The fruitful vine in the margin has been taken as a symbol of "Christ and Christian joy" (Wicksteed 1910: 129), as a symbol related to art, which is "the sacrificial wine of the Eucharist" (Damon 1966: 50), and as an emblem of Job's family love (Lindberg 1973: 342). Among the branches are two pairs of angels, who are taking the communion of art according to Damon (1966: 50), displaying affection according to Lindberg (1973: 340). Most commentators emphasise that the plate proclaims the value of the arts as a means of awakening from the fallen state: the uppermost inscription celebrates the gift of divine inspiration (Damon 1966: 50), and Wicksteed (1924: 203) believes that the room is inside the Gothic cathedral of true art of pls. 1 and 4, while Damon (1924: 235-36) suggests that the spectator is here admitted to "Los's Halls" (*J* 16:62—Wicksteed quotes the passage *in extenso* [1910: 127]). Frye (1947: 434) is convinced that the design represents Job in Eternity, where the room is his body and "the shadows of Possibility" (*J* 92:18) are projected on the walls of his mind. The musical instruments in the margin add a third art to the verbal and visual arts of the central design (Lindberg 1973: 342), and the room adds the fourth, architecture (Gillespie 1983: 61).

pl. 21   The bliss portrayed in this engraving leaves little room for disagreement. What disputable comment there is concerns matters of detail. Do the daughters carry a scroll of verse, an art book and a lyre to represent poetry, painting and music (Damon 1966: 52)? Does the ram in the margin represent Innocence and the bull Experience, a reversal of their meanings in pl. 1 (Wicksteed 1910: 131)? Is the cathedral not restored because the redeemed need no external church, as Rev. xxi.22 (A. Wright 1972: 51) and John iv.21 and 23-24 (Raine 1982: 261) should reveal to us? The uppermost inscription, being from "the song of Moses the servant of God and the song of the

Lamb" (Rev. xv.3), shows that Blake was satisfied that he had unified the doctrines of the Old and New Testaments (Damon 1924: 236).

Works Cited in Notes on Criticism

Ackland, Michael. "The Embattled Sexes: Blake's Debt to Wollstonecraft in *The Four Zoas*." *BIQ*, XVI (Winter 1982-83), 172-83. (Cited as 1982.)

Ackland, Michael. "Blake's Critique of Enlightenment Reason in *The Four Zoas*." *CLQ*, XIX (Dec. 1983), 173-89.

Adams, Hazard. *Blake and Yeats: The Contrary Vision*. Ithaca: Cornell UP, 1955.

————. *William Blake: A Reading of the Shorter Poems*. Seattle: U of Washington P, 1963.

————, ed. William Blake, *Jerusalem, Selected Poems and Prose*. New York: Holt, Rinehart and Winston, 1970.

————. "Blake, *Jerusalem*, and Symbolic Form." *BS*, VII.2 (1975), 143-66.

Adlard, John. "Blake and *Rasselas*." *Archiv für das Studium der neueren Sprachen und Literaturen*, CCI (1964), 47.

————. "Tasso and the Cock and Lion in Blake's *Milton*." *Symposium*, XX (1966), 5-6.

————. "A 'Triumphing Joyfulness': Blake, Boehme and the Tradition." *BS*, I.2 (1969), 109-22.

————. "'The Garden of Love.'" *BN*, IV (Spring 1971), 147-48.

————. *The Sports of Cruelty: Fairies, Folk-songs, Charms and Other Country Matters in the Work of William Blake*. London: Cecil and Amelia Woolf, 1972.

Adler, Jacob H. "Symbol and Meaning in 'The Little Black Boy.'" *MLN*, LVII (1957), 412-15.

Altizer, Thomas J. J. *The New Apocalypse: The Radical Christian Vision of William Blake*. N.p.: Michigan State UP, 1967.

Anderson, Mark. "Oothoon, Failed Prophet." *Romanticism Past and Present*, VIII (Summer 1984), 1-21.

Ansari, Asloob Ahmad. "Blake and the Kabbalah," in *WBED*, 1969. 199-220.

Armstrong, Isobel. "Blake's Simplicity: *Jerusalem*, Chapter I," chap. 3 of *Language as Living Form in Nineteenth-century Poetry*. Sussex: Harvester Press; New Jersey: Barnes and Noble, 1982. 90-112.

Ault, Donald D. *Visionary Physics: Blake's Response to Newton*. Chicago and London: U of Chicago P., 1974.

Baine, Rodney M. "Thel's Northern Gate." *PQ*, LI (1972), 957-61.

———. "Bromion's 'Jealous Dolphins.'" *BIQ*, XIV (Spring 1981), 206-07.

———. "Blake's Sons of Los." *PQ*, LXIII (1984), 239-54.

Baine, Rodney M., and Mary R. Baine. "Blake's *The Marriage of Heaven and Hell*, Plate 9." *Ex*, 32 (Mar. 1974), item 50.

———. "'Then Mars Thou Wast Our Center.'" *ELN*, XIII (1975), 14-18.

Bass, Eben. "*Songs of Innocence and of Experience*: The Thrust of Design," in *BVFD*, 1970. 196-213.

Bateson, F. W., ed. *Selected Poems of William Blake*. 1957; rpt. London: Heinemann, 1963. (Cited as 1957.)

———. "An Editorial Postscript." *EC*, XI (1961), 162-63.

Beer, John. *Blake's Humanism*. Manchester: Manchester UP; New York: Barnes and Noble, 1968.

———. *Blake's Visionary Universe*. Manchester: Manchester UP; New York: Barnes and Noble, 1969.

Behrendt, Stephen C. "'The Worst Disease': Blake's *Tiriel*." *CLQ*, XV (Sep. 1979), 175-87.

Bentley, Gerald E., Jr. "The Failure of Blake's *Four Zoas*." *Texas Studies in English*, XXXVII (1958), 102-113.

———, ed. William Blake, *Vala or The Four Zoas*. Oxford: Clarendon Press, 1963.

———. ed. William Blake, *Tiriel*. Oxford: Clarendon Press, 1967.

———. *Blake Records*. Oxford: Clarendon Press, 1969.

———, ed. *William Blake: The Critical Heritage*. London and Boston: Routledge and Kegan Paul, 1975.

———. *Blake Books*. Oxford: Clarendon Press, 1977.

Bidney, Martin. "*Cain* and *The Ghost of Abel*: Contexts for Understanding Blake's Response to Byron." *BS*, VIII.2 (1979), 145-65.

Bindman, David. *Blake as an Artist*. Oxford: Phaidon; New York: Dutton, 1977.

Bindman, David. *The Complete Graphic Works of William Blake*. 1978; rpt. London: Thames and Hudson, 1986. (Cited as 1978.)

Bindman, David. *William Blake: His Art and Times*. N.p.: Yale Center for British Art; Art Gallery of Ontario, 1982.

Binyon, Laurence. *The Engraved Designs of William Blake*. 1926:
rpt. New York: Da Capo Press, 1967. (Cited as 1926.)

Blackstone, Bernard. *English Blake*. 1949; rpt. Hamden, Conn.:
Archon Books, 1966. (Cited as 1949.)

Bloom, Harold. "Dialectic in *The Marriage of Heaven and Hell*."
PMLA, LXXIII (1958), 501-04.

————. *Blake's Apocalypse: A Study in Poetic Argument*. New
York: Doubleday, 1963.

————. "Commentary." 1965; rpt. in David V. Erdman, ed., *The
Complete Poetry and Prose of William Blake*. Berkeley and
Los Angeles: U of California P, 1982. 894-970. (Cited as
1965.)

————. "Blake's *Jerusalem*: The Bard of Sensibility and the Form
of Prophecy." *The Ringers in the Tower: Studies in Romantic
Tradition*. Chicago and London: U of Chicago P, 1971. 65-79.

Blunt, Anthony. "Blake's 'Ancient of Days': The Symbolism of
the Compasses." 1938; rpt. *VH*. 71-103.

————. *The Art of William Blake*. New York and London: Col-
umbia UP, 1959.

Bogan, James. "Blake's City of Golgonooza in *Jerusalem*:
Metaphor and Mandala." *CLQ*, XVII (Jun. 1981), 85-98.

Bogen, Nancy. "Blake's Debt to Gillray." *American Notes &
Queries*, VI (Nov. 1967), 35-38.

————. "A New Look at Blake's *Tiriel*." *BNYPL*, LXXIV (1970),
153-65.

————, ed. William Blake, *The Book of Thel: A Facsimile and a
Critical Text*. Providence: Brown UP; New York: New York
Public Library, 1971.

Bouwer, Izak, and Paul McNally. "'The Mental Traveller': Man's
Eternal Journey." *BIQ*, XII (Winter 1978-79), 184-92. (Cited
as 1978.)

Bracher, Mark. "The Metaphysical Grounds of Oppression in
Blake's *Visions of the Daughters of Albion*." *CLQ*, XX (Sep.
1984), 164-76.

Brisman, Leslie. "Re Generation in Blake," chap. 6 of *Romantic
Origins*. Ithaca, and London: Cornell UP, 1978. 224-75.

Bronowski, J. *William Blake 1757-1827: A Man Without a Mask*
[London]: Secker and Warburg, [1944].

————. ———— ———— ————. Rev. ed. Harmondsworth, Mid-
dlesex: Penguin, 1954.

Bullough, Geoffrey. "William Blake: *The Book of Thel*," in *Versdichtung der Englischen Romantik*, ed. Teut Andreas Riese and Dieter Riesner. Berlin: Erich Schmidt Verlag, 1968. 108-23.

Butlin, Martin. *The Paintings and Drawings of William Blake*. 2 vols. New Haven and London: Yale UP, 1981.

Butter, Ph. H. "Blake's *Book of Urizen* and Boehme's *Mysterium Magnum*," in *Le romantisme Anglo-Américain: Mélanges offerts à Louis Bonnerot*. Paris: Didier, 1971. 35-44.

Butter, Peter. "*Milton*: The Final Plates," in *InB*, 1978. 145-63.

Carr, Stephen Leo. "William Blake's Print-Making Process in *Jerusalem*." *ELH*, XLVII (1980), 520-41.

Carothers, Yvonne M. "Space and Time in *Milton*: The 'Bard's Song,'" in *BT*, 1978. 116-27.

Chayes, Irene H. "Plato's *Statesman* Myth In Shelley and Blake." *CL*, XIII (1961), 358-69.

————. "Little Girls Lost: Problems of a Romantic Archetype." 1963; rpt. *BCCE*. 65-78.

————. "Blake and Tradition: 'The Little Girl Lost' and 'The Little Girl Found.'" *BN*, IV (August 1970), 25-28. (Cited as 1970a.)

————. "The Presence of Cupid and Psyche," in *BVFD*, 1970. 214-43. (Cited as 1970b.)

————. "The Marginal Design on *Jerusalem* 12." *BS*, VII.1 (1974), 51-84.

Cherry, Charles L. "The Apotheosis of Desire: Dialectic and Image in *The French Revolution*, *Visions of the Daughters of Albion*, and the *Preludium* of *America*." *Xavier University Studies*, VIII (Jul. 1969), 18-31.

Connolly, Thomas E. "The Real 'Holy Thursday' of William Blake." *BS*, VI.2 (1975), 179-87.

Cooper, Andrew M. "Blake's Escape From Mythology: Self-mastery in *Milton*." *SR*, XX (1981), 85-110.

Cramer, Patricia. "The Role of Ahania's Lament in Blake's *Book of Ahania*: A Psychoanalytic Study." *JEGP*, LXXXIII (1984), 522-33.

Crehan, Stewart. *Blake in Context*. Dublin: Gill and Macmillan; Atlantic Highlands, N. J.: Humanities Press, 1984.

Cross, F. L., and E. A. Livingstone, ed. *The Oxford Dictionary of the Christian Church*. 2nd. ed. London: Oxford U. P., 1974.

Curran, Stuart. "The Mental Pinnacle: *Paradise Regained* and the Romantic Four-Book Epic," in *Calm of Mind: Tercentenary Essays on* Paradise Regained *and* Samson Agonistes *in Honor of John S. Diekhoff*, ed. Joseph Anthony Wittreich, Jr. Cleveland and London: Press of Case Western Reserve University, 1971. 133-62.

————. "Blake and the Gnostic Hyle: A Double Negative." *BS*, IV.2 (1972), 117-33.

————. "The Structures of *Jerusalem*," in *BSA*, 1973. 329-46.

Damon, S. Foster. *William Blake: His Philosophy and Symbols.* 1924; rpt. Gloucester, Mass.: Peter Smith, 1958. (Cited as 1924.)

————. *Blake's* Job: *William Blake's* Illustrations of the Book of Job. Providence: Brown UP, 1966.

————. *A Blake Dictionary: The Ideas and Symbols of William Blake.* Rev. printing. 1967; rpt. Hanover and London: UP of New England for Brown UP, 1988. (Cited as 1967.)

Damrosch, Leopold, Jr. *Symbol and Truth in Blake's Myth.* Princeton: Princeton UP, 1980.

Davies, J. G. *The Theology of William Blake.* Oxford: Clarendon Press, 1948.

Deen, Leonard W. *Conversing in Paradise: Poetic Genius and Identity-as-Community in Blake's Los.* Columbia and London: U of Missouri P., 1983.

De Luca, V. A. "Ariston's Immortal Palace: Icon and Allegory in Blake's Prophecies." *Cr* XII (1970), 1-19.

————. "Proper Names in the Structural Design of Blake's Mythmaking." *BS*, VIII,1 (1978), 5-22.

————. "Blake and the Two Sublimes." *SECC*, XI (1982), 93-105.

————. "The Changing Order of Plates in *Jerusalem*, Chapter II." *BIQ*, XVI (Spring 1983), 192-205.

Digby, George Wingfield. *Symbol and Image in William Blake.* Oxford: Clarendon Press, 1957.

Dilworth, Thomas. "The Hands of *Milton*: Blake's Multistable Image of Self-Annihilation." *Mosaic*, XVI (Summer 1983), 11-27.

DiSalvo, Jackie. *War of Titans: Blake's Critique of Milton and the Politics of Religion.* Pittsburgh: U of Pittsburgh P, 1983.

Dorfman, Deborah. "'King of Beauty' and 'Golden World' in Blake's *America*: the Reader and the Archetype." *ELH*, XLVI (1979), 122-35.

Doskow, Minna. "William Blake's *America*: The Story of a Revolution Betrayed." *BS*, VIII.2 (1979), 167-86.

————. *William Blake's* Jerusalem: *Structure and Meaning in Poetry and Picture.* Rutherford: Fairleigh Dickinson UP; London and Toronto: Associated University Presses, 1982.

Douglas, Dennis. "Blake's *'Europe'*: A Note on the Preludium." *AUMLA: Journal of the Australasian Universities Language and Literature Association*, No. 23 (May 1965), 111-16.

Duerksen, Roland A. "A Crucial Line in *Visions of the Daughters of Albion*." *BN*, VI (Winter 1972-73), 72. (Cited as 1972.)

————. "Bromion's Usurped Power—Its Sources, Essence, and Effect: A Replication." *BN*, VIII (Winter 1974-75), 95-96. (Cited as 1974.)

————. "The Life of Love: Blake's Oothoon." *CLQ*, XIII (Sep. 1977), 186-94.

Duplantier, F. R. "Method in Blake's 'Mad Song.'" *BIQ*, XIII (Fall 1979), 102-04.

Easson, Roger R. "William Blake and His Reader in *Jerusalem*," in *BSA*, 1973. 309-27.

Eaves, Morris. "A Reading of Blake's *Marriage of Heaven and Hell*, Plates 17-20: On and Under the Estate of the West." *BS*, IV.2 (1972), 81-116.

————. "The Title-page of *The Book of Urizen*," in *WBEK*, 1973. 225-30.

Ehrstine, John W. *William Blake's* Poetical Sketches. [Seattle]: Washington State UP, 1967.

Emery, Clark, "Introduction" to William Blake, *The Marriage of Heaven and Hell*, ed. Clark Emery. 1963; rpt. Coral Gables, Fla.: U of Miami P, 1972. 1-104. (Cited as 1963.)

————. "Introduction" to William Blake, *The Book of Urizen*, ed. Clark Emery. 1966; rpt. Coral Gables, Fla.: U of Miami P, 1973. 1-54. (Cited as 1966.)

England, Martha Winburn, and John Sparrow, *Hymns Unbidden: Donne, Herbert, Blake, Emily Dickinson and the Hymnographers.* New York: New York Public Library, 1966. (Only England's contributions cited.)

Enscoe, Gerald E. "The Content of Vision: Blake's 'Mental Traveller.'" *PLL*, IV (1968), 400-13.

Erdman, David V. "Blake; the Historical Approach," in *English Institute Essays 1950*, ed. Alan S. Downer. New York: Columbia UP, 1951. 197-223. (Cited as 1951a.)

————. "Lambeth and Bethlehem in Blake's *Jerusalem*." *MP*, XLVIII (1951), 184-92. (Cited as 1951b.)

————. *Blake: Prophet Against Empire: A Poet's Interpretation of the History of His Own Times*. Princeton: Princeton UP, 1954. (Cited as 1954a.)

————. "William Blake's Debt to Joel Barlow." *American Literature*, XXVI (1954), 94-98. (Cited as 1954b.)

————. "The Suppressed and Altered Passages in Blake's *Jerusalem*." *Studies in Bibliography*, XVII (1964), 1-54. (Cited as 1964a.)

————. "The Binding (et cetera) of *Vala*." *Library*, Fifth Series, XIX (1964), 112-29. (Cited as 1964b.)

————, ed. *The Poetry and Prose of William Blake*. Garden City, New York: Doubleday, 1965.

————. Review of S. Foster Damon, *A Blake Dictionary*, in *JEGP*, LXV (1966), 606-12.

————. "A Temporary Report on Texts of Blake," in *WBED*, 1969. 395-413. (Cited as 1969a.)

————. *Blake: Prophet Against Empire: A Poet's Interpretation of the History of His Own Times*. Rev. ed. New York: Anchor Books/ Doubleday, 1969. (Cited as 1969b.)

————. "*America*: New Expanses," in *BVFD*, 1970. 92-114.

————. "The Steps (of Dance and Stone) that Order Blake's *Milton*," *BS*, VI.1 (1973), 73-87.

————, ed. *The Illuminated Blake*. New York: Anchor Press/ Doubleday, 1974.

————, "Errors in the 1973 Edition of *The Notebook of William Blake* & in the First Printing of *The Illuminated Blake*." *BN*, IX (Fall 1975), 39-40.

————, ed. *The Notebook of William Blake: A Photographic and Typographic Facsimile*. Rev. ed. New York: Readex Books, 1977. (Cited as 1977a.)

————. "The Symmetries of *The Song of Los*." *SR*, XVI (1977), 179-88. (Cited as 1977b.)

————. *Blake: Prophet Against Empire: A Poet's Interpretation of the History of His Own Times*. 3rd ed. Princeton: Princeton UP, 1977. (Cited as 1977c.)

————. "Night the Seventh: the Editorial Problem." *BIQ*, XII (Fall 1978), 135-39.

————. "Art Against Armies." *BRH*, LXXXIV (Autumn 1981), 296-304.

Essick, Robert N. "Blake and the Traditions of Reproductive Engraving." *BS*, V.1 (1972), 59-103. (Cited as 1972a.)

————. Contributions to "Brief Notices," *BS*, IV.2 (1972), 170-75. (Cited as 1972b.)

————. "The Altering Eye: Blake's Vision in the *Tiriel* Designs," in *WBEK*, 1973. 50-65.

————. *William Blake Printmaker*. Princeton: Princeton UP, 1980.

Evans, James C. "The Apocalypse As Contrary Vision: Prolegomena to an Analogical Reading of THE FOUR ZOAS." *TSLL*, XIV (1972), 318-28.

Ferber, Michael. "Mars and the Planets Three in *America*." *BIQ*, XV (Winter 1981-82), 136-37. (Cited as 1981.)

Ferguson, James. "Prefaces to *Jerusalem*," in *InB*, 1978. 164-95.

Fisch, Harold. "Blake's Miltonic Moment," in *WBED*, 1969. 36-56.

Fisher, Peter F. "Blake and the Druids." 1959; rpt. *BCCE*. 156-78.

————. *The Valley of Vision: Blake as Prophet and Revolutionary*. 1961; rpt. Toronto and Buffalo: U of Toronto P, 1971. (Cited as 1961.)

Fox, Susan. *Poetic Form in Blake's* Milton. Princeton: Princeton UP, 1976.

————. "The Female as Metaphor in William Blake's Poetry." *CI*, III (1977), 507-19.

Freeman, Rosemary. *English Emblem Books*. London: Chatto and Windus, 1948.

Frosch, Thomas R. *The Awakening of Albion: The Renovation of the Body in the Poetry of William Blake*. Ithaca and London: Cornell UP, 1974.

Frost, Everett C. (with Edward W. Tayler). "The Source of 'Bring out number, weight & measure in a year of dearth." *BN*, V (Winter 1971-72), 213. (Cited as Frost 1971.)

Frye, Northrop. *Fearful Symmetry: A Study of William Blake.* 1947; rpt. Boston: Beacon Press, 1962. (Cited as 1947. Page numbers of first edition unchanged.)

————. "Blake's Treatment of the Archetype," in *English Institute Essays 1950*, ed. Alan S. Downer. New York: Columbia UP, 1951. 170-96.

————. "Blake's Introduction to Experience." 1957; rpt. *BCCE.* 23-31. (Cited as 1957a.)

————. *Anatomy of Criticism.* 1957; rpt. New York: Atheneum, 1966. (Cited as 1957b.)

————. "Notes for a Commentary on *Milton,*" in DV. 97-137. (Cited as 1957c.)

————. "The Keys to the Gates." 1966; rpt. Frye, *The Stubborn Structure: Essays on Criticism and Society.* Ithaca: Cornell UP, 1970. 175-99. (Cited as 1966).

————. "Blake's Reading of the Book of Job," in *WBED*, 1969. 221-34.

Fuller, David. "*Milton*, and the Development of Blake's Thought," in *An Infinite Complexity*, ed. J. R. Watson (n. p.: Edinburgh UP, 1983). 46-94.

Gallant, Christine. *Blake and the Assimilation of Chaos.* Princeton: Princeton UP, 1978.

Gardner, Stanley. *Infinity on the Anvil: A Critical Study of Blake's Poetry.* Oxford: Blackwell, 1954.

Gardner, Stanley. *Blake.* London: Evans Brothers, 1968.

George, Diana Hume. *Blake and Freud.* Ithaca and London: Cornell UP, 1980.

Gilchrist, Alexander. *Life of William Blake*, ed. Ruthven Todd. Rev. ed. London: Dent; New York: Dutton, 1945.

Gillespie, Diane Filby. "A Key to Blake's *Job*: Design XX." *CLQ,* XIX (Jun. 1983), 59-68.

Gillham, D. G. *Blake's Contrary States: The 'Songs of Innocence and of Experience' as Dramatic Poems.* Cambridge: Cambridge UP, 1966.

————. *William Blake.* Cambridge: Cambridge UP, 1973.

Glausser, Wayne. "*Milton* and the Pangs of Repentance." *BIQ,* XIII (Spring 1980), 192-99.

Gleckner, Robert F. "Blake and Wesley." *NQ*, CCI (Dec. 1956), 522-24. (Cited as 1956a.)

————. "Irony in Blake's 'Holy Thursday.'" *MLN*, LXXI (1956), 412-15. (Cited as 1956b.)

————. "Point of View and Context in Blake's Songs." 1957; rpt. *BCCE*. 8-14.

————. *The Piper and the Bard: A study of William Blake.* Detroit: Wayne State UP, 1959.

————. "Blake's *Thel* and the Bible." *BNYPL*, LXIV (1960), 573-80.

————. "William Blake and the Human Abstract." *PMLA*, LXXVI (1961), 373-79.

————. "Blake and the Senses." *SR*, V (1965), 1-15.

————. "Blake's Swans." *BIQ*, XV (Spring 1982), 164-69. (Cited as 1982a.)

————. *Blake's Prelude*: Poetical Sketches. Baltimore and London: Johns Hopkins UP, 1982. (Cited as 1982b.)

Glen, Heather. *Vision and Disenchantment: Blake's* Songs *and* Wordsworth's Lyrical Ballads. Cambridge: Cambridge UP, 1983.

Goslee, Nancy M. "'In Englands green & pleasant Land': The Building of Vision in Blake's Stanzas from *Milton.*" *SR*, XIII (1974), 105-25.

Grant, John E. "Misreadings of 'The Fly.'" *EC*, XI (1961), 481-87. (Cited as 1961a.)

————. "The Art and Argument of 'The Tyger.'" 1960; revised version rept. in *Discussions of William Blake*, ed. John E. Grant. Boston: Heath, 1961. 64-82. (Cited as 1961b.)

————. "Interpreting Blake's 'The Fly.'" 1963; rpt. *BCCE*. 32-55.

————. "Apocalypse in Blake's 'Auguries of Innocence.'" *TSLL*, 5 (1964), 489-508.

————. "Mothers and Methodology (continued)." *BN*, II (Dec. 1968), 50-54. (Cited as 1968a.)

————. "Review article: Blake's *Songs of Innocence and of Experience.*" *PQ*, XLVII (1968), 571-80. (Cited as 1968b.)

————. "'With intellectual spears, & long winged arrows of thought.'" *BN*, II (Sep. 1968), 29-32. (Cited as 1968c.)

————. "Two Flowers in the Garden of Experience," in *WBED*, 1969. 333-67.

————. Editorial note in *BVFD*, 1970. 420-21. (Cited as 1970a.)

————. Editorial note in *BVFD*, 1970. 63-64. (Cited as 1970b.)

————. "The Fate of Blake's Sun-flower: A Forecast and Some Conclusions." *BS*, V.2 (1974), 7-64.

————. "The Female Awakening at the End of Blake's *Milton*: A Picture Story, with Questions," in *Milton Reconsidered: Essays in Honor of Arthur E. Barker*, ed. John Karl Franson. Salzburg: Institut für Englische Sprache und Literatur, Universität Salzburg, 1976. 78-102.

Greenberg, Mark. "Blake's Vortex." *CLQ*, XIV (Dec. 1978), 198-212.

Grimes, Ronald L. "Time and Space in Blake's Major Prophecies," in *BSA*, 1973. 59-81.

Hagstrum, Jean H. "William Blake's 'The Clod & the Pebble,'" in *Restoration and Eighteenth-Century Literature: Essays in Honor of Alan Dugald McKillop*, ed. Carroll Camden. Chicago and London: U of Chicago P, 1963. 381-88.

————. *William Blake: Poet and Painter*. 1964; rpt. Chicago and London: U of Chicago P, 1969. (Cited as 1964.)

————. "Blake's Blake," in *Essays in History and Literature Presented by Fellows of the Newberry Library to Stanley Pargellis*, ed. Heinz Bluhm. Chicago: Newberry Library, 1965. 169-78.

————. "The Fly," in *WBED*, 1969. 368-82.

————. "Christ's Body," in *WBEK*, 1973. 129-56. (Cited as 1973a.)

————. "Babylon Revisited, or the Story of Luvah and Vala," in *BSA*, 1973. 101-18. (Cited as 1973b.)

Hall, Mary S. "Blake's *Tiriel*: A Visionary Form Pedantic." *BNYPL*, LXXIV (1970), 166-76.

Halliburton, David G. "Blake's *French Revolution*: The *Figura* and Yesterday's News." *SR*, V (1966), 158-68.

Halloran, William F. "*The French Revolution*: Revelation's New Form," in *BVFD*, 1970. 30-56.

————. "Blake's *Tiriel*: Snakes, Curses, and a Blessing." *SAQ*. LXX (1971), 161-79.

Harding, Eugene J. "Jacob Boehme and Blake's 'The Book of Urizen.'" *Unisa English Studies: Bulletin of the Department of English, University of South Africa*, VIII (June 1970), 3-11.

Harper, George Mills. "The Source of Blake's 'Ah! Sun-flower.'" *MLR*, XLVIII (1953), 139-42.

————. "Blake's Neo-Platonic Interpretation of Plato's Atlantis Myth." *JEGP*, LIV (1955), 72-79.

————. *The Neoplatonism of William Blake*. Chapel Hill: U of North Carolina P, 1961.

————. "Apocalyptic Vision and Pastoral Dream in Blake's *Four Zoas*." *SAQ*, LXIV (1965), 110-24.

————. "The Divine Tetrad in Blake's *Jerusalem*," in *WBED*, 1969. 235-55.

————. "The Odyssey of the Soul in Blake's *Jerusalem*." *BS*, V.2 (1974), 65-80.

Hartman, Geoffrey H. "Blake and the 'Progress of Poesy,'" in *WBED*, 1969. 57-68.

Helms, Randel. "Ezekiel and Blake's *Jerusalem*." *SR*, XIII (1974), 127-40.

————. "Why Ezekiel Ate Dung." *ELN*, XV (1978), 279-81.

————. "Blake's Use of the Bible in 'A Song of Liberty." *ELN*, XVI (1979), 287-91.

Henry, Matthew. *Commentary on the Whole Bible*. 1708-14; rpt. 6 vols. Iowa Falls: World Bible Publishers, [c. 1980]. (Cited as 1708-14.)

Heppner, Christopher. "'A Desire of Being': Identity and *The Book of Thel*." *CLQ*, XIII (Jun. 1977), 79-98.

Herrstrom, David Sten. "Blake's Transformations of Ezekiel's Cherubim Vision in *Jerusalem*." *BIQ*, XV (Fall 1981), 64-77.

Herzing, Thomas W. "Book I of Blake's *Milton*: Natural Religion as an Optical Fallacy." *BS*, VI.1 (1973), 19-34.

Hilton, Nelson. "The Sweet Science of Atmospheres in *The Four Zoas*." *BIQ*, XII (Fall 1978), 80-86.

————. "Blake and the Mountains of the Mind." *BIQ*, XIV (Spring 1981), 196-204.

————. "Some Sexual Connotations." *BIQ*, XVI (Winter 1982-83), 166-71. (Cited as 1982.)

————. *Literal Imagination: Blake's Vision of Words*. Berkeley: U of California P, 1983.

Hinkel, Howard H. "From Energy and Desire to Eternity: Blake's *Visions of the Daughters of Albion*." *PLL*, XV (1979), 278-89.

Hirsch, E. D., Jr. *Innocence and Experience: An Introduction to Blake*. New Haven and London: Yale UP, 1964.

Hirst, Désirée. *Hidden Riches: Traditional Symbolism from the Renaissance to Blake*. London: Eyre and Spottiswoode, 1964.

Hoagwood, Terence Allan. "*The Four Zoas* and 'The Philosophick Cabbala.'" *BIQ*, XII (Fall 1978), 87-90. (Cited as 1978a.)

———. "Holbach and Blake's Philosophical Statement in 'The Voice of the Devil.'" *ELN*, XV (1978), 181-86. (Cited as 1978b.)

Hobsbaum, Philip. "A Rhetorical Question Answered: Blake's Tyger and Its Critics." 1964; rpt. William Blake, *The Tyger*, ed. Winston Weathers. Columbus, Ohio: Merrill, 1969. 74-79. (Cited as 1964.)

Holloway, John. *Blake: The Lyric Poetry*. London: Edward Arnold, 1968.

Howard, John. "An Audience for *The Marriage of Heaven and Hell*." *BS*, III.1 (1970), 19-52.

———. *Blake's* Milton: *A Study in the Selfhood*. Rutherford: Fairleigh Dickinson UP; Cranbury, N. J.: Associated University Presses, 1976.

———. *Infernal Poetics: Poetic Structures in Blake's Lambeth Prophecies*. Rutherford: Fairleigh Dickinson UP; London and Toronto: Associated University Presses, 1984.

Hungerford, Edward B. "Blake's Albion." *Shores of Darkness*. 1941; rpt. Cleveland and New York: Meridian Books, 1963. 35-61. (Cited as 1941.)

Ives, Herbert. "The Trial of William Blake for High Treason." *Nineteenth Century*, LXVII (1910), 849-61.

Jackson, Mary V. "Prolific and Devourer: From Nonmythic to Mythic Statement in *The Marriage of Heaven and Hell* and *A Song of Liberty*." *JEGP*, LXX (1971), 207-19.

———. "Additional Lines in *VDA*." *BN*, VIII (Winter 1974-75), 91-93. (Cited as 1974.)

James, David E. *Written Within and Without: A Study of Blake's Milton*. Frankfurt am Main: Peter Lang, 1978.

———. "Angels Out of the Sun: Art, Religion and Politics in Blake's *America*." *SR*, XVIII (1979), 235-52.

Jewkes, W. T. "Blake's Creation Myths as Archetypes of Art," in *Directions in Literary Criticism: Contemporary Approaches to Literature*, ed. Stanley Weintraub and Philip Young. University Park and London: Pennsylvania State UP, 1973. 127-40.

Johnson, Mary Lynn. "The Devil's Syntax and the O. E. D." *BN*, III (May 1970), 94-96. (Cited as 1970a.)

————. "Beulah, 'Mne Seraphim,' and Blake's *Thel*." *JEGP*, LXIX (1970), 258-77. (Cited as 1970b.)

————. "'Separating What Has Been Mixed': A Suggestion for a Perspective on *Milton*." *BS*, VI.1 (1973), 11-17.

———— and John E. Grant, ed., *Blake's Poetry and Designs*. New York and London: Norton, 1979.

———— and Brian Wilkie. "The Spectrous Embrace in *The Four Zoas*, VIIa." *BIQ*, XII (Fall 1978), 100-05.

Johnston, Kenneth R. "Blake's Cities: Romantic Forms of Urban Renewal," in *BVFD*, 1970. 413-42.

Jones, Edward Terry. "Another Look at the Structure of *The Marriage of Heaven and Hell*." *BN*, X (Spring 1977), 115-16.

Kauvar, Elaine. "Los's Messenger to Eden: Blake's Wild Thyme." *BN*, X (Winter 1976-77), 82-84. (Cited as 1976.)

————. "The Sorrows of Thel: A Freudian Interpretation of *The Book of Thel*." *Journal of Evolutionary Psychology*, V (1984), 210-22.

Kazin, Alfred, ed. *The Portable Blake*. 1946; rpt. New York: Viking, 1966. (Cited as 1946.)

Keith, William J. "The Complexities of Blake's 'Sunflower': An Archetypal Speculation," in *BCCE*, 1966. 56-64.

Kemper, F. C. "Blake, Wicksteed, and the Wicked Swan." *NQ*, CCV (Mar. 1960), 100-01. (Cited as 1960a.)

————. "The Interlinear Drawings in Blake's *Jerusalem*." *BNYPL*, LXIV (1960), 588-94. (Cited as 1960b.)

Keynes, Geoffrey. *A Bibliography of William Blake*. 1921; rpt. New York: Kraus Reprint, 1969. (Cited as 1921.)

————, ed. *The Writings of William Blake*. 3 vols. London: Nonesuch Press, 1925.

————. "Blake's Trial at Chichester." *NQ*, CCII (Nov. 1957), 484-85.

————. "Description and Bibliographical Statement," in William Blake, *The Marriage of Heaven and Hell*. A facsimile. Clairvaux: Trianon Press, 1960.

————. "Description and Bibliographical Statement," in William Blake, *America: a Prophecy*. A facsimile. Clairvaux: Trianon Press, 1963.

————, ed. William Blake, *Songs of Innocence and of Experience*. A facsimile. London: Hart-Davis, 1967. (Cited as 1967a.)

————. "Description and Bibliographical Statement," in William Blake, *Milton: a Poem in 2 Books*. A facsimile. Clairvaux: Trianon Press, 1967. (Cited as 1967b.)

————. "Commentary," in William Blake, *The Gates of Paradise*. A facsimile. 3 vols. Clairvaux: Trianon Press, 1968. I, 7-22.

————. "Description and Bibliographical Statement," in William Blake, *Europe a Prophecy*. A facsimile. Clairvaux: Trianon Press, 1969.

————. "Description and Bibliographical Statement," in William Blake, *All Religions Are One*. A facsimile. Clairvaux: Trianon Press, 1970.

————. "Description and Bibliographical Statement," in William Blake, *There Is No Natural Religion*. A facsimile. Clairvaux and Paris: Trianon Press, 1971.

————. "Description and Bibliographical History," in William Blake, *The Book of Ahania*. A facsimile. Clairvaux and Paris: Trianon Press, 1973.

————. "Commentary and Bibliographical History," in *The Song of Los*. A facsimile. Clairvaux and Paris: Trianon Press, 1975. (Cited as 1975a.)

————, ed. William Blake, *The Marriage of Heaven and Hell*. A facsimile. London and New York: Oxford UP, 1975. (Cited as 1975b.)

————. "Commentary and Bibliographical History," in William Blake, *The Book of Los*. A facsimile. Clairvaux and Paris: Trianon Press, 1976.

———— and Edwin Wolf 2nd, *William Blake's Illuminated Books: A Census*. 1953; rpt. New York: Kraus Reprint, 1969. (Cited as 1953.)

Kilgore, John. "The Order of Nights VIIa and VIIb in Blake's *The Four Zoas*." *BIQ*, XII (Fall 1978), 107-13.

Kiralis, Karl. "The Theme and Structure of William Blake's *Jerusalem*." 1956; rpt. *DV*. 139-62.

————. "A Guide to the Intellectual Symbolism of William Blake's Later Prophetic Writings." *Cr*, I (1959), 190-210.

————. "'London' in the Light of *Jerusalem*." *BS*, I.1 (1968), 5-15.

————. Letter to the Editor. *BS*, I.2 (1969), 212-14.

Kirschbaum, Leo. "Blake's 'The Fly.'" *EC*, XI (1961), 154-62.

Kittel, Harald A. *"The Book of Urizen* and *An Essay Concerning Human Understanding,"* in *InB*, 1978. 111-44.

Klonsky, Milton. *William Blake: The Seer and His Visions.* New York: Harmony Books, 1977.

Kmetz, Gail. "A Reading of Blake's *The Gates of Paradise*." *BS*, III.2 (1971), 171-85.

Knights, L. C. "Early Blake." 1971; rpt. in his *Explorations* 3. London: Chatto and Windus, 1976. 52-63. (Cited as 1971.)

Kowle, Carol P. "Plate III and the Meaning of *Europe*." *BS*, VIII.1 (1978), 89-99.

Kreiter, Carmen S. "Evolution and William Blake." *SR*, IV (1965), 110-18.

Kroeber, Karl. "Graphic-poetic Structuring in Blake's *Book of Urizen*." *BS*, III.1 (1970), 7-18.

———. "Delivering *Jerusalem*," in *BSA*, 1973. 347-67.

La Belle, Jenijoy. "Words Graven with an Iron Pen: The Marginal Texts in Blake's *Job*," in *VH*, 1973. 527-50.

Latané, David E., Jr. "The Door into Jerusalem." *Romanticism Past and Present*, VII (Summer 1983), 17-26.

Leader, Zachary. *Reading Blake's* Songs. Boston, London and Henley: Routledge and Kegan Paul, 1981.

Lefebvre, Mark S. "A Note on the Structural Necessity of Night VIIb." *BIQ*, XII (Fall 1978), 134.

Leonard, David Charles. "Erasmus Darwin and William Blake." *Eighteenth-century Life*, IV (1978), 79-81.

Lesnick, Henry. "The Function of Perspective in Blake's *Jerusalem*." *BNYPL*, LXXIII (1969), 49-55.

———. "Narrative Structure and the Antithetical Vision of *Jerusalem*," in *BVFD*, 1970. 391-412.

Levinson, Marjorie. "'The Book of Thel' by William Blake: A Critical Reading." *ELH*, XLVII (1980), 287-303.

Lewis, C. S. *The Discarded Image: An Introduction to Medieval and Renaissance Literature.* Cambridge: Cambridge UP, 1964.

Lincoln, Andrew. "The Revision of the Seventh and Eighth Nights of *The Four Zoas*." *BIQ*, XII (Fall 1978), 114-33.

———. "Blake's Lower Paradise: The Pastoral Passage in *The Four Zoas*, Night the Ninth." *BRH*, LXXXIV (1981), 470-78.

Lindberg, Bo. *William Blake's Illustrations to the Book of Job.* Åbo, Finland: Åbo Akademi, 1973.

Lipking, Lawrence. "Blake's Inititiation: *The Marriage of Heaven and Hell*," in *Woman in the 18th Century and Other Essays*, ed. Paul Fritz and Richard Morton. Toronto and Sarasota: Samuel Stevens, Hakkert, 1976. 217-43.

Lowery, Margaret Ruth. *Windows of the Morning: A Critical Study of William Blake's* Poetical Sketches, *1783*. New Haven: Yale UP; London: Oxford UP, 1940.

Majdiak, Daniel, and Brian Wilkie. "Blake and Freud: Poetry and Depth Psychology." *Journal of Aesthetic Education*, VI (Jul. 1972), 87-98.

Margoliouth, H. M. "Notes on Blake." *RES*, XXIV (Oct. 1948), 303-16.

————. *William Blake*. London: Oxford UP, 1951.

————, ed. *William Blake's* Vala: *Blake's Numbered Text*. Oxford: Clarendon Press, 1956.

Marks, Mollyanne. "Self-sacrifice: Theme and Image in *Jerusalem*." *BS*, VII.1 (1974), 27-50.

————. "Structure and Irony in Blake's 'The Book of Urizen.'" *SEL*, XV (1975), 579-90.

————. "Renovation of Form: Time as Hero in Blake's Major Prophecies." *SECC*, V, (1976), 55-66.

Mathews, Lawrence. "Jesus as Saviour in Blake's *Jerusalem*." *ESC*, VI (1980), 154-75. (Cited as 1980a.)

————. "'The Value of the Saviours Blood': The Idea of Atonement in Blake's *Milton*." *Wascana Review*, LV (Spring 1980), 72-86. (Cited as 1980b.)

McClellan, Jane. "Dramatic Movement as a Structuring Device in Blake's *Jerusalem*." *CLQ*, XIII (Sep. 1977), 195-208.

McCord, James. "Historical Dissonance and William Blake's *The Song of Los*." *CLQ*, XX (Mar. 1984), 22-35.

McGann, Jerome J. "The Aim of Blake's Prophecies and the Uses of Blake Criticism," in *BSA*, 1973. 3-21.

McGowan, James. "The Integrity of the *Poetical Sketches*: A New Approach to Blake's Earliest Poems." *BS*, VIII.2 (1979), 121-44.

McNeil, Helen T. "The Formal Art of *The Four Zoas*," in *BVFD*, 1970. 373-90.

Mellor, Anne Kostelanetz. *Blake's Human Form Divine*. Berkeley: U of California P, 1974.

————. "Blake's Portrayal of Women." *BIQ*, XVI (Winter 1982-83), 148-55. (Cited as 1982.)

Middleman, Louis. "'Bring out number, weight & measure in a year of dearth.'" *BN*, IV (Spring 1971), 147.

Mills, Alice. "The Spectral Bat in Blake's Illustrations to *Jerusalem*." *BS*, IX.1-2 (1980), 87-99.

Miner, Paul. "William Blake: Two Notes on Sources." *BNYPL*, LXII (1958), 203-07.

————. "The Polyp as a Symbol in the Poetry of William Blake." *TSLL*, II (1960), 198-205.

————. "William Blake's 'Divine Analogy.'" *Cr*, III (1961), 46-61.

————. "'The Tyger': Genesis & Evolution in the Poetry of William Blake." *Cr*, IV (1962), 59-73.

————. "Visions in the Darksom Air: Aspects of Blake's Biblical Symbolism," in *WBED*, 1969. 256-92.

————. "Visionary Astronomy." *BRH*, LXXXIV (1981), 305-36.

Mitchell, W. J. T. "Style and Iconography in the Illustrations of Blake's *Milton*." *BS*, VI.1 (1973), 47-71. (Cited as 1973a.)

————. "Blake's Radical Comedy Dramatic Structure as Meaning in *Milton*," in *BSA*, 1973. 281-307. (Cited as 1973b.)

————. *Blake's Composite Art: A Study of the Illuminated Poetry*. Princeton: Princeton UP, 1978.

Morton, A. L. *The Everlasting Gospel: A study in the sources of William Blake*. London: Lawrence and Wishart, 1958.

Murray, E. B. "*Jerusalem* Reversed." *BS*, VII.1 (1974), 11-25. (Cited as 1974a.)

————. "'Bound Back to Back in Bromion's Cave.'" *BN*, VIII (Winter 1974-75), 94. (Cited as 1974b.)

————. "Thel, *Thelyphthora*, and the Daughters of Albion." *SR*, XX (1981), 275-97.

Murry, John Middleton. "A Note" in William Blake, *Visions of the Daughters of Albion, Reproduced in Facsimile*. London and Toronto: Dent; New York: Dutton, 1932.

————. *William Blake*. 1933; rpt. London and Toronto: Cape, 1936. (Cited as 1933.)

Nanavutty, Piloo. "'Puzzling Names in Blake.'" *TLS*, 3 Jul. 1937, p. 496.

————. "A Title-page in Blake's Illustrated Manuscript." 1947; rpt. *VH*. 127-46.

———. "Blake and Emblem Literature." *JWCI*, XV (1952), 258-61.

———. "William Blake and Hindu Creation Myths," in *DV*, 1957. 163-82.

———. *"Materia Prima* in a Page of Blake's *Vala*," in *WBED*, 1969. 293-302.

Nathan, Norman. "Blake's 'Head Downwards.'" *NQ*, CXCV (Jul. 1950), 302-03.

Nelms, Ben F. "Text and Design in *Illustrations of the Book of Job*," in *BVFD*, 1970. 336-58.

———. "'Exemplars of Memory and of Intellect': *Jerusalem* plates 96-100." *BS*, V.2 (1974), 81-95.

Nelson, Cary. "Blake's *Jerusalem*: a fourfold vision of the human body." *The Incarnate Word: Literature as verbal space.* Urbana: U of Illinois P, 1973. 129-59.

Nurmi, Martin K. "Blake's Revisions of *The Tyger*." 1956; rpt. William Blake, *The Tyger*, ed. Winston Weathers. Columbus, Ohio: Merill, 1969. 34-51. (Cited as 1956.)

———. "Blake's 'Ancient of Days' and Motte's Frontispiece to Newton's *Principia*," in *DV*, 1957. 207-16. (Cited as 1957a.)

———. *Blake's* Marriage of Heaven and Hell: *A Critical Study*. Kent, Ohio: Kent State University Bulletin, 1957. (Cited as 1957b.)

———. "Joy, Love, and Innocence in Blake's 'The Mental Traveller.'" *SR*, III (1964), 109-17. (Cited as 1964a.)

———. "Fact and Symbol in 'The Chimney Sweeper' of Blake's *Songs of Innocence*." 1964; rpt. *BCCE*. 15-22. (Cited as 1964b.)

———. "Negative Sources in Blake," in *WBED*, 1969. 303-18.

———. *William Blake*. N.p.: Kent State UP, 1976.

Orel, Harold. "Blake's Hostility to the Enlightenment" in *Studies on Voltaire and the Eighteenth Century*, CIII (1973), 37-59.

Ostriker, Alicia, ed. William Blake, *The Complete Poems*. Harmondsworth, Middlesex: Penguin, 1977.

———. "Desire Gratified and Ungratified: William Blake and Sexuality." *BIQ*, XVI (Winter 1982-83), 156-65. (Cited as 1982.)

Ott, Judith. "The Bird-Man of William Blake's *Jerusalem*." *BN*, X (Fall 1976), 48-51.

Owen, A. L. *The Famous Druids: A survey of three centuries of English literature on the Druids*. Oxford: Clarendon Press, 1962.

Paley, Morton D. "The Female Babe and 'The Mental Traveller.'" *SR*, I (1962), 97-104.

———. "Method and Meaning in Blake's *Book of Ahania*." *BNYPL*, LXX (1966), 27-33.

———. "Cowper as Blake's Spectre." *ECS*, I (1968), 236-52.

———. "Thomas Johnes, 'Ancient Guardian of Wales.'" *BN*, II (Apr. 1969), 65-67.

———. *Energy and the Imagination: A Study of the Development of Blake's Thought*. Oxford: Clarendon Press, 1970.

——— and Deirdre Toomey. [Separate contributions to] "Two Pictorial Sources for *Jerusalem 25*." *BN*, V (Winter 1971-72), 185-90. (Cited as 1971.)

———. "William Blake, The Prince of the Hebrews, and The Woman Clothed with the Sun," in *WBEK*, 1973. 260-93. (Cited as 1973a.)

———. "The Figure of the Garment in *The Four Zoas, Milton* and *Jerusalem*," in *BSA*, 1973. 119-39. (Cited as 1973b.)

———. "'Wonderful Originals'—Blake and Ancient Sculpture," in *BT*, 1978. 170-97. (Cited as 1978a.)

———. *William Blake*. Oxford: Phaidon, 1978. (Cited as 1978b.)

———. "'A New Heaven is Begun': William Blake and Swedenborgianism." *BIQ*, XIII (Fall 1979), 64-90.

———. "The Fourth Face of Man: Blake and Architecture," in *Articulate Images: The Sister Arts from Hogarth to Tennyson*, ed. Richard Wendorf. Minneapolis: U of Minnesota P, 1983. 184-215. (Cited as 1983a.)

———. *The Continuing City: William Blake's Jerusalem*. Oxford: Clarendon, 1983. (Cited as 1983b.)

Parisi, Frank M. "Emblems of Melancholy: *For Children: The Gates of Paradise*," in *InB*, 1978. 70-110.

Pearce, Donald R. "Natural Religion and the Plight of Thel." *BS*, VIII.1 (1978), 23-35.

Pechey, Graham. "*The Marriage of Heaven and Hell*: A Text and its Conjuncture." *Oxford Literary Review*, III (1979), 52-76.

Percival, Milton O. *William Blake's Circle of Destiny*. 1938; rpt. New York: Octagon Books, 1964. (Cited as 1938.)

Peterfreund, Stuart. "Blake and Newton: Argument as Art, Argument as Science." *SECC*, X (1981), 205-26.

Peterson, Jane E. *"The Visions of the Daughters of Albion*: A Problem in Perception." *PQ*, LII (1973), 252-64.

Phillips, Michael. "Blake's Corrections in *Poetical Sketches.*" *BN*, IV (Fall 1970), 40-47.

———. "Blake's Early Poetry," in *WBEK*, 1973. 1-28.

———. "William Blake and the 'Unincreasable Club': The Printing of *Poetical Sketches.*" *BNYPL*, LXXX (1976), 6-18.

Pierce, Frederick E. "Etymology as Explanation in Blake." *PQ*, X (1931), 395-99.

Pinto, V. de S. "William Blake, Isaac Watts, and Mrs. Barbauld," in *DV*, 1957. 65-87.

———. "A Neglected Poem of William Blake," in *Critical Essays on English Literature Presented to Professor M. S. Duraiswami on the occasion of his Sixty-first birthday*, ed. Dr. V. S. Seturaman. Bombay: Orient Longmans, 1965. 19-31.

Plowman, Max. *An Introduction to the Study of Blake*. London and Toronto: Dent, 1927.

———. "Note," in William Blake, *The Marriage of Heaven and Hell, Reproduced in Facsimile*. London and Toronto: Dent; New York: Dutton, 1927. 5-24.

Plowman, Dorothy. "Note," in William Blake, *The Book of Urizen, Reproduced in Facsimile*. London and Toronto: Dent; New York: Dutton, 1929. 11-25.

Poole, Matthew. *A Commentary on the Holy Bible*. 1685; rpt. 3 vols. Edinburgh: Banner of Truth Trust, 1979. (Cited as 1685.)

Pottle, Frederick A. "Blake's *The Tyger.*" 1950; rpt. *The Explicator Cyclopedia*. Chicago: Quadrangle Books, 1968. II, 44. (Cited as 1950.)

Preston, Kerrison. *Blake and Rossetti*. 1944; rpt. Folcroft, Pennsylvania: Folcroft Press, 1969. (Cited as 1944.)

Price, Martin. "Blake: Vision and Satire," chap. 13 of *To the Palace of Wisdom: Studies in Order and Energy from Dryden to Blake*. 1964; rpt. New York: Anchor Books/ Doubleday, 1965. (Cited as 1964.)

Quasha, George. "Orc as a Fiery Paradigm of Poetic Torsion," in *BVFD*, 1970. 263-84.

Raine, Kathleen. "Who Made the Tyger?" *Encounter*, II (June 1954), 43-50.

————. "The Little Girl Lost and Found and The Lapsed Soul," in *DV*, 1957. 17-63. (Cited as 1957a.)

————. "Blake's Cupid and Psyche." *The Listener*, LVIII (21 Nov. 1957), 832-35. (Cited as 1957b.)

————. "A Traditional Language of Symbols." *The Listener*, LX (9 Oct. 1958), 559-60.

————. "Blake's Debt to Antiquity." *Sewanee Review*, LXXI (1963), 352-450.

————. *Blake and Tradition*. 2 vols. Princeton: Princeton UP, 1968. [Publication delayed till 1969.]

————. *The Human Face of God: William Blake and the Book of Job*. [London]: Thames and Hudson, 1982.

Read, Dennis M. "Blake's 'Tender Stranger': *Thel* and Hervey's *Meditations*." *CLQ*, XVIII (Sep. 1982), 160-67.

Riede, David G. "The Symbolism of the Loins in Blake's *Jerusalem*." *SEL*, XXI (1981), 547-63.

Rieger, James. "'The Hem of Their Garments': The Bard's Song in *Milton*," in *BSA*, 1973. 259-80.

Reiman, Donald H. and Christina Shuttleworth Kraus. "The Derivation and Meaning of 'Ololon.'" *BIQ*, XVI (Fall 1982), 82-85.

Reisner, Thomas A. "Cain: Two Romantic Interpretations." *Culture*, XXXI (1970), 124-43.

Rix, Donna S. "*Milton*: Blake's Reading of Second Isaiah," in *Poetic Prophecy in Western Literature*, ed. Jan Wojcik and Raymond-Jean Frontain. Rutherford: Fairleigh Dickinson UP; London and Toronto: Associated University Presses, 1984. 106-18.

Rose, Edward J. "The Structure of Blake's *Jerusalem*." *Bucknell Review*, XI (1963), 35-54.

————. "'Mental Forms Creating': 'Fourfold Vision' and the Poet as Prophet in Blake's Designs and Verse." *JAAC*, XXIII (1964), 173-83. (Cited as 1964a.)

————. "Blake's TO THE ACCUSER OF THIS WORLD." *Ex*, XXII (Jan. 1964), item 37. (Cited as 1964b.)

————. "Blake's Hand: Symbol and Design in JERUSALEM." *TSLL*, VI (1964), 47-58. (Cited as 1964c.)

————. "The Symbolism of the Opened Center and Poetic Theory in Blake's *Jerusalem*." *SEL*, V (1965), 587-606.

———. "Visionary Forms Dramatic: Dramatic and Iconographical Movement in Blake's Verse and Designs." *Cr*, VIII (1966), 111-25.

———. "The Meaning of Los." *BN*, I (Dec. 1967), 10-11.

———. "Circumcision Symbolism in Blake's *Jerusalem*." *SR*, VIII (1968), 16-25. (Cited as 1968a.)

———. "Blake's Human Insect: Symbol, Theory, and Design." *TSLL*, X (1968), 215-32. (Cited as 1968b.)

———. "Blake's *Milton*: The Poet as Poem." *BS*, I.1 (1968), 16-38. (Cited as 1968c.)

———. "Blake's Illustrations for *Paradise Lost*, *L'Allegro* and *Il Penseroso*: A Thematic Reading." *Hartford Studies in Literature*, II (1970), 40-67. (Cited as 1970a.)

———. "Blake's Fourfold Art." *PQ*, XLIX (1970), 400-23. (Cited as 1970b.)

———. "'Forms Eternal Exist For-ever': The Covenant of the Harvest in Blake's Prophetic Poems," in *BVFD*, 1970. 443-62. (Cited as 1970c.)

———. "The Spirit of The Bounding Line: Blake's Los." *Cr*, XIII (1971), 54-76. (Cited as 1971a.)

———. "Blake's Metaphorical States." *BS*, IV.1 (1971), 9-31. (Cited as 1971b.)

———. "Wheels Within Wheels in Blake's *Jerusalem*." *SR*, XI (1972), 36-47. (Cited as 1972a.)

———. "Good-bye to Orc and All That." *BS*, IV.2 (1972), 135-51. (Cited as 1972b.)

———. "Los, Pilgrim of Eternity," in *BSA*, 1973. 83-99.

Rosenberg, Marc. "Style and Meaning in *The Book of Urizen*." *Style*, IV (1970), 197-212.

Russell, Archibald G. B. *The Engravings of William Blake*. 1912; rpt. New York: Benjamin Blom, 1968. (Cited as 1912.)

Salemi, Joseph S. "Emblematic Tradition in Blake's *The Gates of Paradise*." *BIQ*, XV (Winter 1981-82), 108-24. (Cited as 1981.)

Sandler, Florence. "The Iconoclastic Enterprise: Blake's Critique of Milton's Religion." *BS*, V.1 (1972), 13-57.

Saurat, Denis. *Blake & Modern Thought*. 1929; rpt. New York: Russell and Russell, 1964. (Cited as 1929.)

Schleifer, Ronald. "Simile, Metaphor, and Vision: Blake's Narration of Prophecy in *America*." *SEL*, XIX (1979), 569-88.

Schorer, Mark. *William Blake: The Politics of Vision*. New York: Holt, 1946.

Schotz, Myra Glazer. "On the Frontispiece of *The Four Zoas*." *BN*, X (Spring 1977), 126-27.

Sethna, K. D. "Blake's Tyger: A New Interpretation," in *Critical Essays on English Literature Presented to Professor M. S. Duraiswami on the occasion of his Sixty-first birthday*, ed. Dr. V. S. Seturaman. Bombay: Orient Longmans, 1965. 170-213.

Simmons, Robert E. "*Urizen*: The Symmetry of Fear," in *BVFD*, 1970. 146-73.

────── and Janet Warner. "Blake's 'How Sweet I Roam'd': from Copy to Vision," *Neohelicon*, I.iii-iv (1973), 295-304.

Sloss, D. J. and J. P. R. Wallis, ed. *The Prophetic Writings of William Blake*. 2 vols. (Oxford: Clarendon Press, 1926).

Smith, J. C. "A Blake Head-piece." *TLS*, 20 Apr. 1933, p. 276.

Spector, Sheila A. "Death in Blake's Major Prophecies." *Studia Mystica*, VII.3 (1984), 3-28.

Spicer, Harold. "Biblical Sources of William Blake's *America*." *Ball State University Forum*, VIII (1967), 23-29.

Stavrou, C. N. "A Reassessment of *The Marriage of Heaven and Hell*." *SAQ*, LIV (1955), 381-85.

Stevenson, W. H. "The Shaping of Blake's 'America'." *MLR*, LV (1960), 497-503.

──────. "Two Problems in *The Four Zoas* (continued)." *BN*, I (Mar. 1968), 6-8.

──────, ed. *The Poems of William Blake*. London: Longman; New York: Norton, 1971.

Stuart, Simon. *New Phoenix Wings: Reparation in Literature*. London, Boston and Henley: Routledge and Kegan Paul, 1979.

Summerfield, H. "Blake and the Names Divine." *BIQ*, XV (Summer 1981), 14-22.

Sutherland, John H. "Blake's 'Mental Traveller.'" *ELH*, XXII (1955), 136-47.

──────, "Blake and Urizen," in *BVFD*, 1970. 244-62.

──────, "Blake's *Milton*: The Bard's Song," *CLQ*, XIII (June 1977), 142-57.

Tannenbaum, Leslie. "Lord Byron in the Wilderness: Biblical Tradition in Byron's *Cain* and Blake's *The Ghost of Abel*." *MP*, LXXII (1975), 350-64.

──────. "Blake and the Iconography of Cain," in *BT*, 1978. 23-34.

————. "Transformations of Michelangelo in William Blake's *The Book of Urizen.*" *CLQ*, XVI (Mar. 1980), 19-50.

————. *Biblical Tradition in Blake's Early Prophecies: The Great Code of Art.* Princeton: Princeton UP, 1982.

Tayler, Irene. "Say First! What Mov'd Blake? Blake's *Comus* Designs and *Milton,*" in *BSA*, 1973. 233-58. (Cited as 1973a.)

————. "The Woman Scaly." *Bulletin of the Midwest Modern Language Association*, VI (Spring 1973), 74-87. (Cited as 1973b.)

Taylor, Gary. "Blake's Proverb 67 (from *The Marriage of Heaven and Hell*)." *Ex*, XXXII (Oct. 1973), item 8.

————. "The Structure of *The Marriage*: A Revolutionary Primer." *SR*, XIII (1974), 141-45.

Taylor, Peter Alan. "Providence and the Moment in Blake's *Milton.*" *BS*, IV.1 (1971), 43-60.

Teitelbaum, Eve. "Form as Meaning in Blake's *Milton.*" *BS*, II.1 (1969), 37-64.

Thompson, E. P. "London," in *InB*, 1978. 5-31.

Tinker, Chauncey Brewster. "Blake: 'The Gates of Paradise.'" *Painter and Poet: Studies in the Literary Relations of English Painting.* Cambridge: Harvard UP, 1939. 100-120.

Todd, Ruthven. "William Blake and the Eighteenth-century Mythologists." *Tracks in the Snow: Studies in English Science and Art.* London: Grey Walls Press, 1946. 29-60.

————. "'Poisonous Blues,' and Other Pigments." *BIQ*, XIV (Summer 1980), 31-34.

Tolley, Michael J. "*The Book of Thel* and *Night Thoughts.*" *BNYPL*, LXIX (1965), 375-85.

————. "Remarks on 'The Tyger.'" *BN*, I (Oct. 1967), 10-13.

————. "Blake's Blind Man" and "Reply" [to Hagstrum's "Rebuttal"]. *BS*, II.1 (1969), 77-84, 86-88.

————. "*Europe*: 'to those ychain'd in sleep,'" in *BVFD*, 1970. 115-45. (Cited as 1970a.)

————. "*Jerusalem* 12:25-29—Some Questions Answered." *BN*, IV (August 1970), 3-6. (Cited as 1970b.)

————. "Blake's Songs of Spring," in *WBEK*, 1973. 96-128.

———— and Michael Ferber. "'Thel's Motto': Likely & Unlikely Sources." *BN*, 10 (Summer 1976), 35-38.

Toomey, Deirdre. See Paley, Morton D. and Deirdre Toomey.

Twitchell, James B. "'The Mental Traveller,' Infinity and the 'Arlington Court Picture,'" *Cr*, XVII (1975), 1-14.

Van Doren, Mark. *Introduction to Poetry*. 1951; rpt. New York: Holt, Rinehart and Winston, 1962. (Cited 1951.)

Wagenknecht, David. *Blake's Night: William Blake and the Idea of Pastoral*. Cambridge: Belknap Press of Harvard UP, 1973.

Ward, Aileen. "The forging of Orc: Blake and the idea of revolution," in *Literature in Revolution*, ed. George Abbott White and Charles Newman. New York: Holt, Rinehart and Winston, 1972. 204-27.

Wardle, Judith. "'Europe' and 'America.'" *NQ*, CCXIII (Jan. 1968), 20-21.

———. "'For Hatching ripe': Blake and the Educational Uses of Emblem and Illustrated Literature." *BRH*, LXXXI (1978), 324-48.

———. "William Blake's Iconography of Joy: Angels, Birds, Butterflies and Related Motifs from *Poetical Sketches* to The Pickering Manuscript." *BS*, IX.1 and 2 (1980), 5-44.

Warner, Janet A. "Blake's Use of Gesture," in *BVFD*, 1970. 174-95.

———. "Blake's Figures of Despair: Man in His Spectre's Power," in *WBEK*, 1973. 208-24.

———. "Blake and the Language of Art: From Copy to Vision." *CLQ*, XIII (Jun. 1977), 99-114.

———. "Blake's 'Auguries of Innocence.'" *CLQ*, XII (Sep. 1976), 126-38.

———. *Blake and the Language of Art*. Kingston and Montreal: McGill-Queen's UP; Gloucester: Alan Sutton, 1984.

Warner, Nicholas O. "Blake's Moon-ark Symbolism." *BIQ*, XIV (Fall 1980), 44-59.

Wasser, Henry H. "Notes on the *Visions of the Daughters of Albion* by William Blake." *MLQ*, IX (1948), 292-97.

Weathers, Winston. "William Blake's *The Book of Thel*: A Transaction," in *The Nature of Identity: Essays Presented to Donald E. Hayden by the Graduate Faculty of Modern Letters, the University of Tulsa*. Tulsa, Oklahoma: University of Tulsa, 1981. 71-91.

Webster, Brenda S. *Blake's Prophetic Psychology*. London and Basingstoke: Macmillan, 1983.

Weiskel, Thomas. "Darkning Man: Blake's Critique of Transcendence," chap. 3 of *The Romantic Sublime: Studies in the Structure and Psychology of Transcendence*. Baltimore and London: Johns Hopkins UP, 1976. 63-79.

Welch, Dennis M. "*America* and Atlantis: Blake's Ambivalent Millenialism." *BN*, VI (Fall 1972), 50.

————. "Center, Circumference, and Vegetation Symbolism in the Writings of William Blake." *SP*, LXXV (1978), 223-42.

Wenger, A. Grace. "Blake's *The Four Zoas*, Night the Ninth." *Ex*, XXVII (Mar. 1969), item 53.

Wicksteed, Joseph H. *Blake's Vision of the Book of Job*. London: Dent; New York: Dutton, 1910.

————. ———— ———— ————. 2nd ed. London: Dent; New York: Dutton, 1924.

————. *Blake's Innocence and Experience: A Study of the Songs and Manuscripts "Shewing the Two Contrary States of the Human Soul."* London and Toronto: Dent; New York: Dutton, 1928.

————. *William Blake's Jerusalem*. n. p.: Trianon Press For The William Blake Trust, London, [1954].

Widmer, Kingsley. "The Marriage of Heaven and Hell," chap. 3 of *The Literary Rebel*. Carbondale and Edwardsville: Southern Illinois UP, 1965. 35-47.

Wilkie, Brian. "Epic Irony in *Milton*," in *BVFD*, 1970. 359-72.

————. "Blake's *Innocence and Experience*: An Approach." *BS*, VI.2 (1975), 119-37.

———— and Mary Lynn Johnson. *Blake's* Four Zoas: *The Design of a Dream*. Cambridge and London: Harvard UP, 1978.

Wilson, Mona. *The Life of William Blake*. London: Nonesuch Press, 1927.

Witke, Joanne. "*Jerusalem*: A Synoptic Poem," *CL*, XXII (1970), 265-78.

Wittreich, Joseph Anthony, Jr. "The 'Satanism' of Blake and Shelley Reconsidered." *SP*, LXV (1968), 816-33.

————. *Angel of Apocalypse: Blake's Idea of Milton*. Madison and London: U of Wisconsin P, 1975.

Worrall, David. "William Blake and Erasmus Darwin's *Botanic Garden*." *BNYPL*, LXXVIII (1975), 397-417.

————. "Blake's Derbyshire: A Visionary Locale in *Jerusalem*." *BIQ*, XI (Summer 1977), 34-35. (Cited as 1977a.)

————. "Blake's *Jerusalem* and the Visionary History of Britain." *SR*, XVI (1977), 189-216. (Cited as 1977b.)

————. "The 'Immortal Tent.'" *BRH*, LXXXIV (1981), 273-95.

Wright, Andrew. *Blake's* Job: *A Commentary.* Oxford: Clarendon Press, 1972.

Wright, Thomas. *The Life of William Blake.* 1929; rpt. 2 vols. in 1. Chicheley: Paul P. B. Minet, 1972. (Cited as 1929.)

Wyatt, David M. "The Woman Jerusalem: *Pictura* Versus *Poesis.*" *BS*, VII.2 (1975), 105-24.

Yeats, William Butler. *A Vision.* London: privately printed, 1925.

Indexes

Italicised page numbers refer to passages in the Notes on Criticism. The main purpose of the Selective Index is to provide ready access to the principal significances of the names and terms.